RODALE'S
ALL-NEW
ENCYCLOPEDIA
OF **ORGANIC**
GARDENING

RODALE'S
ALL-NEW
ENCYCLOPEDIA
OF ORGANIC
GARDENING

The Indispensable Resource for Every Gardener

Edited by Fern Marshall Bradley and Barbara W. Ellis

Rodale Press, Emmaus, Pennsylvania

This edition published by Barnes & Noble, Inc., by arrangement with Rodale Press, Inc. 1998 Barnes & Noble Books

M 10 9 8 7 6 5 4 3 2 1

ISBN 0–7607–0791–X

Printed in the United States of America on acid-free ∞, recycled paper ♻

Senior Managing Editor: Margaret J. Lydic
Senior Editor: Barbara W. Ellis
Editor: Fern Marshall Bradley
Contributing Editors: Ellen Phillips, Sally Roth, Nancy J. Ondra, Jean M. A. Nick, Deborah L. Martin
Editorial Assistant: James E. Farrell
Copy Editor: Laura Quaglio
Indexer: Ed Yeager
Senior Research Associate: Heidi A. Stonehill
Editorial Production Coordinator: Stacy A. Brobst
Editorial/Administrative Assistant: Karen Earl-Braymer
Book Designer: Linda Jacopetti
Cover Designer: Darlene Schneck
Illustration Direction: Denise M. Shade
Associate Designer: Linda Bossard
Cover Illustration: Phyllis and Monroe Stevens
Illustrations: Kathy Bray, Pamela and Walter Carrol, Rae D. Chambers, Jean Emmons, Leslie Flis, Frank Fretz, Elayne Sears

To Robert Rodale, whose ideas and spirit live on in all of our gardens.

Contents

Introduction

Thirty years ago, a remarkable book appeared—*The Encyclopedia of Organic Gardening*. Edited by J. I. Rodale, the encyclopedia was a unique book that became a classic. Well-worn copies, some carefully preserved in handmade covers, are part of collections across North America in garden sheds, homes, and libraries.

In the decades since the encyclopedia's first publication, organic gardening has grown from a fringe movement into the mainstream of American gardening. True to the vision of J. I. and Robert Rodale, organic gardening has emerged as the safest, most economical, and most practical method for home gardeners.

In 1989, we decided to rejuvenate the encyclopedia. We wanted to create a resource book that would reflect heightened awareness of organic methods and new breakthroughs in organic pest control. We laid plans for an encyclopedia that would include not only raising food crops but also maintaining perennials, annuals, trees, shrubs, and lawns without chemicals.

To realize our plans, we gathered ideas from many gardeners, writers, and editors. Robert Rodale lent his unique insights, including suggesting an Organic Pest Management entry to present a holistic approach to managing all garden problems with only organic methods. Then we called on a broad range of garden experts and writers to draft entries in their areas of interest. A team of editors carefully blended and refined their work. Our goal, as for the original encyclopedia, was a comprehensive, easy-to-use book that provides *practical* information on the entire realm of organic gardening.

How to Use This Book

The organization of this book reflects the way you garden. We've grouped information into useful, complete entries that will provide all you need to know about a particular topic, rather than spreading out facts in thousands of short entries. For example, the instructions you need to plan, plant, and care for a vegetable garden are in one entry: Vegetable Gardening. The Composting entry tells you everything you need to know to make and use compost. Entries on Annuals, Perennials, and Trees describe how to get started, how to use these plants in your landscape, and how to keep them flourishing. They include lists of specific plants for specific environmental conditions and uses.

Individual food crops and ornamentals entries provide additional specialized information. For example, the Tomato entry offers lots of tips for growing the biggest, best, earliest tomatoes and includes suggested cultivars. Dozens of special entries—including Dried Flower Gardening, Edible Landscaping, Phenology, Rock Gardens, and Wildlife—will stimulate your gardening imagination and curiosity.

How to Find It

If you scan the table of contents, you'll get a general picture of the encyclopedia's range and focus. Under each letter is a list of the entries that begin with that letter. It's fun and informative to flip to interesting entries that catch your eye. We've included lots of illustrations, tips, and unusual entries that we hope will liven up your browsing sessions.

But if you want information on a narrow subject, such as how to control Japanese beetles, turn to the back pages to a vital, if often unappreciated part of a book: the index. Flip to the Japanese beetle listing in the index, find the subentry for "control of," and you'll be referred directly to page 345, where you'll find a description of the beetles and the damage they cause and a list of the best organic control methods. You'll find the index is an important tool in getting the most from your encyclopedia.

There are also special features that help you find the information you need on a topic. Throughout the book, you'll find cross-references to other entries that contain information related to the subject you're reading about. Look especially for the heading "More On," which lists related entries, and also in some cases lists books or organizations you can refer to for more information on a topic. The "Key Words" heading is your cue to look for essential gardening terms that will aid in your understanding of an entry. And "Smart Shopping" is the flag for tips on finding and buying the best plants and supplies for your garden.

Plant Names

All plants have a botanical name and a common name. Scientists create botanical names, usually derived from Latin words, to help categorize plants. Common names are the ones we use in casual speech or writing about plants.

We list food plants—fruits, herbs, nuts, and vegetables—by common name, so you can look up the Apple, Peach, Pepper, or Tomato entries and find just what you're looking for. However, we list ornamental plants by botanical names, because they frequently have more than one common name. Using botanical names eliminates possible confusion. For example, if you turn to the Amelanchier entry, you'll see that these beautiful spring-blooming trees and shrubs have several common names, including serviceberry, shadbush, and Juneberry. But to be sure

you're getting the plant you want, use the botanical name, *Amelanchier,* so there's no confusion. For more information on plant names, see the Botanical Nomenclature entry.

If you're not familiar with the botanical names of ornamentals, look in the index for the common name of the plant that interests you. The index listing will refer you to the correct botanical name. Or try "Common and Botanical Names" on page 644, where you'll find a list of common names and the corresponding botanical names for all the plants that have individual entries in the encyclopedia.

The Heart of the Matter

There are 26 entries that form the core of the encyclopedia. Together, they are a handbook of organic gardening basics. When you read an entry about a specific plant, you may need to refer to core entries, where we've compiled lots of basic information that applies to specific plants. Core entries fall into four categories:

Gardening Techniques: Garden Design, Landscaping, Planting, Propagation, Pruning and Training, Seeds and Seedlings

Organic Garden Management: Animal Pests, Beneficial Insects, Composting, Disease, Fertilizers, Insects, Organic Pest Management, Soil

Food Crops: Fruit, Fruit Trees, Herbs, Nut Trees, Vegetable Gardening

Ornamental Plants: Annuals, Biennials, Bulbs, Groundcovers, Perennials, Shrubs, Trees

You may find it valuable to read most of these entries soon after getting this book. If you're an experienced gardener, it will be an interesting refresher course. If you're a beginner, the core entries are a great first step to a lifelong enjoyment of your organic garden.

Fern Marshall Bradley
Barbara W. Ellis

Abelia

Abelia. Semi-evergreen, spring- and summer-flowering shrubs.

Description: *Abelia × grandiflora,* glossy abelia, attains a mature height of 4'-6'. It has a rounded habit and purplish red, loosely arching branches. Delicate, lightly fragrant, pale pink or white flowers bloom profusely in late spring, then sporadically until frost. Glossy, opposite, oval leaves turn burgundy red in winter. Leaves may fall in very cold weather. New foliage is rich red, maturing to green. Zones 5-8.

How to grow: Plant in full sun or partial shade; full shade results in sparse growth and few flowers. Abelia grows in a variety of soils but must have good drainage. Plant in fall or spring in Zones 5-7, fall or winter in Zone 8. Flowers appear on new wood, so prune in winter to encourage vigorous growth. Don't shear or leave stubs. Rejuvenate old, overgrown abelias by cutting to the ground. On younger plants, remove ⅓ of the oldest growth each year.

Landscape uses: Abelia makes a charming, low, informal hedge. Its manageable size makes it ideal for foundation plantings, and its spreading form makes it a good groundcover massed on a bank.

Best cultivars: 'Prostrata' is a low-growing form with purple-green winter color. 'Sherwoodii' is a semidwarf, 1½'-2' tall. ❖

Abies

Fir. Needle-leaved evergreen trees.

Description: Firs are native to the evergreen forests and mountain regions of North America. Most are large, pyramidal trees with fragrant needles.

Abies balsamea, balsam fir, performs best in cool climates and may grow to 75' in its native range. Its 1" long, rounded needles release a pleasant fragrance when crushed or rubbed. The brown buds appear to be coated in wax, and the cones grow about 2½" long. Zones 2-5.

A. concolor, white fir, is native to mountainous regions from southern Oregon and Idaho to southern California and into neighboring Mexico, so it handles some summer heat better than other firs. It may reach a height of 50' in the landscape and 100' in its native range. Flattened, 2" long needles give off an orange-peel smell when crushed. Buds are light brown and waxy; cones may grow to 5". Zones 4-7.

A. fraseri, Fraser fir, is a popular Christmas tree in the South; it's grown commercially in the mountains of the Carolinas. Fraser fir may grow 30'-40' tall in the landscape. The needles are about 1" long; cones grow to about 2" long. Zones 5-6.

How to grow: Firs require full sun and well-drained but evenly moist acid soils. Don't plant firs in urban areas where they will suffer from polluted air. These mountain natives do poorly in hot conditions and are not good choices for most Southern landscapes. White firs suffer few pest problems. Watch for balsam woolly adelgid, an aphidlike insect with a waxy, white body coating. These woolly pests remain attached to a host tree throughout their life cycle; severe infestations give the trunk a flocked appearance and cause gradual decline. Control adelgids with soap or dormant oil sprays; beneficial insects such as lady beetles and syrphid fly larvae limit adelgid populations. Spruce budworm, a dark, red-brown, ½"-¾" caterpillar with yellow spots and a black head, disfigures trees by feeding on new growth but rarely disturbs landscape trees.

Landscape uses: Use firs for focal points, groupings, or screens. *A. concolor* is as handsome as Colorado blue spruce (*Picea pungens* 'Glauca') and can replace it in the landscape. ❖

Acer

Maple. Deciduous trees with single or multiple trunks.

Description: *Acer barbatum,* Florida maple, is a small (to 25' in the landscape) tree with a single-trunked, rounded habit. A native of the southeastern United States, it should probably be used more widely there for its reliable fall color and heat tolerance. Zones 7-9.

A. buergeranum, trident maple, can have single or multiple trunks supporting an oval or rounded crown. It normally attains a height of 20'-25' in the landscape but can grow twice as tall. Like many maples, it has three-lobed leaves borne in pairs; the lobes all point in the same direction, away from the base of the leaf. Red or orange fall color may develop in some years. The bark of trident maple is gray and brown, sometimes with orange tones, becoming scaly with age. Zones 6-7.

A. ginnala, Amur maple, grows 15'-20' tall in the landscape. While most maples' flowers are neither fragrant nor showy, Amur maple bears highly fragrant blooms in early spring.

The three-lobed leaves have an extended center lobe and may turn scarlet in the fall. Zones 3-7.

A. japonicum, full-moon maple, is another small (20'-30') maple with considerable landscape value. Full-moon maple's leaves are palmately compound and nearly circular in outline. Flowers are purplish or red. Fall color is crimson and/or yellow in most years and is more reliable in Northern areas. Zones 5-8.

A. negundo, box elder, is a North American native often disdained for its weediness and soft wood, yet it grows where most other trees can't. It has multiple stems, a rounded crown, and a mature height of 50'-70'. Yellow-green flowers appear in early spring before its compound leaves unfold; fall color is a soft yellow. Abundant winged fruits can be messy and lead to numerous seedlings. Zones 2-9.

A. palmatum, Japanese maple, normally grows 15'-20' tall; its branches may spread as wide as the tree is tall, creating a layered appearance unlike the more upright form of other maples. The many cultivars offer countless options of twig and leaf color, gnarled or mounded habits, and lacy threadleaf forms. Protect from direct wind in the North and direct sun in the South. Zones 5-8.

A. pensylvanicum is known as moosewood or striped maple. The green chalk-striped bark of this 15'-20' Northeastern woodland native has considerable landscape interest. Look for yellow fall color. Striped maple performs best in cool climates under partial shade. Zones 3-6.

A. platanoides, Norway maple, is a popular street tree with its round, dense crown, regular form, and tolerance for difficult urban conditions such as air pollution and poor soil. It grows 40'-50' tall and holds its leaves late into the fall. Norway maple generally casts deep shade, making it difficult to grow turfgrass under this type of tree. Zones 4-6.

A. rubrum, red or swamp maple, is a North American native that reaches heights of 40'-60'. Pyramidal in youth, red maple sprawls and arches with age. The smooth gray trunk and branches are distinctive, particularly when trees are

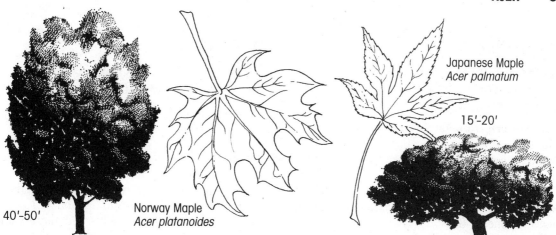

Specimen and shade maples. *Acer palmatum,* Japanese maple, is a small tree with fine branches and a layered, spreading habit—perfect for a specimen. Its palmate leaves are often deeply dissected. *Acer platanoides,* Norway maple, has a strongly upright form with a dense, rounded crown that casts deep shade. It has broadly palmate, sycamorelike leaves.

grouped. Red flowers open before the leaves and are a softly colorful sign of spring. Fall color is bright red and/or orange. Hardiness and heat tolerance vary within the species; choose a cultivar suited to your location. Zones 3-8.

A. saccharinum, silver maple, is touted for its fast growth, but it's also weedy and weak-wooded and may be prone to breakage. Growing 50'-70' high, silver maple is upright, with spreading branches and a rounded crown; its leaves are deeply lobed and silvery beneath. The pale pink flowers appear before the leaves in spring. Look for yellows or reds in the fall foliage, and a gray, furrowed trunk. Zones 3-8.

A. saccharum, sugar, rock, or hard maple, gets its names from the maple sugar derived from its rising spring sap and from the durability of its wood. It has a single trunk and a rounded crown, gray-black furrowed bark, and a mature height of 50'-70'. Sugar maple's fall color is legendary; in good years the trees turn gold, orange, and scarlet. Zones 3-7.

How to grow: With the exception of large maples, like red, sugar, silver, and Norway, used as shade trees, most maples benefit from light shade. Generous mulch and a shaded root zone are also advantages. Most maples require acid soils that are evenly moist but well-drained,

although red maple and box elder occur naturally on swampy sites. Given the conditions they prefer, maples are relatively problem-free trees. Scorched leaf margins may occur on trees suffering from drought or reflected heat from pavement or cars. Watch red and silver maples on high-pH soils for yellowed foliage caused by manganese deficiency. Box elders attract box elder bugs, which like to overwinter indoors. In the fall, groups of these black-and-orange insects move into buildings and become household pests.

Landscape uses: Japanese, full-moon, and Amur maples make fine focal points in small-scale settings; larger areas might call for trident maple or sugar maple. Red, striped, and sugar maples are good choices for naturalizing; Norway maple makes a tough street tree. Use box elders for shade on difficult sites.

Best cultivars: *A. japonicum* 'Aconitifolium', feathery leaves. *A. negundo* 'Variegatum', white-margined leaflets. *A. palmatum:* 'Atropurpureum', dark red foliage through the growing season; 'Bloodgood', red foliage that opens a rosy shade and deepens through the season; 'Dissectum', lacy, threadlike leaves. *A. platanoides* 'Crimson King', dark red foliage through the growing season. *A. rubrum:* 'October Glory', late fall color; 'Red Sunset', superior early fall color. ❖

Achillea

Yarrow. Summer- and sometimes fall-blooming perennials; herbs; dried flowers.

Description: Yarrows bear profuse 2″-6″ flat-topped heads of tiny flowers in shades of white, yellow, gold, pink, and red on 2′-5′ stems. Soft, finely cut, aromatic foliage is green or gray. *Achillea* × 'Moonshine' bears 3″ soft yellow clusters on 1′-2′ stems atop striking gray, dense leaves. Zones 3-8.

A. × 'Coronation Gold' holds its 3″-4″ golden blooms on stems 3′ or taller over greener, looser, larger foliage. Zones 3-8.

A. millefolium, with small white flower clusters rising 1′-2′ above mats of ferny green leaves, has produced many colorful cultivars and hybrids. Zones 3-8.

How to grow: Plant or divide yarrows in spring or fall. Divide every 2-3 years to keep plants vigorous and less likely to lean over when in bloom. Plant in full sun in average, well-drained soil. Generally tough and adaptable, yarrows tolerate poor soil and drought well. In very humid regions, yarrows with gray or silvery leaves may succumb to leaf diseases within a year or two, so grow green-leaved yarrows in those areas. You may want to stake the taller cultivars, especially if you grow them in more fertile soil.

Landscape uses: The flat flower heads of yarrows provide a pleasing contrast to mounded or upright, spiky plants in a border. Try them alone in a hot, dry area. Fresh or dried, yarrows are wonderful as cut flowers. For long-lasting dried flowers, cut the heads before they shed pollen and hang them upside down in a warm, well-ventilated, sunless room.

Best cultivars: The 'Galaxy' series, hybrids between *A. millefolium* and *A. taygetea,* grow 2′-3′ tall and bloom in red, pink, salmon, and yellow shades that are attractive and unusual for yarrows. ❖

Aesculus

Horse chestnut, buckeye. Deciduous flowering trees or shrubs.

Description: The trees and shrubs in this genus are noteworthy for their abundant pyramidal flower clusters. All have opposite compound leaves, composed of five or more coarse leaflets fanning out from a central petiole.

Aesculus × *carnea,* red horse chestnut, is a cross between *A. hippocastanum* and *A. pavia.* This round-headed tree bears red flowers in mid-spring, followed by spiny fruits; mature height is about 40'. Zones 5-7.

A. glabra, Ohio buckeye, is a native tree of rounded habit and a mature landscape height of 20'-40'. Pale yellow flowers appear mid-spring, followed by spiny fruits and yellow or orange fall color. Zones 4-6.

A. hippocastanum, common horse chestnut, is a rounded tree that grows 50'-75' tall. The mid- to late-spring flower clusters are white, blotched with red and yellow, and are followed by large, very spiny fruits. Zones 4-6.

A. octandra, yellow buckeye, grows 60'-70'. Yellow flowers appear in mid- to late spring, followed by smooth fruits. Zones 5-7.

A. parviflora, bottlebrush buckeye, is a spreading shrub that bears white flowers in summer. This native has a rounded form, smooth fruit, and a height of 8'-12'. Zones 5-8.

A. pavia, red buckeye, is a red-flowered Southern native of 10'-20' tall. Zones 4-9.

How to grow: Horse chestnuts grow in full sun or light shade, performing best in acid, well-drained, and evenly moist soils. Leaf blotch may disfigure Ohio buckeye and common horse chestnut; both red horse chestnut and yellow buckeye resist this disease problem.

Landscape uses: Use common horse chestnut, red horse chestnut, and yellow or Ohio buckeye as shade trees in medium- to large-scale sites. Red buckeye naturalizes well in a woodland garden; plant bottlebrush buckeye in large clumps. ❖

Ageratum

Ageratum, flossflower. All-season annuals.

Description: Ageratums bear clouds of small, fuzzy, blue or white flowers on 1' mounds of rather large, rough, dark green leaves.

How to grow: Start from seeds in March or buy transplants. After all danger of frost is past, set out in full sun or partial shade and average soil. Space dwarfs about 6" apart; taller cultivars need 10".

Landscape uses: Ageratums look best massed in beds and borders or as an edging for taller plants. The blue cultivars combine beautifully with yellow marigolds.

Best cultivars: 'Blue Danube' and 'Madison', both 8", medium blue; 'Blue Mink', 10", powder blue; 'Summer Snow', 8", white; 'Bavaria', 14", white with blue edge. ❖

Ajuga

Ajuga, bugleweed. Perennial groundcovers.

Description: *Ajuga reptans,* ajuga or common bugleweed, forms attractive dark green rosettes 2"-3" wide, and spreads by runners 3"-10" long. Cultivars may have bronze, purple, or variegated foliage. Sturdy blue, white, or pink flower spikes bloom in May and June, reaching 4"-6" tall. Zones 4-8.

How to grow: In the spring, set young plants 6"-12" apart in moist, well-drained soil in full sun or partial shade. Ajugas will tolerate heavy shade, but are not heat- or drought-resistant. Feed lightly—overfeeding encourages fungal diseases.

Landscape uses: Use this groundcover to brighten up your garden with carpets of spring color. It is attractive planted under trees or along borders. Don't plant ajuga next to your lawn unless you use a sturdy edging; the ajuga can take over. ❖

Albizia

Albizia, mimosa, silk tree. Deciduous flowering trees.

Description: *Albizia julibrissin,* mimosa, is a single- or multiple-trunked tree with a sprawling, vase-shaped habit. Mimosas normally grow to 15'-25' in the landscape, although larger, older trees have reached 40'. The alternate leaves are compound with numerous small leaflets that create a fine-textured, tropical look. These fernlike leaves fold up on summer nights. Mimosas bloom in silky pink puffs of stamens as early as May in the South and as late as July in the North; flowering continues sporadically through the summer. Dark seedpods, 5"-7" long, appear in late summer; the leaves drop with little or no fall color. Zones 5-9.

How to grow: Plant these trees in sunny, well-drained sites, and water during the first one or two summers until established. Mimosas are very drought-tolerant and will also endure saline and alkaline soils. Vascular wilt and mimosa webworm are common problems. Caused by a soil fungus that enters trees through the roots, vascular wilt has destroyed many Southern mimosas. In the North, the fungus seems unable to overwinter in the soil, and wilt is less of a problem. Remove infected trees; don't plant mimosas where others have grown. To control webworms, penetrate webs with a forceful spray of BTK (*Bacillus thuringiensis* var. *kurstaki*). Spray weekly until feeding stops. Mimosa itself can be a pest as it reseeds easily and resprouts from stumps. Use it with discretion.

Landscape uses: Mimosa makes an interesting and exotic-looking focal point and can serve admirably as a shade tree. Its size and fine texture make it useful in small-scale landscapes. Use mimosas to dress up areas where other trees languish in poor, dry soil.

Best cultivars: *A. julibrissin:* 'Alba' has white flowers; 'E. H. Wilson', also called 'Rosea', is somewhat hardier than the species. ❖

Alcea

Hollyhock. Summer-blooming biennials.

Description: *Alcea rosea,* hollyhock, is an old-fashioned favorite that bears its 3″-5″ rounded blooms in two forms: saucerlike singles with a central, knobby yellow column, or double puffs strongly reminiscent of tissue-paper flowers. Colors include shades of white, pink, red (sometimes so dark it appears almost black), and yellow. The blooms decorate much of the 2′-9′, upright, leafy stems that rise above large masses of rounded or scalloped, rough leaves on long stems. Zones 3-8.

How to grow: Set out larger, nursery-grown plants in spring for summer bloom or smaller ones in fall for bloom next year. You can also start them from seed: Sow in midwinter for possible bloom the same year, or start them after the hottest part of summer for planting out in fall. Most hollyhocks self-sow readily if you let a few flowers go to seed. They prefer full sun to light shade in average to rich, well-drained, moist soil. Water during dry spells, and stake the taller cultivars.

Hose off spider mites and handpick Japanese beetles, which eat both flowers and leaves. Aptly named rust disease shows up as reddish spots on the leaves and stems and can quickly disfigure or destroy a planting. Removing infected leaves and all dead leaves may help, or grow plants in out-of-the-way spots where the damage is less noticeable.

Landscape uses: Hollyhocks look their best in very informal areas such as cottage gardens, along fences and foundations of farm buildings, and on the edges of fields. Try a small group at the rear of a border.

Best cultivars: 'Majorette', 3″ lacy double flowers on 2′-3′ stems; 'Powderpuff', 4″ double blooms on 4′-5′ stems; 'Chater's Double', mostly double 3″-4″ flowers on 6′ plants; 'Nigra', 3″ red-black single blooms on 5′ stems; 'Singles', classic single-flowered form in white, yellow, pink, or red on 6′-7′ plants. ❖

All-America Selections

Have you ever wondered what the All-America Selections Winner symbol printed on seed packets, plant labels, or garden catalogs means? It's a sign that the nonprofit organization All-America Selections (AAS) has tested and evaluated the plant and selected it as a superior cultivar suitable for home gardens.

AAS tests new cultivars each year at more than 30 flower and 20 vegetable test gardens throughout the United States and Canada. Test gardens are located at universities, botanical gardens, and other horticulture facilities.

Plant breeders initiate testing by sending seeds of their new and different plants to AAS. The new entries are grown next to past winners and standard cultivars. Volunteer judges approved by AAS evaluate the cultivars.

The judges look for flowers with attractive, long-lasting blossoms. They also evaluate uniformity, fragrance, and resistance to disease, insects, and weather stress. Vegetables are judged for yield, flavor, texture, pest resistance, space efficiency, nutritional value, and novelty effect.

ALL-TIME WINNERS

In 1984 in conjunction with its fiftieth anniversary, AAS selected the All-American Selections All-Time Winners. These outstanding cultivars were chosen from past winners by garden writers and home gardeners across North America. Topping the All-Time Winners list are:

- First Place Vegetable: 'Sugar Snap' pea, 1979 AAS Winner
- Runner-Up Vegetable: 'Green Comet' broccoli, 1969 AAS Winner
- First Place Flower: 'First Lady' marigold, 1968 AAS Winner
- Tied Runner-Up Flowers: 'Queen Sophia' marigold, 1979 AAS Winner, and 'Scarlet Ruffles' zinnia, 1974 AAS Winner

The All-America Selections shield identifies cultivars honored by All-America Selections for excellence in home gardens.

Judges score plants numerically, and AAS selects potential winners based on judges' scores. Only about 5 percent of the seeds entered each year win awards.

Gold Medal winners are flowers and vegetables that represent a breeding breakthrough, such as 'Sugar Snap' peas, the first edible-pod shell pea.

Flowers that garner All-America Selections Bedding Plant awards are evaluated both in test greenhouse and garden. In the greenhouse, seeds from test and comparison plants are evaluated on earliness, flower quality, uniformity, and size. After the plants are transplanted to test gardens, they undergo the standard evaluation for all AAS categories.

There are more than 200 AAS display gardens in North America. These gardens showcase past, present, and future AAS winners in a landscape setting. Visiting display gardens is a great way to get ideas for using AAS plants in your garden and landscape.

For more information on AAS, write to: All-America Selections, 1311 Butterfield Road, Suite 310, Downers Grove, IL 60515.

All-America Rose Selections (AARS) is a separate nonprofit organization that evaluates roses and recognizes outstanding new cultivars. For more information on AARS, write to All-America Rose Selections, 221 North LaSalle Street, Chicago, IL 60601. ❖

Allium

Allium, ornamental onion. Spring- and summer-blooming perennial bulbs.

Description: Don't let the "onion" in "ornamental onion" scare you off from growing these showy cousins of garlic and leeks. Their beautiful flowers more than make up for the oniony aroma they give off when bruised or cut. All bear spherical or nearly round heads of loosely to densely packed starry flowers on wiry to thick, stiffly upright stems. The grassy or straplike leaves are of little interest. In fact, the foliage on most ornamental onions starts dying back before, during, or soon after bloom and can detract from the display.

Allium aflatunense, Persian onion, bears 4″ wide, tightly packed, lilac globes on 2½′-3′ stems in mid-spring. Zones 4-8.

A. caeruleum, blue globe onion, produces 2″, medium blue balls up to 2½′ above grassy leaves in late spring; it multiplies quickly. Zones 2-7.

A. christophii, star of Persia, bears spidery lilac flowers in globes to 1′ wide on 1′-2′ stiff stems in late spring to early summer. Zones 4-8.

A. giganteum, giant onion, lifts its 4″-6″ crowded spheres of bright lilac flowers 3′-4′ or more above large, rather broad and flat leaves in late spring. Zones 4-8.

A. moly, lily leek or golden garlic, bears its sunny yellow blooms in 2″-3″ clusters on slightly curving, 10″ stems in late spring. Zones 3-9.

A. oreophilum and *A. ostrowskianum* are often confused in the nursery trade, but both are attractive in mid- to late spring. The former bears loose clusters of purple blooms on 4″ stems; the latter carries rather large rose stars on stems from 6″-12″. Zones 2-8.

A. sphaerocephalum, drumstick chives, blooms in midsummer with tiny purple-red flowers in 2″ oval heads on stems up to 2′ tall above grassy foliage. Zones 3-8.

How to grow: Alliums are easy to grow in full sun or very light shade. Site them in average,

---

CHIVES IN THE FLOWER BED

Two alliums normally confined to the herb garden make great choices for borders. Clumps of common chives (*Allium schoenoprasum*) add grasslike foliage and bright spots of light violet flowers. The cultivar 'Forescate' bears pretty rose pink blooms on shorter, neater plants to 1½'. Try garlic chives (*A. tuberosum*) in a sunny or partly shady border. Its lovely 2"–3" heads of white, rose-scented flowers bloom on 2' stems above handsome dark green, narrow, strappy leaves in dense clumps. Cut flower stalks before garlic chives set seed, or the plants will self-sow and become weedy.

---

well-drained soil that you can allow to become completely dry when the alliums are dormant in summer. Plant them with their tops at a depth of about three times their width. Don't try to grow alliums in heavy clay soil. Give Persian onions, stars of Persia, and giant onions a few inches of loose winter mulch.

Landscape uses: Plant alliums in borders, cottage gardens, and among rocks. Grow them with low- or open-growing annuals and perennials, which will disguise the unsightly leaves as they die down. Combine stars of Persia with tall bearded irises and old-fashioned roses for a spectacular show. Small masses of the giant onion blooming among green clouds of asparagus foliage makes an unforgettable and unusual picture. All alliums last a long time as cut flowers; many dry well in silica gel. Harvest the seed heads before they become completely dry and brown.

Best cultivars: Few cultivars exist, though catalog writers have created colorful names for many of the species. Look for the brighter purple *A. aflatunense* 'Purple Sensation', the large-flowered *aflatunense* hybrid 'Gladiator', and the carmine-pink *A. ostrowskianum* 'Zwanenberg'. ❖

Amaranth

Amaranthus tricolor
Amaranthaceae

This quick-growing, heat-loving crop is ideal for small gardens, producing generous quantities of tender, nutritious leaves. Some types of amaranth are grown for the edible seed; for more information, see the Grains entry.

Planting: Vegetable amaranth grows well in fertile soil with plenty of sun. Start seeds in pots in mid- to late June; transplant young seedlings to the garden, spacing them 6" apart.

Growing guidelines: Maintain even soil moisture to keep the plants growing quickly.

Problems: Chewing insects such as cucumber beetles may damage leaves. Protect plants with floating row covers.

Harvesting: Plants are ready for harvest in 30-40 days. Cut the young, tender leaves once or twice a week until plants start to set seed. ❖

Amaranthus

Amaranth, Joseph's-coat. Summer- and fall-foliage annuals.

Description: Flamboyant *Amaranthus tricolor*, Joseph's-coat, bears large leaves in rich and brilliant shades of red, yellow, bronze, and green on erect, stately plants reaching 6' tall.

How to grow: Sow seeds only a few weeks before the last frost and transplant carefully when the soil has warmed up, or sow directly in the garden when the soil is warm. Space at least 1' apart. Plants grow well in sunny, well-drained, dry, average soil, but they do best with some extra water and light fertilizing.

Landscape uses: Joseph's-coat makes a bold show in large beds and borders. Try a few in pots.

Best cultivars: 'Joseph's-Coat', to 4' with top leaves splashed red and yellow; taller 'Illumination', top leaves yellow turning red; 'Flaming Fountain', 4' with narrow scarlet leaves. ❖

Amelanchier

Serviceberry, shadbush, juneberry.
Deciduous, single- or multiple-stemmed
spring-blooming trees or shrubs.

Description: *Amelanchier arborea,* downy
serviceberry, is a multi-stemmed, round-headed
tree that can reach a height of 20′ at maturity. Its
1″-3″ egg-shaped leaves are alternate, deeply
veined, and finely toothed, much like those of a
rose. New foliage opens silvery gray, turning
medium to dark green. Fragrant white flowers
with narrow petals appear in upright 2″-4″ clusters in early spring. Fruits form in late spring or
early summer and ripen from green to red to
black. If you can beat the birds to the ripe fruits,
enjoy them like blueberries. Fall color of this
small tree ranges from orange to red. Zones 3-8.

A. laevis, Allegheny serviceberry, is similar to downy serviceberry in character and landscape attributes except that it is taller (mature
height of about 40′) and lacks the silvery sheen
on new foliage. The leaves of Allegheny serviceberry are reddish as they unfurl. Zones 3-7.

A. × grandiflora, apple serviceberry, is a
cross between *A. arborea* and *A. laevis.* It reaches
a mature height of 25′ and bears longer clusters
of larger white flowers that open from pink-tinged
buds. Zones 4-8.

How to grow: Found in the wild along
riverbanks and forest edges, serviceberries require
full sun or partial shade. Provide evenly moist,
well-drained soil, and plant in spring (in Zone 6
and north) or fall and winter (in Zone 7 and
south). Fire blight, a bacterial disease that causes
twigs to look burnt or water-soaked or to sag into
"shepherd's crooks," can occasionally pose a
problem if the spring has been wet and warm.
Fortunately, weather favoring fire blight rarely
occurs in successive years, so infected plants are
able to recover. If you have a tree with fire blight,
sanitation is the best defense. Prune diseased
twigs back to healthy wood. Be sure to sanitize
your pruners between cuts. Gather and dispose
of all fallen leaves, twigs, and branches around a
diseased tree.

Landscape uses: Serviceberries make fine
focal points in the woodland garden, providing
berries for both animals and people. They also
look good in shrub borders. Their fine-textured
leaves give them a delicate look when they color
up in fall.

Best cultivars: *A. arborea:* 'Autumn Sunset',
single-trunked form with pumpkin orange fall
color; *A. laevis:* 'Prince Charles', upright form
with bronze-red new foliage and orange-red fall
color; *A. × grandiflora:* 'Autumn Brilliance', glow-
ing red fall color; 'Forest Prince', heavy flowering and orange-red fall color; 'Princess Diana',
stunning red fall color. ❖

Anemone

Anemone, windflower, pasque flower.
Spring-blooming and late-summer- to
fall-blooming tubers and perennials.

Description: *Anemone blanda,* Grecian
windflower, produces cheerful daisylike flowers
to 2″ wide in shades of white, pink, red-violet,
and blue on 3″-6″ plants with ferny leaves.
Once established, they multiply to form low
spreading carpets. They die back completely
several weeks after blooming stops. Zones 5-8.

A. coronaria, poppy anemone, bears 3″-5″
single or double blooms in white, pink, red,
blue, and purple shades. Most of the singles
display a cluster of striking black stamens within
a central white ring. All bloom above mounded,
cut foliage that grows to 1′ or more. They are
hardy in Zones 8-9; they may survive under
thick mulch in Zone 7. They also die back after
flowering. Both Grecian windflowers and poppy
anemones bloom in spring and grow from tubers.

A. × hybrida, Japanese or hybrid anemone,
is a group of related late-summer- to fall-blooming
perennials. They bear 2″-3″ single, semidouble,
or double blooms in white or shades of pink.

The flowers appear on leafless stems 2'-5' above mounded, cut leaves. Zones 4-8.

Spring-blooming *A. pulsatilla,* pasque flower, bears charming 2" goblets in white, pink, reddish purple, and blue shades. This perennial forms 6"-10" mounds of almost threadlike, fuzzy leaves that disappear in summer after producing silvery seed heads. Zones 4-8.

A. vitifolia, grape leaf anemone, is a late-summer and fall-blooming perennial with single white flowers held 2' above vigorous clumps of dark green, lobed leaves. Zones 5-8.

How to grow: Plant Grecian windflowers in mid-fall, about 2" deep and no more than 4" apart, where the foliage of other plants will hide the yellowing leaves in summer. Grecian windflowers thrive in a sunny to partly shady spot with average, well-drained soil containing some organic matter. Water in spring if the weather is dry. Mulch with compost or leaf mold to hold moisture in the soil and encourage self-sown seedlings to grow and produce colonies.

In the zones where they are hardy, plant poppy anemones in the same way as Grecian windflowers, but slightly deeper. Farther north, start inside in late winter in a cool place and plant out after the last heavy frost, or grow in pots. Many people prefer to grow poppy anemones as annuals outside or in a cool greenhouse.

Divide or plant Japanese and grape leaf anemones during spring in partial shade, or in full sun if the soil is quite moist. They thrive in deep, fertile, moist but well-drained soils enriched with plenty of organic matter. Poorly drained sites, which may promote rot, can be fatal in the winter. Water during drought. Keep plants out of strong wind, or be prepared to stake them. Cover with several inches of oak leaves or other light mulch for the first winter in the North.

Plant and divide pasque flowers in early spring; they prefer full sun and average, very well drained, slightly alkaline soil with some organic matter. Provide extra water during dry periods in warmer zones.

Landscape uses: Grow Grecian windflowers in masses in the light shade of tall trees or with other woodland plants and bulbs. Also try them toward the front of borders (sow sweet alyssum on top of them to hide the dying leaves), or among rocks or paving stones. Poppy anemones do best in beds or in the cutting garden where they are hardy; grow several in a 12" pot for a spring show. Japanese and grape leaf anemones are glorious in borders and woodland plantings where they will colonize, providing flowers to cut. Combine pasque flowers with spring bulbs and rock plants, or naturalize them in a meadow garden.

Best cultivars: *A. blanda:* dark blue 'Blue Star'; purplish pink 'Pink Star'; vivid red-violet, white-centered 'Radar'; and 'White Splendor'. Mixes of these and others are widely available. *A. coronaria:* single 'De Caen' hybrids and semi-double 'St. Brigid' hybrids, both in the full color range. *A. × hybrida:* 'Honorine Jobert', single, white, 3'-4'; 'Prince Henry', smallish, semidouble, rose, 3'; 'Queen Charlotte', semidouble, pink, 3'; 'Margarete', semidouble, deep pink, 2'-3'; 'September Charm', single, pink with darker outsides, 2'-3'; and 'Whirlwind', 4" semidouble, white blooms, 3'-5'. *A. pulsatilla:* several color variants are available, including white 'Alba' and purplish red 'Rubra'. *A. vitifolia:* 'Robustissima', late-summer-blooming, very hardy, with semi-double, medium pink blooms on 3' plants. ❖

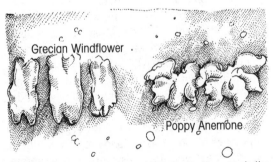

Planting anemone tubers. Before planting, soak the dead-looking tubers in warm water overnight to plump them up. Plant poppy anemone tubers with the clawlike projections pointing downward; place Grecian windflower tubers on their sides.

Animal Pests

Four-footed creatures and birds can cause more damage than insects in many suburban and rural gardens. They may ruin your garden or landscape overnight, eating anything from apples to zinnias. Most animal pests feed at night, so you may have to scout for signs such as destroyed plants, tracks, tunnels, or excrement to figure out who the culprits are.

Follow these guidelines for coping with animal pests:

• Identify the pest. Tracks are often a good clue to the pest's identity. Learn scientific names, because most mammals have more than one common name. Read books on wildlife. Perhaps you'll find an easy control solution, based on the animal's habits.

• Assess the damage. If it's only cosmetic, you may decide your plants can tolerate it. If the damage threatens harvest or plant health, control is necessary. If damage is limited to one plant type, consider dropping it from your landscape or garden plans.

• Determine the best way to prevent or control damage. Combining several tactics may be most effective. Fences and barriers are two of the best control methods. If fencing is impractical, you can use humane traps to catch pests and then release them in a natural habitat at least one mile from your property. Homemade or commercial repellents can give inconsistent results, so use them experimentally. Scare tactics such as scarecrows and models of predator animals may frighten pest animals and birds. Flooding tunnels, trapping, and shooting require killing the pests. It's up to the gardener to decide if the damage is severe enough to warrant these methods.

Deer

Deer have a taste for a wide range of garden and landscape plants. A few deer are a gentle nuisance; during a hard winter, a large herd will eat almost every plant in sight. Deer are nocturnal, but may be active at any time. Watch for deer tracks or deer droppings in your yard.

Fences: Electric fencing is the most effective way to keep deer out, but may not be practical for the home garden. Conventional fences should be 8′ high for best protection. A second, inner fence about 3′ high will increase effectiveness because double obstacles confuse deer. They're also not likely to jump a high, solid fence, such as one made of stone or wood. For small areas, snow fencing may be effective.

Barriers: If deer are damaging a few select trees or shrubs, encircle the plants with 4′ high cages made from galvanized hardware cloth, positioned several feet away from the plants.

Repellents: For minor deer-damage problems, repellents may be effective. Buy soap bars in bulk and hang them from strings in trees. Or nail each bar to a 4′ stake and drive the stakes at 15′ intervals along the perimeter of the area.

Some gardeners report that human hair is an effective repellent. Ask your hairdresser to save hair for you to collect each week. Put a handful of hair in a net or mesh bag (you can use squares of cheesecloth to make bags), and hang bags 3′ above the ground and 3′ apart.

Farmers and foresters repel deer by spraying trees or crops with an egg-water mixture. Mix 5 eggs with 5 quarts of water for enough solution to treat ¼ acre. Spray plants thoroughly. You may need to repeat application after a rain. Commercial repellents are available at garden centers. Be sure to ask if a product contains only organic ingredients. You may have to experiment to find one that offers good control.

Experiment with homemade repellents by mixing blood meal, bonemeal, exotic animal manure, hot sauce, or garlic oil with water. Recipes for concocting these repellents differ, and results are variable. Saturate rags or string with the mixtures, and place them around areas that need protection. Under the pressure of a scarce food supply, deer will learn to tolerate these repellents and will even use them as guides to choice food sources.

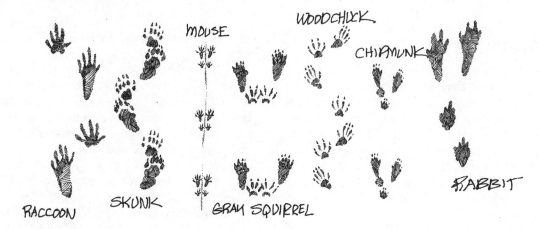

MOUSE

WOODCHUCK

CHIPMUNK

RACCOON

SKUNK

GRAY SQUIRREL

RABBIT

Ground Squirrels and Chipmunks

Ground squirrels and chipmunks are burrowing rodents that eat seeds, nuts, fruits, roots, bulbs, and other foods. They are similar, and both are closely related to squirrels. They tunnel in soil and uproot newly planted bulbs, plants, and seeds. Ground-squirrel burrows run horizontally; chipmunk burrows run almost vertically.

Traps: Bait live traps with peanut butter, oats, or nut meats. Check traps daily.

Habitat modification: Ground squirrels and chipmunks prefer to scout for enemies from the protection of their burrow entrance. Try establishing a tall groundcover to block the view at ground level.

Other methods: Place screen or hardware cloth over plants, or insert it in the soil around bulbs and seeds. Try spraying repellents on bulbs and seeds. Domestic cats are effective predators.

Mice and Voles

Mice and voles look alike and cause similar damage, but they are only distantly related. They are active at all times of day, year-round. They eat almost any green vegetation, including tubers and bulbs. When unable to find other foods, mice and voles will eat the bark and roots of fruit trees. They can do severe damage to young apple trees.

Barriers: Sink cylinders of wire mesh or ¼″ hardware cloth several inches into the soil around the bases of trees.

Traps and baits: Some orchardists place snap traps baited with peanut butter, nut meats, or rolled oats along mouse runways to catch and kill them. A bait of vitamin D is available. It causes a calcium imbalance in the animals, and they will die several days after eating the bait.

Other methods: Repellents such as those described for deer may control damage. You can also modify habitat to discourage mice and voles by removing vegetative cover around trees and shrub trunks.

Moles

In some ways, moles are a gardener's allies. They aerate soil and eat insects, including many plant pests. However, they also eat earthworms. Their tunnels can be an annoyance in gardens and under your lawn. Mice and other small animals also may use the tunnels and eat the plants that moles have left behind.

Traps: Harpoon traps placed along main runs will kill the moles as they travel through their tunnels.

Barriers: To prevent moles from invading an area, dig a trench about 6″ wide and 2′ deep. Fill it with stones or dried, compact material such as crushed shells. Cover the material with a thin layer of soil.

Habitat modification: In lawns, soil-dwelling insects such as Japanese beetle grubs may be the moles' main food source. If you're patient, you can solve your mole (and your grub) problem by applying milky disease spores, a biological control agent, to your lawn. However, if you have a healthy organic soil, the moles may still feed on earthworms once the grubs are gone.

Other methods: You can flood mole tunnels and kill the moles with a shovel as they come to the surface to escape the water. Repellents such as those used to control deer may be effective. Unfortunately, repellents often merely divert the moles to an area unprotected by repellents.

Pocket Gophers

These thick-bodied rodents tunnel through soil, eating bulbs, tubers, roots, seeds, and woody plants. Fan- or crescent-shaped mounds of soil at tunnel entrances are signs of pocket-gopher activity.

Fences and barriers: Exclude gophers from your yard with an underground fence. Bury a strip of hardware cloth so that it extends 2' below and 2' above the soil surface around your garden or around individual trees. A border of oleander plants may repel gophers.

Flooding: You can kill pocket gophers as you would moles, by flooding them out of their tunnels.

Rabbits

Rabbits can damage vegetables, flowers, and trees at any time of year in any setting. Their favorite vegetables are beans, beet tops, carrots, lettuce, and peas. They also eat spring tulip shoots, tree bark, and buds and stems of woody plants.

Fences: The best way to keep rabbits out of a garden is to erect a chicken-wire fence. Be sure the mesh is 1″ or smaller so that young rabbits can't get through. You'll find instructions for constructing a chicken-wire fence in the Fencing entry.

Barriers: Erect cylinders made of ¼″ hardware cloth around young trees or valuable plants. The cages should be 1½'-2' high, or higher if you live in an area with deep snowfall, and should be sunk 2″-3″ below the soil surface. Position them 1″-2″ away from the tree trunks. Commercial tree guards are also available.

Other methods: Repellents such as those used for deer may be effective. Commercial inflatable snakes may scare rabbits from your garden.

Raccoons

Raccoons prefer a meal of fresh crayfish but will settle for a nighttime feast in your sweet corn patch. Signs that they have dined include broken stalks, shredded husks, scattered kernels, and gnawed cob ends.

Habitat modification: Electric fencing is the best way to prevent raccoon damage, but

LOOK, DON'T TOUCH

While we may wish that solving animal pest problems were as easy as posting a "Look, Don't Touch" sign, we should heed the warning ourselves when dealing with animal pests. Wild animals are unpredictable, so keep your distance. They may bite or scratch and, in doing so, can transmit serious diseases such as rabies. Any warm-blooded animal can carry rabies, a virus that affects the nervous system. Rabies is a threat in varying degrees throughout the United States and Canada. Among common garden animal pests, raccoons and skunks are most likely to be infected. It's best never to try to move close to or touch wild animals in your garden. And if you're planning to catch animal pests in live traps, be sure you've planned a safe way to transport and release the animals *before* you set out the baited traps.

may be impractical or too expensive for home gardens. Try lighting the garden at night or planting squash among the corn—the prickly foliage may deter the raccoons.

Barriers: Protect small plantings by wrapping ears at top and bottom with strong tape. Loop the tape around the tip, then around the stalk, then around the base of each ear. This prevents racoons from pulling the ears off the plants. Or try covering each ear with a paper bag secured with a rubber band.

Woodchucks

Woodchucks, or groundhogs, are large, lumbering animals found in the northeast United States and Canada. You are most likely to see woodchucks in the early morning or late afternoon, munching on a variety of green vegetation. Woodchucks hibernate during the winter. They're most likely to be a pest in early spring, eating young plants in your gardens.

Fences: A sturdy chicken-wire fence with a chicken-wire-lined trench will keep out woodchucks. See instructions for constructing one in the Fencing entry.

Barriers: Some gardeners protect their young plants from woodchucks by covering them with plastic or floating row covers.

Other Animal Pests

A few animal pests usually cause only minor damage to gardens or are only pests in a limited area of the country.

Armadillos: These animals spend most of the day in burrows, coming out at dusk to begin the night's work of digging for food and building burrows. Their diet includes insects, worms, slugs, crayfish, carrion, and eggs. They will sometimes root for food in gardens or lawns. Armadillos cannot tolerate cold weather, which limits their range to the southern United States.

A garden fence is the best protection against armadillos. You also can trap them with live or box traps.

Prairie dogs: Prairie dogs can be garden pests in the western United States. They will eat most green plants. If they are a problem in your landscape, control them with the same tactics described for ground squirrels and pocket gophers.

Skunks: Skunks eat a wide range of foods. They will dig holes in your lawn while foraging and may eat garden plants. Skunks can be a real problem when challenged by pets or unwary gardeners.

Keep skunks out of the garden by fencing it. You can try contolling them indirectly by treating your lawn with milky disease spores to kill grubs.

Squirrels: Squirrels eat forest seeds, berries, bark, buds, flowers, and fungi. Around homes, they may feed on grain, especially field corn. Damage is usually not serious enough to cause concern.

Trap squirrels with live traps baited with corn, nut meats, peanut butter, sunflower seeds, or rolled oats. Try using repellents such as those suggested for deer control to protect small areas.

Bird Pests

To the gardener, birds are both friends and foes. While they eat insect pests, many birds also consume entire fruits or vegetables or will pick at your produce, leaving damage that invites disease and spoils your harvest.

In general, birds feed most heavily in the morning and again in late afternoon. Schedule your control tactics to coincide with feeding times. Many birds have a decided preference for certain crops. Damage may be seasonal, depending on harvest time of their favorite foods.

You can control bird damage through habitat management, physical controls, or chemical controls. For any method, it is important to identify the bird. A control effective for one species may not work for another. Also, you don't want to mistakenly scare or repel beneficial birds.

Try these steps to change the garden envi-

SCARE TACTICS

Birds can be a mild nuisance or a major pest in home gardens. Some of the birds likely to raid your gardens are the American robin, blackbird, blue jay, cedar waxwing, common starling, grackle, gray catbird, house finch, oriole, sparrow, and warbler.

You can scare birds by fooling them into thinking their enemies are present. Try placing inflatable, solid, or silhouetted likenesses of snakes, hawks, or owls strategically around your garden to discourage both birds and small mammals. They'll be most effective if you occasionally reposition them so that they appear to move about the garden. Kites and balloons that startle birds by moving in the breeze and mimicking predators are also available.

Unusual noises can also frighten birds. Try putting up a humming line or fastening aluminum pie plates to stakes with strings in and around your garden. Leaving a radio on at night in the garden can scare away some pests. Blinking lights may work, too.

Another tactic that may annoy or scare birds is to coat surfaces near the garden where they might roost with Bird Tanglefoot.

And don't forget two tried-and-true methods: making a scarecrow and keeping a domestic cat or dog on your property.

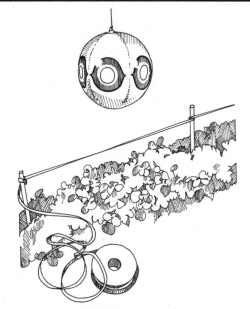

Scare devices. Hang "scare-eye" and hawklike balloons and kites that mimic bird predators in large plantings. Use 4-8 balloons per acre in orchards or small fruit or sweet corn plantings.

A humming line works well in a strawberry patch or vegetable garden. The line, made of very thin nylon, vibrates in even the slightest breeze. The movement creates humming noises inaudible to us, but readily heard and avoided by birds.

ronment to discourage pesky birds:
- Eliminate standing water. Birds need a source of drinking water, and a source near your garden makes it more attractive.
- Plant alternate food sources to distract birds from your crop.
- In orchards, prune to open the canopy, since birds prefer sheltered areas.
- In orchards, allow a cover crop to grow about 9″ tall. The growth will be too high for birds who watch for enemies on the ground while foraging.

- Remove garden trash and cover possible perches to discourage smaller flocking birds like sparrows and finches that often post a guard.

You can also use a variety of physical control devices to prevent birds from reaching your crops. The most effective way is to cover bushes and trees with lightweight plastic netting, and to cover crop rows with floating row covers. You can also use a variety of commercial or homemade devices to frighten birds away from your crops. See "Scare Tactics" above for suggestions. ❖

Annuals

When most people think of annuals they think of color, and lots of it. Annuals are garden favorites because of their continuous season-long bloom. Colors run the spectrum from cool to hot, subtle to shocking. Plants are as varied in form, texture, and size as they are in color.

Many plants are classified as annuals. In the strictest sense, an annual is a plant that completes its life cycle in one year—it germinates, grows, flowers, sets seed, and dies in one growing season. Many plants that we grow as annuals, such as zonal geraniums and lantana, are actually tender perennials. They are treated like annuals because they're not hardy in most climates and are killed by winter's cold.

Key Words
ANNUALS

Annual. A plant that germinates, grows, flowers, sets seed, and dies in one growing season.

Hardy annual. An annual plant that tolerates frost and self-sows. Seeds winter over outside and germinate the following year. Examples: annual candytuft, cleome.

Half-hardy annual. An annual plant that can withstand light frost. Seeds can be planted early. Plants can be set out in the fall and will bloom the following year. Often called winter annual. Examples: pansies, snapdragons, sweet peas.

Tender annual. An annual plant from tropical or subtropical regions, easily killed by light frost. The seeds need warm soil to germinate. Most annuals are in this category. Examples: marigolds, petunias.

Tender perennial. A plant that survives more than one season in tropical or subtropical regions, but that is easily killed by light frost.

Annuals have as many uses as there are places to use them. They are excellent for providing garden color from early summer until frost. They fill in gaps between newly planted perennials. They are popular as cut flowers. Annuals can make even the shadiest areas of the late-summer garden brighter. And since you replace them every year, you can create new designs with different color schemes as often as you want.

Landscaping with Annuals

Annuals are beautiful additions to the home landscape. You can use them alone or in combination with other kinds of plants. Bedding out is the traditional way of using annuals. The Victorians created extensive, colorful displays, usually with intricate patterns against emerald lawns, called bedding schemes. That's why annuals are often called bedding plants.

You can take a tip from the Victorians and create formal or informal designs in island beds or in borders. Fences, hedges, and brick or stone walls all make attractive backdrops for annual gardens. Annuals are also a good choice for outlining or edging garden spaces. Petunias (*Petunia* × *hybrida*), marigolds, begonias, and zinnias are ideal for beds in the sunny garden. Here are some of the best ways to landscape with annuals.

Mixed plantings: Many perennials are slow-growing by nature, so the average perennial garden takes up to three years to look its best. Annuals are perfect for carrying the garden through the first few seasons. Fill in the gaps between those slowpoke plants with the tall spikes of snapdragons (*Antirrhinum majus*), flowering tobacco (*Nicotiana alata*), and blue cupflower (*Nierembergia hippomanica* var. *violacea*). Take care not to crowd or overwhelm the permanent plants—try mid-season pruning or staking of overly enthusiastic annuals.

ANNUALS WITH STRIKING FOLIAGE

These annuals all have outstanding foliage. Some, like wax begonias, zonal geraniums, and morning-glories, also have cheerful flowers. Use foliage annuals to complement annuals grown for flowering display, or as accents on their own.

Alternanthera ficoidea (copperleaf)
Amaranthus tricolor (Joseph's-coat)
Begonia × semperflorens-cultorum (wax begonia)
Beta vulgaris (Swiss chard)
Brassica oleracea (ornamental kale)
Caladium × hortulanum (caladium)
Coleus × hybridus (coleus)
Euphorbia marginata (snow-on-the-mountain)

Foeniculum vulgare 'Redform' (ornamental fennel)
Hibiscus acetosella (mallow)
Hypoestes phyllostachya (polka-dot plant)
Impatiens New Guinea hybrid (New Guinea impatiens)
Ipomoea spp. (morning-glories)
Iresine herbstii (bloodleaf)
Kochia scoparia (summer cypress)
Ocimum basilicum (basil)
Pelargonium × hortorum (zonal geranium)
Perilla frutescens (perilla)
Ricinus communis (castor bean)
Senecio cineraria (dusty miller)
Silybum marianum (holy thistle)
Tagetes filifolium (Irish lace marigold)
Zea mays var. *japonica* (ornamental corn)

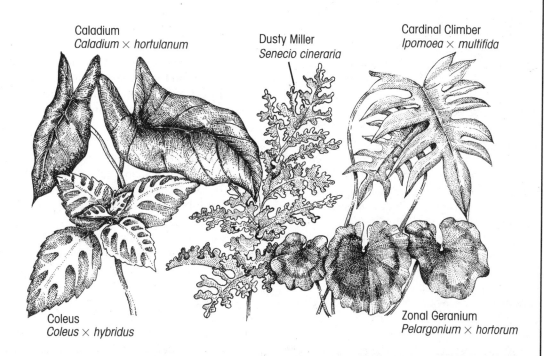

Caladium
Caladium × hortulanum

Dusty Miller
Senecio cineraria

Cardinal Climber
Ipomoea × multifida

Coleus
Coleus × hybridus

Zonal Geranium
Pelargonium × hortorum

Other annuals that are perfect for mixed plantings are annual ornamental grasses. They add elegance to the garden, with clean, simple lines and soft textures. Annual grasses are wonderful to combine with bold-textured plants like *Sedum* 'Autumn Joy' and coneflowers (*Rudbeckia* spp.). Good annual grasses include large quaking grass (*Briza maxima*), fountain grass (*Pennisetum setaceum*), and hare's-tail grass (*Lagurus ovatus*). They're especially valuable for drying.

Shade gardens: After spring wildflowers fade, gardeners often abandon the shaded garden. We tend to think of ferns and hostas as the only plants for the summer shade garden, but annuals can thrive there too. A moist, shaded spot that glows with multicolored impatiens is a welcome summer sight. Use caladiums, begonias, or wishbone flowers (*Torenia fournieri*) in pots around a shaded patio or deck. Caladiums are also nice under trees to perk up beds of pachysandra, periwinkle (*Vinca* spp.), and other groundcovers. Begonias make a colorful edging for a patio or walk. Blue browallia is great for a formal border in the dappled shade at the edge of a lawn.

Trellises and posts: Annual vines make fast-growing screens, providing privacy and shade. They help create garden "rooms." They hide unattractive garden workstations and compost bins. These vines don't need a formal trellis or extensive training. Morning-glories (*Ipomoea tricolor*), climbing nasturtiums, fragrant sweet peas, and haunting moonflowers (*Ipomoea alba*) will easily grow up any support.

You can cover a pillar or lamppost with chicken wire for quick and easy support. Store the wire at the end of the season. Branches made into a tepee frame make a unique trellis. Garden centers even sell collapsible trellises that can be moved from place to place for a temporary screen.

A fence festooned with bright blue morning-glories is a beautiful sight. But if you think about it, what would the morning-glory be without its bright green, heart-shaped foliage, especially in the afternoon when the flowers fade? Don't neglect foliage when you select annual vines. Cardinal climber (*Ipomoea × multifida*) has fingerlike foliage like a tropical philodendron. The round foliage of nasturtiums is attractive and edible, too.

Many vines combine flowers, foliage, and showy fruits. Gourds are very decorative. Their huge yellow flowers are edible, and the multicolored fruits have many craft uses. Whatever your gardening style may be, annual vines deserve a place scrambling up a trellis, post, or pillar.

Containers: Annuals are perfect container plants. Their fast growth, easy culture, and low cost make them irresistible for pots, window boxes, and planters. Best of all, you can move them around the garden to mix and match your display.

Select as large a container as you can comfortably manage. Small containers dry out far too quickly and create extra work. Choose a light soil mix that drains well but holds moisture. Don't overplant. Annuals grow fast and will quickly fill a container. Crowded plants don't bloom well and require constant watering. Fertilize containers regularly with a balanced organic fertilizer.

You can start container gardening in early spring with pansies. Summer and fall bring endless choices for sun or shade. Zonal geraniums, ornamental cabbages, and snapdragons remain attractive until hard frost. Tender annuals such as zonal geraniums, coleus, and lantana (*Lantana* spp.) can also be pruned and brought indoors for the winter.

Hanging baskets were made for annuals. They signal the arrival of summer. Use seasonal displays of fuchsias (*Fuchsia* spp.), ivy geraniums (*Pelargonium peltatum*), trailing lantana (*Lantana montevidensis*), and trailing petunias to highlight a porch, breezeway, or gazebo. Grow

ANNUALS FOR SHADE

If trees, walls, or buildings plunge part of your yard into gloom, don't despair. Count on cheerful annuals to perk things up. The jewel-like tones of impatiens or coleus will brighten even the darkest areas under trees. It's surprising how many annuals do tolerate shade. Plants in this list will grow in partial shade. An asterisk (*) indicates a plant that will tolerate full shade.

Anchusa capensis (summer forget-me-not)
Begonia × semperflorens-cultorum (wax begonia)
Browallia spp. (sapphire flowers)
Caladium × hortulanum (caladium)
Catharanthus roseus (Madagascar periwinkle)

Coleus × hybridus (coleus) *
Impatiens wallerana (impatiens) *
Lobelia erinus (lobelia)
Mimulus × hybridus (monkey flower)
Myosotis sylvatica (forget-me-not)
Nemophila menziesii (baby-blue-eyes)
Nicotiana alata (flowering tobacco)
Nierembergia hippomanica var. *violacea* (blue cupflower)
Omphalodes linifolia (navelwort)
Salvia splendens (scarlet sage)
Thunbergia alata (black-eyed Susan vine)
Torenia fournieri (wishbone flower) *
Viola × wittrockiana (pansy)

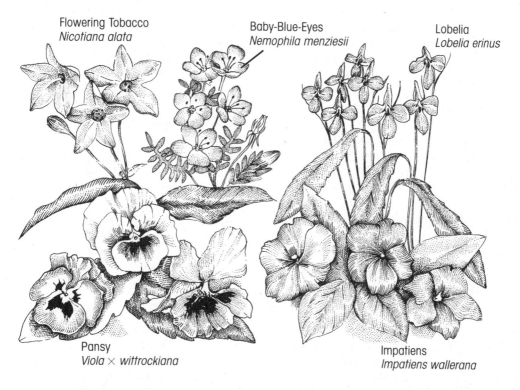

Flowering Tobacco
Nicotiana alata

Baby-Blue-Eyes
Nemophila menziesii

Lobelia
Lobelia erinus

Pansy
Viola × wittrockiana

Impatiens
Impatiens wallerana

plants singly or in combination to create eye-catching displays. Vines are especially nice in hanging baskets and are easily controlled. Choose a medium-weight potting soil that holds moisture. Remember to water often. In midsummer, baskets may need watering 2-3 times a day. Fertilize regularly with a balanced organic fertilizer. See the Container Gardening entry for more information on growing annuals in containers.

Cut flowers: Annuals are popular for cutting because they flower enthusiastically throughout the growing season. Grow them in a special cutting garden or mix with other flowers. Salpiglossis (*Salpiglossis sinuata*), cosmos, sages, and pot marigolds (*Calendula officinalis*) are excellent cutting annuals.

Traditionally, the cutting garden is set off from the rest of the garden. This approach has certain advantages. Plants can be arranged in rows by species, much like a vegetable garden. This provides easy access for cutting and weeding and allows the most sunlight to reach the plants.

Cutting flowers won't spoil the effect of the garden—in fact, it stimulates continued flower production. Choose plants with sturdy stems, showy flowers, and good colors you can use. Fragrance is also an asset, since you'll be bringing the flowers indoors. You may have to stake tall plants for straight stems and disbud to increase flower size. Remember to keep up with maintenance. Weeds compete with your plants for sunlight, water, and nutrition. For more on creating your own cutting garden, see the Cut Flower Gardening entry.

Creating a Design

When designing with annuals, remember that a little color goes a long way. Most annuals are noted for their intense, saturated coloration. Bright oranges, pinks, and reds may clash. Choose annuals with care, and make sure you create a pleasing color combination. A quick and easy way to visualize your garden is to create it on paper with catalog cutouts.

First, choose the area or areas of your yard where you want to plant annuals. Make sure you pick a site with the right amount of sun for the plants you want to grow. Sun-loving annuals need 6-8 hours of direct sun. Situate your annual beds where they receive adequate light, good air circulation, and shelter from strong winds. If your garden is shaded, choose shade-tolerant plants.

A practical but important point that's often overlooked is to make sure you site your garden within hose length of a water spigot. And as with shade tolerance, check the growth requirements of your plants, and group plants with similar requirements.

When you've picked a site, outline the shape and size of your proposed bed right on the spot with a garden hose or string. Next draw a rough sketch showing the shape of the bed, then measure and record the dimensions. Indicate north on your sketch with an arrow. Next, draw the shape of your bed or border to scale on a piece of graph paper. A good scale to begin with is 1″ on paper equals 1′ of garden area. If your garden is extremely large, use 1″ equals 2′, or 1″ equals 3′.

Look through seed catalogs and pick the annuals you would like to use. Keep in mind the colors you like. Think about which colors look good together. Consider the shape and size of the plants: spiky, mounded, or flat and short or tall. Don't forget light requirements; choose plants that match the conditions you can offer. List the plants you choose on a separate sheet and note their color, size, and shape. Cut out pictures from a catalog, clipping a 1″ × 2″ strip of each plant.

Now you are ready to arrange the plants in your paper garden. First, decide if you want a formal or informal pattern with sweeping or straight lines. To visualize your garden, refer to your list of plants. Read the descriptions of the plants and decide which plants will look best

ANNUALS FOR DRY SITES

Unlike most annuals, these plants are adapted to dry soils. Grow them in areas you don't want to water often, or in beds where the soil stays very dry.

Amaranthus tricolor (Joseph's-coat)
Arctotis stoechadifolia (African daisy)
Centauria cyanus (cornflower)
Convolvulus tricolor (dwarf morning-glory)
Coreopsis tinctoria (calliopsis)
Dimorphotheca sinuata (cape marigold)
Dorotheanthus bellidiformis (livingstone daisy)
Dyssodia tenuiloba (Dahlberg daisy)
Eschscholzia californica (California poppy)
Euphorbia marginata (snow-on-the-mountain)

Eustoma grandiflorum (prairie gentian, formerly *Lisianthus russellianus*)
Felicia spp. (blue marguerites)
Gazania spp. (treasure flowers)
Gomphrena globosa (globe amaranth)
Kochia scoparia (summer cypress)
Limonium spp. (statice, sea lavender)
Lobularia maritima (sweet alyssum)
Mirabilis jalapa (four-o'clock)
Pennisetum setaceum (fountain grass)
Portulaca grandiflora (moss rose)
Salvia spp. (sages)
Sanvitalia procumbens (creeping zinnia)
Senecio cineraria (dusty miller)
Tithonia rotundifolia (Mexican sunflower)
Verbena × *hybrida* (garden verbena)

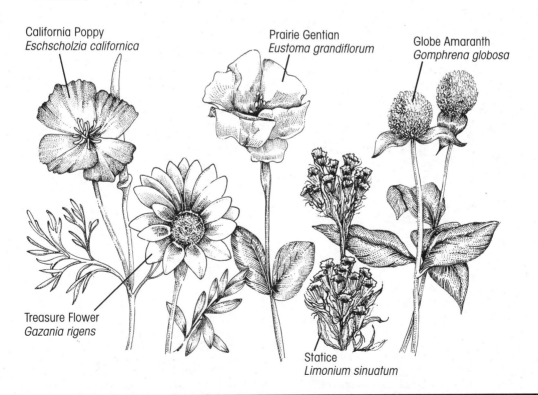

California Poppy
Eschscholzia californica

Prairie Gentian
Eustoma grandiflorum

Globe Amaranth
Gomphrena globosa

Treasure Flower
Gazania rigens

Statice
Limonium sinuatum

together. Referring to the size and height information for guidance, draw a profile of the garden. Place a sheet of tracing paper over the graph paper. Using the size and shape of the garden on your graph paper as an outline, draw the shapes of the plants you plan to use on the tracing paper. Draw spikes, mounds, lumps, and mats as appropriate, keeping the heights and widths in scale with the other plants. For example, a clump of spider flower would be much taller and wider on your plan than a clump of marigolds. When you've outlined the blocks of plants, paste the strips of catalog photographs in the appropriate places. Then you can decide whether or not your colors, shapes, and sizes are in the right places.

Designing with annuals. Mark the shape and dimensions of your garden bed or border on graph paper, drawing to scale (standard is 1" on paper equals 1' of garden). Make a list of annuals you'd like to grow. Include important features such as mature height and width and flower color. To determine how many plants you can fit in your design, see "Figuring the Fit" on the opposite page. Mark out groups of annuals on the graph paper, using the widths on your list as a spacing guide. Put the tallest annuals at the back of a bed or border, unless it's a freestanding or island bed; then, put them in the bed center. Next, using the heights on your list, draw projections up from the graph paper to mark relative heights of the groupings. Finally, cut out 1" × 2" blocks of the flowers from plant catalogs and arrange them as shown on your design to check color compatibility. Rearrange them or choose cultivars with different flower colors until you have what you want.

Figuring the fit: The next step is to decide how many of each cultivar you will need. First, figure the square footage of your garden bed. For example, a 10' × 5' bed is 50 square feet. Next, check the recommended spacing for each plant. Remember to space annuals according to their ultimate size. Seed packets and catalogs will tell you the spacing recommendations for each plant. If you use three different plants with different spacings, divide the square footage into three appropriate sections.

In the practice example, use a 50-square-foot bed with 10" spacing for all plants. Convert 50 square feet to square inches by multiplying by 144 (144" per square foot), which gives you 7,200 square inches. Then square 10" to get 100 square inches. This gives you 7,200 square inches of bed divided by 100 square inches per plant, which results in 72 plants. So you'll need 72 plants spaced 10" apart to fill a 50-square-foot bed.

Choosing What to Buy

With so many different species and cultivars on the market, you'd think it would be impossible to decide which plants to buy. It's easier to narrow your choices if you keep a checklist of what you're looking for and stick to it.

First, choose plants that match your garden design: If you need a tall plant with pastel flowers, don't be swayed by a flat of endearing French marigolds. They may look great in the flat, but they won't look so wonderful stuffed willy-nilly into your bed. Think of it as a simple rule: Don't buy plants unless you have a place for them. This will save you money and frustration, and your garden will look a lot better for your restraint.

Next, when it comes to which deep red petunia cultivar to buy, look at the mature size, rate of growth, how long it takes to bloom, and special considerations (for example, you may not like heavily veined petals). You'll have many

Smart Shopping
ANNUALS

A smart shopper never leaves home without a list—choose the annuals you want to grow and know how many you need before you get to the garden center. Then, before you buy, check the plants carefully, keeping these guidelines in mind:

● Make sure the plants are well rooted. Gently tug on the stem; a plant with damaged or rotten roots will feel loose.
● Choose plants with lush but compact foliage.
● Avoid leggy and overgrown plants. The crown should be no more than three times the size of the container.
● Never buy wilted plants. Under-watering weakens plants and slows establishment.
● Check for insects on the tops and undersides of leaves and along stems.
● Avoid plants with yellow or brown foliage. They have either dried out or have disease problems.
● Don't buy big plants. They are expensive, and smaller plants will quickly catch up once they are planted.
● If you can't plant immediately, keep plants well watered and away from frost.

Buying seeds is easier, since seed quality is usually the same for all companies, but keep these hints in mind:

● Compare costs of seeds from different companies and check seed counts per package. Prices per package may be the same, but one may have less seed than another.
● Buy seeds by named variety or cultivar. Make sure you get exactly what you want.
● Check the date on the back of the package. Make sure you buy fresh seeds. Last year's seeds are a waste of money.
● Mail-ordering requires trust, so start small. Order from a few companies, and see which seeds give the best results.
● Avoid special deals and unbeatable bargains.

more cultivars to choose from if you buy seed instead of plants, because mail-order catalogs offer more choices than garden centers do. And most annuals are easy to grow from seed.

Growing Your Own Annuals

It's better to start most annual seeds in pots or flats indoors rather than to direct-seed in the garden. Indoor planting gives you more predictable results since wind, rain, insects, slugs, compacted soil, and other hazards can combine to reduce outdoor germination below acceptable levels. There is an advantage to direct-seeding, though: With so many gardening chores, you may welcome the opportunity to get things into the ground and be more or less done with them.

If you're trying to decide whether to sow annual seeds indoors or in the garden, remember that direct-seeding works best with larger seeds that are less likely to be washed away or buried too deeply. Also, certain plants like poppies, morning-glories, and sweet peas don't like to be disturbed and should be planted where they are to grow. For seed-starting basics, see the Seeds and Seedlings entry.

Some plants such as portulaca, spider flower, and impatiens may self-sow in the garden. Their seeds survive the winter and germinate in the spring when the soil warms up. If seedlings grow in the right place, you have it made. But more than likely you'll have to transplant your volunteers to the spot where you want them to grow. They tend to come up between rocks, in the middle of other plants, and in the lawn.

Certain annuals such as cosmos, sweet peas, and ornamental grasses produce seeds that you can collect and sow the next year. However, most annuals are hybrids and will not come true from seed. If you tried to save seed of hybrid plants, the seedlings would not resemble their parents and would be of inferior quality.

You can grow many annuals easily from cuttings. A cutting is a portion of the stem that is cut off and rooted to form a new plant. Take cuttings from tender perennials that are grown as annuals. Coleus, begonias, geraniums, fuschias, and impatiens are some common annuals that root easily. Cuttings are a great way to save a favorite color of impatiens or rejuvenate an old geranium that has gotten too big for its container. Cuttings also let you start new plants for planting out next year. You'll get a nice houseplant for the winter and a jump on the spring planting season.

Working the Soil

Annuals prefer a loamy soil that's well drained and moisture-retentive, with plenty of organic matter. If your soil tends to sand or clay, you can bring it closer to the ideal by incorporating lots of compost and other organic materials like shredded leaves. Annuals are heavy feeders. Their rapid growth requires a ready supply of available nutrients. If the soil is well prepared and fertilized prior to planting, most annuals won't need additional feeding.

A complete soil analysis from your local extension office or a soil-testing lab is very useful. It will tell you the nutrient availability and pH of your soil. The pH range for annuals is 6.0-7.5, or slightly acid to slightly alkaline. For more on soil and soil testing, see the Soil entry.

Once you know your soil needs, you are ready to work. The best way to prepare soil for planting is by double digging. The job requires a strong back and a large dose of persistence. But the arduous task has its rewards: Plants will grow with unbelievable gusto. Incorporate a balanced organic fertilizer according to directions. For details on digging, see the Double Digging entry; for more on organic fertilizers, see the Fertilizers entry.

If you don't have time or inclination to double dig, turn the soil evenly to a shovel's depth. Incorporate soil amendments and fertilizers as necessary. Break up all large clods and even out the planting bed.

ANNUALS FOR DAMP SITES

If you're trying to garden in a low area where conditions stay fairly boggy, don't despair. You can grow some of the most beautiful annuals on a damp site. In fact, one of the most striking annuals of all—the towering castor bean—doesn't mind wet feet. All the annuals in this list tolerate moist soil. An asterisk (*) indicates a plant that thrives in very moist soil.

Caladium × *hortulanum* (caladium)
Catharanthus roseus (Madagascar periwinkle)

Cleome hasslerana (spider flower)
Coleus × *hybridus* (coleus)
Exacum affine (Persian violet)
Hibiscus spp. (mallows)
Impatiens wallerana (impatiens)
Limnanthes douglasii (meadow foam) *
Mimulus × *hybridus* (monkey flower) *
Myosotis sylvatica (forget-me-not) *
Ricinus communis (castor bean)
Torenia fournieri (wishbone flower)
Viola × *wittrockiana* (pansy)

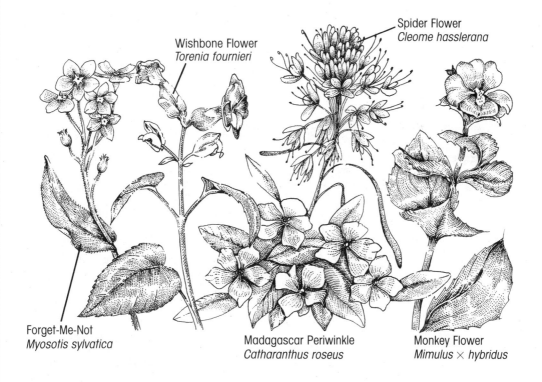

Wishbone Flower
Torenia fournieri

Spider Flower
Cleome hasslerana

Forget-Me-Not
Myosotis sylvatica

Madagascar Periwinkle
Catharanthus roseus

Monkey Flower
Mimulus × *hybridus*

Planting

The first warm days of spring draw droves of gardeners to the nurseries. It's tempting to buy annuals early and get them into the ground. While early shopping may be advisable to ensure the best selection, don't be too hasty. Know the last frost date for your area, and don't plant tender annuals until after this date.

Planting is easy in well-prepared soil. With cell packs, push out the plant from below into your waiting hand. The roots will usually be tightly packed in the ball of soil. Don't be afraid to break them up a bit—otherwise, plants may be stunted. Fast-growing annuals will quickly recover from the shock of transplanting.

Remove the rims and bottoms of peat pots before planting. If there are not too many roots sticking through, remove the whole pot. This allows maximum contact of the garden soil and the potting soil. Slice the outside of peat pellets at least three times to cut the net that encircles them.

Take plants from flats or pots one at a time so you don't dry out the root balls. If soil in the flats is dry, water the plants before planting. Be careful not to plant too deeply—set out your plants at the same depth as they were growing in the flat or pot. Firmly pack the soil around the stem. Water thoroughly and deeply as soon as planting is done. Don't plant during the heat of the day, or plants may wilt and die before you get water to them.

If you're planting a formal design, you'll want the annuals spaced evenly in your bed or border and you may want to use a spacing board. Making a spacing board is simple; directions are given in the Planting entry. Common spacing for most annuals is 10″-12″ apart.

Informal designs do not require such careful attention to placement, and spacing can be estimated using the length of your trowel as a guide.

Maintaining Annuals

If you've prepared the soil well before planting, maintenance chores are pretty basic. Keep the soil evenly moist throughout the growing season. An inch of water per week is standard for most garden plants, though some annuals will thrive in drier soils.

Weeding is important in any garden, and the annual garden is no exception. Turning the soil for planting is likely to uncover weed seeds. Regular hand weeding will ensure that annuals aren't competing with weeds for light, moisture, and fertilizer. Frequent cultivation helps control seedling weeds and breaks up the soil surface, allowing water to penetrate. Put down a light mulch that allows good water infiltration to help conserve water and keep down weeds. Shredded leaves, buckwheat hulls, cocoa shells, and bark mulch are good choices.

Today's annual hybrids have been selected for compact growth, so you usually won't have to pinch and stake them. However, some older cultivars and annuals grown for cut flower production may benefit from thinning or disbudding. This will increase the size of the flowers and the strength of the stems. Tall plants such as 'Rocket' snapdragons and salpiglossis may need staking, especially in areas with strong winds or frequent thunderstorms.

Removing spent flowers keeps annuals in perpetual bloom. If you want to save seed, stop deadheading in late summer to allow ample seed set. Remove yellowing foliage during the growing season to keep down disease. If plants get too dense, remove a few of the inner stems to increase air circulation and light penetration.

Coping with Problems

Annuals are a tough group of plants, but they do get some pests and diseases. The best way to avoid problems is with good cultural practices, good maintenance, and early detection.

More On
ANNUALS

You'll find descriptions, growing information, best uses, and best cultivars in the entries for the following annuals: Ageratum, Amaranthus (amaranth), Antirrhinum (snapdragon), Begonia, Calendula (pot marigold), Callistephus (China aster), Celosia (cockscomb), Centaurea (cornflower), Coleus, Coreopsis, Cosmos, Fuchsia, Gaillardia (blanket flower), Gypsophila (baby's-breath), Helianthus (sunflower), Heliotropium (heliotrope), Iberis (candytuft), Impatiens, Lantana, Lathyrus (sweet pea), Lobelia, Lobularia (sweet alyssum), Lupinus (lupine), Nicotiana (flowering tobacco), Nigella (love-in-a-mist), Papaver (poppy), Pelargonium (zonal geranium), Petunia, Portulaca, Rudbeckia (coneflower), Salvia (sage), Scabiosa (pincushion flower), Tagetes (marigold), Tropaeolum (nasturtium), and Zinnia.

Healthy plants develop fewer problems. Here are a few simple tips:

• Water early in the day to enable plants to dry before evening. This helps prevent leaf spot and other fungal and bacterial problems.

• Don't overwater. Waterlogged soil is an invitation to root rot organisms.

• Remove old flowers and yellowing foliage to destroy hiding places for pests.

• Remove plants that develop viral infections and dispose of them.

• Never put diseased plants in the compost.

• Early detection of insects means easy control.

Many insects that attack annuals can be controlled by treating the plants with a spray of water from a hose. Treat severe infestations with appropriate organic control such as an insecticidal soap. Follow label recommendations. For more on natural pest and disease control, see the Organic Pest Management entry. ❖

Antirrhinum

Snapdragon. Summer- and fall-blooming annuals.

Description: Snapdragons have flowers in all major colors except blue, plus bi- and tricolored flowers. Most bear the typical "little dragon mouth" flowers, but there are also single, open (penstemon-flowered) and double (azalea-flowered) cultivars. Upright cultivars grow 1'-3' tall, with long flower spikes atop stiff stems bearing small leaves. Dwarf cultivars grow 4"-12" tall with almost equal spread.

How to grow: Sow seeds of taller cultivars in early February for bloom beginning in mid-summer, or in June for plants to winter over for bloom late next spring. You can also buy transplants for setting out after hard spring frosts. Pinch plants when they are 3"-4" tall for more bloom spikes. Stake or hill them up with 4" of soil as they grow. After bloom, cut them back halfway, and feed them for a second bloom. Sow seeds of dwarf cultivars a month before the last frost, or sow directly after the danger of hard frost is past.

Snapdragons provide color all season and beyond light frosts in fall. They do best in a sunny spot with light, sandy, humus-rich soil with a neutral pH. Rust, a fungal disease, can cause brown spots on leaves, flowers, and stems, followed by wilting and death of the plant. Grow only rust-resistant cultivars.

Landscape uses: Grow the tall cultivars in a cutting garden for superb cut flowers, but don't overlook their temporary use as tall spikes in beds and borders. The dwarfs make colorful groundcovers and fill gaps left by withering bulb foliage.

Best cultivars: Mixes: 'Rocket', 2'-3'; 'Princess', 1½'; 'Little Darling', 1'; 'Floral Carpet', 8"; 'Magic Carpet', 6". Also try penstemon-flowered 'Bright Butterflies', 2½' and azalea-flowered 'Madame Butterfly', 2½'. ❖

Apple

Malus pumila and other spp.
Rosaceae

Biting into a crisp apple picked fresh from your own tree is like eating sweet corn straight from your garden. You may never taste anything quite so delicious. Growing apples organically takes perseverance, but it can be done. Apple trees come in a wide range of sizes to suit any yard and make good landscape trees.

The Fruit Trees entry covers many important aspects of growing apples and other tree fruits; refer to it for additional information on planting, pruning, and care.

Selecting trees: Since apple trees take at least several years to bear fruit, it pays to select trees carefully before you invest time and energy in them. Consider these factors:

• Apples are subject to many serious diseases such as apple scab. Choose resistant cultivars; new ones are being released every year.

• Tree size is an important consideration. Standard trees can reach 30′ and take 6 years to bear first fruit. Most home gardeners prefer dwarf and semidwarf trees, which are grafted on a rootstock that keeps them small, grow 6′-20′ tall (depending on the rootstock used), and produce full-sized apples in just a few years. See "A Range of Rootstocks" on this page for more information on advantages and disadvantages of various rootstocks. The final height of your tree will also depend on what cultivar you select, because some cultivars are more compact than others. Tree size will also depend on growing conditions and pruning and training techniques.

• Some cultivars bear fruit on short twigs called spurs, while others produce fruit along branches. Spur-bearing cultivars have more fruiting twigs than nonspur trees do, and produce more apples. Cultivars that have a strong, horizontal branching habit are easy for beginners to prune.

• Most cultivars need to be pollinated by a second compatible apple or crab apple within

A RANGE OF ROOTSTOCKS

All apple trees you buy from catalogs or nurseries are made by grafting small pieces of the cultivar onto rootstocks.

There are many fine apple rootstocks available. Shop around until you find a nursery that offers cultivars you want grafted onto the rootstock that best suits your growing conditions.

Different rootstocks have a greater or lesser dwarfing effect. Some don't have strong roots and need staking, while others are very strongly rooted. An interstem is a cultivar grafted between the rootstock and fruiting cultivar. Using an interstem can be the most successful way to achieve a dwarfing effect. The following list gives soil, disease, and size information for some common apple rootstocks.

• 'Seedling': strong roots, full size
• 'M.27': good for containers, needs staking; makes a bush 15 percent of full size
• 'M.9': does well in moist, well-drained soil or even clay, poorly in light, dry soil, needs staking, susceptible to fire blight, resistant to collar rot, 25–35 percent of full size
• 'M.26': likes well-drained, slightly dry soil, needs staking, 30–40 percent of full size
• 'MARK': doesn't usually need staking, resistant to collar rot and fire blight, very cold-hardy, 30–40 percent of full size
• 'M.7': does well in deep, somewhat wet soil, susceptible to root rot and crown gall, 40–60 percent of full size
• 'MM.106': does well in well-drained soil, susceptible to collar rot and winter damage, 45–65 percent of full size
• 'MM.111': tolerates a wide range of soils, drought resistant, resistant to fire blight and collar rot, 65–85 percent of full size
• 'Interstem M.9/MM.106': strong, well-anchored tree, resistant to collar rot, about 50 percent of full size
• 'Interstem M.9/MM.111': tolerates extremes in soil drainage, needs staking the first few years, about 50 percent of full size

40'-50' that blooms at the same time. Some cultivars, such as 'Mutsu' and 'Jonagold', produce almost no pollen and cannot serve as pollinators. A few cultivars including 'Golden Delicious' are self-fruitful. If you only have space for one tree, improve fruit set by grafting a branch of a suitable pollinator onto the tree.

• When choosing apple trees, consider your climate. Your tree will produce more fruit and live longer if it is suited to your area.

• Antique apples can be fun to grow but require careful selection because many are susceptible to diseases. Since many were selected for keeping quality, not flavor, taste before you plant.

• Sample the fruit before you choose. Find some less familiar cultivars at farmers' markets and orchards, or order a collection from a mail-order sampler company. The range of aroma, taste, flesh texture, shape, color, and size of apples is far greater than a trip to your local supermarket would even begin to suggest.

Planting: Buy dormant one-year-old un-branched grafted trees, sometimes called whips. Plant apples in the early spring in most areas, or in late fall in the Deep South. Space standard trees 20'-30' apart, semidwarfs 15'-20', and dwarfs 10'-15'. Start training immediately. See the Fruit Trees entry for instructions on planting and training.

Fertilizing: Healthy apples grow 8"-12" per year. Have the soil tested if growth is less. Low levels of potassium, calcium, or boron may cause reduced growth and poor-quality fruit.

Apples thrive with a yearly mulch of 2" of compost. Cover crops of buckwheat and fava beans are good, too. They provide weed control, encourage beneficial insects, and help improve soil structure.

Apples also benefit from foliar feeding. Spray seaweed extract when the buds show color, after the petals fall, and again when young fruits reach ½"-1" diameter to improve yields. If testing shows calcium is low, spray 4 more times at two week intervals. Gypsum spread on the soil also raises calcium levels.

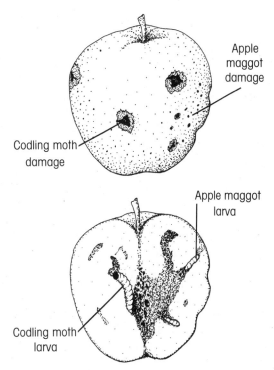

Apple maggot damage

Codling moth damage

Apple maggot larva

Codling moth larva

Common apple pests. Small discolored spots and pits on the apple surface are a sign of apple maggots; in severe infestations, whole fruits are misshapen and gnarled. When codling moth larvae tunnel into fruits, they often leave large, obvious entrance scars.

Pruning: Begin training your trees to a central leader shape immediately after planting. Prune trees yearly, generally in late winter or early spring. Illustrated instructions for the central leader system are on page 253.

Thinning: Once your tree starts bearing, you need to remove excess fruit if you want large and flavorful apples. Thinning also helps prevent trees from bearing fruit every other year. Remove the smaller apples in each cluster before they reach 1" in diameter. Leave one fruit per spur on dwarf trees, two per spur on larger trees.

Problems: Insects and diseases are a major frustration for organic apple growers, but new resistant cultivars and pheromone-bated insect traps make it easier to grow apples organically.

Common apple pests include apple maggots, codling moths, green fruitworms, leafhoppers, mites, and plum curculios. For descriptions and control methods see "Fruit Tree Insects and Diseases" on page 256. "Common Apple Pests" on page 29 shows the damage caused by codling moths and apple maggots. Plum curculio is illustrated on page 119.

Aphids, scale, and tarnished plant bugs can also cause problems; "The Top Ten Garden Insect Pests in America" on page 344 gives descriptions and controls for each.

Fall webworms and tent caterpillars spin webs in branches and munch on leaves. Remove and destroy webs as soon as you see them. Spray BTK (*Bacillus thuringiensis* var. *kurstaki*) where caterpillars are feeding.

Leafrollers pull leaves together and spin small webs. They feed on buds, leaves, and developing fruit. Native beneficial insects such as parasitic wasps help control them. Spray dormant oil just before bud break to kill eggs. Monitor with pheromone traps, and spray with BTK or neem before they spin webs; handpick after webs appear.

To help prevent disease problems, burn all prunings as well as fallen leaves and fruit, or put them in sealed containers for disposal with household trash. Here are some common diseases to watch for:

• Fire blight is illustrated on page 447. "Fruit Tree Insects and Diseases" on page 256 lists fire blight controls.

• Apple scab is illustrated on this page. Plant resistant cultivars to avoid it. Rake up and dispose of fallen leaves, apples, and prunings where it overwinters. Scab likes damp weather. Spray sulfur or lime-sulfur as soon as the buds show green, and every week until midsummer if the weather is dry, or until 30 days before harvest if the weather is wet. Use lime-sulfur sparingly after leaves expand fully, because lime-sulfur can burn leaves, especially in hot weather.

• Black rot causes small brown spots on

Apple scab. Apple scab shows up on leaves as olive green spots with rough, feathery edges. The leaf spots later become raised and look velvety. Raised, dark green areas appear on developing apples; the areas turn black as the misshapen fruits mature.

fruit, which may expand in zones of brown and black. Black dots appear on the spots, and apples shrivel and mummify. It also causes cankers on twigs. Remove and destroy cankers and mummified fruit. Spray with sulfur to control.

• Cedar apple rust causes bright orange spots on leaves and fruit. Fruits may drop prematurely. Eastern red cedar (*Juniperus virginiana*) and other junipers are alternate hosts for the rust fungi; remove any of these trees growing within 300 yards. Also remove susceptible flowering crab apples and hawthorns. Plant resistant cultivars. Spray with sulfur or copper every week until symptoms disappear. Don't spray with copper more than two times during the summer because it may interfere with formation of the following year's fruit buds.

• Powdery mildew covers leaves and shoot tips with a white to pearly gray velvety layer. It kills buds at the shoot tips, causing deformed trees. Plant resistant cultivars. Prune out infected shoots during dry conditions. Spray as for apple scab.

APPLE CIDER

In past centuries, apples were used for making cider, both alcoholic and sweet, as well as for baking, drying, and eating fresh. If you have some extra apples or some that are not top-quality, you can make cider, too. Wash well, remove any rotten parts, and grind the whole apples into pulp. Then squeeze out the juice. For small quantities, you can put the apple pulp in a coarse cloth bag and hang it over a bucket to let the juice drain out. For a large amount, you'll need a cider or fruit press. Put the cider into jugs and let the particulates settle to the bottom. Carefully pour or siphon the finished cider off the muck. Refrigeration will keep your cider from fermenting, or "going hard", for a week or so. Freeze or pressure-can it to keep it sweet longer.

• Bitter pit, small pockets of brownish, corky tissue just under the skin that often only appear after harvest, is due to calcium deficiency. If bitter pit has been a past problem, spray leaves with seaweed extract to help correct it. Or spray soluble boron or foliar calcium in a seaweed base at full bloom and again when petals fall. High nitrogen levels increase the problem.

• Collar rot is encouraged by winter injury. The cankers form near the soil line and can girdle and kill trees. Choose resistant rootstocks and plant in well-drained soil.

Harvesting: Apples ripen from midsummer through late fall. Early apples tend to ripen unevenly over several weeks. Late apples can all ripen the same day. If you have room for a few trees, you can select cultivars that ripen at different times and pick apples all season.

Taste apples to decide when they are ready to pick. Skin color and the first fallen apple may be good clues, but taste is surest. If they taste starchy, they are still green. Some apples are ideal picked early. Others improve as they linger on the branch. You may have to experiment to find when each cultivar tastes best.

Lift each fruit in the palm of your hand and twist the stem. If ripe, it will part easily from the twig without tearing. Handle apples with care so they don't get bruised.

Storage: Apples vary greatly in their keeping quality. In general, late apples are better keepers than summer apples. Store apples in a humid refrigerator at temperatures just above 32°F. If you have several trees full of fruit, you might want to invest in an apples-only refrigerator. Remember to check regularly for that one bad apple that really *will* spoil the barrel.

Best cultivars: There are hundreds of apple cultivars to choose from. Here are a few with particular characteristics:

• Disease resistance: New resistant cultivars are being released every year; check nursery catalogs to find out what's new. Two good cultivars immune to apple scab are 'Red Free' with medium-sized, dark red, slightly tart fruit and 'Williams Pride' with sweet, medium-sized, dark red fruit. Both mature in mid- to late August.

'Liberty' produces dessert-quality apples, is immune to scab, and resists cedar apple rust, powdery mildew, and fire blight, and it ripens in September. 'Sir Prize', another scab-immune cultivar, bears fruit similar to 'Golden Delicious' but bruises easily and is susceptible to cedar apple rust. Two antique apples with good disease resistance are 'Summer Rambo' from sixteenth-century France and 'Yellow Transparent' from Russia.

• Ease of pruning: Cultivars that have a strong, horizontal branching habit such as 'Haralson' and 'Honey Gold' are easy for beginners to prune. Those with upright habits, like 'Red Delicious', are harder.

• Keeping quality: 'Fuji', 'Granny Smith', 'Mitsu', and 'Newtown Pippin' keep their fresh-picked quality for months. 'Jonathan', 'Priscilla', and 'Springold' begin to lose quality within weeks. 'Idared' improves in flavor after a short time in storage. ❖

Apricot

Prunus armeniaca
Rosaceae

Growing apricots can be challenging, but the sweet, aromatic fruit makes it well worth your effort.

The Fruit Trees entry covers many important aspects of growing apricots and other tree fruits; refer to it for additional information on planting, pruning, and care.

Selecting trees: Some apricots are self-fruitful, others need a second tree for cross-pollination. They are quite winter-hardy but tend to break into flower rapidly in the spring; the flowers are often damaged by frosts. Many cultivars don't do well in high-humidity areas.

Select trees grafted to seedling apricot rootstock. Avoid those grafted to peach or to dwarfing rootstocks, because they don't grow as well.

Planting: Space 20'-25' apart, or a little closer for better pollination.

Pruning: Apricot trees can grow up to 30' tall. Train them to an open center shape, as illustrated on page 254. Where diseases are a problem, limit pruning cuts, and slow growth by spreading young limbs.

Thinning: If your tree escapes frost, it may set too many fruit, and you'll need to hand-thin. Remove smaller, damaged, or misshapen fruits before the pits harden. Where summers are moist, space so the fruits won't touch.

Harvesting: Apricots bear fruit in 4-5 years. Harvest when the skin turns a beautiful orange and the fruit is soft. They dry well.

Problems: Apricots suffer from many of the same problems as peaches, see the Peach entry for more information.

Best cultivars: If you have spring frosts and humid summers, look for late-blooming, disease-resistant cultivars such as 'Jerseycot', 'Harcot', and others starting with "Har-" including 'Harglow', 'Hargrand', 'Harlayne', 'Harogem', and 'Harval'. ❖

Aquilegia

Columbine. Spring- and early-summer-blooming perennials.

Description: Unique, elaborate flowers resemble a star within a star. Each flower has five spurs, either long and delicate or short and knobby, curving behind the outer star. Flowers in shades of white, yellow, pink, red, blue, purple, and bicolors are borne above mounded, fanlike, green or blue-green foliage.

Aquilegia canadensis, wild or Canadian columbine, bears 1"-1½" graceful, hanging red and yellow flowers on 1'-2' plants. Zones 3-9.

A. vulgaris, European columbine, has 1", knobby-spurred blooms in shades of pink, blue, and purple on 1'-3' plants. Zones 3-9.

A. × hybrida is a hybrid group, with mostly spurred flowers up to 4" long in all colors on 1½'-3' plants. Zones 3-9. (Columbines are often grown as annuals or biennials in Zones 8-9.)

How to grow: Columbines grow best in partial shade and average to richer, well-drained, moisture-retentive soil. They all reseed prolifically. Two or more species or cultivars grown together will hybridize and produce seedlings with many shape and color variations, so keep them apart if you wish to preserve your favorites. Small plants, including self-sown seedlings, transplant well in spring or fall. Mature plants are difficult to transplant. You can try to divide your favorites in late summer, taking care not to disturb the fleshy roots too much, but expect mixed results. Leaf miners often make disfiguring tunnels in the foliage. Cut off and discard infested leaves; new leaves will replace them.

Landscape uses: Mass columbines in borders, woodlands, informal beds, or cottage gardens. Use wild columbine in shady wildflower gardens. Allow self-sown seedlings to fill gaps and cracks in rock gardens and walls.

Best cultivars: Hybrids: 'McKana', all colors; 'Crimson Star', red and white; 'Snow Queen', pure white; 'Biedermeier', all colors, only 1'. ❖

Arabis

Rock cress. Spring-blooming perennials; groundcovers.

Description: Rock cresses bear ½" four-petalled white or pink blooms in open clusters up to 1' tall above low, spreading, 1"-3" spatula-like leaves. The leaves of *Arabis caucasica* are soft and grayish. Zones 4-7. The leaves of *A. procurrens* are shiny and green. Zones 4-9.

How to grow: In spring or fall, set plants or divisions in a sunny, well-drained spot. They tolerate some shade but bloom less. Poorer soil encourages compact growth. Cut back trailing stems after bloom.

Landscape uses: Often elbowing out more delicate plants, *A. caucasica* is best as a groundcover or filler in larger borders. *A. procurrens* is more restrained.

Best cultivars: *A. caucasica:* 'Flore Pleno', double, longer-lasting blooms; 'Snow Cap', 6", white ; 'Spring Charm', 6", pink. ❖

Arctostaphylos

Bearberry, manzanita. Broad-leaved evergreen groundcover or large shrubs.

Description: *Arctostaphylos uva-ursi* is known as bearberry or kinnikinick. It is a prostrate, mat-forming plant that grows to a height of 6"-12" and spreads to a width of 15'. Glossy green leaves turn bronze in winter. White to light pink, urn-shaped flowers bloom in the spring, followed by red berries in autumn. Zones 2-6.

A. glauca, big-berry manzanita, is a tree-like shrub, reaching 18' tall. It has twisting branches and burgundy red bark. Leathery, gray-green, oblong to oval leaves are 1¾" long. Clusters of white or pale pink flowers appear in early spring, producing brownish berries. Zones 7-9.

How to grow: Acidic sandy or poor soils that are constantly moist are best for bearberry, which is native to sandy beaches and bogs. In the southern end of its hardiness range, use bearberry mostly where summers are relatively cool, in high altitudes, or on north-facing slopes. Provide full sun or partial shade, plus protection from wind, and you'll have a rampant grower where few other plants will perform. Plant in fall or spring, using only container-grown plants. Big-berry manzanita prefers dry soil in full or partial sun with wind protection.

Landscape uses: Bearberry is a good groundcover choice for the woodland or seashore garden or a sandy bank needing stabilization. Big-berry manzanita's picturesque growth habit and colorful bark make it a striking specimen. It's also lovely combined with madrone trees (*Arbutus menziesii*), which also have colorful bark.

Best cultivars: *A. uva-ursi:* 'Big Bear' has large, shiny leaves and large red fruits; 'Massachusetts' is flat-growing, with plentiful pinkish white flowers; 'Vancouver Jade' has shiny dark green foliage and deep red winter color. ❖

Armeria

Thrift, sea-pink. Spring- and repeat-blooming perennials.

Description: *Armeria maritima,* common thrift, bears 1" balls of small flowers in shades of white, pink, rose pink, and lilac on thin, wiry stems less than 1' tall. Plants have dense, spreading clumps of 2"-4" grasslike evergreen foliage. Zones 4-8.

How to grow: Plant or divide armerias in early spring or fall. Plants thrive in full sun and well-drained, average soil; they tolerate sandy, seaside, and poor soil conditions. Excess fertility and moisture cause the centers to die out.

Landscape uses: Plant closely for a tight edging or small group at the front of a border. Thrifts mix well with other small plants in a rock garden or between stones.

Best cultivars: 'Alba', 6", white; 'Laucheana', 6", crimson; 'Vindictive', 6", pink. ❖

Artemisia

Artemisia, sagebrush, mugwort, wormwood. Primarily foliage perennials.

Description: Rarely grown for their flowers, artemisias make up for their scarcity of showy blooms by producing striking gray to almost silver (or, in the case of *Artemisia lactiflora*, green), usually aromatic foliage. *A. ludoviciana*, white sage, grows 2'-3' tall and spreads rapidly, bearing coarsely toothed, 4" elongated gray leaves. Zones 4-8.

A. × 'Powis Castle', a shrubby hybrid, also grows 2'-3' but spreads its branches of very fine gray foliage 3'-4'. Zones 5-8.

A. schmidtiana, silvermound artemisia, resembles a 1' high and wide rounded pile of silver feathers. Zones 3-7.

A. lactiflora, white mugwort, flaunts its large but lacy green leaves and summer-blooming 1'-2' long, creamy flower clusters 6' above its quieter cousins. Zones 5-8.

How to grow: Set out white sage and white mugwort plants or divisions in spring or fall. It's better to start with small plants of 'Powis Castle' and silvermound artemisia in spring, rooting cuttings in summer for overwintering to provide insurance for next year. All of the gray-foliaged artemisias luxuriate in sunny, very well drained (or even dry) sites with average to poor soil. Their foliage will turn greenish and/or the plants will flop open in shade, rich soil, and extreme humidity. Control the sometimes rampantly spreading white sage cultivars by dividing often and by cutting back hard in late spring. White mugwort tolerates some shade and requires a more moist and fertile soil. It often needs a strong support.

Landscape uses: Artemisias provide some of the best grays for sunny borders, beds, and large difficult areas, such as near driveways and swimming pools. Their gray tones can separate and make peace between two strong colors in a border or liven up sometimes monotonous all-pastel combinations. Edge a formal bed with 'Silver Mound' or group it in irregular masses in the front of a border. Let 'Powis Castle' cozy up to a rock or hide dying bulb foliage. Giant white mugwort commands a spot at the back of a border. Its gentle foliage and flower colors tone down the bright golds and yellows of tall daisy-family members.

Best cultivars: *A. ludoviciana*: both 'Silver King' and 'Silver Queen' grow 2'-3' tall, with 'Silver Queen' being a bit shorter and more silvery than 'Silver King'; their foliage dries nicely if cut and hung before the rather homely flowers open; 'Latiloba' is a 1'-2' tall cultivar with gray-green, lobed foliage. *A. schmidtiana*: 'Nana' is a dwarf cultivar, growing only a few inches tall. ❖

Artichoke

Cynara scolymus
Compositae

Artichokes are unusual perennial vegetables grown for their edible flower buds. Although mostly produced in the mild, humid climates of California and Florida, artichokes are adaptable to other areas. All it takes is 100 frost-free days, the proper site, and some winter protection or indoor winter storage.

Planting: The large, thistlelike plants can produce well for 3-7 years, so give them plenty of room in a sunny area. In warm areas, provide some afternoon shade; hot spells can stunt and toughen the delicious buds.

Many gardeners plant dormant root divisions from nurseries. In short-season areas, seed-grown artichokes are better because they mature earlier. Before sowing, refrigerate seeds in damp peat moss for two weeks to promote germination. Plant them ½" deep in 4" pots, 6-8 weeks before the last frost. Place in a warm, south-facing window and keep the soil moist.

Prepare the artichoke bed several weeks

before planting. Double dig the bed, incorporating compost and aged manure to promote fast growth and tender buds. When the earth warms, dig 6″ deep trenches and line with compost or aged manure. Plant roots 4″ deep and seedlings at the level at which they grew in the pot. Space 4′-6′ apart in rows 7′ apart. Protect from late frosts.

Growing guidelines: As the weather warms, mulch to keep soil moist, cool, and weed-free. Water frequently when temperatures exceed 75°F; feed monthly with manure tea. For instructions on making and using manure tea, see the Manure entry.

In Zones 7-8, you may want to try overwintering the plants in the ground. After the first killing frost, strip off the dead foliage. Pile leaves over the plants and cover them with upside-down boxes; top with a thick layer of soil and mulch for insulation. In spring, when the ground has fully thawed, uncover promptly to prevent plants from sprouting too soon.

In most areas, it is best to treat globe artichokes as annuals. Dig up the roots, brush off the soil, and cut stems 2″-3″ above the crown. Store roots in mesh bags in a cool but frost-free place; replant in spring.

Renew plants every three years by cutting rooted suckers from parent plants. Replant the suckers in a new bed, and water them immediately to get them off to a good start.

Problems: Watch for aphids, caterpillars, slugs, and snails. For more information about aphids and caterpillars, see "The Top Ten Garden Insect Pests in America" on page 344. See the Slugs and Snails entry for control methods for these pests. To prevent disease, plant in well-drained soil and practice good garden sanitation.

Harvesting: Cut orange-size buds before they open, with 1″ of stem. Use quickly for best flavor, or refrigerate up to a month.

Best cultivars: 'Green Globe', best for warm climates; 'Grande Beurre' for cold climates. ❖

Asarum

Wild ginger. Spring-blooming deciduous or evergreen perennial groundcovers.

Description: Subtle ½″ urn-shaped, three-pointed blooms in purplish green and maroon hug the ground beneath spreading mounds or mats of kidney-shaped leaves. *Asarum canadense,* Canadian wild ginger, bears dull green, fuzzy 4″ deciduous leaves to 10″ tall. Zones 3-8.

A. europaeum, European wild ginger, produces darker, smooth, shiny evergreen foliage to 6″. Zones 4-8.

How to grow: Shallowly cover the creeping rhizomes of potted plants or divisions in spring or early fall. Plant in shade or morning sun in humus-rich, well-drained, moisture-retentive soil, preferably with a pH of 5.5-6.5. Water in dry spells.

Landscape uses: Grow in masses between taller perennials and shrubs. Wild ginger is beautiful among large rocks or at the base of a tree. ❖

Asclepias

Milkweed, butterfly weed. Summer-blooming perennials.

Description: *Asclepias tuberosa,* butterfly weed, bears ¼″ starlike bright orange flowers in dense flat-topped clusters 6″ or wider over 2′-3′ erect mounds of 2″-6″ dark green elongate leaves. Zones 3-9.

How to grow: Set out container-grown plants during the growing season or bareroot plants in spring. When dividing clumps in spring, take care not to break the long, brittle older roots. Milkweed grows lustily in full sun in average, well-drained soil. It tolerates hot, dry sites.

Landscape uses: Mass in borders and cottage gardens; naturalize in a meadow. With age, single clumps make imposing specimens.

Best cultivars: 'Gay Butterflies', orange, red, and yellow flowers, less hardy. ❖

Asparagus

Asparagus officinalis
Liliaceae

Asparagus is a lovely, fernlike perennial vegetable grown for its delicious young shoots. Rich in B vitamins, vitamin C, calcium, and iron, asparagus is the first spring vegetable you can harvest, and fresh-picked spears are far more tender and tasty than store-bought ones.

Asparagus thrives in any area having winter ground freezes or dry seasons. The mild, wet regions of Florida and the Gulf Coast are about the only places where it's difficult to grow.

Planting: Select and prepare the asparagus bed with care; this crop will occupy the same spot for 20 years or more. It can tolerate some shade, but full sun produces more vigorous plants and helps minimize disease. Asparagus does best in lighter soils that warm up quickly in the spring and drain well; standing water will quickly rot the roots. To prepare the site, remove all perennial weeds and roots, and dig in plenty of aged manure or compost.

Fifty plants are usually adequate for a family of four, but ardent asparagus lovers recommend tripling that amount. Starting asparagus from one-year-old crowns gives you a year's head start over seed-grown plants. Two-year-old crowns are usually not a bargain: They tend to suffer much more from transplant shock and won't produce any faster than one-year-old crowns. Buy crowns from a reputable nursery that sells fresh, firm, disease-free roots. Plant them immediately if possible; otherwise, wrap them in slightly damp sphagnum moss until you are ready to plant. Purchased asparagus crowns may be either male or female. Female plants are less desirable, because they put a lot of their energy into forming berries; this leads to lower yields and lots of unwanted seedlings.

Seed-grown plants require more patience but don't suffer from transplant trauma like nursery-grown roots, and you can buy a packet of seed for the cost of one crown. Most seed-grown asparagus plants eventually out-produce those started from roots. Growing from seed also allows you to eliminate female plants. A bed of all male plants can produce as much as 25-30 percent more spears than a mixed bed of male and female plants.

In the North, start seedlings indoors in late February or early March. Sow single seeds in peat pots, place the pots in a sunny window, and use bottom heat to keep them at 77°F. When the seeds sprout, lower the temperature to 60°-70°F. Once the danger of frost is past, plant the seedlings (which should be about 1' tall) 2"-3" deep in a nursery bed.

When tiny flowers appear, observe them

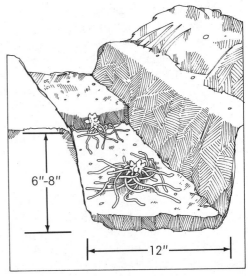

Planting asparagus. Dig 12" wide planting trenches 6"-8" deep and 4' apart. Set the crowns with their tentaclelike roots draped over small mounds of soil or compost 1½'-2' apart in the trenches; top with 2" of soil. Plant seedlings the same way, but pinch off any branches covered by soil. In two weeks, add another 2" of soil. Continue adding soil every two weeks until the soil is slightly mounded above surface level to allow for settling.

with a magnifying glass. Female flowers have well-developed, three-lobed pistils; male blossoms are larger and longer than female flowers. Weed out all female plants. The following spring, transplant the males to the permanent bed.

In milder climates, plant seeds directly into a nursery bed as soon as you can work the ground. Sow two seeds to the inch in rows 1½' apart. They take about 30 days to germinate, so mark the rows with quick-growing radishes. When asparagus shoots are 3" tall, thin them to 4" apart, and at the end of August, transplant the male plants to their permanent home.

"Planting Asparagus" on the opposite page shows you how to set crowns in trenches at planting time. Plant seedlings the same way.

Growing guidelines: Apply mulch to smother weeds, which compete with the young spears and reduce yields. Carefully remove any weeds that do appear. Water regularly during the first two years after planting. As asparagus matures, it crowds out most weeds and sends long, fleshy roots deep into the earth, so watering is less critical. Fertilize in spring and fall by top-dressing with liquid fertilizer (such as manure tea) or side-dressing with aged manure. For instructions on making and using manure tea, see the Manure entry.

Leave winter-killed foliage, along with straw or other light mulch, on the bed to provide winter protection. Remove and destroy the foliage before new growth appears in the spring; it can harbor diseases and pest eggs. Over the years, the crowns will push closer to the soil surface, resulting in smaller and less-tender spears. To remedy this, mound 6" of soil over the rows each spring. If you want white asparagus instead of green, blanch the shoots by continuing to heap up soil or mulch around the emerging stalks.

Problems: Healthy asparagus foliage is necessary for good root and spear production. Asparagus beetles, which chew on spears in the spring and attack summer foliage, are the most preva-

lent problem. The ¼" long, metallic blue-black pests have three white or yellow spots on their backs. They lay dark eggs along the leaves, which hatch into light gray or brown larvae with black heads and feet. Control by handpicking; spray or dust seriously infested plants with rotenone. These methods also control the 12-spotted asparagus beetle, which is reddish brown with six black spots on each wing cover. Asparagus miner is another foliage-feeding pest; it makes zig-zag tunnels on the stalks. Destroy any infested ferns.

Avoid asparagus rust, which produces reddish brown spots on the stems and leaves, by planting resistant cultivars. Minimize damage from Fusarium wilt, which causes spears, leaves, and stems to be small with large lesions at or

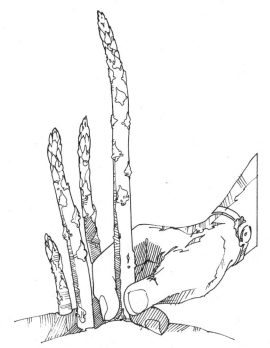

Harvesting asparagus. Don't cut asparagus spears with a knife—you may injure the crowns. It's safer to snap off spears at, or right below, ground level with your fingers.

SALT YOUR CROWNS

For healthy asparagus, add sodium chloride rock salt (NaCl) to beds more than one year old. Apply 2.5 lb. per 100' row either before spears appear or around July 4. Research shows this treatment helps asparagus resist crown and root rot diseases caused by Fusarium fungi and also improves overall growth. Don't use iodized table salt or rock salt made of calcium chloride (CaCl). Pickling salt, however, is fine for the job.

below the soil line, by purchasing disease-free roots and using good garden sanitation. Crown rot causes spears to turn brown near the soil line. Prevent crown rot by planting in raised beds, maintaining good drainage, and keeping soil pH above 6.0. If your asparagus bed does become infected by disease organisms, your best option is to start a new bed in a distant part of the garden, using newly purchased or grown plants.

If young spears turn brown and become soft or withered, they may have been injured by frost. Cover spears with mulch or newspaper when freezing nights are predicted.

Harvesting: Don't harvest any spears during the first two years plants are in the permanent bed. They need to put all their energy into establishing deep roots. During the third season, pick the spears over a four-week period, and by the fourth year, extend your harvest to eight weeks. In early spring, harvest spears every third day or so; as the weather warms, you might have to pick twice a day to keep up with production.

Best cultivars: 'Jersey Giant', 'Mary Washington', and 'Waltham Washington', all rust-resistant; 'Rutgers Beacon', good for the East and Midwest; 'U.C. 157' and 'U.C. 500', developed for the West Coast; 'U.C. 72' and 'U.C. 800', Fusarium-wilt-resistant. ❖

Aster

Aster, Michaelmas daisy. Late-summer- and fall-blooming perennials.

Description: Most asters bear clouds of daisylike, ½"-3" wide flowers in shades of white, pink, red-violet, blue, purple, and lavender. The bushy, mounded to upright plants have uninteresting elongated leaves. *Aster × frikartii* produces 2"-3" yellow-centered blue daisies on 2'-3' open, airy mounds beginning in midsummer. Zones 5-8.

A. novae-angliae, New England aster, sports smaller (to 1½") but more numerous violet blooms in late summer. Flowers are borne in dense clusters atop upright, arching stems from 3'-5' tall. Cultivars offer nearly the entire color range. Zones 4-8.

A. novi-belgii, New York aster, blooms in late summer with flowers usually 1" across on plants ranging from 1' dwarf mounds to impressive 4' giants. Colors are nearly identical to New England asters. Zones 4-8.

How to grow: Set out new plants or divisions in early spring, or in fall after bloom, in a sunny, well-drained but moisture-retentive spot with average fertility. Most resent drought and will show their displeasure by dropping their lower leaves prematurely, by not reaching their full height, and by blooming over a briefer season. On the other hand, avoid wet soil, especially for *A. × frikartii,* or it won't survive the winter. Pinch back all but the dwarf forms in early summer so they'll branch out and produce more blooms, though they'll flower slightly later than if left unpinched. If not pruned, the taller asters tend to fall over as they bloom, so stake them or allow them to arch over and through other plants. Less-fertile soil promotes slightly shorter, sturdier growth, as does dividing clumps every 2-3 years. Powdery mildew can be unsightly, especially on New York asters. You can usually hold this fungal disease to a bearable level by growing asters in a sunny, open site with good air circulation. Cultivars of New England asters tend to be mildew-resistant.

Landscape uses: Mass asters in the front and middle of mixed borders, or devote a bed entirely to early, mid-season, and late-blooming cultivars. Their billowy habit and masses of blue, pink, purple, or white flowers are mainstays of the autumn garden. Their cool flower colors contrast beautifully with the warm yellows, golds, and reds of chrysanthemums, goldenrods, late-season annuals, and fall foliage. New England asters bring rich color to moist meadows and other naturalized sites. Asters and ornamental grasses are an excellent combination. Or for a cool, sophisticated look, combine *A.* × *frikartii* with silver-leaved artemisias and pink- to rust-flowered *Sedum* 'Autumn Joy'.

Best cultivars: *A.* × *frikartii:* 'Wonder of Staffa' and 'Monch' are very similar, both 2½'-3' tall with lavender-blue flowers, but 'Monch' has flowers that are slightly purer blue and more perfectly formed. *A. novae-angliae:* 'Alma Potschke' in bright pink, 'Hella Lacy' in violet-purple, 'September Ruby' in rose red, and 'Harrington's Pink' in salmon pink, all 3'-4' tall. *A. novi-belgii:* 'Professor Kippenberg' has vivid violet-blue flowers and grows 12"-15" tall; 'Alert' bears red flowers on 10"-12" plants. ❖

Astilbe

Astilbe, false spirea. Summer-blooming perennials.

Description: Astilbes have tiny, fuzzy flowers in many shades of white, pink, and red. Flowers are borne in open or dense plumes above shiny, attractive, fernlike foliage clumps often tinged with red. *Astilbe* × *arendsii* includes the entire color range on plants growing from 1½'-3'. Zones 4-8.

A. chinensis 'Pumila', Chinese astilbe, bears deep pink flowers on stiffly upright stems to 1' tall above low, tight foliage. Zones 4-8.

A. taquetii 'Superba', the giant of the group, bears clear pink flowers in foot-long, narrow plumes that rise to 4' above large, imposing foliage. Zones 4-8.

How to grow: Plant or divide astilbes during spring or fall, barely covering the new pink shoots. Astilbes grow best in partial shade (except in areas with cool summers, where they take full sun) in moist, slightly acid, humus-rich soil. Provide extra water in drier soils to prevent leaf scorch. Chinese astilbe tolerates drier soils better than most. Scatter a little organic fertilizer around the crowns in spring to help them increase steadily. Handpick or trap slugs and snails, which abound in the moist conditions astilbes prefer.

Landscape uses: Grow astilbes in large drifts in semishady borders, woodlands, low spots, and along streams. Astilbes look magnificent at the base of a wall or among large rocks. Smaller types, especially Chinese astilbe, are ideal for the front of borders, in rock gardens, or as edgings. Leave flower spikes on the plants for winter interest.

Best cultivars: *A.* × *arendsii:* 'Bridal Veil', 2½', white; 'Deutschland', 2', white; 'Europa', 2', light pink; 'Finale', 2'-2½', light pink; 'Ostrich Plume', 3', bright pink; 'Rheinland', 2', clear medium pink; 'Fanal', 2', blood red; 'Spinell', 3', salmon red. ❖

Astrological Gardening

Since our ancestors first poked a seed into the ground, astrology has played a role in gardening and farming. Today it's easy to scoff at people who plant by moon signs and phases, but in truth, we don't know whether the idea is valid or not. The moon's position in the sky does appear to influence plant and animal behavior. People who plant and garden by zodiac signs claim they mark the cyclical movement of the planets and are, therefore, good indicators of natural rhythms in the universe.

Even those who don't believe that planting by signs of the zodiac makes any difference can understand why the sun, moon, and stars were so important to ancient peoples. They were constants in our ancestors' daily lives. Men and women used the pattern made by the stars' regular cycles in the heavens as a calendar, a way of keeping track. Then they saw that crops fared better when planted at certain times than at others. The moon was believed to be the mistress of growth. During a certain period of time (which lasts 29½ days on average), the moon passed through 12 constellations that, to the ancients, resembled animals and people. This was the zodiac, or circle of animals, also thought to influence plants and planting.

As centuries passed, ancient civilizations learned that some of the celestial objects they had called stars were actually planets. The planets also were given characteristics, and all living things were placed under both the sign of a planet and a zodiac sign. These beliefs gave rise to elaborate systems of gardening, whereby every task was thought to be best accomplished under a certain planet and constellation, ideally when the moon was in a complementary phase.

Enough first-rate farmers and gardeners follow the signs to make us take notice. Maybe they would do just as well if they didn't garden by the signs. We don't know. We *do* know that planting by the moon signs and moon phases does no harm. Why not try an experiment? Plant half your garden by the signs; the other half as you normally would. See for yourself which plot does best. Be fair and let common sense be the overriding factor. Even the most devout "sign planters" take weather and temperature into account before undertaking a gardening project.

Planting by Moon Phases and Signs

To plant by the moon phases and signs, you will need an almanac or calendar that lists the exact time and date of the moon's phases and its passage from one zodiac sign into the next. These are two different occurrences. The term *phase* refers to the moon's apparent shape as viewed from earth during the month. Due to the relative positions of the earth, moon, and sun in this period, the moon appears to change shape.

The lunar month starts with the new moon, also called "the dark of the moon." From the new moon to the first quarter and from the first quarter to the full moon, the moon appears to grow from nothing to a crescent and then to a full circle at mid-month. These are the increasing or waxing phases. The decreasing or waning phases are from the full moon through the last quarter and back to the new moon. Gardening lore holds that aboveground crops should be planted during the increasing phases of the moon, belowground ones in a decreasing phase.

As the moon makes its monthly journey around the earth, it passes through each of the constellations comprising the 12 signs of the zodiac. The moon's path is divided into 12 sections of 30°. Each section takes its name from a constellation. "The moon is in Pisces" means the moon is in the same part of the sky as the constellation Pisces. The moon moves into a new constellation every 2-3 days.

The fruitful signs: Signs of the zodiac vary in their fruitfulness, and gardening tasks seem to be accomplished best when the moon is in certain signs. The following signs are listed in order of most to least fruitful.

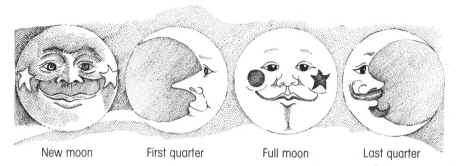

| New moon | First quarter | Full moon | Last quarter |

• Cancer is an excellent sign for planting, transplanting, budding, and grafting.

• Scorpio is a good sign for planting, transplanting, and budding, especially with vines.

• Pisces favors plants requiring strong root development.

• Taurus is semi-fruitful but good for root and leaf crops.

• Capricorn is not quite as fruitful as Taurus but suitable for root crops and tubers.

• Libra is semi-fruitful, good for root crops, vines, lettuce, cabbage, and corn.

The barren signs: Although they don't favor planting, the barren signs are good for accomplishing other gardening tasks. The following signs are listed from most to least barren.

• Leo is the most barren sign. Avoid planting when the moon is in it, but do weed and cultivate.

• Virgo is almost as barren as Leo. It is also good for weeding and cultivating.

• Aquarius is another sign for weeding and cultivating, as well as for killing pests.

• Gemini has attributes similar to Aquarius.

• Aries is barren, but onions and garlic do well when planted in it. It's good for weeding and cultivating.

• Sagittarius is the sign for seeding hay crops, planting onions, and cultivating.

For best results, planting should occur when the moon is in both an appropriate phase and a fruitful zodiac sign.

New moon to first quarter: Plant aboveground crops with seed you can see, such as asparagus, broccoli, brussels sprouts, cabbage, cauliflower, celery, grains, leeks, lettuce, parsley, and spinach. Do so in Cancer, Scorpio, Taurus, Libra, or Pisces, picking the most appropriate sign for the specific crop.

First quarter to full moon: Plant aboveground crops with seed you can see, those that contain seed within a fruit or pod, and flowers. This is the quarter for beans, grains, melons, squash, cucumbers, tomatoes, and peppers. The best signs are Cancer, Scorpio, and Pisces, followed by Taurus, Capricorn, and Libra.

Full moon to last quarter: Plant bulbs and root crops, along with biennials and perennials, because they need strong roots. Beets, carrots, turnips, garlic, onions, radishes, strawberries, and grapes do well when planted in Pisces, Taurus, Capricorn, or Libra. Harvest in Aquarius, Aries, Gemini, Leo, and Sagittarius.

Last quarter to new moon: If you must plant, do so in a fruitful sign. Undertake weeding, cultivating, and pest control in a barren sign. Harvest in one of the signs listed for the third quarter. ❖

More On
ASTROLOGICAL GARDENING

There are many systems for gardening by the moon and stars, each with elements that contradict the others. For more information on astrological gardening, pick up a planting almanac. Louise Riotte has written two books on the subject: *Planetary Planting* and *Astrological Gardening*.

For more on gardening lore, see the Folklore and Companion Planting entries.

Avocado

Persea americana
Lauraceae

Avocado trees are attractive, broad-leaved evergreens. The yellow-green flesh of the fruits is rich in oil and protein. They are easy to grow outdoors in most of California, Florida, and Texas. They also make attractive houseplants but will not bear fruit indoors.

Selecting trees: Avocado trees mature to 15'-45' and are as wide as they are high, so give them plenty of space. Mexican types have dark, rough skins and are hardy to about 22°F. Guatemalan × West Indian hybrids have smooth, green skins and are less hardy. Not all cultivars are self-fertile; check pollination requirements before you plant.

Planting: Purchase a grafted tree of a named cultivar and plant it slightly higher than it was growing in the original container. Choose full sun and very well drained soil with a pH of 5.5-6.5. If you have poor drainage, plant your tree in a large raised bed or mound. Avoid windy locations, as the trees are prone to breakage.

Care: Water young trees weekly, mature trees every other week, or often enough to prevent wilting. If your water contains a lot of salts, flood the tree every fourth watering to flush out built-up salts and lessen possible root damage. Apply a thick layer of organic mulch out to the drip line to conserve water and protect roots. Keep the mulch 1' away from the trunk.

Avocados don't require much fertilizer. If a young tree is not growing vigorously, an application of compost in early spring to midsummer is helpful. If new leaves yellow, have the soil tested. Add the necessary nutrients to soil, or use foliar sprays for quick results.

Pruning: Avocados need very little pruning. Pinch back upright shoots to control the height. Other than that, limit pruning to damaged branches, as heavy pruning will reduce yields and will expose the trunk to sunburn damage.

Problems: The most common avocado problem is root rot. Symptoms include no new growth, very small fruit, and leaf yellowing and wilting. In advanced cases, a tree may die or survive in poor health for many years. Prevent root rot by providing good drainage and not overwatering.

Avocados are sometimes attacked by fungal diseases such as anthracnose, scab, and powdery mildew. They all thrive in high humidity. Control fungal diseases by spacing trees widely and trimming back surrounding trees to increase sunlight.

Insects do very little damage to avocado trees unless the tree is weakened by disease.

Some cultivars naturally tend to fruit lightly, then heavily in alternate years.

Harvesting: Avocados bear in about three years. They ripen almost year-round depending on cultivar and location. Avocados stay hard on the tree and soften only after they are picked. They are ready to harvest when they reach full size and the skin starts to change color. Pick one and let it sit indoors for a day or two. If the stem end doesn't shrivel or turn dark, you can pick others the same size. You don't need to pick them all at once, but don't leave them on the tree too long or they'll begin to lose flavor.

Harvest avocados by cutting the fruit from the tree, leaving a small piece of stem attached. Handle carefully to avoid bruising. Avocados are ready to eat when they yield slightly when squeezed. ❖

Azalea

Azaleas (*Rhododendron* spp.) are beautiful deciduous or evergreen spring-blooming shrubs. They range in size from 1' to over 10' high. Like rhododendrons, azaleas prefer moist, acid soil in partial shade. For more information, see the Rhododendron entry. ❖

Bamboo

For many people, the word *bamboo* conjures up images of dense thickets of rampant spreading canes. While this is true of many types of bamboo, some species are not invasive. Evergreen members of the grass family, bamboos range from petite miniatures to massive giants. There are over 100 species of bamboo, found from the tropics to mountaintops. While most bamboos are tropical or subtropical, there are hardy bamboos that can survive temperatures of −10° to −20°F.

There are two main types of bamboos: running and clumping. Running types send out far-reaching rhizomes and can colonize large areas. Control running bamboos with 3'-4' deep barriers of sheet metal or heavy plastic, or cut off new shoots at ground level. Clumping types stay in tight clumps that slowly increase in diameter.

As they grow, bamboos store food and energy in roots and rhizomes. At the start of the growth cycle, the canes grow out of the ground rapidly to their maximum height. The leaves and canes produce food, which is stored in the rhizomes for the next growth cycle. Young bamboos are usually slow to establish, while older plants have more stored food and therefore grow more quickly.

Plant or divide bamboos in spring. Most enjoy full sun or partial shade. Bamboos tolerate a range of soil conditions as long as moisture is present, but they usually don't like boggy or mucky soils. They are seldom bothered by pests. A carefully chosen bamboo is a beautiful addition to any garden. Low-growers, such as pygmy bamboo (*Arundinaria pygmaea*), are ideal as groundcovers or for erosion control. Small clumping bamboos like hardy clump bamboo (*Fargesia nitida*) can serve as delicate accents; taller species, such as clumping giant timber bamboo (*Bambusa oldhamii*), make good screens or windbreaks. Some, like black bamboo (*Phyllostachys nigra*), make excellent specimens for pots and tubs, both indoors and outdoors. ❖

THE BEST BAMBOOS

Here's a list of some of the best bamboos and their characteristics:

Arundinaria pygmaea (pygmy bamboo): 1'-1½' tall; running growth habit. Zones 5–10.

Bambusa oldhamii (clumping giant timber bamboo): 25'-40' tall; clump-forming habit. Zones 9–10.

Fargesia nitida (clump bamboo): 8'-10' tall; graceful, clump-forming habit. Zones 4–9.

Phyllostachys aurea (golden bamboo): 20'-25' tall; running habit. Zones 7–10.

Phyllostachys nigra (black bamboo): 10'-15' tall; jet-black canes with green foliage and a running growth habit. Zones 7–10.

Baptisia

Baptisia, false indigo, wild indigo.
Late-spring-blooming perennials.

Description: *Baptisia australis*, blue false indigo, bears 1″ pealike purple-blue flowers in loose 1′ spikes. The 3′-4′, dense, bushy plants bear handsome 3″, cloverlike, gray-green leaves. Black 2″-3″ seedpods dry well and rattle when ripe. Zones 3-8.

How to grow: Set out small plants or divisions in spring. These long-lived plants won't need division for many years. Move self-sown seedlings when small. Grow in sunny, well-drained, average soil; allow plenty of room. Partial shade and rich soil promote weaker stems that need staking. Baptisias are drought-tolerant and pest-resistant.

Landscape uses: Feature single specimens in a border, or mass several baptisias as a foliage background for other plants. Allow plants to naturalize in a meadow. ❖

Basil

Ocimum basilicum
Labiatae

Description: Sweet basil is a bushy annual, 1′-2′ high, with glossy opposite leaves and spikes of white flowers. Many cultivars are available with different nuances of taste, size, and appearance. One of the most popular herbs in the garden, it adds fine flavor to tomato dishes and pesto.

How to grow: Plant seed outdoors when frosts are over and the ground is warm. Or start indoors in individual pots. Heating cables are helpful, since this is a tropical plant that doesn't take kindly to cold. Plant in full sun, in well-drained soil enriched with compost, aged manure, or other organic materials. Space large-leaf cultivars 1½′ apart and small-leaf types 1′ apart. Basil needs ample water. Mulch to retain moisture after the soil has warmed. Pinch plants frequently to encourage bushy growth.

Make a second sowing outdoors in June in order to have small plants to pot up and bring indoors for winter. Or as frost nears, you can cut off some end shoots of the plants in the garden and root them in water, to be potted later.

Japanese beetles may skeletonize plant leaves; control pests by handpicking.

Harvesting: Begin using the leaves as soon as the plant is large enough to spare some. Collect from the tops of the branches, cutting off several inches. Handle basil delicately so as not to bruise and blacken the leaves.

You can air-dry basil in small, loose bunches, but it keeps most flavorfully in an oil base. Mash the leaves with a bit of oil to make a paste, and freeze in ice-cube trays for a quick addition to sauces and soups. Or put mashed leaves in a jar, cover with olive oil, and place in the refrigerator. Pesto (a creamy mixture of pureed basil, garlic, grated cheese, and olive oil) will keep for a long time in the refrigerator with a layer of olive oil on top.

Uses: This widely used herb enhances the flavor of tomatoes, peppers, and eggplant. It is also great for fish or meat dishes, combining well with lemon thyme, parsley, chives, or garlic. Try it in green pea, bean, or oxtail soup or in vegetable casserole dishes. Basil vinegars are good for salad dressings; those made with opal basil are colorful as well as tasty.

Best cultivars: Basil cross-breeds easily. Two dozen kinds are offered in the form of seeds or plants, including broad-leaf, lettuce-leaf, and fine-leaf basil; lemon, anise, and cinnamon basil; and basil with either green or purple leaves.

Sweet basil is the classic plant for flavoring. Also try 'Minimum', a small-leaved bush basil; 'Citriodorum', richly lemon-scented; 'Genova Profumatissima', or perfume basil, with intense aroma and taste; and 'Purple Ruffles' or 'Purpurascens', purple-leaved cultivars that are also ideal as ornamentals. 'Spicy Globe' forms a tight mound, making it a great edging plant. ❖

Bean

Phaseolus spp. and other genera
Leguminosae

Dried or fresh, shelled or whole, beans have been a vegetable-garden favorite for many years. They are easy to grow, and the range of plant sizes means there is room for beans in just about any garden. Among the hundreds of cultivars, there are types that thrive in every section of the country.

Types: All beans belong to the legume family. Snap and lima beans belong to the genus *Phaseolus,* while mung, adzuki, garbanzo, fava, and others belong to different genera. In general, there are two main bean types: shell beans, grown for their protein-rich seeds that are eaten both fresh and dried; and snap beans, cultivated mainly for their pods.

The two groups are further divided according to growth habits. Bush types are generally self-supporting. Pole beans have twining vines that require support from stakes, strings, wires, or trellises. Runner beans are similar to pole beans, although runners need cooler growing conditions. Half-runners, popular in the South, fall somewhere in between pole and bush beans.

With the exception of a few types (as noted in the following paragraphs), most beans require similar cultural conditions. For more details, see "Planting" in this entry.

Adzuki beans, which come from Japan, are extremely high in protein. The small plants pro-duce long, thin pods that are eaten like snap beans. When mature at 90 days, they contain 7-10 small, nutty-tasting, maroon-colored beans that are tasty fresh or dried.

Black beans, also called black turtle beans, are a Central and South American staple. The jet-black seeds need 85-105 warm, frost-free days to mature. The dried beans are popular in the Deep South for soups and stews. Most are sprawling, half-runner-type plants, but some newer cultivars, like 'Midnight Black Turtle Soup', have more upright growth habits.

Black-eyed peas, also called cowpeas or southern peas, are cultivated like beans. They need long summers with temperatures averaging 60°-70°F. Use fresh pods like snap beans, shell and cook the pods and seeds together, or use them like other dried beans.

Fava beans, also known as broad, English, Windsor, horse, or cattle beans, are one of the world's oldest cultivated foods. They are second only to soybeans as a source of vegetable protein. In this country, they are mostly grown for animal feed, but there are a number of delicately flavored and very easy-to-grow cultivars available. They take about 75 days to mature and are the only bean that thrives in cold, damp weather. Cook young pods like green beans, shell and eat the fresh beans, or dry and use like dried limas.

Garbanzo beans, also called chick-peas, are bushy plants that need 65-100 warm days. When dried, the nutty-tasting beans are good baked or cooked and chilled for use in salads.

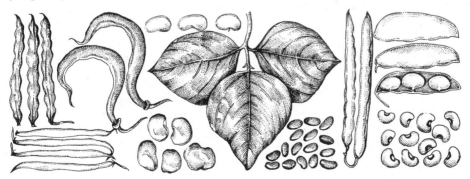

Great Northern white beans are most popular dried and eaten in baked dishes. In short-season areas, you can harvest and eat them as fresh shell beans in only 65 days. Bush-type Great Northerns are extremely productive.

Horticultural beans are also known as shell, wren's egg, bird's egg, speckled cranberry, or October beans. Both pole and bush types produce a big harvest in a small space and mature in 65-70 days. Use the very young, colorful, mottled pods like snap beans, or dry the mature, nutty, red-speckled seeds.

Kidney beans require 100 days to mature but are very easy to grow. Use these red, hearty-tasting dried seeds in soups, stews, chilies, and salads.

Lima beans, including types called butter beans or butter peas, are highly sensitive to cool weather; plant them well after the first frost. Bush types take 60-75 days to mature. Pole types require 90-130 days, but the vines grow quickly and up to 30' long. Limas are usually green, but there are also some speckled types. Use either fresh or dried in soups, stews, and casseroles.

Mung beans need 90 frost-free days to produce long, thin, hairy, and edible pods on bushy 3' plants. Eat the small, yellow seeds fresh, dried, or as bean sprouts.

Pinto beans, found frequently in Mexican cuisine, need 90-100 days to mature. These large, strong plants take up a lot of space if not trained on poles or trellises. Use fresh like a snap bean, or dry the seeds.

Scarlet runner beans produce beautiful, climbing, ornamental vines with scarlet flowers. The beans mature in about 70 days. Cook the green, rough-looking pods when they are very young; use the black- and red-speckled seeds fresh or dried.

Snap beans are also known as green beans. While many growers still refer to snap beans as string beans, a stringless cultivar was developed in the 1890s, and few cultivars today have to be stripped of their strings before you eat them. Most cultivars mature in 45-60 days. This group also includes the flavorful *haricots verts* and the mild wax or yellow beans. For something unusual, try the yard-long asparagus bean. Its rampant vines can produce 3' long pods, though they taste best when 12"-15" long. Grown mainly for their low-calorie pods, snap beans are loaded with vitamins A, B_1, B_8, and C, as well as some calcium, phosphorous, and iron. Once the pods have passed their tender stage, you can shell them, too.

Soldier beans, whose vinelike plants need plenty of room to sprawl, are best suited to cool, dry climates. The white, oval-shaped beans mature in around 85 days. Try the dried seeds in baked dishes.

Soybeans were, at one time, primarily used as animal feed and as a green manure crop. Today, there are a number of garden cultivars, like 'Fiskeby V', 'Prize', and 'Okuhara', that are delicious to eat fresh or dried. The bush-type plants need a three-month growing season but are tolerant of cool weather. Soybeans lack only one amino acid to make them a complete protein. They are also rich in calcium and have now become a staple of the vegetarian diet. They also have many commercial uses.

Planting: In general, beans are very sensitive to frost. (The exception is favas, which require a long, cool growing season; sow them at the same time as you plant peas.) Most beans grow best at air temperatures of 70°-80°F, and soil temperature should be at least 60°F. Soggy, cold earth will cause the seeds to rot. Beans need a sunny, well-drained area rich in organic matter. Lighten heavy soils with extra compost to help seedlings emerge.

Plan on roughly 10-15 bush bean plants or 3-5 hills of pole beans per person. A 100' row produces about 50 quarts of beans. Beans are self-pollinating, so you can grow cultivars side by side with little danger of cross-pollination. If you plan to save seed from your plants, though, separate cultivars by at least 50'.

Bean seeds usually show about 70 percent

germination, and the seeds can remain viable for three years. Don't soak or presprout seeds before sowing. If you plant in an area where beans haven't grown before, dust them with a bacterial inoculate powder called *Rhizobium phaseoli* that's available from garden centers.

Beans generally don't transplant well, but bean lovers with very short growing seasons can try starting them indoors in peat pots about four weeks before the last average frost.

Outdoors, plant the first crop of beans a week or two after the date of the last expected frost. Sow the seeds 1″ deep in heavy soil and 1½″ deep in light soil. Firm the earth over them to ensure soil contact.

Plant most bush cultivars 3″-6″ apart in rows 2′-2½′ apart. They produce the bulk of their crop over a two-week period. For a continuous harvest, stagger plantings at two-week intervals until about two months before the first killing frost is expected.

Bush beans usually don't need any support unless planted in a windy area. In that case, prop them up with brushy twigs or a strong cord around stakes set at the row ends or in each corner of the bed.

Pole beans are even more sensitive to cold than bush beans. They also take longer (10-11 weeks) to mature, but they produce about three times the yield of bush beans in the same garden space and keep on bearing until the first frost. In the North, plant pole beans at the beginning of the season—usually in May. If your area has longer seasons, you may be able to harvest two crops. To calculate if two crops are possible, note the number of days to maturity for a particular cultivar, and count back from the fall frost date, adding a week or so to be on the safe side.

Plant pole beans in single rows 3′-4′ apart or double rows spaced 1′ apart. Sow seeds 2″ deep and 10″ apart. When planting in hills around teepee-type poles, space the hills 3′-5′ apart; sow

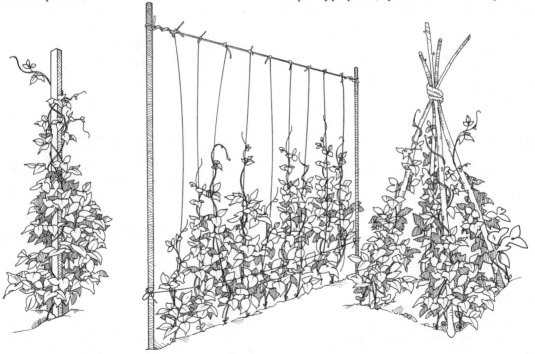

Staking methods. Staking pole and runner beans helps produce a clean, high-yielding crop in a small space. Use a single stake or a string-and-stake trellis. A bean "teepee" can be a great place for kids to play.

6-8 seeds per mound, and thin to 3-4 plants. Provide vertical supports at planting or as soon as the first two leaves of the seedlings open.

Growing guidelines: Bush beans germinate in about 7 days, pole beans in about 14. It's important to maintain even soil moisture during this period and also when the plants are about to blossom. If the soil dries out at these times, your harvest may be drastically reduced. Water deeply at least once a week when there is no rain; be careful not to hose off any of the plants' blooms. Apply several inches of mulch (after the seedlings emerge) to conserve moisture, reduce weeds, and keep the soil cool during hot spells that can cause blossom-drop.

Beans generally don't need extra nitrogen for good growth. Beneficial bacteria that live in nodules on bean roots help to provide nitrogen for the plants. In fact, excessive nitrogen produces leaves instead of blossoms and beans. To speed up growth, give beans—particularly long-bearing pole beans or heavy-feeding limas—a mid-season side-dressing of potassium or a seaweed-extract solution.

Problems: Soybeans, adzuki, and mung beans are fairly resistant to pests. Insect pests that attack other beans include aphids, cabbage loopers, corn earworms, European corn borers, Japanese beetles, and—the most destructive of all—Mexican bean beetles. You'll find more information on these pests in "The Top Ten Garden Insect Pests in America" on page 344.

Leaf miners are 1/10" long, black flies that usually have yellow stripes. Their yellowish larvae tunnel inside leaves and damage stems below the soil. Remove affected parts.

Striped cucumber beetles are 1/4" long, yellowish orange bugs with black heads and three black stripes down their backs. These pests can spread bacterial blight and cucumber mosaic. Apply a thick layer of mulch to discourage them from laying their orange eggs in the soil near the plants. Handpick adults, which tend to hide on the undersides of leaves, or release soldier beetles, tachinid flies, and braconid wasps to prey on

them. Interplant with catnip, tansy, radishes, goldenrod, or nasturtiums to repel cucumber beetles. Plant later in the season to help avoid infestations of this pest.

Spider mites are tiny red or yellow creatures that generally live on the undersides of leaves; their feeding causes yellow stippling on leaf surfaces. Discourage spider mites with garlic or soap sprays. Don't use water sprays to knock mites off plants, because you may knock off blossoms at the same time.

To minimize disease problems, buy disease-free seeds and disease-resistant cultivars, rotate bean crops every one or two years, and space plants far enough apart to provide air flow. Don't harvest or cultivate beans when the foliage is

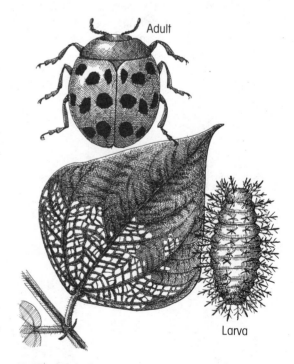

Adult

Larva

Mexican bean beetles. The first signs of these troublesome pests are small clusters of yellow eggs; these hatch into 1/3" long, spiny-looking but soft-bodied yellow larvae. Adults look like larger tan versions of ladybugs. Check the plants daily for eggs, larvae, and adults; squash or remove any you find.

wet, or you may spread disease spores. Here are some common diseases to watch for:

• Anthracnose causes black, egg-shaped, sunken cankers on pods, stems, and seeds and black marks on leaf veins.

• Bacterial blight starts with large, brown blotches on the leaves; the foliage may fall off and the plant will die.

• Mosaic symptoms include yellow leaves and stunted growth. Control aphids and cucumber beetles, which spread the virus.

• Rust causes reddish brown spots on leaves, stems, and pods.

• Downy mildew causes fuzzy white patches on pods, especially of lima beans.

If disease strikes, destroy infected plants immediately, don't touch other plants with unwashed hands or clippers, and don't sow beans in that area again for 3-5 years.

Harvesting: Pick green beans when they are pencil-size, tender, and before the seeds inside form bumps on the pod. Harvest almost daily to encourage production; if you allow pods to ripen fully, the plants will stop producing and die. Don't pull off the pods, or you may uproot the plants. Pinch bush beans off with your thumbnail and fingers; use scissors on pole and runner beans. Also cut off and discard any overly mature beans you missed in previous pickings.

Serve or freeze beans the day you harvest them to preserve the fresh, delicious, homegrown flavor. To turn green beans into old-fashioned "leather britches," use a large-eyed needle to string fresh pods on white crochet thread. Hang them in full sun for 2-3 days until they're dry, then remove the thread and spread the beans in a single layer on cookie sheets. Place in a warm oven for about 5 minutes, then store in glass jars. To cook, break into bite-size pieces, and soak overnight. Pour off the water, add fresh water, bring the beans to a boil, and simmer for several hours until tender.

Pick shell beans for fresh eating when the pods are plump but still tender. The more you pick, the more the vines will produce. Consume

KITCHEN-FRESH SPROUTS

Producing a tasty crop of nutritious bean sprouts right in your kitchen is quick and easy. Buy seeds for sprouting at a health food store or from companies that sell organically grown seeds. Seeds packaged for planting are often treated with fungicides; don't use them for sprouting.

To grow sprouts, you need a jar, some cheesecloth, and seeds. Cover the bottom of the jar with a single layer of seeds and add several inches of warm water. Cover the jar opening with a piece of cheesecloth secured with a rubber band. Let seeds soak overnight. The next day, turn the jar over and drain out the water. Place the upside-down jar on a plate; prop the jar up slightly so the remaining water drains freely. Rinse and drain seeds 2-3 times a day, and keep in a warm place. In 3-5 days, your sprouts will be ready to eat or store in the refrigerator. Mung beans are one of the best-known sprouts, but you can use just about any untreated grain or vegetable seeds.

or preserve them as soon as possible. Unshelled, both they and green beans will keep for up to a week in the refrigerator.

To dry beans, leave the pods on the plants until they are brown and the seeds rattle inside them. Seeds should be so hard you can barely dent them with your teeth. If the pods have yellowed and a rainy spell is forecast, cut the plants off near the ground and hang them upside-down indoors to dry. Put the shelled beans in airtight, lidded containers. Add a packet of dried milk to absorb moisture, and store the beans in a cool, dry place. They will keep for 10-12 months.

Best cultivars: There are hundreds of green and wax bean cultivars from which to choose. Bush types take around 47-57 days to mature, and pole beans need at least 65 days. Select those best suited to your climate and, if necessary, pick ones resistant to area diseases. ❖

Bees and Beekeeping

All bees gather and feed on nectar and pollen, which distinguishes them from wasps, hornets, and other members of the Order *Hymenoptera*. As they forage for food, bees transfer stray grains of pollen from flower to flower and pollinate the blooms. Different kinds of bees favor different flowers, and some are better pollinators than others. There are some 20,000 species of bees worldwide. Of the nearly 5,000 in North America, several hundred are vital to the pollination of cultivated crops. Many others are crucial to wild plants.

Widespread pesticide use and loss of habitat have vastly reduced wild and domestic bee populations. Wise gardeners encourage bee colonies on their property.

Honeybees

Keeping honeybees (*Apis mellifera*) boosts your garden and orchard productivity and provides honey to eat—plus extra to sell or give away.

Hive location: Place a hive so it's protected from prevailing winds and exposed to morning sun, but partially shaded in the afternoon. Bees will forage from a variety of pollen- and nectar-bearing plants. They also need a source of water nearby. Make sure the bees' flyway (the path they follow between the hive entrance and forage areas) doesn't interfere with people or livestock. Also, check local zoning laws.

Honey production: You can get as much as 100-200 lbs. (30-60 gallons) per hive! The national average is only 50 lbs.—plenty for most families.

Time: Caring for three healthy hives takes just a few hours per year, but certain chores must be done at certain times. The busiest seasons are spring, when you need to keep the hive healthy and prevent swarming, and fall, when most honey is harvested.

Equipment: A typical beginner's beekeeping kit includes a complete hive body, ten movable frames with comb foundation, a smoker, a hive tool, gloves, and a veil. This is enough to give you and a colony of bees a start, but only barely. It's better to add a second hive to give the bees more room and at least one "super"—a shallow hive section from which you can easily harvest surplus honey. Later you may also want a honey extractor, but you don't need one immediately. A beginner's kit costs upwards of $100, and the additional supering kit almost as much.

Bees: Buy bees by mail from a reputable source. A 3 lb. package of bees includes about 10,000 workers, a mated queen, and sugar water to feed the colony en route. Once they arrive, they are easily transferred to the hive.

Diseases: Bacterial infection, also known as American foulbrood, is the chief disease problem in honeybees. It attacks brood (reproductive) comb cells and causes bee larvae to die and rot. There is no cure, and infected bees and hives must be destroyed. To avoid problems, buy only clean, inspected bees and equipment.

Pests: In the late 1980s two types of mites became a serious threat to honeybees in North America. Tracheal mites (*Acarapi woodi*) attack the respiratory systems of bees, which weakens the bees and causes the death of whole overwintering colonies. Varroa mites (*Varroa jacobsoni*) are extremely destructive external parasites on adult and pupal-stage bees. They kill pupal-

---

More On BEES AND BEEKEEPING

There is a wealth of literature on the how-to of beekeeping. *Starting Right with Bees, First Lessons in Beekeeping,* and *The ABC and XYZ of Bee Culture* are standard texts. The periodicals *Gleanings in Bee Culture* and *American Bee Journal* also are good sources and carry ads for bees and equipment. For supplies for orchard bees, including paper soda straws, write to: Orchard Bees, 2100 Wayne Street, Auburn, IN 46706.

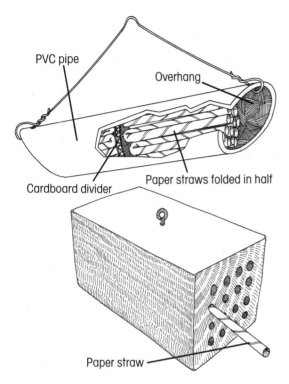

Making orchard bee houses. To make a nesting block for attracting orchard bees, drill ⅜" holes 6" deep in a 4 × 4 wooden block about 8" long. Line each with a paper soda straw cut to length. You can replace the straws as needed to keep the nest clean and free of molds or fungi. One-foot sections of light-colored, 2"–3" diameter PVC pipe also work well for making nests. Put a disk of cardboard in the middle of the pipe as a divider, and fill the pipe with bundles of paper straws folded in half. Mount nests on posts or trees so they are level, and orient them east-west. It's a good idea to provide shelter from rain with an overhang.

stage bees and eventually destroy the whole colony. While there are no known organic controls for mites, work is underway to develop honeybee strains resistant to tracheal and varroa mites.

Bee stings: You *will* get stung if you keep bees, but only infrequently if you wear protective clothing, move about the hive calmly, and pacify bees with smoke as you work them. Honeybees are not dangerous unless you're highly allergic to bee venom. If you are, choose another pastime.

Africanized bees: The northward migration of so-called killer bees has been a subject of much debate. Africanized honeybees are not killers, but they are more aggressive when provoked. Since they are the same species, domestic queen bees mate with wild Africanized bees and hives become Africanized. Only time will tell what impact this will have on beekeeping in North America.

Wild Bees

Many wild bees will pollinate during inclement weather when domestic honeybees won't. Encourage wild bees on your property by providing nectar-bearing plants and nesting sites. White clover and alfalfa are excellent forage. Pithy-stemmed plants such as sumac and elderberry make good nesting habitat. Soil-nesting bees need small areas of bare soil.

An especially desirable wild species is the blue orchard bee (*Osmia lignaria*), a blue-black, flylike bee native to North America. Orchard bees visit up to 1,600 flowers daily and pollinate 90-99 percent of them. A honeybee visits only about half as many flowers, and pollinates only a few dozen. USDA studies indicate that 250-300 orchard bees can do the same job of pollinating fruit and nut trees as a hive of 30,000-40,000 honeybees.

Female orchard bees will pack pollen and nectar into the far end of a long narrow hole, deposit an egg, seal the cell with mud, and repeat until the hole is filled. You can attract orchard bees by making artificial nests such as the ones shown on this page. Hang nests at least 3' off the ground on the sunny side of trees, fence posts, or outbuildings. The more nests you put out, the better your chances are of attracting orchard bees. Keep them in place year-round unless winter temperatures in your area drop below 0°F. If so, move the nests to an unheated (30°-40°F) place late in the fall and return them to the orchard about a week before the first fruit bloom. ❖

Beet

Beta vulgaris
Chenopodiaceae

Attractive and versatile beets are a high-yield addition to any vegetable garden. They thrive in almost every climate and in all but the heaviest soils. The delectable greens contain vitamins A and C, and more iron and minerals than spinach. Beet roots are rich in potassium and contain protein, fiber, iron, calcium, phosphorus, niacin, and vitamins A and C. Bake, boil, steam, or pickle them for use in soups, salads, and side dishes.

Planting: Beets can grow in semishade but prefer full sun. They like a loose, well-drained, root- and rock-free soil. Like all root crops, beets benefit from hilled-up rows or beds. Dig in plenty of compost to lighten heavy soil. Avoid freshly manured areas, which can produce forked roots.

Beets are most productive at temperatures of 60°-65°F. Where summers are hot, use them as an early spring, fall, or late-winter crop. Sow this hardy vegetable directly in the garden a full month before the last expected frost or as soon as you can work the soil. When planting in summer or fall during hot and dry weather, soak seeds for 12 hours to promote germination.

Sow seeds ½" deep and 2" apart with at least 1' between rows. Except for a few mono-germ (single-seeded) types, each beet seed is actually a small fruit containing up to eight true seeds. This means you'll have to thin the resulting cluster of seedlings. Transplant thinnings or enjoy the tiny, tender leaves in salads or as cooked greens. Plant successive crops every two weeks until the weather begins to turn hot.

Growing guidelines: Early weeding is critical to success with any root crop. If you're not willing to do a couple of good weedings early on, you'll never get a good crop of beets. Hand-pull weeds carefully to avoid damaging the easily bruised beet roots. Once the beet seedlings are 2"-4" tall, thin until individual plants are 4"-6"

apart. When the roots are 1" in diameter, pull every other one, water well, and mulch to keep down weeds and conserve moisture. Be sure to provide about 1" of water a week. Otherwise, plants bolt (go to seed), and the roots will crack or become stringy and tough. Quick growth is the secret of tender roots, so water with compost tea or liquid seaweed extract every two weeks. For instructions on making and using compost tea, see the Composting entry. Side-dress with compost at least once halfway though the growing period.

Problems: Well-cultivated beets are usually insect- and disease-free. The most common pests are leaf miners and flea beetles, but they seldom cause serious damage. Leaf miners are tiny black flies whose larvae tunnel within the beet leaves; control them by removing affected leaves. For more information on flea beetles, see "The Top Ten Garden Insect Pests in America" on page 344.

Boron deficiency can cause brown hearts, black spots in the roots, or lack of growth. Apply a foliar spray of liquid seaweed extract every two weeks until the symptoms disappear. Avoid the problem in future crops by adding granite dust or rock phosphate to the soil.

Harvesting: You can harvest up to ⅓ of a plant's leaves without harming the roots. Beet roots are best when 1½"-3" in diameter. Deterioration sets in if you leave them in the ground for more than 10 days after they reach their full size. Hand-pull carefully to avoid bruising them. Shake off the soil, and twist off—don't cut off—the tops, leaving an inch or so of stems to keep the roots from bleeding. To keep them for up to six months, layer undamaged roots between sand, peat, or sawdust in boxes; store in a cool place. Can or freeze beet roots or leaves.

Best cultivars: Try 'Lutz Green Leaf', great for beet tops, and 'Winter Keeper' and 'Detroit Dark Red' for winter storage. For extra color, try 'Golden', with yellow flesh, or 'Chioggia', with pink-and-white flesh. ❖

Begonia

Begonia. Tender perennials grown as summer- and fall-blooming annuals or houseplants; one hardy perennial.

Description: The genus *Begonia* contains hundreds of species and thousands of cultivars, grown for their beautiful flowers or attractive leaves. Begonias generally fall into one of three major groups—fibrous-rooted, tuberous-rooted, or rhizomatous—each with different habits and needs.

Begonia Semperflorens-Cultorum Hybrid, wax begonia, is a tender perennial commonly grown as a reliable annual. The male flowers normally have four petals (two rounded and two narrow) with showy yellow stamens in the center; the females have 2-5 smaller rounded petals around a tight, curly yellow knob. Female blooms occur in pairs, one on either side of each male.

Flowering begins when plants are small and continues until frost. Wax begonias bloom in shades of white, pink, and red, plus blended and edged combinations, on plants that can reach 15″ or more by autumn. The shiny, thick, 1½″-4″ leaves may be green, reddish to bronze, or speckled with yellow. Zone 10.

HARDY BEGONIAS

If you're looking for something to amaze your gardening friends, why not try growing hardy begonia (*Begonia grandis*)? Winter-hardy to Zone 6, this plant bears large, open sprays of pink or white blooms from late summer into early fall on 2′–2½′ arching clumps of striking leaves. It thrives in partial shade (out of hot afternoon sun) and fertile, moist but well-drained soil with plenty of organic matter. Plant or divide in spring when it emerges, which is later than most plants. They look stunning in a bed of common periwinkle (*Vinca minor*) or in woodland plantings with hostas and ferns.

Another type of fibrous-rooted begonia is the cane-stemmed group, including the popular angelwing begonias. Representing several species and cultivars, these houseplants produce plain green or mottled leaves and clusters of brightly colored flowers. Upright cultivars can grow several feet tall; plants with drooping branches are ideal for hanging baskets.

Hybrid tuberous begonias (*B.* Tuberhybrida Hybrids) are commmonly used as outdoor plants. Compared to wax begonias, tuberous begonias are stingy with their display, but they make up for that with larger and far more colorful blooms. Single or double male flowers can grow to 6″ or more across, blooming in bright and pastel shades of white, pink, red, yellow, and combinations. The upright plants grow to about 2′ tall. Zone 10.

Rex begonias (*B. rex*) are perhaps the most widely grown rhizomatous begonia. They produce green or reddish leaves, often attractively patterned with silver or black markings. Enjoy the many cultivars as indoor foliage plants.

How to grow: Set wax begonias out after the last frost in partial to dense shade; they'll grow in full sun in the North if kept evenly moist. Plant in average, moist but well-drained soil; water during drought.

Buy plants or start wax begonias from seed, allowing four months from sowing to setting out transplants after the frost date. Take cuttings of particularly nice plants toward the end of summer to grow as houseplants through the winter; root cuttings from them in early spring for planting out after frost.

Start tuberous begonias indoors, planting them about 8-10 weeks before your frost-free date in a loose growing medium. Barely cover tubers with the concave side up (it should have little pink buds coming out of the center) and moisten lightly. Give lots of water and light after the shoots emerge.

Move tubers to individual 4″ or 5″ pots when shoots are 1″-3″ tall. After all danger of frost is past, plant in partial shade in fertile,

Nonstop (tuberous)

Camellia-flowered (tuberous)

Carnation-flowered (tuberous)

Cascade (tuberous)

Crispa (tuberous)

Wax

Rex

Angelwing

Beguiling begonias. Begonias are generally grown for their stunning array of flower forms and colors, but some, such as the rex begonia, are popular for their brightly colored leaves.

moist but well-drained soil with plenty of organic matter. Water liberally in warm weather; douse every three weeks or so with manure tea or fish emulsion. (For instructions on making manure tea, see the Manure entry.) Stake plants to prevent them from falling under the weight of the flowers.

For container-grown tuberous begonias, choose larger pots (8″ is a good size) and fill with a loose, rich potting mix. Care for them as you would plants in the ground. For hanging baskets, plant no more than three tubers in a 12″ basket, and water frequently. To promote branching, pinch plants when they are about 6″ tall.

When the leaves turn yellow and wither in the fall, lift plants out of the ground with soil still attached. After a week or so, cut the stems to within a few inches of the tuber. Once the stem stub dries completely, shake the soil off the tubers and store in dry peat or sharp sand at 45°-55°F. Leave pot-grown plants in their soil during the winter, or store as you would those grown in the ground. Start them again next spring, replacing the soil for those in pots.

Angelwing and rex begonias need plenty of bright but indirect light. Grow them indoors in a rich, well-drained potting mix. In the summer, they appreciate some extra humidity, along with evenly moist soil and a dose of fish emulsion every two weeks. In winter, water more sparingly and do not feed.

Indoors, begonias are usually pest-free. In the garden, slugs may be a problem; see the Slugs and Snails entry for details on controlling these pests. Stem rot will almost certainly occur on tuberous begonias in poorly drained soil; mildew will whiten the leaves in breezeless corners and pockets. Flower buds may drop in humid weather or if the soil is too dry.

Landscape uses: Outdoors, grow begonias anywhere you want some color in shady beds and borders or in pots for portable color. ❖

Beneficial Animals

Threatening their friends with a shovel while shouting threats is not a common quirk of gardeners. But even mild-mannered folks get violent when they find bats, snakes, spiders, or skunks in their yards. And these animals really are a gardener's friends because they eat insects, rodents, and other garden pests. In summer, a toad can put away 3,000 grubs, slugs, beetles, and other insects every month. A bat can catch 1,000 bugs in one night. You'll find information on the more lovable beneficial animals in the Birds, Earthworms, Toads, and Beneficial Insects entries.

These helpful animals have gotten bad press over the years. A lot of people blame the wrong animal for damage. Skunks are often blamed for raccoon damage, moles for mouse damage, and so on. It's hard to tell the difference, so don't be too quick to condemn animals you don't like.

Bravo for Bats

With the exception of Batman, bats are reviled. They supposedly tangle in women's hair, suck blood, and spread rabies. This is largely nonsense. Bats have no interest in human hair, male or female. North American bats eat bugs and sometimes fruit, but no blood.

As for rabies, scientists once blamed bats for much of the spread of the disease, but have since decided that was an overreaction. Only about 1 percent of bats get the disease themselves, and far fewer pass it on to humans. In 30 years of record-keeping, only 12-15 cases of human rabies have been traced to bats. Most of these incidents could have been avoided: The victim was not attacked by a swooping bat, but instead picked up a diseased bat flapping around on the ground. To avoid a bite, don't handle bats bare-handed. If you must move them, use a shovel.

Healthy bats perform astonishing feats in the air, catching insects with their wings. The little brown bat, a common U.S. species, eats moths, caddis flies, midges, beetles, and mosquitoes. Big colonies of bats, like the Mexican free-tails that cluster in groups of 20 million, can catch 100,000 lb. of bugs in a night.

One way to attract bats is to put up a bat house, a wooden box like a flattened birdhouse with an entrance slot in the bottom. You can buy bat houses or make your own. Make the entrance slot of your homemade bat house ¾" wide. Scribe grooves in the inside back wall about 1/16" deep and ½" apart so the bats can hang on. Fasten it 15'-20' above the ground on the east or southeast side of a building. Then be patient. If there are many roosts available in the neighborhood, bats may take several years to move into yours.

All-Star Spiders

Cars, cigarettes, and high-fat diets kill far more people every year than U.S. spiders have in a whole century. Yet more people panic at the sight of a spider than at more legitimate threats.

Actually, spiders are a lot of fun to watch. The gold-and-black garden spider spins a new web each day, gluing 1,000 to 1,500 connections among strands to form the pattern it has made

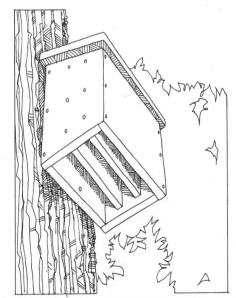

Bat house. From the outside, bat houses look like bird houses, but instead of using a door in the front, bats fly in and out through the bottom. They cling to the partitions inside to roost.

perfectly since its first try. The spinner eats the old web before making a new one, recycling the silk proteins. As you brush by leaves in the garden, jumping spiders will leap aside in fast, basketball-style arcs.

You may also see spider family life: a mother with a layer of offspring hanging onto her back or scurrying for cover when she sounds the alarm with a harsh pluck of a cobweb strand. If she wants to call them to a meal, she just tickles the strands.

Most spiders have a trace of venom, but only two spiders in the United States—the black widow and the brown recluse—have enough to injure a human. The female black widow has a glossy black body a little smaller than a garbanzo bean, marked on the underside with a red hourglass. It weaves a small matted web that it rarely leaves. These spiders are placid and bite only if extremely provoked. The bites are painful, but can be treated.

The brown recluse or violin spider, lives only in the Southern half of the United States (south of Kansas). Its distinguishing feature is a dark violin-shaped patch on the top of the orangish yellow body segment behind its head. Its bites form deep sores that can linger for months.

To avoid mishaps with either of these spiders, don't reach bare-handed into dark crevices of wood piles, tool sheds, and the like. Shake out clothing and towels, especially in rustic cabins or garages, before putting them on or holding them against your body. Avoiding those two unpleasant spiders leaves almost 3,000 species in the United States to enjoy without alarm. Some of these also bite if teased or startled, but they don't do more damage than mosquitos.

The Scoop on Snakes

Of the 115 species of snakes in North America, only four kinds are poisonous: rattlesnakes, copperheads coral snakes, and cottonmouths, also called water mocassins. Most of the snakes that find their way to a backyard will only bite if handled or stepped on, and even then

the bite is harmless. In fact, garden pests, especially insects and rodents, are the real prey of snakes.

Beneficial backyard snakes include the common garter snake, eastern ribbon snake, western terrestrial garter snake, green or grass snake, and brown snake, all of which eat slugs, snails, and insects. The corn snake, black rat snake, and milk snake eat mice and rats. Most of these beneficial snakes are beautiful, too.

How can you tell if a snake is poisonous? Rattlers, copperheads, and cottonmouths are all thick-bodied snakes with large, triangular heads. A rattlesnake will rattle a warning if threatened. The position of the bands on the red, black, and yellow coral snake tells its story: "Red next to yellow kills a fellow."

If you don't like the idea of snakes patrolling your garden, take a few simple precautions. First, don't mulch your plots. Mulch provides shelter and attracts mice, a favored food. Keep your yard cleaned up and stack wood away from the house: Cordwood, junk, brush piles, and other debris will attract snakes to your yard. So will dog or cat food set outdoors and left unattended.

Skunks Earn Their Stripes

At the turn of the century, hops growers in New York state pushed for regulations protecting, of all things, the skunk. The growers claimed that skunks were controlling the dreaded hop grub. Modern gardeners have been less enthusiastic, since in addition to spraying, skunks dig holes in lawns. Actually, the skunks are digging for grubs of Japanese beetles and other pests.

Skunk texts state that the animals take alarm at menaces within 25' and that they can spray accurately at 12'-15'. Yet skunks seem inclined to mind their own business and ignore all but loud, blatant menaces like cars and charging dogs.

The bigger concern with skunks is rabies. They're the number one carriers of the disease, followed by raccoons. Stay away from skunks that seem disoriented or too bold, and have pets vaccinated. ❖

Beneficial Insects

Our insect allies far outnumber the insect pests in our yards and gardens. Bees, flies, and some moths pollinate flowers; predatory insects eat pest insects; parasitic insects lay their eggs inside pests, eventually killing them; dung beetles, flies, and others break down decaying material; and many species of insects are food for birds and other animals.

Bees and Wasps

Honeybees are called the "spark plugs" of agriculture because of their importance in pollinating crops, but other wild bees and wasps are also important pollinators and natural pest control agents. For more on bees, see the Bees and Beekeeping entry.

Parasitic wasps: Most species belong to one of three main families: chalcids, braconids, and ichneumonids. They range from pencil-point-size *Trichogramma* wasps to huge black ichneumonid wasps. Parasitic wasps inject their eggs inside host insects; the larvae grow by absorbing nourishment through their skins. Commercial insectaries sell several parasitic wasp species for control of whiteflies, aphids, and some pest caterpillars.

Yellow jackets: Most people fear yellow jackets and hornets, but these insects are excellent pest predators. They dive into foliage and carry off flies, caterpillars, and other larvae to feed to their brood. So don't destroy the gray paper nests of these insects unless they are in a place frequented by people or pets, or if a family member is allergic to insect stings.

Beetles

While some beetles, such as Japanese beetles and Colorado potato beetles, can be serious home garden pests, others are some of the best pest-fighters around.

Lady beetles: This family of small to medium, shiny, hard, hemispherical beetles includes more than 3,000 species that feed on small, soft pests such as aphids, mealybugs,

and spider mites. (Not all species are beneficial—for example, Mexican bean beetles also are lady beetles.) Both adults and larvae eat pests. Most larvae have tapering bodies with several short, branching spines on each segment; they resemble miniature alligators. Convergent lady beetles (*Hippodamia convergens*) are collected from their mass overwintering sites and sold to gardeners, but they usually fly away after release unless confined in a greenhouse.

Ground beetles: These swift-footed, medium to large, blue-black beetles hide under stones or boards during the day. By night they prey on cabbage root maggots, cutworms, snail and slug eggs, and other pests; some climb trees to capture armyworms or tent caterpillars. Large ground beetle populations build up in orchards with undisturbed groundcovers and in gardens under stone pathways or in semipermanent mulched beds.

Rove beetles: These small to medium, elongated insects with short, stubby top wings look like earwigs without pincers. Many species are decomposers of manure and plant material; others are important predators of pests such as root maggots that spend part of their life cyle in the soil.

Other beetles: Other beneficial beetles include hister beetles, tiger beetles, and fireflies (really beetles). Both larvae and adults of these beetles eat insect larvae, slugs, and snails.

Flies

We usually call flies pests, but there are beneficial flies that are pollinators or insect predators or parasites.

Tachinid flies: These large, bristly, dark gray flies place their eggs or larvae on cutworms, caterpillars, corn borers, stinkbugs, and other pests. Tachinid flies are important natural suppressors of tent caterpillar or armyworm outbreaks.

Syrphid flies: These black-and-yellow or black-and-white striped flies (also called flower or hover flies) are often mistaken for bees or

Beneficial Bugs to Buy

Many species of beneficial insects and mites are now available from commercial insectaries. The following list includes those that are most effective for release in home greenhouses or gardens.

Beneficial Species	Pests Controlled	Notes and Tips
INSECTS		
Aphid midge (*Aphidoletes aphidimyza*)	Aphids, many species	Release 3–5 pupae per plant; two releases may provide better results. Good in greenhouses, shade trees, orchards, gardens, rose bushes.
Braconid wasp (*Aphidius matricariae*)	Green peach and apple aphids	Buy the minimum order for a garden. Plant parsley-family flowers to provide a food source.
Convergent lady beetle (*Hippodamia convergens*)	Aphids	Release minimum order in greenhouses with screened vents; will hibernate in cool greenhouses.
Lacewings (*Chrysoperla carnea,* *Chrysoperla rufilabrus*)	Any small, soft pests including aphids, thrips	Shipped as eggs; distribute widely through garden; apply 1–3 eggs per plant.
Mealybug destroyer (*Cryptolaemus* *montrouzieri*)	Mealybugs	Use in greenhouses or cage them on houseplants; use 2–5 per plant. Nymphs look like mealybugs.
Minute pirate bug (*Orius tristicolor*)	Thrips, mites	Release 1–3 per plant. Plant pollen-rich flowers to entice them to stay in your garden.

yellow jackets. They lay their eggs in aphid colonies; the larvae feed on the aphids. Don't mistake the larvae—unattractive gray or transluscent sluglike maggots—for small slugs.

Aphid midges: Aphid midge larvae are tiny orange maggots that are voracious aphid predators. The aphid midge is available from commercial insectaries for use in the garden, greenhouse, and yard.

Other Beneficials

Dragonflies: Often called "darning needles," the dragonflies and their smaller cousins, the damselflies, scoop up mosquitoes, gnats, and midges, cramming their mouths with prey as they dart in zig-zag patterns around marshes and ponds.

Lacewings: The brown or green, alligator-like larvae of several species of native lacewings prey upon a variety of small insects, including aphids, scale insects, small caterpillars, and thrips. Adult lacewings are delicate, ½"-1" green or brown insects with large, transparent wings marked with a characteristic fine network of veins. They lay pale green oval eggs, each at the tip of a long, fine stalk, along the midrib of lettuce leaves or other garden plants. Lacewings are produced commercially for release in home gardens.

True bugs: True bug is the scientifically correct common name for a group of insects. This group includes several pest species, but there are many predatory bugs that attack soft-bodied insects such as aphids, beetle larvae,

Beneficial Species	Pests Controlled	Notes and Tips
Scale predator beetles (*Chilocorus* spp., *Lindorus* spp.)	Soft scales	Use in greenhouses, or on houseplants or citrus or ornamental trees; minimum order is usually enough to treat the problem.
Spined soldier bug (*Podisus maculiventris*)	Colorado potato beetle, Mexican bean beetle	Try releases of 5 per square yard; similar in appearance to stink bugs.
Whitefly parasite (*Encarsia formosa*)	Greenhouse whiteflies	Release 5 per plant at first sign of whitefly; best in warm, bright conditions such as greenhouses, or gardens in warm regions.
NON-INSECTS		
Predatory mite (*Geolaelaps=Hypoaspis* spp.)	Fungus gnats, thrips	Release a minimum order to establish population early in season; good in greenhouses or on houseplants or ornamentals.
Predatory mite (*Phytoseiulus persimilis*)	Spider mites	Release 2–5 per plant, once, in greenhouses or on strawberries or houseplants; survive best in moderate temperatures (65°–75°F).
Western predatory mite (*Metaseiulus occidentalis*)	European red mite	Release 50–100 mites per tree to establish population, 1,000 per tree to control outbreaks; also useful on strawberries.

small caterpillars, pear psylla, and thrips. Assassin bugs, ambush bugs, damsel bugs, minute pirate bugs, and spined soldier bugs are valuable wild predators in farm systems.

Spiders and mites: Although mites and spiders are arachnids, not insects, they are often grouped with insects because all belong to the larger classification of arthropods. Predatory mites are extremely small. The many native species found in trees, shrubs, and surface litter are invaluable predators. Phytoseiid mites control many kinds of plant-feeding mites, such as spider mites, rust mites, and cyclamen mites. Some also prey on thrips and other small pests. There are many families of soil-dwelling mites that eat nematodes, insect eggs, fungus gnat larvae, or decaying organic matter.

It's unfortunate that so many people are scared of spiders, because they are some of the best pest predators around. We are most familiar with spiders that spin webs, but there are are many other kinds. Some spin thick silk funnels; some hide in burrows and snatch insects that wander too close, while others leap on their prey using a silk thread as a dragline.

Encouraging Beneficials

Attracting and conserving natural enemies of insect pests is an important part of managing your garden organically. The best way to protect beneficial insects is to avoid using toxic sprays or dusts in the garden. Even botanical insecticides kill beneficial species, so use them only

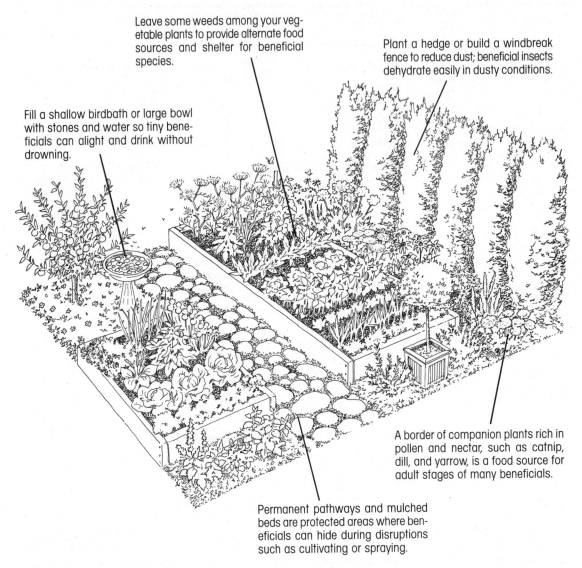

Leave some weeds among your vegetable plants to provide alternate food sources and shelter for beneficial species.

Plant a hedge or build a windbreak fence to reduce dust; beneficial insects dehydrate easily in dusty conditions.

Fill a shallow birdbath or large bowl with stones and water so tiny beneficials can alight and drink without drowning.

A border of companion plants rich in pollen and nectar, such as catnip, dill, and yarrow, is a food source for adult stages of many beneficials.

Permanent pathways and mulched beds are protected areas where beneficials can hide during disruptions such as cultivating or spraying.

Attracting beneficial insects. Making your garden a haven for beneficial insects is easy and fun. It's also one of the cheapest and most environmentally sound ways to help prevent insect pests from getting the upper hand on your food crops and ornamentals.

when absolutely necessary to preserve a crop and then only on the plants being attacked. Be careful when you handpick or spray pest insects, or you may end up killing beneficial insects by mistake. While many beneficials are too small to be seen with the unaided eye, be sure you can identify the larger common beneficials. For illustrations of lacewings, tachinid flies, and lady beetles, see "Insect Diversity" on page 343

You can make your yard and garden a haven

for beneficials by taking simple steps to provide them with food, water, and shelter. For suggestions on how to entice beneficial insects to take up residence on your property, see "Attracting Beneficial Insects" on the opposite page.

Buying Beneficial Insects

Before ordering beneficial insects, make sure you identify the target pest, because most predators or parasites only attack a particular species or group of pests. Find out as much as you can by reading or talking to suppliers before buying beneficials. You'll find a summary of commercially available beneficials listed in "Beneficial Bugs to Buy" on page 58.

Once you receive your order, don't open the package unprepared. There may be insects loose inside the container. Read the directions on the label for handling and releasing: Every species is unique and must be treated differently.

Shipping and being confined in packaging is stressful for insects. Release the beneficials in your garden or greenhouse as soon as you can after they arrive. If you can't release the insects right away, keep them cool (usually 45°-50°F). The door shelf of a refrigerator is suitable for storing most species. Don't keep them in the packaging for more than 24 hours.

Get a good look at the beneficials before releasing them so that you'll be able to recognize them in the garden. You don't want to mistakenly kill them later on, thinking them to be pests. A magnifying glass is useful for seeing tiny parasitic wasps and predatory mites. Release some of the insects directly on or near the infested plants; distribute the remainder as evenly as possible throughout the rest of the surrounding area.

Once you have let out your hired killers, give them time to become established; it usually takes 2-5 weeks before there is an obvious effect on the pests. The key to remember is that biological controls provide a long-term solution to pest problems, not a quick fix. ❖

Berberis

Barberry. Thorny evergreen or deciduous shrubs.

Description: *Berberis julianae,* wintergreen barberry, grows to an upright 3'-6' and has deep green, shiny oblong leaves bearing spines at each serrated point. The evergreen foliage may turn rich red during a cold winter. Zones 6-8.

B. thunbergii, Japanese barberry, has a spreading habit and grows to a height of 4'-6'. The egg-shaped leaves are deciduous. Young leaves are green, gradually darkening to red in fall. Zones 4-8.

Both wintergreen and Japanese barberries produce small yellow flowers in the spring, followed by berries in the summer and fall. Wintergreen barberry has blue-black berries; Japanese barberry has red.

How to grow: Barberries tolerate a wide range of soil conditions, though they must have full sun. In the North, plant wintergreen barberry in fall or spring in a spot that's protected from winter wind; in the South, site it out of summer wind and plant in fall or winter. Plant Japanese barberry in fall or spring. The main problem in growing barberries is the accumulation of debris among the thorny branches; carefully remove the trash at spring clean-up time. Some barberries are alternate hosts for black stem rust, a serious fungal disease of wheat. Check with your Cooperative Extension office before planting barberries in an area where wheat is grown.

Landscape uses: Barberries are excellent choices where low maintenance is important. Use them in hedges or barrier plantings, in shrub borders, or as foundation shrubs.

Best cultivars: *B. julianae* 'Compactum' grows slowly to a mature height of 5'. *B. thunbergii* var. *atropurpurea* 'Crimson Pygmy' grows to about 2' and produces leaves that blush to rich red in full sun; inner or shaded leaves remain chartreuse. ❖

Bergenia

Bergenia. Early-spring-blooming perennial, evergreen groundcovers.

Description: *Bergenia cordifolia,* heartleaf bergenia, bears dense, irregular clusters of five-petalled ½" bells in white, pink, and red on thick stalks up to 2' tall. The 1' long, broadly heart-shaped, shiny evergreen leaves are often tinged with red or purple in colder weather. Zones 4-8.

How to grow: In spring, plant or divide the slowly spreading rhizomes in humus-rich, moisture-retentive soil in partial shade. Bergenias tolerate more sun farther North. Mulch lightly to protect from winter wind. Handpick or trap slugs and snails.

Landscape uses: Plant bergenias on the edges of beds, along patios and walls, at water's edge, with shrubs, or in pots.

Best cultivars: 'Purpurea' has purple-red flowers on red stalks. ❖

Betula

Birch. Single- or multiple-trunked deciduous trees.

Description: Birches offer year-round landscape interest with their peeling bark, graceful branches, and magnificent fall color.

Betula lenta, sweet birch, is a handsome native with red-brown, cherrylike bark and a pyramidal habit in youth. Like the other birches, it bears drooping flower spikes called catkins in spring; these are interesting but not showy. The leaves stay freshly green and unmarred through the summer, turning yellow in the fall. Crushed or scratched twigs yield a rich root-beer aroma. Where it grows wild, sweet birch has been a source of the oil for making homemade root beer. Zones 4-6.

B. nigra, river birch, is a native tree found growing along river banks and rich bottomlands in much of the eastern United States. Pyramidal in youth, this multi-trunked tree reaches heights of 30'-40' in the landscape; the occasional old-timer approaches 100'. River birch features shredding, papery bark in shades of cream and pale salmon, and clear yellow autumn leaf color in most years. 'Heritage' is a nearly white-barked cultivar that can replace the popular but insect-prone *B. papyrifera* in the landscape. Zones 4-8.

B. papyrifera, paper or canoe birch, is a native of the Northern evergreen forests and performs best in cooler climates. Best known for its white bark with dramatic black markings, this tree develops a rounded outline with age. Most paper birches hold their lower branches; allow space for them in your landscape plans. The yellow fall color combines well with its bark and with the reds and oranges of other trees. Plan on a mature height of 50'-70'. Zones 4-8.

B. pendula, European white birch, is similar in many ways to paper birch. Its branches have a drooping habit, and its bark splits into black fissures toward the base. Zones 3-6.

B. populifolia, gray birch, is a workhorse among birches. Thriving in almost any soil, it has grayish white bark with black markings and a multi-trunked habit. A good birch for minimal-maintenance situations. Zones 4-6.

How to grow: Most birches require light shade and evenly moist, humus-rich soil, a shaded root zone, and plenty of mulch. River birch tolerates some standing water. Planted out of their element, birches soon begin to decline and, if they haven't already, attract insects such as the bronze birch borer and the birch leaf miner. Stressed trees most often feature the D-shaped holes left in the bark by borers and the brown paperlike leaves caused by leaf miners; reduce both problems by selecting an appropriate planting site. Gray and river birches, especially 'Heritage', show resistance to these devastating insects.

Landscape uses: Naturalize sweet or paper birch in the shade of taller trees. Use gray or river birch in clumps or masses. ❖

Biennials

Some of our most popular garden flowers are biennials, but you probably think they're annuals. Adding to the confusion, many biennials are grown and treated as annuals. But by definition, a biennial is a plant that completes its life cycle in two years. In the first growing season, the plants germinate and produce a mound of foliage, called a rosette, which is a circular cluster of leaves usually borne at or just above the ground. They winter over in rosette form. In the second season, they send up a flower stalk. After blooming, biennials produce seeds and die at the end of the season.

True biennials, such as Canterbury bells, standing cypress, and sweet William, are winter-hardy. They usually have fleshy taproots. Plants such as pansies, forget-me-nots, and English daisies may also winter over with some protection, but they are short-lived or tender perennials grown as biennials. They are usually fibrous-rooted.

Biennials like foxglove (*Digitalis purpurea*) and forget-me-nots (*Myosotis* spp.) will self-sow, so if you plant them two years in a row, you'll have plants in bloom every year from then on. Just remember to allow some flowers to mature and set seed for next year's plants.

Biennials in the Landscape

Use biennials in your annual designs or in the mixed border with annuals and perennials. If you buy plants, you will have bloom the first season. If you are starting your own seeds, plan ahead, since it will take two seasons to get the floral display you want. The first year, the rosettes provide foliage interest. During the second season, the flowers may last several weeks before fading. Some biennials, including honesty (*Lunaria annua*) and mullein (*Verbascum* spp.), have attractive seed heads that you can use in dried arrangements.

Buying and Starting Plants

Popular biennials like pansies and hollyhocks are sold by nurseries along with the annual bedding plants in the spring. They have been grown for the first season by the nursery and are offered at a stage where they will bloom in the current season. Plant and maintain them as you would annuals.

Purchase only healthy, bright green, well-rooted plants. Avoid overgrown, leggy, or wilted plants—they'll be disappointing. Some biennials, including pansies and foxglove, are offered for fall planting. Plant them in early fall to allow ample time for the roots to get established. Mulch the rosettes after hard frost. This protects the crown and prevents repeated freezing and thawing of the soil that can cause roots to heave out of the ground.

Many choice biennials are not offered by nurseries as plants. If you want them, you'll have to grow them from seed. Mail-order catalogs are usually the best source.

Sow seeds indoors in individual peat pots, pellets, or cell packs. Use a sterile commercial soil mix. Start seeds of true biennials in early summer so they can be planted out in the fall. Sow seeds of pansies, English daisies, and other perennials treated as biennials in August. Protect the young plants with mulch or keep them in a cold frame until early spring.

You can also direct-seed biennials into well-prepared outdoor beds. Keep the seedbed evenly moist but not wet. Take care to protect the seeds from disturbance until they germinate and become well established. Sow thickly and clip off unwanted seedlings with a small scissors. When seedlings are established, mulch the beds to conserve water.

Planting and Maintenance

Before planting biennials, check your soil's fertility and pH. Your local extension agent or a soil-testing lab can provide a detailed report.

BIENNIALS FOR SUN AND SHADE

As these lists show, there are more biennials than you think—including such beloved favorites as hollyhocks, Canterbury bells, sweet Williams, forget-me-nots, evening primroses, and foxgloves. Some are best suited for sun, some prefer shade, and a few thrive in both conditions. Perennials grown as biennials are also included here.

Biennials for Sunny Sites

Alcea rosea (hollyhock)
Campanula medium (Canterbury bells)
Campanula spicata (bellflower)
Cynoglossum amabile (Chinese forget-me-not)
Dianthus armeria (Deptford pink)
Dianthus barbatus (sweet William)
Echium lycopsis (viper's bugloss)
Echium vulgare (viper's bugloss)
Glaucium flavum (horned poppy)
Ipomopsis rubra (standing cypress)
Lavatera arborea (tree mallow)
Lunaria annua (money plant)
Malva sylvestris (high mallow)
Matthiola incana (stock)
Myosotis spp. (forget-me-nots)
Oenothera spp. (evening primroses)
Onopordum acanthium (cotton thistle)
Silene armeria (sweet William catchfly)
Verbascum spp. (mulleins)

Biennials for Shady Sites

Campanula medium (Canterbury bells)
Digitalis purpurea (foxglove)
Lunaria annua (money plant)
Myosotis spp. (forget-me-nots)
Phacelia bipinnatifida (phacelia)

Biennials prefer a loamy soil with ample organic matter and a pH between 6.0 and 7.5. For more on soils, soil testing, and pH, see the Soil entry.

If you can, double dig the garden bed; otherwise, turn the soil to at least a shovel's depth. Thoroughly incorporate the appropriate organic soil amendments and fertilizers. For more on digging the bed, see the Double Digging entry; for more on soil amendments and organic fertilizers, see the Fertilizers entry.

Plant biennials with their crowns at or just below the soil surface. If you're transplanting biennials from peat pots, remove all or a portion of the pots. Gently break up the roots of plants grown in cell packs. Many biennials have taproots. Take care not to damage the taproot when planting.

Keep plants well watered until they're established. An inch of water per week is ade-quate for plants that are growing in well-prepared soil. The fertilizer you added before planting will be all that the plants need throughout the growing season. Weed the beds regularly so that your biennials won't have to compete for light, water, and nutrients.

Pinching the plants may help control the height and spread of some biennials, but it is generally unnecessary. Removing spent flowers prolongs the blooming season. You may have to stake certain tall plants such as standing cypress, stocks, and mallows, especially in areas with high winds.

As a rule, biennials are fairly pest-free. Good cultural practices are the best prevention for both insects and diseases. If problems do arise, spray with an appropriate organic control. Plants with viral diseases should be destroyed. For more on pest and disease control, see the Organic Pest Management entry. ❖

Bio-Dynamic Gardening

Bio-dynamics is both a philosophy and a method of agriculture. Bio-dynamics was developed during the 1920s by Rudolph Steiner, a teacher, writer, and researcher, to help people work with nature to grow more healthful food.

In some ways, bio-dynamic and organic gardening share common goals. Both approaches avoid using synthethic chemicals; instead, they strive to produce vigorous, healthy plants that naturally are less susceptible to pest damage. The recycling of nutrients through composting is also common to both methods. Organics and bio-dynamics share many techniques, including raised beds, crop rotation, and companion planting.

What sets bio-dynamics apart from similar gardening practices is the philosophy behind it. Bio-dynamic gardeners attempt to understand the true nature of their crops and livestock: in other words, what each plant and animal really needs to grow to its potential. In bio-dynamic terms, an ideal farm is a self-supporting system. Livestock feed off the land and supply manure. Composted manures fertilize the soil and provide nutrients for new plant growth, completing the cycle of life. Rather than emphasizing measurable yields, bio-dynamic supporters seek a healthful product produced with minimal environmental impact.

The bio-dynamic concept also incorporates the theory of planetary influences on plant growth. Bio-dynamic gardeners believe these forces manifest themselves in plant characteristics such as vigor and nutrient content. Calendars of cosmic rhythms, such as moon phases and planetary events, guide these gardeners in determining ideal times to complete certain tasks, such as planting and cultivation. If you'd like to learn more about "planting by the signs," see the Astrological Gardening entry. For more information on bio-dynamic practices, contact the Bio-Dynamic Farming and Gardening Association, P.O. Box 550, Kimberton, PA 19442. ❖

Biological Control

Using living organisms ranging from bats to viruses to combat pests is one of the most exciting and promising fields of research for organic gardening. Widely used biological controls include insects such as parasitic wasps and the bacterium *Bacillus thuringiensis* (BT), which infects mosquito and fly larvae and many chewing caterpillars.

Biological control happens naturally in your garden. You can encourage beneficial animals and insects by providing appropriate habitat and alternate food sources. Biological controls are also commercially available: insectaries raise parasitic and predatory insects, and garden centers and catalogs offer sprays and dusts of fungi, bacteria, and viruses that infect garden pests. For more information on biological controls, see the Beneficial Animals, Beneficial Insects, Insecticides, and Organic Pest Management entries. ❖

Biotechnology

Screening plants for viruses gives us healthier, more productive plants. Growing plants from single cells or small bits of tissue allows new cultivars to be propagated rapidly. These techniques are examples of biotechnology, or applied biological science.

Genetic engineering is another highly publicized type of biotechnology. It has the potential to help create cultivars that are hardier, more productive, and more resistant to diseases and pests. It may also help create new strains of naturally occurring biological control organisms such as *Bacillus thuringiensis* (BT).

Make an effort to understand and evaluate biotechnology objectively, rather than letting media reports dictate your opinion. For more information about biological controls, see the Insecticides and Organic Pest Management entries. ❖

Birds

Birds are most gardeners' favorite visitors, with their cheerful songs, sprightly manners, and colorful plumage. But birds are also among nature's most efficient insect predators, making them valuable garden allies. In an afternoon, one diminutive house wren can snatch up more than 500 insect eggs, beetles, and grubs. Given a nest of tent caterpillars, a Baltimore oriole will wolf down as many as 17 of the pests per minute. More than 60 percent of the chickadee's winter diet is aphid eggs. And the swallow lives up to its name by consuming massive quantities of flying insects—by one count, more than 1,000 leafhoppers in 12 hours.

Unless your property is completely bare, at least some birds will visit with no special encouragement from you. Far more birds, however, will come to your yard and garden if you take steps to provide their four basic requirements: food, water, cover, and a safe place in which to raise a family. Robins, nuthatches, hummingbirds, titmice, bluebirds, mockingbirds, cardinals, and various sparrows are among the most common garden visitors.

Food and Feeding

Food is the easiest of the four basic requirements to supply. Even if you live in a city apartment, you can attract birds by putting a feeder filled with seed on your balcony. If your landscape is mostly lawn and hard surfaces, you can use feeders as the main food supply while you add plantings of fruiting trees and shrubs. And if your yard is a good natural habitat, where plants are the primary food source (as they should be), feeders can provide crucial nourishment during winter, drought, and other times when the natural food supply is low. Besides, carefully placed feeders allow you and your family to watch and photograph birds.

Some birds, including juncos, mourning doves, and towhees, feed on the ground, while others, including finches, grosbeaks, nuthatches, titmice, and chickadees, eat their meals higher up. In order to attract as many different birds as possible, use a variety of feeders—seed tubes, broad platforms, and shelf and hanging types. Place them at varying heights, widely separated from one another, and near the protective cover of a tree or shrub if possible. No matter what the style, the feeder should resist rain and snow, and it should be easy to fill and clean. It should hold enough birdseed that you don't have to refill it every day, but not so much that the food spoils before it can all be eaten.

Best birdseeds: You can attract virtually all common seed-eating birds with just two kinds of birdseed: white proso millet (the food of choice among ground-feeding species) and black oil-type sunflower seed (the smallest of the sunflower types and a favorite of many birds). Some birds have special favorites: goldfinches, pine siskins, and purple-finches love niger thistle; white tufted titmice and chickadees enjoy peanut kernels. To attract the greatest possible diversity of birds, use the two basic seed types in most of your feeders, and round out the menu with such nourishing but more species-specific seeds as red proso millet, black- and gray-striped sunflower seeds, peanut kernels, niger thistle, and milo. These are available from mail-order specialty suppliers and from nature centers and farm and garden stores.

Suet: In cold weather, beef suet can help birds maintain their body heat. Woodpeckers especially appreciate suet. Hang the fat in a plastic mesh bag or wire holder (to keep large birds from stealing the entire chunk), or dip pinecones in melted suet and hang the cones from branches.

Special feeding: Supplemental feeding is crucial in the winter and early spring, when natural food supplies are low. But summer feeding is also rewarding. Fruits such as oranges,

Creating a bird garden. Diversity is the key to attracting birds to your yard. Offer a variety of seed in feeders placed at varying levels to cater to the needs of different species. When adding plants, use as many different food-bearing trees and shrubs as possible. Mix short trees and shrubs with tall trees, and combine open spaces with dense plantings. Put birdbaths in the open, so birds will have a clear view when drinking, but near cover to permit a fast escape.

LANDSCAPING FOR BIRDS

To attract birds to your landscape, look at plants from a bird's point of view. Do they provide food and shelter? Nest sites? Try to plant a variety to provide birds with protective cover and a varied diet throughout the year. The following trees and shrubs are excellent food sources—producing berries, nuts, or seeds that birds will flock to. Evergreen species provide food but are also especially important for winter cover. These species will grow in most regions of the country.

Deciduous Shrubs

Berberis thunbergii (Japanese barberry)
Cornus sericea (red-osier dogwood)
Myrica spp. (bayberries)
Prunus pumila, P. besseyi (sand cherries)
Pyracantha spp. (pyracanthas)
Rhamnus cathartica (common buckthorn)
Rubus spp. (raspberries and blackberries)
Sambucus canadensis (American elder)
Vaccinium spp. (blueberries)
Viburnum spp. (viburnums)

Evergreen Shrubs

Cotoneaster spp. (cotoneasters)
Mahonia aquifolium (Oregon grape)
Ilex cornuta (Chinese holly)
Taxus cuspidata (Japanese yew)

Deciduous Trees

Amelanchier spp. (serviceberries)
Carya spp. (hickories)
Celtis spp. (hackberries)
Cornus florida (flowering dogwood)
Crataegus spp. (hawthorns)
Diospyros virginiana (common persimmon)
Elaeagnus angustifolia (Russian olive)
Fagus grandifolia (American beech)
Fraxinus americana (white ash)
Prunus spp. (cherries)
Malus spp. (crab apples)
Morus spp. (mulberries)
Sorbus spp. (mountain ashes)
Quercus spp. (oaks)

Evergreen Trees

Ilex opaca (American holly)
Juniperus virginiana (Eastern red cedar)
Picea spp. (spruces)
Pinus spp. (pines)
Pseudotsuga menziesii (Douglas fir)
Tsuga canadensis (Canada hemlock)

---

apples, and bananas attract many species, including robins, tanagers, mockingbirds, and orioles. Simply cut the fruit in half and stick it on tree branches.

Use your vegetable garden as a source of food for birds. Grow a few rows of sunflowers, wheat, sorghum, and millet just for them. In the fall, let late-maturing vegetables and flowers go to seed. And don't till under cover crops such as buckwheat and rye until spring.

Hummingbirds: Hummingbirds are popular summer visitors in almost all parts of the country and can be attracted with feeders that dispense a sugar-water solution. Sugar water, however, provides only a quick energy boost and no real sustenance, so it's best to hang hummingbird feeders near natural nectar sources such as bee balm (*Monarda didyma*), trumpet vine (*Campsis radicans*), fuchsias (*Fuchsia* spp.), and honeysuckles (*Lonicera* spp.).

You can buy syrup for hummingbird feeders or make your own by mixing 4 parts water to 1 part sugar. Boil the water first, then add the sugar and let the solution cool before pouring it into the feeder. Be sure to clean the dispensers in very hot water and refill them with fresh syrup every 3-4 days to keep molds from developing. Don't use honey to make the syrup—it can foster a fungal growth on the hummingbirds' beaks.

Squelching squirrels and bigger birds: Hungry squirrels and chipmunks can be a problem at feeders. They can get into even hard-to-reach feeders and, once there, quickly empty them. Keep them away from pole-mounted stations by attaching a metal collar or an upside-down flowerpot on the pole just beneath the feeder. If the thieves are climbing a tree or branch to get at the food, wrap a 2' section of sheet metal around the trunk or limb. You can also distract these entertaining but pesky rodents by offering them their own snacks: Stick an ear of corn on a nail in a tree or scatter peanuts on the ground near cover.

You can use the same tactic if large or aggressive birds like grackles and pigeons dominate your feeders while the smaller songbirds are frightened away. Toss some cracked corn or stale bread on the ground several yards from the stations to draw the bigger birds away. (But clean it up nightly so you don't also attract rats or other unwelcome hungry visitors.) One effective solution is to simply add more feeders to reduce the competition.

Water All Year

Under normal conditions, most birds get all the water they need from the food they eat, from dew, and from rain. Nonetheless, a reliable water source makes life easier for birds—and can be critical during drought or in arid regions such as the Southwest.

Set a birdbath or shallow pan in the open and at least 3' off the ground. A spot near shrubs or overhanging branches to provide an escape route from cats or other predators is ideal. The water in the bath should be no deeper than 3". Birds are particularly attracted to the sound of moving water, so it helps to hang a dripping hose (or a leaky can or jug, filled with water daily) from a branch over the bath.

Birds need water in winter, too. Commercial immersion water heaters will keep the water in birdbaths thawed in winter. They are available from stores and mail-order supply houses that sell bird supplies. You can try to keep water from freezing by pouring warm water into the baths as needed, but on very cold days this requires a lot of pouring.

Cover and Nest Sites

Cover is any form of shelter from enemies and the elements. Different bird species favor different kinds of cover: Mourning doves, for example, prefer evergreen groves; others prefer the refuge of densely twiggy shrubs. Likewise, most species require a particular kind of cover in which to raise a family. Some birds, including red-winged blackbirds, nest in high grass; others, such as cardinals, nest in dense foliage; and still others, such as woodpeckers, need wooded land.

You can add more nest sites and attract many types of birds to your yard with birdhouses. Different species have different housing requirements, but there are ready-made birdhouses, and build-your-own plans, for everything from bluebirds to barn owls. Whichever birdhouse you choose, make sure that it is weather-resistant, that its roof is pitched to shed rain, and that there are holes in the bottom for drainage and in the walls or back for ventilation. A hinged or removable top or front makes cleaning easier. Position birdhouses with their entrance holes facing away from prevailing winds, and clean out the boxes after every nesting season.

Landscaping for Birds

Feeders, birdbaths, and birdhouses play important roles in attracting birds. But trees, shrubs, and other vegetation can do the whole job naturally. Plants provide food, cover, and nest sites, and because they trap dew and rain and control runoff, they help provide water, too.

When adding plants to your landscape, choose as many food-bearing species as possible, with enough variety to assure birds a steady diet of fruit, buds, and seeds throughout the year. Mix plantings of deciduous and evergreen species in order to maintain leafy cover in all seasons. Species that are native to your region are generally best, because the local birds evolved with them and will turn to them first for food and cover. Combine as many types of vegetation as possible: tall trees, shorter trees, shrubs, grasses, flowers, and groundcovers. The greater the plant diversity, the greater the variety of birds you will attract.

Hummingbirds have their own landscape favorites. Preferred trees and shrubs include tulip tree (*Liriodendron tulipifera*), mimosa (*Albizia julibrissin*), cotoneasters (*Cotoneaster* spp.), orange-eye butterfly bush (*Buddleia davidii*), flowering quinces (*Chaenomeles* spp.), and rose-of-Sharon (*Hibiscus syriacus*). A trumpet vine (*Campsis radicans*) is a gorgeous sight in bloom, with its showy scarlet flowers, and it is a hummingbird favorite, as are annual climbing nasturtium (*Tropaeolum majus*) and morning-glory (*Ipomoea tricolor*). Favored perennials include columbines (*Aquilegia* spp.), common foxglove (*Digitalis purpurea*), alumroots (*Heuchera* spp.), cardinal flower (*Lobelia cardinalis*), penstemons (*Penstemon* spp.), torch lilies (*Kniphofia* spp.), sages (*Salvia* spp.), and delphiniums (*Delphinium* spp.).

Of course, there is the flip side of landscaping for the birds, especially if you grow berries for your family. Bird netting may be a necessity if you don't want to share your cherries and blueberries with your feathered friends. Fortunately, netting and other simple techniques will prevent or minimize damage. For more on controlling birds, see the Animal Pests entry. But most seed- and fruit-eating birds favor wild food sources and are drawn to gardens only for their relative abundance of insects. ❖

Blackberry

Rubus spp.
Rosaceae

Blackberries taste like summer vacation. The rich-tasting, black fruit brings back memories of lazy summer days and quiet country lanes. Blackberries make superb preserves and baked goods. The newer, thornless cultivars are far easier to live with than their clawed sisters. To learn how to tell the difference between blackberries and black raspberries, see "Blackberries and Raspberries" on page 78. Blackberries can be grown in almost all areas of the country. There are cultivars that thrive in the far South, as well as ones that weather the wintry blasts of the Northern states.

Blackberry plants have perennial roots and biennial canes. They are the largest of the bramble fruits, and most require a trellis or other support. For information on growing blackberries, see the Brambles entry. ❖

Blanching

Gardeners blanch some crops in the garden, others in the kitchen. In the garden, blanching is a technique that keeps light from reaching certain plant parts and prevents them from developing green color. To blanch crops such as cauliflower and celery, tie up leaves or other plant parts around the area to be blanched, or place boards or soil over it. See the Cauliflower, Celery, Endive, and Leek entries for specific information on blanching these vegetables.

In the kitchen, blanching vegetables means exposing them to boiling water or steam for a few minutes and then immediately cooling them in ice-cold water. Blanch vegetables just before freezing to prevent the development of unpleasant flavors or odors and the loss of vitamin C. See the Freezing entry for detailed information on preserving vegetables by freezing. ❖

Blueberry

Vaccinium spp.
Ericaceae

Blueberries are among North America's few cultivated native fruits. They have become one of the most popular fruits for home gardeners for their ornamental value, pest resistance, and delicious berries. Only their soil requirements keep them from being more widely planted.

Types of Blueberries

Northerners grow two species of blueberries: *Vaccinium corymbosum,* highbush, and *V. angustifolium,* lowbush. Southern gardeners tend to raise *V. ashei,* rabbiteye blueberry. All three species and their cultivars bear delicious fruit on plants with beautiful white, urn-shaped flowers and bright fall color.

Lowbush blueberries: Although the fruit of the lowbush blueberry is small, many people consider its flavor superior to that of other blueberries. These extremely hardy plants are good choices for the North. They bear nearly a pint of fruit for each foot of row. Lowbush plants spread by layering and will quickly grow into a matted low hedge. Native lowbush blueberries are the most hardy, especially with snow to protect them in Northern locations. Zones 2-6.

Highbush blueberries: Highbush are the most popular home-garden blueberries. Growing 6'-12' or more in height, each bush may yield 5-20 lb. of large berries in mid- to late summer. Crosses between highbush and lowbush species have resulted in several hardy, large-fruiting plants. They grow 1½'-3' tall, a size that is easy to cover with bird-proof netting or with burlap (for winter protection). Highbush blueberries vary in hardiness, but many cultivars grow well in the North if you plant them in a sheltered spot. Some growers raise them in large pots and store them in an unheated greenhouse or cold frame for the winter. Zones 3-8.

Rabbiteye blueberries: Rabbiteyes are

ideal for warmer climates. They'll tolerate drier soils than highbush plants can, although they may need irrigation during dry spells. The plants grow rapidly and often reach full production in 4-5 years. They grow from 10' to more than 25' high and may yield up to 20 lb. of fruit per bush. Rabbiteyes and their hybrids are not reliably hardy north of Zone 7. They do not grow well in areas that are completely frost-free, however, because they need a chilling period of a few weeks to break dormancy and set fruit. Zones 7-9.

Planting

Blueberries are particular about their growing conditions, so be sure to choose a suitable spot. They need a moist but well-drained, loose, loamy, or sandy soil with a pH of 4.5-5.2. If your soil test indicates a pH higher than 6.2, it's probably not worth the trouble and expense to lower the pH and keep the soil acidic. If your soil tests 5.5-6.0, you can reduce it to the required 4.5-5.2 by mixing sphagnum peat moss with the soil around new plants. You might also plant them in composted pine needles or oak leaves, or in compost made from pine, oak, or hemlock bark. Avoid using the commonly prescribed aluminum sulfate because it's toxic to many soil organisms and changes the flavor of the fruit. For more information on adjusting soil pH, see the pH entry.

Because most blueberries are not self-fertile, you must plant at least two different cultivars to get fruit, and three are even more effective for good cross-pollination. Plant different cultivars near each other, as the blossoms are not especially fragrant and do not attract bees as readily as many other flowers. If you have a large plot set aside for blueberries, try interplanting the cultivars. Blueberries grow slowly and don't reach full production until they're 6-8 years old, so get a head start with two- or three-year-old plants.

After enriching the soil and making sure it's acid enough for blueberries, cultivate it thoroughly to allow the roots to penetrate easily.

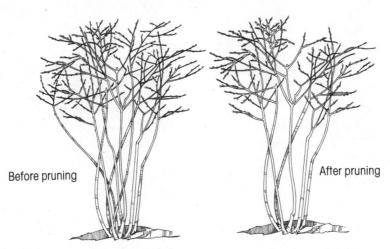

Before pruning

After pruning

Pruning rabbiteye blueberries. After plants begin to produce well, cut out a few of the thick older canes each year. Thin out branches that are crowding each other, and the twiggy ends of canes if they seem too thick. Cut back any plants that are growing too high to harvest conveniently. This system also works for highbush plants in Zones 5–8.

Blueberries are shallow-rooted, so all the nutrients and moisture the plants need must be available in the top few inches of soil.

In spring or fall, set highbush and rabbiteye blueberries 5' apart in rows spaced 7'-9' apart. Set lowbush plants 1' apart in rows 3' or more apart. Water your plants with a liquid organic fertilizer such as manure tea or fish emulsion directly after planting and once a week for the next 3-4 weeks. (For instructions on making manure tea, see the Manure entry.)

Maintenance

Keep plants weed-free, but avoid cultivating or hoeing around them; it's easy to damage the shallow roots. Maintain a thick layer of organic mulch around the plants, and hand-pull any weeds that emerge. Pine needles, oak leaves, or shavings from oak, pine, or hemlock are great mulches that help to maintain soil acidity. Even with a mulch, though, blueberries can dry out quickly, so water often during dry seasons.

Nitrogen is very important for healthy blueberries. Plants lacking nitrogen have stunted growth and yellow leaves that later become a reddish color. Each spring, apply cottonseed meal, soybean meal, dried manure, or a balanced, high-nitrogen, organic fertilizer under the mulch around

each plant. Use ½-1 lb. per plant, depending on the size of the plant and how well it is growing.

Pruning

Like most bush fruits, blueberries benefit from pruning as they become older. Yearly pruning helps to encourage large fruits and maintain productivity. Proper pruning also lets sunshine into the bushes, which aids in ripening the berries. Late winter is the ideal time for pruning.

In general, both highbush and rabbiteye plants respond to the same type of pruning. For the first 3-4 years, prune only to make sure each bush is growing in a strong upright shape. If the fruit buds are too numerous, remove some of them to get fewer but larger berries. (You can distinguish fruit buds on the dormant plants because they are fatter than leaf buds.) For information on pruning established rabbiteye plants, as well as established highbush plants in Zones 5-8, see "Pruning Rabbiteye Blueberries" above for details.

In Zones 3 and 4, highbush blueberries need a different type of pruning because they grow more slowly and don't get as tall. The severe pruning that is necessary farther south would be likely to reduce production drastically for many years. See "Pruning Highbush Blueberries" below for details.

Lowbush plants naturally form low, open-growing shrubs. Prune to remove injured branches and thin out the older canes. For details, see "Pruning Lowbush Blueberries" on page 74.

Problems

Although commercial growers encounter a variety of insects, home gardeners rarely have any problems. The blueberry maggot and cherry fruitworm are the most troublesome insects that are likely to appear. The larvae tunnel in the fruit, making it unsuitable for consumption. Reduce the chances of damage by cleaning up all the old fruit in a planting before winter. If there is a serious infestation, cover the bushes with screen in spring to prevent egg laying.

Diseases are seldom a concern in the North but tend to be more common in the South. Botrytis tip blight kills new growth, and stem canker causes cracks in the canes. Cut away any growth that shows signs of abnormal appearance. Mummy berry makes the fruit rot and fall off. To prevent it, plant resistant cultivars, keep the berries picked, and clean up any dropped fruit.

Viral diseases, such as stunt, are difficult to control and invariably result in the gradual deterioration of the plant. Buy from a reputable nursery to get disease-free plants.

Birds are unusually fond of blueberries. To prevent damage, cover the bushes with tightly woven netting before the berries begin to ripen.

Harvesting

Blueberries ripen over a long season, and you don't need to pick them daily like strawberries. Different cultivars ripen to various shades of blue, so be careful not to pick them too early if you want the best flavor; taste them to determine when they're at their peak. Don't pull berries from the stem; instead, gently twist them off with your fingertips. If the berries don't come off with slight pressure, they're not ready for harvest. Blueberries keep for several days after picking if you keep them cool and dry. They are also ideal for freezing.

Selecting Cultivars

Cross-pollination of blueberries is very important for good fruit production. Keep good records of your plantings, so that if you lose a cultivar

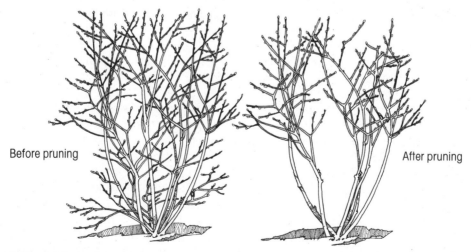

Before pruning   After pruning

Pruning highbush blueberries. In Zones 5–8, prune highbush plants as you would rabbiteyes. In Zones 3 and 4, it is usually only necessary to thin out the twiggy ends of the branches and cut out any wood that is broken or winter-damaged. When the bush is about 20 years old, it is beneficial to remove some of the older wood and gradually renew the plant.

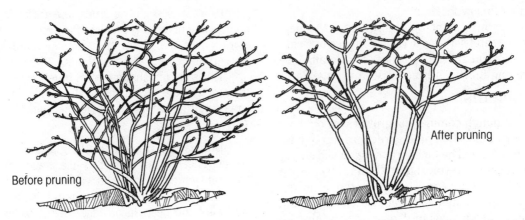

Before pruning

After pruning

Pruning lowbush blueberries. Cut up to half of the older canes to the ground each year, and harvest berries from the uncut stems. The next year, remove the stems you left the previous year, and harvest fruit from the new stems.

you'll be able to replace it with a kind that's different from the surviving plants.

Lowbush: 'Augusta', 'Blomidon', 'Brunswick', 'Chignecto', and 'Putte'. The last, a 1' tall plant from Sweden, is very productive.

Highbush: 'Atlantic', a heavy bearer of high-quality, large, light blue berries; 'Berkley', large, sweet berries, mid-season, moderately hardy; 'Bluecrop', light blue fruit, a bit tart, moderately hardy, reliable; 'Bluejay', crack-resistant fruit, pleasant tart flavor; 'Blueray', early-ripening, firm, sweet fruit, fairly hardy; 'Coville', large berries, tart until fully ripe, vigorous plants, late; 'Earliblue', 4'-6' plants, fruit ripens early, moderately hardy; 'Elliott', medium-sized fruit, tart until fully ripe, very late; 'Herbert', heavy crops of large, flavorful berries in mid-season; 'Ivanhoe', early-ripening, light blue with good flavor, productive; 'Jersey', popular, large, fair-quality berry, late; 'Olympia', large-sized, medium blue berries, popular in the Pacific Northwest; 'Rubel', heavy producer of small berries, good for processing, late; 'Spartan', very large fruit, vigorous, fairly hardy, early; 'Weymouth', older cultivar, ripens very early.

Especially hardy cultivars, growing 2'-5'

tall, include 'Early Bluejay', early-bearing, vigorous; 'Northblue', heavy-bearing, superhardy, 2' plant, high-quality fruit; 'Northland', early-ripening fruit on 4' spreading bush; 'Patriot', large, early-ripening, rich-flavored fruit, 4' bush.

Rabbiteye: 'Aliceblue', early-ripening, medium to large fruit; 'Beckyblue', medium to large, light blue fruit, upright grower; 'Bluebelle', extra-large flavorful fruit in mid-season; 'Bonita', vigorous grower, medium-large light blue fruits, early; 'Briteblue', large clusters of late-ripening, firm, sweet berries; 'Climax', vigorous plant, early ripening with medium-sized berries; 'Powderblue', heavy producer of large, dark blue fruit, late; 'Premier', large, early-ripening fruit on spreading bushes; 'Southland', one of the hardiest of the group; 'Tifblue', good quality, sweet berries, mid- to late season, a popular cultivar; 'Woodard', early-ripening, large, good, but slightly tart fruits.

Hybrids: 'Northsky', grows to 1½' high with a 2'-3' spread, medium-sized light blue fruit, very cold-hardy; 'Top Hat', very compact (to 16") dense growth, medium-sized light blue berries, self-fruitful (needs no cross-pollination), great for containers. ❖

Bog Gardens

If your property has a low, wet spot that drowns lawn grass and is a misery to mow, or if you'd like a graceful landscape around your water garden, try a bog garden. With a little effort, you can turn an unused area into a garden feature. You'll find a design that includes a bog garden in the Water Gardens entry.

Building a Bog Garden

Even if you don't have a low wet spot, you can still have a bog garden. All you need to do is to excavate a hole and line it with a plastic pool liner. The larger you make your bog garden, the better, since small excavations dry out quickly. Choose a level spot in sun or shade, depending on the plants you wish to grow. Excavate a bowl-shaped hole 1½'-2' deep at the center. Line the hole with a commercial pool liner or a sheet of 6-mil plastic.

Unless you have sandy soil, don't use the soil you dig out of your future bog garden. The best mix for a bog is 50 percent sand and 50 percent peat or compost. Fill the excavation with soil mix until it mounds in the center, packing it down as you go. Fill your new bog garden with water. Wait at least a month before planting to let the soil settle. Keep the soil wet at all times.

Choosing Bog Plants

Natural bogs contain plants that are adapted to wet, acid soils. Perennial bog plants you can grow include water arum (*Calla palustris*), creeping snowberry (*Gaultheria hispidula*), twinflower (*Linnaea borealis*), and bog bean (*Menyanthes trifoliata*). Woody plants for backyard bogs include winterberry (*Ilex verticillata*), sheep laurel (*Kalmia angustifolia*), rhodora (*Rhododendron canadense*), and blueberries and cranberries (*Vaccinium* spp.).

Many bog plants, such as pitcher plants (*Sarracenia* spp.) and sundews (*Drosera* spp.), are becoming rare in the wild. If you choose to plant them, buy only from reputable dealers who propagate their plants. For tips on how to avoid buying wild-collected plants, see the Endangered Plant Species entry.

If your soil is neutral rather than acid or if you'd like to grow a more colorful collection of plants, your choices are wider than if you're duplicating true bog conditions. There are quite a few plants that enjoy wet feet. Perennials that grow well in wet garden soils in full sun include swamp milkweed (*Asclepias incarnata*), Joe-pye weed (*Eupatorium maculatum*), rose mallow (*Hibiscus moscheutos*), Siberian iris (*Iris sibirica*), blue flag iris (*I. versicolor*), rodgersias (*Rodgersia* spp.), and globeflowers (*Trollius* spp.). Perennials for a partially shaded bog site include Jack-in-the-Pulpit (*Arisaema triphyllum*), marsh marigold (*Caltha palustris*), turtleheads (*Chelone* spp.), ligularias (*Ligularia* spp.), cardinal flower (*Lobelia cardinalis*), forget-me-not (*Myosotis scorpioides*), and Japanese primrose (*Primula japonica*). Woody plants for soggy soils include red-osier dogwood (*Cornus sericea*), willows (*Salix* spp.), swamp azalea (*Rhododendron viscosum*), and blueberries.

Bog Garden Maintenance

The most important maintenance job for a bog garden is watering, especially if it is an artificial bog. *Never* allow the soil to dry out. Dry soil is sure death for water-loving plants. If you're re-creating an acid-soil bog, grow a living mulch of sphagnum moss (available from biological supply houses). Mulch your bog garden with pine straw or oak leaves in the winter to protect delicate plants. Remove the mulch in spring to allow the sphagnum to grow. If you don't have sphagnum, leave the mulch in place to rot into the soil. Remove weed seedlings before they become a problem. Since bogs are naturally low in nutrients, bog plants don't need fertilizing. ❖

Bonsai

The goal of the traditional Oriental art of bonsai (pronounced *bone-sigh*) is to replicate the look of an old tree shaped by time and weather, but dwarfed and grown in a pot. Traditional bonsai trees are not houseplants. They need protection during temperate zone winters, but are kept outside during the growing season and only brought indoors occasionally for display.

Bonsai (which means "tree in a pot" in Japanese) can be created from evergreens and deciduous trees, or from almost any plant with a solid, woody trunk and stout limbs. Bonsai fruit trees—often quince, plum, or crab apple—bear small fruit. The best plants for bonsai have tapering trunks with interesting shapes, bends or twists. Scars, gnarls, and stumps give the tree an aged look.

There are five basic training styles: formal upright, informal upright, broom-shaped, windswept, and cascade. The formal and informal upright styles are for conical, tightly branched trees. The branches of a broom-shaped tree are more spreading, so that the tree resembles an upside-down broom. Windswept tree trunks grow nearly horizontally. Cascading trees fall away over the pot rim, as trees growing on cliffs or rock outcroppings often do.

Bonsai artists develop the styles through a combination of pruning, pinching, and wiring. The trunk is the primary focus of a bonsai tree, and asymmetrical patterns in the branches complement the trunk. Experienced bonsai artists sometimes scar or strip the tree's bark as well.

The container for a bonsai tree is like the frame of a picture: It should enhance the effect without distracting the viewer from the main attraction. In general, earth-tone containers flatter evergreens, while glazed pots complement deciduous or flowering trees.

If you're intrigued by the art of bonsai and want to learn how to create your own, refer to *Bonsai: The Complete Guide to Art and Technique* by Paul Lesniewicz or *The Beginner's Guide to American Bonsai* by Gerald P. Stowell. ❖

Botanical Gardens

A botanical garden is an institution established for the display and maintenance of living collections of plants. Many botanical gardens began as arboreta (collections of trees arranged for education and research), then expanded to include display gardens featuring herbaceous perennials and annuals for education and enjoyment. You'll often find botanical gardens that are still called arboreta, like the U.S. National Arboretum in Washington, D.C.

There's more to botanical gardens than groups of plants, however. A botanical garden may feature conservatories, research greenhouses, nurseries, an arboretum, display gardens, trial gardens, a library, and an herbarium (where dried plant specimens are kept as a record). Many botanical gardens, like the Brooklyn Botanic Garden, also produce publications related to plants and the garden. Another important aspect of botanical gardens today is management of endangered plant species and education concerning natural areas.

A botanical garden may be affiliated with a university, a state or federal agency, or a municipality, or it may be privately funded. There's bound to be at least one botanical garden or arboretum in your state. Plants are clearly labeled and often beautifully displayed. Visiting a botanical garden is a great way to learn about new and interesting plants that will grow well in your area. You may pick up a few design ideas or wonderful combinations as well. ❖

Botanical Insecticides

Botanical insecticides, such as pyrethrins and neem, are derived from plants. Since they occur naturally, they tend to break down faster in the environment than synthetic chemicals do. This does not mean they are harmless. Many are toxic to nontarget insects and other animals, including humans. For more information on botanical insecticides, see the Insecticides entry. ❖

Botanical Nomenclature

Rose, Iris, Daisy, Fern—there are many wonderful plant names that are also used as names for people. The crossover of human and plant names is fun. However, sorting out confusing and overlapping common plant names isn't fun for puzzled gardeners trying to figure out what to order from a garden catalog or how to find the plants they want at a nursery. Some plants have several common names. For example, the popular shade-tolerant annual many gardeners call impatiens is also known as patient Lucy, Zanzibar balsam, patience plant, busy Lizzy, sultana, and sultan snapweed.

Fortunately, gardeners can keep the names and the plants straight by learning about and using botanical nomenclature. Botanists developed this systematic way of naming plants so they could precisely classify every plant they study. This system gives a plant a two-part name, which identifies the plant and classifies it in relation to other plants. The two parts of the name are the *genus* and the *species*. A species is a group of individual plants that share common attributes and are able to breed together. A genus is a group of one or more species with closely similar flowers, fruits, and other characteristics.

Genus and species names are analagous to people's first names and surnames. The genus name is like a surname: It indicates a group of plants that have some shared characteristics, just as a surname links a group of related human beings. Genus names are often derived from Greek or Latin words, or from the names of people. For example, *Allium* (the genus of onions and their kin) is the Latin word for garlic, and *Nicotiana* (the genus of tobacco) was named for Jean Nicot, who introduced tobacco to Europeans. It's usually easy to see the shared traits of plants in a genus. Gardeners often refer to plants by using the generic name (the name of the genus) as a common name. When gardeners talk about irises, dahlias, and anemones, they use the generic names *Iris, Dahlia,* and *Anemone* as common names.

The species name is like a person's first name. By itself, a species name won't help you identify a particular plant. For example, many plants bear the specific name *odorata* because they are fragrant, so the name *odorata* alone doesn't refer to any one kind of plant. It takes both names, the genus and the species, to identify a plant as, for example, *Viola odorata* (sweet violet). Together, the two parts of a botanical name specify a particular kind of plant and distinguish it from all other kinds of plants.

In nature, most members of a species look pretty much the same, aside from differences due to age or growing conditions. Minor but consistent variations that occur within a species in nature are called subspecies or varieties. For example, doublefile viburnum is *Viburnum plicatum* var. *tomentosum*. It bears flat, showy flowers in rows on top of the branches, unlike the species, Japanese snowball viburnum (*Viburnum plicatum*), which bears round snowball flowers.

Among cultivated plants, however, there can be wide variation within a species. Gardeners have always singled out and propagated individual plants with noteworthy form, color, fragrance, or flavor. Any cultivated plant with particular features that are passed along when the plant is reproduced by seed or by asexual propagation is called a cultivar, short for *culti*vated *vari*ety. To be proper, cultivar names should follow the species name, as in *Salvia officinalis* 'Tricolor'. (Botanical varieties can also have cultivars—for example, *Viburnum plicatum* var. *tomentosum* 'Mariesii' is a large-flowered form of doublefile viburnum.) For convenience, though, most gardeners refer to vegetables, fruits, and annual flowers by the cultivar name and common name, such as 'Silver Queen' sweet corn.

Botanical names and groupings sometimes change, as botanists correct past errors or achieve new understanding. Usually a specialist will grow, observe, and study all the plants in a genus for many years before publishing a revised classification. Several more years may pass before such changes are widely adopted. ❖

Brambles

Rubus spp.
Rosaceae

Raspberries and blackberries are among the most delicious and desirable berries you can grow. They are frequently treated as gourmet fruit, not because they are hard to grow, but because they don't ship well.

Selecting Brambles

Brambles can produce fruit for 10-25 years. It's important to choose cultivars that have the characteristics you want and suit your climate.

Raspberries: There are two types of raspberries: summer-bearing and fall-bearing. In some areas of the country, their bearing season may overlap, so you can harvest raspberries from early summer until frost. Red and yellow cultivars are summer- or fall-bearers. Black and purple raspberries are all summer-bearers.

Red and yellow raspberries are the easiest raspberries to grow. Their fruit is sweet and fragrant. Yellow raspberries are mutations, or *sports,* of reds, and tend to be very sweet. The color is less attractive to birds, too.

Black raspberries are not as winter-hardy as red ones, but tend to tolerate more summer heat. They also are more prone to viral and fungal diseases and have stiffer thorns. The berries are seedy but have a very intense flavor. They are good eaten fresh or in preserves.

Purple raspberries are hybrids resulting from crosses between reds and blacks. The canes are generally more winter-hardy than the black parents. They tend to be very spiny and productive with large, intensely flavored berries.

Blackberries: In general, blackberries are less winter-hardy than most raspberries. In Northern areas, the roots may survive without protection, but the overwintering canes are often killed above the snow line. But because blackberries tend to be extremely vigorous, even a very short portion of surviving cane will often produce a surprising amount of fruit.

Blackberries can be divided into three general groups: erect, semi-erect, and trailing.

The erect type has strong, upright canes that are usually thorny and don't require support. They tend to be more winter-hardy than the other types and produce large, sweet berries.

Semi-erect blackberries are thornless and more vigorous and productive than the erect type. Most of them grow better if supported. The fruit is tart and large. The plants bloom and mature later than the erect type.

Trailing blackberries, or dewberries, are the least winter-hardy. They need support, are early ripening, and have large wine-colored to black fruit of distinctively good flavor.

Hybrids: Raspberry-blackberry hybrids combine the characteristics of their parents. Most

Blackberries and raspberries. Each berry is made up of a cluster of drupelets, each of which contains a single seed. Raspberries are shaped like little caps, with a hollow where the stem was. Blackberries have a solid core.

of them are very winter-tender. Some are thornless. The fruit resembles blackberries.

Planting and Care

Brambles prefer deep, sandy-loam soil, but they will grow in almost any soil with adequate drainage and a pH range of 6.0-7.0, preferably near 6.5. Choose a site with good air drainage. Avoid low-lying areas and frost pockets. Full sun is preferred. In Southern areas, partial midday shade will prevent sunscalded fruit. In exposed locations, give your berries a windbreak.

Soil Preparation

Brambles thrive in soils with high organic content. Incorporate as much organic matter as you possibly can. Have the soil tested, and amend it if necessary. If you have perennial weeds, eradicate them before planting brambles because the young plants do not compete well with weeds. Cultivate repeatedly or use a thick, organic mulch to smother out the weeds.

Planting

Plant brambles in very early spring. The exception is plants produced by tissue culture, which have young, tender leaves. Plant them after all chance of frost has passed, or provide frost protection. Set bareroot plants 1″-2″ deeper than they were in the nursery. Dig a large enough hole so the roots will fit without bending. Don't let roots dry out while planting. Cut the canes off at ground level and burn or dispose of them to reduce the possibility of introducing diseases.

Plant Spacing

Row spacing should be wide enough to allow sunlight and air to reach all plants and to allow you to walk or mow between the rows without damaging yourself or the plants. For home gardeners this means at least 5′ between rows for raspberries and 7′ for blackberries.

Some types of brambles produce suckers. Red and yellow raspberries spread 12″-15″ a year, so plant 1′-2′ apart, depending on how soon

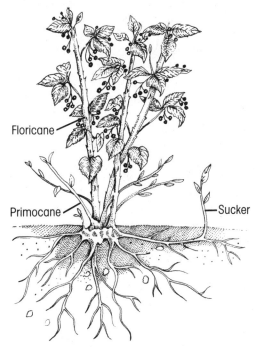

Bramble plant. Primocanes are new shoots that arise from the main plant or new suckers that rise from roots away from the main plant. In their second year they are called floricanes. Most brambles bear fruit only on floricanes. Fall-bearing raspberries fruit on primocanes.

you want a solid hedgerow. Blacks and most purples don't sucker but form clusters of canes from their crowns. Plant them 2½′-3′ apart. Blackberries sucker vigorously; space them 5′-6′ apart in rows.

Trellising

Though many brambles can be grown without a support system, all are best grown on a trellis. Trellising reduces disease problems, saves space, and speeds pruning and picking.

T trellis: Summer-bearing raspberries do well on a T trellis like the one illustrated on page 80. Construct it as follows:

1. Set a sturdy 4″ post at each end of the row and about every 20′ in between. Post should be set at least 2′ deep and extend 4′-6′ aboveground.

2. Add a 2″ × 4″ cross arm, with notches cut on each arm, to hold wires. The height of the cross arms will depend on how vigorous your brambles are. Try putting them about 3′ high, and move them if necessary.

3. Cut two lengths of #12- or #14-gauge wire or synthetic baling twine a little longer than the trellis, and fasten the ends to either side of the endpost cross arms.

4. After pruning, put the wires in the outer notches, and arrange the canes outside the wire. Tie each cane individually to the wire. Or use two sets of wires on each side of the cross arm, and sandwich the canes between them. After harvest, move the wires to the inside notch to keep the new canes upright.

Hedgerow trellis: All types of bramble fruit do well when supported by a hedgerow-type trellising system like the one shown on this page. To construct it:

1. Set a sturdy 4″ post at each end of the row and about every 20′ in between.

2. Hammer upward-slanting nails into both sides of each post 3′ and 4′ above the ground.

3. Cut four lengths of wire slightly longer than the trellis and twist the ends of the wires into a loop to fit over the end nail.

Hedgerow trellis. This easy-to-build trellis system gives good support to any type of brambles.

4. After pruning, lift the wires onto the nails to hold the canes upright between them. (Future pruning is easier if you can remove the wires, so don't staple them to the posts, just rest them on the nails.) Tuck new canes between the wires. A variation of this trellis uses 1′ cross arms to hold the wires farther apart.

Pruning

For pruning purposes, let's divide the brambles into four categories: fall-bearing raspberries, summer-bearing raspberries, black and purple raspberries, and blackberries. Since each site and cultivar is different, you will want to adjust cane densities to fit your needs.

Fall-bearing raspberries: Mow or cut off these brambles as close to ground level as possible after leaf drop in the fall. Pruning fall-bearing raspberries is easy because you don't have to decide which canes to save. The most common problem is not cutting the canes low enough to the ground. If stubs are left, some of the buds on them will sprout in the spring and grow into weak, unproductive branches. Pruning fall-bearers is illustrated on page 82.

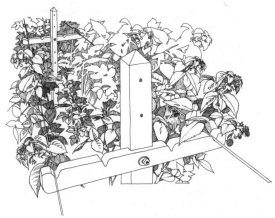

T trellis. This trellis bends the fruiting canes outward and lets the new primocanes grow straight and strong in the center without competition from the floricanes.

Summer-bearing raspberries: Summer-bearing raspberries and erect blackberries bear fruit on second-year canes called floricanes. Prune bearing canes off at ground level immediately after the harvest has finished. To avoid spreading diseases, do this when the canes and leaves are dry.

Dormant-prune every year in very early spring before growth starts. Drop any trellis wires out of the way. If you didn't remove the spent floricanes after harvest, cut them off at ground level now. Cut off any spindly canes, and thin the remaining ones to leave 2-4 of the largest, straightest canes per foot of row. Cut off any suckers that are sprouting outside the row as well. Cut the remaining canes back to 4'-5' and reinstall the trellis wires, or tie the canes to your support system. Pruning summer-bearers is illustrated on this page.

Black and purple raspberries: These brambles bear fruit on second-year canes, with most of their fruit on sideshoots. During the summer, cut the tip off each cane when it's about 2½'-4' high. This will force it to develop sturdy side branches the first year. After harvest, cut the spent floricanes back to the ground.

Dormant-prune every year as for summer-bearing reds, thinning the remaining canes to leave 6-9 of the largest, straightest ones per hill. Prune back the side branches to 8"-12", and remove any spindly ones. Pruning black and purple raspberries is illustrated on page 83.

Blackberries: Trailing and semi-erect blackberries are usually left to grow on the ground along the row during the first season. Blackberries bear fruit on second-year canes. Prune spent floricanes off at ground level immediately after the harvest has finished.

In very early spring, select the thickest 6-9 canes per hill, cut them back to about 7', space along the trellis and tie them. Shorten side branches to 10"-15", remove spindly ones.

Harvesting

Brambles ripen in early summer. Red raspberries tend to ripen first, followed by blacks, and even later by blackberries. Berries do not keep ripening after harvesting. For best flavor and ease of picking, wait until they are fully ripe. Some raspberries offer a slight resistance to picking even when fully ripe. Let your taste tell you when to pick. Red raspberries vary in color at maturity from light to dark red. Some

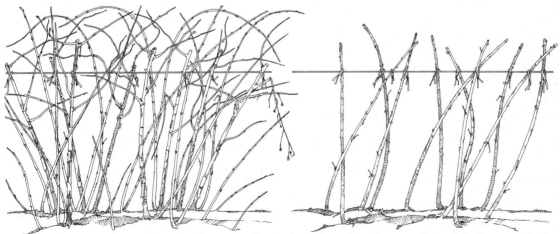

Pruning summer-bearing raspberries. Prune raspberries in early spring. Remove all spent floricanes and thin remaining canes to 2-4 per foot of row.

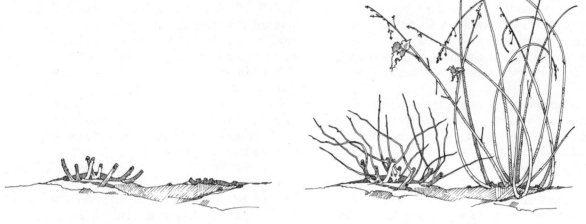

Pruning fall-bearing raspberries. After the plants drop their leaves, cut all canes off at ground level. Don't leave stubs—they will produce short, unproductive sprouts.

purple ones change from red to purple to almost black, with sugar levels increasing as the color darkens. Blackberries, though they also vary in color, are typically shiny black when not quite ripe and dull black when fully ripe. They come off the vines more easily when fully ripe.

Pick your berries as early in the morning as possible while they are cool. If the berries are wet, let them dry before picking. Handle them gently and place, don't drop, them into a shallow container. Refrigerate immediately.

It's easier to pick berries with both hands free. Tie two long strips of sturdy cloth like apron ties to a large tin can or small bucket. Tie your picking can around your waist, or hang it around your neck. Put your berry basket in the bottom if you like. Carry an extra basket to put overripe or moldy berries in as you pick; removing these berries will help prevent rot problems from occurring later.

Problems

While there are many insects and diseases that can attack brambles, there are few bothersome pests in any given area. See the Organic Pest Management entry for more information on control methods.

Insects

Certain common garden pests attack brambles. Aphids can spread viruses. Japanese beetles feed on ripe fruit. Tarnished plant bugs feed on buds, blossoms, and berries. "The Top Ten Garden Insect Pests in America" on page 344 lists descriptions and controls for all three. Keep surrounding areas weed-free to limit tarnished plant bugs.

Picnic or sap beetles sometimes damage ripening fruit. This is the same black beetle that is attracted to potato salad (hence its name) and any overripe or fermenting fruit. To control them, pick all ripe berries promptly. Trap the beetles by putting out overripe muskmelons.

If leaves turn pale and speckled, you may have a spider mite problem. Hot, dry climates and seasons encourage them. "Fruit Tree Insects and Diseases" on page 256 lists controls.

The small green larvae of the raspberry sawfly feed on young leaves, often leaving only the leaf skeleton. Handpick the larvae or spray with BTK (*Bacillus thuringiensis* var. *kurstaki*).

Tiny, light yellow worms feeding on the fruit are Eastern raspberry fruitworm larvae. They overwinter in the ground; adult beetles emerge in the spring. The larvae feed on leaves, flower buds, and berry cores. Berries may drop before they ripen. Remove and destroy infested fruits. Cultivate in late summer to reduce overwintering insects. The following season, spray pyrethrins when blossom buds appear and again just before they open.

Cane borers cause shoot tips or whole canes to wilt and die during the growing season. They puncture two parallel rings of holes around the cane. To control them, cut off wilted canes about 6" below the holes or swelling and destroy. They overwinter inside canes, so collect and burn prunings.

Crown borers feed on the base, roots, and sometimes shoots of plants, causing whole shoots to wilt and die. Cut wilted shoots back to below ground level and destroy. Squash rust-colored egg masses you see on the leaves in late summer.

Sometimes leaves will develop many small punctures, or even large tears, but no obvious insect culprit is seen. The problem may be the wind. Windblown leaves can be rapidly shredded by thorns on the canes. Trellises and windbreaks reduce damage.

Diseases

These diseases can affect brambles:
• Raspberry mosaic, blackberry sterility, and leaf curl are major bramble viruses. Mosaic stunts plants and causes yellow-blotched, puckered leaves. Sterility results in vigorously growing plants that produce only nubbins—tiny, crumbly, malformed berries—or no berries at all. Leaf curl causes dark green, tightly curled and malformed leaves. Viruses can drastically reduce yields. There is no cure. Infected plants should be dug up and disposed of immediately.

Plant virus-resistant cultivars and purchase plants only from nurseries which market virus-free tissue culture or certified bareroot plants. Remove all wild brambles within 500'-1000', especially upwind, and keep aphids off your brambles because they spread viruses. Plant black raspberries away from red and yellow ones, because blacks are more susceptible to viruses.

• Anthracnose causes leaves and canes to develop round sunken purple spots that enlarge to oval shapes with gray centers and raised borders. It also causes black, sunken spots on fruit.

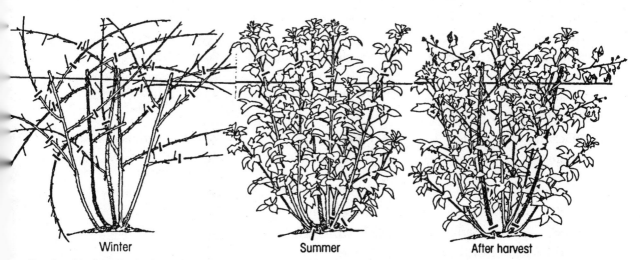

Winter   Summer   After harvest

Pruning black and purple raspberries. Each winter or early spring, remove all but the strongest 6-9 canes, and shorten side branches. Tip-prune in summer, and cut spent floricanes to the ground after harvest.

Raspberry Cultivars

84

There are many fine raspberry cultivars to choose from. This table lists the season of bearing, flavor and size of fruit, hardiness zone, noteworthy characteristics, and known disease resistance or susceptibility of selected cultivars. **R** indicates resistance; **S** indicates susceptibility.

Cultivar	Season	Flavor/Size	Hardiness/Comments
SUMMER-BEARING REDS			
'Algonquin'	Middle	Excellent/medium	Zone 4/ **R:** mosaic
'Boyne'	Early	Good/medium	Zone 3/ productive
'Canby'	Early	Excellent/large	Zone 5/ few thorns; **R:** mosaic
'Chilliwack'	Middle	Excellent/very large	Zone 6/ **R:** mosaic, root rot; **S:** crown gall
'Haida'	Late	Excellent/medium	Zone 4/ few thorns; **R:** mosaic, spur blight
'Killarney'	Middle	Good/medium	Zone 3/ sturdy canes, productive
'Newburgh'	Middle	Excellent/medium	Zone 5/ **R:** mosaic, root rot
'Nordic'	Early	Good/medium	Zone 3/ **R:** mosaic, fungal diseases
'Nova'	Middle	Excellent/large	Zone 4/ **R:** cane diseases
'Sentry'	Middle	Excellent/medium	Zone 4/ tolerates winter temperature swings
'Tulameen'	Late	Excellent/very large	Zone 6/ long season; **R:** mosaic
FALL-BEARING REDS			
'Amity'	Early	Excellent/medium	Zone 4/ **R:** root rot, mosaic, spur blight
'Autumn Bliss'	Very early	Excellent/large	Zone 3/ **R:** mosaic
'Bababerry'	Very late	Good/large	Zone 7/ heat-tolerant
'Heritage'	Late	Good/medium	Zone 4/ **R:** powdery mildew
'Redwing'	Very early	Excellent/medium	Zone 3/ **R:** heat
'Ruby'	Late	Good/very large	Zone 4/ **S:** root rot, crown gall
'Summit'	Very early	Excellent/medium	Zone 3/ **R:** root rot
BLACK RASPBERRIES			
'Black Hawk'	Late	Good/medium	Zone 5/ **R:** anthracnose
'Bristol'	Late	Good/medium	Zone 5/ **R:** powdery mildew; **S:** anthracnose
'Cumberland'	Late	Excellent/medium	Zone 5/ **S:** anthracnose
'Haut'	Middle-late	Good/medium	Zone 5/ long season
'Jewel'	Early	Excellent/large	Zone 5/ **R:** most diseases
PURPLE RASPBERRIES			
'Brandywine'	Late	Good (tart)/large	Zone 4/ **S:** crown gall
'Royalty'	Late	Excellent/large	Zone 4/ **R:** mosaic; **S:** crown gall

• Cane blight causes shoot tips to wilt and die in midsummer. Canes are often purple or brown. Summer tipping black raspberries gives the disease organism a natural opening; be sure to do it on a dry day.

• Orange rust attacks black raspberries and some blackberries. In spring, the underside of the leaves are covered with bright, orange fungal growth. Dig up and burn infested plants.

• Verticillium wilt causes canes to turn bluish black from the soil line upward, and leaves to yellow and drop. The fungus also attacks vegetables such as tomatoes and peppers. Avoid planting brambles where Verticillium-susceptible crops have been grown previously.

• Phytophthora root rot causes stunted plants, yellow leaves, or scorched leaf margins. Avoid it by providing good drainage.

• Fruit rots are caused by various fungi. Wet weather during maturity can cause severe problems. Pick the berries as soon as they are ripe, and remove any moldy ones immediately.

• Powdery mildew shows up as a white powder on the lower sides of leaves and can spread to shoot tips. Fruit may be stunted. Baking soda sprays can help control it.

• Crown gall causes lumpy, corky swellings on the roots and bases of canes. Avoid wounding when cultivating, or use mulch instead.

Fungi need warm temperatures and humid conditions to thrive. Anything you do to keep the aboveground parts of the plants dry will be to your advantage. Select a planting site with good air circulation and drainage. Avoid overhead watering. Keep rows narrow, and thin canes to recommended densities. Avoid excessive nitrogen. Trellis canes for best air circulation. Remove spent canes right after harvest. Collect and destroy all prunings. If fungal diseases were a problem in previous years, apply lime-sulfur spray in the spring when the first leaves are $\frac{1}{4}$"-$\frac{1}{2}$" long.

Best Cultivars

Raspberries: There is a wide range of raspberry cultivars available. See "Raspberry Cul-

> ## More On
> ### BRAMBLES
>
> For more detailed information about growing brambles, contact the North American Bramble Growers Association, 19060 Manning Trail N., Marine, MN 55047-9723, or the North American Fruit Explorers, Route 1, Box 94, Chapin, IL 62628.

tivars" on the opposite page for a listing of some of the best.

There are only a few yellow raspberry cultivars. 'Fallgold' is a very sweet, soft, low-yielding, medium-sized, fall berry. 'Amber' is a summer-bearer with similar characteristics. Both are quite susceptible to bushy dwarf virus.

Blackberries: The hardiest blackberries are erect cultivars like 'Darrow' (−20°F), and 'Illini Hardy' (−24°F). 'Chester' is the hardiest semi-erect thornless cultivar (Zone 5).

Many blackberries grow well in Zones 6-8. 'Cherokee', 'Cheyenne', 'Choctaw','Navaho', and 'Shawnee' are erect cultivars. 'Black Satin', 'Dirksen Thornless', 'Hull', 'Smoothstem', and 'Thornfree' are semi-erect.

'Brazos', 'Comanche', and 'Rosborough' are erect cultivars suited to Zones 7-9. Trailing blackberries like 'Flordagrand', 'Marion', 'Olallie', and 'Waldo' are often most suited to one region, so check with your supplier.

Hybrids: Raspberry-blackberry hybrid cultivars combine the characteristics of both parents, but many of them resemble trailing blackberries. Boysenberry and loganberry are thornless and hardy in Zones 8-9 and produce large, wine-colored fruit. 'Sunberry', 'Tummelberry', and 'Youngberry' are cold-tender cultivars.

Tayberry is hardy in Zones 5-8 and produces purple, unique, sweet-tart fruit. ❖

Broccoli

Brassica oleracea, Botrytis group
Cruciferae

Increased interest in healthful foods has made broccoli a regular feature of most Americans' diets. Broccoli is delicious cooked or raw, it freezes well, and it contains large amounts of vitamins A and C, as well as B vitamins, calcium, and iron.

Planting: Broccoli prefers full sun, but partial shade can prevent plants from bolting (going to seed) in areas with warm spells. Provide a rich, well-drained soil, with plenty of compost.

Cool days and nights are essential once the flower heads start to form. Different cultivars can take from 45 to 85 days to mature, so pick a cultivar that will mature before the weather in your area turns hot. Gardeners in most temperate areas can harvest both spring and fall crops. In areas without ground freezes, try growing a third crop by planting a slow-maturing cultivar in winter.

You can sow the spring crop directly in the garden about two months before the last expected frost. Extreme temperatures, though, may affect the quality of your harvest. A prolonged period of nights around 30°F and days in the 50°-60°F range can produce tiny, immature heads called buttons. Protect plants with cloches or row covers during cool weather. Unexpected warm spells will cause the heads to "rice," or open too soon.

To avoid temperature-related problems, sow your spring crop indoors in sterilized soil 7-9 weeks before the last expected frost. Plant each seed ¼" deep in its own 1' deep pot. Place pots in a sunny area and maintain the temperature at 60°-65°F; keep the soil moist but not wet. The seeds should germinate in 4-5 days.

To avoid premature heading, it's important to transplant seedlings into the garden when they are the proper size. They should be about 6" tall, with 2-4 leaves. Before planting in the garden, harden them off for a week by putting them outdoors during the day and bringing them in at night.

Set the young plants 1"-2" deeper in the garden than they grew in the pots or flats. Space them 1'-2' apart in rows 2'-3' apart. Closer spacing will produce smaller heads. Firm the soil and water well.

Sow fall crops directly in the ground in July or August. In mild winter climates, plant in the late fall for a spring harvest.

Growing guidelines: The trick to producing good broccoli is to keep it growing steadily. Two to three weeks after transplanting, top-dress with manure tea or side-dress with blood meal or fish emulsion, and water deeply. (For instructions on making and using manure tea, see the Manure entry.) Repeat monthly until a week before harvesting the flower head. This regimen also encourages large and tender sideshoots, which you can harvest until hot weather or a heavy ground freeze ends the broccoli season.

Cultivate around young plants to get rid of weeds and keep the soil loose. When daytime temperatures exceed 75°F, put down a thick layer of organic mulch to cool the soil and conserve moisture. Broccoli needs 1"-1½" of water a week. A lack of water will make the plants produce tough stems, so soak them extra well during dry spells. Fall crops need steady (but slightly less) water.

Problems: Of all cabbage-family plants, broccoli is the least affected by pests, and fall crops have even fewer problems than spring ones. Possible pests include aphids, cabbage loopers, imported cabbageworms, cabbage maggots, cutworms, and flea beetles. See "The Top Ten Garden Insect Pests in America" on page 344 for more information on controlling these insects.

Other pests include slugs, mites, and harlequin bugs. Slugs chew holes in plant leaves; see the Slugs and Snails entry for controls. Mites are tiny red or black pests; their feeding causes yellow stippling on the leaves. Knock them off the plant with a strong blast of water, or spray with insecticidal soap. Control harlequin bugs, black insects with red markings, by handpicking or applying soap spray.

Diseases are seldom a problem. Black leg produces dark spots on leaves and stems. Symptoms of black rot include yellowing leaves and dark, foul-smelling veins. Prevent these diseases with good cultivation and crop rotation. In case of club root, which shows up as weak, yellowed plants with deformed roots, boost the pH to 7.0 with lime.

Leaf spot shows up as enlarging, water-soaked spots that turn brown or purplish gray. Fusarium wilt, also known as yellows, causes lower leaves to turn yellow and drop off and makes broccoli heads stunted and bitter. Destroy plants afflicted with leaf spot or Fusarium wilt to prevent these diseases from spreading.

Harvesting: Harvest before the florets start to open and turn yellow. Cut just below the point where the stems begin to separate. Once you've harvested the main head, just-as-edible sideshoots will form in the leaf axils and all over the lower stalk. Keep picking, and broccoli will keep producing until the weather gets too hot or too cold. Can, freeze, or pickle broccoli, or keep it refrigerated for up to two weeks. Green cabbage loopers and imported cabbageworms often go unnoticed on harvested heads and can end up in your cooked broccoli. To prevent this, drive them out by soaking the heads in warm water with a little vinegar added for 15 minutes before cooking.

Best cultivars: For a harvest that lasts six weeks or more, look for cultivars that produce large heads and many sideshoots; good choices include 'Bravo', 'Gem', 'Bonanza', and 'DiCicco' (also called 'Italian Green Sprouting'). In areas with early warm spells, use fast-maturing types like 'Cleopatra', 'Spartan Early', and 'Green Comet Hybrid'. 'Green Duke' does well in Southern climates. Broccoli raab produces small, tender, delicious branches and edible leaves instead of heads. ❖

Brussels Sprouts

Brassica oleracea, Gemmifera group
Cruciferae

Brussels sprout plants yield a large harvest from a small area. The mini-cabbages, which form along 2'-3' stems under umbrella-like foliage, need up to 100 days to mature.

Planting: The hardiest cabbage-family crop, brussels sprouts survive freezing temperatures better than hot spells. For a spring crop, start seeds indoors early enough for transplants to mature before hot weather sets in. Fall crops are often more successful. Direct-sow around July, timing plantings to mature when days are still warm but when night frosts bring out the sprouts' flavor. In mild-winter areas, time the crop for a winter-to-spring harvest.

Whether planting indoors or out, sow seeds ½" deep and 2" apart. When seedlings are 5"-7" tall, space or thin them to 2' apart. Set transplants deeper than they grew originally, with the lower leaves just above the soil. Firm the ground around the plants, and water well.

Growing guidelines: Mulch to retain soil moisture, and hand-pull any weeds to avoid damaging the shallow roots of the sprout plants. Foliar-feed lightly once or twice a month with manure tea or seaweed extract. (For instructions on making and using manure tea, see the Manure entry.) Stake in areas with strong winds. The leaves that grow below each sprout turn yellow as sprouts mature; remove these leaves to give sprouts room to develop.

Problems: See the Cabbage entry for insect and disease control information.

Harvesting: Small sprouts are the most tender. Harvest them as they mature from the bottom of the stalk upward. Remove sprouts by twisting them from the stem. Pinching off the plant tops forces sprouts to mature faster. Just before a severe freeze or summer heat wave, pull plants up and hang them upside down in a cool place for a few more weeks of harvesting. ❖

Budding

All plants have buds, small undeveloped shoots laying in wait for a signal to grow into new stems and leaves. The propagation technique called budding involves cutting a bud off of one plant and inserting it in the stem of another plant, called the rootstock. Budding is a type of grafting, a propagation method in which a piece of plant stem is wedded to another plant.

Many plants can be either grafted or budded. Budding is a common practice for fruit trees and roses. In ideal conditions, a budded plant can grow 2'-6' in its first season.

When you graft a bud onto another plant, the cambium, or inner growing tissue, of the plant produces a special thin wall of cells called callus. These callus cells eventually develop into new cambium cells. These cells form a continuous path from the plant to the grafted bud, so that water and nutrients can pass between the plant and the bud. Good contact between the bud and rootstock is essential for this growth and merger of cambium and bud to occur.

Nursery growers and gardeners bud plants in order to change plant characteristics or improve plant performance. For example, a desirable but tall-growing apple cultivar might be budded onto a dwarfing rootstock. Rootstocks can also lend vigor, hardiness, and insect or disease resistance. For successful budding, the bud plant and the rootstock must be compatible; that is, it must be possible to join the two pieces and grow the new plant to maturity. In general, closely related plants are compatible. Roses, for example, are budded onto other roses, apple cultivars onto other apples. Rootstocks for budding are usually ½" or larger in diameter. See the Grafting entry for more information on choosing and planting rootstocks.

A thin, sharp knife is essential for budding. For a few bud grafts, a sharp pocketknife or razor blade is sufficient. If you plan to do many bud grafts, consider investing in a good-quality budding knife, which curves upward at the tip.

Look for them in plant supply catalogs. You'll also need some type of wrapping material, such as electrical tape, to cover the union.

Season: Budding is usually done in late summer (August or September). For successful budding, the bark must slip, or lift easily; this occurs when the cambium layer is active. When buds are inserted toward the end of the growing season, the union heals in a few weeks. The buds remain dormant until the following spring. If they do start to grow early, the buds may winter-kill.

Getting started: Use only healthy and vigorous plants for budding. In dry weather, water the rootstock plant thoroughly a few days before budding. Collect bud sticks—pieces of stem from which you'll cut buds—in the morning of the day you plan to graft. Prepare them from the midsections of ¼" diameter branches with buds from the current season's growth. Avoid immature branch tips and the dormant buds at the branch base. Cut the leaf blades off of the stem, leaving ½" of the petiole (the stalk that joins the leaf to the stem). This piece of petiole will serve as a "handle," making it easier to hold the bud after you cut it out of the stem. Keep the bud sticks moist by putting them in a plastic bag lined with wet paper towel or damp peat moss. Remove the lower leaves from the rootstock.

Method: "T-budding" on the opposite page illustrates the steps of this common budding technique:

1. Make a shallow 1"-1½" vertical cut in the bark close to the base of the rootstock, 1"-2" above the soil. At the top of this cut, make a horizontal cut about 1" long to form the top of the T.

2. Prepare the bud. Be sure to select a leaf bud, which is usually narrow and pointed, and not a plump, round flower bud. Make a shallow horizontal cut above a suitable bud. Place the knife blade ¾" below the bud, and make a shallow upward cut that meets the first cut.

3. Slide the bud piece off the stem. Dip the severed bud in water and keep it moist until you

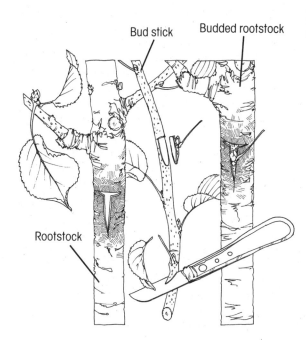

T-budding. This technique involves cutting a single bud from a plant and inserting it in a T-shaped cut near the stem base of the rootstock plant. Be careful to insert the bud right-side up, or the two parts will not unite.

are ready to insert it into the graft.

4. Use the tip of your knife to pry open the two flaps of bark. Gently slide the bud under the bark flaps. Wrap the union with masking tape or electrical tape, but don't cover the bud itself.

Aftercare: Check the buds 3-4 weeks after grafting, and cut the wrapping material. If the buds you inserted look dry and brown instead of green and vigorous, try rebudding on another part of the stem. Keep the soil around the budded stem free of weeds, and protect the stem from animals. In the spring, remove the top of the rootstock plant by making a clean, sloping cut just above the successful bud. Stake the developing shoot to encourage straight growth. Remove any suckers that grow from the rootstock. ❖

Buddleia

Butterfly bush. Deciduous summer-blooming shrubs.

Description: Arching branches give *Buddleia alternifolia,* fountain buddleia, a fountain-like appearance; it grows to a mature height of 12'. It bears alternate, silvery gray leaves. Lavender-colored flowers bloom in the leaf axils of last year's growth. Zones 4-8.

B. davidii, orange-eye butterfly bush, matures at 5'-8'. Opposite, silvery gray leaves are borne on stems that are upright on a young plant and arching with age. Flowers are white, red, pink, or purple, and bloom on the current season's growth. Zones 6-8.

Both species are intensely fragrant in bloom.

How to grow: Butterfly bushes require full sun and fertile, loamy soil. South of Zone 6, plant them in fall or winter; plant in fall or spring in Zones 4-6. Annual pruning keeps plants growing vigorously and blooming like mad. Prune orange-eye butterfly bush in winter, by either cutting all stems to the ground or removing the oldest ⅓ at ground level. Leave no stubs! Prune fountain buddleia immediately after it blooms. If you want a smaller shrub, prune to the ground; otherwise remove ⅓ of the oldest branches. A particularly cold winter will kill some stems to the ground. Cut out dead wood anytime.

Landscape uses: Butterfly bushes offer great summer color and fragrance in a sunny spot. They make a fine focal point when grown in a mass and are a good deciduous hedge. Add butterfly bushes to the perennial border for height and fountains of bloom. In a butterfly garden, they're indispensable.

Best cultivars: *B. alternifolia* 'Argentea' offers very silvery foliage. *B. davidii* 'Black Knight' produces dark purple flowers. 'Lochinch' bears 1' panicles of lavender-blue flowers with orange eyes. 'White Profusion' blooms are white. ❖

Bulbs

In spring, most gardeners' fancies turn to thoughts of bulbs—clusters of crocuses, oceans of daffodils, kaleidoscopes of tulips. But bulbs light up the garden throughout the year. Dahlias, lilies, glads, and many other familiar flowers are classified as bulbs. Bulbs are a diverse group of perennial plants, including true bulbs, corms, rhizomes, and tuberous roots—all structures that store nutrients to support growth and bloom.

Landscaping with Bulbs

We've all seen lines of tulips or daffodils stuck beside a drive or path. But we've also seen how large groups of daffodils and tulips can electrify a spring landscape. Summer bulbs like lilies, dahlias, and glads are mainstays in the flower garden. Here are some effective ways to use bulbs in your landscape.

Bulbs with groundcovers: Bulbs grow beautifully in groundcovers. There's nothing like a dark green groundcover background to make daffodils sparkle. Daffodils look great massed in pachysandra, with the silver-white foliage of spotted lamium (*Lamium maculatum*), the green-black leaves of English ivy, or growing through prostrate junipers. Daffodils and small bulbs look lovely growing through common periwinkle (*Vinca minor*).

One popular groundcover that does not combine well with tall spring bulbs like daffodils is lawn grass. The reason is simple: Bulb foliage needs 8-12 weeks to ripen after bloom so the bulb can store enough food for the following season. By the time the daffodil or tulip foliage is ripe, the grass would be knee-high! If you enjoy the sight of blooming bulbs in your lawn, plant low-growing species like crocuses, because their foliage generally matures before grass needs cutting.

Bulbs with perennials: With the exception of tender bulbs like cannas (*Canna* spp.) and dahlias that must be dug every year or treated as annuals, bulbs are perennial and should be used like perennial flowers. In fact, they're ideal companions for perennials. In spring, bulbs add color to the perennial garden when little else is in bloom, and perennials hide unsightly bulb foliage while it ripens. Spring bulbs prefer dry shade in summer, when they're dormant, and perennial gardens provide these conditions. Peonies, hostas, daylilies, irises, and asters are especially good with bulbs. You can create a simple but effective bed with nothing but daylilies and daffodils—choose cultivars of both that bloom early, mid-season, and late to extend the bloom season.

Use tender bulbs to enhance a planting of perennials the same way you'd plug in annuals. The beautifully mottled leaves of caladiums add summer beauty to groupings of shade-loving perennials like astilbes (*Astilbe* spp.) and hostas. Dahlias, with their huge, showy blooms and large, shrubby habit, can be used as accent plants in the back of a perennial border.

Bulbs with wildflowers: Another great place for bulbs is with wildflowers in either meadow or woodland settings. Spring bulbs will give the meadow show a head start while the wildflowers are coming up, and the mature wildflowers will hide ripening bulb foliage as spring and summer progress. Bulbs also complement woodland wildflowers. Use clumps of daffodils or any of the little bulbs like snowdrops (*Galanthus nivalis*) in a woodland wildflower garden. Daffodils and Virginia bluebells (*Mertensia virginica*) bloom at the same time and look gorgeous planted together. When their foliage begins to die back in summer, overplant with annuals like wax begonias. Also try daffodils with azaleas and woodland wildflowers.

Bulbs with trees and shrubs: Don't forget the beautiful show spring-blooming bulbs make under deciduous trees and shrubs. (For best results, avoid planting bulbs under trees such as beeches and some maples that have aggressive surface roots, which will outcompete the bulbs.) Daffodils under magnolias are a breathtaking sight—especially white, pink, or pale yellow cultivars to complement the whites, roses, and

Key Words
BULBS

True bulb. True bulbs, like onions, have layers of food-storing scales surrounding the central leaves and flowering stem. Often, the bulbs are covered with a papery skin, called the tunic. Daffodils, tulips, lilies, and hyacinths are all true bulbs.

Corm. A corm is a rounded, swollen stem covered with a papery tunic. Unlike true bulbs, corms are solid, with a bud on top that produces leaves and flowers. Crocuses and gladioli are corms.

Tuber. Like Irish potatoes, tubers are fleshy underground stems that have eyes or buds from which leaves and flowers grow. Some tubers, such as caladiums and tuberous begonias, are cormlike. But unlike corms, which sprout roots only from the bottom, tubers also sprout roots from the sides and top. Other tubers are woody, like anemones.

Tuberous root. Tuberous roots are swollen, fleshy roots. They have a pointed bud on top and roots that sprout from the bottom. Dahlias have tuberous roots.

Rhizome. Rhizomes masquerade as roots, but are actually thick, horizontal stems. Roots grow from the bottom of the rhizome; leaves and flowers sprout from the top. Callas, cannas, and bearded irises have rhizomes.

Perennialize. To come up year after year.

Naturalize. To spread naturally in the landscape like a wildflower.

Little bulbs. A general term used to refer collectively to the many species of small, hardy bulbs, especially spring-blooming ones. These include crocuses, snowdrops, winter aconites, squills, and grape hyacinths.

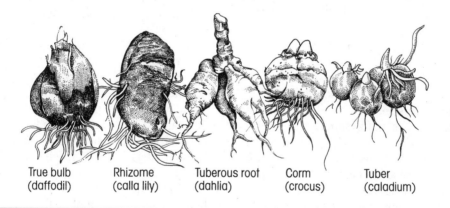

True bulb (daffodil) Rhizome (calla lily) Tuberous root (dahlia) Corm (crocus) Tuber (caladium)

plums of magnolia blooms. White daffodils set off early rhododendrons, and daffodils and grape hyacinths (*Muscari* spp.) sparkle in front of a green hedge.

Tender bulbs can set off trees, shrubs, and hedges, too. Use dahlias to create a dense, dark green annual hedge. Tuberous begonias appreciate the cooler air under trees and shrubs, as long as you give them plenty of water.

Bulbs with annuals: Annuals are perfect plants for covering dying bulb foliage or gaps in the flower border left by dormant bulbs. Mari-

golds, snapdragons, wax begonias, zinnias, and spider flower (*Cleome hasslerana*) are all good "filler" annuals. Plant impatiens to fill in around bulbs in a shady or partially shaded spot. Smaller cultivars of daffodils are lovely with pansies, biennials commonly grown as annuals.

Bulbs with other bulbs: Don't forget about planting bulbs with bulbs. Clumps of mixed daffodils, or scatterings of other spring-blooming bulbs such as tulips or crocuses are well-known signs of spring. You can create an unforgettable garden picture by planting a "river" of grape hyacinths, with daffodils and tulips planted along its "banks."

Bulbs in containers: You can also enjoy bulbs in pots, planters, or window boxes. Pots of bulbs make a great show indoors on the patio, deck, or doorstep. Combining container-grown bulbs with groundcovers, annuals, or perennials can take your bulb pot through several seasons. For more on growing bulbs in containers, see "Forcing Bulbs" on page 96.

Growing Hardy Bulbs

Hardy bulbs like daffodils, tulips, crocuses, and lilies can stay in the ground year after year like perennials. Their care requirements are different from those of tender bulbs like dahlias, which must be dug every winter or treated as annuals north of Zone 9. For information on growing these bulbs, see "Growing Tender Bulbs" on page 95.

Planting Hardy Bulbs

Planting hardy bulbs is easy when you do it right. Here are steps to foolproof planting.

Selecting a site: Almost all bulbs are sun lovers and grow best in full sun. However, this is only true when they're actively growing. By the time spring-blooming bulbs go dormant, they can tolerate full shade. That's why spring bulbs like daffodils and crocuses grow well under deciduous trees and shrubs—their active growing season occurs before the trees leaf out. Some bulbs, like pink daffodils, will have better color if they're grown in partial shade.

Bulbs need loose, humus-rich soil for best performance; they won't bloom well in poor, compacted soils. Most bulbs also need well-drained soil, and will appreciate the addition of decomposed organic matter like composted pine bark. If you have poorly drained or compacted soil, try growing bulbs in raised beds, which will enhance drainage and make for easier planting. Of course, bulbs will thrive in beds that have been double-dug, for they thrive in well-worked soil, but in most soils this extra effort isn't essential. Bulbs prefer a pH of 6.0-7.0, but will tolerate slightly more acidic soils.

Determining planting times: Plant spring- and early-summer-flowering bulbs in fall so they can develop a root system and meet their cold requirements. (Hardy bulbs usually need a certain number of hours of cold temperatures to bloom.) It's best to wait until soil temperatures are below 60°F at 6″ deep before planting. Follow these rules of thumb: In Zones 2-3, plant bulbs in September; in Zones 4-5, September to early October; in Zones 6-7, October to early November; in Zone 8, November to early December; and in Zone 9, December. In Zone 9, pre-cooling may be necessary; see "Forcing Bulbs" on page 96 for more on this technique.

You can plant bulbs later in the fall, as long as they're planted before the onset of hard freezes. Late-planted bulbs tend to bloom several weeks later and on shorter stems, and there is the possibility of aborted blooms or bulbs freezing before roots are established.

Soak anemone (*Anemone* spp.) and winter aconite (*Eranthis hyemalis*) tubers overnight in warm water before planting to bring them out of dormancy. Plant anemones in fall in Zones 7-9, or in the spring for summer bloom in Zones 4-9. Because it is difficult to tell the top from the bottom of anemone tubers, plant them on edge.

Spacing bulbs: Place bulbs in your flower bed and space according to flower stalk height. For greatest impact, plant in clusters of ten or more rather than singly in rows. Plant large bulbs 5″-6″ apart and small bulbs 1″-3″ apart. Leave room to interplant with perennials, groundcovers, or annuals.

You can use 6″ concrete reinforcing wire as a template to make a uniform bulb bed. Put the hardware cloth flat on the ground and place bulbs in the centers of the squares. Remove the hardware cloth before planting.

Planting techniques: The general rule for planting depth is 3-4 times the height of the bulb. This depth will help to protect the bulbs against frost, animals, and physical damage from hoeing. Deeper planting will also help bulbs naturalize and perennialize.

The thought of planting a boxful of bulbs can be daunting, but with the right tools and techniques, bulb planting is easy. A heavy-duty tubular bulb planter large enough for daffodil bulbs is the ideal tool for prepared beds. It's a cup-shaped steel cylinder with a foot bar and long handle on top. Insert the bulb planter in the soil by stepping on the foot bar. Twist the planter, lift it out, then place the bulb in the bottom of the hole. Fill hole with dirt from the planter, then repeat with the next bulb. For planting bulbs in unworked soil, around tree roots, and in ground-covers, you need a stronger tool. Choose a naturalizing tool (a straight steel blade with a forked end, topped by a foot bar and long handle), a crowbar, or a narrow spade with a sharp cutting edge and a foot bar. Push the blade halfway into the soil and pull back, then push down hard so the blade goes completely into the soil. Push forward so the blade lifts up the soil to make a planting slot. Put in a bulb, remove the tool, step down to firm the soil, and repeat with the next bulb.

There's a special trick to planting small bulbs. Using a narrow trowel, one person can easily plant several hundred small bulbs in an hour. (See "Planting Bulbs in a Lawn" on page 94 for an illustration and discussion of this technique.)

Caring for Hardy Bulbs

For the most part, bulbs are undemanding plants. Plantings of daffodils, for example, can thrive for years with little, if any, care. But bulbs do benefit from basic routine care, and they'll reward your efforts with more vigorous growth and spectacular bloom displays.

Mulching: Mulch newly planted bulbs with a light organic mulch like pine needles to aid moisture retention and offer protection from frost heaving. Mulch will help keep down weeds in established plantings during the growing season.

Smart Shopping
BULBS

Whether you buy bulbs from a garden center, mail-order catalog, or specialist grower, bear these tips in mind:

● Buy the biggest bulbs you can afford— you get what you pay for. Look for categories like "exhibition size," "jumbo," "top size," and "double- (or triple-) nosed" for the best bloom. Smaller bulbs, often called "landscape size," are less expensive and good for naturalizing.

● Inspect bulbs as soon as you get them in the mail or before you buy them at a garden center. Healthy bulbs are sound, solid, and heavy. Lightweight, pithy, soft bulbs won't grow well. If you are in doubt, heft the bulbs in your hand. Healthy bulbs are solid and heavy for their size.

● Small nicks and loose skins do not affect the development of the bulb. In fact, loose skins (tunics) make it easier for the bulb to sprout. However, don't buy bulbs (especially tulips) that completely lack the protective tunic.

● Bulbs should not have mold or show signs of rot. Powdery mildew, a blue-gray fungus, is a sign that the bulbs have become damp. Basal rot is a fungal disease that shows up as brown streaks near the base of the bulb.

● If you receive damaged or diseased bulbs through the mail, call or write the company immediately. A reputable bulb dealer will replace them or give you a refund.

● Plant bulbs as soon as they arrive. If you can't plant them at once, store bulbs in a dry place with good ventilation and get them in the ground as soon as you can.

● If you buy species bulbs rather than cultivars, make sure they are nursery-propagated, not collected from the wild, a practice that endangers native populations. See the Wildflowers entry for buying tips.

It will also help maintain even moisture levels in the soil. Most bulbs can emerge through 2"-3" of light mulch. Keep a layer of light mulch such

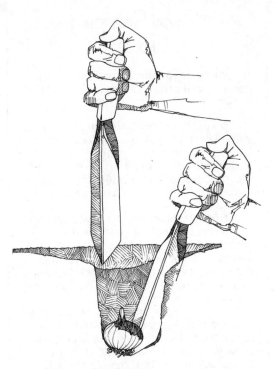

Planting bulbs in a lawn. Crocuses and grape hyacinths (*Muscari* spp.) brighten spring lawns and are easy to plant. Here's a fast, effective method: Stab a bulb trowel into the soil like a dagger and pull toward you to make a hole for the bulb. Drop in a bulb, and step on the spot to close the slot.

as pine needles, salt hay, weed-free straw, or ground composted bark on established plantings. Renew as needed.

Feeding: For many years bonemeal was considered the best food for bulbs. But bonemeal is not a complete bulb food—it is only a good source of phosphorus and calcium. Start your bulbs off right with a topdressing of a complete organic fertilizer, dried manure, or compost in the fall after planting. (Don't put fertilizer in the holes with the bulbs.) This will provide the bulbs with nutrients from the time root growth begins until the foliage matures.

To give your bulbs the complete nutrition they need for top-notch performance, mix 2 lb. of dried blood (for nitrogen), 2 lb. of bonemeal (for phosphorus and calcium), and 3 lb. of greensand or wood ashes (for potash) per 100 square feet of garden bed. If your soil is acid, wood ashes will raise the pH; if it's already near neutral, use greensand. Unfortunately, bonemeal tends to attract rodents and dogs, which may dig up your bulbs to get to it. For established plantings, apply your homemade bulb food as a topdressing in early spring when the foliage is just beginning to emerge from the ground, followed by 2 more pounds of dried blood in early fall. (If you wait to fertilize until after bloom, it's too late—the foliage will have died by the time the nutrients reach the bulb's roots.)

If you don't want to mix your own bulb food, a simpler alternative is to top-dress with ¼" of dried manure (about 2 bushels) per 100 square feet in spring and fall, or 2 bushels of compost in fall and 2 lb. of dried blood in spring. Whichever source of nutrients you use, don't scratch the fertilizer into the soil surface—you might damage the bulbs, and rains will wash in the nutrients without further help from you.

Watering: When your bulbs are actively growing, they'll need to be watered if they don't receive ½" of rain per week. This is especially important in the fall to assure good root growth before freezing weather sets in, in spring when active top growth starts, and especially in April and May when the foliage is out and bulbs are manufacturing food for next year's bloom.

Handling bulb foliage: Allow bulb foliage to die naturally rather than mowing or cutting it off. Bulbs need at least 8 weeks of leaf growth after bloom in order to produce food for the next season's blooms. When the foliage begins to turn yellow and fall over, you can cut it. Don't braid foliage or bind it with rubber bands while waiting for it to ripen. This actually harms the bulbs—it cuts off sunlight and air, hampers flower production, and encourages rot.

Deadheading: After tulip flowers bloom and fade or fall off, remove seed heads to conserve the bulb's resources. Deadhead other bulbs only if they look unsightly; seed formation won't weaken them significantly.

Dividing: Hardy bulbs—especially daffodils—can become overcrowded after many years in the same site. Clumps that cease blooming or produce few or undersized flowers are probably overcrowded. When this happens, dig and divide the bulbs when their foliage is half-yellowed. By then, the bulbs will have ripened but will still be easy to find. Separate the bulbs and replant immediately in well-drained soil; top-dress with compost. Be sure you set each species at the proper depth and spacing. Transplant bulbs you'd like to move to another site in the same manner.

Propagating hardy bulbs: The easiest way to propagate hardy bulbs—especially the ones that are good for naturalizing such as daffodils—is to dig them when the foliage yellows, separate the offsets on each bulb, and replant. You can plant them at the same depth and location as the mature bulbs, but they might reach flowering size sooner if you grow them in a nursery bed for 2-3 seasons first.

Propagate crocuses and other bulbs that arise from corms in much the same way; dig them and separate the small new corms, called cormels, that form alongside the parent corm.

There are two ways to propagate lilies: Pick the small bulbils that form along the stem above the leaves or the bulblets that form at the base of the stem. Then plant them in a nursery bed, where they'll need to grow for several years to attain blooming size. You can also scale lily bulbs to propagate them. Remove the scales one at a time, and place them in a shallow flat or pot filled with moist vermiculite or peat moss. Bury the scales about halfway, and keep them moist. Small bulblets, which can be transplanted to a nursery bed, will form at the base of each scale.

Coping with pests: Hungry rodents are almost certain to be your bulbs' worst problem. Protect bulbs like crocuses and tulips from voles by adding a handful of fine crushed gravel to each planting hole on top of the bulb. Fine marble chips or crushed road gravel the size of peas (but sharp, rather than round) are best.

Some bulbs are naturally rodent-proof. Daffodils are poisonous, so rodents leave them alone. The skunklike odor of fritillaria (*Fritillaria* spp.) bulbs repels hungry voles, mice, and squirrels.

Try interplanting bulbs with a groundcover to deter rodents. Woody plants like cotoneasters and junipers are particularly effective—the rodents don't like fighting their way through the fibrous roots. If you have a serious rodent problem, protect larger bulbs like tulips and lilies by planting the bulbs in a hardware cloth cage. When you prepare the planting bed, dig a 12″ deep trench around the bed and line it with ½″ wire mesh.

Growing Tender Bulbs

If hardy bulbs need the same basic care as perennials, tender bulbs need to be treated like annuals: Set them out in late spring when the soil warms, and give them rich soil and lots of food and water. Like annuals, tender bulbs are big feeders. When fall frosts threaten, you can dig your tender bulbs, cure them, and store them until spring, or consign them to the compost heap with your other annuals.

Planting Tender Bulbs

To get your tender bulbs off to a good start, start by selecting a well-drained site in full sun; exceptions are callas (*Zantedeschia* spp.), caladiums, and tuberous begonias, which prefer partial shade.

Plant tender bulbs like cannas, callas, dahlias, and glads after all danger of frost is past in spring. These bulbs are frost-tender and won't start growth in the ground until the soil warms above 60°F. Set these bulbs out directly in the garden, or start them indoors and transplant them.

Plant tender bulbs in a well-worked bed enriched with plenty of organic matter. Dahlias, tuberous begonias, cannas, and caladiums all prefer evenly moist soil, so keep them watered and mulch well after planting. Make sure plants are spaced far enough apart to allow good air circulation; tuberous begonias and dahlias may develop powdery mildew if they're planted too close together or in a spot with still air.

Starting bulbs indoors: Give tuberous begonias and caladiums a head start by potting them up indoors in early spring and transplanting them when the soil warms outside. Start them in flats or pots in a peat-based potting soil. Set the tubers near the top of the pot, barely covering them with soil. Keep the soil mix evenly moist but not wet. Put the flats or pots in a warm, bright place. When the new shoots are several inches tall, pot up the plants or plant them outdoors at the same level as they grew in the pots.

Caring for Tender Bulbs

Tender bulbs need the same basic conditions as other summer flowers: humus-rich soil, ample water, mulch, and periodic topdressings. (The larger dahlia cultivars are heavy feeders and appreciate supplemental feedings to support their lush growth.) However, tender bulbs need special storage and propagation techniques. For more on general care, see the Annuals entry.

Storing tender bulbs: If you live north of Zone 9, tender bulbs like dahlias, glads, caladiums, and tuberous begonias won't normally survive the winter if left outdoors. However, you can dig these bulbs, keep them indoors over winter, and replant them in spring—a worthwhile technique if you grow special cultivars. Lift tender bulbs that you wish to save in the fall as the foliage begins to die. Let the bulbs dry in a cool, dry place with plenty of air movement (best under a fan). Then store them at 50°-60°F in wood shavings, dry peat moss, or another suitable porous, dry material. Check several times during the winter and discard any damaged, soft, or rotten bulbs.

Dahlias are hardy in Zones 9-10; elsewhere, dig and store them for the winter. Glads are reliably hardy in Zones 9-10 but can be successfully overwintered in protected locations as far north as Zone 6. (If you want to experiment, leave a few bulbs well mulched in a sheltered site and dig the rest.)

Propagating tender bulbs: You can increase your stock of favorite dahlia cultivars in the fall when you've dug the tuberous roots and allowed them to dry, or store the clumps whole and divide them in spring. Use a sharp, sterile knife. Make sure that each division has a piece of stem attached; new shoots sprout only from that part of the plant. Discard any thin or immature roots. Divide tubers like tuberous begonias and caladiums in spring. Cut them into pieces, making sure each piece has an eye or bud. Let the pieces dry for two days and then plant them. Gladiolus corms produce small cormels, which you can grow to flowering size in 2-3 years. Dig, cure, and store the cormels the same way you treat the mature corms. In spring, plant the cormels in a nursery bed at the same time you put the mature corms out in the garden.

Forcing Bulbs

There's nothing mysterious about forcing hardy bulbs into bloom out of season. It's all a matter of giving them a compressed life cycle: a cool fall for root growth and a cold winter dormancy, followed by the warmth and water of spring. The trick is in manipulating the seasons to shave off a few weeks and get early bloom. (Some mail-order catalogs offer precooled bulbs, which have already had their cold treatment and are ready for forcing.)

Start in the fall with the biggest, fattest, healthiest bulbs you can find. Check bulb catalogs for cultivars that are recommended for forcing. Tulips, daffodils, hyacinths, crocuses, grape hyacinths, snowdrops, miniature irises (*Iris reticulata* and *I. danfordiae*), and glory-of-the-snow all force well.

The best containers for forcing are shallow, wide pots, often called bulb pans, because they won't tip over when the bulbs grow tall and top-heavy. Drainage holes are a must.

To make a good basic potting medium, mix equal parts of potting soil, peat moss, and perlite, and then add one part of coarse sand or fine gravel to each two parts of soil mix. If you want to save the bulbs for next year, add a balanced organic fertilizer when planting.

You'll be planting to make a show, so crowd the bulbs into the container, leaving only a little space between. Plant the bulbs shallowly with their noses poking out of the ground to encourage fast growth.

Plant tulip bulbs, which usually have one side less well-rounded than the other, in a circle with the flat sides toward the outside of the pot. That way, the first leaf of each bulb will grow from the flat side, and the flower stems will be bunched in the middle. To squeeze more daffodils into a container, plant them in two layers. Place the bottom bulbs on a 2″ layer of potting mix, cover them to their necks, then set more bulbs between them and cover to the top. Try this with Dutch iris and small spring bulbs, too. Press firmly to settle the bulbs in place and keep them from heaving out.

In addition to the cold period they need to bloom, most spring bulbs need several weeks of darkness and cold temperatures (33°-50°F) to give them time to grow a healthy set of roots *before* freezing weather sets in. Tulips need a total of 14-20 weeks of cold (including the cool fall period). Daffodils need 16-22 weeks. Hyacinths will root at warmer temperatures than others and need 10-14 weeks. Crocuses, snowdrops, and other small bulbs need about 12 weeks of cold.

Keep the bulbs moist during this period. You can leave pots outside under a blanket of mulch or in a cold frame until it's time to bring them indoors. Or you can dig a trench, and store the pots buried up to their rims in coarse sand. Protect the pots from bulb-hungry rodents.

Bring bulbs indoors when the tips have grown about 1″ tall. Put them in a cool but bright place at no more than 50°-55°F. Higher temperatures will rush new growth, making it pale and spindly. Once the flowers start to bloom, move your containers anywhere you want a touch of early spring. They'll last longer in a cool spot. Moving them into a cool room at night will also prolong bloom.

After flowering, give the bulbs a dose of fertilizer, and water regularly to keep the foliage growing. Plant them outside when the ground thaws. With good care, they'll recover and give a good show after 1-2 years of growth.

Bulbs through the Year

We tend to think of bulbs as spring flowers, but that's because few other flowers are competing with spring bulbs for our attention. Actually, bulbs can contribute to the garden's beauty in every season. Here are some of the best bulbs for each season, with tips on how to use them.

Bulbs in Winter

If you live in Zones 7-9, you can enjoy late-winter bloom from bulbs planted in the garden. For gardeners in Zones 6 and north, plant these lovely small bulbs for early spring bloom. These bulbs are also suitable for planting or naturalizing in lawn grass, as their foliage will mature before the grass needs cutting.

Snowdrops (*Galanthus nivalis*), have bell-like green and white flowers, and will form colonies in woodland sites. Use them in rock gardens, in pockets of soil between tree roots, or in groups at the front of the border.

For a bright yellow carpet of buttercuplike, quarter-size flowers, plant winter aconites (*Eranthis hyemalis*). These are sometimes hard to establish, but after several years, they'll self-sow and spread nicely. Other golden additions for the cold months are very early blooming daffodils, such as 'February Gold', or miniature irises such as reticulated iris (*Iris reticulata*) and Danford iris (*I. danfordiae*).

The Bulbs of Spring

Spring is that magical season when our gardens come alive. Among the first bulbs to bloom is glory-of-the-snow (*Chionodoxa luciliae*) in lovely soft blue or pink. These often bloom with the last of the winter bulbs and the darker blue or white Siberian squill (*Scilla sibirica*). Of course, crocuses, daffodils, hyacinths, and tulips are mainstays of the spring garden. See the Crocus, Hyacinthus, Narcissus, and Tulipa entries for more on these plants. By choosing carefully among the many daffodil and tulip cultivars available (there are early, mid-season, and late bloomers) you can plan for blooms all spring in a variety of shapes and colors.

Use anemones to create a spring carpet under larger bulbs. Grecian windflowers (*Anemone blanda*) are available in pink, blue, and white. They have ferny foliage through May. See the Anemone entry for more on these plants.

Plant grape hyacinths (*Muscari* spp.) as edgings, in borders, under trees and shrubs, in "rivers," and as accents. Grape hyacinths have a long bloom season and are very easy to grow. *Muscari armeniacum,* a deep blue, is the most

common and least expensive; 'Blue Spike' is a showy double cultivar. The early dwarf tulips flower in mid-spring, too.

Trout lilies or dog-tooth violets (*Erythronium* spp.) are perfect for woodland gardens. They have lilylike white, yellow, or purplish pink flowers; some species also have beautifully mottled foliage. Fritillaries (*Fritillaria* spp.) also like a rich, well-drained woodland location. Try 8"-10" tall checkered lily (*F. meleagris*) or the stately crown imperial (*F. imperialis*), which has yellow or orange-red flowers, as an accent plant.

Clumps of summer snowflakes (*Leucojum aestivum*) are attractive in perennial gardens. They have glossy daffodil-like foliage and pendulous white-and-green bell-shaped flowers.

Nodding star-of-Bethlehem (*Ornithogalum nutans*) with its silver-green flower spikes is very attractive. You can naturalize *O. umbellatum,* star-of-Bethlehem, in lawn grass, but keep it out

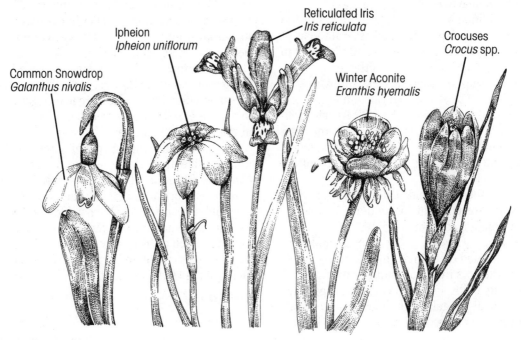

Common Snowdrop
Galanthus nivalis

Ipheion
Ipheion uniflorum

Reticulated Iris
Iris reticulata

Winter Aconite
Eranthis hyemalis

Crocuses
Crocus spp.

Bulbs for naturalizing. Daffodils are perhaps the best-known bulbs for naturalizing because they'll spread as readily as wildflowers. Many of the so-called small bulbs such as winter aconites (*Eranthis hyemalis*), snowdrops (*Galanthus nivalis*), crocuses, and miniature irises also naturalize well. You'll get good stands of these small but cheerful bulbs.

of the garden and wildflower plantings—it is very invasive.

The alliums (also called ornamental onions) make their appearance in early spring and bloom up through June. This diverse and decorative genus ranges from the giant onion (*Allium giganteum*), with 4″-6″ globes of pinkish purple flowers borne on 3′-4′ stems, to the lily leek (*A. moly*), bearing small clusters of bright yellow flowers on 14″ stems. See the Allium entry for more on these plants.

Foxtail lily (*Eremurus stenophyllus*) is one of the tallest bulbs, reaching 2½′-6′. It has brushy flower spikes in white, pink, or yellow. Like the alliums, bloom continues into early summer. Foxtail lilies need very well drained soil. They make wonderful specimens and accents.

Summer-Blooming Bulbs

Lilies, which are hardy bulbs, are among the stars of the summer border. Many tender bulbs also shine at this time of year, including tuberous begonias, cannas, caladiums, dahlias, and glads. These bulbs are usually planted as annuals in Zones 3-7, but they may be stored indoors over winter and replanted the following spring. Many will perennialize in Zones 7-9. See the Begonia, Caladium, Canna, Dahlia, Gladiolus, and Lilium entries for information on these important summer bulbs.

Calla lilies (*Zantedeschia aethiopica*) look best grown in clumps for their decorative foliage and white, pink, yellow, or orange flowers. Callas also can tolerate wet feet; try growing them at the edge of a pond or in a container in the water. Callas are hardy in Zones 7-9 but need winter protection in Zone 7.

Crocosmia (*Crocosmia* × *crocosmiiflora*) is an orange- to red-flowered gladioluslike plant that is hardy in Zones 6-9. Its 2′-3′ tall sprays of fiery flowers are effective in clumps in the border or naturalized in a well-drained wildflower meadow.

Fall-Flowering Bulbs

Dahlias, caladiums, some species lilies, and other summer bulbs extend their summer show

> ## More On
> ### BULBS
>
> You'll find specific bulbs covered in detail in the following entries: Allium, Anemone, Begonia, Caladium, Canna, Convallaria (lily-of-the-valley), Crocus, Dahlia, Gladiolus, Hippeastrum (amaryllis), Hyacinthus (hyacinth), Iris, Lilium (lily), Narcissus (daffodil), Ranunculus (buttercup), and Tulipa (tulip).

into fall. But other bulbs flower only in fall.

Autumn crocus, also called meadow saffron (*Colchicum autumnale*), is a crocus look-alike hardy in Zones 5-9. Plants produce large clusters of purple, pink, or white flowers in September and October. Large, glossy leaves appear in spring.

There are also true crocuses that bloom in fall, including *Crocus speciosus,* showy crocus, with lavender-blue flowers, hardy in Zones 5-9, and *C. sativus,* saffron crocus, with purple flowers, hardy in Zones 6-9. Other fall-flowering species and cultivars are available with lilac-blue, white, or purple flowers. Plant these hardy bulbs in August and September for bloom in October and November.

Spider lilies (*Lycoris* spp.) are a group of hardy bulbs that emerge and bloom in a day or two, earning the name magic lilies. Red spider lily (*L. radiata*) has clusters of bright red flowers with prominent stamens that give them a spidery look. It usually blooms in September and is hardy in Zones 7-10. Magic lily (*L. squamigera*) bears showy, pink, trumpet-shaped flowers on 2′ stems. They are hardy in Zones 6-10 and bloom in July through August.

Hardy cyclamen (*Cyclamen hederifolium*) are beautiful small plants for dry shade (the prevailing condition under trees and shrubs). Their heart-shaped, silver-dollar-size, mottled foliage is as lovely as the uniquely shaped pink flowers they bear in September and October. Plants are hardy in Zones 5-9. Make sure your cyclamen are nursery-propagated. ❖

Butterfly Gardening

Color on the wing is waiting to fill your garden with a fluttering rainbow. Nearly every locale across the country offers some butterflies that you can attract into your garden by meeting just a few of the insects' basic needs.

Every butterfly passes through four distinct life stages: egg, caterpillar, chrysalis, and adult. Of course, you can't attract chrysalises or eggs themselves, but you can entice the adults who start the cycle. Adding flowers like zinnias, cosmos, and other butterfly favorites to your garden is an easy way to attract these nectar seekers.

But in some species, the adult butterfly doesn't eat. Its only function is to reproduce, mating and laying eggs for the next generation. You can still attract these butterflies—as well as those that drink nectar—by supplying suitable food plants for their caterpillars to munch. In most species, when the female is ready to lay her eggs, she seeks out the host plant species that the upcoming caterpillars will need as food.

The caterpillar is an eating/growing machine, but many species will eat only a few types of plants. The caterpillar of the familiar monarch, for example, eats only milkweed (*Asclepias* spp.); black swallowtails may favor your parsley. And as any gardener who's fought off cabbageworms can tell you, the common white cabbage butterflies prefer cole crops for their host plants.

Supplying food for nectar-seeking adults and host plants for egg-laying ones are the best ways to attract butterflies into your garden. Use low-growing groundcovers such as clovers and grasses to provide sunning spots for adults to warm themselves. Shallow depressions that remain moist naturally or through regular watering offer drinking sources. Walls, hedgerows,

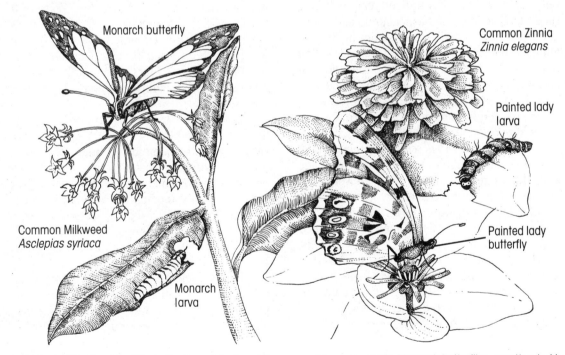

Monarch butterfly

Common Zinnia
Zinnia elegans

Painted lady
larva

Common Milkweed
Asclepias syriaca

Monarch
larva

Painted lady
butterfly

Butterfly gardening. Dancing butterflies add color and movement to your garden. Monarch butterflies are attracted to the flowers of many wildflowers for nectar. They depend on milkweeds for food for their larvae. Painted lady adults and larvae relish flowers and foliage of daisy-family members, including zinnias.

BUTTERFLY PLANTS

Plants may serve as nectar sources for butterflies, as host plants for caterpillars, or as food for both adults and larvae. To increase the number of butterflies flitting about your garden, plant as many host plants and nectar sources as you can in your yard.

Blend butterfly-attracting weeds such as alfalfa, clovers, Queen-Anne's-lace, nettles (*Urtica* spp.), teasel (*Dipsacus fullonum*), or mustard-family members like field mustard (*Brassica rapa*) into a wildflower patch. And plant some extra parsley just for larvae of the beautiful swallowtail butterflies. Some plants that butterflies appreciate are garden pests. These include dandelions and thistles, which will attract lovely painted lady butterflies. But the airborne seeds of these weedy plants will settle in other areas of your garden. Use common sense when creating your butterfly garden.

The list below includes suggestions suitable for all parts of the country.

Perennials and Annuals

Ageratum houstonianum (ageratum)
Alcea rosea (hollyhock)
Asclepias spp. (milkweeds, butterfly weed)
Aster spp. (asters)
Buddleia spp. (butterfly bushes)
Chrysanthemum leucanthemum (oxeye daisy)
Chrysanthemum × *superbum* (Shasta daisy)
Coreopsis spp. (coreopsis)
Echinacea purpurea (purple coneflower)
Erigeron spp. (fleabanes)
Eupatorium spp. (bonesets, Joe-Pye weeds)
Grindelia spp. (gumweeds)
Helenium autumnale (sneezeweed)
Helianthus spp. (sunflowers)
Heliotropium arborescens (common heliotrope)
Hemerocallis spp. (daylilies)
Lavandula spp. (lavenders)
Lobularia maritima (sweet alyssum)
Mentha spp. (mints)
Monarda spp. (bee balms)
Phlox spp. (phlox)
Rudbeckia spp. (coneflowers)
Salvia spp. (sages)
Sedum spectabile (showy stonecrop)
Solidago spp. (goldenrods)
Tagetes patula (French marigold)
Thymus spp. (thymes)
Verbena spp. (verbenas)
Vernonia spp. (ironweeds)
Zinnia spp. (zinnias)

Trees and Shrubs

Chrysothamnus nauseosus (gray rabbit-brush)
Ligustrum spp. (privets)
Lonicera spp. (honeysuckles)
Rhus spp. (sumacs)
Salix spp. (willows)
Syringa vulgaris (common lilac)
Tilia americana (basswood)
Vaccinium spp. (blueberries)

Many of the plants suitable for a butterfly garden are regional. In addition to the plants listed above, gardens in the East and Midwest have many other butterfly-attracting species to consider, including *Allium schoenoprasum* (common chives), *Asclepias tuberosa* (butterfly weed), *Centaurea cyanus* (cornflower), *Cosmos bipinnatus* (cosmos), *Eupatorium perfoliatum* (boneset), *Eupatorium purpureum* (Joe-Pye weed), *Lobelia cardinalis* (cardinal flower), *Nepeta cataria* (catnip), and *Tropaeolum* spp. (nasturtiums). Additional trees and shrubs for the East and Midwest include *Ceanothus americanus* (New Jersey tea), *Cercis canadensis* (Eastern redbud), *Lindera benzoin* (spicebush), *Rubus* spp. (blackberries), and *Philadelphus* spp. (mock-oranges).

In addition to native perennials such as *Astragalus* spp. (milk vetch) and *Dichelostemma pulchellum* (wild hyacinth), Western gardeners have a wealth of butterfly-attracting native shrubs and trees to consider, including *Eriodictyon californicum* (yerba santa), *Ceanothus cordulatus* (snowbush), *Ceanothus cuneatus* (buckbrush), *Ceanothus integerrimus* (deer bush), *Ceanothus thyrsiflorus* (blueblossom), *Cephalanthus occidentalis* (buttonbush), *Eriogonum* spp. (wild buckwheats), *Plumbago auriculata* (cape plumbago), and *Prosopis juliflora* (mesquite).

and similar windbreaks add protected spots that nearly all butterfly species will appreciate.

Planning Your Garden

If you want to add the living color of butterflies to your garden, start by using some of the recommended plants in the lists on page 101. The aptly named butterfly bush (*Buddleia* spp.), for instance, will attract monarchs, swallowtails, fritillaries, metalmarks, and many other nectar drinkers to its fragrant flower clusters.

If your aim is to attract a particular species, you'll need to do a bit of homework to find out its favorite nectar plants or caterpillar host. Milkweed makes an unusual addition to the wild garden or middle border, though it's a good idea to contain its vigorous roots in a buried bottomless bucket. The oddly shaped, sweet-smelling flowers will attract a variety of feeding butterflies, and from summer through early fall, monarchs ready to lay eggs will seek out your planting. If you're extra lucky, you may find a delicate chrysalis hanging below a milkweed leaf like a jade pendant, decorated with shining gold dots.

A field guide to butterflies is helpful in planning the butterfly garden. Look for a book with information about the plants that caterpillars eat, the plants from which the adults take nectar, and the drinking, sunning, or other unique habits of the adults. Detailed, full-color illustrations of both the caterpillar and adult stages, and information about the geographical area in which the insects are found, are also valuable.

Spring and summer butterfly-watching expeditions in your neighborhood are a good way to establish your own checklist of local species. Use your list to develop a custom-tailored butterfly garden of food and host plants. *Butterflies: How to Identify and Attract Them to Your Garden* by Marcus Schneck is a good guidebook that includes color illustrations of many species plus information on habitat, host plants, and nectar sources. A local natural history museum, college entomology department, or butterfly club can give you more pointers. ❖

Buxus

Boxwood. Evergreen shrubs or trees.

Description: *Buxus microphylla*, littleleaf boxwood, is a compact, dense, rounded shrub about 3' tall at maturity. Glossy green leaves are arranged in pairs on the angled twigs. Early spring flowers are inconspicuous. Hardiness varies; select cultivars adapted to your location. Most cultivars grow in Zones 6-8.

B. sempervirens, common boxwood, is a shrub or small tree of 6'-15' at maturity. The leaves are dark green above and light green below, turning brown or bronze in the winter, and are borne in pairs. Common boxwood grows best in warm, moist situations. Zones 6-8.

How to grow: Boxwoods are healthiest when protected from direct sun and wind; the drying effects of these elements cause discolored foliage and dieback of late-season growth. Avoid exposed sites and fertilize in spring or very late fall after plants are dormant. Plant in evenly moist, humus-rich soil and mulch well to keep roots cool. Plan to give winter protection to boxwoods in open areas or at the northern extremes of their hardiness.

Landscape uses: A staple of formal gardens, boxwood's dense compact shape, fine foliage, and slow growth make it useful in landscape situations ranging from small borders to large hedges. Boxwood is a favored plant for topiary, where its slow growth and tolerance of severe pruning allow gardeners to trim it into fantastic shapes. Dwarf boxwoods make excellent edgings for herb gardens. Some people find the odor of boxwood foliage offensive; smell before you plant.

Best cultivars: *B. microphylla:* 'Compacta', slow-growing with dark green foliage; var. *koreana*, yellow-brown winter foliage, hardy to Zone 4; 'Wintergreen', retains color well in winter; *B. sempervirens:* 'Curly Locks', contorted branches; 'Northern Find', low-growing and blue-green in color; 'Suffruticosa', compact and slow-growing; 'Vardar Valley', nice for edging, stays below 1½' until it is quite old. ❖

Cabbage

Brassica oleracea, Capitata group
Cruciferae

Cabbage thrives in cool weather. In most areas, you can plant an early crop for fresh consumption and a late crop—usually the more problem-free and tasty of the two—primarily for winter storage. Choose from early, mid-season, and late-season cultivars with green, red, or purple heads that weigh 2-50 lb. Loose-leaf versions include Chinese cabbages, like bok choy, and ornamental cabbages.

Planting: You can buy nursery transplants, but cabbage is easy to grow from seed. Plan to set out early types four weeks before the last expected frost date. Sow seeds indoors, ¼″ deep and 2″ apart, around mid-January or February in the South and in March in the North. Place in a sunny spot with temperatures between 60° and 70°F, and keep the soil uniformly moist. When daytime temperatures reach 50°F and seedlings have three leaves, plant them outdoors.

Plant seedlings in the garden slightly deeper than they grew in flats. Make planting holes wide enough to accommodate spread-out roots; firm soil around each seedling and water thoroughly. Space 6″-12″ apart in rows 1′-2′ apart. Wide spacings produce bigger heads, but young, small cabbages are tastier. To get both, plant 6″ apart and harvest every other one before maturity.

Stagger plantings at two-week intervals for a longer harvest.

Start your late crop in July, sowing seeds in flats or directly in the garden. Space these seedlings farther apart than the spring crop, and place them so a tall crop, such as corn or pole beans, provides some afternoon shade.

Plant Chinese cabbage in fall about ten weeks before the first average frost date.

Growing guidelines: Soil texture is not critical, but early cabbages do best in a sandy loam, while later types need a heavier, moisture-retaining soil. Side-dress seedlings with well-rotted manure three weeks after planting. Hand-pull weeds to avoid damaging cabbage's shallow roots; use a mulch to keep the soil moist. Uneven watering can cause a sudden growth spurt that will make the developing head split. If you see a cabbage head starting to crack, twist the plant a half turn and pull up to slightly dislodge the roots and thus slow the plant's growth. Or use a spade to cut the roots in one or two places 6″ below the stem. This also helps to prevent cabbage from bolting (producing a flower stalk).

Don't water foliage during cool weather or periods of high humidity, because constantly wet leaves are prone to disease. Cut back on water as cabbage matures. If leaves start to yellow, provide a mid-season nitrogen boost with manure tea. (For instructions on making and using manure

103

tea, see the Manure entry.) This type of feeding can also encourage a slow-growing crop to mature before hot weather or a winter freeze sets in.

Problems: Major cabbage pests include cabbage maggots, imported cabbageworms, cabbage loopers, and cutworms. You'll find information on controlling them in "The Top Ten Garden Insect Pests in America" on page 344. The harlequin bug, a black insect with red markings, causes black spots and wilting leaves; control by handpicking or applying insecticidal soap. Slugs may chew ragged holes in leaves; see the Slugs and Snails entry for controls.

Black leg, a fungal disease, forms dark spots on leaves and stems. Black rot symptoms include black and foul-smelling veins. Club root prevents water and nutrient absorption. Fusarium wilt, also known as yellows, produces yellow

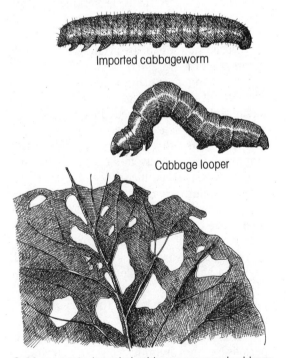

Imported cabbageworm

Cabbage looper

Cabbage pests. Imported cabbageworms and cabbage loopers chew large ragged holes in the leaves of cabbage and related crops. Both are small green caterpillars; cabbage loopers have a characteristic humpbacked appearance.

leaves and stunted heads. Remove and burn plants affected by these diseases; if club root is a problem, rake in extra lime.

Good growing conditions, crop rotation, and the use of disease-resistant cultivars are the best defenses against cole crop problems. Also, thoroughly clean up the garden at the end of the season, removing all remaining leaves and roots.

Harvesting: Use a sharp knife to cut heads when they are firm. Leave stalks and roots in place to produce tasty little cabbages; eat them like brussels sprouts or let them develop into a second crop of small heads. Fresh cabbage has the best taste, but late-season cultivars keep well in a moist, cool place (32°-40°F) for 5-6 months. Turn split heads into sauerkraut.

Best cultivars: Cabbages take 60-180 days to mature. Only early types like 'Grenadier' are suitable for areas with short growing seasons. In areas with hot spells, pick a heat-resistant cabbage such as 'Savoy King'. Tight-headed cultivars, such as 'Danish Ballhead', keep well over winter. 'Golden Acre', 'Stonehead Hybrid', and 'Early Jersey Wakefield' are among the most disease-resistant cultivars. ❖

Cacti

It's a long way from the saguaro forests of Arizona to a Northeastern backyard. But cacti are also East Coast natives, growing as far north as Canada. Why grow cacti in the landscape? Their spring profusion of large, luminous flowers in shades of yellow, peach, and scarlet is reason enough. But in our water-conserving times, these tough dryland succulents are perfect plants for xeriscaping.

Cacti for the North

Choosing cacti. There are close to 2,000 species of cacti in the New World, but only about 100 species and varieties will grow outside arid areas. The prickly pears, *Opuntia* spp., are the most adaptable cacti for Northern gardens. *O.*

fragilis, brittle prickly pear, is a small, hardy species that may produce up to 100 large yellow flowers per plant. *O. basilaris* var. *basilaris,* purple beavertail cactus, has bluish purple pads and deep pink flowers. Other cold-hardy cacti include *Echinocereus triglochidiatus,* claret cup cactus, a small clump-forming cactus with large red flowers and fruits; *Coryphantha vivipara,* spiny star, which is small and clumping, with dense white spines and pink flowers; and *Opuntia darwinii,* Darwin's cactus, with cigar-shaped pads and yellow flowers. These cacti will survive outdoors in Zone 6 (possibly Zone 5).

Preparing the soil. When growing cacti in the North, the critical factor isn't cold (many cacti are hardy to −40°F), it's good drainage. Rock garden conditions—good drainage in full sun—are ideal. If you want to grow cacti but have soil that drains poorly, try a raised bed. Cacti prefer humus-rich soil with compost or well-rotted manure worked in. Add plenty of coarse sand, limestone chips, and pea gravel. Remember to site your beds in full sun—cacti need at least 5-6 hours daily.

Planting cacti. Plant cacti in spring. Wear leather gloves and use tongs or newspaper rolled and bent like tongs to protect yourself from the spines. Note that prickly pears have two kinds of spines, large ones you can see and tiny hooked barbs called glochids. So-called "spineless" prickly pears lack the large spines, but are well armed with glochids, which can easily work their way through gloves. Prickly pears can spread 1½'-2', so give young plants room to grow. The other cacti are more restrained; plant them about 1' apart. After planting, mulch the bed with 2" of gravel so plants won't rot.

Maintenance. Once you've prepared the bed and planted your cacti, maintenance is a snap. Apply manure tea each spring when growth resumes. (For instructions on making manure tea, see the Manure entry.) You don't have to water—in fact, watering can be fatal in fall, when plants must shrivel in order to survive the winter. And cacti are virtually pest-free.

Landscaping with cacti. Cacti look wonderful combined with other succulent plants like sedums, hens-and-chickens (*Sempervivum* spp.), and yuccas (*Yucca* spp.)—a combination especially useful for hot, sunny sites where many other plants will not thrive. Prickly pears will also add an exotic touch to a well-drained perennial border, where their shape, low habit, and large, exquisite flowers make a striking contrast to bold-textured perennials like daylilies and irises. But where they are happy, these cacti will spread—a problem when you have to extract them. Unless you have nerves (and gloves) of steel, keep them out in the open where they're easy to reach.

Cacti for the Southwest

Arid, rocky, alkaline soil and hot winds make gardening in the Southwest a challenge. Creating the artificial environment needed for lawns, trees, and flowers takes lots of water and fertilizer. But cacti call these inhospitable conditions home. It makes sense to include them in the backyard landscape.

Landscaping with cacti. When choosing cacti for your landscape, pick species that are native to your area or to places with similar conditions. Think of the plant's size at maturity, and space accordingly. Before you plant, con-

---

More On
CACTI

One of the best books on cacti is *The Encyclopedia of Cacti.* If you want to grow cacti outdoors in the North, look for these two magazine articles: "Spiny Gems for Northern Gardens" by John N. Spain (*Fine Gardening,* July/August 1989) and "Cactus Gardens for the Snow Belt" by Mel Hunter (*Garden,* January/February 1986).

sider what you want the plant to do. If it's a barrier, choose a tall, hedging cactus. But if it's an ornamental planting, site your cacti away from walks, driveways, and other areas where passersby could come to grief.

In Southwestern gardens, cacti mix beautifully with native shrubs like desert willow (*Chilopsis linearis*), mesquite (*Prosopis*), and palo verde (*Cercidium floridum*), as well as other succulents like agaves (*Agave* spp.), aloes (*Aloe* spp.), and yuccas, and a host of desert wildflowers like penstemons (*Penstemon* spp.), evening primroses (*Oenothera* spp.), and sand verbenas (*Abronia* spp.).

Edible landscaping. Southwesterners can also grow a cactus "orchard," harvesting the beautiful, sweet fruits of the prickly pear. Marketed as cactus pears, the fruits are produced abundantly on a shrubby cactus called the Indian fig (*Opuntia ficus-indica*). Cultivars bear pear- or fig-shaped maroon, peach, or green 2″ fruits that are as sweet as watermelon. Handle cactus pears with care; they bear tiny barblike glochids that must be removed before eating or marketing these fruits. ❖

Caladium

Caladium. Summer or fall tuberous plants grown for foliage.

Description: *Caladium* × *hortulanum*, fancy-leaved caladiums, light up shady areas with their 6″-12″ pointed, heart-shaped leaves marked with white, pink, red, and green. Leaves are borne in 1′-2′ loose, arching bunches. Hooded, off-white flowers are inconspicuous. Hardy only in frost-free soil. Zone 10.

How to grow: Start caladiums indoors about 4-6 weeks before all danger of frost is past. Plant tubers in a loose, fast-draining mix such as peat, sand, perlite, vermiculite, and compost, barely covering the tops. (The end with tiny buds is the top.) Plant the tubers in shallow boxes, flats, or pots. Keep warm (70°F is ideal), and give plenty

of water once growth begins. Plant out after the soil is warm, in partial shade with a few hours of morning sun, or under tall trees. Caladiums grow best in fertile, well-drained, moist, humus-rich soil. Apply fish emulsion or manure tea every 3-4 weeks to encourage new leaves and bright colors. (For instructions on making manure tea, see the Manure entry.) Handpick or trap slugs and snails. Dig up caladiums after the first frost, remove the soil after it has dried, and store the tubers almost dry at around 65°F in peat or vermiculite. Start them again in spring.

Landscape uses: Mass on 8″ centers in shady beds and corners, or tuck groups of 3-5 as accents between larger plants such as ferns, hostas, or shrubs. Show off several in a gray pot or wood planter.

Best cultivars: 'Candidum', white with green veins; 'Fanny Munson', bright pink with red veins and green edge; 'John Peed', red flames on green; 'Pink Beauty', green-splashed pink; 'Pink Symphony', pink with green veins; 'White Queen', white with red veins and green markings. ❖

Calendula

Pot marigold. Spring- and fall-flowering annuals; edible flowers; herbs.

Description: Pot marigolds bear daisylike 2″-4″ flowers in shades of yellow and orange on 1′-2′ tall open mounds of rough, straplike leaves.

How to grow: Start indoors in late winter or plant seeds directly where they are to bloom. Lightly cover the seeds in sunny, well-drained, average soil as soon as frost leaves the ground. Transplant or thin to stand no more than 1′ apart. Pot marigolds will also self-sow.

Landscape uses: Mass them in mixed annual and perennial plantings or in a cutting garden. Use them to conceal the dying foliage of spring bulbs.

Best cultivars: 'Pacific Beauty', 1½′ plants with double blooms. ❖

Callistephus

China aster. Summer- and fall-blooming annuals.

Description: Pompon, button, daisy, or shaggy flowers, 2″-6″ across, bloom in shades of white, pink, red, blue, and violet. Some grow in 6″ mounds; others form bushy 2′ "bouquets" on upright stems with narrow leaves.

How to grow: Transplant April-sown seeds outdoors after frost; this is also a good time to direct-seed another crop. Full sun and average soil produce the best flowers. Plant wilt-resistant cultivars.

Landscape uses: Grow successive cut-flower crops of early, mid-season, and late cultivars. Try the dwarfs in pots.

Best cultivars: Mixes: 'Ostrich Plume', 1′-2′; 'Powderpuffs', 2′-2½′. ❖

Camellia

Camellia. Evergreen, fall- or winter-blooming shrubs or small trees.

Description: *Camellia japonica* is a dense, evergreen, upright tree, with a pyramidal or oval crown and one or many trunks; it reaches 8′-15′ tall. Oval leaves are large, shiny, and deep green, with a serrated margin and pointed tip. Bloom begins in late fall; some cultivars bloom through the winter. The pink, red, or white flowers are single or double, sometimes waxy, and may have showy stamens. Some cultivars have been selected for their splotched and streaked petals, usually caused by a virus. Zones 7-8.

C. sasanqua shares the same shrubby or treelike characteristics as *C. japonica* but has a more open habit. It can reach 15′ but is usually closer to 4′-6′. It bears smaller leaves and smaller flowers, which are white or pink, single or double. Zones 7-8.

How to grow: All camellias require humus-rich, acid soil, light to medium shade, good drainage, and wind protection. Flowering is sparse in dense shade. Plant camellias in the fall or winter. Camellias are shallow-rooted; if you plant them too deeply, they'll die. For this reason, be sure to plant "high," leaving some room for the soil to settle. Water camellias during establishment and during dry summer weather to promote good flowering. Flower buds form during the summer, so moisture availability in these months is crucial. Mulch generously. The dense foliage can inhibit flowering and reduce air circulation. To open the plant to light and air and to retain its upright, oval form, prune after flowering and before next year's flower buds are set.

Landscape uses: For winter interest in the right climate, there are few better choices for a focal point, screen, or hedge. ❖

Campanula

Bellflower, harebell. Late-spring- and summer-blooming perennials or biennials.

Description: All bellflowers produce lovely single blue, purple, or white star- or bell-shaped flowers above deep green, often toothed foliage. There are many species and cultivars to choose from. All are usually longer-lived in cooler areas. The following are among the best.

Campanula carpatica, Carpathian harebell, bears a profusion of upward-facing, open 1″ bells in white and blue shades. These blooms are held individually on threadlike stems, usually 8″ above tight mounds of shiny green 2″ leaves; flowers appear in early summer and sporadically throughout the growing season. Zones 3-8.

C. glomerata, clustered bellflower, has dense 4″ clusters of narrower, more pointed purple bells on 1′-2½′ erect stems above spreading masses of dark green, rough, fuzzy leaves in late spring and early summer. Zones 3-8.

C. persicifolia, peach-leaved bellflower, carries open, 1½″ widely spaced white or blue bells on upright stalks to 3′ above matlike, slender, 8″ glossy leaves during summer. Zones 3-8.

LOW-GROWING BELLFLOWERS

Though tall bellflowers are striking, the shorter species can be stunning in the front of a border, in rock gardens, and as ground-covers. Try spiral bellflower (*Campanula cochlearifolia*), Dalmatian bellflower (*C. portenschlagiana*), Serbian bellflower (*C. poscharskyana*), and bluebell (*C. rotundifolia*). These species range from 4″ to 12″ tall, with graceful bell- or star-shaped flowers in sky blue, blue-violet, lilac blue, purple, or white.

C. medium, Canterbury bells, is a biennial usually grown as a hardy annual. It bears loose spikes of showy, 2″ long violet-blue bells on plants 2′-4′ tall. Zones 3-8.

How to grow: Plant or divide bellflowers in spring in sunny, average, well-drained soil. Carpathian harebell especially needs good drainage. Provide some afternoon shade in warmer zones. Clustered bellflower tolerates wetter sites but not boggy conditions. Remove flowers soon after bloom to encourage rebloom on Carpathian harebell and peach-leaved bellflower. Most come relatively true to type from self-sown seed. Handpick or trap slugs and snails.

Landscape uses: Mass taller bellflowers in borders, cottage gardens, and naturalized areas. The cool blue and white shades of peach-leaved bellflowers contrast nicely with pink and red old-fashioned roses. Carpathian harebells look better in small-scale settings, such as rock gardens, walls, and among cracks in paving stones. Avoid *C. rapunculoides,* the creeping or rover bellflower, an invasive plant that is almost impossible to control once it gains a foothold.

Best cultivars: *C. carpatica:* var. *alba* and 'White Clips', clean white; 'Blue Clips', 6″-9″, medium blue; 'China Doll', 9″, lavender-blue. *C. glomerata:* 'Joan Elliott', to 1½′, deep violet-blue; 'Superba', 2½′, violet, more heat-tolerant. Choose from many single or rarer double cultivars of *C. persicifolia* in white and blue shades. ❖

Canna

Canna. Summer- and fall-blooming tender perennials.

Description: *Canna* × *generalis,* hybrid cannas, bear 4″-6″ irregularly shaped blooms in cream, yellow, pink, red, orange, and combinations. The flower clusters appear above substantial clumps of broad green or rich purple-bronze leaves on upright plants 2′-8′ tall. Lift to overwinter in the North; leave in the ground in Zones 8-10.

How to grow: Start cannas about a month before all danger of frost is past. Plant the rhizomes horizontally with the tips pointing up; cover with about 1″ of potting mix. When the weather warms, plant out in full sun and fertile, well-drained, moist, humus-rich soil. Mulch with compost, shredded bark, or pine needles when the shoots are about 1′ tall to control weeds and conserve moisture. Give cannas plenty of water during hot weather and drench liberally with fish emulsion or manure tea during the first 6-8 weeks. (For instructions on making manure tea, see the Manure entry.) Handpick Japanese beetles. Remove spent flowers if you can reach them. To overwinter them, dig the clumps after frost blackens the foliage and cut them back to 6″ stubs. Allow the soil to dry, shake it off, and store the clumps in barely moist peat at 45°-50°F. In spring, cut the clumps into pieces with 1-3 eyes (buds) and start again.

Landscape uses: Grow small groups in a border, or devote a bed to one or several cultivars. The dark-leaved cultivars contrast boldly with red, gold, and orange flowers, and all the tall cannas can temporarily screen out an unsightly view. Try a smaller cultivar in a 12″ pot.

Best cultivars: Green-leaved Pfitzer cannas, from 1½′-3′ tall, include 'Crimson Beauty', 'Chinese Coral', 'Primrose Yellow', and 'Salmon Pink'. Others: 'The President', scarlet, 4′; 'Red King Humbert', red with bronze foliage, 5′; 'Wyoming', orange with bronze foliage, 6′; and 'City of Portland', salmon pink, 4′. ❖

Canning

You can count on canning—just as generations of gardeners have—to preserve fruits and vegetables safely for months.

The secret to canning's success is simple: heat and an airtight seal. Food is packed in jars, then heated to very high temperatures to destroy enzymes, bacteria, and other food-spoiling microorganisms. During heating, air is driven from the jars. As the jars cool, a vacuum seal forms. The seal prevents air—which is laden with microorganisms—from reentering the jars and spoiling the contents.

If you're a budget-minded gardener, canning is an economical choice. Most canning equipment need be bought only once. And, unlike frozen produce, canned foods need no electricity to keep them at their peak. All you need is an empty shelf in a cool, dark, dry spot.

Mason-type jars are best for canning. They come in regular and widemouthed styles; sizes range from half-pints to quarts. Each takes a two-piece top—a flat metal disc, or lid, with a self-sealing compound and a metal screw band that helps hold the lid tight.

Before each use, wash the jars and screw bands with hot, soapy water and rinse them well. Check the jar rims and the bands for nicks, dents, and other irregularities. Discard damaged jars or bands; they may not seal. The flat discs must be tossed out once used, because the sealing compound is good for only one time around. When using the tops, follow the manufacturer's directions.

Safe Canning

Canning is a very safe process *if* you adhere to all recommended procedures. Do not experiment!

All low-acid foods, such as vegetables, meats, poultry, and seafood, must be processed under pressure at 240°F; otherwise, spores from *Clostridium botulinum,* a harmful bacteria, can survive and thrive in the airless conditions of the sealed jars. As the spores grow, they produce a

---

CANNING APPLESAUCE

To make applesauce, wash, core, pare, and slice apples. Cook them in a small amount of water in a covered saucepan over medium heat, stirring occasionally, until tender. Press the apples through a food mill, then sweeten the sauce to taste. Return the sauce to the stove, and heat it to boiling. Pack the sauce into hot pint or quart jars, leaving ¼" head space. Remove bubbles with a rubber spatula and wipe the jar rims. Add the lids. Process in a boiling water bath for 20 minutes.

---

deadly toxin, but the tainted foods show no obvious signs of spoilage. Fortunately, the spores do not grow in high-acid foods, such as fruits, tomatoes, pickles, and jams, which can be processed at 212°F in a boiling water bath.

For water-bath processing, you can use either a specially made water-bath canner or a large stockpot. Be sure the pot has a flat bottom, a tight-fitting lid, and a rack to hold the jars off the bottom. For two-tier canning, add a second rack. If you have a tall pressure canner, it can double as a water-bath canner. Leave the lid unfastened and the vent open.

The pot must be deep enough to cover the jars with 1"-2" of water, plus another 2" allowance for briskly boiling water. The pot should hold at least five jars, not touching. But the pot must be no more than 4" wider than the diameter of your stove's burner.

If you're in the market for a pressure canner, it's best not to buy one made before 1970. These older canners may lack important safety features, and replacement parts are hard to find. Modern canners usually have a lid that turns to lock in place, a jar rack, a gasket, a dial or weighted gauge, an automatic vent/cover lock, a steam vent with a counterweight, and a safety fuse. Before buying a used canner, be sure all parts work properly. For best results with your canner,

> ## CAN IT!
>
> Use only fresh, top-quality foods for canning. Try these garden choices for tasty eating all winter.
>
> **Fruits:** apples, berries, cherries, grapes, nectarines, peaches, pears, plums
>
> **Vegetables:** asparagus, beets, carrots, corn, green beans, hot peppers, okra, onions, peas, potatoes, pumpkin, rhubarb, tomatoes, wax beans, winter squash

follow the manufacturer's instructions for use and care.

Preparing and Packing Food

Consult a reliable, up-to-date cookbook for canning procedure details and processing times. Here are some basic guidelines:

• Food can be packed into jars raw or slightly cooked. Hot packing is preferable, because more air is forced out of food tissues. To hot pack, simmer food for 2-5 minutes in water, juice, or syrup. Then pack the food into canning jars, and pour in enough hot liquid to fill around the food and cover it. To raw pack, put raw fruit or vegetables in jars and fill the jars with boiling water, juice, or syrup. Use enough liquid to fill around the food and cover it.

• To prevent apples, pears, peaches, and other light-colored fruits from darkening, use an antidarkening agent. Drop slices into a solution of 1 teaspoon (3000 mg) of ascorbic acid to 1 gallon of water. Or you can use lemon juice — ¾ cup juice to 1 gallon water. Remove the slices from the solution and drain them before packing.

• Leave the recommended space between the top of the food or liquid and the lid. Too little space can result in food boiling out during processing; too much can allow air to remain in the jar after processing. Either can mean a poor seal.

• After packing each jar, remove air bubbles by inserting a plastic spatula between the

food and the jar. Move the spatula up and down while slowly turning the jar. Wipe the jar rim. Add the flat lid and screw band. Tighten the band.

Processing

Consult a thorough, modern cookbook before you begin. Allow yourself plenty of time; canning 10 lb. of beans, for instance, can take about 3½ hours from start to finish.

Water-bath canning: Use this method to can high-acid foods only. Fill the canner halfway with water. Add the closed jars packed with food. Pour boiling water into the canner until the water level is 1″-2″ above the tops of the jars.

Turn the heat to high, and bring the water to a boil. Cover the canner and lower the heat, maintaining a gentle boil during processing. Add boiling water, if needed, to maintain the level. When the processing time is up, remove jars with specialized tongs called a jar lifter.

Pressure canning: Use this method to safely can low-acid foods. Put 2″-3″ of water in the canner; add filled, closed jars. Fasten the canner lid, but leave the vent open. Heat at the highest setting until steam escapes from the vent. Allow 10 minutes, then close the vent.

Start timing when the dial gauge reaches the proper pressure or when the weighted gauge starts rocking. Regulate the heat to maintain constant pressure. When the processing time is up, take the canner off the burner and let the pressure drop. This takes about 45 minutes. Carefully open the vent. About 2 minutes later, open the lid. Remove the jars, using a jar lifter.

Storing

Let the jars cool at room temperature for 24 hours. Then test the seals: Press the middle of each lid with your finger. Release. Do any lids spring back? Those that do are *not* sealed. Refrigerate unsealed jars and use them within several days. Store sealed jars in a cool, dark, dry place.

Do not taste any food showing signs of spoilage, such as mold, discoloration, foaming, or other suspicious characteristics. When in doubt, throw it out. ❖

Carpinus

Hornbeam. Deciduous trees.

Description: *Carpinus betulus,* European hornbeam, has an upright oval form and grows to about 50′ at maturity. Zones 5-7.

C. caroliniana, American hornbeam, has a more open branching pattern. Its bluish gray trunk and older branches have a sinewy, muscular look; it usually reaches 20′-30′ and may even reach 50′. Zones 5-8.

Both species have sharply serrated, oblong green leaves.

How to grow: Plant in loose, well-drained, humus-rich soil. Water diligently for the first two summers and in hot, dry weather. European hornbeam prefers full sun; American hornbeam does better in partial shade.

Landscape uses: European hornbeam makes an impressive focal point, hedge, or shade tree. American hornbeam looks best in a loose, informal planting. ❖

Carrot

Daucus carota var. *sativus*
Umbelliferae

Variations on the four basic carrot shapes, plus a host of hybrids, provide a wide variety of carrot types for the home vegetable garden. The white, yellow, crimson, or orange roots can be fat, slender, or round; they come in early and late cultivars and may be disease- and crack-resistant. A single root supplies more than the recommended dietary allowance of vitamin A; it also contains vitamins B, C, D, E, and K.

Planting: Success with carrots depends on deep, loose, rock-free soil. To produce the best crop possible, thoroughly prepare the planting bed by double-digging. Adding plenty of compost can help loosen a heavy soil, but avoid using fresh manure; too much nitrogen produces poor-tasting carrots with many side rootlets.

Make your first sowing of this cool-weather crop three weeks before the last expected frost; plant again every 2-3 weeks after that. Plant in fall or winter in subtropical regions. Most cultivars take 70-80 days to mature, so make the last planting 2-3 months before the last expected frost.

Rake the soil free of lumps and stones. Plant on raised beds, spaced far enough apart so you can walk without compacting the soil near the carrots. Broadcast the tiny seeds, or for easier weeding, plant in rows. Put a pinch of about six seeds to the inch. They will take 1-3 weeks to sprout, so mix in quick-growing radish seeds to mark the rows. Cover with ¼″-½″ of loose soil or sand—a little more in warm, dry areas—to make it easier for the delicate seedlings to emerge. Water gently to avoid washing seeds away; keep the soil moist, so seeds will germinate.

Growing guidelines: Thin to 1″ apart when the tops are 2″ high, and be ruthless; crowded carrots will be deformed. Thin again two weeks later to 3″-4″ apart.

As the seedlings develop, gradually apply mulch to maintain an even moisture level and reduce weed problems. If the soil dries out completely between waterings, gradually remoisten the bed over a period of days; a sudden drenching may cause the roots to split. Carrots' feeder roots are easily damaged, so hand-pull any weeds that get through the mulch, or cut them off just below the ground. Cover carrot crowns, which push up through the soil as they mature, with mulch or soil to prevent them from becoming green and bitter.

Problems: The biggest threats to carrots are such pests as deer, gophers, woodchucks, and rabbits. For controls, see the Animal Pests entry. Otherwise, carrots are fairly problem-free.

Keep an eye out—particularly in the Northwest—for carrot rust flies, which look like ¼″, green houseflies with yellow heads and red eyes. Their eggs hatch into whitish larvae that burrow into roots, turning them dark red and turning leaves black. Infestations usually occur in

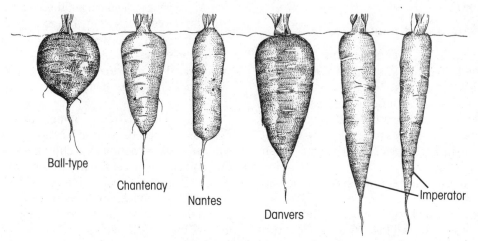

Ball-type

Chantenay

Nantes

Danvers

Imperator

Carrot shapes. Compact ball-type carrots are ideal for container growing. The stout Chantenay and hefty Danvers are good for heavy soils. Slender Nantes and long, thin Imperator are best suited for deep, loose soils.

the early spring, so one solution is to delay plantings until early summer when damage is less likely. Or cover plants with a floating row cover to keep flies away.

Parsleyworms—green caterpillars that turn into black swallowtail butterflies—have black stripes, white or yellow dots, and little orange horns. They attack carrot foliage. Handpick or apply BT (*Bacillus thuringiensis*), or dust with rotenone for severe infestations.

The larvae of carrot weevils, found from the East Coast to Colorado, tunnel into carrot roots, especially in spring crops. Discourage grubs by rotating crops.

Nematodes, microscopic wormlike animals, make little knots along roots that result in stunted carrots. Rotate crops and apply plenty of compost, which is rich in predatory microorganisms. To treat serious nematode problems, plant the area with French marigolds (*Tagetes patula*) the year before growing carrots.

Leaf blight is the most widespread carrot disease. It starts on leaf margins with white or yellow spots that turn brown and watery. Plant resistant cultivars.

Hot, humid weather causes a bacterial disease called vegetable soft rot. Prevent it by rotat-

ing crops and keeping soil loose. The disease spreads in storage, so don't store bruised carrots.

Mosaic mottles leaves with light to dark shades of green. Aphids spread the disease, so control them to reduce the spread of the virus. See "The Top Ten Garden Insect Pests in America" on page 344 for details on aphid control.

Harvesting: Carrots become tastier as they grow. You can start harvesting as soon as the carrots are big enough to eat, or leave them to all to mature for a single harvest. Dig your winter storage crop before the first frost on a day when the soil is moist but the air is dry. Since spading forks tend to bruise roots, hand-pull them; if necessary, loosen the soil with a trowel. Watering the bed before harvesting softens the soil and makes pulling easier.

To save carrots for winter use, twist off the tops. Layer undamaged roots (so they're not touching) with sand or peat in boxes topped with straw. Storing carrots in this manner retains more flavor and nutritional value than canning or freezing.

Best cultivars: Short-rooted 'Orbit' or thick-shouldered 'Goldinhart' for heavy soil; 'King Midas', disease- and crack-resistant; 'Tip Top', perfect for juicing. ❖

Cauliflower

Brassica oleracea, Botrytis group
Cruciferae

The sweet and mild taste of homegrown cauliflower more than justifies the extra care it requires. In general, cauliflower is not difficult to grow, but it is sensitive to extreme temperatures. Primarily a cool-weather crop, cauliflower won't produce heads in hot weather and is frost-tolerant only as a mature fall crop. Most cultivars need about two months of cool weather to mature, though some require as little as 48 days and others over 95 days. Success, therefore, lies in choosing the right cultivar for your climate, planting it at the proper time, and providing a steady supply of moisture.

Planting: Like other cabbage-family members, cauliflower needs a soil rich in nitrogen and potassium, with enough organic matter to retain moisture. In warm climates, plant in the fall or late winter for an early-spring harvest. In colder areas, cauliflower usually performs best as a fall crop.

To avoid disturbing roots, start spring crops indoors in peat pots. Plant seeds ¼"-½" deep, 4-6 weeks before the last average frost. Set the pots in a south-facing window and provide constant moisture; use bottom heat, if necessary, to keep the soil temperature around 70°F.

About two weeks before the date of the last frost, harden the plants off before transplanting to the garden. Make sure each transplant has a small developing bud in the center; otherwise, it won't produce a head. Set the seedlings 15"-24" apart. Make a saucerlike depression around each plant to help hold water. Firm the soil, and water seedlings thoroughly.

Sow crops for a fall harvest in garden beds 2-3 months before the first expected frost. To avoid seed rot in soggy soil, plant in small hills spaced 2' apart. Sow about five seeds per hill. A month later, thin to the sturdiest seedling in each hill.

Growing guidelines: Provide at least 1" of water a week, soaking the soil to a depth of 6". Cauliflower requires constant moisture to produce large, tender heads; soil that dries out between waterings will cause heads to open up and become "ricey." Use a thick layer of compost or organic mulch to cut down on evaporation and weeds and to cool the soil. Be careful not to disturb cauliflower roots when weeding, because damaged roots produce uneven growth. Give young plants monthly light feedings with fish emulsion fertilizer or manure tea. If you want to speed up growth, feed every two weeks. For instructions on making and using manure tea, see the Manure entry.

When the flower heads (curds) of white-headed cultivars are about egg-size, blanch them by shading out the sunlight. Otherwise they'll turn green, yellow, or brown and become, if not less tasty, certainly less appetizing. Prepare plants for blanching on a sunny afternoon when the plants are totally dry, because damp heads will be more susceptible to rot. Just bend some of the plants' own leaves over the head and tuck them in on the opposite side, or secure the leaves at the top with soft twine, rubber bands, or plastic tape. Use enough leaves to keep out light and moisture, but allow room for air circulation and for the heads to grow.

Once the blanching process begins, water only the roots of the plants, not the heads or leaves. Unwrap occasionally to check on growth, to look for pests, or to allow heads to dry out after a rain. In hot weather, heads can be ready to harvest in a matter of days. In cool periods, the maturing process can take as long as two weeks. This technique is not necessary with purple-headed and self-blanching types, which have leaves that naturally curl over the head.

Problems: Pests—such as aphids and flea beetles—tend to attack cauliflower more in the spring than in the fall. Cabbage maggots, sometimes called root maggots, can also be a serious problem. Caterpillars, such as cabbage loopers and imported cabbageworms, are other common cauliflower pests. For more details on these insects and appropriate controls, see "The Top Ten Garden Insect Pests in America" on page 344.

Other pests include harlequin bugs and weevils. Harlequin bugs, black insects with red markings, attack many cabbage-family crops. Handpick these pests or spray with insecticidal soap. Weevils are brown beetlelike insects that feed on foliage at night and hide in the ground during the day. For serious infestations, spray pyrethrins over the whole plant to reduce feeding. Minimize damage by keeping the garden clean to eliminate hiding places.

In boron-deficient soil, cauliflower heads turn brown and leaf tips die back and become distorted. If this occurs, foliar-feed with liquid seaweed extract immediately, and repeat every two weeks until the symptoms disappear. For subsequent crops, provide boron by adding granite dust or rock phosphate to the soil, or plant fall cover crops of vetch or clover.

Crop rotation, good garden sanitation, and using resistant cultivars will prevent most cauliflower diseases. These include black leg, black rot, club root, and Fusarium wilt (yellows). See the Cabbage entry for more information on these problems.

Harvesting: Mature heads can range in size from 6" to 12" across. Harvest when the buds are still tight and unopened. With a sharp knife, cut them off just below the head, along with a few whorls of leaves to protect the curds. Use or preserve right away. If you don't get the crop harvested before a heavy frost, remember that the heads are still edible unless they thaw and freeze again. To store plants for about a month, pull them up by the roots and hang them upside down in a cool place.

Best cultivars: 'All-the-Year-Round', keeps longer than most cauliflowers; 'Snow King', suitable for winter culture in the South and on the West Coast; 'Snow Crown', particularly tasty eaten raw; 'Alert' and 'Self-Blanche' provide their own protection from the sun. ❖

Cedrus

Cedar. Needle-leaved evergreen trees.

Description: The true cedars are attractive, tufted evergreens, pyramidal in youth, then taking on a flat-topped form when mature, often with strongly horizontal branching. With age, the gray-brown bark takes on a pebbled look. Waxy cones are borne upright on the branches, like candles.

Cedrus atlantica, atlas cedar, is a handsome tree of 40'-60'; it occasionally reaches 100' in height. The bluish to dark green 1" needles radiate from spurs on the branches; the 3" cones are waxy and squat. Zones 6-8.

C. deodara, deodar cedar, has gently pendulous branches that weep dramatically; 2" needles are silvery dark green and provide a soft texture. It grows to heights of 40'-70', sometimes to 150', with a top that nods to one side and 5" long cones. Zones 6-7.

C. libani, cedar-of-Lebanon, is the hardiest of all true cedars. It has a horizontally layered habit and low branches that may sweep the ground. The solid green 1" needles are borne on spurs. Cedar-of-Lebanon reaches heights of 40'-60' in the landscape, but may grow to 100'. Zones 5-7.

How to grow: Plant cedars in sunny sites with well-drained to slightly dry soil. Set them out in spring as small balled-and-burlapped or container-grown plants. Select a site protected from direct wind and allow ample space for the tree's mature size. Unlike cedar-of-Lebanon, atlas cedar tolerates partial shade.

Landscape uses: Use any of these cedars as a graceful focal point; they are also attractive when massed and can be used for screening.

Best cultivars: *C. atlantica:* 'Glauca', blue atlas cedar, striking blue-gray foliage and cones; 'Glauca Pendula', a weeping, blue-needled tree. *C. deodara* 'Shalimar', hardy to Zone 5. *C. libani* var. *stenocoma,* hardiest of the cedar-of-Lebanons and best for the northernmost reaches of Zone 5. ❖

Celery

Apium graveolens var. *dulce*
Umbelliferae

Contrary to popular belief, celery is not all that difficult to grow. The main things this former marsh plant requires are rich soil, plenty of water, and protection from hot sun and high temperatures. Grow celery as a winter crop in the South, a summer crop in the far North, or a spring or fall crop in most other areas.

Planting: You can buy transplants from nurseries, but cultivar choices expand enormously when you grow celery from seed. For a late-summer crop, sow seeds indoors 8-10 weeks before the last average frost. Soak the tiny seeds overnight to encourage germination. Fill flats with a mix of ⅔ compost and ⅓ sand, and plant in rows 1″ apart. Cover the seeds with a sand layer ⅛″ deep, then cover the flats with damp sphagnum moss or burlap until seeds sprout.

Place in a bright place out of direct sun, and keep the temperature at 70°-75°F during the day and about 60°F at night. Provide plenty of water and good drainage and air circulation. Transplant the seedlings into peat pots when they are about 4″ tall. At 6″, harden off the plants for about 10 days, and then transplant them into the garden.

Space the plants 6″-8″ apart in rows 2′-3′ apart. Set them no deeper than they grew in pots. Water immediately, and fertilize each seedling with manure tea. For instructions on making and using manure tea, see the Manure entry.

For a fall crop, sow seeds indoors in May or June, and follow the same directions, transplanting seedlings in June or July. Provide shade in hot, humid weather.

Growing guidelines: Apply several inches of mulch, and provide at least 1″ of water a week. Gently remove any weeds that might compete for nutrients with celery's shallow roots. Feed every 10-14 days. If night temperatures are consistently below 55°F, protect plants by covering them with cloches; otherwise, the stalks become weak.

Blanching celery destroys some nutrients but prevents stalks from becoming bitter. It also protects fall crops against heavy frosts. Try any of these methods:

• Gradually pull the soil up around the plants as they grow, keeping the leaves exposed.

• Two weeks before harvest, tie the tops together, and mound soil up to the base of the leaves.

• Cover the stalks with large cans, drain tiles, or sleeves made out of paper or other material.

• Line up boards, secured with stakes, along each side of a celery row to shut out the sun.

Problems: Celery's main enemies are parsleyworms, carrot rust flies, and nematodes. See the Carrot entry for more information on these pests. Celery leaf tiers are tiny yellow caterpillars marked with one white stripe; control by handpicking. Attacks of tarnished plant bugs show up as black joints or brown, sunken areas. See "The Top Ten Garden Insect Pests in America" on page 344 for controls.

Common diseases include early and late blight, which both begin as small dots on the leaves, and pink rot, which shows up as water-soaked stem spots and white or pink coloration at stalk bases. Crop rotation is the best control.

Distorted leaves and cracked stems can indicate a boron-deficient soil; correct by spraying plants with liquid seaweed extract every two weeks until symptoms disappear.

Harvesting: Cut the plant off just below the soil line, or cut single stalks of unblanched celery as needed. To preserve a fall crop, pull up the plants and place them in deep boxes with moist sand or soil around the roots. Store in a cool place; they will keep for several months.

Best cultivars: 'Giant Pascal', blight-resistant, produces long, tender, stringless stalks; 'Florida 683', withstands cracking, a good choice for hot climates. ❖

Celosia

Crested cockscomb, plumed cockscomb. Summer- and fall-blooming annuals; dried flowers.

Description: Crested cockscombs are available in cream, yellow, orange, red, and red-purple shades. The wavy, velvety flower heads reach 4"-12" across on thick, 6"-24" tall stems with long, narrow, green or dark red leaves. Feathery plumed cockscombs share the same color range and plant habits, producing 4"-12" long flame-like heads.

How to grow: Start seeds about four weeks before the last frost, or direct-seed outdoors after the ground warms up. Plants resent root disturbance, so transplant carefully into a sunny, well-drained spot with average to fairly rich soil. They tolerate infertile soil and drought very well, but for the largest flower heads, water regularly, side-dress with a high-phosphorus fertilizer such as bonemeal, and stake the taller cultivars. Wide spacing (8"-12" apart for dwarfs, 1½' for tall types) produces larger heads.

Landscape uses: Dwarf crested cockscombs lend interest to beds, edgings, and pots. Keep tall, large-headed plants in the cutting garden. Plumed cultivars are excellent for massing in beds and borders. For drying, cut either type when in peak color and hang upside down in a warm, well-ventilated place out of direct sun.

Best cultivars: Crested mixes: 'Jewel Box', 6"-9"; 'Floradale', 16"-24". Plumed mixes: 'Fairy Fountains', 15"; 'Century', 2'-2½'. Also try 'Apricot Brandy' and red-leaved, red-flowered 'New Look', both 16". ❖

Plumed
Cockscomb

Crested
Cockscomb

Centaurea

Knapweed, cornflower. Late-spring- to early-summer-blooming annuals and perennials.

Description: *Centaurea cyanus,* cornflower or bachelor's-button, is a popular summer-blooming annual that bears shaggy, 1½", circular, swollen-based blooms in shades of white, pink, red-violet, blue, and violet. The 1'-3' upright or slightly floppy plants are clad in long, skinny, grayish fuzzy leaves that become much smaller toward the top.

C. montana, mountain bluet, resembles its annual cousin but is a perennial, offering 2"-2½", more finely cut buttons, almost always in a deep, rich blue, on 1'-2' open mounds of broader, greener foliage. Zones 3-8.

How to grow: Plant both types in full sun to very light shade in average to less fertile, well-drained soil to keep plants compact.

You can start cornflowers a few weeks ahead of the last hard frost and plant them out as small plants before the last frost; however, they settle in much better if sown directly after frost leaves the soil or in early fall.

Plant mountain bluets in early spring or early fall. Divide often to keep plants vigorous, or allow the usually abundant self-sown seedlings to replace them. Plants deteriorate soon after bloom, so you may want to cut them back nearly to the ground, leaving a few to produce seeds.

Landscape uses: Grow both types in masses in informal borders, cottage gardens, cutting gardens, or meadow plantings. Site with other plants that can fill the gaps left after bloom. Both naturalize readily.

Best cultivars: Cornflowers come in a range of colors and sizes, from the 1' blue 'Jubilee Gem' and the slightly taller 'Polka Dot' mixture to the 2' white 'Snowman' and the tallest 'Blue Boy' at 2½'-3'. Unique 2½' 'Frosty' mix has lighter-tipped petals. ❖

Chaenomeles

Flowering quince. Deciduous, late-winter- or early-spring-blooming shrubs.

Description: *Chaenomeles speciosa* is a round, spreading shrub, 4'-8' tall. It produces showy single or double flowers in white or shades of red or pink. Yellow, 2", aromatic fruits form on the thorny branches in summer, ripening in fall. Zones 4-8.

How to grow: Flowering quince must have good drainage and full sun. Plant in fall or spring in Zone 7 and north, and in fall or winter south of Zone 7. Prune plants after flowering. Rejuvenate old, overgrown plants by pruning to within 5" of the ground. Since flowering quince is a rose-family member, fire blight can be a problem.

Landscape uses: Useful as a focal point, massing, or barrier plant for early spring color, this plant is uninteresting when out of bloom. Use the fruits to make jelly. ❖

Chard

Beta vulgaris, Cicla group
Chenopodiaceae

Grow mild-flavored, prolific Swiss chard for its huge, succulent leaves. It withstands cold and heat better than most greens.

Planting: Chard tolerates partial shade and a range of soils. In spring, broadcast seeds directly in the garden 2-3 weeks before the last expected frost; rake to cover seeds. Plant in late summer for a fall crop.

Growing guidelines: Water during dry spells and keep weed-free. Thin gradually until plants are 8"-10" apart.

Problems: See the Spinach entry for disease and insect control.

Harvesting: Pick outer leaves as needed.

Best cultivars: 'Rhubarb' or 'Ruby' chard, bright red stems and veins. ❖

Cherry

Prunus spp.
Rosaceae

Do you enjoy sweet cherries despite their steep price? Do you love hot cherry pie or the sight of a cherry tree in full bloom? If so, why not try growing your own sweet and tart cherries?

The Fruit Trees entry covers many important aspects of growing cherries and other tree fruits; refer to it for additional information on planting, pruning, and care.

Selecting trees: Tart cherries (*Prunus cerasus*), also called sour or pie cherries, are easy to grow. Use the tangy fruit for baking, or let it overripen on the tree for fresh eating. Sour cherries are self-fertile and will set fruit alone. They grow only 20' tall and bear fruit at an earlier age than sweet cherries. Sour cherries are hardy to −30°F.

Sweet cherries (*P. avium*) do best in mild, dry climates, but some cultivars will do well in other climates with a little special care. Most sweet cherries need a second compatible cultivar for pollination. Certain sweet cherries can't pollinate other specific cultivars, so check before you plant. If you can only plant one tree, buy one grafted with two cultivars, or try one of the newer self-fertile cultivars. Sweet cherries can grow into trees 35' or taller. They are hardy to −20°F.

Sweet cherries come in purple, red, and yellow. There are bigarreau (firm-fleshed) types and guigne (tender, soft-fleshed) types. Soft-fleshed types tend to be less prone to cracking.

Duke cherries are hybrids between sweet and tart cherries, and tend to be sweet/tart.

Bush cherries (*P. besseyi, P. tomentosa,* and *Prunus* spp.) bear small cherrylike fruit and grow in areas where cherry trees will not.

Rootstocks: Tart cherries are small trees no matter what rootstock they are grafted on. Standard sweet cherries are grafted on seedling rootstocks such as 'Mazzard' (*P. avium*) and

'Mahaleb' (*P. mahaleb*). If your soil is heavy, try 'Mazzard'. For lighter soils, choose 'Mahaleb' for a smaller tree that bears in 2-4 years. 'Mahaleb' also adapts well to irrigation and slightly alkaline soil. 'Damil' rootstock makes a sturdy dwarfed tree and appears even more tolerant of wet soil than 'Mazzard', but some of the dwarfing rootstocks available give disappointing results.

Planting and care: Tart cherries grow well throughout much of the United States. They need about 1,000 chill hours below 45°F in the winter. This limits their range to the Carolinas and northward through Zone 5. Although all cherries need well-drained soils, tart cherries tolerate moderately heavy soils better than sweet cherries. Space tart cherries 20'-25' apart, sweet cherries 25'-30' apart. Dwarf trees can be planted with closer spacing.

Sweet cherries are not as winter-hardy as tart cherries. Early autumn frosts also can damage sweet cherry trees. Commercially, sweet cherries grow best in the West, where the summers are dry but the roots are irrigated regularly.

Cherries bloom early and are susceptible to frost damage. Sweet cherries bloom earlier than sour cherries. For site selection and frost protection ideas, see the Peach entry.

Once the fruit sets, watch soil water levels. Cherry fruit matures early and fast. It is particularly sensitive to moisture availability in the last two weeks of ripening. If the soil is too dry, the swelling cherries will shrivel. If it is too wet, they will crack and split. There is not much you can do about excessive rainfall other than to plant cultivars that resist cracking. Spread a thick organic mulch out to the drip line to help maintain soil moisture at a constant level. Irrigate as necessary to keep the soil evenly moist.

Healthy cherry trees will grow about 1' a year. If your tree's progress is slower or the new leaves are yellow, have the soil and/or foliage tested for nutrient deficiencies. See the Soil entry for instructions on taking a soil sample. Mulch each spring with a thin layer of compost out to the drip line. Don't fertilize after midsummer. This could encourage new growth that won't harden before fall frosts.

Pruning: Tart cherries tend to have a naturally spreading shape; train them to an open center form. Sweet cherries naturally grow more upright, so train them to a central leader. Spreading the branches while they are young will help control height and encourage earlier bearing. After the trees reach bearing age, prune to let light penetrate to the interior of the tree. Prune tart cherries lightly each winter to stimulate new growth and thin tangled branches. Prune sweet cherries less frequently, only every third or fourth year. Cut back heavy tops on overgrown sweet cherry trees to force new fruiting wood to develop on lower branches.

Problems: Fruit cracking and hungry birds are two of the biggest problems when raising cherries. Most insect and disease problems are less severe on tart cherry trees than on sweet. For information on pest control methods, see the Organic Pest Management entry.

Birds can strip a few trees of all of their cherries in a short time. Covering trees with netting before the fruit starts to ripen is the most effective way to stop bird damage. You can also try planting a mulberry tree nearby that fruits at the same time as your cherries to lure birds away from the harvest. See the Animal Pests entry for more ways to discourage feathered scavengers from stealing your cherries.

Cherry fruit fly, green fruit worm, peach tree borer, mites, and plum curculio all attack cherries. "Fruit Tree Insects and Diseases" on page 256 describes and lists controls for all of them. Plum curculio is illustrated on the opposite page. Aphids and scale can also cause problems; "The Top Ten Garden Insect Pests in America" on page 344 lists descriptions and controls for both. Sawfly larvae (pearslugs) sometimes skeletonize cherry leaves; see the Pear entry for

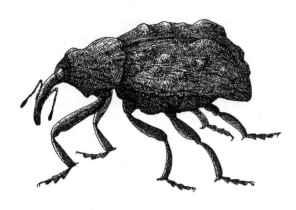

Plum curculio. These small, dark brown or steely gray beetles with distinctive snouts and four humps on their backs attack cherries, plums, peaches, apricots, apples, and pears. Developing fruits that have been attacked show crescent or half-circle scars and often drop prematurely.

description and controls.

Shothole borers can attack cherries and other fruit trees. They make small holes in the bark of twigs and trunk. The holes are often covered with gum. The larvae are pinkish white and about 1/8″ long. Prevent the tiny black adults from laying eggs by painting trunk and large branches in spring, summer, and fall with white latex paint diluted 1:1 with water. Applying BT (*Bacillus thuringiensis*) or pyrethrins can also provide control.

Pear thrips can cause disfigured leaves and blossoms. Predatory mites usually provide control, as do insecticidal soap sprays.

Diseases can be a serious problem on cherries. Watch for these:

• Brown rot and perennial canker attack cherries and other stone fruit. "Fruit Tree Insects and Diseases" on page 256 describes and lists controls for each of them.

• Black knot can attack cherries; see the Plum entry for details.

• Cherry leaf spot appears as small purple spots on upper leaf surfaces. The spots later turn brown, and their centers may fall out. Leaves turn yellow and drop before autumn. Clean up and dispose of fallen leaves each winter. Plant resistant cultivars. If leaf spot is a problem in your area, plan a preventive spray program with lime sulfur or sulfur. Lime sulfur may discolor fruits, so don't use it after young fruits begin to develop.

• Powdery mildew can be a problem on cherries. See the Apple entry for description and control.

• A number of viruses attack cherries. Buy virus-free stock and avoid planting in old cherry orchards or near wild chokecherries.

Harvesting: When the fruit begins to drop, it is ready to pick. Tart cherries can be left to sweeten on the tree for a day or two.

To pick cherries, gently pull off clusters, keeping the stems on the fruit. Be careful not to tear the branch.

Best cultivars: Sweet cherry trees: 'Stella', self-fertile, resists cracking; 'Angela', 'Bada', 'Hardy Giant', 'Hudson', 'Sam', 'Sweet Ann', 'Valera', 'Van', and 'Viva' all resist cracking; 'Gold', 'Lambert', 'Hedelfingen', 'Schmidt Bigarreau', 'Valera', and 'Viva' resist cherry leaf spot; 'Bada', 'Sam', 'Sue', 'Corum', and 'Early Burat', some resistance to bacterial canker; 'Windsor', resistant to brown rot.

Tart cherry trees: 'Northstar' resists cracking, cherry leaf spot, powdery mildew, and brown rot. 'Meteor' resists cherry leaf spot.

Cultivars with yellow fruit may be less attractive to birds than those with red fruit.

Tart cherries of the amarelle or Kentish types, such as 'Meteor' and 'Montmorency', have light-colored flesh and colorless juice. Morello or griotte types, such as 'North star', have red juice and darker fruit. ❖

Children and Gardening

Gardening is pure fun for children. They love to dig, plant, and water from a very young age. Planning your garden with children in mind means designing it for active use—a space where children can learn and romp.

Children learn by watching, so explain what you are doing and why. Keep it simple, and ask them questions, too. Encourage them to examine the soil, feel a leaf, and look closely at a flower. Plant some magic—children love spectacular plants that grow big and fast, like giant sunflowers, sprawling pumpkins, and ornamental gourds. Capture their interest and, through your patience and guidance, a child will become fascinated by the miracle of growing things.

Getting Started

For children, it is the process of gardening that is exciting, not the final product. Keep it easy and fun.

Looking through seed catalogs together is a good way to start. Select tougher-than-usual plants that can endure a little extra watering or abuse on occasion. Give suggestions for easy-growing vegetables and flowers, but let your child help make the choices.

Choose plants with large seeds, such as nasturtiums, beans, pumpkins, sunflowers, and peas, for the younger child. Children of all ages enjoy planting a neat row of onion sets. Planting potato eyes is easy and satisfying, even for the youngest gardener. Fast-growing lettuce, spinach, carrots, and radishes are other good "starter" plants. Marigolds, zinnias, cosmos, and other dependable annual flowers are a nice addition.

Set up a plan on paper to show how much room each plant will take. Children enjoy cutting out shapes of colored paper or using coins of different sizes to indicate the space requirements of each plant. It's fun to clip and paste pictures from seed catalogs onto the garden plan.

Growing seeds indoors in containers is a good activity if you have sunny windows and the space to spare. Remember that transplanting can be a little tricky for children; choose plants that don't mind some root disturbance. Tomatoes are a good first choice for indoor gardening. See the Seeds and Seedlings and Transplanting entries for instructions.

Preparing the Garden

A beginner's garden can be an extension of the main garden or a separate small plot. Layout of the garden is one of the most important aspects in planning. Choose a sunny, level spot. If the children's garden is part of the family garden, avoid locating it near plants with prickles, such as raspberries, cucumbers, or squash.

Start small. A plot measuring 6' × 10' is big enough for a first garden. Make sure it is accessible on all four sides; add a 1½' wide path down the center. Allow room for a bean or morning-glory teepee, or put a path into the corn patch for a special secret place.

Fence the boundaries of the garden to help the child recognize it as his or her own space. Use flowers, bricks, or small stones to define the edges. Clearly mark the paths with grass or boards.

Turning over the soil the first year may be too hard for children to do, but let them help break up the clumps of soil by whatever means they want to use. Even very small children can collect stones in a box to be emptied later. Use hand tools so everyone can participate. The loud noise of rotary tillers and the constant warnings to stay clear will frighten youngsters.

Tools

The best tools for children are their own hands. But since children love to imitate their parents, tools are desired objects from an early

Morning-glory teepee. To construct a plant teepee, insert eight bamboo poles or stakes around a 4' circle, leaning them toward the center. Secure at the top with twine. Continue the twine down the poles, wrapping around and between poles until you have a teepee shape. Plant 4–5 morning-glory or runner bean seeds at the base of each pole. As the vines grow, direct them up the poles and strings. Remember to leave space for a doorway!

age. Young children are capable of digging with a rounded trowel and enjoy it so much that it makes sense to have a few on hand. Most grown-up tools are too large and too heavy for young gardeners, even if handles are cut down. Weight is as important as height for a rake or a hoe, so invest in a set of children's-size tools. Avoid plastic tools that are designed for the sandbox. They are too flimsy for the garden, and children will be happier, and more successful, with real tools like your own.

You'll want to set a few rules about tools, though: Designate the purposes for which they should be used. Show children by example that tools should be cleaned and put away after use.

Planting and Maintenance

Keep the garden rows short, not more than 3'-4' long. Use a string stretched between two sticks to mark the rows. With a hoe, mark a furrow where the seed is to go. Count out enough seed for the row, and show the child how thinly to sow. Small children can plant big seeds, like beans, peas, and sunflowers, one at a time. Graduate to medium-sized seeds, such as spinach and radishes, showing how to tap the seeds out in a well-spaced line. Some children like to do their own measuring, with their fingers as a guide. Or you can prepunch holes for seeds with a dibble.

Seed sowing takes a lot of practice, so have

patience. If the seeds pour out all at once (oops!), spread them by hand or hoe to fill the furrow. Remember, the goal is to make gardening fun, not to have perfectly spaced radishes.

If you like to be in the garden, your children will, too. Your participation is important in making the garden a successful experience. Help the children with weeding and maintenance. Encourage them to do the chores they can handle. The smallest gardeners enjoy spreading handfuls of mulch. Young children love watering cans and hoses — and mud.

To many children, harvest is the best part and will need no encouragement. Offer some advice, a basket, and a garden hose or washtub nearby for rinsing. Your delight in the harvest will encourage a sense of pride and self-esteem.

In the kitchen, you can find simple recipes to make together: breads, cakes, pickles, and much more. The younger child will enjoy making animals out of overgrown squash, using toothpicks to attach flowers for eyes and cherry tomatoes for a nose. Older children can set up a farm stand at the foot of the driveway or enter their harvest in the fair.

Garden Projects

When the children tire of picking off Japanese beetles or pulling weeds, try one of these projects:

• Take a close look at the soil. What is it made of? Who lives in it? Talk about how earthworms live. An older child may be interested in how a soil test works. Collect soil from different parts of the garden. Try growing the same kind of plant in different soil conditions.

• Study seeds. Look at their size, how they are formed, and how they grow. Sprout seeds on a damp paper towel, or make a production out of it: Roll a piece of black construction paper and fit it inside a clear glass. Fill the center with a crumpled paper towel. Place several kinds of seeds between the black paper and the glass. Pour in enough water to moisten the paper towel.

When the seeds start to germinate, flip the glass upside down and watch as the roots find their way downward again.

• Help a child keep a garden journal. Clip pictures from a seed catalog and attach the seed packet to the journal page for easy reference. Chart when the seed is started, note the weather as it grows, add the dates when it bears flowers and fruit.

• Make edible necklaces by collecting a harvest of peas, beans, and edible flowers. String a doubled piece of strong thread onto a needle, and sit in the shade of the porch to make edible jewelry.

• Cornhusk dolls are a big hit. The cornhusks can be fresh or dried. (Soak dried husks in warm water until they bend without cracking.) Put several husks together, then fold over in half. Tie a piece of yarn a few inches down from the fold to form a head. Fold a few more pieces of husk lengthwise, then slip horizontally through the body for arms. Let them stick out on either side. Tie at the wrists and cut the ends (hands) to even up the lengths. To make a dress, slip a husk across each shoulder, cross in the middle, and tie with yarn at the waist. Fluff out the lower part of the skirt. Glue cornsilk for hair, and draw on a face with markers.

• Try making vegetable dyes. This project needs adult supervision, but the results are satisfying and memorable. You'll need several pots of boiling water. In separate pots, simmer beets, cabbage leaves, onion skins, or flowers such as tansy or marigold. Strain the liquid and soak white yarn or fabric in the colored water. Use for decorative artwork; dyes will not be colorfast.

• Older children enjoy a theme garden. Try a cutting garden of only pink flowers. Visit a nursery or garden center and start a patch of several kinds of mints. Or try a patchwork-quilt design of salad greens: Place stakes at 1' intervals on all four sides of a 2' wide garden bed. Run twine between stakes to form a grid. Broadcast seeds, a different salad green in each plot. ❖

Christmas Trees

With as little as a 10' × 20' plot of land, you can grow eight Christmas trees in your backyard. Start by planting small trees from one- or two-gallon pots. In 6-8 years, you can harvest your own beautiful 6' Christmas tree. In addition to the personal pleasure of harvesting your fresh-cut tree, you'll be saving the dollars you'd have paid at a tree lot.

Choosing the right tree: Think about the kind of Christmas tree you usually buy. Is it fat and full-branched, or tall and spindly with plenty of room for ornaments to hang? Many commercial trees, especially the firs and pines, are carefully clipped for years to achieve the perfect Christmas tree look. Other species, such as balsam fir or Eastern red cedar, are enjoyed imperfections and all.

Here are some popular Christmas tree types to get you started:

- Long-needled: Scotch pine (*Pinus sylvestris*), Eastern white pine (*Pinus strobus*), red or Norway pine (*Pinus resinosa*), Austrian pine (*Pinus nigra*).
- Short-needled: Balsam fir (*Abies balsamea*), Douglas fir (*Pseudotsuga menziesii*), Southern balsam fir or Fraser fir (*Abies fraseri*), Colorado blue spruce (*Picea pungens* 'Glauca'), Norway spruce (*Picea abies*).
- Scaled needles: Cypresses (*Cupressus* spp.), Eastern red cedar (*Juniperus virginiana*).

Some Christmas trees like it hot. But some like it cold, some like it moist, and some like it dry. Ask your local nursery owner or extension office to recommend species that thrive in your area.

Planting and care: Plant your trees in an area of full sun, about 6' apart. Remember, you will harvest them before they reach mature size. Evergreen trees require little or no fertilizer for healthy growth. Mulch with well-rotted manure around the selected tree a year before cutting for deep green color.

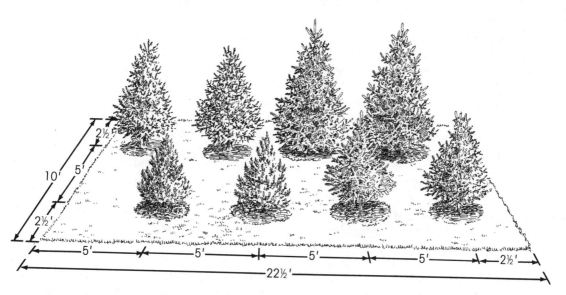

Christmas tree spacing. Plant trees in staggered rows for best use of space. The first year, plant two or three trees. Then plant another tree or two each year until you've planted eight trees. In 6-8 years, cut the first tree. The following spring, remove the stump and plant a new young tree.

A LIVING CHRISTMAS TREE

Decorate a balled-and-burlapped evergreen for Christmas, and then plant it outside to enjoy the memories of Christmas past. Sounds simple, yet the stress on the plant is so great that many ex-Christmas trees end up in the chipper.

The tree's chances for a successful transition from your living room to your yard are best if it remains indoors for only a few days. A longer stay will make the tree break dormancy and produce tender new growth. If this happens, keep your tree in a cool, sunlit room through the winter, and treat it as a giant houseplant.

Follow this plan of action:

1. Dig a planting hole in late fall before the ground freezes. Fill with loose straw. Save the soil—needed for later planting—in an area where it's protected from freezing.

2. For best selection, choose your tree early. Store it in an unheated garage or outdoors.

3. A few days before Christmas, place the tree indoors, well away from heat sources. Check soil moisture daily.

4. After Christmas, remove the straw from the hole and plant the tree, using the reserved soil. Water thoroughly, and spray with an antidesiccant.

If you want to shear your trees to encourage the classic Christmas tree shape, do so in spring. See the Evergreens entry for instructions on pruning and shearing.

Pine-tip moths and sawflies feed on and distort new growth. Check your trees closely for their caterpillar-like larvae, which may appear May through September. Snip off damaged branch tips and destroy them. You can spray sawflies with insecticidal soap, or with pyrethrins or neem for severe infestations.

For more information on growing Christmas trees, write to: Christmas Tree Growers Association, 611 E. Wells St., Milwaukee, WI 53202. Ask for the name of the regional contact in your area. ❖

Chrysanthemum

Chrysanthemum, garden mum. Fall-blooming perennials, cut flowers.

Description: *Chrysanthemum* × *morifolium*, garden or hardy mums, can bring brilliance to your autumn garden. They fall roughly into two groups: the 1'-1½' mounded cushion mums sold in bloom seemingly everywhere in fall, plus some 2'-3' upright types; and a huge range of specialist-favored exhibition cultivars. Florist's mums, grown as pot plants, are frequently not hardy, and they need such a long season to flower that even where they'll survive the winter, they often won't bloom before the first fall freeze. By far the best choices for most gardeners are those from the first group. Ranging in size from ½" to 4", the mostly double, rounded flowers, in white, yellow, orange, red, rust, lavender, and purple, harmonize beautifully with their dark green, aromatic foliage. Zones 5-9.

C. × *superbum*, Shasta daisies, are perhaps the ultimate daisies, with their large, abundant cheerful blooms. In early summer, plants display single to double, 2"-4" white or cream flowers borne on stiff 1'-3' stems atop elongated, shiny dark green leaves. Zones 4-9.

C. coccineum, painted daisy, named for its bold flower colors, is also known as pyrethrum, a familiar botanical insecticide. However, it is not the garden ornamental but its relative, *C. cinerariifolium,* that is the best source of pyrethrins. For the gardener, painted daisies are lovable for their flowers alone. Plants bear single to double 2"-4" blooms in shades of white, pink, and red in early summer. The weakly upright, 2'-3' flower stems rise above delicate lacy leaves up to 10" long. Zones 3-7.

How to grow: Start garden mums with rooted cuttings bought in spring, or divide last year's clumps, replanting only the most vigorous pieces. You also can buy plants in bloom in fall and plant them directly into borders. Plant in full sun in average to slightly rich soil with excellent drainage; water during drought. Add a little extra fertilizer in late spring and midsummer. For dense plants with lots of flowers, pinch out the tips one or two times before July 15 in the North and August 15 in the South. Hose regularly to deter aphids and mites. To avoid nematode problems, don't grow mums in the same place for more than a few years.

Plant or divide Shasta and painted daisies in spring or early fall in a sunny, average to slightly rich, very well drained soil. Shasta daisies grow easily and quickly from seed, but seed-grown painted daisy plants may produce misshapen flowers. Painted daisies don't ship well, so buy locally grown plants.

After the flowers fade, cut plants back and fertilize lightly to promote rebloom. You may need to support painted daisies with twiggy branches when in bloom.

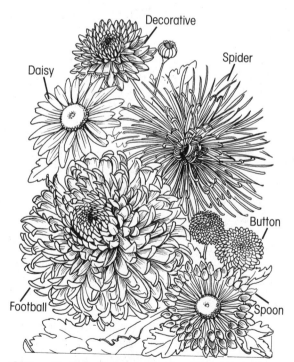

Chrysanthemum flower forms. Hundreds of years of selective breeding have created these distinctive bloom shapes. Only decorative, button, and daisy types are reliably hardy in the garden.

Landscape uses: Plant garden mums in borders with other fall-blooming perennials like asters and goldenrods for a stunning autumn show. Their ornamental foliage and bushy habit make mums good foliage plants in a spring, summer, or mixed border, too. Mums are bold plants that make an impressive display in a bed by themselves or in containers on a patio or deck.

Grow Shasta daisies in masses throughout sunny borders and in cottage and cutting gardens. Their round flowers contrast nicely with spiky or mounded blooms. Grow painted daisies in informal settings and cottage gardens.

Best cultivars: *C. × morifolium*: Choose from hundreds of colorful chrysanthemum cultivars; be sure your selections are hardy in your area. In the North, look for names with 'Minn' in them; these are particularly hardy. *C. × superbum*: single-flowered 'Alaska', to 3'; fringed and double 'Aglaya', to 2'; and semidouble 'Little Miss Muffet', growing under 1'. ❖

Cimicifuga

Bugbane, snakeroot. Summer- to fall-blooming perennials.

Description: These plants' skyrockets of small white flowers light up the garden above large, fernlike leaves. *Cimicifuga racemosa*, black snakeroot, grows 3'-8' tall, bearing 1'-2' fuzzy wands in summer; sideshoots extend the bloom into early fall. *C. simplex*, Kamchatka bugbane, is a bushier plant that blooms in mid-fall and seldom exceeds 5'. Zones 3-8.

How to grow: Plant in spring or fall in partial shade and fairly rich, moist but well-drained soil. Divide for more plants.

Landscape uses: Let black snakeroot tower over a border or wood's edge; feature Kamchatka bugbane in a woodland setting. Their upright form breaks the monotony of a shrub planting.

Best cultivars: *C. simplex* 'White Pearl' ('The Pearl') grows to 4'. ❖

Citrus

Citrus spp.
Rutaceae

Citrus trees have shiny, evergreen leaves, fragrant flowers, and attractive fruit that hangs for months without dropping. In Northern climates, you can grow dwarf citrus trees in tubs and bring them indoors during the winter. "Northland Citrus" on the opposite page has more information about how to grow citrus trees in containers.

Selecting trees: There are so many types of citrus that you may have trouble deciding which to grow. Edible types include calamondin (× *Citrofortunella mitis*), citrange (× *Citroncirus webberi*), citron (*Citrus medica*), grapefruit (*C.* × *paradisi*), lemon (*C. limon*), lime (*C. aurantiifolia*), limequat (× *Citrofortunella swinglie*), kumquat (*Fortunella* spp.), mandarin orange or tangerine (*Citrus reticulata*), orange (*C. sinensis*), rangpur lime (*C.* × *limonia*), shaddock or pummelo (*C. maxima*), sour or Seville orange (*C. aurantium*), tangelo (*C.* × *tangelo*), and temple orange (*C.* × *nobilis*).

Consider the yearly range of temperatures and possible frost when making your selection. Local nurseries usually stock citrus trees that grow well in the area. The fruit of all types is easily damaged by frost, but the leaves and wood of some are more cold-resistant. In general, limes are the least hardy, oranges slightly hardier, and calamondins and kumquats are the most hardy, withstanding 12°-15°F. Trifoliate orange (*Poncirus trifoliata*) is hardy into sheltered areas of Zone 5. The thorny, deciduous tree bears small, inedible, yellow-orange fruit and makes an interesting ornamental.

A single mature citrus tree yields more than enough fruit for a family. If you plant more than one tree of the same type, select cultivars with different harvest times, or plant different types of citrus so you won't be overwhelmed with one kind of fruit. Almost all citrus are self-pollinating.

A few hybrids are not; be sure to check for the kind you want when you buy.

Select sturdy nursery-raised trees. A one-year-old tree should have a trunk diameter of ¾". A two-year-old plant should have a diameter of at least 1". Those with fewer fruits and flowers are better because they have put more energy into sturdy top and root growth.

Rootstocks: Most commercially grown citrus fruits are grafted onto rootstocks. Trifoliate orange and sour orange are both good rootstocks where cold-hardiness is important. Sour orange is susceptible to nematode attacks and shouldn't be used where they are a problem. 'Milam' lemon is a nematode-resistant rootstock. Your local extension office can tell you what rootstock is best in your region.

Planting: Citrus do best at pH 6.0-6.5. They are not fussy about soil but do require good drainage. If drainage is a problem, plant in a raised soil mound about 1½' high.

Select a sheltered area with full sun, such as a sheltered, south-facing alcove of a building. Citrus flowers attract bees, so don't plant them in high-traffic areas.

Plant citrus in late winter or early spring. Keep the graft union 6" above the soil surface when planting. Full-sized trees require at least 25' between trees; smaller trees need less.

Citrus bark is thin and easily sunburned. Wrap the trunk with commercial tree wrap or newspaper for the first year, or paint it with diluted white latex paint.

Care: In dry areas, water newly planted trees at least once a week for the first year. Once established, trees need less-frequent watering, but never wait until leaves wilt to water. Water stress can cause developing fruit to drop; prolonged drought causes leaf drop and may kill the tree. Water slowly and deeply; shallow sprinkling does more harm than good. In drought areas, construct a shallow watering basin that extends from 6" away from the trunk to 1' beyond the drip line. Or install drip irrigation under a

NORTHLAND CITRUS

Beyond their northern range, citrus trees make fine patio/sunroom plants. Indoors, they need a well-ventilated area with high humidity and at least half a day of full sun. During the summer, a sheltered, partially shaded spot outdoors is ideal.

Select a container that is deep and wide enough for the tree you choose. A calamondin will fruit in a 10" pot, a 'Meyer' lemon will grow to 6' in a 5-gallon pot. If you plan to move them in and out, choose containers you can handle easily. Or mount wooden planters on casters; set other heavy containers on wheeled stands. Citrus need a loose, well-drained potting mix and benefit from the addition of bonemeal. The Container Gardening entry gives guidelines for selecting suitable containers, preparing planting mixes, and caring for plants.

Citrus need warm days (70°–75°F) and cool nights (45°–55°F) during the winter. During the summer, they like it as warm as possible. If you move your trees indoors during the winter and outdoors during the summer, acclimatize them by setting containers in an intermediate area for a few days so they can adjust gradually. Leaf burn may occur with sudden climate changes.

Don't let the potting mix dry out. Water whenever the top ½" of potting mix starts to dry out. Water thoroughly until water drains from the bottom, but don't let the plant sit in water. At least once a month, water with liquid fertilizer such as seaweed extract. Mist leaves frequently and group plants to conserve humidity.

If your citrus flowers indoors, you'll need to pollinate it by hand for a good fruit set. Take a small artist's brush or a cotton swab and transfer pollen from one blossom to another. Giving the plant a slight shaking also transfers pollen.

Container-grown citrus need a light yearly pruning. Thin out branches rather than shortening them, or you'll get a flush of new branches sprouting below the cut. When plants become rootbound, repot in fresh potting mix in a larger container. To keep the plant small, prune off circling roots and cut back some of the remainder. Shake out as much of the old potting mix as you can, repot in fresh mix, and cut back top growth by about one-fourth.

Many citrus are naturally dwarf and adapt well to container culture. Suitable types and cultivars include calamondin, 'Owari Satsuma' mandarin, 'Meyer Improved' lemon, 'Eureka' lemon, 'Ponderosa' lemon, 'Bears Seedless' lime, 'Mexican' lime, 'Eustis' limequat, 'Washington Navel' orange, 'Nagami' kumquat, 'Meiwa' kumquat, 'Moro' blood orange, 'Oro Blanco' grapefruit, and 'Rangpur' lime.

thick layer of mulch to conserve water and protect shallow feeder roots. Keep mulch 6" away from the trunk.

In citrus-growing areas, soils often lack organic matter and nitrogen. Spread compost, well-rotted manure, blood meal, or cottonseed meal on the soil surface out to the drip line four times a year, beginning in February.

Pruning: Most citrus trees need little pruning beyond removing dead or broken branches. Limit the tree's size by thinning out energetic shoots that outgrow other branches. Thin branches rather than shortening them. Remove suckers as soon as they emerge from the ground. See the Pruning and Training entry for instructions on correct pruning technique.

You can revitalize an old and unproductive citrus tree by pruning severely in early spring. Wear thick gloves if the tree has thorns. Cut off all branches 2" or larger in diameter flush to the trunk, and feed and water heavily for the next year. Very severe pruning may stop fruiting for up to two years.

Winter protection: Citrus are usually grown

outdoors in climates where frost is rare: Zones 9-10 and the warmer parts of Zone 8. While some types of citrus are more cold-hardy than others, all citrus fruit is vulnerable when frost does occur. In areas where mild frosts are common, don't plant cultivars that bear in winter and early spring. Since succulent new growth is more prone to frost injury, withhold fertilizer and extra water in late summer to limit new growth. When frost does threaten, cover trees with large fabric sheets. Use fans to keep air circulating around the trees. Symptoms of frost damage include yellow wilting leaves or greenish shriveled leaves. Should frost damage appear, wait until spring growth starts to see the true extent of damage. A tree that loses all its leaves can still rejuvenate. If damage is severe, dieback may continue during the growing season.

Harvesting: Citrus trees usually bear in 3-4 years. It can be hard to tell when citrus fruit is ready to pick. Color is not a good indicator. Fruit can have ripe coloration several months before being ready to harvest or may remain green and unappealing even when ripe and juicy inside. Use the taste test to determine when fruit is at its peak flavor. Allow fruit to ripen on the tree before picking.

Use pruning shears to cut stems close to the fruit when harvesting. Don't just pull fruit off the tree. Ripe citrus fruit can remain on the tree for up to three months. Once harvested, citrus can be stored in the refrigerator for three or more weeks.

Problems: Citrus trees in the home garden are relatively untroubled by pests. Much of the damage that does occur is cosmetic and has no effect on the internal fruit quality. In dry climates, insects such as scale, whiteflies, mealybugs, thrips, and mites may cause problems. In humid climates, fungal diseases are more likely to cause problems.

Scale insects appear as small, hard bumps on leaves, twigs, and fruit. Sooty mold may be present. Predatory lady beetles attack scale. Summer oil spray also controls them.

Whiteflies suck leaf sap. Clouds of tiny white flies appear when foliage is disturbed. Fruit is pale and stunted. Leaves are dry and yellowing and may show black sooty mold, which grows on the honeydew excreted by the pests. Ladybugs, lacewings, and parasitic wasps help control whiteflies. Repeated strong water sprays knock whiteflies off trees. For added control, spray with insecticidal soap.

Thrips cause distorted, yellow-streaked new growth in spring. Blossoms turn brown, and developing fruit shows a ring at the blossom end. To reduce chances of thrips infestation, keep citrus adequately watered. Lacewings help control thrips. For severe infestations, apply insecticidal soap or pyrethrins.

Mites cause pale leaves, sometimes with yellow spots. Fruit may have dark brown markings, and leaves may drop. Spray leaves with cold water regularly to remove dust, and provide adequate water. Ladybugs, lacewings, and predatory mites attack mites.

Mealybugs are white, cottony or waxy insects that feed on sap. They secrete honeydew, which attracts ants and encourages sooty mold. They are controlled by the mealybug destroyer, a ladybug type of beetle. Horticultural oil sprays also provide control.

Snails may climb trees and feed on leaves. Encircle tree trunks with a copper barrier strip to prevent snail problems.

Root rot can damage citrus trees. Too much fertilizer, cultivation, and gopher gnawing all can encourage the disease. Avoid injuring roots.

Dead bark near the soil line and large amounts of gummy sap indicate foot rot. Keep the tree base dry and remove discolored wood. Foot rot problems can be avoided by providing good drainage at planting.

Viral diseases are a major problem in some areas. Purchase only virus-free trees. ❖

Clematis

Clematis. Perennial or woody vines.

Description: Clematis are mostly twining woody vines, growing 5'-18' long. Most are deciduous with heart-shaped leaves. Feathery seed heads follow the blooms and linger into early winter. The large-flowered hybrids, familiar to many gardeners, have large 3"-6" flat blooms and come in every color except true yellow. Zones 4-9. The species clematis are less widely grown, but also desirable. Their delicate blooms, shaped like saucers, stars, or bells, are delightfully different from common garden flowers. Many of them are vigorous enough to use for screening.

Clematis armandii, Armand clematis, is one of the few evergreen clematis with large leaves. It is fast-growing (to 10') with fragrant white star-shaped blooms in late spring. Zones 7-10. Grow *C. heracleifolia,* a perennial (herbaceous) clematis, with light staking for support. It bears clusters of fragrant blue 1" flowers in late summer. Zones 3-8. *C. macropetala,* big-petal clematis, is a vigorous vine (to 12'), with nodding double blooms of blue, pink, or white in spring. Zones 3-7.

C. maximowicziana (also known as *C. paniculata*), sweet autumn clematis, is a vigorous vine (to 7') that is covered with fragrant white 1" blooms from August through October. Zones 4-9. *C. montana,* anemone clematis, is also a vigorous vine (to 20'), with white or pink 2½" open flowers in May and June. Zones 6-8.

C. tangutica, golden clematis, is a strong climber (to 15') with bright yellow, 3"-4" nodding flowers borne in June and July. Zones 2-8. *C. texensis,* scarlet or Texas clematis, is a vigorous vine (to 9') with scarlet 1" bell-shaped blooms from midsummer through frost. Zones 4-8.

How to grow: Transplant container-grown clematis plants in spring or fall. Plant in moist, well-drained soil. Give the roots cool conditions, but plant in full sun. (To achieve this seemingly contradictory goal, plant clematis where the roots will be shaded by a nearby shrub, or mulch well). Research has found that clematis don't need additional lime; ignore advice to the contrary. Plant where a support is available for the vine to twine around—a pillar, tree trunk, or trellis will work well. Clematis stems break easily, so install your trellis or stake before planting.

Clematis wilt is the only serious problem of clematis. When the fungus attacks, the entire plant or afflicted branch will droop and shrivel. Remove all diseased parts, even if it means cutting the plant to the ground. Plants may recover, resprouting from the roots. Good sanitation is important, as the fungal spores can overwinter on dead leaves. Do not add infected material to the compost heap—burn or otherwise destroy it. Do not replant a clematis in a site where wilt has been a problem.

Some clematis bloom on old wood, while others bloom on the current year's growth. Lightly prune the clematis that bloom on old wood to thin or shape after flowering; heavily prune clematis that bloom on new wood in late winter or early spring before bud break. (Ask your nurseryman which type of clematis you're buying.) Remove all dead shoots and trim vines back to the first pair of plump buds. Untangle vines growing on walls and tie them to a trellis in a fan pattern.

Landscape uses: Large-flowered clematis are ideal for growing on walls, fences, arbors, and posts, or through shrubs. Most of the species are very vigorous and create good screens. You can use the herbaceous perennial clematis in a perennial or mixed border.

Best cultivars: Large-flowered clematis: 'Duchess of Edinburgh', double white; 'Ernest Markham', ruby red; 'General Sikorski', dark lavender; 'Hagley Hybrid', shell pink; 'Henryi', cream; 'Jackmanii', deep purple; 'Lincoln Star', raspberry pink; 'Mrs. Cholmondeley', lavender-blue; 'Niobe', red; 'Ramona', deep blue; 'Ville de Lyon', crimson; 'Vyvyan Pennell', deep violet-blue. ❖

Cloches

The term *cloche* applies to a broad range of light-permeable plant covers, primarily used to protect plants from frost. The first cloches were glass bell jars—heavy, unventilated, and breakable, but useful in extending the growing season. Today, many types of cloches exist, ranging from individual plant covers to row covers, formed from a variety of materials. You can either make cloches or buy them ready-made.

Cloches work much like greenhouses. Short ultraviolet rays from the sun pass through the translucent cover and warm the soil and air inside. The soil collects and stores the heat, then releases it slowly, creating a greenhouselike atmosphere and protecting plants from frost. The warmer conditions under a cloche also encourage growth. You can use cloches to harden off transplants or to protect seeds and seedlings from wind, insects, birds, and small animals. You'll find basic guidelines for using cloches and other season extenders in the Season Extension entry. ❖

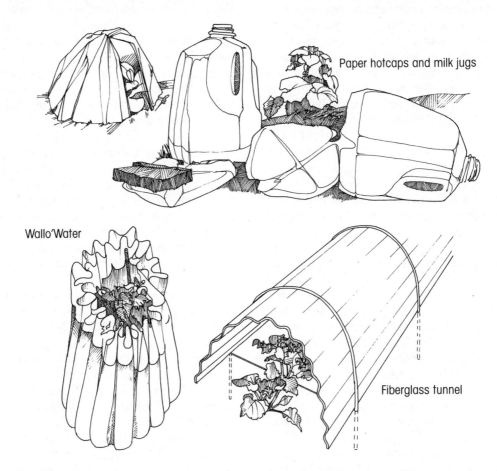

Paper hotcaps and milk jugs

Wallo'Water

Fiberglass tunnel

Cloches in the garden. Several types of cloches are available for season extension. Commercial products include paraffin-treated paper hotcaps and Wallo'Water; the latter surrounds plants with an upright ring of narrow plastic tubes filled with water. For a homemade cloche, cut along three sides of the bottom of a plastic milk jug. Or create a tunnel cloche out of 4' long translucent corrugated fiberglass. Small cloches heat up quickly on sunny days, so remove cloches or tip them up during good weather so you don't "cook" your plants.

Cold Frames

Cold frames and hotbeds give gardeners some control over the one thing most beyond their control—the weather. By creating an area of close-to-ideal conditions right where the plants need them, cold frames and hotbeds enable gardeners to stretch the seasons and to grow plants accustomed to warmer climates.

Gardeners most commonly use cold frames in early spring for starting or hardening off seedlings destined for the garden. However, there are many other uses for cold frames. A moist, shady frame provides a good start to fall crops in the dry heat of summer; in winter, the same frame offers a spot for cold-treating spring bulbs for forcing. Some models are also useful for rooting cuttings of woody plants or perennials.

Form and Function

Cold frames are rectangular, boxlike structures with glass sash on top. Most have slanting sash "roofs," with the high end toward the north, so the sun's rays strike the glass at about a 90° angle, and water and snow slide off the lids easily. A lid with a slope of 35°-45° catches the most sunlight year-round, although a 55° slope traps more autumn sun, which has a lower angle. Glass window sash are most often used to cover frames, but you can substitute fiberglass, Plexiglas, or heavyweight polyethylene.

A white or light-colored frame interior increases the amount of light reflected onto the plants. Use blocks or sticks to prop the lids open for ventilation.

Cold frames are essentially passive solar collectors; to get maximum benefit from the heat and light of the sun, they should face south—southeast or southwest exposures are the next best choices. Ideally, the site should receive full sun from mid-morning to mid-afternoon during the winter and early spring months. Hotbeds need a full-sun exposure as well.

The site should also be fairly level and well drained. For protection from winter winds, try to locate your frame with a building, fence, or hedge on the north side. Select a site that is near a water supply and is easy to monitor year-round. Deciduous trees overhead aren't necessarily bad; they'll provide summer shade without blocking winter sun.

Permanent or Portable?

There are two types of frames to consider: permanent and portable. Permanent models are built over foundations that are either dug into the ground or constructed on the surface. Above-ground models provide less frost protection than ones built over a dug foundation, but both provide more reliable protection from the cold than portable frames. Permanent frames are generally sturdier and last longer.

Portable frames, which are basically bottomless boxes with clear lids, function in much the same way as permanent frames. Many models are collapsible for storage when not in use. However, their reduced insulating capacity makes them subject to wider temperature fluctuations. In the vegetable garden, portable frames can extend the season for spring or fall crops such as lettuce or spinach, or keep frost off late-ripening crops. In areas with mild winters, use them to grow winter crops of cold-tolerant vegetables. Placed over garden beds, portable frames will provide adequate winter protection for many perennials. In summer, use portable frames to create a cool, shady spot for seedlings.

Hot or Cold?

Hotbeds and cold frames are structurally identical, except that hotbeds contain a source of artificial heat. Traditionally, rotting manure served as the heat source, but today, electric heating cables provide the warmth. Because hotbeds have a regular source of heat, they can be used earlier in the season than most cold frames, and they create ideal conditions for starting most types of seeds.

Make any frame with a dug foundation into a hotbed by adding an electric heating cable. You can use portable frames, although they don't conserve heat as well as permanent frames, but you need a pit at least 1' deep to hold the heating cable. For best control over temperatures within the frame, select a heating cable with a thermostat.

To make a hotbed, spread a 2" layer of vermiculite on top of a gravel layer at the bottom of your pit or dug foundation. Spread the cable on the vermiculite, using long loops to provide an even source of heat. Don't let the cable wires cross; keep loops at least 8" apart and 3" away from the frame edges. Cover the cable with 1" of sand, followed by a layer of screen or hardware cloth to protect it from being damaged by sharp objects. Cover the screen with 4"-6" of coarse builder's sand in which to sink pots.

Frame Management

Ensure success by carefully monitoring the conditions inside your frames, hot or cold. As with any gardening situation, the plants require proper light, moisture, and temperature levels.

Temperature control: On a bright, sunny day, whatever the outdoor temperature, the temperature in an unvented, insulated frame can rise to 100°F or more. A thermometer, placed in a shaded spot in the frame, is a must for determining when to vent. Solar-powered automatic openers, triggered by temperature, will vent the frame when you aren't home, but it's best to learn the temperature nuances of your frame as well.

In unusually cold weather, or if you have an uninsulated, aboveground frame, bank leaves, bales of hay, or soil around the frame. Be aware that this may attract unwanted rodents. Stack bricks or plastic gallon jugs filled with water against the north wall as passive solar collectors; enhance the heat absorption of either with a coat of black paint. Both will absorb heat during the day and release it at night.

Spring and summer. Harden off seedlings in your cold frame in the spring before planting them out in the garden. In the summer, root woody and herbaceous cuttings in a lath-shaded frame. The controlled environment provides ideal rooting conditions.

Watering: Until you become familiar with the conditions in your frame, check plants frequently to be sure they have enough water. This is especially important in warm weather when plants are actively growing. Check the moisture of the soil between 1″ and 1½″ deep; for most plants, soil should remain moist, but not soggy, at all times. Water whenever plants look droopy, but avoid watering on cold, cloudy days. To discourage fungal diseases, water early in the day. Use water about the same temperature as the growing medium, because cold water can shock plants and slow their growth. If you're using your frame to store dormant plants over winter, water well before the onset of cold temperatures, then check moisture every few weeks.

Containers: Growing plants in containers has several advantages over planting directly in soil in the frame. Plants in containers can easily be added, moved about, or removed without disturbing the frame's other inhabitants. Soil mixes can be made to suit individual plants, as can watering and fertilizing schedules, so the frame can hold a variety of plants. Also, using individual pots helps control diseases, which can spread quickly in frames. Place pots on the layer of gravel at the frame's bottom, or sink to the rims in 4″-6″ of sand over the gravel.

Pests and diseases: Check your frame regularly for evidence of disease or insect infestation. In mild weather, uncontrolled insects, slugs, or other pests will thrive in a cold frame or hotbed. Before placing a pot in the frame, check it for hitchhiking pests. The warm, moist conditions inside a frame may also encourage plant diseases. Generous spacing and proper ventilation can help prevent disease problems. Remove and discard infested, diseased, or sick-looking leaves and plants as soon as you spot them, because problems spread rapidly. If serious problems

Fall and winter. Late-fall leaf crops like lettuce and spinach thrive in a cold frame well after the first frost. When winter comes, save your refrigerator space for food and use your cold frame for giving spring bulbs their cold treatment before forcing.

develop, remove all plants and sterilize the inside of the frame. To sterilize, pour boiling water into the gravel and/or sand at the bottom of the frame, or leave the glass lids tightly closed during the summer to allow heat to build up inside the frame. If you grow plants directly in soil at the bottom of your frame, it is also a good idea to dig it out completely every 2-3 years and replace it with fresh soil.

Frame maintenance: The moist, warm environment inside a frame subjects it to rapid deterioration. When paint starts flaking, repaint as soon as the frame is free of plants. Let a newly painted frame air for several weeks before putting plants in it, because paint fumes may harm plants. Recaulk as necessary to maintain airtight conditions. Keep the sash and inside of the frame clean to increase the amount of light available to plants.

Year-Round Uses

The uses you find for your frame depend upon not only what your gardening needs are, but also where you live, what exposure you have available, and what type of frame you select. Experiment to find the best way to use your cold frame and/or hotbed, as well as the best seasonal schedule for your area.

Spring: To harden off seedlings started indoors, move them to a cold frame a week or two before they're scheduled for transplanting. Gradually open the vent for longer periods each day. To keep the seedlings from burning, shade them at first by using wood lath or burlap or by painting the glass with a mixture of clay soil and water. Expose them gradually to full sun.

Cold frames are also good places to germinate seeds in early spring—especially those of cold-tolerant vegetables, perennials, and annuals. Sow seed in flats or pots placed directly in the frame about 2 months before the last spring frost date. For an even earlier start, sow seeds in a hotbed or indoors, and move seedlings to a cold frame after their first transplanting. This frees up space for more tender plants indoors and eliminates the succulent, rank growth of seedlings grown in warm temperatures. Later in the season, sow tender annuals in the frames.

Where the growing season is short, use a cold frame to start long-season plants such as melons that otherwise might not mature, or plant very early spring crops of lettuce or spinach.

Summer: During the summer, store the glass sash that cover your cold frames and replace them with screens or other coverings to keep out leaves and debris. In late summer, use frames shaded with a grid of wood lath over the screens to start fall crops of heat-sensitive vegetables such as lettuce. Raise seedlings in pots or flats, then transplant to the garden when temperatures begin to cool. Summer-sown perennials or biennials can be germinated in pots or flats, held over their first winter under the cold frame, and moved to the garden the following year. Cold frames can also be used for rooting cuttings taken any time of year.

Fall and winter: As the days shorten and temperatures drop, replace the glass sash, and your cold frames become ideal places to sow seeds of hardy annuals, perennials, wildflowers, shrubs, or trees. With seed sown in fall or early winter, the object is not to germinate the seed immediately but to provide a cold treatment so it will germinate the following spring. Sow seed just before the ground freezes so it won't germinate before winter arrives.

Fall crops of lettuce and spinach prosper in cold frames. Fall is also the time to move perennials, herbs, and container-grown plants that might not be quite hardy outdoors under cover for winter protection. Dig semihardy herbs such as lavender from your garden and keep them in a cold frame over the winter. Also, use your cold frame for forcing pots of hardy spring bulbs. See the Bulbs entry for complete instructions. ❖

Coleus

Coleus, flame nettle. Tender perennials grown as foliage annuals.

Description: Coleus leaves brighten semi-shady spots with their many hues of green, white, pink, red, yellow, and almost black. Choose from 8″ mounded midgets to bushy 2½′ giants with pointed, scalloped, lacy, or oaklike leaves.

How to grow: Sow seeds as early as February; plant out after frost. They grow best in semishade in average, fairly moist soil. Pinch taller types at 6″; remove flower buds as they appear. Cuttings root easily in water.

Landscape uses: Mass one color pattern or many in beds, borders, and pots. Match their colors with nearby flowers.

Best cultivars: Mixes: 'Wizard', 10″; 'Carefree', 8″, oaklike leaves; 'Saber', 8″, slightly scalloped, pointed leaves. ❖

Collard

Brassica oleracea, Acephala group
Cruciferae

Often considered a Southern vegetable, collards also grow well in cooler areas. They are cold-resistant, like kale and cabbage, but can tolerate more heat.

Planting: Sow seeds ¼″ deep in spring, four weeks before the last expected frost. Space seedlings 1′ apart in rows 3′ apart. For a fall crop, broadcast seed 8-10 weeks before the first expected frost; thin to 12″ apart.

Growing guidelines: Foliar-feed with liquid seaweed extract 2-3 times during the growing season.

Problems: See the Cabbage entry for disease- and insect-control measures.

Harvesting: Start picking outer leaves when plants are 1′ tall. Frosts improve flavor. ❖

Community Gardens

Sharing land and water for gardening first became popular in the United States during World Wars I and II, when growing food in "victory gardens" was a patriotic duty. At peak production in 1944, 20 million victory gardeners grew 40 percent of America's fresh produce.

Over the past few decades, renewed interest in energy and environmental conservation, rising food prices, and growing concern about chemical additives and residues in processed foods have made homegrown produce more appealing and have reawakened the community spirit of the victory garden.

The American Community Gardening Association (ACGA), a national not-for-profit organization of gardening and open space volunteers and professionals, was started in 1979 to encourage community gardening and greening. The ACGA offers guidelines to help gardeners understand how community gardening works. Community gardens develop gradually; some steps occur concurrently, while others occur as time and people power become available.

Forming a group: A community garden starts as a gathering of individuals willing to share time, space, and labor to garden. Make the most of human resources such as knowledgeable mature gardeners and energetic kids.

A planning committee allocates group resources and should accomplish these tasks:

- Identify the need and desire for a garden.
- Involve the people who are to benefit from the garden in all phases of the program.
- Organize a meeting of interested people.
- Select a well-organized garden coordinator.
- Approach sponsors, if necessary.

Getting organized: Once a committee has addressed the initial issues, involve all participants in setting rules, electing officers, and determining dues and their uses. Community gardens run best when managed by the gardeners. New gardening groups need structure, especially the first year, to make sure work is divided equally and responsibilities are clear.

Topics covered by garden rules may include conditions of membership, assignment of plots, maintenance of common areas, and even ways of enforcing the rules. Leave room for rules to grow along with membership.

Finding a site: A 1982 Gallup Survey found that 78 percent of the public would like to garden if space were available in their neighborhoods. Finding land is often a matter of persistently pursuing a variety of sources. If you see a potential site for a garden, find out who owns it and convince them that gardens make great tenants.

Municipal agencies that may grant access to garden space include park commissions and public housing and community development offices. State departments of transportation, agriculture, or housing may also have land to offer.

Schools, churches, railroads, nature centers, community colleges, utility companies, senior centers, and community centers are other potential garden space providers.

Look for a site that will contribute to gardening success. Desirable features include full sun with nearby shade for weary gardeners; a water source; neighborhood support; visibility for safety and publicity; safe soil (not polluted by former uses); long-term availability; access for gardeners, volunteers, and delivery trucks; and nearby restrooms, telephone, and parking. Few sites have all the amenities; decide which are most important for your gardening group.

Acquiring the land: Once your group finds a site, get permission and a written lease to use it. If your garden plan includes physical improvements such as fencing, creating raised beds, or adding soil, try to obtain at least a three-year lease. Your group should be able to use the site long enough to justify its investments.

Your group may need to have public liability insurance before a lease is granted. Garden insurance is new to many insurance carriers, and their underwriters hesitate to cover community

---

MAKING IT FORMAL

A statement of purpose helps to finalize decisions made by garden members and makes rules clear. Here is an example from Green Chicago, Chicago Botanic Garden:

Our purpose is to improve the neighborhood and provide a place to garden for food and recreation. Membership is open to everyone in the neighborhood. People within a two-block radius will be given priority in the case of a waiting list. Our three leaders are elected annually, two months before the garden season begins. Meetings are held three times per year and decisions are made by the majority. Attendance at spring and fall work days is mandatory for all members. If you cannot attend, you must send a friend in your place or complete a task assigned by the officers. Membership dues are $10 per year for a 10' × 20' plot.

---

gardens, despite their risk-free history. Decide what you want before talking to agents, and use an agent who handles several carriers.

Making a plan: Analyze what the group wants before touching the site. Develop a clear plan, including plot sizes, common area maintenance, and group activities. Evaluate your group's resources—what do you have? What do you need? Assign members to gather missing elements *before* gardening begins.

A few final tasks will improve garden relations during the growing season. Plan a work day for site cleaning and plot assignments. Keep records of plot locations and users; mark plots clearly with gardeners' names. Identify and prepare paths and common areas, then open for planting. Use a rainproof bulletin board to hold announcements and a garden map.

Getting help: If your group needs horticultural information or other gardening support, try local resources such as the Cooperative Extension Service, garden clubs, or garden centers. For organizational help, write to the ACGA, 325 Walnut Street, Philadelphia, PA 19106. ❖

Companion Planting

Mixing marigolds and herbs in the vegetable garden to confuse or repel plant pests is a well-known example of the practice of companion planting. Hundreds of examples of plant companions are recorded in garden lore. Modern research substantiates the effectiveness of some companion plants in repelling pests or attracting pest predators and parasites. However, the mechanisms that cause a plant to repel or attract pests remain largely unverified, and many companion planting practices continue to combine folklore and fact.

It's interesting to find scientific justification for companion planting, and it's fun to try your own companion planting experiments. See the Folklore entry for a discussion of companion planting as part of garden lore.

"Evidence" from scientific studies and gardeners' experimentation indicates several possible benefits from companion planting:

• Masking or hiding a crop from pests
• Producing odors that confuse and deter pests
• Serving as trap crops that draw pest insects away from other plants
• Acting as "nurse plants" that provide breeding grounds for beneficial insects
• Providing food to sustain beneficial insects as they search for pests
• Creating a habitat for beneficial insects

Repel with Smell

Experiments demonstrate that night-flying moths (parents of many destructive cutworms and caterpillars) approach flowers by flying upwind. If netting is placed over flowers, the moths will still land and feed, indicating that they react to flower odor. However, moths won't land on colored flowers that don't have noticeable aroma. Can masking odors from plants such as marigolds work, too? If pests can't smell your prize plants, or if the scent isn't right, maybe they'll go elsewhere.

Common sources of repellent or masking fragrances include the following plants.

Marigolds: Plant them as thickly as you can in a vegetable garden, but keep in mind that unscented marigolds won't work for this trick. French marigolds (*Tagetes patula*) offer a second benefit—their roots emit a substance that repels nematodes in the immediate area.

Mints: Cabbage pests and aphids dislike catnip and some other members of this fragrant family. Since mints can grow out of control, set potted mints around your garden or plant in areas where growth can be controlled.

Rue: Oils from the leaves of rue (*Ruta graveolens*) give some people a poison-ivy-like rash, so use this low-growing plant with care. However, what annoys people also deters Japan-

SCIENTIFIC SUPPORT

Research into the facts behind companion planting folklore shows that many practices derive their success from naturally occurring compounds within the plants. As these compounds are isolated and identified, the preferred companion plants of past gardens may become the source of modern-day botanical controls.

Here are some results of recent studies of companion plants and natural compounds:

● A potato plant grafted onto a tobacco plant root becomes resistant to the destructive Colorado potato beetle.
● A mustard oil extracted from turnip roots effectively deters pea aphids, Mexican bean beetles, and spider mites.
● The presence of asparagus roots in soil leads to a decline in the stubby root nematode population.
● Specially treated seeds of the tung-oil tree (*Aleurites fordii*) give off a substance that deters boll weevil feeding.
● Boston fern leaves contain a feeding deterrent effective against Southern armyworm.
● A chemical found in tomato plant leaves is toxic to some weevil species.

ese beetles. Grow rue as a garden border or scatter leaf clippings near beetle-infested crops.

Sweet basil: Interplant *Ocimum basilicum* in vegetable or flower gardens, or chop and scatter the leaves to repel aphids, mosquitoes, and mites. It also acts as a fungicide and slows the growth of milkweed bugs.

Tansy: Used as a mulch, tansy (*Tanacetum vulgare*) may cause cucumber beetles, Japanese beetles, ants, and squash bugs to go elsewhere for a meal. It attracts imported cabbageworms, however, limiting its appeal as a repellent.

Other interplanting possibilities exist. Try the following combinations in your garden:

• Plant basil among your tomatoes to control tomato hornworms.

• Combine thyme or tomatoes with cabbage plantings to control flea beetles, cabbage maggots, white cabbage butterflies, and imported cabbageworms.

• Sow catnip by eggplant to deter flea beetles.

• Set onions in rows with carrots to control rust flies and some nematodes.

• Grow horseradish with potatoes to repel Colorado potato beetles.

• Grow radishes or nasturtiums with your cucumbers for cucumber beetle control.

• Alternate double rows of corn with double rows of snap beans or soybeans to enhance the growth of the corn.

• Interplant peanuts with corn or squash to increase the yields of both crops.

• Plant spinach, lettuce, or Chinese cabbage at the base of trellised peas, where they benefit from the shade and wind protection.

• Grow tomatoes, parsley, or basil with asparagus to help control asparagus beetles.

Nasturtiums also deter whiteflies and squash bugs, but they are more often used as a trap crop for aphids, which prefer nasturtiums to other crops. Planting a ring of them around apple trees limits woolly aphid damage to the trees (although the nasturtiums won't look too great).

Support Beneficials

The idea of gardening to *attract* insects may seem odd, but in the case of beneficial insects, this companion planting technique can really pay off. Although some beneficials feed on pests, host plants provide food and shelter during some or all of their life cycle.

Beneficial insects have short mouthparts. They can't reach deeply into flowers for food. Plants with numerous, small flowers, containing easy-to-reach pollen and nectar, provide the necessary high-protein and high-sugar meals that maintain beneficial insect populations.

Help beneficial insects get a jump on early spring aphid activity by planting gazanias, calendulas, or other small-flowered plants that will grow in your area despite early-season cool weather. Beneficial insects need a series of blossoms to sustain them from spring until fall.

Herbs such as fennel, dill, anise, and coriander are carrot-family members that produce broad clusters of small flowers attractive to beneficials. Grow these culinary items near your vegetables to keep parasitic wasps nearby. Composite flowers such as sunflowers, zinnias, and asters also attract beneficials and have a longer season of bloom than carrot-family herbs.

Use this list of plants and the beneficials they attract to lure such insects to your garden:

• *Achillea* spp. (yarrow): bees, parasitic wasps, hover flies

• *Angelica archangelica* (angelica): lady beetles, lacewings

• *Iberis* spp. (candytuft): syrphid flies

• *Ipomoea purpurea* (morning-glory): lady beetles

• *Nemophila menziesii* (baby-blue-eyes): syrphid flies

• *Oenothera biennis* (evening primrose): ground beetles

• *Solidago* spp. (goldenrod): lady beetles, predaceous beetles, parasitic wasps ❖

Composting

Inside a compost pile, billions of decay organisms feed, grow, reproduce, and die, recycling household and garden wastes into an excellent organic fertilizer and soil conditioner. This process of decomposition occurs constantly and gradually in nature. When you build a compost pile, you intervene to speed things up and create a valuable soil amendment.

Compost systems range in size from small, home-built bins used to recycle one household's food scraps to industrial systems capable of handling hundreds of tons of municipal wastes daily. Your choice of a composting method depends on what materials you plan to use, how much money you're willing to spend, how much space you have available, and how much time and effort you want to devote to it.

Composting offers benefits to both the environment and your pocketbook. By making compost, gardeners create a source of high-quality nutrition for their garden and eliminate the need to buy commercial fertilizers. Compost improves soil structure and moisture retention, and can actually protect plants from certain diseases. As an alternative to landfills and incinerators, composting attracts interest even from nongardeners seeking to reduce their trash-collection bills. As much as ¾ of a household's waste is compostable. On the farm, composting is a practical, cost-effective way to conserve the nutrients in manure. The composting process also allows the farmer to make use of free sources of soil fertility such as municipal yard waste and food processing wastes.

Good compost starts at home. Begin your search for compost ingredients in your own backyard, kitchen, and neighborhood. What organic wastes could you divert from the trash stream into your compost pile? Most of us don't have to travel far to find a wealth of nutrient-rich materials such as grass clippings, pine needles and cones, hay, manure, kitchen scraps, coffee grounds, and dried leaves to turn into soil-nourishing compost.

Key Words
COMPOSTING

Aerobic. Describes organisms living or occurring only in the presence of oxygen.

Anaerobic. Describes organisms living or occurring when oxygen is absent.

Composting. The art and science of combining organic materials under controlled conditions so that the original raw ingredients are transformed into humus.

C/N ratio. The proportion of bulky, dry, high-carbon materials to dense, moist, high-nitrogen materials. The ideal C/N ratio for stimulating compost organisms is 25:1–30:1; finished compost's C/N ratio is about 10:1.

Cold, slow, or passive pile. A compost pile that receives little or no turning, allowing some anaerobic decomposition to occur; composting proceeds at cooler temperatures over a longer period of time.

Hot, fast, or active pile. A compost pile that is turned or otherwise aerated frequently, creating high temperatures and finished compost in a relatively short time.

Sheet composting. A method of spreading undecomposed organic materials over the soil's surface, then working them into the soil to decompose, rather than piling them and spreading the resulting compost.

Windrow. A long, low, broad compost pile often used in large-scale composting systems; dimensions are limited only by the equipment available to turn the pile and the weight of the materials being composted.

Building a Compost Pile

Your goal in building a compost pile is to provide the best possible conditions for the proliferation of a hardworking microherd of composting organisms. Introduce organisms to your compost pile with a starter culture of rich garden soil or finished compost, or apply a commercial compost activator. Composting organisms'

needs are simple: a balanced diet, water, air, and warmth. Understanding a few basic composting principles will help you get the best possible results from the labors of your microherd.

Ingredients: Anything of living origin can be composted, but the quality and quantity of the materials you use affects the process and determines the nutrient value of the finished compost. Compost organisms require the correct proportion of carbon for energy and nitrogen for forming protein—called the C/N ratio—to function efficiently. If the C/N ratio is too high (excess carbon), decomposition slows down and nitrogen is depleted. Too low a C/N ratio (too much nitrogen) wastes nitrogen by letting it escape into the air, causing unpleasant odors, and into the water, creating pollution problems.

The ideal C/N ratio of 25-30:1 is readily reached by building your pile in alternating layers of high-carbon materials, such as sawdust, and high-nitrogen materials, such as fresh grass clippings. "C/N Ratios of Common Compost Ingredients" on the opposite page illustrates the ratio of carbon to nitrogen in some compostable materials. In general, high-carbon materials are brown or yellow, dry, and bulky. High-nitrogen materials tend to be green, moist, and often sloppy. If you find you have an abundance of either high-nitrogen or high-carbon wastes on hand, make the effort to locate ingredients that provide your microherd with the right nutrient balance.

Most organic materials supply a wide range of the other nutrients needed by compost organisms and plants. The greater the variety of materials you include in your compost, the greater your certainty of creating a nutritionally balanced product. Use additions of mineral-rich materials such as rock phosphate or greensand to tailor the nutrients in your compost to match the needs of your soil and plants. See the Fertilizers entry for information on mineral sources you can add to your compost pile.

Although lime is often used to moderate pH and odors in compost, it is not always a desirable addition to the compost pile. Particularly when

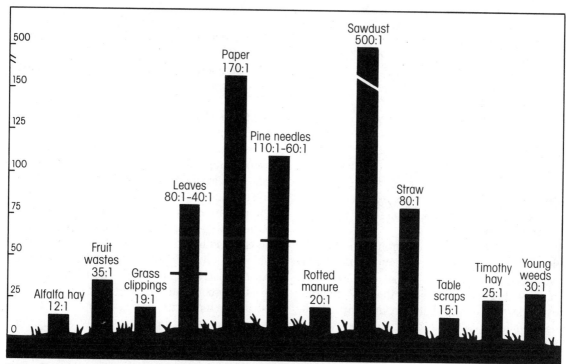

C/N ratios of common compost ingredients. Composting organisms need carbon for energy and nitrogen for growth. It's the composter's job to supply both kinds of materials in roughly the proportions the microorganisms prefer. Carbonaceous ingredients are almost always plant materials; many nitrogen sources, such as manure and blood meal, come from animals, although fresh plant matter is also nitrogenous.

manure is being composted, lime causes the release of nitrogen into the atmosphere in the form of ammonia, reducing the nitrogen available to compost organisms and plants. Replace the calcium supplied by lime with crushed eggshells, bonemeal, or wood ashes, which also provide potash. Like lime, wood ashes are alkaline and will raise the pH of your compost. Use wood ashes in moderation to avoid high pH levels that inhibit microorganism activity and limit nutrient uptake by some plants.

There are some organic materials to avoid or use only with caution when composting. Human and pet feces may carry disease organisms; meat scraps and fatty materials break down very slowly and attract animals. Some municipal or industrial wastes are contaminated with high levels of heavy metals, pesticide residues, or other highly toxic substances. If your composting plan includes industrial waste products, obtain a complete laboratory analysis for possible contaminants before you add such waste products to your pile.

Moisture: All living organisms need water, but too much moisture drives out air, drowns the pile, and washes away nutrients. Good compost is about as damp as a moist sponge. There are several ways to control moisture levels in compost piles:

• Build your pile on a site that is well drained. If necessary, start with a bottom layer of sand or gravel to make sure the pile never sits in a puddle.

• Sprinkle each layer with a watering can or garden hose as you construct the pile. The composting process requires water; check the moisture level every few days and, if necessary, add water when you turn your compost.

• Layer very wet, sloppy materials such as fruit wastes with absorbent ingredients such as sawdust or shredded dry leaves.

• Turn your pile to release excess moisture that prevents proper heating.

• Protect your pile from the weather. Compost in a covered bin, or place a layer of hay or straw over your pile.

• Shape your pile to work with weather conditions. In humid climates, a pile with a rounded, or convex, top repels excess water; a sunken, or concave, top lets the pile collect needed water in dry climates.

Aeration: Supplying enough air to all parts of a compost pile to encourage thorough decomposition is perhaps the key to successful composting. Frequent turning is the most straightforward way to do this, but there are other aerating techniques to use in addition to or even in place of turning:

• Build a base of coarse material such as brush or wood chips under your pile to allow air penetration from below.

• Shred leaves, hay, and garden debris before composting. Use materials such as paper and grass clippings sparingly, because they tend to form impermeable mats when wet.

• Insert sticks into the pile when building it, then pull them out later to open air passages. You can also poke holes in the compost with a garden fork or crowbar.

• Bury perforated drainpipe at intervals in a passive compost pile as an excellent way to improve aeration. Sunflower stalks and straw also conduct air into compost; cornstalks don't hollow out as they decay and won't work for this purpose.

• Limit both the height and width of the pile to 5'-6' to avoid compression. There is no limit on length—large-scale compost systems frequently employ windrows hundreds of feet long.

Temperature and critical mass: Too large a pile interferes with aeration, but a minimum size of 3' in each dimension is needed in order for heating to occur. Given the proper C/N ratio, moisture, and aeration, your compost will heat up even in cold winter weather. A hot pile can reach temperatures of 160°F but will produce satisfactory results if it cooks along at about 120°F. Northern composters sometimes insulate their piles with hay bales or leaves to help composting continue throughout the winter.

Structures: The type of structure used for composting can vary greatly, depending on the materials available, the needs of the composter, and the climate. A structure isn't essential—many composting methods employ freestanding piles or heaps. As long as the volume of materials is at least 3 cubic yards, the container is relatively unimportant. Compost bins are made of wood, plastic, concrete, bricks, or just about any durable, weatherproof material. Whether permanent or portable, bins can protect compost from the weather, conserve heat during composting, and keep out scavenging animals. They are also more aesthetically pleasing. Composting structures made of wire fencing or wood and wire frames are sometimes called pens. Pens may be somewhat more portable than bins, but the terms are often interchangeable.

Making Hot Compost

Methods that meet the requirements of compost organisms range from quick, hot composting that requires effort and attention to slow, cool techniques that take less trouble. Many people perceive quick, hot composting as the only way to compost, but such methods have drawbacks as well as advantages.

Quick compost is generally ready to use in less than eight weeks and can be finished in as little as two weeks. Frequent turning is the secret: It keeps the compost well aerated so that decomposer organisms can work efficiently. Keep your compost working properly by monitoring the temperature and turning the pile again as soon as the temperature drops. The object is to maintain temperatures of 113°-158°F until decomposition is complete. A thermometer is helpful but not essential; you can stick your hand down into the pile to see how hot it is. Or insert a metal rod into your compost. If the rod feels hot to the touch after a few minutes in the pile, your compost is heating properly.

The main advantage of hot composting is its speed—even in cooler climates you can process six or more batches in a season. It's the most effective way to build fertility when you are just starting out in a new location or have limited room for composting. The other major benefit of this method is its heat. Hot composting temperatures, maintained over several weeks, kill most weed seeds and pathogens. Perfect your hot-composting skills before you include diseased plants or seed-bearing weeds on your list of compost ingredients. Weeds such as Canada thistle that sprout readily from small pieces of root also are better left out of the compost bin. It's better to miss out on some plant material than to risk putting weed- and disease-carrying compost on your garden.

The major disadvantage of quick composting is the labor involved in turning the compost every few days. It is also a less forgiving process than others; if the moisture level or C/N ratio is wrong, you have to make adjustments. Another drawback is that the whole pile must be built at once. If your compost pile is also your household garbage disposal system, compostables must be saved up until you're ready to start a new pile.

Hot composting conserves less nitrogen than cooler methods because fast bacterial growth requires extra nitrogen, some of which inevitably drifts off in the form of ammonia. Finally, studies have shown that compost produced at high temperatures is less able to suppress soil-borne diseases than is cool compost, since the beneficial bacteria and fungi that attack pathogens can't survive the higher temperatures.

Small-Scale Composting

You don't need a lot of space to compost successfully. If you have a small yard, a single 3'

diameter circle of rigid wire fencing is all that is necessary. Even apartment dwellers can make compost indoors with the help of earthworms. A worm box, with air holes, drainage, and a healthy earthworm population, helps turn food wastes into compost with very little effort and little or no odor. A general rule of thumb suggests that 1 square foot of surface area is needed to digest each pound of waste material generated per week—a box 3' square and 1' deep can accomodate most of a family's food wastes. You can also use a plastic garbage can, modified to allow drainage and aeration, as a worm-powered indoor composter. Read the Earthworms entry to learn more about composting with earthworms.

Make a simple outdoor composter by cutting out the bottom of a trash can and setting the can firmly into the ground to prevent tipping. Use several such cans for continuous waste composting; simply wait six months to a year, depending on your climate, for the finished product. Chopping your wastes first speeds up the process, as does occasional turning or fluffing of the can's contents. Air holes, drilled into the sides and lid, provide aeration to keep the system working and encourage earthworms to inhabit your garbage can composter.

Compost tumblers, also called barrel or drum composters, offer many of the benefits of hot composting, while virtually eliminating the effort of turning. Compost tumblers work quickly; used properly, they produce finished compost in about two weeks. Their capacity tends to be limited, however; once the drum is full, you have to wait until composting is complete before adding new materials. Store kitchen wastes in plastic buckets with tight-fitting lids during this time, using sawdust or similarly absorbent materials to minimize odors.

Municipal Composting

Ever-decreasing landfill capacity and escalating waste disposal costs continue to spur interest in composting among municipal solid waste managers. By 1990, more than 1,000 municipal

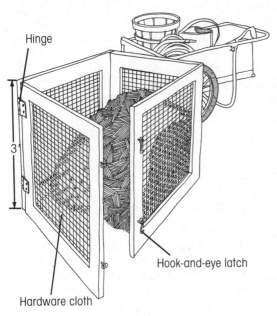

Hinge

3'

Hardware cloth

Hook-and-eye latch

Wood and wire compost bin. Construct a 3' × 3' portable bin using four sides made of 3' × 3' pieces of ½" hardware cloth fastened to 2 × 4s. Hinge one of the sides and place hooks and eyes on the edge opposite the hinges, creating a door for your bin. Set up this bin close to your garden; when the bin is full, move it to another convenient location and begin a new pile.

composting facilities were operating in the United States. Most of these facilities handled only yard waste (brush, leaves, and sometimes grass clippings), about 200 composted sewage sludge, and fewer than 10 processed mixed municipal solid waste. New legislative limits on waste disposal and public demands for environmentally safe waste handling can only lead to increases in all types of composting operations.

Municipal compost operations range from small leaf-composting facilities to huge systems capable of turning 800 tons per day of waste into compost. Most facilities use windrows that are either turned every few days with mechanized compost turners or aerated using forced-air methods. A few are fully enclosed, automated "in-vessel" compost systems that take in refuse

GARDENING IN COMPOST

Nowhere is it written that gardeners have to till, spade, and generally churn up more soil than an army of earthworms to have successful gardens. Several well-known and respected organic gardeners like Ruth Stout advise just the opposite. They are firm advocates of no-dig gardening.

So how do you garden without regular digging or cultivating? Easier than you might think. Simply start collecting all manner of organic wastes—leaves, grass clippings, kitchen scraps, shredded tree trimmings, even weeds—and compost them. Many municipalities now collect yard wastes and even make compost, which is available free or at low charge.

Spread all of this material evenly on your garden plot, sprinkle on organic high-nitrogen substances such as cottonseed meal, and if the weather is dry, sprinkle it with water. Then mix it up with a garden fork, or till shallowly and simply let it rot.

This combination of heavy mulching and sheet composting is especially helpful if you have heavy clay soil. Experienced gardeners advise first working up the soil for better drainage and then letting nature and earthworms work their magic on the smorgasbord of organic materials you'll heap on the soil surface.

Other gardeners don't even till the compost into the soil. They leave it on the soil surface, continuing to apply organic materials in strips to form raised beds. They then plant seeds or transplants into the beds, rather than into the soil, and cover them with finished compost or heavy mulch.

at one end and sort, grind, mix, moisten, and aerate it on its way to the other end of the process, where it arrives as finished compost.

Municipal compost facilities often make their product available to area residents at little or no cost. To locate nearby composting facilities, contact local governing bodies responsible for solid waste management; most states maintain listings of operating or planned compost facilities as well. The quality of compost produced by municipal operations can vary considerably, depending on the nature of the materials composted, the skill of the facility's operators, and how long the product has been allowed to mature. Most states prohibit distribution of compost containing heavy metals or other toxic contaminants to the public.

Using Compost

Finished compost is a versatile material that you can apply freely at any time of year without fear of burning plants or polluting water. For most garden applications, use compost that is well finished—aged long enough so that the decomposition process has stabilized. Unfinished compost retards the germination and growth of certain plants, although others, such as corn and squash, seem to thrive on partly finished compost. Try these tips for using compost around your garden and yard.

Vegetables and annuals: Incorporate compost liberally into the top inch or two of all annual beds (including your vegetable garden) before seeding or transplanting. Apply compost during the growing season as a mulch or side-dressing, and work it into the soil when you turn under cover crops.

Trees and shrubs: If your soil is poor, avoid backfilling the planting hole with compost-enriched soil, since roots will tend to ball up inside the hole instead of branching out in search of nutrients. Top-dress with compost around the root zone and bore plugs of compost into the soil around the drip line.

Lawns: Spread compost when establishing new seedings and rejuvenating your lawn in spring. Add fine compost when you aerate, so it comes in contact with roots.

Potting mixes: Compost provides an excellent medium for starting seeds and growing houseplants. Contrary to popular belief, pasteurization is unnecessary—heating compost actually suppresses disease-fighting microbes,

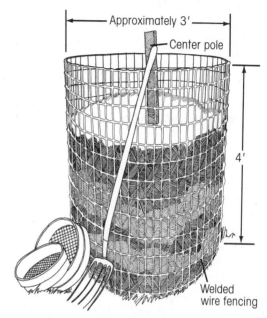

Compost pen. A 10' length of 4' wide welded wire fencing forms a circular compost pen slightly larger than 3' in diameter. Fasten the ends of the fencing together with wire or reusable clips. Turn the compost by unfastening the fencing and setting up the pen next to the freestanding pile; turn into the now-empty pen. To direct moisture into the center of your compost pile, drive a pole or length of pipe into the ground in the center of your pen so that it extends slightly above the top edge of the pen and your compost.

allowing airborne pathogens to populate the growing medium. Simply screen your compost to remove large pieces and mix the fine compost with sand, peat moss, or other amendments to create a custom potting mix. (Use the large pieces you screen out as mulch or to "seed" a new compost pile.)

Compost tea: When plants need some immediate care, perk them up with nutrient-rich water made by soaking a cloth bag full of compost in a watering can or barrel for a couple of days. Dilute the resulting solution to a weak-tea color; reuse your compost "tea bag" a few times, then apply the remaining solids to your garden. ❖

Container Gardening

Gardening in containers is ideal for those with little or no garden space. Container plants also add versatility to large gardens. They lend instant color, provide a focal point in the garden, or tie in the architecture of the house to the garden. Place them on the ground or on a pedestal, mount them on a windowsill, or hang them from your porch.

Choosing Containers

Pots and planters come in a wide range of sizes, shapes, materials, and styles. You can also modify everyday containers such as bowls or barrels to be planters.

Drainage: Drainage holes are essential. Without drainage, soil will become waterlogged and plants may die. The holes need not be large, but there must be enough so that excess water can drain out. If a container has no holes, try drilling some yourself. A container without holes is best used as a cache pot, or cover, to hide a plain pot. Self-watering, double-walled containers are available.

Size: When choosing a container, keep in mind what plant you want to grow in it. The size and shape of a plant's root system, and how rapidly it grows, will determine how large and deep the container must be. A rootbound plant will dry out rapidly and won't grow well. Large containers hold more soil, stay moist longer, and are less subject to rapid temperature fluctuations. Small hanging baskets are especially prone to drying. Light-colored containers keep the soil cooler than dark containers. The maximum size (or weight) of a container is limited by how much room you have, what will support it, and whether or not you plan to move it.

Materials: Each type of container has merits and disadvantages:

• Clay or terra-cotta containers are attractive but breakable and are easily damaged by freezing and thawing.

• Cast concrete is long-lasting and comes in a range of sizes and styles. You can even make attractive ones yourself. Plain concrete is heavy, but concrete mixed with vermiculite or perlite, or concrete and fiberglass blends are much lighter.

• Plastic and fiberglass are lightweight, relatively inexpensive, and available in many sizes and shapes. Choose sturdy and somewhat flexible pots. Avoid thin, stiff pots—they become brittle with cold or age.

• Wood is natural-looking and protects roots from rapid temperature swings. You can build wooden planters yourself. Choose a naturally rot-resistant wood such as cedar or locust, or use pine treated with a nontoxic preservative. (Don't use creosote, which is toxic to plants.) Molded wood-fiber containers are sturdy and inexpensive.

• Metals are strong, but they conduct heat, exposing roots to rapid temperature fluctuations. Metal must be lined with plastic for growing edibles.

Preparing Your Container

While your container must have drainage holes, it's not necessary to cover them with pot shards or gravel. It doesn't improve drainage, and pot shards may actually block the holes. Prevent soil from washing out by placing a layer of paper towel or newspaper over the holes before adding soil. If your container is too deep, you can put a layer of gravel or Styrofoam in the bottom to reduce the amount of soil required.

Plain garden soil is too dense for container plantings. For containers up to 1 gallon in size, use a houseplant soil mixture; see the Houseplants entry for a recipe. For larger containers, use a relatively coarse soilless planting mixture to maintain the needed water and air balance. Buy a commercial planting mix or make your own from equal parts of compost or sphagnum peat, pulverized pine or fir bark, and perlite or vermiculite. For each cubic foot of mix add 4 oz. dolomitic limestone, 1 lb. rock phosphate or colloidal phosphate, 4 oz. greensand, 1 lb. granite dust, and 2 oz. blood meal.

CONTAINER PLANTS FOR SHADE

Many plants grow well in containers in full sun. Try these plants for shady spots.
Light shade: Asparagus fern (*Asparagus setaceus*), browallia, foxgloves (*Digitalis* spp.), Johnny jump-ups, New Guinea impatiens, pansies, wishbone flowers (*Torenia* spp.), and yellow loosestrife (*Lysimachia punctata*).
Medium shade or a northern exposure: Allegheny foamflower (*Tiarella cordifolia*), aluminum plant (*Pilea cadierei*), begonias, coleus, European wild ginger (*Asarum europaeum*), fuchsias, hostas, impatiens, lungworts (*Pulmonaria* spp.), periwinkles (*Vinca* spp.), self-heals (*Prunella* spp.), and violets.

You may want to mix in one of the special super-absorbent polymers—synthetic substances that hold large amounts of water available for plants. They will improve water availability without making the soil soggy. While these products are not naturally occurring substances, they appear to be inert and to have no toxic breakdown products.

Plant in containers as you would in the garden. For trees and shrubs, trim off any circling roots and cover the root ball to the same level as it was set at the nursery. Firm the planter mixture gently and settle by watering thoroughly. Don't fill pots level to the top with soil mixture, but leave space for watering.

Selecting Plants

Almost any vegetable, flower, herb, shrub, or small tree can be grown in a container. Dwarf and compact cultivars are best. Select plants to suit the climate and exposure. Use your imagination, and combine upright and trailing plants, edibles, and flowers for pleasing and colorful effects.

Container gardens can be enjoyed for one season and discarded, or designed to last for years. When designing permanent containers, remember plants are less hardy because their roots are more exposed to air temperatures. Nonhardy plants will need to have winter protection or to be moved to a sheltered space. So consider how heavy the container will be and decide how you will move it before choosing a nonhardy plant.

Caring for Container Plants

Water container plants thoroughly. How often depends on many factors such as weather, plant size, and pot size. Don't let soil in containers dry out completely, as it is hard to re-wet.

Container plants need frequent feeding. Fertilize them by watering with diluted fish emulsion, seaweed extract, or compost tea. Or foliar-feed by spraying the leaves with doubly diluted preparations of these solutions. Start by feeding once every two weeks; adjust the frequency depending on plant response. ❖

Convallaria

Lily-of-the-valley. Perennial groundcovers.

Description: *Convallaria majalis,* lily-of-the-valley, bears arching, 6"-8" sprays of fragrant white bell-shaped flowers in early spring. By fall, the broad, green basal leaves slowly turn shades of golden yellow, then disappear completely, leaving the ground bare. Zones 2-8.

How to grow: Lily-of-the-valley prefers partial shade in moderately rich, acid, moist but well-drained soil. In the fall, top-dress with leaf mold or rotted manure. Divide clumps every 3-5 years when plants are dormant, and transplant the pips (new shoots) 4" apart in early spring.

Landscape uses: Plant lily-of-the-valley in clumps, or use as a groundcover in difficult northern exposures where most plants can't survive. Lily-of-the-valley is spectacular interplanted among low shrubs and ferns or around deciduous trees. ❖

Cooperative Extension Service

Ever wonder if those wonderful English roses will grow in your garden? Or do you hanker for homegrown watermelon, but garden where summers are short? All the know-how you need to select and grow ornamentals, vegetables, and fruits is available from the Cooperative Extension Service.

A unique partnership between college and government, the extension service was established in 1914 to provide an educational link between the public, the United States Department of Agriculture (USDA), and land-grant colleges, state colleges built on land donated by the government. Extension offices provide gardening advice tailored to your particular climate, soil, and growing conditions through publications, classes, and workshops. The Master Gardener program provides special training for volunteers interested in teaching as well as learning; see the Master Gardeners entry for a full description. Staff, volunteers, or computers are often available to answer your gardening questions.

State extension offices are housed at the land-grant college (often the state university or the home of the state agricultural school). Local offices are scattered throughout the state. The type and cost of services provided may vary. Check with your local office to find out what's available in your area. Keep in mind that extension agents may not always offer advice with the organic gardener foremost in mind. If you ask for pest control or soil fertility information, be sure you specify that you want recommendations for organic control methods or fertilizers.

How do you find your extension office? Most offices are listed in the government section of the phone book. Look for the headings Cooperative Extension, Extension, or University Extension under the county government listing, or check for the same headings under the listing for your state land-grant college. ❖

Coreopsis

Coreopsis, calliopsis, tickseed.
Summer-blooming annuals; late-spring-to fall-blooming perennials.

Description: *Coreopsis tinctoria*, annual calliopsis, bears loads of single 1"-2", broad-petalled daisies in shades of yellow, gold, red, brown, and combinations. The 1'-2' erect plants are scantily clad in fine, threadlike leaves.

Perennial hybrid coreopsis—from *C. grandiflora* and *C. lanceolata*—bears single to double, 1½"-3", mostly gold daisies on long, leafless stems above loose sheaves of long, medium green leaves; plants grow 10"-36" tall.

C. verticillata, threadleaf coreopsis, produces many 1"-2", starlike blooms in yellow and gold shades atop 1'-3' spreading mounds of delicate, airy foliage. Zones 3-8.

How to grow: Sow annual calliopsis in spring (in fall in the South) where they are to bloom in a sunny, average to less fertile, well-drained spot. Although their bloom season is short, they tolerate heat and drought very well, and will self-sow freely for the next year or perhaps for a second crop in fall.

Give perennial coreopsis similar conditions, dividing them every few years in spring or fall. Taller hybrids need staking; prompt deadheading will prolong bloom throughout much of the growing season. Cut back threadleaf coreopsis after the main flush of bloom to encourage another heavy bloom in fall. Or let it continue to bloom unchecked, although it will bloom less spectacularly.

Landscape uses: All make an important contribution to borders and cottage gardens. Hybrids provide plenty of cut flowers.

Best cultivars: *C. tinctoria* is nearly always offered as a mix. Hybrid coreopsis: tufty 10"-12" single 'Goldfink', and 1½'-2' semidouble 'Early Sunrise', which blooms in 12 weeks from seed. *C. verticillata*: 1'-1½' gold 'Zagreb' and 1½'-2' soft yellow 'Moonbeam'. ❖

Corn

Zea mays
Gramineae

Corn is more American than apple pie. It was cultivated by New World civilizations for more than 4,000 years, and settlers from the Old World soon made maize a staple in their own diets. Today, even though most of our own corn production is fed to livestock, it remains—in the forms of popcorn, cornmeal, grits, and sweet corn—one of America's favorite foods. Despite its need for a large share of garden space, many gardeners find room for sweet corn because of the superior taste of fresh-picked ears.

In the past, the sugar in corn kernels started changing to starch almost as soon as you picked the ears. Now, breeders have developed dozens of new and ever-sweeter cultivars that retain their sugar content for days. Even with these improvements, though, sweet corn that goes straight from stalk to stove or freezer offers a special flavor that makes raising corn in your backyard extremely worthwhile.

Hundreds of cultivars are on the market today, but most belong in one of the four major categories: popcorn, a low-calorie, nutritional snack; dent (field) corn, used mostly for corn meal and animal feed; multicolored, ornamental Indian (flint) corn; and the home-garden favorite, sweet corn, in white, yellow, and bicolor types.

Planting: Corn is very susceptible to frosts. You can lose a crop if you plant too early. Corn doesn't transplant well, either, so if you garden in a short-season area and want to start corn indoors, use peat pots to avoid disturbing the roots at transplanting time. It's better to wait until all danger of frost is past and the soil warms up to the 60°F needed for seed germination. If the weather stays cool, spread black plastic on the planting area to speed up ground-warming.

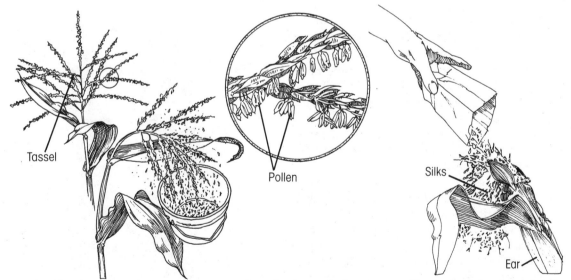

Tassel

Pollen

Silks

Ear

Hand-pollinating corn. If you only have room for a few corn plants, you can still get a well-developed crop by hand-pollinating the silks. Collect pollen as soon as the silks develop and the tassels have a loose, open appearance. In the morning of a calm day, shake the tassel over a dry container to release the pollen; collect from several plants. Immediately transfer the pollen into a small paper bag and sprinkle the powdery material onto the silks. Repeat once or twice on subsequent days to ensure complete pollination.

Typically, corn produces only two ears per stalk, except for some dwarf cultivars that have four ears per plant. If you want corn only for fresh eating, plant a minimum of 10-15 plants per person. To extend your harvest, sow an early-maturing type every two weeks for six weeks, or plant early, mid-season, and late types at the same time. To avoid cross-pollination, keep different corn cultivars 400 or more yards apart, or plant them so they tassel two weeks apart. To make good use of garden space, interplant with a crop like half-runner beans, pole beans, pumpkins, or squash.

Site your corn patch in a sunny, wind-protected area. Corn is an extremely heavy feeder, especially on nitrogen, so it thrives in a place where earth-enriching crops like beans, alfalfa, or clover grew the previous season.

In order to produce kernels, wind must deposit pollen from the tassels (plant tops) onto each of the silks on the ears. Every unpollinated silk results in an undeveloped kernel. To promote complete pollination, plant corn in blocks rather than a few long rows, or try hand-pollination.

For early plantings, sow seeds only 1" deep; in the hot weather of midsummer, plant them 4" deep. The germination rate is only 75 percent, so plant three seeds together every 7"-15". They should germinate in 7-10 days. Thin to one plant every 15". To avoid disturbing remaining plants, remove unwanted seedlings by cutting them off at soil level. Plant dwarf cultivars 1" deep; thin to 8" apart.

Growing guidelines: Corn can't compete with weeds, so cultivate thoroughly around the stalks for the first month of growth. After that, the shallow, easily damaged roots will spread 1' out from the plant; be careful not to disturb these roots. Instead, control weeds by applying mulch. Corn needs about 1" of water a week, particularly when the stalks begin to tassel. Water by flooding soil surface rather than by spraying from above, which could wash pollen off the flowering tops.

When the stalks are 6" tall, side-dress them with blood meal or a diluted fish-based fertilizer, and repeat the feeding when they are about knee-high. Don't remove any sideshoots or suckers that appear; they won't harm production, and cutting them might damage roots.

Problems: The most common pests include corn borers, flea beetles, and cutworms. You'll find details on controlling these pests in "The Top Ten Garden Insect Pests in America" on page 344.

Corn earworms, which also attack tomatoes, are most prevalent in the South and Central states. The yellow-headed, striped adults are about 2" long with yellow, green, or brown bodies. If you catch heavy infestations before the worms crawl too far inside the ear, treat with BT (*Bacillus thuringiensis*), rotenone, or pyrethrin. Another remedy (also good for coping with ear-drilling, ⅛" long black sap beetles) is to put a few drops of mineral oil into the top of each ear *after* the silks wilt and start to turn brown (indicating that the ears were pollinated).

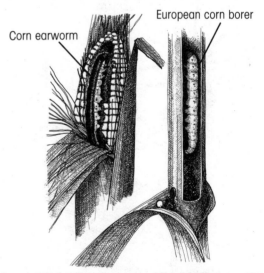

Corn earworm

European corn borer

Corn pests. Corn earworms usually attack ear tips when plants begin to tassel. If damage is minor, cut tips off after harvesting. European corn borers attack stalks below tassels; look for small piles of sawdustlike material beside small holes. Squeeze the stalk to destroy the borer.

European corn borers are 1″ long, flesh-colored worms marked with tiny black dots. BT is an effective control; use rotenone as a last resort for severe infestations. Corn borers overwinter as full-grown larvae in weed stems and old cornstalks. Pull up and destroy such winter refuges to break their life cycle.

Cucumber beetle larvae, also known as corn rootworms, cause plants to weaken and collapse. Adults are yellow beetles with black stripes or spots. Minimize damage by rotating crops; control severe infestations with rotenone.

Seed-corn maggots attack kernels planted too deeply in cool soil. These yellowish white maggots are ¼″ long, with pointed heads. If they attack, wait until warmer weather to plant another crop at a shallower level.

Animal pests can seriously reduce your corn yields. Birds may be a problem at both seeding and harvesting time, while raccoons are fond of the ripening ears. For information on discouraging these creatures, see the Animal Pests entry.

Clean garden practices, crop rotation, and planting resistant hybrids are the best defenses against most diseases, including Stewart's wilt, a bacterial disease that causes wilting and pale streaks on leaves.

Corn smut makes pale, shining, swollen galls that burst and release powdery black spores. Cut off and dispose of galls before they open. If necessary, destroy affected plants to keep smut from spreading. It can remain viable in the soil for 5-7 years.

Harvesting: Three weeks after corn silks appear, start checking ears for peak ripeness. Pull back part of the husk and pierce a kernel with your thumbnail. If "milk" spurts out, rush those ears to the table, refrigerator, or freezer. Ears on the same stalk usually ripen a few days apart. A completely dry silk or a yellow or faded-green sheath means the ear is past its prime.

Leave field corn, ornamental corn, and popcorn on the stalks to dry until the first hard frost. If the weather is cloudy and wet, cut and stack stalks in a cool, dry place until the corn dries.

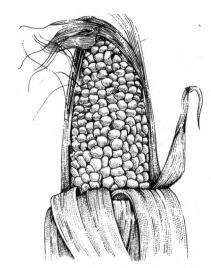

'Country Gentleman' corn. A longtime favorite, 'Country Gentleman' produces ears of irregularly spaced kernels.

Best cultivars: Early cultivars (58-70 days to mature, good for areas with cold, damp springs): large-eared 'Spring Gold' and white 'Silver Sweet'; 'Aztec', resists some strains of wilt and tolerates smut.

Mid-season cultivars (mature about a week later than early types): 'Gold Rush', good for a variety of climates; 'Kandy Korn', retains its sugary taste for up to two weeks on the stalk; 'Honey and Cream', a bicolor, has a tight husk that discourages earworms and other insects; 'Platinum Lady', a delicious, disease-resistant white cultivar.

Late-season cultivars: 'Golden Bantam' and 'Country Gentleman', developed decades ago, remain among the most popular; 'Silver Queen', disease-resistant, tasty white kernels are still a favorite.

Dwarf: popular 'Golden Midget', 2½', produces 4″ long ears that freeze well.

Popcorn: 'White Cloud' and 'Japanese Hulless' pop well and have no hulls.

Roasting: 'Hickory King', a field corn, good if picked before it becomes tough.

Indian or ornamental (needs a long, hot growing season of well over 100 days): 'Indian Ornamental Pop', decorative and tasty. ❖

Cornus

Dogwood, cornel. Single- or multiple-stemmed deciduous spring-flowering trees or shrubs; herbaceous ground-covers.

Description: The many plants in this genus share characteristic foliage and flowers. The simple, ovate leaves come to a point at the end, paired veins extend lengthwise from the midrib toward the leaf tip. The flowers, noteworthy in many species, feature petal-like bracts that surround the small, true blossoms. Some dogwoods have showy, brightly colored bracts, while others bear less-noticeable leaflike bracts.

Cornus canadensis, bunchberry, is native to the woods of North America and grows best in cool regions. This herbaceous groundcover grows to 9″ and has greenish white bracted flowers in spring that resemble those of flowering dogwood. Red berries appear in the fall. Zones 2-5.

C. florida, flowering dogwood, grows in the shade of other trees in the forests of the eastern United States. In the landscape it reaches heights of 20′-40′ and has a graceful, layered branching habit. Heart-shaped white bracts surround the true flowers in early spring. Red berries and leaf color in shades of burgundy, scarlet, orange, and yellow appear in fall. Choose your dogwood from a nursery offering cultivars for your region because heat, drought, and cold tolerance vary within the species. Zones 5-8.

C. kousa, kousa dogwood, has a vase-shaped habit, layered branching, and a maximum height of 20′ in the landscape. The flowers appear in late spring and are surrounded by white, pointed bracts. Raspberrylike fruits are green through the summer, coloring pink when the leaves turn reddish in the fall. Shedding bark reveals patches of tan and cream. Zones 5-7.

C. sericea, red-osier dogwood, is a native North American shrub. Its habit is loose and broadly rounded. The red stem color intensifies during dormancy, becoming strongest in the weeks just prior to bud break. White flowers bloom in flat-topped clusters; white berries contrast nicely with reddish fall foliage. Zones 2-7.

How to grow: Dogwoods usually require partial shade, although some tolerate full sun in cooler climates. Provide evenly moist, humus-rich soil, good drainage, and mulch to shade the roots. (Swamp-dwellers like red-osier dogwood tolerate some standing water.) Dogwoods have little tolerance for air pollution, reflected heat, and other urban conditions. Insects and diseases that afflict dogwoods include dogwood borer, anthracnose, and stem canker on the shrub dogwoods. Provide an appropriate planting site, and minimize environmental stresses on the tree; for example, water during dry spells and protect from mechanical enemies such as lawn mowers.

Although common across the Eastern states, flowering dogwoods grown as specimens rarely prosper in full sun in the middle of lawns. Flowering is abundant for a few years, but soon you see dead wood, sucker shoots at the tree's base, and unthrifty growth. If decline doesn't finish off such trees, borers will. However, solitary trees do seem less likely to suffer anthracnose, a fungal disease that causes patches of dead tissue in the leaves and prospers in warm, wet weather and is transmitted by splashing rain. Full sun and good air circulation around single trees limit anthracnose's spread.

Landscape uses: Plant dogwoods for wildlife food and in woodland gardens. Shrubby dogwoods are appropriate for grouping and screening. Use the red- or yellow-twigged shrubs where they can be seen on snowy days. Tree dogwoods make nice focal points but work better (visually and culturally) in groups. Try kousa dogwood as a replacement for flowering dogwood in sunny, dry locations.

Best cultivars: *C. florida:* 'Cherokee Chief', red bracts; 'Cloud 9', large white bracts; 'Rainbow', tricolor leaves. *C. kousa* 'Milky Way', abundant flowers. *C. sericea* 'Flaviramea', bright yellow twigs in winter. ❖

Cosmos

Cosmos. Midsummer- to fall-blooming annuals.

Description: *Cosmos bipinnatus* bears 2″-4″ broad-petalled, daisylike flowers in red, pink, and white, on mounds of light green, feathery foliage up to 5′. *C. sulphureus* has 2″ orange, red, or yellow flowers and fernlike, dark green leaves on plants up to 3′.

How to grow: Direct-seed in full sun in loose, average, well-drained soil. If necessary, transplant only when very small. Cut fading flowers for more blooms. Tall cultivars may need staking.

Landscape uses: Mass the tall cultivars by themselves or at the back of a border; use shorter cultivars in midborder clumps. Cosmos also make excellent cut flowers.

Best cultivars: *C. bipinnatus:* 'Early Wonder' mix, 3½'; 'Sensation' mix, 4'; 'Sea Shells', 3½', with fluted petals. *C. sulphureus:* 'Bright Lights' mix, 3'; 'Sunny Red', 1'. ❖

Cotoneaster

Cotoneaster. Deciduous or evergreen spring-blooming shrubs or groundcovers.

Description: *Cotoneaster apiculatus,* cranberry cotoneaster, is a low (to 20″), spreading groundcover with round, deep green, glossy leaves. Small pink flowers appear in spring, followed by red cranberry-like fruits. Fall foliage turns reddish before it drops. Zones 5-7.

C. divaricatus, spreading cotoneaster, eventually grows wider than tall, with a mature height of about 5′. Its purplish stems bear glossy oval leaves and pale pink spring flowers. Red berries appear in fall, accompanied by red foliage in most situations. Zones 5-8.

C. horizontalis, rockspray cotoneaster, is a spreading, mounding, layered plant with a func-

tional height of 2′-3′ and a wider spread. It bears glossy green, rounded foliage that occasionally turns red before falling, revealing a herringbone branching structure. Zones 5-8.

C. multiflorus, many-flowered cotoneaster, is a deciduous shrub that attains a mature height of 8′-12′. The broadly oval foliage is dull rather than glossy, with little fall color. This cotoneaster is known for its abundance of small white flowers in spring. Bright red berries are borne in the fall. Zones 4-6.

C. salicifolius, willowleaf cotoneaster, grows to a height of 8′-12′. Its gracefully arching branches bear slender, glossy, leathery leaves that usually persist through the winter and may blush to a handsome red if the weather turns unusually cold. Small white flowers, largely hidden by the foliage in spring, are followed by slightly more visible red berries in autumn. Zones 6-8. Note that in spite of appearances, cotoneaster is pronounced "kuh-tow-nee-AS-ter."

How to grow: Cotoneasters thrive in a variety of soils, and most can tolerate wind exposure. Provide full sun and good drainage. North of Zone 8, plant in spring and fall; in Zone 8, plant in fall or winter. Once established, most cotoneasters will thrive without additional watering. Fire blight is a major concern and severely limits the use of these plants in the South. This disease causes new shoots to wilt suddenly, turn dark, and die back. It eventually spreads, killing the whole plant. Lush new growth is particularly susceptible, so avoid overfertilizing.

Landscape uses: Because of their spreading shape, cotoneasters are ideal as groundcovers, borders, barriers, screens, and massed plantings. They're also good in mixed borders and foundation plantings. Rockspray cotoneaster makes an effective espalier.

Best cultivars: *C. horizontalis:* 'Robusta' has dark green foliage that turns purple-red in fall. It bears pink flowers in spring. 'Variegatus' has white-edged leaves. *C. salicifolius:* 'Scarlet Leader' is low-growing, with good fall color. ❖

Cottage Gardening

Cottage gardening originated during the Middle Ages, when people cultivated gardens outside the doorsteps of their thatched stone and wood cottages. They grew a patchwork of herbs, flowers, vegetables, and fruit trees. These joyful cottage gardens can still be found along the lanes of English villages.

Even if you don't live in a cottage, you might want your own cottage garden—its cheerful disorder looks surprisingly contemporary. For the most authentic look, locate the garden in a sunny plot surrounding a path to the front or kitchen door, and enclose the yard, or part of it, with a rustic fence. A decorative gate or arbor at the garden's entrance would add a charming touch. A cottage-style garden could also work well along the side of the house or beside a garage, barn, or toolshed.

The delightful informality of a cottage garden makes it a perfect place for accessories. A swing or bench is at home there, and so is a sundial, beehive, windchime, or other ornament. Add a birdbath to welcome the many birds and butterflies that will visit your profusion of herbs and flowers, or a rustic birdhouse on a pole. Remember not to overload your cottage garden with ornaments, though—the emphasis should always be on the flowers.

Traditionally, the path leading through a cottage garden proceeded in a straight line from the lane to the door—its purpose was functional, not decorative. However, you might prefer to make a meandering path through your garden. Cover the path with bark chips, old paving bricks, or cobblestones. Or create a fragrant path with stepping stones nestled among scented "path plants" such as chamomile, woolly thyme (*Thy-*

BEST COTTAGE GARDEN PLANTS

These cheerful flowers will give your cottage garden a joyful, exuberant look. The annuals self-sow freely, returning to your garden each year. And many of these spreading perennials have adorned cottage gardens for hundreds of years. Cottage garden plants aren't fussy; they prefer full sun and average soil.

Annuals

Browallia spp. (browallias)
Calendula officinalis (pot marigold)
Centaurea cyanus (cornflower)
Cleome hasslerana (spider flower)
Consolida ambigua (rocket larkspur)
Cosmos bipinnatus (cosmos)
Delphinium spp. (delphiniums)
Ipomoea spp. (morning-glories)
Lobularia maritima (sweet alyssum)
Lunaria annua (honesty)
Mirabilis jalapa (four-o'clock)
Myosotis sylvatica (garden forget-me-not)
Nemophila menziesii (baby-blue-eyes)
Nigella damascena (love-in-a-mist)
Papaver rhoeas (corn poppy, Shirley poppy)
Viola tricolor (Johnny jump-up)

Perennials

Achillea millefolium (common yarrow)
Achillea ptarmica (sneezeweed)
Alchemilla mollis (lady's-mantle)
Anchusa azurea (Italian bugloss)
Artemisia ludoviciana 'Silver King' ('Silver King' artemisia)
Chrysanthemum parthenium (feverfew)
Coreopsis verticillata (threadleaf coreopsis)
Hemerocallis spp. (daylilies)
Lathyrus latifolius (perennial pea)
Lychnis coronaria (rose campion)
Monarda didyma (bee balm)
Oenothera pilosella (sundrops)
Phlox subulata (moss pink)
Viola sororia (woolly blue violet)

mus pseudolanuginosus), or Corsican mint (*Mentha requienii*).

Plants for Cottage Gardens

If you have room, consider a small flowering tree or two along the fence for year-round structure—perhaps a crab apple or fruit tree. Old-fashioned fragrant flowering shrubs such as lilacs, sweet mock oranges (*Philadelphus coronarius*), and shrub roses in the corners add structure and enhance the garden's homey feeling. And don't forget a butterfly bush (*Buddleia* spp.) for the butterflies.

Choose flowers that fit the casualness of the cottage garden style, like self-sowing annuals and spreading perennials. Mix flowers right in with your favorite herbs. Dill, parsley, and coriander will self-sow and look pretty with the flowers. If you want to add mints to your garden, keep in mind that they are very invasive; add them to your garden in pots.

To complete the effect, drape climbing roses, goldflame honeysuckle (*Lonicera* × *heckrottii*) or Jackman clematis (*Clematis* × *jackmanii*) over a fence or arbor. Pop in vegetables wherever you find a spot, and use herbs such as lavender and parsley as edging plants along the walk.

Caring for Your Cottage Garden

Because part of its charm comes from its informal design, a cottage garden requires less work to maintain than more manicured gardens. But weeding can be a challenge in spring, when you have to decide which are self-sown annual and herb seedlings and which are weeds. Thin or transplant flower seedlings as needed.

Add a topdressing of compost and mulch each year after seedlings are well established. Pick off spent flowers of annuals early in the season to encourage more blooms, but allow flowers to ripen into seed heads in late summer so they can disperse seeds to start next year's garden. ❖

Cover Crop

Cover crops are plantings of grasses or legumes that cover the soil surface. Cover crops help prevent soil erosion and stop weeds from taking over unplanted garden beds. Gardeners often use the term *cover crop* interchangeably with the term *green manure crop,* although their technical definitions are not the same. For complete information on cover crops and green manures, see the Green Manure entry. ❖

Crafts from the Garden

Your garden can be a rich source of craft projects for you and your family. Flower beds and herb gardens can yield plants for wreaths, potpourri, fresh and dried arrangements, candles, pressed-flower crafts, and beauty products like soaps, shampoos, and lotions. You'll find more on herb and flower crafts in the Cut Flower Gardening, Dried Flower Gardening, Flower Arranging, Herbs, Potpourri, and Wreathmaking entries.

Other plants around your yard will provide a wealth of crafts materials: vines for wreaths and baskets; foliage, pods, and berries for arrangements; pinecones for ornaments, wreaths, and fire starters; leaves for cards or stationery; and evergreens for wreaths and swags. If you have an apple tree, you can make clove-studded pomanders, dried-apple dolls, and apple-slice wreaths.

Even the vegetable garden has the raw materials for some fun projects. For example, garlic braids and dried-pepper wreaths make great gifts. If you grow some of the dried bean cultivars with beautiful colors and patterns, you can make a seed-jar lamp. Just fill a clear ginger-jar lamp with dried beans.

You can also fill a lamp with colorful Indian corn. And don't forget cornhusk crafts! Harvest your corn when the kernels are hard and the husks dry. Use the husks plain or dyed to make cornhusk dolls, wreaths, and even chair seats.

Wheat also makes beautiful crafts, from wreaths and swags to intricate wheat weavings.

Gourds are another great source of craft projects. You can make gourd birdhouses and bird feeders, dippers, and ornaments. Harvest gourds before the first frost and spread them on newspapers in a warm, dry, well-ventilated place to dry. Turn the gourds daily to expose all sides to the air. Small gourds will cure in about a month; large gourds may take six months. For more on growing gourds, see the Gourd entry. ❖

Crataegus

Hawthorn. Deciduous flowering trees.

Description: Attractive small trees with flowering and fruiting interest, hawthorns have traditionally been used as hedges because of their thorny branches. White flowers in late spring, followed by persistent glossy red fruits, present other landscape options.

Crataegus crus-galli, cockspur hawthorn, has a broad, rounded outline, horizontally layered branches, and a height of about 30'. The rounded leaves are glossy and turn a purplish bronze before falling in autumn. Zones 4-7.

C. phaenopyrum, Washington hawthorn, is a broadly oval, single-trunked tree that grows to about 25' in height. Lobed leaves turn orange, scarlet, or purple in the fall. Zones 4-8.

C. viridus, green hawthorn, grows to 25'. Fall color is purple or scarlet. Zones 5-8.

How to grow: Provide a site with full sun, good drainage, and some air movement to reduce the risk of fire blight infection. Cedar-hawthorn rust also afflicts most hawthorns: Green hawthorn resists rust better than other species; Washington hawthorn is somewhat resistant. Plant hawthorns away from red cedars and other junipers, cedar-hawthorn rust's alternate hosts.

Landscape uses: Hawthorns are useful as hedges, but their long, sharp thorns make them undesirable in activity areas. Plant as screens, in masses, or singly. ❖

Crocus

Crocus. Spring- or fall-blooming corms.

Description: Crocuses bear nearly stemless, 1"-2" wide starry goblets in white, cream, yellow, gold, and purple, many marked or brushed with a contrasting color. Grassy leaves, usually quite short when in bloom, elongate to 4"-6". The familiar spring-blooming Dutch hybrid crocuses produce relatively large blooms in white, yellow, and purple shades, plus purple stripes on white, to 6" tall. Zones 3-8.

Species crocuses include spring-blooming *Crocus chrysanthus,* golden crocus, which grows to 2". Zones 4-8. Fall-blooming *C. speciosus,* showy crocus, bears blue-violet flowers and can reach 6" or more. Zones 5-8.

How to grow: Plant crocuses in fall at a depth 2-3 times their width in a sunny or partially shady spot with average, well-drained soil enriched with organic matter. Plant fall-blooming crocuses as soon as they are available in mid- to late summer. Do not remove leaves until they have yellowed, when you can also lift and divide the corms. Rodents may eat the corms unless a resident dog or cat keeps them at bay. Slugs sometimes devour the flowers of fall-blooming species.

Landscape uses: Grow massed in thin grass (do not mow until the foliage has died off), in rock gardens, or in clumps along a path or at a doorstep. In borders, overplant with low-growing annuals like sweet alyssum so you won't disturb them later in the season. Grow fall-blooming species in low groundcovers such as common periwinkle to help support the flower stems. ❖

Crop Rotation

Crop rotation is the practice of shifting crop locations in the garden from year to year to avoid crop-specific diseases and pests and to balance soil nutrients. For more on crop rotation, see the Green Manure, Organic Pest Management, and Vegetable Gardening entries. ❖

Cucumber

Cucumis sativus
Cucurbitaceae

Cool and juicy cucumbers are popular for both eating fresh and preserving as pickles. These frost-sensitive tropical natives need warm, humid weather and at least 8 hours of sun a day. But since they require only 55-60 days from planting to picking, cucumbers will grow in most areas of the country as long as rain or water supplies are adequate.

Types: Cucumbers range in size from little lemon-shaped types to thin "yard-long" ones; there are also seedless and disease-resistant cultivars. Others no longer have the bitterness that can cause stomach upsets in some people. These burpless cucumbers require no peeling—a nutritious advantage, since most of the vegetable's vitamins A and C, along with a large number of minerals, are located in its skin.

New bush cultivars produce vines that are more compact and require less space. For high yields, try a gynoecious cultivar; instead of the usual male and female flowers, these plants produce only female blooms and, thus, more cucumbers.

In seed catalogs, cucumbers are often divided into slicing types, used for salads or cooking, and smaller, fast-growing pickling kinds. Sometimes a cultivar is labeled "dual-purpose," meaning that you can harvest them small for pickling or larger for slicing. You'll also see the terms "white-spined" and "black-spined" applied to cucumbers. Spines are the miniature stickers that protrude from young fruits and disappear as the cucumbers mature. Overripe white-spined cucumbers are creamy white; black-spined ones turn a yellow-orange.

Planting: Cucumber yields are highest in fertile clay soil with plenty of humus, but they will grow well in most good vegetable garden soils. The plants hate to stand in water, so the site must drain well.

The biggest mistake most cucumber growers make is planting too early. It's best to wait 3-4 weeks after the date of the last frost. Spreading black plastic over the planting area will promote the soil warmth cucumbers need.

When you start seeds indoors, keep the air temperature at 70°-80°F during the day and no colder than 60°F at night. Use peat pots instead of flats to avoid disturbing the cucumber roots during transplanting. Sow 3-4 seeds ½" deep in each pot, about two weeks before the last frost. When 2-3 true leaves have developed, snip off (don't pull) all but the most vigorous seedling. If the soil or air remains cool, harden off the plants before transplanting by putting them outdoors during the day and bringing them in at night.

Plant a minimum of 6-9 vines per person. You can grow them either in hills or in rows next to a fence or trellis. Make hills 3' wide; space hills or rows 4'-5' apart (3' apart for bush cultivars). In each hill, place three transplants or sow 7-8 seeds; thin to the best three seedlings when they are a few inches tall by cutting the unwanted ones at ground level. If you're planting in rows, plant seedlings 1' apart, or sow seeds 1" deep with 3-5 seeds per foot of row and thin seedlings to 1' apart.

If you're growing gynoecious cultivars, remember to plant a few of the specially marked male seeds. Mark them well to make sure you don't thin them by mistake. Plants from these seeds will bear male flowers, which provide the pollen necessary for fertilization. One or two male plants will provide enough pollen for all of the female flowers.

To make good use of garden space, consider interplanting cole crops, such as cabbage, cauliflower, and broccoli, with your cucumbers; they should be producing around the time cucumbers come up. Radishes, bush beans, and lettuce are other good choices for intercropping. Just plan ahead when planting the early crops so that you leave enough space to plant the cucumber seeds or plants around them.

Growing guidelines: Cucumbers are 95 percent water, so adequate moisture is vital to a good cucumber crop. A thirsty plant simply stops growing, and its fruits are likely to be deformed, bitter, or tasteless. Soak the soil deeply when the weather turns dry. Soaker hoses along rows are good for this purpose. Or punch a few very small holes in a coffee can, and bury it up to the rim in the middle of each hill. Keep it filled with water to maintain the even moisture the plants need. Avoid handling or brushing up against foliage when it's wet to keep from spreading diseases. If you use overhead irrigation, water in the morning so the leaves can dry out before evening; this will also minimize disease problems.

Weed by hand until the seedlings are 1' tall; then side-dress with blood meal or aged manure, water well, and lay down at least 2" of an organic mulch, such as straw, hay, grass clippings, or leaves. In addition to conserving moisture and suppressing weeds, the mulch will help to keep fruits clean and healthy.

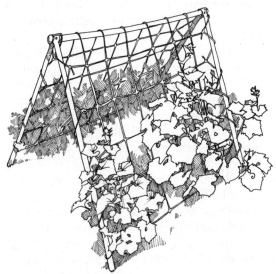

A-frame trellis. To save garden space, grow cucumbers on a vertical structure such as this A-frame trellis. Such supports produce healthier, cleaner fruits by keeping the crop off the ground and allowing for air circulation.

Male flowers appear first, followed by female blooms about a week later. Bees will spread the pollen from one to the other. If long periods of cloudy, rainy weather keep the bees inactive, you can do the job yourself by carefully picking a male flower and—after removing the petals—brushing its pollen-covered anthers against the stigmas in the center of the female blossoms. (If you're not sure how to tell the male and female flowers apart, see the Squash entry for an illustration.) Unpollinated blooms will produce tiny, curled, seedless cucumbers.

Problems: Cucumber beetles are a common pest on this vegetable. They not only chew on plants, particularly young seedlings, but also spread diseases like bacterial wilt and mosaic. There are a number of ways to battle them:

• Inspect the foliage and insides of flowers daily; handpick and destroy any beetles you find.

• Lure striped cucumber beetles away from the cucumbers by planting radishes nearby.

• Plant later in the season when the beetles are less prevalent.

• Cover young plants with a fine netting, such as cheesecloth, or with a floating row cover. Remember that a cover will also keep bees out; if you leave the cover on after flowering begins, you'll have to hand-pollinate the flowers to get a crop.

• Plant nonbitter cultivars, because cucurbitacins, chemical compounds that cause bitterness in cucumbers, also attract the beetles.

• As a last resort, apply pyrethrins to control large infestations.

Squash vine borers—1" long, white caterpillars—burrow into the plants' main stems, leaving sawdustlike droppings and causing the vines to wilt. At the first sign of this pest, cut a slit along the stem of the affected plant, remove the larvae, and cover the injured area and several close-by vine joints with soil. This enables the plant to put out new roots to help it recover. You can also attack the borers by injecting the stems with BTK (*Bacillus thuringiensis* var. *kurstaki*).

Spotted cucumber beetle   Striped cucumber beetle

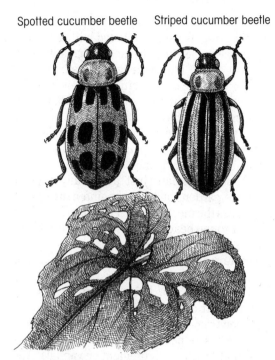

Cucumber beetles. Adult cucumber beetles are ¼" long with black heads and greenish yellow wings; they chew large ragged holes in plant leaves. There are actually two versions of this pest: the spotted cucumber beetle and the striped cucumber beetle.

Handpick green melon worms that feed on foliage and occasionally munch their way inside a fruit. Handpicking and keeping the garden clean will also help control young pickleworms, pale yellow caterpillars with black spots that turn green- or copper-colored as they grow.

Other cucumber pests include cutworms, aphids, and spider mites. For information on controlling cutworms and aphids, see "The Top Ten Garden Insect Pests in America" on page 344. Spider mites are tiny creatures that feed on the undersides of leaves, causing yellow stippling on leaf surfaces; control by spraying the plants with water to knock off the pests.

Prevent cucumber diseases by planting resistant cultivars and rotating crops on a 3-4 year basis. Minimize the spread of disease spores by keeping cucumbers away from melons, pumpkins, and squash; never handle wet vines. Keep the garden clean and free of perennial weeds, particularly ragweed and ground cherry, that can harbor disease. Here are some common diseases to watch for:

• Anthracnose produces hollow, water-soaked spots on the leaves that enlarge and turn brown. It can also blacken and pit the fruits, making them inedible.

• Bacterial wilt, spread by the cucumber beetle, starts with a single, wilted leaf, followed by the wilting of the entire plant.

• Downy mildew is brought on by damp weather and results in irregular yellow or purplish spots on the leaves, which soon curl up and die.

• Mosaic, spread by both aphids and cucumber beetles, shows up as rough, mottled leaves, stunted plants, and whitish fruit.

If these diseases do occur, immediately destroy affected vines, or put them in sealed containers for disposal with household trash.

Harvesting: Pick cucumbers frequently, before they mature. With some cultivars, especially small pickling types, it may be necessary to harvest daily. If the seeds of even *one* fruit are allowed to mature, the whole vine will quit producing. Pick regularly, and you can extend the harvest to around six weeks. Gently twist or clip off the cucumbers, being careful not to break the rather delicate vines. Cucumbers keep refrigerated for 1-2 weeks, but pickling is the best method for long-term storage.

Best cultivars: For slicing: 'Sweet Slice', gynoecious, nonbitter skin, burpless, disease-tolerant; 'Slicemaster', gynoecious; 'Sweet Success', somewhat disease-resistant, seedless, and burpless.

For pickling: 'Saladin' and 'Country Fair', prolific, burpless, and disease-resistant, less attractive to cucumber beetles.

Oddities include a disease-resistant white cucumber, a serpent-shaped Armenian type, and a yellow, lemon-shaped cucumber. ❖

Cultivation

Working the soil is important to prepare fine, smooth seedbeds and to remove weeds. However, digging and turning soil can damage plant roots, have detrimental effects on soil life, and disrupt soil structure. Never cultivate soils that are too wet or too dry, or you can turn your soil into a dusty or clodded disaster area. Avoid working around wet plants, too, to reduce the chance of spreading disease spores.

Mulching the soil reduces the need for cultivation by keeping down weeds and helping prevent soil compaction. To learn more about cultivation, see the Soil, Tools and Equipment, and Weeds entries. For more information on using mulches to protect the soil, see the Green Manure and Mulch entries.

One method organic gardeners use to cultivate is double digging. This method lifts and loosens the top 1'-2' of soil. For more information, see the Double Digging entry. ❖

Cultural Controls

Making plants less attractive to pests is one of the easiest ways to produce chemical-free crops. The various steps you can take to manipulate the environment around your plants are known as cultural controls. Keeping plants healthy and vigorous, for example, will discourage pests while promoting high crop yields. Sometimes diseases and pests need two kinds of plants to complete their life cycles, so removing one of the hosts can eliminate the problem. Rhubarb curculio, for instance, lays its eggs on wild dock, so destroying these plants will lessen the chance of crop damage. Keeping the garden free of dropped fruit and other plant residue reduces breeding and overwintering sites. Crop rotation and tillage are other ways to prevent the buildup of pests and diseases. For complete information on using cultural controls, see the Organic Pest Management entry. ❖

Curbside Gardens

The strip of ground between a sidewalk and the street is usually planted with a patch of unused lawn. Technically, the municipality owns the 2'-4' strip, but homeowners usually must care for it. Some communities plant street trees in this area, but if you want to use that space more creatively, check local ordinances to see if they have specific planting regulations. Regulations usually involve plant height (for safety reasons), but may be more restrictive.

You could plant just about any type of curbside garden, but a low-maintenance planting makes the most sense. Select plants not only for year-round beauty but also for toughness and durability; they'll be subjected to all kinds of mistreatment, including trampling by kids and people getting in and out of cars, and spraying of road salt and sand. Near the street, it's also hotter and drier than in other parts of your yard.

Don't choose trees with very smooth bark, like beeches, or peeling bark, like birches, since both kinds invite disfigurement by vandals. Also avoid trees like silver maples with large surface roots, which eventually break the sidewalk. Plant trees and shrubs with branching structures that won't interfere with pedestrians or traffic— weeping willows and other trees with drooping branches aren't for curbside gardens. See "Street Trees" on page 586 for a list of trees for curbside plantings.

The best plants for curbside gardens withstand drought, compacted soil, and other problems. Also, they don't have messy seedpods, thorns, or overhanging branches. Consider low shrubs such as rockspray cotoneaster (*Cotoneaster horizontalis*), St.-John's-worts (*Hypericum* spp.), dwarf mugo pine (*Pinus mugo* var. *mugo*), shrubby cinquefoil (*Potentilla fruticosa*), or some of the many dwarf or prostrate junipers, including cultivars of creeping juniper (*Juniperus horizontalis*). Groundcovers such as English ivy, blue lilyturf (*Liriope muscari*), and common periwinkle (*Vinca minor*) are ideal for curbsides, as are perennials such as daylilies, sundrops (*Oenothera fruticosa*),

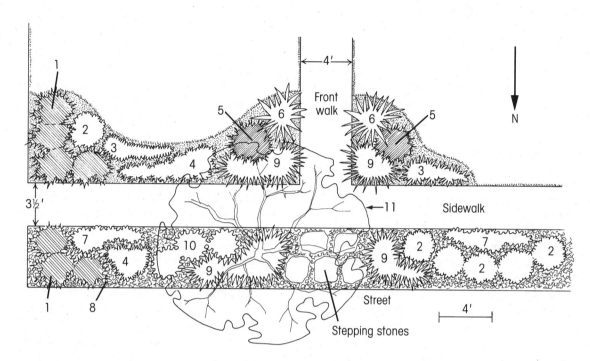

A care-free curbside garden. This design features tough but attractive plants that withstand drought, compacted soil, and other problems. Repeating the plants in the front of the yard ties the curbside planting to the house.

1. Prostrate Chinese juniper (*Juniperus chinensis* var. *procumbens*)
2. Shrubby cinquefoil (*Potentilla fruticosa*)
3. 'Moonbeam' threadleaf coreopsis (*Coreopsis verticillata* 'Moonbeam')
4. 'Hidcote' lavender (*Lavandula angustifolia* 'Hidcote')
5. 'Repandens' English yew (*Taxus baccata* 'Repandens')
6. Daylilies and daffodils (*Hemerocallis* and *Narcissus* cultivars)
7. Barren strawberry (*Waldsteinia fragarioides*)
8. Woolly thyme (*Thymus pseudolanuginosus*)
9. Variegated blue lilyturf (*Liriope muscari* 'Variegata') and crocuses
10. 'Harbor Dwarf' heavenly bamboo (*Nandina domestica* 'Harbor Dwarf')
11. 'Shademaster' honey locust (*Gleditsia triacanthos* var. *inermis* 'Shademaster')

'Goldsturm' black-eyed Susan (*Rudbeckia* 'Goldsturm'), and 'Autumn Joy' sedum. Try low-growing ornamental grasses, too, including blue fescue (*Festuca caesia*) and fountain grass (*Pennisetum alopecuroides*).

Successful Curbside Gardening

Begin your design where your front walk meets the sidewalk, laying down paving stones to extend the front walk on the other side of the sidewalk to the street. You can extend the planting to the apron of the driveway, mirroring it on each side, and repeat elements of the design along the opposite edge of the sidewalk rather than having lawn abut the pavement.

To plant your curbside garden, first strip off the lawn by cutting just beneath the roots with a shovel. Then add plenty of compost or other organic matter to the soil. Next install the stepping stones, then add the plants. Finish with a thick layer of organic mulch to discourage weeds and keep the soil moist. Shredded bark is a good choice. ❖

Currant

Ribes spp.
Saxifragaceae

It's hardly surprising that currants have been cultivated for centuries; these easy-to-grow plants produce generous quantities of tasty fruit with very little maintenance. Currants are deciduous shrubs with an upright or spreading habit, growing 3'-7' high and wide. They bear ¼"-¾" black, red, pink, green, golden yellow, or creamy white fruit. The black fruits are the most intensely flavored, while the pale whites have a more delicate taste.

These cold-hardy plants begin growth in very early spring. They flower and fruit on wood that is one or more years old. Each bush can continue to yield over a period of 15-20 years. When deciding how many bushes to plant, remember that currants can be prolific producers. Five-year-old black currant bushes often yield 10 lb. or more of fruit per bush; red and white types yield more than 15 lb. Currants are mostly self-fertile, but many cultivars benefit from cross-pollination, so it's wise to plant several different cultivars if you have room. Zones 3-5.

Types: Currants represent several species and hybrids of *Ribes*. Black currants are *R. nigrum* (European black currant), *R. americanum* (American black currant) and *R. odoratum* (buffalo currant). Black currants are commercially important for preserves, juices, wine making, and fresh eating. Red and white currants were developed from *R. rubrum* (red currant), *R. sativum* (common currant), *R. petraeum*, and their hybrids. Red currants are popular for making intensely colored and flavored jellies and juices.

Planting: Choose a protected site with full sun if possible. Currants do well in partial shade, but the fruit will be more acidic. Moist but well-drained loamy soil is ideal; clay soils loosened with organic matter are also good. Avoid poorly drained soils and frost pockets.

Plant red, white, and buffalo currants with the topmost root 1" below the surface; other black currants should be 3"-4" deeper than they grew in the nursery. Conditions permitting, plant currants from November to early March; early fall planting is best. Black currants need 8' all around them. Space bushes of other currants 5'-6' apart in rows at least 6' apart. Rows should run north to south when possible, to allow maximum sunlight to reach each plant.

Care: Currants are shallow-rooted plants, so avoid cultivation after planting. Maintain a 2"-3" mulch layer to hold in moisture and smother weeds; hand-pull any that do emerge. Currants benefit from regular applications of high-nitrogen organic fertilizer. Keep the soil evenly moist; water deeply in dry weather.

Pruning: For red and white currants, the usual form is an open, cup-shaped bush on a 6' main stem. See "Pruning Red Currants" on the opposite page for more information on training the bush form. Another pruning style is vertical cordons (upright, single-stemmed plants spaced 2' apart), ideal for small gardens. Establish cordons by training a single vertical stem up a 6' stake. At planting, remove all but one of the leaders; cut back the remaining stem by half and its side branches to a few buds. Keep mature cordons at their desired height by summer-pruning the leader to one bud.

Black currants are grown as multi-stemmed bushes. Cut each cane back to only two buds above the soil at planting time. In the years after planting, prune back leaders to ½ or ⅓ of their length and laterals to 1-3 buds. After the second or third year, also cut a few of the oldest stems to the ground each year to encourage vigorous new growth.

Problems: Imported currantworms have green caterpillarlike larvae that feed on leaf edges. Control by handpicking; for severe infestations, apply pyrethrins. Gooseberry fruitworm attacks both currants and gooseberries. Larvae burrow into the fruit just before it ripens, eat the pulp, and then spin a silken webbing joining fruits and leaves. Destroy affected fruit; dust with rotenone when you find the first webbing. Currant borers cause stems to wilt suddenly; prune off affected stems below the entrance hole, and burn them or place them in sealed containers for disposal with household trash.

Diseases include American gooseberry mildew, which causes white powdery patches on leaves and shoots. Control by pruning shoot tips back by ⅓ and spraying the plant with sulfur fungicide or baking soda. Leaf spot causes brown patches on leaves, with early defoliation. Apply a sulfur- or copper-based spray for control.

A major concern when growing currants is white pine blister rust. This disease needs both a species of *Ribes* and a white or other five-needled pine to complete its life cycle. While it has little effect on *Ribes* species, it causes fatal cankers on pine trees. In the early 1920s, the federal government established a ban on growing and selling any *Ribes* species. In the 1960s, the federal restrictions were removed as white pines became less important as timber trees. Some areas, though, still have state restrictions, so contact your Cooperative Extension Service for information on your locality's status. If you have white pines on your property, site *Ribes* species at least 200′ away from the trees, or choose rust-resistant cultivars.

Harvesting: Early cultivars are ready for picking in mid-June; later ones, especially some black currants, ripen into September. Pull off entire fruit clusters, rather than the individual fruits. Ripe fruit will stay on the plant for several

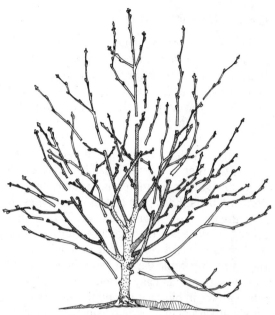

Pruning red currants. Cut back leaders by half and laterals to 1–3 buds at planting and thereafter every fall. Make cuts just above a downward- and outward-facing bud; remove all suckers from the bottom 6″ of the stem.

days. Once picked, though, they don't keep well, so use them as soon as possible.

Although you can eat the fruit fresh when it's fully ripe, currants are most often used in preserves, jellies, and juices. Fruit from mild, sweet black currants also makes excellent wine. White currants are best eaten fresh or canned whole in light syrup. All currants freeze well.

Best cultivars: Black currant: 'Ben Sarek', dwarf, very heavy bearing; 'Consort', rust-resistant; 'Crandal', scented flowers; 'Laxton's Giant', very large, sweet fruit; 'Silvergeiter's Black', great for wine; 'Strata', sweet fruits.

Red currant: 'Jonkheer van Tets', excellent fresh or preserved; 'Red Lake'; 'Malling Redstart', heavy-bearing.

White currant: 'White Versailles', excellent for a variety of uses; 'White Imperial', good flavor, reliable producer. ❖

Cut Flower Gardening

With the cost of cut flowers these days, it makes more sense than ever to grow your own. With your own cutting garden, you can grow the flowers you love in the colors you want, and make sure you have a selection of flowers for cutting year-round.

There are two ways you can grow flowers for cutting: with all the plants of each species grown together in rows or raised beds, as in a vegetable garden, or mixed in ornamental borders and beds. Each plan has its advantages. If you already grow vegetables, you'll find that adding cut flowers to the vegetable garden makes it glow with vivid colors. You probably never thought a vegetable garden could be so pretty! Cut flowers are as easy to tend as vegetables when grown in blocks, too, and it's easy to compare cultivars planted side by side to see which you like better or which grow better for you.

If you want to grow cut flowers in an ornamental garden, interplant annuals and perennials, including ornamental grasses, with bulbs, roses, and herbs to create spectacular mixed beds and borders. To make sure the flowers you cut won't leave holes in your border, grow at least three plants of each perennial and six or seven of each annual. When you design mixed flower beds and borders, group the plants of one species or cultivar in masses for the most striking visual effect.

Use the rest of your landscape to supplement your cutting garden. Grow roses with other shrubs in a foundation planting, as a border or screen at the edge of the property, or around a deck or patio. Train vines on arbors, trellises, or fences to supply graceful stems for arrangements. Trees and shrubs provide foliage, flowers, berries, and branches for cutting. You can turn a shady spot into a lovely garden of ferns and hostas that will supply foliage for arrangements.

When you're deciding which plants to include in your garden, remember to grow a variety of plant shapes, so you'll always have the right shapes for any arrangement. Satisfying arrangements generally have three primary elements: tall, spiky flowers and foliage for line; large, flat, round flowers and foliage for focal points or mass; and small, airy flowers and foliage for fillers. To learn how to prepare cut flowers and make arrangements, see the Flower Arranging entry.

Choose plants that bloom for a long period and hold up well as cut flowers. Many annuals bloom almost nonstop during the summer; most perennials flower for a week to well over a month. Make sure you grow flowers that bloom at different seasons to have bouquets indoors throughout the year. Other important considerations are color, height, and fragrance.

Think first about color when selecting the flowers you'll grow. The most effective arrangements coordinate with the colors in your home—you wouldn't want orange flowers in a pink room. If one color predominates in the house, grow flowers that complement that color.

Height also matters when choosing plants for cutting. For flower arrangements, it is easier to use longer stems. New cultivars of annuals and perennials frequently are shorter, more compact-growing plants. As you choose plants, note the mature or blooming height.

Growing fragrant flowers makes both gardening and flower arranging more pleasurable. Scented flowers that are good for cutting include hyacinths, lilies, lilies-of-the-valley, peonies, and phlox. Nicotiana (*Nicotiana* spp.), pinks (*Dianthus* spp.), stocks (*Matthiola* spp.), sweet peas (*Lathyrus odoratus*), and tuberoses (*Polianthes tuberosa*) are also good choices. Don't overlook trees and shrubs like lilacs, magnolias, and roses.

Most herb foliage, flowers, and seed heads provide fragrance as well as form to arrangements. Consider angelica, artemisia, basil, comfrey, costmary, dill, fennel, hyssop, lavender, lemon balm, lemon verbena, mint, parsley, rosemary, rue, sage, savory, sweet cicely, and sweet woodruff for cut flowers and foliage.

Among the best hardy bulbs for cutting are daffodils, hyacinths, irises, lilies, tulips, alliums

BEST FLOWERS FOR CUTTING

Annuals and perennials can provide months of cut flowers. Most cutting-garden flowers prefer full sun with average soil and moisture. Plant different colors and shapes, so you'll have a variety of flowers to work with. Flower shapes can be grouped by their use in arrangements: linear, for line and height; round, for mass or a focal point; and filler, to unify and add an airy look. Plant names are followed by flower shape and color.

ANNUALS

Antirrhinum majus (snapdragon): linear; white, pink, red, orange, yellow
Calendula officinalis (pot marigold): round; yellow, orange
Callistephus chinensis (China aster): round; white, yellow, pink, red, blue
Coreopsis tinctoria (calliopsis): round; yellow, red
Cosmos spp. (cosmos): round; white, pink, red, yellow
Limonium sinuatum (statice): filler; white, pink, purple-blue, yellow
Matthiola incana (stock): linear; white, pink, rose, lavender
Zinnia elegans (zinnia): round; white, pink, red, yellow, orange

PERENNIALS

Achillea spp. (yarrows): round; yellow, pink, white
Artemisia spp. (artemisias): filler, linear; silver gray
Aster spp. (asters): round; white, pink, red, lavender, blue
Campanula spp. (bellflowers): round, linear; white, pink, blue
Chrysanthemum spp. (chrysanthemums): round; white, pink, red, orange, yellow
Delphinium spp. (delphiniums): linear; white, blue, purple
Dianthus spp. (pinks): round; white, pink
Echinacea purpurea (purple coneflower): round; mauve, white
Echinops spp. (globe thistles): round; blue
Gaillardia spp. (blanket flowers): round; yellow, red, orange
Gypsophila paniculata (baby's-breath): filler; white
Hesperis matronalis (sweet rocket): round; white, purple
Liatris spp. (gayfeathers): linear; white, purplish pink
Phlox spp. (phlox): round; white, pink, red, orange, lavender
Rudbeckia spp. (coneflowers): round; yellow
Salvia spp. (sages): linear; purple-blue

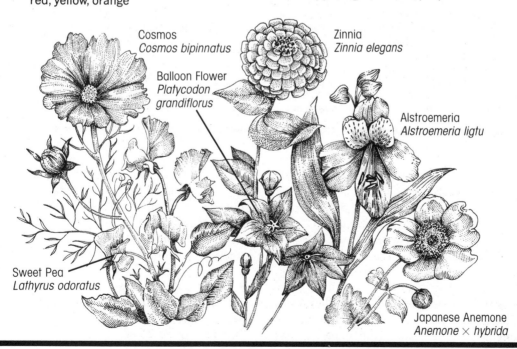

Cosmos
Cosmos bipinnatus

Zinnia
Zinnia elegans

Balloon Flower
Platycodon grandiflorus

Alstroemeria
Alstroemeria ligtu

Sweet Pea
Lathyrus odoratus

Japanese Anemone
Anemone × hybrida

FOLIAGE FOR CUTTING

Don't overlook foliage when you're out cutting flowers for arrangements. Adding beautifully colored, textured, shaped, or variegated foliage can integrate the different shapes and colors of your flowers and give an arrangement added charm and sophistication.

Herbs are a great choice for arrangements. Their delightfully scented leaves add a special dimension to a vase of flowers. Scented geraniums (*Pelargonium* spp.) come in a variety of scents and leaf patterns. The silvery foliage of artemisias blends beautifully into any arrangement. Try pungent, sprucelike rosemary, cool blue rue (*Ruta graveolens*), or fuzzy gray lavender cotton (*Santolina chamaecyparissus*) in your next arrangement.

Many perennials produce interesting foliage along with their flowers. Low-growing lady's-mantle (*Alchemilla mollis*) bears beautifully scalloped, pleated leaves. Ligularias (*Ligularia* spp.) form clumps of bold heart-shaped foliage. For a soft, silver gray leaf, choose lamb's-ears (*Stachys byzantina*).

Shade-loving plants such as ferns, hostas, pachysandra, and bergenias (*Bergenia* spp.) are easy to grow and offer a range of texture and leaf shapes. In addition, some hostas and pachysandras have variegated foliage, which can add color and drama to any arrangement.

Don't neglect your trees and shrubs when scouting for foliage to enhance arrangements. Evergreens such as boxwoods (*Buxus* spp.), false cypresses (*Chamaecyparis* spp.),

Feature foliage in arrangements. Many types of foliage are good counterpoints for flowers in an arrangement. Here, leaves of artemisias, hostas, rue (*Ruta graveolens*), and scented geraniums (*Pelargonium* spp.) add contrasting shapes and subtle fragrance to the carnations.

spruces (*Picea* spp.), yews (*Taxus* spp.), and hemlocks (*Tsuga* spp.) supply attractive foliage all year. Hollies (*Ilex* spp.) and Japanese aucubas (*Aucuba japonica*) have evergreen foliage and colorful berries, while cherry-laurels (*Prunus laurocerasus*) and magnolias (*Magnolia* spp.) produce wonderfully fragrant flowers as well as lustrous foliage.

(*Allium* spp.), and grape hyacinths (*Muscari* spp.). Tender bulbs that make great cut flowers include caladiums, dahlias, gladioli, tuberous begonias, agapanthus (*Agapanthus* spp.), and montbretias (*Crocosmia* spp.)

To grow cut flowers successfully, choose the planting site carefully and prepare the soil well. Most of your plants will thrive if you site your cutting garden where they'll get well-drained, humus-rich soil and full sun. Check the cultural requirements of the plants you want to grow;

group plants with similar needs together.

Give your plants the care they need: adequate watering and fertilizing, diligent weeding and deadheading (removal of faded flowers), and winter protection and pest control when necessary. An organic mulch, such as compost or shredded leaves, conserves moisture, inhibits weeds, and keeps flowers and leaves clean and mud-free. Commonsense care and careful plant selection will give you a constant supply of beautiful cut flowers all season. ❖

Cuttings

Plants have the amazing capacity to regenerate from small pieces of tissue called cuttings. These small portions of stems, leaves, or roots will form new roots and shoots if given the right treatment.

Taking cuttings is the most common way to propagate many types of ornamental plants. Because raising plants from cuttings is an asexual type of reproduction, the new plants will look exactly like the parent.

Materials and Methods

There are several ways to make cuttings, but all types of cuttings need a medium to support them while they grow roots and some type of structure to protect them during the rooting period. It's also important to observe good sanitation to minimize disease problems.

Media: The best media for taking cuttings are moisture-retentive but well drained and free of insects, diseases, and weed seeds. Commonly used media are sand, perlite, vermiculite, and peat moss. No one medium or combination is ideal for all plants, but an equal mixture of peat and sand or perlite is useful in most situations. Soil is not a good propagation medium, especially in containers. Unlike the other materials, soil is not sterile and can compact severely from frequent waterings. Only very hardy cuttings are planted directly into soil.

Some plants, such as African violets, coleus, and willows (*Salix* spp.), will root directly in water. This method is fun to try, but if you want to save the cutting, plant it in potting soil while the roots are still small. Plants may have difficulty adapting to soil if their roots are in water too long.

Structures: Cuttings need a protected, high-humidity environment while they root. Cuttings don't have roots to take up water, but they still lose moisture through their leaves. By keeping the surrounding air moist, you minimize water loss and help cuttings survive until they can support themselves.

On a small scale, plastic bags are great for protecting cuttings. Support the bag so plastic does not rest on the cuttings and encourage rot. Provide ventilation by occasionally opening the bag for an hour or two. In most cases, you won't have to add water until the cuttings form roots. To harden off rooted cuttings, gradually open the bag for longer periods.

For large numbers of cuttings, a cold frame or greenhouse is more practical. You can set pots of cuttings on the soil or plant directly in the soil inside a cold frame. Close the frame and cover the glass with shading material, such as cheesecloth or wooden laths (like snow fencing or lattice); gradually remove the shading when roots form. Ventilate and harden off by gradually opening the cold frame for longer periods.

Sanitation: Use a clean, sharp tool (such as a knife or scissor-type pruning shears) to collect and prepare cuttings. Crushed plant tissue is an invitation to rot. Never propagate from diseased or insect-infested plants. Plant cuttings in fresh, sterile propagation mix that is stored in closed containers. Pots and propagation areas should be scrubbed clean and, if possible, sanitized by rinsing with a 10 percent bleach solu-

---

ROOTING HORMONES

Rooting hormones—synthetic versions of natural plant hormones—can encourage root formation on stem cuttings of difficult plants and increase the number of roots on others. Commercial rooting hormones are usually available in garden centers in powder form; be aware that some products contain chemical fungicides. Product labels will suggest uses, or experiment with treated and untreated cuttings.

A solution known as *willow water* can also encourage rooting. Cut willow stems into 1'' pieces and place them in a small container; add about 2'' of water, cover, and let stand for 24 hours. Remove the stems, insert cuttings, and let them soak overnight before planting.

tion (1 part bleach to 9 parts water). Check plants often during rooting and remove any fallen leaves or dead cuttings. Don't overwater; do provide adequate ventilation.

Softwood Stem Cuttings

Take softwood cuttings from succulent spring growth of woody plants such as azaleas and magnolias. Treat stem cuttings of herbaceous plants, including geraniums and impatiens, like softwood cuttings. Because these cuttings are from young tissue, they form roots easily but need high humidity to prevent wilting.

Season: Take softwood cuttings from April through June, when new leaves are fully expanded but stems are still soft. Take houseplant cuttings anytime.

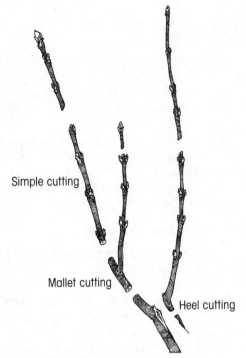

Simple cutting

Mallet cutting

Heel cutting

Hardwood cuttings. Take simple cuttings from the midsections of branches. For difficult-to-root plants, take a heel or mallet cutting, each with a bit of older wood at the base.

Getting started: Water the parent plant a day or two before taking cuttings. Fill a container with moist propagation mix.

Method: Collect cuttings in the morning or on cloudy, cool days, and keep them moist until planting. Cuttings should be 3"-6" long; they usually include a terminal bud. Remove leaves from the lower half of the stem, and apply rooting hormone if desired. Insert the cutting to about ⅓ its length, firm the medium with your fingers, and water to settle the cutting. Enclose the container in plastic, or place it under a mist system in a cold frame or greenhouse.

Aftercare: Ventilate plants; water as needed to keep the medium moist but not wet. Softwood and herbaceous cuttings root quickly, often in 2-4 weeks. When roots appear, harden off the cuttings and plant in the garden or in a pot.

Softwood and herbaceous cuttings. Take these cuttings from stems that snap when bent. Remove the cutting just below a node; discard the stem piece left on the parent down to the uppermost node.

Hardwood Stem Cuttings

Take hardwood cuttings from woody plants during their dormant period. Hardwood cuttings don't require high-humidity conditions. This method is effective for some types of woody plants and vines, including grapes, currants, willows, and some roses.

Season: Take cuttings after leaf fall and before new growth begins in spring. Mid-autumn is often the best time to collect and plant cuttings, so they can form roots before the buds begin to grow.

Getting started: For potted cuttings, fill the container with moist propagation mix. If you are planting cuttings outdoors or into a cold frame, prepare a deep, well-drained nursery bed.

Method: Collect 4''-8'' cuttings from vigorous, one-year-old wood, a few inches below the terminal bud. Make a straight cut at the top, slightly above a bud, and a sloping cut at the base, slightly below a bud. Stick cuttings 2''-4'' apart in the medium, with the top bud about 1'' above the surface. Be sure the cuttings point upward: double-check that you've stuck the ends with sloping cuts into the medium. Plant fall cuttings soon after they are taken, or store them upside down in moist peat moss or perlite and plant right-side up in spring. Cover fall-planted cuttings with 6''-8'' of mulch to prevent frost heaving; remove mulch in spring. Plant late-winter cuttings directly into pots or soil.

Aftercare: Keep cuttings moist. They usually root rapidly in spring, but it is best to leave them at least until fall. Transplant rooted cuttings to the garden or into pots.

Evergreen Cuttings

Broad-leaved and needled evergreens are often propagated by stem cuttings. Try this method on plants such as arborvitae, hollies, and boxwood.

Season: Collect broad-leaved cuttings in late summer. Take needled cuttings in fall or

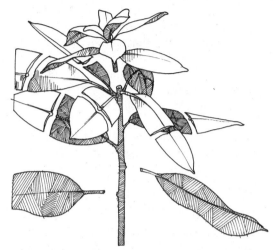

Broad-leaved evergreen cuttings. To save space in flats, you can remove up to half of the leaves from a cutting. Some broad-leaved evergreen cuttings benefit from wounding. Use a sharp knife to make a shallow 1'' cut at the stem base.

winter; yew and juniper cuttings should have had some frost.

Getting started: Fill a container with moist propagation mix, or prepare a well-drained bed in the base of a cold frame.

Method: Collect 4''-6'' tip cuttings in the proper season. Some cuttings benefit from a piece of older wood—a heel—left at the base of the stem. To take a heel, pull sharply downward on the base of a sideshoot as you remove it from the parent plant; trim the excess with a knife.

Wounding is another way to encourage the rooting of difficult plants. Create a wound by cutting a shallow sliver on the side of the cutting near the base. This process stimulates cell division and enhances water uptake but also increases the chance of disease problems.

Before planting, remove lower leaves and sideshoots. To save space with large broad-leaved cuttings, cut each remaining leaf in half. Apply rooting hormone if desired. Plant cuttings to about ⅓ of their length, firm the soil, and water to settle the cuttings. Place potted cuttings indoors in a plastic bag or in a greenhouse; alternately, set pots in a cold frame, or plant directly into the frame.

Aftercare: Ventilate and water if necessary. Once roots appear, gradually harden off the cuttings. The new plants are best left in place until autumn and then planted in the garden or in a pot.

Leaf Cuttings

Some plants with thick or fleshy leaves can produce roots and shoots directly from leaf pieces. This is a popular method for houseplants such as African violets and snake plants.

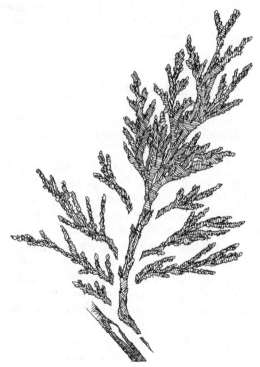

Needled evergreen cuttings. Leaving a small bit of the main stem—called a heel—at the base of the cutting stem enhances rooting of needled evergreen cuttings.

PROPAGATION POINTERS

Try these tips for best success with cuttings:

● Plant large numbers of cuttings in wooden or plastic flats; use pots for small quantities.
● Cuttings are usually 4″–6″ long, but they can be shorter if the stock plant is small; get at least two nodes (leaf-stem joints). Nonflowering shoots are best. Remove flowers and flower buds from unrooted cuttings.
● Soil warmth encourages root formation. Place containers of cuttings on a propagation mat, a board over a radiator, or the top of your refrigerator.
● Don't tug on cuttings—check the bottom of the container to see if roots are visible.
● Be adventurous! Try different techniques on a range of plants to see what works for you. Label your experiments and record results for future reference.

Season: Take cuttings any time of year. Use healthy, young but fully expanded leaves.

Getting started: Thoroughly water the parent plant a day or so before collecting cuttings. Fill a container with moist propagation medium.

Method: Cut snake plant and streptocarpus leaves into 2″ long pieces. Plant the pieces rightside up, about 1″ deep. Peperomias and African violets are reproduced by leaf-petiole cuttings. Detach a leaf along with 1½″-2″ of its petiole. Plant vertically or at a slight angle, so the petiole is buried up to the leaf blade. After planting, water the cuttings to settle them in the soil.

Aftercare: If excessive condensation occurs, ventilate the cuttings. When new leaves appear, usually in 6-8 weeks, gradually harden them off. Sever plantlets from the parent leaf if it has not already withered away; transfer rooted plants to pots. ❖

Dahlia

Dahlia. Summer- and fall-blooming tender perennials.

Description: Dahlia flowers come in many forms, sizes, and colors, in solids and mixes, often brushed or speckled. Single flowers have one row of petals around a yellow center. Semidoubles have a few rows of petals around the center. The anemone form resembles a single, but also has a tuft of petals around the center; collarettes have a collar of petals instead of a tuft. Cactus dahlias are double flowers with tubular, almost pointy petals. Formal decoratives are double flowers with broad petals in a neat pattern, while informal decoratives are doubles that look less neat, and often have twisted petals. Ball dahlias have double, ball-shaped flowers with cupped petals turned toward the center; pompons are like balls, but are less than 2" wide.

Most dahlias grow 2'-6' tall and may spread almost as wide, bearing thick bamboolike stems and lush green or dark purple-red foliage resembling giant celery leaves. The foliage may be only 3"-4" long or it may exceed 1½'. Dahlias are hardy in Zones 8-11 if soil is well drained and not allowed to freeze; otherwise lift them for winter.

How to grow: You can start dahlias indoors before planting them out, treating them like cala-

diums (see the Caladium entry), or plant them directly into the open ground after it has warmed up. After all danger of frost is past, plant them in full sun and deep, fertile, moist but well-drained soil enriched with plenty of organic matter. Whether plants are already in leaf or not yet growing, set the roots horizontally 3"-6" below the soil surface. If already started, carefully break off the lowest leaves to encourage additional roots to form. Don't cover unsprouted tuberous roots completely at planting time—gradually fill in the holes as the plants grow. After setting out each plant, immediately drive a sturdy stake 6" from the growing point, especially for tall cultivars. Don't wait until the plants are up and growing, or you may destroy the tuberous roots. Mulch thickly with pine needles, straw, or compost after plants are at least 6" tall and the soil is warm. Water often and fertilize liberally throughout summer with fish emulsion, manure tea, bonemeal, or other fertilizers not excessively high in nitrogen. For instructions on making manure tea, see the Manure entry.

When plants are about 6"-10" tall, pinch out the center to promote branching and more flowers. You can pinch them again after they put out another 6" of growth. Tie the shoots to the stake as they grow long enough. When the flower buds reach the size of a pea, remove the side buds to allow the center one to grow as large as

Dahlia flower forms. Showy dahlias range in size from 1″ to well over 1′ and are available in all colors except blue and green. Be sure to note flower form when you order by mail, so you won't be surprised at bloom time.

possible for its type, or leave the side buds on for more but smaller flowers.

Handpick slugs and snails when the plants are small, and apply soap sprays to control spider mites in summer. Corn stem borers may attack dahlias, so be on the lookout for wilting shoots and cut them back until you find the borer. Cucumber beetles and grasshoppers relish the flowers; control with pyrethrins. To help keep viruses from spreading, destroy immediately any plants that produce yellow-streaked, twisted leaves or stunted plants.

After frost blackens the plants, cut them back to a few inches above ground level, lift the clumps from the ground, and store them on their sides while waiting for the soil on the tubers to dry. Label them with their cultivar names, using an indelible pen or attachable tag. Store as entire clumps with the soil remaining on them, or remove the soil and store the root clumps in barely moist peat or vermiculite in a cool (45°-50°F) spot, sprinkling a little water on the peat or vermiculite to plump up withered tuberous roots. Cut the clumps up in spring, making sure each piece has a small pinkish "eye" attached to it.

Landscape uses: Many of the shorter and medium-height dahlias make excellent additions to the late-summer and fall border. Taller dahlias can temporarily screen out an unpleasant view. They're also colorful in front of a tall hedge (leave a few feet between the hedge and the dahlias). Or grow dahlias in a bed by themselves. ❖

DAHLIAS FROM SEED

Some dahlias grow and bloom heavily the first year from seed. They bear semi-double to double, 2″–3″ flowers in white, pink, red, yellow, and orange on plants about 1′ tall, often with dark reddish leaves. Sow in late winter for summer bloom, or sow directly after frost for later bloom. Although not as glorious as most of their taller relatives, these dahlias are much easier to grow. Give them the same soil conditions you would any dahlia. Grow as annuals or store tuberous roots of your favorites for next year. All do well in borders, beds, and pots. Try red-leaved 'Redskin' with 3″ flowers, green-leaved 'Rigoletto' with slightly smaller flowers, or the unusual single 'Piccolo' with 2½″ blooms. All three come in a range of colors.

Daphne

Daphne. Evergreen or semi-evergreen, winter- or spring-blooming shrubs.

Description: *Daphne × burkwoodii,* Burkwood daphne, grows 2'-5' with a spreading habit; blue-green leaves are semi-evergreen in the South and deciduous in the North. Pink buds open to fragrant, creamy white flowers. Zones 4-7.

D. odora, winter daphne, is low and spreading (2'-5'), with very fragrant rosy purple flowers and glossy evergreen foliage. Zones 6-8.

How to grow: Provide partial shade, even moisture, a deep mulch, and well-drained gravelly or sandy soil. Don't overfeed daphnes. Plant in fall or spring. (In Zone 8, plant winter daphne in fall or winter.)

Landscape uses: Daphne makes a stunning focal point, foundation, or rock garden plant. Note that daphnes are poisonous.

Best cultivars: *Daphne × burkwoodii* 'Carol Mackie' has pink flowers and cream-edged leaves. ❖

Delphinium

Delphinium. Summer- and repeat-blooming perennials.

Description: *Delphinium × elatum,* hybrid delphiniums, bear 2"-3" single, starlike or semi-double, rounded flowers in white, pink, lavender, blue, purple, and combinations on dense spikes that rise 2'-8' above maplelike leaves on long stems. *D. × belladonna,* belladonna delphiniums, have 1½"-2" single blooms in white and blue, borne loosely on numerous spikes above smaller leaves; plants grow 3'-4'. Zones 3-7.

How to grow: Set out plants or rooted cuttings in spring; sow seeds in winter for summer bloom or in midsummer for bloom next year. Plant in a sunny site in fertile, humus-rich, moist but well-drained soil. Delphiniums prefer regions with cool summers; if you have hot summers, try them in a partly shady, moist area.

Feed and water hybrid delphinium cultivars regularly. They'll also need staking. Deadhead, water, and fertilize all cultivars immediately after flowering to promote rebloom. Wide spacing increases air circulation, reducing disease problems. Hose off spider mites regularly if they appear.

Landscape uses: Use tall cultivars as exclamation points in borders, near buildings and hedges, or in beds alone. Mass shorter cultivars in borders or a cutting garden. Delphiniums are ideal for cottage gardens.

Best cultivars: *D. × elatum:* 5'-7' 'Pacific Giant' series (also known as the 'Round Table' series), dubbed with Arthurian names such as 'Galahad' and 'Guinevere', bloom in the entire color range. *D. × belladonna:* light blue 'Belladonna'; darker 'Bellamosa'; white 'Casa Blanca'. The 'Connecticut Yankee' series bears numerous dense spikes on 2½', bushy plants in the entire color range. ❖

Deutzia

Deutzia. Deciduous spring-blooming shrubs.

Description: *Deutzia gracilis,* slender deutzia, is a broad, mounding plant (2'-5') with arching branches, lance-shaped leaves, and clusters of white flowers in late spring. Zones 5-8.

D. × lemoinei, lemoine deutzia, a *gracilis* hybrid, has showier white flowers. Zones 4-8.

D. scabra, fuzzy deutzia, has an upright, fountainlike form and grows 5'-8' tall. The medium green leaves are covered with small tufts of hair. White or pink flower clusters appear in late spring or early summer. Zones 6-8.

How to grow: Provide well-drained soil, even moisture, and full sun. Plant in fall or spring north of Zone 8, fall or winter in Zone 8. Prune deutzias after flowering.

Landscape uses: Use as a focal point, in borders, or in foundation plantings. ❖

Dianthus

Pinks, carnations. Spring- and summer-blooming perennials.

Description: Cheerful pinks offer a variety of single to double flowers in shades of white, pink, and red, often banded and richly clove-scented, on thin stems above tufted or matlike grassy leaves. *Dianthus* × *allwoodii,* Allwood pinks, produce mostly double 1"-2" blooms in summer, 12"-15" above attractive gray-green mounds of foliage. Zones 4-8.

D. deltoides, maiden pinks, bear masses of ¾" flowers 6"-12" above spreading mats of leaves for several weeks in summer. Zones 3-8.

D. gratianopolitanus, cheddar pinks, bear ½"-¾" flowers up to 1' above small mounds of narrow, gray-green leaves in spring and sporadically through the season. Zones 3-9.

D. caryophyllus, florist's carnations, need greenhouse conditions and are not suitable for the garden.

How to grow: Plant or divide in spring or fall in a sunny spot with average to low fertility and well-drained, slightly alkaline soil. Although maiden pinks tolerate very light shade, anything less than full sun usually results in weak, floppy stems and dead central leaves. Maiden and cheddar pinks will rebloom if promptly deadheaded. To avoid crown rot disease, don't plant pinks in poorly drained soil.

Landscape uses: Perfect for edgings and in rock and cottage gardens, pinks are also delightful in groups in the front of borders or filling gaps in stone paths. Grow maiden pinks as a groundcover; try the tiny ones in shallow pots. Cheddar pinks make good groundcovers, too. Allwood pinks make good cut flowers.

Best cultivars: *D.* × *allwoodii:* 'Aqua', white; 'Doris', salmon pink; 'Ian', red; and the single-flowered 6"-10" 'Alpinus' mix in pink and red shades, hardy to Zone 3. *D. deltoides:* 'Albus', white; 'Brilliant', bright red. *D. gratianapolitanus:* tiny pink 'Petite', to 4"; 'Spotti', red and white; 'Tiny Rubies', deep pink, to 6". ❖

Dicentra

Bleeding heart. Spring- and recurrent-blooming perennials; wildflowers.

Description: Bleeding hearts bear heart-shaped flowers above mounded leaves. *Dicentra eximia,* fringed bleeding heart, blooms in late spring and sporadically through the season, with clusters of narrow, ¾" pink flowers on 1'-1½' slender stems. Its blue-green leaves are delicate and ferny, often with a grayish sheen. Zones 3-8.

D. spectabilis, common bleeding heart, blooms in spring. It bears 1½" pink-and-white flowers in rows from gracefully curving stems up to 2' long, above a 2'-3' mass of blue-green leaves. Zones 2-8.

How to grow: Carefully set out bleeding hearts in early spring. Plant either pot-grown specimens or divisions, but handle them with care, since bleeding hearts have brittle roots that are easily damaged and generally resent disturbance. Grow them in partial shade and well-drained, humus-rich soil. Most reseed prolifically where conditions suit them. Water all bleeding hearts during drought. Common bleeding heart tolerates full sun if given plenty of moisture during active growth. It dies back to the ground in summer or even sooner in hot, sunny spots; remove the leaves when they start to turn brown and unsightly.

Landscape uses: Grow fringed bleeding hearts in woodland plantings, shady rock gardens and walls, and even in the shade of larger plants in sunny borders. Common bleeding hearts are one of the best plants for spring borders and combine well with tulips. Grow common bleeding hearts with hostas, ferns, and astilbes to fill in blank spots when the foliage dies in summer, or overplant carefully with annuals.

Best cultivars: *D. eximia:* soft pink 'Boothman's Variety', with blue-green leaves; 'Snowdrift', white flowers. Hybrids of *D. eximia:* deep pink 'Bountiful', with blue-green leaves; near red 'Luxuriant', with green leaves; *D. spectabilis:* 'Pantaloons' has pure white flowers. ❖

Dictamnus

Gas plant. Late-spring-blooming perennials.

Description: *Dictamnus albus,* gas plant, bears 1″ flowers, with white or pink petals and boldly sweeping threadlike stamens. The 1′ flower spikes top the 2′-3′ dense, spreading mound of dark green, sharply lemon-scented compound leaves. Zones 3-8.

How to grow: Plant in spring in a sunny or lightly shaded spot with fertile, well-drained soil. This long-lived plant will take a few years to establish; divide only when necessary.

Landscape uses: Grow as a specimen in a border or as a bold mass. The foliage is attractive all season, blending well with shrubs and as a backdrop for other flowers.

Best cultivars: Plants sold as *D. ruber,* 'Ruber', 'Rubra', and 'Purpureus' are all pink-mauve with darker veins. Try the handsome white form 'Alba'. ❖

Digitalis

Foxglove. Late-spring- to early-summer-blooming biennials and summer-blooming perennials.

Description: *Digitalis purpurea,* common foxglove, is a biennial that carries long spikes of 2″-3″, tubular, open-faced bells in shades of white, pink, and red-violet (usually spotted inside), on 2′-5′ upright, leafy plants. In the first year, young plants form a tight rosette of oblong leaves to 1′ or more; the next spring and early summer the bloom spikes emerge, set with progressively smaller leaves stopping just below the flowers. Zones 4-8.

Perennial *D. grandiflora* (also sold as *D. ambigua*), yellow foxglove, is similar to common foxglove, bearing 2″ yellow flowers marked with brown inside on 2′-3′ open clumps of dark green, narrower, more pointed leaves. Zones 3-8.

D. × *mertonensis,* strawberry foxglove, is a short-lived perennial that offers 2½″ rosy pink blooms patterned with coppery lines on 3′-4′ oval-leaved plants. Zones 4-8.

How to grow: For biennial foxgloves, set out nursery-grown plants in late summer, or start from seeds sown in midsummer. Outdoors, sow in a protected spot away from strong sun and wind, scattering the seed into lightly raked open ground. Or start in flats, lightly pressing the fine seed into the growing medium. Foxgloves grow best in partial shade and average to fertile, moist but well-drained, humus-rich soil. They tolerate full sun farther north if kept moist. Water if the soil is dry, especially in spring. Keep stakes handy, particularly if the plants are growing in windy areas. After the ground freezes, place pine needles, straw, or other light mulch *under* the leafy crowns to help prevent root damage in winter.

After bloom, cut the flower stems off to encourage possible bloom the next year, or remove the entire plant. If you allow some plants to go to seed, foxgloves will self-sow readily and form impressive stands where conditions suit them.

Grow perennial foxgloves in similar conditions, dividing every 2-3 years in spring to keep them vigorous.

Landscape uses: The dramatic vertical spires of foxgloves add height and contrast to more rounded and spreading shapes in a border or cottage garden. Allow them to naturalize in lightly shady, moist woodland settings. Plant in the cutting garden for stunning cut flowers.

Best cultivars: *D. purpurea:* old, reliable 'Shirley' mix bears its flowers on one side of the stem like the species, whereas the 'Excelsior' mix bears spikes set all around with bloom. Both grow to 5′. 'Foxy' mix is an All-America Selections award winner and the only cultivar that blooms the first year from seed. Blooms appear on 3′ bushy plants. For first-year bloom, sow seed indoors in winter and allow 5-6 months from sowing to flowering. Many gardeners prize the 4′-5′ white 'Alba' as a contrast to the colored forms or as a pure stand of unspotted blooms. ❖

Disease

Vigorous, well-nourished plants have a natural ability to resist diseases. Organic gardening practices, such as composting and improving soil organic matter content, tend to keep disease organisms in check by producing stronger plants and by encouraging a wide range of beneficial soil organisms.

You can use simple preventive controls to keep disease problems from developing or to limit their severity. In a few instances, you may have to resort to spraying organically acceptable substances such as copper or sulfur fungicides to control diseases on your plants.

Causes of Disease

Plant diseases are caused by living organisms. Disease-causing microorganisms include fungi, bacteria, viruses and viruslike organisms, and pathogenic nematodes.

In many cases, plants may show symptoms such as yellowing leaves or black spots on fruits that look like disease but aren't caused by living organisms. The cause may be a plant disorder such as salt injury, or a nutrient imbalance such as lack of nitrogen. While technically these are not diseases, it's helpful to consider them as possible causes of problems when you're trying to figure out what's wrong with your plants. Diagnosing problems that have symptoms common to both diseases and disorders can be tricky. "Diagnosing Plant Problems" on page 419 may help you decide whether the symptoms on your plants are due to insects, disease, a plant disorder, or a nutrient imbalance. You can also refer to the Plant Disorders and Plant Nutrition entries for more information about nondisease plant problems.

Identifying Diseases

Identifying specific plant diseases also can be difficult. Fortunately, precise identification isn't always necessary, since many similar diseases respond to the same controls.

When identifying a disease, rule out cultural problems and insect damage first. Review the symptoms of nutrient deficiencies, and consider recent unusual weather patterns and nearby sources of pollution. Inspect the plant carefully, using a magnifying lens to examine suspect areas. Become familiar with the general types of disease and the common disease problems in your area. Plant-disease books often are organized by plant and list the diseases that each can get.

If you are familiar with the types of organisms that cause disease, and some of the common diseases they cause, you will have a good chance of identifying and controlling most prob-

---

Key Words
DISEASE

Pathogen. An organism that causes disease.

Host. A plant or animal that a parasite or pathogen depends on for sustenance.

Fungus. A plant that lacks chlorophyll.

Spore. A one- or many-celled reproductive unit.

Bacteria. A single-celled microorganism that reproduces by simple cell division.

Nematode. A microscopic, unsegmented, threadlike worm; also called an eelworm.

Virus. A group of ultramicroscopic organisms that consist of genetic material in a protein coat.

Parasite. An organism that obtains nourishment from cells of another living organism without contributing anything toward the host organism's survival.

Inoculum. The portion of a pathogen that can be transferred to a susceptible site on a host.

Inoculation. Contact between the inoculum of a disease-causing organism and a host.

Infection. Entry or growth of a disease-causing organism into a host.

lems you encounter. If you run into a problem that you can't identify or control, submit a fresh plant sample to a diagnostic laboratory or your local extension office for identification.

Types of Pathogens

There are four major types of microorganisms that cause plant diseases: fungi, bacteria, viruses, and nematodes.

Fungi: Fungi are primitive plants that lack chlorophyll, the pigment that allows green plants to convert sunlight and air into food. Fungi obtain nutrients by inserting special rootlike organs called haustoria into host plants or dead organic matter. Most fungi can be seen with the naked eye at some point in their life cycle. Often the spore-producing structures are visible as dots on discolored areas. These spore-producing structures are one of the best ways to distinguish fungal diseases from other plant problems.

Many fungi live on and decompose dead organic materials. These beneficial fungi are an important ally in the organic garden.

Parasitic fungi, on the other hand, are a leading cause of plant disease. Most disease-causing fungi live on a host plant, soil, and organic matter at various times during their life cycle. Some attack only one species of plants, while others attack a wide array of plants.

Fungi produce tiny spores that are spread by wind, water, insects, and gardeners. Spores germinate to form mycelia—the body of the fungus. Mycelia rarely survive winter, but spores easily survive from season to season.

Bacteria: You need a microscope to see bacteria, but the disease symptoms they cause in plants are easy to see with the naked eye.

Most bacteria break down dead organic matter and are considered to be beneficial. A few, however, cause plant diseases. Bacteria usually reproduce by splitting in half. Bacteria spread via wind, water, insects, garden tools, and gardeners' hands. Bacterial diseases are more diffi-

cult to control than fungal diseases are.

Nematodes: Nematodes swim freely in the film of moisture surrounding soil particles and plant roots. A few types are barely visible to the naked eye. Many nematodes do not cause plant diseases and are important members of the soil community. In fact, beneficial nematodes often prey on the nematodes that attack plants.

Parasitic nematodes can be very destructive. They lay eggs that hatch into tiny larvae. Larvae molt several times before maturing to adults. Nematodes puncture plant cell walls, inject saliva, and suck out the cell's contents. Some species move from plant to plant to feed; others attach themselves permanently to one root. They can travel short distances on their own but are spread through the garden by water and on tools or gardeners' hands.

Viruses: Viruses are so small, they're difficult to see even with a microscope. Viruses are not complete cells and must be inside living cells of a host in order to reproduce. Viruses are transmitted by vegetative propagation, in seeds and pollen, and on tools and gardeners' hands. Viruses are also transmitted by aphids and other insects, mites, nematodes, and parasitic plants.

Disease Development

Microorganisms that cause plant disease are widespread. There may be hundreds of species of disease organisms in your garden soil or living in weeds in and around your yard.

Disease-causing organisms can be carried by the wind to host plants or splashed up from the soil by raindrops. Insects carry disease organisms from plant to plant. And all too often, the gardener spreads disease with his hands or tools when working in the garden.

The presence of disease-causing organisms doesn't always mean a plant will develop disease. Untold millions of potential diseases never develop because conditions aren't favorable for their development.

Plant defenses: Plants have many physical defenses that help protect them from infection. Leaves have a waxy coating called the cuticle that prevents them from staying wet, making it hard for disease-causing organisms to survive. The leaf cuticle may also prevent spore germination and slow the penetration of disease-causing organisms. Leaf hairs trap spores and hold them away from the surface of the leaf. Some leaf hairs actually secrete sticky substances that help catch disease organisms, and insects that spread them, or chemicals that prevent spores from germinating.

Plants may react to attack by walling off the infected area in order to stop further invasion and the spread of pathogen toxins. Some plants respond to infection by forming a corky layer of tissue around it. Other plants may respond by sealing off the diseased part, which then dies along with the disease organisms.

Plants also have a wide variety of natural chemical defenses, some of which are present all the time and some of which are turned on when disease-causing organisms are present. These natural defense mechanisms are one factor plant breeders select for in developing disease-resistant cultivars.

Infection: Infection occurs when the disease-causing organism makes contact with susceptible tissues of the host and begins drawing nutrients from them. The pathogen grows and reproduces inside or on the host plant, and disease symptoms appear.

Overwintering: Disease-causing organisms have many ways of surviving the winter or other unfavorable seasons. They may spend the winter inside insects, on tools in the gardening shed, in infected plant debris, seeds, or plant tissue, or in the soil. Many have specialized structures that resist environmental extremes.

Environmental Influences

Plants are more prone to disease problems when conditions are not optimum for the plant. Just as humans are more prone to getting sick when they are stressed, plants that don't get enough water or nutrients are more likely to develop disease problems. Be on the lookout for factors such as these that may leave your plants open to disease.

Moisture stress: Plants need a steady supply of moisture in the soil for proper growth. Too little and plants wilt. Too much and the roots become stunted from lack of oxygen. Either way, the plants are less able to resist disease-causing organisms.

Nutrient imbalance: Deficiencies can stunt plants and make them less resistant to disease. Too much fertilizer can also increase disease problems. For example, too much nitrogen can stimulate young succulent growth that is susceptible to powdery mildew, rusts, and fire blight. Such growth is also susceptible to cold injury, which in turn can lead to other diseases. Nutrient imbalances also cause symptoms that can be mistaken for disease symptoms.

Lack of beneficial microorganisms: Natural environments are home to a diversity of good and bad microorganisms that tend to regulate their own population growth. The balance, however, can be upset by the improper use of herbicides, insecticides, and fungicides. When the balance is upset, the disease-causing organisms often bounce back faster than the beneficial organisms that normally keep them in control.

Weather: The climate, weather conditions, and exposure also have major effects on plant growth. Cold injury, sunscald, hail, and wind can injure plant tissues, leaving openings for infection. Too much shade can result in weak growth. High humidity and lack of air movement encourages many plant diseases.

Mechanical damage: Lawn mower damage to bark and other types of injuries weaken plants and, more important, provide openings in a plant's protective layers. Many diseases gain access to plants through wounds.

Chemical damage: Air pollutants, road

salt, and herbicide drift are added insults that can weaken plants and leave them open to disease.

Controlling Diseases

You can control most plant diseases in your garden with a combination of cultural and physical control measures. A few may require the judicious use of organically acceptable chemicals for satisfactory control. Remember to use chemical controls only as a last resort, not as a substitute for preventive measures. You'll find detailed discussion of cultural and physical control methods in the Organic Pest Management entry.

Cultural controls: Choose resistant or tolerant cultivars, and make sure all plants and seeds you plant are free of disease. Build up soil organic matter content, and correct nutrient imbalances. Find out what requirements your plants have for best growth, and make sure they get it.

Do an annual fall cleanup. Clean and disinfect tools, hands, and feet regularly, whether you are working with diseased material or not. Stay out of your garden when the leaves are wet because disease organisms spread easily in wet conditions. Avoid damaging plants, as every wound is an opening for disease to enter. Interplant crops and use crop rotation to reduce problems. Some problems can be avoided by planting earlier or later than usual.

Physical controls: Dispose of diseased material throughout the season. Pull up plants or prune off infected portions, and get rid of them by burning, putting them in sealed containers for disposal with household trash, burying them deeply, or putting them in the center of a hot compost pile.

Soil solarization can control soilborne diseases in the garden. You can heat-sterilize seed starting mixes or greenhouse soil, or add compost, which reduces disease problems. Presoaking seeds in a disinfecting solution can clean up contaminated seed. For more information on how to solarize the soil in a garden bed, see "Solarizing Soil" on page 430.

Control insects such as leafhoppers and cucumber beetles that spread disease. Row covers and traps protect plants from insects.

Chemical controls: Sprays of seaweed extract, horsetail tea, and compost tea can help prevent plant diseases. To some extent they work by improving the overall health of the plant. They also have some direct effect on disease-causing organisms. Sprays of baking soda or garlic also offer some disease control. For instructions on making compost tea, see the Composting entry.

Sulfur, copper, and lime can also be used to control diseases. They can damage plants and beneficial organisms and should be used as a last resort. For more detailed information on chemical controls, see the Fungicides entry.

Common Plant Diseases

Diseases are often classified by the type of symptom they cause. If you can identify the symptoms, you may be able to successfully control the disease, even if you don't know the specific pathogen causing the infection.

Blights

When plants suffer from blight, leaves or branches suddenly wither, stop growing, and die. Later, plant parts may rot.

Fire blight: This bacterial disease affects apples, pears, fruit trees, roses, and small fruits. Infected shoots wilt and look as if they had been singed by fire. For further description and controls, see the Pear entry.

Alternaria blight: This fungal blight infects ornamental plants, vegetables, fruit trees, and shade trees worldwide. On tomatoes, potatoes, and peppers, it is called early blight. On leaves, brown to black spots form and enlarge, developing concentric rings like a target. Heavily blighted leaves dry up and die as spots grow together. Lower leaves are usually attacked first. Targetlike, sunken spots will develop on tomato branches and stems. Both fruits and tubers also develop dark, sunken spots. Spores are carried by air currents and are common in dust and air everywhere. They are a common cause of hay fever allergies. Alternaria fungi spend the winter on infected plant parts and debris, or in or on seeds. Control this disease by planting resistant cultivars and soaking seed in a disinfecting solution before planting. Dispose of infected plants and use a three-year rotation.

Phytophthora blight: Lilacs, rhododendrons, azaleas, and holly infected by Phytophthora fungi suffer dieback of shoots and develop stem cankers. Prune to remove infected branches and to increase air movement.

On peppers, potatoes, and tomatoes, Phytophthora infection is known as late blight. The first symptom is water-soaked spots on the lower leaves. The spots enlarge and are mirrored on the undersurface of the leaf with a white downy growth. Dark-colored blotches penetrate the flesh of tubers. These spots may dry and appear as sunken lesions. During a wet season, plants will rot and die. The pathogen overwinters on infected tubers and in plant debris. To control, dispose of all infected plants and tubers, presoak seed in a disinfecting solution, and plant resistant cultivars. Sprays of Bordeaux mixture can help control outbreaks during wet weather.

Bacterial blight: This bacterial disease is particularly severe on legumes in eastern and southern North America. Foliage and pods display water-soaked spots that dry and drop out. On stems, lesions are long and dark-colored. Some spots may ooze a bacterial slime. To control, plant resistant cultivars, remove infected plants, and dispose of plant debris. Use a three-year rotation and don't touch plants while they are wet, as you may spread the disease.

Cankers

Cankers usually form on woody stems and may be cracks, sunken areas, or raised areas of dead or abnormal tissue. Sometimes cankers ooze conspicuously. Cankers can girdle shoots or trunks, causing everything above the canker to wilt and die. Blights and diebacks due to cankers look quite similar. Cold-injury symptoms may look like, or lead to the development of, cankers and diebacks.

Cytospora canker: This fungal disease attacks poplars, spruces, and stone fruits. The cankers are circular, discolored areas on the bark. To control, plant resistant trees and cut out branches or trees with cankers.

Nectria canker: This fungus attacks most hardwoods and some vines and shrubs. It is most damaging on maples. Small sunken areas appear on the bark near wounds, and small pink spore-producing structures are formed. It kills twigs and branches and may girdle young trees. Control by limiting pruning cuts and removing diseased branches.

Rots

Rots are diseases that decay roots, stems, wood, flowers, and fruit. Some diseases cause leaves to rot, but those symptoms tend to be described as leaf spots and blights. Rots can be soft and squishy or hard and dry. They are caused by various bacteria and fungi. Many are very active in stored fruits, roots, bulbs, or tubers.

Fruit rots: Grapes infected with black rot turn brown, then harden into small, black, mummified berries. Brown rot of stone fruits causes whole fruit to turn brown and soft. Control fruit rots by planting resistant cultivars, removing and destroying infected fruit, and pruning to increase air movement. Sulfur sprays throughout the season help, too.

Root and stem rots: Control these troublesome rots by providing good drainage and good air circulation. Start cuttings in sterilized mix, and plant only healthy plants. Dispose of all infected plant material. Winter injury may invite problems on woody plants.

Mushroom and wood rots: These rots can damage or kill trees. Some of them form obvious mushrooms or other fungal growths. Cutting out infected areas can provide control. Keep soil well drained, and plant resistant species and cultivars where problems are severe.

Rusts

Rusts are a specific type of fungal disease. Many of them require two different plant species as hosts to complete their life cycle. Typical rust symptoms include a powdery tan to rust-colored coating or soft tentacles.

Asparagus rust: This disease appears as a browning or reddening of the small twigs and needles, and a release of rusty, powdery spores. It overwinters on stalks and infects new shoots as they emerge the following spring. Rust is also carried to other plants by wind. To control, space plants to allow air circulation. Plant resistant cultivars. Remove infected plants and burn them in the fall.

Other rusts: Wheat rust, cedar-apple rust, and white pine blister rust require alternate hosts. Wheat rust needs barberry to survive, cedar-apple rust needs both juniper and an apple relative, and white pine blister rust needs a susceptible member of the currant family. Removing the alternate hosts in the area can control outbreaks.

Wilts

Plants wilt when they don't get enough water. When fungi or bacteria attack or clog a plant's water-conducting system, they can cause permanent wilting, often followed by the death of all or part of the plant. Wilt symptoms may resemble those of blights.

Stewart's wilt: This bacterial disease is widespread on sweet corn in eastern North America. It overwinters in flea beetles and infects corn when they begin feeding on its leaves. Infected leaves wilt and may have long streaks with wavy margins. Bacterial slime will ooze out if the stalks or leaves are cut. Plants eventually die or are sufficiently stunted that no ears are produced. To control, plant resistant cultivars and eliminate flea beetles. Destroy infected plants.

Fusarium and Verticillium wilt: These fungal wilts attack a wide range of flowers, vegetables, fruits, and ornamentals. Plants wilt and may turn yellow. To control, plant resistant cultivars. Rotate crops, or do not replant in areas where problems have occurred. If wilt only affects a branch, it may help to cut it out well below the wilt symptoms. Destroy infected branches or plants.

Other Diseases

Anthracnose: Anthracnose, or bird's-eye spot, is a fungal disease. It causes small dead spots that often have a raised border and a sunken center, and that may have concentric rings of pink and brown.

Bean anthracnose infects beans and other legumes. The symptoms are most obvious on the pods as circular, black, sunken spots that may ooze pink slime and develop red borders as they age. To control, buy disease-free seed, rotate crops, turn under or hot-compost infected plants, and avoid touching plants when they are wet so you won't spread the disease.

Club root: Club root affects vegetables and flowers in the cabbage family. Plants infected by the fungus wilt during the heat of the day, and older leaves yellow and drop. Roots are distorted and swollen. To control, select resistant cultivars, buy clean seedlings, and rotate related crops.

Damping-off: Damping-off is caused by a variety of soilborne fungi. Seeds rot before they germinate, or seedlings rot at the soil line and fall over. Control-damping off by keeping soil moist, but not waterlogged. Provide good air movement. Wait until soil is warm enough for the specific plant before seeding. Sterile seed-starting mix or mix with compost can help prevent problems, too.

Downy mildew: Downy mildews are fungal diseases that attack many fruits, vegetables, flowers, and grasses. The primary symptom is a white to purple, downy growth, usually on the underside of leaves and along stems, which turns black with age. Upper leaf surfaces have a pale color. Lima bean pods may be covered completely, while leaves are distorted. The disease overwinters on infected plant parts and remains viable in the soil for several years. It is spread by wind, by rain, and in seeds. To control, buy disease-free seeds and plants, follow a three-year rotation, and remove and dispose of infected plants.

Galls: Galls are swollen masses of abnormal tissue. They can be caused by fungi and bacteria as well as certain insects. If you cut open a gall and there is no sign of an insect, suspect disease.

Crown gall is a serious bacterial disease that infects and kills grapes, roses, fruit trees, brambles, shade trees, flowers, and vegetables. Galls are rounded with rough surfaces and are made up of corky tissue. They often occur on the stem near the soil line or graft union but can also form on roots or branches. To control, buy healthy plants, and reject any suspicious ones. Don't replant in an area where you have had crown gall. Avoid wounding stems, and disinfect tools between plants when pruning. Remove and destroy infected plants, or cut out galls.

For more information on galls, see the Galls entry.

Leaf blisters and curls: Leaf blister and leaf curl are fungal diseases that cause distorted, curled leaves on many trees. Oak leaf blister can defoliate and even kill oak trees. Blisters are yellow bumps on the upper surface of the leaves, with gray depressions on the lower surface. Peach leaf curl attacks peaches and almonds. New leaves are pale or reddish and the midrib doesn't grow along with the leaves, so the leaves become puckered and curled as they expand. Fruit is damaged, and bad cases can kill the tree. Both diseases are controlled with a single dormant spray just before buds begin to swell.

Leaf spots: A vast number of fungi can cause spots on the leaves of plants. Most of them are of little consequence. A typical spot has a definite edge and often has a darker border. When lots of spots are present, they can grow together and become a blight or a blotch.

Blackspot is a common disease on roses. The spots appear on the leaves and are up to ½″ across with yellow margins. Severe cases cause leaves to drop. To control, plant resistant cultivars, and destroy all dropped leaves and prunings. Mulch to prevent dirt and spores from being splashed up onto plants. Weekly copper or sulfur sprays provide control.

Molds: Molds are characterized by a powdery or woolly appearance on the surface of the infected part.

Gray mold, or botrytis, is a common problem on many fruits and flowers. It thrives in moist conditions and is often seen on dropped flower petals or overripe fruit. It appears as a thick, gray mold or as water-soaked blighted regions of petals, leaves, or stems. In most cases it first infects dead or dying tissue, so removing faded flowers and blighted buds or shoots will control the problem. Peonies, tulips, and lilies can be severely damaged in wet seasons. Destroy infected material, and space, prune, and support plants to encourage good air movement.

Nematodes: Nematodes themselves are described earlier in this entry. Symptoms of nematode invasion include reduced growth, wilting, and lack of vigor.

Some nematodes cause excessive branching of roots, rotted roots, or enlarged lumps on roots. Other nematodes attack leaves, causing triangular wedges of dead tissue.

Root knot nematodes attack a variety of plant root systems, including most vegetable and ornamental crops. Carrot plants will be stunted with yellowed leaves, and roots may be distorted. Roots of other plants will have swollen areas. Remember that legumes are supposed to have swellings on their roots that are caused by nitrogen-fixing bacteria.

Prevent nematodes from invading your plants by maintaining your soil organic matter. Repel nematodes by interplanting with marigolds or asparagus, which repel the pest. Rotate susceptible crops. Adding products containing chitin to the soil can help reduce problems.

Heat greenhouse soil to about 125°F for 30 minutes to kill most nematodes and their eggs. Hot-water dips can eradicate nematodes from within roots, bulbs, and the soil on them.

Powdery mildew: Mildews are one of the most widespread and easily recognized fungi. They are common on phlox, lilac, melons, cucumbers, and many other plants. Mildew forms a white to grayish powdery growth, usually on the upper surfaces of leaves. Small black dots appear and produce spores that are blown by wind to infect new plants. Leaves will become brown and shrivel when mildew is extensive. Fruits ripen prematurely and have poor texture and flavor. To control, prune or stake to improve air circulation. Dispose of infected plants before spores form. Apply sulfur weekly to susceptible plants.

Scabs: Scabs are fungal diseases that cause fruits, leaves, and tubers to develop areas of hardened, overgrown, and sometimes cracked tissue. Fruit scab can be a major problem on apples and peaches. Control by disposing of fallen leaves, pruning to increase air movement, and spraying with sulfur in spring and summer.

Smuts: Smuts are fungal diseases. They are most commonly seen on grasses, grains, and corn. Enlarged galls are soft and spongy when young but change to a dark, powdery mass as they age.

Corn smut can form on kernels, tassels, stalks, and leaves. Smut galls ripen and rupture, releasing spores that travel through the air to infect new plants and overwinter in the soil, awaiting future crops. To control, select resistant cultivars. Remove and burn galls before they break

open, and follow a four-year rotation.

Viruses: Infected plants often grow slowly and yield poorly. Leaves may cup or twist, and develop mottling, streaking, or ring-shaped spots. Identification is often the elimination of all other possible causes. Professional growers use heat treatments and tissue culture to control viral disease. Purchase certified plants to avoid problems. Control insects that spread viruses. Remove and burn all plants with viral disease to prevent disease from spreading.

Cultural Disorders

Many unhealthy-looking plants are not actually suffering from disease. Extreme weather conditions, nutrient imbalances in the soil, and chemical or physical damage can produce symptoms similar to those of diseases. You'll find more information on nutrient imbalances in the Plant Nutrition entry. Chemical and physical damage are discussed in the Plant Disorders entry.

Cold injury: Freezing injury can cause death or dieback. Symptoms of cold stress are stunting, yellowing, bud or leaf drop, and stem cracking. Fruit may form a layer of corky tissue or be russeted if exposed to cold when young.

Heat injury: Temperatures that are too high cause sunscald of fruits, leaves, or trunks on the sunny side of the plant. Discoloration, blistering, or a water-soaked and sunken appearance are other symptoms of heat stress.

Moisture imbalance: Plants need a relatively constant supply of water. If they don't have enough, they will wilt. Long periods of wilting, or repeated wilting, can cause stunting, pale color, and reduced flowering and fruit production. Plant roots also need oxygen. Too much water in the soil damages roots and will cause symptoms like frequent wilting, pale color, root decay, leaf dropping, and lack of vigor.

Wind: High winds also take their toll on plant appearance. Silvery discoloration and tattered leaves are symptoms of wind damage. ❖

Division

Division is a quick and reliable way to propagate many types of multi-stemmed plants with almost guaranteed success. Dividing—separating a plant into several smaller new plants—works well for increasing groundcovers, clump-forming perennials, bulbs, and tubers. You can also divide ornamental grasses and suckering shrubs, as well as houseplants and herbs.

Season: The best time to divide garden plants is when they are dormant. In general, divide spring- and summer-blooming plants in the fall, and fall-blooming plants in the spring. If possible, divide houseplants in the spring as new growth starts. Divide plants with tubers and tuberous roots, such as dahlias and tuberous begonias, before planting in the spring.

Getting started: The key to division is

Dividing fleshy crowns. Divide plants with fleshy crowns, such as astilbes and hostas, with a sharp knife. Make sure each new piece has its own roots.

starting with a vigorous parent plant. If the soil is dry, water the plant thoroughly the day before. Whenever possible, wait for cool, cloudy weather (or at least evening) to reduce moisture loss from the plant during the process.

Method: To divide a hardy plant, lift it from the soil with a fork or spade. Separate small clumps by pulling off the vigorous young plantlets; discard the woody center growth. Cut apart iris rhizomes with a knife. When dividing plants, make sure that each piece you remove has its own root system. Otherwise, new divisions won't grow.

Lift hardy bulbs after the foliage yellows and dies down. Separate the bulbs and replant them at the proper depth and spacing. Divide tubers and tuberous roots in early spring. Cut dahlia crowns apart with a knife. Make sure that each swollen root has at least one bud where the root joins the crown. Cut begonia and caladium tubers into two or three sections, each with a visible bud or sprout. Expose the cut areas to air for a day or two before planting.

Aftercare: Replant divisions as quickly as possible, to the same depth as the original plant, and water them thoroughly. Mulch fall divisions well to protect the developing roots from frost heaving. ❖

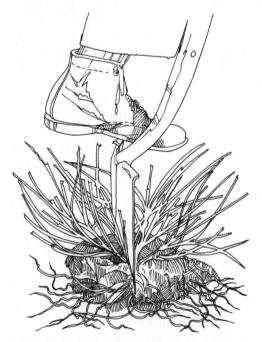

Dividing herbaceous plants. Use a sharp spade to divide perennials or tough clumps of ornamental grasses. Don't chop at the roots, though; try to make single, clean cuts.

Double Digging

Double digging a garden bed takes considerable time and effort, but it's work well rewarded by more vigorous, higher-yielding plants. The process improves the structure and fertility of the top 2′ of the soil.

When you double dig, you remove a spadeful of topsoil from a garden bed, loosen the soil layer below the topsoil, and then restore the topsoil layer. During the process, you can incorporate organic matter into the soil. Lavish most of the organic material on the topsoil. Add only small amounts of compost or chopped leaves to the lower soil layer because the rate of decay is much slower in the second 6″ of soil than it is in the top 6″. Double digging your beds will raise them about 3″-4″ because it thoroughly loosens and aerates the soil.

Double digging is hard work. If you have back problems, it's probably best not to double dig your garden. And if you've never double dug a bed before, start small. Try working a 3′ × 3′ bed, and build up from there. ❖

Topsoil

Loosened subsoil

Topsoil

How to double dig. 1. Several days in advance, mark off the area you plan to dig, and soak the soil with water. A few days later, remove weeds or sod, and loosen the top 1′ of soil with a spading fork.

2. The next day, begin digging, starting from one end of the marked area. With a spade, dig a 1′ wide, 1′ deep trench. Pile the topsoil from that trench onto a ground cloth or garden cart.

3. To loosen the exposed subsoil, stick your spading fork deeply in the soil and twist and wiggle the fork to loosen up the clumps. Spread a shovelful of organic matter over the surface of the exposed subsoil.

4. Slide the topsoil from the next 1′ section of the bed onto the subsoil in the first trench. Loosen the subsoil in the second trench.

5. Continue systematically down the bed, shifting the topsoil and loosening the subsoil.

6. When you reach the end of the bed, use the reserved topsoil from the first trench to fill in the last trench.

7. Spread compost or other organic matter over the entire bed, and use a spading fork to work it into the top 4″-6″ of the soil.

Dried Flower Gardening

Capture the beauty of your garden for year-round enjoyment by drying flowers to use indoors. Having a variety of dried flowers, foliage, and pods makes it easy to put together gifts for the holidays or to change the look of a room as often as you want. For more on using dried flowers, see the Flower Arranging and Wreathmaking entries.

Tips for Top Flowers

Choose the most perfect flowers and other plant material for drying, since drying magnifies even the smallest flaw. Pick flowers at different stages, from buds to almost fully opened blooms. Each stage will open further as it dries.

Pick plant material in late morning, when it is thoroughly dry but not wilted from the hot sun. Choose a time when you can continue the drying procedure immediately. If it must be delayed, put the flowers in a bucket of lukewarm water in a cool, dark place.

Flower colors often change as blooms dry. Reds and purples darken or turn blue; yellows and greens fade; white turns cream or beige; rust turns brown; flowers grown in the shade or picked past their prime turn brown; oranges can turn red. Blues, oranges, and pinks retain their color best.

Easy Air Drying

Air drying is the simplest and cheapest method—all you need is a warm, dark, dry place with gentle air circulation. An attic is the classic place for air drying, but a large closet, unused room, garden shed, or garage are fine, too.

Air drying works well with plant materials that tend to dry and retain their form naturally, such as "everlasting" flowers, grasses, weeds, reeds, pods, seed heads, grains, cones, lichens, and mosses. Some flower spikes also air dry well, including delphiniums (*Delphinium* spp.), larkspurs (*Consolida* spp.), goldenrods (*Solidago* spp.), monkshoods (*Aconitum* spp.), and violet sage (*Salvia* × *superba*).

Air dry most plant materials by hanging them upside down in bunches. Make sure the plants are not wet; remove the leaves from the stems unless the leaves also dry well. Gather 6-10 stems together and wrap a rubber band around them at least twice, about 2" from the stem ends. Hang the bunches so they are not touching. Air drying usually takes from less than a week to three weeks or more. Material is thoroughly dry when the stems snap readily.

Some plants dry better right-side up. Place the fresh stems in tall, cylindrical containers, such as widemouthed jars or coffee cans. Try this method for baby's-breath, poppy seed heads, Chinese lanterns (*Physalis alkekengi*), and globe thistles (*Echinops* spp.). It's also the best way to give grains, grasses, and other plants gracefully curving stems.

Some plants that dry best right-side up need ½" of water in the container to start with. The water will evaporate as the plants dry. Try this with ageratums, hydrangeas, and yarrows. Alliums (*Allium* spp.), bells-of-Ireland (*Moluccella laevis*), and heather (*Calluna vulgaris*) also perform well this way. Pick them just as they start to dry naturally on the plant.

To dry round, flat flowers, place the stems through a screen, such as ¼" hardware cloth. The stems hang loose below, and the flowers are supported face up by the screen. Use this method with fennel, dill, Queen-Anne's-lace, and edelweiss (*Leontopodium alpinum*).

Some everlastings have weak stems when they dry, so remove the stem before drying and replace it with a wire "stem." Use this method with globe amaranth (*Gomphrena globosa*), strawflower (*Helichrysum bracteatum*), and immortelle (*Xeranthemum annuum*). To make wire stems, cut the plant stem off ½" below the flower and insert a length of #22-gauge floral wire up through the remaining plant stem and out through the center of the flower. Make a small hairpin hook in the top of the wire and gently pull it back down through (but not entirely out of) the flower. The flower and stem will shrink and dry tightly

BEST PLANTS FOR DRYING

Whole books have been written about plants for drying, there are so many. Flowers and plants suitable for drying generally thrive in full sun with average soil and moisture. Their shapes can be grouped into three main categories for use in arrangements: linear, for line and height; round, for mass or a focal point; and filler, to add an airy look and unify the other elements. These are among the most reliable plants for drying. Plant name is followed by flower shape and color.

ANNUALS

Ammobium alatum (winged everlasting): round; white

Celosia cristata (cockscomb): round, linear; yellow, pink, red

Gomphrena globosa (globe amaranth): round; white, pink, red, magenta

Helichrysum bracteatum (strawflower): round; white, pink, red, yellow

Helipterum roseum (helipterum): round; white, pink, red

Lunaria annua (honesty): round, filler; white

Moluccella laevis (bells-of-Ireland): linear; green

Nigella damascena (love-in-a-mist): round; brown

Xeranthemum annuum (immortelle): round; white, pink, rose-purple

PERENNIALS

Achillea spp. (yarrows): round; yellow, pink, white

Anaphalis margaritacea (pearly everlasting): round; white

Artemisia spp. (artemisias): filler, linear; silver gray

Delphinium spp. (delphiniums): linear; white, blue, purple, pink

Echinops ritro (globe thistle): round; blue

Eryngium spp. (sea hollies): round; blue

Gypsophila paniculata (baby's-breath): filler; white

Lavandula spp. (lavenders): linear; purple

Limonium spp. (statice): filler; white, pink, purple-blue, yellow

Physalis alkekengi (Chinese lantern): round; orange

Rosa spp. (roses): round; white, pink, red, yellow

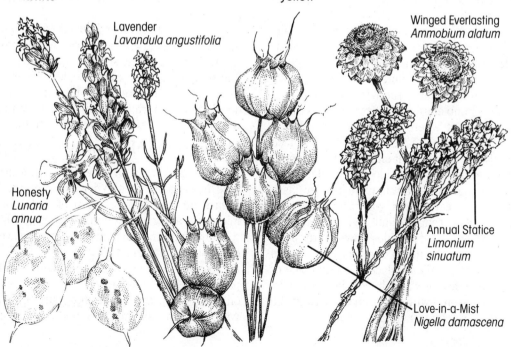

Honesty
Lunaria annua

Lavender
Lavandula angustifolia

Winged Everlasting
Ammobium alatum

Annual Statice
Limonium sinuatum

Love-in-a-Mist
Nigella damascena

187

around the wire. Tape the wire stem with floral tape by stretching the tape as you wrap it around the wire.

Store air-dried flowers and plants where they were dried, or place loosely in shoe or suit boxes lined with tissue paper. Place tissue paper between layers, making no more than three layers. To keep the flowers from shattering, lightly coat dried flowers and grasses with hair spray, clear plastic craft spray, or clear lacquer spray. Store the boxes in a dry location.

Dependable Desiccant Drying

Desiccants absorb moisture from their surroundings. Flowers dried with desiccants generally retain their color and shape better than air-dried materials. Silica gel is the most popular desiccant. Sold under various brand names, it is available at hobby and craft stores and garden centers. Start by purchasing 5 or 10 lb.; you can reuse it indefinitely. When silica gel has absorbed as much moisture as it can, reactivate it by heating in an oven or microwave, following manufacturer's directions.

To dry with (and store) silica gel, use airtight containers, such as cookie tins, plastic food-storage containers, or a shoe box and masking tape. You'll also need floral wire, stretchy ½" wide green floral tape, and wire cutters.

Gather unblemished flowers in various stages of development when the dew has completely dried. Cut the stems 1"-2" long. Cut a 6" piece of floral wire and insert it either straight up into the base of the flower (on blooms like daisies or pansies), or crosswise through the heavier bases on flowers like roses. If you insert the wire crosswise, leave it straight until drying is complete, and then bend the two sides down so they are parallel. When the flowers are dry and you are ready to arrange them, place a longer piece of wire alongside the wire already in the flower. Wrap this "stem" with floral tape, twirling the stem and stretching the tape as you work.

To dry flowers and leaves, spread a ½"-1" layer of silica gel on the bottom of your drying container. Lay leaves and ferns flat, with several inches of silica gel between layers. For daisy-type flowers, make a small mound of gel and lay the flower face down. Place flowers with many petals like roses and marigolds face up. Lay long, spiky flowers like delphiniums sideways, with inverted V's of cardboard supporting the stems every 2". Leave several inches of silica gel between each flower, and place only one kind of flower in each container. When all the flowers are in place, carefully cover each flower with ½"-1" of silica gel. Sift the silica gel around the petals of many-petalled flowers like roses and peonies so they're not crushed.

Seal the container and label it with the date and contents. Check in 2-3 days by gently tilting the container until a few petals are exposed. If they are crisp and papery, the flowers are dry. Carefully pour the silica gel into another container as you remove each flower. Use a fine, soft artist's brush to remove any silica gel clinging to the petals.

Put a drop of clear household cement or other clear-drying glue at the center and base of the flower to prevent shattering. Spray with a dull-finish clear plastic craft sealer or hair spray to protect the flowers from humidity. Store the dried flowers upright in an airtight container with dry sand or silica gel in the bottom.

Miraculous Microwave Drying

The microwave oven reduces plant-drying time to several minutes. When using this method, always be sure to put a cup of water in the microwave along with your plant material. Drying without water may damage your microwave. To dry both green and fall-colored leaves in the microwave, put one or several inside a folded paper towel. Set a microwave-proof cup or dish on top to keep the leaves from curling. Microwave on high for 2 minutes, and then check; if leaves are dry and crisp, they are done. If they're almost dry, heat them another minute or so. If too dry, try again with new leaves and halve the cooking time. To dry everlastings in a microwave, put flowers inside a paper towel or napkin. Dry for 2 minutes on high as a test, then adjust the time if necessary. ❖

Drying Food Crops

There's nothing mysterious about the way drying preserves food: It deprives food-spoiling organisms of the moisture they need to grow. And the way it's done is fairly energy-efficient and inexpensive. Small pieces of food are exposed to warm, dry, moving air until 75-95 percent of the food's moisture has evaporated.

The results are splendid: Lightweight, compact foods with chewy textures and concentrated flavors. Familiar dried apple slices are easy to make. Try thin zucchini slices; they're quick to dry and pleasantly crunchy. Dried foods keep well, too. They'll last 4-12 months stored in airtight containers in a dry, cool place.

There's one hitch. Drying foods takes time. For example, peaches can take up to five days to dry in the sun, up to 30 hours to dry in the oven, or up to 20 hours in a dehydrator. After that, they need several days of conditioning.

Sun Drying

Drying food in the sun is the simplest method, and the cost is nil. But it works only if you live where the humidity is low and the days are long, sunny, and breezy. The procedure is simple: Put out the food on trays early in the morning. At night, or during rain, cover the trays or bring them in so dampness doesn't reenter the food.

You can make your own drying trays using a wooden frame and nylon mesh. Put the trays on blocks for good air circulation. Cover the food with cheesecloth to keep out dirt and insects. To speed drying, place everything under glass or clear plastic. But watch carefully. If temperatures are too high, the food will cook instead of dry.

Fruits are the best choice for sun drying because their high levels of sugar and acid protect them from becoming moldy as they dry.

Indoor Drying

Where the humidity is high, it's wise to dry food indoors. Indoor drying is your best bet for vegetables, which have low acid levels and mold readily when drying conditions aren't ideal.

You can use your oven for drying, as long as it can be set to a low temperature, between 125°F and 160°F. Too much heat will cook the food. Electric convection ovens and gas ovens both provide for air circulation, but you will need to leave the door of an electric oven ajar to let air circulate. Air circulation is important for good drying. A microwave oven is handy for drying herbs, but it doesn't work for denser foods; they will be cooked instead of dried. See the Herbs entry for instructions on drying herbs in the microwave.

For oven drying, disconnect the broiler element, or place a metal tray on the top rack to deflect the heat. Heat should come from the bottom only. Cover the racks with nylon netting or mesh.

Unfortunately, oven drying isn't energy-efficient for drying large quantities. If you'll be processing lots of food, consider purchasing a dehydrator. Ranging in price from $50 to $250, commercially made dehydrators have electric heating elements, fans, and air vents. Some dehydrators have a horizontal air flow, with a heating element and fan on the side instead of on the bottom, allowing several different foods to be dried at once without mixing flavors. A dehydrator is fairly simple to construct. If you're inclined to build one yourself, check books on drying food for designs or plans. A word to would-be users: Dehydrators can put out a lot of humidity. Be sure to use yours in a well-ventilated area.

GOOD FOR DRYING

Try some of these suggestions for home drying.

Fruits: apples, bananas, cherries, grapes, nectarines, peaches, pears, plums, rhubarb, strawberries

Vegetables: beans, beets, carrots, celery, garlic, mushrooms, onions, parsnips, peppers, pumpkin, tomatoes, zucchini

Food Preparation

Wash, core, peel, and slice or chop foods before drying. Make the pieces uniformly sized, so that they dry at the same rate. Thin slices dry quickly; bigger, thicker pieces take longer to dry.

Fruits and vegetables hold their colors and flavors well if you pretreat them before drying. To prevent light-colored fruits such as apples and peaches from darkening, soak slices for 3-5 minutes in orange, lemon, or pineapple juice or ascorbic acid solution (1 tablespoon of ascorbic acid powder in 1 quart of water). Drain the fruit before transferring it to trays. If you enjoy sweetened fruit, use a honey dip to inhibit darkening. Dissolve ½ cup of honey in 1½ cups of boiling water. Let the mixture cool to lukewarm; use as you would the juice dip.

To halt the enzyme action that produces color and flavor changes in vegetables, blanch them with steam or boiling water. Blanching also hastens drying and rehydration. Use water blanching to crack the skins of small whole fruits, such as cherries or plums, and to speed up drying.

To water-blanch, place vegetable pieces in a wire basket. Submerge them briefly in boiling water; then dip them quickly in cold water. Spread them on drying trays.

To steam-blanch, place vegetables no more than 2½″ deep in a wire basket. Suspend the basket over rapidly boiling water; cover the pot and blanch for the recommended length of time. Cool the vegetables on racks or trays.

Drying Tips

Here are some ideas for successful home drying. For more details, check a comprehensive cookbook.

• Use fresh-picked fruits and vegetables in the best condition.

• Lightly coat drying trays with nonstick vegetable spray for easy removal of dried foods.

• Spread food in a single layer on the trays. Stir food and rotate the tray positions occasionally during drying time.

• Foods dried outdoors may contain tiny insects and their eggs, which you can destroy by heating or freezing. Spread food on baking sheets and warm in a 175°F oven for 10-15 minutes. Or pack the food in freezer bags, and freeze for at least 48 hours.

Storing

Properly dried fruit should be pliable, but not sticky. You can test fruit for dryness by slicing several pieces in half. There should be no visible moisture. Vegetables should feel tough, hard, or brittle.

At the end of drying, some pieces of food will have more moisture than others. To distribute the moisture evenly among the pieces, place in a large uncovered bowl in a warm, dry area for 7 days. Stir the contents daily.

Store dried foods in small containers impervious to chewing rodents and insects. You can also freeze dried foods.

Dried fruits are delicious when eaten just as they are, but if you'd like to rehydrate them, simmer in a small amount of water until tender. Rehydrate dried vegetables the same way, or add them directly to soups and other dishes with lots of liquid. ❖

Earthworms

Earthworm ancestors survived the Ice Age. More than 3,000 species now exist, and they live almost everywhere. One acre of cultivated land may be home to as many as 500,000 earthworms, each making your soil a better place for plants. Earthworms are among a gardener's best allies, so whenever you work the soil, consider how your actions affect the worms below its surface.

The 4″ long, pale red garden worm is often called "nature's plow." The earthworm pushes through soft earth with the point of its head. If the soil is hard, the worm eats its way through, forming interconnected burrows, some several feet deep. Burrows loosen the soil, admitting air and water and helping roots grow.

As an earthworm feeds, organic matter passes through its body and is excreted as granular dark castings. You may see these small casting piles in your garden. An earthworm produces its weight in casts daily. Wormcasts are rich in nutrients otherwise unavailable to plants. When you add nitrogen-rich compost to your soil, you help worms. An earthworm's body is 72 percent protein, so it requires lots of nitrogen (the building block of proteins) to maintain itself. However, adding *synthetic* nitrogen fertilizers may repel earthworms. Worms are very sensi-tive to physical and chemical changes and will flee the salty conditions that result from an application of chemical fertilizer.

Life Cycle: In cold weather, a soil search will turn up mature and young earthworms as well as eggs. By late spring, most worms are mature. As temperatures rise, activity slows; many lay eggs and then die. By midsummer, most worms are very young or protected by egg capsules. As the weather cools, young worms emerge. With wet weather, they grow active, making new burrows and eating extra food, resulting in more wormcasts. Egg laying again occurs. Activity continues as long as soil stays damp.

After a heavy rain, earthworms often appear aboveground. They haven't drowned. Fresh water doesn't disturb earthworms—they need ongoing skin moisture to breathe—but stagnant or contaminated water forces them from their burrows.

You may have seen a bird tugging on an earthworm. Sometimes the worm escapes. A worm crawls by digging tiny bristles into the soil and pulling or stretching forward. When a bird tries to pull it from the ground, the worm swells up, pushing its bristles into the soil so firmly that the bird may get only half a worm. The remaining worm grows a new head if no more than the first 7-8 body rings are missing.

Earthworms can survive in soil that freezes gradually, but sudden freezing can kill them. Protect earthworms against sudden freezes with mulch or a cover crop, both of which also provide worms with food.

Earthworm bins: You can raise earthworms indoors in a modified garbage can, washtub, or wooden box. Kept in a cool, dark place, a worm bin provides a composting system for kitchen scraps, as well as a source of worms for the garden. To keep conditions moist but well-drained, make a drainage area in the bottom of the bin; use a rigid divider to separate it from the worms' living quarters. A loose cover keeps flies and light out and moisture in.

Fill the bin with 2 parts commercial steer manure, 2 parts sawdust, and 1 part shredded leaves. Garden soil may also be added. Mix this well in advance and dampen thoroughly; if the mixture heats up, wait a few days before adding worms or the heat may kill them. Introduce earthworms, purchased or from your garden, to their new home. If you buy worms, use them for composting only—most commercially available worms are species that live only in manure or very rich soil and will not survive in average garden soil.

Feed your worms well-chopped vegetable matter mixed with a bit of water. Soft foods are best for the first few days; if food doesn't disappear in 24 hours, reduce the amount. Good earthworm foods include oatmeal, peanut hulls, toast, fruit and vegetable trimmings, and coffee grounds. Run the food through a blender; worms don't have teeth to tear off large chunks. The population should double in about a month; after 60 days, your bin should be full of rich compost.

Save some earthworms for another session. Place compost outdoors on a sheet of heavy plastic or fabric, and let it sit for about an hour; the worms will cluster together to stay cool and moist. Dig in and find the cluster. Return some worms to the bin; put the rest in your garden or start a second bin. ❖

Echinacea

Purple coneflower. Summer-blooming perennials; wildflowers; medicinal herbs.

Description: *Echinacea purpurea,* purple coneflower, bears 3″-6″ daisies with prominent pointed orange centers. Flowers are borne in shades of rose, purple, mauve, and white on 3′-4′ upright plants with rough, dark green foliage. Zones 3-8.

How to grow: Plant or divide in spring or early fall in full sun and average, well-drained soil. Once established, water only during severe drought. Pick off Japanese beetles.

Landscape uses: Mass in meadows; grow along a sunny wall or fence. Coneflowers combine well with larkspurs and phlox. They also are attractive in perennial borders.

Best cultivars: Choose 'The King', 'Bright Star', or 'Magnus' in rose red. White-petalled 'White Lustre' provides contrast. ❖

Echinops

Globe thistle. Summer-blooming perennials; dried flowers.

Description: *Echinops ritro,* globe thistle, bears 2″ balls of small, gray-blue flowers on 3′-5′ upright masses of dark green, 8″ thistlelike leaves. Zones 3-8.

How to grow: Plant or divide the thick, tangled crowns in spring. Grow in full sun and average, well-drained soil. Globe thistles tolerate heat and drought. Avoid shade and excess fertility, which cause weak stems and flopping.

Landscape uses: Mass globe thistles toward the rear of a border, along a fence, or in dry, sunny spots. The blooms attract butterflies and bees. Cut and hang just before flowers open for dried arrangements.

Best cultivars: Try 'Taplow Blue' or the slightly darker 'Veitch's Blue'. ❖

Edible Landscaping

While many gardeners would like to grow their own fresh produce, not all have time or space for a separate food garden. Edible landscapes do double duty—they produce food and make our yards attractive at the same time. An edible landscape is also convenient. Slogging out to the vegetable garden on a rainy evening after work is a chore. Picking a few ripe tomatoes on your way in from the car or gathering a handful of fragrant herbs from a small garden beside the back door is a pleasure.

The concept of edible landscaping is not new. Ancient Egyptian pleasure gardens included fish ponds, flowers, grape arbors, fruit trees, and places to sit and enjoy the serenity. But by the Renaissance, gardeners began to exclude edible plants from their formal ornamental gardens. They planted separate herb gardens, vegetable gardens, and orchards. Edible landscaping concepts came to the fore in the 1980s. Gardeners recognized that many edible plants are also beautiful, and reintroduced them to the general landscape.

Making the Transition

Only those who move into newly built homes have the luxury of designing the landscape from scratch. Most likely, your yard already has many permanent plantings. While you won't want to redesign and uproot your whole yard overnight, there are many ways to gradually transform your existing plantings into an edible landscape. Keep in mind that an edible landscape is one in which *most,* but not all, of the plantings are food-producing plants.

Start by including some edibles with your annual flowers. Remember, you don't have to plant vegetables in rows—they'll grow just as well interplanted among ornamentals and herbs. Use the same design rules you would with flowers alone. Try accenting a flower bed with deep green rosettes of corn salad, small mounds of 'Spicy Globe' basil, or crinkly red leaf lettuce.

Plant perennial herbs and vegetables in your existing ornamental borders—make room by relocating or replacing existing plants. For example, lavender and rosemary have upright forms with thin leaves and will add four-season interest to a border. Artichokes are perennial in Zones 9 and 10; their silvery, spiky foliage makes an interesting foil for other plants.

If you need to remove an existing tree or shrub that has died or outgrown its site, consider a fruit or nut tree as a replacement. A nut tree (pecan, hickory, English walnut, hazelnut—whatever is suitable for your climate) can replace a large shade tree. A full-sized fruit tree might be a good replacement for a medium-sized tree. Many of the spring-flowering pears, cherries, and crab apples used in landscaping are sterile hybrids that do not produce fruit. Their fruiting cousins are equally attractive in bloom and do produce fruit.

There are several other special ways to incorporate edibles into your existing landscape:

• Convert areas of lawn into new garden beds and include edibles in the design.

• Replace grass with food-producing groundcovers in some areas. Alpine strawberries produce fruit all summer and tolerate light shade.

• Make use of existing walls and fences, or add new ones. Train dwarf fruit trees against them, or use them to support raspberries, blackberries, or vegetables. You'll find directions for training dwarf fruit trees to a fence or trellis in the Espalier entry.

• Plant a fruiting hedge. Shrub roses such as rugosa roses (*Rosa rugosa*) make a lovely and intruder-resistant barrier.

• Build an arbor or trellis. Grapes are traditional, but hardy kiwi would also be a good choice for a large arbor. Vegetables like cucumbers, melons, and beans work well too, but some need special support for the fruit.

• Add containers to your landscape. Many dwarf fruit trees are now available and can be grown in large tubs. Dwarf citrus will grow even in northern climates if the trees are moved to a cool, sunny, indoor location during the winter. Strawberry jars are good for strawberries or herbs. For more suggestions on incorporating edibles in your container plantings, see "Colorful and Tasty, Too" on this page.

Selecting Plants

When you become an edible landscaper, you'll find that bringing vegetables and fruit trees out of hiding and into the total landscape makes your gardening even more rewarding.

There are food-producing plants to satisfy every need in your landscape. Fruit and nut trees come in a wide range of sizes and shapes, provide shade, and may provide spring blooms and/or fall color. Berry-producing shrubs, such as blueberries and wild plums, also provide flowers and fall color. Some blueberries even have attractive red branches in the winter. The flowers of certain annual and perennial flowers, such as nasturtiums and chives, are edible. Many herbs and vegetables have interesting foliage, and some have showy flowers or brightly colored fruit. Fruiting vines such as grapes, melons, and climbing beans will cover fences and trellises. Some edibles, such as creeping thyme and alpine strawberries, make good groundcovers.

Your personal taste and how much space you have available will determine what you plant. Consider these factors as you select plants:

• What foods do you like and use most? You're defeating the purpose of an edible landscape if you plant crops you won't eat.

• How big is each plant and how much will it produce? Fresh homegrown sweet corn is a treat without comparison, but those large cornstalks yield only two or three ears apiece.

• Do you have a location suitable for growing edibles? Many fruit and vegetable crops will only thrive if they have direct sun for at least 6 hours daily. Your choice will be limited if you have a shady yard.

• What fresh foods can you buy locally, and which are expensive or difficult to find? You may decide to plant raspberry canes and forego zucchini plants. Good raspberries are next to impossible to buy at the grocery store, while zucchini in season is cheap (or available free from friends).

A Gallery of Edibles

Almost all food-producing plants have ornamental value. The following listings are only a small sampling of the many excellent edible landscape plants.

Trees: In warm climates, citrus (orange, lemon, lime, grapefruit) are versatile trees. They are large enough to provide good shade, cooling the house or an area of the garden during the heat of the day. They retain their shiny deep green leaves through the winter, and have fruit in various stages of development and ripeness

---

COLORFUL AND TASTY, TOO

Once you begin working with edible landscaping designs, you'll discover there are nearly limitless possibilities for attractive combinations of food-producing and ornamental plants. The combinations listed below are suitable for container plantings or for garden beds.

• Curly parsley and yellow pansies (*Viola* spp.)
• Red leaf lettuce with dwarf yellow marigolds (*Tagetes erecta*)
• Red chard and New Zealand spinach
• 'Spicy Globe' basil with 'Nantes' carrots and dwarf orange marigolds (*Tagetes erecta*)
• Dwarf curly kale with dusty miller and pink nemesia (*Nemesia versicolor*)
• Sorrel with curly parsley, trailing lobelia (*Lobelia erinus*), and alpine strawberries
• Eggplant and ageratum
• Yellow zucchini and coreopsis (*Coreopsis* spp.)
• 'Royal Burgundy' bush beans with 'Royal Carpet' alyssum and oregano
• Red geraniums (*Pelargonium* × *hortorum*) with white alyssum and trailing blue lobelia

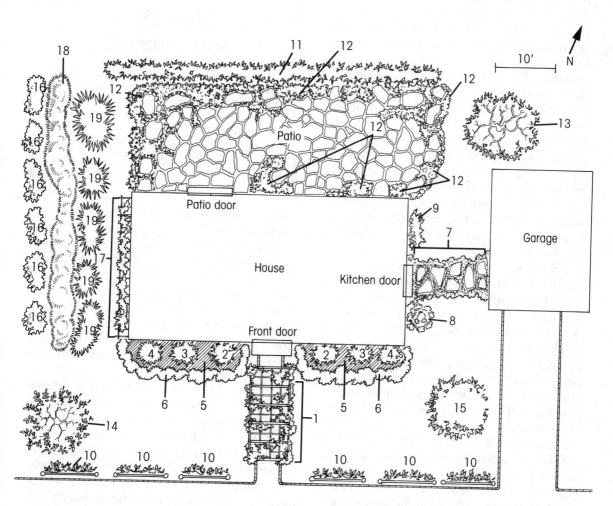

Edible landscaping possibilities. Try adapting some of the ideas from this edible landscape design in your yard.

1. Hardy kiwi and pole beans climbing on arbor, with red leaf lettuce planted at base
2. Fig trees
3. Highbush cranberries
4. Blueberries
5. Sorrel and mache
6. French marigolds (*Tagetes patula*) interplanted with basil
7. Chamomile and lemon thyme planted between flagstones

8. Lettuce, oriental greens, and Johnny jump-ups planted in a tower-shaped planter
9. Cherry tomato on trellis with pansies at the base
10. Espaliered dwarf apple, pear, apricot, and peach trees trained against sections of fence
11. Blackberry/raspberry bushes forming a living hedge
12. Herbs and edible flowers (alpine strawberries, calendula, chervil, dianthus [*Dianthus* spp.], dill, fennel, French marigolds, lavender, marjoram,

mint, oregano, pansies, parsley, sage, thyme) planted in cracks and islands between stones of flagstone patio
13. Crab apple tree
14. Walnut tree
15. Beech tree
16. Rugosa roses (*Rosa rugosa*) forming a living hedge
17. Sugar snap peas followed by tomatoes, trained on trellis
18. Asparagus
19. Tulips and violets followed by daylilies (*Hemerocallis* sp.)

on their branches year-round. When in flower, their fragrance perfumes the air. The flowers of the orange tree are extremely sweet and can be used to flavor honey, sugar, and tea, or as a beautiful garnish.

In the East, if your flowering dogwood (*Cornus florida*) trees are in decline, replace them with Korean dogwood (*Cornus kousa*). It blooms in June (later than the flowering dogwood), the flowers are longer-lasting, and it has brilliant fall foliage. The edible fruit resembles a pale strawberry. It is tartly sweet, with a pearlike, mealy texture, and is favored by birds and wildlife. Figs make interesting foundation plants but they need a sheltered location and winter protection in the North. Dwarf fruit trees work well in small areas.

Shrubs: A blueberry bush makes a good foundation plant, but must have acid soil to thrive. Bush cherries, wild plums, gooseberries, currants, hazelnuts, and highbush cranberries (*Viburnum trilobum*) make good hedges. Tightly planted raspberries or blackberries create a living fence. Some shrub-type roses, such as rugosa roses, produce large, bright orange or red, edible rose hips with 60 times the vitamin C of an orange. The hips can be used to make tea, jam, or jelly.

Ornamentals: Leaves of amaranth (especially 'Love Lies Bleeding', 'Red Stripe Leaf', and 'Early Splendor'), leaves and flowers of anise hyssop (*Agastache foeniculum*), young leaves of balloon flower (*Platycodon grandiflorus*), seeds of love-in-a-mist (*Nigella damascena*), and leaves and flowers of nasturtium and violets are edible.

Edibles with showy flowers and foliage: The following edibles have colorful and attractive flowers: amaranth (green, purple, red), artichokes (lavender), beans (red, purple, white), cardoon (lavender), chives (lavender, white), dill (yellow-green), eggplant (lavender), garlic (white), Jerusalem artichoke (yellow), nasturtiums (orange, red, yellow), okra (white, yellow), rosemary (pale blue), salsify (blue), and sugar snap peas (purple, white). The foliage of edibles also comes in

> ## *More On*
> ## EDIBLE LANDSCAPES
>
> If you'd like in-depth information for planning and planting an edible landscape, try reading Kate Rogers Gessert's *The Beautiful Food Garden*, Rosalind Creasy's *The Complete Book of Edible Landscaping*, or Robert Kourik's *Designing and Maintaining Your Edible Landscape Naturally*.

many interesting colors and forms. Various cultivars of artichokes, cabbage, cardoon, kale, lavender, leeks, marjoram, onions, rosemary, and sage feature shades of gray and blue. Beets, purple basil, red cabbage, red chard, purple ornamental kale, red lettuces, and purple mustard feature pink and red shades. Carrots, endive, white ornamental kale, variegated lemon balm, nasturtiums, and thyme feature light green, yellow, and white. Asparagus has attractive green fernlike foliage.

Vines: Peas are lovely trained on a fence and can be followed by cucumbers or squash as the season progresses. Hardy kiwi is a vigorous climber. 'Scarlet Runner' beans have bright red-orange flowers and are pretty planted with white-flowering cultivars of beans. Indeterminate tomatoes can be trained on a trellis or arbor; let the sideshoots grow in for maximum coverage.

Groundcovers: Alpine strawberries produce tasty fruit. Many herbs are low-growing and vigorous and can be used as groundcovers.

Fragrant edibles: Certain fragrances may be attractive to some people and annoying to others. The most fragrant edibles include basil, chamomile, chives, fennel, mint, oregano, parsley, sage, strawberry, thyme, and tomato. Creeping varieties of thyme and oregano are low-growing and work well planted between stepping stones where they may be lightly stepped on, releasing their fragrance. ❖

Eggplant

Solanum melongena var. *esculentum*
Solanaceae

Most people, when they think of eggplant, visualize large, purple, pear-shaped fruits, but that's just the beginning. Eggplants can produce glossy black, green, yellow, or white fruits, too, in a variety of shapes and sizes. Even as annuals, most eggplants need 100-150 warm—or at least frost-free—days to produce a crop.

Planting: Give eggplants a head start on the growing season by starting them indoors, 6-9 weeks before the average last frost. Soak seeds overnight to encourage germination; sow them ¼″ deep in a loose, fine medium, such as vermiculite. Use bottom heat to maintain a soil temperature of 80°-90°F for the 8-10 days required for sprouting. Transplant seedlings to individual peat pots once they reach 3″. When outside nighttime air temperatures are above 50°F, gradually expose them to the outdoors to harden them off. You can keep transplanting into larger and larger pots while waiting for both air and soil to warm up to at least 70°F.

Try growing eggplants in raised beds, which heat up quickly in the spring. Plants given plenty of room are healthier and more productive, so space them 2½′-3′ apart in all directions. Water well, pour 1-2 cups of manure tea around each plant, and firm the soil gently. (For instructions on making manure tea, see the Manure entry.) Eggplants are also good for container growing, with one plant per 5-gallon pot.

Growing guidelines: Mulch immediately after transplanting, and gently hand-pull any invading weeds. Interplant an early crop, such as lettuce, between the eggplant transplants. When the eggplants bloom, apply more liquid fertilizer and repeat monthly. For best production, plants need 1″-1½″ of water a week.

Problems: Flea beetles, which chew many tiny holes in leaves, are eggplant's worst pest. To avoid this problem, keep plants indoors until early summer, or cover outdoor plants with cheese-

Flea beetles. These tiny black beetles jump like fleas when disturbed. Flea beetles attack many different vegetables, especially those in the seedling stage. These pests can quickly wipe out a crop by chewing hundreds of tiny holes in the leaves.

cloth or a floating row cover. Combat severe infestations with pyrethrins.

Handpick and destroy yellow-and-black-striped Colorado potato beetles and the yellow masses of eggs they lay on leaf undersides. Handpicking is also effective for tomato hornworms, 4″ green caterpillars with white stripes. Don't destroy those covered with tiny white cocoons; these contain the parasitic offspring of the beneficial braconid wasp. Tiny spider mites cause yellow-stippled leaves; control these pests by knocking them off the plant with a spray of water. For details on controlling aphids and cutworms, see "The Top Ten Garden Insect Pests in America" on page 344.

The most common eggplant disease is Verticillium wilt. Avoid it by planting resistant cultivars and by rotating crops.

Harvesting: Pick eggplant when the skin takes on a high gloss, at ⅓-⅔ of the fully mature size. To test, press the skin. If the indentation doesn't spring back, that fruit is ready for harvest. When the seeds inside turn brown, it's past the good-eating stage. To harvest, cut the stem with a knife or pruning shears. Eggplants will keep for two weeks if refrigerated.

Best cultivars: 'Black Beauty', deep purple-black; 'Dusky', glossy black, early; 'Casper', ivory white; 'Easter Egg', egglike white fruit. ❖

Elderberry

Sambucus spp.
Caprifoliaceae

For centuries Europeans have valued elderberries, both for the rich flavor of the fruit and for their reputed ability to prevent and cure many illnesses. Although they're not as widely grown in North America, elderberries are worth growing for their beautiful—and edible—flowers and the unique taste of the fruit: a medley of grape, raspberry, and blackberry. Just be sure you have plenty of room for these large, spreading plants; they're not for small gardens!

Types: *Sambucus nigra,* European elder, reaches 10'-30' tall. It bears large clusters of yellowish white flowers in June, followed by shiny black berries in September. Zones 5-8.

S. canadensis, American or sweet elder, grows 6'-12' tall. It produces similar clusters of flowers in late June and, later, purple-black berries. Several cultivars of American elder produce large berries that ripen over a long season. Northern gardeners often raise them as substitutes for grapes where the latter are not hardy or fail to ripen before frost. Zones 3-9.

Planting: Elderberries like a sunny location with lots of room to spread. They thrive in a deep, moist soil well supplied with organic matter. Set young plants 5' apart in rows at least 8' apart, and keep them 10' from other plantings. Elderberry flowers are self-pollinating, but the plants are more productive if two or more cultivars are planted near each other.

Care: Apply a thick layer of organic mulch to conserve moisture. If plants aren't growing well, apply an organic plant food containing nitrogen under the mulch; otherwise, fertilization usually isn't needed. Water in dry seasons.

Pruning: Prune away dead canes in spring, and cut out all the old canes whenever bushes become crowded. Vigorous elderberries produce an abundance of suckers, so keep plants in neat rows by frequent clipping or mowing. Dig and transplant suckers if you want new plants.

Problems: Elderberries are remarkably free from disease and insect pests, but birds love the fruit, and it is not easy to cover the tall bushes with netting at harvest time. If birds aren't too numerous and you have the space, plant extra bushes. When berries are abundant, birds tend to tire of them after a few days and leave the ones that ripen later. Or pick berries a day or two before they are ripe, and set them in a warm room, where they'll continue to ripen.

Winter damage can be a problem some years. The plant's roots are very hardy, but extreme cold sometimes injures the canes. Fortunately, the fruit forms on new growth, so even when damage is severe, it seldom affects the crop. Since blooms don't appear until summer, late spring frosts never hurt them. If, however, you live where fall frosts come early, plant early-ripening cultivars for the best results.

Harvesting: The clusters of tiny white flowers in summer are not only beautiful but delicious. Pick them as soon as they open, and make them into wine or dip them in a batter and fry them. To make a tasty "tea," add a few flower clusters to a gallon glass jar filled with water and a bit of lemon juice and sugar. Set it in the sun for a day, then strain out the flowers.

Soon after blooming, green fruits form and ripen to a rich dark color. Pick the whole fruit cluster and strip off the berries later when you're ready to use them. Most people do not eat elderberries out of hand, but instead make them into tarts, pies, and other desserts or process them into jelly, juice, or wine. They're a great substitute for blueberries in many recipes.

Best cultivars: 'Adams', early-ripening, medium-sized berries, heavy bearer; 'Johns', vigorous, with large fruits that ripen late; 'Nova', large-fruited, productive, slightly later than 'Adams'; 'York', similar to 'Nova', but berries are larger and later. ❖

Endangered Plant Species

Nature is a series of interconnected events — a puzzle of sorts where each piece is dependent upon all others. If a single piece is missing, the picture fails. The extinction of any one plant species affects not only man but ultimately the entire puzzle we call earth.

As gardeners, it's easy to understand the value of plants. They beautify our gardens with exquisite color and fragrance and provide us with shelter, food, and tranquility. Plants also supply food for wildlife, provide us with energy sources, and play a vital role in medical research. A plant's function in the environment is sometimes taken for granted, but every species is valuable to the balance of nature.

Plant species that have reached the point of near-extinction throughout their range are classified as endangered. A large number of endangered plants are wildflowers. For example, there are native cacti, orchids, asters, and goldenrods on the U.S. Fish and Wildlife's list of endangered plants. Some of the most beloved wildflowers such as trilliums (*Trillium* spp.), trout lilies (*Erythronium* spp.), and lady's slipper orchids (*Cypripedium* spp.) are rare throughout their natural ranges, although technically not in danger of extinction. Local pressures such as overcollecting can threaten populations of these plants, and eventually the entire species, with extinction. Trees and shrubs can suffer the same fate — franklinia (*Franklinia alatamaha*), a native tree, is not known to exist outside cultivation.

Plants become endangered for two major reasons. The first is a result of the destruction of a species' natural habitat. This destruction can come in many forms — overgrazing of cattle, natural or man-induced fire, deforestation, or the never-ending development of land for industrial, residential, and commercial purposes.

The second factor that can threaten a species' existence — most pertinent to home gardeners — is the collection of plants from the wild. Wild collecting — even on a homeowner scale — can decimate local populations of wildflowers. In the case of small local populations, or if too few plants of a particular species remain, it can hamper cross-pollination and therefore reproduction. Eventually this can limit genetic diversity and, with it, a species' ability to adapt and survive.

Large-scale wild collection still occurs within the nursery trade. Many nurseries are now propagating native plants from seed, cuttings, or spores or by other methods that do not disturb wild populations. Yet there are a number of nurseries and distributors that continue to wild-collect and offer collected plants for sale to the public. Commercial wild collection usually occurs in large quantities (providing for the world market), and such collection threatens the plants' natural ability to reproduce.

What can you do to help protect endangered and threatened plants?

• When purchasing plants or seeds, be sure to question their origin. If you know or suspect that a nursery or distributor is selling wild-collected plants, don't buy them. Plant societies and botanic gardens often have sales of propagated wildflowers, trees, and shrubs.

• Before selecting plants for your home garden, get to know your site and select plants that will thrive in the conditions your garden has to offer. Also, avoid invasive non-natives such as Japanese honeysuckle (*Lonicera japonica*) and purple loosestrife (*Lythrum salicaria*) that may overrun desirable plants. See the Wildflowers entry for more on gardening with native plants.

• To protect the plant's ability to reseed, do not collect plants or plant parts from the wild unless they are commonly abundant in your area.

• If you know of any individuals or organizations that wild-collect plants or if a local area is threatened by development, contact a local plant-preservation society or botanical garden. ❖

Endive

Cichorium endivia
Compositae

Curly endive is a lacy, loose, slightly bitter green often labeled *chicory* in the supermarket. It looks nothing like its close relation, a less-frilled, broad-leaved endive known as escarole. They both, however, have the same growing requirements. Although you can grow them as spring crops, they are ideal for fall harvesting; frost improves the plants' flavor and makes them less bitter.

Belgian endive, also known as witloof chicory, is entirely different from curly endive and escarole. Under normal growing conditions, Belgian endive produces bitter greens, but when grown indoors out of season, it makes a delicious winter salad crop. "Forcing Belgian Endive" on this page shows how.

Planting: Both curly endive and escarole prefer humus-rich soil in full sun.

For an early-summer harvest, sow seeds indoors in flats two months before the last frost date; thin to 6" apart. Four weeks after sowing, plant the 4"-5" seedlings 1' apart, slightly deeper in the soil than they were in flats. Provide shade if the weather turns hot.

For fall crops, seed in July, about 90 days before the date of the first frost; stagger plantings every two weeks to extend the harvest. Water the ground thoroughly before sowing three seeds per inch; cover the seeds with ⅓" of sand, soil, or peat. Thin the seedlings to at least 1' apart in all directions. Overlapping leaves can cause the plants to rot.

Growing guidelines: Water regularly, because leaves will be tough and bitter if the soil dries out. Endive needs about 1" of water per week. Wet plants tend to rot, though, so soak the soil, not the foliage.

Blanching keeps light out of the interior and turns the heart a creamy yellow color. You can blanch endive during the last 2-3 weeks of growth by tying the leaf tops together with rub-

Forcing Belgian endive. In late spring, sow seeds of Belgian endive (*Cichorium intybus*) outdoors in deep loose soil. Dig the roots in fall, and cut off the tops 2' above the crown. Trim the roots and set in an upright position in boxes or flowerpots. Fill the containers with potting mix to the tops of the roots; add 6"-8" of sand on top of that. Keep moist and at a temperature of 60°-70°F. Harvest the heads when their tips peek up through the sand.

ber bands or twine. Make sure the leaves are dry when you do this, or the head may rot. Blanching produces a milder, less bitter taste, but it also reduces endive's vitamin content.

Problems: Unless water stands in the hearts of the plants (promoting rot), endive is usually problem-free. To avoid rot, untie plants after a rainstorm, and let the leaves dry before retying. For details on controlling the few aphids or cutworms that may attack, see "The Top Ten Garden Insect Pests in America" on page 344.

Harvesting: Harvest individual leaves or an entire plant when needed. Cut the plants with a knife at ground level. If you leave undamaged roots and 1" of stem, new growth may occur in warm weather.

Best cultivars: 'Salad King', a curly endive, slow to bolt, resistant to tipburn and frost; 'Batavian Full Heart', escarole, slightly crinkled dark green leaves. ❖

Environment and Gardening

Put a seed into good soil, give it warmth and sunlight, air and water, and it will burst forth with flower and fruit. Withhold any one of the things a seed needs, and it withers and dies. All life, whether that of a seed or a human, depends on the gifts of nature.

The famous naturalist John Muir, founder of the Sierra Club, wrote about the "interconnectedness" of the natural world: Each part, however small or seemingly insignificant, is connected to the next in such a way that it's impossible to affect one without affecting the other. His point is amply illustrated by many of the environmental problems that face the planet today.

Acid rain, for example, begins as an air-pollution problem. Oxides of sulfur and nitrogen enter the air from industrial boilers and vehicle exhaust. High aloft, they are changed chemically into acidic compounds and fall to earth as acid rain or snow, sometimes hundreds of miles from the original pollution source. Normal rain is nearly neutral—around 7.0 on the pH scale. Storms in some U.S. areas have produced rain with a pH as low as 2.0—more acidic than vinegar.

Acid rain runs into streams and lakes, which then become acidic. Unable to adapt to the higher acidity, fish and other aquatic animals die. Soils may also become more acidic, killing trees and other plants or making them more vulnerable to disease and insects. Mammals and birds that relied on the streams and forests for food and shelter are the next to be affected. As the environment loses its capacity to renew itself, we are the ultimate victims.

Power in Numbers

The United States, with less than 5 percent of the world's population, consumes more than ¼ of its energy resources. Not all of that goes into our automobiles or oil furnaces; some of it is turned into chemicals, plastics, and other products. Too often, these products are not designed to be recyclable. When they are worn out, they are thrown out, adding to environmental problems.

Thoughtful people have grappled for decades with the problems posed by our increasing demands on natural resources. Historically, responses have come from the government, in the form of antipollution rules and laws aimed at protecting the environment. Today, the most important action may be coming from the home and the backyard.

There are many ways individuals can help relieve the strain on the environment: choosing nontoxic and recycled or recyclable products, and using energy and water resources prudently. One of the best is planting and tending a garden, whether for food production, ornamental beauty, or wildlife habitat. A homegrown tomato saves the energy (and pollution) required to truck it from faraway farm to wholesaler to retailer to your kitchen. The effect of each action may be small, but the collective effect of many millions of individual actions can be powerful.

Environmentalism

Until the middle of the twentieth century, much of the nation's work on behalf of the environment was in the realm of conservation—setting aside areas of particular scenic beauty or value to wildlife as parks and nature preserves.

Rising concern about air and water pollution in the 1960s led to Earth Day in 1970 and the passage of laws aimed at protecting the environment more broadly. From that era came the Clean Water Act, the Clean Air Act, and the Environmental Protection Agency, the federal office directly responsible for controlling pollution. Other federal agencies play important roles in such areas as wildlife protection, soil conservation, and health standards. See the Government Agencies entry for information on the areas with which these organizations are concerned.

More laws have been added as the nation became aware of the extent of environmental problems. Toxic chemicals and the pollution of underground water supplies, for example, were scarcely considered in the early days of the envi-

ENVIRONMENTAL ORGANIZATIONS

Environmental organizations are good sources of information about problems, laws, and regulations. Many also can offer practical guidance on ways to avoid wasting or damaging natural resources. Here are some of the national groups and the issues they follow most closely:

● Clean Water Action Project, 1320 18th Street NW, Washington, D.C. 20036. (Also regional and state offices.) Water quality and toxic-chemical control.
● Environmental Defense Fund, 257 Park Avenue South, New York, NY 10010. (Also regional offices.) Many issues, including energy and resource conservation, air quality, and wildlife.
● Friends of the Earth, 218 D Street SE, Washington, D.C. 20003. Many issues, including energy, water, agriculture, and toxic substances.
● National Audubon Society, 950 Third Avenue, New York, NY 10022 (Also chapters and regional offices). Land, water, and wildlife conservation.
● National Coalition Against the Misuse of Pesticides, 701 E Street SE, Suite 200, Washington, D.C. 20003. Agricultural chemicals and groundwater problems.
● National Wildlife Federation, 1400 Sixteenth Street NW, Washington, D.C. 20036. (Also regional and state offices.) Many issues, including wildlife, air, water, forests, and soil resources.
● Natural Resources Defense Council, 40 West 20th Street, New York, NY 10011. Many issues, including pesticides, air and water quality, and urban environment.
● The Nature Conservancy, 1815 North Lynn Street, Arlington, VA 22209. Preservation of critical wildlife habitat and natural areas.
● Sierra Club, 730 Polk Street, San Francisco, CA 94109. (Also chapters and field offices.) Many issues, including resource conservation.

ronmental movement. Today, there are many laws regulating these and many other environmental concerns.

In the United States as well as other nations, environmentalism has become a potent political force. The so-called "green movement," begun in West Germany in the late 1970s to promote environmental as well as social and economic concerns, has official political parties in more than a dozen countries. Some of the "green parties" have successfully fielded candidates. Others have used their base of popular support to influence policy, such as winning more funds for environmental research.

In this country, the green movement is more diverse and less formal. The political momentum tends to come from concerned and knowledgable citizens, often working through local or national environmental organizations. Some of these groups are broad-based membership organizations with a wide field of interests; others are concerned with specific issues. You can add your voice by joining those groups that focus on the issues that concern you most.

Protecting the Air

When the environmental movement was young, cleaning up the air meant getting rid of the sooty plumes coming from America's smokestacks and tailpipes. In 1970, sooty emissions, or *particulates,* as the government calls them, amounted to more than 18 million metric tons a year. By 1985, they were down to 7.3 million tons—a drop of nearly 60 percent. But that's not all that comes out of the smokestack. The following figures explain why air quality is still a major concern:

● Sulfur dioxide: 28.2 million metric tons in 1970; 20.7 million in 1985. A drop of about 26 percent.
● Nitrogen oxides: 18.1 million tons in 1970; 20 million in 1985. A 10 percent increase.
● Hydrocarbons: 27.2 million tons in 1970;

21.3 million tons in 1985. A 21 percent decrease.

Acid Rain

Sulfur dioxide and nitrogen oxides play a major part in the formation of acid rain. Sulfur dioxide also leads to the formation of *sulfate haze*—a type of air pollution that is gradually obscuring many of our most scenic vistas. Nitrogen oxides and hydrocarbons are involved in the formation of ozone in the lower atmosphere, leading to the familiar form of air pollution that we know as smog.

All of these pollutants are damaging to health, particularly the lungs and respiratory systems of both humans and animals. They also can damage vegetation, including the plants in your garden. Scientists have recorded yield reductions of up to 30 percent in agricultural crops subjected to ozone pollution. In some urban areas, plants for landscaping must be carefully chosen to avoid species that cannot tolerate pollution, such as the eastern white pine.

Poor air quality can hamper growth and weaken plants, making them more susceptible to disease and weather stress and more vulnerable to insect predators. Acid rain, if acidic enough, can "scorch" the foliage of some sensitive crops such as beans; it also makes it more difficult to maintain soil pH at the near-neutral levels many cultivars need to thrive.

The Greenhouse Effect

The earth's atmosphere contains moisture and gases that trap solar energy, like a greenhouse cover that holds in the sun's heat. If it did not, the earth would be more than 90°F colder than it is now and life as we know it would not be possible.

However, in the industrial era, the heat-trapping gases, especially carbon dioxide, have become more concentrated. Carbon dioxide is a natural product of life processes. When you exhale, you breathe out carbon dioxide. Decaying plant material gives off carbon dioxide. Burning wood

MUSCLE POWER

Each gasoline-powered piece of equipment, from your car to your lawn mower, adds to pollution problems—not only exhaust fumes and gases, but noise as well.

Replace your noisy, polluting, energy-draining machines with people-powered tools whenever you can. If your lawn is small, consider using a hand-powered reel mower to cut it. Replace demanding lawn grass with naturalistic landscaping. Try a scythe or a pair of grass shears instead of a string trimmer; a hoe and shovel instead of a rotary tiller. Use a rake instead of a leaf blower, a shovel instead of a snow blower. You get the idea—good old-fashioned muscle power instead of internal combustion or electricity.

Keep the machines you can't live without well maintained for better efficiency.

If you find yourself spending more time on outdoor maintenance than you'd like, it may be time to rethink your landscaping. You'll find a good selection of tips for reducing maintenance in the Groundcovers, Landscaping, Mulch, Natural Landscaping, and Xeriscaping entries.

and fossil fuels—oil and coal, the carbon-rich remnants of ancient plants—also produces carbon dioxide.

Of all the carbon dioxide added to the atmosphere during human history, half was added in the last 30 years. As the earth's atmosphere traps more of the sun's heat, we appear to be headed for major climate change—global warming.

Estimates are that the earth could be as much as 9°F warmer, on average, by the year 2040. If that sounds like only a slight difference, consider that the earth was only 9°F colder, on average, during the coldest part of the last Ice Age than it is today.

The change won't affect all areas equally; some parts of the globe will heat up more than others, and some might actually get colder if the change affects the course of ocean currents. The big unknown is what global climate change will do, not just to daily temperatures, but to weather patterns. With the help of computers, scientists are guessing now that winters in North America will be colder, wetter, and shorter; summers will be hotter, drier, and longer.

By current calculation, the earth is warming 5-10 times faster than it did at the end of the last Ice Age. That may be much faster than native plants and animals can adapt. Instead of hardwood and pine forests, we may end up with shrubby woodland. Many species of insects, birds, and other animals could perish along with their habitat.

It may not be possible to halt the greenhouse effect entirely, but slowing it would make it easier for plants and animals—and humans—to adapt to global warming. Conserving energy is an important step; burning fossil fuels is the chief source of the problem. Another way to slow down global warming is by protecting forests, which store vast amounts of carbon in their living tissue. Tropical rainforests, for example, are being cut down at the rate of more than 54 acres every minute; their decaying vegetation may account for $1/5$ of the excess carbon dioxide in the atmosphere.

Solvents such as dry cleaning fluid and paint thinners are sources of hydrocarbons, so use them sparingly if at all. Buy the least amount you need, and keep the container tightly sealed between uses to minimize evaporation. Avoid buying products made from exotic tropical woods, such as teak, unless they are plantation-grown. Reputable manufacturers proudly label their products. The demand for redwood increases pressure for logging of large, old-growth trees. Substitute easily grown pine instead. Recycle paper products and patronize manufacturers who use recycled paper. See "Recycling in the Garden" on the opposite page for ideas on items you can reuse in your garden.

The Ozone Layer

In the lower atmosphere, ozone is an air pollutant. But in the stratosphere, miles above the earth, ozone shields the earth from the sun's most harmful rays—the ultraviolet rays. Certain man-made chemicals are destroying stratospheric ozone, allowing more ultraviolet radiation to strike the earth.

Exposure to ultraviolet radiation can damage eyes and skin, increasing skin cancers and cataracts. The effect on plant and animal life is less understood, but research has found that about $2/3$ of more than 200 plant species tested are sensitive to ultraviolet radiation. Among them are peas and beans, squash and melons, and cabbage-family members. Increased ultraviolet radiation most often stunted the plants and caused their leaves to grow abnormally small. Research on soybeans also suggests that excess ultraviolet radiation makes plants more susceptible to pests and disease.

Many nations have joined together in an effort to halt the release of chemicals most destructive to the ozone layer. Chief among these are the chlorofluorocarbons (CFCs), a family of chemicals that have been used for decades in our industries and in our homes. CFCs are used in refrigerators, freezers, and air conditioners. The computer industry uses them as solvents to clean delicate microchips. CFCs put the fizz in aerosol cans and the bubbles in plastic foam products such as insulation, disposable cups, and fast-food containers.

Chlorofluorocarbons are extremely stable; they do not degrade in the environment on earth. Instead, they float gradually up to the stratosphere and come apart only under intense solar radiation. Molecules of ozone are destroyed by chlorine atoms flung out in the process.

Many industries, including McDonald's restaurants, have started using substitutes that pose less environmental risk. But the ozone problem is likely to worsen as the CFCs already manufactured make their way to the stratosphere.

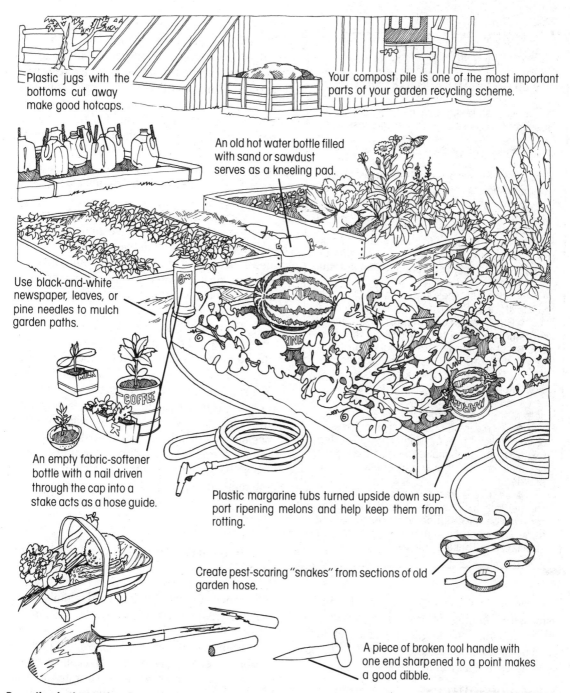

Plastic jugs with the bottoms cut away make good hotcaps.

Your compost pile is one of the most important parts of your garden recycling scheme.

An old hot water bottle filled with sand or sawdust serves as a kneeling pad.

Use black-and-white newspaper, leaves, or pine needles to mulch garden paths.

An empty fabric-softener bottle with a nail driven through the cap into a stake acts as a hose guide.

Plastic margarine tubs turned upside down support ripening melons and help keep them from rotting.

Create pest-scaring "snakes" from sections of old garden hose.

A piece of broken tool handle with one end sharpened to a point makes a good dibble.

Recycling in the garden. Recycling and gardening go together as naturally as soil and seeds. Look for opportunities to recycle household materials in your garden, as well as recycling as much of your yard and garden waste as possible.

Smart Shopping
ENVIRONMENT AND GARDENING

Responsible shopping can help conserve resources and ease environmental pressures.

● Buy locally grown produce, organic if possible. This saves energy used in transportation. Organic production reduces chemical pollution that can damage water supplies.

● Buy grocery items in bulk, and use your own storage containers. This saves packaging and reduces the waste stream.

● Make it a habit to carry a string sack in pocket or purse. Use it instead of the store's paper or plastic bags for incidental purchases.

● Take last week's grocery bags along to the store to hold this week's groceries.

● Buy items in returnable or recyclable containers—and return or recycle them.

● Look for items that are made from recycled materials. This can help build the market for recycled products, encouraging even more recycling.

● Read labels carefully and choose products that are low in toxicity.

● Try old-fashioned remedies instead of commercial preparations that are often toxic. Baking soda makes a fine all-purpose cleanser; ordinary borax is an effective roach powder.

● Shop at stores that specialize in "environmentally friendly" merchandise, such as recycled paper products and energy-saving items; there are also mail-order firms that specialize in these products.

You can protect yourself and your family by using sunscreening lotions when you work or play outdoors; don't forget that small children need protection, too. Protect your eyes with good sunglasses and a visored hat.

Water Resources

Only 3 percent of the earth's water is fresh; the rest is salt water. Fresh water is a renewable resource, cycled continuously through the processes of evaporation and rainfall, but it is no longer one we can take for granted. In the 1980s, prolonged periods of drought drained reservoirs and forced many cities to adopt water conservation measures. Underground water supplies are under pressure as well. One-fourth of the irrigated farmland in the United States is watered by drawing from underground sources; in some areas, the demand of water by agriculture has lowered the water table by as much as 4' every year.

Part of the problem is population growth, creating water demands that cannot be met with existing supplies and delivery systems. Even if new reservoirs and pipelines are built, however, there is no guarantee of enough water to fill them, especially if the greenhouse effect significantly changes rainfall patterns.

There are many ways to save water in the garden. For landscaping, choose native plants that require little or no water beyond what nature provides. See the Natural Landscaping and Xeriscaping entries for suggestions. Minimize lawn areas in favor of less-thirsty groundcovers. Mulching conserves soil moisture; watering methods such as drip irrigation or soaker hoses can reduce evaporation by directing water to plant roots. The Irrigation entry will help you choose the method that's right for you.

Water Purity

In the past, most water-quality rules were aimed at keeping sewage and industrial wastes from fouling streams and lakes. Now it appears that much of what is contaminating our water is coming from our farms, our yards, and our city streets.

Runoff from farmland can contain high levels of nutrients from fertilizers and animal wastes, particularly nitrates. Excessive nitrates in drinking water may cause birth defects and a serious type of blood poisoning in infants, high blood pressure in children, and gastric cancers in adults.

GRAY WATER

Chronic water shortages in some areas have increased interest in recycling so-called gray water—that is, household wastewater from sources other than the toilet. Water from the washing machine or dishpan may be suitable for use on ornamental plants and some edible crops such as fruit trees, but you should avoid using it on seedlings, leafy vegetables, or root crops that you eat uncooked.

Because wastewater is alkaline, avoid using it on acid-loving plants such as hollies and rhododendrons. Alternate gray water with fresh water to cleanse the soil of sodium salts from soaps and detergents; do not use gray water if your household water is treated with sodium-based softeners. If you use washing-machine water, avoid bleach and do not use boron-based detergents; boron can be toxic to plants.

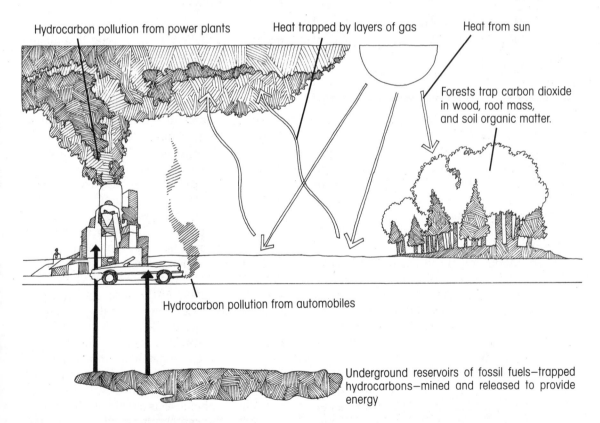

Hydrocarbon pollution from power plants

Heat trapped by layers of gas

Heat from sun

Forests trap carbon dioxide in wood, root mass, and soil organic matter.

Hydrocarbon pollution from automobiles

Underground reservoirs of fossil fuels—trapped hydrocarbons—mined and released to provide energy

Plants and the greenhouse effect. Help stave off global warming by planting new trees. Plants remove carbon dioxide from the air and use it to build tissue. Annual plants and herbaceous perennials release much of that carbon each year as they die and decay, but woody, long-lived plants like trees can store it for many decades.

THE POWER OF THE PEN

What can one person do to save the Earth? When environmental problems seem overwhelming, pick up your pen. To find out names of executives and corporate addresses, ask your library for a directory of corporations. To whom should you write?

● Your representatives in local, state, and national government. Your library has their names and addresses—and their phone numbers.
● Manufacturers and users of agricultural chemicals.
● Auto manufacturers.
● Companies that use excess packaging materials.
● Manufacturers and users of plastic-foam cups and containers.
● Mail-order firms that use foam "peanuts" for packing.
● The editor of your local newspaper.

Nitrates also seep into the soil, where they can contaminate well-water. When combined with pesticides, nitrates can form cancer-causing compounds called nitrosamines.

Because there is less open land to absorb water, runoff from urban areas can be even more polluted. Storm drains collect rainwater laden with heavy metals and hydrocarbons from traffic emissions, chemicals from road de-icers, and home-use pesticides and fertilizers. In some areas, water has been contaminated by toxic-waste dumps and chemicals leaking from industrial storage tanks. Many household products contain dangerous chemical compounds that can contaminate water supplies if they are poured down the drain or emptied into the nearest storm sewer.

Farmers are being encouraged—and sometimes ordered—to handle fertilizers, pesticides, and animal wastes in ways that reduce the poten-

tial for pollution. Urban dwellers can help reduce pollution by not using synthetic chemicals in their homes or yards. Handle all potentially hazardous chemical products with caution. Contact local waste authorities for advice on disposing of unwanted chemical products.

Reduce runoff and erosion in your yard by planting groundcovers and using loose mulches. Soils rich in organic matter have more capacity to absorb water; this reduces runoff while retaining more moisture in the soil where plants can use it. See the Soil entry for more information on improving soil organic matter and reducing soil erosion.

Biodiversity

Biodiversity is the term used to refer to the multitude of life forms and species that inhabit the earth, from the smallest microorganism to the largest mammal. The ecological significance of many of these life forms has yet to be discovered—in fact, some life forms themselves are still undiscovered—but it is known that many species are disappearing or shrinking in numbers. To find out more about plants in trouble, see the Endangered Plant Species entry.

The chief reason for loss of species is loss of habitat. As forests, marshlands, and other species-rich areas are developed or converted to other human uses, wildlife is lost. The most threatened habitat is tropical forestland, which makes up only 6 percent of earth's land surface but is home to an estimated 50-90 percent of all species. The effect of this loss can be seen in your own backyard—fewer migratory songbirds, for example, as species lose their wintering habitat in Central America and Mexico.

A healthy environment needs a diversity of life forms. In a garden, for example, destructive insects can be kept in control with the help of predators—other insects or animals that prey on the pests. You can encourage diversity by providing habitat. Attract insects and birds with plants that produce nectar, seeds, or berries; a moist shelter, such as an overturned clay pot or shady nook, may attract an insect-devouring toad to your garden. For ideas on attracting these helpful species, see the Beneficial Animals, Beneficial Insects, Birds, Toads, and Wildlife entries.

Recycling Waste

Municipal waste in the United States amounts to more than 178 million metric tons every year, more than 3 lb. a day per person. Industrial waste amounts to another 613 million metric tons; 250 million metric tons of that is considered hazardous waste. Hundreds of toxic-waste dumps have leaked poisons into groundwater or contaminated soils and streams. Municipal landfills also can release pollutants, some of them toxic. Landfills are filling up, and finding new dump sites is increasingly difficult.

The economic and environmental cost of waste disposal has led to new interest in waste reduction and recycling. In many areas, over half of municipal garbage consists of compostable yard waste such as prunings, clippings, and leaves. By composting the waste instead of burying it, cities save money and produce valuable organic material. The Composting entry will show you how to compost your own yard waste.

Recycling glass, aluminum, paper, and other materials reduces the waste stream; it also saves resources and energy. Making new aluminum cans from recycled ones requires 96 percent less energy than producing new aluminum. Switching from nondegradable packaging materials such as plastic to degradable papers, cellophane, and cardboard can help ease the waste problem. Remember, though, that even paper does not break down easily in the oxygen-free conditions of a landfill; to be beneficial to the environment, such materials must be recycled or composted.

To reduce your own waste stream, buy fewer disposable items. Look for products with the least amount of unnecessary packaging. A little imagination can turn many other throwaways into useful items for the garden. ❖

Epimedium

Epimedium, bishop's hat. Deciduous, evergreen, or semi-evergreen perennial groundcovers.

Description: *Epimedium grandiflorum,* long-spurred epimedium, grows 1' tall. Leaves are divided into leathery, heart-shaped leaflets to 3" long. New leaves are tinged with pink, maturing to green, then turning bronze in autumn. In May, plants bear loose sprays of small spurred flowers in white, pink, or violet. Zones 3-8.

How to grow: Epimediums thrive in humus-rich, well-drained, acid soil in sun or shade. Mulch plants with leaf mold to retain moisture. Divide after flowering, setting plants 8"-10" apart. Cut off old leaves in spring before flowering. Plants are evergreen in the South with protection, deciduous or semi-evergreen in the North.

Landscape uses: Epimediums are grown primarily for their striking foliage. Because they can tolerate dry shade, you can use them under trees and among shrubs. ❖

Erosion

Soil erosion occurs in nature; man's "improvements" to nature accelerate this wearing away of soil and cause worldwide environmental damage. Land covered by vegetation loses about an inch of soil every 100-250 years. This loss is offset by new soil formation. But many human activities —including clear-cutting forested slopes, repeated monocropping using only chemical fertilizers, and driving heavy machinery over unpaved ground—hasten erosion by damaging soil structure and reducing soil organic matter content. Without the binding effects of humus, organic matter, and microorganisms, soils are more vulnerable to the damaging effects of rain and wind. Drops of water that would have been easily absorbed by soil organic matter become torrents that erode soil by the ton. For methods to reduce erosion, see the Soil and Environment and Gardening entries. ❖

Espalier

An espalier (pronounced is-PAL-yuhr) is a fruit tree or an ornamental shrub that is pruned to grow in a flat plane. Although sometimes free-standing, an espaliered plant is generally attached to a framework against a wall, and is usually trained in a well-defined pattern.

Espalier plants are ideal for those who want fruit, but have limited space. Although you get less fruit per plant with espaliers than with orchard trees, the fruit develops more perfectly because each one is better exposed to sunlight and air. The heavy pruning espaliers require also encourages larger fruits.

Espaliers are more attractive than many foundation plantings, but they will take a few years to grow and establish their pleasing patterns. Trained plants can add interest to plain surfaces along the side of a building or in front of a wall. They can create a beautiful living fence between properties or garden areas.

Before deciding to start an espalier, remember that it needs one of the trickier kinds of pruning. The process is time-consuming, and it's only for fearless pruners. All espaliers require persistent attention to direct growth where it is wanted. Unwanted growth has to be removed before it weakens the plant and strays from the pattern. If you like a manicured look and having a project that needs regular attention, then espaliers could be right for you.

Selecting Plants

To create an espalier, it's best to start with a young, unbranched tree. A young tree has an abundance of energy and can withstand vigorous pruning without damage to its health. An older tree that's been allowed to grow normally is difficult to convert to an espalier. It would require radical pruning that could weaken it and make it susceptible to disease and insects. You may be able to get a head start with espalier-trained trees from a garden center or nursery.

They're more expensive, but the basic pattern is already started; you'll still have to train them regularly after planting.

In general, slow-growing dwarf plants are best for espalier. In cold climates, pick the hardiest cultivars available. Choose fruit trees that produce their fruit on spurs (short twigs along the stems), such as apples, and not on the branch tips, like peaches. Remember that you may need more than one plant to get good pollination for the fruit.

Recommended plants for espalier include: camellias, citrus fruits, crab apples, figs, forsythias, dwarf fruit trees, fuchsias, evergreen magnolias, cotoneasters (*Cotoneaster* spp.), flowering quince (*Chaenomeles speciosa*), fragrant viburnums (e.g., *Viburnum carlesii* and *V.* × *carlcephalum*), ginkgos (*Ginkgo biloba*), hawthorns (*Crataegus* spp.), pyracanthas or firethorns (*Pyracantha* spp.), sweet bay (*Laurus nobilis*), and yews (*Taxus* spp.). Avoid standard (full-size) fruit trees, hydrangeas, lilacs, and honeysuckles (*Lonicera* spp.). Plums, cherries, peaches, apricots, and nut trees are also difficult to train.

Sites

Like most plants, espaliers generally thrive in rich, well-drained soil. If you want to plant an espalier close to the foundation of your house, you may find that the soil there is infertile, compacted, or alkaline. Carefully consider these conditions and improve the soil before planting. Be ready with some kind of irrigation that won't flood your basement or foundation wall when you water the espalier. Also, avoid planting along a driveway or walkway where you use salt to melt ice in winter. For more information on soil improvement, see the Soil entry. For more on watering, see the Irrigation entry.

In the South, an espalier will get too hot in a spot that receives direct sun all day. A nonreflective background surface is better there since it gives off less heat. To modify the temperature, you

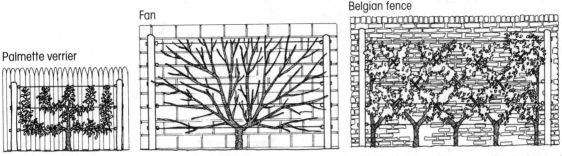

Classic espalier patterns. The formal palmette verrier pattern is ideal for plants that flower on spurs, like apples and pyracantha. Plants that flower on vigorous one-year-old shoots, such as peach, or on current growth, such as citrus, are better suited to more informal or upright patterns, such as a fan. Belgian fence makes a beautiful living screen.

can train the espalier onto a framework that stands away from the wall or keep more leaves on the espalier to shade the wall.

In cooler summer areas, you can safely place an espalier along a south-facing wall. The fruit ripens earlier because it's sheltered. If your area is usually too cold for grapes, you may find that they will bear fruit as espaliers on the south side of a building. A wall color and material that gives off heat is a better background for espaliers in the North.

All plants should have at least 6″ between them and a wall. It is not a good practice to tie branches directly to a wall, because pruning is difficult when the branches lie flat. It also makes repainting the building nearly impossible. The fruit will not be able to develop naturally on one side. And air circulation, which is crucial to avoiding fungal diseases, is hampered by the closeness of the wall. Plants that need spraying for pests should not be espaliered on wooden walls, painted or unpainted, because sprays can discolor or stain the surface.

Types of Supports

For espaliers, you need strong supports. You can use a lattice, trellis, or wire fence. Wire is easiest and usually the most practical support for fruit trees. Wooden trellises are common, but you can also use metal supports if your summers are not too hot. It looks good to use a support that has the same pattern as the espalier will have, but a simple rectangular grid will also do.

For a wire fence, set 4″ × 4″ × 8′ posts at the expected outside spread of each plant. In the North, place them deep enough to avoid frost heaving. If you're using wires, brace the posts to prevent them from sagging.

Next, staple smooth, #10-gauge wire from one support to the other. String the first wire horizontally about 3′ from the ground, or lower if you have a certain pattern in mind. Place the next horizontal strand of wire 1′-2′ above the first strand, and so on. You'll need at least three strands, but you may use more, depending upon the pattern you want to achieve.

Patterns

There are many patterns for training espaliers. "Classic Espalier Patterns" above shows three of the most popular patterns: palmette verrier, fan, and Belgian fence. In addition to the usual ones, you can also establish an informal pattern to suit a more naturalistic garden and plants that don't form spurs. Train the branches (or at least the tips) of informal, fruit-bearing espaliers at an angle of at least 30° above the horizontal to encourage branch vigor and flower production.

Planting and Training

Plant your young tree about 1' away from the framework, to allow room for the trunk to expand as it grows. Space it midway between the two posts.

Start careful pruning early in the life of the tree, and continue it at regular intervals during the whole life of the espalier. As an espalier gets older, less and less pruning is needed. It may take several years of training to "finish" a pattern. Once the main framework of branches is established, little or no tying is necessary, but you will always need to do some pruning. This is the only way to achieve and retain an attractive pattern.

The specific techniques you will use depend on the pattern you've chosen. In general, strive for a balanced pattern as well as balanced plant health. The balanced pattern is achieved by encouraging weaker branches and discouraging branches that are too vigorous. Do this by pruning the strong branches shorter and allowing weaker ones to grow longer. Rub off side buds on the stronger branches right away, but leave the buds on weaker branches. Tie the more vigorous branches frequently and closely to the supports. (Sisal twine is an excellent material for tying espalier, because it will break before it girdles the branch. Don't use plastic twine, which might girdle the branches as they expand.) Leave weaker branches growing freely a little while longer. Remove some leaves from the stronger ones, and remove all fruit from the weaker ones.

Early in summer, pinch back each lateral branch as soon as it has made 3-4 leaves. Also pinch back terminal shoots when they have made a few inches of growth. If a lot of leafy growth

> ## More On
> ### ESPALIER
> To learn more about creating espalier and other exciting topiary projects, check out *The Complete Book of Topiary* by Barbara Gallup and Deborah Reich.

occurs as summer progresses, nip out a few shoots entirely. This sort of maintenance preserves the pattern and reduces the amount of growth. Remember, you are trying to achieve a balance, and only by keeping your espalier small will it be healthy.

Throughout the growing season, remove branches that are not growing in the right direction. Remember that you want the espalier to be flat against the support, so remove shoots that start growing out and away from the framework. Don't let fruiting spurs develop more closely than 5"-7" apart. When very old spurs bear repeatedly, either prune the spur or plan to thin out the fruit in early summer. Spur wood is fragile, so take great care in pruning.

During the dormant season (late winter is better in the North), cut back every lateral branch to 2-3 buds. If laterals are close together, remove some to prevent a bunchy look. At the same time, shorten every vertical shoot. If there has been moderate growth (from 4"-8"), just cut back each tip to a healthy-looking side bud. If growth has been vigorous (more than 9"), remove up to ⅔ of the shoot. Also cut back the leader if it is growing above the desired height.

Prune evergreen espaliers throughout the growing season. Start early in spring just before growth begins. Remove crowding branches entirely. Cut back terminal shoots to within a few inches of the previous year's wood. ❖

Eucalyptus

Eucalyptus, gum tree. Evergreen or deciduous flowering trees or shrubs.

Description: *Eucalyptus cinerea,* silver-dollar tree, grows 20'-30' in the landscape with an open, irregular form. The aromatic juvenile foliage is round, gray-green, and arranged in pairs on the branch; like many eucalyptus, young leaves are attached directly onto branches and without petioles. Reddish brown fibrous bark is typical of the group of eucalyptus Australians call "stringybarks." Zones 8-10.

E. gunnii, cider gum, has a mature height of 15'-40'. Cider gum has shedding, green-and-white mottled bark and yellow fall flowers. The evergreen leaves are opposite, round, and blue-green when young, maturing to a darker green lance shape. Zones 8-10.

How to grow: Native to Australia, eucalyptus trees perform best as landscape plants on the West Coast of the United States where conditions are similar to those of their native habitat. The Southeast's warm autumns force these trees into late-season growth, and cold injury soon follows. Grow eucalyptus in full sun and dry, extremely well drained soil. High fertility and excess moisture cause root rot and rank top growth. Provide support, such as stakes, when necessary. Bees visit the flowers of most eucalyptus, and excellent honey results.

Landscape uses: Eucalyptus trees are good choices for dry, infertile sites where screening or bank stabilization might be necessary. Some gardeners grow eucalyptus strictly for the juvenile foliage, which is used in floral arrangements. Such trees are cut back close to the ground each year (known as coppicing); this practice prevents the development of adult foliage, and the resulting juvenile shoots are harvested. Because of their fragrant foliage, some eucalyptus are grown as houseplants; these are also pruned to maintain juvenile traits. ❖

Euonymus

Euonymus, spindle tree. Evergreen or deciduous shrubs or small trees; evergreen groundcovers or vines.

Description: *Euonymus alata,* burning bush or winged spindle tree, is a deciduous shrub with an upright, eventually spreading habit. It reaches 12'-15'. Distinctive thin wings of bark form on its branches. The 1"-3", medium to dark green foliage turns bright red in fall, fading to shades of pink before falling. This shrub is commonly used in its wide range of adaptability. Zones 4-8.

E. bungeana, winterberry euonymus, is a tree-form euonymus that grows to a mature height of about 18'. As the tree ages, interesting striations appear on its trunk. This tree has yellow fall color and pink fruits, which open to expose bright red-orange seed coats that persist into the winter. Zones 4-7.

E. fortunei, wintercreeper, has countless cultivars, which range from groundcovers to vines to tall shrubs. The foliage is evergreen, usually glossy, sometimes variegated, and subject to wintertime bronzing. Although this euonymus will grow in Zones 4-9, scale insects severely limit its use in Zones 8-9.

E. japonica, Japanese euonymus, is an evergreen shrub that grows to a mature height of 6'-10' with an upright form. The dark green, serrated, leathery leaves often display dramatic variegated patterns. Zones 8-9.

How to grow: Site deciduous species in full sun to promote robust growth and fully developed fall color. Plant evergreen euonymus in a spot protected from sun and wind. North of Zone 8, plant in fall or spring; in Zones 8-9, plant in fall or winter. Euonymus thrives in humus-rich soil with even moisture and good drainage. The deciduous species appear to be less susceptible to scale than the evergreens, but they do sometimes get it—usually on the branches rather than the leaves. Control scale with oil sprays. Crown gall, a fungal disease, may also be serious on wintercreeper and Japanese euonymus. Deer with few other food sources will eat deciduous euonymus; where deer are a problem, choose another shrub.

Landscape uses: Burning bush makes an attractive hedge, massed planting, or screen; it is stunning in fall. Use winterberry euonymus and Japanese euonymus as eye-catching focal points. Depending on the cultivar, use wintercreeper as a groundcover, vine, or shrub.

Best cultivars: *E. alata* 'Compactus' is rounded, reaching 10', without the notable corky bark wings of the species; 'Rudy Haag' is even more compact, growing only 4'-5' tall, with lovely pinkish red fall foliage; 'October Glory' has outstanding red fall color. *E. bungeana* var. *pendula* is a weeping form. *E. fortunei:* many, including var. *coloratus,* a groundcover with plum-colored fall foliage; 'Gold Prince', 2' mound with gold-tipped new foliage. ❖

Euphorbia

Spurge. Spring-blooming perennials.

Description: *Euphorbia epithymoides,* cushion spurge, bears small flowers in 2"-3" heads surrounded by showier greenish yellow leafy bracts. Plants form symmetrical 1'-1½' mounds of 2" leaves that turn orange and red in fall. Zones 3-8.

How to grow: Set out small plants or carefully separated divisions during early spring in full sun and average to poor, well-drained or dry soil. To avoid leaf diseases, provide afternoon shade in areas with long, hot summers.

Landscape uses: Plant as a specimen or group in borders, rock gardens, and walls; allow to self-sow. Interplant with red tulips in spring; contrast with dwarf blue or purple asters in fall. ❖

Evergreens

Many people think "Christmas tree" at the mention of evergreens. Since all plants that retain their green color throughout the year can properly be called evergreens, there is a broad range of shapes and sizes. Evergreen can mean a 60' fir tree—or the diminutive groundcover common periwinkle.

Evergreens are divided into two groups according to the general shape of their leaves. Narrow-leaved or needle evergreens include plants such as junipers, pines, and yews. Most needle evergreens are very hardy and can be successfully grown over much of the United States.

Broad-leaved evergreens, which usually have showy flowers or fruit, are generally not as cold-hardy. But some types, such as azaleas and

Key Words
EVERGREENS

Evergreen. A plant that retains its leaves year-round.

Deciduous. A plant that drops all of its leaves in the fall.

Semi-evergreen. A plant that keeps some of its leaves year-round. Many semi-evergreens, such as cotoneasters, are evergreen in mild climates and semi-evergreen in colder regions.

Needle drop. The natural shedding process of narrow-leaved evergreens. The life of a needle may be 1–10 years, depending on species. Some old needles are dropped each year.

Candles. New shoots that grow from the branch tips of needle evergreens in a flush of spring growth.

Conifer. A cone-bearing plant, often an evergreen. Not all conifers are evergreens; Larch (*Larix* spp.), dawn redwood (*Metasequoia glyptostroboides*), and bald cypress (*Taxodium distichum*) are conifers, but all drop their needles in autumn.

rhododendrons (*Rhododendron* spp.), hollies (*Ilex* spp.), and Japanese barberry (*Berberis thunbergii*) are widely adaptable. Tender evergreens, such as gardenias (*Gardenia* spp.), are grown only in the warmest regions of the country.

Low maintenance and moderate water use are two of the most important advantages of evergreens. To reduce the lawn area in your yard, use shade-tolerant species to create small woodlands, which are an attractive low-care alternative to lawn grass. Spreading species like low-growing junipers cover ground quickly and eliminate grass-cutting chores.

Evergreens are always a popular choice for foundation plantings. Select species with similar form for foundation plantings to avoid a spotty appearance. For example, try grouping

soft flowing types of evergreens such as spreading junipers, yews (*Taxus* spp.), or hollies. They are most attractive when allowed to grow naturally and blend together.

Be sure to learn the mature height and spread of the foundation plants you are considering. The rule is patience: Allow time for your new small plants to mature and fill the space you have planned. If you make the mistake of planting cute little arborvitaes (*Thuja* spp.) under the window, or a white pine close to the house, you'll be continually pruning or cutting them down when they outgrow their space.

Try a background of evergreens to provide contrast and showcase your flowering shrubs and perennials. Plant a living privacy fence to screen deck, pool, or lawn. For an accent plant,

WHICH IS WHICH?

Sorting out the needle evergreens takes close-up detective work. Here are the clues:

● Arborvitae (*Thuja* spp.). Scalelike needles in fan-shaped sprays; soft to the touch.
● Fir (*Abies* spp.). Needles are flat, soft, two-sided, 1''–2½'' long.
● Hemlock (*Tsuga* spp.). Needles are flat, ¼''–1'' long, with two white-band markings on underside.

● Juniper (*Juniperus* spp.). Sharp awl-shaped needles, as well as fans of scalelike needles; both types harsh to the touch.
● Pine (*Pinus* spp.). Needles are thin, 2''–5'' long, in bundles of two, three, or five.
● Spruce (*Picea* spp.). Needles are thin, ½''–1¼'' long, with four sides and sharp points. Feel the edges by rolling between thumb and finger.
● Yew (*Taxus* spp.). Needles are flat, lustrous, dark green, ½''–1½'' long. Young twigs have green bark.

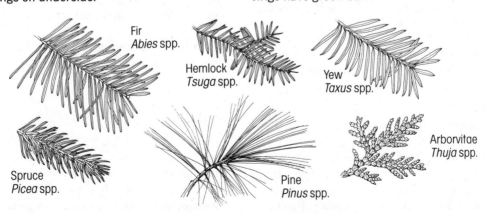

Fir
Abies spp.

Hemlock
Tsuga spp.

Yew
Taxus spp.

Spruce
Picea spp.

Pine
Pinus spp.

Arborvitae
Thuja spp.

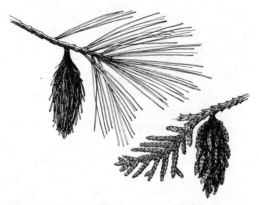

Bagworms. These moth larvae chew leaves of many kinds of evergreens. They spin silken bags studded with bits of needles; the bags may resemble pinecones. Handpick and destroy the bags in winter. Spray BTK (*Bacillus thuringiensis* var. *kurstaki*) for larvae in spring; catch adult moths in pheromone traps in summer.

choose a weeping Norway spruce such as *Picea abies* 'Pendula', or a blue Atlas cedar such as *Cedrus atlantica* 'Glauca'. Evergreens can even help save money on fuel bills: Plant them as a hedge to break the force of winter winds.

Planting and Care

Most evergreens like rich, humusy, moist but well-drained soil. Cypress, junipers, and pines tolerate dry soil once their roots are established. Some evergreens, such as azaleas, heathers, and rhododendrons, prefer acid soil. See the pH entry for information on how to alter soil pH in the planting area for these plants.

Carry an evergreen by its root ball or container, never by the trunk or branches. For planting and staking instructions, see the Planting entry.

Pruning

Evergreens that are the proper size for their location need very little pruning. Their natural growth habit is interesting and attractive. To remove unhealthy or errant growth, use a thinning cut, pruning off branches nearly flush against the branch from which they originate. For information on how to make pruning cuts correctly, see the Pruning and Training entry.

> ## More On
> ### EVERGREENS
>
> You can read more about broad-leaved evergreens in the Shrubs entry. Pachysandra and other evergreens are discussed in Groundcovers. For tips on using evergreens in home landscapes, see the Christmas Trees, Hedges, Landscaping, Natural Landscaping, Rock Gardens, and Trees entries.

Unlike broad-leaved evergreens, needle-leaved evergreens aren't quick to resprout after pruning. Take care to prune them properly. Follow these steps when pruning evergreens:

• Thin evergreens by removing branches any time of the year. Cut stray branches far enough to the inside to hide the stub. Branches cut back beyond the green needles will not sprout new growth.

• Don't cut the central leader at the top of the tree—an evergreen without its central leader will have a drastically different shape.

• Prune arborvitae, hemlocks, junipers, and yews throughout the growing season.

• Cut back firs, pines, and spruces only in spring when "candles" of new growth appear at the tips of the branches. To encourage denseness or shape the tree, cut off about $\frac{1}{2}$ or $\frac{2}{3}$ of the candle.

•Trim your evergreens gradually. If you cut off more than $\frac{1}{3}$ of the total green on the plant, it may die. ❖

Everlastings

Making dried flower arrangements is a wonderful way to bring the beauty of plants into your home year-round. Everlastings are common dried flowers that are a staple of these arrangements. For information on growing and using everlastings, see the Dried Flower Gardening entry. ❖

Fagus

Beech. Large deciduous trees.

Description: *Fagus grandifolia* is the handsome American beech. Massive with age, this North American native grows 50'-70' tall and almost as wide in the landscape. Its habit is upright in the forest, where it may reach heights of 100'-120' and spreading when in the open. Specimens are often short-trunked with densely pyramidal crowns. The alternate leaves are toothed and deeply veined, opening silvery green and maturing to a glossy dark green. Fall turns the foliage golden bronze; leaves persist on the tree through the winter. The bark is smooth and gray, becoming wrinkled like elephant hide with age. Zones 4-8.

F. sylvatica, European beech, is a similarly massive tree, 50'-60' tall in the landscape, with a rounded form and low branches that sweep the ground. Light green, deeply veined leaves with few or no marginal teeth emerge in late spring, becoming darker green in summer and turning bronze in autumn. Zones 5-7.

How to grow: Beeches have extensive, shallow root systems that are extremely sensitive to disturbances such as digging, changes in soil level, and soil compaction; protect them from such abuses. The combination of dense shade from the canopy and numerous shallow roots makes survival beneath a beech tree's branches virtually impossible for other plants; most lawn grasses quickly succumb. Plant beeches in full sun (they tolerate some shade) in well-drained, evenly moist soil; don't plant deeper than the depth at which they were grown in the nursery.

Landscape uses: Plant American or European beeches as focal points in the landscape, leaving plenty of room for their low, spreading branches and substantial mature size. American beech fares better in Southern heat and Midwestern winter exposure than does European beech, so choose it for those areas. Beeches are excellent for large-scale natural plantings, since edible beechnuts make good wildlife food, attracting squirrels and a variety of birds to the trees. European beeches withstand heavy pruning and can be shorn into an attractive deciduous hedge.

Best cultivars: *F. sylvatica:* 'Asplenifolia', fernleaf beech, has finely dissected foliage; 'Atropunicea' (sometimes offered as 'Purpurea'), purple beech, has young leaves that open very dark and turn purple-green with time; 'Cuprea', copper beech, related to purple beech but with coppery green leaves; 'Pendula' has weeping branches that sometimes take root, forming concentric rings of trees around the main trunk on very old specimens; 'Rotundifolia' has rounded, shiny, dark green leaves. ❖

Fencing

No matter how fond of animals you may be, there is nothing heartwarming about the sight of some furry creature munching away on your garden's bounty. Repellents, traps, and scare devices can help discourage or fend off hungry wildlife. But in many cases, especially in rural areas, a fence may be the only effective way to keep marauding mammals away from your landscape plantings and food crops.

The size and type of fence to use depends largely on the kind of animal you're trying to stave off. A simple 2' high chicken-wire fence will discourage rabbits, but a more formidable barrier is necessary to deal with such garden burglars as deer, raccoons, skunks, or woodchucks.

Cost and appearance are also important considerations. A solid or picket-style wooden fence is attractive but is expensive and difficult to install. Wooden fences also tend to shade the perimeter of the garden, and require regular maintenance. Wire fencing and electric fencing are less costly, but are by no means inexpensive, particularly in the case of a large area.

You may be able to forego fencing off your entire garden or orchard by erecting barriers around only those beds or crops most vulnerable to animal pests. A fenced plot for corn and melons is a good idea where raccoons are a problem. You'll find more information about making barriers for individual plants, as well as suggestions for using traps and repellents, in the Animal Pests entry.

Chicken-Wire Garden Fence

A simple 3' high chicken-wire fence and a subterranean chicken-wire barrier can protect your garden from nearly all small and medium-sized animals, including the burrowing types.

Chicken wire comes in a variety of widths and mesh sizes, and is sold in 50' rolls. The 1" mesh is best for excluding animal pests.

Building the fence: The first step in building a fence is to decide where you want it to run.

Mark the corners with small stakes and measure the perimeter. You will need two lengths of 1" mesh chicken wire, one 3' wide for the fence itself, and another 1' (or more) wide to line an underground trench; or one length wide enough to do both.

You also need one 5' post for each corner, additional posts for long sections, and one post for each side of the gate(s). Steel T-posts are inexpensive, can be driven into the ground with a hammer or sledge, and come with clips for attaching the fencing. Rot-resistant wooden posts such as locust provide excellent support, but you'll need a post-hole digger to set them. Also, nailing or stapling fencing to dense wood can be difficult.

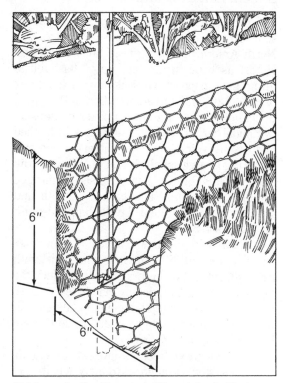

Chicken-wire lined trench. A 6" trench lined with chicken wire provides protection against animals that try to burrow underground to get into the garden.

Stretch string between the small stakes to mark the fencing line. Dig a trench 6″ deep and at least 6″ wide along the outside of the string. Line the trench with the 1′ wide chicken wire bent into the shape of an L, so that the wire covers the the bottom of the trench as well as the side nearest the fence, as shown on the opposite page. Be sure the wire extends an inch or so above ground level.

Set the posts 2′ deep along the marked fence line. Stretch the 3′ wide chicken wire between the posts and attach it to them. The fencing should overlap the chicken wire lining the trench by 2″ or 3″. Use wire to fasten the two layers together. (If you use one wider length of chicken wire you save this last step.) Then refill the trench with soil.

Altering the design: If woodchucks are a serious problem, make the wire-lined trench a foot or more deep and up to 3′ wide. If you're trying to keep gophers out, dig the trench 2′ deep and 6″ wide, line it with ¼″ mesh hardware cloth, and/or fill it with coarse gravel.

Raccoons are good climbers. To foil them, don't attach the topmost 1′ of fencing to the posts. When the burglars clamber up, the loose section will flop backward and keep the raccoons from climbing over the top.

If pests continue to raid your garden despite the chicken-wire barrier, you can add a single-strand electric fence, as shown on this page.

Most garden supply stores sell easy-to-install electric fence kits, including a plug-in or battery-powered charger, 100′ of wire, and plastic posts. Or check mail-order gardening catalogs, which carry a variety of electric fence products designed with the home gardener in mind.

Deer Fencing

Deer are more difficult to control with fences. A six-strand high-voltage electric fence, with the wires spaced 10″ apart and the bottom one 8″ off the ground, is an effective deterrent. But it is an impractical choice for many small-scale grow-

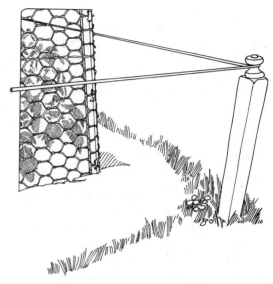

Animal-proof fence. Adding a low single-strand electric fence just outside a nonelectric fence should put an end to problems with virtually any animal pest except deer. Set up the electric fence 6″ outside the chicken-wire fence, with the wire 4″-6″ off the ground.

ers because of the high cost and complex installation.

Another alternative is to build a fence that is simply too high for a deer to jump over. The absolute minimum height for a jump-proof nonelectric deer fence is 8′. Standard woven-wire farm fencing comes 4′ tall, so it's a common practice to stack one course on top of another to create an 8′ fence. This method is neither inexpensive nor easy.

An easier approach is to erect two fences, 3′ or 4′ high and spaced 3′ apart, of welded-wire or snow fencing. Deer seldom jump a fence when they can see another fence or obstacle just on the other side. If you already have a fence around your garden and deer become a problem, add a 3′ nonelectric or a 2′ single-strand electric fence 3′ outside the existing one. ❖

Ferns

Ferns are the quintessential shade plants. Their graceful, arching fronds conjure up images of shaded retreats and cool walks by wooded streams. Ferns will grow in the deepest, darkest woodland. They will grow in moist soil or even standing water. However, not all ferns are limited to the shade. Marsh fern, cinnamon fern, and bracken fern grow in full sun. Most ferns prefer moist soil and partial shade.

Ferns in the Landscape

Use large ferns as foundation plantings along with or instead of shrubs. Plant them along fences or walls to break up the flat expanse. They hide the "bare ankles" of sparse shrubs or perennials. Large hostas and ferns will draw attention to a shaded spot. Mass plantings of ostrich ferns (*Matteuccia* spp.) and osmundas (*Osmunda* spp.) are very effective for filling bare spaces or adding depth in the shade of tall trees. They also form a perfect backdrop for annuals and perennials.

Use medium-sized ferns such as New York fern (*Thelypteris noveboracensis*), lady fern (*Athyrium filix-femina*), and maidenhair fern (*Adiantum pedatum*) in combination with spring wildflowers. Their unfurling fronds are a beautiful complement to spring beauty (*Claytonia virginica*), wild blue phlox (*Phlox divaricata*), and others. Fronds will fill in the blank spots left when wildflowers and spring bulbs go dormant.

Try ferns along the border of a shaded walk to define the path, or ferns with creeping rhizomes on a slope to hold the soil. Mix textures and add evergreen ferns such as wood ferns (*Dryopteris* spp.) and Christmas ferns (*Polystichum acrostichoides*) for late-season and winter interest.

Crown-forming ferns like interrupted fern (*Osmunda claytoniana*) and cinnamon fern (*O. cinnamomea*) have a graceful vase shape and make excellent accents alone or in small groupings. They grow slowly, so they won't take over the garden like some running ferns such as hay-scented ferns (*Dennstaedtia punctilobula*). Plant rampant growers where they can spread to form groundcovers and fill in under shrubs. For low, wet areas, chain ferns (*Woodwardia* spp.), osmundas, and marsh ferns (*Thelypteris palustris*) are stunning. Combine them with the spiky foliage

---

FERNS FOR SPECIAL USES

Not all ferns are made for the shade— some can take full sun and dry soil. And many ferns are evergreen, enhancing the garden all year. These ferns are all hardy to at least Zone 6; many are hardy to Zone 4, and some to Zone 3.

Ferns for Sunny Sites

Unlike most ferns, deer fern (*Blechnum spicant*), hay-scented fern (*Dennstaedtia punctilobula*), fragrant shield fern (*Dryopteris fragrans*), and shield ferns (*Polystichum* spp.) can stand at least a half day of sun. For full sun and moist soil, choose water clover (*Marsilea quadrifolia*), sensitive fern (*Onoclea sensibilis*), marsh fern (*Thelypteris palustris*), and chain ferns (*Woodwardia* spp.). Ferns that thrive in full sun and dry soil include lip ferns (*Cheilanthes* spp.), parsley fern (*Cryptogramma crispa* var. *acrostichoides*), polypody ferns (*Polypodium* spp.), bracken (*Pteridium aquilinum*), and rusty woodsia (*Woodsia ilvensis*). You can grow interrupted fern (*Osmunda claytoniana*) in either full sun and moist soil or shade and dry soil.

Evergreen Ferns

Evergreen ferns add color and structure to the garden all year. The best include spleenworts (*Asplenium* spp.), grape ferns (*Botrychium* spp.), parsley fern (*Cryptogramma crispa* var. *acrostichoides*), wood ferns (*Dryopteris* spp.), hart's-tongue fern (*Phyllitis scolopendrium*), polypody ferns (*Polypodium* spp.), shield ferns (*Polystichum* spp.), and chain ferns (*Woodwardia* spp.).

Key Words
FERNS

Fern. A nonflowering vascular plant that reproduces by spores borne on the underside of its fronds.

Frond. The leaf of a fern, including the blade and the stipe.

Blade. The flattened leafy portion of a frond.

Stipe. The stalk of a frond that supports the blade.

Rhizome. The creeping underground stem of a fern from which fronds and roots arise.

Fiddlehead. The young, unfurling frond of a fern.

Spore. An asexual reproductive cell.

Spore case (Sorus, *pl.* **sori).** The spore-bearing structures on the underside of fronds.

Prothallus. Usually a flat, heart-shaped green structure that grows from a spore and bears the fern's sexual reproductive cells.

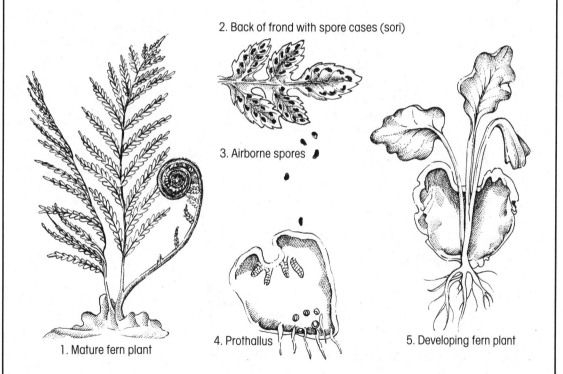

2. Back of frond with spore cases (sori)

3. Airborne spores

4. Prothallus

5. Developing fern plant

1. Mature fern plant

Fern life cycle. The life cycle of a fern, unlike seed-bearing plants, includes both asexual and sexual phases.

of yellow flags (*Iris pseudacorus*) and arrowheads (*Sagittaria* spp.).

Since foliage is the fern's major attraction, consider the color and texture of the fronds. The blue-gray fronds of Japanese painted fern (*Athyrium goeringianum* 'Pictum') look great with blue hostas and *Heuchera* 'Palace Purple'. Chartreuse-colored interrupted fern combines well with dark ferns and other foliage. The shiny fronds of ferns such as autumn fern (*Dryopteris erythrosora*), deer fern (*Blechnum spicant*), and maidenhair fern glisten in filtered sunlight.

Preparing the Soil

Ferns generally require rich, moist soil with extra organic matter. Some require a drier, less-fertile soil. Have your soil tested by your local extension service or a soil-testing lab to determine soil fertility and pH. Some ferns are extremely fussy about pH. It's important to know the requirements of the plants and to prepare the soil accordingly. For more on soils, soil testing, and pH, see the Soil and pH entries.

For large and medium-sized ferns, prepare the bed by double digging, or at least by turning the soil to a spade's depth. Sprinkle on organic fertilizer, if needed, when you add soil amendments. For details on digging, see the Double

Digging entry; for more on organic fertilizers, see the Fertilizers entry.

Buying and Planting Ferns

Garden centers offer a few ferns, but you can find more through mail-order. No matter where you buy, make sure plants are nursery-propagated, not collected from the wild. Large plants at low prices usually mean wild-collected plants. Don't be afraid to ask the vendor's sources.

Plant ferns in fall or early spring. Garden-center plants will be potted, but mail-order plants are likely to arrive bareroot. Remove potted plants from their containers, cutting the plastic if necessary. Very carefully score the root ball with a sharp knife. Make 3-5 shallow cuts lengthwise down the root ball. This breaks up the solid mass of fibrous roots that often forms along the container wall. Plant the fern at the same level at which it was growing in the pot. Planting too deeply will kill plants with single crowns.

Set bareroot plants with creeping rhizomes ½"-1" below the surface. Large rhizomes can be planted deeper. Set single-crowned ferns like osmundas and ostrich ferns with the crown above soil level. Place the upper part of the rhizome above the soil surface, with the crown 3"-5" above the soil, depending on the plant's size. Finally, don't plant too thickly, since most ferns spread rapidly.

Continuing Care

Ferns are a care-free group of plants. Mulch with shredded leaves or bark to help control weeds and conserve moisture. Ferns never need staking, pinching, or pruning. You may have to remove an occasional damaged frond.

Each spring, remove last fall's leaves from the fern bed, shred them, and return them to the bed. Clear the bed early to avoid damage to emerging fiddleheads. Don't rake the beds, or you may damage crowns and growing tips. You won't need fertilizer if you leave the mulch to rot into the soil. ❖

More On
FERNS

For an in-depth look at these fascinating plants, read David L. Jones's *Encyclopaedia of Ferns*, F. Gordon Foster's *Ferns to Know and Grow*, and Barbara Joe Hoshizaki's *Fern Growers Manual*. Also, *A Field Guide to Ferns and Their Related Families* in the Peterson Field Guide Series provides clear field identification.

Fertilizers

Organic gardeners use fertilizers like seasonings: they add the finishing touch that brings out the very best in plants. Because an organically managed soil is biologically active and rich in nutrients, organic gardeners don't need to pour on fertilizers to get good plant performance.

Chemical vs. Organic

Many organic materials serve as both fertilizers and soil conditioners—they feed both soils and plants. This is one of the most important differences between a chemical approach and an organic approach toward soil care and fertilizing. Soluble chemical fertilizers contain mineral salts that are readily available for uptake by plant roots. However, these salts do not provide a food source for soil microorganisms and earthworms, and will even repel earthworms because they acidify the soil. Over time, soils treated only with synthetic chemical fertilizers will have decreased organic matter and altered biological activity. And as soil structure declines and water-holding capacity diminishes, a greater proportion of the soluble chemical fertilizers applied will leach through the soil. Ever-increasing amounts of chemicals will be needed to feed the plants.

Most chemical fertilizers are synthesized from non-renewable resources, such as coal and natural gas. Others are made by treating rock minerals with acids to make them more soluble. Fortunately, there are more and more truly organic fertilizers coming on the market. These products are made from natural plant and animal materials or from mined rock minerals. However, there are no national standards regulating the content of organic fertilizers. Read labels to be sure that commercial fertilizers labeled "organic" contain only safe, natural ingredients. Look for products labeled "natural organic," "slow release," and "low analysis." Be wary of products labeled organic that have an NPK ratio that adds up to more than 15.

Using Organic Fertilizers

If you're a gardener who's making the switch from chemical to organic fertilizers, you may be afraid that using organic materials will be more complicated and less convenient than using pre-mixed chemical fertilizers. Not so! Commercially formulated organic fertilizer blends can be just as convenient and effective as blended synthetic fertilizers. You don't need to custom-feed your plants unless it's an activity you enjoy. So while some experts will spread a little blood meal around their tomatoes at planting, and then some bonemeal just when the blossoms are about to pop, most gardeners will be satisfied to make one or two applications of general-purpose organic fertilizer throughout the garden.

If you want to try a plant-specific approach to fertilizing, you can use a variety of specialty organic fertilizers that are available from mail-

Key Words
FERTILIZERS

Fertilizers. Materials that feed growing plants.

Soil conditioners. Materials added to feed and enrich the soil.

NPK ratio. A ratio of three numbers that identifies the percentage of three major nutrients—nitrogen (N), phosphorus (P), and potassium (K)—in fertilizers.

Top-dress. To apply fertilizer evenly over a field or bed of growing plants.

Side-dress. To apply fertilizer alongside plants growing in rows.

Broadcast. To spread fertilizer evenly across an area, by hand or with a spreading tool.

Foliar-feed. To supply nutrients by spraying liquid fertilizer directly on plant foliage.

Leaching. The downward movement or runoff of nutrients dissolved in the soil solution.

order supply companies or at many well-stocked garden centers. For example, you can use blood meal, chicken-feather meal, or fish meal as nitrogen sources. Bonemeal is a good source of phosphorus, and kelp or greensand are organic sources of potassium. "Common Organic Fertilizers for Home Gardens" on page 226 lists average nutrient analysis and suggested application rates.

Dry Organic Fertilizers

Dry organic fertilizers can be made from a single material, such as rock phosphate or kelp, or can be a blend of many ingredients. Almost all organic fertilizers provide a broad array of nutrients, but blends are specially formulated to provide balanced amounts of nitrogen, potassium, and phosphorus, as well as micronutrients. There are several commercial blends, but you can make your own general-purpose fertilizer by mixing individual amendments, as suggested in "Mix and Match" below.

Applying dry fertilizers: The most common way to apply dry fertilizer is to broadcast it and then hoe or rake it into the top 4"-6" of soil. You can add small amounts to planting holes or rows as you plant seeds or transplants. Unlike dry synthetic fertilizers, most organic fertilizers are nonburning and will not harm delicate seedling roots.

During the growing season, boost plant growth by side-dressing dry fertilizers in crop rows or around the drip line of trees or shrubs. It's best to work side-dressings into the top inch of the soil.

Liquid Organic Fertilizers

Use liquid fertilizers to give your plants a light nutrient boost or snack every month or even every two weeks during the growing season. Simply mix a tankful of foliar spray, and spray all your plants at the same time.

Plants can absorb liquid fertilizers through both their roots and through leaf pores. Foliar feeding can supply nutrients when they are lacking or unavailable in the soil, or when roots are stressed. It is especially effective for giving fast-growing plants like vegetables an extra boost during the growing season. Compost tea and seaweed extract are two common examples of organic foliar fertilizers.

Some foliar fertilizers such as kelp are rich in micronutrients and growth hormones. These foliar sprays also appear to act as catalysts, increas-

---

MIX AND MATCH

If you want to mix your own general-purpose organic fertilizer, try combining individual amendments in the amounts shown here. Just pick one ingredient from each column. Because these amendments may vary in the amount of the nutrients they contain, this method won't give you a mixture with a precise NPK ratio. The ratio will be approximately between 1-2-1 and 4-6-3, with additional insoluble phosphorus and potash. The blend will provide a balanced supply of nutrients that will be steadily available to plants and encourage soil microorganisms to thrive.

Nitrogen (N)	Phosphorus (P)	Potassium (K)
2 parts blood meal	3 parts bonemeal	1 part kelp meal
3 parts fish meal	6 parts rock phosphate or colloidal phosphate	6 parts greensand

ing nutrient uptake by plants. You can make your own liquid fertilizer by brewing up compost or manure in water. See the Composting and Manure entries for directions.

Applying liquid fertilizers: With flowering and fruiting plants, foliar sprays are most useful during critical periods (such as after transplanting or during fruit set) or periods of drought or extreme temperatures. For leaf crops, some suppliers recommend biweekly spraying.

When using liquid fertilizers, always follow label instructions for proper dilution and application methods. You can use a surfactant, such as coconut oil or a mild soap (¼ teaspoon per gallon of spray), to ensure better coverage of the leaves. Otherwise the spray may bead up on the foliage and you won't get maximum benefit. Measure the surfactant carefully; if you use too much, it may damage plants. A slightly acid spray mixture is most effective, so check your spray's pH. Use small amounts of vinegar to lower pH and baking soda to raise it. Aim for a pH of 6.0-6.5.

Any sprayer or mister will work, from hand-trigger units to knapsack sprayers. Set your sprayer to emit as fine a spray as possible. Never use a sprayer that has been used to apply herbicides.

The best times to spray are early morning and early evening, when the liquids will be absorbed most quickly and won't burn foliage. Choose a day when no rain is forecast and temperatures aren't extreme.

Spray until the liquid drips off the leaves. Be sure to concentrate the spray on leaf undersides, where leaf pores are more likely to be open. You can also water in liquid fertilizers around the root zone. A drip irrigation system can carry liquid fertilizers to your plants. Kelp is a better product for this use, as fish emulsion can clog the irrigation emitters.

Using Growth Enhancers

Growth enhancers are materials that help plants absorb nutrients more effectively from

More On
FERTILIZERS

You'll find more information about specific fertilizers and soil amendments in the Green Manure, Manure, Mulch, and pH entries. The Soil entry explains how to test your soil to determine what soil amendments you need to apply. The Plant Nutrition entry explains how to diagnose nutritional problems based on the appearance of your plants.

the soil. The most common growth enhancer is kelp, which has been used by farmers for centuries.

Kelp is sold as a dried meal or as an extract of the meal in liquid or powdered form. It is totally safe and provides some 60 trace elements that plants need in very small quantities. It also contains growth-promoting hormones and enzymes. These compounds are still not fully understood, but are involved in improving a plant's growing conditions.

Applying growth enhancers: Follow the directions for spraying liquid fertilizers when applying growth enhancers as a foliar spray.

You can also apply kelp extract or meal directly to the soil; soil application also stimulates soil bacteria. This in turn increases fertility through humus formation, aeration, and moisture retention.

Apply 1-2 lb. of kelp meal per 100 square feet of garden each spring. Apply kelp extract once a month for the first four or five months of the growing season.

If fresh seaweed is available, rinse it to remove the sea salt and apply it to your garden as a mulch, or compost it. Seaweed decays readily because it contains little cellulose. Furthermore, there's no need to worry about introducing weed seeds with seaweed mulch. ❖

Common Organic Fertilizers for Home Gardens

Use this table to select the appropriate fertilizers and application rates for your garden. The table lists the nitrogen-phosphorus-potassium (NPK) ratio, where relevant, as well as the content of other significant nutrients. It also lists the primary benefit of each fertilizer: Some supply particular nutrients, some help balance soil minerals, and others primarily enrich the soil with organic matter.

Use suggested application rates based on your soil's fertility. If your soil fertility is low, you'll need to add more of an amendment than you would for medium or adequate fertility. Determine soil fertility in conjunction with an assessment of your soil by a soil-testing laboratory, as well as your personal observations and the specific requirements of the crops you are growing.

Organic Amendment	Primary Benefit	Average NPK Ratio or Mineral Analysis	Average Application Rate Per 1,000 Sq. Ft.	Comments
Alfalfa meal	Organic matter	5-1-2	Low: 50 lb. Med: 35 lb. Adq: 25 lb.	Contains triaconatol, a natural fatty-acid growth stimulant, plus trace minerals.
Blood meal	Nitrogen	11-0-0	Low: 30 lb. Med: 20 lb. Adq: 10 lb.	—
Bonemeal (steamed)	Phosphate	1-11-0 20% total phosphate 24% calcium	Low: 30 lb. Med: 20 lb. Adq: 10 lb.	Higher grades contain as much as 6:12:0.
Coffee grounds	Nitrogen	2-0.3-0.2	Incorporate in compost	Acid-forming: needs limestone supplement.
Colloidal phosphate	Phosphate	0-2-0 18-20% total phosphate 23% calcuim	Low: 60 lb. Med: 25 lb. Adq: 10 lb.	—
Compost (dry commercial)	Organic matter	1-1-1	Low: 200 lb. Med: 100 lb. Adq: 50 lb.	—
Compost (homemade)	Organic matter	0.5-0.5-0.5 to 4-4-4 25% organic matter	Low: 2,000 lb. Med: 1,000 lb. Adq: 400 lb.	—
Compost (mushroom)	Organic matter	Variable	Low: 350 lb. Med: 250 lb. Adq: 50 lb.	Ask supplier whether the material contains pesticide residues.
Cottonseed meal	Nitrogen	6-2-1	Low: 35 lb. Med: 25 lb. Adq: 10 lb.	May contain pesticide residues.

Organic Amendment	Primary Benefit	Average NPK Ratio or Mineral Analysis	Average Application Rate Per 1,000 Sq. Ft.		Comments
Eggshells	Calcium	1.2–0.4–0.1	Low:	100 lb.	Contains calcium plus trace minerals.
			Med:	50 lb.	
			Adq:	25 lb.	
Epsom salts	Balancer, magnesium	10% magnesium 13% sulfur	Low:	5 lb.	–
			Med:	3 lb.	
			Adq:	1 lb.	
Fish emulsion	Nitrogen	4–1–1 5% sulfur	Low:	2 oz.	–
			Med:	1 oz.	
			Adq:	1 oz.	
Fish meal	Nitrogen	5–3–3	Low:	30 lb.	–
			Med:	20 lb.	
			Adq:	10 lb.	
Granite meal	Potash	1–4% total potash	Low:	100 lb.	Contains 67% silicas and 19 trace minerals.
			Med:	50 lb.	
			Adq:	25 lb.	
Grass clippings (green)	Organic matter	0.5–0.2–0.5	Low:	500 lb.	–
			Med:	300 lb.	
			Adq:	200 lb.	
Greensand	Potash	7% total potash plus 32 trace minerals	Low:	100 lb.	–
			Med:	50 lb.	
			Adq:	25 lb.	
Gypsum	Balancer, calcium	22% calcium 17% sulfur	Low:	40 lb.	Do not apply if pH is below 5.8.
			Med:	20 lb.	
			Adq:	5 lb.	
Kelp meal	Potash, trace minerals	1.0–0.5–2.5	Low:	20 lb.	Contains a broad array of vitamins, minerals, and soil-conditioning elements.
			Med:	10 lb.	
			Adq:	5 lb.	
Limestone, dolomitic	Balancer, calcium, magnesium	51% calcium carbonate 40% magnesium carbonate	Low:	100 lb.	–
			Med:	50 lb.	
			Adq:	25 lb.	
Limestone, calcitic	Balancer, calcium	65–80% calcium carbonate 3–15% magnesium carbonate	Low:	100 lb.	–
			Med:	50 lb.	
			Adq:	25 lb.	

(continued)

Common Organic Fertilizers for Home Gardens—*Continued*

Organic Amendment	Primary Benefit	Average NPK Ratio or Mineral Analysis	Average Application Rate Per 1,000 Sq. Ft.		Comments
Oak leaves	Organic matter	0.8-0.4-0.1	Low: Med: Adq:	250 lb. 150 lb. 100 lb.	—
Peat moss	Organic matter	pH range 3.0-4.5	As needed		Use around acid-loving plants.
Rock phosphate	Phosphate	0-3-0 32% total phosphate 32% calcium	Low: Med: Adq:	60 lb. 25 lb. 10 lb.	Contains 11 trace minerals.
Sawdust	Organic matter	0.2-0-0.2	Low: Med: Adq:	250 lb. 150 lb. 100 lb.	Be sure sawdust is well rotted before incorporating.
Soybean meal	Nitrogen	7.0-0.5-2.3	Low: Med: Adq:	50 lb. 25 lb. 10 lb.	—
Sul-Po-Mag	Potash, magnesium	0-0-22 11% magnesium 22% sulfur	Low: Med: Adq:	10 lb. 7 lb. 5 lb.	Do not use with dolomitic limestone; substitute greensand or other potassium source.
Wheat straw	Organic matter	0.7-0.2-1.2	Low: Med: Adq:	250 lb. 150 lb. 100 lb.	—
Wood ashes (leached)	Potash	0-1.2-2	Low: Med: Adq:	20 lb. 10 lb. 5 lb.	—
Wood ashes (unleached)	Potash	0-1.5-8	Low: Med: Adq:	10 lb. 5 lb. 3 lb.	—
Worm castings	Organic matter	0.5-0.5-0.3	Low: Med: Adq:	250 lb. 100 lb. 50 lb.	50% organic matter plus 11 trace minerals.

SOURCE: Reprinted with permission of Necessary Trading Company, New Castle, VA 24127.

FIG 229

Fig

Ficus carica
Moraceae

If you'd like to try growing an unusual fruit crop that's delicious and nearly trouble-free, consider figs. These trees will grow well unprotected in Zones 8-10, and also in colder areas if given proper winter protection.

The Fruit Trees entry covers many aspects of growing figs and other tree fruits; refer to it for more information on planting and care.

Selecting trees: There are more than 200 cultivars grown in North America, with a broad range of fruit shapes and colors. It's important to select a cultivar adapted to your climate; also look for self-pollinating cultivars.

Planting and care: Plant trees as you would any young tree. Mulch trees well with compost, and apply foliar sprays of seaweed extract at least once a month during the growing season.

Pruning: Use a shovel to disconnect suckers that sprout from the roots throughout the growing season; replant or share them with friends. Figs don't require formal training; thin or head back as needed to control size.

Problems: Generally, figs do not suffer from insect or disease problems in North America. Keep birds away with netting; spread wood ashes around the base of trees to keep ants from climbing up to fruits.

Harvesting: In warm climates, you can harvest twice, in June and again in late summer. In colder areas, expect one harvest in late summer to fall. Check trees daily for ripe fruit in season. Ripe fruits are soft to the touch; skin may begin to split. Figs will keep up to one week in the refrigerator, but spoil easily. Cook figs by simmering them with a dash of lemon and honey for about 20 minutes, mashing them as they cook. Then puree in a food processor, blender, or food mill. The puree freezes well and makes an excellent cookie filling, sauce for ice cream or poached pears, or spread for toast.

Cultivars: 'Alma', amber flesh, good for containers; 'Brown Turkey', sweet pink flesh, best in Texas and the Northeast; 'Black Mission', sweet, rich, pale red flesh, good for California. ❖

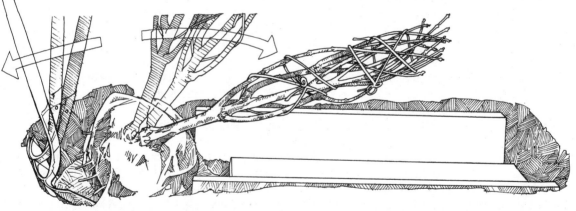

Burying fig trees. Protect figs from cold in nature's insulator—the soil. In late fall, prune trees back to about 6', and head back horizontally spreading branches. Tie branches with rope or twine to make a tight cylinder. Dig a 2' deep trench as long as the tree is tall, starting at the root ball of the tree. Place boards on the bottom and sides of the trench. Dig out soil from the roots opposite the trench until the tree is free enough to be tipped into the trench. Wrap the tree in heavy plastic, bend it into the trench (this will take some effort), and fill around it with straw or dried leaves. Put a board over the tree, and shovel the soil over it. You'll know you buried your tree properly if a neighbor enquires whether you have a body buried in your yard. Resurrect trees in spring after danger of hard frost is past.

Flower Arranging

Anyone can make attractive arrangements with garden-grown flowers. No fancy materials or special classes are required. All you need is a bucket, pruning shears, household scissors, a knife, and a container.

You can use just about any container to hold an arrangement, as long as it doesn't compete with the flowers. If the container doesn't normally hold water, such as a basket, place a plastic or glass container inside. For a more shapely arrangement, use floral foam, marbles, or a florist's frog to hold stems in position.

Cutting and Conditioning Flowers

A few simple steps prolong the life of cut flowers and foliage: Cut the flowers early in the morning or late in the afternoon or evening. Carry a bucket of water with you and plunge the stems into the bucket as soon as they are cut. For more on flowers for cutting, see the Cut Flower Gardening entry.

Indoors, cut another 1"-2" from stems under water and transfer to a clean container of tepid water, immersing stems almost up to the flower itself. For plants with fuzzy leaves, remove the bottom 1/3 of the foliage and immerse to this depth. With woody-stemmed plants, remove the lower 1"-2" of bark and slit the stem several times with a knife or pruning shears. Sear the stem ends of flowers with milky sap, such as oriental poppies, with a candle or gas flame.

Place the containers of flowers and foliage in a basement or other dark, cool, humid place for 6-8 hours to complete conditioning. When ready to arrange, remove all foliage that would be under water or in floral foam and recut stems under water to desired length.

Prolong vase life by changing water daily. You can also use a commercial cut flower preservative or make your own with 1/4 teaspoon of bleach and 1 tablespoon of granulated sugar per gallon of water. Displaying the arrangements out of direct sunlight and away from drafts and heat keeps them fresh longer.

Styling Principles

Styles in flower arranging vary, but a good arrangement is more than a matter of taste. The best arrangements make the best use of balance, rhythm, scale, and color.

Balance: A balanced arrangement seems secure and stable. Balance your arrangement by putting the heavier-looking flowers toward the center and lower parts of the arrangement.

Rhythm: Rhythm is how your eyes are led from the focal point throughout the arrangement. Get rhythm in your arrangements with repetition of shapes and colors and by using branches and stems to create a continuous flow of line.

Scale: Scale is the size relationship of the various elements. Good scale means that the proportions of each element are pleasing and in harmony with the others. A basic guideline is that your arrangement should be 1½ times as high or as wide as the container.

Color: Color contributes to the balance, rhythm, and scale of an arrangement. Dark flowers look heavier and farther away; pastels seem lighter and closer. You can use variations of one color, complementary colors, or contrasting colors in an arrangement.

Remember the principles of style as you create your arrangement. First, establish the shape of your arrangement by building a framework with linear materials like branches and long, thin leaves. Next, add fuller, rounder elements to create a focal point. Finally, use filler material like baby's-breath and fern fronds to camouflage the base and connect the other elements.

Most arrangements are some variation of a handful of basic shapes. "Floral Arrangement Styles" on the opposite page shows you four of the most popular styles. ❖

Form the basic outline of a round arrangement with linear material. Use stems of various lengths to give depth. Next, fill in with round flowers. Finally, add filler material to soften the transition between linear and round materials.

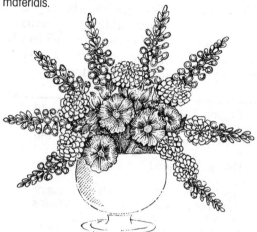

To make a vertical arrangement in a tall, deep vase, start with one tall, spike-shaped flower, bud, or leaf. On each side, put progressively shorter spikes to form a tapering outline. Use rounder, fuller flowers and foliage near the base.

Use linear material to establish the tallest point and the two base points of a triangular arrangement. Use slightly shorter elements for the base points. Fill in with additional linear materials. Add rounder, darker flowers in the center, then buds of the same flower at other points in the arrangement. Finish with filler material.

For a horizontal arrangement, position a short-stemmed round flower in the center of a piece of floral foam. Add longer horizontal spikes of flowers on each side. Complete the outline by adding shorter pairs of spiky flowers. Place progressively smaller round flowers from the center out to the edges, facing them in all directions. Add filler materials to blend the various elements.

Floral arrangement styles. Round arrangements can be viewed from all sides or only one side. Triangular and vertical arrangements are effective, easy-to-make arrangements. A horizontal arrangement in a low bowl is ideal for a dining room centerpiece.

Flowers

Flowers are more than pretty faces; they're the reproductive organs of plants. A flower's main role is to produce seeds; its color or fragrance is only a reflection of its need to attract visits from pollinating insects, birds, or animals. We may admire showy, colorful, fragrant flowers like lilies and roses, but vegetables, weeds, grasses, and trees all make flowers, too, in order to reproduce by seed.

Some flowers contain all four basic parts: sepals, petals, pistils, and stamens. Others are lacking some parts. For example, tiny beet and spinach flowers don't have petals. Often one set of sexual parts is missing. Melons bear separate male and female flowers on the same vine; hardy kiwifruit vines are either all-male or all-female. For more information on pollination of flowers, see the Seeds and Seedlings entry. ❖

Key Words
FLOWERS

Petals. Leaflike flaps, often colorful, on a flower.

Sepals. Leaflike flaps, often green, at the base of a flower.

Stamen. The male reproductive part of a flower.

Pistil. The female reproductive part of a flower.

Anther. A pollen-bearing capsule borne on a slender stalk; part of the stamen.

Stigma. The sticky, top part of the pistil that is receptive to pollen.

Style. A tubelike structure below the stigma.

Ovary. The seed-bearing base of the pistil.

Ovules. Unpollinated seeds in the ovary.

Complete flower. A flower that contains sepals, petals, stamens, and pistils.

Incomplete flower. A flower that lacks one or more parts found in a complete flower.

Monoecious. Producing male and female flowers on the same plant.

Dioecious. Producing male and female flowers on separate plants.

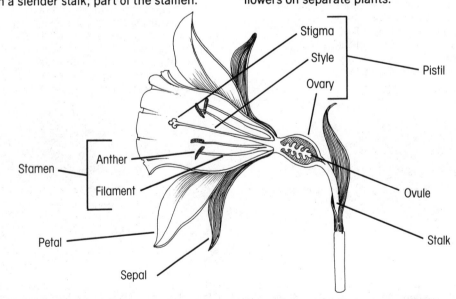

Folklore

When your neighbor leans over the fence and says, "'Round here, 'tis Easter for spinach, May 30 for tomatoes," he's passing along local gardening folklore, just as the first gardeners did thousands of years ago.

Gardening folklore refers to the beliefs, customs, stories, and sayings about plants and how to grow them that have been preserved orally among various peoples. The definition sounds dry, but the lore is a lively mix of axioms based on careful observation, common sense, myth, legend, and magic, often seasoned with astrology.

To see how fact and fancy mingle, let's look at some familiar notions about potatoes. First, the jingle, "When you hear the cuckoo shout, 'tis time to plant your tetties out." In ancient myths the cuckoo possessed great wisdom. Cuckoos were (and still are) messengers of spring, but not because of their brainpower. Like other migratory birds, they leave the southern hemisphere and head north to arrive in time for warmer weather.

The idea that people should plant potatoes on Good Friday involves the moon. To ancient peoples, the moon was the White Goddess, the Earth Mother who had dominion over agriculture. The moon's lover or son died after each harvest and was reborn the next spring. In the Christian world, Easter supplanted the pagan moon festival, Eostre, that celebrated this event.

By the time the potato was brought to England in the late 1600s, the Church had long since banned pagan rituals, but the idea of planting by the moon had not lost its grip on farmers and gardeners (and it still hasn't). Someone decided that a potato buried in the ground was a fitting symbol for the death of Christ and its green shoots an appropriate symbol for the Resurrection. Planting potatoes on Good Friday became a way of paying homage to Christ while subconsciously acknowledging the White Goddess. The custom also followed moon lore, which says that root crops should be planted during a waning moon. (Easter usually falls during one.) Now, what happens when Easter falls during a waxing moon? People plant their tetties anyhow. Why? Another bit of lore holds that breaking a rule every so often enhances its strength.

In our high-tech world, it's easy to debunk this myth and magic. But much of it expresses truths about the fundamental rhythms of life—the cycles of the seasons and the role of the sun, moon, and stars in day-to-day affairs. It is part of our collective unconscious, as valuable to our psyches as to our gardens.

Weather Lore

Our ancestors understood the role weather played in growing food. They saw that nature gave ample warning of approaching rain, storms, and frost. The sky is filled with weather indicators, especially cloud formations. For example, "When ye see a cloud rise out of the west, straightway cometh the rain" (Luke 12:54) refers to the fact that weather fronts usually move from west to east.

"Rainbow at night, shepherd's delight. Rainbow in morning, shepherd's warning" refers to the same phenomenon. A rainbow seen in the evening to the east is caused by the setting sun shining from the west, indicating fair weather in that direction. A morning rainbow, caused by the rising sun from the east, indicates rain to the west, heading your way.

"If the sun goes pale to bed, 'twill rain tomorrow, it is said" is another saying that involves cloud patterns. High cirrus clouds in the west give the setting sun a veiled look. When appearing as bands or mares' tails, they signal an approaching storm.

Finally, who among us will argue with "Clear moon, frost soon"? Cloud cover acts like a blanket over the earth, keeping temperatures from dipping as low as they would on a clear night.

The skies are not the only aspect of nature

filled with weather signs. Animal and plant behavior also indicates changes. Some of this lore bears up well under scientific scrutiny; some does not. That which falls into the latter category is still often reliable, but no one knows why. Here belong all the sayings about the thickness and color of an animal's coat, the bark on a tree, or the skin of a vegetable, such as "When the corn wears a heavy coat, so must you." A related saying is "The darker the color of a caterpillar in fall, the harder the winter."

Certain animals and plants do respond in a consistent way to a change from a high- to a low-pressure system, which often brings rain. This is why a saying such as "When the sheep collect and huddle, tomorrow will become a puddle" is reliable. "The higher the geese, the fairer the weather," a saying that applies to all migratory birds, also refers to this phenomenon.

Many plants are sensitive to drops in temperature and to high humidity. "When the wild azalea shuts its doors, that's when winter tempest roars" refers to the fact that azaleas and rhododendrons draw their leaves in when the temperature drops.

Plant Lore

Weather lore merges easily into plant lore. Not only do the sun, moon, and stars herald changes in the weather, but also they affect every phase of plant culture, from sowing seed to harvesting. Much of the lore is pure common sense, garbed in charming language. Snow, for example, is "the poor man's fertilizer." It acts as mulch, protecting plants and keeping nutrients in the soil that rain would otherwise wash away. Frost is "God's plough" because it breaks up ground and kills pests.

The lore about the effects of rain, wind, and snow is reliable information based on centuries of careful observation. But magic and myth lie behind most planting lore involving the sun and moon. Planting by the phases of the moon, as well as by the signs of the zodiac, is an age-old tradition that remains popular today. Some scientific evidence suggests planting near a full moon does encourage growth, probably because of changes in the earth's electromagnetic field. For more information on these practices see the Astrological Gardening entry.

For the most part, the sun takes a backseat to the moon in gardening lore. But Sol controls a few things. In parts of Kentucky and Illinois, people say that aboveground crops grow best when planted in the morning as the sun rises, the converse for root crops. And in many places it is still taboo to plant on "the Sun's Day" (Sunday).

Magic and superstition: Gardening folklore is filled with ways to encourage plant growth by practicing magic or placating the gods. Some of these practices have beneficial effects on their recipients, while others are pure superstition. Imitative magic is often at work in sayings about planting specific vegetables. For example, when sowing turnip seed, one is supposed to say, "As long as my arm, as thick as my wrist." Ever wondered why children are often asked to participate in tree-planting ceremonies? By imitative magic they supposedly give a tree their energy.

The best-known ceremony regarding fruit production is wassailing. In Old English "wes hal" means "in good health." Sometime between December 25 and January 18 each year, farmers carried a jug of mulled cider into their orchards and toasted their best trees. As Robert Herrick wrote, "Wassail the trees, that they may beare,/ You many a Plum and many a Peare;/ For more or less Fruits they will bring,/ As you doe give them Wassailing." People tossed cider around the bases of the trees and set pieces of toast on the branches for the tree robin (the robin may have started out as Pomona, the tree goddess). Next, someone fired a shot or two into the trees. This actually was a helpful practice, because it dislodged dead branches and overwintering insect pests.

Over the centuries, farmers and gardeners saw that some substances promoted growth or repelled insects. The idea of appeasing the gods or destroying evil spirits disappeared, but the traditions survived because of their favorable effects. For example, tannin is good fertilizer. That's why spreading tea leaves around plants does help their growth, as does the Ozark custom of burying old leather boots near fruit trees.

Companion planting: Early gardeners also noted that some plants fared better when planted near others. So began companion planting. Was parsley first planted among carrots, tomatoes, or asparagus because of its reputed supernatural powers? Perhaps it was because someone observed that carrot beetles avoid carrots planted with parsley or that tomatoes and asparagus were more vigorous in its presence. We will never know the answer, but we do know that companion planting often is helpful, just as we know some plants are natural enemies to others. For more on this subject, see the Companion Planting entry.

Symbolism

Ancient peoples anthropomorphized plants —they thought of them as having human characteristics. Specific plants had a spirit and symbolized either a god or goddess or an abstract idea. The meanings changed from culture to culture. For example, to the Greeks the rose was a woman named Rhodanthe and the carnation belonged to Jupiter. By the Middle Ages, pink carnations symbolized "mother love" to Christians and the rose belonged to Mary. If a plant had a distinctive characteristic—having a lovely fragrance or an appealing flower, being edible, or having medicinal value—a body of lore about its qualities or powers evolved alongside the lore about growing it.

For reasons no one can fathom, more lore exists about parsley than any other plant, and much of it is contradictory. As it has in many cultures, parsley symbolized both life and death to the ancient Greeks. They strewed it on tombs. "To be in parsley" was to be near death. Yet they crowned victors at games with it and wore parsley crowns at feasts. In England, parsley was an aphrodisiac and indicated the real head of a household. It only thrived "where the Missus was master." Throughout Western Europe it was a plant of death. To render its effects powerless, people sowed it on Good Friday. To speak a person's name while picking it meant death was sure to follow in 7 days.

A plant's growing habits and physical appearance are the basis for much lore. Ivy's tenacious growth accounts for its dual reputation as an evil omen and a symbol for immortality. In the Victorian era it stood for friendship and fidelity. Ivy is a "lightning" plant, along with holly, ferns, parsley, hawthorns, elders, gooseberries, mistletoe, oaks, and rowan (*Sorbus aucuparia*). Throughout the world, these plants are regarded as possessing supernatural powers, perhaps because they bear some resemblance to flashes of lightning. Curiously, most have flowers or leaves with a rank odor. In early cultures, those with white flowers represented the White Goddess. In all cultures, the red berries represented blood (life) and were therefore able to ward off evil.

The Language of Flowers

Food was more important than beauty to our ancestors, which explains why far more folklore exists about edible plants than those prized for beauty alone. Some flowers, such as the rose, have always attracted lore, but flower lore didn't come into its own until people had the time and money to grow flowers strictly for beauty. It reached its apex in the Victorian-era "Language of Flowers." Every flower acquired a meaning, which enabled people to convey feelings with them. In a straitlaced period, people used posies to express passion and other strong emotions they could not speak freely about in words. See

"Say It with Flowers"on this page for more on this tradition.

Herbs

The Language of Flowers may be the most charming aspect of gardening lore, but historically, the lore about herbs has proven the most beneficial. Our ancestors used herbs to season food and mask flavors and aromas. For centuries, they were the only medicines. Many late twentieth century medications are still herb-based. The first herbals were compiled by the Chinese in 3000 B.C. Traders took that knowledge to the West, and the Greeks wrote herbals of their own. Like other early gardening lore, these herbals contained common sense, but also much fanciful material.

Galen, a Greek doctor born in 130 A.D., saw that various parts of the body often needed outside help if they were to get well. He came up with the notion that like heals like, which seemed logical, especially at a time when white magic was still practiced. His idea developed into the Doctrine of Signatures, which called for treatment of an ailment or body part with a plant that looked like the malady or organ. Help for a mental problem? A walnut, because the shell and meat resemble the brain. Treatment for heart disease? Clovers, with their trefoil leaves. A cure for jaundice? Turmeric, because of its yellow color.

The reason many of these remedies worked, of course, was due to the chemical composition of the herb, not its appearance, but Galen and his successors didn't know that. Many looked to astrological botany for answers not supplied by the Doctrine of Signatures. By the early seventeenth century, a plant's resemblance to a body part or ailment was the simplest part of the Doctrine of Signatures.

According to many herbalists, every plant was under the sign of a planet and a sign of the zodiac, and embodied the Four Elements (Fire, Air, Earth, and Water). The parts of the body

---

SAY IT WITH FLOWERS

The Victorian language of flowers was complex. How a flower was held, where it was worn, and what color it was affected meaning. If you wanted to tell the recipient something about yourself, you tilted the flower to the left; turning it upside down gave the flower the opposite of its normal meaning. A flower worn in the hair indicated caution; on the heart, love. Even the position of the knot on a bouquet delivered a message. The following are some of the meanings of common flowers and plants.

Plant	Meaning
Apple	Temptation.
Bay leaf	I change only in death.
Daisy	Small double: I reciprocate your affection.
Holly	Foresight. Am I forgotten?
Rose	Love. Beauty.
Tulip	Red: Declaration of love. Yellow: Hopeless love.
Violet	Purple: You occupy my thoughts.
Zinnia	Thoughts of absent friends.

---

were also under signs. The trick was to match the plant signatures and signs to the ailment.

Not all herbalists believed in the Doctrine of Signatures. The theory fell into disrepute, and astrology and the notion of like helping like disappeared from herbals. Today herb lore is still evolving. The emphasis has switched to a scientific approach as we try to discover why old standbys have curative powers and to find new plants with healing properties. For more information about using herbs as remedies, see the Herbs entry. ❖

Food and Nutrition

Food alone can't make you healthy, but eating right helps you feel well and maintain good health. When you grow your own fruits and vegetables, you know you're getting fresh, wholesome food.

Gardening organically means you can sink your teeth into a sun-warm tomato without wondering whether you're also getting a mouthful of unwanted chemicals. Organic produce has no toxic residues on leaf or fruit. The quality of the crop can only be as good as what it is fed. Organically grown produce is fed by biologically active soil full of rich and complex nutrients.

The less time from garden to table, the better. Fruits and vegetables harvested at their peak provide far more vitamins and nutrients than food that is trucked in from afar.

Nutritional Bounty

Gardening puts you in charge of a vital part of your food supply. Fruits and vegetables are rich in fiber, so important to a healthy diet. Lettuce, celery, apples, and others are excellent sources of fiber, or roughage. Fresh-picked fruits and vegetables are high in vitamins, especially vitamins A and C and the B-complex vitamins, and supply necessary elements such as potassium and calcium.

Legumes such as peas, beans, and lentils can be combined with grains (or homegrown corn or buckwheat) to make healthy protein—without the added fat and cholesterol of meat. Many Americans still consume nearly twice as much animal protein as necessary. A simple dish of rice and beans is just as nutritious as a well-marbled steak. And its combination of high fiber and low fat is much healthier for your body.

Vitamin-Rich Foods

Orange-fleshed fruits and vegetables, particularly carrots, melons, apricots, winter squash, and sweet potatoes, are high in vitamin A. Researchers have found that carrots with deeper, more intense orange color are higher in vitamin A. Dark green vegetables, like broccoli and spinach, are also high in this vitamin.

Citrus fruits, such as oranges and grapefruits, are well known for their vitamin C content. But other fruits are also brimming with goodness. Loganberries, raspberries, and other bramble fruits are high in vitamin C. And a single half-cup serving of strawberries provides about 2/3 of an adult's Recommended Dietary Allowance (RDA) of vitamin C.

If you think only of fruit for vitamin C, think again. Green peppers contain more than twice as much vitamin C as oranges! A half cup of white cauliflower gives you 1½ times the RDA of vitamin C. Other good sources of this essential vitamin are broccoli, brussels sprouts, and tomatoes.

For a helping of B-complex vitamins such as thiamine, niacin, and riboflavin, eat beans, peas, and leafy greens. Broccoli, kale, and collards supply calcium. (Spinach is high in calcium but also in oxalic acid, which prevents your body from absorbing the calcium.) Fruit, pumpkins, and squash all supply good amounts of potassium.

What's Wrong with Store-Bought?

Modern life has introduced us to the convenience of a supermarket—and to tasteless tomatoes, watermelon in January, and apples and cucumbers coated with wax. For convenience, supermarkets can't be beat. But for flavor and health, there's nothing like homegrown.

Some homegrown foods, such as celery or snap beans, may cost you more in time and money than supermarket produce. Stores can buy in volume from large growers. But fresh herbs, tender lettuces, baby squash, and other produce with a short shelf life can be home-grown for far less than high-priced supermarket specialties.

Many fruits and vegetables bound for markets across the country are harvested before they're ripe, when vitamins and nutrients haven't reached their highest levels. Even crops picked at maturity, such as broccoli or cabbage, lose many nutrients during shipment from coast to coast. When the vegetable leaves the vine, it doesn't stop biological activity; the enzymes that ripen it will continue to affect the nutrition levels as well as the flavor. If you've ever eaten just-picked sweet corn, you know the reason why fresher is better.

Many vitamins are destroyed if produce is allowed to wilt or exposed to heat. Fruits and vegetables from your home garden are picked and used at the peak of goodness. Garden-ripened tomatoes, for instance, may have up to 30 percent more vitamin C than those in the supermarket bin—and much better flavor.

Because supermarket produce needs to travel long distances and survive plenty of handling, growers have developed extra-tough cultivars. The "cardboard" tomato has been around long enough to become the butt of jokes, yet it's still the tomato of choice at most markets because it ships well, keeps well, and shrugs off rough handling.

Many old-time cultivars have been lost due to the demand for vegetables that were uniform and easy to ship. Oftentimes flavor was bred out in favor of endurance and disease resistance. But seed sources for heirloom fruits and vegetables are resurfacing for American gardeners. The importance of seed saving is once again being recognized by gardeners looking to preserve cultivars that are treasured for flavor.

Good-looking produce is a big factor, too, in the supermarket trade. Organic gardeners are willing to trade a few holes or blemishes for wholesome eating. Commercial growers aim for picture-perfect good looks, using an arsenal of

MEET YOUR PRODUCE MANAGER

As a consumer, you have power. Get to know the produce manager of your supermarket. Tell her or him what you want in fresh fruits and vegetables.

If you're intrigued by unfamiliar foods, ask for cooking and serving suggestions. If you want better-tasting, organically grown food, say so. Suggest a supermarket display: one side, chemically grown food; the other side, organically grown. Ask the store to label the display, and see which side sells the most.

Here are some other questions to ask your produce manager:

● Where was the food grown? Would the store consider country-of-origin signs or stickers?
● Is there a local source for supermarket produce? Can the local source be used, even if only for part of the supply?
● When was the crop harvested? How long was it in transit?
● What pesticides or herbicides were used to grow the food? Are they legal in the United States as well as the country of origin?
● What preservatives or fungicides were used? What would the shelf life be without those chemicals?
● What is the best way to remove chemical residues from produce?

chemicals to repel insects and disease and produce smooth-skinned beauty. After harvest, a residue of chemicals keeps molds at bay.

Imported produce may contain even more pesticides than domestically grown produce, because other countries are not limited by the same restrictions on chemicals. That South American-grown melon you slice for a December dessert may have been doused with chemicals banned in the United States.

Even canned or frozen foods are better homemade. The food you "put by" is carefully and promptly picked and handled, so it's fresher and in better condition to start with. And home processing eliminates the extra salt, sugar, and preservatives used by commercial canners and freezers.

Keeping the Goodness

Just how much nutritional value fresh fruits and vegetables provide depends not only on how they are grown but also on how they are harvested and prepared. To preserve vitamins and minerals and prevent loss of nutritional value, take extra care when harvesting and preparing garden foods.

It's better to harvest in the afternoon of a sunny day than early in the morning or after several days of cloudy weather. The amount of light a plant receives directly affects the quality of vitamin C a crop produces. Studies have shown that a food crop still on the vine loses vitamin C in darkness or reduced light, but often regains what is lost when exposed to strong light again.

Treat your produce tenderly. Avoid bumps and bruises. Harvest greens directly into a bowl of cool water; keep peas in their pods until ready to use. The skins and outer leaves of fruits and vegetables are often especially high in valuable vitamins. Homegrown carrots and new potatoes need no scraping of their tender skins. Keep the nutrient-rich, darker green outer leaves of lettuce and cabbage for a healthy salad. Tuberous vegetables store nutrients in their skins. Wait until you're ready to cook before chopping or dicing; these techniques expose more cut area, and enzymes are released that can cause vitamin loss.

To get the full benefit of your garden-grown foods, eat them raw, soon after picking. Cooking is the natural enemy of vitamins: The water leaches out valuable water-soluble nutrients, and the heat destroys many others. Choose cooking methods like steaming or stir-frying that cook vegetables lightly; boiling can destroy up to ⅔ of a raw vegetable's vitamins B and C, potassium, iron, and other minerals. Use a minimal amount

SMALL SPACE, BIG RETURNS

As gardeners increase their appetite for vegetables and combine their talent for cooking, the garden can become the source for many hard-to-find vegetables as well as traditional favorites.

If you have limited time or space for a garden, it's important to plan your crops carefully. Corn, for instance, takes up a lot of precious room; perhaps you'd be satisfied with a dozen ears from the local farm stand. Pumpkins are rampant sprawlers, but they may be worth the space if your children eagerly await the harvest.

Plant vegetables you and your family enjoy eating. Kohlrabi may be high in vitamins, but if your family won't eat it, it's better to give up the space to sugar peas or cherry tomatoes. Comb the catalogs for selections described as high in flavor. Here are some favorites, old and new:

● Leafy crops, such as lettuce, spinach, and salad greens, are at their peak of flavor and nutrition immediately after harvest. Plant a variety to liven up salads.

● It's true: There's nothing like a homegrown tomato. One or two plants will provide enough for summer salads. Some of the older heirloom tomatoes, such as 'Big Rainbow' or 'Brandywine', are still prized for their superb flavor.

● Commercially grown broccoli, cauliflower, and carrots often contain a high percentage of chemical pesticides. These vegetables rank high on the vitamin scale, so it makes sense to plant your own.

● Fresh herbs make vegetable dishes something special. Start your own collection.

● Garlic and shallots are easy to grow. Try a few snips of their green tops for flavoring.

● Tasty and unusual vegetables that are not usually available through supermarkets add a new dimension to your gardening pleasure. If you're a squash fan, try 'Ronde de Nice', a little round zucchini perfect for stuffing, or 'Sunburst', a star-shaped summer squash with fine flavor.

of water, and cook for a short time. Wait until water is boiling to add vegetables. Use vitamin-rich cooking water in soups and sauces.

The Winter Food Supply

How can a home gardener keep wholesome foods available all year long? Winter storage is the answer. Some vegetables can be stored as is, with no processing needed. Make braids of garlic and onions, and dry herbs in small bunches. Keep root crops, such as carrots or potatoes, in boxes of soil or shredded newspapers in an unheated garage or basement. Your vegetable bin in the refrigerator will keep cabbage and carrots for a month or more. When frost threatens, pick all your tomatoes—even the green ones. Wrap each one loosely in newspaper. They'll go on ripening for weeks.

Home-preserved foods are the highest in nutrition you can get next to fresh, since the harvest is promptly taken from garden to kitchen kettle or freezer. The Canning, Drying Food Crops, and Freezing entries will help you choose a method to preserve that garden goodness.

If You Can't Grow Your Own

If your yard is too small or too shady to grow fruit and vegetables, or your free time too little to tend a big garden, there are alternatives. Container gardening is one way to make the most of your space and time. A tomato plant in an old bucket or a window box of leaf lettuces is simple and low-care. See the Container Gardening entry for more ideas.

Look to local farm stands and farmers' markets for fresh fruits and vegetables in season. Be sure to ask what crops they grew themselves; some produce may have been bought for resale. Small farmers are often willing to pick custom orders. Let them know if you want a hundred ears of fresh sweet corn for canning, or a bushel of garden peas. Support your local agriculture system and help keep small farms alive.

Pick-your-own fruit and vegetable farms are

> ## More On
> ### FOOD AND NUTRITION
>
> For more information about community-supported agriculture, write CSA/Bio-dynamic Association, P.O. Box 550, Kimberton, PA 19442.
>
> Government agencies and representatives welcome your input. Write to them with suggestions or questions about healthy food. To find the appropriate organization, refer to the Government Agencies entry. For names and addresses of your local, state, and federal government representatives, ask at your public library.

popular in some areas for strawberries, blueberries, cherries, peas, beans, and a variety of other foods. Check your local newspaper, especially the classified-ad section, for advertisements of crops and picking dates.

Community-supported agriculture (CSA), sometimes known as subscription farming, is also a growing idea in many regions. Becoming a member means you invest in a farm operation and as a dividend receive fresh vegetables. Members prepay a yearly fee to the farmer. It's an investment, putting up money in January for vegetables to follow later in the year. The privilege of participating in the farming is sometimes an option.

Food cooperatives, a way of purchasing food as a group, have been active in many communities for decades. Co-ops, in which members combine their food orders, were established to provide food at better prices with less packaging. Larger food co-ops are set up much like small supermarkets, with a wide range of food products available in bulk quantities or packaged by members. In these co-ops, members and non-members are welcome to buy food. Co-ops are a good place to find organically grown food. ❖

Forcing

For centuries gardeners have used a variety of techniques to force flowers to open, vegetables to sprout, and fruits to ripen out of season. On the long dark days of late winter, nothing lifts the spirits as much as the sight of a few branches of golden forsythia or coral-colored quince, or a pot of fragrant purple hyacinths. And if you use row covers or have a home greenhouse, you can extend the harvest period for many fruits and vegetables beyond the usual growing season.

Branches of spring-flowering trees are easy to force for indoor display. You can force almost any spring-blooming tree or shrub from mid-January or early February on. Earlier than this, most forcing fails because buds have not had sufficient chilling to break their natural winter dormancy.

Experiment with a variety of things from your garden, cutting heavily budded branches on a mild day. Select stems of medium thickness or better, since these contain large quantities of stored sugars needed to nourish flower buds. Use a sharp knife or pruning shears to cut the branches; slice diagonally just above a bud. Cut branches at least 2'-3' long; shorter branches are less effective in arrangments. Keep plant health and form in mind as you harvest branches for forcing: Cut as carefully as you would when pruning. To ensure a steady supply of flowers, cut fresh branches every week or so.

After you bring the branches indoors, strip flower buds and small twigs from the bottom few inches of the stems. Slit up the stem ends a few inches or crush slightly with a hammer to encourage water absorption. Some may bloom faster if you submerge them completely in a tepid water bath for a few hours before making your arrangement. Recut stems and change the water in the containers every few days.

Besides forsythias, pussy willows, and fruit trees such as apples, cherries, plums, and almonds, some proven favorites for forcing are flowering quinces (*Chaenomeles* spp.), lilacs (*Syringa* spp.), witch hazels (*Hamamelis* spp.), hawthorns (*Crataegus* spp.), mock oranges (*Philadelphus* spp.), spireas (*Spiraea* spp.), wisterias (*Wisteria* spp.), spicebush (*Lindera benzoin*), alders (*Alnus* spp.), and horse chestnuts (*Aesculus hippocastanum*). Most of these will burst into bloom within 2-6 weeks of cutting if forced at temperatures between 60° and 70°F. The closer it is to the plant's natural blooming period when you cut the branches, the less time it will take for them to open. You can control blooming time to some extent by moving branches to a cooler room to hold them back, or placing them in a warm sunny window to push them ahead.

When arranging forced branches in containers, keep in mind the beauty of stems as well as flowers. Don't crowd them together so tightly that the interesting tracery of the branches is obscured.

For more information on forcing, see the Bulbs, Cloches, Cold Frames, Endive, Greenhouse Gardening, and Season Extension entries. ❖

Forsythia

Forsythia. Deciduous spring-flowering shrubs.

Description: *Forsythia × intermedia,* border forsythia, grows to 8'. It produces bright yellow flowers in early to mid-spring, followed by 3"-5" medium green leaves on arching branches. Often it has good yellow-purple fall color. Zones 4-8.

F. viridissima 'Bronxensis', Bronx green-stem forsythia, is a low (10"-12") groundcover with bright green foliage and primrose yellow early spring blooms. Zones 5-8.

How to grow: Forsythia grows best in full sun. Provide water in summer to help it get established. Prune after blooming to encourage vigorous growth. Every year, remove about ⅓ of the stems at ground level.

Landscape uses: Use for spring color in a massed planting or as a hedge. ❖

Fraxinus

Ash. Deciduous shade trees.

Description: *Fraxinus americana,* white ash, is widely admired for its fall display of muted reds, yellows, and purples. It is a broad-spreading tree with a rounded crown and a single, gray-barked trunk, growing to heights in the landscape of 50'-80' (occasionally to 120'). The opposite leaves are compound with 5-9 dark green 2"-6" leaflets. Zones 4-9. *F. pennsylvanica,* green ash, is a somewhat similar species with yellow fall foliage.

How to grow: Provide a site with full sun, even moisture, and good drainage. These plants tolerate a broader soil pH range than many trees. Plant nonfruiting (male) cultivars to avoid having ash seeds and seedlings everywhere.

Landscape uses: Use ash as a shade tree.

Best cultivars: *F. americana* 'Rosehill' is a pyramidal, male tree resistant to many of the diseases common to ash. *F. pennsylvanica* 'Marshall's Seedless' is a vigorous male cultivar that has fewer insect problems than the species. ❖

Freezing

If you're looking for a simple, quick way to preserve fruits and vegetables at home, freezing is your best bet. By relying on extreme cold (0°F or less) to inhibit the growth of bacteria, molds, and yeasts, freezing keeps foods safe for eating. It does a remarkable job of capturing the best colors, flavors, and textures of garden-fresh foods while preserving nutrients.

The one disadvantage to freezing is its high cost. A freezer can cost several hundred dollars, and electricity for its continuous operation adds to the bill.

Wraps and containers: Flexible bags and wraps are a good choice for fruits and vegetables packed without liquid. Choose among heavy plastics, heavy foil, and laminated papers. Be sure you use materials specifically made for the freezer.

You'll need rigid freezer containers for sauces and fruits packed in liquid. Look for containers made from plastic, foil, or glass (dual-purpose canning jars) or cartons lined with air-moisture barriers. Cardboard ice-cream or milk containers lack good barriers and are not suitable. Straight-sided containers pack better in the freezer. Wide openings allow easy removal of frozen foods. Check to see that lids fit tightly; if not, reinforce the seal with freezer tape.

Freezing produce: Some vegetables freeze better than others, retaining good flavor and texture. Vegetables recommended for freezing include asparagus, broccoli, brussels sprouts, carrots, cauliflower, corn, lima beans, peas, peppers, summer and winter squash, and tomatoes (as sauce). Celery, cucumbers, lettuce, and radishes do not freeze well.

Freezing garden produce is a simple process. Refer to a reliable, up-to-date cookbook for complete details. Follow these guidelines:

• Harvest ripe but firm fruits and vegetables in tip-top condition.

• Wash and dry produce quickly; do not soak. (Cauliflower, broccoli, and brussels sprouts are the exceptions: Soak them to remove insects.)

• Remove cores, seeds, stems, and skins with a stainless-steel knife.

• You can pack fruits dry, in water or fruit juice, or in a light syrup of water and honey. To prevent darkening, add ascorbic acid to sliced apples and peaches.

• Blanch vegetables in boiling water or steam, then cool and dry them. Pack in suitable containers.

• Remove as much air as possible from containers after filling them. Gently press excess air from bags and wraps. "Burp" rigid containers by lifting the lid from one side, then pushing back down. ❖

Fruit

To the gardener, a fruit is a succulent part of a plant, usually eaten raw or as a dessert. The botanist, however, defines a fruit as the ripened ovary of a flower, including its contents and any closely adhering parts, or as something with a seed. The botanical and common definitions of fruit do not always concur. Rhubarb, for example, is generally considered to be a fruit because it's eaten in desserts, even though we use only the leaf stalk. Many plants we commonly call vegetables, like sweet corn, tomatoes, and peas, are, in fact, fruits.

Fruits commonly are subdivided into categories. *Tree fruits* are those that grow on trees, such as apples and peaches. *Small fruits* refers either to fruits that are small or fruits that are borne on small plants. Strawberries and blueberries are familiar small fruits. Some fruits, though, are difficult to place in a particular category. Mulberries and juneberries are examples of this: Both bear soft, small fruits, but they're produced on full-sized trees. Nuts are actually dry fruits with woody shells.

To develop fruit, most plants need to have their flowers pollinated. When flowers on a plant produce fruit after being dusted with their own pollen, that plant is self-pollinating. Strawberries are self-pollinating, so if you plant only one cultivar, you still get fruit. Flowers that need pollen from a plant of a different cultivar to develop fruit need cross-pollination. Apples, for example, require cross-pollination, so a 'McIntosh' tree needs a 'Golden Delicious' tree (or some other cultivar besides 'McIntosh') nearby to supply pollen. To learn more about pollination, see the Pollination and Plant Breeding entries.

There are some very good reasons to grow your own fruit. First of all, you can harvest your crop at the peak of perfection. You also can grow the best-tasting cultivars, not necessarily the ones that are most attractive or ship best. By

> ## More On
> ### FRUIT
>
> You'll find more information about individual fruits in the following entries: Apple, Apricot, Avocado, Blueberry, Brambles, Cherry, Citrus, Currant, Elderberry, Fig, Fruit Trees, Gooseberry, Grape, Kiwi, Peach, Pear, Persimmon, Plum, Quince, Strawberry. Also see entries on fruiting plants grown as ornamentals: Amelanchier (serviceberry), Cornus (dogwood), Rosa (rose), and Viburnum.

choosing the right cultivars, gardeners all over the country can enjoy fresh fruit, beginning in spring with strawberries and going through winter with the last of the apples that ripen in cold storage.

Don't overlook the ornamental value of fruit-bearing plants. A peach tree, for example, is transformed into a cloud of pink blossoms in spring. The crimson red color of blueberry leaves in fall rivals that of the sugar maple. And strawberries make an attractive, herbaceous edging.

Fruit plants do need care. Almost all of them need annual pruning of some sort. And with the exception of plants such as gooseberry, currant, and pawpaw, fruit plants need full sunlight for best quality and production.

Tree fruits such as apples, peaches, and plums are the greatest challenges, since they are susceptible to pests that must be controlled. To avoid problems, plant resistant cultivars on a well-chosen site and employ good cultural practices such as cleaning up dropped fruit. Pests rarely pose problems with strawberry, raspberry, and other small fruits, as long as you give them a good site and annual pruning. The easiest fruits to grow are cornelian cherry, jujube, feijoa, and other unusual fruits (see the table "Unusual Fruits" on page 244), all of which provide tasty fare with little or no attention. ❖

Unusual Fruits

As you choose fruit-bearing plants for your property, don't forget to look past the usual apples and peaches. There are also many lesser-grown plants that provide wonderfully flavorful fruits. Here you'll find descriptions of a variety of unusual plants and their fruits, as well as notes on their culture. Some of these, such as cornelian cherry, hardy kiwi, rugosa rose, and serviceberry, also have great ornamental value.

Name/Cultivars	Fruit	Plant Type	Culture
Banana (*Musa acuminata, M. × paradisiaca*): 'Apple', 'Cavendish', 'Gros Michel', 'Lacatan', 'Lady-Finger', 'Red Jamaica'.	Besides the familiar, large, yellow banana of our markets, there also are cultivars with red fruits, and cultivars with small, finger-size fruits. As with other fruits, cultivars vary somewhat in flavor. Bananas ripen without regard to season.	A treelike, perennial herb with velvety leaves 4'–8' long and 1' or more across. Depending on cultivar, height varies from 8'–25'. Suckers grow up from around base of stem, enlarging and eventually replacing stems that fruit, then die.	Plant in full sun, but sheltered from strong winds, in rich, well-drained soil. Depending on vigor of the cultivar, set plants 10'–15' apart. No pollination is needed for fruiting. Prune off some of the suckers from around the base of the plant so that ony one or two will be fruiting at a time. Zone 10.
Cornelian cherry (*Cornus mas*): Currently available cultivars have been selected for their ornamental rather than edible qualities. Yellow-fruited 'Flava' is sweeter than most seedlings available.	Fruits are usually oval, fire-engine red, with a single stone. Some cultivars have barrel- or pear-shaped fruits; color may vary from yellow through dark purple. Flavor is tart, with varying degrees of sweetness, depending on the cultivar and how long fruit is left hanging. Fruits ripen from summer through autumn, depending on the cultivar.	Cornelian cherry is a long-lived, oval-headed tree or large shrub, growing up to 25' tall. The bark is attractive, flaking off in muted shades of tan and gray. Masses of yellow flowers appear on leafless branches in very early spring, but they rarely are damaged by frost. Leaves turn mahogany red in autumn.	Cornelian cherry tolerates a wide range of soils. Though it will grow in partial shade, full sun is needed for best fruiting. The flowers are self-fertile, but cross-pollination may further increase yield. The plant rarely needs pruning, only enough to shape it and keep it in bounds, if necessary. Zones 4–8.
Cranberry (*Vaccinium macrocarpon*): 'Early Black', 'Howes', 'Searles', and 'McFarlin' are commercial cultivars.	The ½"–¾", tart red berries ripen in autumn. Fruits usually are eaten cooked.	Evergreen vine with long, thin stems rising about 1' off the ground. The vines creep along the ground and root to form a solid mat of plants. Leaves are small and leathery, and a glossy, dark green.	Cranberries need a sunny site with a soil that is very acidic (pH 4.0–5.0), very high in organic matter, and moist year-round. The ideal site is a bog that is flooded in winter. Fertilize with an acid-type fertilizer. No cross-pollination needed. Zones 3–8.

Name/Cultivars	Fruit	Plant Type	Culture
Feijoa (*Feijoa sellowiana*): Also known as pineapple guava. 'Mammoth', 'Triumph', 'Pineapple Gem', 'Choiceana', 'Superb'.	Fruits are torpedo-shaped or round, 1"–3" long, and have a green skin and yellowish, jellylike interior. The sweet-tart flavor is reminiscent of pineapple, strawberry, and mint. Ripens in autumn.	Evergreen tree or small shrub about 10' high and wide. Leaves are glossy green above with silvery undersides. Edible flowers appear on new growth. Petals are white, tinged with purple.	Tolerates part shade, but does best in full sun in a variety of soil types. Thrives in dry climates. Needs cross-pollination. Prune lightly each year to prevent over-crowding of branches. Harvest fruits as they drop to the ground. Zones 8–10, but fruit flavor is best in cooler summer climates.
Highbush cranberry (*Viburnum trilobum*): Also known as Pembina. 'Andrews', 'Manitou', 'Phillips', 'Hahs', 'Wentworth'.	Fruits are ⅓" across and borne in clusters that are ready for harvest in autumn. The tart berries make excellent preserves and jellies. Except for a single, hard seed, the fruit is similar to that of the true cranberry.	Deciduous, round-topped bush 8'–12' high. Bushes are covered in spring with large clusters of white flowers. The large, three-lobed leaves turn red in August; fruits decorate plants through winter if not harvested.	Moist, well-drained soils in full sun or partial shade. Keep plants productive by removing one or two of the oldest stems each year and thinning new stems. Zones 2–7.
Jostaberry (*Ribes nidigrolaria*): 'Jostagranda', 'Jostina', and others.	The ⅝" black fruits of this hybrid have a taste somewhat reminiscent of its parents: black currant and gooseberry. Jostaberries are borne in clusters of 3–5 berries on wood at least one year old. Fruit ripens in summer.	This bush produces vigorous upright branches that can grow up to 6' tall. The glossy dark green leaves are deciduous, although they hang onto the plant late into the fall.	Jostaberries prefer well-drained, moderately fertile soil. Mulch to keep roots cool. Plant in a sheltered site to protect early-spring blooms from frost. Keep plants productive by removing one or two of the oldest stems each year. Some cultivars, such as 'Jostina' and 'Jostagranda', need cross-pollination. Zones 4–7.
Jujube (*Ziziphus jujuba*): Also known as Chinese date. 'Lang', 'Li', and many others.	Fruits range from cherry- to plum-size. Just-ripe fruit has mahogany skin, and a white flesh that is crisp and sweet like an apple. Left to ripen longer, the fruit dries and wrinkles, and the flesh becomes beige and concentrated in flavor. Fruits ripen in late summer and autumn.	Small, deciduous tree with small, glossy leaves and a naturally drooping habit. Young trees and some clones have spines. Trees sometimes send up many suckers. Masses of yellow flowers are present for an extended period.	Thrives in the sunniest and warmest possible locations. Not finicky as to soil. Avoid cultivating ground around trees because this increases tendency of plants to sucker. Blossoms late enough to escape spring frosts, but yield in some areas increases with cross-pollination. Zones 6–10.

(continued)

245

Unusual Fruits—*Continued*

Name/Cultivars	Fruit	Plant Type	Culture
Lingonberry (*Vaccinium vitis-idaea* and *V. vitis-idaea* var. *minus*): Also called cowberry, partridge-berry, whortleberry, mountain cranberry, and foxberry. 'Erntesgen', 'Koralle', 'Scarlet'.	Lingonberries are slightly smaller than, but otherwise similar to, cranberries in appearance and flavor. An early crop ripens in summer, but the main crop ripens in autumn.	Sprawling, ever-green shrub with leathery, oval leaves. The plant grows from a few inches to 1' in height. Spreads by under-ground rhizomes. Blooms in spring and again in summer.	Grows best in full sun or partial shade, and in acidic soil (pH 4.0–5.0). Set plants 1' apart in all directions to eventually form a solid mat of plants. Plants enjoy an organic mulch. Cross-pollination increases yields. Zones 1–6.
Medlar (*Mespilus germanica*): 'Nottingham', 'Dutch', 'Royal'.	Fruit resembles a small, russeted apple. It ripens in late autumn but must be allowed to soften indoors. Ripe fruit has a baked-apple texture and a brisk winelike flavor—much like old-fashioned applesauce with cinnamon.	Small, deciduous tree. Flowers appear in late spring, after shoots have grown a few inches, and are white or slightly pink.	Grows best in a sunny loca-tion in any soil that is well-drained and reasonably fertile. Plants are self-fertile. The tree needs little prun-ing beyond shaping, when young. On older trees, prune out diseased or interfering wood. Zones 5–8.
Mulberry (*Morus alba, M. nigra, M. rubra*): 'Illi-nois Everbearing', 'Wellington', 'Black Persian', 'Noir'.	Fruits are shaped like blackberries, but may be white, lavender, dark red, or black. Flavor may be sweet or a pleasant balance of acidity and sweet-ness. Ripening begins midsummer and con-tinues for a few weeks or more, depending on the cultivar.	Deciduous 20'–40' tree. Leaves are 2"–5" long and may be pointed or divided into two or more lobes—even on the same tree. Male and female flowers may be borne on the same or sepa-rate trees.	Needs full sun, but not fin-icky as to soil. Don't plant near walkways or driveways, where stains from fallen fruits would be tracked indoors. Most cultivars are self-fertile. No pruning is needed once young trees have been trained to a sturdy framework. Birds compete avidly for the fruit. Zones 5–10, depending on the cultivar.
Pawpaw (*Asimina triloba*): Also called Hoosier banana, Michigan banana, and poor man's banana. 'Overleese', 'Sunflower', 'Taytwo'.	Greenish yellow skin becomes speckled brown as the fruit ripens. Flesh inside is creamy white and custardy, tasting like banana with hints of vanilla, pineapple, and mango. Embedded in the soft pulp is a row of large brown seeds. Fruit ripens in late summer and autumn.	Small, pyramidal, deciduous tree with long, drooping leaves. Trees pro-duce suckers. Flow-ers are lurid purple, though not promi-nent, and appear late enough in spring to escape frosts. Leaves turn an attractive yellow in autumn.	Full sun or partial shade in any well-drained soil. Young trees benefit from shade. Trees do not need pruning. Most cultivars ('Sunflower' is an exception) need cross-pollination. Zones 5–9.

Name/Cultivars	Fruit	Plant Type	Culture
Pomegranate (*Punica granatum*): 'Foothill Early', 'Granada', 'Ruby Red', 'Sweet Spanish' ('Papershell'), 'Wonderful'.	Fruit is round and the size of a large apple. Inside the hard shell are numerous seeds, each surrounded by a sweetish tart juice sac. Fruit color ranges from off-white to purplish or crimson. Fruit ripens in late summer.	Deciduous or semi-deciduous small tree or shrub, 15'–20' high. Flowers are brilliant orange-red and are borne periodically from spring through the summer toward the ends of branchlets.	Plant tolerates a wide range of soil conditions. Train to a single or multiple stem, then every winter prune by thinning out crowded areas and removing interfering branches and some of the suckers. Zones 8–10, but yields best-quality fruits in dry, hot climates.
Prickly pear (mostly *Opuntia ficus-indica*, but other species also): Also known as Indian fig or tuna. Luther Burbank's superior selections included 'Bijou', 'Elegant', 'Superb', and 'Whitefruit'.	Fruits are 1"–3" across, pear or fig-shaped, and yellowish green to dark purple in color. Except in some cultivars, skin is covered with spines that must be rubbed off. Pulp is sweet, seedy, and red.	Plants grow 3'–15' tall. Cacti with flat pads covered with thorns, except for certain thornless cultivars. Flowers are very showy, orange or yellow.	Plant in full sun in well-drained soil or sand. Zones 5–10, depending on species. For more on growing cacti, see the Cacti entry.
Rose hips (*Rosa rugosa*): Commonly known as the rugosa, or Japanese, rose.	Orange or yellow, urn-shaped fruit good for jelly or fruit soup. Ripe flavor is good raw, but fruits are very seedy. The fruits (hips) ripen in late summer.	Deciduous shrub 4'–8' tall with prickly stems and wrinkled leaves. Blooms heavily in spring and sporadically until frost. Flowers are 2" across, with a row of white or pink petals, depending on the cultivar.	Tolerates almost any soil, even beach sand near the ocean. Full sun preferred. For maximum flowering and fruiting, prune away very old wood at or near ground level each winter. Self-fertile. Zones 2–7.
Serviceberry (*Amelanchier* spp.): also known as June-berry 'Honeywood', 'Pembina', 'Regent', 'Smoky', 'Success', 'Thiessen'.	Fruits are the size of blueberries, and dark blue, purple, or, in the case of a few cultivars, white. Flavor is sweet and juicy, with a hint of almond from the seeds. Fruits ripen in June or July, but the harvest season is very short for an individual plant.	Serviceberries with tasty fruits are represented by plants ranging in size from low-growing, spreading shrubs to small trees. In early spring, the plants are covered with white blossoms. Autumn color can be spectacular, as the leaves turn shades of purple, orange, and yellow.	Grows in sun or partial shade in a wide range of soil types. Tree species need little pruning. Bushy species should be pruned each winter, cutting away at their bases any shoots more than four years old, and thinning out the previous season's shoots so only a half dozen of the most vigorous ones remain. Birds are very fond of serviceberries. Zones 3–8.

Fruit Trees

Fruit trees make great landscape plants, blooming abundantly in spring and trimmed with colorful fruit in summer and fall. But unlike strictly ornamental trees, their fruit is not only attractive but also a succulent edible treat. The flavor of tree-ripened apples, peaches, and other fruits is unmatched, and you'll appreciate the savings in your grocery bills. However, to reap good quality fruit, you must make a commitment to pruning, monitoring, and maintaining your trees.

Selecting Fruit Trees

Before you buy, determine which fruit trees can survive and fruit in your climate. Northern gardeners should choose cultivars that will survive winter cold, blossom late enough to escape late-spring frosts, yet still set and mature fruit before the end of the growing season. Southern gardeners need cultivars that will tolerate intense summer heat and humidity. For organic gardeners, choosing disease-resistant trees is especially important. Check with local fruit growers or with your local extension service office to see which cultivars have a good track record in your area. You should also do some independent research on your climate and consider your fruit needs.

Temperature: Fruit trees need a dormant period during which temperatures are below 45°F. Trees that don't get sufficient winter chilling will not fruit properly. Low-chill cultivars flower and fruit with as little as half the usual cold requirement, stretching deciduous fruit production into Texas, northern Florida, and parts of California. Extra-hardy, high-chill cultivars for the far North require longer cold periods and flower a week later than most.

If winter temperatures in your area drop below −25°F, stick with the hardiest apple and pear cultivars; between −20° and 0°F, you can try most apples and pears, sour cherries, European plums, and apricots; if miniumum temperatures stay above −5°F, you can consider sweet cherries, Japanese plum, nectarines, and peaches. If minimum temperaures in your area are above 45°F, be sure to select low-chill cultivars.

Spring frosts: Freezing temperatures can kill fruit blossoms. If you live in an area with unpredictable spring weather and occasional late frosts, look for late-blooming or frost-tolerant cultivars, especially for apricots and plums.

Humidity: In humid regions, select disease-resistant cultivars whenever possible. Diseases such as apple scab and brown rot are more troublesome in humid conditions.

Usefulness: If you are fond of baking, top your list with sour cherries and cooking apples, which make excellent pies. For canning, look for suitable cultivars of peaches, nectarines, and pears. For jellies, try apricot, plum, and quince. If you're interested in fruit for fresh eating, think about how long the fruit will last in storage. Some apples stay good for months if kept cold, but soft fruits must be eaten within about one week or they will spoil.

Choosing a Tree Type

Fruit trees come in shapes and sizes for every yard. Most home gardeners prefer dwarf or semidwarf trees, which fruit at a younger age and are easier to tend.

Standards: Standard fruit trees can reach 30′ or taller, becoming small shade trees that can be underplanted with flowers or groundcovers. They are long-lived and hardy but can be more difficult to maintain and harvest.

Grafted semidwarfs: Apples grafted on size-controlling rootstocks grow well. However, stone fruit trees grafted onto dwarfing rootstocks often are not long-lived. In just a few years, perhaps when the young tree is burdened with a heavy crop of fruit, the graft can unknit and the tree will die. For more information on the effects of rootstocks on grafted fruit trees, see the Grafting entry.

Genetic dwarfs: Genetic dwarf or miniature trees are naturally compact trees grafted on standard-sized root systems. They reach about 7′

may be preferable to standard trees because they need less winter cold to flower.

Older genetic dwarf cultivars had poor-quality fruit, but modern types approach the flavor of their full-sized counterparts. However, none of the modern genetic dwarfs are disease-resistant. They need diligent thinning, because foliage and fruit can become overcrowded.

Pollination requirements are another important factor to consider when selecting trees. Most apples, pears, sweet cherries, and Japanese plums are not self-fruitful. You must plant a second compatible cultivar nearby to ensure good pollination and fruit set. Peaches, nectarines, tart cherries, and some European plums are self-fruitful. Some cultivars of apples, pears, sweet cherries, and European plums are somewhat self-fruitful but set better crops when cross-pollinated. Individual fruit tree entries provide details about pollination requirements.

Planting Fruit Trees

Plant fruit trees in a small traditional orchard, or intersperse them in borders, mixed beds, or a vegetable garden. You can even put a dwarf apple at the end of a foundation planting. Some will grow in lawns, but most perform better in a prepared bed.

Site Selection

Be certain the site you choose has the right growing conditions for fruit trees.

Sunlight: Even 1 or 2 hours of daily shade may make fruit smaller and less colorful. Envision the mature size of trees and shrubs close to your planned site. If their shadow will encroach on your fruit trees in years to come, you may want to select a different site, or remove the neighboring plants. Sour cherries tolerate a bit of shade better than other tree fruits do.

Shaded soil in early spring can be beneficial. A cool soil can delay flowering, perhaps until after late killing frosts.

Soil: Fruit trees need well-drained soil. Sandy soils can be too dry to produce a good crop of

---

Key Words
FRUIT TREES

Standard. A full-sized fruit tree, usually maturing to at least 20' in height.

Dwarf and semidwarf. Fruit trees grafted on size-controlling rootstocks. Dwarf trees often mature to 8'–10' in height. Semidwarfs mature to 12'–18'.

Genetic dwarf. A fruit tree that stays quite small without a dwarfing rootstock.

Rootstock. A cultivar onto which a fruiting cultivar is grafted. Rootstocks are selected for strong, healthy roots or for dwarfing effect.

Whip. A young tree, often the first-year growth from a graft or bud.

Scaffolds. The main structural branches on a fruit tree.

Pome fruit. Fruit that has a core containing many seeds, such as apples and pears.

Stone fruit. Fruit with a single hard pit, such as cherries, plums, and peaches.

Low-chill. Requiring fewer hours of cool temperatures to break dormancy.

High-chill. Requiring more hours of cool temperatures to break dormancy.

Self-fruitful. A tree that produces pollen that can pollinate its own flowers.

Compatible cultivars. Cultivars that can successfully cross-pollinate.

Crotch. The angle of emergence of a branch from the trunk.

Suckers. Shoots that sprout out of or near the base of a tree.

Watersprouts. Upright shoots that sprout from the trunk and main limbs of a tree.

---

and bear about ⅕ as much normal-sized fruit as a standard tree. Genetic dwarfs tend to be shorter-lived than standard trees and are not hardy in Northern areas. They can be grown in planters and moved to a protected area where temperatures remain between 30°F and 45°F in winter, such as an unheated storage room. Genetic dwarfs are ideal for the Pacific Northwest or the southern United States. In fact, in those areas they

Smart Shopping
FRUIT TREE CATALOG SHOPPING

If you can't find the kind of fruit trees you want locally, turn to catalogs. Your best choice is a mail-order nursery that specializes in fruit trees, located in a climate similar to your own.

Most of the information you need to make the proper selection, such as chilling requirements and insect and disease resistance, should be listed in the catalog. However, you may have to call the nursery to find out what rootstock is used and make your own decision about its compatibility and potential in your area. Also, if the catalog doesn't list pollination requirements, inquire whether a particular cultivar is self-fruitful. If it's not, be sure to ask for names of compatible cultivars.

If you do decide to buy trees at a local garden center, be wary of trees offered in containers. These trees may have been shipped to the garden center bareroot, had their roots trimmed to fit a container, and been potted up just for the sake of appearance. This treatment will not help the tree grow any better, and the stress to the roots may actually set the tree back.

fruit. Wet, clayey soil encourages various root rots. See "Soil Preparation" on this page to learn how to cope with less-than-ideal soil.

Slope: Plant near the top of a gentle slope if possible. Planting on a north-facing slope or about 15′ from the north side of a building helps slow flowering in spring and protect blossoms from late frosts. Planting on a south-facing slope can hasten flowering and lead to frost damage. Sheltered alcoves on the south side of a house protect tender trees. Planting in a frost pocket, as shown in "Frost Pockets" on the opposite page, can increase the risk of spring frost damage to flowers and young fruit.

Wind: Blustery winds in open areas or on hilltops can make training difficult, knock fruit

off trees early, or topple trees. Staking will help trees resist the force of prevailing winds. Where wind is a problem, you can slow it by erecting a hedge or fence. However, don't box the tree in and stifle the breeze. Air circulation is helpful for reducing diseases.

Tree Spacing

The amount of room your trees will need depends on their mature height and width, how they are trained, their soil fertility level, and tree vigor. Give every tree plenty of space to grow without impinging on neighboring plants or spreading into shady areas. Small trees, such as dwarf peaches and nectarines, require only 12′ between trees, while standard apple trees need 20′-30′ between trees.

Soil Preparation

To make the effort and expense of planting fruit trees worthwhile and to maximize yield and fruit quality, it pays to prepare the soil properly. Plan ahead, and take these steps in the season preceding the year you plan to plant:

• Test the soil and follow recommendations to correct deficiencies. Keep in mind that fruit trees prefer soil high in calcium, magnesium, and potassium, with balanced levels of nitrogen, phosphorus, and other micronutrients. Excessive nitrogen can lead to lush growth that is more susceptible to certain insect and disease problems.

• Raise soil organic matter content by adding compost or planting a green manure crop.

• Clear out all roots of perennial weeds. To reduce the number of annual weed seeds, lightly cultivate the top 6″ of soil several times and, if possible, plant a cover crop the season before you plant.

• Amend clayey or sandy soils throughout the area where the roots will extend. A good rule of thumb is to amend the area out to where you estimate the branch tips of the full-grown tree will reach. Add up to 50 percent organic matter, preferably leaf mold and compost. Make a raised

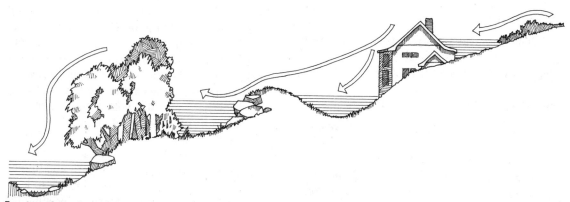

Frost pockets. In spring and fall, cold air sinks to the bottom of a slope, creating a frost pocket, a localized area of below-freezing temperature. Trees planted in frost pockets are more susceptible to frost damage. Buildings, small rises, and trees on a slope stop cold air flow but can create frost pockets on their uphill side.

growing bed if necessary to improve drainage. Break up any subsoil hardpan and add drainage tiles to eliminate standing water.

After planting, you can plant annual green manures such as buckwheat beneath the tree. These crops will smother weeds and provide shelter for beneficial insects that help control pest insects. Annual cover crops die with frost and decompose to humus over winter.

Planting Instructions

Plant fruit trees while dormant in early spring, or in the fall where winters are quite mild. Fall planting gives roots a head start, because they continue to grow until the soil freezes. However, fall planting is risky in areas where the soil freezes, because the low temperatures may kill the newly grown roots.

Most nurseries stock bareroot fruit trees. Plant the young trees as you would any bareroot tree. See the Planting entry for full instructions. "Determining Planting Depth" on this page shows how to determine the proper depth to set a fruit tree at planting.

You may be able to speed a young tree's establishment by dipping the roots in powdered bonemeal before you plant. Also apply compost tea or manure tea at planting. Allow the tea to sit

for several days before applying, or it may burn roots. See the Composting and Manure entries for instructions on making compost or manure tea.

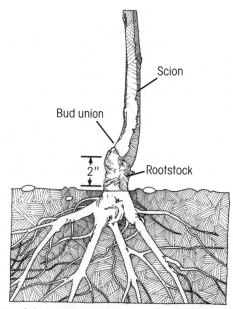

Determining planting depth. Plant a tree growing on standard roots at the same depth or slightly deeper than it grew at the nursery. If the tree is budded or grafted, set the bud union—the crooked area where the scion and rootstock join—2" above soil level. Scions can root if trees are set too deeply, and the trees can lose rootstock effects, including size control.

Aftercare

Follow-up care each year is critical to your ultimate goal in planting fruit trees: a harvest of plentiful yields of healthy fruit.

Pruning

To grow top-quality fruit, and to have easy access for harvesting, you need to establish a sturdy and efficient branching framework. For home gardens, the two best training methods are open center and central leader. Some commercial fruit producers also use a training system known as modified central leader. All three systems encourage the growth of branches with wide crotches that are less likely to split when burdened with a heavy fruit load. However, modified central leader trees can become top-heavy if not carefully maintained, and fruit on lower branches will be shaded out.

It's important to establish the main branches while the tree is young. You'll then maintain tree shape of your bearing trees each year with touch-up pruning. Central leader trees produce more fruiting spurs, important for spur-type apple and pear cultivars. For nectarines, peaches, and Japanese plums, use open center training to maximize air circulation and sunlight penetration among the branches, which will help reduce disease. Illustrated instructions for the central leader system are on the opposite page, and for open center training, page 254.

Spread young branches so they will develop broad crotch angles. Use clothespins to hold branches out from the trunk, or insert notched boards in the crotch angle. Branches that aren't spread may develop a strip of bark called a bark inclusion in the crotch angle, making the crotch weaker and more likely to break.

In certain circumstances, it's best not to train. Some fruit trees, including apricots and pears, are particularly susceptible to disease, which can invade through pruning cuts or attack young growth that arises near the cuts. If disease is a problem in your area, you may want to limit pruning to general maintenance or renewal of fruiting wood. In the far North, keep training to a minimum, since new growth is more susceptible to winter injury. However, leave some young suckers on main scaffolds to act as renewal wood in case main branches are injured by cold.

Whether you train your trees or not, you should prune off shoots that emerge low on the trunk and any branches that cross and rub. Where one limb grows above and shades another, or when two branches of equal length and diameter arise at one fork, select one branch to keep and prune off the other. During the summer, remove suckers that sprout near the tree base, watersprouts that shoot out from the trunk or main limbs, and any dead or diseased wood. For instructions on how to make correct pruning cuts, see the Pruning and Training entry.

When to prune varies with the tree type. You can prune apples and pears in early spring before the trees break dormancy. For stone fruits that are susceptible to cankers caused by disease organisms, wait until bud break, when they are less likely to be infected. Prune away dead and diseased branches on all kinds of fruit trees as the growing season continues. Stop pruning by the end of August in areas where winter injury is a concern. Late pruning can stimulate a flush of new growth that could be damaged when cold weather sets in.

Fertilizing

Even with thorough advance soil preparation, your fruit trees may need fertilizing. Nutrient consumption varies with tree type and age, soil, and growing conditions. For instance, you will have to fertilize a fruit tree growing in the lawn more frequently than if the soil around the tree is cleared and mulched. But don't simply fertilize on a set schedule. Overfertilizing can encourage soft new growth that is susceptible to disease attack and winter injury.

Monitor tree growth to determine when trees need fertilizing. Nonbearing apple trees should grow 1½'-2' per year; those producing fruit aver-

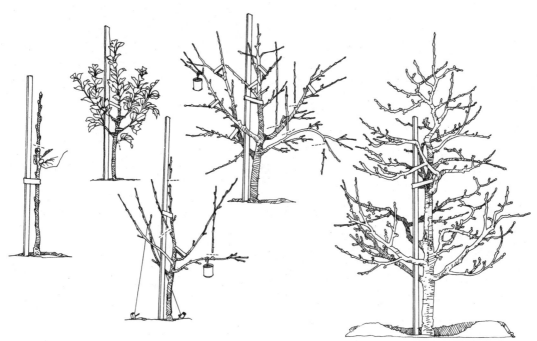

Central leader training. Follow these instructions for training a young fruit to a central leader form:

1. Head back a one-year-old whip to 2½′ at planting.
2. In mid-June, select four branches that emerge in different directions and are spaced several inches apart along the trunk as scaffolds. The strongest-growing, upper-most shoot will be the central leader, which becomes the trunk. Pinch off all other shoots.
3. For the following few years, repeat this process by heading back the central leader in early spring about 2′ above the previous set of scaffolds. Then in June, select an additional layer of scaffolds. Choose branches that are at least 1½′ above the last set of scaffolds. Scaffolds should spiral up the trunk so each branch will be in full sun.

age 8″-12″. Mature peach trees should grow 1′-1½′ each year. If your trees seem to be lagging, have the nutrient levels in the leaves analyzed. Call your local extension office for information about leaf analysis.

Fertilize only in the spring. Spread materials on the soil surface in a circle around the trunk out to the edge of the leafy canopy. If the tree is growing in the lawn, make holes with a crowbar around the perimeter of the branches and drop fertilizer below the grass roots. Avoid high-nitrogen fertilizers. The best fertilizer for fruit trees is compost because it has a good balance of nutrients. Foliar seaweed sprays improve tree health, increase yields, and increase bud frost resistance. Spray trees when buds start to show color, when petals drop, and when fruit is ½″-1″.

Mulching

Mulched trees will have access to more water and nutrients, especially if you use soil-enriching mulch such as compost or shredded leaves. Mulch also will keep down weeds that compete with trees for water and nutrients. It prevents excessive evaporation of soil moisture, a necessity around young or weak trees, in dry climates, and in sandy soils. In areas with fluctuating winter

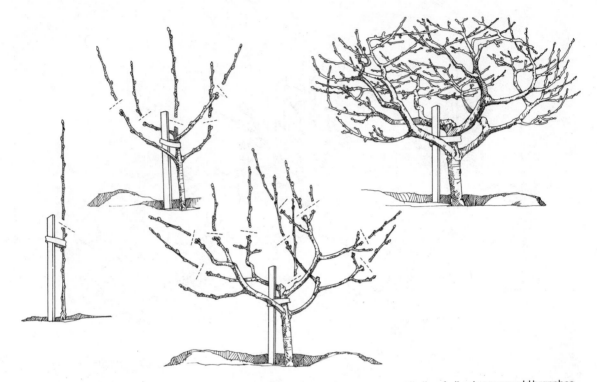

Open center training. Follow these steps to train a fruit tree to the open center form:

1. After planting, cut the whip back to 2'-2½' and head back all side branches.
2. At the beginning of June, choose three scaffolds that emerge in different directions and are separated along the trunk by about 4". Cut off all others.
3. In the third and fourth years, thin as lightly as you can to avoid delaying fruiting.
4. Once peach, nectarine, and Japanese plum trees begin to bear, they fruit only on year-old branches. To have plenty of fruiting wood, cut the scaffolds back to the same height every year, encouraging the growth of 1'-1½' of new fruiting wood. Thin overly crowded or short and weak fruiting spurs.

temperatures, mulch will eliminate damage from frost heaving. Mulch can keep the soil cooler in spring and delay flowering of early-spring bloomers such as apricots or peaches, hopefully beyond the threat of frost.

The drawback of mulching is that it can make heavy soils too wet and can harbor pests, especially mice and voles.

Where mulch is warranted, apply a 3"-6" layer of organic mulch in an area from 1'-2' away from the trunk out to just beyond the branch tips. Fluff the mulch with a spading fork occasionally so it doesn't compact. Check the soil moisture level occasionally. If the soil is staying overly wet, rake the mulch back to prevent root rot. You also may want to push the mulch out from under the tree boughs during leaf fall if disease is a problem. Afterward, rake up the fallen leaves and respread the mulch.

Watering

Ideally, the soil around fruit trees should be evenly moist, neither dry nor waterlogged. Moisture is especially important to young trees and to trees bearing ripening crops. Thoroughly soak the root system of newly planted trees, and repeat whenever the soil becomes dry for the next few months.

After the tree is growing well, your watering schedule will depend on the weather and climate. If the weather has been dry, even during a midwinter warm spell, stick your little finger down in the soil around the drip line. If you do not feel moisture below the surface, water the tree thoroughly. A trickle irrigation system is ideal for watering fruit trees. In cold climates, stop watering by early fall to harden the plant for winter.

Winter Protection

Protect your trees against winter sunscald, frost heaving, and pest damage, all of which can

injure or kill fruit trees. Sunscald occurs when sun-warmed wood is killed by nighttime cold. The damaged area becomes dry, sunken, and attractive to borers and diseases. Prevent sunscald by wrapping the trunk with a white plastic tree guard or painting it up to the first scaffold branch with white latex paint diluted 1:1 with water.

To minimize frost heaving—shifting of soil when it freezes and thaws—mulch *after* the soil freezes to keep it frozen. This is especially important for young trees that can suffer extensive root damage due to frost heaving.

Flower and Fruit Care

Once your trees reach maturity, there are some extra activities involved in their seasonal care. Some trees may require hand-pollinating, others may need young fruit thinned, and all will have to be harvested.

Hand-pollinating: Early-flowering fruit trees can suffer partial to full crop loss if the weather is not mild when the tree is in bloom. If temperatures aren't high enough for insect activity, flowers won't be pollinated and fruit won't develop. If there's a cold spell when your trees are blooming, you can save your crop by hand-pollinating. Simply collect pollen from one tree by rubbing flowers gently with an artist's brush or cotton swab, and then brush the pollen onto the flowers of a compatible cultivar.

Be sure nights are frost-free if you plan to hand-pollinate. If you expect a late frost, you can cover small trees with plastic or spray them with a frost-protecting product. As a last resort, try sprinkling water on trees all night. Use care, as the weight of ice that forms on the trees can break branches.

Thinning: Because fruit trees tend to be overburdened by young fruit, you should thin off the excess on all trees except those with cherry-size fruit. Without your intervention, the weight of the fruit may actually break limbs. The stress from the excessive fruit load may also reduce the number of flower buds the tree produces the

(continued on page 258)

RESTORING OLD TREES

If a fruit tree goes without regular care, it will become overgrown, minimally productive, and home for hoards of pests and diseases. Should you save the old tree or start over with a new one? If the tree has a lovely shape, vital position in your landscape, or sentimental value, it may be worth keeping. Here's how to restore it:

● If the tree is suffering from diseases such as scab, black knot, or fire blight, begin a spray program to help lessen damage.
● Remove dead and diseased branches.
● Check for trunk or root rot and, in warm climates, nematodes.
● Prune back any neighboring trees and shrubs that shade the fruit tree.
● Take a leaf analysis for nutrient levels, and correct soil nutrient deficiencies. Use a foliar seaweed spray to restore tree vigor while the soil comes back into balance.
● When the tree is reasonably healthy, you can begin to prune it into a productive shape. Gradually thin out unproductive branches to open the canopy to sunlight. To minimize watersprout and sucker regeneration, take no more than ¼–⅓ of the new wood on the tree or on a particular branch any year.

Fruit Tree Insects and Diseases

Pest control is serious business when it comes to fruits. There are many disease organisms and insects just waiting to eat your fruit before you do. Fortunately, home gardeners now benefit from an increasing range of alternatives to the regimented programs of synthetic chemical sprays used to prevent pest damage on fruit trees. Here you'll find descriptions of the most persistent tree fruit pests, the damage they cause, and the methods used to control them.

Problem	Hosts	Damage	Control
INSECTS			
Apple maggot (*Rhagoletis pomonella*) Adults: ¼″ black flies with yellow legs. Larvae: white maggots.	Apple, blueberry, plum; related flies attack cherry, peach, and walnut. Found in eastern and northwestern United States and Canada.	Larvae tunnel through fruit, which drops early; early cultivars usually most damaged.	Collect and destroy fallen fruit daily; hang baited red sticky ball traps in trees (1–6 per tree), remove traps when fruit colors; plant white clover groundcover to attract predators.
Codling moth (*Cydia* [=*Laspeyresia*] *pomonella*) Adults: gray-brown moths, ¾″ wingspan. Larvae: pink or white caterpillars, brown heads. Eggs: white eggs laid on leaves, twigs, fruit.	Apple, pear. Found throughout North America.	Larvae burrow into fruit. Entry holes are surrounded by dead tissue and sawdust-like material. Fruit interior is dark and rotted. Young fruit may drop.	Sow or encourage cover crop to support predators and parasites, especially ground beetles. Band trunks with sticky-trap glue to intercept larvae.
Green fruitworm (*Lithophane antennata*) Adults: Fuzzy-looking gray or purple moths, 1½″ wingspan. Larvae: light green, with lengthwise stripe on sides, 1″. Eggs: tiny, pale grey, sand-dollar shaped, laid singly on branches.	Apple, apricot, cherry, peach, pear, plum, quince. Found in northern states and southern Canada.	Larvae chew leaves, flower buds, and green fruits. May cause premature fruit drop. Developed fruits show healed-over brown depressions or holes.	Monitor with pheromone traps. Spray BT (*Bacillus thuringiensis*) when larvae are feeding. Spray neem for severe infestations. Plant wild carrot and dill to encourage parasitic wasps. These controls are also effective for leafrolling pests.
Mites (*Panonychus ulmi*) Adults: pale brown or reddish, spider-shaped insects, visible with hand lens. Eggs: tiny, reddish, laid in groups around bases of buds and fruit spurs.	Apple, apricot, cherry, peach, pear, plum, quince. Found in most fruit growing areas of North America.	Heavy infestations cause off-color, bronzed foliage, reduced tree growth, and fewer flower buds the next season.	Spray dormant oil when buds show pink if you've had problems in past. Check leaves with hand lens; spray insecticidal soap or horticultural oil if more than 10 mites per leaf. Plant groundcover to encourage predators.

Problem	Hosts	Damage	Control
Peach tree borers (*Synanthedon exitiosa* and *S. pictipes*) Adults: Steel blue, clear-winged moth with yellow or orange markings, 1″ wingspan. Larvae: white with brown head, 1″. Eggs: tiny, brown or gray, laid in bark crevices.	Apricot, cherry, peach, plum. Found throughout North America.	Borers enter bark on lower trunk and injured limbs. Masses of gummy sawdust appear around entrance holes. Branches or whole trees may be stunted and die.	Keep bases of trunk clear. Monitor moths with pheromone traps. Probe holes with wire to kill borers. Cut out damaged areas to healthy wood and paint with a 1:1 mix of lime-sulfur and white latex paint.
Plum curculio (*Conotrachelus nenuphar*) Adults: gray or brown ⅓″ beetles with a prominent snout. Larvae: ½″ grayish white grubs. Eggs: tiny, white, laid under skin of fruit.	Apple, blueberry, cherry, peach, pear, plum, quince. Found throughout eastern North America.	Small semicircular scars left on green fruit. Larvae burrow and feed on interior of fruit. Fruits drop prematurely.	Monitor with light green sticky ball traps hung in trees. Knock weevils out of tree onto sheet and destroy. If severe, spray with pyrethrins in early spring.

DISEASES

Problem	Hosts	Damage	Control
Bacterial leafspot (*Xanthomonas pruni*) Overwinters in small cankers on twigs.	Apricot, peach, plum. Common east of the Rocky Mountains.	Many small, dark spots on leaves; centers dry and drop out, leaving shot-holes. Small, sunken dark spots or cracks on fruit.	Spray copper when buds open until temperatures reach 85–90°F in wet weather. Limit high-nitrogen fertilizers.
Brown rot (*Monolinia fructicola, M. laxa*) Overwinters in dried fruit on tree or ground.	Apricot, peach, plum. Found throughout the United States and Canada.	Flowers and new growth wilt and decay. Developing or mature fruit show soft, brown spots that enlarge rapidly, and may grow gray mold.	Remove and destroy dried fruit, cultivate soil before bloom. Cut out infected twigs. Spray sulfur in summer and lime-sulfur when trees are dormant.
Canker, perennial (*Valsa leucostoma* and *V. cincta*) Overwinters in cankers and dead wood.	Apricot, cherry, peach, plum. Found in all areas except the western United States.	Sunken, oozing cankers on trunk or twigs. May cause wilting or death of branches or trees.	Avoid mechanical injury: Cut out cankers and paint wounds with a 1:1 mix of lime-sulfur and white latex paint.
Fire blight (*Erwinia amylovora*) Overwinters in cankers.	Apple, pear, quince. Found throughout North America.	Young, tender shoots die back suddenly. Leaves turn brown or singed looking and remain on the twig. Bark may become water soaked and ooze.	Select resistant cultivars. Cut off blighted twigs at least 12″ below decay on a dry day. Sanitize pruning tools between cuts. Limit high-nitrogen fertilizers.

next year. Disease problems such as brown rot can spread quickly among crowded fruits, ruining the crop before it ripens. In addition to avoiding problems, thinning lets you channel all the tree's resources into fewer but bigger and more beautiful fruit.

Thin when the fruit is young, the smaller the better. First clip or twist off all insect-damaged or deformed fruits. Then remove the smaller fruits. Leave only the biggest and best.

If you can't reach the upper limbs of large trees, tap the limbs with a padded pole to shake loose some of the extras. On small apple, nectarine, and peach trees with big fruit, thin fruit to 6″-8″ apart. Plums and apricots can be more closely spaced, about 3″-5″ apart.

Even after thinning, fruit may become heavy enough to tear a branch. For extra support, prop branches up with a forked stick. On central leader trees, you can secure branches to the central leader with a rope or with a chain covered with garden hose.

Harvesting: Most fruit is ready to harvest when the green undercolor changes to yellow or the fruit softens and drops. Grasp the fruit in the palm of your hand and twist it off the stem carefully so you don't damage the branch. Handle the ripe fruit gently so it does not bruise.

Pests and Diseases

It's not easy to grow fruit trees using only organic pest control methods. Fruit is so succulent and tasty that it attracts a wide range of pests, from mites to deer. Watch diligently for pests, and control them before they damage the tree or the fruit.

Insects and diseases: Take as many preventive steps as possible to avoid insect and disease problems on your fruit trees. Your best first choice is to plant insect- and disease-resistant cultivars. Pick up and destroy infested fruit that falls prematurely. Prune out diseased or pest-infested wood.

Learn to identify particular pests, and know their life cycles. When pest problems arise, select

More On
FRUIT TREES

You'll find information on selecting trees, planting and care, pest problems, and winter protection in the entries for the following tree fruits: Apple, Apricot, Avocado, Cherry, Citrus, Fig, Peach, Pear, Persimmon, Plum, and Quince.

the most environmentally gentle method of control, such as encouraging or releasing predatory insects. Move on to the use of horticultural oil, soap sprays, and BT (*Bacillus thuringiensis*). Reserve botanical insecticides such as pyrethrins or neem for a last resort. While they break down rapidly in the environment and are generally less toxic than synthetic chemical pesticides, they should still be used with caution. See "Fruit Tree Insects and Diseases" on page 256 for pest control recommendations for specific fruit tree pests. The Organic Pest Management entry offers details on control methods.

Animal pests: Deer will eat young shoots, twigs, and fruit. Raccoons will harvest ripe peaches the night before you plan to pick them yourself. Rodents and rabbits will chew on bark during the winter. Birds are especially troublesome pests of cherries and plums. For control suggestions, see the Animal Pests entry.

Propagating Fruit Trees

Most fruit trees consist of a preferred fruit-producing cultivar grafted onto the rootstock of a different cultivar. Dwarfing rootstocks are successful for apples but unreliable for stone fruits.

Home gardeners can try their hand at budding or grafting fruit trees. For information on these techniques, see the Budding, Grafting, and Propagation entries. You'll find recommendations for propagating specific fruits in the individual fruit tree entries. ❖

Fuchsia

Fuchsia, lady's eardrops. All-season tender perennials grown as annuals or houseplants.

Description: *Fuchsia × hybrida,* fuchsia, bears distinctive 1″-3″ earringlike flowers in shades and combinations of white, pink, red, and purple that seem to dance upon upright or hanging stems ranging from 1'-5' and bearing ¾″-3″ green or reddish purple leaves.

How to grow: Plant in the ground or in large pots in partial shade (morning sun is best) and fertile, moist but well-drained, humus-rich soil. Water and fertilize often in summer. Before frost, take the plant inside, reduce watering, and allow leaves to drop. Water very lightly until spring, then cut stems back to a few inches. Repot if rootbound, and resume watering.

Landscape uses: Use in hanging baskets, window boxes, or containers. ❖

Fungicides

Fungicide use dates back to the late 1800s, when sulfur was used to kill fungi and other disease-causing organisms on both plants and people. Organic gardeners use certain organic fungicides to help control disease problems, but they are a method of last resort. See the Disease and Organic Pest Management entries for ways to avoid disease problems.

How Fungicides Work

Fungicides can be classified as protectants or eradicants. A protectant fungicide stops disease organisms from infecting a plant. Eradicant fungicides can destroy disease organisms or inhibit their development after initial infection. Virtually all fungicides used by organic gardeners are protectants with little or no eradicant action. They must be applied before infection occurs and before symptoms appear. For example, once blackspot appears on roses, no amount of spraying will remove it.

Antibiotics and certain synthetic chemical fungicides are eradicants. There is a wide range of synthetic chemical fungicides available for home gardens, but none of these compounds are considered acceptable for use by organic gardeners. The potential environmental and health hazards of these products are too great.

Fungicides may act locally or systemically. Almost all fungicides used by organic gardeners are localized or contact fungicides, which are not absorbed by the plant. These fungicides can wash off plants or break down into simpler, nonfungicidal forms. They must be reapplied for protection to continue. Some synthetic fungicides are systemic. They are absorbed by the plant and thus can even kill fungi in plant parts that were not treated.

Using Fungicides

Applying fungicides on a regular basis is often recommended to prevent disease. To use protectant fungicides efficiently, keep records of the disease problems that occur in your garden, or ask fellow gardeners what diseases to expect in your area and when to expect them. By learning about diseases common to your area, you can reduce fungicide use, spraying or dusting only during the seasons and weather conditions when infection is likely to occur.

Few fungicides are available to organic gardeners, and their drawbacks often outweigh their benefits. Rather than relying on fungicides, discourage diseases from developing by using preventive cultural practices and by keeping the garden clean. Choose resistant or less-susceptible cultivars of plants whenever possible. Accept some level of disease symptoms as tolerable, rather than striving for a 100 percent disease-free garden. For more about steps you can take to prevent and limit disease problems, see the Organic Pest Management entry.

If you decide to apply a fungicide, select the least toxic substance that will prevent or control the problem. Always take appropriate safety precautions when applying fungicides; see the Insecticides entry for guidelines.

The following list of fungicides is arranged from least to most toxic.

Microbial fungicides: These fungicides contain benign organisms that establish themselves on or in plants and prevent disease-producing organisms from gaining a foothold. For example, Binab T, a mixture of beneficial fungi, is painted on fresh tree wounds to prevent decay.

Barriers: A thorough spray of vegetable or light horticultural oil coats plant surfaces, acting as a barrier to infection. Oils seem to help prevent fungal rusts and mildews. For application rates, see the Insecticides entry.

Antitranspirants such as Wilt-Pruf, designed to prevent leaves from losing moisture, may also prevent powdery mildew. Follow label directions, and don't treat heat- or drought-stressed plants.

Plant products: Garlic appears to be a fungicide as well as an insecticide. Mix 5-10 cloves with 1 pint of water in a blender, strain, and spray on plants. Horsetail (*Equisetum arvense*) infusion sprayed on plants may help prevent fungal diseases. For more information on making homemade sprays see "Home-Brewed Pest Controls" on page 339.

Some research indicates that a compost tea spray may have possibilities for combating disease. Fungicides based on natural vitamins and amino acids also are being developed.

Baking soda: Baking soda (sodium bicarbonate) prevents fungal spores from establishing themselves on plants and may even prevent established fungi from continuing to develop. Dissolve 1 teaspoon of baking soda and a few drops of soap in 2 quarts of water, and spray on plants.

Sulfur: Direct contact with sulfur prevents the development of disease organisms. However, it also damages important soil microorganisms and beneficial insects and is moderately toxic to mammals, including humans. Apply sulfur sparingly, and always take appropriate safety precautions.

Both a plain spray mix of elemental sulfur and mixtures of sulfur and other substances are effective preventive fungicides. Powdered sulfur is almost insoluble in water. Wettable sulfur has been finely ground with a wetting agent and is easier to use. Liquid sulfur is the easiest to dissolve. Sulfur also can be applied as a dust or as a fumigant.

Adding lime to sulfur increases its effectiveness as a fungicide. Lime allows the sulfur to penetrate leaves and kill recently germinated disease spores. However, lime sulfur sprays are more likely to damage plant tissue than are plain sulfur sprays.

At temperatures above 85°F, sulfur becomes highly phytotoxic and will injure plants. Combining sulfur and oil also causes damage to growing plants. A combination of oil and lime sulfur is safe to use on dormant trees; see the Insecticides entry for details.

Copper: Copper is a powerful, nonspecific fungicide that kills disease organisms. It damages beneficial soil microorganisms and beneficial insects and is more toxic than sulfur to plants. Copper sulfate has been used as an herbicide to control annual weeds. Repeated applications of any copper product will stunt plants. Copper sulfate is classified as very toxic to humans. Organic gardeners often choose to avoid copper fungicides when possible because of their negative effects on nonpest species.

Copper is available as a powder or liquid. Fixed-copper fungicides are available from organic suppliers as dusts or sprayable solutions. Bordeaux mixture is a combination of hydrated lime and copper sulfate that can be applied as a dust or spray. Bordeaux mixture is a strong fungicide. To prevent leaf damage, spray only when it will dry rapidly. On edibles, use it at half the rate recommended for ornamentals. ❖

Gaillardia

Blanket flower. Summer- to fall-blooming annuals and perennials.

Description: Blanket flowers bear 2″-4″ single or double daisies in shades of red, yellow, and orange (often red tipped with yellow). The long, curved or leaning stems grow to 3′ above loose mounds of hairy, gray-green leaves to 1′ long. *Gaillardia pulchella,* annual blanket flower, usually grows a bit more upright and is smaller in all its parts than *G.* × *grandiflora,* perennial blanket flower, hardy in Zones 4-8.

How to grow: Start annual blanket flowers from seed about three weeks before the last frost, or direct-sow into a sunny spot with average to less fertile, well-drained soil. They take heat and drought very well. Deadhead to promote more blooms. Give perennials the same conditions, making certain the soil drains well in winter. Plant or divide every few years in spring.

Landscape uses: Mass in perennial borders and cutting gardens, or naturalize in dry, sunny spots. Try dwarf perennial cultivars as edgings; they look at home among rocks or in containers.

Best cultivars: *G. pulchella:* double 'Lollipops' to 1½′, blooms in many color combinations. *G.* × *grandiflora:* 8″ 'Baby Cole' and 1′ 'Goblin' both bear single blooms of red tipped with yellow. ❖

Galls

Galls can stump even the snappiest gardeners. Everyone has seen them. In fact, if you grow peas or beans, you depend on them. But few gardeners know what galls are or how they are caused.

Galls come in many shapes and sizes, including tiny nipplelike bumps on leaves, swellings on the stems of goldenrods and other meadow plants, and fluffy cottonball-like masses on oak twigs. These unusual formations come in many colors, too, including green, pink, red, brown, and purple. Galls are actually tumors on plants caused by a gall-forming microbe or insect. They usually don't grow uncontrollably like animal cancers. Instead, many have very predictable shapes and sizes. (To see an illustration of a typical type of gall, turn to page 423.)

If you cut through a gall, you'll see that it is made of plant tissue, similar in consistency to apple flesh. Gall growth is directed by the plant *and* the gall former, so if the gall former dies or leaves, the gall stops growing. Some experts believe galls are the plant's way of walling off attacking intruders. If that's the case, then the gall former has turned a plant defense to its advantage, because a gall provides its inhabitants with both food and shelter. Most cecidologists (scientists who study galls) believe that galls are exquisite examples of how plants and their enemies have co-evolved to accomodate each other.

Take time to admire and examine galls when you see them. Galls can be found on all kinds of plants: seaweeds, mushrooms, mosses, pines, cacti, orchids, grasses, oaks, and others. Galls can form on all plant parts, too, but are especially common on leaves and stems. There are even galls that form on galls.

In North America, oaks are a favorite gall plant for tiny wasps called cynipids. The gall wasp *Amphibolips confluenta* causes one type of oak apple gall commonly found in the East. The developing larva lives in the center of the large, greenish yellow gall, which later turns brown.

Other examples of galls include club root of cabbage, which is a fairly common garden gall caused by slime mold fungi. Another kind of fungus turns azalea leaves into small white balloons. Tomatoes are favorites for gall-forming root knot nematodes.

Some types of galls can damage plants, others don't. As a general rule, galls that occur on roots or stems can disrupt the flow of nutrients and cause the plants to be stunted or to die. On the other hand, galls on leaves are rarely considered pests because they don't seem to affect plant vigor. Surprisingly, some galls are extremely valuable. For example, plants and gardeners depend on the nitrogen-fixing galls (called nodules) on legume roots for soil nutrient enhancement. Some types of galls have been sold for centuries as sources of dyes and medicines. Others have recently been used for the biocontrol of invasive field weeds.

Control measures vary depending on the type of gall. The best way to avoid root galls on vegetables or fruit trees is to select resistant cultivars. For example, tomatoes bred for resistance to root knot nematodes are denoted by an *N* after the cultivar name. Crown-gall-resistant fruit trees are available at most nurseries. Crop rotation discourages buildup of gall-forming microbes in the soil. The best way to get rid of leaf galls, if you don't want to just enjoy them, is to prune them out of the plant in spring. ❖

Garden Design

The best and most satisfying gardens are the result of careful planning and sound design. Whether you want to design a flower garden or plant a shrub border to add privacy to an outdoor patio, there are some basic aesthetic principles that will help you make decisions as you plan.

Design Styles

There are two general types of garden design styles—formal and informal. Formal gardens exhibit classical symmetry. Flower beds, terraces, pools, and other features are generally rectangular (or sometimes round), and walks are straight. Formal gardens are not necessarily grand, though, for gardens designed in this manner can be unfussy and simple.

Informal gardens feature curved, free-form flower beds that sweep along the land's features. Lawns, terraces, walkways, and other features are also irregularly shaped, with one gentle arc

Smart Shopping
MAKE A NURSERY BED

Making a nursery bed is a great way to save money on plants. If your design calls for lots of groundcovers or hostas, for example, buy only a plant or two. Then systematically propagate them for a year or more by division, cuttings, or layering, depending on the species, until you have a small nursery of plants to move to your garden. A nursery bed is perfect for young seedlings, too. Keeping the young plants together ensures they get the care they need, for they're easier to water and weed en masse. Transplant to the garden when the plants are large enough to thrive on their own.

To make a nursery bed, prepare the soil and add plenty of compost or leaf mold; a raised bed is ideal. Shade with wood lath if the bed is in hot sun.

Formal design. Because they can be unfussy and simple, formal designs are often very effective on a small lot. Rectangular beds filled with herbs and edged with dwarf shrubs, straight walks, and symmetrical design are all characteristic of a formal garden.

Informal design. Even a rectangular lot can have an informal design. Parts of the garden— terraces, lawn areas, beds of groundcovers, flower gardens, or plantings of shrubs and trees— all have free-form shapes that flow together in a unified, informal design.

leading to another. Natural-looking woodland wildflower gardens or free-form island beds of perennials are both examples of informal style. If the lay of your land is irregular, it will lend itself to an informal design.

Basic Design Principles

Regardless of style, all well-designed gardens make use of three essential principles—balance, proportion, and repetition—to blend the various parts of the garden into a harmonious whole.

Balance: When elements on two sides of a central point are similar in size or visual weight, they are balanced. Balanced design gives the viewer a peaceful, restful feeling; unbalanced, lopsided, design is unsettling. Balance doesn't necessarily mean symmetry; you don't need mirror-image plantings to accomplish it. Several

good-sized clumps of a plant can balance one large one, for example. Symmetrical balance is a hallmark of formal gardens, and asymmetrical balance of informal gardens.

Proportion: Garden features (plants, flower beds, terraces, etc.) are in proportion when their scale is in good relationship to their surroundings. For example, a large clump of 9′ tall giant reed planted in a bed with low-growing, 2′-3′ perennials creates a picture that is out of proportion. Similarly, a huge shed would be out of proportion in a small yard.

Repetition: Repeating an element—color, texture, shape, or even building materials like landscape timbers—throughout a garden adds unity and harmony to a design, so the parts of the garden fit together more closely. For example, repeating the color red at intervals in a flower bed leads the eye through the design and creates

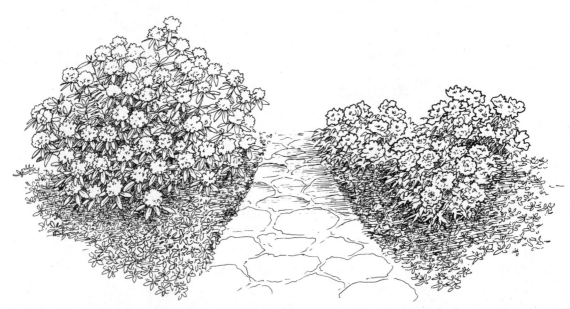

Balance. Asymmetrical balance can be accomplished by placing two different types of plantings on either side of a central point. Several good-sized clumps of peonies will balance one large shrub, but a single peony paired with a large shrub would be out of balance.

Proportion and repetition. Plants in a design are in proportion when they are all in scale with one another and with nearby garden elements such as fences or other structures. Repeating a flower color or foliage texture throughout will unify a design.

a feeling of wholeness and rhythm. You can repeat the same plant, or use different species with similarly colored blooms to achieve the same effect.

Plants and Design

The color, height, form, and texture of plants play a vital role in any garden. All plants change from season to season and year to year. They may grow taller than planned, spread too vigorously, or not bloom when expected. Balancing and working with these changes is what makes gardening an art. Even the most carefully designed gardens are never static; their owners adjust and develop the design over time.

Color: In a garden, color can be used in many different ways. One gardener may prefer bright reds and yellows, another soft pinks, blues, and lavenders. Color can influence the mood of a garden. Hot colors—vibrant reds, oranges, and yellows—are cheerful and bright. Cool colors—greens, blues, and purples—are more serene.

Color can influence perceived perspective.

Hot or warm colors appear to bring an object or scene closer. Cool colors tend to recede and push the object farther away, so they're a good choice for making a small garden seem larger. Use them in large clumps to catch the eye, and remember they can be easily overwhelmed by warm colors.

Use balance, proportion, and repetition to design your color scheme. Strive for balanced distribution of color. A large planting of one color can overwhelm a design. Repeating a color at intervals can unify the design. Use clumps of a single plant or several different species with the same flower color.

Height: Plant height should also be balanced and in proportion. In a planting in front of a fence or other backdrop, plant the tallest plants in the back, the shortest in front. If the shape is free-form, put the tallest plants at the widest parts of the border. In island beds, which can be viewed from all sides, plant the tallest plants in the center, with shorter plants around the edges.

Form: This term refers to shape—round,

vertical, creeping, or weeping, for example. It's used to describe the entire plant or just the flowers. For example, delphiniums are vertical plants with spike-shaped bloom stalks; marigolds are mound-shaped with round blooms. Intersperse different plant forms throughout a design for balance and interest. Form can be used like color, although it's more subtle. Repeating a form at intervals strengthens unity and harmony. You needn't repeat the same plant to achieve this effect; several plants with similar forms will do.

Texture: Plant leaves can look coarse, crinkled, glossy, fuzzy, or smooth. Flowers can be feathery and delicate or waxy and bold. Using plants with a variety of textures—and repeating interesting textures at intervals—adds interest and appeal. Like form, texture is a subtle characteristic.

Planning Considerations

Before you start buying and planting plants, take time to decide what role you want the garden to play in your overall landscape. Flower or shrub borders can be used to edge walkways or terraces, to define a work or play area, embellish a fence, or provide privacy. See the Landscaping entry for details on how to make a plan for your property.

Site characteristics: Learning everything you can about the site you've chosen is an essential step for designing a garden that will grow and thrive. Take time to learn about the soil: Is it sandy or clayey? Well drained or boggy? Is it rich in organic matter or does it need improvement? Is the site in full sun, dappled shade, or deep shade? Once you know what conditions exist, you can look for plants that will thrive there naturally. Matching plants to the site is more practical than trying to modify the site to match the requirements of the plants. Why? Plants matched to site will perform well from the start; routine gardening practices such as soil improvement and mulching will only improve their performance.

Size: Several factors play a role in determining the best size for your garden. Available space may be the main consideration, but keep in mind what landscape purpose the garden is to serve. For example, if you need a shrub border to screen an unattractive view or create a private patio space, determine the size by walking around your yard and studying where the largest plants need to be planted to accomplish your purpose. Smaller shrubs and perennials that connect these larger plants into a continuous border can be filled in later, as time and budget permit. The beauty of having an overall plan is that nothing is planted haphazardly and you'll be able to work gradually toward your goal.

For a flower garden that blooms all season, you'll need enough space to accommodate a variety of plants that will provide an extended bloom period. About 125 square feet will give you enough room to mass flowers for a succession of

More On
GARDEN DESIGN

You'll find designs you can use in your own garden in several entries in this encyclopedia. Under Perennials we've included a sunny perennial border. Under Natural Landscaping you'll find a shady woodland border. For details on designing with annuals, see Annuals. Birds, Butterfly Gardening, and Beneficial Insects contain design ideas or plant lists for attracting these creatures to your yard. Food gardeners will find garden designs or design ideas in the Herbs, Edible Landscaping, and Vegetable Gardening entries. Water Gardens contains a bog and water garden design.

There are many lists of plants suitable for growing in particular conditions in the Annuals, Biennials, Curbside Gardens, Ferns, Groundcovers, Perennials, and Shade Gardening entries.

color. For a formal garden, a 5′ × 25′ rectangle, two 5′ × 12½′ beds, or a 12′ diameter circle all provide about 125 square feet. In an informal garden, make the shapes free-form, or plan several related beds divided by paths. In general, don't plan gardens that are less than 4′ or 5′ wide if you want a lush effect. Don't plan them any wider if you want to be able to tend the plants without stepping into the bed, or plan on an access path on either side.

Time and money: These last considerations are critical: How much time and money do you want to spend? You can plan for features that reduce maintenance, but any garden will require basic care—especially in the early stages. Consider how much time you want to devote to such tasks as weeding, staking, watering, and pruning. Look for tough, low-maintenance plants if you want to keep these chores to a minimum.

Plants and supplies also cost money; decide how much you want to spend before you start to dig. (See "Smart Shopping: Make a Nursery Bed" on page 262 for a tip on minimizing your plant investment.) If you're not realistic about what size garden you can control, it will end up controlling you. Once you have a garden plan, you can plant each area as time and budget permit. Plan your garden so you'll have time to enjoy it.

Selecting Plants

Once you've decided on the type of garden you want and studied your site, it's time to make a plant list and develop the design. For this, you'll need regular and colored pencils or crayons, a tablet of paper (for plant lists), graph paper, tracing paper, and a soft eraser. Use graph paper with a scale of ½″ equals 1′. Tape two sheets together, if necessary.

To get an idea of how many plants you'll need, consider the approximate size at maturity of the types of plants you want. Perennial plants generally need 2-4 square feet at maturity; that means you can fit from 30 to 60 of them in a 125-square-foot garden. Shrubs and small trees may need from 9 to 25 or more square feet.

Making a plant list: Selecting the plants for any garden is a challenge. There are literally thousands to choose from and a confusing array of flower colors, sizes, shapes, and textures. Start with a list of favorite plants, then add ones you've admired in other gardens, nurseries, photographs, books, magazines, and nursery catalogs. Leave plenty of space between plants for notes. Jot down plant descriptions, growing tips, bloom time, height, color, hardiness, and culture.

Keep an eye out for perennials with good foliage and long season of bloom. Trees and shrubs with winter interest—like evergreens or ones with ornamental bark or branching habits—are also invaluable. Don't worry about making your list too long.

Periodically review your list and cross off plants that won't grow well in the site and don't fit your needs. If you have only shade to offer, cross off plants that need full sun. Do you want only easy-care plants? Eliminate those that need staking or deadheading to look their best. Do you want to save on water bills? Cross off any that may need supplemental watering.

Charting selections: Next, make a chart to help identify plants that will add the most to your design. On a clean sheet of paper, make a column on the left labeled "Plant Names/Bloom Season." Draw lines across the page at intervals to indicate sections for each season of bloom (see the example on page 268). If you have a large garden, you can use a separate sheet for each bloom season. Write down the bloom seasons you want in the first column—early, mid-, and late summer, for example. Leave enough space under each season to list plant names.

Divide the right side of the paper into several columns for plant heights and colors. You'll need three or four to indicate various heights and as many for flower colors. Add an extra

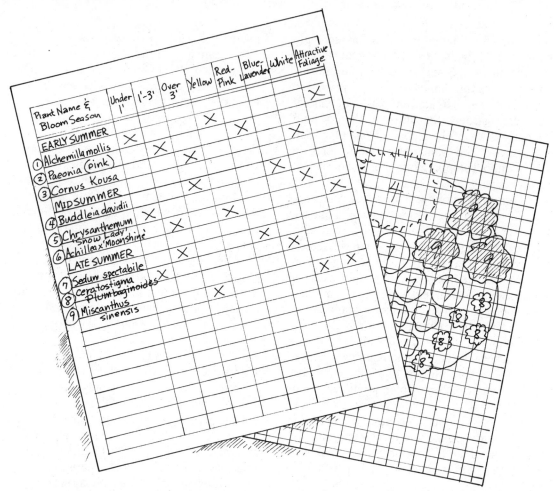

Plant Name & Bloom Season	Under 1'	1'-3'	Over 3'	Yellow	Red-Pink	Blue-Lavender	White	Attractive Foliage
EARLY SUMMER				X	X		X	X
① Alchemilla mollis	X	X						
② Paeonia (pink)		X	X				X	
③ Cornus Kousa				X			X	X
MIDSUMMER								
④ Buddleia davidii	X				X			
⑤ Chrysanthemum 'Snow Lady'		X				X		
⑥ Achillea x 'Moonshine'		X					X	
LATE SUMMER							X	X
⑦ Sedum spectabile		X						
⑧ Ceratostigma plumbaginoides	X				X			
⑨ Miscanthus sinensis								

Drawing your design. Make a chartlike plant list that's organized according to season of bloom, and indicate plant height and color. Then use the list to locate plants on your design.

column to indicate plants with attractive foliage or winter interest.

Starting with the first plant on your list, enter it under the appropriate bloom season on your chart. Then indicate height and color with an "X" in the appropriate columns. Repeat this process for each plant on your list. When you finish, look the chart over to make sure you have a fairly equal representation of "X's" under each column. Will some flowers of each color be bloom-ing in each season? Are there are a variety of heights? Add and subtract plants until you have a balance in all the categories and a manageable number of plants to grow. Last, number the plants on your list. Use these numbers to fill in the spaces as you draw your garden design.

Drawing Your Design

Draw an outline of your garden to scale on graph paper. Use tracing paper over the graph paper, so you can start over easily if you need to. Begin drawing shapes on the paper to indicate where each plant will grow. (Try to draw them to scale, based on the sizes you determined.) Instead of drawing neat circles or blocks, use oval or oblong shapes placed in horizontal drifts that will flow into one another.

Arrange plants, especially perennials and small shrubs, in clumps of several plants. Because of the basic design principles of balance and repetition, you'll want to repeat clumps of at least some species. So, as a general rule you'll probably want half as many plants on your list as you can fit in your border. In our example, that would mean 15 to 30 plants.

Beginning with the first plant on your list, study its "profile" and decide where you want to plant it. Transfer its name or number to the corresponding shape—or shapes if you want to repeat it in more than one spot—on your diagram. Do this with all the plants on your list.

As you work, you'll have to decide how many of each plant you want to grow. You may wish to follow the "rule of three" for perennials that are relatively small at maturity. Three plants will make an attractive clump when mature. For large plants, such as peonies, you may want only one plant; for others, two.

Place the tallest plants in the back of your diagram. It's a good idea to mix up heights somewhat to create interest. Let some tall plants extend forward into the middle group, and medium-sized ones up front. Also try to mix shapes and textures throughout, planting glossy, dark green-leaved plants next to ones with gray-green, fernlike foliage, for example.

Also consider color combinations as you work, and avoid large masses of single colors. To visualize how your garden will look at each season, put a sheet of tracing paper over your completed design. Check your plant list to find out which plants bloom in early summer, for example. Trace the plants blooming at that time on your tracing

paper. Then color them the appropriate color. Do the same for the other seasons of bloom, using a separate sheet of tracing paper for each.

Strive for a balanced composition in every season, with the color evenly distributed throughout the border during each bloom period. Are all the reds or yellows off to one side so that the design looks lopsided? Are the color combinations pleasing to you? Are major color combinations repeated at rhythmic intervals to tie the border together? Would it help to add more plants of a particular color?

As you grapple with these problems and refine your design, be sure to make changes on both tracing paper and master diagram. Expect to have to redo your design several times before you feel you have it right. Think of it this way: each sheet of crumpled paper brings you closer to your goal of creating a beautiful garden, tailor-made by and for you. ❖

Gardenia

Gardenia, cape jasmine. Evergreen spring-flowering shrubs.

Description: *Gardenia jasminoides,* common gardenia or cape jasmine, grows 3'-5' tall with a spreading habit. Thick, dark green, 2"-4" leaves have a shiny surface. Creamy white, waxy, 2"-3½" wide, sometimes double, intensely sweet flowers appear in late spring and early summer. Zones 8-9.

How to grow: Provide moist, well-drained, humus-rich soil and light shade. Plant in fall or winter. Water to establish, and when needed in dry weather. Scale, whitefly, mealybugs, and nematodes can limit use of gardenias in parts of the South.

Landscape uses: Use gardenias around foundations and patios and in borders where you will enjoy their stunning fragrance. ❖

Garlic

Allium sativum, A. ophioscorodon
Liliaceae

Garlic should be a staple of every organic garden. Garlic cloves are great for seasoning all kinds of foods or for roasting and eating whole. Another part of the plant, the robustly flavored young greens, are prized in many cuisines. Start by using them as a chivelike garnish for numerous dishes, or try making garlic pesto. You may decide to devote part of your garlic patch solely to greens production. An added benefit of garlic growing is that homemade garlic oil spray is an effective deterrent for many garden pests. For a recipe, see "Home-Brewed Pest Controls" on page 339.

Types: There are two types of garlic, one commonly called soft-neck (*Allium sativum*) and the other hard-neck (*A. ophioscorodon*). Hard-neck garlic is also known as seedstem (or top-setting or bolting) garlic because in late spring, just before bulb expansion, it will shoot up a flower stem that should be removed for best yields. Hard-neck garlic yields larger cloves and usually tastes better but is harder to prevent from sprouting in long-term storage. Soft-neck garlic has a longer shelf life, is a little easier to grow (especially in warmer regions), and may have slightly higher yields than hard-neck garlic. Soft-neck bulbs have an inner row of frustrating hard-to-work small cloves on the inside of each head—hard-neck bulbs don't. Almost all garlic sold in supermarkets is soft-neck.

Planting: Garlic grows best in deep, rich soil and full sun. Plant garlic in the fall, on or around Columbus Day in most of the country, a little later in the deep South. The bulbs should have a little root growth before winter, so that they won't be heaved out of the ground by frost. Spring-planted garlic rarely provides satisfactory yields.

Select large cloves for planting, and plant only healthy cloves. Space the cloves 4"-6" apart and 1"-2" deep in rows no closer than 1' apart. Be sure to set the cloves root-end down. Cover loosely with soil, then mulch lightly or interplant with a cover crop that will winter-kill in your area. You can expect to harvest 5-10 lb. of bulbs per 20' of row.

Growing guidelines: In the spring, encourage vigorous leaf growth by applying foliar seaweed or fish emulsion sprays every two weeks. Watering is important during the bulb-forming stage, provide extra water if conditions are dry in early summer. Weeds are probably garlic's biggest enemy, so weed beds regularly.

Problems: Diseases can generally be prevented by avoiding excessive standing moisture, and viruses, sometimes a problem, usually do nothing worse than diminish yield. See the Onion entry for information on controlling insect pests.

Harvesting: Check plants frequently once the leaves begin to turn brown. If you lift the bulbs too early, you'll be giving away size. Lift them too late, and the outer wrapper will be more likely to tear, resulting in lower quality and poor keeping ability. Cure garlic in a hot, dry, dark, and airy place for a few weeks. Trim roots and neck, or braid if you wish.

Best cultivars: Don't plant cloves from supermarket garlic—they may have been treated with an antisprouting chemical. For excellent garlic-growing information and carefully tested planting stock, write to: Garlic Seed Foundation, c/o Rose Valley Farm, Rose, NY 14542, or Filaree Farm, Route 1, Okanogan, WA 98840. ❖

Geranium

Cranesbill. Spring- and summer-blooming perennials.

Description: Don't confuse these perennials with the popular annual geraniums, which are in the genus *Pelargonium*. Cranesbills bear many ¾"-2" rounded flowers in shades of white, pink, magenta, blue, and violet. Plants form 6"-36" spreading, mounded, or slightly upright plants with scalloped to deeply cut 1"-8" foliage, sometimes tinged red or orange in fall. Zones 3-8.

How to grow: Plant or divide in spring or fall. Grow in a sunny spot with average, well-drained but moisture-retentive soil. Give partial shade in hotter, drier areas. Excess fertility leads to floppy growth. Generally easy to grow and trouble-free.

Landscape uses: Mass cranesbills in borders, informal gardens, and lightly shaded woodlands, or as a colorful groundcover.

Best cultivars: 'Claridge Druce', 1½'-2', mauve-pink with grayish leaves; 'Johnson's Blue', 1½', purple-blue. ❖

Geum

Avens. Spring- and summer-blooming perennials.

Description: Avens bears rounded, single to double 1" flowers in reds, oranges, and yellows. Plants have 2', open clumps of basal, fuzzy leaves. Zones 5-7.

How to grow: Plant in spring or divide in early fall. Grow in a sunny site in fertile, moist, well-drained, humus-rich soil. These plants do best in cool Northern areas, often growing as biennials farther South. Many self-sow readily.

Landscape uses: Mass avens 10" apart in borders, or let them squeeze into tight spots between other plants in borders or cottage gardens. Showy with irises.

Best cultivars: 'Lady Stratheden', yellow semi-double; 'Mrs. Bradshaw', scarlet double; 'Starker's Magnificent', 1½', apricot semi-double. ❖

Ginkgo

Ginkgo, maidenhair tree. Broad-spreading deciduous trees.

Description: *Ginkgo biloba* is a single-trunked tree that is pyramidal in youth and broadly rounded at maturity. It has a mature height of 50'-80' but can reach a height of 120'. Fan-shaped, two-lobed leaves turn bright yellow in fall and seem to drop in unison. The 1" fruits are tan to orange with a waxy bloom. While the nut inside is edible (it's considered a delicacy by some Asian cultures), the flesh has a rancid, repulsive odor. Zones 4-7.

How to grow: Provide a site with full sun, good drainage, and ample space. Ginkgos perform well under such adverse conditions as air pollution and heat. Unless you are willing to endure the pungent fallen fruit or want to try the seeds, purchase a male cultivar. Nearly all named cultivars are male; avoid plants identified simply as *Ginkgo* with no cultivar name.

Landscape uses: Plant ginkgo as a shade or street tree. They also make excellent large specimen trees.

Best cultivars: 'Autumn Gold' is a male cultivar with excellent yellow fall color. ❖

Gladiolus

Gladiolus, glads. Summer- and fall-blooming corms.

Description: *Gladiolus × hortulanus,* glads, bear 2"-5" triangular blooms, many with ruffled edges, in an enormous range of colors (except true blue) in solid shades and combinations. The blooms are arranged neatly and closely up one side of stiffly upright stems from 1½'-5' tall that rise out of a fan of swordlike leaves. Many are hardy in Zones 7-10.

How to grow: Because an individual plant's flowers last in good condition for about 10 days, begin planting the corms after the last severe frost and continue at 10-day to two-week intervals until midsummer for a longer bloom season. Full sun encourages strong growth and vigorous corm production for next year, but the plants also tolerate light shade. Depending on the height of the cultivar, cover with 3″-6″ of fertile, well-drained, moist soil. Add organic matter like compost if your soil is heavy. Plant closely (3″-6″ apart) to save space and to make staking easier. Mulch with pine needles, straw, or other light material when the leaves are about 6″ tall. Water well during dry spells. Give plants an application of fish emulsion or manure tea as the fans begin to elongate in the center and as the flower spike becomes visible within the leaves. For instructions on making manure tea, see the Manure entry.

Most glads grow tall and may blow over in storms or even fall under their own weight when in bloom, so stake them individually if you grow only a few. If you're growing clumps of glads, provide a corset of stakes and twine running in all directions between them. Or grow them in rows with two parallel strings on either side tied firmly to strong stakes.

Thrips cause streaky leaves and deformed flowers; control them in spring before planting by soaking the corms in very hot water (hotter than you can bear but not boiling). To help control Fusarium wilt and viruses, immediately lift and destroy any plant which turns yellowish and looks stunted. In fall, or after the foliage is quite yellow, dig up the corms and store in a dry place until the soil clinging to them is dry. Shake off the soil, cut the foliage off to 1″-2″ above the corm, and break off the shriveled dead corm under the new one(s). Store the new corms dry and cool (around 45°F) in plastic mesh bags.

Landscape uses: Grow a few small masses between other border plants that can disguise the fading foliage, or remove glads after they bloom. Glads make excellent cut flowers, so grow bunches of them in a cutting garden where you can attend to their special needs. ❖

Gleditsia

Honey locust. Deciduous shade trees.

Description: *Gleditsia triacanthos* is a native North American tree with a vase-shaped habit. Honey locust leaves are finely compound with tiny ½″ leaflets, giving the spreading crown of this tree an open, airy feeling and casting light, dappled shade. Honey locust grows 30′-40′ in the landscape; an occasional old-timer will reach 80′. This tree also bears stout, simple or three-branched spines on its trunk and branches, and quantities of brown-black, 7″-8″ straplike seedpods. Wild-edible enthusiasts consider the sweet inner pulp of the pods to be a good field snack. Both thornless and seedless cultivars are available and strongly recommended over the species, because the thorns can be quite dangerous, and unwanted seedlings are a nuisance. *G. triacanthos* var. *inermis* is thornless honey locust, from which most cultivars have been selected for landscape use. Zones 4-9.

How to grow: Plant honey locust where there is full sun and good drainage. Watch foliage for signs of mimosa webworm activity; select cultivars that show resistance to these tent-forming caterpillars. If problems occur, penetrate webs with a forceful spray of BTK (*Bacillus thuringiensis* var. *kurstaki*). Continue to spray weekly until feeding stops.

Landscape uses: Use thornless honey locust as a street or shade tree. Open branches and fine foliage make growing grass easier beneath honey locust than under many shade trees.

Best cultivars: The following are seedless cultivars of *G. triacanthos* var. *inermis:* 'Moraine', golden yellow fall color, good resistance to mimosa webworm; 'Shademaster', strong terminal leader and upright habit, some resistance to mimosa webworm; 'Sunburst', spring foliage opens a golden yellow that persists at twig tips when the remaining leaves turn to green for the summer, little resistance to mimosa webworm. ❖

Gooseberry

Ribes spp.
Saxifragaceae

Gooseberries come in a kaleidoscope of colors—golden yellow, green, orange, pink, red, purple, and almost black—with a corresponding diversity of flavors. They are wonderful for preserves and refreshing summer wines; some are at their best eaten fresh at full ripeness.

Gooseberries are deciduous shrubs that grow 3'-6' high and wide. The arched branches are usually armed with long, sharp spines. They fruit on wood a year or more old; each plant can produce for more than 30 years. Five-year-old bushes yield 6-9 lb. of fruit on early cultivars and 12 lb. or more on later ones. Gooseberries perform best in Northern climates, where cool, moist summers favor slow ripening that brings out the fruit's subtle flavor. Zones 3-6.

Types: Gooseberries belong to two species of *Ribes*: *R. uva-crispa* (from Europe) and *R. hirtellum* (from America). European dessert gooseberries rival the finest grapes and other fruits in taste and appearance. They are, however, often less heat-tolerant and more mildew-susceptible than small-fruited American types.

Jostaberries are a hybrid of gooseberry and black currant. The black fruits are ½" and larger, and the bushes resist many pest and disease problems.

Planting: Gooseberries require similar planting, pruning, and nutritional treatments as their close relatives, red and white currants, which also belong to the genus *Ribes*. See the Currant entry for details. For gooseberries, be sure to choose a protected, sunny site; gooseberries also do well in partial or dappled shade. Jostaberries are grown like red currants, but leave 8' all around at planting.

Care: Maintain a 2"-3" mulch layer to conserve moisture and reduce weeds. Keep the soil evenly moist. Gooseberries need lots of potassium and magnesium and low amounts of nitrogen. Leaf margin scorching and weak wood are symptoms of potassium deficiency. If your soil is deficient in potassium, fertilize with granite dust. For a magnesium deficiency, apply dolomitic limestone or Epsom salts.

Thinning is only necessary if you want large fruits or if a plant has set an exceptionally heavy crop; if necessary, remove every other fruit in late May. Never let the ground dry out once fruit starts to ripen, as a heavy rain or watering might cause the berries to burst.

Pruning: Summer-prune gooseberries starting in July. Cut back laterals of the new season's growth to 3-5 leaves, leaving leaders unpruned. Always prune just above an upward- and outward-facing bud. In fall, cut out any crossing, broken, or unproductive canes.

Problems: The federal ban on planting any species of *Ribes* (because of its role in the disease cycle of white pine blister rust) was lifted in the 1960s, leaving a patchwork of state regulations. Contact your Cooperative Extension Service for information on your locality's status. See the Currant entry for more information on common problems.

Harvesting: Gooseberries ripen over a 2-3 week period, so bushes must be picked over several times. Be sure to wear gloves to protect your hands from spines as you pull off the fruit. Pick early cultivars when fruit is not yet ripe (in early June) for culinary use or processing. Late cultivars ripen in mid-July through early August. Dessert berries keep for up to two weeks after harvesting, refrigerated in a sealed container. All kinds freeze well.

Best cultivars: For all-around use: pale green 'Whitesmith' and the dark red 'Whinham's Industry', both with excellent flavor and large fruit. Yellow-green, culinary: 'Careless', 'Jubilee', and 'Invicta'. Yellow-green, dessert: 'Early Sulphur', 'Langley Gage', and 'Leveller'. Red, dual purpose: 'Poorman', 'Clark'. ❖

Gourd

Cucurbita spp. and others
Cucurbitaceae

For a crop that's both fun and practical, try growing gourds. You can transform the sturdy, colorful fruits into a variety of unique and useful items, including bottles, bowls, spoons, musical instruments, birdhouses, and sponges.

Botanically speaking, there are a number of edible gourds that most people think of as squash or pumpkins. However, the plants we call gourds — with their multitude of sizes, colors, and shapes — are usually grown for crafts and other decorative purposes.

Gourd enthusiasts commonly divide gourds into hard- and thin-shelled types. Hard-shelled fruits are produced by white-flowered gourds (*Lagenaria siceraria*); these are the gourds to use for crafts such as bird homes. Yellow-flowered gourds (*Cucurbita pepo* var. *ovifera*) produce colorful, decorative, thin-shelled gourds.

Planting: Grow this crop in hills or on fences or trellises. Provide a deeply worked, well-drained soil to which you've added one heaping shovelful of compost per plant.

Large gourds can take up to 140 days to mature; start long-season types indoors several weeks before the last frost. Soak seeds overnight to promote germination. Grow the seeds in peat pots to avoid disturbing the sensitive roots at transplanting time. Plant the seedlings outdoors after the last frost date.

Sow shorter-season gourds directly after the last frost, following the seed-packet directions for each specific cultivar. Place about five seeds each in hills spaced 5' apart; thin to one strong seedling. Or plant in a row along a fence or trellis, thinning the plants to 2'-3' apart.

Growing guidelines: Gourds will flatten on the side in contact with the ground as they mature. Flat-bottomed gourds make good con-

GOURDS FOR THE BIRDS

Looking for a great garden project? Try growing your own birdhouses! Bottle gourds (*Lagenaria siceraria*) can be ideal homes for a variety of birds, including purple martins, swallows, chickadees, and wrens. Besides bringing beauty to your garden, these birds can eat thousands of insects a day.

Bottle gourds are available in many garden seed catalogs. Planting and growing requirements for bottle gourds are the same as for other gourds. Bottle gourds can tolerate light frosts, so let them ripen on the vines; mature bottle gourds have hard, light brown shells. Bring them indoors and allow them to cure for several months in a cool, dry place until you hear the seeds rattle inside as you shake the gourd.

Drill a 1''-2½'' hole in the side of each gourd; make the smaller-sized hole for small birds like wrens, the larger-sized hole for large birds like martins. Also drill a few small holes in the bottom of the gourd for drainage. Drill two more holes in the top, and thread a piece of waterproof cord or wire through

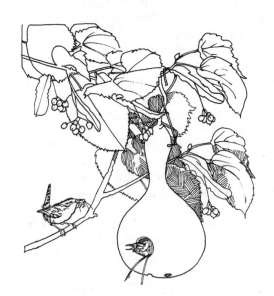

these holes to hang the house. You may want to varnish the gourd house before you hang it, although it should last about two years if untreated.

tainers, but slow-maturing gourds that rest on soil for a long time can rot. Avoid this problem by growing them on a trellis or by spreading several inches of mulch around plants before the stems begin to sprawl. Besides protecting the developing gourds, the mulch also conserves soil moisture and helps keep weeds down. Side-dress in midsummer with a mix of compost and aged manure, and keep the soil evenly moist.

Problems: See the Squash entry for insect and disease control.

Harvesting: Let gourds ripen on the vines until the stems are brown, but be aware that any frost will soften and ruin the fruits of some types of gourds. Always handle gourds carefully, because they bruise easily. Harvest by using a sharp knife to cut through the stems 2″-3″ away from the gourd. Dry off any moisture.

Gourds are dry when the seeds rattle around inside. Some, like sponge gourds (*Luffa aegyptica*), may dry sufficiently on the vine; others you'll need to harvest and dry indoors. To reduce the chances of spoilage, wipe gourds with a mild vinegar or bleach solution.

Place hard-shelled types on a rack with good air circulation. Smaller gourds can dry in less than a month, but large types may take up to six months. Use a knife to scrape off any mold that appears. To prepare gourds for display, remove the thin outer shells with steel wool.

To dry thin-shelled gourds, place them on trays in an airy place, or hang them in mesh bags. You can wax, varnish, or shellac thin-shelled types, but don't cut or carve them until the protective coating is completely dry.

Grow sponge gourds, or Luffas (loofahs), for their spongelike, fibrous interiors. Pick them young and green for a soft sponge; fruits with yellow or brown skins produce hard, scratchy sponges. Soak the gourd in water for several days, then peel off the skin. Cut off one end, and shake out the seeds; your sponge is now ready for use.

For more on growing and preserving gourds, contact the American Gourd Society, Box 274, Mount Gilead, Ohio 43338. ❖

Government Agencies

It may surprise you to discover that there's plenty of good gardening advice available from local, state, and federal governments. The type of services provided and fees charged vary with location and agency. You'll find addresses and phone numbers in the government listings in your phone book. If you're writing or calling for information, be specific. For example, if you're planning to plant street trees, ask for a list of good choices for street trees, not for general publications about trees.

• Ask your municipal health department about nuisance animals, compost regulations, or water quality.

• Consult your county or municipal department of public works or forestry about tree planting, maintenance, and related ordinances. Ask whether free compost or wood chips are available in your area.

• Your local Cooperative Extension Service offers a wealth of gardening information through pamphlets, workshops, and classes. See the Cooperative Extension Service entry for more information about this agency.

• Check with state departments of natural resources, conservation, or wildlife for advice and regulations on trees, compost, wildlife attraction (or control), pesticide use and disposal, and water quality.

• Write to the United States Department of Agriculture (USDA) Soil Conservation Service to find out about your soil type or to ask about drainage and erosion control.

• Request a list of lawn and garden publications from your local government printing office or the Superintendent of Documents, U.S. Government Printing Office, Washington, D.C. 20402. The USDA breeds, collects, and researches plants, and shares the results through these publications.

• For questions about gardening practices that affect the environment, such as the application or disposal of pesticides or other chemicals, contact the Environmental Protection Agency (EPA). ❖

Grafting

Many gardeners who routinely propagate plants in other ways view grafting—attaching a piece of living plant onto another plant—as an almost mystical technique, beyond the ability of the average "green thumb." Grafting does require some advance planning and the proper tools, but with a little practice, you can learn to graft.

Grafting is commonly used to propagate woody plants that produce few or no seeds. It is also useful for propagating named plant cultivars that do not come true from seed.

Grafting can help you get the most from limited garden space. For example, if you want to grow fruit trees that need cross-pollination, graft a branch or two of the needed pollinator onto the desired plant. You can also, within limits, graft several fruit cultivars onto one rootstock; the resulting plant will yield different fruits on a single trunk. Grafting produces large plants quickly and can encourage early bearing on fruit trees. In general, grafting is suitable for propagating many types of ornamental trees, roses, and fruit trees, and some conifers.

Grafting Basics

Before you grab a knife and head for your favorite tree, it's helpful to understand how grafting works. When you graft, your aim is to join the cambium—the actively growing tissue that produces cells that conduct water and nutrients—of two plant stems. The stem of the parent plant is the rootstock; the stem you are joining to it is called the scion.

When you cut and join the scion and rootstock, the cambium of each part produces wound tissue called callus. Eventually the two areas of callus meet, and the cells intermingle. Some of the callus develops into cambium cells, which form a bridge between the cambium of the scion and that of the rootstock. Once there is a continuous connection between the two cambium layers, the graft is successful and the parts can continue to grow normally.

The key to success with grafting is practice. Collect prunings from less-desirable plants, bring the pieces indoors, and practice the appropriate cuts before attempting to graft a valuable specimen. Make clean, flat grafting cuts so there is maximum contact between scion and rootstock; also, make your cuts quickly, and don't allow the surfaces to dry out.

Try to choose a scion and rootstock that have the same diameter, so there is maximum cambial contact. If the rootstock is larger than the scion, matching the cambium layers on one side of the union is sufficient. Wrap the joint firmly to press the cuts together and to protect the finished graft from being knocked out of alignment. Besides adding support, wrapping and waxing a graft protects the union from drying.

Scions: Scions are one-year-old stem pieces, generally 3"-6" long with a diameter of ⅛"-¼". Be sure scions have leaf buds, which are usually narrow and pointed; avoid plump, round flower buds. Scions should be dormant when grafted, because actively growing leaves will draw mois-

Key Words
GRAFTING

Grafting. The process of joining a stem piece to another plant in such a way that the parts are united by living tissue and continue to grow.

Rootstock. The plant that supplies the root system for the grafted plant.

Scion. The stem piece joined to the rootstock in a graft.

Cambium. A thin layer of actively growing tissue between the bark and the wood.

Callus. A mass of plant cells that have not yet developed a specific function; produced in a wounded area.

Compatible. A given scion and rootstock are compatible when they can be successfully grafted and grown to maturity.

ture out of the scion and inhibit the healing process. Collect scion material in early or late winter, a few weeks or months before you plan to graft. Don't use frozen wood or wood that shows signs of winter damage. For evergreens, collect scions from the previous year's shoots. The stem should be mostly green, with a bit of brown bark at the base. For deciduous plants, take scion material from the middle portions of suitable stems, because branch tips are low in stored nutrients and the buds near the base of the stem may be slow to produce new shoots.

Cut the stems you collect into 6"-12" pieces, bundle them together, and store in a plastic bag containing damp peat moss. If you will be grafting in a few weeks, store the bag in your refrigerator (about 40°F). To store for longer periods, keep the stem pieces at temperatures closer to 33°F. Before grafting, remove the pieces from storage and soak them in water until you are ready to prepare the scions.

Rootstocks: In most cases, you can grow your own rootstocks, although some types (such as dwarfing stocks) are not readily available. The rootstock can be a seedling, a cutting, or a mature tree. Seedling rootstocks are easy and inexpensive to produce. They often have deeper root systems than cuttings and are less likely to have virus problems. Because seeds are genetically variable, though, they may not all produce the same effect on the grafted plant. If you want a rootstock for a specific trait, such as disease resistance, cuttings provide more uniform results. The process known as top-working, which uses mature trees for rootstocks, is most commonly practiced in orchards. Top-working involves cutting back the limbs of an undesirable tree and grafting on scions of a more useful cultivar.

A rootstock can influence a scion in many ways. Apple scions, for example, are grafted onto a range of rootstocks, producing dwarf, semi-dwarf or full-sized versions of the scion cultivar. Some plants, such as hybrid tea roses, may produce weak root systems if you grow them from cuttings; graft them onto rootstocks of other rose types to get more vigorous plants.

Besides regulating the size of the grafted plant, rootstocks can also provide pest resistance or tolerance to less-than-ideal soil conditions. Species and cultivars that are adaptable to a wide range of conditions often make good rootstocks. *Rhododendron* 'Cunningham's White', for example, can tolerate a pH up to 7.0, so other normally acid-loving rhododendron cultivars are often grafted onto that rootstock. These new plants can adapt to a wider range of soil pH. Some rootstocks extend the range of a given plant by providing a hardier root system.

Two-year-old seedlings or two- to three-year-old cuttings make the best rootstocks. Outdoors, graft onto rootstocks planted in a nursery area or directly in the garden. In autumn, about 18 months before you want to do spring grafting, plant the rootstocks in your chosen site. For a single garden specimen, follow normal transplanting procedures. If you confine your grafting projects to a specific area, prepare a deep, well-drained, fertile nursery bed. Plant rootstocks 1'-3' apart in rows, with 2'-3' between the rows.

For indoor grafting, grow the rootstocks in pots, or transplant one-year-old seedlings into pots the autumn before grafting, and store them in a cold frame. Bring them into the greenhouse 4-6 weeks before you plan to graft. Make sure all rootstock plants are clearly labeled, so you'll know exactly what they are when you need them.

Materials: The most important grafting tool is a razor-sharp knife. A penknife will serve for grafting, but for best results, a special grafting knife is a good investment. Grafting knives have strong, straight steel blades that can be sharpened to a fine edge. They are often available through plant and seed catalogs. You'll also need a sharp pair of pruning shears to collect scion material and to cut back rootstock tops. Scissor-type shears make clean cuts without crushing delicate plant tissues.

Grafting ties provide support for the union,

hold in moisture to provide humidity, and protect the wounds from disease organisms. Cut rubber bands, waxed string, masking tape, and electrical tape are all suitable for grafting. Apply the wrapping material in a single layer, to about 1″ on each side of the union. When using tape, overlap the edges slightly as you cover the stem. Check wrapped grafts after a month or two, and carefully cut the tie if necessary. If an uncut tie does not break down on its own, it may girdle and kill the rapidly growing stem of an otherwise successful graft.

Grafting waxes serve a purpose similar to that of ties; the two are often used together. Waxes are important for protecting exposed cuts, such as the upper tips of scions and the surfaces of cleft grafts. Commercial grafting wax is sometimes available in garden centers or through plant supply catalogs. Instead of wax, you can apply a commercial tree paint. This material is applied in a liquid form that eventually solidifies. If it rains within 24 hours of use, make another application. With either type of covering, check the treated area 2-3 days after grafting, and apply more wax or paint if any cracks have appeared.

Graft failure: You can minimize the chances of graft failure by making the right cuts, providing the proper callusing conditions, and protecting the finished grafts. But in some cases these precautions aren't enough to ensure success. If either the stock or scion is infected with a plant virus, the union may not heal properly. Compatibility between the stock and scion also is important for creating and keeping a successful graft. To be compatible, the two parts must be from closely related plants. You can generally graft one cultivar onto another of the same species with a high success rate; this is usually also true of different species within a genus. In certain cases, you can graft plants from different genera, such as pears (*Pyrus* sp.) on quince (*Cydonia* sp.), or tomato (*Lycopersicon* sp.) on potato (*Solanum* sp.). It's uncommon to get successful grafts between plants in different families.

Sometimes incompatibility causes immediate graft failure; in other cases, it becomes visible only after several years of growth. Symptoms of incompatibility include slow healing of the graft union, lack of vigor, early fall color, or branch dieback; a clean break at the graft union is an obvious sign. There isn't much you can do if these problems occur. Fortunately, delayed incompatibility is uncommon.

Planting and maintenance: Placement of the graft union relative to the soil surface is important. In general, if you choose a rootstock for a particular trait, such as a dwarfing effect, set the union above soil level. If you don't, the scion may produce its own roots, and the rootstock will lose its influence on the scion.

In other cases, the purpose of the rootstock is to provide roots for scions that are slow to form their own. Hybrid lilacs (*Syringa* spp.), for example, are sometimes grafted onto privet (*Ligustrum* spp.) seedlings. Once the parts unite, the rootstock supports the plant until the scion produces its own roots. In this case, plant the graft union slightly below the soil surface. When buying a grafted plant, you may want to ask the salesperson for planting advice.

Another special maintenance aspect is the removal of shoots and suckers growing from the rootstock. Vigorous rootstocks may produce many suckers, which can shade out and kill a weaker scion. Check your grafted plants several times a season, and remove any suckers. Scions sometimes grow up to several feet during the first season. Stake these shoots or head them back; otherwise, they are prone to breakage.

Whip-and-Tongue Graft

Whip-and-tongue grafting is used for many types of ornamental and fruit trees. It is best for small plant material, from ⅛″-¼″ in diameter. The major advantage of this method is the high level of cambium contact; one disadvantage is the degree of advance planning involved. Before grafting, rootstocks should be allowed to establish themselves for at least a year after you plant them. Once grafted, it will take 3-4 years to produce a garden-sized tree.

Season: Whip-and-tongue grafting is done outdoors in early spring, before bud break. If possible, choose a warm day; it's hard to make a good grafting cut when your fingers are numb!

Getting started: Remove your stem pieces from storage and let them soak in water until you are ready to make your cuts.

Method: First, prepare the scion. If possible, choose a stem that is the same diameter as the rootstock stem. Cut a 4″-5″ section, with at least 2-3 leaf buds, from the scion stem. Make the top cut just above a bud, and the bottom cut about 1″ below a bud. Holding the piece upside down, use a sharp knife to make a long, sloping cut on the base of the scion, on the side opposite the bottom bud. To make the tongue, position the knife blade across the angled cut, about ⅓ of the way from the point of the cut; make a downward cut about ½″ into the stem.

Next, prepare the rootstock. With pruning shears, cut the rootstock stem to about 4″ above the ground. Use the knife to make a sloping cut similar to that on the scion, putting the blade above a bud and cutting upward. Also make a ½″ deep vertical cut downward into the stem, ⅓ of the way down from the point of the cut.

To join the two pieces, align the cuts, and push the tongue of the rootstock into that of the scion. "Joining a Whip-and-Tongue Graft" on this page illustrates this technique. If the two stems are the same diameter, you will get good cambium contact all around; otherwise, match the cambium layers on one side of the union. To secure and protect the graft, carefully wrap the area with a grafting tie such as electrical tape. Cover the wrapped area and the cut top of the scion with commercial grafting wax or wound paint.

Aftercare: Check the graft in a few days; if any cracks have appeared in the wax or paint coating, make another application. The scion should begin to grow in 3-4 weeks. If the tie does not disintegrate on its own, carefully cut and remove it about a month after grafting. Stake

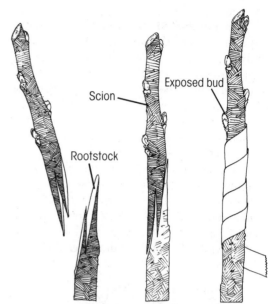

Scion

Exposed bud

Rootstock

Joining a whip-and-tongue graft. Prepare the rootstock and scion with equal, sloping cuts. Make vertical cuts into the stems to create the "tongues." Carefully push the two pieces together. The tongues should interlock, forming a secure union. Wrap the joint, but don't cover the bottom bud on the scion. Cut the tape after a month or so, when new growth has started.

the graft if necessary, and remove shoots and suckers from the rootstock.

Side Veneer Graft

Use side veneer grafts on Japanese maples and evergreens, especially dwarf conifers that are very slow-growing or difficult to root. This technique is carried out indoors, on potted one- or two-year-old seedlings generally ¼″-½″ in diameter. A greenhouse or a temperature-controlled propagation case is ideal. Bottom heat, from a propagation mat or a board resting on a radiator, is very helpful. Soil warmth promotes root growth and callus formation, but warm air encourages vigorous shoot growth that may inhibit healing.

Season: Late winter is the best time to do side veneer grafts.

Getting started: In December and January, gather and store scion material. When you are ready to graft in February, remove the material from storage and soak the pieces in water until you need them. If possible, the scions should be 4″-6″ long, but they can be shorter if you are working with dwarf conifers. In January, about six weeks before grafting, bring the potted rootstock into the greenhouse.

Method: Prepare the rootstock by stripping the leaves off a few inches of stem near the base of the plant. Use a sharp knife to make a shallow downward cut, 1″-1½″ long, starting about 3″ above the soil surface. Make another short downward cut in from the other side of the

rootstock to meet the first cut; remove the chip of wood. To prepare the scion, select a piece with a stem diameter equal to or smaller than the rootstock. Use a knife to cut the base of the scion, with a long sloping cut on one side and a short inward and downward cut on the other. "Making a Side Veneer Graft" below shows how to join the scion and rootstock.

Aftercare: High humidity is helpful for callus formation, so you may want to mist the grafted plant frequently. Keep soil on the dry side; water lightly but frequently. The graft will take 6-8 weeks to unite; if necessary, cut the tie about two months after grafting. Harden off the plant by gradually exposing it to cooler temperatures and lower humidity. Cut back the top of the rootstock in stages, removing about half when the graft

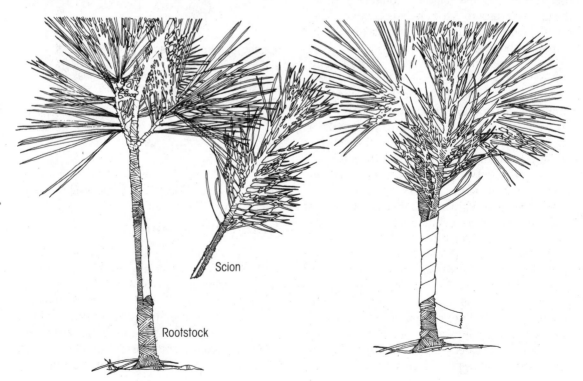

Scion

Rootstock

Making a side veneer graft. Prepare the scion and rootstock by making a 1″-1½″ downward cut near the base of the stem, and another short slice inward to meet the base of the first cut. Remove the chip of wood. To join the two pieces, fit the base of the scion into the notch on the rootstock stem, so that the long cuts are next to each other. Match the cambium layers on one or both sides, and wrap the graft with tape, waxed string, or rubber ties.

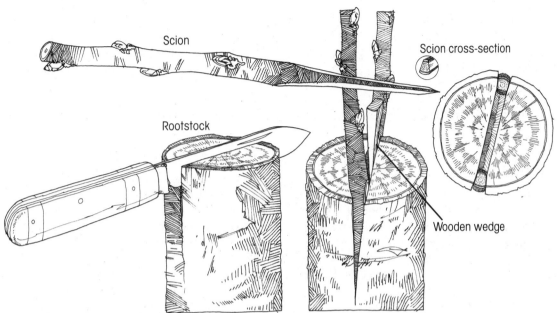

Scion

Scion cross-section

Rootstock

Wooden wedge

Preparing a cleft graft. To prepare a cleft graft: (1) Use a sharp knife to split the rootstock stem. (2) Tap a large knife (not your grafting knife) into the wood with a mallet to make a 2″ cleft. (3) Pull out the knife, and use the mallet to tap in a wooden wedge or the pointed end of a screwdriver to hold the cleft open. (4) Cut two scions from stem pieces about ¼″ in diameter, each about 4″ long, with 2-3 buds. (5) With your knife, make two long sloping cuts on each scion, one on each side of the stem. Angle the cuts so one side of the scion is slightly thicker than the other. The bottom bud should be on the wider side, just above the cuts forming the wedge. (6) Insert the scions, matching the cambium layers. Remove the wedge.

has been hardened off and the rest a month or so later.

Cleft Graft

Try cleft grafting on more mature rootstocks, at least 1″ in diameter. This method is often used in top-working fruit trees, resulting in a newly productive tree in as little as three years.

Season: Use cleft grafting in spring, when the buds on the rootstock plant start to swell.

Getting started: Remove previously collected scions from storage, and soak them in water until you need them. Prepare the rootstock by cutting the end of a stem or branch cleanly with a sharp saw.

Method: "Preparing a Cleft Graft" above shows how to prepare the scion and rootstock for this type of graft. To join the pieces, insert the

scions into the cleft on the rootstock. Make sure the wider side of the scion is toward the outside. Match the cambium layers by settling the scion slightly within the edge of the rootstock bark. Carefully remove the wedge or screwdriver from the cleft. Cleft grafts usually don't need tying or wrapping, because the pressure of the split stock should hold the scions firmly, but be sure to wax or paint the cut surfaces.

Aftercare: Check the graft a few days later; rewax if necessary. If both scions grow, cut the weaker one back by half the first season, and remove it completely the next year; in the meantime, the weaker scion will produce tissue that helps to heal the cleft. Remove shoots and suckers from the rootstock. If a scion makes excessively vigorous growth, either brace it or prune it back to avoid breakage. ❖

Grains

You can raise grains such as wheat, oats, rice, buckwheat, barley, millet, and rye in your backyard without special machinery, and in surprisingly little space.

A typical family uses about a bushel of wheat (60 lb.) a year, plus about ¼-½ bushel of other grains. Given reasonably good conditions, you should be able to grow a bushel of wheat in a 20′ × 50′ plot (1,000 square feet).

Planting and Growing

Grains are easy to plant: Simply work the soil into a good seedbed and broadcast the seed by hand or with a crank-type seeder. Rake the soil lightly to work the seed into the top 2″ of ground. Spread a 2″-4″ layer of loose straw mulch after seeding to help conserve moisture and control weeds.

You can purchase small amounts of common grain seed at most farm stores. Some general garden seed catalogs carry a few types, too. See "More On: Grains" on page 284 for other sources of information.

Wheat: Wheat (*Triticum spp.*) is the most widely consumed grain in North America. It makes excellent bread, pasta, sprouts, and tasty whole or cracked kernels.

Wheat prefers a nearly neutral (about 6.4 pH) soil, and does best with a cool, moist growing season followed by warm, dry weather for ripening.

Winter wheat is planted in the fall, stays green until early winter, then goes dormant until spring. The onset of warm weather causes rapid new growth, and seed heads develop within two months. Winter wheat ripens about the first week of June in the South, later to the north.

Spring wheat is planted at the beginning of the growing season and ripens in mid- to late summer. It tolerates drier conditions than winter wheat, but doesn't yield as well.

Hard red winter and hard red spring wheat are used for bread baking. Soft red winter and white wheat are used primarily for pastry flour. Durum wheat is used for making pastas. Regardless of their commercial use, all the wheats make good bread. There are many cultivars; choose those commonly grown in your area.

Plant spring wheat at about the same time as the average last killing frost. Plant winter wheat at about the time of the average first fall frost. If Hessian fly, a common wheat pest, is a problem in your area, be sure to plant after the "fly date." Check with your local extension office for this date. Use about 4 lb. of seed per 1,000 square feet.

Rye: Rye (*Secale cereale*) adds a rich flavor to bread or rolls. Cracked rye can also be used in baked goods or served as a cooked grain. Rye sprouts are sweet and crunchy.

Rye grows better than wheat in cold, wet climates. It also grows in poor soils that won't support wheat, but yields about 30 percent less.

Plant rye in the same manner and at the same rate as winter wheat any time from late summer to late fall. Rye ripens 7-10 days before winter wheat.

Oats: Oats (*Avena sativa*) are highest of all cereal grains in protein and lowest in carbohydrates. Oats make tasty table fare, but most cultivars have a tough hull that's hard to remove. 'Freedom' oats are virtually hull-free.

Oats need lots of moisture, and favor a cool climate and fertile, well-drained soil. In the South, plant oats in the fall for harvest the following summer. But in general, it's best to plant oats in very early spring. Plant about 2-3 lb. of seed per 1,000 square feet.

Corn: As home gardeners, we think of corn (*Zea mays*) as sweet corn, but fresh ground cornmeal is wonderfully fragrant and tasty, too. Choose a dent or flint type for cornmeal, and a flour type for a finer meal, rather than a sweet corn cultivar. Indian corn and field corn are familiar drycorn types.

SUPERGRAINS

Amaranth and quinoa are both grown extensively in other parts of the world for their seed and edible leaves. Both seeds contain about 16 percent protein and are high in fiber and in amino acids often absent in cereal grains.

Amaranth: Grain amaranth (*Amaranthus* spp.) is a relative of the familiar ornamental amaranth. Amaranth seed is white to yellow, round, and very small. Amaranth seed makes a tasty porridge and can be toasted to make a crunchy topping. The flour must be mixed with other flour for baking.

Grain amaranth matures in about 120 days. Start the plants indoors, or direct-seed in rows and thin to 1''–3'' apart. Seed is ready to harvest when it starts to dry. Cut the whole seed heads and hang them in clusters or in a cloth sack to dry. Thresh by beating the bag; sift chaff from seed with a fine screen.

Quinoa: Pronounced "ki-NO-uh", quinoa (*Chenopodium quinoa*) seed is the staple grain of the Andean highlands. It is a close relative of the potherb Good King Henry. Quinoa seed is tiny and, when cooked, has a delicate flavor and a fluffy texture. It can be used like rice—just be sure to rinse the raw seed first or it will be bitter. Quinoa flour gives a moist texture to baked goods when mixed with other flours.

Quinoa is adapted to high mountainous areas, and most cultivars will not make seed in areas where temperatures reach 95°F. Plant seed ½''–1'' deep in cool soil; the crop is easy to grow. Its culture and appearance is similar to amaranth.

Grow dry corn as you would sweet corn; see the Corn entry for details. Remember to separate it from sweet corn cultivars, so they won't cross-pollinate. Dry corn is normally left on the plant until after frost, but can be picked after the husks begin to dry. Bring husked ears under cover to finish drying.

Barley: Barley (*Hordeum vulgare*) is a delicious, nutty-tasting cereal grain, especially good in casseroles, soups, and pilaf. The grain has an outer hull that should be removed. Pearl barley has been milled to remove the tough husks. Barley flour is low in gluten and is mixed with other flours for making bread.

Plant 4 lb. of seed per 1,000 square feet. Spring-sown barley matures in about 70 days, while fall-planted barley ripens about 60 days after growth resumes in the spring.

Rice: Although we commonly think of rice (*Oriza sativa*) as a tropical crop, there are early-maturing cultivars that will grow in most parts of North America. Rice is often grown in flooded fields, but it will also thrive under the same conditions as corn. Wild rice (*Zizania aquatica*) is native to North America and grows in ponds and slow-moving water.

Soak seed for 24 hours and plant in flats of moist, mucky soil about a month before your last frost. Prepare raised beds with plenty of organic matter and cover with a thick organic mulch. Transplant on 9'' centers, pushing the mulch aside. Water rice once or twice a week so that it gets about 1''–1½'' from rain and irrigation combined. When rice flowers, make sure it gets plenty of water; cut back once the grain starts to harden. Rice is hard to hull.

Millet: Millet is a catchall name for at least five different genera and assorted species of cereal grains native to Asia and Africa, where the hulled grain is a staple food in many countries. We are most familiar with it as the shiny, little, round, yellow or orange-brown seeds in bird seed mixes. It is higher in essential amino acids than other cereal grains and has a subtle, nutlike flavor when baked or cooked. To bring out its full taste, roast the grain in a pan with a little oil before using.

Millet will tolerate poor soils. The plants mature very quickly—some in just 30 days. You can sow millet almost any time from spring through late summer. Plant about 1 lb. of seed per 1,000 square feet.

Buckwheat: Buckwheat (*Fagopyrum esculentum*) isn't a cereal grain. It belongs to the family Polygonaceae, as do rhubarb and garden sorrel. It is commonly grown as a green manure crop and as a bee forage plant. The amino acid composition of the seed tops that of all other cereal grains, and the flour's earthy flavor makes it a welcome addition to treats such as flapjacks and breads. The seed matures in just 70-80 days; it makes a good second crop in a two-crop rotation.

You can plant buckwheat almost any time from spring to late summer, in almost any type of soil. Generally, late-June or July plantings yield the most seed. Sow about 2½ lb. per 1,000 square feet. Buckwheat seeds ripen at varying rates, so watch the crop carefully and harvest when most of the seed is ripe.

Harvesting and Using

Harvest cereal grains about 7-10 days before they're fully mature and dry. The grain heads should still be greenish or just turning yellow, the stalks mottled with green. Pinch a kernel with your thumb and index finger. It should be soft enough to be dented by your thumbnail, but not so soft that it squashes.

Cut the stalks just aboveground, and gather and tie them into bunches. The traditional tool for cutting grains is a scythe. See "Classic Tools" on page 576 for directions on using a scythe. Stack or hang the bunches in the field or under cover to dry. The grain will cure in 10-14 days. When you bite a kernel between your teeth, it should be hard and crunchy.

Threshing: To thresh, put a bundle or two on a sheet spread over a hard surface, such as a patio or floor. Beat the seed heads with a length of rubber hose or an old mop handle to knock the seeds from the stalks.

Winnowing: Next, clean the grain of chaff

More On
GRAINS

For more information on growing grains in your backyard, and for seed sources, contact:

● The Grain Exchange, c/o The Land Institute, 2440 East Water Well Road, Salina, KS 67401.
● Southern Exposure Seed Exchange, P.O. Box 158, North Garden, VA 22959.
● Seed Savers Exchange, R.R. 3, Box 239, Decorah, IA 52101.

and hulls. Pour the grain slowly from one bucket to another in front of a fan. The breeze should be strong enough to blow the chaff away, but not to take the kernels with it. Repeat until clean.

Storing: Keep small quantities of cereal grains in a refrigerator or freezer. You can also store thoroughly dry grain in a cool, dark place in sealed jars to protect it from insects.

Hulling: Hulling grain with tough hulls is one of the biggest stumbling blocks for home gardeners. You can hull small quantities by roasting the grain in an oven at 180°F for 60-90 minutes, and then running the kernels lightly through a blender and picking out the cracked hulls. For larger quantities, you can adapt a grain grinder by replacing the steel burr disk with a gum rubber one. Plans are available from I-Tech, P.O. Box 795, Davis, CA 95617.

Milling: Grains can be cracked or ground into flour in a good household blender. Grind ¼ cup at a time, taking care not to let the motor labor too much. If you make a lot of flour, you may want to buy a hand-cranked or electric flour mill. Grind only as much as you will use in a few weeks, and store prepared grains in the refrigerator or freezer; they go rancid rapidly. ❖

Grape

Vitis spp.
Vitaceae

Grapes make a wonderful treat straight from the vine, or preserved as jelly, juice, or wine. They thrive in full sun, with good drainage and protection from late frosts.

Selecting Grapes

There are four main types of grapes grown in North America: European, or wine grapes (*Vitis vinifera*); American, such as 'Concord' (*V. labruscana*); hybrids between European and American; and muscadine (*V. rotundifolia*).

Early settlers to North America found native grapes growing rampantly. Many good fresh-eating and juice grapes have been selected from the native species, including 'Concord' and 'Niagara'. American grapes have a strong grape or "foxy" flavor and slipskins, which means that the berries can easily be squeezed out of the skins.

Vinifera (European) grapes produce most of the world's table grapes, wine, and raisins. They are not as hardy as their American cousins, are much more susceptible to diseases, and require more work to harvest a satisfactory crop.

Plant breeders have crossed and recrossed vinifera and American species and created grapes to satisfy almost every taste and use. Many of them are as hardy as their American parent, to about −10°F, and have good disease resistance.

If you grow seedless cultivars, you probably won't get grapes as large as those on bunches for sale at the market. Commercial growers dip or spray clusters with synthetic growth regulators so they'll produce big berries.

If you live in the far South, you may only be able to grow muscadine grapes. They make good jelly and juice and a distinctive, sweet wine.

Rootstocks: American and hybrid grape cultivars can be grown on their own roots. Vinif-era grape roots are very susceptible to phylloxera, a sucking insect native to the eastern and southern United States and now spread throughout the world. Choose vines grafted on American rootstocks. Certain American rootstock cultivars are also resistant to nematodes and the virus diseases they transmit.

Planting and Care

Begin preparing your site a year before you plant your vines. Eliminate perennial weeds from your planting site; see the Weeds entry for methods. Have the soil tested. Your best bet is to double dig the site prior to planting, adding lots of organic matter and any amendments needed to correct deficiencies. Grapes do best at pH 5.0-6.0. Nitrogen, potassium, and magnesium are most likely to cause deficiencies. Iron and boron can cause toxicity symptoms in the West.

Plant dormant, one-year-old vines in the spring before their buds begin to swell and open. Soak roots for 1-2 hours before planting, in a pail of water with a handful of bonemeal.

Prune each vine back to leave two live buds before planting; also cut back long roots so they'll fit easily into the hole without bending. Leave 1″-2″ of trunk above ground and make a shallow basin around the vine to hold water. If you are planting grafted vines, be sure to keep the graft union above ground level.

Pruning and Training

There are many ways to train grapes. Three of the most common methods for home gardeners are cane pruning, spur pruning, and head training. If you are new to grapes, don't let talk about training and pruning scare you. Grapevines are very forgiving. You can train cane- and spur-pruned vines on an existing fence or wall. If you're planning to plant several vines, you'll probably need to build a trellis; "Trellising Grapes" on page 289 shows how.

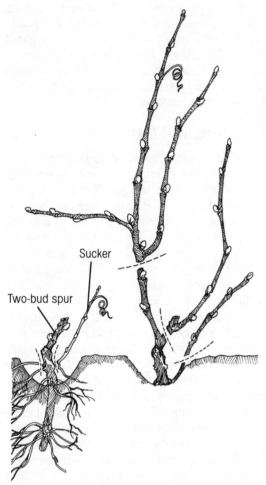

Sucker

Two-bud spur

Early pruning. Prune newly purchased vines back to two buds before planting. The first winter, select the strongest, straightest shoot and cut it back to two buds. Prune off all other shoots. The vine will look very much like the little vine you planted the previous spring.

The training method you select depends on where you live and what cultivars you grow. Cane pruning is a good choice for cultivars in which the first few buds on a cane are not fruitful, such as 'Thompson Seedless', and for people who want a heavy crop, because cane pruning results in long vines with many buds.

Head-trained plants stand alone like little trees. They need sturdy, individual stakes until the trunks get strong enough to support the vine. Head-trained vines are simple to prune, but fruit and foliage bunch around the head, which can create a favorable environment for pests and disease, especially in humid climates. Head training is primarily used for wine grapes in dry areas.

Early Training

No matter what training method you plan to use, all vines are treated the same until the second winter after planting.

First growing season: During their first summer, the vines need to grow a strong root system. Use drip irrigation or a soaker hose if needed to keep the soil damp but not soggy. From mid-August on, water only if the leaves wilt so the vines will harden off for winter. Mulch or cultivate to control weeds.

You can let the vines sprawl on the ground the first year, or tie them loosely to a small stake to keep them out of harm's way.

First winter: Any time from midwinter on, select the strongest, straightest shoot and prune off all the others. Cut the chosen shoot back to two live buds. The result will look very much like the little vine you planted the previous spring. But remember, the first season is for growing roots. Go ahead and cut off all that top growth; you'll have a better plant in the long run. If cold injury is a problem in your area, wait until the buds start to swell so you can see which ones are alive. You may want to select two shoots rather than one as insurance against injury.

Second growing season: If you haven't done so already, place a stake in the ground as close as possible to the vine. When new shoots are 6"-12" long, select the sturdiest, most upright shoot and tie it loosely to the stake. Break off the remaining shoots with your fingers. If you are developing two trunks, save one shoot on each. As the shoot grows, tie it to the stake at 12" intervals to form a straight trunk.

If you're growing grapes on a trellis, mark

the stake at a point about 6″ below the first permanent trellis wire. This will be the height of the vine head—the top of the trunk. Side arms will grow out from here, and the lateral shoots will grow up to the higher trellis wire. For vines growing against a fence or wall, you can choose to make the vine head at about 3′, or let the trunk grow taller and allow the vines to cascade down from the side branches.

When the shoot reaches the desired height, break off the small shoots that are growing above each leaf near the base of your trunk-to-be, but don't remove the leaves. Let the sideshoots grow on the five leaf nodes just below the vine head; cut the tip off the main shoot when it grows a few inches or so above the vine head. Prune off any suckers below the soil line as close to the trunk as possible.

If your vine doesn't reach the desired height by the end of the second season, it probably hadn't developed enough roots to produce the size plant you wanted. Cut the vine back to two buds, and let it try again the next summer.

Second Winter Pruning

Any time from midwinter on, remove any shoots from the trunk or roots.

Cane- or spur-pruned vines: Select two sturdy, pencil-size canes from near the mark you made to show the top of your trunk. Tie them to the training wire. Buds should be spaced about every 4″-5″ along the canes; rub off any extras. Shorten the canes so each has ten buds.

Head-trained vines: Select five pencil-size canes just below the mark on the stake and prune them back, leaving two buds on each. Cut off the main shoot just above the head.

Third Growing Season

Now that your vine has a strong root system, it shouldn't need watering very often unless your soil is very sandy. Tie up or pinch back shoots in danger of breaking. Clip off all or most of the flower clusters this year.

Third Winter Pruning

Continue to prune off any shoots or suckers on the trunks or roots.

Cane-pruned vines: Select a pencil-size shoot from near the base of each of the previous season's canes or from the top of the trunk. Cut off and remove all other growth from the previous season. Cut the new canes back to ten buds, and tie them securely to the wire.

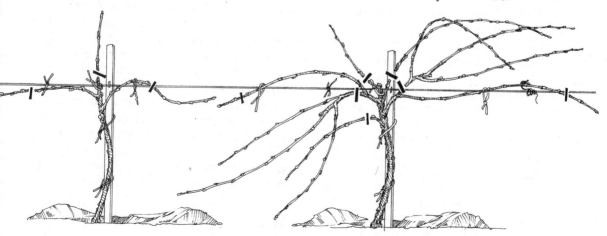

Cane pruning. During the second winter of growth, tie two sturdy, pencil-size canes near the top of the trunk to the training wire. Rub off buds to leave buds spaced 4″-5″ apart. Shorten the canes so each has ten buds. The third winter, select a pencil-size shoot from near the base of each of the previous season's canes or from the top of the trunk.

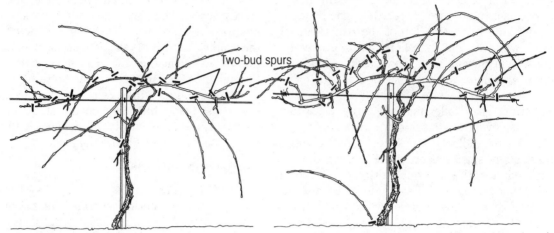

Two-bud spurs

Spur pruning. Treat spur-pruned vines like cane-pruned vines during the second winter. The third winter, cut each upright shoot along the horizontal arms back to two buds. Leave a two-bud spur every 4"-5". The fourth and subsequent winters, select a pencil-size shoot from near the base of each spur, and cut it back to two buds.

Spur-pruned vines: Cut each upright shoot along the horizontal arms back to two buds. There should be a two-bud spur every 4"-5"; remove any extras.

Head-trained vines: Cut each of the five canes back to two-bud spurs.

Training Bearing Vines

In the fourth growing season, vines are ready to bear a normal crop. For large table grapes, give vines 1" of water per week. For small, highly flavored wine grapes, don't water unless the vine is wilted.

Fourth winter: In the fourth and subsequent winters, you may want to add a few new spurs and keep a few more buds on each cane for the next season. The vigor of a vine will tell you how many buds and spurs it can support. If your vine has many spindly shoots and little fruit, try leaving fewer total buds the next winter. If it has long, thick shoots and few clusters, leave more buds the next winter. For cane-pruned vines, select new canes as for third winter.

Spur-pruned and head-trained vines need different treatment. Select a pencil-size shoot from near the base of each spur, and cut it back to two buds. You will need to develop replacement spurs every few years because the original ones become unwieldy. Select shoots on the main arm or base of the spur, cut them back to two buds, and remove the old spurs.

Subsequent growing seasons: During the spring through mid-July, position shoots so light penetrates through the foliage. On short-trunk, trellised vines, tuck the shoots behind the catch wires above the training wire. If shoots reach the top of the trellis and hang down, they will shade the fruit and the canes where next year's flower buds are forming. Prune off the tips if they get too long. Especially on head-trained vines, pick off leaves and small shoots near fruit clusters to let in light. This is important because it promotes ripening and discourages pests. You may want to remove or thin clusters to increase berry size or improve quality. If you have too heavy a crop, the fruit may be slow to ripen as well.

Winter Protection

There are grape cultivars that will tolerate severe winter cold. You can grow cultivars beyond their normal northern limit by training trunks

TRELLISING GRAPES

While a trellis requires some effort to build and maintain, it's the best way to manage your vines. Each vine you grow will need about 8' of trellis. To construct a trellis, set 8' posts 24' apart and 2' into the ground (one post set every third vine). Install guy wires from the end posts to keep them from being pulled over. Secure the guy wires with a block of concrete set into the ground or with an earth screw.

Stretch #9- or #10-gauge galvanized wire between the end posts, 2½' above ground level, and clamp it securely. Then staple it to the other posts. Add another trellis wire at the top of the posts, and one or two additional wires between them.

Hammer large nails into both sides of each post about halfway between each pair of trellis wires. These nails will support catch wires, used to lift the vines up to the permanent trellis wires during the season. To make catch wires, cut two pieces of lighter-gauge wire that are as long as the full trellis. Connect short pieces of chain to each end of the catch wires. Hook the chains over the end post nail, and let the wire rest on all the other nails.

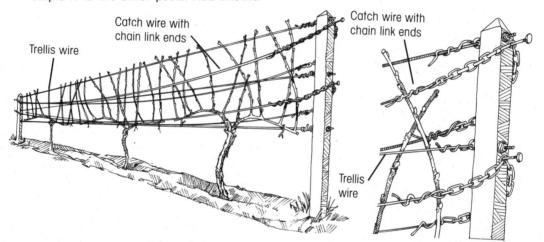

Catch wire with chain link ends

Trellis wire

Catch wire with chain link ends

Trellis wire

Grape trellis. Grape shoots will climb permanent trellis wires on their own, or they can be tucked through by hand during the season. Movable catch wires go around the trellis like a giant rubber band and keep shoots pointing up. Drop the catch wires to the nails below the vine heads when you prune each winter. Once growth starts and shoots are about 2' long, raise the catch wire to the nails above the vine head; as you lift it, the wire will pick up any shoots that are straying from the trellis. Raise the wire to the next set of nails as the shoots grow, or use a second catch wire.

only 1' high and covering vines with mulch during the winter, or by bending whole vines over and burying or mulching them for the winter.

Once grape buds begin to swell in the spring, they become more frost-tender. All species are susceptible to frost damage at temperatures below 31°F. See the Fruit Trees entry for more information on site selection and frost protection. Autumn frosts seldom cause damage because the high sugar content of the berries keeps them from freezing and the outer canopy protects both the foliage and fruit beneath it. If you live in an area with short seasons, plant an early-ripening cultivar.

Fertilization

On most sites, careful soil preparation before planting eliminates the need for heavy fertilization. Mulch lightly with compost in late winter each year. Overfertilizing can cause vines to grow rampantly and produce little fruit. When in doubt, don't fertilize. Compost tea and dilute seaweed extract sprays are a good general foliar fertilizers. (For instructions on making compost tea, see the Composting entry.) If you suspect you have a specific nutrient problem, have a leaf analysis done; see the Soil entry for information on this procedure.

Harvesting

Grapevines bear by their third or fourth growing season. Harvest when the fruit tastes ripe. Support the cluster with one hand and cut its stem with pruning shears. Handle clusters gently, and lay them in a basket or flat. Harvest large quantities in the morning, small amounts any time of day. Move picked fruit to a cool, protected place as soon as possible.

Problems

Insects: Grape berry moths lay eggs on flower clusters. The greenish or purplish larvae spin silver webs and feed on buds and flowers. Control grape berry moth with mating disruption pheromone dispensers.

Many caterpillars can feed on grape leaves. Control by spraying BT (*Bacillus thuringiensis*). Japanese beetles are fond of grapes. A few won't hurt the vine, but complete defoliation will. See "The Top Ten Garden Insect Pests in America" on page 344 for ways to control them.

Diseases: Prevention and good housekeeping are the best ways to avoid disease problems. Mulch or cultivation will help prevent spores from splashing up from the soil and infecting new growth. Keep the area under the vine weed-free to increase air movement and reduce disease problems. Fungal diseases thrive in dark, humid environments, so arrange shoots in the leaf canopy so some light falls on all foliage. Cut off leaves shading clusters. Remove infected parts immediately, and collect prunings and fallen leaves and dispose of them.

Sulfur dust or spray helps prevent disease. If you've had past problems with disease, you may want to consider a regular preventive spray program. Coat all parts of the vines, including the undersides of leaves, before symptoms appear. Apply when canes are 6", 12", and 18" long, then every two weeks until 4-6 weeks before harvest.

Common grape diseases include the following:

• Black rot causes rusty brown leaf spots, which develop small, black, spore-producing dots in moist weather. It turns green berries into hard, black "mummies."

• Botrytis bunch rot can cause leaf spots, but primarily attacks the flower or fruit clusters. Infected berries turn brown and soft, and whole areas of the cluster become covered with powdery brown mold.

• Downy mildew first shows up as lighter blotches on leaves, which are covered with a fine white powder on the underside. Young shoots and fruit clusters may be covered with white powder in severe cases. If infection occurs early in the season, fruit clusters may ripen unevenly.

• Powdery mildew appears first as a gray moldy-looking material on canes, then on the leaves, and finally on the berries, which split or stop developing.

• Crown gall and cane dieback can be problems. Avoid damaging bark when cultivating, and sanitize pruning shears between vines. Winter injury can make vines more prone to problems.

• Viruses can cause ring-shaped spots or mottling on leaves, and other symptoms. Buy only certified virus-free vines. Dig up and burn or destroy any vines that become infected.

Cultivars: Disease-resistant cultivars include American grapes 'Canadice' (seedless), 'Concord', 'Steuben'; muscadine grape 'Carlos'; French hybrids 'Aurore', 'Baco Noir', 'Seyval'. ❖

Grasses

Containing over 8,000 species, the grass family is the most economically important plant group in the world. Many species are cultivated for food, turf, or ornamental uses. In the home garden, the most common use of grasses is for lawns. To learn more about lawns and how to care for them, see the Lawns entry. Some grasses have special decorative value, with luxurious foliage, showy flowers, or vivid fall color. This group, known as ornamental grasses, contains true annual and perennial grasses as well as sedges, rushes, and other grasslike plants.

Ornamental grasses vary widely in their growth habits. Some, such as oriental fountain grass (*Pennisetum orientale*), form clumps of foliage that grow straight upright or arch gracefully. Others, including ribbon grass (*Phalaris arundinacea* var. *picta*), spread rapidly from underground stems called rhizomes or aboveground stems called stolons. Spreading grasses are ideal for naturalizing or erosion control.

Grasses are divided into two main groups: cool-season growers and warm-season growers. Cool-season grasses grow from fall into spring. They tend to be evergreen and are generally more moisture-tolerant. Cool-season grasses usually flower in late winter and spring and grow rapidly during these times; they often slow down or even stop growing in summer.

Warm-season grasses are dormant in winter. They begin growth in spring, bloom during summer and fall, and go dormant with the onset of cool temperatures. Warm-season grasses often display brilliant fall colors, including orange, red, and purple. During the winter, the dried foliage and seed heads can be quite attractive.

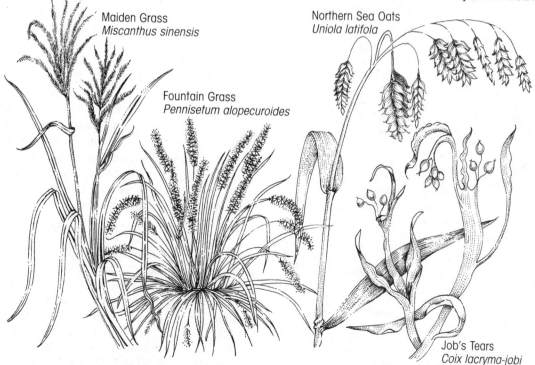

Maiden Grass
Miscanthus sinensis

Northern Sea Oats
Uniola latifola

Fountain Grass
Pennisetum alopecuroides

Job's Tears
Coix lacryma-jobi

Ornamental grasses. These plants add an elegant touch to any garden. Their often-vertical growth habits add interest to a planting of mounded and spreading herbaceous plants. Though the individual flowers may not be showy, they are combined into eye-catching spikes or feathery plumes that often develop into interesting seed heads.

EIGHT GREAT GRASSES

The plants listed below are eight of the best perennial clump-forming grasses.

Briza media (quaking grass): A cool-season grass that grows 1'–1½' high with an equal spread. Showy flowers appear in spring over tufts of green foliage. Zones 4–9.

Calamagrostis acutiflora var. *stricta* (feather reed grass): A warm-season grass growing 3'–4' high and wide. Flowers bloom in summer over arching clumps of medium green foliage that turns orange-brown in fall. Zones 4–9.

Cortaderia selloana var. *pumila* (compact pampas grass): A cool-season grass growing 4'–6' high and wide. Flowers bloom in fall over mounds of gray-green foliage. Zones 7–9.

Helictotrichon sempervirens (blue oat grass): A cool-season grass that grows 1½'–2' high and wide. Flowers bloom in spring over tufts of blue foliage. Zones 5–9.

Miscanthus sinensis 'Morning Light' ('Morning Light' miscanthus): A warm-season grower reaching 4'–6' high and 3'–4' wide. Flowers appear in late summer over upright arching clumps of gray-green foliage with white margins; orange-brown fall color. Zones 5–9.

Pennisetum alopecuroides (fountain grass): A warm-season grass growing 3'–4' high and wide. Flowers bloom in summer over mounds of green foliage with yellow-brown fall color. Zones 5–9.

Stipa gigantea (giant feather grass): A cool-season grass growing 2'–3' high and wide. In spring, showy flowers appear over mounds of gray-green foliage. Zones 7–9.

Uniola latifolia (northern sea oats): Sometimes called *Chasmanthium latifolium*, this warm-season grass grows 2'–3' high with an equal spread. Flowers appear in summer over upright arching clumps of light green foliage that bronzes in winter. Zones 4–9.

Growing Ornamental Grasses

Grasses can adapt to a variety of soil textures, from sand to clay. Most grasses are drought-tolerant. A site with moist but well-drained, loamy soil of average fertility will suit most of these plants. At least a half day of full sun is usually ideal, although some grasses, such as hakonechloa grass (*Hakonechloa macra*), grow well with more shade. In general, those with thin, wide leaves accept more shade and are less drought-tolerant.

Grasses require very little maintenance. Fertilize only if you have very sandy soil. Pests and diseases are rarely a problem. You may want to cut the plants back close to the ground once a year (generally in early spring). If you leave seed heads for winter interest, the grass may self-seed. Cultivate lightly around clumps in spring to uproot unwanted seedlings.

Grasses are easy to propagate by seed or division. Sow seed of annuals indoors about four weeks before the last frost. Transplant (or sow seeds directly) into the garden after danger of frost is past; thin to 6"–12" apart. Seed is also an inexpensive way of increasing many perennial species.

To propagate cultivars or renew old clumps, divide existing plants. Lift plants from the ground, separate them into smaller clumps, and replant. To learn more about this technique, see the Division entry. Divide or plant warm-season growers in spring, just as they are starting to grow; move cool-season grasses in spring or fall.

Using Ornamental Grasses

Grasses can add a new dimension to any garden design. The airy foliage and flower heads bend and rustle with the slightest wind, adding the elements of sound and movement to the garden. Try adding grasses to an herbaceous border, as individual specimens or in a mass. In the landscape, use a tall grower like eulalia grass (*Miscanthus sinensis*) as a windbreak or to screen an unpleasant view. Grasses also make beautiful, low-maintenance groundcovers. ❖

Green Manure

Green manure crops can be a great supplement to an organic soil improvement program. If you can't get animal manures, or if your compost supply isn't equal to demand, try planting green manures in the garden areas you till annually, such as vegetable or annual flower beds. Many gardeners plant a green manure crop such as buckwheat or clover in the fall, after finishing the harvest and clearing debris from the beds. Others make green manures part of a crop rotation, and plant them during the growing season.

A green manure crop sown in the fall and grown through the winter also functions as a cover crop, protecting the soil from erosion and compaction. Plan to till or dig the crop into the soil in early spring, about 3-4 weeks before you begin your vegetable garden. In soils that are wet in early spring, dig the green manure into the soil late in the fall and let it decompose over the winter. Otherwise, the damage done by working soil when it's wet could outweigh the benefit of the green manure.

"Green Manures for Home Gardens" on page 294 will guide you in choosing the green manure crop that is best suited to your garden. If you select a legume, it's a good idea to apply a bacterial inoculant so your soil will get maximum benefit from the crop's nitrogen-collecting ability. Different crops require different strains of inoculant. Use the specific strain required by the legume you're planting or a product that's a blend of many types of nitrogen-collecting bacteria. You'll find inoculants at well-stocked garden centers, or order them by mail.

Planting Green Manures

If possible, sow seed when rain is forecast. The stand will not establish well if the soil surface dries during the germination period. Remove all crop residues and rake the soil free of clumps before sowing. You can sow seed with a manually powered seeder that consists of a bag or reservoir for holding seed connected to a crank-operated seed broadcaster. For small areas, try broadcasting seed by hand. If you're sowing less than 1 lb. of seed per 1,000 square feet, mix the seed with fine sand, organic fertilizer, or screened soil before spreading. When sowing fine seed by hand, rake the seedbed afterward to cover the seed. Cover larger-seeded crops, such as Austrian peas or soybeans, with 1/4"-1/2" of soil.

After seeding, tamp the soil with the back of a hoe or spade to ensure good contact between soil and seed. You can cover the newly seeded area with loose straw or grass clippings to help prevent drying. For large plots (1 acre or more), a small seed drill pulled by a farm or garden tractor will plant and cover the seed in one pass.

Planting Living Mulches

Some gardeners plant green manures such as alsike or white clover between rows of young squash or corn to add nitrogen to the soil and to help control weeds. The green manure acts as a living mulch—it's a growing crop, but serves all the functions of a standard mulch. You can plant

Key Words
GREEN MANURE

Green manure. A crop that is grown and then incorporated into the soil to increase soil fertility or organic matter content.

Cover crop. A crop grown to protect and enrich the soil, or to control weeds.

Nitrogen fixation. The capture and conversion of atmospheric nitrogen gas into nitrogen compounds, stored in soil, that can be used by plants.

Legume. A plant whose roots form an association with soilborne bacteria that can capture atmospheric nitrogen.

Inoculant. A seed treatment medium that contains the symbiotic rhizobial bacteria to capture nitrogen when in contact with legume roots.

Green Manures for Home Gardens

One of the best ways to improve your soil is to grow green manure crops. Incorporating green manures into the soil increases organic matter content, improves tilth, and feeds earthworms and soil microorganisms. Try combining plantings of more than one species for best results.

Crop	When to Sow	Rate per 1,000 sq. ft.	Cultural Requirements	Comments
LEGUMES				
Alfalfa (*Medicago sativa*)	Spring	1–2 lb.	Needs good drainage and pH higher than 6.5.	Significant nitrogen contribution. Perennial.
Alsike clover (*Trifolium hybridum*)	Spring or late summer	½–1 lb.	Tolerates poor drainage and acid soils.	Low-growing perennial.
Austrian peas (*Pisum arvense*)	Late summer or fall	2–5 oz.	Prefers well-drained soils.	Winter legume for warmer climates. Annual.
Crimson clover (*Trifolium incarnatum*)	Spring or fall	8–12 oz.	Likes neutral, well-drained soils.	Tall clover with dense root system. Annual.
Hairy vetch (*Vicia villosa*)	Late summer or fall	1–2 lb.	Tolerates moderate drainage. Winter cover with rye.	Good nitrogen capture; grows well in Northern climates. Annual.
Ladino clover (*Trifolium repens* var. *latum*)	Early spring or fall	4–8 oz.	Needs well-drained soil.	Best sown in fall. Plant with oats in spring. Perennial.
Red clover (*Trifolium pratense*)	Spring or late summer	4–8 oz.	Somewhat tolerant of acidity and poor drainage.	Good phosphorus accumulation; grows quickly for incorporating during same season. Biennial.
Soybeans (*Glycine max*)	Spring or summer	2–3 lb.	Tolerate poor drainage.	Inoculate for nitrogen fixation. Annual.
White clover (Dutch) (*Trifolium repens*)	Spring or late summer	4–8 oz.	Tolerates droughty soils.	Good for undersowing in row crops as a living mulch. Perennial.
White sweetclover (*Melilotus alba*)	Spring or summer	½–1 lb.	Intolerant of acid soils and poor drainage.	Extensive root mass accumulates phosphate from rock powders. Biennial.
Yellow sweetclover (*Melilotus officinalis*)	Spring or summer	½–1 lb.	Intolerant of acid soils and poor drainage.	Similar to white sweetclover, but less root mass and faster growing. Biennial.

Crop	When to Sow	Rate per 1,000 sq. ft.	Cultural Requirements	Comments
NONLEGUMES				
Annual ryegrass (*Lolium multiflorum*)	Spring	1–2 lb.	Tolerates a wide range of soils.	Provides fast cover; good for establishing slow-growing crops. Annual.
Buckwheat (*Fagopyrum esculentum*)	Spring or summer	2–3 lb.	Tolerates infertile and acid soils.	Accumulates phosphorus. Annual.
Oats (*Avena sativa*)	Spring or summer	2–3 lb.	Prefer well-drained loamy soil. Tolerate some acidity.	Quick-growing summer crop. Provides quick cover for helping establish clover. Annual.
Rape (*Brassica napus*)	Spring or summer	6–8 oz.	Prefers moderately well-drained loam.	Good cover for short growing periods in summer. Annual.
Sudan grass (*Sorghum vulgare* var. *sudanense*)	Spring or summer	1–2 lb.	Will tolerate somewhat poorly drained soils.	Produces very large mass of root and top growth in summer. Annual.
Winter rye (*Secale cereale*)	Late summer or fall	2–3 lb.	Prefers well-drained soil.	Very winter-hardy, grows well in early spring. Annual.

living mulches between many vegetable row crops.

This system only works well if you seed the green manure plant in a weed-free seedbed. After planting the main crop, keep both areas between rows and between plants clear of weeds for about one month. Till or dig just before planting the mulch crop and pick out any exposed weed roots to prevent rerooting. Work carefully to avoid disturbing the root systems of your vegetable plants. The annual green manure will die down at frost or can be tilled or dug in when you prepare the soil for winter cover.

Late-season plantings of broccoli and cauliflower can benefit from underseeding with a winter-hardy green manure such as hairy vetch. To underseed, let the vegetable crop get established for about one month, keeping the area weed-free. Then broadcast the green manure seed over the entire area, not just between the rows, when the vegetable plants are 6″-8″ tall. By the time the plants are ready to harvest, you will be able to walk on the green manure without damaging it. Till or dig it several weeks before planting the following spring. Don't let vetch go to seed or it could become a nuisance.

Oats are also effective as an undersown or living mulch crop. Planted anytime from the middle to the end of summer, the crop will suppress weeds, but won't set seed itself. The oats will die down during winter, leaving a thick layer of mulch to prevent soil erosion and suppress late-fall and early-spring weeds. Shallowly till or dig in the oats two weeks before planting the following spring. Or to conserve time and effort, hand-pull the mulch back in spots and transplant established seedlings into it. It will retard weed growth until it decomposes, by which time the plant's leaves will be shading the area. ❖

Greenhouse Gardening

No matter what kind of greenhouse you choose, you'll discover the joys of a warm, bright spot on sunny winter days and the pleasures of gardening well beyond each end of the normal frost-free season. Depending on the type of greenhouse you choose, it's possible to enjoy colorful flowers, cultivate gourmet vegetables such as European seedless cucumbers, or start seedlings for the outside garden. A greenhouse can even add needed heat, humidity, and oxygenated air to your home.

Greenhouses can be attached to your home or stand alone. Your choice will depend on many factors, including your house design and gardening needs. Talk to other greenhouse owners and comparison-shop thoroughly before choosing the style and model you'd like to buy.

Kits of modular prefabricated sections are available for both freestanding and attached structures. Look for advertisements for these kits in the back of most gardening magazines. Some people prefer to build their greenhouse from scratch. Check your library or bookstore for useful references about designing and building an attached, energy-conserving greenhouse.

Tending a Greenhouse

Greenhouse gardening is similar in many ways to gardening outside. The plants still need adequate nutrients and water, and protection from insect pests and diseases. You still must tie, prune, and tend to them.

But the greenhouse environment is also very different than a backyard garden. The very things that make greenhouse growing more controlled and convenient also make it more demanding. In a greenhouse, you control temperature, humidity, soil aeration, drainage, nutrient- and moisture-holding qualities, and if you've invested in the appropriate equipment, even light levels and photoperiods. This degree of environmental control gives you a tremendous amount of latitude as well as some new responsibilities.

Temperature: Heaters, vents, and fans are your allies in temperature control. Even in a well-designed solar-efficient greenhouse, outside conditions are sometimes so cold and cloudy that auxiliary heat is needed to keep plants growing at an optimum rate.

Vents and fans help to cool the greenhouse. On a sunny day, even at 20°F below zero, greenhouse air can heat well beyond healthful levels. If the greenhouse is attached, you can move this air into your home. But in a freestanding unit, hot air must have a way to exit, and cool air a way to enter. Passive vents allow for this sort of movement, as do thermostatically controlled exhaust fans and intake vents. Manually operated vents are relatively inexpensive, but you'll need to check them at least twice a day, and open or close them as necessary. Automatic ventilation systems are more costly, but they save time and reduce the chances of excessive cooling or heating.

Adjust air temperature in the greenhouse according to the level of light. In general, summer crops grow best at temperatures of about 75°-85°F in the daytime and 60°-75°F at night. On cloudy days, these temperature ranges should be somewhat lower, since the plant is not manufacturing as many sugars as usual.

Winter air temperatures can go as low as 45°F at night without damaging most leafy green crops and shouldn't go much above 65°-70°F during the day. Spring seedlings vary in their temperature preferences. Cool-weather crops, such as broccoli and lettuce, grow most vigorously at 50°F nights and 60°-65°F days, while warm-weather plants such as tomatoes and squash require nights at a minimum of 55°F and days of at least 65°F but no higher than 80°F.

Air circulation: Air circulation is extremely important to plant health. Good air circulation strengthens the woody tissue in stems and decreases the opportunities for fungi to attack your plants. Dense plant growth can interfere with air circulation and contribute to excessive relative humidity. Leave adequate space between plants and prune so that leaves from adjacent

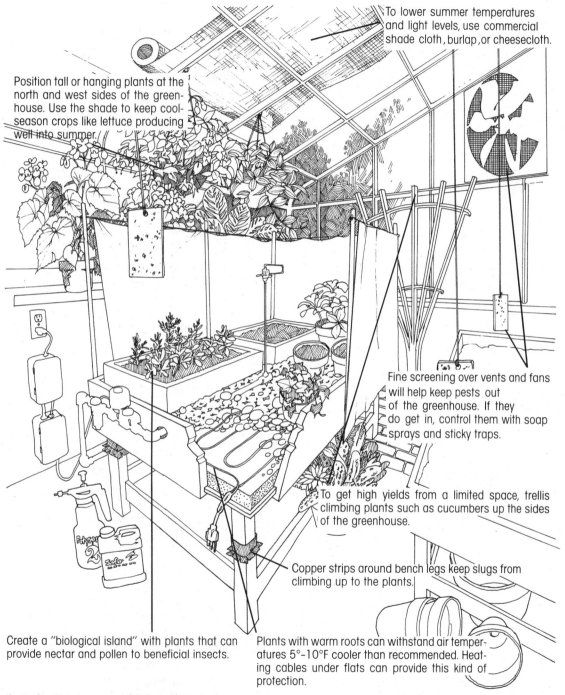

To lower summer temperatures and light levels, use commercial shade cloth, burlap, or cheesecloth.

Position tall or hanging plants at the north and west sides of the greenhouse. Use the shade to keep cool-season crops like lettuce producing well into summer.

Fine screening over vents and fans will help keep pests out of the greenhouse. If they do get in, control them with soap sprays and sticky traps.

To get high yields from a limited space, trellis climbing plants such as cucumbers up the sides of the greenhouse.

Copper strips around bench legs keep slugs from climbing up to the plants.

Create a "biological island" with plants that can provide nectar and pollen to beneficial insects.

Plants with warm roots can withstand air temperatures 5°–10°F cooler than recommended. Heating cables under flats can provide this kind of protection.

Organic greenhouse gardening. Greenhouses provide year-round enjoyment for the serious gardener. You can grow vegetables and flowers, propagate new plants, and overwinter tender ones. The controlled environment is an ideal place to use organic pest control measures, such as insect predators and parasites.

plants don't touch each other.

Plants use carbon dioxide from the air to manufacture sugars. In a closed greenhouse, carbon dioxide can be so depleted that plant growth is slowed. Remember to ventilate to change the air supply at least once each morning, even if you have to add extra heat.

Humidity: Greenhouses that feel like rainforests don't produce sturdy, healthy plants. Relative humidity should be close to 75-80 percent during high growth periods. At levels of 90-95 percent, plant growth is sappy, early bolting occurs, and fungal diseases become a real problem. Decrease humidity levels by venting or exhausting humid air and watering only when necessary. Growers in arid climates can increase humidity levels in the greenhouse by spraying water on the floor.

Light: Light levels in a greenhouse are partially determined by the design. When planning a greenhouse, check shade patterns from roof overhangs at the summer solstice in June and modify the plan if the shade is too great. Artificial lights are very useful when you're growing spring seedlings, particularly in cloudy regions. They can also give a boost to midwinter greens and the last of the fall-fruiting crops.

Soils and fertility: Commercial growers sometimes amend the soils under their greenhouses and plant right in them. Home greenhouse growers usually find it easier to use benches with individual pots set on them or growing beds filled with a soil mix.

Soil mixes for containers, benches, and beds should be lighter and more fertile than most garden soils. Good soil mixes drain fast, hold moisture well, contain balanced and slow-release nutrients, and have a slightly acid pH. For more on soil mixes, see the Houseplants entry.

It's best to make your own potting soil; commercial mixes don't have long-lasting fertility and they easily become too acid. A common recipe is 2 parts soil, 2 parts finished compost, 1

GOOD GREENHOUSE CROPS

Many great garden vegetables also adapt well to greenhouse culture. The healthiest, highest-yielding greenhouse plants are grown close to their natural season. With artificial lights and a good heater, you can get tomatoes in December, of course, but the plants will be more prone to insect and disease problems and won't yield as well as they do in May or October.

Succession planting makes sense for all quickly maturing green crops. For example, you'll have tender young lettuce all through the spring if you plant a few seeds each week rather than a season's supply all at once. If you want to harvest cold-resistant leafy greens through the winter months, plant them by October.

Crop	When to Plant
Beet greens, chard, oriental greens, lettuce, mustard, other leaf crops	Mid-February to May; August to mid-October
Herbs	Mid-February to mid-October
Tomatoes, peppers, and eggplants	Mid-February to March
Squash-family crops	March to late April

part peat moss, and 1 part vermiculite or perlite. If the soil is clayey, add sand; if it's too sandy, use vermiculite instead of perlite and increase the proportion of peat moss. Test the pH and adjust it if necessary.

Add compost and other amendments such as vermiculite each spring and fall. Good midseason fertilizers include compost tea and side-dressings, manure tea, liquid fish emulsion, and seaweed. Foliar-feed plants by spraying leaves with dilute compost tea, nettle tea, or liquid seaweed for extra nutrients and some disease resistance. Fertilize less in winter, when cool soil temperatures inhibit microbial activity. (For instructions on making compost and manure teas, see the Composting and Manure entries.)

Pests and Diseases

Good plant health, through good nutrition and environmental control, is the first line of defense against both pests and diseases. But even in the best circumstances, some pests may bother your plants.

Aphids, mites, and whiteflies are the most common serious insect problems. Use mechanical controls such as vacuuming, squashing, and washing at the first sign of trouble. If pest populations continue to grow, soap sprays or appropriate botanical controls such as neem may be useful.

Biological control with predatory insects such as green lacewings and parasites such as *Encarsia formosa* are extremely effective. Set up a small "biological island" in a warm, bright spot with pots of parsley-family members (Umbelliferae), such as chervil and dill, and small-flowered ornamentals, such as scented geraniums, lobelias, and salvias. Kept in bloom for the entire greenhouse season, these plants provide nectar and pollen for the beneficial insects.

Tempting as it is to bring outdoor peppers, eggplants, and herbs into the greenhouse at summer's end, you'll be running the risk of importing pests with them. If you decide to take the risk, quarantine the plants inside sacks made of tightly woven translucent material for at least 7-10 days. Aphids and damage from such pests as mites and thrips will be easier to see after this time. If problems appear, it's generally best to throw the plant out.

Fungal diseases are usually the greatest disease problems in a greenhouse. Preventive sprays help minimize disease incidence. Fermented nettle tea and dilute compost tea, sprayed on leaves at weekly intervals from the seedling stage onward, inhibit many diseases while also providing trace elements. Sanitation is important, too; isolate or dispose of sick plants, and clean up spilled soil and dropped leaves in the aisles and under benches.

Using a Greenhouse

For many gardeners, the prospect of growing vegetables year-round is a powerful incentive for building a greenhouse. Tomatoes, cucumbers, and lettuce are some of the most popular greenhouse crops. If your plants don't produce fruit, keep in mind that the protected greenhouse environment excludes natural pollinators like insects and wind. You may have to gently shake the plants (like tomatoes) or hand-pollinate them (as for squash) to get fruit. See "Good Greenhouse Crops" on the opposite page to learn more about growing vegetables indoors.

Growing flowers is probably the most common use of a greenhouse. You can encourage potted plants to bloom, for enjoyment in the greenhouse or your home. If you like flower arranging, try raising plants such as sweet peas for a constant supply of fresh cut flowers. A greenhouse is also an ideal place to force potted bulbs and to overwinter frost-tender potted plants. (Be sure, though, to inspect any outside plant for insects and disease before bringing it indoors). For more information on forcing bulbs, see the Bulbs entry.

Besides protecting established plants, a greenhouse can provide the perfect environment for many propagation techniques. Growing your own vegetable and flower transplants can save money while allowing you to grow less-common cultivars, and you'll know that they were raised without chemical pesticides and fertilizers. Herbaceous cuttings root quickly in the warm, moist conditions. And you can bring potted plants indoors in late winter to get them ready for grafting. See the Budding and Grafting entries for more details. ❖

Groundcovers

Groundcovers are the original landscape problem solvers. Where lawn grass won't grow easily or well, groundcovers come into their own. You can use plants like pachysandra to cover bare spots in the dense shade and dry soil under trees. Choose tough, deep-rooted groundcovers like daylilies to stabilize slopes. Plant Chinese astilbes (*Astilbe chinensis*) or Japanese primroses (*Primula japonica*) in wet, boggy sites instead of mowing a quagmire.

For weed control and reduced yard maintenance, groundcovers can't be beat. But they're also excellent for covering up plants that are past their peak. For example, hostas will mask dying daffodil foliage so it can ripen in peace without becoming an eyesore. You can also use groundcovers like periwinkle (*Vinca* spp.) under spring bulbs, ferns, and perennials—its uniform green will set off taller and more colorful plants.

You can use any low-growing plant as a groundcover as long as it meets certain requirements: It should look attractive all season, spread quickly to carpet the ground, require a minimum of maintenance, and keep down weeds. Don't limit your choices to the obvious ivy, pachysandra, and periwinkle, though all three make excellent evergreen groundcovers. Wildflowers, perennials, ornamental grasses, annuals, and low shrubs can all be used as groundcovers. For most situations, choose plants that hug the ground or grow up to 3' tall; the most useful groundcovers are generally 6"-18" tall.

How to Use Groundcovers

Why use groundcovers when you can just grow grass? For adaptability, resilience, and uniformity, you can't top lawn grasses. They withstand heavy foot traffic, rough play, and all the abuse a family can muster. However, it can require a lot of effort to keep lawn grasses healthy and attractive. They won't grow well under trees and shrubs or in wet sites. You'll save yourself time and work, and create a more dynamic landscape, if you reduce your lawn to the smallest size you need for outdoor activities and turn the rest of your yard over to groundcovers, decks, patios, and ornamental plantings.

Another good way to use groundcovers is to grow them in islands under trees. With a planting of groundcovers around your trees, you won't injure the trunks by scraping them with the lawn mower or waste precious gardening time hand-trimming around each trunk. A mixed planting of hostas, with their beautiful leaf patterns and colors, looks wonderful under trees. So do ferns and astilbes (*Astilbe* spp.), or try blue-green lilyturf (*Liriope* spp.) for a cool contrast to the lighter lawn grass.

Underplanting trees with groundcovers makes your landscape more interesting, too. You can tie individual plants together by surrounding them with an island of groundcover plants, or tie separate groups of plants together by underplanting them with the same groundcover. Try uniform or mixed plantings of groundcovers under shrubs and next to lawn areas, too. You'll find that your yard looks more appealing when everything looks connected—suddenly it will look like a landscaped garden, and all because of a few groundcovers!

You can also grow groundcovers instead of lawn grass where you want to limit water use. As everyone who's spent their evenings or weekends holding a hose knows, lawns are very thirsty. Xeriscaping, a landscape philosophy based on water conservation and minimizing damage to the landscape, uses extensive plantings of tough, drought-resistant groundcovers. These adaptable plants reduce environmental impact, save water, and cut maintenance time. For more on water-wise gardening techniques, see the Xeriscaping entry.

Groundcovers also can perk up the landscape in the off season. Think about fall and winter in your garden. Many groundcovers take on beautiful hues as cool weather returns. Some, like lilyturf and bearberry (*Arctostaphylos uva-*

ursi), display colorful fruits. Seed heads of ornamental grasses are loveliest late in the season. Evergreen foliage shines against light snowfalls.

Don't forget to go beyond problem solving when you're using groundcovers—after all, you have to look at them, too. A yardful of pachysandra may get the ground covered, but it's not nearly as appealing as a combination of groundcover plants. Think about mixing shape, texture, and color in exciting combinations. Feathery ferns with white-variegated hostas and low, glossy-leaved European wild ginger (*Asarum europaeum*) will make a shady site much more interesting than any one of the three alone. A mix of ajugas (*Ajuga reptans*)—perhaps 'Pink Beauty' (a pink-flowered, green-leaved cultivar) with the bronze-leaved 'Bronze Beauty' and large-leaved, blue-flowered 'Catlin's Giant'—will add more sparkle to a sunny spot than a single cultivar.

Don't be afraid to try something new if a combination falls flat. If a plant doesn't work where you've put it, just move it: Your best design tool is your shovel. For inspiration on using groundcovers in the landscape, see the garden design in the Curbside Gardens entry.

Choosing the Best Groundcovers

The cardinal rule in gardening is to match the plant to the site. To get the best performance from a groundcover, you must give it the growing conditions it needs. Plant shade-loving, shallow-rooted Bethlehem sage (*Pulmonaria saccharata*) to cover a bare area in the shade of a maple tree, and sun-loving, deep-rooted yarrows (*Achillea* spp.) to stop erosion on a dry, sunny bank.

Don't forget maintenance. Plant rampant growers like ivies or sedums where you need dense cover to control weeds, not in a small space where they would quickly get out of control. For a small space that's not weed-prone, choose airy plants like Allegheny foamflower (*Tiarella cordifolia*) or chamomile (*Chamaemelum nobile*) that won't be in a hurry to overgrow the site.

GROUNDCOVERS FOR DRY SHADE

Dry shade—the kind usually found under shade trees and shrubs—is one of the most difficult conditions gardeners face. Other places that dry shade is often a problem are under eaves and on shaded slopes, where rainwater often runs off. Plenty of plants grow in damp shade or in dry, sunny sites, but what usually grows under water-hogging trees and shrubs are bare spots. Fortunately, groundcovers can come to the rescue and create lush plantings to replace the eyesores. Here are a variety of good perennial groundcovers for dry shade. Plant heights range from creeping to 1½'.

Aegopodium podagraria (bishop's weed)
Ajuga reptans (ajuga)
Bergenia cordifolia (heartleaf bergenia)
Convallaria majalis (lily-of-the-valley)
Cornus canadensis (bunchberry)
Epimedium spp. (epimediums)
Euonymus fortunei (wintercreeper)
Festuca caesia (blue fescue)
Hakonechloa macra (hakonechloa grass)
Hedera spp. (ivies)
Lamiastrum galeobdolon (yellow archangel)
Lamium maculatum (spotted lamium)
Liriope spp. (lilyturfs)
Mahonia repens (creeping mahonia)
Ophiopogon spp. (mondo grasses)
Polygonatum spp. (Solomon's seals)
Vinca spp. (periwinkles)
Waldsteinia fragarioides (barren strawberry)

In both cases, a well-chosen groundcover will reduce your yard work, while a badly chosen groundcover will pitch you into a losing battle.

When you're looking for a good groundcover, let your needs limit your choices. Focus on the plants that suit your garden and your design. First, define your needs by asking yourself a few key questions:

• Is your site shaded, partially shaded, or in full sun?

GROUNDCOVERS FOR WET SITES

Trying to grow a lawn on a boggy site is an effort doomed to failure. Rather than living with a muddy weed patch, landscape the area with some of these attractive perennial groundcovers. You can create a beautiful wetland garden by mixing drifts of plants with different foliage and a wide range of flowering times. Here are some perennial groundcovers that can grow in wet soil. Plant heights range from creeping (strawberry geranium) to 2' (sedges), so match the plant to the scale of your site.

Acorus gramineus (Japanese sweet flag)
Alchemilla mollis (lady's-mantle)
Anemone canadensis (meadow anemone)
Astilbe chinensis (Chinese astilbe)
Brunnera macrophylla (Siberian bugloss)
Carex spp. (sedges)
Galium odoratum (sweet woodruff)
Hosta spp. (hostas)
Lysimachia nummularia (creeping Jenny)
Primula spp. (primroses)
Pulmonaria spp. (lungworts)
Saxifraga stolonifera (strawberry geranium)
Tiarella cordifolia (Allegheny foamflower)
Viola canadensis (Canada violet)

• Is your site moist or dry?
• Do you need a ground-hugging plant for the site, or would a taller plant look better?
• Do you want bold or fine texture?
• How important are flowers? Flower color?
• Can you use variegated foliage to brighten things up?
• Should the plant be evergreen or deciduous?
Read more about how to choose plants in the Garden Design entry.

Planting and Maintenance

When you're trying to grow a good ground-cover, thorough soil preparation is essential, espe-

cially in difficult sites. Plants will take off and grow faster if you give them a head start, so you'll have less trouble with weed competition. If you haven't had a soil test, consider it; you'll learn a lot about your gardening conditions. (To find out about soils and soil testing, see the Soil entry.)

First remove existing sod or undesirable growth from your site. Double dig the soil to a minimum depth of 18"-20". (For more on this technique, see the Double Digging entry.) Spread a generous layer of compost, shredded leaves, or other organic matter over the soil. Add an organic fertilizer and other amendments as needed. (You

---

GROUNDCOVERS FOR SLOPES

If you've ever tried to mow grass on a slope—sliding down after the mower, struggling to push it back up, or hauling it up and down on a rope—you know why a care-free groundcover is a better idea. Good ground-covers for slopes should transplant readily, provide cover quickly, and send down deep, soil-anchoring roots to keep the soil from eroding. Choose plants that can take the full sun and drought conditions on most slopes. Here's a selection of the best perennial groundcovers for slopes. They range in height from ground huggers to 3' shrubs, so match the groundcover to the scale of your slope.

Achillea spp. (yarrows)
Alchemilla mollis (lady's-mantle)
Arctostaphylos spp. (manzanita, bearberries)
Arundinaria pygmaea (pygmy bamboo)
Coronilla varia (crown vetch)
Cotoneaster spp. (cotoneasters)
Euonymus fortunei (wintercreeper)
Hypericum calycinum (St.-John's-wort)
Juniperus cultivars (creeping junipers)
Pteridium aquilinum (bracken)
Sedum spp. (sedums, stonecrops)
Verbena spp. (verbenas)

Planting groundcovers on a slope. 1. Where the ground slopes gently, you can plant groundcovers directly in the bank, then mulch around them until they're established. 2. On a steep slope, begin planting from the top down. Put up a wooden barrier where you want a plant, pile soil behind the barrier, and put in the plant. Once the plants are established, remove the barriers.

can find out more about fertilizers in the Fertilizers entry.) Turn the soil again, incorporating all the amendments thoroughly. Level the soil surface with a garden rake. Break up any remaining clods. Water to settle the soil, and you're ready for planting.

Space plants according to their growth rate and size at maturity. Plant fast-growing perennials, ornamental grasses, and other herbaceous plants 1'-3' apart, depending on the mature size of the plant. Plant junipers and other large woody plants 3' apart. Plant slow-growing woody plants like wintergreen (*Gaultheria procumbens*) 1' apart.

Arrange the plants within the bed according to your design. Dig a hole for each plant large enough to accommodate the loosened root ball. If you're using container plants, make sure the plants are positioned at the same level at which they grew in the containers. Soak the roots of bareroot plants for several hours before planting. Remove the plants from the water one at a time and spread the roots evenly over a

dome of soil in the bottom of the planting hole. Check the level of the crown to make sure it's at the right planting depth. (For more how-to-plant techniques, see the Planting entry.)

Mulch the site after planting to control weeds and reduce moisture loss. Water newly set plants thoroughly. Groundcovers need regular watering until they are well established, which will take an entire growing season for woody plants. Pull weeds early to avoid competition.

Groundcovers as a group are tough, trouble-free plants. But some pest and disease problems are inevitable in any garden situation. Prevention is the best control. Keep plants healthy, well watered, and mulched. Remove weeds that can harbor pests. If problems arise, consult the Organic Pest Management entry.

Growing Your Own Groundcovers

Groundcovers are a diverse group of plants. Propagation techniques vary according to whether

---

More On
GROUNDCOVERS

You'll find details on how to grow specific groundcovers in the following entries: Achillea (yarrow), Ajuga, Astilbe, Bergenia, Convallaria (lily-of-the-valley), Cotoneaster, Epimedium, Euonymus, Grasses, Hedera (ivy), Hosta, Juniperus (juniper), Lamium, Liriope, Pachysandra, Sedum, Sempervivum (hens-and-chickens), Vinca (periwinkle), and Viola (violet).

---

you're dealing with a shrubby, vining, or perennial groundcover. Most groundcovers can be grown from seed started indoors or direct-seeded outdoors. But you'll get quicker results from fast-growing groundcovers if you take cuttings or divide them.

Take cuttings from perennial groundcovers like English ivy (*Hedera helix*), spotted lamium (*Lamium maculatum*), leadwort (*Ceratostigma plumbaginoides*), pachysandra, periwinkle, and sedum in early to midsummer. You can divide groundcovers in spring or fall. If the plant is a vine or creeper like ajuga, creeping phlox (*Phlox stolonifera*), English ivy, Allegheny foamflower, periwinkle, or wintercreeper (*Euonymus fortunei*), sever rooted plantlets from the parent stem. Lift clumps of perennials like astilbe, bergenia (*Bergenia* spp.), blue fescue (*Festuca caesia*), crested iris (*Iris cristata*), daylily, and hosta, and separate the crowns.

A slow but easy method of propagating woody groundcovers like cotoneasters (*Cotoneaster* spp.) and junipers is layering—encouraging branches to root where they touch the ground. For more on propagation, see the Cuttings, Division, Layering, and Seeds and Seedlings entries. ❖

Gypsophila

Baby's-breath. Summer-blooming annuals and perennials.

Description: Most kinds of baby's-breath resemble earthbound clouds when in bloom, with hundreds of tiny five-petalled single or double flowers in white and pink shades. The open, much-branched plants bear narrow, gray-green leaves 1"–4" long. *Gypsophila elegans,* annual baby's-breath, blooms for a short season and rarely exceeds 2'. *G. paniculata,* perennial baby's-breath, blooms over a longer season and can grow to 3' tall and wide. Zones 3–8.

How to grow: Both kinds of baby's-breath need a sunny site with average to less-fertile soil that is neutral or slightly alkaline and moderately moist but well drained. Sow annual baby's-breath once the weather is warm directly where it is to grow. Make several sowings two weeks apart for a longer bloom season. Plant perennial baby's-breath in spring and divide only if necessary; the long, fleshy roots resent disturbance. Double cultivars are sometimes propagated by grafting, so plant the graft union below the surface of the soil to encourage new roots to form. Perennial baby's-breath tolerates heat quite well. Cut it back immediately after bloom to encourage fresh new growth and possible rebloom. Stake tall cultivars.

Landscape uses: Both annual and perennial baby's-breaths are beautiful in borders, cottage gardens, and other informal plantings. Fill the gaps they leave after bloom with asters and other fall-blooming plants. Grow baby's-breaths in a cutting garden for bouquets; blooms can be used either fresh or dried. To dry them, gather some stems in full bloom and hang them upside down to dry.

Best cultivars: *G. elegans:* 'Covent Garden' with rather large single flowers on 1½'–2' plants. *G. paniculata:* double white 'Bristol Fairy', to 3' tall; similar but larger-flowered 'Perfecta'; and double 'Pink Fairy', to 1½' tall. ❖

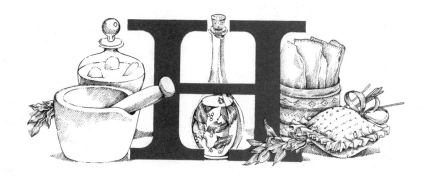

Halesia

Silverbell. Deciduous spring-flowering trees.

Description: *Halesia carolina,* Carolina silverbell, is an upright tree with branches held horizontally. It has a mature height of 30'-40', though it has been known to grow to 80' in the wild. Native to the understories of damp forest slopes in the Smoky Mountains, Carolina silverbell produces bell-shaped pink to white flowers, suspended from its branches in spring. Its alternately arranged leaves are simple and turn yellow in the fall. Zones 5-8.

H. diptera, two-winged silverbell, is a small rounded tree reaching 20'-30' in height. It resembles Carolina silverbell but bears its white, bell-shaped blooms approximately 1-2 weeks later.

H. monticola, mountain silverbell, is similar in many ways to Carolina silverbell, but it has larger leaves, flowers, and fruits. It also grows much larger—50'-60' in the landscape or to 100' when conditions are right. Zones 5-7.

How to grow: Grow silverbells on sites with rich, humusy, moist soil that is slightly acid. Silverbells require well-drained soil and full sun to partial shade (especially in areas with hot summers). Few pests and diseases bother these trees.

Landscape uses: Silverbells are lovely trees with year-round interest. They are effective used as focal points, as lawn trees, and in shrub borders, or naturalized in a woodland garden. ❖

Hamamelis

Witch hazel. Deciduous fall- or winter-flowering shrubs and small trees.

Description: *Hamamelis vernalis,* vernal witch hazel, grows 6'-10' tall and can spread wider than its height. Fragrant yellow to red flowers appear in late winter to early spring and are showy for almost a month. Golden yellow fall foliage color is very showy. Zones 4-8.

H. virginiana, common witch hazel, grows 15'-20' tall and wide. Its spicy-scented, saffron yellow flowers unfurl as its clear yellow fall foliage is dropping. Zones 4-8.

H. mollis, Chinese witch hazel, reaches 10'-15' tall and wide. It is spectacular in the landscape because its blooms appear in midwinter, often against a backdrop of snow. Zones 5-8.

All species have dull green, 2"-6" leaves. In autumn, seed capsules can catapult seeds many feet.

How to grow: Grow witch hazels in partial shade, especially in the southern end of their range. Common witch hazel grows best in moist, humus-rich soil, with plenty of mulch. Prune only to remove branches that are dead, dying, crossing, or rubbing.

Landscape uses: Witch hazels make good specimens. Common witch hazel is lovely in a native planting.

Best cultivars: *H. × intermedia* 'Arnold Promise' is a *H. mollis* hybrid with bright yellow flowers and reddish fall foliage. *H. mollis* 'Brevipetala' has orange flowers. ❖

Hedera

Ivy. Evergreen woody vines.

Description: *Hedera helix,* English ivy, is a vigorous evergreen vine with shiny 3- to 5-lobed leaves, 2″-5″ long. Black, inconspicuous berries appear in summer and persist through the fall and into winter. It is hardy in Zones 5-9, although some cultivars are hardy to Zone 4. *H. canariensis,* Algerian or Canary ivy, is similiar to English ivy but more tolerant of heat and better suited to warm climates. It is hardy in Zones 9-10 and the milder parts of Zone 8. *H. colchica,* Persian ivy, displays large leaves and coarse growth. Zones 6-9.

How to grow: Plant rooted cuttings or transplants of ivy in spring or fall. Plants prefer moist, humus-rich, well-drained soils. They are tolerant of acid or alkaline conditions. Grow ivies in partial or dense shade—they won't tolerate full sun or hot sites. Ivy is relatively free of pest and disease problems.

Landscape uses: Use ivy as a groundcover or climbing vine. It makes an excellent low-maintenance planting with its lush, dark green foliage. Ivy is especially useful in dense shade where little else will grow. The vine has holdfasts on aerial rootlets that allow it to cling to brick and masonry walls. This can be a drawback if the wall is cracked, since the rootlets can work into the cracks and dislodge pieces of brick or stone. Ivy requires little pruning except for an occasional trim to keep it in bounds. Its lush growth will quickly hide and soften harsh walls or edges. The small-leaved ivy cultivars are often used to create unusual topiary shapes or grown in a tree form (called a standard) to ornament a patio. Ivies also make outstanding houseplants.

Best cultivars: *H. helix:* 'Baltica', 'Bulgaria', 'Hebron', and 'Thorndale' (all hardy to Zone 4); 'Goldheart', yellow-centered leaves. *H. canariensis:* 'Variegata', white-variegated leaves. *H. colchica:* 'Dentata', toothed leaves. ❖

Hedges

Plant a hedge for a privacy screen to block out unwelcome views or traffic noise or to add a green background to set off other plantings. Hedges also provide excellent wind protection for house or garden. Thick, tall, or thorny hedges make inexpensive and forbidding barriers to keep out animals—or to keep them in.

A formal hedge is an elegant, carefully trimmed row of trees or shrubs. It requires exacting and frequent pruning to keep plants straight and level. The best plants for formal hedges are fine leaved and slow growing—and tough enough to take frequent shearing. An informal hedge requires only selective pruning and has a more natural look. A wide variety of plants can be used, many of which have attractive flowers or berries.

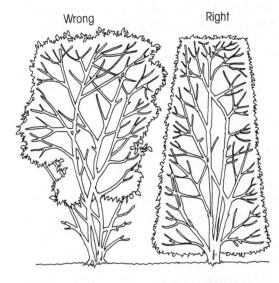

Shaping a hedge. A bare bottom results when your hedge has a wide top tapering to a narrow base. Sunlight doesn't reach lower leaves, causing them to die and drop off. A base wider than the top allows light to reach all sides, keeping your hedge growing vigorously.

HEDGE PLANTS

Many plants make excellent hedges. Even tall or bushy annuals can make a temporary hedge; plant herbs such as lavender for an attractive low hedge. Most hedges are shrub or trees species; this list is a mix of common and uncommon hedge plants. An asterisk (*) indicates a plant for a formal hedge.

Evergreen Trees

Chamaecyparis lawsoniana (lawson cypress)
Juniperus spp. (junipers)
Prunus laurocerasus (English laurel)*
Thuja occidentalis 'Pyramidalis' (pyramidal arborvitae)
Tsuga canadensis (Canada hemlock)*

Deciduous Trees

Carpinus betulus (hornbeam)*
Crataegus spp. (hawthorns)*
Fagus spp. (beeches)

Evergreen Shrubs

Buxus spp. (boxwoods)*
Cotoneaster spp. (cotoneasters)*
Euonymus spp. (euonymus)
Ilex crenata (Japanese holly)*
Ligustrum spp. (privets)*
Lonicera spp. (shrub honeysuckles)*
Mahonia spp. (Oregon grapes)
Pyracantha spp. (firethorns)*
Taxus spp. (yews)*

Deciduous Shrubs

Berberis spp. (barberries)
Chaenomeles speciosa (Japanese quince)
Elaeagnus angustifolia (Russian olive)
Forsythia × *intermedia* (forsythia)
Ligustrum spp. (privets)*
Philadelphus spp. (mock oranges)
Rhamnus spp. (buckthorns)*
Rosa spp. (shrub roses)
Viburnum spp. (viburnums)

Planting and Pruning

It's best to plant young plants when starting a hedge. Full-grown specimens are more apt to die from transplanting stress in the early years, and finding an exact replacement can be difficult. It's easier to fill a gap in an informal hedge.

For an open, airy hedge of flowering shrubs, allow plenty of room for growth when planting. For a dense, wall-like hedge, space the plants more closely. You may find it easier to dig a trench rather than separate holes. To ensure your hedge will be straight, tie a string between stakes at each end to mark the trench before digging. See the Planting entry for details on preparing planting holes and setting plants.

Broad-leaved plants used as a formal hedge need early training to force dense growth. For a thick, uniform hedge, reduce new shoots on the top and sides by ⅓ or more each year until the hedge is the desired size. Cutting a formal hedge properly is a challenge. Stand back, walk around, and recut until you get it straight—just like a haircut. Shear often during the growing season to keep it neat.

Needled evergreens require a different technique. Avoid cutting off the tops of evergreens until they reach the desired height. Shear sides once a year, but never into the bare wood. See the Evergreens entry for more pruning tips.

Prune informal hedges according to when they bloom. Do any needed pruning soon after flowering. Use thinning cuts to prune selected branches back to the next limb. Heading cuts that nip the branch back to a bud encourage dense, twiggy growth on the outside. To keep informal hedges vigorous, cut 2-3 of the oldest branches to the ground each year.

For fast, dense growth, prune in spring. This is also a good time for any severe shearing or pruning that's needed. For more about when and how to prune, see the Shrubs and Pruning and Training entries. ❖

Heirloom Plants

Every fall, gardeners of a special breed harvest the seeds that will keep little bits of history alive for one more year. These are "heirloom" gardeners, and the seeds they gather are those of heirloom plants, cultivars of plants grown in the eighteenth, nineteenth, and early twentieth centuries. Were they not preserved in backyard plots by quietly dedicated heirloom gardeners, many of these old cultivars would not survive today. Competition from hybrid cultivars selected for commercially important characteristics and widely promoted for as long as 50 years has largely driven them from the pages of the seed catalogs. Many survive only because they have been passed, a few seeds at a time, among family members and friends for generations.

Characteristics: Heirloom plants are not suited to large-scale production because they cannot be harvested mechanically or transported long distances to market. But they are often ideal for home gardeners, whose needs and preferences remain unchanged through the generations. Many heirloom crops taste better or are more tender than their hybrid replacements, and many spread their harvest over a longer period. If grown for years in one locality, they have adapted to the climate and soil conditions of that area and may out-produce modern cultivars. Others may be less productive than today's hybrids, but offer greater disease and insect resistance, which is invaluable to organic gardeners. Heirloom plants also add interest to garden and table, with a wide range of shapes, colors, and tastes unavailable in modern cultivars.

Heirloom plants are a tangible connection with the past. Like fine old furniture and antique china, the garden plants of earlier generations draw us close to those who have grown them before us. Some heirloom cultivars have fascinating histories. 'Mostoller Wild Goose' bean, said to have been collected from the craw of a goose shot in 1864 in Somerset County, Pennsylvania, was once grown by the Cornplanter Indians.

More On
HEIRLOOM PLANTS

To get started as an heirloom gardener, try ordering seed from small specialty houses that carry old cultivars. Also, you can contact nonprofit organizations that work with individuals to preserve heirloom plants. One of the best known is the Seed Savers Exchange, R.R. 3, Box 239, Decorah, IA 52101. Another good way to find heirloom plants is to check readers' letters in gardening magazines—many offer homegrown seed for a small fee.

For directions on how to save your own seed, see the Seeds and Seedlings entry.

'Anasazi' corn, found in a Utah cave, is thought to be more than 800 years old. Cultivars like these are eagerly sought by collectors, who maintain them for their historic value just as archivists maintain old papers and books.

Genetic diversity: A more vital reason for growing old cultivars is that heirloom plants represent a vast and diverse pool of genetic characteristics—one that will be lost forever if these plants are allowed to become extinct. Even cultivars that seem inferior to us today may carry a gene that will prove invaluable in the future. One may contain a valuable but yet undiscovered compound. Another could have the disease resistance vital to future generations of gardeners and plant breeders. The federal government maintains a National Seed Storage Laboratory in Fort Collins, Colorado, as part of its commitment to maintaining genetic diversity, but the task of preserving seed is so vast that the government probably cannot do a complete job on its own. Heirloom gardeners recognize the importance of maintaining genetic diversity, and many feel a real sense of urgency and importance about their own preservation work. ❖

Helianthus

Sunflower. Summer- to fall-blooming annuals and perennials.

Description: *Helianthus annuus,* common sunflower, is an annual that lights up gardens with single or double daisies in shades of cream, yellow, orange, and red-brown on plants 2'-10' tall or taller. For more details, see the Sunflower entry.

H. × multiflorus, perennial sunflower, bears 3"-5" golden blooms on upright, bushy plants to 5'. Blooms appear from late summer to fall. Zones 3-8.

How to grow: Start annuals indoors a few weeks before the last frost, or sow directly in full sun and average to rich, moist but well-drained soil. Water and fertilize regularly. Provide similar growing conditions for perennials; plant or divide them in spring.

Landscape uses: Grow in borders, informal gardens, and cutting gardens. ❖

Heliotropium

Heliotrope, cherry pie. Tender perennials grown as summer- and fall-blooming annuals.

Description: Heliotropes bear rich purple, lavender, or white 3"-8" clusters of small, fragrant flowers atop loose mounds of dark green foliage up to 1½' tall.

How to grow: Start seeds in early spring or buy plants to set out after the last frost. With regular watering, they thrive in sun or part shade and in light, rich soil.

Landscape uses: Enjoy heliotrope's fragrance by growing plants in pots, perhaps as a standard, or toward the front of a bed, border, or cottage garden.

Best cultivars: 'Marine', 1½', and 'Dwarf Marine', 8", are both purple. Hunt for fragrant white or lavender selections. ❖

Helleborus

Hellebore. Winter- to early-spring-blooming perennials.

Description: Hellebores bear 2"-3", shallow bowl-shaped flowers and 1' palm-shaped evergreen leaves. *Helleborus niger,* Christmas rose, bears white flowers in winter or early spring among 1' mounds of foliage; *H. orientalis,* lenten rose, blooms in early spring, with white, green, pink, or maroon flowers among handsome, 1½' shiny green leaves. Zones 4-8.

How to grow: Set out pot-grown or small plants in spring or fall. Divide these slow-to-establish but long-lived plants in spring, but only when you want new plants. They thrive in partial to full shade and well-drained, moisture-retentive, humus-rich soil. Keep out of drying winter winds.

Landscape uses: Allow to naturalize in woodland plantings and among shrubs. Feature with early snowdrops and crocuses. ❖

Hemerocallis

Daylily. Mostly summer-blooming perennials; some bloom in spring and fall.

Description: Daylilies bear 2"-8" wide, trumpet-shaped flowers in tones of almost every floral color except pure white and blue. Individual blooms last for only one day, though plants produce many buds, which provides a long display period. Flowers are borne on 2½'-3½' top-branched, strong stems above fountainlike clumps of straplike, roughly 2' long, medium green leaves. Zones 3-9.

How to grow: Plant or divide daylilies any time from spring to fall, though early spring and early fall are best. Divide 4- to 6-year-old clumps by lifting the entire clump from the ground and inserting two digging forks back-to-back, pulling them apart to split the tight root mass. Replant as single, double, or triple "fans." Daylilies grow in sun or partial shade. Plant in average to fertile, well-drained, moisture-retentive soil (though plants will tolerate drought). Routinely deadhead spent blooms, which otherwise collect on the stalks and spoil the display. Watch for thrips, which brown and disfigure the buds; control them with soap spray or by removing infested flowers.

Landscape uses: Grow as specimens or groups in borders, or showcase daylilies in beds of their own. Many tougher, older cultivars make excellent groundcovers and bank plantings to control erosion and weeds.

Best cultivars: Choose from literally thousands. Base your choice on flower color, size, and shape, bloom season (including repeat bloom), height, fragrance, and deciduous or ever-green leaves (evergreens are best in the South). Try to observe plants in bloom locally, or buy award-winning cultivars. ❖

Herbicides

Herbicides are substances that kill weeds. Like other synthetic chemical pesticides, herbi-cides vary in their level of safety and persistence in the environment. Because herbicides work so well, many farmers have become dependent on them to their own disadvantage. Weeds quickly develop resistance to herbicides when farmers fail to rotate their use. Herbicides sprayed on bare soil to prevent weed growth sometimes run off into surface and ground water. And like other pesticides, herbicides may have health and envi-ronmental hazards of which we're not aware. For more information on the hazards of synthetic pesticide use, see the Pesticides entry.

Modern synthetic herbicides are very com-plex in the ways they work. Some herbicides are nonselective, which means they damage nearly any plant on which they're applied. But many synthetic herbicides are highly selective. They kill just one type of weed and leave crop plants unharmed. Some herbicides kill weeds on contact, while others are translocated within the plant before they act.

Before the development of synthetic herbi-cides, farmers dusted or sprayed their fields with ashes, salt, copper sulfate, and various oils to kill unwanted plants. Unfortunately, these prod-ucts aren't much safer than the synthetic herbi-cides that replaced them. The older products were not selective and were as likely to injure neighboring vegetable and ornamental plants as the weeds. They often required high rates of application, persisted in soil for a long time, and created environmental hazards.

There are very few organically acceptable herbicides. For the most part, organic gardeners must rely on preventive cultural controls and mechanical removal to control these plant pests. For more information on developing a complete pest management plan, see the Organic Pest Management entry. For further information on weed control, see the Weeds entry.

There is one natural herbicide available that organic gardeners may want to try. The Safer company has enhanced the phytotoxic prop-erties of its soaps and has used this technology to create a safe herbicide. SharpShooter, com-posed of naturally occurring fatty acids, is non-toxic to mammals and is as easy on beneficial insects as insecticidal soaps are. It is sprayed directly on plants and works best on young or delicate foliage. Complete coverage is important. SharpShooter works well on young seedlings of annual weeds. Perennial plants may need sev-eral applications for effective control.

Boiling water is an effective herbicide for small areas. Pour it directly on the offending plants. It doesn't work very well on established perennial weeds, unless you dig up the roots.

Vinegar and salt can be used as herbicides. Use them only where you will never want to grow anything, such as in cracks between walk-way bricks. ❖

Herbs

Every gardener wants to grow at least a few herbs, even if only in pots on a sunny porch. Herbs contribute to our cuisine and our well-being, serve as decorative additions in gardens, bouquets, and wreaths, and fascinate us with their rich history and lore.

The word *herb* has no neat and final definition. *Webster's Ninth New Collegiate Dictionary* lists two different definitions of the term. According to the first, an herb is "a seed-producing annual, biennial, or perennial that does not develop persistent woody tissue but dies down at the end of a growing season." This definition recognizes the way botanists use the term herb, but *Webster's* second definition is closer to the way gardeners use it: "A plant or plant part valued for its medicinal, savory, or aromatic qualities."

Above all, whether used for flavorings, fragrances, medicines, or teas, herbs are useful plants. They're also among the most familiar garden plants because they have been part of our daily lives since the beginning of time.

Gardening with Herbs

There are nearly as many ways to incorporate herbs into your garden as there are herbs to choose from. Traditionally, they have been grown in gardens devoted to herbs alone. But herbs add interest to flower gardens, too. Although it's sometimes easiest to appreciate them when they're given a spot of their own, they can be mixed into plantings of perennials or annuals, for example. An added advantage of growing herbs apart from ornamentals is that you won't spoil the flower garden display when you harvest your herbs.

Herb growing can be as simple or as complicated as you choose to make it. Most herbs are easy to grow—they demand little and give a lot. You can grow herbs successfully in anything from a simple arrangement of pots to a stylized formal garden. There are, of course, a few prima donnas that demand a bit more coddling than most. Some that are not hardy in the North must be brought indoors for the winter.

Kitchen Gardens

It's a good idea to have a small herb garden easily accessible to the kitchen door so that you can snip a few herbs while cooking—even if it's raining. To grow herbs successfully in a dooryard garden, be sure the soil has good drainage and the area is in sunlight for at least 6 hours per day.

A kitchen garden is the perfect place for thyme, parsley, marjoram, and oregano, as well as coriander (also called cilantro) if you like the flavor of the leaves. You might want to include several kinds of basils—sweet, small-leaved, and purple—since they have such different flavors. This is the place for French tarragon, too; it's not decorative enough for a flower border. Plan on keeping a rigorously controlled mint plant or two close at hand as well. Plant mint in tubs above ground or in bottomless sunken buckets to keep it from crowding out other plants.

Chervil, once started, will seed itself under a shrub, sticking to its spot for the rest of your life. Dill will also show up dependably every spring.

Chives and garlic chives are two more kitchen-garden favorites. Be sure to cut the dying blossom heads from the latter if you expect to grow anything other than garlic chives. This individual is as ruthless a colonizer as the mints, although it spreads only by seed, not by roots. Its umbels of white starry flowers add beauty in the garden, and the flat leaves add interesting flavor when chopped and sprinkled on salads and soups.

You may decide to make your dooryard garden more ambitious and duplicate a colonial garden, complete with the medicinal and culinary herbs that our forebears grew and relied upon. This project would contain different plants

Kitchen garden. Keep herbs for cooking in easy reach with a dooryard kitchen garden. These small gardens are low-maintenance, informal-style collections of your favorite herbs for seasoning food.

than a typical kitchen garden. (Our forebears, for example, wouldn't have grown our basils, French tarragon, or coriander.) Visit historical gardens to get ideas, or check your library for books that provide the historical information necessary to create such a garden.

Vegetable Gardens

If you are going to grow herbs in quantity, you may want to grow them in rows or beds in your vegetable garden for ease of care and harvest. Plants such as oregano, savory, santolina, thyme, culinary sage, and lavender do best in well-drained soils to which lime and grit have been added. Place them on specially prepared ridges or in raised beds. Angelica can be settled into a wettish spot, and dill, coriander, parsley, French tarragon, mints, and basils will do well in well-drained soil containing lots of organic matter.

Herbs are often used as companion plants in the vegetable garden. According to folklore, in some cases backed by scientific studies, certain herbs can either aid or hinder vegetable growth. Herbs also help deter pests. See "Companion Planting" on page 324 and the Companion Planting entry for more details.

Herbs and Flowers

Many herbs are suitable for a mixed border or bed—a flower garden that combines perennials, annuals, and shrubs. You may already have some herbs in your garden, although you think of them as flowers or foliage plants.

English lavender cultivars such as 'Hidcote' or 'Munstead' are always welcome among the flowers in beds or borders. Pure blue, silky flowers on delicate wiry stems make blue flax (*Linum perenne*) a favorite in flower beds. Feverfew (*Chrysanthemum parthenium*) is another herb often used in mixed borders. Its lacy, bright green foliage sets off small, pure white single or double daisies. Catmint (*Nepeta* spp.), with sprays of blue-lavender flowers, pungent, gray-green leaves, and tufted habit, is lovely with lilies and roses.

Many gray-leaved herbs, such as Russian sage (*Perovskia* spp.) with its silvery foliage and misty blue flowers, are useful for separating and blending colors in the garden. Even a culinary workhorse like dill can be used to fine effect in the mixed border. Its delicate, chartreuse flowers and lacy foliage add an airiness to any planting.

Herbs in Containers

Herbs and containers are a happy combination, especially for a gardener short on space, time, or stamina. Maintenance chores—except for watering—are eliminated or much reduced. Even if your garden has plenty of space, a potted collection adds interest to a sunny porch, patio, or deck. An assortment of terra-cotta pots brimming with herbs used for cooking makes a charming—and useful—addition to a kitchen doorstep. Or try a sampler of mints in a wooden half-barrel—the notorious perennial spreaders stay in control, will come back year after year, and are handy when you're ready to brew a pot of tea. For information on potting soil mixes for container plants, see the Container Gardening and Houseplants entries.

Some tender herbs are often grown—or at least overwintered—in containers because they aren't hardy and won't survive Northern winters. These include rosemary (*Rosmarinus officinalis*), sweet bay (*Laurus nobilis*), myrtle (*Myrtus communis*), pineapple sage (*Salvia elegans*), and lemon verbena (*Aloysia triphylla*). See "Overwintering Tender Perennials" on page 317 for directions on keeping these tender herbs from year to year.

HERBS FOR A MIXED BORDER

Many herbs will thrive in a sunny mixed bed or border with average to rich, well-drained soil. These herbs are showy enough to hold their own in any garden. Plants are perennials unless otherwise noted.

Achillea spp. (yarrows): yellow, white, red, or pink flowers; used medicinally and dried for herbal crafts
Calendula officinalis (pot marigold): annual with bright orange or yellow daisylike flowers; used medicinally and in cooking
Digitalis purpurea (common foxglove): biennial with tube-shaped pinkish purple or white flowers; used medicinally (with medical supervision)
Echinacea purpurea (purple coneflower): rosy purple daisies with high, bristly centers; used medicinally by Native Americans
Lavandula angustifolia (lavender): lavender or purple flowers; flowers and foliage used for fragrance and herbal crafts
Linum usitatissimum (flax): blue flowers; used medicinally
Monarda didyma (bee balm): shaggy rose or pink blossoms; dried blossoms and foliage used for tea, fragrance, and herbal crafts
Tropaeolum majus (garden nasturtium): annual with abundant flowers in shades of orange, yellow, and red; used in cooking and as a companion plant

Formal Herb Gardens

Most gardeners would probably include an exquisitely groomed formal herb garden on their wish list. But if you have the impulse to make a formal herb garden, bear in mind that they're not for everyone. These carefully planned gardens with their neatly trimmed, geometric arrangements require both strength and time to keep them looking their best.

Knot gardens, in which miniature hedges in different colors and textures create the look of intertwining strands, are a classic feature of formal herb gardens. Dwarf boxwoods (*Buxus* spp.), lavender (*Lavandula* spp.), lavender cotton (*Santolina virens* and *S. chamaecyparissus*), or germander (*Teucrium chamaedrys*) are popular knot-garden plants. You can also mix textures and colors of mulches—brown cocoa shells, white marble chips, gray-blue crushed granite—to elaborate the knot garden. However, while knot gardens can be an intriguing challenge to plan and plant, even a modest version requires constant maintenance. Everything must be kept under control—constant trimming and shaping are essential, and all the plants must be in top-notch health if the knot pattern is to remain attractive.

If you're ambitious enough to try a formal garden, keep your knot garden small, so that replacements and maintenance aren't overwhelming. You'll need to replace individual specimens in the clipped hedges that don't make it through the winter. Replacements can be hard to find in the same size as the plants that remain intact. If you have space, keep a few extra plants growing in a nursery bed or other out-of-the-way spot for just such emergencies.

Informal Herb Gardens

Perhaps one of the easiest and most rewarding ways to use herbs in the landscape is in an informal herb garden. An informal garden can be a free-form island bed, with the tallest herb plants in the center and the shortest around the edges. Or it could be more like a perennial border, set against a background such as a wall, hedge, fence, or building and defined with either straight or curved lines.

So many flowering plants have been used as herbs that even the most rigid purist—one who wants a garden of only traditional herbs—could have fine color and texture. Such a garden also would have an abundance of fragrances, plus an added bonus of plenty of herbs to use in wreaths, potpourris, or other projects.

An informal garden could feature billows of poppies, yarrows, and lavenders (one herb nursery offers 46 species and cultivars!). Masses of painted daisies (*Chrysanthemum coccineum*), catmints (*Nepeta* spp.), artemisias, and flax (*Linum* spp.) might be backed by white spikes of Culver's root (*Veronicastrum virginicum*), tall foxgloves (*Digitalis* spp.), or Canadian burnet (*Sanguisorba canadensis*). For further textural interest, try the elegant leaves and umbels of angelica (*Angelica archangelica*), the shaggy blossoms of bee balm (*Monarda* spp.), and the fragrant, frothy plumes of white mugwort (*Artemisia lactiflora*), one of the few artemisias with green leaves.

Gray-leaved plants provide good contrast, but avoid the artemisia cultivars 'Silver King' and 'Silver Queen' unless you confine them with a physical barrier. They are determined spreaders and quite invasive. Two large, attractive silver artemisias that do not spread are 'Lambrook Silver' and 'Powis Castle'. 'Powis Castle' is not reliably hardy north of Zone 6, but cuttings root easily during the summer and can be kept in pots indoors during the winter.

Yarrows (*Achillea* spp.) have been used medicinally for ages and belong in any herb garden. They now come in wonderful colors—shades of rose, buff, apricot, and crimson, as well as their usual yellows, white, and pink. Still pretty in the garden are the old 'Coronation Gold', in deep yellow, and the pale lemon 'Moonshine'. The flowers of 'Coronation Gold' dry particularly well for winter bouquets.

Include hyssop (*Hyssopus officinalis*) and anise hyssop (*Agastache foeniculum*) in an informal herb garden, too. Although members of the mint family, they spread by means of seeds instead of stolons. The ordinary hyssop is a bushy, 2′ plant whose flowers come in blue, pink, or white. Anise hyssop is taller and produces dense spikes

HERBS FOR SHADY GARDENS

Although most herbs require a sunny site, there are some herbs that will grow in shade. Provide these shade-loving herbs with loose, rich soil and plenty of moisture. This list includes herbs grown for fragrance, culinary uses, and teas. Many are American natives that were used medicinally. Grow them from seed or buy plants from nurseries that propagate their own stock, rather than gathering them from the wild.

Anthriscus cerefolium (chervil): white-flowered annual; culinary herb

Asarum canadense (wild ginger): attractive groundcover; used medicinally

Caulophyllum thalictroides (blue cohosh): blue berries (poisonous); roots used medicinally

Cimicifuga racemosa (black snakeroot): spikes of small white flowers; roots used medicinally

Coptis groenlandica (common goldthread): small shiny-leaved plant with threadlike yellow creeping roots used medicinally and for dye

Galium odoratum (sweet woodruff): low-growing plant with white flowers; excellent groundcover; dried foliage and flowers used for fragrance

Gaultheria procumbens (wintergreen): creeping evergreen with tasty leaves and berries; used medicinally and for teas

Hamamelis virginiana (common witch hazel): shrub with autumn flowers with petals like small yellow ribbons; used medicinally

Hydrastis canadensis (goldenseal): thick yellow root used medicinally and for dye

Melissa officinalis (lemon balm): white-flowered mint-family member; used for fragrance and teas

Mentha spp. (mints): rampant-growing herbs with pungent foliage used medicinally and for fragrance and teas

Myrrhis odorata (sweet cicely): ferny, fragrant foliage; smells of licorice; culinary herb

Polygonatum spp. (Solomon's seals): dangling bell-like flowers; roots used medicinally

Sanguinaria canadensis (bloodroot): white flowers in early spring; used medicinally

Viola odorata (sweet violet): comes in many colors and will spread; used for fragrance

of bluish lavender flowers in August when perennial flowers are scarce.

Culinary sage and other salvias, rue, and orris (*Iris × germanica* var. *florentina*) are other good choices for an informal garden.

Use low-growing or mat-forming herbs to front the tall and midsized plants. Try clove pinks (*Dianthus caryophyllus*), chives, santolinas (both green and gray), and thymes.

Growing Herbs

Herbs are generally undemanding plants. Given adequate light and good soil, they will produce well and suffer from few problems. Some herbs are perennials; others are annuals. Keep in mind that tender perennial herbs will behave like annuals in the Northern states.

Annual Herbs

Common annual herbs are basil, chervil, coriander, dill, summer savory, and parsley, which is actually a biennial that is grown as an annual. More exotic annuals include Jerusalem oak (*Chenopodium botrys*), safflower (*Carthamus tinctorius*), sweet wormwood (*Artemisia annua*), and sweet marigold (*Tagetes lucida*), a substitute for French tarragon. Sweet marjoram is not hardy north of Zone 6, but it lives through the winter in the South.

Plant seeds for chervil, coriander, and dill outdoors where they are to grow, in spring or fall. These herbs are extremely difficult to transplant successfully. If you want a head start on outdoor planting, sow them in peat pots for minimum root disturbance at planting time. Sow sweet wormwood and Jerusalem oak outdoors in autumn.

Herb seedlings are often tiny and slower-growing than weeds, so it makes sense to start them indoors. Start basil, marigolds, marjoram, and summer savory indoors in flats or pots, and move them to the garden when no more cold weather is expected. Parsley takes so long to come up that you might be better off starting it indoors, too. Outdoors, you will be down on your knees every day trying to sort out the baby parsley plants from the weeds, which germinate quickly and will always have a head start.

Some annual herbs, such as dill, self-sow so generously there is no need to plant them year after year if the plot where they are growing is kept weeded. This makes for convenience and good strong plants as well, because self-sown plants are almost always sturdier than those started indoors under lights. For more information on starting herb seeds, see the Seeds and Seedlings entry.

Perennial Herbs

Perennial herbs can be grown from seed, but they take longer to germinate than the annuals. It's better to start out by buying young plants of perennial herbs such as mints, sages, and thymes. Once you've gotten started, increase your supply by dividing plants such as mint or by taking cuttings, which works well for rosemary and myrtle. For more on propagating herbs, see the Division and Cuttings entries.

Many perennial herbs need no help once they're established in your garden. Sweet woodruff (*Galium odoratum*) will supply you with bushels of foliage for potpourri while it covers the ground. Chamomile, chives, feverfew, garlic chives, lemon balm, and winter savory will self-sow eternally.

Horehound, oregano, and thyme usually sow some seedlings, but fennel and lovage seem to stay in one place without multiplying. Some of the catmints (*Nepeta* spp.) self-sow; others don't.

You may prefer to propagate certain perennial herbs by means of cuttings because they are especially beautiful forms or cultivars. (Plants propagated from seed don't always resemble their parents, whereas those from cuttings do.) If you have a fine lavender such as 'Hidcote' and you would like to have more without paying for more plants from the nursery, take 3"-4" cuttings of the semi-hard tips and gently remove the lower leaves. Press the cuttings into a mixture of damp peat and sand in a light but not sunny spot, cover with a cloche or jar, and start yourself some new plants. You can also do this with thymes, taking cuttings from a silvery or variegated plant or any one that you especially like. Lemon verbena is sterile and must be propagated this way. Luckily, it roots readily.

French tarragon (*Artemisia dracunculus* var. *sativa*) must be purchased as a plant, since it never sets viable seed. The so-called Russian tarragon offered as seed has no culinary value. When French tarragon is grown in sun or part sun and in light, well-watered but well-drained soil, it usually thrives and spreads enough to divide one plant into many each spring. It is hardy at least through Zone 5. However, if you do not succeed with it, due to severe cold or to high summer temperatures in your area, try the annual marigold from Mexico and South America called sweet marigold (*Tagetes lucida*). It makes an excellent substitute.

General Care

Like nearly all plants, herbs require well-drained soil. While most do best in full sun, they will accept as little as 6 hours of sunlight a day. Incorporate compost or other organic matter into the soil regularly. Cultivate carefully to keep out weeds. Mulch everything except the Mediterranean plants (marjoram, oregano, rosemary, sage, winter savory, and thyme) with a fine, thick material that neither acidifies the soil nor keeps out the rain. Avoid pine bark (chipped or shredded) and peat. Mediterranean plants prefer being weeded to being mulched, since they are used to growing on rocky hills with no accumulation of vegetable matter around their woody stems. In the colder areas of the country, protect your plantings of catmint, horehound, lavender, rue, thyme, winter savory, and sage with evergreen boughs in the winter.

Gardeners who grow their plants out in the sun and wind will have little trouble with disease or insect damage. Basil is sometimes subject to attack by chewing insects, but if you follow good cultural practices and grow enough plants, the damage can be ignored. You'll rarely have the need to take measures to control insect pests on herbs. It's best never to apply botanical insecticides to culinary herbs.

Overwintering Tender Perennials

To overwinter frost-tender herbs such as rosemary (*Rosmarinus officinalis*), sweet bay (*Laurus nobilis*), myrtle (*Myrtus communis*), pineapple sage (*Salvia elegans*), and lemon verbena (*Aloysia triphylla*), you can either grow them permanently in pots or take cuttings of plants at the end of the season, root them, then pot them and hold them over the winter indoors until the following spring. This method works well for nonwoody herbs like basils and pineapple sage.

Shrubby or woody plants, like sweet bay or rosemary, are best grown in pots so they can be moved indoors when winter cold threatens. In summer, set them in a spot outdoors where they get morning but not afternoon sun. Some gar-

deners take their tender herbs out of the winter pots and put them into the ground for the summer. However, this is an extremely stressful procedure for the plants, because the roots they send out in garden soil have to be chopped back in fall and forced into pots for the winter.

During the winter months indoors, keep herbs in a cool, sunny window. Make sure they don't ever dry out. Rosemary especially must be watered frequently, although never left to sit in water. Verbenas will shed most or all of their leaves during the winter. Water them very sparingly until early spring, when tiny leaf buds begin to appear along their branches.

These plants don't really object to being grown in pots, but they don't tolerate being in-

Drying herbs. Tie herbs in loose bunches and hang from a folding rack in an airy but dark room. They'll air dry in about two weeks.

doors very well. You may have to help them fight off bugs and diseases during the winter months. Potted herbs in the house may become afflicted with scale, aphids, or other pests. (Scented geraniums are the exception; these plants tend to shrug off pests.) Keep a close watch for signs of infestation. See the Houseplants entry for information on controlling these pests. In spring, move the plants outside. Within a few days, their relief will be visible, and they'll start growing happily again.

Before bringing herbs in for the winter, turn them out of their pots and put them into larger ones, adding new soil mixed with compost. When, after some years, the pots have reached the limit of what you want to lift, turn out the plants and root-prune them. If the roots form a solid, pot-shaped lump (as they certainly will in the case of rosemary), take a cleaver or large kitchen knife and slice off an inch or two all the way around. Fill in the extra space with fresh soil and compost. Cut back ¼ to ⅓ of the top growth to balance what you have removed from the bottom.

Harvesting and Storing

Cut and use your herbs all summer while they are at their very best. The flavor of herb leaves is at its peak just as the plants begin to form flower buds. Cut herbs in midmorning, after the sun has dried the leaves but before it gets too hot. You can cut back as much as ¾ of a plant without hurting it. (When harvesting parsley, remove the outside leaves so that the central shoot remains). Remove any damaged or yellow foliage. If the plants are dirty, rinse them quickly in cold water and drain them well.

You will want to save some herbs for the winter months. Drying is an easy way to preserve herbs, although you can also freeze them in plastic bags or preserve them in olive oil.

Air drying: Dry herbs as quickly as possible in a dark, airy place. Attics and barns are ideal, but any breezy room that can be kept dark will do. Hang the branches by the stems, or strip off the leaves and dry them on racks through which air can circulate. Drying on racks is the best way to handle large-leaved herbs such as sweet basil or comfrey. It's also good for drying rose petals or other fragrant flowers for potpourris.

To keep air-dried herbs dust-free and out of the light while drying, you can cover them with brown paper bags. Tie the cut herbs in loose bunches, small enough so that they don't touch the sides of the bag, then tie the bag closed around the ends of the stems. Label the bag.

After a few weeks, test for dryness. When the leaves are completely dry and crisp, rub them off the stems and store them in jars out of the light.

Oven drying: You can also dry herbs on racks made of metal screening in a gas oven that has a pilot light. Turn twice a day for several days. Or dry in an oven at very low heat—150°F or lower. When herbs are crisp, remove the leaves from the stems and crumble them into jars.

Microwave drying: Microwave-dried herbs retain excellent color and potency. Start by laying the herb foliage in a single layer on a paper towel, either on the oven rack or on the glass insert. Cover the leaves with another paper towel and microwave on high for 1 minute. Then check the herbs, and if they are still soft, keep testing at 20- to 30-second intervals. Microwave ovens differ in power output, so you'll have to experiment. Keep track of your results with each kind of herb.

Microwave drying is a bit easier on plant tissue than oven drying, because the water in the herb leaves absorbs more of the energy than the plant tissue does. The water in the leaves gets hot and evaporates—that's why the paper towels get damp during the drying process—leaving drying plant tissue behind. The plant

CULINARY HERBS

There's a broad range of herbs for adding flavors to everything from salad dressing to dessert. This list includes popular herbs for livening up your meals.

Angelica (*Angelica archangelica*): in salads, soups, stews, desserts

Caraway (*Carum carvi*): with vegetables or in soups, stews, or bread

Chervil (*Anthriscus cerefolium*): in soups and stews, or with fish or vegetables

Chives (*Allium schoenoprasum*): add to soups, salads, and sandwiches

Coriander (*Coriandrum sativum*): in salad, stew, or relish; popular in Thai cooking

Dill (*Anethum graveolens*): with fish or vegetables; in salads or sauces; seed used for pickling

French tarragon (*Artemisia dracunculus* var. *sativa*): in salads or sauces; with meat, fish, or vegetables

Garlic (*Allium sativum*); with all kinds of foods, except desserts

Garlic chives (*Allium tuberosum*): add to soups, salads, and sandwiches

Lovage (*Levisticum officinale*): use like celery, in soups, stews, salads, or sauces

Mint (*Mentha* spp.): in jellies, sauces, or teas; with meats, fish, or vegetables

Oregano (*Origanum heracleoticum*): in sauces, or with cheese, eggs, meats, or vegetables

Parsley (*Petroselinum crispum*): use with all kinds of foods, except desserts

Rosemary (*Rosemarinus officinalis*): with meat or vegetables; in soups or sauces

Sage (*Salvia officinalis*): with eggs, poultry, or vegetables

Savory (*Satureja* spp.): in soups or teas, or with vegetables

Sweet basil (*Ocimum basilicum*): with meats or vegetables, in sauces

Sweet bay (*Laurus nobilis*): in soups, stews, or sauces

Sweet marjoram (*Origanum majorana*): use like oregano

Thyme (*Thymus vulgaris*): with meat or vegetables

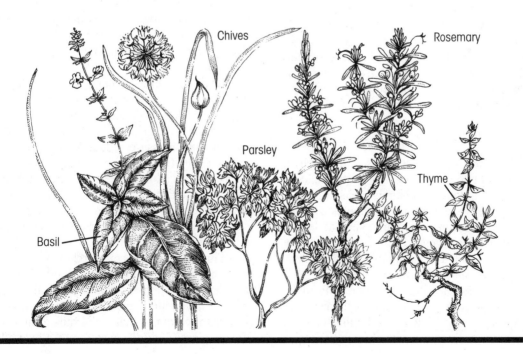

Chives

Rosemary

Parsley

Thyme

Basil

tissue heats up a little because of contact with the water, but the water absorbs most of the heat. In a conventional oven, all the plant material gets hot, not just the water.

Using Herbs

If you have only a tub or two in which to grow herbs, you might plant a few culinary herbs or lavender for fragrance. If you have a big garden, you can experiment with medicinal plants as well as with material to dry for winter bouquets, wreaths, and potpourris.

Herbs for Cooking

If you're not accustomed to using herbs in cooking, start out by exercising restraint. If you overdo it, you might find you have overwhelmed the original flavor of the meat or vegetable whose flavor you meant to enhance. Remember that dried herbs are more powerful, ounce for ounce, than fresh ones. Study herb cookbooks, and when you've learned the usual combinations (French tarragon with fish or chicken, or basil with tomatoes and eggplant, for instance), experiment on your own. You could invent some new and wonderful dishes. See "Culinary Herbs" on page 319 for a list of herbs to get you started.

Herbs for Teas

While you're gathering herbs for the kitchen, include some to use for tea. Herbal teas can be soothing, stimulating, or simply pleasant. Many of them are wonderful aids to digestion or for allaying cold symptoms. Some, such as lemon balm, pineapple sage, and lemon verbena, make refreshing iced tea or additions to iced drinks.

You can make herb tea with dried or fresh leaves, flowers, or other plant parts. To make herb tea, place leaves into an earthenware or china pot or mug. Start with 1 tablespoon of dried herbs or 2 tablespoons of fresh herbs per cup, and adjust the quantity to suit your own taste as you gain experience. Then add boiling water, and steep for 5-10 minutes before straining.

One word of caution: Not all herbs are suitable for making tea. If you're interested in experimenting with herbal-tea making, remember that some herbs can make you ill if ingested. Research before you drink. See "Tea Herbs" on the opposite page for a list of herbs you can safely brew and sip.

Herbs as Medicines

Until quite recently in human history, herbs were the only medicines available. Herbal medicine has a rich and fascinating history. For example, the Doctrine of Signatures theorized that the shape of a leaf or flower indicated the human organ a plant was designed to heal; thus, hepatica, having liver-shaped leaves, was thought to cure diseases of that organ. Pliny listed 70 diseases for which leeks were used as medicine. While we wouldn't agree today with the old Roman doctors as to the great healing power of leeks, it is astonishing to find how many of the herbs we use in cooking have medicinal as well as culinary value.

Marjoram, mint, oregano, sage, and thyme all help in digestion. Garlic is antiseptic, as well as being an effective aid in the treatment of colds, influenza, and bronchitis. Onions are said to lower blood pressure, reduce blood cholesterol, and aid circulation. Coriander, parsley, rosemary, savory, and sorrel have been and are still being used as remedies for minor ills. It's comforting to think that as we add herbs to our food to enhance the flavor, we are promoting our health at the same time.

Through centuries of searching and experimenting, we have found certain plants that contain elements to help heal many of our ills. Some of them have long been part of our pharmacopoeia and remain so today; digitalis, from common foxglove (*Digitalis purpurea*), for example,

TEA HERBS

Of all the uses that herbs have, the one people most enjoy is making and drinking herb tea. Historically, herb teas were used as medicine, and many people still brew and drink them today for medicinal effect. For others, herb tea is simply the beverage of choice. Brew a tasty pot from any of the following herbs. Herb name is followed by parts to be used for brewing.

Angelica (*Angelica archangelica*): leaves
Bee balm (*Monarda didyma*): leaves
Catnip (*Nepeta cataria*): leaves and flowers
Chamomile (*Chamaemelum nobile*): flowers

Costmary (*Chrysanthemum balsamita*): leaves
Elderberry (*Sambucus* spp.): flowers
Lemon balm (*Melissa officinalis*): leaves
Lemon thyme (*Thymus × citriodorus*): leaves
Lemon verbena (*Aloysia triphylla*): leaves
Mints (*Mentha* spp.): leaves
Roses (*Rosa* spp.): hips and petals
Rosemary (*Rosmarinus officinalis*): leaves
Sage (*Salvia officinalis*): leaves
Scented geraniums (*Pelargonium* spp.): leaves

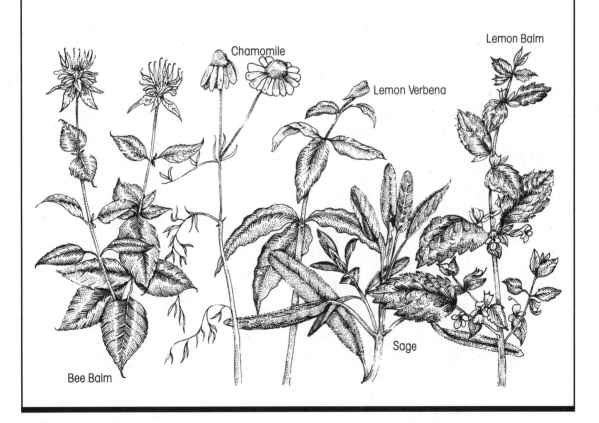

Chamomile

Lemon Balm

Lemon Verbena

Sage

Bee Balm

COMMON HOME REMEDIES

Home remedies can save money, and some are very effective. Be sure to check and double-check the identity of a plant before using it as a remedy.

Aloe (*Aloe barbadensis*): Juice of cut leaves soothes small burns and insect stings.

Broadleaf plantain (*Plantago major*): Crushed leaves soothe insect bites and poison ivy.

Chamomile (*Chamaemelum nobile*): Tea from flowers aids digestion and upset stomachs.

Cranberry (*Vaccinium macrocarpon*): Drinking cranberry juice helps prevent/cure bladder infection; taking 2–4 cranberry capsules with lots of water is also effective.

Dandelion (*Taraxacum officinale*): Leaves are a rich source of vitamins. Dried root is a mild laxative.

Flax (*Linum usitatissimum*): Crushed seed wrapped in a cloth may be used as poultice for sores or insect bites.

Garlic (*Allium sativum*): Raw garlic or the juice from crushed cloves mixed with hot water or honey is a cold and sore throat remedy.

Hens-and-chickens (*Sempervivum* spp.): Juice from cut leaves soothes burns and insect stings.

Horehound (*Marrubium vulgare*): Tea from dried leaves helps soothe coughs and acts as an expectorant.

Peppermint (*Mentha × piperita*): Tea made from leaves can soothe an upset stomach.

Rosemary (*Rosmarinus officinalis*): Tea made from leaves and flowers is good for colds and indigestion.

Roses (*Rosa* spp.): Tea made from rose hips is high in vitamin C and good for colds. It also acts as a laxative.

Sage (*Saliva officinalis*): Tea made from the foliage is good for indigestion and cold symptoms.

Sweet fern (*Comptonia peregrina* var. *asplenifolia*): Juice from crushed stems stops itching of poison ivy.

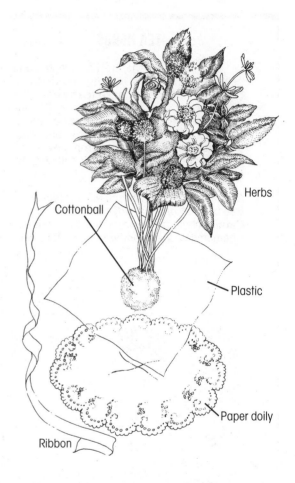

Herbs

Cottonball

Plastic

Paper doily

Ribbon

Fashion a tussie-mussie. In Victorian days, people used these pretty little bouquets to exchange greetings in the language of flowers—a rose or two (for love) combined with southernwood (constancy) might speak of enduring love, for instance. Today, dainty tussie-mussies are still fun to make and give. Collect a handful of herbs of different textures—a strong accent of color or shape in the center, surrounded by leafy and wispy snippings, and framed with an outer ring of attractive leaves. Remove any unsightly bits and strip off lower leaves. Put a moist cotton ball in the middle of a small square of plastic wrap. Fold the plastic around the stems, and wrap at top with florist's tape. Insert the bouquet through a paper doily and secure with a florist's pin. Decorate with a twist of ribbon.

has been used to treat heart disorders for hundreds of years. In Europe and America, herbs are usually used only by healers outside the mainstream of Western medical practice; in Asia, herbs are still an important element in all healing. Since so many of our medicines come from plants, the search goes on for substances that will help our bodies fight afflictions. This is one of the reasons scientists are so alarmed at the rapid destruction of unique plant communities such as the rain forests.

While amateur herbalists may safely soothe their digestive systems by drinking mint tea, beware of doctoring yourself or others with extracts or infusions of plants whose properties you do not fully understand. A "remedy" from a wild plant is not necessarily safe, because "natural" substances are not automatically benign. Overdoses or even small doses of a plant such as foxglove can kill rather than save. See "Common Home Remedies" on the opposite page for suggestions for safe herbal treatments.

Herbs for Fragrance

Flowers release their perfume into the air so freely, you need only walk past to enjoy the scent of roses, lilacs, honeysuckle, clove pinks, or any other highly fragrant flower. Occasionally, we can detect the scent of lavender or thyme when they are baking in the hot sun. But plants with aromatic leaves do not, as a rule, release the odor of their oils unless you rub a leaf or walk on the plant or brush against the branches while working around them.

The leaves of scented geraniums (*Pelargonium* spp.)—just one example of the many fragrant-foliaged herbs—are wonderful to rub. They come in a wide variety of scents, including lemon-rose, lemon, mint, nutmeg, rose, and ginger. Their many different fragrances, and leaf and flower variations, make them fascinating to collectors and gardeners alike.

Lavender, lemon balm, lemon verbena,

FRAGRANT HERBS

Rub a leaf and use your nose to find what smells best to you! Here are some of the herbs that can be used, fresh or dried, for herbal crafts such as wreaths, potpourri, sachets, or arrangements. Plant name is followed by common uses.

Aloysia triphylla (lemon verbena): highly prized for potpourri and tea

Artemisia abrotanum (southernwood): dried branches traditionally hung in closets to repel moths

Artemisia annua (sweet wormwood): sweetly aromatic flowers and foliage make good filler material for herbal wreaths

Chenopodium botrys (Jerusalem oak): fluffy gold branches good for herb wreaths

Galium odoratum (sweet woodruff): leaves especially fragrant when dried; used in potpourri, wreaths, and as a tea

Lavandula angustifolia (lavender): flowers and foliage used in many herbal crafts

Melissa officinalis (lemon balm): used in teas, food, potpourri, and commercially in soap and toilet water

Mentha spp. (mints): fragrant foliage used in teas, potpourris, wreaths, and other herbal crafts; orange mint probably best for fragrance

Monarda didyma (bee balm): blossoms and foliage used in wreaths, potpourris, and teas

Pelargonium spp. (scented geraniums): fragrant leaves used in sachets and potpourris

Rosmarinus officinalis (rosemary): fragrant, needlelike leaves used for tea, cooking, and winter sachets

Salvia elegans (pineapple sage): wonderfully fragrant leaves and scarlet flowers used in wreaths and other herbal crafts

Santolina chamaecyparissus (lavender cotton): used in herb wreaths; odor of gray foliage may be too medicinal for sachets or potpourri

Thymus spp. (thymes): leaves and tops used in sachets and wreaths

Training an herb standard. Choose a young, straight, single-stemmed plant for making an herb standard. Follow these steps to create a rounded-head standard, like a miniature tree, from your herb plant. (1) Insert a slim bamboo stake of the height you want your standard to attain, pushing in the stake until it touches the bottom of the pot. (2) Cut back all side branches below the desired height to 1½". Allow leaves that grow from the main stem to remain. (3) Tie the stem to the stake with slender strips of raffia at 2" intervals. (4) As new shoots appear at top, clip the tips to encourage branching and to make a bushy head. (5) When your plant reaches the desired height, pinch off the tip of the top shoot and remove all the lower leaves and branch stems to within 4"–5" of the top. Shape the head with clippers to form a rounded globe.

scented geraniums, and sweet woodruff are among the best-known herbs grown for fragrance. All can be preserved by air drying (see "Harvesting and Storing" on page 318 for directions). For more suggestions of herbs to grow for fragrant flowers, foliage, or fruit, see "Fragrant Herbs" on page 323.

Sachets and potpourri are two good ways to preserve the scent of herbs for winter. Sachets are made with combinations of dried herb leaves and frequently rose petals, crumbled or ground. You can dry rose petals by spreading them on sheets or screens in a dark, airy place. Petals of apothecary's rose (*Rosa gallica* var. *officinalis*)

are the most fragrant.

Potpourri is a mix of petals and leaves used whole; it can be made with fresh or dried leaves and petals. Some potpourris include dried orange or lemon peel and spices such as cloves and allspice. Experiment with different combinations and see which ones you prefer. The fragrance is usually set with a fixative, such as orris root. See the Potpourri entry for more information.

Companion Planting

Companion planting is nothing new — plants have been doing it on their own since the world

HERBS FOR REPELLING INSECTS

Planting herbs as companion plants in the vegetable and flower garden is a time-honored but not infallible way of helping to deter some pests. See if your most troublesome pests are on this list.

Allium sativum (garlic): useful against aphids, Japanese beetles

Artemisia spp. (artemisias): repels flea beetles, cabbageworms, slugs

Calendula officinalis (pot marigold): deters asparagus beetles

Chrysanthemum cinerariifolium, C. coccineum (pyrethrums): dried flower heads can be used as insect repellent

Chrysanthemum parthenium (feverfew): repels many insects

Coriandrum sativum (coriander): discourages aphids

Lavandula spp. (lavenders): repels moths; combine with southernwood, wormwood, and rosemary in an antimoth sachet

Mentha spp. (mints): deters aphids, cabbage pests, flea beetles

Nepeta cataria (catnip): useful against ants, flea beetles

Ocimum spp. (basils): deter flies and other insects

Pimpinella anisum (anise): repels aphids

Rosmarinus spp. (rosemary): repels moths; use in sachets

Satureja hortensis (summer savory): protects beans against Mexican bean beetles

Tanacetum vulgare (common tansy): discourages Japanese beetles, ants, flies

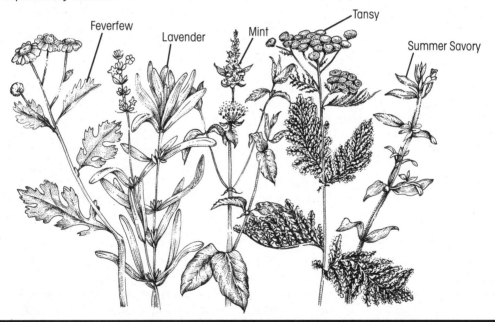

Feverfew Lavender Mint Tansy Summer Savory

began. By studying the ways that plants in the wild manage to be mutually beneficial, we can use some of their systems in our gardens. We can try to give a plant the kind of neighbor that suits it best.

There are many factors to consider when

selecting plants as companions. Some plants are heavy feeders; these might match well with plants that prefer a spare diet. Shallow-rooted plants may grow well near a deep-rooted companion. There are plants whose roots add to or take from the soil elements that are beneficial or harmful to their neighboring plants. Other plants have odors that repel or attract beneficial or harmful insects. Research studies in this field are ongoing, but for some aspects of companion planting, no hard scientific evidence yet exists. No one yet knows for sure why certain plants growing next to one another seem to be mutually beneficial or mutually harmful.

Many herbs are used as companion plants for vegetables and ornamentals. The herbs may help ward off harmful insects, or they may even attract harmful insects, which can then be picked off and destroyed. Companion herbs may be used to attract bees for pollination or because of a benign effect on neighboring plants. You may want to try planting your basil by your tomatoes; mint by the cabbages; and catnip, which discourages flea beetles, by the eggplant. Or try putting a few garlic plants near roses or anything else victimized by Japanese beetles.

Some plants may be detrimental to another's growth; keep dill away from the carrots, fennel away from beans, and garlic and onions away from all legumes. As you carry out experiments in your garden, keep records for your own benefit and perhaps for that of other gardeners. See "Herbs for Repelling Insects" on page 325 and the Companion Planting entry for more suggestions about helpful and harmful plant companions.

Herbs as Standards

A standard plant is one trained to a single stem, with leaves and branches only at the top. Standard roses, sometimes called tree roses, are used in formal gardens or designs. Herbs are sometimes trained as standards to serve as accents in herb gardens, particularly in formal ones. Standard herbs make charming table decorations, especially at holiday time.

A simple design of rounded head atop a single stem is a classic. "Training an Herb Standard" on page 324 gives step-by-step instruc-

More On HERBS

Look for the individual entries on popular herbs for more about using and growing these interesting plants. For more on culinary herbs, see Basil, Garlic, Mint, Onion, Oregano, Parsley, Sage, and Thyme. Herbs often grown for their flowers or other features are listed by botanical name. See Achillea (yarrow), Artemisia (sage), Asarum (wild ginger), Digitalis (foxglove), Echinacea (purple coneflower), Hamamelis (witch hazel), Hibiscus (mallow), Lavandula (lavender), Monarda (bee balm), Pelargonium (geranium), Rosa (rose), and Viola (pansy).

tions for obtaining this shape. You can also create multilayered standards or train herbs into upright wreath shapes.

Choose herbs with a sturdy stem that can support the weight of the full, rounded head. Lemon verbena, myrtle, rosemary, scented geraniums, and sweet bay can be trained into attractive standards. The main stem will thicken with age, but standards should remain tied closely to their stakes to protect them from damage. Running children, animals, or high winds can easily tip them over.

Scented geraniums with a compact growth habit and tightly packed leaves make excellent candidates. With the small-leaved types, aim for a tight globe of foliage and nip off the flowers. The larger-leaved ones are suitable for a less-formal effect; allow them to decorate themselves with flowers if they wish. In fact, they look splendid when blooming.

If you want a scented geranium standard to be 3' tall, remove all sideshoots from the bottom 2' of stem. When the central stem has reached 3', pinch the tip. As the crown burgeons, keep it trimmed to encourage branching. ❖

Heuchera

Alumroot, coral bells. Spring- to summer-blooming perennials.

Description: *Heuchera sanguinea,* coral bells, bear clouds of delicate, ½″ hanging bells in shades of white, pink, red, and green. Flowers are borne on thin, 1½′ stems above low mounds of rounded to maplelike 2″ evergreen leaves. Zones 3-8.

How to grow: Plant or divide in spring when the centers die out. Grow in partial shade in moist but very well drained, humus-rich soil. Plants tolerate full sun in the North if kept moist. Good drainage and loose mulch help reduce freeze-and-thaw winter damage to the fragile roots. Support weak stems with thin, twiggy branches.

Landscape uses: Mass in thin woodlands, in borders, and among rocks. Contrast with hostas, ferns, columbines, or wildflowers.

Best cultivars: 'Bressingham' hybrids in many colors; 'Chatterbox', rose pink; 'June Bride', white; 'Pluie de Feu', red. ❖

Hibiscus

Mallow. Deciduous summer-flowering perennials, small trees, or shrubs.

Description: *Hibiscus coccineus,* scarlet rose mallow, is grown as a shrub in Zone 9 and a perennial in Zones 5-8. It is multi-stemmed, 6′-12′ tall, with 5″-6″ red flowers. *H. syriacus,* rose-of-Sharon, is a shrub or small tree reaching 12′, with 3″-5″ blooms in white, red, pink, or violet. Zones 5-8. Both bloom all season.

How to grow: Hibiscus must have full sun, good drainage, and steady moisture. North of Zone 8, plant in fall or spring; plant in fall or winter for Zones 8-9. Hibiscus bloom on the current season's wood, so prune in the winter for vigorous new growth.

Landscape uses: Scarlet rose mallow is a striking addition to a sunny border. Rose-of-Sharon is best in shrub borders and informal hedges. ❖

Hippeastrum

Amaryllis. Winter- and spring-blooming bulbs for pots.

Description: *Hippeastrum* hybrids, commonly called amaryllis, bear flamboyant 4″-12″ wide, trumpet-shaped blooms in white, pink, red, and salmon, usually in clusters of four on leafless stems normally rising 1′-3′. Arching fans of broad, straplike leaves appear during or after flowering. Hardy only in Zones 9-10, amaryllis are great indoors as flowering, container-grown plants.

How to grow: Choose a pot that will allow about 1″ of growing space between the bulb and the rim. For a suitable soil mix, see the House-plants entry. Plant with ⅓-½ of the bulb above the soil line. Water slightly until growth starts, then water often. Grow in a warm (65°-70°F) spot in a sunny window, especially after the leaves develop. Most bloom 4-8 weeks after growth begins. Once the flowers open, moving the plant to a cool spot out of direct sun will lengthen the life of the flowers.

When the flowers fade, cut off the flower stalk close to the bulb. Return the plant to a sunny window and water regularly. You may keep the plant inside all year, feeding every 2-3 weeks with liquid seaweed, fish emulsion, or other organic fertilizer. You can put your amaryllis outside after frost in a spot with morning sun or under the shade of tall trees, or knock them out of their pots and grow them in the open ground. Gradually reduce water in late summer to encourage dormancy. After a few months' rest, replace the top few inches of soil or repot and begin again.

Best cultivars: 'Dazzler' and 'White Christmas', white; 'Susan' and 'Rose Marie', pink; 'Liberty' and 'Red Lion', red; 'Rilona', salmon; 'Appleblossom', white brushed with pale pink; 'Minerva' and 'Star of Holland', red star on white. Also try the smaller-flowered (4″) red 'Scarlet Baby' and the slightly orange 'Pamela'. ❖

Historical Gardens

Historic sites are popular destinations for school field trips and vacation groups. But most people think of buildings and battlefields, rather than gardens, when they want to see a bit of history. However, there are many historical gardens in North America, and home gardeners may find visits to them to be both fun and educational.

The concept of preserving historical gardens has been slower to develop than the idea of maintaining historical buildings. As early as 1853, a plan was launched to buy and maintain George Washington's Mount Vernon home. It was not until 1936, however, that its kitchen garden was restored.

Many historical gardens are interpretations of the *type* of garden that existed in a particular place and time. These include gardens on the grounds of historical societies, living history farms, and museums. They are an effective way to present gardening styles and methods of past generations, even though they are not restorations of actual gardens.

Other historical gardens are reconstructions. The gardens at Mount Vernon and Monticello were restored and are maintained from detailed plans and notes kept by their illustrious owners.

A few historical gardens have been consistently maintained since they were established. The gardens at Biltmore House in Asheville, North Carolina, designed by nineteenth century landscape architect Fredrick Law Olmsted, remain largely as he designed them.

It's also possible to pick up organic gardening tips at historical gardens, since early growers gardened without benefit of chemical fertilizers or pesticides. For example, at the National Colonial Farm in Accokeek, Maryland, you can see companion plantings of corn, beans, and pumpkins. Corn plants serve as trellises for the beans, beans help build soil nitrogen, and pumpkins cover the ground, shading soil and providing natural weed control. Also, vegetable gardens and orchards at historical sites are good places to see and learn about old-fashioned food plants, known as heirloom plants or heirloom cultivars.

To locate historical gardens in your area — or an area that you plan to visit — consult local historical societies, the chamber of commerce, or garden clubs. Read more about heirloom cultivars in the Heirloom Plants entry. ❖

Horseradish

Armoracia rusticana
Cruciferae

This pungent root crop makes a wonderful sauce for serving with meat and fish, but beware — it's also a vigorous perennial that can quickly spread beyond the boundaries of its planting area and become a difficult-to-eradicate weed.

Planting: Horseradish seldom produces seeds, so you'll need to start plants from root cuttings in moist, rich soil. Horseradish roots can grow several feet deep; good soil preparation will encourage thick, straight roots. Plant root pieces in early spring with the small ends down and the large ends 2″-4″ below soil level; space 1′ apart in rows 3′-4′ apart.

Be aware that horseradish can spread quickly by its roots and will soon fill its space. To control it, either plant it in an out-of-the-way area, or dig it up completely each year and replant only a few of the roots. Another method is to plant it in a bottomless bucket that you've sunk into the soil.

Growing guidelines: Water when needed, particularly in late summer and fall, when the plants do most of their growing.

Harvesting: Pick a few spring leaves as needed for salads; use a spading fork to dig roots in October or November. The hardy roots will keep in the ground for several months; unharvested pieces will sprout the following spring. ❖

Horticultural Therapy

Horticultural therapy involves the cultivation and appreciation of plants and nature to relieve an illness or disability. In a sense, all gardeners practice it when they enjoy working in the garden. People with mild to severe physical, developmental, emotional, and mental disabilities also benefit from the therapeutic effects of plants.

Horticultural therapy is practiced in such diverse settings as rehabilitation and mental health centers, nursing homes, schools, and hospitals. Many older and disabled people practice horticultural therapy in their homes.

Horticultural therapists guide stroke patients through simple tasks such as filling pots with soil. Others may help a recovering alcoholic see how the effects of overwatering plants relate to his or her condition. Some share children's excitement as they watch seeds sprout and grow.

Horticultural therapy programs usually rely on volunteers, including master gardeners. Paid staff usually have a degree in horticultural therapy, occupational therapy, recreation therapy, and/or horticulture. Sometimes teachers do horticultural therapy in the classroom. For more information, contact the American Horticultural Therapy Association, 9220 Wightman Road, Suite 300, Gaithersburg, MD 20879. ❖

Hosta

Hosta, plantain lily, funkia. Summer- and fall-blooming perennials grown primarily for their foliage.

Description: Hostas display 6"-48" wide mounds of lancelike to broad, long-stemmed leaves in green, white, yellow, and bluish solid colors and variegations. Trumpet-shaped flowers, sometimes fragrant but often not very showy, are borne on stalks above the leaves. *Hosta fortunei,* Fortune's hosta, grows into a clump 2'-3' tall and wide of 5"-6" oval leaves. Zones 3-8.

H. plantaginea, August lily, holds 6" sweetly fragrant white trumpets 2' above bold, 8" light green leaves on 3' wide clumps in late summer. Zones 3-8.

H. sieboldiana, Siebold's or seersucker hosta, bears quilted bluish 1' leaves on 2'-3' mounds up to 4' wide. Zones 3-8.

Grow *H. ventricosa,* blue hosta, for its 3" hanging violet bells on 3' stalks above rich green, 8" leaves in 2' wide mounds. Zones 3-8.

How to grow: Plant or divide hostas in spring or fall. They prefer partial to deep shade and moist, well-drained soil with some organic matter. Some can take full sun in the North if kept moist. Yellow- and blue-leaved cultivars color better if given morning sun. Some older cultivars of Fortune's hosta and blue hosta withstand very dry soil and deep shade. Slugs and snails can chew holes in emerging leaves in spring; otherwise, hostas are easy, tough plants.

Landscape uses: Grow in groups or, with showy cultivars, as specimens. Hostas cover dying bulb foliage and lighten up dark, shady areas under trees or in corners.

Best cultivars: There are many fine species and cultivars, including *H. sieboldiana:* 'Frances Williams', yellow-edged; *H. plantaginea:* 'Royal Standard', more sun-tolerant; *H. fortunei:* 'Gold Standard', light gold edged in green. ❖

Hotbed

Hotbeds are boxlike structures with a regular source of heat. Gardeners use hotbeds to protect their plants from harsh weather conditions. Traditionally, the heat source for hotbeds was rotting manure in a pit underlying the hotbed frame. Today, most gardeners rely on electric cables to provide heat. See the Cold Frames entry for information on making and using a hotbed. ❖

Houseplants

Houseplants offer beautiful foliage, brilliant flowers, and enticing fragrances. You can assure your plants will thrive if you understand their basic needs.

Starting Off Right

When you buy a new plant, it should include a label with information about its light, moisture, soil, and temperature requirements. Check this *before* you buy the plant—some need high humidity or other conditions that may be difficult for you to provide. Buy plants from a reputable plant store. Choose plants that look well taken care of and vigorous. Inspect plants closely for signs of insects or disease; be sure to check the underside of the leaves and stems. If you see any insects or signs of insect feeding such as holes, punctures, or deposits of leaking sap, don't buy. Portions of the plant that are wilted, yellowish, reddish, or brownish, have speckled leaves, or have dead areas also may indicate disease or insect damage. If you see anything suspicious, don't buy the plant. If you do not know what the plant should look like, ask a knowledgeable salesperson. Keep in mind that many commercial houseplants have been treated with systemic pesticides. If you buy a treated plant, or if you're not sure whether it's been treated, wear rubber gloves when you first repot it to be safe.

Light Is the Key

All plants need light, some much more than others. When selecting a plant, be sure its light requirements match your proposed location. A plant that needs direct sun will slowly die in a dim corner.

The number and position of the windows in a room and the location of a plant determine the amount of light it gets. Light intensity drops off rapidly as you move away from a window. Plants that aren't receiving enough light often become elongated and pale. Or they may just fail to grow at all and drop their lower leaves. (A plant moved

---

BEST PLANTS FOR LOW-LIGHT LOCATIONS

Try these low-light houseplants.

Aglaonema commutatum (Chinese evergreen)
Aspidistra elatior (cast-iron plant)
Chlorophytum comosum (spider plant)
Cissus antarctica (kangaroo vine)
Cissus rhombifolia (grape ivy)
Dracaena marginata (dragon tree)
Philodendron spp. (philodendrons)
Spathiphyllum wallisii (spathe flower)

---

from a greenhouse into your home may also drop some leaves at first as it adjusts to the lower light levels.) Too much light, on the other hand, may burn the leaves of low-light plants.

Most houses have many good locations for plants that need low light and fewer suitable locations for plants that need moderate to bright light. Add shelves or plant hangers to windows or provide plant growth lights to increase the amount of space you have available. Rotate two plants that need moderate light between a low and a high-light location every few days.

An excellent way to increase the amount of light your plants receive is to use them to decorate your patio or garden in summer. Direct sunlight can easily burn leaves of houseplants accustomed to low light levels. *Always* place them in the shade at first and gradually move only those that like direct light out into sunnier locations. You may need to water smaller plants daily during hot spells, especially those in clay pots.

Watering

Various factors including size of containers, season, rate of growth, light, and temperature will affect how much water each plant requires. Some plants need water only when the soil surface has dried out, while others need to be kept constantly moist. You shouldn't follow a strict schedule year-round, because you may overwater or underwater. Learn each plant's preference, and check each pot before you water.

There are various ways of determining how much moisture is in the soil. Don't wait until the plant wilts to water it. Looking at the surface color helps, but doesn't tell the whole story. Learn to judge how moist the soil is by hefting the pot. Or push your finger into the soil an inch or so and feel for moistness. Avoid overwatering; if in doubt, wait.

Always water thoroughly, until water seeps out the bottom of the pot. Use pots with drainage holes and saucers, but never allow plants to sit in water. If the soil becomes very dry, it may shrink away from the pot sides, allowing water to run through rapidly without being absorbed. If this happens, add water slowly until the soil is saturated, or set the pot in a tub of water for a few minutes. Water will also run out rapidly if the plant is rootbound.

Feeding

Plants growing in a rich potting mix containing organic matter and bonemeal need little additional fertilizer if repotted regularly. During active growth in spring and summer, most plants appreciate regular doses of a liquid organic fertilizer such as fish emulsion. Mix at half the strength recommended on the label, and apply at the recommended frequency or more often as needed. Fertilize less during the winter, when lower temperatures and light levels slow most plants' growth.

Temperature and Humidity

Many popular houseplants are well suited to the warm, dry conditions found in most homes. Others, such as many ferns, will only do well if you provide extra humidity. Place a large saucer filled with water and pebbles under the pot, but be sure the pot doesn't sit in water. Mist plants often, run an electric humidifier, or group several plants together to increase humidity.

It's important to know what temperature your plants prefer. Some plants require cool winter temperatures to either bloom or to overwinter successfully. South African plants like clivias need a cool, dry rest period to bloom. Overwintering plants such as rosemary and sweet bay do best with cool winter temperatures.

Natural light. Light-loving plants should be placed as close to windows as possible. Remove sheer curtains and keep windows clean to maximize light. Wash plants regularly to remove dust. If your windowsills are narrow, install shelf brackets under the sills and add boards to widen the windowsills. You can also install several shelves across a window and create a curtain of plants. Heavy plexiglass is good for upper shelves. Use wood screws to mount brackets to wooden window frames. To mount brackets on the wall next to the window, use appropriate wall anchors.

Organic Potting Soil

Good soil structure and fertility are maintained outside by the addition of organic matter, and by freezing, thawing, and earthworm activity—conditions that don't occur in the soil of indoor plants. For that reason a good organic potting mix is important for houseplants. As they grow, your plants should be repotted into fresh soil in larger containers. Use commercial potting soil (be aware that it may contain synthetic chemical fertilizers and very little organic matter) or blend your own. If you have a lot of plants, you may want to make your own mix, both to save money and to provide a rich organic soil.

To prepare a good potting mix, combine: 1-2 parts commercial potting soil or good garden soil; 1 part builder's sand or perlite; and 1 part peat moss, compost, or leaf mold. Add 1 tablespoon of bonemeal per quart of mix.

Each of these components provides specific benefits to the plants: Soil contains essential minerals. Sand and perlite assure good drainage, which prevents disease and allows air to reach the roots. Sand will make the mix much heavier. Perlite, an expanded volcanic rock with many tiny air spaces, will make it lighter.

Compost or leaf mold (organic matter) makes the mix rich. They release nutrients slowly, help maintain proper soil pH, improve soil drainage, and hold moisture. Peat moss is acidic and has few nutrients but greatly increases the water-holding capacity of a mix.

For plants that need extra-rich soil, double the amount of compost or leaf mold. If the plant needs acid soil, double the amount of peat moss. For cacti and succulents that like drier conditions, add an extra ½-1 part coarse sand.

You may want to add other organic amendments such as blood meal, cottonseed meal, rock phosphate, or greensand. See the Fertilizers entry for specific nutrient content of each. See the Container Gardening entry for more information on adding soil amendments to potting mixtures and for blending potting mixtures to use in large pots.

Repotting

Repotting—moving a plant into a larger pot—keeps the root system in balance with the foliage and adds fresh soil and nutrients. Generally, the best time to do your repotting is in the spring when most plants resume active growth. It's a great outdoor activity for a sunny spring day. Remember not to put your newly repotted plants in full sun right away though. Move a plant to a pot only a few inches larger in diameter—enough to allow about 1" (or 2" for larger plants) of fresh soil around the root ball in the new container. If you repot in too big a pot, the extra soil may hold too much moisture, or the plant may not flower.

To determine if it's time to repot, place one hand on the surface of the soil with the stem between your fingers, flip the pot upside down, and tap the bottom of the pot to loosen the root ball. If lots of roots are visible on the root ball and beginning to circle the pot, it's time to repot. For large plants that are harder to remove from their pots, check for roots coming up to the surface—this is also a sign that the plant is due to be repotted.

To repot, work the circling roots loose. Place the plant's root ball in the new pot, and fill around it with fresh potting mix. Keep the plant at the same depth in the soil, placing it so that the soil surface is 1" below the pot rim. Don't push the new soil down too firmly, just water thoroughly after repotting to firm it.

Containers

Whatever containers you choose, be sure they have holes in the bottom, and use saucers to catch the excess water. If you use unglazed clay saucers, be sure to use plastic liners to protect furniture and floors. Or set pots and saucers on trivets or trays for protection.

Clay pots are porous. Air can pass through them to plant roots, and excess moisture can evaporate more easily. They are a good choice for plants that like dry conditions. They are heavy, which can help prevent top-heavy plants from tipping over but makes larger plants difficult to move.

Plastic is lightweight and a good choice for plants that might dry out too easily in clay pots. It also stays clean looking, while clay pots may become discolored with use. Air can't pass through plastic to roots, but this won't be a problem if you use plenty of sand or perlite to ensure good soil aeration.

Pests and Diseases

If you grow your plants in a good organic potting mix, give them the correct amount of water and light, and repot regularly, you shouldn't have many insect or disease problems. Avoid bringing problems in on new plants.

It's a good idea to inspect your plants regularly so that if a problem develops, you catch it early. Isolate suspect plants. Yellowing or discolored leaves may mean disease or incorrect light or watering practices. Overwatering probably kills more houseplants than anything else does. Double-check the plant's requirements, remove damaged areas, and watch for developments.

Damaged or deformed plants or sticky deposits may indicate insect problems. These pests are common on indoor plants:

Mealybugs: These insects look like tiny tufts of white cotton. They are often found under leaves and in sheltered areas of stems. Both the immature stage and the adults can crawl, but often cluster together in one place. Remove each insect with rubbing alcohol on a cotton swab, or spray with insecticidal soap.

Whiteflies: These ubiquitous pests are about 1/16" long. They fly around in a cloud whenever an infested plant is disturbed. Wipe crawling young off of the underside of leaves, vacuum up the flying white adults, spray with insecticidal soap, or place a yellow sticky trap on a stake in each pot to catch them.

Mites: Mites are tiny pests about the size of a grain of salt. You are likely to notice plant symptoms before you actually see the pests themselves. Leaves attacked by mites are stippled or mottled; flowers may be deformed. Wash plants with a hose or shower to remove pests, mist daily, and spray with insecticidal soap.

Aphids: Aphids are small, translucent, pear-shaped insects. They may be many colors including white, green, and black. Sticky deposits of plant sap in growing tips may indicate aphid activity. Remove these soft-bodied sucking insects by hand or wash them off with sprayed water.

Whatever treatment you use for any of these pests, repeat it several times to control later hatchings. ❖

Hyacinthus

Hyacinth. Spring-blooming bulbs.

Description: *Hyacinthus orientalis,* hyacinths, bear many 1" starry flowers in white, pink, red, yellow, blue, and violet. The sweetly fragrant flowers are borne in loose to dense clusters about 1' above straplike leaves. Zones 3-8; give winter protection in Zones 3-5.

How to grow: Plant bulbs with the tops about 5" below ground in a sunny spot with average, well-drained soil enriched with rotted manure or compost. Fertilize lightly when shoots emerge in spring. After flowering, allow the foliage to yellow before removing it. If rodents dig and eat the bulbs, plant bulbs in wire mesh cages.

Landscape uses: The biggest bulbs produce the largest, densest spikes for formal beds and forcing in pots. Smaller bulbs produce more graceful stems that are lovely in borders, shrub plantings, and woods. ❖

Hydrangea

Hydrangea. Deciduous summer-blooming shrubs or small trees.

Description: *Hydrangea arborescens,* smooth hydrangea or hills-of-snow, forms a 2'-5' spreading mound. It has large (3"-6"), deep green oval leaves. Dense, flat or rounded flower clusters grow on the current season's wood. Zones 4-8.

H. macrophylla, bigleaf hydrangea or florist's hydrangea, reaches 3'-6' tall. It bears pink flowers when grown in near-neutral soils and blue in acidic soils. There are two types of cultivars: Hortensia types form round flower clusters; lacecap types have flat clusters of small, fertile flowers surrounded by an outer circle of larger, showier sterile flowers. Both types bloom on the previous year's wood. Zones 6-8.

H. paniculata, panicle hydrangea, grows in tree or shrub form to a height of 4'-15'. It blooms on the current season's wood, with pyramidal clusters of creamy white, mostly sterile flowers. Zones 4-9.

H. quercifolia, oakleaf hydrangea, reaches 6' tall and has rich, cinnamon brown, layered bark when mature. Showy 10" flower panicles change from white to pink to brown. Large, lobed leaves turn red to burgundy in fall. Zones 5-8.

How to grow: Hydrangeas prefer evenly moist, humus-rich soil with good drainage. They will grow in partial shade or in full sun, provided they receive adequate soil moisture. Prune bigleaf hydrangea after blooming and the others in winter. Unless you have a tree form, cut older branches to the ground.

Landscape uses: Smooth hydrangea and oakleaf hydrangea are most at home in a woodland garden; they also look attractive in massed plantings and foundation plantings. Large plants make striking specimens. Bigleaf hydrangea and panicle hydrangea have strong form and color; use them sparingly as specimens. ❖

Hydroponics

Even the richest garden soil is useless to plants unless its nutrients are dissolved in water so they can be absorbed by roots. That's the idea behind hydroponics, the science of growing plants without soil: As long as plants get the right mix of essential elements, and the proper light and temperature, they grow just as well in trays of swirling nutrient solutions as in a rain-washed garden.

The old-fashioned habit of keeping rooted coleus clippings in a jar of water is a simple hydroponic system. Modern hydroponic methods, which produce high-quality crops of tomatoes, squash, cucumbers, lettuce, and other vegetables, call for carefully orchestrated mixtures of pure chemicals. Light, humidity, and temperature are all closely regulated. An inert growing medium, such as pea-size gravel or perlite, supports the roots. Nutrient solution is pumped or soaked through the medium, then drained and collected for reuse.

Commercial hydroponic systems rely on chemicals mixed according to a precise formula: nitrogen, phosphorus, and potassium, plus calcium, zinc, iron, and an assortment of others. Organic hydroponics relies on nutrient teas, home-brewed from manure or compost, and seaweed concentrate, which supplies essential trace minerals. A few commercial products tailored to organic hydroponics are available, such as a blend of bat guano and worm castings.

Organic hydroponics, just as organic gardening, is an intuitive approach that depends on the gardener's eye rather than the chemical scale. The commercial world has left organic hydroponics to inventive home gardeners and other researchers and to Third World countries. In India and New Guinea, organic hydroponic systems that make use of pragmatic ingredients like hoof meal and rusty nails have been producing good food for years. ❖

Iberis

Candytuft. Spring- and summer-blooming annuals and perennials.

Description: *Iberis umbellata,* annual candytuft, produces 1″ clusters of tiny flowers in shades of white, pink, red-violet, and purple through much of the summer on upright plants to 15″.

I. sempervirens, perennial candytuft, is actually an evergreen shrub that bears similar white flowers on 6″-12″ spreading mounds of narrow, dark green leaves. Most cultivars bloom only in spring. Zones 4-8.

How to grow: Sow the annual type where it is to bloom in a sunny or lightly shaded spot with average, moist but well-drained soil; allow to reseed for bloom next year. Plant or divide perennial candytuft in spring or fall; give it similar conditions. Cut back partway after bloom for compact growth and possible rebloom in fall. Water during drought. Mulch in summer, and lightly cover with pine needles or straw in winter to prevent sun and wind damage.

Landscape uses: Plant at the front of borders, among rocks, or in cottage gardens.

Best cultivars: *I. umbellata* mix: 'Dwarf Fairyland', 9″-12″. *I. sempervirens:* reblooming 8″ 'Autumn Snow'; tiny 6″ 'Little Gem'. ❖

Ilex

Holly. Evergreen or deciduous shrubs or trees.

Description: *Ilex × attenuata* is an evergreen with an upright, narrowly pyramidal form, growing 20′-30′ tall. The leaves are small, dark green, and glossy. The fruits, which are red and rounded, appear on the current year's growth. Zones 6-8.

I. cornuta, Chinese holly, is twiggy, dense, and rounded, with flowers blooming on the previous year's growth. Fruits are red and rounded; the evergreen leaves are glossy green and five-spined, with the terminal spine pointing downward. Zones 6-8.

I. crenata, Japanese holly, is a densely layered, compact evergreen with small, notched leaves and black fruit. Many cultivars exist; most are much smaller than the species, which grows to 15′ tall in the landscape. Zones 6-8.

I. × meserveae, blue holly, bears spiny blue-green leaves, purplish stems, and red berries. This evergreen grows about 7′ tall. Zones 5-7.

I. opaca, American holly, is pyramidal in youth, open and irregular with age. Growing to heights of 15′-30′ in the landscape, this native may reach 50′ in the wild. The evergreen leaves are spiny, dull dark green above, and yellow-green beneath. Dull red berries form on the current year's growth. Zones 5-9.

I. verticillata is the swamp-dwelling native winterberry. It has a twiggy, rounded habit and grows 6'-10' tall. Plumlike leaves fall in the autumn, exposing plentiful brilliant red berries that are very effective in massed plantings. Zones 4-9.

I. vomitoria, yaupon, is a southeastern native with an upright, irregular tree form and mounded shrub form. Yaupon has smooth gray twigs, notched evergreen leaves, and translucent red berries. The shrub form grows 3' tall; the tree form grows 15'-30'. Zones 7-9.

How to grow: Hollies are dioecious, meaning that individual plants are either male or female. Therefore, with few exceptions, you must have a male holly in the vicinity in order to have a nice crop of berries. Purchase hollies from a reliable source to ensure that you get both male and female plants. Hollies need full sun to partial shade and evenly moist, well-drained, humusy soil. Avoid windy sites and (except for winterberry) poor drainage.

Landscape uses: Plant hollies in groups for hedges, barriers, screens, or a mass effect. A single specimen makes a stunning focal point. Hollies are also good in natural landscapes, since their berries provide food for wildlife.

Best cultivars: *I. × attenuata:* 'Foster #2', narrowly pyramidal with small, dark green leaves; 'East Palatka', loose form, light green foliage; 'Savannah', light green foliage, good crops of berries most years. *I. cornuta:* 'Burfordii', rounded leaves with a single spine; 'Burfordii Nana', compact and slow-growing; 'D'Or', yellow berries; 'Carissa', low, rounded, seems to tolerate hot, dry conditions well. *I. crenata:* 'Compacta', dark green leaves, grows to about 3'; 'Helleri', compact and layered, small leaves, grows to about 3'; 'Microphylla', small leaves, upright form. *I. × meserveae:* 'Blue Prince', dark green foliage, low profile; 'Blue Princess', more upright, female. *I. vomitoria:* 'Pendula', irregular, weeping habit; 'Schelling's Dwarf', low and layered. ❖

Impatiens

Impatiens, patient Lucy, garden balsam. Tender perennials used as annuals.

Description: Two species are commonly grown, *Impatiens wallerana*, impatiens, and *I. balsamina*, garden balsam. Both bear 1"-3" flat or roselike flowers in white, pink, rose, red, orange, lavender, purple, or spotted and banded combinations. The succulent-stemmed plants can grow 8"-36" tall. *I. wallerana* cultivars cover the entire height range on spreading, green-leaved plants, while *I. balsamina* types resemble 2' trees with longer green leaves. New Guinea hybrids have large flowers and elongated green or multicolored leaves.

How to grow: Sow seeds indoors in early spring for planting after danger of frost is past, or buy transplants, especially of New Guinea hybrids, which are often grown from cuttings. Plant in partial shade and average soil. Water during droughts. New Guinea hybrids will grow in full sun if soil is kept constantly moist. Root cuttings of your favorites in late summer for overwintering indoors. Spider mites can cause yellow-stippled leaves; control by applying soap spray every 3-5 days for two weeks.

Landscape uses: Impatiens are superb for beds, in masses among shrubs, as edges for plantings or structures, and in pots. White- or pastel-flowered impatiens will light up the gloomy areas under trees and other shady sites with their bright blooms. In warmer areas, self-sown seeds may naturalize to form a dramatic groundcover. Impatiens, especially the New Guinea hybrids, also make lovely houseplants.

Best cultivars: Mixes: *I. wallerana:* 'Elfin' and 'Futura', both 8"-12"; 'Accent', 10"; and 'Blitz', 12"-16". *I. balsamina:* 'Tom Thumb', 1', and 'Camellia Flowered', 1½'-2', both double-flowered. New Guinea hybrids: 'Spectra', 1'-1½', or cutting-grown cultivars like the 'Circus' group. Also try 'Fluffy Ruffles', with giant 6" flowers on 1½' plants. ❖

Insecticides

Insecticides kill insects. They're a quick and seemingly simple solution for pest problems in houses, office buildings, restaurants, farm fields, and backyard gardens. However, organic gardeners prefer to use control techniques that are less toxic and less environmentally damaging to manage insect pests whenever possible. Even botanical poisons—organically acceptable insecticides—pose environmental risks and should be used only when all other control methods fail. For more information on cultural, physical, and biological insect control methods, see the Organic Pest Management entry.

How Insecticides Work

Insecticides destroy or inhibit the development of insects and related pests. The insect's multilayered external skeleton is a formidable barrier to insecticides. Even if something gets through, insects are often able to detoxify it. Some insecticides are contact poisons that kill by suffocation or dehydration. Other insecticides paralyze, poison, or sicken the insects after they eat treated plants.

Many natural and synthetic insecticides are nonselective; they kill any insect they come in contact with, pest or not. They are often highly toxic to other animals and humans. Some synthetic insecticides are designed to be systemic. They move around inside the plant and are active even in parts of the plant that were not originally treated.

Many products that kill insects also have significant health and environmental consequences. Even botanical insecticides must be used cautiously to avoid problems. See the Pesticides entry for more information on the possible health and environmental hazards.

Using Insecticides

The first step in controlling an insect problem is to identify the pest and learn about its life cycle. By identifying the times when the pest is most susceptible and how and where it lives, you can plan the best controls.

If you decide to apply an insecticide, always follow the appropriate safety precautions. See the Pesticides entry for safety instructions.

The list of natural insecticides has grown long enough to be confusing to even experienced gardeners. Knowing how these substances work may help you decide when to use them, if at all. The following list is arranged from least to most toxic. For maximum effect, be sure to spray both the upper and lower surfaces of the leaves. When using commercial products, follow the directions on the label. Caution: Do not mix pesticide products together or add activators or boosters unless the label directs you to do so.

Microbial insecticides: Microbial insecticides cause pests to get sick. Just like people, insects sometimes get diseases caused by bacteria, fungi, viruses, and other microorganisms. Microbial insecticides make use of these often highly specific insect diseases. These products do not kill pests as quickly as some chemical insecticides do, but there are virtually no harmful side effects.

BT (*Bacillus thuringiensis*) bacteria produce crystals and spores that paralyze the digestive tract of certain insect larvae. BT products are nontoxic to mammals, are specific to the target pest, do not harm beneficial insects, and may be used right up to harvest. There are several BT varieties. BTK (*B.t.* var. *kurstaki*) controls cabbage looper, cabbageworm, tomato hornworm, fruitworms, European corn borer, and similar larvae. BTSD (*B.t.* var. *san diego*) controls small larvae of the Colorado potato beetle. BTI (*B.t.* var. *israelensis*) controls mosquitoes, black flies, and fungus gnats.

Milky disease (*Bacillus popilliae* and *B. lentimorbus*) infects the grubs of the Japanese beetle and its close relatives. The disease will persist in the soil for many years.

Nosema locustae provides long-term control of grasshoppers. About half the grasshoppers that eat the bait containing the organisms will die within 3-4 weeks. Surviving grasshoppers will infect the following year's generations.

Some nematodes parasitize larvae and grubs. They attack an insect and release bacteria that paralyze and kill the insect within 2-4 days. The nematode then feeds on the dead insect and reproduces rapidly. About 10-20 days later, huge numbers of nematodes leave the dead insect in search of new victims. Their larvae can survive for long periods in the soil, but for the greatest effect you need to release more each year. Because nematodes perish in sunlight or dry places, they are most useful against pests in soil or hidden locations. Use a syringe or an oil can to inject nematodes into borer holes.

Some interesting new insecticides make use of toxins produced by naturally occurring organisms. Avermectins are derived from the antibiotics made by a common soil bacterium, *Streptomyces avermitilis*. Thuringiensin is derived from the BT toxins, which seem to have very low toxicity to animals but are toxic to some degree to a wide range of insects and mites—including beneficial ones. More research is needed to determine the side effects new pesticides like these may have and if they have a place in organic pest contol.

Pheromones and growth regulators: Pheromones are hormonelike chemicals produced and emitted by insects and other animals to communicate with other members of their species. They are highly specific and can attract insects from great distances. Pheromone products are available for many pests, including peachtree borers, codling moths, corn earworms, cabbage loopers, apple maggots, and Japanese beetles.

Traps baited with pheromones are used to keep track of specific pest populations. Small capsules containing pheromones are placed inside cardboard traps coated with a sticky material. The species attracted to the pheromone flies into the trap and gets caught in the glue. Gardeners and orchardists may also be able to control certain pests by hanging large numbers of traps. Pheromone lures without traps confuse pests and keep them from finding food or mates.

Insect growth regulators (IGRs) are chemical mimics of insect hormones. IGRs disrupt feeding, development, or reproduction of a specific insect, and present little risk to nontarget species. They are currently available for controlling aphids, whiteflies, fleas, and fungus gnats. IGRs are synthetic compounds. While they appear to be free of side effects, more research is needed to determine what place they have in organic pest control.

Insecticidal oils: Petroleum and plant oils have long been used to kill eggs and immature stages of insects. Oils block the insect's supply of oxygen and are especially effective because they spread well over surfaces. Oils may also poison or repel some insects. They break down quickly and are more toxic to pests than to beneficial insects.

Dormant oils are heavy petroleum oils that can be sprayed on dormant orchard trees and ornamental plants to control overwintering stages of mites, scales, aphids, and other insects. Spray a 1-3 percent mixture of oil in water when the air temperature is above 40°F. Certain plants such as Japanese maple are very sensitive and can be severely damaged by dormant oil. It also removes the blue "bloom" from blue spruce. Before spraying the whole plant, spray a small area and see if yellowing occurs.

Summer oils, also called superior or supreme oils, are lighter petroleum oils that contain fewer of the impurities that make dormant oils toxic to plants. Spray up to a 2 percent mixture of summer oil and water even on fully leafed plants as long as the air temperature is below 85°F and the plants are not drought or heat stressed. Summer oil controls aphids, spider mites, scales, psylla, mealybugs, and some caterpillars. It is slightly toxic to mammals and registered for ornamental and greenhouse use. Oils may cause leaf damage to some plants under certain conditions. Spray a small area and wait a few days. If the plants are unharmed, spray thoroughly.

Vegetable oils provide similar control. Mix 1 cup of cooking oil with 1 tablespoon of liquid soap. Use 2½ teaspoons per cup of water to spray.

Diatomaceous earth: Diatomaceous earth (DE) is a nontoxic mineral product, mined from fossilized shell remains of an algae known as *diatoms.* This fine powder has microscopic, sharp edges that pierce soft-bodied insects and cause them to dehydrate.

Apply natural-grade DE as a dust, preferably after a light rain, in order to make it stick better. Or to spray DE, mix 1 ounce of DE with ¼ teaspoon liquid soap, and add 1 gallon of water. To protect trees and shrubs from caterpillar attack, paint a thicker mix on their trunks.

Insecticidal soaps: Insecticidal soaps are specially formulated solutions of fatty acids that kill insect pests like aphids, mites, and whiteflies. Insecticidal soap is a contact insecticide that paralyzes insects, which then die of starvation. Spray plants every 2-3 days for two weeks for bad infestations. Mix with soft water. Soaps may damage plants if applied too strongly or if plants are drought or heat stressed. Soaps break down within 1-2 weeks.

Many organic gardeners use 1-3 teaspoons of household soap (not detergent) per gallon of water as a garden insecticide.

Sulfur: You can use sulfur to control mites and chiggers. Sulfur is gentle on large predaceous insects but will kill tiny parasitic wasps. See the Fungicides entry for more details.

Neem oil: Neem oil is extracted from the neem tree, *Azadirachta indica,* native to India. The oil is extracted from seed kernels, leaves, bark, flowers, and wood. Neem oil is a broad-spectrum insect poison, repellent, and feeding deterrent. It also stops or disrupts insect growth and sterilizes some species. Research is ongoing, but neem oil appears to be easy on beneficials

and of very low toxicity to mammals.

Neem oil solution can be used as a spray to control many insects and as a soil drench to control soil stages of pests. Spray when the leaves will remain wet for as long as possible.

Pyrethrins: Pyrethrins are derived from the flowers of pyrethrum daisies (*Chrysanthemum cinerariifolium* and *C. coccineum*). The dried flowers are finely ground to make an insecticidal dust. Pyrethrins are extracted from the dust and used in sprayable solutions. Pyrethrins attack an insect's central nervous system, providing the rapid knockdown that gives many gardeners a satisfying feeling of revenge. At low doses, however, insects may detoxify the chemical and recover. The addition of synthetic synergists, like piperonyl butoxide (PBO), prevent insects from detoxifying insecticides. Synergists may be toxic themselves, so you may wish to avoid products with them. Pesticide manufacturers have also created synthetic pyrethrinlike

HOME-BREWED PEST CONTROLS

Organic gardeners have long relied on homemade sprays that are safe to use and easy to prepare. Results aren't guaranteed, so monitor the plants after treating them.

Bug juice: Collect ½ cup of a specific pest and mash well. Mix with 2 cups of water, and strain. Mix ¼ cup of this bug juice and a few drops of soap with 2 cups of water, and spray. Don't make yourself sick, too! Use nonfood utensils and wear plastic gloves.

Garlic oil: Finely chop 10–15 garlic cloves and soak in 1 pint of mineral oil for 24 hours. Strain and spray as is, or dilute with water and add a few drops of soap.

Hot-pepper spray: Blend ½ cup of hot peppers with 2 cups of water. Strain and spray. Caution: Hot peppers burn skin and eyes.

insecticides call pyrethroids. Check labels to be sure you're getting a plant-derived, organically acceptable product.

Pyrethrins are effective against a broad spectrum of pest insects, including flies, mosquitoes, and chewing and sucking insect pests. You can apply it up to one day before harvest because it breaks down rapidly in heat and light. Pyrethrins are moderately toxic to mammals and highly toxic to fish. Don't apply them around ponds or waterways.

Pyrethrins are available in many commercial dusts and sprays, some of which also contain soap and/or other natural insecticides. Apply pyrethrins in the early evening. Two applications 2 hours apart may provide better control.

Rotenone: Rotenone occurs naturally in more than 65 species of plants; however, most commercial supplies come from Peruvian cubé, Malaysian derris, or Brazilian tembo plants. When fewer pest-control options were available, rotenone was a common item on the organic gardener's shelf since it was considered safer than synthetic insecticides. But recent research has highlighted the deadliness of this natural poison, and safer organic practices have been discovered.

Rotenone's insecticidal property is broad spectrum, so beneficial insects are killed on contact along with the pests. It is moderately toxic to people and most animals and very toxic to swine, birds, and fish. Some people are highly allergic to rotenone on food crops and suffer from violent reactions even after a week-long post-spray period, sometimes even after the food has been cooked. New evidence suggests that rotenone may cause growth abnormalities in laboratory animals.

For all of these reasons, rotenone is no longer recommended for use in organic gardens. Rely on safer options, such as row covers to keep pests off plants or sprays of neem or pyrethrins to deal with infestations that do occur.

Ryania: Ryanodine is the active, insecticidal ingredient of a tropical shrub (*Ryania speciosa*). For years, this botanical insecticide has been recommended for use against citrus thrips, corn earworms, European corn borers, codling moths, and a variety of other pests. However, ryania is also quite toxic to mammals and water life. For this reason, it's better to rely on safer pest control measures, such as insecticidal soap, neem, or pyrethrins.

Nicotine: Nicotine is a highly poisonous alkaloid, extracted from special tobacco selected for its high nicotine content. As insecticides, nicotine products are poisonous to most plant pests, including aphids, mealybugs, scales, and spider mites. Nicotine is also highly toxic to mammals when taken internally or absorbed through the skin—more toxic than many synthetic pesticides. It remains toxic on leaf surfaces for several weeks after an application. Also, nicotine products may contain the pathogen that causes tobacco mosaic virus in related plants, including eggplant, peppers, tomatoes, and potatoes. For these reasons, nicotine sprays and dusts are no longer recommended for use in organic gardens. Instead, choose safer control measures, such as insecticidal soap or neem sprays, to control garden pests.

Sabadilla: Like nicotine and ryania, sabadilla owes its insecticidal powers to several poisonous alkaloids. It is made from the seeds of *Schoenocaulon officinale,* a lilylike plant found in Venezuela.

This powerful botanical insecticide has been used to control a variety of garden pests, including aphids, flea beetles, tarnished plant bugs, and thrips. Unfortunately, sabadilla is also moderately toxic to mammals and causes violent allergic reactions in susceptible individuals. It is toxic to honeybees, too. For these reasons, it's better to stick with milder control measures, such as insecticidal soap, neem, or pyrethrin sprays. ❖

Insects

Insects are the most numerous animals on earth. Four out of every five animals are insects. There are more species of beetles than there are of all other animals, including insects, put together. And while estimates of the number of insect species range from 2 to 10 million, no one knows how many more species are yet to be discovered, especially in remote regions such as the tropics.

People are largely unaware of insects until they find holes in the leaves of their favorite plants or until the mosquitoes start biting. Then they rush to exterminate the offenders without realizing that they could also be harming beneficial insects that naturally keep the pests in check. As organic gardeners, we should learn as much as we can about the behavior and biology of the insects in our yards and gardens. Frequently, a little knowledge about how insects function can help us prevent pest damage without using invasive and potentially toxic control methods.

Life Cycles

Some insects have strange and complicated life cycles. The best-known example is the tranformation of a wormlike caterpillar into a sensationally beautiful butterfly. In general, insects follow one of two main patterns of development.

Complete metamorphosis: In this pattern, the immature insect is transformed during a resting stage into an adult that looks like a completely different organism. The adult insect usually inhabits a different environment and eats different food than it did at the immature stage. In some cases, one stage may be a pest, while the other is harmless. For example, parsleyworms, which feed on carrots and related plants, are the larvae of black swallowtail butterflies.

As the larva grows, it periodically sheds its skin until it reaches its full size. It then forms a pupa and enters a resting stage. When the adult has finished forming inside, it splits open the pupa and emerges, expands its wings, and when its outer skeleton has hardened, it flies away to search for food and mates.

Incomplete metamorphosis: Insects that follow this pattern develop from immature to adult in gradual stages without forming a pupa. The insect starts life as an egg, which hatches into a nymph. The nymph sheds its skin several times as it grows, becoming more and more like the adult with each molt. It gets progressively larger, its body lengthens, and wing pads appear where its wings will grow. The last molt is to the adult stage, with fully formed wings and reproductive organs. The nymph and adult usually have the same type of diet.

Winter Survival

Knowing how and where pest insects spend the winter can give you important clues about how to control them. Most insects in the temperate zones sense the shortening day length and cooler temperatures of autumn. Their bodies prepare for winter by building up energy reserves and by undergoing chemical changes so that their blood won't freeze. Many adult insects cannot survive winter, but at least one of their life stages, such as egg, larva, or pupa, can withstand the long cold period in a state of hibernation (called *diapause* in insects). The overwintering stages of many pests, including armyworms and sawflies, burrow deep into the soil or into litter on the ground. Cultivating the soil in early spring can expose these hidden hibernators to predators such as birds. Other pests, such as leafrollers and tent caterpillars, pupate or lay eggs in cracks and crevices in tree bark. Scraping egg masses off of bark and spraying trees with dormant oil can help to eliminate these pests.

Feeding Habits

Insects have a wide variety of feeding habits: some are vegetarians, others are carnivores.

Key Words

INSECTS

Arthropods. Cold-blooded animals that have an armoured skeleton, called an exoskeleton, on the outside of their bodies. This group of animals includes crustaceans, insects, mites, spiders, millipedes, and centipedes.

Metamorphosis. A change in form during the development of an insect.

Larva. An immature stage of an insect.

Caterpillar. The larva of a moth or butterfly.

Grub. The larva of a beetle.

Maggot. The larva of a fly.

Pupa. A hardened shell formed by a larva, within which the adult stage develops.

Cocoon. A protective cover for a pupa.

Chrysalis. The pupa of a butterfly.

Nymph. An immature stage of an insect that does not form a pupa.

Parasite. An animal or plant that lives in or on and draws nourishment from another organism.

Parasitoid. An insect that parasitizes another insect.

Predator. An animal that attacks and feeds on other animals.

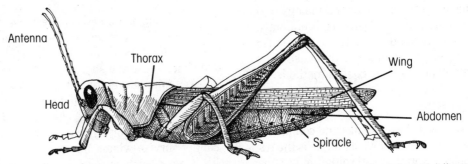

Parts of an insect. Insects have six legs, and their bodies are divided into three sections: the head, thorax, and abdomen. Insects have two antennae, which aid in sensory perception. Most adult insects have two pairs of wings located on the thorax—flies have only one pair. Insects breathe through spiracles, small air tubes located along the length of their bodies and branching throughout their tissues.

Some eat nearly anything, while others can eat only one species of plant. But only a minority of insects feed on our crop or ornamental plants.

Plant eaters: These insects chew or suck on leaves, stems, or roots for food. They are usually pests—aphids, gypsy moth caterpillars, and Colorado potato beetles are good examples. Some are considered beneficial and have been used in biological control programs to combat weeds.

Parasites: Some insects, such as mosquitoes and blackflies, suck blood from birds and mammals; others, like lice and fleas, are skin parasites on animals. Parasitoid insects are generally beneficial from the gardener's standpoint. Parasitoid larvae such as those of *Encarsia formosa* live and grow inside host insects until the hosts eventually die. The adults of many parasitoids feed on pollen and nectar.

(continued on page 346)

Insect diversity. Insects have the longest history of evolution and the greatest range of habitats of all animals on earth today. Even in an area as small as your yard, there is a remarkable diversity of insects—in both appearance and function. While gardeners usually regard insects as potential trouble, as much as 90 percent of the insects in their gardens are actually beneficial insects such as bees, lacewings, tachinid flies, and lady beetles and their larvae.

343

The Top Ten Garden Insect Pests in America

Every gardener has his or her personal list of most troublesome garden pests. The following list of pest descriptions and control measures may not match yours pest for pest, but it will provide a good starting point for tackling pest control in gardens throughout the United States and Canada. Control solutions are listed in order of environmental friendliness. Botanical pesticides, which can have detrimental effects on beneficial insects and other animals, are listed as a last resort.

Pest	Host/Range	Damage	Control
Aphids (many species). Tiny, pear-shaped; long antennae; two tubes projecting rearward from abdomen.	Most fruits and vegetables, flowers, ornamentals, shade trees. Found throughout North America.	Aphids suck plant sap, causing foliage to distort and leaves to drop; honeydew excreted on leaves supports sooty mold growth; feeding spreads viral diseases.	Wash plants with strong spray of water; conserve native predators and parasites; release aphid midges, lacewings, or lady beetles; spray with garlic spray, insecticidal soap, dormant or summer oils, alcohol, pyrethrins, neem.
Cabbage maggot (*Delia radicum*). Adults: ¼″ gray flies. Larvae: white, tapering maggots.	Cabbage-family crops. Found throughout North America.	Maggots tunnel in roots, killing plants directly or by creating entryways for disease organisms.	Apply floating row covers; set out transplants through slits in tar-paper squares; avoid first generation by delaying planting; apply parasitic nematodes around roots; burn roots from harvested plants; mound wood ashes, diatomaceous earth, red pepper dust around stems.
Caterpillars (many species). Soft, segmented larvae with distinct, harder head capsule; six legs in front, fleshy false legs on rear segments.	Many fruits and vegetables, ornamentals, shade trees. Range varies with species.	Caterpillars chew in leaves or along margins; droppings soil the produce; some tunnel into fruits.	Encourage native predators, parasites; handpick; apply floating row covers; spray with BT (*Bacillus thuringiensis*), pyrethrins.
Colorado potato beetle (*Leptinotarsa decemlineata*). Adults: yellow-orange beetles with 10 black stripes on wing covers. Larvae: orange, hump-backed grubs with black spots along sides. Eggs: yellow ovals, laid in upright clusters.	Potatoes, tomatoes, eggplant, petunias. Found throughout North America.	Beetles defoliate plants, reducing yields or killing young plants.	Apply floating row covers; spray with BTSD (*B.t. var. san diego*); handpick; use deep straw mulches; attract native parasites and predators; spray with neem or pyrethrins.

344

Pest	Host/Range	Damage	Control
Cutworms (several species). Fat, 1" long, gray or black segmented larvae; active at night.	Most early vegetable and flower seedlings, transplants. Found throughout North America.	Cutworms chew through stems at ground level; they may completely devour small plants; most damaging in May and June.	Use cutworm collars on transplants; delay planting; handpick cutworms curled below soil surface; scatter bran baits mixed with BTK (*B.t.* var. *kurstaki*) and molasses before planting.
Flea beetles (several species). Small, dark beetles that jump like fleas when disturbed.	Most vegetable crops. Found throughout North America.	Adults chew numerous small, round holes in leaves; most damaging to young plants; larvae feed on plant roots.	Apply floating row covers; apply parasitic nematodes to soil; spray with neem or pyrethrins.
Japanese beetle (*Popillia japonica*). Adults: metallic blue-green, ½" beetles with bronze wing covers. Larvae: fat, white grubs with brown heads.	Many vegetables and flowers, small fruit. Found in all states east of the Mississippi River.	Adults skeletonize leaves, chew flowers, may completely defoliate plants; larvae feed on lawn and garden plant roots.	Shake beetles from plants in early morning; apply floating row covers; set out baited traps throughout community; apply milky disease spores to soil; spray sod with neem to control larvae.
Mexican bean beetle (*Epilachna varivestris*). Adults: oval, yellow-brown, ¼" beetles with 16 black spots on wing covers. Larvae: fat, dark yellow grubs with long, branched spines.	Cowpeas, lima beans, snap beans, soybeans. Found in most states east of the Mississippi River; also parts of Arizona, Colorado, Nebraska, Texas, Utah.	Adults and larvae chew on leaves from beneath, leaving characteristic lacy appearance; plants defoliated and killed.	Apply floating row covers; plant bush beans early; handpick; plant soybean trap crop; release spined soldier bugs; spray neem or pyrethrins.
Scales (more than 200 species). Adults: females look like hard or soft bumps on stems, leaves, fruit; males are minute flying insects. Larvae: tiny, soft, crawling larvae with thread-like mouthparts.	Many fruits, indoor plants, ornamental shrubs, and trees. Found throughout North America.	All stages suck plant sap, weakening plants. Plants become yellow, drop leaves, and may die. Honeydew is excreted onto foliage and fruit.	Prune out infested plant parts; encourage native biological controls; scrub scales gently from twigs with soft brush and soapy water, rinse well; apply dormant or summer oil sprays; spray with pyrethrins.
Tarnished plant bug (*Lygus lineolaris*). Fast-moving, mottled, green or brown bugs, forewings with black-tipped yellow triangles. Nymphs: similar to adults, but wingless.	Many flowers, fruits, vegetables. Found throughout North America.	Adults and nymphs suck plant juices, causing leaf and fruit distortion, wilting, stunting, and tip dieback.	Apply floating row covers; encourage native predatory insects; spray pyrethrins.

Predators: Predators such as lady beetles and ground beetles can eat hundreds of insects during their life cycles. Many predators, such as pirate bugs, are also adapted to survive by sucking plant juices or eating pollen when prey is scarce.

Omnivores: Some insects have evolved the ultimate survival strategy: They eat almost anything. Cockroaches and earwigs are omnivores; they eat many sorts of animal or vegetable material—even soap, glue, and paper bindings.

Scavengers: Dung beetles, carrion beetles, fly larvae, and other insects live on decaying vegetable or animal material, breaking down the dead tissues or organic matter and hastening their decay.

Fungus feeders: The larvae of fungus gnats and some obscure species of lady beetles feed on fungi.

Insect Control

The first step in controlling pests is knowing what they look like. You should recognize all the life stages of a pest, not just the adult form. For example, if you know what Colorado potato beetle egg clusters look like, you can scout for them on your plants and crush any you find. This will minimize damage and help you avoid later problems that might require the use of more drastic control measures.

Becoming familiar with the appearance of the insects in your yard and garden also helps you to avoid mistaking beneficial insects for pests. Predatory insects are often attracted to damaged plants, because they expect to find their food (the caterpillar or larva that is eating your plant) there. For details about these good bugs and how they can help in your organic garden, see the Beneficial Insects entry.

Learn to diagnose problems based on the type of damage you find. If you find leaves with holes in them, look closely, especially on the undersides, for larvae or grubs. Leaf distortion

can be a sign of aphid damage, and leaf speckling may be the result of feeding by tiny pests such as thrips or spider mites. If you don't find a pest, it could be that the culprits feed only at night, or have finished eating and left your plants. We often don't notice the damage until the pest is gone, because most caterpillars and beetle larvae do the most noticeable damage during the final days of their development, just before they stop feeding and pupate. If the new leaves on the plant are undamaged or the edges of the chewed hole are dry and brown, it is likely that the pest has been gone for several days. In contrast, freshly cut leaf edges and exuding sap are a clue that the critter is still around. Once you have found a suspect, try referring to an insect field guide to identify it, or contact your local extension office for information about species common in your area. You may be able to get further help from local extension agents, university entomologists, or pest management services.

Once you've identified your pest, you have many options for controlling them organically. The cheapest and safest pest management strategy is to protect and attract the myriad of wild beneficial insects to your garden by planting attractive flowers, giving them a water source, and by maintaining refuges of permanent plantings around the garden. You can also use other passive preventive measures, such as planting resistant cultivars or putting fine screen over the plants to keep insects away. The next step is to release beneficial insects or set traps for the pests. Spraying natural pesticides, such as pyrethrins and neem, should be your last resort. Although these sprays are derived from plants, they are quite poisonous and are rarely needed in a home garden. You'll find recommendations for controlling some of the most common pests in "The Top Ten Garden Insect Pests in America" on page 344. For complete information on how to use various control methods, read the Organic Pest Management entry. ❖

Integrated Pest Management

Integrated Pest Management (IPM) is a method of managing a specific pest on commercial crops by monitoring pest populations and applying a combination of preventive and control techniques, including applying synthetic pesticides. Its goal is acceptable crop yield, crop quality, and profit with the least environmental disruption. IPM was developed for commercial growers in response to the problems and high costs associated with synthetic pesticides. Unfortunately, some IPM programs are little more than modifications of traditional chemical spray programs. The many problems associated with the use of synthetic pesticides are described in the Pesticides entry.

IPM programs start by identifying the problem or pest and gathering information on it. A threshold level of tolerable damage is set, and the kinds of controls that can or must be used to maintain that level are selected. Four categories of controls are considered: cultural, physical, biological, and chemical.

A grower then develops a complete management plan. The plan is integrated because it depends on many controls, each of which contributes to overall success. Some controls are used routinely, others only when specific conditions occur.

Monitoring is a critical part of implementing an IPM program. Growers examine plants at regular intervals and count the number of insects or disease units. Controls are used only when problems reach a predetermined level, such as a certain number of aphids per leaf.

In the home organic garden, synthetic chemicals are not an option. Integrated pest management modified to eliminate synthetic pesticides is organic integrated pest managment, which we term Organic Pest Management. See the Organic Pest Management entry for complete instructions on developing an organic pest management system for your yard and garden. ❖

Intensive Gardening

Intensive horticulture has been practiced for centuries in many parts of the world, particularly Asia. In Europe and America, the best-known methods are bio-dynamic, French intensive market, and bio-dynamic/French intensive gardening. Each has its own disciplines, but all use basic practices that set intensive gardening apart from traditional row-crop growing: raised growing beds, close spacing between plants, careful attention to building and maintaining soil fertility, and a schedule of succession planting and crop rotation that maximizes production by making best use of available growing space.

Applied skillfully, intensive growing methods can (and consistently do) produce harvests 4-10 times greater than might be expected from a conventional garden. But intensive gardening also demands more initial work, planning, and scheduling. If you wish to convert to intensive methods, it's best to start gradually. For example, you could try building one or two raised beds each gardening season for a few years.

Raised Growing Beds

A keystone of intensive gardening is the raised growing bed. Gardeners prepare a raised bed by first tilling, digging, or double digging the plot. Then they add more earth, compost, manure, and other amendments to create a mound of loose soil 4"-8" high. Raised beds improve drainage and aeration, plant roots penetrate readily, and weeds are easy to pull up. Also, the raised bed's rounded contour provides more actual growing area than does the same amount of flat ground.

Preparing a raised bed garden, however, requires a strong back and substantial labor. It can take 8 hours to double dig one $5' \times 20'$ bed. Tilling the site saves time, but doesn't loosen the subsoil as well. The bed still must be built up with soil and compost—a good 2 hours' work.

Close Plant Spacing

A traditional garden planted according to seed-packet guidelines uses only about 30 percent of the total soil area for growing crops. Pathways and spaces between crop rows make up the remainder. Intensive gardening puts as much as 80 percent of a garden's surface area into crop production. Plants are placed close together over the entire bed, usually in a triangular or staggered pattern, so that their leaves overlap slightly at maturity. This allows for more plants per square foot, and produces a continuous leafy canopy that shades the bed, moderates soil temperature, conserves moisture, and discourages weeds. Close spacing also means plantings must be carefully planned according to each crop's growing habits, including root spread, mature size, and water and nutrient needs.

High Soil Fertility

Intensive plantings require fertile, well-balanced soil rich in organic content. Soil amendments such as greensand and rock phosphate help. So do green manure crops, such as buckwheat and alfalfa, which intensive gardeners often grow and work into the soil between plantings. But the quintessential soil-building ingredient in intensive gardening is compost, applied copiously throughout the entire grow-ing season. Without it, intensively gardened soil soon loses its vitality.

Succession Planting

Succession planting is the practice of rapidly filling the space vacated by a harvested crop by planting a new crop. This can be as simple as following harvested cool-season spring vegetables, such as peas or spinach, with a planting of warm-season summer crops, such as beans or squash. Once harvested, those crops could be followed by a cold-tolerant fall crop such as spinach. Another technique is to stagger plantings at 1- or 2-week intervals to prolong the harvest. Advanced intensive gardeners also interplant compatible short-, mid-, and full-season vegetables in the same bed at the same time. They then harvest and replant the faster-growing plants two, three, or even four times during the season.

Timing succession plantings and interplantings requires a considerable understanding not only of each kind of crop, but of each cultivar's germination rate, days to maturity, compatibility with other crops, rooting patterns, and light and shade tolerance.

Crop Rotation

Different crops have different nutrient requirements, and affect soil balance differently. Some, like corn and tomatoes, are heavy feeders that quickly deplete soil nitrogen and phosphorus. Intensive gardeners carefully rotate the crops in order to keep soil nutrients balanced from harvest to harvest.

The general rule of thumb is never to plant the same kind of crop (root, leaf, legume, and fruiting) successively in the same place. It's best to follow nitrogen-fixing legumes such as peas or beans with nitrogen-loving leaf or fruiting crops such as lettuce or tomatoes. Replace heavy-feeding leaf crops with light-feeding root crops. Try not to plant crops from the same botanical family in the same bed two years in a row, in order to discourage crop-specific diseases and insect pests. ❖

Ipomoea

Morning-glory, moonflower. Annual or tender perennial vines.

Description: *Ipomoea alba,* moonflower, is a twining, 8'-10' vine with heart-shaped leaves. The fragrant, white, trumpet-shaped flowers open only at night. *I. nil, I. purpurea,* and *I. tricolor,* all called morning-glory, are similar. All are twining vines with heart-shaped leaves. The funnel-shaped blue, white, blue-purple, or crimson blooms open in the morning and close at night. All are tender perennial vines grown as annuals.

How to grow: Plant morning-glory seed after all danger of frost is past. Nick the hard seed coat for faster germination. Grow in full sun to partial shade. Morning-glories prefer cool weather.

Landscape uses: Plant morning-glories to climb up fences, porch rails, and arbors. ❖

Iris

Iris, flag. Mostly spring- to early-summer-blooming perennials and bulbs.

Description: Irises offer a huge range of colors and patterns, heights, and bloom times, with variations on a common theme of flower shape and plant form. The basic flower shape consists of three inner (often erect) petals, called *standards,* surrounded by three outer petals (usually arching out), called *falls.* Leaves are almost always flat and long, resembling swords or blades of grass; they grow in rather open to quite dense upright or arching clumps from bulbs or creeping rhizomes.

By far the most popular group is the large collection of hybrids termed the "bearded" irises, named for the hairy caterpillarlike tuft creeping out of the center of each fall. Flowers range from barely 2" wide to 7" giants in what is probably the widest color range of any plant group, lacking only pure red. They bloom in early summer, from 2" to nearly 5' above stiff, swordlike leaves. Zones 3-8.

In place of a beard, "beardless" irises flaunt a colorful spot, called a *signal,* or an intricate pattern of lines. Blooms on *Iris sibirica,* Siberian iris, rarely exceed 3" wide and are more open and graceful than most bearded irises; they occur in shades of white, red-violet, blue, and purple (plus a few rare pinks and yellows) on upright, grassy clumps averaging 3' tall. They bloom toward the end of the bearded's season. Zones 3-8. *I. ensata* (formerly *I. kaempferi*), Japanese irises, bear 4"-10", six-petaled flattish or more double flowers in shades of white, pinkish lavender, red-violet, blue, and violet, often exotically edged, lined, and speckled. Most grow to about 3' and are broader-leaved and less dense than Siberians, blooming a few weeks later. Zones 5-8. Very early spring-blooming, bulbous *I. reticulata* hybrids, reticulated irises, produce narrow-petalled, sweetly scented 3" blooms, mostly in blue and purple shades with orange or yellow signals, among sparse, four-sided leaves which may grow to 1½' after bloom. Zones 5-8.

How to grow: Most bearded irises are easy to grow, but they do have specialized needs. Plant and divide every 3-4 years in summer or early fall, splitting them into individual "fans" with the rhizome attached, or into divisions with a few fans. Trim leaves back before planting to make up for root loss. They grow best in full sun or very light shade and average to rich, well-drained soil. Barely cover the rhizome and point the leafy end in the direction you want it to grow, ideally out from the center of a group of three to five of a kind.

Bearded irises tolerate drought very well when dormant (usually beginning about six weeks after bloom), but water them well up to the time dormancy sets in and after division. Fertilize routinely in spring and early fall, keep weeds and other plants away from the rhizomes, mulch loosely the first winter after division, and be ready to stake the tall ones in bloom.

Soft rot attacks during wet seasons in poorly drained soil, entering through wounds in the rhizome made from premature leaf removal or

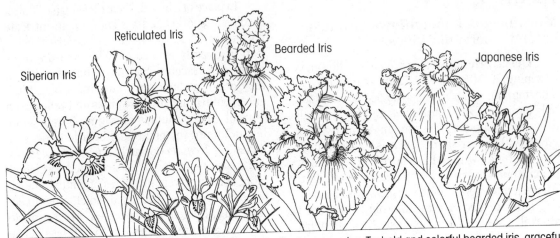

Reticulated Iris

Bearded Iris

Japanese Iris

Siberian Iris

Iris flower forms. Many wonderful irises are available for the home garden. Try bold and colorful bearded iris, graceful moisture-loving Siberian iris, elegant Japanese iris, or dainty reticulated iris.

too-close cultivation, or it is carried on the body of the iris borer. The eggs of this pest hatch in spring, producing 1″-1½″ long, fat, pinkish larvae. The larvae enter a fan at the top and tunnel down toward the rhizome where they may eventually eat the whole interior without being noticed.

In fall, remove dead, dry leaves, which often carry borer eggs, and destroy badly infested fans in spring. You can also crush borers in the leaves by pinching toward the base of the telltale ragged-edged leaves or by running your thumb between the leaves and squashing any borers you find. They are also vulnerable when you divide the clumps; check every rhizome for this pest. If you find a few borers, try cutting them out; destroy badly infested rhizomes.

Siberians enjoy similar conditions as beardeds, tolerating wetter soil and requiring less-frequent division in spring or fall. Be certain to replant as soon as possible after dividing them. Rot and borers seldom plague them.

Grow Japanese irises in much the same way, providing shade from the hottest sun. Water well before and during bloom. They need acid soil and benefit from a few inches of mulch in summer.

Plant reticulated irises in fall about 3″ deep and a few inches apart in average to more fertile, very well drained soil. Grow with annuals and perennials to fill the gaps left by their leaves, which wither by summer.

Landscape uses: Smaller bearded irises are perfect in rock gardens and along paths and beds. For mid- to late-spring bloom, plant taller ones in a perennial border, or in a separate bed to provide optimum conditions. They also look splendid among garden ornaments and along patios. Siberian and Japanese irises are good choices for borders and wet sites, although they prefer slightly drier conditions in winter. Reticulated irises look at home among rocks, naturalized in thin grass, or at the front of borders.

Best cultivars: For bearded types, *I. sibirica* and *I. ensata,* you can choose from hundreds of cultivars. Try to observe plants growing locally to identify your favorites. *I. reticulata* hybrids: light blue 'Cantab'; medium blue 'Harmony'; red-violet 'J. S. Dijt'; dark purple 'Violet Beauty'. ❖

Irrigation

At one time or another, most of us have run into a water shortage. We couldn't wash our cars, water our lawns and gardens, or let the children play in the sprinkler. It lasted maybe a few weeks; then it rained and life returned to normal. Or so it seemed. Running on empty is becoming a way of life in state after state in the United States and in a growing number of countries around the world.

There is lots of water. But it has a way of not always being in the right place at the right time. There always seems to be too much or too little water. Flood or drought is the aquatic version of feast or famine.

Water Use

A big part of the problem lies in the fact that when people moved into places that are naturally deserts—California, Arizona, and many states in the Great Plains—they brought along plants native to humid climates. These plants are accustomed to growing in areas that receive about 40″ of rain each year. In arid climates, yearly precipitation may be 12″.

Another problem is the shift in agricultural production to arid areas. A major portion of United States agriculture depends on irrigation. In California, agriculture uses 85 percent of all available water in the state. Irrigating alfalfa alone uses more water in a year than the combined household needs of the state's 30 million residents.

Water quality is also an increasing concern. In coastal areas with shallow water tables, for example, heavy pumping of groundwater allows salt water to seep into wells. In heavily agricultural areas, pesticides and fertilizers are tainting both surface and groundwater supplies. We've all heard of acid rain, of course. Now the Iowa Department of Natural Resources has found traces of herbicides in rainfall during spring planting. And "toxic fog" containing a witch's brew of farm chemicals has been reported in California by the United States Department of Agriculture (USDA).

While we can't as individuals change patterns of water use in commercial agriculture, we can all take steps to reduce water usage in our homes and yards.

Conserving Water in the Garden

As organic gardeners, we know that we can grow good crops without chemicals. We can also have good gardens, beautiful lawns, and landscaping that need very little supplemental watering. The first step, of course, is to increase the water-holding capacity of your soil by adding organic matter. In deep, rich soil protected by mulch, plants find it much easier to develop the strong, deep root systems necessary to find water during dry periods. This won't "drought-proof" your plants, but research has shown that crops grown in organically managed soils withstand drought much better than those in unimproved soil. Cultivating the soil between row crops also helps water filter into the soil. For more information on soil improvement, see the Soil entry.

There are many other things you can do to reduce watering needs, without sacrificing the beauty or pleasure of your yard and gardens:

• Mulch trees, shrubs, and other plants with up to 3″ of mulch. See the Mulch entry for suggestions of materials to use.

• Water less frequently, but water deeply, making sure to soak the root zone rather than the whole yard.

• Select native plants that require less water. The Natural Landscaping entry offers many tips on using native plants in your yard.

• In arid climates, follow the principles of xeriscaping in planning and maintaining your yard. See the Xeriscaping entry for details.

• Limit the size of your lawn. That doesn't mean you have to cover your yard with cement,

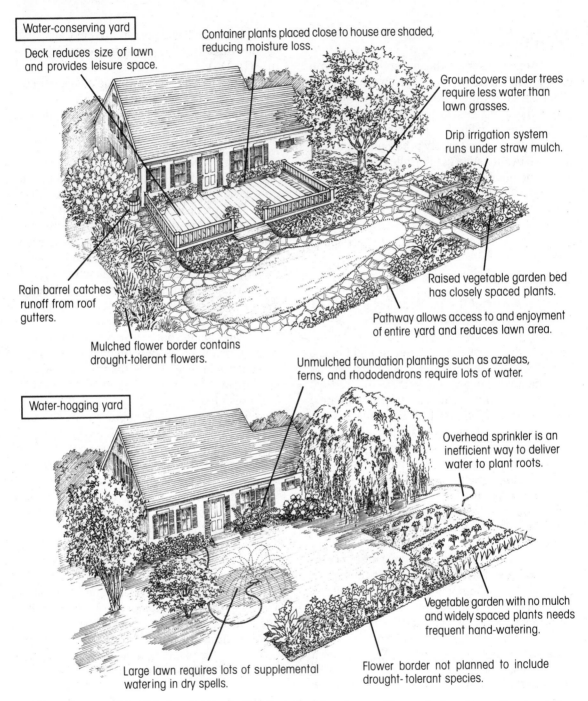

Water-conserving yard

Deck reduces size of lawn and provides leisure space.

Container plants placed close to house are shaded, reducing moisture loss.

Groundcovers under trees require less water than lawn grasses.

Drip irrigation system runs under straw mulch.

Rain barrel catches runoff from roof gutters.

Raised vegetable garden bed has closely spaced plants.

Pathway allows access to and enjoyment of entire yard and reduces lawn area.

Mulched flower border contains drought-tolerant flowers.

Unmulched foundation plantings such as azaleas, ferns, and rhododendrons require lots of water.

Water-hogging yard

Overhead sprinkler is an inefficient way to deliver water to plant roots.

Large lawn requires lots of supplemental watering in dry spells.

Vegetable garden with no mulch and widely spaced plants needs frequent hand-watering.

Flower border not planned to include drought-tolerant species.

Is your yard a water hog? Dull and unimaginative, the typical American yard is a water hog. Conventional sprinklers waste water needed by thirsty plants. With a little advance planning and thoughtful plant selection, any yard can be transformed into a water-efficient Eden that is as pleasing to the eye as it is friendly to the environment.

asphalt, or stones. You can add a new measure of beauty and enjoyment to your yard with ground-covers, mulches, and shade trees to help you and your yard keep cool. The Groundcovers entry includes many suggestions for incorporating groundcovers in your landscape.

• Add a walkway, deck, or patio to help reduce water consumption while adding more enjoyment to your yard.

• Set out a rain barrel. Connected to a down-spout on your house, it will give you a ready source of water for your plants.

• Recycle household waste water from the kitchen sink, bath, or dishwasher. You can also water plants with water from the washing machine if you limit use of chlorine bleach and detergents that contain boron. Household water should be diverted before it reaches sanitary waste lines.

Drip Irrigation

For those situations where you have to water, always strive for the most efficient method. When you water with the hose or an overhead sprinkler, some water is immediately lost to evaporation from plant surfaces, through surface runoff, or by falling in areas that don't need water, such as a street or walkway.

Southwestern Indians buried a large, un-glazed clay pot with its neck level with the soil near each of their plants. The pots were kept filled with water, which slowly seeped out through the porous clay. For a modern-day substitute, poke one or two tiny holes in the bottom of a gallon-size milk jug, set it on the ground near the plant, and keep it filled with water.

A more convenient method is a custom-designed drip irrigation system that will water all or any part of your landscape, including trees and shrubs, patio container gardens, and flower gardens. Also called "trickle" or "weep" irrigation, drip systems are as beneficial for dryland gar-deners in the arid Southwest as for those in the northern, eastern, and southern parts of the country. They more than make up for the cost and effort involved in design and installation in water savings and increased plant growth.

A drip irrigation system delivers water directly to the root zone of a plant, where it seeps slowly into the soil one drop at a time. Almost no water is lost through surface runoff or evaporation, and soil particles have plenty of opportunity to absorb and hold water for plants. It also means very few nutrients leach down beyond the reach of plant roots. Furthermore, since drip irrigation delivers water directly to the plants you want to grow, less is wasted on weeds. The soil surface between plants also remains drier, which discourages weed seeds from sprouting. All these benefits add up to the fact that drip irrigation systems can save a great deal of water—and money in terms of reduced water bills. Studies show that well-designed drip systems use at least 30 percent, and in some cases 50 percent, less water than other methods of watering such as sprinkling.

For busy gardeners, the main benefit of installing a drip irrigation system is the savings of both time and effort. Drip systems eliminate the need to drag hoses and sprinklers around. For systems that use a timer, gardeners need only spend a few seconds to turn the system on; the timer automatically turns it off.

Plants watered with drip systems grow more quickly and are more productive, because they have all the water they need and their growth isn't slowed by water stress. (This is especially true when drip irrigation is used in conjunction with mulch.) These systems also keep water off the foliage, which helps prevent some foliage diseases such as powdery mildew.

Basic Components

Drip irrigation systems move water at low pressure through a series of tubes and other hardware and deliver it to precise locations and specific plants of the gardener's choosing. Although each system is different, water gener-ally flows out of your faucet through a timer (which is optional), a filter, a pressure regulator, and into a series of hoses or pipes that carry water to emitters that release water drop by drop to the plants. Some systems use soaker hoses, which leak water all along their length, instead of emitters. A complex system may contain two or more individual lines as well as valves that allow for watering specific parts of the garden.

Designing a System

The first decision to make in designing a drip irrigation system is what you want to water. Do you want a system only for your vegetable garden or for your entire landscape? Topography is also a consideration: If your garden is hilly, you'll probably need to use emitters that compensate for pressure changes in the line.

You can design your own system, but most companies that sell drip irrigation equipment will design systems for you if provided with a scale drawing of your garden, information on what you're growing, your soil type, and garden topography. Their design will come complete with a list of parts and spacing for emitters. Whatever method you choose, start by making a fairly accurate drawing of your garden to determine how many feet of tubing you'll need.

Plants can become "addicted" to drip irrigation, because roots will concentrate in the area where the water is available. When designing a drip system to carry water along the rows of a vegetable garden or to the roots of a prized rhododendron, it's important that the water be spread uniformly throughout the irrigated area so root growth will be uniform. For example, if you are irrigating larger plants such as trees and shrubs, place emitters on two or more sides of each plant to encourage roots to grow out in all directions rather than clustering on one side. Using your system for frequent, short waterings, rather than long, slow ones, isn't a good idea for the same reason; the water doesn't have a chance to spread far in the soil, and consequently the roots will form a tight, ball-like mass around the emitters.

Beginner's Kits

An easy way to get started with drip irrigation is to buy a starter kit. Most companies have kits for both small and large gardens, which come with the essential components necessary to set up the system. However, they often don't include parts such as pressure regulators, timers, backflow preventers, and line filters. Be sure to buy a kit that can be added on to, so you can expand your system.

Soaker Hoses

Soaker hoses are another type of drip irrigation system that provide many of the advantages of emitter drip systems at a fraction of their cost. Some ooze water over their entire length, others spurt water through tiny holes. When using soaker hoses with holes, be sure to face the holes downward so the water doesn't squirt up in the air like a sprinkler. Systems using these hoses need no assembly; it's easy to lay out the hoses between small plants and along narrow rows.

Soakers save water, reduce loss through evaporation, and keep leaves dry. However, since water emerges evenly along the length of the hose, water delivery can't be directed as precisely as with an emitter system. Soaker hoses can be used for short runs (100'-200') over flat surfaces. They're useful for crops such as carrots that are closely spaced.

Also known as dew hoses, soaker hoses can be made of canvas, various types of plastic, or rubber. Hoses made of rigid plastics or rubber can be hard to lay flat and difficult to bend around corners. Plastic and rubber soakers are resistant to fungal attack and seldom develop leaks at couplings or seams, so they can be left in the beds for long periods of time without deterioration. In contrast, canvas hoses are susceptible to mold and mildew and should be drained and dried after each use. ❖

Jasminum

Jasmine. Winter- or spring-blooming shrubs or vines.

Description: *Jasminum nudiflorum,* winter jasmine, is a twiggy, 4'-5' tall shrub. It has green arching stems and opposite leaves, each bearing three 1" leaflets. In winter, its fragrant, ¾"-1" lemon yellow flowers bloom directly on the stems. Zones 6-9.

J. officinale, common white jasmine, is a deciduous or semi-evergreen vine that can climb about 10'-15'. Fragrant ¾"-1" white flowers appear in spring, then sporadically until frost. Leaves are opposite and compound, with five to nine ½"-2½" leaflets per leaf giving a lacy texture. Zones 7-9.

How to grow: Both jasmines benefit from full sun. Provide a well-drained soil, and water during the first two growing seasons. Once established, the jasmines need little supplemental watering. Overgrown winter jasmines benefit from post-bloom rejuvenation pruning; cut them right to the ground.

Landscape uses: Winter jasmine is especially useful for grouping on banks and walls, and as a foundation plant. Common white jasmine is a good vine for posts and arbors. (Be sure to provide attachments during the first growing season or two.)

Best cultivars: *J. officinale:* 'Affine' has pink-tinged flowers; 'Grandiflorum' has larger flowers, to 1⅓" wide. ❖

Jerusalem Artichoke

Helianthus tuberosus
Compositae

Despite its name, this hardy perennial is a native of North America. Prepare the vitamin- and mineral-rich roots as you would potatoes. Or enjoy their sweet nutty flavor by slicing raw Jerusalem artichokes into a salad or a stir fry.

Planting: Plant whole tubers or large pieces in spring or fall in loose, fertile soil. Allow them plenty of room because the root systems can spread widely. Place Jerusalem artichokes 1' apart in 4" deep furrows spaced 3' apart. The plants will grow into 6'-10' single stalks topped with 3" rough-looking sunflowers.

Growing guidelines: Apply a layer of mulch in late spring to keep weeds down and retain soil moisture. This vegetable spreads rapidly if not controlled. Dig up all the tubers and replant a few in the spring, or let the plants multiply naturally in an out-of-the-way place.

Problems: Jerusalem artichokes are usually free of insect and disease problems. The only problem you may have with this crop is keeping it under control. The invasive root and top growth can overwhelm neighboring crops.

Harvesting: Once the foliage has died down (after the first frost), dig roots with a spading fork as needed. The tubers are thin-skinned, so keep them moist until you're ready to eat them, otherwise they will shrivel. Roots keep best in the ground, even over winter. ❖

Juglans

Walnut. Deciduous, nut-bearing trees.

Description: The trees in this genus produce edible nuts; you'll find more information on care and culture in the Nut Trees entry.

Juglans nigra is the native North American black walnut. It has an upright oval form and a trunk that displays an interlacing diamond pattern in its brown-black bark. Normally growing 50'-75' tall, black walnut occasionally reaches more than 100'. Its alternate compound leaves consist of 15-23 dull green, 2"-5" long leaflets that show little or no fall color before dropping in autumn. Green husks, each with seams defining four quadrants, form in the fall; the walnut and shell are inside. Zones 5-7.

J. regia, Persian or English walnut, shares many characteristics with black walnut, but only grows to 40'-60' in the landscape. The nuts of English walnut are more easily freed from their fleshy outer husks than those of black walnut, and the inner shells are thinner, simplifying removal of the nut meat. English walnuts are widely grown in California for nut production; these are the walnuts most often sold in stores. Hardiness varies. Zones 5-8.

How to grow: Provide a site with full sun, good drainage, and deep, rich, moist soil. Walnuts can retard the growth of plants around them through a chemical competition known as allelopathy. The trees' roots exude a substance called juglone that may be toxic to plants growing nearby, although not all plants are affected by it. Tomatoes are especially susceptible to juglone injury. As a general rule, maintain a distance equal to at least 1½ times a walnut tree's height between it and other plants.

Landscape uses: Walnuts make a coarse-textured shade tree for large-scale situations. Wood and nut production are also desirable.

Best cultivars: *J. regia* 'Carpathian', Carpathian walnut, is cold-hardy well into Zone 5. ❖

Juniperus

Juniper. Needle- or scaly-leaved evergreen trees, shrubs, or groundcovers.

Description: *Juniperus chinensis,* Chinese juniper, can be either a mounded shrub growing 4'-6' tall or an erect, conical tree that can reach a mature height of 50'. The blue- or gray-green evergreen foliage can be scaly or needlelike, often with both forms on the same plant, and rather prickly. Zones 4-8.

J. horizontalis, creeping juniper, has a low, prostrate, horizontally layered form that grows no more than 2' tall. Foliage may spread to 4'-8' per plant at maturity. Its blue-gray or green scaly foliage turns a soft plum purple in winter. Zones 2-8.

J. virginiana, Eastern red cedar, is a tree that reaches a mature height of 10'-50' with an upright, pyramidal form. The silvery to deep blue-green foliage droops slightly with age and bears waxy blue-gray berries. Zones 3-8.

How to grow: All junipers require full sun and well-drained soil. Chinese juniper and Eastern red cedar benefit from evenly moist soil conditions. Creeping juniper tolerates dry soils, seaside or alkaline conditions, and de-icing salts. Prune junipers only to control the size of spreading shrubs; never shear. Phomopsis twig blight can pose problems during a wet spring; prune and destroy diseased twigs. Bagworms can infest junipers at any time; handpick and destroy the larvae. If you are in or near an apple-growing area, be aware that juniper is the alternate host for cedar apple rust, a disease that overwinters on Eastern red cedar and severely injures apple trees.

Landscape uses: Junipers are a good choice for hot, dry, sunny spots that are out of reach for regular watering. There are hundreds of cultivars in many colors, shapes, and sizes. Choose appropriate cultivars for specimens, massed plantings, foundation plantings, groundcovers, screens, hedges, and windbreaks. ❖

Kale

Brassica oleracea, Acephala group
Cruciferae

Frost sweetens the taste of this vitamin- and mineral-packed cooking green. Kale can thrive in semishade and in cloudy climates; hot weather turns it tough and bitter.

Planting: Rich soil promotes a faster-growing and more tender crop. Where summers are cool, sow seeds in early spring, ½″ deep in rows 2½′ apart. For a sweeter fall-winter crop, broadcast seed at least six weeks before the first frost; rake to cover.

Growing guidelines: Thin plants to 2′ apart. Keep the soil moist. Mulch established plants to control weeds.

Problems: See the Cabbage entry for insect and disease controls.

Harvesting: Harvest outer leaves as needed; use young, tender leaves for salads and older leaves for cooking. ❖

Kalmia

Laurel. Spring-blooming broad-leaved evergreen shrubs.

Description: *Kalmia latifolia,* mountain laurel, can grow to 15′. Rounded when young, plants develop a handsome bare-trunked tree form at maturity. Dark green, leathery, 2″-5″ oval leaves are evergreen. Showy clusters of late spring flowers are white with banded markings in shades of pink. Zones 5-8.

How to grow: Mountain laurel requires evenly moist, well-drained, humus-rich soil and deep mulch. Plant in fall or spring in Zones 5-6 and shield from winter sun and wind. In Zones 7-8, plant in fall or winter in partial shade. Pruning is rarely needed.

Landscape uses: Mountain laurel is a good choice for a native planting, woodland garden, or Southern wetland garden. ❖

Kiwi

Actinidia spp.
Actinidiaceae

Kiwis are a gourmet treat eaten fresh or in preserves, baked goods, and ice cream. They also contain ten times the vitamin C of oranges. Hardy kiwis can be grown throughout most of the United States. Southern gardeners can grow the larger Chinese kiwi. Kiwi vines are ornamental and require little care except pruning. Untrained, the vines grow rampantly and will clamber over anything in their paths, strangling trees or forming a tangled waterfall of vines. Trellised, they are beautiful and high-yielding.

Selecting vines: Hardy kiwis are the size of a large grape. They have smooth skin and are eaten unpeeled, unlike their fuzzy cousins. *Actinidia arguta* survives to −25°F (Zone 4); its vines can reach 40′ long. *A. kolomikta,* sometimes called 'Arctic Beauty' kiwi, is hardy to −40°F (Zone 3). It leafs out later than *A. arguta* and so is less susceptible to frosts. Male 'Arctic Beauty' plants have lovely pink-and-white variegated foliage.

Chinese kiwis, *A. chinesis,* are the fuzzy fruits found in supermarkets. They are hardy only to 10°F, and trunks need winter protection.

Most kiwis produce male and female flowers on separate plants; plant one male for every 3-4 females to ensure fruit set. A few cultivars, such as 'Issai' (*A. arguta*) and 'Blake' (*A. chinesis*) can produce fruit without another vine. They are also less vigorous and easier to control.

Planting and care: Kiwis do best at a pH of 6.0-6.5, and prefer well-drained soil. They like full sun but will tolerate partial shade. *A. kolomikta* prefers shade in hot climates.

Kiwis need support. Grow them on a trellis, arbor, or sturdy fence. A mature, bearing vine is very heavy, so build a strong arbor.

Plant vines in the spring. Prune back newly planted vines to 4-5 buds. When these buds grow, select a sturdy shoot to be the main trunk. Tie it to the support, encouraging it to grow to the top of the arbor. When it does, cut off the tip to stimulate side branches.

Once a month each summer, prune all new growth back to 4-5 buds. This produces a dense, twiggy vine which bears large clusters of fruit. Prune overgrown vines back severely.

Kiwis tolerate drought but produce better if they get at least 1″ of water a week. They are heavy feeders; apply 30 lb. of rotted manure or compost to each vine in early spring.

Harvesting: Vines bear in 2-3 years. The fruits ripen in late summer. Pick them just before they are fully ripe and allow them to soften at room temperature. It may take some experimentation to get the ripening right, so keep trying. Kiwis keep in the refrigerator for two months if stored before softening.

Problems: Kiwi vines suffer from few if any insect or disease problems. ❖

Kniphofia

Torch lily, red-hot poker. Summer- to fall-blooming perennials.

Description: Torch lilies bear dense, foot-long, shaggy spikes of 1″-2″ hanging, tubular flowers in shades and combinations of ivory, yellow, orange, and red. Flowers are borne on thick stalks 2′-4′ above grassy foliage to 3′ long. Zones 6-9.

How to grow: Plant or divide (infrequently) in spring in a sunny spot with rich, very well drained soil. Sandy soils are best. Tie the leaves together in fall in Zone 6 to prevent water from collecting in and freezing the crowns.

Landscape uses: Use as a specimen or a small mass in a border or for cut flowers. They are striking with daisies, daylilies, and lilies, or in a cloud of baby's-breath.

Best cultivars: 'Earliest of All', coral, 2½', one of the hardiest. ❖

Kohlrabi

Brassica oleracea, Gongylodes group
Cruciferae

Kohlrabi resembles an aboveground turnip. It's a cabbage-family member, so it's no surprise that the edible white, green, or purple "bulbs" (which are actually swollen stems) have a cabbage-turnip taste. Kohlrabi is, however, milder and sweeter than either of those vegetables.

Kohlrabi is more tolerant of heat than other cole crops, but cool weather is still essential for a good harvest. Seed directly in the garden in early spring, or in warm regions, grow it as a fall or winter crop. The harvest can be extended with successive plantings where growing seasons are long and cool.

Planting: Kohlrabi grows in loose, average soil. For a spring crop, direct-sow seeds 4-6 weeks before the last average frost; plant ¼″ deep, 10 seeds per foot. Or start the crop indoors 6-8 weeks before the last average frost. When seedlings are around 4″ tall, thin plants to (or set out transplants at) 5″ apart in rows 1′ apart.

Plant fall crops outdoors ten weeks before the first frost. Light frosts will enhance flavor.

Growing guidelines: Keep plants well watered and free of weeds; put down a mulch to help accomplish both tasks. Cultivate carefully to keep from damaging the delicate, shallow roots.

Problems: See the Cabbage entry for insect and disease controls.

Harvesting: Use young leaves in salads. Harvest immature "bulbs" when they are no more than 2″ in diameter, cutting the stems 1″ below the swollen stem. Remove the leaf stems and leaves, and use the remaining stem as you would turnip roots. Kohlrabi will keep for several weeks in the refrigerator and for several months in a moist root cellar.

Best cultivars: 'Kolpak', early, white, tender flesh; 'Early Purple Vienna', purplish skin with greenish white flesh. ❖

Lagerstroemia

Lagerstroemia. Deciduous, summer-flowering trees or shrubs.

Description: *Lagerstroemia indica,* crape myrtle, flowers on new growth in white, pink, or watermelon red. When grown as a tree, it has an upright, narrowly vase-shaped, multi-trunked form, and a mature height of about 20′. Some cultivars feature dark bark that peels away to expose lighter patches. When grown as a shrub, plants may reach 2′-12′ in a season. Northern gardeners grow dwarf forms of crape myrtle as a semi-woody perennial that sprouts from the roots each year. Fall color varies. Zones 7-9.

How to grow: Give lagerstroemias full sun and good drainage. Shade promotes powdery mildew, which can be a serious problem. A National Arboretum breeding program produced many mildew-resistant cultivars; look for these selections when buying lagerstroemias. Prune in winter to promote vigorous growth for good flowering. Cut shrub forms entirely to the ground, or remove ⅓ of the oldest stems at ground level. Shape tree forms by pruning out sucker shoots, water sprouts, and rubbing branches. Prune away spent flowers and seed heads; in Zones 8-9, midsummer deadheading results in a second bloom in fall.

Landscape uses: Lagerstroemias work beautifully as screens, street trees, or focal points. ❖

Lamium

Lamium, dead nettle. Trailing perennial groundcovers.

Description: *Lamium maculatum,* spotted lamium or spotted dead nettle, has 1″-2″ long, heart-shaped, trailing leaves. Cultivars have beautiful white or silver variegated foliage. The small, hooded pink, magenta, or white flowers open in whorls on stalks 6″-8″ high. Plants bloom from April through June and again in September. Zones 3-9.

How to grow: Spotted lamium prefers partial shade and average, moist soil. It tolerates full sun and even poor soil. Don't fertilize these plants, or they may become invasive weeds. Propagate by seeds, cuttings, or root division in the spring.

Landscape uses: Spotted lamium is prized for its lengthy flower display and for its interesting silvery foliage. It's an excellent choice for a shady site and can be used as a contrast to a solid green planting. Plants provide an unusual background for taller ornamentals. Spotted lamium looks attractive under trees, in rock gardens, in hanging baskets, or in drifts.

Best cultivars: 'Beacon Silver', pink flowers and silver leaves with green margins; 'White Nancy', white flowers and silver-variegated leaves; 'Variegatum', leaves with silver stripes down the center. ❖

Landscaping

You don't have to be an artist to create an attractive and useful environment around your home. Landscaping is a form of personal expression, an extension of the care you put into arranging the inside of your house. There is no "right" landscape; what works for your neighbor may not suit your needs or look good on your site.

Having a beautiful and unique property depends on four basic steps: gathering ideas, creating a design, installing plants and structures, and maintaining the landscape. Attractive landscaping will help you enjoy your home and increase its value as well.

Gathering Ideas

Before putting anything on paper, start the design process by looking around for ideas. Great landscaping ideas are all around you. Look at homes in your community and take note of landscapes that catch your eye. See if a garden club in your area sponsors tours of local gardens; these "open gardens" are a great way to get a close view of plants and design ideas that are appropriate for your area. Public parks and botanical gardens can also give you planting ideas. Check out the wide variety of gardening books available; they're packed with photographs and tips about other people's success stories.

When you look at a landscape, try to visualize it as a series of garden "rooms." Like a room in a house, each part of the landscape has walls, a floor, and a ceiling. The walls could be a hedge, a row of trees, a fence, or a trellis. The floor might be turf, mulch, groundcover, crushed stone, or wooden decking; the sky or an arbor may serve as the ceiling.

Breaking a landscape down into rooms makes it easier to identify the elements you need to add or change. For example, if you want to separate the vegetable garden from the rest of your yard, you need some sort of wall. If you don't want to see the garden, you could plant a hedge or install a solid wood fence. If you are enclosing the garden to protect it from animals, you might try a woven wire fence planted with attractive vines. These rooms need doorways too—don't forget to think about gates or openings in the walls.

When you view a landscape as a combination of these solid elements, the whole process of planning a design is much more manageable. If you see a landscape that you particularly like, try to figure out what makes it special. Is there an attractive fence that makes a nice backdrop for the plants? Is there a beautiful tree or shrub you would just love to have for your own property? Has your neighbor come up with a clever way to screen the front yard from the street? You may not want to copy any of these ideas exactly, but they will give you some idea of what is possible for your own home. The unlimited combinations of these elements make it easy to create a landscape that is unique to your property. And that's what landscaping is all about: making the best of your site.

Creating a Design

Creating a design starts with a wish list, based on the ideas you've gathered from books and neighboring properties. This list should include design ideas, garden structures, and specific plants. This isn't the time for you to be realistic—go ahead and put down anything that you'd like to see in your yard.

The next step is figuring out what you really need in the landscape. If you have children, a play area may be the most important use of the yard. If you do a lot of entertaining, a shady arbor might be just the place for parties. For a large family, parking may be a major consideration. Besides play areas, entertaining, and parking, think about privacy, security, noise reduction, pets, flowers, and food production.

Compare your wish list with your needs list. Some things will probably appear on both lists. The rose hedge on your wish list, for example, may match your need to keep romping pets out of the vegetable garden. Other wants and needs may be totally incompatible. If your yard is a popular place for neighborhood football or volleyball games, a delicate rock garden might be out of the question. Discuss the lists with your family, and decide which elements are acceptable to everyone. Also, don't forget to consider maintenance needs. A lovely perennial border can quickly deteriorate into a tangled mess if you don't have time to take care of it.

Your site will also determine some of your choices. The style of your home may influence the feel of the design. If you have a brick house, the landscape might include formal brick paths and clipped evergreen hedges. A house with natural wood siding lends itself to wood-chip paths and rail fencing. You'll also need to plan access areas, such as paths, steps, and ramps.

Take note of wet, shady, and rocky spots, and try to take advantage of them. A wet spot may not be desirable in a play area, but it could be a good place for a group of moisture-loving plants. Also, think of the landscape as it changes through the seasons. Evergreens and berried shrubs, along with a bench in a sunny spot, can make your yard a pleasant winter retreat. A little careful planning can give the landscape four-season appeal. Don't forget details like specimen plants, interesting rocks, or sculpture to give the garden character.

Start the actual design by making a basic plan of your property and plotting it on paper. Nothing will inspire you to look more closely and critically at your landscape. Make as accurate a plan as possible, and include all your garden's features—paths, trees, buildings, fences, and walkways. Draw it to scale, measuring distances with a 100' tape measure and transferring this information to graph paper. A scale of ¼" = 1' is workable; tape sheets together if your property is large. This will make a valuable permanent record you can work from and give you the best idea of where your landscape is heading.

Use sheets of thin tracing paper as overlays to sketch in ideas and see how they fit while you

REDUCING LANDSCAPE MAINTENANCE

Keep these time-saving pointers in mind when designing and caring for your yard:

● Apply a generous layer of mulch to keep weeds down and reduce watering needs.

● On a steep, hard-to-mow slope, build terraces to break the slope into steps or plant the incline with groundcovers.

● Use the right tool for the job. A good tool can make a tiresome chore a pleasure.

● Keep up with yard maintenance by doing a little bit at a time. Fifteen minutes a day can take the place of a whole afternoon of yard work once a week.

● Don't struggle with sparse, weedy grass under trees; surround trees with beds of shade-loving plants.

● Brick or stone mowing strips placed around trees and flower beds will keep out grass and make mowing easier.

● Avoid using sharp angles or fussy curves when laying out flower beds; mowing around them is less difficult along straight lines and smooth curves.

● Reduce lawn area and cut down on mowing time by installing decking or low-maintenance groundcovers.

● If you really want to grow fruit, try easy-to-grow bush cherries, blueberries, strawberries, or raspberries.

● Minimize fall leaf-raking chores by planting small-leaved trees such as black locust (*Robinia pseudoacacia*).

● Plant slow- and smaller-growing trees and shrubs to reduce pruning chores.

● Plan on informal hedges, which rely on natural shrub shapes; formal hedges require repeated shearing to keep their shape.

● Choose disease- and insect-resistant plants to reduce pest control problems.

work on the design. That way, you can use your master plan again and again until you decide on the best arrangement of pathways, flower beds,

FOUNDATION PLANTING

Foundation planting is one of the most misunderstood landscaping concepts in America. This planting idea became popular many years ago, when homes were built with high foundations that detracted from the rest of the house. Today, the foundations on most homes are hardly visible, yet the plantings continue in the name of tradition.

Many homeowners make the mistake of buying small plants at the nursery without considering the mature size of the plants. When this happens, the inevitable result a few years later is either a tangled mess of shrubs and trees blocking the windows, path, and doorway, or a home surrounded by overpruned, unhealthy plants hacked into stiff geometric forms.

There is, however, a happy medium. Make a plan before you buy the plants, and choose among the many low-growing and dwarf cultivars of trees and shrubs that mature at the size you'd like. Providing plants with the room they need to develop properly allows them to display their natural beauty, and you won't need to shear them into cubes or cones in an attempt to keep them in bounds. If the planting looks too sparse, fill in spaces with annuals, perennials, or bulbs until the shrubs develop.

Remember, the ultimate goal of landscaping is to integrate house and landscape in a harmonious arrangement. Foundation planting can be a start, but you also need to continue the planting areas out into the yard. With some planning, your landscape will be a source of year-round enjoyment, rather than boredom and drudgery.

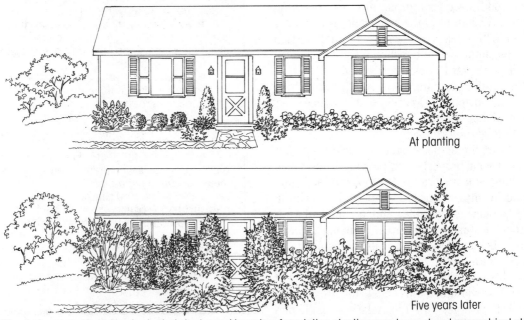

At planting

Five years later

Plan before you plant. Newly planted shrubs and trees in a foundation planting may be neat and symmetrical at planting time, but they will inevitably smother a house in greenery unless they're properly selected. Plan a planting featuring species of low-growing shrubs or small trees, and also take advantage of the many dwarf cultivars of trees and shrubs that are available.

and other landscape features. You can then transfer the final design to your master plan.

Whether you design your home landscape yourself or leave it to a professional, make sure that the finished plan fits your needs. Don't add a deck just because all your neighbors have them if what you really want is a dooryard herb garden. And while you don't want to copy your neighbors exactly, try to keep the general theme of the area in your design. A woodland garden in the Southwest would look as out of place as a cactus garden in New England. By using plants that are best adapted to your area, your landscape will have the appropriate regional look. Your plants also will be healthier and will require less special care.

Installing Plants and Structures

Once you actually have a plan, the next step is to carry it out. The first consideration in installation is often the cost. If you can't or don't want to do everything at once, consider carrying the plan out over several years. It's usually best to start with any structures, such as fences and buildings. Next, add the trees and hedges. Eventually, add smaller shrubs, flowers, and groundcovers. This approach makes it fairly easy to install the landscape on your own.

If you do want to carry out the plan all at once, it may be best to hire a professional; this is especially true if the plan includes grading and drainage changes or irrigation and lighting systems. For your protection, get three bids for large projects, and make sure you have signed contracts before work begins. Also, don't forget to check local regulations and get necessary permits before starting.

Maintaining the Landscape

After you have spent all this time developing and installing your landscape, you'll certainly want to take good care of it. In new landscapes, watering is probably the most important task. Regular watering for the first year or two helps plants to settle in. After that, water your plants less frequently to encourage strong root systems. Pruning, applying mulch and fertilizer, and controlling insects and diseases are all routine maintenance tasks that keep your landscape looking its best. ❖

More On
LANDSCAPING

With some research and a lot of thought, you can create a beautiful, healthy landscape. As you gather ideas for your property, keep in mind the many types of theme gardens that can add appeal to your yard. For more information, see the following entries: Bog Gardens, Butterfly Gardening, Container Gardening, Cottage Gardening, Curbside Gardens, Cut Flower Gardening, Dried Flower Gardening, Edible Landscaping, Meadow Gardens, Natural Landscaping, Raised Bed Gardening, Rock Gardens, Shade Gardening, Vegetable Gardening, Water Gardens, and Xeriscaping. You may also want to read Beneficial Animals, Beneficial Insects, Birds, and Wildlife for details on attracting these creatures to your garden.

As you create your plan, see the Garden Design entry for information on specific design styles and principles; you'll also learn more about planning considerations and plant selection. For details on other landscape elements, see the Fencing, Hedges, Lawns, and Walkways and Paths entries.

If you are looking for specific plant ideas, see: Annuals, Biennials, Bulbs, Evergreens, Fruit Trees, Grasses, Groundcovers, Herbs, Nut Trees, Perennials, Shrubs, Trees, Vines, and Wildflowers.

For more information on landscape installation and maintenance, see the entries on Fertilizers, Irrigation, Organic Pest Management, Planting, Pruning and Training, Soil, Staking, and Tools and Equipment.

Lantana

Lantana. Tender perennials grown as all-season annuals.

Description: *Lantana camara* sports 1″ flower heads in white, yellow, orange, red, or combinations. The spreading, 2′-4′ bushes have rough, dark green leaves. *L. montevidensis* (*L. sellowiana*), weeping lantana, bears lavender or white flower heads on trailing stems with paler leaves.

How to grow: Buy plants in bloom and set out after frost in full sun. Rich soil encourages foliar growth at the expense of flowers. Lantana is drought-tolerant. Control whiteflies with soap spray.

Landscape uses: Mass *L. camara* in a bed or border, or train into a standard. Try weeping lantana in a hanging basket.

Best cultivars: *L. camara*: 'Semantha', yellow and red; 'Dwarf Yellow', 3′. *L. montevidensis*: 'Alba', white. ❖

Larix

Larch. Deciduous needled conifers.

Description: *Larix decidua,* European larch, is a single-trunked, pyramidal tree with horizontal primary branches and smaller branchlets hanging from them. It grows to 70′-100′. The needles turn yellow in autumn and drop, leaving the tree bare in the winter except for the cones and dangling branchlets. Zones 3-6.

L. laricina, tamarack, resembles *L. decidua* but is a slightly shorter (40′-80′) tree. Tamarack is native from the northern Great Lakes region across Canada and into Alaska. Zones 2-4.

How to grow: Plant larches in sunny sites with moist, acidic, humusy soil like that found in the cool forests to which they are native.

Landscape uses: Use specimen larches to provide light shade and fine texture in large-scale Northern landscapes. ❖

Lathyrus

Sweet pea. Cool-weather annuals.

Description: Sweet peas bear short spikes of fragrant, butterflylike 1″ blooms in white, pink, red, orange, cream, or purple plus bi- and tricolors. The flowers appear on weak 6′ vines or 15″ mounds of pealike foliage.

How to grow: Sweet peas grow and bloom best in cool weather. Plant seeds outdoors 2″ deep in late fall or early spring, in a sunny spot with rich, moist, slightly alkaline soil. Provide support for vining cultivars. Pick flowers often for more bloom. Control aphid infestations with soap spray.

Landscape uses: Vines make temporary screens. Bushy plants brighten edges, beds, pots, and window boxes.

Best cultivars: Mixes: vining 'Galaxy'; bushy 'Knee Hi' resists some heat. ❖

Lavandula

Lavender. Evergreen summer-blooming perennial herbs.

Description: The species most commonly grown for its fragrant oil is English lavender, *Lavandula angustifolia* (also sold as *L. officinalis, L. spica,* or *L. vera*). English lavender bears narrow, grayish, aromatic leaves on woody stems growing 1′-3′ tall. In summer, 2″ long spikes of fragrant purplish blue flowers appear above the foliage. Zones 5-8.

How to grow: Lavender needs a sunny site with good drainage and average soil. Take stem cuttings to renew plants that are getting too woody. Prune regularly to promote bushy growth.

Landscape uses: Plant in containers, borders, or rock gardens; dry the flowers for use in crafts.

Best cultivars: 'Hidcote', deep purple flowers; 'Munstead', compact habit. ❖

Lawns

Healthy green turf makes everything near it look better. A carpet of green grass also makes a great place to play or relax, while preventing soil erosion and enhancing the value of your home. A good lawn is the result of conscientious gardening practices, whether you're starting a new lawn with a carefully selected cultivar or rejuvenating an existing lawn of unknown parentage.

Build a strong lawn by using grass species adapted to your climate. Encourage healthy growth naturally by letting light grass clippings remain where they fall and by applying compost or other organic material. Relying on high-nitrogen chemical fertilizers can lead to problem-prone, shallow-rooted turf that needs mowing more often. These are some of the most widely grown lawn grasses:

• Bermudagrass (*Cynodon dactylon*), a fine-textured, drought-resistant grass popular in warmer climates. Becomes buff brown in the winter. Numerous runners create a wear-resistant turf. Open-pollinated strains are extremely aggressive; modern hybrids are much easier to keep from invading flower beds.

• Buffalo grass (*Buchloe dactyloides*), a creeping, warm-season grass. Tolerates drought and will grow in alkaline soil. Good wear tolerance. Brown in midsummer and fall.

• Centipede grass (*Eremochloa ophiuroides*), a coarser-leaved, warm-season, creeping grass with good drought tolerance. Plant in low-wear areas.

• Fine fescues (*Festuca* spp.), dark green, fine-textured, creeping, cool-season grasses with good shade tolerance, often mixed with Kentucky bluegrass.

• Kentucky bluegrass (*Poa pratensis*), a lush, dark green turfgrass with narrow blades that requires substantial sunshine. Favored cool-season lawn grass. May become dormant during summer droughts or during winter freezes. Creeping stolons knit a tough turf.

• Turf-type tall fescue (*Festuca arundinacea*), a coarse, medium green grass good for sun or shade, increasingly popular in the central United States. Updated cultivars remain green most of the year. Drought-resistant. Grows in low clumps and doesn't creep, so is often mixed with other grasses.

• Zoysia grass (*Zoysia* spp.), a medium green, creeping, fine-textured grass for full sun. Green in warm weather, tan in winter.

Fertilizing

You don't need to know every grass plant in your yard by name to grow a healthy lawn. The most important thing to note is the time of year when the grass begins to grow rapidly. This is the ideal time to apply a good organic fertilizer. In the North where cool-season grasses have a growth spurt in spring and another in fall, plan to fertilize twice. For warm-season grasses, fertilize in late spring, just as your lawn greens up, and again a few weeks later.

Choose a finely pulverized, weed-free organic fertilizer, such as processed manure or sifted compost, and spread evenly over the lawn just before rain is expected. Mow the grass about a week after you fertilize. Let the nitrogen-rich clippings remain on the lawn. For more ideas on what to feed your grass, see the Fertilizers entry.

Maintaining Lawns

Mowing: Sharpen your mower blade at the beginning of each season to make sure the grass blades are cut, rather than torn, when you mow. Remove only ⅓ of the grass's topgrowth. The exact height for mowing depends on the species of grass. Cut low-growing grasses, such as bermudagrass and zoysia grass, no shorter than 1″. Cut taller grasses, such as bluegrass and tall fescue, no shorter than 2″. Mow high during

Key Words
LAWNS

Cool-season grass. A grass that grows strongly in spring and fall, often remaining green in winter but tending to go dormant when the hot days of summer come. Examples: Kentucky bluegrass, fine fescues.

Warm-season grass. A grass that grows well in summer, even in hot, dry climates, and is usually dormant in winter. Examples: bermudagrass, centipede grass, zoysia grass.

Stolon. A specialized stem that creeps below the surface of the soil, rooting and sprouting new plants along the way.

Sod. Strips of living grass that have been peeled, roots and all, from the soil.

Plugs. Small pieces of sod used to start a lawn of creeping types of grass. Plant plugs in scooped-out holes, 6''–12'' apart.

Sprigs. Pieces of rooted grass stem or stolon, extricated from shredded sod. Plant sprigs 6'' apart to start a lawn of creeping types of grass.

Thatch. A layer of grass clippings and other dead plant parts that accumulate in a lawn.

summer droughts. To cut very tall grass, set your mower blade at its highest setting. In the course of the next two mowings, lower the blade until you are cutting at the usual height.

If you mow regularly, let your grass clippings lay where they fall. They will eventually rot and add organic matter to the soil beneath. Large clumps of clippings sitting on your lawn block sunlight and promote disease. Gather them up and use as mulch in other parts of your yard.

Dethatching: All lawns have thatch, a layer of clippings and stems that gradually decomposes and feeds the roots. There's no need to remove it if the layer is no thicker than about ¼''. Thatch problems often start with overuse of synthetic chemical fertilizers, which make grass grow fast and lush. As clippings build up into a thick layer of thatch, grass plants are unable to get enough air for healthy growth. Use a thatch rake to break up thatch in a small lawn; rent a vertical mower to dethatch a larger area.

Aerating: Since lawns often bear heavy foot traffic, the soil below them becomes compacted over time. Grass roots have trouble growing down and out and instead concentrate their growth at the surface. Prevent or fix compacted lawns by aerating every 2-3 years. Aerating a lawn consists of poking tiny holes through the turf into the soil below. Use a step-on core cultivator for small areas; rent a power aerator machine for larger lawns. Mow the lawn and spread a thin layer of organic fertilizer. Aerate in one direction; repeat crosswise. Water deeply.

Repairing Lawns

Ruts left by heavy vehicles or scars created when shrubs or trees are removed call for prompt spot repairs. If damage occurs in winter, prepare the soil and cover it with a mulch until spring.

Loosen the soil in the damaged site, setting aside any grass plants that seem healthy. Keep them damp and shaded as you work. Add a ½'' layer of compost or peat moss to condition the soil, along with enough good topsoil to raise the level of the damaged area 1'' above the soil level of the surrounding turf. Lightly walk over the spot, and fill in any holes or low places. Reseed or replant, matching the primary species in your yard. Water regularly for a month.

Planting New Lawns

All lawn grasses require at least 4'' of good topsoil in which to stretch their roots. If your new yard has been scraped down to the subsoil, you will have to spread new topsoil. Site prepa-

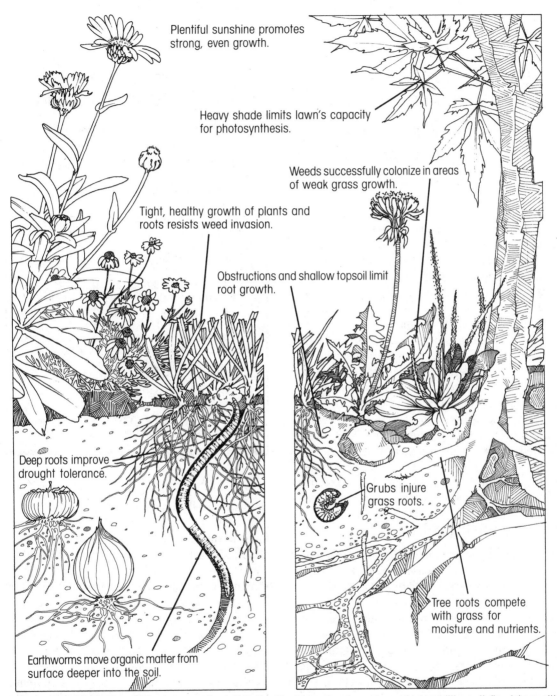

Plentiful sunshine promotes strong, even growth.

Heavy shade limits lawn's capacity for photosynthesis.

Weeds successfully colonize in areas of weak grass growth.

Tight, healthy growth of plants and roots resists weed invasion.

Obstructions and shallow topsoil limit root growth.

Deep roots improve drought tolerance.

Grubs injure grass roots.

Earthworms move organic matter from surface deeper into the soil.

Tree roots compete with grass for moisture and nutrients.

Healthy lawn/sickly lawn. The lawn on the left is healthy because of good growing conditions. It flourishes with minimum care. The lawn on the right is sparse and sickly, struggling along in poor condition. It needs renovation. Better soil preparation, the use of a shade-tolerant grass cultivar, and regular maintenance would improve the lawn. A bed of groundcovers or mulch beneath the tree would be a better choice than grass.

ration is the same whether you plan to begin with seed or sod: Cultivate new or existing topsoil thoroughly, adding a 1″ layer of peat moss, compost, or other organic matter. Rake out all weeds and roots, cultivate again, and rake smooth. Use a roller to evenly compact the site and make it level.

Be picky when shopping for grass seed. Improved cultivars of the best lawn grasses cost more than their open-pollinated cousins, but they offer superior performance. Choose named cultivars that have been specially bred for drought tolerance, insect and disease resistance, adaptability to shade, or other traits. Use a mechanical seeder for even distribution. Roll after seeding. Keep constantly moist for two weeks. Start mowing three weeks after seeding.

Sod is the fastest way to an attractive lawn, though the cost is higher than seed. It's ideal for spot repairs, especially in high-traffic areas or on slopes. Plant cool-season species in early spring or from late summer to early fall; plant warm-season grasses in late spring to early summer. Use only fresh, green strips. Keep them shaded and damp until planted. Work crosswise along slopes. Roll or walk on the strips after planting to push the roots into the soil. After planting, water every 2-3 days for three weeks.

Coping with Problems

A healthy lawn is naturally more resistant to weed, insect, or disease problems. A tight cover of vigorous grass will outcompete weeds. Loose, well-drained soil helps prevent disease problems. Proper fertilization goes a long way toward preventing lawn problems since it encourages growth of strong, healthy turf. Most updated turfgrass cultivars offer genetically improved resistance to diseases and some insects. If you have lawn areas that are chronically problematic, consider replanting them with an improved cultivar or trying an alternative to lawn grass. See the Groundcovers entry for suggestions of plants

---

BEST BETS FOR LOW MAINTENANCE

For the best lawn in the least time, follow these tips:

● Limit the amount of lawn in your landscape.

● Keep lawn in large, continuous swaths. Join trees and shrubs with a bed of mulch or groundcovers instead of mowing around and between. Don't plant lawn in hard-to-mow corners.

● Replace aggressive old strains with an improved cultivar or mixture.

● Use lawn edgings and mulch to separate grass from flower beds and trees.

● Accept clovers as beneficial nitrogen-fixers in your lawn, not weeds.

● Where conditions are too steep, too shady, or otherwise unsuitable for good lawn, choose alternatives such as ornamental grasses or groundcovers.

● During droughts, water modestly once a week. Provide sufficient water to keep your grass alive, but not enough to coax it out of heat-induced dormancy.

---

that work well as substitutes for lawns.

There are a few simple steps to take if your lawn develops weed or pest problems. Use a small, sharp knife to slice off any established weeds about 1″ below the soil surface. If more than half of the plants in your lawn are weeds, it is best to renovate the lawn by replanting.

Subterranean insect larvae, such as white grubs, occasionally cause serious damage when they feed on grass roots. Apply milky disease spores for long-term control of these pests. Biological insecticides that utilize parasitic nematodes control numerous insects likely to feed beneath your lawn. For more ideas on reducing pests and disease, see the Organic Pest Management entry. ❖

Layering

Layering is a way of propagating plants by encouraging sections of stems to sprout new roots. The rooted stems are cut from the mother plant and planted. This simple and reliable method produces good-sized new plants in a relatively short time.

Simple Layering

Simple layering involves bending a low-growing branch to the ground and burying several inches of stem. It is used to propagate many types of vines and woody plants, including grapes and magnolias.

Season: Spring is the best time to start simple layers. Choose flexible, vigorous one-year-old shoots about as thick as a pencil.

Getting started: Thoroughly water the soil around the plant. The next day, bend a shoot down to the soil. Measure back 9″-12″ from the tip of the shoot, and mark the spot where that point on the stem touches the ground. Release the shoot, and dig a 4″ hole at the marked point. The hole should have three straight sides, with the fourth side sloping toward the parent plant. Work in several handfuls of finished compost.

Method: Remove leaves and sideshoots along the chosen stem from 6″-15″ behind the stem tip. Wound the stem by making a shallow 2″ long cut at a point about 9″ behind the tip. Insert a toothpick or small pebble in the cut to keep it open. Dust the cut with rooting hormone. Bend the prepared stem down into the hole, and use a wire pin to keep the wounded area in contact with the soil. Stake the stem tip if it doesn't stay upright by itself. Cover the pinned stem with the soil you removed earlier, and water the area thoroughly.

Aftercare: Keep the layered area moist and weeded. The stem may root by fall; check by uncovering the stem, removing the wire pin, and tugging lightly. If the stem feels firmly anchored, it has rooted. Sever it from the parent plant, but

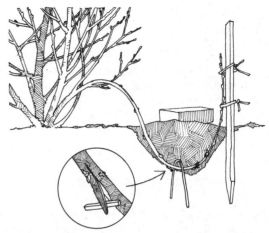

Simple layering. Use a piece of wire, bent into a hairpin shape, to hold the wounded stem in the trench. A brick over the buried stem helps to retain moisture.

leave it in place until spring. Then pot it up or transplant it. If the stem is not well rooted, replace the soil and wait a year before separating it from the parent plant.

Tip Layering

Shoot tips of certain plants root when they touch the ground. This phenomenon, called tip layering, happens naturally in black and purple raspberries.

Season: Plant tip layers in late summer, using the ends of the current season's growth. Make sure you use healthy, vigorous canes.

Getting started: Prepare a hole as you would for simple layers; judge the placement of the hole by the tip of the stem.

Method: Bend the stem tip down to the prepared planting hole. Lay the cane against the sloping side and place the tip against the farthest edge of the hole. Replace the soil, and water the area well.

Aftercare: By early autumn, shoots will appear and roots will have formed; cut the original cane where it enters the soil. In mid-autumn or the following spring, carefully dig up the rooted tip, and plant it in its new position.

Air Layering

Air layering is similar to simple layering, but the stem is covered with long-fibered (unmilled) sphagnum moss rather than soil. You can air-layer upright stems of trees, shrubs, and indoor plants such as philodendrons and weeping fig trees.

Season: Outdoors, start air layers in early fall with young wood, or in spring with the previous season's growth. Indoors, air layers can be done any time, but it's best to start when plants begin growing actively in spring.

Getting started: Soak the sphagnum moss in water for a few hours or overnight. Before using, wring the excess water out of the moss, so it is moist but not dripping wet.

Method: Start with a healthy, vigorous stem. Decide where you want the roots of the new plant to be, anywhere from 6″-18″ behind the tip. Remove all leaves and sideshoots for 3″ on either side of that point. Wound the stem by making a shallow 2″ long cut into it. Dust the wounded area with rooting hormone. Wrap the ball of moist sphagnum moss around the wound and tie it with string. Next, cover the moss ball

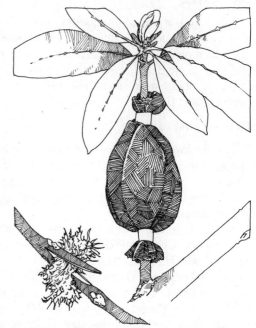

Air layering. Wound the stem and tuck a bit of moss into the wound. Wrap the remainder around the stem, and cover with plastic. If the moss looks dry during rooting, open the plastic, moisten the moss, and reseal.

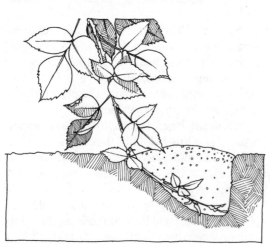

Tip layering. Keep the soil moist to promote rooting. Sever the rooted layer from the parent plant in early fall; wait at least a few weeks before moving the new plant.

with a piece of clear plastic about 6″ square. For indoor plants, tie the plastic at both ends with string or twist ties. Use waterproof tape to secure the ends on outdoor air layers; make sure the ends are completely sealed. For outdoor plants, also cover the plastic wrap with foil or black plastic and tie or tape it to the stem; this will keep the layered area from getting too hot in the sun.

Aftercare: Indoor plants can produce roots in a few months; outdoor plants may take one or two growing seasons. You'll be able to see the roots growing in the moss. Cut off the top of the plant below the new roots and remove the plastic. Soak the root ball for 3-4 hours, pot it up, and place it in a sheltered spot for a few days. Let outdoor plants grow in their pots for a few months before planting them out. ❖

Leaves

Leaves come in a wonderful array of sizes, shapes, textures, and colors, but whatever the form, they all serve a common function. Leaves manufacture the sugars and other compounds that serve as food for plants. To perform this manufacturing process, called photosynthesis, leaves need several ingredients: light, chlorophyll, carbon dioxide, and water.

To intercept as much light as possible, most leaves are flat and face broadside to the sun. Also, they are positioned to avoid shading other leaves on the same plant. When light strikes a leaf, much is reflected—on a sunny day, leaves sparkle like mirrors—but some enters and is captured by chlorophyll, the pigment that gives leaves their green color. (The colors of fall foliage and of variegated plants come from other pigments,

Key Words
LEAVES

Alternate. Having one leaf or bud at each node along a stem.

Opposite. Having two leaves or two buds at each node along a stem.

Simple leaf. A leaf with an undivided blade.

Compound leaf. A leaf whose blade is divided into distinct leaflets.

Pinnate. Having similar parts arranged along the opposite sides of an axis.

Palmate. Resembling a hand with the fingers spread; having lobes that radiate from a common point.

Whorled. Having three or more buds or three or more leaves at a node.

Trifoliate. Having three leaflets.

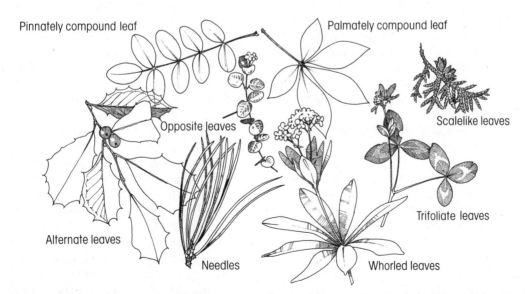

Pinnately compound leaf

Palmately compound leaf

Scalelike leaves

Opposite leaves

Trifoliate leaves

Alternate leaves

Needles

Whorled leaves

Leaf types. Looking at leaf shapes and arrangments is an important way to identify plants. Botanists have their own vocabulary of technical descriptive words that describe leaves. Learning a few basic leaf terms will help increase your knowledge of and ability to identify plants.

some of which also help in photosynthesis.)

Carbon dioxide is part of air. It makes up about 1/30 of 1 percent of the atmosphere. Air enters leaves through microscopic pores called stomates. Stomates are tiny but number as many as 200,000 or more per square inch. Usually stomates are located on the bottom surfaces of leaves, where they are less likely to be blocked by dust, but on upright leaves like blades of grass, corn, or daffodil leaves, stomates occur on *both* sides.

Roots absorb water, which is drawn upward to the leaves, but most of it—as much as 98 percent—is lost when it transpires (evaporates) through the open stomates. This may seem wasteful, but transpiration is a cooling process that keeps leaves from overheating in the sun. And fortunately, the stomates close quickly to stop further water loss if a leaf starts to wilt.

Photosynthesis takes place when chlorophyll molecules trap energy from light and use the energy to split water molecules into hydrogen and oxygen. The oxygen flows out through the stomates; the hydrogen combines with carbon dioxide to make glucose and other sugars. Glucose molecules are later joined together to make starch and a fibrous material called cellulose. In combination with nitrogen and other nutrients, sugars are also the primary ingredient from which plants make proteins, oils, vitamins, pigments, and other compounds.

Although most plant nutrients are absorbed through the roots, plants can also absorb nutrients through the leaves, apparently via the stomates. Sometimes this happens in nature—rain water, particularly during thunderstorms, contains small amounts of dissolved nitrates and other nutrients readily absorbed by plant leaves. Gardeners can foliar-feed by spraying leaves with dilute solutions of fish emulsion, seaweed extract, manure tea, or other fertilizers. Plants respond rapidly to such treatment, looking greener and healthier within days. For more information on foliar feeding, see the Fertilizers entry. ❖

Leek

Allium ampeloprasum
Liliaceae

The sweetest and most delicately flavored of all onions, leeks are easy to grow. They are resistant to pests and diseases, and in many places, you can harvest throughout the winter.

Planting: Leeks love a crumbly, rich loam, but they will do well in any well-prepared vegetable garden soil.

Sow seeds indoors in flats 2-3 months before the last average frost. Keep them at a temperature of 65°-70°F during the day and 55°-60°F at night. When seedlings are 3″ tall, thin to 1″ apart; at 5″ tall, thin to 2″ apart. At about 8″ tall, transplant to the garden, placing them in 6″ deep holes spaced 6″ apart in rows at least 1½′ apart. The tips of the plants should be just a few inches above the surface. Water the seedlings, and replace the soil loosely around the plants.

Growing guidelines: Keep the soil evenly moist, and feed with manure tea once a month during the growing season. (For instructions on making manure tea, see the Manure entry.) When leeks are pencil-size, bank soil or mulch around the lower 2″-3″ of stem to cut out sunlight and elongate the edible stem. Many gardeners think such blanching also improves the look and flavor of leeks.

Problems: See the Onion entry for insect and disease controls.

Harvesting: Leeks take 70-110 days to mature; their flavor is best after a light frost. In climates where the temperature stays above 10°F, harvest leeks throughout the winter as needed. In colder areas, pull the entire crop when extremely cold temperatures are expected. Leeks will keep a few weeks if refrigerated; to store them longer, pack them in a box with moist soil or vermiculite and store in a cool, dry place. Use leeks in any recipe that calls for a delicate onion flavor. ❖

Lettuce

Lactuca sativa
Compositae

Crispy lettuce greens are easy to grow and demand little space. Grow lettuce in the vegetable garden, tuck it into flower beds, or cultivate it in containers. With a little care, you can enjoy homegrown lettuce almost year-round in much of the country.

Types: Home gardeners can choose from dozens of different cultivars, each with its own special taste and texture.

Cabbagelike crisphead, or iceberg, lettuce stands up to hot weather and ships well; it is the type most often found in stores. Iceberg lettuce is also the least nutritious type, lacking the high amounts of vitamins A and B found in other types.

The crunchy, spoon-shaped leaves of romaine, or cos, lettuce are much more nutritious. In addition to being heat-tolerant and easy to grow, the big-leaved types also produce crisp, white hearts that can substitute for celery.

Butterhead, or Boston, lettuce has soft, tender, rich green outer leaves and white to yellowish hearts. It is also high in nutrition, and its taste and texture are excellent. Many butterheads, particularly the quick-maturing cultivars, require cool weather and an excellent soil to produce well.

Fast-growing, nutritious leaf lettuce tolerates much warmer temperatures than head lettuce. Most cultivars have loose, open growth habits and leaves that range from smooth to frilly. Harvest the outer leaves of leaf lettuces, and the plants will grow new ones for later picking.

Planting: Lettuce needs a humus-rich, moisture-retentive but well-drained soil with plenty of nitrogen.

Broadcast the seeds and rake lightly to cover them, or sow seeds ¼″ deep and as thinly as possible in rows 1½′ apart. A small seed packet will plant a 100′ row and produce some 80 heads, or about 50 lb. of leaf lettuce. Germination rate is over 80 percent.

Although lettuce is primarily considered a cool-season crop, it is possible to extend the harvest with some careful planning. If you're a real lettuce lover, try the following schedule:

• Start cos or head lettuce indoors 4-6 weeks before the last frost date, making three small sowings at weekly intervals. Set out the seedlings successively as soon as the ground is workable. If the soil temperature is at least 35°F, germination should take place in 6-12 days. At the same time, direct-seed leaf lettuce outdoors at two-week intervals. Or if you plan to harvest only outer leaves as the plants grow, you can sow the entire loose-leaf crop at once.

• As the weather warms, plant heat-resistant cultivars. If you place them in shady areas and give them adequate water, they are less likely to bolt and go to seed during hot spells. If the earth is very warm, try presprouting the seeds to get better germination. Place the seeds on wet blotting paper or mix them with a little damp peat moss and perlite; store in the refrigerator for 5 days before sowing.

• In midsummer, switch back to head or cos types, making successive sowings—again, in shady areas—for a fall harvest that can last until frost. In milder climates, cover immature heads with cloches to prolong the harvest; in cold-winter areas, transplant a few heads into pots and let them continue growing in a greenhouse or sunny window.

Growing guidelines: When the seedlings have four leaves, thin head or romaine lettuce to 12″-16″ apart. Do the same for leaf lettuce unless you plan to harvest entire plants instead of leaves; in that case, 4″ spacing is adequate. Thin butterheads 3″-5″ apart.

Lettuce is 90 percent water and has very shallow roots, so keep the soil surface moist but not soggy. Make sure the crop gets at least 1″ of water a week from rain or irrigation. To help prevent disease, try to water on sunny mornings, so the leaves can dry by evening. After a good rain or watering, apply a thick layer of mulch to conserve moisture, suffocate weeds around the easily damaged roots, and keep lettuce leaves free of dirt. To promote quick growth, side-dress with manure tea or fish emulsion once or twice during the growing season. For instructions on making manure tea, see the Manure entry.

Just before bolting, lettuce plants start to elongate and form a bitter sap. To keep this from happening, pinch off the top center of the plant. Pull up and discard any plant that goes to seed. If you are a seed saver, choose the last plants to bolt, since quickness to bolt is a bad trait. Seed savers should also be aware that different lettuce cultivars can cross with each other and with wild lettuce.

Problems: The most likely pests are aphids, cutworms, and slugs. For details on controlling these pests, see "The Top Ten Garden Insect Pests in America" on page 344 and the Slugs and Snails entry.

Soggy soil and crowded plants can encourage bottom rot, a disease that turns lettuce plants black and foul smelling. Crop rotation is the best preventive measure.

Gray mold makes grayish green or dark brown spots on lower leaves and is usually brought on by damp, overcast weather. Injured seedlings are particularly vulnerable. Pull up any infected plant and dispose of it far from the garden.

Harvesting: Pick lettuce in the morning to preserve the crispness it acquires overnight. Watch your crop closely, as mature plants deteriorate quickly. To test the firmness of heading types, press down gently on lettuce hearts with the back of your hand; don't pinch them, as this can bruise the hearts. Use a sharp knife to cut heads below the lowest leaves, or pull plants out by the roots. Harvest leaf types as needed. Lettuce tastes best when eaten fresh but will keep up to two weeks when refrigerated. ❖

Liatris

Gayfeather, blazing-star. Summer-blooming perennials.

Description: Gayfeathers bear small, shaggy flowers in white, pink, purple, and magenta along dense spikes from a few inches long to 2' or more. Plants have grasslike leaves. *Liatris aspera,* rough gayfeather, grows 3'-6'; *L. spicata,* spike gayfeather, rarely exceeds 3'. Zones 3-8.

How to grow: Plant or divide (infrequently) in spring in a sunny spot with average, moist but well-drained soil. They tolerate both drought and excess moisture in summer, but standing water in winter is fatal.

Landscape uses: Feature small groups in a border or meadow. It is also fine for the cutting garden. Tone down magenta gayfeathers with pale yellow, medium blue, and cream flowers.

Best cultivars: *L. aspera:* 'September Glory', purple, and 'White Spire', both 5'; *L. spicata:* 'Kobold', mauve, 1½'-2'. ❖

Light

Plants have the remarkable capacity to use sunlight as the energy source for making their own food. All animals, including humans, ultimately rely on this process, called photosynthesis, for their food. See the Leaves entry for an explanation of photosynthesis.

While many plants thrive in full sun, others do better in shade. The amount of light striking a plant affects its leaf size, shape, color, and texture, as well as its overall size and form, growth rate, and yield.

Some plants have internal biochemical clocks that measure the photoperiod, or hours of daylight, and use this information to time growth responses. Many perennials and woody plants sense shortening daylength in late summer and fall as a signal to drop their leaves, harden their buds, and prepare for winter dormancy. ❖

Ligularia

Ligularia, golden-ray. Summer-blooming perennials.

Description: *Ligularia dentata,* bigleaf ligularia, has yellow-orange 2″-5″ blooms in loose clusters held above impressive mounds of dark green, kidney-shaped 1½′ leaves. *L. stenocephala* 'The Rocket', rocket ligularia, bears 1″-1½″ yellow blooms in 1½′ spikes on erect, 4′-6′, dark stems. Medium-green foliage is 1′ wide, rounded with pointed teeth. Zones 5-7.

How to grow: Plant or divide (infrequently) in spring in a site with morning sun and afternoon shade. Grow in fairly rich, moist soil. Even in these conditions, the leaves may wilt, but normally recover at night.

Landscape uses: Feature a clump or group by a stream or pool. Grow in a plastic-lined area of a border, and water often.

Best cultivars: *L. dentata:* 'Desdemona' has rich green leaves with purple undersides and is more heat-tolerant than the species. ❖

Ligustrum

Privet. Deciduous or evergreen shrubs or small trees.

Description: *Ligustrum amurense,* Amur privet, is an upright deciduous shrub reaching 15′ tall. It has glossy green, oblong leaves, small white flower clusters in spring, and inconspicuous black berries developing through the summer. It may suffer from winter injury at the Northern reaches of its range. Zones 4-7.

L. japonicum, Japanese privet, can be grown as a shrub or tree; it grows 8′-12′ tall. Glossy evergreen 3″-4″ oval foliage is a lustrous dark green. Pyramidal white flower clusters bloom in spring, followed by black berries. Zones 7-9.

L. obtusifolium, border privet, is an upright, deciduous shrub that grows 10′-12′ tall, with 1″-2″ oblong medium to dark green leaves and clusters of small white flowers in early summer

followed by black berries. Zones 4-7.

How to grow: Privets thrive in a variety of soils, climates, and light levels, but they do require good drainage. Amur privet and border privet can be planted bareroot, which is cost-effective when many plants are needed, as with a hedge. Plant bareroot stock while it is completely dormant, in late fall or early spring. North of Zone 8, plant container-grown privets in fall or spring; plant in fall or winter in Zone 8 and south. Shear formal hedges during the growing season to keep them tidy. Informal hedges may need occasional rejuvenation pruning; tree forms may need pruning to open or shape them.

Landscape uses: Use privet for screens, hedges, or focal points (tree forms only). ❖

Lilium

Lily. Late-spring- to late-summer-blooming bulbs.

Description: Lilies have 3″-12″ usually bowl- or trumpet-shaped flowers in white, pink, red, yellow, orange, lilac, and green, many dotted in maroon or near-black. Plants bear a few to two dozen or more blooms on 2′-7′ stems with narrow leaves. Most lilies are hardy in Zones 3-8. Give winter protection in the North, especially during the first winter.

There are three major groups of hybrid lilies. By choosing some cultivars from each group, you can have lilies blooming all summer. The early-summer-blooming Asiatics normally grow 2′-4′ and bear bowl- or cup-shaped, 3″-5″ flowers in nearly the entire color range. The summer-blooming trumpets and Aurelians grow 4′-7′, producing large clusters of trumpet- to bowl-shaped, often fragrant 4″-6″ blooms in all colors but bright red. Last to bloom are the spicily fragrant 3′-6′ Orientals in the white-pink-red range, some with distinct yellow stripes; blooms may be 1′ wide and almost flat.

Besides the popular hybrid lilies, there are many beautiful species. Among the best are

Lilium candidum, Madonna lily, with pure white, lightly fragrant blooms in summer on 2'-4' stalks. *L. regale,* regal lily, bears fragrant white flowers on majestic 4'-6' stalks in summer; flowers have wine-red shading on the outside. *L. speciosum,* Japanese lily, bears 15-30 fragrant flowers on 4'-5' stalks in late summer; flowers are white, flushed pink, with pink or red spots. *L. superbum,* Turk's-cap lily, bears 20-40 nodding flowers on 4'-7' stalks in late summer; flowers are orange-red and heavily spotted.

How to grow: Lilies thrive in sun or partial shade in deep, fertile, moist but well-drained, humus-rich soil out of strong winds. Lilies never go completely dormant, so plant the fragile bulbs carefully soon after you receive them. Fall planting is best. Prepare the soil to 1½' deep and mulch the site heavily to keep the soil unfrozen and ready for planting in very late fall, which is when many dealers ship. Most lilies produce roots along the below-ground part of their stems; therefore, plant the bulbs with no less than 6" of soil above the top of the bulb. (Madonna lilies are the exception; they need just 1" of soil.) Mark the site to avoid injuring emerging shoots in spring.

Mulch with several inches of compost or finely shredded bark to keep the soil cool. Water during dry spells and douse with manure tea, compost tea, or fish emulsion monthly from late spring to early fall. (For instructions on making compost tea and manure tea, see the Composting and Manure entries.) Stake tall lilies and deadhead after bloom. After the tops die, cut the stems to a few inches above the ground.

Aphids spread devastating viral diseases; dig and destroy any plants with yellow-streaked or deformed leaves or dramatically stunted growth. Deer and woodchucks relish lilies; see the Animal Pests entry for control measures.

Landscape uses: Plant specimens or groups throughout borders and light woodlands. Some of the larger, more robust lilies grow happily near shrubs if given a few feet of their own space. ❖

Lime

Lime is a mineral substance that provides calcium, helps alter soil pH, and improves the efficiency of sulfur as a fungicide. You can buy lime as ground limestone, dolomitic limestone, or gypsum, or in other forms. See the pH, Fertilizers, and Fungicides entries for more information about using lime. ❖

Linum

Flax. Late-spring- to summer-blooming perennials.

Description: *Linum perenne,* blue flax, produces hundreds of 1" clear blue saucerlike blooms in 1½'-2' V-shaped bunches. The thin stems are gently arched at the tips and sparsely clad in 1" needlelike bluish green leaves. Zones 5-8.

How to grow: Set out small plants in spring or let self-sown seedlings come up in a sunny spot with average to lean, very well drained, light soil. Self-sown plants tolerate drought.

Landscape uses: Allow flax to naturalize in borders, meadows, and cottage gardens. They mix nicely with yellow coreopsis, pink dianthus, and white alyssum.

Best cultivars: 'Saphyr' is more compact than the species; grow it from seed sown in early spring. White 'Album' gives contrast. ❖

Liquidambar

Sweet gum. Deciduous shade trees.

Description: *Liquidambar styraciflua,* sweet gum, is pyramidal when young and matures to an upright oval shape. Maximum height can range from 60' to 120'. The alternate leaves are star-shaped with 5-7 lobes and are sweet-smelling when crushed. The bark is furrowed and grayish brown. Fall colors of yellow, purple, red, and orange can be excellent. Small seeds are borne within 1½" spiky round capsules and are a minor food source for wildlife. Some of the numerous seed capsules persist on trees into the winter; the rest fall to the ground, creating a long-lasting litter problem. Zones 5-8.

How to grow: Provide a site with full sun, even moisture, good drainage, and lots of room.

Landscape uses: Sweet gum makes a fine shade tree or focal point.

Best cultivars: Look for 'Rotundiloba', which does not produce the spiny seed capsules. ❖

Liriodendron

Tulip tree, tulip poplar, yellow poplar. Large, deciduous shade trees.

Description: *Liriodendron tulipifera,* tulip tree, is an upright tree with a sturdy, straight trunk and furrowed gray-brown bark. This massive native tree grows 70'-90' in the landscape, to 200' in nature. Its tuliplike flowers have yellow-green petals with an orange base. These unusual flowers are hard to see because they blossom high in the branches after the leaves open. Winged fruits turn brown in fall and persist through the winter. Fall color appears gradually, changing the leaves from green to yellow one by one. Zones 5-8.

How to grow: Plant tulip trees on a site with plenty of room to spread, full sun, and deep, moist, loamy soil.

Landscape uses: Naturalize tulip trees in a woodland or use them as shade trees. ❖

Liriope

Liriope, lilyturf. Evergreen perennial groundcovers.

Description: *Liriope muscari,* big blue lilyturf, and *L. spicata,* creeping lilyturf, form dense, dark green mats of tufted, grasslike leaves. Big blue lilyturf is taller, with clumps 1'-1½' wide and leaves ½" wide and 2' long. The showy, violet-blue blossoms resemble grape hyacinths

and bloom from July to September. The flower spikes rise above the leaves. Shiny black berries persist through winter. The narrow leaves of creeping lilyturf measure ¼" across and 8"-12" long. Flowers are pale lavender to white, with black berries appearing after the blossoms have faded. Unlike big blue lilyturf, the leaves of creeping lilyturf turn yellow and are unsightly through winter. Both are hardy in Zones 6-10.

How to grow: Liriopes can grow in deep shade to full sun in rich, acid, well-drained but moist soil. However, they prefer filtered sunlight in protected locations. Plants are tolerant of drought and salt spray. Add leaf mold or other organic matter to your soil if it isn't humus-rich. Divide clumps in the spring or fall and plant them 1' apart. In late fall, mow or clip back plants to encourage new growth. Handpick or trap slugs and snails.

Landscape uses: Liriopes are excellent groundcovers for difficult locations, including seashore areas. They are also attractive along paths, around the edges of flower gardens, and in rock gardens. ❖

Lobelia

Lobelia. All-season annual and mid-summer to early-fall perennials and wildflowers.

Description: *Lobelia erinus,* edging lobelia, produces intricate blooms in shades of white, red-violet, and blue (many with a striking white "eye"). Plants produce spreading clumps to 6" or trailing forms that may reach a few feet long by the end of the season. Small leaves often assume rich bronzy purple shades.

Perennial *L. cardinalis,* cardinal flower, bears brilliant red, almost insect- or birdlike flowers on long spikes above unbranched to more bushy plants reaching 3'-4'. Rich green leaves provide a sharp contrast. Zones 3-8.

How to grow: Start edging lobelia from

seed indoors in late winter in the North or sow directly farther south. Provide full sun in cooler areas and part shade in warmer areas to prolong bloom in average, moist but well-drained soil. A light mulch is also beneficial.

Plant or divide cardinal flowers every few years in spring or after bloom. They prefer a partially shaded spot (full sun in the North if soil is constantly moist) in average to rich, moist to wet, humus-rich soil. Water freely in summer if they're in a traditional border setting. Mulch in summer with bark or chips; replace with straw or hay in winter in the North (Zones 3-5).

Landscape uses: Mass edging lobelia at the front of borders, along paths, and in pots, especially cascading types. Feature a clump of cardinal flower in a moist border or naturalize by a stream or pond. Hummingbirds love them.

Best cultivars: *L. erinus:* dark blue, bronzy-leaved 'Crystal Palace' and light blue 'Cambridge Blue', both to 6". Cascading types: 'Sapphire', dark blue, and the 'Cascade' mix, also available in separate colors. ❖

Lobularia

Sweet alyssum. Long-season annuals.

Description: Tiny white, rose, or purple flowers cover creeping, 4" cushions of small, narrow leaves.

How to grow: Sow seeds thinly in spring where they are to grow. Pick a sunny or lightly shaded spot with well-drained, average soil. Make later sowings or shear plants in midsummer to extend bloom into fall. Plants withstand heat and drought.

Landscape uses: Edge a path or bed with one or more colors, or use to fill in between paving stones and along walls. They soften the edge of a pot or window box.

Best cultivars: 'Carpet of Snow' and 'Snow Crystals', white; 'Rosie O'Day', rose-purple; 'Royal Carpet', deep purple; 'Wonderland' and 'Easter Bonnet', mixes. ❖

Lonicera

Honeysuckle. Deciduous, semi-evergreen, or evergreen shrubs or vines.

Description: Most honeysuckles are deciduous (some are semi-evergreen or evergreen) shrubs or vines. They are valued for their sweetly fragrant and showy trumpet-shaped, 1"-3" flowers. Berries appear in late summer or fall; they are usually red and sometimes very showy. The shrubs have loose upright or rounded growth habits. Honeysuckles have opposite, roundish leaves that range in color from dark green through blue-green to apple green.

Lonicera × *brownii,* Brown's honeysuckle, is a vining honeysuckle that looks and behaves much like its parent, *L. sempervirens,* but it is more cold-tolerant. It has red or orange-red flowers and blooms summer through fall. Zones 3-9.

L. fragrantissima, winter honeysuckle, is a 6'-10', open, semi-evergreen shrub with fragrant white blooms appearing before the leaves in very early spring. It is one of the most fragrant early-blooming shrubs. Zones 5-9.

L. × *heckrottii,* goldflame honeysuckle, is an outstanding evergreen or semi-evergreen vine, reaching 10'-20' long. It has blue-green leaves and bears abundant, slightly fragrant flowers that are magenta with yellow interiors. Plants flower in late spring and summer. Zones 4-9.

L. mackii, Amur honeysuckle, is a large (10'-15'), rangy, upright deciduous shrub. In late spring it bears fragrant flowers that open white then turn yellow and sports showy red fruit in autumn. Zones 3-8.

L. morrowii, Morrow honeysuckle, is a 6'-8', rounded deciduous shrub with bluish green foliage. In late spring it bears fragrant flowers that open white and turn yellow, followed by showy red berries. Zones 5-8.

L. nitida, boxleaf honeysuckle, is a dense shrub to 6' with small, shiny, dark green leaves that are nearly evergreen. The fragrant flowers are inconspicuous and are followed by dark blue fruit. Useful for hedges. Zones 6-9.

L. pileata, privet honeysuckle, is very similar to boxleaf honeysuckle, but has a prostrate habit. Zones 6-9.

L. sempervirens, trumpet honeysuckle, is a semi-evergreen to evergreen twining vine that grows to 20' long. The showy scarlet and yellow-orange flower clusters bloom in summer and are followed by bright red berries in the fall. Zones 4-9.

L. tatarica, Tatarian honeysuckle, is a large (10'-12'), upright deciduous shrub with blue-green foliage. The showy blooms are red, pink, or white, depending on the cultivar, and are not fragrant. Plants bear attractive red berries in late fall. Zones 3-8.

A HAZARDOUS HONEYSUCKLE

Japanese honeysuckle (*Lonicera japonica*) is a very vigorous semi-evergreen or evergreen twining vine, growing to 30' long. It has dark green foliage with fragrant blooms from June to September. Flowers open white and turn yellow. This familiar roadside honeysuckle is decorative in bloom, but be warned: It is very invasive, requiring vigorous pruning to keep it in bounds. Unless you're up to a constant war against uncontrolled spread, pick another vining honeysuckle (trumpet honeysuckle, *L. sempervirens,* is a well-behaved alternative) or the cultivar 'Aureo-Reticulata', which has leaves with yellow netting and is not invasive like the species. Resist the urge to plant this attractive vine in mild climates, where it really runs rampant. Japanese honeysuckle is hardy in Zones 5–9.

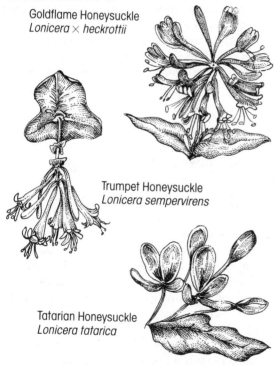

Goldflame Honeysuckle
Lonicera × heckrottii

Trumpet Honeysuckle
Lonicera sempervirens

Tatarian Honeysuckle
Lonicera tatarica

Honeysuckle habits and flower forms. Most of us picture a tangle of Japanese honeysuckle when we think of these delightful vines, but there are many to choose from that are equally decorative and far less invasive. Tatarian honeysuckle, trumpet honeysuckle, and goldflame honeysuckle are among the best.

How to grow: Honeysuckles transplant easily. Plant in good, well-drained soil in full or partial sun. They tolerate a range of soil types and pH. Prune after flowering by cutting the oldest wood to the ground and gently shaping the shrub. If plants have become overgrown, cut to the ground and allow them to resprout.

Landscape uses: Use shrub honeysuckles as hedges and screens, or as part of a shrub border where their flowers and berries can be enjoyed. They do not make strong specimen plants because of their loose or rounded forms. Use the vines to cover banks, fences, walls, or arbors. Remember that they require a support to twine around.

Best cultivars: *L. × brownii:* 'Dropmore Scarlet', bright red, long-blooming. *L. sempervirens:* 'Magnifica', bright red, long-blooming; 'Sulphurea', yellow; 'Superba', bright red. *L. tatarica:* 'Alba', white; 'Arnold Red', dark purplish red; 'Rosea', rosy pink. ❖

Lupinus

Lupine. Late-spring- to early-summer-blooming annuals and perennials.

Description: Perennial *Lupinus* Russell hybrids are most common and bear spectacular spikes of pealike flowers in a wide color range to 4' above large clumps of palmlike leaves. Zones 4-7. *L. texensis* and *L. subcarnosus,* Texas bluebonnets, are native annuals that produce spikes of blue flowers on plants to about 1'.

How to grow: Set out nursery-grown perennials in spring, or start seeds in late winter to plant out after frost. Grow in full sun to partial shade in moist but well-drained, acid, humus-rich soil. They grow poorly in hot, humid summers and dry soil. Direct-sow annuals onto a sunny site with average to less-fertile soil.

Landscape uses: Mass hybrids in borders. Annuals look best in natural settings. ❖

Lychnis

Campion, catchfly. Late-spring- to summer-blooming perennials.

Description: *Lychnis chalcedonica,* Maltese cross, bears bright orange-red stars in 3"-4" clusters atop 2'-3½' clumps of green leaves. Zones 4-8.

L. coronaria, rose campion, offers 1", vivid magenta blooms on branched stems above a rosette of felty gray leaves. Zones 4-8.

How to grow: Plant or divide Maltese cross in spring or fall into a sunny spot with average to less fertile, moist but well-drained, loose soil. Short-lived rose campion grows under the same conditions, though it tolerates some shade. Let it self-sow to keep new plants coming along.

Landscape uses: Grow in borders and informal plantings. Use with similar strong colors or next to gray or green foliage as a contrast.

Best cultivars: *L. coronaria:* 'Abbotswood Rose', pink flowers; var. *alba,* white flowers. ❖

Lysimachia

Loosestrife. Summer-blooming perennials.

Description: *Lysimachia clethroides,* gooseneck loosestrife, bears ½" starry white flowers in dense, tapered, arching 6" spikes. Flowers are borne atop 3' upright spreading colonies of 3"-6", dull green leaves. Zones 3-8. *L. punctata,* yellow loosestrife, displays its 1" bright yellow stars in neatly arranged rings around 2½'-3' stems bearing 3" medium green leaves; it also spreads widely. Zones 4-8.

How to grow: Plant or divide in spring or fall in a sunny or partly shady spot with average, fairly moist soil. Loosestrifes tolerate drier soil in shady sites and spread less rapidly. They can become weedy.

Landscape uses: Plant loosestrifes in a low wet spot such as a ditch, or along ponds and streams. Give plants plenty of room and divide often if you plant them in borders. ❖

Lythrum

Purple loosestrife. Summer- to early-fall-blooming perennials.

Description: *Lythrum salicaria,* purple loosestrife, and *L. virgatum,* wand loosestrife, bear starlike ½" flowers in purple, pink, and magenta. Flowers appear in clusters that can elongate into curved 2' wands. The 1½'-5' plants have dark green, pointed 3"-6" leaves. Zones 3-8.

How to grow: Plant or divide in spring in full sun and average, wet to fairly dry soil. Pick off Japanese beetles. Grow named cultivars only, and cut plants to the ground when blooms fade to keep them from overrunning wetlands.

Landscape uses: Grow in small groups in a border; mass in a wet spot.

Best cultivars: *L. salicaria:* 'Firecandle', 3', bright pink. *L. virgatum:* 'Dropmore Purple' and 'Morden Pink', both 3'-4'. ❖

Magnolia

Magnolia. Evergreen or deciduous, single- or multiple-trunked flowering trees.

Description: Few plants rival the dramatic beauty of the South's magnolias in bloom. Available in a wide variety of sizes, shapes, and flower colors, magnolias have alternate, usually glossy foliage and gray bark; large, softly fuzzy, silver-gray buds form in summer for the following year's bloom.

Magnolia grandiflora, Southern magnolia or bull bay, is a native evergreen with leathery and glossy green leaves and waxy white, heavily fragrant flowers. It is pyramidal in form and attains heights of 50'-75' in the landscape, 100' in nature. The flowers can be as wide as 15"; they bloom abundantly in late spring and sporadically through the summer. Conelike seed pods form in summer and fall, splitting open to reveal bright red seeds that fall out and hang from threads. Zones 6-9.

M. × soulangiana, saucer magnolia, is a multi-stemmed, deciduous tree or shrub that grows to 25'. The flowers bloom in shades of pink and magenta in spring before the dark green leaves appear. Zones 5-8.

M. stellata, star magnolia, is a small (6'-12'), deciduous, multi-stemmed shrub that produces white flowers in early spring before the leaves. The blossoms are composed of several long, strap-shaped petals that give a starlike effect. Leaves are 2"-4" long, entire, and dark green above with lighter green undersides. Zones 4-8.

M. virginiana, sweet bay, is a semi-evergreen, multi-stemmed, native tree that has an upright, open, loose habit. The leathery, oblong leaves are dull green with silvery white undersides. Small white flowers are waxy and fragrant, appearing in a flush in late spring, then sporadically through the summer. Seedpods resemble those of Southern magnolia. Zones 6-9.

How to grow: With the exception of sweet bay, which benefits from the light shade of taller trees, magnolias perform best in full sun. Choose a site with humusy, well-drained soil with even moisture. Pest problems are minimal. Spring frosts almost always ruin the flowers of star and saucer magnolias; avoid giving these early bloomers a southern exposure that encourages premature bud break. Star magnolia is prone to suckering shoots that grow up through the plant and detract from its structure; remove them. Prune after flowering before buds are set for the next year's bloom. Some gardeners object to the deep shade cast by Southern magnolia and the difficulty of growing anything amid shade, surface roots, and old, slow-to-decompose leaves.

Landscape uses: Use magnolias in groups,

for naturalizing, or as specimens. Star magnolia is especially useful in small-scale situations.

Best cultivars: *M. grandiflora:* 'Edith Bogue', exceptionally cold-hardy; 'Little Gem', a compact, upright plant with 3″-4″ white flowers. *M. × soulangiana* 'Alexandrina', large flowers with petals purplish rose outside, white inside. *M. stellata* 'Royal Star', pink buds open to many-petalled, fragrant white blooms. ❖

Mahonia

Mahonia, Oregon grape. Evergreen, winter- or spring-blooming shrubs.

Description: *Mahonia aquifolium,* Oregon grape, is 3′-6′ tall, with upright stems and compound, hollylike evergreen leaves. Spikes of yellow flowers appear in spring, followed by clusters of blue-purple berries. Zones 6-8.

M. bealei, leatherleaf mahonia, is larger (to 12′), with leathery foliage and good winter color. Zones 6-8.

How to grow: Mahonias will thrive in almost any well-drained soil. Shelter them from direct wind in the North and direct sun in the South. Prune after flowering; cut ⅓ of the oldest stems to the ground each year to keep plants from looking straggly.

Landscape uses: Mahonias are useful in a massed planting; leatherleaf mahonia can also make an eye-catching specimen. ❖

Malus

Crab apple. Deciduous spring-flowering trees or shrubs.

Description: This genus also includes apples; you'll find more information on culture, pruning, and pest control in the Apple entry.

Malus floribunda, Japanese flowering crab apple, is a shrub or tree with a broad, arching form and a mature height of about 25′. The flowers are deep red in bud, opening rose; the fruits are yellow. Zones 4-7.

M. hupehensis, tea crab apple, is a vase-shaped tree that grows 25′ tall. Fragrant flowers are pink in bud, opening white, and heavy in alternate years. Fruit is greenish yellow with a reddish blush. Zones 4-7.

M. sargentii, Sargent crab apple, is a shrub or small tree that grows about 6′ tall. Gnarled with age (and possibly thorny), this plant grows wider than tall and produces pink flower buds that open white. It tends to flower heavily in alternate years. The fruits are red. Zones 4-7.

M. sieboldii, Toringo crab apple, is an arching shrub that grows about 12′ tall. Flowers are pink in bud, fading to white when open; fruits are red to yellow-brown. Zones 4-7.

How to grow: Give crab apples full sun and well-drained, evenly moist, acid soil. Prune to remove dead wood any time; prune in winter (when you can get a good look at the tree's structure) for water sprouts and crossing or rubbing branches. Do shaping and size-reduction pruning when flowering finishes and before the next year's flower buds are set in June or July.

Fire blight, apple scab, and cedar-apple rust are common crab apple problems. Fire blight, a bacterial disease, spreads to trees when they are in bloom. Infected blossoms shrivel and turn brown; later, young branches turn black and wilt into a characteristic cane-handle shape. Olive green spots on the undersides of leaves are the first signs of apple scab. Spots on upper leaf surfaces and blossoms and corky "scabs" on fruit follow as this fungus progresses. Cedar-apple rust is a fungus that needs both *Malus* and *Juniperus* "cedar" species to complete its life cycle. On crab apples, it causes yellow spots that turn orange on leaves and fruits. All three of these diseases disfigure flowering crab apples, often defoliating trees and causing gradual decline. Avoid disease problems by planting resistant species and cultivars; exclude susceptible *Juniperus* species from *Malus* plantings. Japanese flowering crab apple shows good resistance to apple scab, but is moderately susceptible to fire blight. Sargent crab apple resists fire blight and apple scab. Both Toringo and tea crab apples are resistant to scab and rust; tea crab apple is somewhat susceptible to fire blight.

Landscape uses: Crab apples are impressive in groups or individually as focal points in the landscape. Few trees rival them for showy spring blossoms. Use crab apples to add flowering interest to a wildlife feeding area; the abundant fruits will attract birds and animals. Some trees produce excellent fruits for jelly making.

Best cultivars: The following are noted for their resistance to scab, fire blight, and cedar-apple rust: 'Adams' has red buds opening pink; fruits are red. 'Autumn Glory' is deep red in bud, opening blush pink, then full white. This 12' tall upright tree bears glossy orange-red fruits. 'Callaway' has pink flower buds opening white and red fruits and is a good choice for Southern gardens. 'Centurion' has red flowers and rose red leaves that turn green. The fruits are cherry red on this columnar tree. 'Christmas Holly' has bright red buds opening white. Fruits are red; fall color is yellow. 'Donald Wyman' is a 15' tall tree with deep pink flower buds opening white; fruits are bright red. 'Indian Summer' has rose red flowers and cherry red fruits. 'Molten Lava' is a yellow-barked, weeping form, red in bud, opening white, with red-orange fruits. 'Professor Sprenger' has pink buds opening white; fruits are orange-red. ❖

Malva

Mallow, musk mallow. Summer-blooming perennials.

Description: *Malva alcea,* hollyhock mallow, bears 2″ saucerlike blooms in white or pink along nearly the entire length of 2'-4', nearly upright stems. Zones 4-8.

M. moschata, musk mallow, produces slightly larger, fragrant white or rose pink blooms with notched petals on bushier plants with nearly palmlike leaves. Zones 3-6.

How to grow: Plant or divide in spring in a sunny or partly shady spot with average, well-drained, slightly alkaline soil. They tolerate some drought in the North (where they may self-sow freely) but need extra water in the South.

Landscape uses: Both look best in informal settings such as cottage gardens, along fences, and in naturalized areas. ❖

Manure

In the days when most families kept a milk cow or small chicken flock, manure was a primary garden fertilizer. But with changes in food production practices and the advent of synthetic fertilizers, many gardeners stopped using manure. Organic gardeners have rediscovered the benefits of manure as a fertilizer, soil conditioner, and compost ingredient.

The best places for home gardeners to get manure are local farms. While many farmers spread manure on their fields, they may be willing to give—or sell—you some, provided you do the hauling. Other good sources are local stables or feedlots. Urban gardeners can contact the city zoo or visit a fairground or circus after the animals have left town. Don't use manure from dogs or cats—it may carry disease organisms that can be particularly dangerous to children.

Most garden centers now sell bagged composted manure. These products are more expensive, but save you the time and effort of locating, hauling, and composting.

Using Manure

Don't put raw manure in or on garden soils. Raw manure generally releases highly soluble nitrogen compounds and ammonia, which can burn plant roots and interfere with seed germination. Also, don't incorporate raw manure into unplanted garden beds. Raw manure often is filled with weed seeds, so spreading it on soil can create serious weed problems.

You can use manure as a fertilizer by adding it to the compost pile or by making manure tea.

Manure is a prime source of nitrogen, potassium, and phosphorus, and is rich in bacteria. Manure is important in a rapid composting method that requires a high-nitrogen, high-bacteria heat-up material. See the Composting entry for directions on making hot compost.

Manure tea: To make manure tea, place one or two shovelfuls of fresh or dried manure in a permeable bag. The finer the holes in the bag, the less likely it is that weed seeds from the manure will get into your tea. Burlap bags are best, but perforated plastic or mesh bags will work. Tie the bag closed, then place it in a barrel or other large container filled with water. Make sure the bag is submerged. Allow your "teabag" to steep for about one week.

You can apply manure tea at full strength for periodic feedings or dilute it and use it whenever you water your plants. Do not apply undiluted manure tea directly onto plant foliage—it will injure plant tissue.

Manure and pesticides: Manure from non-organic farms may contain pesticides or pesticide residues. Some farmers spray manure piles with pesticides to kill fly larvae. Manure may also contain residues from antibiotics or other livestock medications. These chemicals can suppress microbial populations in compost. It's best to ask the farmer whether the manure or the animals that produced it have been treated with medications or pesticides. ❖

Master Gardeners

If you like working with plants and people, you can become a Master Gardener. Master Gardeners are trained volunteers who assist the Cooperative Extension Service, a government agency that provides gardening advice to the public.

As a Master Gardener candidate, you'll receive in-depth training in horticulture and backyard gardening from university and extension specialists. You'll learn about the basics of vegetable and ornamental gardening, as well as landscaping, plant diseases, and insects.

After you complete your training, you can volunteer to serve at your local extension office. The Cooperative Extension staff will help match your talents and interests with the needs of the extension office and gardening public. You might teach small groups through classes and workshops at libraries, botanical gardens, or fairs and other events. Or you may answer individual gardeners' questions by phone, by mail, or in person.

Once you become a Master Gardener, you can receive updates and training through your local extension office, participate in statewide or regional meetings, and even attend a biennial national conference for Master Gardeners.

The Washington State Extension office developed this program in 1972 to help handle the overwhelming number of home gardening questions. Today, Master Gardeners can be found throughout the United States, and a similar program exists in Canada. To become a Master Gardener, contact your local Cooperative Extension Service office. ❖

NUTRIENTS IN MANURES

While all animal manures are good sources of organic matter and nutrients, specific sources vary in nutrient content. It's useful to know whether the manure you're using is rich or poor in a particular nutrient such as nitrogen. In this list, NPK analysis refers to percentages of nitrogen (N), phosphorus (P), and potassium (K).

Kind of Manure	NPK Analysis
Chicken	1.1–0.8–0.5
Cow	0.6–0.2–0.5
Duck	0.6–1.4–0.5
Horse	0.7–0.3–0.6
Pig	0.5–0.3–0.5
Rabbit	2.4–1.4–0.6
Sheep	0.7–0.3–0.9
Steer	0.7–0.3–0.4

Meadow Gardens

Meadow gardening fiction: All you need do to create a beautiful wildflower meadow is to scatter wildflower seeds over an established lawn and stop mowing. Meadow gardening fact: Seeds of any kind—even of hardy wildflowers—need some help to grow into established plants. And typical turfgrasses will overwhelm meadow flowers because their mat-forming roots crowd out other plants.

Fortunately, it's also a fact that it's easier to create a beautiful, self-perpetuating meadow than a flower bed. To make your own meadow, just follow the same soil preparation, timing, sowing, and watering methods you'd use to establish a new lawn.

A meadow garden mimics the beauty of a natural meadow, and part of that beauty comes from meadow grasses. The meadow grasses—mostly clumping, warm-season species that grow slowly in spring and fall, thrive in the heat of summer, and go dormant in winter—stabilize the soil and provide support for the flowers. The grasses add color and texture to the meadow, especially when they change color in fall.

Evaluating Seed Mixes

A meadow garden should be composed of native warm-season grasses and flowering annuals, biennials, and perennials that will spread and self-sow to create a self-maintaining field of flowers and foliage. Unfortunately, most of those lavish packaged meadows sold in shaker cans contain no grass seed at all. If grass seed isn't in your mix, purchase it separately; you can find sheep's fescue (*Festuca ovina*) at many farm supply centers, and it works well in meadow gardens in most areas of the country if sown at 1 lb. per 1000 square feet.

Choosing a seed mix can be tricky. Don't let the pretty pictures seduce you—read the label. Don't purchase any meadow mix that doesn't list the species in it—all of them. And be sure the mix is a regional one that has been specially formulated for your area of the country.

Many commercial seed mixes include both annuals and perennials. The annuals will bloom the first year and make a pretty meadow that first growing season, but they rarely reseed as expected. For splashy annual color every year, overseed with annuals each spring. Meanwhile, during that first season the perennials are sprouting, putting down sturdy roots, and just getting themselves established. The perennials should flower the second season and get even better as the years pass, particularly if mixed with protective grasses. They may even self-sow. If you're impatient for perennial flowers— and have the funds—plant container-grown or bareroot perennials in a newly seeded or established meadow, or grow your own transplants.

Sowing Seeds and Fighting Weeds

Natural meadows occur in full sun—make sure you site your wildflower meadow in full sun, too. The meadow soil can be average, and you don't have to fertilize or improve it at all—

MEADOW-GROWING BASICS

Follow these guidelines and your wildflower meadow will be off to a good start:

● Clear the soil of all vegetation and then till to prepare a seedbed.
● Use a mixture of perennial and annual flowers along with native clump-forming grasses. Sow at a heavy application rate, as much as twice the rate on the package directions, and cover thinly with soil.
● Mix seed with equal portions of clean river sand to facilitate even spreading.
● Keep the seedlings moist. You may need to irrigate during the first year.
● Weed diligently the first year.
● Cut the meadow to 6'' high in late winter to prevent invasion by woody plants and to help disperse flower and grass seed.
● Sow seeds of annual flowers every year for a good show. This means some yearly soil preparation when sowing.

BEST PLANTS FOR MEADOW GARDENS

These wildflowers and grasses are the most dependable native annuals and perennials for meadows across the country. Look in a wildflower gardening book, check with a wildflower society, or refer to wildflower seed catalogs to find the plants that do best in your area. Plants marked with an asterisk (*) are non-native species that can be successfully naturalized.

Wildflowers for Meadow Gardens

Achillea millefolium (common yarrow)*
Asclepias tuberosa (butterfly weed)
Aster novae-angliae (New England aster)
Baptisia australis (blue false indigo)
Centaurea cyanus (cornflower)*
Chrysanthemum leucanthemum (oxeye daisy)*
Coreopsis spp. (coreopsis)
Cosmos sulphureus (yellow cosmos)*
Dodecatheon meadia (shooting-star)
Echinacea purpurea (purple coneflower)
Gaillardia pulchella (blanket flower)
Helenium autumnale (common sneezeweed)
Heliopsis helianthoides (ox-eye sunflower)
Liatris spicata (spike gayfeather)
Lilium canadense (Canada lily)
Lupinus perennis (wild lupine)
Monarda didyma (bee balm)
Oenothera speciosa (showy evening primrose)
Penstemon digitalis (foxglove penstemon)
Ratibida pinnata (yellow coneflower)
Rudbeckia hirta (black-eyed Susan)
Solidago spp. (goldenrods)
Trifolium incarnatum (crimson clover)*

Grasses for Meadow Gardens

Andropogon virginicus (broomsedge)
Bouteloua curtipendula (sideoats grama grass)
Festuca spp. (fescues)
Koeleria cristata (June grass)
Miscanthus spp. (miscanthus)
Panicum virgatum (switchgrass)
Schizachyrium scoparium (little bluestem)

unless it is extremely sandy or clayey. Ordinary soil will give you the best meadow, because meadow plants feed lightly.

Your greatest adversary in establishing a successful meadow garden will be weeds. The battle begins at planting time and continues for at least 1-2 seasons. An established meadow garden, especially one with grasses, should have thick enough foliage to shade out most weeds *if* you get rid of aggressive species like johnsongrass, thistles, and bindweeds early on.

The fight is most fierce at the start because the newly cleared soil offers an open invitation to airborne seed and because weed seed lying dormant in the soil springs to life when the ground is cleared. Soilborne weeds are particularly troublesome if you till the soil when sowing the meadow mixture, because dormant seed lying too deep to germinate comes to the surface and sprouts. One way to handle this is to till the soil (either by hand or with a power tiller), wait several weeks until weed seeds have sprouted, and then till, hoe, or disk the soil *shallowly* to disrupt the weed seedlings. (Shallow disking is essential, because deeper tilling brings up more weed seed.) You may have to repeat the process.

Once the soil is tilled and weeded several times, sow the meadow garden. Do this in either spring or fall, depending on your climate: in the South and Mid-Atlantic, fall sowing works best; in the North, spring sowing is better. It is essential to sow the seed thickly—often at twice the recommended rate on the package—to keep out weeds. Rake over the area 2-3 times to settle the seeds into the soil. Once the meadow is up and growing, hand-weed as needed. Keep your meadow watered throughout the first growing season to help the plants get established.

To keep woody plants from taking over your wildflower meadow and shading out the flowers, mow it back to about 6″ from the ground each year in late winter. A regular lawn mower won't do the job because it cuts too low—use a scythe or a small tractor. ❖

Melon

Cucumis melo and other genera
Cucurbitaceae

Despite some demanding requirements, the superior taste of vine-ripened melons is worth the effort it takes to grow them. Melons pack up on sugar during their final days of growth; this sweetness is noticably missing in commercial melons picked green for shipping.

Most melons need nutrient-rich soil, plenty of sunshine, and at least 3-4 months of warm weather. Melons can take up lots of space. A single watermelon vine, for example, can sprawl across 100 square feet and only produce two fruits; muskmelons, on the other hand, can provide at least dozen fruits in a 16-square-foot area. If you have limited space, try the more compact bush cultivars, or grow standard types vertically on a strong fence or trellis.

Types: What we call cantaloupes are actually muskmelons. This class of melon has a pumpkinlike ribbing and skin covered with a netting of shallow veins. Its fragrant flesh ranges from salmon to green. True cantaloupes, grown mostly in Europe, have orange flesh and rough, scaly skin with dark, distinct veins.

Winter melons (also a type of muskmelon) ripen as the weather starts to turn cool and will keep for fairly long periods if stored properly. This group includes honeydews, crenshaws, casabas, and Persians. These larger, more oval fruits—grown mostly in the interior valleys of California—have waxy skins that can be smooth or wrinkled, with less-fragrant flesh.

Winter melons require a growing season of well over 100 days and are more susceptible to diseases, but they're certainly delicious. Honeydews have smooth, creamy white skins and lime green flesh that takes on a slight golden tinge when mature. Crenshaws have salmon pink flesh with a distinctive flavor. The tenderness of their dark green skins make them difficult to ship. Casabas have wrinkled, golden skins and white flesh that stays sweet and juicy over a long period. Large, round Persian melons have thick, orange flesh.

Watermelons fall under a different botanical classification, *Citrullus lanatus,* but they thrive under the same cultural conditions that other melons require. Once limited to large farm gardens, watermelons are now available in compact-growing cultivars that are perfect for smaller home gardens. There are also seedless cultivars that produce firm, sweet fruits.

Planting: Melons need the sunniest spot possible with plenty of air circulation to help them dry out quickly after rain and prevent diseases. Melon roots usually extend from 2″ to 10″ into the earth, but some go as deep as 4′-5′. Therefore, the soil must be loose and moisture-holding but well drained. Since melons will be one of the last things you plant in your vegetable garden, you might want to give them an extra boost by working 2″-3″ of aged manure or compost into the planting area.

Vines may not set fruit if they are chilled as seedlings, so don't plant until the soil has warmed to 70°-80°F. Get a head start by planting seeds indoors in 4″ peat pots. Start them just 2-4 weeks before transplanting, because seedlings that develop tendrils or more than four leaves may have difficulty later in establishing roots. Sow several seeds ½″ deep in each pot, and place the pots in a south-facing window or other sunny spot. Provide bottom heat if necessary to bring the soil temperature to 75°F. Thin 2″ tall seedlings to the strongest plant by cutting the others off at soil level. A few days before planting, harden off the seedlings by setting them outdoors in a sunny area during the day and bringing them in at night.

You can grow large crops in rows, but most melons seem to do better in hills. For most cultivars, space hills 4′-6′ apart; vigorous growers, like watermelons, may require 6′-12′ between hills, while some bush types need only 2′.

When planting directly in the garden, sow

six seeds per hill no earlier than two weeks after the last frost date. Thin to 2-3 plants per hill, or in short-season areas, thin to only one plant per hill, so it won't have to compete with the other vines for nutrients.

In colder climates, put down a sheet of black plastic a few weeks prior to planting or transplanting to warm up the soil and keep it warm once the plants are in the ground. Anchor such sheets securely to keep them from shifting and covering young plants. You can also use hotcaps to keep seedlings warm.

Growing guidelines: A mulch, several inches thick, will keep down weeds and help keep the melons clean and disease-free; apply as the plants begin to vine. Provide generous

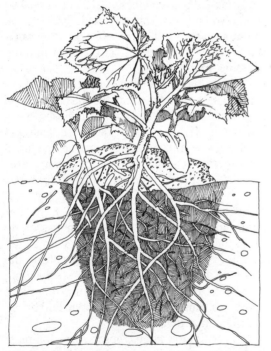

Hill planting. Raised mounds or "hills" provide warm soil and good drainage for your melons. Even in good garden soil, work an extra shovelful of compost or well-aged manure into each 1' high, 2'-3' wide hill just before planting. Or to really baby your crop, dig a 1' deep hole, fill it with compost or aged manure, and build the planting hill on top.

amounts of water, particularly right after transplanting and as the fruits develop.

Male flowers appear first, at leaf joints on the main stem and on larger sideshoots. Around a week later, fruit-producing female flowers form on secondary sideshoots. Despite the many female blossoms, each vine will produce only 3-4 melons. Most young melons will grow to the size of eggs, then shrivel as they put their nutrients back into the vines. Fertilize with manure tea when the fruits set and again two weeks later. For instructions on making manure tea, see the Manure entry.

Though the vines look very robust, they are actually quite delicate and must be handled carefully. If they start to sprawl outside the area where you wish them to grow, gently guide them back toward the center of the planted area.

After midsummer, remove flowers and smaller fruits from the vines; these won't have time to mature before frost, and they use up energy that should go into ripening the 2-3 larger fruits you've left on each vine.

Problems: Striped and spotted cucumber beetles can be serious pests. The beetles, which spread bacterial wilt as they feed, tend to be more destructive to direct-seeded plants than to transplants. They often attack around the time the plants flower. Tents of cheesecloth, mosquito netting, or floating row covers are the best protection from beetles, but you must remove these coverings when female flowers form so that bees can pollinate them. Control severe cucumber beetle infestations with pyrethrins.

Melon aphids can also be a problem. For more information, see "The Top Ten Garden Insect Pests in America" on page 344.

Squash vine borers, which eat their way up the stem of a plant and cause the leaves to wilt, may also attack melons. See the Squash entry for information on this pest.

Resistant cultivars and crop rotation are the best defenses against melon diseases, including downy and powdery mildews. Mildews are common in wet weather. Downy mildew produces

Supporting trellised melons. Melons on fences or trellises need support as they ripen, otherwise their weight may drag down the vines. Put them in a sling made from pantyhose, mesh onion bags, nylon bird netting, or similar material. Use soft cloth strips to tie the vines to the supports.

yellow spots on leaf surfaces, with purplish areas on the undersides. Powdery mildew causes powdery white areas on leaves and stems. Even a small amount of mildew can affect the sweetness of melons because the fungus will siphon off the vine's sugar to fuel its own growth. Cut off and destroy any affected branches.

Bacterial wilt produces limp leaves and stems that secrete a white sticky substance when cut. Remove and destroy affected plants. Reduce the chances of bacterial wilt by controlling cucumber beetles and aphids.

Harvesting: The stem of a vine-ripened fruit should break cleanly with no pressure at all on the stem; just picking up the fruit should be sufficient. You can often judge the ripeness of cantaloupes and muskmelons by scent alone.

Some gardeners determine the ripeness of a watermelon by thumping it, with a resulting ringing sound if it's green and a dull or dead sound if it's ripe. However, a dull or dead sound can also mean that the fruit is overripe. Other growers harvest when the "pig's-tail" curl where the watermelon attaches to the vine turns brown, but on some cultivars this tail dries up a 7-10 days before the fruit is ripe. Instead, look at the bottom surface or "ground spot" on a watermelon. If it has turned from a light straw color to gold, orange, or rich yellow, it's ripe for the picking.

Storage time for various melons kept in a cool place can vary from two weeks for a cantaloupe to eight weeks for a casaba.

Best cultivars: Cantaloupes and muskmelons: 'Ambrosia Hybrid', extra-sweet, salmon-fleshed, resistant to powdery mildew; 'Alaska', good in the North; 'Musketeer', 5"-6" split-resistant fruits, 2'-3' diameter plants, good for small gardens; 'Chieftain', disease- and pest-resistant, 6-8 lb. fruits with orange flesh.

Honeydews: 'Amber', 8-10 lb. melons with pale orange flesh, resistant to powdery mildew; 'Ogen Hybrid', 5½"-6" fruits with pear-flavored flesh; 'Passport', 6 lb. fruits with pale green flesh that grows sweeter the longer it's on the vine; 'Earlidew', green-fleshed, good for short growing seasons.

Crenshaw: 'Early Crenshaw', large fruits that taste like a cantaloupe-honeydew cross.

Watermelon: 'Moon & Stars', speckled foliage, yellow moon- and star-shaped splashes on dark green skin and bright red, sugary sweet flesh; 'Charleston Gray' and related cultivars, dependable, disease-resistant; 'Honey Red Seedless', small, 8" diameter, round, light green melons with bright red flesh; 'Jack of Hearts Hybrid', green-striped, 11-15 lb. fruits with firm, red flesh and small edible seeds; 'Golden Crown Hybrid', early-maturing, golden-skinned, 7 lb. melons with red flesh, 'Yellow Baby Hybrid', 7" diameter fruits, sweet yellow flesh. ❖

Mertensia

Bluebells. Spring-blooming perennial wildflowers.

Description: *Mertensia virginica,* Virginia bluebells, bear graceful hanging clusters of pink buds that open into sky blue bells. The 1'-2' arching clumps have 8" broad, blue-green leaves. Zones 3-8.

How to grow: Plant container-grown bluebells in early spring or divide the brittle roots in fall. Bluebells prefer sun or partial shade and humus-rich soil with even moisture during growth. They go dormant soon after bloom, and then established plants will tolerate dry soil. Self-sown plants can multiply quickly.

Landscape uses: Bluebells are at their best with bulbs in borders or woodland settings. Grow with annuals, perennials, ferns, and other plants to disguise dying foliage.

Best cultivars: 'Alba' has white flowers. ❖

Mint

Mentha spp.
Labiatae

Description: Mints have squared, four-sided stems with opposite leaves and lipped flowers. All parts of the plants are pungent. Most mints are rampant spreaders, forming a thick mat of spreading stolons just under the surface of the ground. Aboveground, plants produce 2'-3' upright stems.

The genus *Mentha* has many species and cultivars. *Mentha* × *piperita,* peppermint, and *M. spicata,* spearmint, are the most familiar. Herb gardeners can also grow *M. suaveolens,* the furry apple mint, *M.* × *piperita* var. *citrata,* exotic orange mint, *M. requienii,* the creeping, mosslike Corsican mint, and various hybrids or variegated forms.

How to grow: All mints prefer a cool, moist spot in part shade but will also grow in full sun. Mint is extremely variable from seed. Order plants from a reputable source, or visit a nursery to find plants whose flavor and aroma appeal to you. One plant of each cultivar you select will soon provide more than enough mint for home use—the big problem is to keep them from overrunning all neighboring plants. Plant mints in deep, bottomless containers sunk in the ground, or plant above ground in tubs and barrels.

Harvesting: Snip leaves or sprigs as needed. To harvest in quantity, cut stems to within an inch or so above the ground. You can make several harvests, depending on the length of the season. Hang mint in loose bunches to air dry, or freeze in self-sealing bags.

Uses: Enjoy aromatic mint teas hot or iced. Peppermint tea, a centuries-old remedy, can calm an upset stomach. Add chopped leaves to lamb, rice, salads, or cooked vegetables. Corsican mint is an attractive creeper, good between paving stones or in the rock garden. ❖

Monarda

Bee balm. Summer-blooming perennials; wildflowers; herbs.

Description: *Monarda didyma,* bee balm, bears shaggy 2"-3" flowers in white, pink, red, and purple. Spreading colonies of 2'-3½' upright plants bear 3"-6" fragrant leaves on square stems. Zones 4-8.

How to grow: Plant or divide in spring or fall in a sunny site with average, well-drained, moisture-retentive soil. Shade produces floppy stems and mildewed leaves. Divide bee balm often to curb its spread and reduce disease problems; cut back nearly to the ground after bloom for a new crop of healthy leaves.

Landscape uses: Group in borders and herb gardens; allow to naturalize in moist meadows. Hummingbirds love them.

Best cultivars: 'Cambridge Scarlet', bright red; 'Croftway Pink'; 'Mahogany', dark purple-red; 'Snow Queen', white; 'Violet Queen'. ❖

Mulch

The most time-saving measure you can take in a garden is to mulch it. This goes for every garden site, from vegetable garden to flower bed. Mulched gardens are healthier, more weed-free, and more drought-resistant than unmulched gardens, so you'll spend less time watering, weeding, and fighting pest problems.

There are two basic kinds of mulch: organic and inorganic. Organic mulches include formerly living material such as wood chips, shredded bark, chopped leaves, straw, grass clippings, compost, sawdust, pine needles, and even paper. Inorganic mulches include gravel, stones, black plastic, and geotextiles (landscape fabrics).

Both types discourage weeds, but organic mulches also improve the soil as they decompose. Inorganic mulches don't break down and enrich the soil, but under certain circumstances they're the mulch of choice. For example, black plastic warms the soil and radiates heat during the night, keeping heat-loving vegetables such as eggplant and tomatoes cozy and vigorous.

Using Organic Mulches

There are two cardinal rules for using organic mulches to combat weeds: First, be sure to lay the mulch down on soil that is already weeded, and second, lay down a thick enough layer to discourage new weeds from coming up through it. It can take a 4"-6" layer of mulch to completely discourage weeds, although a 2"-3" layer is usually enough in shady spots where weeds aren't as troublesome as they are in full sun.

The best organic mulch is compost, a mixture of decomposed organic materials. For directions on making compost, see the Composting entry.

You can purchase bags of decorative wood chips or shredded bark from the local garden center to mulch your flower garden and shrub borders. A more inexpensive source of wood chips might be your tree-care company or the utility company. They may be willing to sell you a trunkload of chips at a nominal price. Many communities are also chipping yard debris or composting grass clippings and fall leaves, then offering the result back to the community for free or for a small charge.

If you have a lot of trees on your property, shredding the fallen leaves creates a nutrient-rich mulch for free. You can use a leaf-shredding machine, but you don't really need a special machine to shred leaves—a lawn mower with a bagger will collect leaves and cut them into the perfect size for mulching.

You can spread a wood chip or shredded leaf mulch anywhere on your property, but it looks especially attractive in flower beds and shrub borders. Of course, it's right at home in a woodland or shade garden. Wood chips aren't a great idea for vegetable and annual flower beds, though, since you'll be digging these beds every year and the chips will get in the way.

Grass clippings are another readily available mulch, but they aren't particularly attractive. Some people pile the nitrogen-rich clippings under shrubs or on flower beds, but they are more appropriate on vegetable beds, where appearance is less critical. Your vegetables will thank you for the nitrogen boost!

Another great mulch for the vegetable garden is straw, salt hay, or weed-free hay. It looks good and has most of the benefits of mulches: retaining soil moisture, keeping down weeds, and adding organic matter to the soil when it breaks down. But be sure the hay you use is weed- and seed-free, or you'll just be making trouble for your garden. And don't pull hay or straw up to the stems of vegetables or the trunks of fruit trees or you'll be inviting slug and rodent damage.

Using Plastic Mulch

Mulching a vegetable garden with sheets of black plastic film can do wonders. The plastic heats up in the sun, warming the soil and radiating heat during the night, effectively creating a microclimate about 3°F warmer than an unmulched garden. Because the plastic film remains warm and dry, it protects the fruits of vining crops such as strawberries, melons, and cucum-

ORGANIC MULCHING MECHANICS

An organic mulch is sort of like compost, only instead of working it into the soil, you lay it down on top. The mulch saves labor and nurtures plants by:

● Preventing most weed seeds from germinating and making pulling those that do pop through easy.

● Keeping the soil cool and moist in summer, reducing the need to water.

● Decomposing slowly, releasing nutrients into the soil.

● Encouraging earthworm activity, improving soil tilth and nutrient content.

● Keeping dirt from splashing on flowers and vegetables.

● Preventing alternate freezing and thawing of the soil in winter, which can heave plants from the soil.

Nothing, unfortunately, is perfect. When using organic mulches, keep in mind the following facts:

● As low-nitrogen organic mulches such as wood chips and sawdust decay, nitrogen is temporarily depleted from the soil. Fertilize first with a high-nitrogen product such as cottonseed meal, blood meal, or chicken manure to boost soil nitrogen levels.

● An organic mulch retains moisture, which can slow soil warming; in spring, pull mulch away from perennials and bulbs for faster growth.

● A wet mulch piled against the stems of flowers and vegetables can cause them to rot; keep mulch about 1″ away from crowns and stems.

● Mulch piled up against woody stems of shrubs and trees can cause them to rot and encourages rodents, such as voles and mice, to nest in the mulch. Keep deep mulch pulled back about 6″–12″ from trunks.

● In damp climates, organic mulches can harbor slugs and snails, which will munch on nearby plants; don't mulch near slug-susceptible plants.

● Organic mulches are usually more or less acidic, depending on their content; mix some lime with the mulch beneath plants that prefer neutral or slightly alkaline soil.

bers from rotting and keeps them clean. And of course, the mulch prevents weed growth and retains soil moisture.

In raised bed gardens, lay down a sheet of plastic over the entire bed. Bury it at the edges or weigh the plastic down with rocks. Then punch holes in it for the plants. A bulb planter makes quick work of hole cutting. Sow seeds or plant transplants in the holes. You should be able to reuse the plastic for several years if you take it up and store it over winter.

Because water can't permeate the plastic, the mulch retains soil moisture but can also keep rainwater from soaking the planting bed. That means you'll have to water the garden yourself, with a drip irrigation system or soaker hoses placed beneath the plastic. The simplest method is to shove the end of the hose through a hole in the plastic and turn it on.

Don't use black plastic as a mulch under shrubs. Although it keeps out weeds and can be camouflaged with decorative mulch, black plastic destroys the shrubs' long-term health. Because water and air cannot penetrate the plastic, roots grow very close to the soil surface—sometimes right beneath the plastic—seeking moisture and oxygen. The shallow roots suffer from lack of oxygen and moisture and from extremes of heat and cold. Eventually the plants decline and die. Stick to organic mulches such as shredded leaves, bark, wood chips, or compost under your trees and shrubs.

Unlike black plastic, geotextiles or landscape fabrics let air and water through to the soil beneath while keeping weeds from coming up. But geotextiles have some of the same drawbacks as black plastic. If exposed to light, they'll degrade, so you have to cover them with a second mulch (they're ugly, so you'd want to, anyway). Some studies have found that shrub roots may grow up into the geotextile mulch, creating real problems if you want to remove it. And weeds that germinate in the mulch on top of the geotextile can send roots down into the fabric, tearing it when you pull them out. ❖

Narcissus

Daffodil, narcissus, jonquil. Spring-blooming bulbs.

Description: Daffodils, the first showy flowers of the season, bear blooms with a cup- or trumpet-shaped corona surrounded by six outer petals collectively called the perianth. Flowers measure from less than 1″ to over 6″ wide. Colors include shades of white, yellow, orange, pink, and red. Heights vary from species a few inches tall to sturdy hybrids reaching 2′. Flowers are borne singly or in clusters above straplike or, rarely, reedlike leaves. Thousands of cultivars are available, and the American Daffodil Society has established 11 daffodil classes, based on flower shape, to organize the many types. To add variety and lengthen your bloom season, plant cultivars from several classes. See "Daffodil Flower Forms" on page 394 for some of the most popular flower forms. Most are hardy from Zones 3-8.

Species worth considering include: *N. cyclamineus,* bearing strongly swept-back golden perianths and prominent trumpets growing to 1′, Zones 6-9; *N. jonquilla,* the classic jonquil, with multiple flattish, fragrant golden flowers on 1½′ stems among rushlike leaves, Zones 7-9; *N. poeticus,* the poet's narcissus, with a rounded white perianth and tiny, fragrant, red-and-green cup, blooms at the end of daffodil season and reaches 1′, Zones 4-9; and *N. triandrus,* angel's-tears, bearing multiple hanging white blooms on 1′ stems, Zones 4-9.

How to grow: Plant in early fall (or late summer in the far North) in a spot that receives sun in spring. Set the bulbs at a depth 2-3 times their width in average, well-drained soil containing organic matter. (Daffodils tolerate less-fertile soils but will probably not bloom as well.) Add some cottonseed meal, bonemeal, and wood ashes, scratching them in around the bulbs. Water if fall rains are scanty. Cover with a few inches of light mulch in the North after the ground begins to freeze. Remove the mulch in early spring and scatter more fertilizer, again watering if rain falls short. After bloom, deadhead daffodils if they set seed, provide water if necessary, and let the foliage turn yellow before cutting it off near the soil line. Never tie it up in bunches, because sun must reach the leaves for them to manufacture food for next year's flowers.

With good culture, after several years one bulb will multiply into a large, tight mass that will bloom less freely. Dig up the entire clump after the leaves turn yellow but before they disappear and separate out the largest bulbs for replanting immediately, or store them in a shady, well-ventilated spot until fall planting time. Plant

Daffodil flower forms. Daffodils are available in many flower forms and sizes, from the clusters of tiny, fragrant flowers borne by tazetta types to the 4″ wide trumpet types with their large tubular coronas. Some of the most popular are shown here.

the smaller bulbs in a nursery area for growing into blooming-size bulbs or naturalize them. Fertilize each year in fall as you would for newly planted bulbs. Don't plant soft or squishy bulbs, and destroy any with virus-streaked foliage, which indicates viral infection.

To naturalize daffodils, plant them in thin, rough grass that you can leave unmowed until the leaves have yellowed. Then leave them to their own devices, perhaps adding a little fertilizer to boost them along.

Landscape uses: Plant sweeping masses or small groups in thin grass or in woodlands, or grow them in borders and beds, allowing companion plants to partially disguise the foliage. Site them close to the house and near windows for easy viewing indoors on cold days; bring some indoors for cut flowers. Many cultivars are excellent for forcing in winter. ❖

Native Plants

Plants that grow in the specific habitats in which they evolved are called native plants. Plants from outside a specific habitat or area are non-native or exotic plants. A plant from Europe growing in North America is exotic. So is a plant from Virginia growing in Alaska. It is native to North America but not to Alaska.

Use native plants in informal or formal landscapes. Shade gardens are perfect for woodland wildflowers, ferns, and shrubs. Create your own woodland with a canopy of native trees. Showcase unusual native perennials like Joe-Pye weed (*Eupatorium purpureum*) and Culver's root (*Veronicastrum virginicum*) in perennial borders with familiar native garden plants like phlox (*Phlox* spp.) and bee balm (*Monarda didyma*). For more on landscaping with native plants, see the Natural Landscaping entry. ❖

Natural Landscaping

Picture this: a yard with birds singing from flowering dogwoods and redbuds nestled under the taller trees of a small woods. At the back of the yard is a clearing where ferns and rocks frame a lovely pool. You can see the native yellow water lily blooming on the pool's surface; nearby, a frog is calling. A leaf-covered path leads you quietly to the woods' edge. Shrubs that have colonized the brighter area at the foot of the trees give way to a colorful wildflower meadow. This natural paradise could be your own backyard—*if* you've replaced some of the lawn with natural landscaping.

Natural landscaping is designing all or part of your yard with the aim of re-creating the feel of a natural scene. That doesn't mean stomping into the woods, digging up everything in sight, and plunking it down in your yard just the way it was. What it does mean is *looking* at the woods— or the prairie, or the Alaskan tundra, or whatever natural scene appeals to you most—and bringing back ideas.

To get started on your own natural landscaping adventure, follow these simple steps:

- Pick the natural landscape that has the strongest appeal for you.
- Spend a couple of minutes drawing the scene. You don't have to draw anything elaborate; just make it clear enough so when you look at the drawing, you'll remember the major elements of the natural landscape.
- Look at what you've drawn. If you took away one thing from the picture, what element would make the most difference? By finding that element, you'll find the key to what makes the scene a woodland, meadow, or bog to you. For example, you might find that a line of trees, old hedgerow, or fence—the juxtaposition of light and dark—was what defined a meadow. In a prairie, the horizon line serves as the edge. Tall, vertical tree trunks tend to define a woodland.
- When you decide what it is that makes an area special, you're ready to choose plants that will give your landscape the same feeling. The sections that follow will tell you how to get started.

Seeing Nature

When you've chosen a natural landscape that has strong appeal for you and worked through the basic exercise to get a grasp of the essentials of the scene, you still have to decide how to use plants in it. To do that, you need to go back to the natural area and look around. The first step in analyzing a natural scene is to determine the topography, exposure, and soil. Is the area flat, rolling, or hilly? Does it face east or west? Is it in sun or shade? For how much of the day? What about moisture and soil type? Is it a well-drained, sandy slope or a mucky bottom? Think about how these conditions match those in various parts of your yard.

Next, look at the way the plants are arranged or layered. Do tall trees shelter small flowering trees, which in turn rise above a diversity of deciduous and evergreen shrubs, ferns, and wildflowers? Is there mostly a cover of grasses, with an occasional wildflower, shrub, or tree? The way plants grow with others is part of the distinctive look of a site. It's a look you'll want to bring to your own yard, if you want your woods or meadow to look "real."

Now identify the dominant species. If you removed all the oaks, for example, would the woodland be radically altered? If a particular groundcover were gone, would the look of the woods change? These key species will be vital to reproducing the scene in your garden. Note other showy or abundant species that will add interest and variety to your design.

Another important consideration is how the plants grow. Some plants grow in masses or drifts; others are sprinkled sparingly across the land. Look at the spacing. Are plants clumped, or do they grow singly? Do they cluster at the bases of trees? Make notes, take photographs, or sketch the patterns you see.

As you look, you'll see that repetition of key elements—like the brown tree trunks in a forest— unifies the landscape. While you see the tree trunks, you think, "forest." In a prairie, unity comes from the continuous background of grasses and the virtual absence of trees and shrubs. To make a recognizable natural landscape at home, you have to give it a unified look. But balance unity with diversity. The unexpected in nature is what keeps us excited. Think of the wonder we feel when we round a bend in a woodland path and stumble on a clump of yellow lady's-slippers in bloom under a tree. Choose a variety of plant forms, textures, and colors to keep your landscape exciting.

Finally, consider the boundaries in your natural scene. Boundaries exist in natural and in human landscapes. Since your garden will have boundaries, it is important to study nature's edges. Fencerows, agricultural fields, stream banks, and hedges provide gradual transitions from open sun to some form of shade. Let a hedge, tree line, or wall create the same transition in your garden.

Natural Landscaping Styles

Once you've gotten a good idea of the kinds of plants that make up your natural scene and the way they grow there, you need to consider specific plants to grow in your own natural landscape. There are two ways to create a natural landscape: by using only native plants in your garden or by creating a naturalistic design using both native and exotic plants.

If you garden exclusively with plants native to your region of the country, choose trees, shrubs, wildflowers, and ferns that suit your design and grow in your area. Most people use their state boundaries as cut-off points for plant selection. Others consider any plant native to North America to be acceptable.

The second approach uses plants to create a natural effect without regard to their origins. The plants may be native to your area or exotic— brought in from other countries or (if you're a purist) states. When you use exotic plants, choose plants that are hardy in your area. And don't buy rampant spreaders that may escape from your garden and become established in the wild, endangering native ecosystems.

Designing the Garden

Now you're ready to start designing. Remember that when you design a natural garden, you're not trying to make an exact copy of a natural scene. Instead, you want to reproduce the *feel* of a favorite place. Follow these points to successfully translate nature's lessons to your garden.

Understanding your site: Sun, shade, soil, moisture, and exposure determine the kind of landscape you create and the plants you grow there. Watch the movement of the sun across your yard daily and throughout the season. Where are the shady spots? Which areas remain in sun all day? Check for wet spots after a good rain. Disturbed soils around houses seldom resemble what you find in nearby woods or meadows. You must find plants adapted to the soil conditions you have, or amend your soil to accomodate the plants you wish to grow.

Organizing garden spaces: Next, decide how large an area to develop. Start small! A few choice trees, shrubs, and groundcovers can be the beginning of a woodland garden; a 2' × 3' pond can be a focal point for a future bog garden. You can always add to your garden. Decide where to place the beds and where the paths will go. Keep the paths under 4' wide to maintain intimacy. In a prairie or meadow, a 3' path allows the plants to brush you as you pass, providing a direct experience of the landscape.

Create the illusion of depth by layering the vegetation away from the path. Place low plants close for easy inspection. Use shrubs to close off views or to fill empty spaces. Vertical tree trunks will pull your eye upward. If your yard is small, borrow views from your neighbors. Create an opening between trees on your property so it frames a distant tree and makes it seem like it's part of the garden.

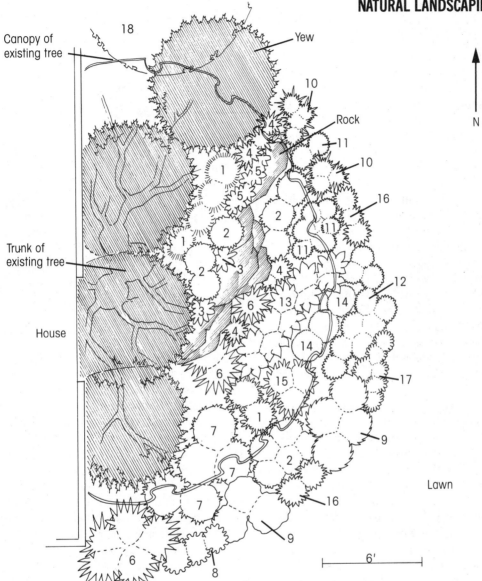

Canopy of existing tree

18

Yew

10

Rock

11

10

16

Trunk of existing tree

1

1

2

5

5

4

5

4

4

1

2

2

2

3

3

16

11

11

4

12

14

6

13

14

House

4

17

6

15

14

1

7

9

7

2

7

16

7

9

6

8

N

Lawn

6'

Shady woodland garden. This design will bring the feeling of the woods into your backyard. An asterisk (*) indicates a plant that's native to the United States.

1. Lady fern (*Athyrium filix-femina*)*
2. Fringed bleeding heart (*Dicentra eximia*)*
3. Bloodroot (*Sanguinaria canadensis*)*
4. Maidenhair fern (*Adiantum pedatum*)*

5. Canada wild ginger (*Asarum canadense*)*
6. Siberian iris (*Iris sibirica*)
7. Goat's beard (*Aruncus dioicus*)*
8. Chinese astilbe (*Astilbe chinensis* 'Pumila')
9. Bergenia (*Bergenia* spp.)
10. Crested iris (*Iris cristata*)*
11. 'Palace Purple' coralbells (*Heuchera* 'Palace Purple')
12. Allegheny foamflower (*Tiarella cordifolia*)*

13. Hostas (*Hosta* spp.)
14. Long-spurred epimedium (*Epimedium grandiflorum*)
15. Fragrant Solomon's seal (*Polygonatum odoratum*)
16. 'Beacon Silver' lamium (*Lamium maculatum* 'Beacon Silver')
17. Purple-leaved ajuga (*Ajuga reptans* 'Atropurpurea')
18. Allegheny serviceberry (*Amelanchier laevis*)*

Plant placement: Place plants in the garden as they would grow in nature. Situate them at the top, middle, or bottom of a slope, in a low spot or edging a garden pool, based on what the plants require for best growth. Try to space the plants randomly—after all, plants tend to grow in clumps in nature, not in uniform rows or singly. When grouping, place plants close together at the center of the planting and more loosely at the edges. Add a small clump or single plant separate from the main planting to give the look of a chance seedling.

Punctuate low plantings and groundcovers with vase-shaped ferns or upright plants like baneberries (*Actaea* spp.). Accent straight tree trunks with the arching stems of wildflowers like Solomon's seal (*Polygonatum* spp.). Use the bold foliage of hostas in combination with more delicate phlox, foamflower (*Tiarella cordifolia*), or barrenworts (*Epimedium* spp.). Just a few well-placed plants can make your natural garden successful.

Plant selection: Choose plants to match the conditions of the site and the requirements of your design. If you are using only natives, base your plant selection on the natural site your design is modeled on. In a mixed planting, select harmonious colors, forms, and textures. Foliage is more important than flowers because it is effective all season. Don't forget to work with the plants that are already on your site.

Towards maturity: As conditions change in the garden, the composition will also change. Aging trees produce more dense shade; a dead tree opens a sunny spot. Plants will grow too large and need division. Seedlings will come up at random. Nature is always at work. Enjoy and use the opportunities she provides.

Maintaining the Garden

The natural garden needs care and maintenance like any other garden. Water whenever rainfall is insufficient. Weed to remove unwanted

More On
NATURAL LANDSCAPING

Natural landscaping is so interesting, and there are so many natural scenes that you can try in your yard, that you may want to read more about it. Good books on natural landscaping include *Landscaping with Nature* by Jeff Cox, *The Natural Garden* by Ken Druse, and *Livable Landscape Design* by John F. Collins and Marvin I. Adelman. For more on natural landscaping styles, see the Bog Gardens, Meadow Gardens, Shade Gardening, Water Gardens, and Wildflowers entries. For more on landscaping techniques, see the Landscaping and Garden Design entries.

plants and control those that spread aggressively. Mulch beds for winter protection, water conservation, and weed control. Shredded leaves are excellent in woodland gardens.

Leave dried meadow and prairie plants standing throughout the winter. Mow them in early spring to make room for new growth. Prune trees and shrubs as needed to keep them healthy and vigorous. Tasks such as pinching, deadheading, and staking are seldom necessary, since the garden should look natural. If you've matched plants to your conditions, you should have minimal pest and disease problems. Should problems arise, however, see the Organic Pest Management entry for tips on how to control them. ❖

Nectarine

Prunus persica
Rosaceae

Nectarines are smooth-skinned peaches. The fruit is often more susceptible to pest and disease problems than fuzzy-skinned peaches are. See the Peach entry for growing information. ❖

Nematodes

Nematodes, also called eelworms, are microscopic, slender, translucent roundworms. They live in moist areas such as soil, decaying organic matter, water, and the insides of other animals. Beneficial nematodes hasten the decay of organic matter in compost. Parasitic nematodes control Japanese beetle grubs and other root pests. Plant-feeding nematodes suck plant juices from roots and leaves, and root knot nematodes attack roots of tomatoes, peppers, lettuce, and other plants, causing distorted, knotty roots. Affected plants grow poorly and may die.

To control nematodes in home gardens, rotate crops, plant nematode-resistant cultivars, plant a fallow crop of African marigolds (the roots of *Tagetes* spp. are toxic to nematodes), or solarize the soil in affected areas. For more on controls, see the Organic Pest Management entry. ❖

Nepeta

Catmint. Spring- to summer-blooming perennials.

Description: *Nepeta* × *faassenii,* catmint, produces a profusion of ½″ blue-violet blooms borne in clusters over 1′-2′ spreading mounds of 1″-1½″ fragrant, gray-green, scalloped leaves. Zones 4-8.

How to grow: Plant in spring or fall or divide in spring in a sunny spot (partial shade in the South) with average, well-drained soil. Cut back by half and fertilize lightly after flowering for fall rebloom. Buy cutting-grown plants to make sure you get *N.* × *faassenii* rather than its less attractive parent, *N. mussinii,* which can be grown from seed.

Landscape uses: Group near the front of borders; grow as an edge or low hedge or among rocks. Combine with roses, pinks, and gray-leaved plants in a cottage garden. ❖

Nicotiana

Flowering tobacco. Summer- and fall-blooming annuals.

Description: Star-faced, 2″ blooms in white, pink, rose, red, and green are fragrant at night. Leafless, sticky stems rise up to 2½′ from flat rosettes of paddle-shaped, medium green leaves.

How to grow: Sow the tiny seed indoors in March for planting out after frost danger is past. You can also buy transplants, or direct-seed after the ground warms up. Ordinary, well-drained soil is fine. Partial shade enhances the red and green flowers.

Landscape uses: Tall cultivars are a mainstay of cottage gardens and borders; the dwarfs do well in beds and pots.

Best cultivars: Mixes: 'Sensation' and 'Daylight Sensation', both 2½′; the 'Nicki' series, 2′; 'Domino', 1′. 'Lime Green' has fragrant, pale green flowers and can reach 5′; 'Affinis' is pure white, 2½′. ❖

Nigella

Love-in-a-mist, fennel flower. Short-season annuals, dried flowers.

Description: Intricate, jewel-like, 1″ flowers in white, rose, blue, and lavender nestle atop 1′-1½′ mounds of delicate, misty green foliage.

How to grow: Sow seeds directly in a sunny, well-drained spot with average soil and moisture. Make several sowings three weeks apart for longer bloom. Thin 8″-10″ apart for mounds; closer spacing produces upright stems. Seedpods dry well when cut green or as they take on a red blush.

Landscape uses: Use to disguise dying bulb foliage. Allow self-sown plants to grow throughout borders and cottage gardens.

Best cultivars: 'Persian Jewel', 15″, mix; 'Miss Jekyll', 1½′, blue. ❖

Nut Trees

Reliably long-lived, often simply gargantuan in size, and possessing many unique physical attributes, nut trees have become an important part of American culture. Grown since colonial times, nut trees are truly a multi-purpose crop, providing shade, beauty, edible nuts, building materials, and wildlife habitats.

Nuts are excellent sources of the proteins and fats commonly found in meats. Many nuts contain up to 30 percent protein by weight, while fresh beefsteak contains less than 20 percent. Except for chestnuts, which are nearly 50 percent carbohydrate, most nuts also contain 50-70 percent fat. Nearly all of this fat is unsaturated. Nuts are also good sources of certain vitamins, and of minerals, mined by the deep root systems of the trees.

Nut trees also provide us with some of our finest building materials. Black walnut trees are especially prized for their exceptional, beautifully grained lumber. An ideal single specimen can sell for as much as $30,000. Lumber cut from nut trees is some of the most valuable wood known to humans.

The natural beauty of nut trees is enhanced by the abundance of wildlife that makes full use of their generous bounty. Squirrels, partridges, wild turkeys, deer, and other enjoyable creatures enrich our suburbs and small towns with their presence while gleaning America's nut crops. Nut trees are a natural choice for gardeners who want to attract local wildlife.

Although they respond best with ideal growing conditions, many nut trees are wonderfully adaptable to a range of sites. You can plant them on steep slopes to stop soil erosion, or in soils too rocky to be plowed. Once established, the trees send their roots deep into the earth, garnering minerals and stability from the rocks below. And nut-producing plants come in a range of sizes, from bushy filberts to towering hickories, so there's one to fit in almost every garden.

Selecting Nut Trees

People often ask whether they should plant cultivars or seedling nut trees. Named cultivars are produced vegetatively, usually by grafting or budding, yielding genetically identical clones. The advantage of grafted trees is that you know exactly what you are going to get with respect to hardiness, cracking quality, flavor, size, and other crop characteristics. Seeds, on the other hand, are always somewhat different genetically. This genetic diversity can make a stand of seedlings less susceptible to serious insect or disease problems than a stand of genetically identical cultivars.

Where high-quality nut production is of greatest importance, as with pecan or English walnut, stick to named cultivars where available. For trees such as black walnut and butternut, where timber value may be as important as the nut quality, plant a few grafted trees and use high-quality seedlings to fill out the rest of the planting. The resulting forest will be much healthier, and the cost of seedling trees is also a fraction that of grafted ones.

Planting and Care

These low-maintenance plants can adapt to a range of sites. They generally need very little extra care once established. Keep in mind that many nut trees, including pecans and most black and English walnuts, need cross-pollination; be sure to plant more than one cultivar or seedling of each kind.

Planting: Soil requirements vary among the trees; "Nut Trees for Home Use" on page 402 tells about the particular cultural conditions each kind of tree prefers. In general, though, nut trees thrive in deep, rich, moist, loam or clay loam soil. Top-grade soils bring out the best in nut trees; one well-documented study identified an entire grove of black walnuts which had reached an average height of 100' in only 26 years!

Planting nuts directly into the ground is a

nice idea, but experience has proven that planting high-quality seedlings is far more successful. Squirrels and other rodents have an uncanny ability to sniff out planted nuts. In addition, most reputable nurseries will screen their seedlings, discarding weak and unhealthy trees, so you'll get better plants.

Most nut trees have a deep anchoring taproot, making them a bit more difficult to establish than other trees. Whenever possible, start with small, young trees; they will often adjust more quickly and begin growing sooner than larger trees. Make sure you dig the planting hole deep enough to accommodate the taproot.

Aftercare: Water the planted tree thoroughly and top-dress with 6''-8'' of compost or mulch to help keep the soil underneath moist. (Keep the mulch away from the trunk, though, to avoid rodent damage.) Failure to keep the moisture level high around the newly planted tree can cause the soil in the hole to shrink away from the taproot during hot, dry weather. Insufficient water during the first year is probably the leading cause of death in newly planted nut trees. Water young trees deeply once a week during dry spells until they are established.

Once they have settled in, the trees should grow rapidly, producing crops anywhere from 3 to 7 years after planting, depending on the type of nut and the local climate.

Pruning: Unlike fruit trees, most nut trees don't require special pruning techniques to produce good crops. Prune nut trees as you would any shade tree, removing dead, diseased, or crossing branches regularly. If you've planted grafted trees, be sure to prune off any suckers that may arise from the rootstock. For trees that are eventually intended for timber, keep side limbs pruned off to about 12'-16' up the trunk.

Problems

Although a host of pests and diseases can attack nut trees, none of these are usually lethal. The best pest-control program is to maximize

More On
NUT TREES

The Trees entry includes information on general care and maintenance of trees that also applies to nut tree culture. You'll find descriptions, suggested uses, and cultural information about specific nut trees in the following entries: Fagus (beechnut), Ginkgo, Juglans (butternut, walnut), Pinus (pine), Prunus (almond), and Quercus (oak).

If you're interested in learning more about growing nut trees, contact: Northern Nut Growers Association, Kenneth Bauman, 9870 South Palmer Road, New Carlisle, OH 45344. Association members receive a quarterly newsletter.

trees' natural resistance by keeping them healthy. Applying BT (*Bacillus thuringiensis*) is an effective control for many leaf-eating caterpillars. Resistant cultivars are available for some pests and diseases. Pick up fallen leaves, twigs, husks, and nuts regularly to remove possible overwintering sites for pests and diseases.

Chestnut blight (*Cryphonectria parasitica*) is a serious fungal disease on American chestnut trees. Since the early 1900s, it has wiped out almost all American chestnuts. Until effective control measures or resistant cultivars are available, try growing a Chinese chestnut–American chestnut hybrid, or choose another type of nut.

Harvesting

Most nuts are best gathered as soon as they become ripe. Remove the outer husk as soon as possible to prevent mold or darkening of the nut kernel. Store the husked nuts in their shells in a cool, dry, rodent-free area. Allow the nuts to cure (dry) for 1-3 months. After curing, most nuts will keep in the shell for at least a year. ❖

Nut Trees for Home Use

Besides producing a tasty crop, many nut trees are beautiful, long-lasting landscape specimens. You may want to try planting one or several of the nut trees described below in your home landscape.

Plant Name	Cultural Requirements	Size and Zone	Comments
Almond (*Prunus amygdalus*)	Rich, well-drained soil. Blossoms cannot withstand late spring frosts.	Small (20'–30'); Zone 7–9.	Beautiful flowers, blooms very early, drought-tolerant; limited range. Cultivars: 'Hall's Hardy' (Zones 5–8), 'Nonpareil', 'Peerless', 'Mission'.
Alpricot (*Prunus armeniaca*)	Rich, light loamy soil. Protect from late frosts.	Small (15'–30'); Zones 5–8.	Attractive flowers, edible fruit and kernels; dropped fruit can be messy. Commonly planted from seed.
Beechnut (*Fagus grandifolia*)	Rich, moist, rocky upland soil. Prefers a wooded site, especially when young.	Large (50'–100'); Zones 2–8.	Smooth blue-gray bark, long-lived; slow grower. Commonly grown from seed. Cultivar: 'Jenner'.
Buartnut (*Juglans cinerea* × *J. ailantifolia*)	Prefers rich, deep soil, but will tolerate a range of conditions.	Medium (40'–70'); Zones 4–8.	Prolific producer, nuts are attractive; may be toxic to some plants, nuts will stain pavement. Mostly grown from seed. Cultivars: 'Fioka', 'Dunoka', 'Mitchell Hybrid', 'Pierce'.
Butternut (*Juglans cinerea*)	Prefers rich, deep soil, but will tolerate a range of conditions.	Medium (40'–70'); Zones 3–7.	Graceful tree; may be toxic to some plants; susceptible to disease, nuts will stain pavement. Cultivars: 'Chamberlin', 'Craxezy', 'George Elmer', 'Ayers', 'Weschcke'.
Chestnut, Chinese (*Castanea mollissima*)	Light, upland, sandy loam soil.	Small (10'–20'); Chinese-American crosses will be taller; Zones 5–8.	Ideal for small sites; prickly burrs surround nuts. Many Chinese-American crosses available. Cultivars: 'Crane', 'Eaton', 'Nanking', 'Orrin'.
Chestnut, European (*Castanea sativa*)	Rich, upland, loamy soil.	Large (50'–90'); Zones 5–8.	Long-lived, stately tree; prickly burrs surround the nuts, needs a pollinator. Mostly grown from seed.
Filbert, hazelnut (*Corylus* spp.)	Rich, light, well-drained soil.	Small (10'–40'); Zones 2–8.	Crimson fall foliage; husks litter the ground. Grow as a hedge, a multi-stemmed bush, or a small tree. Can be grown from seed. Cultivars: 'Barcelona', 'Bixby', 'Royal', 'Hall's Giant'.

Plant Name	Cultural Requirements	Size and Zone	Comments
Ginkgo (*Ginkgo biloba*)	Rich, moist, heavy soil.	Medium (40'–70'); Zones 4–8.	Stately tree, beautiful foliage; grows slowly, foul-smelling fruit on female trees. Grow nut-bearing female trees from seed.
Heartnut (*Juglans ailantifolia* var. *cordiformis*)	Deep, rich soil.	Medium (30'–60'); Zones 5–8.	Light-colored bark, lacy foliage, fast-growing; may be toxic to other plants, nuts can stain pavement.
Hickory, shagbark and shellbark (*Carya ovata* and *C. laciniosa*)	Rich, upland soil; tolerates a wide range of sites.	Large (60'–120'); Zones 3–8.	Stately, long-lived; husks will litter the ground. Cultivars: *Shagbark:* 'Weschcke', 'Porter', 'Bridgewater'; *Shellbark:* 'Fayette', 'Mackinaw'.
Oak (*Quercus* spp.)	Rich soil on a range of sites. Very adaptable.	Large (50'–120'); Zones 3–8.	Stately, nice shape, long-lived; oak cup litter. Most oaks are grown from seed. Cultivar: *Q. macrocarpa* 'Ashworth'.
Pecan (*Carya illinoinensis*)	Deep, rich, moist bottomland is required.	Large (70'–150'); Zones 6–9.	Stately, long-lived; husks litter the ground. Grow strongly once established. Cultivars: 'Major', 'Peruque', 'Stuart', 'Colby'.
Pine (*Pinus* spp.)	Poor, sandy soil. May require 60–70 percent shade for several years.	Large (60'–100'); Zones 2–9.	Beautiful blue-green foliage; slow-growing, cones litter the ground. Commonly grown from seed.
Walnut, Eastern black (*Juglans nigra*)	Rich, deep soil; tolerates a range of sites.	Large (60'–120'); Zones 4–8.	Stately tree, lacy foliage; may be toxic to other plants, nuts may stain pavement. Often grown from seed. Cultivars: 'Bicentennial', 'Weschcke', 'Thomas Black', 'Snyder'.
Walnut, Persian (*Juglans regia*)	Rich, deep soil.	Large (50'–90'); Zones 5–9.	Stately tree, fast-growing; may be toxic to other plants, nuts may stain pavement. Cultivars: 'Ashworth', 'Broadview', 'Colby', 'Hansen'.

Nymphaea

Water lilies. Summer-blooming aquatic perennials.

Description: Hardy water lilies bring fragrant beauty and mystery to pools and ponds with their 3″-6″ starburst blooms in white, pink, red, or yellow, most with yellow brushlike centers. They float on the water or rise just above it, opening in the morning and closing by afternoon. The floating, rounded, 3″-8″ shiny leaves may extend outward in a circular pattern to 6′ in diameter. Zones 3-10. Be sure to buy species and cultivars that are labeled as hardy; many water lilies are tropical, and must be grown as annuals or overwintered indoors.

How to grow: Plant in spring a few weeks after the last hard frost in still or very slow-moving water that receives at least 6 hours of sun; full sun is best. Depending on eventual size, plant in a 5-30 quart (1′-4′ wide and about half that deep) bucket, tub, or basket. Partially fill the container with a 3:1 mix of rich clay loam and well-rotted manure. Place the plant in the container, with the knobby crown about 2″ below the rim. Add more soil to just below the crown; then cover the soil (not the crown) with 1″ of pea gravel to keep the soil from floating away in the water. Moisten the soil completely, and then slowly sink the container into the water. Gradually lower the plant as it adjusts to its new home until there are 6″-18″ of water above the crown. You can grow water lilies in bottom mud, but container-planting makes the adjustment process easier, the plants won't become rampant spreaders, and fish won't stir up water-clouding mud. Cut off yellow leaves and dead flowers regularly. Leave the plants outside during winter if the water doesn't freeze to the level of the crowns. Otherwise, remove the plants from the water and keep them moist and above freezing in their containers in a cellar or shed. Repot into fresh soil in spring. Divide when the plants become crowded, usually every 2-3 years. Mammals, birds, fish, and turtles may feed on the leaves, but new leaves appear regularly from below to replace them. If insects, especially aphids, infest the leaves, submerge the entire plant for a few days to drown the pests, or remove the worst leaves.

Landscape uses: Grow a few or many water lilies in a natural pool or pond, or enjoy a choice cultivar in an in-ground plastic pool. The smallest cultivars will thrive in a watertight half-barrel. If there's room, landscape your pool with lotuses and other water plants, and surround the pool with water-loving perennials such as astilbes and Japanese iris for a finished look. For more on landscaping a water garden, see the Water Gardens entry.

Best cultivars: Specialty catalogs and some nurseries carry many lovely cultivars. Usually the less expensive cultivars and those with Latin-sounding names are the older tried-and-true ones, such as yellow 'Chromatella' (a good choice for small pools and barrels), pink 'Fabiola', and white 'Virginalis'. ❖

Nyssa

Tupelo. Deciduous shade trees.

Description: *Nyssa sylvatica*, black tupelo or sour gum, is an upright, pyramidal tree with horizontal branches. Though it reaches a height of up to 100′ in the wild, count on 40′-80′ in the landscape. The alternate leaves are oblong and pinnately veined, displaying spectacular fall color in yellows, reds, and oranges. Flowers and small blue fruits are inconspicuous. Zones 4-9.

How to grow: Plant in a sunny to semishady site with humusy, acid soil, even moisture, and good drainage. Black tupelo tolerates wet soil and needs little attention once established.

Landscape uses: Black tupelo provides nectar for honeybees and fruits that are sought by wildlife. Use it as a shade tree or focal point, or naturalize it with other trees. ❖

Oenothera

Evening primrose, sundrops. Late-spring- to summer-blooming perennials.

Description: *Oenothera speciosa,* showy evening primrose, bears 2″, cuplike four-petalled flowers in white turning to pink, or uniformly pink. Blooms are borne one to a stem on 6″-15″ masses of elongated 3″ weedy-looking leaves in summer. Zones 5-8.

O. tetragona, common sundrops, flaunts similarly shaped, slightly smaller bright yellow blooms in small clusters in late spring. The 1½′ upright reddish stems bear similar dark green leaves which turn purple in fall. Zones 3-8.

How to grow: Plant or divide in spring or fall. Both thrive in full sun or very light shade in average to less-fertile, moist but well-drained soil, tolerating dry soil quite well. Fertile soil encourages rapid spread, especially with showy evening primrose.

Landscape uses: Both are well suited to borders if their spreading ways are not a problem. Otherwise enjoy them in low-maintenance masses in hot, dry, infertile areas.

Best cultivars: *O. tetragona* 'Fireworks' (also sold as 'Illumination') has larger flowers (to 3″), may repeat-bloom, and spreads more slowly; 'Yellow River' has deep yellow, 2″-2½″ wide flowers. ❖

Okra

Abelmoschus esculentus
Malvaceae

Okra, native to Africa and a beautiful relative of hibiscus, was brought to America in the 1600s. This tropical plant quickly became popular in the Deep South both as a side dish and as a thickening for gumbos and stews. It can, however, thrive in any climate where corn will grow. Depending on the cultivar, the large-flowered, fast-growing plants reach a height of 2′-6′ and make attractive garden borders.

Planting: Okra needs full sun. It will grow in ordinary garden soil but does best in fertile loam, particularly where a nitrogen-fixing crop, such as early peas, grew previously.

In the South, plant the first crop in the early spring and a second crop in June. In short-season areas, start plants indoors six weeks before setting them out (3-4 weeks after the last frost date). Put two seeds to a peat pot and clip off the weaker seedling.

When seeding okra directly in the ground, wait until after the soil has warmed and the air temperature is at least 60°F. Use fresh seed, and soak it overnight or nick each seed coat with a file to encourage germination. Sow seeds ½″ deep in light soil and 1″ deep in heavy soil. Space them 3″ apart in rows 3′ apart. Thin seedlings to 2′-3′ apart, always leaving the strongest of the young plants. Put collars around stems to deter cutworms.

Growing guidelines: When okra is 4″ tall, mulch to keep out weeds and conserve moisture. Water during dry spells. Every 3-4 weeks, side-dress with aged manure or give a heavy feeding of manure tea. (For instructions on making manure tea, see the Manure entry.) In hot, long-season areas, cut the plants back almost to ground level in midsummer and fertilize to produce a second crop.

Problems: Okra seldom succumbs to pests or diseases. Handpick any stinkbugs that appear; these light green, shield-shaped bugs cause mis-shapen pods. To control corn earworms, cabbage loopers, aphids, or flea beetles, see "The Top Ten Garden Insect Pests in America" on page 344. Fusarium wilt, a soilborne disease, is sometimes a problem in hot regions. If the disease causes leaves to yellow and wilt, pull and destroy affected plants. Crop rotation is the best preventive measure.

Harvesting: About 50-60 days after planting, edible pods will start to appear. They are tough when mature, so harvest daily with a sharp knife when they are no more than finger-size and when stems are still tender and easy to cut. Pick frequently and the plants will keep producing until killed by frost. Be sure to remove and compost any mature pods you might have missed earlier.

Many people find their skins are sensitive to the pods' prickly spines, so wear gloves and long sleeves when harvesting, or plant spineless cultivars.

Best cultivars: 'Clemson Spineless', 7″-9″, straight, grooved pods; 'Emerald Spineless', smooth, round pods, good for areas with short growing seasons; 'Dwarf Green Long Pod', no more than 2½′ tall; 'Burgundy', an ornamental-looking plant with burgundy stems, burgundy-ribbed leaves, creamy yellow blooms, and 8″ pods. ❖

Onion

Allium cepa and other species
Liliaceae

These pungent bulbs have been part of the human diet since antiquity. Onions are easy to grow and have medicinal qualities, although they're best known for their use in all types of cooking. Dried or fresh, raw or cooked, onions are an indispensable ingredient in a variety of soups, salads, breads, and casseroles.

Types: Onions come in a wide variety of shapes, sizes, and colors. The white, yellow, or red bulbs range in size from small pickling onions to large Spanish cultivars; they can be globe-, top-, or spindle-shaped.

Most onions can be pulled young as green onions called scallions, but there is also a perennial bunching type (*Allium fistulosum*) that produces superior scallions and is practically disease- and insect-proof. Another perennial—the multiplier or potato onion (*A. cepa* Aggregatum group)—is propagated by a division of underground bulbs, with each bulb multiplying into a bulb cluster.

The Egyptian or top onion (*A. cepa* Proliferum group) produces a bulb cluster at the end of a long stem with a second cluster frequently forming on top of the first. It also has an underground bulb, which is often too pungent to eat. Other tasty plants include early spring, grass-like chives (*A. schoenoprasum*), garlic chives (*A. tuberosum*), and expensive-to-buy but easy-to-grow shallots (*A. cepa* Aggregatum group). For information on other onion relatives, see the Garlic and Leek entries.

Planting: You can grow onions from seeds, transplants, or sets. Growing from seeds offers the greatest choices in cultivars, but seed-grown plants can take five months to mature and are often susceptible to diseases.

Transplants, which are seedlings started in the current growing season and sold in bunches, are available from nurseries and by mail order.

They usually form good bulbs over a short period of time (65 days or less), but they, too, are subject to diseases.

Sets are immature bulbs grown the previous year and offer the most limited cultivar choices. They are, however, the easiest to plant, the earliest to harvest, and the least susceptible to diseases.

When buying sets, look for ½″ diameter bulbs, because larger ones often go to seed before producing decent-sized bulbs, and anything smaller may not grow well. Onion sets come in white, red, and yellow types. Most growers prefer white sets for green onions.

You should also check a cultivar's daylength requirement. Long-day types, like 'Sweet Sandwich' and 'Southport Red Globe', need 13-16 hours of summer daylight found in more northern latitudes; short-day onions, such as 'Red Hamburger', thrive in Southern climates with only 12 hours of daylight.

Onions like cool weather in the early part of their growth, so plant them in the spring, except in mild-winter areas, where onions are grown as a fall or winter crop. Generally speaking, onions grow tops in cool weather and form bulbs when the weather warms.

Plant onions 4-6 weeks before the last average frost—or even earlier indoors or in a cold frame. When indoor seedlings are 2″-3″ tall, harden them off by exposing them to above-freezing night temperatures.

"Onion Planting Methods" on page 409 explains how to plant seeds, sets, and transplants directly in your garden.

Growing guidelines: The practices you use will depend on the specific crop you're growing. In general, onions grow best if you keep them well weeded. Use a sharp hoe to cut off intruders; pulling or digging weeds up can damage the onions' shallow roots. Once the soil has warmed, put down a mulch around and between the plants to discourage weeds and to hold moisture in the soil.

Dry conditions cause bulbs to split, so water when necessary to provide at least 1″ of water each week; keep in mind that transplants require more water than sets do. If you've prepared your soil well, no fertilizing should be necessary. Always go easy on nitrogen, which can produce lush tops at the expense of bulbs. New growth from the center will stop when the bulbs start forming.

Egyptian onions, chives, and shallots require slightly different cultivation from regular onions. Here are some guidelines for growing these onion relatives:

• Plant Egyptian onions in the fall throughout the country; harvest some in the spring as green or bunching onions. In midsummer or fall, miniature bulbs will form at the stem tip, where most onions form flowers. Pick these tiny bulbs when the tops begin to wilt and dry. Use them fresh or store in the freezer.

• Plant chives and garlic chives in early spring in rich soil. They will tolerate partial shade but prefer full sun. Seeds are very slow to germinate, so most growers prefer to plant clump divisions, which can be harvested after two months. Space the clumps, each of which should contain about six bulbs, 8″ apart.

Cut the grasslike, hollow tops frequently to maintain production. The pom-poms of lavender flowers are very attractive, but always remove the spent flowers to reduce the chances of rampant self-seeding. Dig up, divide, and replant every third year. Transplant to containers and move indoors for winter harvests. Chives are almost as good frozen as they are fresh.

• Shallots, a favorite of French chefs, have a blue-green stem that's used when young. In addition, it has a gray, angular, mild-flavored bulb that's related to the multiplying onion and is used like a mild-flavored garlic. Shallots will tolerate all but the most acid soils, but dig the earth deeply because the plants put down 8″ long feeder roots. However, they have no lateral roots, so space them 2″-3″ apart.

Propagate shallots by dividing bulb clusters. Each clove, in turn, will produce 4-8 new bulbs. In February or March, plant them 1″ deep, barely covering the tip of the clove. Keep the soil weed-free and slightly moist, but don't fertilize. In early summer, draw the soil away from the bulbs. Harvest shallots as green onions at any time. Cutting the tops off near soil level will produce new tops, and such harvesting actually increases bulb production. Bulbs mature in about five months. Pull and store like onions.

Problems: You can generally expect a disease- and insect-free crop. One possible pest is onion maggots: ⅓″ long, white, legless larvae that travel in line from one bulb to the next and burrow upwards to feed on the stems. To reduce the chances of extensive damage, scatter-plant onions throughout the garden. (This interplanting can also benefit other garden plants; many *Allium* species will ward off pests—such as aphids, Japanese beetles, and carrot flies—from roses, lettuce, carrots, beets, parsnips, and members of the cabbage family.) Placing a thin layer of sand around onion bulbs may discourage adult flies from laying their eggs at the bottoms of the plants.

Barely visible onion thrips tend to attack during hot, dry weather in July or August. They produce deformed plants with silvery blotches on the leaves. Thrips overwinter in weeds, so reduce pest populations by keeping the garden clean. Try releasing predatory mites to control thrips. Combat serious infestations by applying insecticidal soap or pyrethrins.

In May and June, onion crops are sometimes hit by the lesser bulb fly. Protect the plants by covering them with a floating row cover during this period. You can also fight these flies and the garden springtail, a tiny purple insect with yellow spots, with homemade garlic sprays (add ½ cup of finely chopped garlic to 1 pint of water; steep, strain, and spray the liquid on infested plants).

A disease called smut causes a swelling or hardening of leaves just above the neck, which eventually bursts and spills powdery black spores over the plant. Downy mildew, a purplish mold, shows up in midsummer during warm, humid weather. Onions are also subject to pink root, which causes roots to turn various colors and then shrivel, and neck rot, which causes tissues at the neck to become soft and brown and later to form a hard, black crust. All these problems are caused by fungi in the soil and can be avoided by rotating crops and by working humus into the onion bed to provide good drainage.

Harvesting: Once onion tops turn yellow, use the back of a rake to bend them over horizontally. This stops the sap from flowing to the stems and diverts the plants' energy into maturing the bulb. A day or so later, when the tops turn brown, pull or dig the bulbs on a sunny

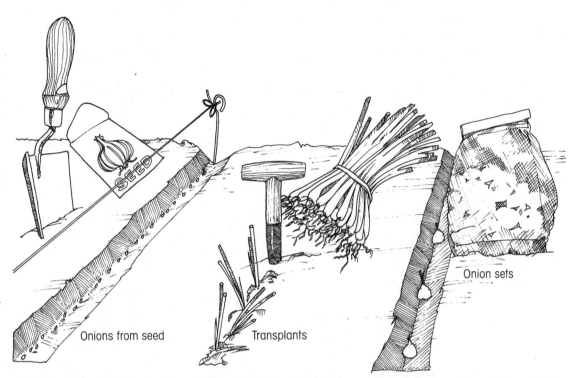

Onions from seed   Transplants   Onion sets

Onion planting methods. (1) Outdoors, sow seeds thickly about ½" deep, mixing in radish seeds to mark the planted area and to lure any root maggots away from the onions and to the radishes. If planting in rows instead of raised beds, space the rows about 2½' apart. Thin seedlings to 1" apart, and thin again in four weeks to 6" apart. At the same time, pull the soil back a little to expose the tops and sides of the bulbs; this will induce them to develop. (2) Space transplants or sets 2" deep and 4"-6" apart. Use the closer spacing if you plan to harvest some young plants at about five weeks as green onions. (3) A pound of sets, which should be planted carefully with the stem end up, is enough for a 50' row.

day, and leave them to dry in the sun. Lay the tops of one row over the bulbs of another to help prevent sunscald.

When the outer skins are thoroughly dry, wipe off any soil and remove the tops—unless you intend to braid them. Store in a cool, dry place; hang braided onions or those kept in mesh bags in an airy spot. Such dried bulbs will keep from about four months to one year.

Best cultivars: 'Yellow Sweet Spanish' and 'Yellow Globe Danvers' perform well in all zones; 'White Sweet Spanish', best in the North and West, mild and sweet; 'Southport White Globe', grown for green bunching onions or excellent-quality white onions, good for fall planting in the South; 'Carmen Hybrid', for red onions; 'White Portugal' and 'Crystal Wax Pickling', good for pickling; 'Sweet Sandwich' and 'Copra', best for storage; 'Red Beard', a bunching onion with red stalks and white roots. ❖

Orchard

Commercial orchards cover hundreds of acres, but your backyard orchard may have only 3-5 trees in it. Whatever the scale, fresh-picked fruit is a gardener's delight. You'll find information about growing fruit trees in the Apple, Apricot, Avocado, Cherry, Citrus, Fig, Fruit Trees, Peach, Pear, Persimmon, Plum, and Quince entries. ❖

Orchids

If you can grow houseplants, you can grow orchids. Many orchids are tough, durable plants that will bloom year after year on a windowsill. These sturdy beauties only *look* fragile and exotic!

Getting Started

Before you buy an orchid, think about where you plan to put it. Different species do best at specific light levels and temperature ranges. You'll get the best bloom if you match plant to place. Some of the best windowsill orchids and their preferred conditions include:

• Paphiopedilums: need low to medium light (an east- or west-facing window) and temperatures between 55° and 75°F. Exotic relatives of our familiar lady-slippers.

• Phalaenopsis: need low to medium light and temperatures between 70° and 80°F. The "moth orchid."

• Cattleyas: need medium to high light (a south-facing window) and temperatures of 70°-80°F. The classic corsage orchid.

• Equitant oncidiums: need same conditions as cattleyas. Very compact growers. The "butterfly orchid."

There are two other points to consider when buying orchids. First, although orchids bloom for a long time (sometimes months), when they're not in bloom, they're foliage plants. Some paphiopedilums and phalaenopsis have beautifully patterned foliage that makes them beautiful even

More On
ORCHIDS

The American Orchid Society (6000 South Olive Ave., West Palm Beach, FL 33405) publishes a monthly bulletin and the excellent *Handbook of Orchid Culture*. The best book for windowsill growers is Rebecca T. Northen's *Home Orchid Growing*, also available from the society.

when not in bloom. Second, orchids can take years to reach blooming size. When you buy a plant, specify "blooming size" to make sure it will flower the first year.

Growing Great Orchids

Orchids will *not* grow in garden soil. Instead, use Douglas fir bark, mixing 2 parts bark to 1 part perlite. Use fine-grade bark for paphiopedilums, medium grade for the others. Buy bark where you buy your orchids—at greenhouses and well-stocked garden centers or through mail-order orchid catalogs. For best growth and bloom, repot once a year since fir bark breaks down and orchids need a loose, fast-draining medium.

Thorough watering once a week is enough except for large or very small plants. Household humidity that's comfortable to you (40-60 percent) is fine for orchids. (A humidifier will be good for you *and* your plants!) Or set the pots on pebble-filled trays and add water to the trays to increase the humidity around your plants. Make sure the water doesn't reach the top of the pebbles.

Feed orchids twice a month with a balanced organic fertilizer, and give a nitrogen supplement such as fish emulsion at each feeding.

Orchids are remarkably problem-free. Use insecticidal soap to control the most common pests: mealybugs, scale, and spider mites. If a plant shows signs of disease, isolate it, remove affected parts with a sharp, flame-sterilized knife, and watch for recurrences. ❖

Oregano

Origanum spp.
Labiatae

Description: There are many species of oregano, including the annual *Origanum majorana,* or sweet marjoram, which also goes by the name of *Majorana hortensis.* Seeds and plants of *O. vulgare* are often mistakenly sold as the oregano to use for cooking. It is good as an ornamental, but unfortunately it has almost no flavor to contribute to food. The plants have erect, hairy, square stems with oval, pointed leaves up to 2″ long and small, tubular, rose-purple to white flowers borne on 1″ spikes.

The oregano to buy or grow for kitchen use is *O. heracleoticum* (sometimes called *O. hirtum* or *O. vulgare* subsp. *hirtum*). This small-leaved plant forms low, spreading mounds, with spikes of white flowers rising about 1′ above the foliage. It is marvelously aromatic.

How to grow: Start seeds or buy labeled plants. Site oregano in a raised bed or on a ridge of soil into which you have incorporated some grit or very fine gravel, and lime if your soil tends to be acid. Culinary oregano is not as winter-hardy as the purple-flowered *O. vulgare,* but it will survive in Zone 5 if grown in full sun with good drainage. It often seeds itself, making lots of nice small plants for spring.

Harvesting: Pinch leaves or cut the long stems just as the flower heads are forming. Dry oregano to preserve the sweet, sharp aroma and flavor.

Uses: The purple-flowered oregano is useful as dried flower material, as it has good dark rose-purple flowers that dry well on their wiry stems. You can also plant masses of it to hold up an eroding sunny bank. Some people claim the tea relieves stomach upsets and indigestion. The white-flowered culinary oregano, used sparingly, will contribute just the flavor needed in Italian, Mexican, or Greek cooking. It complements tomato, pepper, and eggplant dishes as well as those made with shellfish and eggs. ❖

Organic Certification

Organic certification is a process that assures consumers that foods labeled organic have been grown, processed, or handled in compliance with standards designed to keep the food, as well as agricultural workers and the environment, free of harmful contaminants. The federal government became involved with regulating organic food production when Congress passed the Organic Foods Production Act as part of the 1990 Farm Bill. As of October 1993, food sold as "organic" has to meet requirements set by the USDA. The law also covers organic livestock and its meat, eggs, or milk.

Prior to this legislation, certification was the initiative of private organizations and some state agriculture departments, a total of about 40 groups with separate but similar requirements for organic food production. Under federal law, these programs may continue to operate and to enforce their standards if they are consistent with federal guidelines.

If you sell organic food or livestock but receive less than $5,000 annually from its sale, you do not need to be certified. If you earn more than $5,000, you must comply with federal standards. This entails keeping detailed records of practices and materials, plus on-farm inspections and periodic residue testing. Acceptable practices and materials are set by the U.S. Secretary of Agriculture and the National Organic Standards Board, a 15-person group of organic farmers, organic food handlers and retailers, environmentalists, and consumers. For example, green manures, beneficial insects, and mechanical weed control are acceptable; synthetic chemical fertilizers, pesticides, and herbicides are not.

For more information about organic certification, contact the USDA Agricultural Marketing Service, Transportation and Marketing Division, P.O. Box 96456, Washington, DC 20090. Or ask your local extension office or state agriculture department for the names and addresses of certification groups active in your area. ❖

Organic Farming and Gardening

Gardening organically is a skill that draws on farming traditions of the past as well as modern scientific discoveries. Simply stated, organic gardening is a method that uses our understanding of nature as a guide for gardening and living, and caring for the plants in our yards and gardens without using synthetic chemical pesticides or synthetic fertilizers.

How Does the Organic Method Work?

Have you ever wondered how a forest or meadow grows and thrives with no added fertilizer? The answer is that natural ecosystems make their own fertilizers. Nature's cycle of growth, death, and decay is continuous. As plants and animals die, rodents, insects, earthworms, and microscopic soil creatures consume their bodies, and nutrients are released. These nutrients feed new generations of plants.

There's no need for synthetic pesticides in a natural ecosystem. Some insects eat plants, but natural predators and parasites help keep their numbers in check. Also, nature tolerates some damage. No one worries whether wild plants and fruits have perfect cosmetic quality.

In organic gardens, similar cycles and natural balances exist. However, gardeners harvest and remove crops from the garden, breaking the cycle. To keep the natural processes that feed plants working, they add organic materials such as compost or purchased organic soil amendments. Also, gardeners may demand better appearance or yield from their food and ornamental plants than they would from those growing in the neighboring woods. But by encouraging biological diversity in their yards and gardens, they can minimize the need for artificial pest control. When organic gardeners do intervene, they choose control tactics that have little impact on natural systems.

Many gardeners choose the organic method because they want to be good stewards of the environment. They are concerned about pollution of air, water, and soil, and about protecting the health of their families and communities. They know that using synthetic pesticides can destroy wildlife, bees, and other beneficial insects, and may have an effect on food quality and safety. Tending an organic garden connects them with the soil and makes them feel close to nature.

The Historical Perspective

The development of organic gardening closely followed that of organic farming, since the practices that farmers used in their fields were often adopted in the home garden. Organic farming can be traced to several historical philosophies that influenced the way farmers raised crops many years ago.

In the mid-1800s, dominance over the environment was the conventional agricultural philosophy in many Western countries. Scientists considered soil a sterile medium, useful only for holding plants in place. Crop production was a matter of chemistry.

In the early 1900s, the discovery of manufacturing processes to produce artificial fertilizers, the development of modern pesticides, the improvement of transportation methods, and the demand for farm products helped pave the way for increased crop specialization. Chemical farming became the predominant method in North America and Europe.

Genesis of the Organic Method

Charles Darwin was one of the first scientists to study living organisms in the soil. As a result of reports he wrote on his work in the 1880s, several new philosophies about the relationships between soil and plants evolved. Only a small number of modern farmers and scien-

ORGANIC IN A NUTSHELL

If you're new to gardening or to the organic method, you may be wondering how to begin. Here are some basic suggestions to help you get started:

● Read about gardening and growing plants, especially using the organic method. Learning about gardening is an ongoing process gardeners enjoy throughout their lives.

● Use a plan and keep records. Find out about the plants you want to grow and which types will grow best in your area. Draw a sketch of your garden and decide what will go where, then revise it as you work. Begin a garden journal for keeping records through the season. Stock up on supplies and tools you may need during the gardening year.

● Learn more about your soil. You may want to have it tested by the Cooperative Extension Service or by a private laboratory. Use the results as a guide to bring your soil into balance with a long-term approach—biological changes aren't instant and may take several years! Add lime, compost, or organic fertilizers as needed. Maintain soil balance by growing green manure crops and adding organic matter each season.

● Start a compost pile. Recycling garden wastes and increasing soil organic matter content are two fundamentals of organic gardening. Composting helps you do both. There are many simple designs for compost enclosures, or you can just make a compost heap in a shaded corner of your yard.

● Prevent pest problems before they happen. Always check plants to be sure they're healthy before you bring them into the garden. Keep plants healthy with timely feeding and watering. Create a diverse ecosystem to encourage beneficial insects. Use row covers to exclude pests; build a fence to exclude animals. Remove diseased and insect-infected plant material from the garden. Handpick insect pests and their eggs. Try biological control techniques. As a last resort, use botanical insecticides.

● Learn to identify weeds, and eliminate them while they're small. Be diligent! A light cultivation several times early in the season may be all you need. Don't let weeds mature and produce seed for the next season.

---

tists accepted these views, which took a holistic approach. They recognized the importance of returning nutrients to the soil, and the roles of soil animals, humus, and organic matter in crop production.

In the early 1920s, Rudolf Steiner, an Austrian philosopher and author, founded the bio-dynamic method of farming. Bio-dynamic farmers embraced the holistic view of the farm as a living system. But unlike many other organic farmers, they used secret preparations of plant and animal materials to stimulate crop production and placed importance on timing farming practices to coincide with phases of the moon.

Bio-dynamic farming remains a separate and specialized method, practiced more widely in Europe than in the United States. You can learn more about Bio-dynamics by reading the Bio-Dynamic Gardening entry.

Two independent schools of thought developed in the early 1900s that promoted the importance of humus in soil. Eventually, both schools merged to form what we call the organic method. The new farmers regarded the agricultural environment as a living system that required recycling of organic wastes. They believed that the new synthetic fertilizers and pesticides were fatal to the environment. An explosion of publications in the 1940s promoted this new, organic method. Among them was *Organic Farming and Gardening,* founded by J. I. Rodale in 1942.

At that time, Sir Albert Howard introduced a special slow-composting system, the Indore method, and wrote eloquently about the importance of humus, soil microbial life, and soil aeration. Lady Eve Balfour, a leader of the organic movement in Great Britain, echoed Howard's ideas in her book, *The Living Soil* (1943). Soon after, Rachel Carson published the environmental classic, *Silent Spring* (1954), which directly questioned the influence of agricultural chemicals on the environment. These books and others helped carry organic farming concepts to farmers and scientists in North America and Europe.

A small segment of farmers adopted the organic methods, and more gardeners became aware of their options. There was no longer only one way to grow crops.

For many years, the organic method was considered radical or unusual, embraced by some home gardeners, but largely ignored by commercial farmers.

Eventually, as their production costs increased and their profits decreased, some large-scale farmers switched to organics. They found that the organic method was a viable way to run a farm, not just a garden. Still, the term organic lacked a definition. Attempts to define it often came out as a long list of what organic gardeners *didn't* do. Everyone knew that organic growers didn't use synthetic pesticides and fertilizers. What exactly *did* they do?

Organics Comes of Age

By 1980, farmers and scientists across the nation were asking questions about organics. The U.S. Department of Agriculture responded by offering this detailed definition of organic farming: "A production system which avoids or largely excludes the use of synthetically compounded

---

MASTERS OF THEIR FIELD

If you want to refine your gardening skills, you may enjoy reading books by or about these great leaders of organic farming and gardening.

Sir Albert Howard (1873–1947). One of the first proponents of a holistic approach to agriculture, Howard believed that soil organic matter, humus, and proper aeration play key roles in soil fertility and plant nutrition because they support soil microbial life. Organic gardeners in the United States largely follow the guidelines and methods established by Howard in the early 1900s and published in his book *An Agricultural Testament* (1940).

Helen and Scott Nearing (1883–1983). These pioneers of self-subsistent organic farming founded the Social Science Institute, a publishing organization for many of their books and articles that influenced the back-to-the-land movement of the 1960s and 1970s. Their books include *The Maple Sugar Book: Together with Remarks on Pioneering as a Way of Living in the Twentieth Century* (1971) and *Living the Good Life: How to Live Sanely and Simply in a Troubled World* (1971). Helen Nearing, born in 1904, currently lives in Maine.

J. I. Rodale (1898–1971) and Robert Rodale (1930–1990). The Rodales brought the organic method to popular knowledge and acceptance by American gardeners through the books and magazines published by Rodale Press in Emmaus, Pennsylvania. Both have authored numerous books about organic gardening, health, and other topics.

Ruth Stout (1891–1980). Known to gardeners as the woman who originated the year-round mulched, no-work garden. Her gardening books include *The Ruth Stout No-Work Garden Book* (with Richard Clemence, 1971), *How to Have a Green Thumb without an Aching Back* (1955), *Gardening without Work* (1961), and *I've Always Done It My Way* (1975).

fertilizers, pesticides, growth regulators, and livestock feed additives. To the maximum extent feasible, organic farming systems rely upon crop rotations, crop residues, animal manures, legumes, green manures, off-farm organic wastes, mechanical cultivation, mineral-bearing rocks, and aspects of biological pest control to maintain soil productivity and tilth, to supply plant nutrients, and to control insects, weeds, and other pests." This definition officially recorded not only what organic growers don't use, but also the special techniques that they do use to raise crops successfully.

Concurrently, J. I. Rodale's son, Robert Rodale, was developing the ideas of a larger organic philosophy—regeneration. He coined the term "regenerative agriculture." Rodale felt that regeneration of renewable resources was essential to achieving a sustainable form of agriculture. He also believed that regenerative agriculture could nurture new ideas for general social leadership in addition to solving problems in agriculture and gardening. You can read more about regeneration, and about the contributions of J. I. and Robert Rodale to the organic farming movement, in the Regeneration and Rodale entries.

An important boost for organic farming came in 1988, when the USDA began a program to fund research and demonstrations on what it named low-input sustainable agriculture (LISA). The goal of the USDA LISA program is to lower the costs of crop production, maintain optimum yields, and increase profits while protecting health and the environment. Since then, LISA money has been used to help both organic and conventional farmers learn how to reach these goals.

Once farmers realized there were alternatives to the conventional method, a new era of farming began that continues to evolve. Both organic farmers and gardeners can expect to see many exciting improvements and discoveries as acceptance of the organic method continues to grow. ❖

Organic Matter

Adding organic matter—various forms of living or dead plant and animal material—to your soil is crucial to successful organic gardening. Organic matter:

• Supplies nutrients for plants by providing surfaces where nutrients can be held in reserve in the soil
• Facilitates better drainage by loosening soil structure
• Stores water in the soil
• Helps increase air drainage
• Increases the activity and numbers of soil microorganisms
• Helps decrease problems caused by plant diseases and insects
• Encourages earthworms

You can increase your soil's organic content by mulching with organic materials such as compost or shredded leaves, or by digging or tilling them into the top several inches of the soil. Then, to maintain a healthy, humus-rich soil, make adding organic matter part of your yearly garden activities. Organic matter does not persist in the soil. Soil microorganisms act to break it down to simpler compounds, and these compounds are then food for your plants.

You can slow the loss of soil organic matter by cultivating soil gently, mulching during the growing season, and mulching or planting a cover crop during the winter.

As a general rule, strive to maintain 5-6 percent organic matter in your soil. Don't overdo it! Adding too much fresh organic matter, such as plant residues and manure, can overstimulate soil microorganisms, which then consume so much nitrogen and other plant nutrients that soil fertility temporarily declines.

You can learn more about the importance of organic matter and about materials you can use to increase soil organic matter content by reading the Composting, Mulch, and Soil entries. ❖

Organic Pest Management

No one wants pests in their yard and garden. Yet at one time or another, we've all had to deal with a disease that ruins beautiful foliage or insects that eat holes in our favorite crop. The simple answer might seem to be to apply a chemical that kills the pest. However, mounting evidence shows that this simple answer has had complex and harmful side effects for our gardens, and for the environment at large. Toxic chemicals, even organically acceptable ones, kill beneficial insects as well as pests. Pests develop resistance after repeated exposure to pesticides. Herbicides accumulate in our water supply. Insecticide residues on food may have detrimental effects on our health.

Clearly it's time for a new approach to fighting pests. Agricultural researchers have responded by developing integrated pest managment (IPM) programs. IPM programs combine a variety of measures to take advantage of weak points in a pest's life cycle or behavior to prevent problems. IPM usually starts with a conventional spray program and integrates other techniques, such as releasing beneficial insects or using traps or barriers, with a goal of reducing or eliminating the use of pesticides.

However, there is no place for synthetic chemical pesticides in the organic home garden. We borrow many of the helpful concepts of integrated pest management and apply them in an organic pest management (OPM) program. Through a combination of organic soil building, proper plant care, and preventive pest control, you can create a garden environment where even organically acceptable pesticides such as pyrethrins or neem are a rarely used last resort.

If you have relied on synthetic or even natural pesticides as your first defense, you may be skeptical about OPM. However, with a little experience, you'll be pleasantly surprised at how well cultural, physical, and biological methods work to control insects, diseases, and weeds, and how simple they are to use.

Preventing Pest Problems

Basic organic gardening practices are an important part of organic pest management. These practices bring your yard and garden into natural balance. You create a stable system where there are no huge population explosions of pests, but rather a diverse ecosystem where pest populations are regulated naturally. If you take good care of your soil and plants, your garden will be healthier and have fewer problems with insects, diseases, and weeds.

Healthy plants attract fewer insect pests, are less susceptible to disease, and beat out weeds. Make soil building a priority. The more organic matter you add to your soil, the better. Have your soil tested, and correct any imbalances. Use organic fertilizers to keep your plants thriving while you work to improve your soil. See the Soil, Composting, Mulch, Green Manure, and Fertilizers entries for more information on soil care and fertilizing.

Good garden sanitation is another prerequisite for a healthy garden. Remove and dispose of garden waste. Every pulled weed represents thousands of seeds that won't take root. Each disease-spotted leaf you remove represents untold numbers of disease spores that won't find their way onto next year's crop.

Don't spread problems on your hands, feet, or tools. Clean your tools regularly, and always after working with diseased plants. Do a fall cleaning of all your garden tools and equipment every year, and you'll reduce the number of problems the following season. Disinfect stakes, plastic mulch, and the like before storing them for the winter.

Making an OPM Plan

An organic pest managment program starts with a plan. Planning ahead will allow you to make full use of preventive control measures and to have the tools and materials you need to fight problems if they arise. Your pest control measures will include cultural, biological, and

Key Words
ORGANIC PEST MANAGEMENT

Organic Pest Management (OPM). An approach to pest control that combines cultural, biological, physical, and certain chemical control measures to prevent problems or to keep them in check. Organically acceptable chemical controls are a last resort used only when all other methods aren't adequate.

Integrated Pest Management (IPM). A pest-control philosophy that combines cultural, biological, and physical controls to supplement chemical (including synthetic) control measures to prevent or eliminate problems.

Cultural controls. Gardening practices that reduce pest problems, including keeping plants healthy, selecting well-adapted cultivars, and keeping the garden clean.

Biological controls. Pest-control measures that use living organisms to fight living organisms, including releasing, attracting, and protecting natural insect predators and parasites, and using microbial sprays to control insects and plant infections.

Physical controls. Control measures that prevent pests from reaching your plants or remove them if they do. Barriers, traps, and handpicking are physical controls.

Chemical controls. Control methods that involve substances that kill pests. Organically acceptable chemical controls are naturally occurring minerals or plant products, and they tend to break down into harmless substances faster than synthetic pesticides. They do have toxic side effects and are used only as a last resort.

physical controls, and as a last resort, organically acceptable chemical controls.

The first step in developing your own specific OPM plan is identifying the problems that you've had in the past or that are common in your area. Make a list of these problems. If you don't know what causes them, try to find out. Then learn as

much as you can about each one. By knowing how pests and diseases overwinter, and when they attack your plants, you will be able to pick effective control methods.

Note the ways you could help to control each of the problems on your list. Also note what times during the pest's life cycle each control is effective. It may help to make a chart of the life cycle and control activities.

Once you have all your options in front of you, make a comprehensive plan. Start by noting what cultural controls are effective, and when they need to be done. Then add the biological controls. Follow with the physical controls. If any supplies are needed, be sure to order them in advance.

Complete your plan by considering chemical control options. Certain problems like brown rot on fruit may require sulfur or copper fungicides. Decide on a spray schedule, and consider how you'll adjust it depending on weather conditions. During a prolonged wet period, which favors fungal growth, you may need extra sprays. In a dry year, you may never have to get out your sprayer. Be sure to order pesticides so you'll have them if needed; not all organically acceptable pesticides are readily available at garden centers.

Garden Patrol

All the planning in the world won't help if you don't keep a watchful eye out for problems. Make it a habit to walk through your garden at least once a week—daily is best—looking carefully at your plants, turning over leaves, and noting overall appearance. See "The Garden Detective" on page 418 for suggestions of what to look for on your patrols.

Look for signs of the problems you listed, and go over your plan to see what steps you need to take. You'll also see a few new problems on occasion. If you aren't sure what is causing the problem you find, refer to "Diagnosing Plant Problems" on page 419 for help.

Keep notes on your program during the

THE GARDEN DETECTIVE

Plant problems fall into three general categories: insects and animals, disease, and cultural problems (water stress, heat or cold, nutrient imbalances). Symptoms caused by different problems may look remarkably similar. You need to investigate a number of possibilities and do some detective work.

1. Look at the entire plant and those around it. Is just one plant or an entire row affected? Is the whole plant affected, or just part of it? Does it seem to be random, or is there a distinct pattern, such as only new growth is affected?

2. Check the undersides of leaves and the stems, flowers, and roots for insects, eggs, webs, or damage such as borer holes. Examine the affected areas with a hand lens, looking for tiny insects or fungal growth.

3. Collect sample insects and samples of damaged leaves for later identification. Put samples in pill bottles or plastic bags.

4. "Diagnosing Plant Problems" on the opposite page can help you decide what type of problem you may have. There are also many good books available that can help you identify pests, diseases, and cultural problems. Some are arranged by plant type and list the common problems for each, which makes finding the answer easier. Ask knowledgeable gardeners, garden center employees, or extension people to help diagnose problems.

5. Once you have identified the problem, find out as much as you can about it. Then develop a plan to control it.

6. Some problems are hard to diagnose. Don't despair; give the plants the best care you can. Plants often recover when conditions improve. But keep an eye on the problem—if more plants develop the same symptoms, put your detective hat back on.

season. Make notes to yourself about what works and what doesn't, what controls you used, how much you used, and where. The more informa-

tion you have, the better you'll be able to refine your plan for the next season.

Cultural Controls

Cultural controls are steps you can take as you plant and care for a garden that make the environment less hospitable to pests. Some cultural controls work by benefiting the plant and making it better able to resist damage, others interfere with a pest's life cycle or behavior.

Resistant Plants

You can make an important contribution to pest control by choosing insect- and disease-resistant cultivars and avoiding susceptible ones. Disease-resistant cultivars of apples, corn, tomatoes, and many other plants are available. Some new cultivars are bred specifically for disease resistance. The resistance will be listed in catalog descriptions, or perhaps as a series of letter codes in the cultivar name. If you can't find a cultivar resistant to a pest that is problematic in your area, choose cultivars that are well adapted to your local climate and soil conditions.

Keep in mind that older cultivars, selected for superior performance before the widespread use of synthetic pesticides, may offer some resistance to specific problems. These resistances may not be noted in catalog descriptions.

Certain physical characteristics of plants make them more or less attractive to pests. Corn cultivars with good husk cover are least damaged by corn earworms. Imported cabbageworms rarely trouble purple cabbage and broccoli.

Healthy Plants

Plants grown on fertile soils with adequate water tolerate insect attack better than plants suffering from nutrient deficiency, water stress, crowding, or low light levels. Healthy plants also mount their own chemical defenses to diseases and insects faster.

(continued on page 424)

Diagnosing Plant Problems

Some plant problems are a cinch to diagnose. If you see a fat green caterpillar feasting on your broccoli, you know immediately who the culprit is. But if your roses have yellowish foliage and just don't seem to be doing well, you may be dealing with a nutritional deficiency, an insect problem, or a disease problem. Use the following key to help pinpoint the cause. While it's not comprehensive, it does include many of the common plant problems you may encounter. Using this key will help you learn how to examine plants carefully and distinguish between problems that look similar at first glance.

The key has five sections: Whole Plant Symptoms, Leaf Symptoms, Stem Symptoms, Fruit/Flower Symptoms, and Root Symptoms. In each section, you'll see categories of symptoms—"Discolored Leaves," for example. Each category is broken down into more specific distinguishing symptoms, such as "Old leaves yellow, turn brown, drop off." In most cases, these specific symptoms are followed by a cause; in the case of this example, the cause is nitrogen deficiency. In a few cases, the key will direct you instead to another section, where you'll find more symptom information.

Begin by finding the section of the key that relates to your plant problem. Then skim the symptom categories and find the one that best matches the problem. Read through the specific symptoms in that category, studying your plant again, if need be, to narrow down the possible causes. Once you've decided what the cause of your problem may be, refer to the page number given in parentheses after the cause for more information and solutions.

Whole Plant Symptoms

Symptom	*Cause*
WHOLE PLANT OR PLANT PART WILTS	
Plant not stunted	
—whole plant or tips wilt; recovers when watered	Water stress (183)
—whole plant or branch wilts; stays wilted	Borers (555), wilts (181), blights (179), viruses (183)
Plant stunted	See Root Symptoms.
ALL FOLIAGE AND STEMS DISTORTED	
Leaves, stems long and narrow; plant stunted	Viruses (183)
Many short branches bunched together	Witch's brooms (639)
New leaves and stems curl, old leaves normal	Calcium deficiency (481)

Sagging, discolored foliage and small flower buds: aster yellows.

Wilted plants: water stress or bacterial infection.

(continued)

Leaf Symptoms

Symptom	*Cause*

DISCOLORED LEAVES

New leaves yellow or light green
  —veins darker — Iron deficiency (481)
  —veins paler; growth rigid — Yellows virus (183)
  —yellow patches on older leaves; stem center brown — Wilts (181)

New leaves dark green
  —purplish red veins and undersides — Phosphorus deficiency (481)
  —new growth curls, edges yellow and die — Calcium deficiency (481)

Old leaves yellow, turn brown, drop off — Nitrogen deficiency (481)

Leaves blotchy light green, yellowish, or white
  —between veins — Nutrient deficiency (481)
  —patterns crossing veins, may be ring-shaped — Mosaic virus (183)

Leaves black or scorched
  —wipes off — Sooty mold (from insect feeding) (344)
  —won't wipe off — Fire blight (257)

Leaves gray or whitish — Mildew (183)

Leaves yellow or pale, stippled
  —fine webbing on underside — Spider mites (256)
  —silvery sheen to damage — Thrips (408)
  —blotchy patterns, spots of excrement present — Lace bugs (510)

Leaf edges brown and dry — Potassium deficiency (481)

HOLES IN LEAVES

Small holes
  —with cleanly cut edges — Flea beetles (345)
  —with dry, dark edges; leaves also have spots — Bacterial leaf spot (257)

Fine webbing: spider mite infestation.

Distorted, discolored leaves: diseases or aphid feeding.

Skeletonized leaves: insect feeding.

Symptom	Cause
Medium to large holes, including veins	
—greenish droppings on leaves	Caterpillars (344)
—shiny trails	Slugs or snails (540)
—no clues	Beetles (345), animals (11)
Leaves skeletonized, only veins remain	Mexican bean beetles (345), Japanese beetles (345)

DISTORTED LEAVES

Symptom	Cause
Puckered, twisted leaves or growing tips	
—honeydew present	Aphids (344)
—no honeydew	Plant bugs (345)
Leaves rolled up	
—webbing inside rolled leaves	Leafrollers (30)
—no webbing	Nutrient deficiency (481), diseases (176)

OTHER SYMPTOMS

Symptom	Cause
Small dark spots on leaves	Scab (30), blackspot (518), other diseases (176)
Curving whitish trails in leaves	Leafminers (552)
Galls on leaves	Gall insects (261), diseases (176)
Sticky coating on leaves	Scale (345), aphids (344)

Root Symptoms

Symptom	Cause

ROOTS DISTORTED, ABNORMALLY THICKENED

Symptom	Cause
Small swollen areas on roots	
—white or gray, hard knots	Root knot nematodes (182)
—round nodules, on legumes	Nitrogen-fixing bacteria (515)
Whole root thickened (on cabbage-family plants)	Club root (181)
Corky lumps on roots and stem near soil line	Crown gall (182)

SHORT OR SPARSE ROOTS, TOPS OFTEN WILTED

Symptom	Cause
Roots brownish or dark-colored	Diseases (176), salt buildup (482)
Roots have soft, water-soaked appearance	Root rots (180)
Roots chewed	Rootworms (151), grubs (368)

OTHER SYMPTOMS

Symptom	Cause
Numerous woody secondary roots (on carrot-family plants)	Yellow virus (183)
Tunnels and rot in roots (cabbage, carrot, onion)	Root maggots (344)
Tree blows over; roots never left planting hole	Windthrow (585)

(continued)

Diagnosing Plant Problems—*Continued*

Fruit/Flower Symptoms

Symptom	*Cause*
FLOWERS DISTORTED	
Petals have silvery patches, or streaks	Aphids (344), viruses (183)
Petals have water-soaked patches	Botrytis rot (182)
FLOWERS APPEAR, BUT NO FRUIT	
Flowers open normally	Lack of pollination (255), cold damage (630), excess nitrogen (482)
Flowers drop before opening	Plant bugs (345)
FRUIT DROPS BEFORE RIPENING, MAY COLOR EARLY	
Fruits with normal exterior	
—interior tunneled and mined	Insect damage (341)
—interior normal	Normal self-thinning (255)
Shriveled fruits, early-ripening cultivars most affected	Fruit maggots (256)
Scarred, distorted fruits	Disease (176), plant bugs (345)
FRUIT DAMAGED, STAYS ON TREE	
Fruits with large, chewed holes	Caterpillars (344), animals (11)
Fruits have discolored areas	
—always at tip end	Blossom-end rot (572)
—also soft areas	Fungal or bacterial rots (180)
Fruits have small, dark scabs or spots	Bacterial or fungal disease (177)
Fruit distorted, puckered	Inadequate pollination (255), plant bugs (345), leaf curl (182)
OTHER SYMPTOMS	
Buds shrivel or rot before opening	Bud blast (434), insects (341)
Chewed flowers	Japanese beetles (345), other insects (341)

Small dark scabs on fruits: apple scab.

Brown, shriveled flowers: bud/flower blast.

Sunken lesions at blossom end of fruits: blossom end rot.

Stem Symptoms

Symptom	*Cause*

BRANCH OR WHOLE PLANT WILTS

Holes in stem or trunk; gummy sap or sawdust	Boring insects (257)
Collapsed areas on stem with soft, watery, brown discoloration	Botrytis (182), soft rots (180)
Raised areas on stems	
—cracks	Temperature injury (183), mechanical injury (479, 593), cankers (180)
—hard growths	Galls (261), cankers (180), graft incompatability (278)
Stems brown or reddish when cut open	Wilts (181)

SEEDLING OR TRANSPLANT STEMS COLLAPSED OR CUT OFF

Cut stem crisp, appears healthy	
—trail of silvery mucus on soil	Slugs or snails (540)
—no mucus trail present	Cutworms (345), animals (11)
Stem soft, watery	Damping–off (181), collar rot (31)

TIPS OF BRANCHES, TWIGS DIE BACK

Growth blackened	Insects (341), frost (630), blights (447)
—also distorted and wilted	Plant bugs (345)
Don't leaf out in spring	Cold injury (630)

OTHER SYMPTOMS

Small bumps on stems and leaf veins; honeydew present	Scale (345), mealybugs (333)
Stems and crowns hollow, corky (on cabbage-family plants)	Boron deficiency (481)

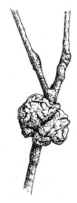

Galls: insect and disease problems.

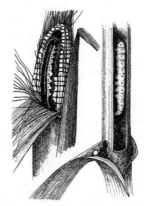

Holes in plant stems, "sawdust" around holes: borer damage.

Wilted, distorted, discolored plant parts: tip blight.

Healthy soil: Healthy soils contain a complex community of soil organisms that are vital to plant health. Mycorrhizal fungi protect fine roots from infections and aid plants in taking up nutrients. Nitrogen-fixing bacteria live symbiotically with roots of legumes, beneficial fungi trap harmful nematodes, and many fungi and bacteria produce antibiotics that suppress pathogens. Nutrient deficiencies and imbalances make plants more attractive to pests. Conversely, overfertilizing with nitrogen can cause soft, lush growth, which is very attractive to sucking pests such as aphids.

Proper moisture: Water-stressed plants are more attractive to pests and susceptible to diseases. For example, aphids and thrips are more likely to attack wilted plants, while wet, waterlogged soil encourages soilborne diseases. Plants usually grow best when moisture is maintained at a constant level. Most plants need about 1″ of water per week from rain and/or irrigation while they are actively growing. Learn your plant's specific likes and dislikes. Some plants have critical times during their development when sufficient water is crucial.

Be sure to water effectively. Apply water to the soil, below mulch if possible. Avoid routinely wetting leaves, because water helps spread many leaf diseases and may burn leaves in full sun. Water thoroughly: A long, slow soak every few days is much better than a short sprinkle every day. For more information on effective watering, see the Irrigation entry.

Mulches: Mulching saves water, controls weeds, and may add organic matter. It provides pest control by acting as a barrier, preventing soilborne problems from reaching plants, or providing a home for beneficial insects. You can mulch with a variety of organic or inorganic materials. A deep straw mulch in the potato patch can help prevent damage caused by Colorado potato beetles. Reflective aluminum mulch confuses aphids and prevents them from landing on your plants. For more information on what materials to use and how and when to apply them, see the Mulch entry.

Spacing and training: Proper spacing, staking, and pruning can reduce pest problems. Crowded plants are weak and spindly and are more prone to disease and insect problems. Staking keeps plants from coming in contact with soilborne diseases, prevents them from being stepped on or damaged, and increases air movement. Pruning plants increases air movement and makes it easier to spot insects before they become a major problem. Leafy crops can be their own living mulch and suppress weeds if spaced so that the plants just touch at maturity.

Sanitation

Keeping the garden clean is a basic principle of organic pest management. Don't bring diseased or infested plants into your garden, and remove pest-ridden plant material from the garden promptly.

Don't bring in problems: Check all new plants for signs of insects, disease, or hitchhiking weeds. Thoroughly inspect leaves, buds, bark, and if possible, roots. Discard, reject, or treat infested plants. Choose certified disease-free plants and seed when possible. Don't buy grass or cover-crop seeds contaminated with weed seeds, don't let weeds or garden plants go to seed, and avoid hay or other mulches that contain weed seed.

Handle plants carefully: Stay out of the garden when it's wet, because disease organisms spread easily on the film of water on wet leaves. Don't step on or bend plants when you work around them. Use mowers and trimmers with care: Any wound provides an entry for disease.

Don't spread problems: Wash your tools, boots, and clothes at the end of every work session. Even if you don't notice disease, you may spread it as you work. If you do touch a diseased plant, sanitize your tools and wash your hands before moving on. Dip or swab with a 10 percent bleach solution (½ cup of bleach plus 4½ cups of water) and let air dry. If you use the bleach solution on metal, be sure to wipe it with a little oil after it dries to prevent rust. Also sanitize plastic mulch and stakes before reusing them. Carry a plastic bag with you to put seed-bearing weeds and sick plants into.

Clean up pest-damaged plants: Pull up diseased plants or prune off damage. Burn them, put them in sealed containers for disposal with household trash, put them in the center of a hot compost pile, or feed them to animals. Picking up and destroying dropped fruit weekly is an effective way to reduce infestations of apple maggots, currant fruit flies, codling moths, and plum curculios.

Clean up crop residues: Good sanitation includes cleaning up all crop residues promptly. Compost them well or turn them under. Cultivating crop residues into the soil after harvest kills pests, including corn earworms, European corn borers, and corn rootworms.

Timed Planting

Seeds planted before the soil has warmed up in the spring are more susceptible to disease. Learn the soil temperature each crop requires to germinate, and use a soil thermometer to determine proper planting time.

Some pests have only 1-2 generations a year. You can reduce damage by planning planting or harvesting times to avoid peak pest populations. For example, plant radishes to mature before the first generation of cabbage root maggots appear to avoid damage, or delay setting out cabbage-family plants until after the first generation of cabbage root maggots has passed.

Crop Rotation

Crop rotation is the practice of shifting the locations of crops within the garden each season so the same crop does not grow in the same place year after year. This technique helps manage soil fertility and helps avoid or reduce problems with soilborne diseases and some soil-dwelling insects, such as corn rootworms.

Nutrient balance: Plants affect the soil in different ways. To keep soil nutrients balanced, avoid planting the same type of crop (leafy, fruiting, root, or legume) in the same place two years in a row.

Leafy and fruiting crops (such as lettuce, cabbage, corn, and tomatoes) are heavy feeders and rapidly use up nitrogen. Root vegetables and herbs are light feeders. Peas, beans, and other legumes add nitrogen to the soil but need lots of phosphorus. Follow a soil-building crop with a heavy-feeding crop, and follow a heavy feeder with a root crop or another soil builder to balance the supplies of nutrients in the soil.

Disease and pest prevention: Many diseases and pests are host-specific: They attack only a certain plant or family of plants. Although it may be difficult in a small garden, it's best to avoid planting the same plants in the same family in the same location year after year. For more information on rotating plant families in the vegetable garden, see "Rotating Vegetable Families" on page 613.

Green manure crops can be included in a rotation plan to discourage specific types of pests and to improve soil. For example, beetle grubs thrive among most vegetables, but not in soil planted in buckwheat or clover. A season of either crop can greatly reduce grub populations and at the same time will increase soil organic matter content.

Lengthy rotations are sometimes necessary to control chronic soilborne problems. Bean anthracnose fungus can persist in soil for up to three years, so a four-year rotation is needed to keep the disease at bay. The same holds true for such fungal diseases as Fusarium wilt and Verticillium wilt. A few problems, such as club root, persist in the soil for even longer, so rotation is less useful for controlling them.

Companion Planting

Neat rows or patches of a single crop make ideal places for pests to thrive. Many organic growers interplant two or more crops or combine certain companion plants with a crop to help reduce pest damage.

A few successful plant combinations work by directly repelling or confusing pests, or by changing the microclimate around the crop. Planting cabbage seedlings among taller plants that provide shade helps protect them from flea beetles who prefer to feed in full sun. Other companion plants attract adult beneficial insects. After eating, the beneficials lay their eggs among the pests on nearby plants. When the predatory offspring hatch, they attack the pests.

Interplanting crops with different harvest dates also makes good use of garden space. One crop is harvested as the second needs more room to spread out and mature. When interplanted with other plants, legumes may help provide them with nitrogen. For more information on what combinations work, see the Companion Planting entry.

Biological Controls

Using living organisms—beneficial insects and animals, parasitic nematodes, and microbial pesticides—to control pests is called biological control. Biological control is the essence of a balanced ecosystem. A good OPM plan takes the fullest advantage of the beneficial species that are naturally present and supplements them with purchased biological controls.

Beneficial insects and animals: Conserving and attracting native beneficial insects, birds, and animals is one of the best and most economical ways for gardeners to control pests. In a well-balanced garden, thousands of beneficial species do most of the work of suppressing pests for you. Learn to identify your helpers and find out what they like. Attract and encourage them to stay by providing food and nesting sites.

Many beneficial insects are raised commercially. You can buy beneficial insects and release them in relatively large quantities, so they'll have an immediate impact on pests. Or you can introduce a small population in your garden, which will become permanently established and suppress future generations of pests.

Choose species that are hardy or otherwise adapted to the climate in your area so they may become permanently established. It's not a good idea to release non-native species in your garden because they could displace a native species doing the same job or become pests themselves.

Not all beneficial insects sold are useful to home gardeners. For example, convergent lady beetles are widely sold for use in home gardens, but their instinct to fly away as soon as they are released makes them a poor investment. For more information on beneficials, see the Beneficial Insects entry; for more on attracting pest-consuming animals, refer to the Beneficial Animals entry.

Microbial insecticides: Just like people, insects suffer from diseases caused by bacteria, fungi, viruses, and other microorganisms. Microbial insecticides make use of these often highly specific insect diseases to kill garden pests. Some of the most widely sold biological controls in the world are strains of *Bacillus thuringiensis* (BT). BT kills many species of caterpillars, beetles, flies, and mosquitoes. Milky disease (*Bacillus popilliae* and *B. lentimorbus*) has been used for 50 years to control the larvae of Japanese beetles. For more details, see "Microbial Insecticides" on page 337.

Beneficial nematodes: Certain nematodes parasitize insect larvae. Because nematodes need moist conditions, they are most useful against pests in the soil or in hidden locations. Look for advances in formulation—nematodes may be useful over a wider range of conditions in the future. For more information on beneficial nematodes, see the Insecticides entry.

Microbial fungicides: Certain harmless fungi can be used to exclude disease-causing organisms. Binab T, a mixture of beneficial fungi, is painted on fresh tree wounds to prevent decay. Development of these highly specific fungicides is an active area of research.

Biological herbicides: Researchers are looking for specific insects that eat, and microbial diseases that kill, problem weeds. Watch for these products in the future.

Physical Controls

Physical controls either keep pests from reaching your plants or remove pests from plants. These controls include old-fashioned hand-weeding and modern insect traps.

Barriers

Barriers are among the most effective ways to prevent pest damage because they stop the pests from reaching the crop in the first place.

Floating row covers: Floating row covers of spunbonded polypropylene material were introduced to improve plant growth and extend the growing season. They have proven to be excellent barriers to such insect pests as carrot rust flies, cabbage maggots, flea beetles, and Mexican bean beetles. They also stop many pests whose feeding transmits plant diseases. Row covers also frustrate some small animals and birds.

Cover newly seeded beds or pest-free transplants with row covers, leaving plenty of slack in the material to allow for growth. Be sure to bury the edges in the soil or seal them in some other way. Otherwise, pests will sneak in and thrive in the protected environment.

You can leave row covers over some crops, such as carrots or onions, all season. Uncover other crops, such as beans or cabbage, once the plants are well grown or the generation of pests is past. Plants such as squash that require pollination by insects must be either uncovered when they start to flower or hand-pollinated. In a hot climate you may have to remove covers to prevent excessive heat buildup.

Fences and netting: Deny larger animal pests access to your garden riches with fences, barriers, repellents, and scare tactics. See the Animal Pests entry for specific ways to frustrate hungry moochers.

Cutworm collars: These collars fit around transplant stems to protect them from nocturnal cutworm raids. To make collars, cut strips of lightweight cardboard about $8'' \times 2\frac{1}{2}''$, overlap the ends to make a tube, and fasten with tape. Or cut sections of cardboard tube to similar dimensions. When transplanting, slip a collar over each plant and press it into the soil around the stem so about half of the collar is below the soil line.

Root fly barriers: Tar-paper squares are an old-fashioned and effective barrier to cabbage root flies, preventing them from laying their eggs around the roots of cabbage-family plants.

Cut tar paper into $6''$-$8''$ squares and make a small X-shaped cut in the center of each. Slide the square over the plant and flat against the soil, press the center flaps firmly around the stem, and anchor it with pebbles.

Tree bands: Tree bands are effective against pests that can't fly, such as snails, slugs, ants, and gypsy moth caterpillars. Some prevent pests from crossing, others actually trap pests.

Make cloth tree bands from strips of heavy cotton cloth or burlap about $15''$ wide, and long enough to form a generous overlap when they are wrapped around the trunk. Tie the band to the trunk with a string around the middle of the cloth, then pull the top section down over the lower half to make a dead end for creatures climbing up the tree. Check daily and destroy any pests trapped in the material.

Make corrugated cardboard tree bands by wrapping long strips around the trunk several times, with the exposed ridges facing in, and tying snugly with string. These bands attract codling-moth caterpillars looking for a sheltered place to spin their cocoons. Check for and destroy cocoons weekly.

Sticky tree bands: Pests get caught on sticky bands when they try to cross them and eventually die. Paint a 3″ band of sticky compound all the way around the trunk of mature trees, reapplying as needed. Younger trees may be damaged by the compound. Wrap a strip of fabric tightly around the trunk and cover that with a strip of plastic wrap. Apply the sticky compound to the plastic wrap. When the barrier loses effectiveness, replace the plastic.

Copper barriers: Strips of copper sheet metal make an excellent and permanent barrier against slugs and snails. Fasten them around the trunks of trees and shrubs, wrap them around legs or edges of greenhouse benches, or use them to edge garden beds. Be sure that there are no alternate routes over the strips for slugs to get to the plants. Pull or cut back leaning or overhanging weeds and plants.

To install a copper barrier around a garden bed, press the edge of a 3″-4″ wide strip about 1″ into the soil around the entire perimeter of the bed. Bend the top edge outward at a right angle to form a ½″ lip. Eliminate slugs from inside the barrier by using slug traps and by leaving the soil bare as long as possible.

Dehydrating dust barriers: Sharp dusts such as a layer of cinders or diatomaceous earth (DE) scratch insects and cause them to die from dehydration. Dusts also act as repellants, although a hungry slug will cross a dust barrier. Dusts work best when dry; renew after a rain.

To deter cabbage root maggots from laying eggs, spread a 6″ circle of wood ashes, talc, DE, or lime around the stem.

Paint a thick slurry made from ¼ lb. DE, 1 teaspoon soap, and water on tree bark to repel ants and deter adult borers from laying their eggs in the bark.

Removal

Removing insects or diseased plants is often an effective way to prevent problems from getting worse. For some pests, it's the only control method needed.

Weeds: Hand-pulling and hoeing weeds are effective physical controls. Be especially vigilant about not letting weeds in or near your garden set seed. Tilling and mowing can help, but don't till perennial weeds that re-grow from small sections of root. For more information on discouraging weeds, see the Weeds entry.

Insects: Handpicking insects is an effective, though rather tedious, way to control light or moderate infestations of large, easy-to-see caterpillars, such as tomato hornworms or cabbage loopers. Dig cutworms out of their daytime hiding place at the base of plants. Pick and destroy spinach or beet leaves with leafminer mines. Scrape gypsy moths' egg masses off tree trunks. Pry newly hatched corn earworms out of the tips of corn ears before they can get very far into the cob.

Shaking pests from plants is a variation of handpicking and works especially well for heavy beetles, such as Japanese or Colorado potato beetles and plum curculios. Shake or beat them off the foliage onto a sheet of plastic, then pour them into a pail of soapy water.

Vacuuming is a high-tech version of handpicking that works well for removing adult whiteflies from tomato plants in a greenhouse. Commercial growers now pull giant bug vacuums behind their tractors to suck up pests. Small hand-held vacuums are available. Just be careful not to suck up your plants, too.

A strong spray of water can physically injure aphids and knock them off plants. Spray plants in early morning or late afternoon to avoid scorching the leaves. If you have problems with diseases that thrive in wet conditions, you may want to choose another control method.

Diseases: Pulling up diseased plants or pruning off diseased shoots and disposing of them can be a good control method. Remove diseased weeds near the garden, too. Some plant diseases rely on alternate hosts for part of their life cycle. Removing the alternate hosts within a certain distance of your garden can reduce or eliminate disease problems.

Dispose of diseased material by placing it in the center of a hot compost pile, burying it, burning it, or putting it in sealed containers for disposal with household trash. See the Composting entry for directions for making a hot compost pile.

Traps

Traps are used to help control insect and animal pests. They generally consist of one or more attractive components or lures (usually a color, odor, or shape) and a trapping component (usually sticky glue, a liquid, or a cage). Traps are used in two ways: to catch so many individuals that the local population is too low to do significant crop damage, or to monitor the emergence or arrival of a pest so that other controls can be timed to have the most impact.

When using traps to control pests directly, judge their effectiveness by the reduction in plant damage, not just by the number of dead insects in the trap. If damage does not decrease, try other controls. Monitoring traps are useful for timing releases of beneficial insects, such as *Trichogramma* wasps, or to time a spray application to hit the peak pest population.

Colored sticky traps: Colored sticky traps are useful to control or monitor a variety of species. Bright blue traps are suitable for monitoring flower thrips numbers; white traps attract tarnished plant bugs, but they also attract beneficial flies, so should be used only early in the season. Yellowish orange traps lure carrot rust flies.

Yellow sticky traps are effective controls for

HOMEMADE TRAPS

Here are a few simple traps you can make yourself.

Sticky traps: You can make sticky traps from wood, cardboard, or stiff plastic. Paint the base with a coat of primer and two coats of bright yellow or medium blue paint. Coat with a sticky compound using a paintbrush, or spread it on with a knife. Use stiff adhesives like Tanglefoot for large insects and thinner glues such as Stiky Stuff or STP oil treatment for small insects. Scrape off insects and recoat as needed. Plastic balls can be painted red to make apple maggot traps. Plastic soda bottles make good cherry fruit fly traps—paint the shoulders of the bottle yellow and fill the bottle with lure.

Traps to use with pheromone lures: You can make a simple trap from a 1-quart, plastic ice-cream or yogurt container. Cut three large holes in the upper half of the sides. Paint the lid, or line it with cardboard to shade the lure. Tape a commercial lure to the inside of the lid. Fasten the trap to a sturdy stake. Fill the bottom half of the container with soapy water and snap on the lid, holding the lure.

Japanese beetle traps: Cut the necks off 1-gallon plastic jugs and fill ⅓ full with fermenting mixtures of water, sugar, crushed fruit, and yeast. Strain out the beetles regularly, and reuse the mixture.

---

whiteflies, fungus gnats, and imported cabbageworms. However, they work only as monitors for thrips and aphids.

Apple maggot traps: Red spheres covered with sticky glue attract female apple maggot flies and are often the only control necessary in a home orchard. Starting in mid-June, hang one trap in a dwarf tree and up to six traps in a full-sized tree, renewing the glue every two weeks. Some research shows that attaching an apple-scented lure to the trap increases its attractiveness, but not necessarily to the target pest—other related species may gum up the trap instead.

Cherry fruit fly traps: Yellow sticky traps catch cherry fruit flies if a small bottle of equal parts water and household ammonia or a commercial apple maggot lure is hung up with the trap. Hang one trap in each tree or four traps in a small orchard, and renew the sticky glue and the ammonia bait as necessary.

Yellow water traps: Fill a bright yellow pan or tray with water, to which a small amount of liquid soap has been added, to attract and drown aphids. These traps are effective monitors, but not controls. They also attract tiny beneficials; remove the traps if this happens.

Traps with pheromone lures: Pheromones are chemical cues that insects use to communicate with others of their species. Sex pheromones are wafted onto the air by females to attract males, who follow the direction of the odor until they find a mate. Synthetic pheromones are available in long-lasting lures and are widely used in sticky traps to monitor pest pop-

ulations, especially the various species of moths that attack fruit trees. When enough pheromone traps are used, they can control the population by trapping so many males that a significant portion of the females go unmated and don't lay eggs.

Commercial lures are long-lasting, and many are available in small quantities for home gardeners, either to be used in commercial traps or incorporated into homemade traps. Set out traps about 2-3 weeks before the target pest is expected to emerge; one trap is usually enough for a home orchard or garden. Check the traps daily or weekly; follow package directions.

Pheromones can also be used without traps to control pests. When large numbers of pheromone lures are put out, the air becomes saturated with aroma and males can't locate females to mate. Twist ties impregnated with pheromones are available for controlling oriental fruit moth and other pests.

Food lures: Japanese beetles are attracted to a fermenting mush of mashed fruit and sugar water or wine, with some yeast to speed fermen-

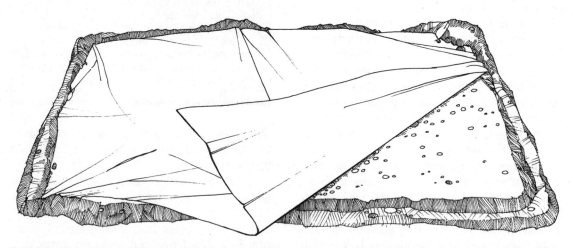

Solarizing soil. Midsummer is the best time to solarize soil to kill soilborne insects and disease organisms, especially in the North. Cultivate and remove crop residues from the soil, rake it smooth, and water it if it is dry. Dig a trench several inches deep around the bed, and spread thin clear plastic film (1-4 mils) over the bed. Press the plastic into close contact with the soil, and seal the edges by filling the trench with soil. Leave in place for 1-2 months, then remove plastic.

tation. See "Homemade Traps" on page 429 for instructions for making food lure traps for these pesky insects. Japanese beetle traps are most effective if used over a wide area of a community and in conjunction with other controls.

Slugs and snails are attracted to stale beer, spoiled yogurt, or a mixture of yeast and water. Set out the bait in saucers or tuna cans, buried with the lip of the container level with the soil surface, so the pests fall in and drown. Put a cover with holes in it on the trap to keep rain from diluting the beer and to keep large animals from drinking it.

Food traps: Control onion maggots by planting sprouted or shrivelled onions between rows of onion seeds in early spring. The onion maggot flies lay their eggs in the soil nearby, and the maggots burrow into the trap onions. About two weeks after the trap onions sprout, pull and destroy them to prevent the next generation of flies from developing.

Reduce the number of wireworms in the soil before you plant. Cut potatoes in half and poke a stick into each to serve as a handle. Bury the pieces of potato in the soil in early spring. Wireworms will be attracted to the trap potatoes; check the traps every few days, and destroy the wireworms or replace the potatoes.

Trap crops: Plants that are more attractive to certain pests than the crop you want to protect are useful as trap crops. For example, dill or lovage lures tomato hornworms away from tomatoes, and early squash is useful to trap pickleworms before late melons are set out. Pull and destroy trap plants as soon as they are infested, or the pests may reproduce on the crop and thus provide a larger pest population.

Soil Solarization

Soil solarization is an effective way to control many soilborne problems. Covering the soil with clear plastic for 1-2 months can generate high enough temperatures in the top 6"-12" of soil to kill pest insects, nematodes, weed seeds, and many disease organisms. This process has proven valuable for home gardeners, because soilborne pests, particularly nematodes, accumulate in crops grown in the same place year after year. The beneficial effects seem to last for several seasons. "Solarizing Soil" on the opposite page shows how to prepare a bed for solarizing.

Chemical Controls

Chemical controls are your last resort, after a combination of cultural, biological, and physical controls have proved inadequate. In some cases, 1-2 well-timed applications of an insecticide while the first generation of a pest is just emerging can reduce the problem to such an extent that no further applications are needed. Careful timing of applications helps make the best use of pesticides and can reduce overall use. Remember that these planned applications are only part of your complete management plan. In conjunction with cultural, biological, and physical controls, they bring down pests or diseases to acceptable levels.

Some organic pesticides are much less toxic than others to nontarget organisms. Always choose the least toxic but most effective method available. Botanical insecticides and copper and sulfur fungicides vary in their effectiveness for different pests. Choose the one best suited to each problem. For detailed information on specific chemical controls, see the Insecticides and Fungicides entries.

Botanical pesticides and naturally occurring minerals break down into more harmless compounds in a relatively short time. But remember: Some of them are very toxic to you and to other organisms at the time they are applied. Use them sparingly or as a last resort. Wear protective clothing, a face mask, and gloves when handling them. See the Pesticides entry for more information on safety. ❖

Ostrya

Hop hornbeam. Small deciduous trees.

Description: *Ostrya virginiana,* American hop hornbeam, is an upright tree with a spreading to rounded crown. A native that lives on dry slopes in the shade of other trees, hop hornbeam grows 25'-40' in most situations. It has alternate, rounded, finely toothed leaves; 1" catkins in groups of three are visible through the winter. Yellow fall color is unimpressive. Shallow vertical fissures in the tan bark create a slightly shredded effect. Zones 4-8.

How to grow: Provide a site with full sun or partial shade and well-drained, evenly moist soil. Mulch generously. Hop hornbeam is relatively pest-free and needs little maintenance.

Landscape uses: Plant hop hornbeam among other trees, or use it as a focal point. Its small to medium size makes this a nice, trouble-free shade tree for lawns and streets. ❖

Overwintering

Many plants grown as perennials in warm climates are not hardy enough to withstand the freezing temperatures in Northern areas. You can choose to let these plants die or to overwinter them until the next growing season. Overwintering involves protecting the plant from the cold, either in the garden or in a sheltered place. There are many overwintering techniques, ranging from covering dormant plants with a thick layer of mulch to moving plants to a cold frame, sunny windowsill, or cool basement. What works for one type of plant might be fatal to another. Check individual plant entries for specific overwintering instructions.

An easy way to overwinter some plants is to grow them in containers year-round and use them as houseplants or on the sun porch during the winter. Slow-growing woody plants such as lavender, rosemary, and tarragon make the transition from outdoor plant to houseplant and back very successfully and can thrive for many years.

You can also save many types of nonhardy plants that are planted outside. Cut back, dig up, and pot them before the first frost. Some plants, such as scented geraniums, suffer from transplant shock. It's easier to overwinter them by taking cuttings and rooting the cuttings inside. Rooted cuttings also take up less space, and there is less chance of inadvertently overwintering diseases or insect pests. Multiply a desirable plant for spring planting by taking cuttings of the overwintering plants in mid- to late winter. Many summer bedding plants, including impatiens, begonias, alyssum, and coleus can be overwintered this way. Their tendency to get leggy indoors as the winter progresses can be avoided by pinching or putting them under plant lights. See the Cuttings entry for instructions on how to take cuttings.

Geraniums and some other plants can be overwintered two ways. Bring them indoors as described above, or force them into dormancy. Forcing dormancy is useful if you're short on space for houseplants or want to save time and effort on winter care. Put the plant, either potted or with newspaper wrapped around its root ball, in a cool (not below 40°F), preferably dark place for the winter. Allow the soil to dry somewhat but not completely; check every few weeks and water sparingly if needed. In spring, replant outside after danger of frost is past or place in a warm, well-lit place and resume watering.

Many tender perennials go dormant by themselves, but need protection. Cover them with a thick layer of mulch, or dig and move to a cold frame or cool basement. Overwinter container plants outdoors by packing them in the center of large boxes full of leaves. Tender bulbs, such as dahlias, gladioli, tuberous begonias, and canna lilies, are dug, dried, and stored. Wrap shrubs and vines that need winter protection, or bury them in trenches. ❖

Pachysandra

Pachysandra, spurge. Evergreen perennial groundcovers.

Description: *Pachysandra terminalis,* Japanese pachysandra or Japanese spurge, has oval, glossy, dark green, 1″-3″ leaves set in whorls 6″-8″ high. Plants have underground creeping stems that spread slowly, producing a thick carpet. In May, fragrant white flower clusters appear on stout, fuzzy spikes. Occasionally, white berries form on older plants. Zones 4-9.

P. procumbens, Allegheny spurge, is native to the Southeast. Leaves are coarsely toothed at the ends and mottled with purple. Flowers are white and borne near the ground. Plants, which are evergreen in the South, are less vigorous than Japanese pachysandra. Zones 5-9.

How to grow: Pachysandras prefer partial shade in rich, moist, slightly acid soil. Although plants can adjust to deep shade, the leaves yellow in full sun. In the fall, top-dress the soil with dehydrated manure, or mulch lightly with compost. Rejuvenate old plantings by mowing in the spring. Propagate in the spring by division or cuttings. Space plants 6″-12″ apart.

Landscape uses: Plant pachysandras under shallow-rooted trees or broad-leaved evergreens. They're also excellent groundcovers along banks, slopes, or any difficult shaded areas.

Best cultivars: 'Silveredge' has silver-white leaf margins and is good for brightening up a shady area. ❖

Paeonia

Peony. Spring-blooming perennials.

Description: *Paeonia lactiflora,* common garden or Chinese peony, cultivars bear 3″-8″ single to double blooms in white, pink, and red shades, many with tufted (and sometimes yellow) centers. Common garden peonies bloom over a 4-6-week season above elegant, 4″-10″, glossy, dark green leaves on mounds averaging 3′ tall and wide. The foliage remains attractive throughout the growing season. *P. officinalis,* common peony, bears 4″-5″ satiny, vivid purplish red blooms on 2′ mounds of medium green, matte foliage resembling the common garden peony's. It blooms about a week before the common garden peony. Zones 3-8.

Tree peonies are derived from several species, including *P. suffruticosa, P. lutea,* and *P. delavayi.* Unlike herbaceous peonies, tree peonies have woody stems that don't die back to the ground in winter. The single, semidouble, or double flowers may be up to 10″ across and come in white, pink, red, salmon, and apricot. The sometimes fragrant blooms appear in mid-spring on sturdy, well-branched, 4′-6′ shrubs with divided dark green leaves. The plants are slow-growing, but they can live for decades with a little extra care once established. Zones 3-8.

How to grow: Plant peonies during late summer in the North or early fall in the South. If you wish to increase a favorite plant, divide herbaceous peonies at the same time. (Expect at least a year for the plant to settle in before blooming again.) Peonies prefer a sunny spot (partial shade in the South and for pastel cultivars) with fertile, well-drained soil. They can remain in the same spot for many years, so prepare the planting hole with lots of compost.

Improper planting is a common reason for failure to bloom. On herbaceous peonies, make sure the tips of the pointed, pinkish new shoots, called eyes, are 1"-2" below the surface. Plant tree peonies with the graft union about 6" below the soil surface.

Remove foliage of herbaceous peonies when it dies down after frost. Tree peonies benefit from a light yearly pruning to promote bushy growth; also, remove all suckers from the rootstock. Both kinds of peonies benefit from a layer of mulch the first winter or two after planting. In early spring, feed plants with a balanced fertilizer; keep soil evenly moist throughout the growing season. Botrytis blight can cause wilted, blackened leaves and make buds shrivel before opening. Remove wilted parts immediately. Cut stems to ground level after frost blackens leaves.

Anthracnose appears as sunken lesions with pink blisters on stems. Pruning off infected areas and thinning stems to improve air circulation will help lessen anthracnose problems. Infection by root knot nematodes can cause plants to wilt, become stunted, and have yellowed or bronzed foliage. Roots may be poorly developed and have tiny galls on them. Dig out and destroy severely infected plants.

Landscape uses: Use as specimens or small groups in borders. Grow peonies alone in beds or in dramatic sweeps along a lawn.

Best cultivars: *P. lactiflora:* Classic double cultivars are 'Festiva Maxima', white with red flecks; 'M. Jules Elie', rose; 'Phillipe Rivoire', dark red; and 'Sarah Bernhardt', light pink. Pink 'Seashell' and 'Krinkled White' are good singles. *P. officinalis:* 'Rubra Plena' is a handsome double with dark red flowers. Tree peonies: often sold by color. ❖

Palms

Palms. Evergreen trees or shrubs.

Description: Approximately 4,000 species of palms are found in the world's tropical and subtropical regions; palm fruits, oils, and building materials make the palms an economically important family. Eight or nine genera of palm are native to the United States, where they occur mostly in the southern coastal regions.

Cycas revoluta, Japanese sago palm, is not a true palm, but is included with palms for practical purposes. It consists of a rosette of stiff, coarse, compound leaves that are a dull dark green and 2'-7' long. Japanese sago palm may develop a trunk after many years but will still stay within the range of 3'-5' tall. The plant bears a conelike male flower and a female flower that may eventually bear fruit. Zones 8-9.

Raphidophyllum histrix, needle palm, forms a low rounded clump with a coarse outline. The 3'-4' long foliage is blue-green and fanlike, with black needlelike sheaths protruding at the bases of leaves. Zones 8-9.

Sabal palmetto, cabbage palmetto, is a Southeast coastal native that can survive temperatures of 10°-20°F in its home habitat. Cabbage palmettos reach 80'-90' tall and bear fan-shaped leaves that are 5'-6' long, 7'-8' wide, and deeply divided. Cabbage palmetto is the state tree of both South Carolina and Florida. Zones 8-9.

Sabal minor, dwarf palmetto, is a mounding, coarse-textured rosette of stiff, fanlike, compound leaves growing 3'-8' long. Small whitish flowers appear on stalks in summer, followed by black fruits in autumn. Often found growing in the shade of taller trees, dwarf palmetto grows 3'-5' tall. Zones 7-9.

Serenoa repens, saw palmetto, is similar to dwarf palmetto in many ways. It has olive to blue-green, fan-shaped foliage with coarse serrations along the edges. Large (up to 3') branches of small, fragrant white blossoms appear in summer and are favorites of bees. Berrylike, bluish black fruits provide food for wildlife. Saw palmetto spreads via rhizomes, making it difficult to transplant or remove. Zones 8-9.

Trachycarpus fortunei, windmill palm, has an erect form with a slender trunk and a head of large, fan-shaped leaves of dull dark green. The texture is coarse and bristly from the stiff crown to the fiber-covered trunk. Look for yellow flowers among the foliage and bluish fruits developing afterward. At heights of 15'-30', windmill palm is a good choice for small spaces, such as courtyards and entryways. Zones 7-9.

Washingtonia filifera, petticoat palm or California fan palm, is a West Coast native that lines streets in southern California and Florida. Petticoat palm, so-named because its persistent foliage hangs down from the crown to form a "petticoat" around the trunk, grows to 50' tall in the landscape; fan-shaped gray-green leaves may be 6' wide on mature plants. Zone 9.

How to grow: Most palms require full sun and fertile, moist, slightly acid soil. Dwarf palmetto is somewhat shade-tolerant and often lives beneath a hardwood canopy; cabbage palmetto will also tolerate partial shade. Fertilize lightly in spring and summer. Palms are extremely susceptible to cold injury, so don't do anything (like heavy or late fertilization) that would cause plants to produce tender new growth in the fall. Cold injury is most damaging when it affects the palm's crown, from which all new growth arises; plants that suffer damage to leaves may look unhealthy but will survive.

Landscape uses: Use low-growing palms for naturalizing, groundcovers, barriers, massed plantings, or foundation plants. Don't plant sharp-leaved saw palmetto or needle palm in high-traffic or play areas, but consider either for a durable hedge. Use windmill and petticoat palms as focal points. Petticoat palms and cabbage palmettos are good street trees in California and Florida. Beyond the coastlines of the Southeast and Southwest, even hardy palms are limited to container growing. ❖

Papaver

Poppy. Spring- to summer-blooming annuals, biennials, and perennials.

Description: Poppies bear saucer- to bowl-shaped blooms with prominent central knobs. Single-, semidouble-, and double-flowered poppies bloom on long stems above masses of hairy leaves; flower colors include solid shades and combinations of white, pink, red, yellow, and orange.

Annual *Papaver rhoeas,* corn poppy, produces 2" blooms on sparse-leaved plants usually reaching 2'.

Biennial *P. nudicaule,* Iceland poppy, bears 2"-6", mostly single blooms on similar plants. Zones 2-7.

Perennial *P. orientale,* Oriental poppy, offers dazzling 6"-10" wide flowers (most with striking black blotches inside) on stems from 2½'-4' above dense, leafy masses. Zones 3-7.

How to grow: All are easy to grow and prefer full sun to very light shade and average to rich, moist but well-drained soil. Direct-sow corn poppies in spring; start Iceland poppies in late summer in the North (fall in the South) for bloom the next year. Allow both to self-sow. Plant container-grown Oriental poppies in spring or in summer after the leaves disappear, which is an ideal time to divide them if necessary. Combine with later-blooming annuals and perennials to fill the large gaps left when the poppies go dormant, but leave room for leaves that reemerge in the fall. Provide light, loose mulch in winter.

Landscape uses: Grow in borders and informal gardens, or enjoy a solid bed or mass of corn or Iceland poppies. Flowers last a few days in water if cut ends are seared in a flame.

Best cultivars: *P. rhoeas* mixes: 'Shirley', in white and shades of pink and red; 'Mother of Pearl' includes unusual peach, lilac, and gray shades. *P. nudicaule:* 12"-16" 'Bubbles' and compact 'Wonderland' cultivars in mixed colors. *P. orientale:* many, including 'Carousel', white with orange edge. ❖

Parasitic Plants

Parasitic plants obtain water and nutrients needed for growth from another plant. They have specially adapted rootlike projections that puncture host plant tissues.

Dodders (*Cuscuta* spp.) are parasitic members of the morning-glory family. The leafless vines wrap tightly around their hosts, which include alfalfa and other legumes. Control it as you would any annual weed: Don't allow it to set seed, and avoid crop seed contaminated with dodder. See the Weeds entry for more controls.

Mistletoes (*Phoradendron* spp.) are semi-parasites on many tree species. Birds spread the seeds. Heavy infestations can damage trees. Remove mistletoe seedlings from trees. You can get a long-handled tool to do the job.

Don't confuse parasitic plants with epiphytes, such as mosses and some orchids, which use other plants for support only. ❖

Parsley

Petroselinum crispum
Umbelliferae

Description: Parsley is a decorative 8″-18″ biennial with much-divided leaves. In its second year, it produces small yellow flowers in flat umbels. To some, the leaves have a bitter taste and smell of camphor; many people, however, enjoy the pleasantly pungent flavor.

There are two distinct kinds of parsley available—curly and flat-leaved. Flat-leaved or Italian parsley (*Petroselinum crispum* var. *neapolitanum*) has luxuriant, shiny leaves and contains more vitamin C than the curly kind. It also has superior flavor. Curly parsley (*Petroselinum crispum* var. *crispum*) has ruffled leaves; it is popular in cooking and as a garnish. All parsley contains three times as much vitamin C, weight for weight, as oranges. It is also a fine source of vitamin A and iron.

How to grow: You can plant parsley outdoors in spring, but since it is slow to germinate (4-6 weeks), it's better to start seeds indoors. In either case, first soak the seeds in warm water for several hours or overnight.

For a reliable supply, sow new parsley plants each year. Although it's hardy, parsley will flower and die the second year unless you remove the flower stalks. Parsley plants that do flower in the garden will often self-sow. Pot up small plants in fall for indoor use.

Harvesting: Pick leaves as you need them. Freeze chopped or whole parsley in self-sealing bags to keep more of its fresh flavor, or dry in an oven or microwave.

Uses: The uses of parsley are endless, since its flavor combines well with most other culinary herbs and nearly all foods except sweets. It is traditionally one of the French *fines herbes* in soups, omelets, and potato dishes and is indispensable in Middle Eastern dishes like tabbouleh. ❖

Parsnip

Pastinaca sativa
Umbelliferae

Parsnips are large carrot-shaped roots with a distinctive nutty-sweet taste. They require 100-120 days to mature and need a bit of extra soil preparation, but parsnip lovers think they're worth the effort. Prepare parsnips like carrots— steamed or sliced into soups or stews.

Planting: Parsnip's cream-colored root grows 8″-24″ long, with 2″-4″ wide shoulders. Take some extra care in preparing the planting area. Loosen the soil to a depth of 2′; remove rocks or clods. Dig in 2″-3″ of compost; avoid high-nitrogen materials that can cause forked roots.

In most areas, sow seed ½″-1″ deep in the spring as soon as the soil can be worked. In the South, plant parsnips in the fall for a spring harvest. Use only fresh seeds, and soak them for several hours to encourage germination. Even then, germination will be slow and uneven, so sow the seed thickly and mark the rows with a quick-maturing radish crop. Firm the soil and water gently; keep the soil evenly moist.

Growing guidelines: Keep young plants free of weeds, and use a light mulch to conserve moisture. Parsnips have long roots and tolerate dry conditions, but your crop will be more successful if watered regularly.

Problems: Parsnips are usually problem-free. See the Carrot entry for details on controlling problems that do occur.

Harvesting: Harvest roots after a hard frost for the best flavor. Dig and store like carrots, or mulch with a thick layer of hay and leave in the ground over winter, harvesting as needed. Pull the entire crop in early spring before new growth spoils its flavor. ❖

Parthenocissus

Woodbine. Deciduous woody vines.

Description: Woodbines are fast-growing vines that can climb 30'-50'. The vines cling to supports with adhesive discs at the end of their tendrils. Their shiny green, lobed or compound alternate leaves display excellent crimson red to purple-red fall color. Their blue-black fruits, borne in fall, are showy after leaves drop. *Parthenocissus quinquefolia,* Virginia creeper or woodbine, has compound leaves with five leaflets. Zones 3-9. *P. tricuspidata,* Boston ivy or Japanese ivy, has three-lobed, maplelike leaves. Zones 4-8.

How to grow: Woodbines are easy to grow. Transplant container-grown plants. Plant in sun or shade. Plants tolerate a wide range of soil conditions.

Landscape uses: Boston ivy and Virginia creeper are excellent for covering stone or brick walls. They are the ivies most often seen on college campuses. ❖

Passiflora

Passionflower. Tender perennial vines.

Description: Colorful, dramatic flowers characterize this genus. The arrangement of the flower parts reminded early missionaries of the story of Christ's crucifixion, giving the plant its common name, passionflower. There are over 400 tropical species in the genus. Passionflowers have alternate three- to five-lobed semi-evergreen to evergreen leaves. The vines climb by twining tendrils to over 20'.

Passiflora caerulea, blue passionflower, has five-lobed leaves and white, pinkish, or light blue summer-blooming flowers up to 4" wide. Zones 8-10; evergreen in Zones 9-10.

P. incarnata, wild passionflower or maypop, blooms from midsummer to early autumn and produces sweet, edible yellow fruits. The purplish pink flowers are 2" across and displayed against the three-lobed leaves. Zones 7-10.

P. lutea, yellow passionflower, is a yellow-blooming native species that is hardy to Zone 6.

How to grow: Passionflowers are easy to grow from seed or cuttings. Grow in well-drained but moist soil in full sun or light shade. Remove old shoots in late winter to encourage bloom. Plants die to the ground in harsh winters but usually resprout. Grow in the greenhouse in cool climates for the colorful blooms. Be sure to provide support for tendrils to twine around.

Landscape uses: Grow passionflowers on a fence, trellis, or post to show off their dramatic blossoms. They will also create a light screen around patios or on the edge of your property. Passionflowers make stunning container plants for balconies and decks; let them twine around the railing. Yellow passionflower is not as showy as the others, but its yellow flowers are attractive in the wild garden.

Best cultivars: *P. caerulea:* 'Constance Elliott', pure white; 'Grandiflora', large-flowered (to 6"). ❖

Pea

Pisum sativum
Leguminosae

Peas, whose crisp, sweet taste embodies spring, are one of the world's oldest crops. They were foraged in the wild long before they were domesticated. Romans, however, believed fresh green peas were poisonous and had to be dried before they could be consumed. It wasn't until the time of King Louis XIV of France that a French gardener developed a green-pea hybrid known as *petits pois*. Fresh peas soon became the rage at the king's court and thereby quickly gained widespread popularity.

Types: Still a garden favorite, peas are one of the first vegetables that you'll plant and harvest in spring. There are extra-early, early, midseason, and late types, taking 7-10 weeks to mature. Vining peas need trellises to grow on, while dwarf types need little or no support. Vining peas usually produce a heavier crop than do dwarfs.

Among green—or English—peas, there are wrinkled-seeded types and smooth-seeded types, both of which must be shelled. While wrinkled green peas are sweeter, smooth ones are hardier and better for super-early spring planting and for autumn and winter crops.

Snow peas and snap peas have edible pods.

Snow peas produce flat pods that you can eat either raw or cooked. Snap peas are eaten either as young flat pods or after the peas have grown and are fat and juicy in the pods. Snow and snap peas are available in both vining and dwarf versions.

Some edible-podded cultivars have strings running down each pod that you must remove before eating; fortunately, "stringless" cultivars have been developed that eliminate this task. Edible-podded peas are perfect for stir-fries and other Oriental dishes.

Field peas or cowpeas—which include black-eyed peas, crowder peas, and cream peas—are, botanically, beans. These plants thrive in areas with long, hot summers. See the Bean entry for information on cultivating these crops.

Planting: Give early peas a sunny spot protected from high winds. Later crops may appreciate partial shade. Some growers have success with fall pea crops by planting them where corn or pole beans will shade them until the weather cools.

Early peas in particular like raised beds or a sandy loam soil that warms up quickly. Heavier soils, on the other hand, can provide cooler conditions for a late pea crop, but you'll need to loosen the ground before planting by working in some organic matter. Being legumes, peas supply their own nitrogen, so go easy on such fertil-

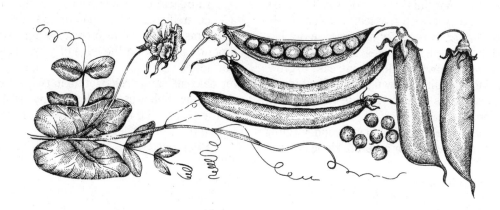

izers as manure. Too much nitrogen produces lush foliage but few peas.

Peas don't transplant well and are very hardy, so there's no reason to start them indoors. Pea plants can survive frosts but won't tolerate temperatures over 75°F. In fact, production slows down drastically at 70°F.

Southern gardeners often sow peas in mid- to late fall so the seeds will lie dormant through the winter and sprout as early as possible for spring harvest. On the West Coast and in Gulf states, you can grow peas as a winter crop. Elsewhere, if the spring growing season is relatively long and cool, plant your peas 4-6 weeks before the last frost, when the soil is at least 40°F. For a long harvest season, sow early, mid-season, and late cultivars at the same time, or make successive sowings of one kind at 10-day to two-week intervals until the middle of May.

Soak seeds for 24 hours before planting to loosen the tough seed coat and speed germination. When planting peas in an area where legumes haven't grown before, it helps to treat seeds with an inoculant powder of bacteria, called *Rhizobia*. This treatment promotes the formation of root nodules, which contain beneficial bacteria that convert the nitrogen in the air into a form usable by plants. To use an inoculant, roll wet seeds in the powder immediately before planting.

Space seeds of bush, or dwarf, peas 1" apart in rows 2' apart. Bush peas are also good for growing in beds. Sow the seeds of early crops 2" deep in light soil or 1" deep in heavy soil; make later plantings an inch or two deeper. Thin to 2"-3" apart. This close spacing will allow bush peas to entwine and prop each other up.

Plant vining types in double rows 6"-8" apart on either side of 5'-6' tall supports made of wire, string, or nylon mesh, with 3' between each double row. The more simple the support, the easier it is to remove the vines at the end of the pea season and reuse it.

Generally speaking, 1 lb. of seeds will plant a 100' row and should produce around 1 bushel of green peas or 2 bushels of edible pods. Another rough guideline is to raise 40 plants per person. Unused seed is good for three years.

To make good use of garden space, interplant peas with radishes, spinach, lettuce, or other early greens. Cucumbers and potatoes are good companion plants, but peas don't do well when planted near garlic or onions.

Growing guidelines: Providing peas with just the right amount of water is a little tricky. They should never be so waterlogged that the seeds and plants rot, and too much water before the plants flower will reduce yields. On the other hand, don't let the soil dry out when peas are germinating or blooming or when the pods are swelling. Once the plants are up, they only need about ½" of water every week until they start to bloom; at that time, increase their water supply to 1" a week until the pods fill out.

Peas growing in good soil need no additional fertilizer. If your soil is not very fertile, you may want to side-dress with compost when the seedlings are about 6" tall.

The vines are delicate, so handle them as little as possible. Gently hand-pull any weeds near the plants to keep from damaging the pea roots. To reduce weeds and conserve moisture, lay down a mulch at least 2" thick once the weather and soil warms. This also helps to keep the roots cool. Soil that becomes too warm can result in peas not setting fruit or can prevent already-formed pods from filling out. Mulch fall crops as soon as they are planted, and add another layer of mulch when the seedlings are 1"-2" tall.

Once a vine quits producing, cut it off at ground level, leaving the nitrogen-rich root nodules in the ground to aid the growth of a following crop, such as brassicas, carrots, beets, or beans. You can compost vines in a hot compost pile, but be careful about plowing them under, because you may be putting undetected viruses or fungi into the soil.

Problems: Aphids often attack developing vines. For information on controlling these pests, see "The Top Ten Garden Insect Pests in America" on page 344.

Pea weevils—tiny brown beetles with black and white spots—chew holes in blossoms and lay eggs on pods; these eggs develop into larvae that bore into the pods and damage the seeds. Rotate crops and clean up plant debris to break the cycle of infestation. If these pests are a serious problem, spray with pyrethrins to control adults.

Thrips—very tiny black or dark brown insects—often hide on the undersides of leaves in dry weather. They cause distorted leaves that eventually die; thrips also spread disease. Control them with an insecticidal soap spray.

See the Animal Pests entry for information on protecting seeds and seedlings from birds.

Crop rotation is one of the best ways to prevent diseases. To avoid persistent problems, don't grow peas in the same spot more than once every five years.

Plant resistant cultivars to avoid Fusarium wilt, which turns plants yellow, then brown, and causes them to shrivel and die.

Root rot fungi cause water-soaked areas or brown lesions to appear on lower stems and roots of pea plants. Cool, wet, poorly drained soil favors development of rots. To avoid root rot, start seeds indoors in peat pots and wait until the soil is frostless before setting out the plants. Provide good fertility and drainage for strong, rapid growth.

Warm weather brings on powdery mildew, which covers a plant with a downy, white fungal coating that sucks nutrients out of the leaves. Sulfur dust, if applied early, can be effective. Destroy seriously affected vines, or place them in sealed containers for disposal with household trash. Avoid powdery mildew by planting resistant cultivars.

Control mosaic virus, which yellows and stunts plants, by getting rid of the aphids that spread it.

Harvesting: Pods are ready to pick about three weeks after a plant blossoms, but check frequently to avoid harvesting too late. You should harvest the peas daily to catch them at their prime and to encourage vines to keep producing. If allowed to become ripe and hard, peas lose much of their flavor. Also, their taste and texture are much better if you prepare and eat them immediately after harvesting; the sugar in peas turns to starch within a few hours after picking.

Pick shell and snap peas when they are plump and bright green. Snow pea pods should be almost flat and barely showing their developing seeds. Cut the pods from the vines with scissors; pulling them off can uproot the vine or shock it into nonproduction.

Preserve any surplus as soon as possible by canning or, preferably, by freezing, which retains that fresh-from-the-garden flavor. To freeze peas, just shell and blanch for 1½ minutes, then cool, drain, pack, and freeze. Snow peas, which are frozen whole, are treated the same way, but don't forget to string them first if necessary. Peas have a freezer life of about one year.

If peas become overripe, shell them and spread them on a flat surface for three weeks or until completely dry. Store in airtight containers and use as you would any dried bean.

Best cultivars: Green peas: 'Maestro', early, dwarf, disease-resistant; 'Green Arrow', high-yielding, easy to pick; 'Lincoln', heat-resistant, great for its fresh-eating quality; 'Wando', heat-resistant, a good choice for Southern growers; 'Laxtonian', sturdy, vigorous vines and sweet, tender peas, excellent for freezing.

Snow peas: 'Dwarf Gray Sugar', early, hardy, compact, and disease-resistant; 'Oregon Sugar Pod II', sweet, tender pods, disease-resistant.

Snap peas: 'Sugar Ann', compact, early; 'Sugar Snap', edible at all stages, freeze well; 'Snappy', very productive; 'Super Sugar Mel', high-yielding, great flavor; 'Sugar Daddy', stringless. ❖

Peach

Prunus persica
Rosaceae

There may be no greater pleasure than biting into a peach fresh from the tree. These wonderful fuzzy fruits are the same species as nectarines. Only a single gene controls whether a cultivar bears smooth- or fuzzy-skinned fruit.

The Fruit Trees entry covers many important aspects of growing peaches and other tree fruits; refer to it for more information on planting, pruning, and care.

Selecting trees: Most peach trees are self-fertile. One tree will set a good crop.

Select cultivars to match your climate. See "Chill Hours" on this page for a more exact way to determine what cultivars to plant. Choose disease-resistant peaches when available.

What you plan to do with your harvest will influence your selection. Freestone fruit are easy to separate from the pit and great for fresh eating, but the melting flesh often gets soft if canned. Clingstone fruit hang onto the pit for dear life, but their firm, aromatic flesh is great for cooking and preserving.

Yellow flesh is standard, but white-fleshed peaches are quite tender and equally tasty.

If you have the space for several trees, pick cultivars that will give you a succession of harvests. Just be sure your growing season is long enough for the fruit to mature.

Rootstocks: Standard peach trees are grafted on seedling rootstocks grown from 'Lovell' and 'Halford' seed, two common commercial canning peaches. Standard trees grow to about 20', but you can keep them to a manageable size with pruning. Grafted dwarf peach trees have been short-lived and unreliable. Avoid trees grafted on cherry or plum rootstocks. Look for the newer dwarfing rootstocks like 'Citation', which make better trees.

Where nematodes are severe, try 'Nema-guard' rootstock. 'Siberian C' rootstock may be a good choice for cold climates where winter temperatures do not fluctuate. If you have warm spells, seedling rootstocks may be less likely to break dormancy prematurely.

Planting: Peaches prefer soil that is well drained and sandy-light on the surface with heavier texture in the subsoil layers. This keeps the crown and roots dry, helping to prevent disease problems, but still gives the tree a deeper reservoir of moisture and nutrients. For best results in any soil, add organic matter and correct any drainage problems before planting. Peaches need a pH of 6.0-6.5. Don't add lime if the pH is 6.2 or higher, since a high level of calcium in the soil reduces absorption of potassium and magnesium by tree roots. Fertilize with compost. Space standard peaches 15'-20' apart,

CHILL HOURS

Like other tree fruits, peach trees need a period of cold-weather rest or dormancy. The number of hours of cold between 32°F and 45°F each cultivar needs before it breaks dormancy is referred to as chill hours. (Cold below 32°F doesn't count toward meeting the dormancy requirement.) Once the number is reached, the tree assumes winter is over, and it starts growing the next warm day. Peaches bloom rapidly once their requirement has been met, which makes them more prone to frost damage than other tree fruits that are slower to burst into bloom.

Call your local extension service to find out how many chill hours your area receives and what cultivars match that requirement. If you choose a cultivar that needs fewer chill hours than you normally receive, it will flower too early and be prone to bud damage. But if you choose one that needs more chill hours, it won't get enough chilling to stimulate normal bloom.

and space dwarfs 12' apart.

Peach blossoms are easily damaged by frost. In areas where late-spring frosts are common, plant peaches on the upper half of a north-facing slope, so cold air will settle below them. A north-facing slope warms slowly, which may delay flowering by as much as 1-2 weeks. Planting about 15' away from the north side of a building may have the same effect. A thick mulch under the trees will help delay flowering by keeping the soil cool.

Peaches ripen best when the sun shines and temperatures hover at about 75°F. If temperatures are consistently cooler, the fruit can develop an astringent flavor or be almost tasteless. Plant your tree in a sheltered location that conserves heat to help the fruit ripen.

Since most peach trees have a maximum productive life of about 12 years, plant replacements periodically. If you plan ahead, you will always have mature trees and fresh fruit. Don't replant in the same location, though. Viruses and nematodes, which will shorten the life of new trees, may have built up in the soil.

Care: Healthy peaches should grow 1'-1½' a year. If growth is slower or the foliage is a light yellow-green or reddish purple, have the leaves and soil tested for nutrient content, and correct deficiencies. The Soil entry gives specifics on soil testing. In cold climates, fertilize only in early spring so wood can be fully hardened before winter. Mulch with compost or other low-nitrogen organic materials to maximize water and nutrient availability.

Peach trees need even moisture around their roots to produce juicy, succulent fruit. If the weather is dry or the soil is sandy, install trickle irrigation over the entire root system out to the drip line. Keep the soil moist, not wet. Mulch to reduce evaporation. See the Irrigation entry for more information on installing a trickle irrigation system.

Sometimes peaches flower when the weather is still too cool for much insect activity. To get a good harvest, you must spread pollen from flower to flower in place of insects. Use a soft brush to dab pollen from one flower onto its neighbor. Hand-pollinate newly opened flowers every day, and you'll have a decent crop. Or attract wild orchard bees, who work even when it's cool. See the Bees and Beekeeping entry for more information.

Frost protection: Winter temperatures of −10°F or lower will kill some or all of the flower buds of most peach cultivars. Some may even suffer cold damage to the wood, branch crotches, or trunk. The closer the cold snap comes to spring flowering time, the more severe the damage will be. Plant cold-tolerant cultivars to minimize losses. Or try letting the tree grow taller than you normally would; the upper boughs may escape frost damage.

If frost is predicted, spray an anti-transpirant the day before for 2°-3°F of extra protection. Or get up and hose down trees with water just before sunrise.

Pruning: Train peaches to the open center system. This makes an attractive, productive tree that is low and spreading and easy to reach. For instructions, see "Open Center Training" on page 254.

Start training your tree when you plant it. The first few years you prune to shape the tree. After that, prune only to keep the tree fruiting and reasonably small. Prune each year just before the tree breaks dormancy. If canker is a problem or spring frosts are common, prune after flowering to minimize disease problems and ensure that you will have a good crop. Dry weather at pruning discourages canker invasion, and you will be able to prune more or less depending on how many buds survived winter. Heading back new growth now reduces the fruit load and your later thinning chores.

Try central leader training if your trees suffer sunscald, or protect trees by painting the

Peach tree borers. Peach tree borers are 1", clear-winged blue moths with a wide yellow-orange belt. Their white larvae burrow into the trunk near the soil line.

larger branches with diluted white latex paint. In very cool climates, try training your peach tree against a stone or brick wall that reflects sun and radiates heat. For training instructions, see the Espalier entry.

No matter what training method you choose, try to minimize the amount of wood you remove the first few years. Rub off unwanted shoots and suckers as soon as they appear during the growing season. Your tree will bear earlier and more heavily if you do.

As the tree gets older, continue to prune each spring for maintenance and renewal. Peaches fruit only on one-year-old wood. Encourage new growth by cutting off old branches that are no longer productive. Head back new growth by ⅓-½ of its length to keep the tree compact. Cut back to just above an outward-facing branch or bud. Heading back also encourages more small side branches, which are the best fruit producers, and keeps the tree from overbearing.

Thinning: Once your tree starts bearing, it may set more fruit than it can handle. Remove some of the green fruit before the pits harden, so the remaining fruit will grow large and sweet and the tree won't break under the weight of the ripe fruit. Leave one peach every 4"-6". If you don't remove enough, prop up heavily laden branches with a forked stick until harvest. Prune and thin harder the next year.

Harvesting: Peach trees bear within three years. As peaches ripen, the skin color changes from green to yellow; the flesh slightly gives to the touch when ripe. Hold the fruit gently in your palm and twist it off the branch. Avoid bruising it. You can store ripe peaches for about a week in a refrigerator.

Problems: Peach trees can be plagued by a number of pests and diseases; the most serious are canker and peach tree borers. Nectarine fruits are even more likely to be attacked by fruit pests than peaches are, perhaps because pests dislike the fuzzy skin on peaches.

Common peach pests include green fruitworms, leafhoppers, two types of peachtree borers, mites, oriental fruitmoth, and plum curculios. For descriptions and control methods see "Fruit Tree Insects and Diseases" on page 256. A peach tree borer moth is illustrated on this page. Aphids, Japanese beetles, scale, and tarnished plant bugs can also cause problems; see "The Top Ten Garden Insect Pests in America" on page 344 for descriptions and controls.

Fall webworms and tent caterpillars spin webs and munch on leaves. Gypsy moth caterpillars also eat leaves. Destroy webs and caterpillars as soon as you see them. Spray BT (*Bacillus thuringiensis*) where they are feeding.

Trees infected by root knot nematodes may have weak growth and yellow leaves. Affected trees won't bear fruit and eventually die. If you suspect a nematode problem, ask your local extension office about having your soil tested for nematodes. To avoid nematode problems, don't replant where peaches have grown previously, solarize soil before planting, and enrich soil with organic matter to encourage natural fungi or apply parasitic nematodes to soil before planting. 'Nemaguard' rootstock is resistant to root knot nematode.

Some common diseases of peaches are bacterial leaf spot, brown rot, powdery mildew, perennial canker (also known as valsa and cytospora), and peach leaf curl. See "Fruit Tree Insects and Diseases" on page 256 for descriptions and controls. Peach leaf curl is illustrated on this page.

Peach scab causes small, olive green spots, usually clustered near the stem end of half-grown fruit about a month after infection. Later the spots turn brown and velvety, and the skin cracks. Twigs and leaves also get peach scab. Remove and destroy infected fruit and clean up fallen leaves and fruit. Weather that is warm and either wet or humid encourages scab. Control as you do brown rot. If you've had problems with scab in previous seasons, spray sulfur weekly from the time the first green shows in the buds until the weather becomes dry.

Certain cankers cause wilting or yellowing of new shoots or leaves and can also girdle limbs. Delay routine pruning until after bud break to reduce the chance of infection by canker organisms. Prune out and destroy any gummy cankers on trees whenever you spot them.

Crown gall and crown rot sometimes attack peach trees; providing good drainage helps to avoid these problems. Use a sharp knife to remove galls that form near the soil line, and paint wounds with a mixture of lime-sulfur and white latex paint.

Virus diseases such as yellows and mosaic may cause leaf distortion, discoloration, and mottling. Buy only certified disease-free stock. Destroy infected trees immediately.

Best cultivars: Late-flowering or cold-tolerant cultivars include 'Clayton', 'Jayhaven', 'Emery', 'Redhaven', 'Jefferson', 'Cresthaven', and 'Nectar'. In Zone 5, try extra-hardy peaches like 'Reliance' and 'Sunapee'.

Heat-tolerant cultivars for Southern growers include 'Florida King' and 'Florida Prince'.

Cultivars that resist bacterial leaf spot include

Peach leaf curl. Leaves are puckered and reddish. Later in the season they may turn pale green, shrivel, and drop. Fruit production is decreased; fruits may have a reddish, irregular, rough surface.

'Raritan Rose', 'Clayton', 'Ouchita Gold', 'Candor', 'Redhaven', 'Biscoe', 'Champion', and 'Nectacrest'.

Canker-resistant cultivars are 'Biscoe', 'Elberta', 'Candor', 'Brighton', 'Raritan Rose', 'Harken', 'Madison', 'Reliance', 'Harbrite', 'Champion', and 'Harbelle'.

Brown rot-resistant cultivars include 'Carmen', 'Elberta', 'Orange Cling', 'Red Bird', and 'Sunbeam'.

Cultivars that resist peach leaf curl include 'Candor', 'Com-Pact Redhaven', 'Correll', 'Clayton', 'Dixiland', 'Elberta', 'Redhaven', and 'Stark EarliGlo'.

'Compact Redhaven' and 'Compact Elberta' are naturally small genetic dwarf trees.

'Springold' and 'Earligrande' are early-season cultivars. 'Derby', ' Redhaven', and 'Raritan Rose' are mid-season, and 'Veteran', 'Redglobe', and 'Canadian Harmony' are late-season.

Little known Chinese Peen-to peaches such as 'Saturn' are as sweet as liquid sugar. They look like a juicy doughnut with a little pit in the center. Since they don't store well, you'll have to plant a tree to enjoy them. ❖

Peanut

Arachis hypogaea
Leguminosae

Contrary to popular belief, the peanut is not a nut; it is actually a vegetable belonging to the legume family, which includes peas and beans. These tropical natives of South America require about 120 days to mature, but fortunately they can withstand light spring and fall frosts. Although peanuts are generally considered a Southern crop, Northern gardeners can also grow them successfully if they choose early cultivars and start plants indoors.

Planting: Peanuts need full sun. If you have heavy soil, ensure good drainage by working in enough organic matter to make it loose and friable.

Peanut seeds come in their shells and can be planted hulled or unhulled. If you do shell them, don't remove the thin, pinkish brown seed coverings, or the seeds won't germinate.

Northern growers should start plants indoors in large peat pots a month before the last frost. Sow seeds 1″ deep, place in the sunniest spot possible, and water weekly. Transplant seedlings to the garden when the soil warms to 60°-70°F. Space transplants 10″ apart, being careful not to damage or bury the crown.

In the South, plant outdoors around the date of the last expected frost. Space seeds 2″ deep and 5″ apart in rows 2′-3′ apart. Firm the soil and water well. Thin plants to 10″ apart.

Growing guidelines: When the plants are about 1′ tall, hill the earth around the base of each plant. Long, pointed pegs (also called peduncles) grow from faded flowers and grow 1″-3″ down into the hills. A peanut will form on the end of each peg. Lay down a light mulch, such as straw or grass clippings, so the pegs will have no difficulty penetrating the soil.

One inch of water a week is plenty for peanuts. Being legumes, peanuts supply their own nitrogen, so don't add nitrogen fertilizers, such as manure, which encourage foliage rather than fruits. Well-prepared soil will provide all

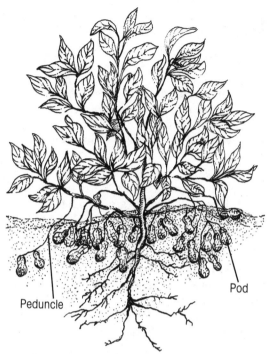

Peanut plant parts. Peanuts have self-pollinated flowers that occur above or just below ground level. Peanut seeds form in pods, which develop underground on the ends of elongated flower stalks known as peduncles or pegs.

the nutrients the plants need.

Problems: Peanuts are usually problem-free. For aphid controls, see "The Top Ten Garden Insect Pests in America" on page 344.

Harvesting: The crop is ready to harvest when leaves turn yellow and the peanuts' inner shells have gold-marked veins. If you wait too long, the pegs will become brittle, and the pods will break off in the ground, making harvesting more difficult. Pull or dig the plants and roots when the soil is moist. Shake off the excess soil, and let plants dry in an airy place until the leaves become crumbly; then remove the pods. Unshelled peanuts, stored in airtight containers, can keep for up to a year.

Best cultivars: 'Jumbo Virginia', large pods, very productive; 'Spanish' cultivars are quick to mature, good for Northern growers. ❖

Pear

Pyrus communis and its hybrids
Rosaceae

Pear trees produce bushels of delicious fruit and make beautiful landscape trees with their glossy leaves and white blossoms. They are long-lived, and less troubled by insect pests and diseases than many tree fruits.

Most gardeners are familiar with European pears, including the familiar 'Bartlett' and 'Bosc' pears. However, Asian pears, which have crisp, juicy, almost round fruits, will also grow well in most parts of the United States and Canada. The Fruit Trees entry covers many important aspects of growing pears and other tree fruits; refer to it for additional information on planting, pruning, and care.

Selecting trees: Pears need cross-pollination to set a good crop. Most European and Asian cultivars pollinate each other. A few cultivars don't produce viable pollen; if you select one, you'll need to plant three different cultivars to ensure good fruit set. Certain cultivars will not pollinate other specific cultivars. Check pollination requirements before you buy.

European pears are hardy to −20°F. If your winters are short, and your summers warm, try the Asian pears derived from the Japanese sand pear, *Pyrus pyrifolia,* such as 'Nijisseiki'; this type needs fewer chill hours than Europeans. (For more information on fruit tree chilling requirements, see "Chill Hours" on page 441.) If you live in the far North, try some of the super-hardy "Chinese varieties" of Asian pears.

Fire blight can be a devastating problem in some regions. Choose resistant cultivars if fire blight is a problem in your area. Asian pears seem to be less appealing to pear psylla, another common problem.

Rootstocks: Standard pear trees are grafted onto seedling rootstocks. They can grow to 40′ if they are not pruned and have strong, hardy roots.

Dwarf pears are grafted onto any of several rootstocks. 'Old Home × Farmingdale' rootstock is resistant to fire blight and pear decline and makes a semidwarf tree.

Planting and care: Pears are quite winter-hardy. They bloom early but tend to be more resistant to frost damage than other fruits. Open pear blossoms can be damaged at 26°F.

Pears will tolerate less-than-perfect drainage but need deep soil. They are vulnerable to water stress. Foliage will brown out, and the fruit will stay small. Mulch with a thick layer of organic matter out to the drip line, and irrigate deeply if the soil dries out.

Pears prefer a pH of 6.0. If pH is higher than 7.0, iron and manganese deficiencies may develop. If pH is too low, the tree may be more susceptible to fire blight. A healthy pear tree grows 1′-1½′ a year. If growth is less, have the foliage tested and correct any deficiencies. The Soil entry gives details on how to get foliage tested. Go easy when fertilizing with nitrogen; it encourages soft new growth that is susceptible to fire blight. If there is too much new growth on the tree, let weeds or grass grow up beneath the tree to consume excess nutrients in the soil. Zinc and boron may be deficient, especially in Western soils. Boron deficiency can cause corky tissue and pitting in the fruit. See the Apple entry for controls.

Pruning: Pear trees are tall-growing. However, you can keep all the limbs within an arm's reach of a ladder by training your young tree. How you choose to prune and train your tree will greatly affect its lifespan as well as its ability to produce large crops. Prune just before the tree breaks dormancy in spring. Or in locations where pears suffer winter bud damage, prune just after flowering.

Start training as soon as you plant your tree. Be sure to spread the branches, because pears tend to grow up, not out, if left on their own. If you develop a strong, spreading framework,

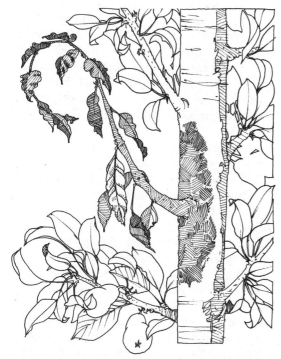

Fire blight damage. Infected blossoms appear water-soaked. Infected twigs wilt suddenly, turn brown or black, dry up, and remain attached. The hooked shoot tip is characteristic. Sunken, slightly cracked cankers may develop at the base of infected shoots.

it will be easier to prune, and the tree will bear earlier. Train European pears to a central leader system and Asian pears to an open center system. In areas where fire blight is severe, you may want to leave two main trunks as crop insurance.

To minimize fire blight attack on susceptible trees, discourage soft young growth, and make as few cuts as possible. Thin out whole branches rather than heading them back. This will reduce the total number of cuts made and won't stimulate the growth of soft, highly susceptible sideshoots. Snip off any flowers that appear in late spring or summer. They are an easy target for fire blight.

Remove unproductive and disease-susceptible suckers that sprout from the trunk and branches. As the tree gets older, you may want to leave a renewal sucker to replace a limb with four- or five-year-old spurs, or one damaged by fire blight. During the summer, select a sucker near the base of the branch to be replaced. Spread the crotch so it will develop a good outward angle. Carefully remove the old branch the next spring so the sucker will have room to develop.

Thinning: Pears are likely to set more fruit than they can handle. Fruits will be small, and the heavy fruit load may break branches or prevent flowering the following year if not thinned. A few weeks after the petals fall, remove all but one fruit per cluster. Prop up heavily laden limbs with a forked stick.

Harvesting: Pears bear in 3-5 years after planting. Pick European pears before the flesh is fully ripe; the fruit will finish ripening off the vine. To test ripeness, cut a fruit open; dark seeds indicate ripe fruit. Also, if you can pull the fruit stem away from the branch with a slight effort but without tearing the wood, the fruit is prime for harvesting. Store pears at just above 32°F. Many European cultivars store well; hard, late-bearing cultivars store better than earlier cultivars. When you're ready to eat them, place them in a 60°-70°F room to soften and sweeten. Pears that won't ripen may have been in cold storage too long, or the ripening temperature may be too high. If a pear is brown and watery inside, it was harvested too late.

Asian pears are sweetest when allowed to ripen on the tree. Watch for a color change, and taste to decide when they are ripe.

Problems: Apple maggots, cherry fruit flies, codling moths, green fruit worms, mites, and plum curculio can attack pears. For descriptions and control methods, see "Fruit Tree Insects and Diseases" on page 256. Codling moth and apple maggot damage is illustrated on page 29. Pears also attract aphids, scale, and tarnished plant bugs; see "The Top Ten Garden Insect Pests in America" on page 344 for descriptions and controls. See the Apple entry for description and control of leafrollers and other leaf-eating caterpillars.

Pear psylla is a major pest in many areas. These tiny sucking insects are nearly invisible to the naked eye. They are often noticed only when the foliage and twigs at the top of pear trees turn black in late summer. The black color is actually a sooty mold that grows in the honeydew produced by the psylla. Left uncontrolled, psylla and sooty mold can reduce fruit production or even kill the tree. Psylla also can carry and infect trees with viruslike diseases such as pear decline. Native beneficial insects can help keep psylla in check. If psylla have been a problem, spray dormant oil in early spring and again when the first green shows in the buds, to smother eggs and overwintering adults. If you see leaves developing brown edges during the season, look for sticky drops of honeydew. Examine the drops with a hand lens. If you see small, yellowish blobs with red eyes (immature stage), spray with insecticidal soap. If you don't find honeydew, or if you see small dark insects (adults) through the hand lens, add pyrethrins to the soap spray for effective control. If your tree has lots of black sooty mold, spray trees with copper fungicide after the leaves drop in fall to reduce problems the following season.

Thrips are tiny insects too small to see, but you can see their small dark droppings on leaves. Leaves will appear bleached and wilted, fruit may show scabs or russeting. Predatory mites will control thrips. Or spray with insecticidal soap, or pyrethrins as a last resort.

Pearslugs are the small sluglike larvae of sawflies. They eat leaf tissue but leave a skeleton of veins behind. Handpick, wash them off leaves with a strong water spray, or spray with insecticidal soap.

Fire blight, a bacterial disease that affects many fruit trees, is especially severe on pears. It can rapidly kill a susceptible tree or orchard in humid conditions. The sooty mold that goes with psylla can also look like fire blight. Sooty mold wipes off; fire blight doesn't. Fire blight symptoms are illustrated on page 447; control measures are described in "Fruit Tree Insects and Diseases" on page 256. Pear trees also suffer from cedar apple rust; see the Apple entry for description and controls.

Pseudomonas blight symptoms resemble fire blight, but it thrives in cool fall conditions when fire blight is less common. Control as for fire blight.

Pear scab looks much like apple scab. See the Apple entry for description and controls.

Fabraea leaf spot causes small, round, dark spots with purple margins. Leaves turn yellow and drop. Fruit develop dark, sunken spots and may be misshapen. If many leaves drop, trees are weakened, and future crops are reduced. Clean up fallen leaves each winter. If leaf spot has been a problem in the past, spray copper just before the blossoms open and again after the petals fall off.

Many viral diseases affect pears, causing leaf or fruit distortion and discoloration. Buy certified virus-free stock, and control insects such as aphids, which may transmit viruses.

Best cultivars: There are many fine pear cultivars to choose from.

'Baldwin', 'Dutchess', 'Garber', 'Orient', 'Shinko', 'Seuri', 'Starking Delicious', 'Ya-Li', 'Kieffer', 'Seckel', 'Moonglow', and 'Magness' are somewhat resistant to fire blight. The last four also produce fruit that is too hard for coddling moth larvae to attack.

'Bartlett', 'Bosc', and 'Clapp' are highly susceptible to fire blight, so avoid them if you live in an area with fire blight problems.

'Magness' doesn't produce viable pollen, so be sure to plant with two other cultivars. ❖

Pelargonium

Zonal geranium, garden geranium.
Tender perennials grown as all-season
annuals or houseplants.

Description: Flower colors include white,
pink, rose, red, and orange shades, plus starred,
edged, banded, and dotted patterns of two or
more colors. Pick from single (five-petalled) or
double forms resembling rosebuds, tulips, cactus flowers, or carnations. The rounded flower
clusters may be very dense or quite open and
airy, measuring 1″-6″ across. Geraniums normally grow 1′-2′ in a single season. Smaller
sizes include miniature (3″-5″), dwarf (6″-8″),
and semidwarf (8″-10″). Upright, mounded, and
cascading habits are available. The soft and fuzzy,
rounded, scalloped, or fingered leaves can grow
from ½″-5″ wide. Leaves may be all green,
banded in darker green, or green combined with
one or more shades of white, red, yellow, or brown.

How to grow: Buy blooming plants of
cutting-grown cultivars from a nursery, or sow
seeds in February for plants that will bloom by
summer. Plant out after all danger of frost is
past. Most prefer full sun, but shade variegated
cultivars from the hottest afternoon sun to prevent leaf browning. Geraniums adapt to most
well-drained soils with average moisture, although
they prefer sandy loam. Avoid high-nitrogen
fertilizers, which encourage leaf growth at the
expense of flowers. Pinch the tips of plants that
are reluctant to branch on their own to avoid tall,
leggy plants with leaves and flowers only toward

SPECIALTY GERANIUMS

Ivy Geraniums

Ivy geraniums (*Pelargonium peltatum*)
bring color to window boxes and baskets
throughout summer and fall. Clusters of
white, red, pink, salmon, lavender, and purple flowers bloom profusely on trailing stems
above shiny, scalloped leaves. Plants can
grow 2′-5′ in a season.

Buy plants in bloom to set in sunny
spots, but provide afternoon shade in summer. Water container plants frequently, but
don't let them stand in water. A rich, well-
drained potting mix is best, with monthly
feedings of liquid organic fertilizer. Pinch
plants back for more flowers.

Besides growing plants in the traditional
window box, try them in a raised planter or
as a flowering groundcover.

Many nurseries sell ivy geraniums only
by color, but you might ask them to offer the
'Balcon' ('Alpine') series. Also look for the
more compact hybrids between the ivy and
garden geranium.

Martha Washington Geraniums

Glamour queens of the genus *Pelargonium,* Martha Washington geraniums (*P.
× domesticum*) take the spotlight in cooler
regions, where their 6″ clusters of azalealike
flowers bloom profusely in white, pink, red,
lavender, and violet. Rounded leaves up to
8″ wide grow thickly on mounded 1′-2′
plants.

Set purchased plants in a sunny, cool
spot with good, slightly alkaline soil. They
require plenty of water while in bloom. Treat
them as true annuals and discard at season's end, or take cuttings or pot up plants
to bring indoors for winter.

Spectacular in beds, they also make
great houseplants and dazzling standards.
If you live where summers are hot, you can
still enjoy these beauties as spring pot plants,
discarding them after bloom.

Martha Washington geraniums are usually sold by color, but some specialty growers offer named cultivars.

the top. In late summer, root 4″-5″ cuttings in clean sand, or dig up your favorites and pot them before frost.

SCENTED GERANIUMS

Although not as colorful as zonal geraniums, scented geraniums (*Pelargonium* spp.) also deserve a place in your garden. A few of them bloom, producing small clusters of pink, white, or lavender flowers, but they're really grown for their fragrant foliage. Leaf form varies from tiny ½″ rounded leaves to 6″ oaklike giants, but all release their powerful aromas with a gentle rub. Habit ranges from loose, spreading plants to strong bushes reaching 4′ or more.

Scented geraniums require much the same care as zonal geraniums, but don't overfeed them or the fragrance won't be as strong. They grow well in pots of loose, well-drained soil, and their scented foliage makes them ideal houseplants. Grow them in your flower borders for a green accent, or show them off in an herb or kitchen garden.

There are many, many scented geraniums available. The following list is only a sample:

Name	Fragrance
P. crispum	Lemon
P. denticulatum	Pine
P. × fragrans	Nutmeg
P. graveolens	Rose
P. × nervosum	Lime
P. odoratissimum	Apple
P. scabrum	Apricot
P. tomentosum	Peppermint

Hybrids between these and other species have given rise to many cultivars, among them 'Grey Lady Plymouth', with rose-scented, gray-green leaves edged in white; 'Mabel Gray', with an intense lemon fragrance and sharply lobed leaves; and 'Prince Rupert Variegated', bearing small, yellow-flecked lemony foliage.

Landscape uses: Mass geraniums in beds of their own, or use them to brighten a mixed border. Plants may live for several years in pots, and look especially handsome if trained into standards. For more information on creating standards, see the Herbs entry. Fill a window box with a single color or a mixture, and brighten slightly shady corners or areas under tall trees with variegated types.

Best cultivars: The cutting-grown cultivars are far too numerous to mention; specialty catalogs list hundreds. Try to buy locally grown cultivars which are suitable for your region, especially in the humid South. Seed-grown mixes include 'Elite', 'Orbit', 'Pinto', 'Sprinter', and 'Ringo', all 1′-2′. ❖

Penstemon

Penstemon, beardtongue. Late-spring-to summer-blooming perennials; wildflowers.

Description: Penstemons produce tubular flowers with scalloped tips and a fuzzy area (beard) inside the throat. Flowers range from white to pink, red, scarlet, orange, wine, and indigo. They bloom at the ends of creeping or 1′-3′ upright stems bearing pointed, often evergreen leaves. Zones 3-8. Many penstemons are common wildflowers in the West; only a few species are native to the eastern United States.

How to grow: Plant or divide in spring in sunny, average, very well drained soil. Provide partial shade in warmer areas. Mulch with gravel or other inorganic material; organic matter holds too much moisture and will rot the crowns.

Landscape uses: Use penstemons as a filler in borders and beds and in rock gardens.

Best cultivars: *Penstemon barbatus:* 'Rose Elf', pink, 1½′; 'Prairie Fire', scarlet, 2′. *P.* 'Husker Red': reddish foliage, pink blooms, 2½′. ❖

Pepper

Capsicum annuum var. *annuum*
Solanaceae

Pepper choices—ranging from crispy sweet to fiery hot, from big and blocky to long and skinny—increase each year. This native American vegetable is second only to tomatoes as a garden favorite, and its cultivation is much the same. Peppers are also ideal for spot-planting around the garden. The brilliant colors of mature fruits, particularly those found in many hot-pepper cultivars, are especially attractive in flower beds and in container plantings. Just remember to keep sweet peppers, often called bell or green peppers, at some distance from hot ones, since the two sometimes cross-pollinate.

Planting: Choose a site with full sun for your pepper plot. Don't plant peppers where tomatoes or eggplants grew previously, because all three are members of the nightshade family and are subject to similar diseases. Make sure the soil drains well; standing water encourages root rot.

Garden centers offer a good variety of transplants, but the choices are greater when you grow peppers from seed. Pepper roots don't like to be disturbed, so plant them indoors in peat pots two months before the last frost date, sowing three seeds to a pot. Maintain the soil temperature at 75°F, and keep the seedlings moist, but not wet.

In 3-4 weeks, when the seeds sprout, move them to a sunny, warm spot, such as a south-facing window, where they can get sun for at least 5 hours a day. Once the seedlings are 2"-3" tall, thin them by leaving the strongest plant in each pot and cutting the others off at soil level.

Seedlings are ready for the garden when they are 4"-6" tall. Before moving the young plants to the garden, harden them off for about a week. To avoid disrupting the growing process when transplanting, make sure the soil temperature is at least 60°F; this usually occurs 2-3 weeks after the last frost. Transplant on a cloudy day or in the evening to reduce the danger of sun scorch; if this is not possible, provide temporary shade for the transplanted seedlings.

When buying transplants, look for ones with strong stems and dark green leaves. Pass up those with blossoms or fruit, because such plants won't produce well. Peppers take at least two months from the time the plants are set out to the time they produce fruit, so short-season growers should select early maturing cultivars.

Space transplants about 1½' apart in rows at least 2' apart, keeping in mind that most hot-pepper cultivars need less room than sweet ones. If the plot is exposed to winds, stake the plants, but put these supports in place before transplanting the seedlings to keep from damaging roots. To deter cutworms, place a cardboard collar around each stem, pushing it at least an inch into the ground. If the weather

turns chilly and rainy, protect young plants with hotcaps.

Growing guidelines: Evenly moist soil is essential to good growth, so spread a thick but light mulch, such as straw or grass clippings, around the plants. Water deeply during dry spells to encourage deep root development. Lack of water can produce bitter-tasting peppers. To avoid damaging the roots, gently pull any invading weeds by hand.

Although peppers are tropical plants, temperatures over 90°F often cause blossoms to drop and plants to wilt. To avoid this problem, plan your garden so taller plants will shade the peppers during the hottest part of the day. If you plant peppers in properly prepared soil, fertilizing usually isn't necessary. Pale leaves and slow growth, however, are a sign that the plants need a feeding of liquid fertilizer, such as manure tea. For instructions on making manure tea, see the Manure entry.

Problems: Since sprays of ground-up hot peppers can deter insects, it's logical that pests don't usually bother pepper plants. There are, however, a few exceptions. The pepper weevil, a ⅛″ long, brass-colored beetle with a brown or black snout, and its ¼″ long larva, a white worm with a beige head, chew holes in blossoms and buds, causing misshapen and discolored fruits. Prevent damage by keeping the garden free of debris. Handpick any pests that do attack; control serious infestations with pyrethrins.

Adult pepper maggots are ⅓″ long yellow flies with brown-striped wings; the white or yellow larvae are small and peg-shaped. Pepper maggots feed on the insides of fruits, causing the peppers to rot and drop off. Destroy any infected fruits. Avoid damage by protecting plants with a floating row cover.

Other occasional pests include aphids, Colorado potato beetles, flea beetles, hornworms, and cutworms. See "The Top Ten Garden Insect Pests in America" on page 344 for information on these insect pests and how to control them.

Crop rotation and resistant cultivars are your best defense against most pepper diseases. Here are some common diseases to watch for:

• Anthracnose infection causes dark, sunken, soft, and watery spots on fruits.

• Bacterial spot appears as small, yellow-green raised spots on young leaves and dark spots with light-colored centers on older leaves.

• Early blight appears as dark spots on leaves and stems; infected leaves eventually die.

• Verticillium wilt appears first on lower leaves, which turn yellow and wilt.

• Mosaic—the most serious disease—is a viral infection that mottles the leaves of young plants with dark and light splotches and eventually causes them to curl and wrinkle. Later on, mosaic can cause fruits to become bumpy and bitter.

Harvesting: Most sweet peppers become even sweeter when mature as they turn from green to bright red, yellow, or orange—or even brown or purple. Mature hot peppers offer an even greater variety of rainbow colors, often on the same plant, and achieve their best flavor when fully grown. Early in the season, however, it's best to harvest peppers before they ripen to encourage the plant to keep bearing; a mature fruit can signal a plant to stop production.

Always cut (don't pull) peppers from the plant. Pick all the fruit when a frost is predicted, or pull plants up by the roots and hang them in a dry, cool place indoors for the fruit to ripen more fully. To preserve, freeze peppers (without blanching), or dry hot types.

Best cultivars: 'Big Bertha' and 'Bell Boy', sweet, green, mature to red; 'Orobelle', sweet, large, blocky, golden when mature; 'Chocolate Bell', sweet, brown when mature, green when cooked; 'Purple Beauty', sweet, dark purple, matures to red; 'Anaheim TMR 23', mildly hot, a stuffing favorite; 'Thai Hot', 1″ long, green and red, one of the hottest. ❖

Perennials

Perennials are part of our lives, even if we're not flower gardeners. Most of us grew up with daylilies, irises, and peonies, and perennials like astilbes and hostas are familiar faces in backyard gardens. But many, less well known perennials have an exotic mystique: We may admire them, but we're not sure we'd know what to do with them in our own gardens.

Actually, most plants grown in the garden are perennial, if you consider every plant that lives more than a year, including trees and shrubs. But to most gardeners, a perennial is a plant that lives and flowers for more than one season and dies to the ground each winter.

Many perennials—including peonies, oriental poppies, and daylilies—are long-lived. Others, like coreopsis and columbines, may bloom just a few years before disappearing, but they are prolific seeders, and new seedlings keep coming back just like their longer-lived cousins. Most popular perennials fall somewhere between the two extremes, and will appear year after year with reassuring regularity.

Landscaping with Perennials

Perennials are all-purpose plants—you can grow them wherever you garden and in any part of your garden. There's a perennial to fit almost any spot in the landscape, and with a little planning, it's possible to have them in bloom throughout the frost-free months. In addition to an endless variety of sizes, shapes, colors, and plant habits, there are perennials for nearly any cultural condition your garden has to offer.

Most perennials prefer loamy soil with even moisture and full sun. Gardeners who have these conditions to offer have the widest selection of plants from which to choose. However, if you have a shaded site, there are dozens of perennials

Key Words
PERENNIALS

Perennial plant. A plant that flowers and sets seed for two or more seasons. Short-lived perennials like coreopsis and columbines may live 3–5 years. Long-lived perennials like peonies may live 100 years or more.

Tender perennial. A perennial plant from tropical or subtropical regions that can't be overwintered outside, except in subtropical regions such as Florida and Southern California. Often grown as annuals. Tender perennials include zonal geraniums, wax begonias, and coleus.

Hardy perennial. A perennial plant that tolerates frost. Hardy perennials vary in the degree of cold that they can tolerate, however, so make sure a plant is hardy in your zone before you buy it.

Herbaceous perennial. A perennial plant that dies back to the ground at the end of each growing season. Most garden perennials fall into this category.

Semiwoody perennial. A perennial plant that forms woody stems but is much less substantial than a shrub. Examples include lavender, Russian sage, and some of the thymes.

Woody perennial. A perennial plant such as a shrub or tree that does not die down to the ground each year.

for you, too. See "Best Perennials for Shade" on page 454 for a list of plants to try. For ideas for other types of sites, see "Best Perennials for Dry Soil" on page 458 and "Best Perennials for Moist Soil" on page 459.

Perennials add beauty, permanence, and seasonal rhythm to any landscape. Their yearly growth and flowering cycles are fun to follow—it's always exciting to see the first peonies push-

BEST PERENNIALS FOR SHADE

There are dozens of choice perennials to brighten a shady site. Most prefer woodland conditions: rich, moist, well-drained soil and cool temperatures. Many plants in this list grow well in partial shade. Plants that tolerate deep shade include species of *Brunnera, Cimicifuga, Epimedium, Heuchera, Hosta, Mertensia, Polygonatum,* and *Pulmonaria.* Plant name is followed by bloom time and color.

Aconitum spp. (monkshoods): summer to early fall; blue

Aquilegia spp. (columbines): spring to early summer; all colors, bicolors

Astilbe spp. (astilbes): late spring to summer; red, pink, white

Bergenia spp. (bergenias): early spring; rose, pink, purple, white

Brunnera macrophylla (Siberian bugloss): spring; light blue

Cimicifuga spp. (bugbanes): summer to fall; white

Dicentra spp. (bleeding hearts): spring; rose pink, white

Epimedium spp. (epimediums): spring; pink, red, yellow, white

Helleborus spp. (hellebores): early spring; white, rose, green, purple

Heuchera spp. (alumroots): spring to summer; pink, red, white, green

Hosta spp. (hostas): early to late summer; violet, lilac, white

Mertensia virginica (Virginia bluebells): spring; blue, white

Polemonium spp. (Jacob's ladders): spring to summer; blue, pink, white, yellow

Polygonatum spp. (Solomon's seals): spring; white, white-green

Pulmonaria spp. (lungworts): spring; purple-blue, blue, red

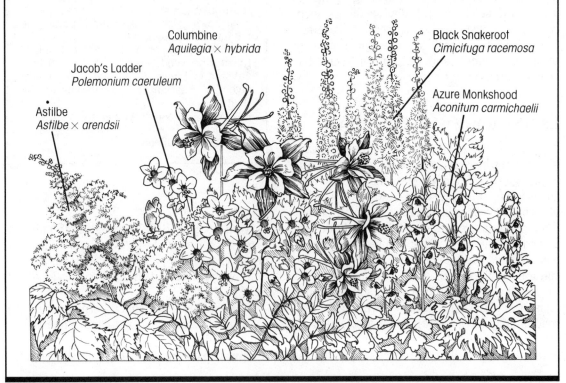

Astilbe
Astilbe × *arendsii*

Jacob's Ladder
Polemonium caeruleum

Columbine
Aquilegia × *hybrida*

Black Snakeroot
Cimicifuga racemosa

Azure Monkshood
Aconitum carmichaelii

ing out of the ground in April or the asters braving another November day. Look at your property and think about where you could add perennials. There are a number of ways to use perennials effectively in your yard.

Borders: If you have a fairly long area that could use some color, like a fence or rock wall or the side of a building, consider a perennial border. Perennial borders are the most popular way to display perennials. Group plants with similar requirements for soil, moisture, and sunlight. Also plan for pleasing color combinations and arrange them by height, form, and texture to create garden pictures. (For more on how to do this, see the Garden Design entry.)

Beds: Another way to use perennials is in beds. A bed differs from a border in that it is freestanding, without an immediate background like a fence or wall. Try beds to add color and drama to the sides of a path. You can use them to define the edge of a patio or deck. Or create an island bed in your lawn to relieve all that green with a bright splash of color. Plant the tallest plants in the center of the bed, using progressively shorter plants toward the edge.

Specimen plants: Larger perennials make

Perennials in the landscape. Most gardens have more than one ideal spot for displaying perennials. Use perennial borders to soften a fence, or set them off against a backdrop such as an outbuilding or a hedge of evergreens or shrubs. Use island beds the way you would an ornamental pool or specimen shrub—floating gracefully in the lawn. Specimen plants work like an exclamation in the landscape, drawing the eye. Choose large, dramatic-looking plants like Siberian iris (*Iris sibirica*).

striking specimen plants. You can use them in the landscape wherever you want an accent but don't want to feature something as large or heavy-looking as a shrub or tree. A large clump of peonies at the corner of the house or a spiky clump of Siberian iris at the edge of a water garden are just two of the many possibilities. You can also use specimen plants to point visitors to specific views of the yard or mark the beginning of a path. Use a bold accent like a very large-leaved hosta, such as 'Krossa Regal', at a bend in a shady garden path to attract attention and pull visitors into the garden.

Shade gardens: Turn problem shady sites where lawn grass won't grow, such as under trees or between buildings, into an asset by creating a shade garden. Many perennials tolerate shade, but remember that shade plants often have brief periods of bloom. For the most successful shade garden, you should count on the plants' foliage to carry the garden through the seasons. The most engaging shade gardens rely on combinations of large-, medium-, and small-leaved plants with different leaf textures. For example, try mixing ferns with variegated hostas, astilbes, Virginia bluebells (*Mertensia virginica*), and shade-tolerant groundcovers like Allegheny foamflower (*Tiarella cordifolia*) and creeping phlox (*Phlox stolonifera*) to create a diverse mix of size, foliage, and texture.

Bog and water gardens: If you have a low area that's always wet, you know that fighting to grow grass there is a losing battle. Instead, turn that boggy patch into a perennial bog or water garden. Some perennials will even grow with their roots submerged in the shallows. For more on making a bog or water garden, see the Bog Gardens and Water Gardens entries; Water Gardens features a bog and water garden design.

Rock gardens: If you have a rock wall that edges a bank or a dry, stony slope in full sun, you have a perfect site for a rock garden. A host of plants thrive in poor soil and relentless sunshine, including yarrows, sedums, and hens-

PERENNIALS FOR THE NORTH

These perennials flourish in the cooler summers of Northern zones and withstand cold winters to Zone 3. Species of *Campanula, Delphinium, Hemerocallis, Papaver, Penstemon, Phlox, Primula,* and *Veronica* are hardy to Zone 2. Many of these same plants will grow as far south as Zone 9, but only a few prosper under hot, humid conditions. Plant name is followed by bloom time and color.

Achillea spp. (yarrows): spring to summer; yellow, white, red
Aquilegia spp. (columbines): spring to early summer; all colors, bicolors
Campanula spp. (bellflowers): spring to summer; blue, white, purple
Cimicifuga racemosa (black snakeroot): late summer; white
Delphinium spp. (delphiniums): summer; blue, red, violet, white
Dianthus spp. (pinks): spring; pink, red, white, yellow
Dicentra spp. (bleeding hearts): spring; rose pink, white
Gypsophila spp. (baby's-breath): summer; white, pink
Hemerocallis spp. (daylilies): spring to summer; all colors except blue
Hosta spp. (hostas): early to late summer; violet, lilac, white
Iris spp. (irises): spring to summer; all colors, bicolors
Papaver orientale (Oriental poppy): early summer; scarlet
Penstemon barbatus (common beardtongue): spring; pink, white
Phlox spp. (phlox): early spring to summer; pink, white, blue
Primula spp. (primroses): spring; all colors
Rudbeckia spp. (coneflowers): summer; yellow
Sedum spp. (sedums): spring to fall; yellow, pink, white
Thermopsis spp. (false lupines): spring; yellow
Veronica spp. (speedwells): spring to summer; blue, white

and-chickens. For more on rock gardening, see the Rock Gardens entry; for a design featuring a rock garden, see the Water Gardens entry.

Containers: To add color and excitement to a deck, patio, balcony, or entryway, try perennials in containers. Mix several perennials together, combine them with annuals, or plant just a single perennial per container. Try a daylily in a half barrel in a sunny spot or hostas with variegated foliage in a shady one. Remember, containers dry out quickly, so choose plants that tolerate some dryness for best results. For more ideas, see the Container Gardening entry.

Designing with Perennials

Designing with perennials may seem overwhelming, since there are so many to choose from. But don't let yourself drift away in a sea of plant names. Chances are, your growing conditions are right for only a fraction of what's available. Let your moisture, soil, and light conditions limit the plants you choose. If you have a garden bed that gets full sun and tends toward dry soil, don't plant shade- and moisture-loving perennials like hostas and ferns. Instead, put in plants that like full sun and don't like wet feet, like daylilies and ornamental grasses. And don't forget to choose only plants that are hardy in your area.

Once you've narrowed your choices to plants that do well in your area and conditions, the key to successful design with perennials is to choose plants that look good both in and out of bloom. Unlike annuals, perennials aren't in bloom all season. Some may bloom for a month or more, but the average perennial is in bloom for 1-2 weeks. This means foliage will be in the spotlight most of the time.

Designing a perennial garden is challenging but fun. Color, form, and texture are the three main ingredients you need to begin. When you're working on your design, aim for a pleasing color scheme, but don't forget to combine
(continued on page 460)

PERENNIALS FOR THE SOUTH

These perennials stand up to the heat and humidity of Southern summers, although most benefit from partial shade in the hottest months. Species of *Achillea, Baptisia, Boltonia, Coreopsis, Echinacea, Helianthus, Hemerocallis, Hibiscus, Iris, Rudbeckia,* and *Verbena* will tolerate full Southern sun. Plant name is followed by bloom time and color.

Achillea spp. (yarrows): spring to summer; yellow, white, red
Asclepias tuberosa (butterfly weed): summer; orange
Baptisia spp. (baptisias): spring to summer; blue, white, yellow
Boltonia asteroides (boltonia): late summer; white, purple, pink
Coreopsis spp. (coreopsis): spring to summer; yellow
Echinacea spp. (purple coneflowers): summer; mauve, white
Helianthus spp. (sunflowers): late summer to fall; yellow
Hemerocallis spp. (daylilies): spring to summer; all colors except blue
Hibiscus moscheutos (common rose mallow): summer; white, pink, red
Hosta spp. (hostas): early to late summer; violet, lilac, white
Iris spp. (irises): early spring to summer; all colors
Liatris spp. (gayfeathers): summer; mauve
Liriope muscari (blue lilyturf): late summer; lilac, white
Platycodon grandiflorus (balloon flower): summer; blue, white
Rudbeckia spp. (coneflowers): summer; yellow
Salvia spp. (sages): summer to fall; all colors
Sedum spp. (sedums): spring to fall; yellow, pink, white
Verbena spp. (verbenas): spring to summer; red, pink, purple
Veronica spp. (speedwells): spring to summer; blue, white

BEST PERENNIALS FOR DRY SOIL

These tough plants tolerate heat *and* dry soil, making them useful for spots that the hose can't reach and nice for sunny meadow gardens. Some actually grow invasive and weedy in rich, moist soils, while others survive drought but suffer in humid conditions. All prefer well-drained soil. Plant name is followed by bloom time and color.

Achillea spp. (yarrows): spring to summer; yellow, white, red

Anthemis tinctoria (golden marguerite): summer; yellow, orange

Armeria maritima (common thrift): summer; pink, white

Artemisia spp. (artemisias): summer; gray, white, yellow

Baptisia spp. (baptisias): spring to summer; blue, white, yellow

Coreopsis spp. (coreopsis): spring to summer; yellow

Dianthus spp. (pinks): spring; pink, red, white, yellow

Echinops ritro (globe thistle): summer; dark blue

Eryngium spp. (sea hollies): summer; blue, silver-blue

Euphorbia spp. (spurge): spring to summer; yellow, red

Gaillardia × *grandiflora* (blanket flower): summer; red, yellow

Hemerocallis spp. (daylilies): spring to summer; all colors except blue

Kniphofia spp. (torch lilies): late spring; red, orange

Liatris scariosa (tall gayfeather): summer; purple, white

Limonium spp. (statice): summer; blue, red, white, lavender

Linum perenne (blue flax): spring; blue

Rudbeckia spp. (coneflowers): summer; yellow

Salvia spp. (sages): summer to fall; all colors

Scabiosa spp. (scabious): summer; blue, pink, yellow, white

Sedum spp. (sedums): spring to fall; yellow, pink, white

Solidago spp. (goldenrods): late summer to fall; yellow

Stachys spp. (lamb's-ears): spring; purple

Yucca spp. (yuccas): summer; white

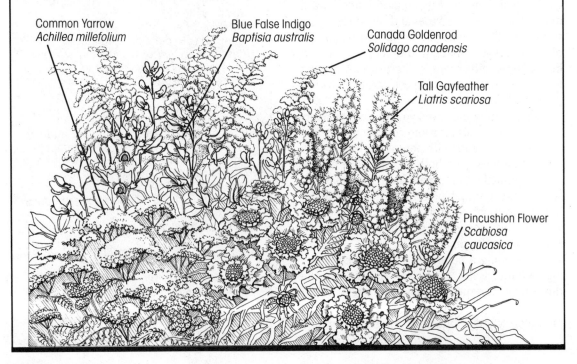

Common Yarrow
Achillea millefolium

Blue False Indigo
Baptisia australis

Canada Goldenrod
Solidago canadensis

Tall Gayfeather
Liatris scariosa

Pincushion Flower
Scabiosa caucasica

458

BEST PERENNIALS FOR MOIST SOIL

Grow these perennials if you have a poorly drained or boggy spot in your yard. True to their streamside origins, most prefer at least partial shade and cool nights. Species of *Caltha, Chelone, Filipendula, Iris, Lobelia, Lysimachia, Rodgersia,* and *Thalictrum* tolerate full sun, while *Hibiscus* and *Tradescantia* demand it. Plant name is followed by bloom time and color.

Aruncus spp. (goat's beards): late spring; creamy white

Astilbe spp. (astilbes): late spring to summer; red, pink, white

Caltha palustris (marsh marigold): spring; yellow

Chelone glabra (white turtlehead): summer; white with red tinge

Cimicifuga spp. (bugbanes): late summer to fall; white

Eupatorium spp. (bonesets): late summer to fall; purple, blue, white

Filipendula spp. (meadowsweets): summer; pink, white

Iris ensata (Japanese iris): summer; pink, blue, purple, white

Iris pseudacorus (yellow flag): early summer; yellow

Iris sibirica (Siberian iris): spring; blue, white, purple, wine red

Ligularia spp. (ligularias): summer; yellow, orange

Lobelia siphilitica (great blue lobelia): late summer; blue

Lysimachia spp. (loosestrifes): early to late summer; yellow, white

Mertensia virginica (Virginia bluebells): spring; blue, white

Monarda didyma (bee balm): summer; red, white, pink, purple

Primula japonica (Japanese primrose): late spring; pink, red, white, purple

Rodgersia spp. (rodgersias): late spring to summer; creamy white, red

Thalictrum spp. (meadow rues): summer; lilac, pink, yellow, white

Tradescantia spp. (spiderworts): summer; blue, pink, white, red

Trollius spp. (globeflowers): spring; orange, yellow

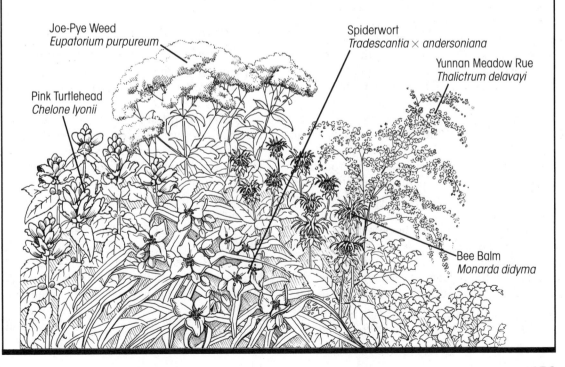

Joe-Pye Weed
Eupatorium purpureum

Pink Turtlehead
Chelone lyonii

Spiderwort
Tradescantia × andersoniana

Yunnan Meadow Rue
Thalictrum delavayi

Bee Balm
Monarda didyma

foliage textures and plant shapes to make the garden interesting all season. The focus of the garden will shift as different combinations in different parts of the garden take center stage.

You can create rhythm in your garden, which will unify the design, by repeating plants with the same color, form, height, or texture at regular intervals.

Don't be afraid to change your design if it doesn't look right, even if the plants are in place. After all, perennials are easy to move. For more on design, see the Garden Design entry.

Color: First, choose your color scheme. Perennial flowers cover the entire range from pastel to intense. Warm colors are in the red, orange, and yellow range. These are bright and bold. Visually, they come forward or jump out at you. Cool colors are the greens, blues, and purples. They are softer, more subtle, and have a calming effect. They retreat from the eye; they seem farther away.

If your garden is distant from your viewing point, choose brighter colors or create more contrast. If you will view the garden at close range, choose a more subtle or harmonious scheme. Create the illusion of depth in a small or shallow garden by using blue and purple flowers toward the back. To add excitement, use bright colors or add a dash of red to a more subdued combination.

Form: Form is the next thing to consider when choosing plants. You'll get the most pleasing composition if you combine flat, rounded, and spiky forms. Consider the shape of the leaves and the flowers. A Siberian iris has stiff, straplike foliage and creates a vertical accent with its spiky form. When the iris blooms, however, the masses of flat flowers give the iris a rounded look. You can use both forms to create a changing look in the garden, but remember that the foliage will dominate during most of the season. Use the iris where you need vertical accent most.

When thinking of overall form, don't forget plant height. Height affects the form of the garden as a whole as well as the forms of individual plants. The general rule is to place low plants at the front of the border, and work upward to tall plants as you go to the back of the planting. This is a good rule to start with, but to add interest, vary plant heights by pulling some tall plants toward the middle of the planting. Spiky forms or other vertical plants like lilies or phlox are best for this.

Texture: Texture is also extremely important. Use the rich diversity of perennial leaf shapes and sizes to add interest when plants aren't in bloom. Think of the rounded, deeply veined leaves of hostas, the straplike leaves of daylilies, the lustrous lobed leaves of peonies, and the ferny foliage of threadleaf coreopsis. Remember that the form and texture of the plants will carry the garden through most of the season. You can also use foliage as a backdrop to display other plants—like low candytuft washing around a clump of daylilies.

Planting Perennials

Because perennials live a long time, it's important to get them off to a good start. Proper soil preparation and care at planting time will be well rewarded.

Soil preparation: The majority of perennials commonly grown in beds or borders require evenly moist, humus-rich soil of pH 5.5-6.5. A complete soil analysis from your local extension office or a soil-testing lab will give you a starting point. For more on soils and soil testing, see the Soil entry.

Double digging is the best way to prepare a perennial bed. Despite the difficulty of the task, the rewards are unparalleled. Plants' roots will be able to penetrate the friable soil easily, creating a strong, vigorous root system. Water and nutrients will also move easily through the soil, and the bed won't dry out as fast. As a result,

PERENNIALS WITH STRIKING FOLIAGE

Most perennials bloom for only a few weeks, so it makes sense to think about what they'll look like the rest of the season. These dual-purpose perennials have especially interesting foliage when not in flower. Try species of *Ajuga, Asarum, Bergenia, Epimedium, Hosta, Lamium, Liriope, Saxifraga, Sedum, Sempervivum, Stachys,* and *Tiarella* as groundcovers in place of grass. Plant name is followed by foliage interest.

Acanthus spp. (bear's-breeches): shiny; lobed or heart-shaped; spiny

Ajuga reptans (ajuga): striking variegations and colors

Alchemilla mollis (lady's-mantle): maplelike; chartreuse

Artemisia spp. (artemisias): silver or gray; aromatic; ferny

Asarum spp. (wild ginger): leathery; glossy; dark green

Bergenia spp. (bergenias): glossy; evergreen; burgundy fall color

Heuchera spp. (alumroots): dark purple to green; lobed; basal

Hosta spp. (hostas): many colors; smooth; puckered; variegated

Houttuynia cordata (houttuynia): heart-shaped; shiny; variegated forms

Lamiastrum galeobdolon (yellow archangel): heart-shaped; green and white variegated

Lamium spp. (lamiums): green-, yellow-, white-variegated

Polygonatum odoratum (Solomon's seal): long, graceful shoots; variegated forms

Pulmonaria spp. (lungworts): dark green; gray- or silver-spotted

Rodgersia spp. (rodgersias): huge; maplelike or buckeyelike; bronze

Saxifraga stolonifera (strawberry geranium): silver-veined; reddish undersides

Sedum spp. (sedums): fleshy; many colors; variegated forms

Sempervivum spp. (hens-and-chickens): fleshy rosettes, some red-tinged

Stachys byzantina (lamb's-ears): white, gray-green, yellow; velvety

Tiarella cordifolia (Allegheny foamflower): heart-shaped; bronze; evergreen

Yucca spp. (yuccas): sharply pointed; large; evergreen

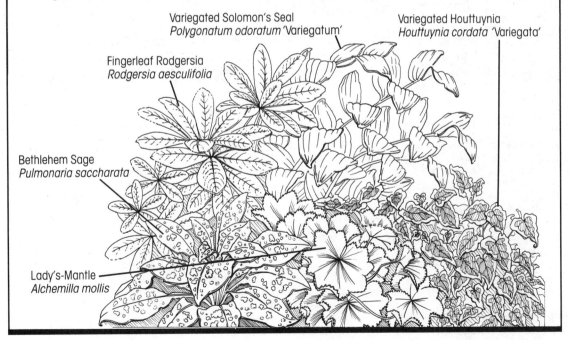

Variegated Solomon's Seal
Polygonatum odoratum 'Variegatum'

Variegated Houttuynia
Houttuynia cordata 'Variegata'

Fingerleaf Rodgersia
Rodgersia aesculifolia

Bethlehem Sage
Pulmonaria saccharata

Lady's-Mantle
Alchemilla mollis

your plants will thrive. Have the necessary soil amendments and organic fertilizer on hand before you start. For more on this technique, see the Double Digging entry.

If you can't double dig before you plant, turn the soil evenly to a shovel's depth at plant-ing time. Thoroughly incorporate appropriate soil amendments and fertilizer as required. Break up all clods and smooth out the bed before planting.

Planting: Plant perennials any time the soil is workable. Spring and fall are best for most

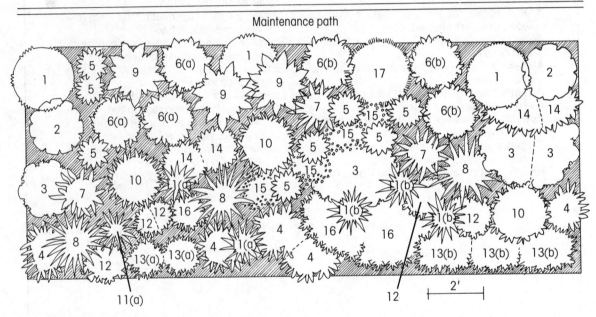

A sunny perennial border. This simple but beautiful flower border has drama and two-season interest. It's a blaze of color from early summer to frost.

1. New England aster (*Aster novae-angliae*)
2. 'Autumn Joy' sedum (*Sedum* × 'Autumn Joy')
3. 'Moonshine' yarrow (*Achillea* × 'Moonshine')
4. Ozark sundrops (*Oenothera missouriensis*)
5. Spike gayfeather cultivar (*Liatris spicata*), mauve-flowered
6. Garden phlox cultivar (*Phlox paniculata*)
   (a) purple-flowered
   (b) white-flowered
7. Balloon flower (*Platycodon grandiflorus*)
8. Daylily cultivar (*Hemerocallis* hybrid), yellow-flowered
9. Purple coneflower (*Echinacea purpurea*)
10. Peony cultivar (*Paeonia lactiflora*), white-flowered
11. Siberian iris cultivar (*Iris sibirica*)
    (a) blue-flowered
    (b) purple-flowered
12. Columbine cultivar (*Aquilegia* × *hybrida*), yellow-flowered
13. Blood red cranesbill cultivar (*Geranium sanguineum*)
    (a) white-flowered
    (b) pink-flowered
14. Obedient plant cultivar (*Physostegia virginiana*), white-flowered
15. Baby's-breath (*Gypsophila paniculata*)
16. Catmint (*Nepeta mussinii*)
17. Switchgrass (*Panicum virgatum*)

Smart Shopping
PERENNIALS

Smart shopping begins at home. Make a list of the plants you intend to buy, then stick to it. You may have to put on blinders to keep from carting home everything in the garden center! Otherwise, you might set out to buy a peony and return home with a carload of mixed plants that looked good in the store, but have no place in your garden.

At the Garden Center

Buying at a garden center has an advantage: You can see what you're getting. Many have display gardens where you can see the mature sizes of the plants. The plants will be larger than those available by mail, and they will become established more quickly. But your selection may be limited. Here are some tips to keep in mind when buying plants at garden centers:

● The best selection is available in spring.

● If you want a specific color, buy a named cultivar.

● Avoid plants that are visibly rootbound. Check the root systems of plants that are leggy or disproportionately large in relation to the size of the pot.

● Choose plants with lush, nicely colored foliage and multiple stems. Avoid plants with dry, pale, or shriveled leaves.

● Check for insects on the tops and undersides of leaves and along stems.

● When buying in the fall, plants will look rough. They have probably been sitting on the bench all summer. Check the root system first. If it is in good shape, the plant is likely to be healthy.

● If you can't plant immediately, keep containers well watered. Check them daily!

Mail-Order Nurseries

Mail-ordering requires trust, since you can't examine the plants until you have purchased them. Start small. Order from a few nurseries at a time until you get the quality you want. Some nurseries ship in containers; others ship bareroot. If you live in the North, specify shipping times when ordering from Southern nurseries. If you don't, they may ship your plants in spring before the ground is ready to be worked, or after the ground has frozen in fall. If a nursery sells bareroot plants, order them in fall. Some plants such as irises, peonies, and poppies are only available in the fall. To get the most from mail-ordering:

● Order early for the best selection.

● Specify desired shipping time when ordering.

● Once they arrive, evaluate containerized mail-order plants in the same way you would evaluate plants at the garden center. Remember that shipping is hard on foliage: The leaves may be broken or bruised. Don't worry—if the plants are healthy, they will recover quickly.

● Examine bareroot plants for pests and diseases. Check the roots, crowns, and stems for hidden pests or signs of pest damage.

● If roots on bareroot plants are not plentiful and in good condition, return the plants.

● Rewrap bareroot plants after examination and store in a cool place until you are ready to plant them.

● Before planting, soak roots of bareroot plants in a bucket of water for a minimum of 1 hour.

● Make all claims of substandard or damaged plants to the supplier immediately.

● Avoid special deals, unbeatable bargains, and unbelievable claims of grandeur. If it sounds too good to be true, it usually is. However, reputable nurseries sometimes offer collections of perennials that are excellent buys (but not *unbelievable* buys).

Perennials from Seed

If you have more time and patience than money to spend on your perennials, buying seed is smart shopping. A packet of seed is much cheaper than the equivalent number of purchased plants (or even one plant!). In exchange for a good buy, though, you must be willing to forgo instant gratification. You'll need to set up a cold frame or nursery bed and care for your seedlings for 2–3 years before they reach blooming size. For more on growing from seed, see the Seeds and Seedlings entry.

plants. If plants arrive before you are ready to plant them, be sure to care for them properly until you can get them in the ground.

Planting is easy in freshly turned soil. Choose an overcast day whenever possible. Avoid planting during the heat of the day. Place container-grown plants out on the soil according to your design. To remove the plants, invert containers and knock the bottom of the pot with your trowel. The plant should fall out easily. The roots will be tightly intertwined. It's vital to loosen the roots—by pulling them apart or even cutting four slashes, one down each side of the root mass—so they'll spread strongly through the soil when planted out. Clip any roots that are bent, broken, or circling. Make sure you place the crown of the plant at the same depth at which it grew in the pot.

Planting bareroot perennials and transplants requires more care. Inspect the roots carefully and prune off any irregularities. Dig a hole large enough to accommodate the full spread of the roots. Build a mound with tapering sides in the center of the hole. Spread the roots of fibrous-rooted plants evenly over the mound and rest the crown of the plant at its apex. Check to be sure that the crown will end up just below the soil surface. Build up the mound to raise the crown if necessary. Do not plant too deeply!

Position rhizomes such as those of iris at or just below the surface, depending on the species. Spread the roots evenly over a mound of soil as described above. Spread tuberous roots like those of daylilies evenly in a similar fashion. Fill in the planting hole with soil, then firm it down and add more soil if necessary before you water the new plant.

Water plants thoroughly after planting so the soil is completely settled around the roots. Give your newly planted perennials a layer of organic mulch to conserve soil moisture. Provide extra water for the first month or so while plants are becoming established.

Maintaining Your Perennials

Perennials benefit from some regular care throughout the growing season. In return, they'll reward you with strong growth and vigorous flowering year after year.

Weeding: Weeds compete for water, nutrients, and light, so weeding is a necessary evil. Catch them while they're small and the task will seem easier. A light mulch of bark or shredded leaves allows water to infiltrate and keeps weeds down. Mulch also helps soil retain water.

Watering: Regular watering is essential. Most plants need 1″ per week for best growth. Bog and pond plants require a continual supply of water. Dry-soil plants are more tolerant of a low water supply, but during the hottest summer months, even they may need watering. Water all your perennials with a soaker hose where possible. If using aboveground irrigation, avoid watering during the heat of the day when the water evaporates quickly, and mulch to conserve soil moisture and cut down on watering.

Staking: Staking may be necessary for thin-stemmed plants such as coreopsis, yarrow, and garden phlox. Extremely tall plants such as delphiniums require sturdy stakes to keep flower spikes from snapping off. Heavy, mounding flowers like peonies may need hoop supports (circular wire supports set up on legs) to keep their faces out of the mud. You can also stake up a clumping perennial by circling the clump with twine, then tying the twine to a sturdy stake. For more ideas, see the Staking entry.

Pinching: Pinching keeps plants bushy. Plants like chrysanthemums and asters have a tendency to grow tall and flop. Pinch them once or twice in the spring to encourage production of side shoots. Early pinching promotes compact growth without sacrificing bloom.

Thinning: Plants like delphiniums and phlox produce so many stems that the growth becomes crowded and vigor is reduced. Cut out excess stems to increase air circulation and promote larger flowers on the remaining stems.

Disbudding: Disbudding is another technique used to increase flower size. Peonies and chrysanthemums produce many buds around each main bud. Simply pinch off all but the largest bud to improve your floral display.

Deadheading: Removing spent flowers will help promote production of new buds in many plants. Just pinch or cut off faded flowers, or shear bushy plants just below the flower heads if the plant blooms at once. Some perennials like baptisias and 'Autumn Joy' sedum will not rebloom, and their seed heads are decorative. Leave these for winter interest in the garden.

Winterizing: In autumn, begin preparing the perennial garden for winter. Remove dead foliage and old flowers. After the first frost, cut down dead stems and remove other growth that will die to the ground. (Leave ornamental grasses and other plants that add winter interest.) After the ground freezes, protect plants from root damage from frost heaving with a thick mulch of oak leaves or marsh hay. Evergreen boughs are also good for this purpose. Snow is the best insulator of all, but most of us can't count on continuous snow cover. Mulching helps keep the ground frozen during periods of warm weather.

Dividing: Sooner or later, even the slow-growing perennials become crowded and need dividing. Divide plants in spring or fall in the North and in the fall in the South. (Some plants such as peonies should only be dug in the fall.) Some fast growers like bee balms, chrysanthemums, and asters should be lifted every 2-3 years. They have a tendency to die out in the middle, while new growth forms a circle of growth around the old center of the clump. Lift the plants in spring or fall to cut away any old or dead growth. Take advantage of the bare spot to work the soil, adding compost and fertilizer. Replant the rejuvenated clump in the center of the freshly worked planting hole.

Lift and pull or cut apart overgrown clumps of irises, daylilies, and hostas. You'll know a clump is overgrown because it looks crowded, doesn't have as large or as many blooms as it used to, and may have died out in the center. You may need to separate large clumps with a shovel; see the Division entry for more on this technique. Replant a reasonably sized clump or group of clumps into freshly prepared soil.

Controlling pests and diseases: On the whole, perennials are tough, durable plants, but they're not completely problem-free. The best way to avoid problems is to give plants the conditions they need to thrive. If you plant a moisture-loving bog plant in a dry, windy site, you're asking for trouble. Poor or inappropriate growing conditions stress plants, and a stressed perennial is more likely to lose the struggle against an invading pest or ailment.

If you know that a perennial is prone to a certain problem, either choose another species or look for a resistant cultivar. Garden phlox (*Phlox paniculata*), for instance, is mildew-prone, and there's nothing like powdery mildew to ruin the appearance of a plant. The best way to avoid this is to plant cultivars of a similar but mildew-resistant species, wild sweet William (*Phlox maculata*). If you must have garden phlox or other mildew-prone perennials, plant in a sunny site with good air circulation, thin plants to the strongest 4-5 shoots so air can circulate in the clump, water from the bottom to keep the foliage dry, and never water at night.

Similarly, when confronted by a pest, start at the low end of the control spectrum rather than rushing for the sprayer. Handpicking insects may not be pleasant, but it's often effective. A simple soap spray will control most pests. If a pest is a major problem on the same perennial every year, it's better to replace it with one of the many pest-free perennials rather than waging a time-consuming and discouraging battle again each season. For more on organic pest and dis-

More On
PERENNIALS

You'll find descriptions, growing and landscaping tips, and best cultivars in individual entries for these perennials: Achillea (yarrow), Anemone, Aquilegia (columbine), Arabis (rock cress), Armeria (thrift), Artemisia, Asarum (wild ginger), Asclepias (milkweed), Aster, Astilbe, Baptisia, Begonia, Bergenia, Campanula (bellflower), Centaurea (cornflower), Chrysanthemum, Cimicifuga (bugbane), Coreopsis, Delphinium, Dianthus (pinks), Dicentra (bleeding heart), Dictamnus (gas plant), Digitalis (foxglove), Echinacea (purple coneflower), Echinops (globe thistle), Euphorbia (spurge), Fuchsia, Gaillardia (blanket flower), Geranium, Geum, Gypsophila (baby's-breath), Helianthus (sunflower), Helleborus (hellebore), Hemerocallis (daylily), Heuchera (alumroot), Hibiscus (mallow), Hosta, Iberis (candytuft), Iris, Kniphofia (torch lily), Liatris (gayfeather), Ligularia, Linum (flax), Lobelia, Lupinus (lupine), Lychnis (campion), Lysimachia (loosestrife), Lythrum (purple loosestrife), Malva (mallow), Mertensia (bluebells), Monarda (bee balm), Nepeta (catmint), Nymphaea (water lily), Oenothera (evening primrose), Paeonia (peony), Papaver (poppy), Penstemon (beardtongue), Phlox, Platycodon (balloon flower), Primula (primrose), Ranunculus (buttercup), Rudbeckia (coneflower), Salvia (sage), Scabiosa (pincushion flower), Solidago (goldenrod), Thalictrum (meadow rue), Tradescantia (spiderwort), Verbascum (mullein), Veronica (speedwell), Viola (violet), and Yucca.

There are many ways to enjoy perennials outside of traditional flower gardens. You can find some of them in the Cut Flower Gardening, Dried Flower Gardening, Ferns, Flower Arranging, Grasses, Meadow Gardens, and Shade Gardening entries.

---

ease control techniques, see the Organic Pest Management entry.

Propagating Perennials

Time and patience are the only requirements for growing your own perennials. Seeds take longer to produce flowering plants than cuttings, but not all perennials can be grown from cuttings. Of course, you can propagate by cutting apart established clumps of perennials. This technique, called division, is described in "Dividing" on page 465.

Seeds: Perennial seeds are available from most major seed companies, though some offer a wider variety than others. Plant societies often have seed exchanges. You can also save seeds of your own plants and trade with friends. Note: Most cultivars cannot be produced from seed. They must be propagated by cuttings or division.

If you leave seed heads to mature in the garden, you'll get self-sown seedlings. Transplant these to appropriate spots or trade them with friends. For more on growing plants from seed, see the Seeds and Seedlings entry.

Cuttings: Cuttings are a quick and easy way to increase a perennial. Unlike seed, which produces seedlings genetically different from the parent plants, all cuttings taken from a single plant will be identical to the parent plant. Take cuttings in late spring or early summer for best results. Cut a 3"-6" section from the stem and strip the leaves off the lower half of the cutting. If the leaves are large, cut them in half. Stick the cuttings in a 1:1 mixture of peat and perlite. Keep them in a high-humidity environment for 1-2 weeks or until they are well rooted. Transplant them to pots or directly into the garden. To learn how to grow cuttings in a nursery bed, see "Smart Shopping: Make a Nursery Bed" on page 262. For more on this technique, see the Cuttings entry. ❖

Permaculture

Combining the best of natural landscaping, edible landscaping, and xeriscaping, permaculture aims for a site that sustains itself *and* the gardener. The ultimate purpose of permaculture is to develop a site until it meets all the needs of its inhabitants, including food, shelter, fuel, and entertainment. While it's the rare home gardener who can follow permaculture principles to that degree, most can borrow ideas from permaculture to create a new way of landscaping based on usefulness.

Permaculture emphasizes use of plants that are native or well adapted to your local area. Plant things you like, but make sure they have a purpose and somehow benefit the landscape. Plants such as berry bushes provide food; others such as nitrogen-fixing Russian olive (*Eleagnus angustifolia*) improve the soil. Beauty and fragrance also deserve consideration but are secondary to tangible benefits. Instead of a border of flowering shrubs, for instance, a permaculture site would have a raspberry or blackberry border.

Disease-prone plants such as hybrid tea roses, or those that require excessive amounts of water or other human input, are not good permaculture candidates. Choose a native persimmon tree that doesn't need spraying and pruning, for example, instead of a high-upkeep peach tree. Work with the materials already on the site, rather than trucking in topsoil or stone. Consider the natural inclinations of your site along with the needs of its inhabitants, and put as much of your site as possible to use. Remember that a permaculture design is never finished, because the plants within a site are always changing.

There is no set formula for developing a permaculture design, but there are practical guidelines. Here are some of them:

• Copy nature's blueprint and enhance it with useful plants and animals. In nature, the canopies of tall trees give way to smaller ones, flanked by large and small shrubs and, finally,

More On
PERMACULTURE

The word *permaculture* was coined in the mid-1970s by Australians Bill Mollison and David Holmgren. To learn more about theory and practice, see Mollison's *Permaculture: A Practical Guide for a Sustainable Future*. Try inquiring about permaculture organizations in your area at nurseries that specialize in native plants. The Edible Landscaping and Natural Landscaping entries also offer ideas for creating a more useful and sustainable home landscape.

by the smallest plants. This natural pattern provides for the greatest diversity of plants. Fruiting shrubs, such as autumn olives or currants, and native grasses, such as beargrass, can be used to create an edge habitat.

• Stack plants into guilds. A guild includes plants with compatible roots and canopies that might be stacked in layers to form an edge. As you learn more about your site, you'll discover groups of plants that work well together. For example, pines, dogwoods, and wild blueberries form a guild for acid soil.

• Make use of native plants and others adapted to the site. Plan for diversity.

• Divide your yard into zones based on use. Place heavily used features, such as an herb garden, in the most accessible zones.

• Identify microclimates in your yard and use them appropriately. Cold, shady corners, windswept places in full sun, and other microclimates present unique opportunities. For instance, try sun-loving herbs like creeping thyme on rocky outcroppings; plant elderberries in poorly drained spots. ❖

Persimmon

Diospyros kaki (Asian); *D. virginiana*
(American)
Ebenaceae

Persimmons are attractive trees with large, leathery leaves that turn bright colors in the fall. The bright orange fruit often hangs on the branches long after the leaves drop. Persimmon fruit can be very astringent before the fruit is mushy-ripe, but some cultivars can be enjoyed while firm. The Fruit Trees entry covers many important aspects of growing persimmons and other tree fruits; refer to it for additional information on planting, pruning, and care.

Selecting trees: American persimmons are hardy to −25°F, bear small fruit, and grow to 40'. Most bear better crops if you have two trees. Buy named cultivars for reliable fruit. 'Meader' has only female flowers and bears seedless fruit if not cross-pollinated. Asian persimmons are hardy to 0°F, bear large fruit, and grow to 30', and most are self-pollinating. Buy young persimmon trees, because older trees have long taproots and don't transplant well. Also check whether you are buying an astringent or non-astringent cultivar.

Planting and care: Persimmons bloom late and usually avoid frost damage. They tolerate a wide range of soils but perform best in fertile, well-drained soil. Give Asian persimmons a sheltered location. Space trees 20' apart to avoid crowding. Persimmons need little fertilizer. A thick organic mulch will conserve water and supply plenty of nitrogen for new growth.

Pruning: Persimmons require only light pruning, but if you want to keep them small, prune each spring before bud break. Train your tree to a central leader as shown on page 253. Cut back long shoots to an outward-facing bud or branch. Spread new scaffolds when they are young to make them stronger and to reduce upward growth. Persimmons flower on current season's wood. Encourage new growth by cutting out old branches periodically and allowing new ones to replace them. Head back longer branches to encourage side branches.

Persimmons produce a lot of root suckers. If not removed, they will form a dark, crowded thicket. Discourage suckers by spreading a thick layer of organic mulch such as compost over the root zone. Avoid cultivating or tramping over the roots, and remove suckers whenever you see them.

Thinning: Young trees may drop immature fruit. However, if an older tree continues to drop fruit, the tree is probably suffering from some kind of stress. Check nutrient levels, winter temperatures, and the severity of your pruning. On Asian cultivars, you may need to hand-thin to encourage larger fruits; American cultivars bear only small fruit.

Problems: Persimmons are reasonably pest-free in the home garden. They can be troubled by scale and borers, and by persimmon psylla and citrus mealybug in the South. See the Pear entry for information on psylla. "Fruit Tree Insects and Diseases" on page 256 and "The Top Ten Garden Insect Pests in America" on page 344 provide descriptions and control measures for other problems. In areas where persimmon wilt is a problem, plant Asian cultivars, which are resistant.

Paint the trunk and main branches with diluted white latex paint to prevent sunscald. If your tree often fruits every other year, you need to thin the fruit more heavily so the tree is not over-stressed.

Harvesting: Persimmons mature in mid-fall. Use pruning shears to clip off the ripe fruits when they are still slightly firm. Let astringent cultivars get very soft before eating. Non-astringent cultivars can be eaten while firm. Ripening often coincides with frost, but chilling is not essential for softening and sweetening. Freezing or drying can remove astringency. Or ripen fruit by putting it in a bag with an apple for a few days. ❖

Pesticides

Sulfur and certain botanical insecticides have been used for centuries, but widespread use of synthetic pesticides is a relatively recent phenomenon. The effects of massive releases of these chemicals on human health and environmental quality is of increasing concern.

The best-known example of the hidden hazards of pesticide use is DDT. This synthetic insecticide was first used extensively during World War II. It appeared to be an effective, inexpensive solution to insect problems. DDT virtually eliminated malaria from parts of the world, and it was hailed as a "wonder insecticide." Other synthetic pesticides quickly followed.

Few people stopped to consider the possible negative side effects. DDT is a nonselective poison. It is very stable and remains poisonous for years. Over time, DDT moved through the food chain and finally ended up concentrated at the highest level—in eagles and other birds of prey. The dramatic result, eggshells so weak that they were crushed before they could hatch, caught the public's attention.

The banning of DDT in the United States on January 1, 1973, marked the beginnings of change. Since then, many studies have documented human health hazards and environmental contamination due to pesticide use. Since pesticides are tested for toxicity to mammals, not to birds or other animals, it is hard to tell what side effects they may have—another reason for avoiding them altogether.

Other problems with widespread dependence on pesticides have also become apparent. Insecticides kill not only pests but also their natural enemies. Some pests have only become a problem since widespread pesticide use. Important pollinators such as bees are also killed. After repeated use, pests develop resistance, and newer, stronger poisons are required.

These concerns, as well as increased costs of synthetic pesticide production and regulation, have led researchers to look for safer, less toxic solutions to pest problems—just as organic gardeners have been doing for years.

Organic gardeners refuse to use synthetic pesticides because of their many health and environmental hazards. Proper cultural methods and sanitation make the routine use of pesticides unnecessary. See the Organic Pest Management entry for more information.

As a last resort, certain naturally occurring elements and plant extracts with pesticidal properties are acceptable. These compounds are considered safer than synthetic chemicals because they break down rapidly into nontoxic substances, so they will not accumulate in organisms or in the environment. For details on acceptable organic pesticides, see the Fungicides, Herbicides, and Insecticides entries.

Pesticide Safety

Some natural pesticides are very toxic, and any control can be damaging if not used properly. Keep the following points in mind:

• Keep all pesticides in original containers with product name and instructions. Read the label. Those marked "Danger" are super toxic, "Warning" very toxic, and "Caution" moderately or mildly toxic.

• Store pesticides tightly closed and away from food and out of reach of children.

• Mix and apply exactly according to directions. Measure carefully, and keep a set of measures just for mixing pesticides.

• Wear protective clothing when mixing, applying, and cleaning up. This may include a long-sleeved shirt and pants, rubber boots, rubber or other waterproof gloves, goggles, and a dust mask or respirator. Read the label for requirements.

• Wash clothing, skin, containers, and sprayers thoroughly when cleaning up.

• Stay out of treated areas until spray is dry or dust has settled. ❖

Petunia

Garden petunia. Summer- and fall-blooming annuals.

Description: Petunias bear abundant 2"-4", often-fragrant trumpets in white, pink, rose, red, yellow, blue, and purple. Single or double-flowered cultivars may have lacy or starred shapes and ruffled or smooth margins. Most grow upright or mounded to 1' tall. Smallish, sticky leaves are unremarkable.

How to grow: Indoors, sow the minute seeds in late winter or early spring for planting out after frost, or choose from the wide selection of bedding plants at garden centers. At 3"-4", pinch out the centers to promote bushiness, even if the plants are in bloom. Grow petunias in full sun or with some afternoon shade in average soil and moisture. They tolerate drought very well, and pests rarely bother them. Cut the plants back hard in midsummer if they grow tall and straggly, and give them a little extra water and fertilizer. They will bloom again in fall. Take cuttings of favorites and overwinter them indoors in a warm, bright spot.

Landscape uses: Grow petunias in beds, borders, pots, hanging baskets, and window boxes. Let them tumble over rocks or a tree stump. Small-flowered blue-purple petunias add a lovely soft touch to the front of the perennial border; they'll self-sow if flowers are allowed to mature in fall. Petunias will look tired by late summer, so grow them where other plants can take over while they recover.

Best cultivars: The 'Cascade' series, including lovely 'Super Cascade Lilac', are perfect for hanging baskets. All-America Selections Winner 'Purple Pirouette' is double with a white edge. Grandifloras (3"-4" flowers): single 'Daddy' and 'Countdown'; double 'Fanfare'. Multifloras (vigorous plants with many 2½" flowers): single 'Polo'; double 'Bonanza'. Floribundas (many 3"-4" flowers): 'Celebrity', 'Madness', and 'Primetime', all single. All of these are mixes. ❖

pH

Soil acidity or alkalinity affects plant growth by influencing the chemical availability of the nutrients in soil for uptake by plants. The measure of acidity or alkalinity, expressed as a number, is called pH. Many gardening books and catalogs list the preferred pH for specific plants. The good news for gardeners is that, with a few exceptions, most plants will tolerate a fairly wide range of soil pH. "The pH Scale" on the opposite page shows how pH values relate to soils.

Nutrient uptake and pH: Plant roots absorb mineral nutrients such as nitrogen and iron when they are dissolved in water. If the soil solution (the mixture of water and nutrients in the soil) is too acid or alkaline, some nutrients won't dissolve easily, and so are unavailable for uptake.

Most nutrients that plants need are readily available when the pH of the soil solution ranges from 6.0 to 7.5. Below pH 6.0, some nutrients, such as nitrogen, phosphorus, and potassium, are less available. When pH exceeds 7.5, iron, manganese, and phosphorus are less available.

Regional differences: Many environmental factors, including amount of rainfall, vegetation type, and temperature, can affect soil pH. In general, areas with heavy rainfall and forest cover such as the Eastern states and the Pacific Northwest have moderately acid soils. Soils in regions with light rainfall and prairie cover such as the Midwest tend to be near neutral. Droughty areas of the western United States tend to have alkaline soils. However, the pH of cultivated and developed soils often differs from that of native soil. During construction, topsoil is frequently removed and may be replaced by a different type of soil. So your garden soil pH could be different from that of a friend's garden across town.

Changing pH: Most horticultural plants grow well in slightly acid to neutral soil (pH 6.0-7.0). Some common exceptions include blueberries, potatoes, and rhododendrons, which prefer moderately acid soil. You can make small

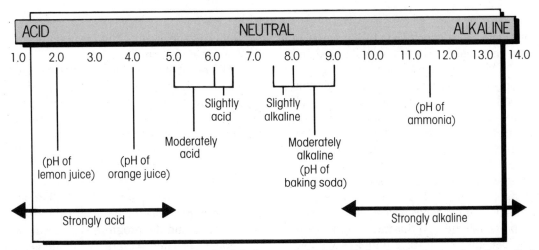

The pH scale. The pH scale ranges from 1.0 to 14.0. Soils are called acid or alkaline, but the degree of acidity or alkalinity in soils is not great enough to pose any hazard to humans. Most soils are less acidic than orange juice and less alkaline than baking soda. Gardeners generally refer to alkaline soils as "sweet" and acid soils as "sour."

changes to soil pH by applying soil amendments. However, you'll have best success if you select plants that are adapted to your soil pH and other soil characteristics. Adding organic matter to the soil also tends to make both acid and alkaline soils more neutral.

If you have your soil analyzed by a lab, the lab report will include soil pH. See the Soil entry for information on how to sample your soil and have it tested. You can also test soil pH yourself with a home soil test kit or a portable pH meter. Home kits and portable meters vary in accuracy but can be helpful in assessing the general pH range of your soil.

The quantity of liming or acidifying material needed to change soil pH depends on many factors, including current pH, soil texture, and the type of material. A soil lab report will contain recommendations on types and quantities of amendments to use.

You can spread liming or acidifying materials with a garden spreader or by hand for small areas. If hand-spreading, be sure to wear heavy gloves to protect your skin.

Correcting acid soil: If your soil is too acid, you must add alkaline material, a process

commonly called liming. The most common liming material is ground limestone. There are two types: calcitic limestone (calcium carbonate) and dolomitic limestone (calcium-magnesium carbonate). In most instances, you'll use calcitic lime. Apply dolomitic lime only if your soil also has a magnesium deficiency.

Ground limestone breaks down slowly in the soil. Apply it to the garden and lawn in the fall to allow time for it to act on soil pH before the next growing season. A rule of thumb for slightly acidic soils is to apply 5 lb. of lime per 100 square feet to raise pH by one point. In general, sandy soils will need less limestone to change pH; clay soils will need more.

The amount of lime you must add to correct pH depends not only on your soil type but also on its initial pH. For example, applying 5 lb. of limestone per 100 square feet will raise the pH of a sandy loam soil from 6.0 to 6.5. It would take 10 lb. per 100 square feet to make the same change in a silty loam soil. However, if 5.6 was the initial pH of the soil, 8 lb. per 100 square feet would be required for the sandy loam soil, and 16 lb. per 100 square feet for the silty loam soil. There is no simple rule of thumb that applies to all soils. The safest approach to take if you plan to apply limestone is to have your soil tested and follow the lab recommendations.

Applying wood ashes also will raise soil pH. Wood ashes contain up to 70 percent calcium carbonate, as well as potassium, phosphorus, and many trace minerals. Because it has a very fine particle size, wood ash is a fast-acting liming material. Use it with caution, because over-applying it can create serious soil imbalances. Limit applications to 25 lb. per 1,000 square feet, and only apply ashes once every 2-3 years in any particular area. At this rate, your soil will get the benefits of the trace minerals without adverse effects on pH.

Correcting alkaline soil: If your soil is too alkaline, add a source of acidity. The most common material to add is elemental sulfur. As with lime, there is no simple rule on how much sulfur to add to change pH by a set amount. Testing your soil and following lab recommendations is the best approach if you want to lower the pH of an entire bed or area of your yard.

Mixing peat moss with the soil will also lower pH. Peat moss can be expensive, so it's generally only a feasible choice for small areas such as flower beds and container gardens. ❖

Phenology

"Plant corn when oak leaves are the size of squirrels' ears." This piece of folk wisdom is an example of phenology, the study of the timing of biological events and their relationships to climate and to one another. Such events include bird migration, animal hibernation, the emergence of insects, and the germination and flowering of plants.

Phenologists have found that many plants and insects within the same region or climate pass through the stages of their development in a consistent, unified sequence. The budding of a given plant, for example, may correlate with the hatching out of a particular pest insect. Variations in weather from one year to the next affect the timing of such events, but the order in which they occur tends to remain the same.

As a result, it's possible to foretell when conditions are right for a crop to germinate or an insect to appear by learning to read the various growth stages of indicator plants. Gardeners can use phenology to help them manage their own crops. Plant a variety of perennials as indicators that will provide a steady succession of blooms throughout a season. Then observe and record the indicators' growth phases, along with weather data, the appearance of insects or diseases in your garden, and the progress of food crops.

Sooner or later, patterns will emerge. You may notice that daffodils always begin to bloom when the soil becomes warm enough to sow peas, or that Mexican bean beetle larvae appear at about the same time foxgloves open. You can then use that information in subsequent years to help you decide when to plant peas or when to start handpicking beetle larvae. ❖

Philadelphus

Mock orange. Deciduous, spring-blooming shrubs.

Description: *Philadelphus coronarius,* sweet mock orange, is an upright, rounded shrub that grows to 12′ tall and wide; the branches arch eventually, giving the plant a fountainlike shape. The bark peels and sheds with age, exposing orange inner bark. Oval, 1½″-4″ leaves are dark green and remain green until they drop. The 1″-1½″ flowers are white and fragrant, appearing in late spring. Zones 4-7.

How to grow: Plant mock oranges in full sun or partial shade with well-drained soil and even moisture. Prune after flowering.

Landscape uses: Mature mock oranges tend to be bare around the base as the spreading top growth shades out the lower foliage, so plant low-growing shrubs or perennials around their feet. Mock oranges are unobtrusive when not in bloom, so use them in the shrub border rather than as specimens. ❖

Phlox

Phlox. Summer-blooming perennials.

Description: *Phlox paniculata*, garden phlox, enjoys star billing in many summer gardens. Hundreds of 1″ rounded blooms crowd into massive, roughly pyramidal clusters of white, pink, red, orange, and purple, many with a contrasting "eye" in the center of each bloom. Most have a sweet, light, musty scent, especially during dusk and early evening. Plants form 1½′-3′ tall upright mounds with pairs of 3″-6″ pointed leaves set at a 90-degree angle to the pair below. Zones 4-8.

How to grow: Plant or divide phlox in spring or fall in a sunny, well-drained spot with fertile, humus-rich soil. Partial shade may prolong bloom in the South. Phlox are heavy feeders and benefit from a scattering of organic fertilizer in early spring. Water frequently in summer. For best growth and reasonable mil-

---

MORE FINE PHLOX

Not all phlox are as imposing as garden phlox, but several are just as useful and attractive in the garden. Native wild blue phlox (*Phlox divaricata,* also called wild sweet William) and creeping phlox (*P. stolonifera*) both bear a profusion of delicate 1″ blooms in shades of white, blue, and lavender on thin stems to 1′ in spring. These gently spreading plants give a misty quality to lightly shaded moist woodlands and provide a cheerful contrast to bulbs and perennials in a border. Lowest growing of all is moss pink (*P. subulata*). Myriad ½″ blooms in white, pink, magenta, and lilac shades hide its spreading 1″-3″ mats of dense, needlelike evergreen leaves in spring. They thrive in sun and lean to rich, well-drained soil. Allow them to fill spaces in rock gardens and walls, or let them carpet a steep bank. All of these phlox are hardy in Zones 3-8 and have many fine cultivars.

---

dew control, divide every other year into renewed soil, and thin to about 6 shoots per plant. Never grow in airless spots or allow the clumps to become dense. If you do, the result will be a mildewed mess of ratty leaves and small flower heads. Remove flower heads before they drop their seeds to prevent vigorous seedlings (usually in vivid magenta shades) from crowding out their more desirable parents.

Landscape uses: Feature a variety of colors in a border, or tie a planting together with shades of a single color. Phlox look good in a bed or cutting garden. Allow reverted seedlings to naturalize in thin woods or a field.

Best cultivars: Choose from many early-, mid-season-, and late-blooming cultivars such as pale pink 'Bright Eyes', lilac 'Franz Shubert', white 'Mt. Fuji', red-orange 'Starfire', and purple 'The King'. ❖

Picea

Spruce. Evergreen trees or shrubs.

Description: Large trees that reach heights of 30′-60′ in the landscape, spruces are pyramidal to conical in habit, with short stiff needles and drooping cones.

Picea abies, Norway spruce, has horizontal limbs and branchlets that dangle with age. Cones grow 4″-6″ long. Norway spruce grows 40′-60′. Zones 2-6.

P. glauca, white spruce, becomes spirelike with age and reaches heights of 40′-60′. White spruce has drooping branchlets, four-sided needles, and 2″ cones. Zones 2-6.

P. mariana, black spruce, is also spirelike with age. It grows 30′-40′ tall. Zones 1-6.

P. omorika, Serbian spruce, is a slim-trunked tree of 50′-60′ with branches that droop but point upward at the tips. The flattened needles are deep green on top and whitish underneath; cones are 2½″ long. Zones 4-6.

P. orientalis, Oriental spruce, is a graceful tree that grows 50′-60′ tall. Four-sided needles are waxy, deep green, and crowded on branches.

Cones are about 3″ long. Zones 5-7.

P. pungens, Colorado spruce, is a stiffly pyramidal tree that grows 30′-60′ tall in the landscape. The four-sided needles are stiff and prickly; branchlets are yellowish brown and smooth. *P. pungens* 'Glauca' is the popular Colorado blue spruce, known for its blue-green or silvery green needles. Zones 2-6.

How to grow: Spruces need a cool climate and plenty of room. They grow quickly (as much as 1′-2′ per year), astounding homeowners with their ability to take up space, especially when they looked so small at planting time. Spruces transplant easily because of their shallow spreading root systems, and even large specimens can be relocated. In addition to space, spruces require evenly moist, well-drained, acid soil and full sun, although they can be grown successfully in

clay soils. Most species will tolerate light shade but grow open and untidy-looking in heavy shade. To encourage dense growth, prune in spring when new growth is nearly half-developed, removing ½ to ⅔ of the candle of new growth. Spruces generally require little pruning; some species tolerate heavy pruning and can be used to form hedges.

Pests that attack spruces include spider mites, sawflies, spruce gall adelgids, and bagworms. Spider mites often afflict trees that are under drought stress, and infestations tend to appear in very hot, dry weather. Avoid spider mite problems with proper culture—plant trees in cool areas and water deeply in dry weather. Use a strong spray of water to knock spider mites from trees, or spray with an insecticidal soap. Sawfly larvae feed on needles and disfigure trees. See the Pinus entry for sawfly control information. Remove and burn spruce galls from the twig tips before the next generation of spruce gall adelgids emerges. If you can't take off all the galls, spray with dormant oil before growth begins or with a summer oil during the growing season. Don't use oil sprays on blue spruces—they discolor the foliage. Sprays of insecticidal soap also give control if applied prior to bud break in early spring or timed to coincide with adelgid emergence from galls in July and August. For information on bagworm control, see the Evergreens entry.

Landscape uses: Use spruces as screens, hedges, and windbreaks. Many are attractive trees that work well as focal points in large-scale situations. Use blue spruces with discretion if color harmony is important to you—their strong blues are often hard to combine with other colors in the landscape.

Best cultivars: *P. glauca* 'Densata', Black Hills spruce, is a slow-growing conical tree, reaching 20′-40′ in the landscape. *P. glauca* 'Conica', dwarf Alberta spruce, is a 3′-6′, tightly conical shrub with fine foliage. Use it for formal effect in small-scale situations. *P. pungens* 'Koster' is known for its powerful blue color. ❖

Spruce gall adelgid. These small, aphidlike insects suck sap from spruce needles, causing a pinecone- or pineapple-shaped gall to form around them at the ends of branches. The gall turns brown and cracks open in summer, releasing mature adelgids that lay powdery egg masses near the base of the tree's buds.

Pieris

Pieris. Spring-blooming, broad-leaved evergreen shrubs.

Description: *Pieris floribunda,* mountain pieris or fetterbush, is a rounded, spreading shrub that grows to 6' tall. This plant bears upright clusters of creamy white flower spikes in spring. Zones 5-7.

P. japonica, Japanese pieris, can reach 10' at maturity. Glossy green foliage forms a background for the creamy white, cascading flower clusters. Zones 6-7.

How to grow: Pieris need partial shade and humus-rich, well-drained, evenly moist, well-mulched soil. Prune after flowering to remove dead wood. Remove spent flowers for good bloom next year. If lace bugs are a problem, control with soap sprays.

Landscape uses: Japanese pieris makes a fine specimen; plant where you can enjoy it at close range. Mountain pieris is a good choice for massed plantings and woodland gardens. ❖

Pinus

Pine. Evergreen trees or shrubs.

Description: *Pinus bungeana,* lacebark pine, is a multi-trunked tree that reaches 30'-50' in the landscape, becoming flat-topped with age. The bark flakes off, revealing attractive olive, gray, and tan patches. The 4" needles grow in bundles of three; the cones are about 3" long. Zones 5-7.

P. densiflora, Japanese red pine, has crooked trunks and horizontal branches. This picturesque pine becomes flat-topped with age and attains a mature height of 40'-60'. The 5" blue-green needles grow in bundles of two. The bark is orangish and the cones are about 2" long. Zones 5-6.

P. flexilis, limber pine, is pyramidal in youth and flat-topped with age, growing to a height of 30'-50'. The twisted, blue-green 3" needles grow in bundles of five; the cones can be 3"-10" long.

This North American native develops deep fissures in its old bark, but its most interesting feature is its rubbery, fun-to-play-with, flexible branches. Zones 5-6.

P. mugo, Swiss mountain pine, is a shrub or small tree that grows 15'-20' tall. Valued for its dwarf cultivars, it has a low, round, bushy habit and 2" needles in bundles of two. Zones 3-7.

P. nigra, Austrian pine, becomes massive and picturesque with age. In youth it's pyramidal, but develops a flat top and gray—almost white—bark with deep fissures forming blocky patterns. It grows 50'-60' tall in the landscape, bearing 6½" needles in bundles of two and cones about 3" long. Austrian pine is one of the few pines that tolerates urban conditions. Zones 4-6.

P. strobus, Eastern white pine, is soft and graceful in texture, pyramidal in youth, and stout with age. The branches appear in whorls on the trunk, with bluish green 5" needles in bundles of five. The cones are 4"-6" long. This native grows 50'-80' tall; it has little tolerance for road de-icing salts. Zones 3-6.

P. sylvestris, Scotch pine, is pyramidal in youth and gnarled with age, reaching a mature height of 30'-60'. The bark of the upper trunk flakes off to reveal a colorful orange inner bark that shows through the stiff, twisted, blue-green needles. The 3" long needles are borne in bundles of two. Scotch pine tolerates poor, dry soils and is grown as a Christmas tree in Northern states. Zones 2-6.

P. taeda, loblolly pine, is a fast-growing Southern native that can reach 60'-90'. Its 6"-10" needles are in bundles of three. Older trees have few lower branches; the exposed trunk's furrowed bark makes a nice background for small trees like *Cornus.* Zones 7-9.

P. thunbergiana, Japanese black pine, is pyramidal in youth, growing irregular, open, and picturesque with age. Its usual mature height in North America is 20'-30', though in its seaside habitat in its native Japan it grows to 130'. The 3"-4½" needles are borne in bundles of two; the bright green, sharp-pointed cones are 2½" long.

Pine needle scale

Sawfly larvae damage

Pine tip moth larvae damage

Insect damage on pines. Pine needle scale appears as small yellowish white bumps on the needles. In large numbers, scales give infested branches a snowy look. Voracious sawfly larvae feed on the needles of evergreens; feeding normally begins on old growth, but severe infestations can defoliate the entire tree. Dying branch tips on pines are the work of pine tip moth larvae. The dark-colored caterpillars bore into needle and bud bases, killing the shoots as they tunnel through them. Damaged trees have brown, slightly curled shoot tips.

Japanese black pine is good for coastal areas because it is resistant to salt spray. Zones 6-7.

P. virginiana, Virginia pine, is a scrubby pine of 15'-40' with paired needles and an irregular branching habit. Virginia pine is not particularly desirable as a landscape plant, but it tolerates poor, dry soils and can be used in difficult sites. Zones 5-9.

P. wallichiana, Himalayan white pine, is a pyramidal tree that becomes massive with age. Soft gray-green needles are 8" long and borne in bundles of five; they droop gracefully from the branches. The cones are 6"-12" long; the tree reaches a height of 50'-80'. Zones 5-6.

How to grow: Somewhat more adaptable to poor soil, exposed sites, and urban conditions than firs and spruces, pines prefer full sun, well-drained soil, and plenty of room. Several pest and disease problems trouble pines, but serious damage is usually limited to stressed trees or those found in large plantings such as Christmas tree farms.

Pine needle scales feed while attached to the needles; eggs mature beneath the scales, and one or two generations of tiny reddish crawlers emerge during the growing season. Infested needles may turn yellow and drop from the tree. Apply dormant oil or lime sulfur spray in late winter before growth begins; spray insecticidal soap or summer oil when crawlers appear in spring and again in early summer.

Sawfly is a name given to several species of nonstinging wasps that insert their eggs into the needles of pines and other evergreens. The larvae emerge to feed on the needles; one generation occurs in the North, but as many as three may attack Southern pines. Pick off any caterpillars that you can reach, or spray with summer oil or neem.

Pine tip and pine shoot borers are the caterpillars of several species of small moths. Remove and destroy infested branch tips; apply sprays of BTK (*Bacillus thuringiensis* var. *kurstaki*) when caterpillars are visible.

Landscape uses: Grow pines as specimen plants, screens, windbreaks, and hedges. They can make glorious focal points in large-scale situations. ❖

Plant Breeding

The enticing photographs you see each year in seed catalogs display the results of plant breeding: the development of new or improved plants, commonly known as varieties, but more properly called cultivars. While professional plant breeders use some complex methods to create new cultivars, the most common method is controlled cross-pollination, a technique you can try at home.

Before you start, you might want to review some basic botany so you can tell which flower parts to remove and which to keep. (The Flowers entry will tell you what you need to know.) For best results, start out with breeding plants that have large flowers, such as melons, daylilies (*Hemerocallis* spp.), irises, or squash. And remember: To cross successfully, the plants you choose need to be closely related (in the same species, at least). You won't have much luck crossing a marigold and a geranium, for example, but you may be able to cross some kinds of squash and pumpkins!

Once you've chosen the flowers you want to pollinate, you'll need to isolate them; otherwise, the wind or insects may pollinate the flowers before you get there. Cover the blossom buds with a paper bag a few days before the flowers open. If the plant to be pollinated has perfect flowers (with both male and female parts), use tweezers to remove the pollen-laden anthers as soon as the blooms open.

To pollinate a newly opened blossom, collect pollen from the desired male flower by brushing the stamens with a fine artist's paintbrush; then knock the pollen off the brush into a small container. Another way to gather pollen is to collect whole anthers from the male flower. Dust some of this pollen, using the brush or the anthers themselves, onto the stigma of the desired female flower. Cover the blossom with the bag again, and tie it underneath to prevent unwanted pollen from reaching the stigma.

Before you leave the plant, make a note of the parents and the date on a weather-resistant label, and attach it loosely to the stem just below the flower. (It's also helpful to keep a written record of the plants, their locations, and the dates of crossings.) After a few days, remove the bag and let the blossom fade and fall apart. Once the seed has formed and ripened, collect and store it in an airtight container in a cool place.

To see what has resulted from the cross, start the seeds by providing the recommended germination conditions for that plant. As the seedlings grow, watch them carefully and record what you observe. Weed out any weak or sick-

Key Words
PLANT BREEDING

Chromosome. A linear structure in the nucleus of a cell that contains and transmits hereditary characteristics.

Gene. A unit with a fixed location on a chromosome, having specific hereditary information and capable of mutating.

Cultivar. A cultivated variety of a plant.

Open-pollination. Pollination that occurs in uncontrolled conditions, as in nature.

Cross-pollination. Pollination in which the pollen source is a different species of plant or a plant of the same species that has a different genetic makeup (e.g., a different cultivar).

Self-pollination. Pollination in which the pollen source is the flower itself, flowers on the same plant, or plants with the same genetic makeup (i.e., of the same cultivar).

Hybrid. A new plant produced from successfully cross-pollinating parent plants that are genetically different.

Mutation. A variant that differs genetically and often visibly from its parent or parents and arises rather suddenly or abruptly. Also called a sport.

Genetic engineering. The manipulation of genes by humans to produce plants with special characteristics.

looking seedlings (a process known as roguing out) to make room for the stronger plants.

When they bloom, the first generation of any cross may not look at all promising. The second or third generation, however, can produce outstanding plants. So be sure to collect seeds from the first generation plants, start them, and let them grow to maturity. Out of hundreds of plants, you may find a few superior plants that will reward all of your efforts.

Although saving and growing the seed of a hybrid is frequently not recommended, it can be worthwhile to cross-pollinate two different hybrids of the same species. Seeds from hybrids will produce plants with a wide range of traits, many of which may be less desirable than those of the parent plant. If you have room and enjoy experimenting, though, try growing on some of the seeds to see what you get.

Plant breeding on a commercial scale is usually more successful than in the home garden. The professionals make hundreds or thousands of crosses, have a good idea of the qualities they are looking for, and take the time necessary to observe the plants with experienced eyes. They look for improved fruit, flower, or leaf color, disease or insect resistance, growth habit, and hardiness, or some combination of these. Once they have found promising plants, breeders have the facilities to reproduce them and evaluate large numbers of plants.

Some breeders also have access to the tools of genetic engineering. This offers many new possibilities for improved plants but carries significant responsibilities for the scientists practicing it. Genetic engineering could result in the release of potentially disruptive organisms, or in increased use of herbicides to kill weeds among crops that have engineered resistance to the herbicide. However, these same techniques can also produce hardier, more productive, and more disease- and insect-resistant plants. It's important to evaluate genetic engineering techniques individually rather than condemning—or approving of—them on a general, uninformed basis.

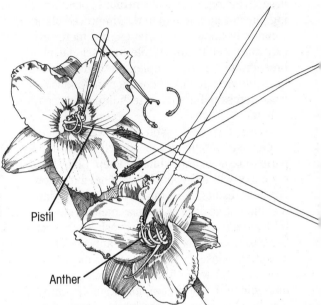

Controlled cross-pollination. Daylilies, with their big, easily visible parts, are ideal specimens for the beginning plant breeder. When the flower you want to pollinate opens, carefully remove the anthers (as shown on the top). Then use a soft brush to transfer pollen from another flower to the stigma of the prepared flower (on the bottom).

Some gardeners are concerned that the marketing of new and different cultivars makes some older, very worthy plants unavailable. It's important to realize, though, that it is in plant breeders' best interest to preserve these treasures. Often the old selections provide valuable genetic material for new and improved cultivars, and organizations such as the Seed Savers Exchange are devoted to preserving these useful plants. To learn more about old-fashioned plants, see the Heirloom Plants entry. ❖

Plant Disorders

People unintentionally cause almost as many plant problems as insects and disease. Selecting a plant well suited to the site is the best way to prevent frustrating, costly, and fatal plant disorders. See the Planting entry for more information on matching plant to site.

If illness does befall your favorite tree, play the detective and sleuth around for clues as to the cause. Don't assume that blight or bugs are to blame, even if such pests are evident—they may only be taking advantage of a plant weakened by environmental conditions.

Growth habits: Know a plant's growth habit before you buy. How high and wide will it be? Will its branches extend into power lines, inviting inexpert or untimely pruning by utility companies? If a tree's branches extend 25′ from the trunk, its supporting roots reach out that far into the surrounding soil. Other plants within its radius will compete for nutrients and water. More aggressive plants often win this battle, while losers grow slowly, have poor appearance, and produce few fruits. Trees with surface roots will destroy sidewalks or invade sewer and water lines within that radius, too.

Construction: Many home buyers ask that large trees on a lot be saved during construction. However, few trees will withstand the rigors of construction—changing grades and drainage, topsoil removal, and soil compaction around roots.

To preserve trees on a new homesite, keep equipment away from trees by erecting fences beyond the drip line before construction begins. For help in preserving trees close to the site, consult a tree specialist. Professional pruning may be necessary to compensate for root loss. For more information on caring for trees at construction sites, see the Trees entry.

Trees vs. lawn: Healthy trees and healthy lawn grass do not necessarily go hand in hand. Lawn mowers often bump and scrape a tree's bark just above ground level; the blades chop into roots rising from the lawn. Shallow watering—soaking only the top 2″ of soil—can cause trees to develop droughtlike symptoms, including small, yellowing leaves, early leaf drop, slow growth, and brittle twigs. Water-seeking tree roots grow upward, cracking concrete paving along the way.

Keep grass out of the area covered by the tree's fully leafed branch spread—plant shade-tolerant groundcovers that don't need mowing instead. During droughts, use a root irrigator to water trees deeply every two weeks.

Salt damage: Ocean spray and road salt, as well as animal urine, can injure plants. Salts can accumulate on leaves, stems, and buds, or build to toxic levels around the roots. Over time, salt burn weakens the entire plant and causes droughtlike symptoms.

Use barriers to protect plants near roads and sidewalks from salt, grow salt-tolerant species, and use water to flush salts from the soil. If visiting dogs are the problem, put up a fence or ask owners to curb their pets.

Air pollution: Motor vehicle exhaust and industrial emissions affect plants as well as people. Symptoms may result from a sudden excess of pollutants in the air or long-term exposure. Grow tolerant species where pollution is a problem, and avoid planting in sites that receive direct, regular exposure to exhaust.

Girdling roots: Sometimes a root wraps around another root or even the entire trunk and gradually strangles the tree as it grows. Above soil level, a girdling root looks like a thick coil wrapped around the trunk at ground level—carefully remove girdling roots with a saw, axe, or chisel. If this girdling occurs underground, it may not be evident until it's too late. See "Planting Trees" on page 584 for information on preventing girdling roots.

Plant disorder symptoms may resemble those cause by nutrient deficiencies, pests, or diseases. See "Diagnosing Environmental Disorders" on page 480. See also the Plant Nutrition entry and "Diagnosing Plant Problems" on page 419. ❖

Grading changes can damage roots and turn a well-drained site into a water basin.

Lawn mower injury to bark invites invasion by insects and diseases.

Lawn grass competes for water and nutrients, reducing tree vigor.

Road salt and salts from pet urine can limit water uptake, causing yellowed leaves and droughtlike injury.

Air pollution can cause slow growth or browning, curling, or odd coloration of leaves.

A girdling root causes small leaves and early leaf drop or fall color on one side of a tree.

Diagnosing environmental disorders. Environmental problems often cause symptoms that mimic those caused by insects or diseases, including early leaf drop, brown or undersized leaves, and general weak growth. Stressed plants are also more open to attack by pests and diseases. If a plant shows signs of stress, take time to look for clues to the cause of the problem. For example, borers, a girdling root, or injury to one side of the trunk can cause early leaf drop or wilting on one side of a tree.

Plant Nutrition

Plants make their own food through the process of photosynthesis, but gardeners play an important supporting role by making sure all the necessary raw materials are available. Organic gardeners do this primarily by enriching their soils with a variety of organic materials. Feeding plants with organic fertilizers can also help to provide optimum nutrition.

At least 60 elements have been found in plants, but only 16 are proven essential for plant growth. Scientists categorize these essential elements as macronutrients or micronutrients.

Plant macronutrients are calcium, carbon, hydrogen, magnesium, nitrogen, oxygen, phosphorus, potassium, and sulfur. Macronutrients generally are part of plant parts such as leaf or root cells. Micronutrients are boron, chlorine, copper, iron, manganese, molybdenum, and zinc. Plants use micronutrients in chemical processes such as photosynthesis or nutrient uptake.

Nutrient Uptake

Carbon, hydrogen, and oxygen: Plants take up carbon, hydrogen, and oxygen from air and water. (All other macro- and micronutrients are taken up as compounds or elements dissolved in the soil solution.) Carbon dioxide, an important ingredient in photosynthesis, supplies carbon and oxygen. Plants also take in oxygen gas through their leaf pores and root hairs. Plants derive hydrogen from water taken up from the soil.

Natural supplies of these three macronutrients are usually, but not always, plentiful. For example, in waterlogged or heavily compacted soil, oxygen gas is not available to root hairs. And in a poorly ventilated greenhouse, plants may use up so much of the available carbon dioxide that their growth will suffer.

Nitrogen: Nitrogen is a major part of proteins that make up plant tissue. Nitrogen is also a component of chlorophyll, the green pigment needed for photosynthesis. Air is 78 percent nitrogen gas, but plants cannot absorb nitrogen gas directly. Instead, plants take up nitrogen compounds from the soil. Synthetic chemical fertilizers supply nitrogen in forms that plant roots can immediately absorb: ammonium, a compound containing nitrogen and hydrogen; and nitrate, a nitrogen-oxygen compound. However, both of these compounds are mobile in the soil and can be lost through leaching or by reconverting to nitrogen gas. Organic gardeners supply nitrogen by applying well-rotted manure or compost, by growing legumes, or by using natural nitrogen fertilizers such as blood meal. Soil microorganisms convert the nitrogen compounds in organic fertilizers to ammonium and nitrate

Key Words
PLANT NUTRITION

Element. A fundamental substance that consists of only one kind of atom, for example, oxygen.

Compound. A substance that contains more than one element. For example, water is a compound made of hydrogen and oxygen.

Essential element. An element needed by a plant to complete its life cycle (e.g., to set seed). Different plant species require different proportions of the essential elements.

Macronutrient. An element used in relatively large quantities by plants.

Micronutrient. An element used in relatively small quantities by plants.

Soil solution. The water containing dissolved nutrients found in the pore spaces of the soil.

Luxury consumption. The uptake of excess quantities of nutrients by plants.

Hidden hunger. A plant nutrient deficiency that has not yet shown itself in any visible symptoms.

Interveinal chlorosis. A condition in which leaf veins remain green while the tissue between veins turns yellow, generally resulting from a nutrient deficiency or from disease.

slowly and steadily, giving plants a long-term, balanced nitrogen supply.

Phosphorus: Phosphorus is an important part of the genetic material in plants and also plays a role in several plant biochemical processes. There is little phosphorus in the mineral portion of most soils. It generally comes from the decay of organic matter. Phosphorus can easily become insoluble in an unbalanced soil. If you're working to improve a problem soil, or one that's low in organic matter, you'll probably need to supplement the natural phosphorus supply. Bonemeal and rock phosphate are good natural sources of phosphorus; rock phosphate will become available slowly, especially in soils with neutral or alkaline pH.

Potassium: Potassium is important in the formation of proteins, carbohydrates, and chlorophyll. Potassium also plays a role in uptake of other nutrients and in the functioning of stomates. Although potassium naturally occurs in most soils, plants will likely need more than is available. Greensand and granite meal are potassium-rich soil amendments.

Other macronutrients: Calcium is a building block of plant cell walls. Magnesium is a component of chlorophyll and aids in the formation of plant fats, oils, and starch. Sulfur becomes part of some proteins, oils, and chlorophyll. Naturally occurring supplies of these three elements in garden soils are usually sufficient for good plant growth. Exceptions include sandy and acidic soils, which are often low in calcium and magnesium.

Micronutrients: Micronutrients play varying roles. Iron is a component of chlorophyll and is also important in other biochemical plant processes. Manganese is also needed for chlorophyll formation. Zinc is important in the formation of enzymes and hormones. Copper is an important component of vitamin A. Boron helps regulate plant metabolism and cell development. Molybdenum helps plants use nitrogen. Chlorine plays a role in photosynthesis.

Plant micronutrients can all be found in the tiny rock fragments in soils. Most micronutrients occur in relatively small quantities in the soil solution, and their availability is affected by soil conditions. Soil pH influences the availability of iron and manganese. In droughty areas, boron and chlorine may accumulate in the soil to the point of becoming toxic to plants.

Nutrient Excesses

Occasionally, some nutrients may be present in large enough quantities to have harmful effects. Excessive uptake of boron, copper, or manganese may be toxic to plants. Luxury consumption of nitrogen can result in excessive production of weak, dark green leaves, and delayed flowering and fruit production. Excess magnesium in the soil can interfere with uptake of other essential elements.

In low-rainfall areas or in overfertilized gardens, various elements generally called "salts" can accumulate to harmful levels. This can also happen in garden soils irrigated with water that contains high quantities of these salts. Excessive salt content can cause plants to show symptoms of drought stress because of direct injury to roots or by interfering with water uptake. Plants grown in containers are at particular risk for salt injury if overfertilized or improperly watered.

Nutrient Deficiencies

The plant nutrition problems gardeners most often face are the result of nutrient deficiencies. If your garden soil is deficient in one or more nutrients, your plants will suffer. At first, plants suffering from hidden hunger will look normal. However, over time, deficiencies will begin to show up as a sometimes bewildering array of symptoms. "Common Nutrient Deficiency Symptoms in Plants" on the opposite page will help you in diagnosing deficiency problems.

Some deficiency symptoms are easy to identify. For example, black, dead areas inside beet roots are due to boron deficiency. However,

Common Nutrient Deficiency Symptoms in Plants

Unfortunately, plants can't tell us what nutrients they may be lacking, and visual diagnosis of deficiencies is an imprecise art. One helpful tip is to remember that some nutrient deficiencies are likely to appear on new growth first, while others appear first on older plant parts. This table groups deficiency symptoms according to where symptoms are likely to show up first.

Nutrient	Deficiency Symptoms
SYMPTOMS APPEAR FIRST ON OLDER OR LOWER LEAVES	
Nitrogen	Lower leaves yellow, overall plant light green, growth stunted
Phosphorus	Foliage red, purple, or very dark green; growth stunted
Potassium	Tips and edges of leaves yellow, then brown; stems weak
Magnesium	Interveinal chlorosis, growth stunted
Zinc	Interveinal chlorosis, leaves thickened, growth stunted
SYMPTOMS APPEAR FIRST ON YOUNGER OR UPPER LEAVES	
Calcium	Buds and young leaves die back at tips
Iron	Interveinal chlorosis, growth stunted
Sulfur	Young leaves light green overall, growth stunted
Boron	Young leaves pale green at base and twisted, buds die
Copper	Young leaves pale and wilted with brown tips
Manganese	Interveinal chlorosis on young leaves with brown spots scattered through leaf
Molybdenum	Interveinal chlorosis, growth stunted

the symptoms of other nutrient deficiencies look very similar to one another. For example, magnesium, iron, manganese, zinc, and boron deficiencies all result in interveinal chlorosis, a yellowing of tissue between the leaf veins. Nonnutritional disorders and diseases can also cause similar symptoms. See the Organic Pest Management entry for more information on keying out plant problems by symptom.

Although some well-established gardens may have a good supply of all the essential elements, most gardens will need some nutrient supplements. See the Fertilizers entry for a complete rundown on organic fertilizers and soil amendments and how to apply them. If you aren't sure whether your soil is providing sufficient nutrients for good plant growth, it's a good idea to have your soil tested and get recommendations for adding amendments. See the Soil entry for information on testing soil. ❖

Planting

One of the best ways to ensure that plants will grow well is to do a good job planting them. Preparing planting areas thoroughly, so roots will quickly extend into the soil surrounding the planting holes, is time well spent.

Matching Plant with Site

Before you dig that planting hole or plant those seeds, try to make a good match between the plant and its environment. Learning to know your soil and growing conditions—and using that knowledge to pick the right plants—is just as important as knowing the best planting techniques. So before you plant:

• Take a close look at your soil. Is it red clay or deep loam? Waterlogged or sandy and dry? Is it acid or alkaline?

• Check the amount of sunlight your site gets. Is it full sun all day or just afternoon sun? Is the shade dappled through the small, shifting leaves of a birch, or deep and heavy, as beneath a fir? A tomato plant must have 6 hours of direct sunlight daily for good fruit set, but the same amount of sun fades and burns ferns.

• Know your hardiness zone. Your local nurseries and garden centers generally stock only plants that are hardy in your area. But if you do any mail-order buying, knowing your zone will save you money and disappointment. If you're not familiar with the concept of hardiness zones, see the Weather entry for an explanation.

• Be aware of seasonal conditions. Is the spot you picked sheltered by a wall or windbreak, or does it get the full blast of winter winds? Is it low-lying and prone to late-spring frost?

• Learn the growth rate and size of your plants. Choose a site where they won't cause problems or overgrow your garden. This is especially important for permanent plants such as trees and shrubs.

Getting Soil in Shape

If you set plants into poorly drained soil, the roots are likely to rot and die. If you plant seeds into poorly drained soil, they may never even germinate. Before you plant a pumpkin seed or a pine tree, be sure that your soil drains well. If drainage is poor, see "Problem Soils" on page 549 for ways to improve it. Or consider growing plants in raised beds. The Raised Bed Gardening entry explains how to make and plant raised beds. For very wet areas, your best bet may be to grow plants that can tolerate wet conditions. See the Bog Gardens and Water Gardens entries for ideas.

If you till the soil for a vegetable garden or dig a hole for a tree when the soil is too wet, you'll destroy the soil's structure. Your soil will compact, causing water to run off or lay in puddles rather than penetrate. Without air, root growth suffers. If your soil is too wet, let it dry before planting. Pick up a handful of soil and squeeze it. If it crumbles, it's perfect for planting. But if it forms a muddy ball, the soil is too wet to be worked.

Most plants pay less attention to pH than gardeners do. If your soil is fertile and well-drained and neither extremely acid nor extremely alkaline, most plants will do just fine. But a number of plants are more demanding. Acid-loving azaleas and blueberries, for instance, will do poorly in soil that's on the alkaline side. If you don't know the soil pH in an area you plan to plant, it's a good idea to test it.

Enrich flower and vegetable beds with lots of aged manure, compost, or leaf mold before planting. For more about soil testing and enriching your soil, see the Composting, Fertilizers, Green Manure, and Soil entries.

Seeds

Plant flowers and vegetables in fertile, well-drained soil that is rich in organic matter. If you're starting a new garden, double digging is worth the effort. This technique loosens the top 2' of the soil, increasing pore space to hold soil and water. For step-by-step directions, see the Double Digging entry.

Prepare the seedbed with a rotary tiller, or turn the earth with a spade or garden fork. If you do the tilling or digging in fall, you'll be one step ahead come spring. Rake the soil to a fine tilth, breaking up clods and removing stones and weeds.

Check seed packages to find out when to sow and if the plants have any special germination requirements. Some plants, such as peas, prefer cool weather; others, such as corn, will rot if planted before soil warms up. Many will produce flowers or fruit earlier if given a head start indoors or in a cold frame. If you're interested in starting seeds early, see the Cold Frames and Seeds and Seedlings entries.

Sow seeds thinly to avoid thinning chores later. Sprinkle flower seeds in long single rows for cutting, or broadcast with a flinging motion over a wider area for a free-form display. Plant small vegetable seeds such as lettuce and spinach in rows, or scatter them in a wide band. Plant

large flower and vegetable seeds individually, spaced according to package instructions. Vining plants such as melons and cucumbers can be planted in hills of 3-5 seeds.

Cover the seeds with fine soil to a depth 2-3 times the diameter—not the length—of the seed. Firm the soil (use the palm of your hand or the back of your hoe) to establish good contact between seed and soil. Some seeds, such as lettuce, petunias, and begonias, must have light to germinate. Lightly press seeds like these onto the surface of moistened soil.

Always water gently after you plant seeds, taking care not to wash the seeds away. A fine, misty spray is best; you can buy a hose attachment at garden centers and hardware stores. Keep the soil evenly moist until you see stems and leaves popping above the ground.

Bulbs and Herbaceous Perennials

Plant bulbs and perennials in prepared beds well enriched with organic matter and having excellent drainage. Bulbs especially are quick to rot in soggy conditions. If you are making a naturalistic bulb planting in a lawn area, add a handful of bonemeal to each planting hole.

Bulbs

Plant bulbs individually, or dig a hole big enough for several bulbs at a time. Even an entire bed can be dug out, then refilled after the bulbs are placed. Dig the planting hole to the depth recommended for each type of bulb, generally 3-4 times their widest diameter. When planting bulbs individually, dig holes just slightly wider than the widest diameter of the bulb. Place bulbs pointed-end up in their holes and cover with soil. If you can't tell which end is up, plant the bulb sideways. Firm the soil, and water. If you're planting in a lawn area for naturalizing, carefully replace plugs of grass atop the holes.

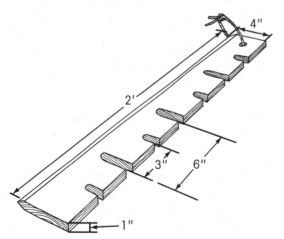

Planting guide. It's easier to plant seeds at the correct spacing than to thin them later. A notched board with a beveled edge makes a helpful guide for even seed sowing.

Perennials

Perennials generally are available either bareroot or growing in containers. There's no time to waste with bareroot perennials—if you can't plant right away, remove packaging and store roots in moist peat. When planting, dig a hole wide enough to allow you to fully spread out the roots and deep enough so the plant is set at the same depth at which it grew previously. Avoid burying the crown, from which new shoots will spring. Water thoroughly and mulch. Put a box over the plant to block light; this allows energy to be put into root growth instead of greenery.

Heeling in. If you can't plant bareroot plants right away, keep the roots moist by heeling them in. Dig a trench with one vertical and one slanted side in a spot sheltered from direct sun and wind. Lay bareroot plants against the slanted side, and cover the roots with soil. Uncover and move to a permanent position while the plant is still dormant.

Container-grown perennials are gratifyingly easy to add to the garden. Dig a hole just a bit wider than and the same depth as the pot. To prevent wilting, make a mud puddle of your planting hole by filling with water. Wait till the water drains away, then fill again. When the water drains the second time, you're ready to plant.

To remove the plant from the container, hold one hand firmly across the soil surface, with the plant stems between your fingers. Then flip the pot over. With a bit of wiggling and gentle tugging, the pot should slide free. If not, give it some encouragement by smacking the bottom with your trowel. Untangle potbound roots, and set the root ball in the hole. Fill, firm the soil, water once more, and mulch.

Trees and Shrubs

Do you know how to dig a proper planting hole? A few minutes of extra preparation can make all the difference. Although some trees' roots may go deep, the small but all-important feeder roots forage mostly through the top 6"-8" of soil. Shape the hole to accommodate the feeder roots. "Planting Do's and Don'ts" on page 488 shows how to shape a planting hole for best root development.

Plant trees and shrubs at the same depth at which they were previously planted. Look for the dark mark on the plant stem that indicates how deep the plant was grown at the nursery. Checking depth by hauling the tree or shrub in and out of the hole is a lot of wear and tear on you and the plant. Here's an easier way: Measure from the stem mark to the bottom of the roots or root ball to find out how deep the hole should be. As you dig, check depth now and then by laying a board across the hole and measuring from the board's center to the bottom of the hole.

Encourage roots to reach out by loosening ground surrounding the hole. Plunge a garden fork in as deep as the tines allow, and wiggle it

SETTLING THEM IN

Your new trees and shrubs may be bare-root, balled-and-burlapped, or planted in a container. For best results, follow these guidelines when planting.

Bareroot plants: As long as you plant bareroot trees or shrubs while the stock is still dormant, your chances of success are good with these generally low-cost plants.

Leave a small cone of undisturbed soil in the center of the hole. Remove any circling, broken, or diseased roots. Spread out the roots over the cone of soil, and fill. Water well and mulch.

Balled-and-burlapped plants: It's best to get balled-and-burlapped (B&B) plants in the ground while they're dormant, so the roots can get a good start before they have to supply food and water to burgeoning top growth. But the B&B method gives you more leeway; even actively growing trees and shrubs can be held until the weekend for planting.

"Planting Do's and Don'ts" on page 488 shows how to set a B&B plant in the planting hole. Remove binding ropes or twine and all nails. Leave natural burlap in place: It will eventually rot. Slit synthetic wrapping material in several places so roots can penetrate it. Try to keep the root ball intact. If the root ball is in a wire basket, cut off the loops on top to keep them from sticking up through the soil, and snip and remove the top few wires. If the tree is large, have a helper hold it in place as you fill the hole. After every few shovelfuls of dirt, add water to help settle air pockets.

Container-grown plants: Remove any labeling tags to keep the tags or wires from cutting into the stems. Support the plant while you turn it upside down and remove the pot. Even fiber pots of compressed peat or paper are best removed; exposed edges wick away moisture, and the walls slow down root growth.

Snip off dead or sickly roots and use your fingers to comb out any potbound roots. Cut through circling roots. Set plant as deep as it grew before, fill, water, and mulch.

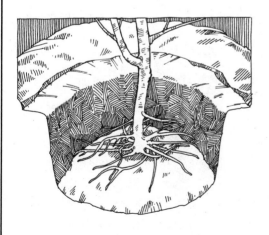

Bareroot plant

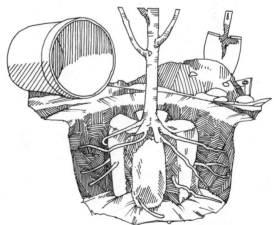

Container-grown plant

Correct Planting Techniques

Diseased, dead, and crossing branches pruned

Incorrect Planting Techniques

No corrective pruning

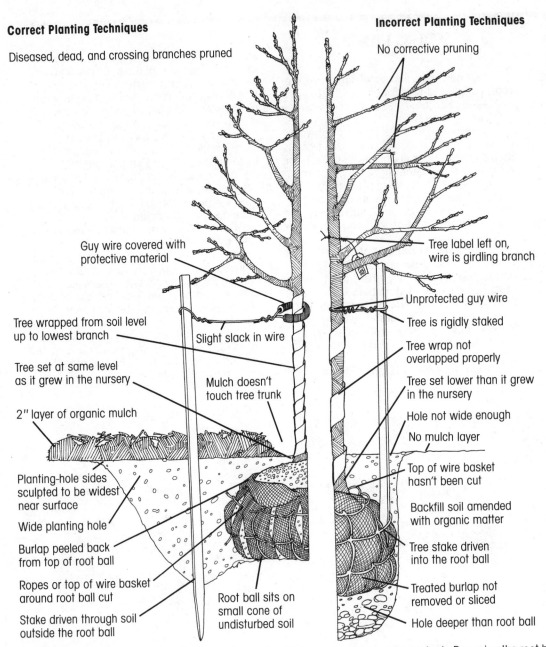

Guy wire covered with protective material

Tree label left on, wire is girdling branch

Slight slack in wire

Tree wrapped from soil level up to lowest branch

Unprotected guy wire

Tree is rigidly staked

Tree set at same level as it grew in the nursery

Mulch doesn't touch tree trunk

Tree wrap not overlapped properly

Tree set lower than it grew in the nursery

2" layer of organic mulch

Hole not wide enough

No mulch layer

Planting-hole sides sculpted to be widest near surface

Top of wire basket hasn't been cut

Wide planting hole

Backfill soil amended with organic matter

Burlap peeled back from top of root ball

Tree stake driven into the root ball

Ropes or top of wire basket around root ball cut

Root ball sits on small cone of undisturbed soil

Treated burlap not removed or sliced

Stake driven through soil outside the root ball

Hole deeper than root ball

Planting do's and don'ts. Take the time for small details when you plant a new tree or shrub. Preparing the root ball, setting the plant properly, mulching, and pruning dead and diseased branches all will contribute to your new plant's health, beauty, and longevity.

DON'T CODDLE THE ROOTS

Standard tree-planting instructions used to include a recommendation to enrich the soil in planting holes with organic amendments and fertilizers. But recent studies show this can hinder, not help, new trees and shrubs as they adjust to your native soil.

A hole filled with peat moss and rotted manure encourages roots to grow only in the hole instead of branching out. These pockets of overly amended soil stay too wet during rainy periods and too dry during drought. This means tree roots can suffocate from too much moisture or can be more prone to wilting during drought. Also, since the roots don't spread and anchor the plant strongly, it will be more susceptible to windthrow—being toppled during high winds.

add soil gradually. For bareroot plants, give the tree or shrub an occasional shake as you refill the hole to sift soil among the roots. Level the soil around the base of the plant. Don't stomp all the air out of your newly filled hole: Instead of using your feet, tamp the soil with your hands or the back of a hoe to settle it and eliminate air pockets.

Soak the soil thoroughly after planting. Apply a 2″-3″ layer of mulch to retain moisture, pulling it back a bit from the trunk. Make it a habit to water new plants once a week during their first year, especially if rainfall is less than 1″ per week. By the time you notice wilting or other signs of stress, it may be too late.

Finishing Touches

You don't need to prune newly planted trees and shrubs, except to remove branches that are broken, diseased, narrow-angled, or overlapping. If you cut back all the branches, you may actually slow your tree's or shrub's establishment, because buds produce chemicals that aid root growth. The exception is young fruit trees, which you must prune promptly if you plan to train them for easier harvesting and care. See the Fruit Trees and Pruning and Training entries for more information.

A tree wrap protects the trunk from sunscald, nibbling rodents, and lawn mower nicks. Wrap the trunk from the base to the lowest branch, and tie in place. Remove wrapping after no more than a year.

Stake trees only if they're located in a windy area or if they're top-heavy. One or two stakes will hold a small tree, while three stakes may be needed for a large tree. Allow a few inches of slack in the wire or other material that you use to attach the tree to the stake so that the tree can sway a bit in the wind. Remove stakes and attaching materials after one year to prevent damage to enlarging stems. ❖

slightly to break up compacted soil. Repeat every 1′-1½′ to a distance of 5′ or more on all sides.

The trees and shrubs you buy will be bareroot, balled-and-burlapped (B&B), or in containers. Many deciduous trees and shrubs, such as apples, maples, lilacs, and roses, are sold as dormant, bareroot plants. Evergreens are usually sold B&B because even when they're dormant, they have leaves that draw water from the roots. Container-grown plants have roots established in the container (sometimes a little too well established!); these plants are easy to add to your garden, even in full growth. "Settling Them In" on page 487 explains how to set each of these types of plants in a planting hole.

After settling the plant in the hole, observe it from all angles to be sure it is positioned straight up and down. There's nothing more frustrating than filling your planting hole and then discovering that the plant is set crookedly. Once you're sure the plant is positioned properly,

Platanus

Planetree, sycamore. Deciduous shade trees.

Description: These massive trees have striking peeling bark with tan, green, and white patches. They bear spreading crowns of broad, 3- to 5-lobed, medium green leaves. Light, feathered seeds form on pendulous 1″ balls.

Platanus × *acerifolia,* London planetree, reaches heights of 50′-80′ in the landscape and tolerates urban conditions. Zones 5-8.

P. occidentalis, American planetree, buttonwood, or sycamore, has a landscape height of 60′-90′ and can surpass 100′. Zones 5-8.

How to grow: Provide a site with plenty of sun, moisture, and space. Blocky, dead areas on smaller-than-usual leaves are signs of anthracnose. Sprays of copper fungicide or lime sulfur offer control but are impractical for large trees. London planetree shows some resistance.

Landscape uses: Plant sycamores as focal points or in groups in spacious locations. ❖

Platycodon

Balloon flower. Summer-blooming perennials.

Description: *Platycodon grandiflorus*, balloon flower, bears inflated, balloonlike buds that open into 2″ starry bowls of violet-blue, white, or pink, on 1½′-3′ plants with attractive 3″ oval leaves. Zones 4-8.

How to grow: Set out small or container-grown plants in spring, or carefully separate the fleshy roots before shoots emerge. Plant in a sunny or lightly shaded spot with average, well-drained soil. Balloon flowers come up late in spring; mark their location so you won't damage them while digging. Stake taller cultivars.

Landscape uses: Balloon flowers are beautiful with *Rudbeckia* 'Goldsturm', daylilies (*Hemerocallis* spp.), and other summer-flowering perennials in beds and borders. ❖

Plum

Prunus spp.
Rosaceae

Plums have greenish, yellow, red, purple, and blue fruit in a wide range of shapes, sizes, and flavors to suit every taste. The Fruit Trees entry covers many important aspects of growing plums and other tree fruits; refer to it for more information on planting, pruning, and care.

Selecting trees: Most European plums (*Prunus domestica*) and damson plums (*P. insititia*) are partly self-fruitful. They are more hardy (Zones 4-9) and tend to bloom and ripen later than Japanese cultivars. They have a high sugar content and can be dried to make prunes.

Most Japanese plums (*P. salicina*) require cross-pollination. In fact, you may need three compatible cultivars for good crop set because some cultivars don't produce much pollen. Early-blooming European cultivars may pollinate Japanese cultivars. Japanese plums are less hardy (Zones 6-10) and tend to have larger fruit than European cultivars. Fruits are quite juicy, with a blend of sweet and tart flavor. European/Japanese hybrids, which combine the characters of both types, are available. Be sure to choose disease-resistant trees to prevent many common problems.

Many native *Prunus* species are sold as bush plums. They tend to have small fruit but tolerate drought and hot summers well. Hybrids of plum and cherry or apricot can be fun to try.

Rootstocks: There are a number of good rootstocks available. 'Myrobalan' seedling roots produce a tree of about 20′. They tend to be hardy and long-lived, resistant to canker and nematodes, and tolerant of clay. Good dwarf and semidwarf rootstocks are available and produce trees as small as 8′.

Planting and care: Space plum trees 20′-25′ apart. Plums don't compete well with grass in lawns. Spread a thick layer of organic mulch out to the drip line to conserve moisture.

Pruning: Generally European plums grow upright and Japanese plums spread. Train European types to central leader as show on page 253 and Japanese to open center as shown on page 254. European plums bear fruit on long-lived spurs in the tree's interior. Thin suckers and overly thick outer growth to let sunlight in to the fruit. Japanese types fruit on older spurs as well as year-old wood. Encourage new growth by pruning off old wood, but leave the still-fruitful inner spurs.

Thinning: Shake limbs to thin or pinch off small, odd-shaped, or overcrowded fruits before the pits harden. Leave 1"-3" between small fruits, 4"-5" between larger ones.

Problems: Plums have many of the same problems as other stone fruits. Expect birds to take their share as well. See the Cherry and Peach entries for common problems. Select resistant trees and prune for good air circulation.

Harvesting: Most plum trees bear in 3-4 years from planting. Harvest plums for cooking when they are slightly immature. For fresh eating, let European types grow sweet and soft on the tree. Pick Japanese plums a little early and let ripen indoors. Leave the stems on the fruit and handle as little as possible, and the plums will store better.

Best cultivars: 'AU-Rosa', 'Crimson', and 'Ozark Premier' resist brown rot, perennial canker, black knot, and bacterial leaf spot.

'Redheart' resists brown rot, perennial canker, and bacterial leaf spot.

'AU-Producer', 'AU-Roadside', and 'Homeside' resist perennial canker, black knot, and bacterial leaf spot.

'AU-Amber' resists perennial canker and bacterial leaf spot. 'President' resists perennial canker and black knot.

'Bradshaw', 'Formosa', 'Homeside', 'Milton', 'Santa Rosa', and 'Shiro' resist black knot.

'Damson', 'Green Gage', 'Simon', and native American plums resist bacterial leaf spot. ❖

Poisonous Plants

Most of us know better than to forage for wild mushrooms for dinner, and we keep hungry children and pets away from poisonous houseplants like dieffenbachia and decorations like mistletoe. But common backyard plants can also pose a hazard. By learning which plants are poisonous, you can avoid growing them while you have small children, or you can make the garden childproof.

Common plants that are poisonous to touch are usually found in wooded or suburban areas. In the eastern United States and Canada, look out for poison ivy (*Rhus toxicodendron*) and its cousin, poison sumac (*R. vernix*). In the western regions of these countries, watch out for poison oak (*R. diversiloba*).

Common vegetables with poisonous leaves are potatoes, tomatoes, and rhubarb.

Many ornamental plants are mildly to fatally poisonous when eaten. All parts of autumn crocus (*Colchicum autumnale*), bittersweet (*Celastrus scandens*), bleeding hearts (*Dicentra* spp.), boxwood (*Buxus sempervirens*), daffodils (*Narcissus* spp.), English ivy (*Hedera helix*), flowering tobacco (*Nicotiana alata*), horse chestnut (*Aesculus* × *carnea*), hydrangeas (*Hydrangea* spp.), mountain laurel (*Kalmia latifolia*), rhododendrons and azaleas (both *Rhododendron* spp.), and Virginia creeper (*Parthenocissus quinquefolia*) are poisonous.

Leaves of foxglove (*Digitalis purpurea*), larkspurs and delphiniums (both *Delphinium* spp.), monkshoods (*Aconitum* spp.), and oleander (*Nerium oleander*) are poisonous. Berries of lily-of-the-valley (*Convallaria majalis*) and hollies (*Ilex* spp.), hyacinth bulbs (*Hyacinthus orientalis*), and lupine seeds (*Lupinus* spp.) are also poisonous.

An excellent resource for identifying poisonous plants is the *AMA Handbook of Poisonous and Injurious Plants* by Dr. Kenneth F. Lampe and Mary Ann McCann. ❖

Pollination

Pollination is the transfer of pollen from the male parts (stamens) to the female parts (pistils) of flowers. Following pollination, sperm from the pollen fuse with eggs in the pistils, and the fertilized eggs develop into seeds.

Many garden plants, such as sweet corn and cucumbers, require the transfer of pollen from male flowers to female flowers. The flowers of other plants, including tomatoes and beans, have both male and female parts, so that one plant, or even one flower, can set seeds by itself. Cultivars of some fruit trees and other plants require pollen from a different cultivar for successful pollination. Insects, wind, and hummingbirds are important pollinating agents.

For more information on flowers and pollination, see the Seeds and Seedlings entry. For instructions on hand-pollinating flowers, see the Plant Breeding entry. ❖

Populus

Poplar, aspen, cottonwood. Deciduous trees.

Description: *Populus alba,* white poplar, is an irregular, wide-spreading tree growing 40'-70' tall at maturity. The three-lobed leaves have white to silvery gray undersides; the twigs are covered with a whitish felt. Zones 3-8.

P. deltoides, cottonwood, is a native tree with a massive, furrowed trunk. It grows 75'-90' tall at maturity. The leaves are triangular, and their flattened stems cause them to flutter in any breeze—a trait of all poplars, striking in species with whitish lower leaf surfaces. In late spring, female trees release large amounts of cottony seed, which are carried by wind and water. Zones 2-7.

P. grandidentata, bigtooth aspen, is a 50'-70' tree known for its coarsely toothed leaves with grayish undersides. It is pyramidal in youth, becoming irregular with age. The gray-green trunk is smooth but warty. Zones 4-6.

P. nigra, black poplar, is a slender tree that grows 70'-90' tall. Its cultivar 'Italica' is the columnar Lombardy poplar. Zones 3-8.

P. tremuloides, quaking aspen, reaches 40'-50' in the landscape. This quick-growing tree is pyramidal when young, rounded with age. Finely toothed leaves have a clear yellow fall color; the bark is a pale olive. Zones 2-6.

How to grow: Poplars perform best in moist, even wet, soils in full sun. Weak wood and a variety of problems, including cankers, powdery mildew, borers, galls, leaf blisters, and rusts, limit poplars' usefulness to a few situations. Invasive roots grow into sewer lines and drain tiles; keep poplars far away.

Landscape uses: Used with an understanding of its limits, quaking aspen's shimmering leaves and fall color make it useful for naturalizing. Use cottonwood for shade on appropriate sites. ❖

Portulaca

Portulaca, moss rose. All-season annuals.

Description: Portulaca's 1" single or double roselike flowers, in white, pink, red, yellow, orange, or magenta bloom freely on sprawling, 4"-6" mats of succulent, needlelike leaves.

How to grow: Sow seeds directly after the soil warms up, or set out transplants no more than 6" apart. Plants thrive in sunny, hot, dry areas with poor soil. Plants self-sow readily, but the flower color may revert to bright magenta.

Landscape uses: Use portulaca as a filler between paving stones and cracks. It also adds color to pots and baskets.

Best cultivars: Double-flowered 'Afternoon Delight' and 'Cloudbeater', both mixes. ❖

Potato

Solanum tuberosum
Solanaceae

The versatile and nutritious potato has been a staple crop for hundreds of years. Native to the Andes mountains of South America, potatoes thrive in the cool northern half of the United States and the southern half of Canada. Growers in other areas, however, can have successful crops by planting potatoes in very early spring or, in warm regions, in fall or winter for a spring harvest.

Planting: Although you can grow a few cultivars from seed, it's easier to plant certified, disease-free "seed potatoes" purchased from garden centers. (Potatoes you buy at the grocery store are often chemically treated to prevent the eyes from sprouting.) You'll need 5-8 lb. of potatoes to plant a 100' row.

Potatoes need space, sunshine, and fertile, well-drained soil. Acid soil provides good growing conditions and reduces the chance of scab.

Plant seed potatoes whole, or cut them into good-sized pieces, each of which should contain 2-3 eyes. Cure the cut pieces by spreading them out in a bright, airy place for 24 hours, or until they are slightly dry and the cut areas have hardened. In wet climates, dust seed potatoes with sulfur to help prevent rot.

Start early cultivars 2-3 weeks before the last spring frost or as soon as you can work the soil. Time the planting of late cultivars so they will mature before the first fall frost.

Plant potatoes in rows spaced 3' apart. Place the seed pieces 6" apart, and cover them with 4"-5" of soil. As the vines grow, hill soil, leaves, straw, or compost over them to keep the developing tubers covered. (When exposed to sunlight, tubers turn green and develop a mildly toxic substance called solanine.) Leaving only a small portion of the growing vines exposed encourages additional root development.

Many growers prefer to plant potatoes in hills. "Potato Planting Methods" below shows potatoes planted in soil hills and mulch mounds. The mulch-planting method is especially good for growing potatoes in containers, such as large barrels. This "dirtless" method makes harvesting extremely clean and easy but can produce a smaller crop of small tubers.

Growing guidelines: Once the plants blossom, stop hilling up the soil, and apply a thick mulch to conserve moisture and keep down weeds. Water deeply during dry spells.

Problems: Climate and growing conditions can create a number of problems. Speckle leaf, a disorder which appears as dark splotches on leaves with sunken areas on the leaf undersides, is apparently caused by too much ozone in the atmosphere. Breeders are developing resistant cultivars. Keeping plants healthy and well cultivated is the best prevention.

Potato planting methods. To plant in hills (left), pile up a 3'-4' wide mound of soil 4"-6" high. Space seed potatoes 6" apart near the center of the hill and bury with 4"-5" of soil; continue covering tubers as they develop. To mulch-plant (right), form hills in the fall with a 3'-4' thick mound of leaves. The next spring, plant the seed potatoes on top of the partially decomposed mound and cover them with with 1' of straw or hay, adding more as the vines mature.

Hollow areas in tuber centers are caused by rapid and uneven growth. To prevent, plant seed potatoes closer together, cut down on watering and fertilizer, and avoid susceptible cultivars.

Potatoes are attractive to a number of common pests, including aphids, Colorado potato beetles, cutworms, and flea beetles. For control measures, see "The Top Ten Garden Insect Pests in America" on page 344.

Other possible pests include blister beetles, leafhoppers, and wireworms. Blister beetles are ¾″ long, slender, dark-colored insects that feed on leaves; reduce damage by handpicking (be sure to wear gloves to avoid blisters). Thin, wedge-shaped, ¼″ long leafhoppers cause leaves to curl and yellow; apply soap spray for control. Wireworms are ½″-¾″ long larvae of the click beetle; these orange "worms" feed on and damage developing tubers. They are most prevalent in newly cultivated areas, so wait a few years before planting potatoes in freshly turned sod; crop rotation and frequent cultivation can also help.

Avoid most potato diseases by rotating crops, providing good air circulation, keeping the garden clean, selecting resistant cultivars, and planting disease-free seed potatoes. If disease does strike, remove and destroy affected plants. Here are some diseases that might occur:

• Black leg, a bacterial infection, begins as yellowing of top foliage and progresses to a black, slimy rot that destroys stems and tubers.

• Early blight, also called leaf spot, is a fungus that shows up on leaves as enlarging brown spots that develop concentric rings. The blight eventually spreads to the tubers, reducing yields and creating puckered skins with discolored spots.

• Late blight hits crops after they've blossomed. It begins with dark, watery spots on leaves and spreads to stems and tubers.

• Ring rot is a highly infectious bacterial disease that is not generally obvious aboveground. Underground, it starts with a ⅛″ ring of decay under a tuber's skin; eventually the whole interior decays, leaving a shell of firm tissue.

• Scab causes rough, corky spots on tubers. It is most commonly a problem in soils that have a near-neutral or alkaline pH or in those that are on the dry side. Keep the pH low and maintain an even moisture level in the soil to avoid scab.

• Verticillium wilt turns older leaves yellow and eventually causes the whole plant to wilt and die.

Harvesting: Blossoming plants are a sign that the first "new" potatoes are ready to harvest. Pull aside the earth around the base of plants and gently pick off cooking-sized tubers, which are delicious boiled with the skins on.

Once the foliage starts to wither and die back, the tubers will be full-grown. If the weather is not too warm or wet, they will keep in the ground for several weeks. Dig them up with a spading fork before the first frost. Potatoes that are nicked or bruised during harvesting won't

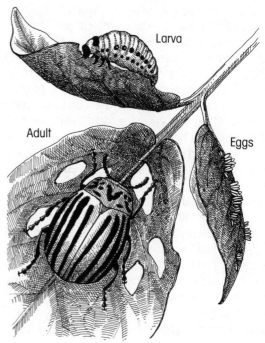

Colorado potato beetles. This well-known garden pest is easy to identify. Control by handpicking adults and larvae; rub the yellowish egg clusters off the undersides of leaves.

store well, so eat them as soon as you can. Clean and dry the crop as quickly as possible, but never expose it to sunlight. Store tubers in a dark place at around 40°F.

Best cultivars: 'Norland', early, medium-sized, oblong, scab-resistant, red tubers with compact tops; 'Norgold's Russet', long, white tubers good for baking but not storing; 'Irish Cobbler', an old-fashioned favorite, non-scab-resistant, does well in heavy soils; 'Red LaSoda', good for warm climates; 'Kennebec', late-maturing, white, blocky tubers, scab- and blight-resistant; 'Red Pontiac', late-maturing, oblong, smooth-skinned, stores well; 'Bintje,' old-fashioned and prolific, with waxy, yellow skin and yellow flesh. ❖

Potentilla

Cinquefoil. Spring- and summer-blooming deciduous shrubs.

Description: *Potentilla fruticosa,* shrubby cinquefoil, is an exceptionally hardy shrub. It has a low, twiggy, rounded form, growing to 2'-4' tall and wide. The compound leaves are a soft gray-green. Lemon yellow, 1″ flowers cover the plant in late spring, followed by sporadic bloom through summer and into fall. Zones 2-7.

How to grow: Cinquefoil does best with full sun in well-drained soil. Once established, it needs little supplemental watering. Prune in late winter before growth begins.

Landscape uses: Because of its compact size, cinquefoil makes a good foundation plant. It is also effective as a specimen or in a massed planting.

Best cultivars: 'Mount Everest' has pure white flowers. ❖

Potpourri

The popularity of potpourri is due to its beauty and fragrance, its usefulness in scenting rooms, closets, and linens, and how much fun it is to make. Early potpourris were damp mixtures of rose petals pickled with salt and spices. Dry potpourri is more popular today because it is easier to make, prettier, and more useful.

Dry potpourri is a mixture of dried herbs and flowers, spices, and essential oils. (See "Plant Materials for Potpourri" on page 497 for ideas.) The blossoms, leaves, and seeds of plants provide texture, color, and some scent. The essential oil adds an intense fragrance. A fixative holds the perfume in the potpourri.

When you're combining mixtures of flowers, leaves, and other plant materials, think about how the various scents go together. Just as in perfumes, there are combinations with floral, woodsy, citrusy, or spicy scents. The rule of thumb for potpourri is to use no more than 4-6 different flowers and leaves and 3-4 spices and other ingredients.

Drying Flowers and Herbs

Cut flowers and herbs for potpourri after the dew has dried on a morning following a few days of clear, dry weather. Pick flowers just as they begin to open and herbs just before they start to flower.

After the flowers are picked, trim off the stems or cut the individual florets from the stalks. Pull rose petals from the flowers and spread them to dry. Dry a few tiny rosebuds, such as those from 'Bonica', 'Cécile Brunner', or any of the miniature roses, for decorating the potpourri. Spread flowers or petals in a single layer on cheesecloth, a nonmetal screen or tray, or a cookie sheet with a nonstick coating. Put in a dark, dry, well-ventilated place to dry. If on a solid tray or sheet, stir occasionally.

Hang herbs upside down in small bunches held together with rubber bands and placed in a dark, dry, well-ventilated place. When the leaves are completely dry, strip them from the stems.

What seems like a great quantity of fresh material will dry to a much smaller amount. You may have to dry several batches before you have enough of the varieties you want to make a certain potpourri. Keep dried flowers and herbs in glass containers with airtight screw-top lids. Label the jars and store in a dark place.

Scenting Potpourri

Use intensely fragrant essential oils to enhance the natural fragrance of potpourris. Choose an oil that has the same fragrance as the plant material used in the greatest quantity. Craft and perfume shops as well as potpourri suppliers usually carry essential oils. If you can't find your first choice, then choose an oil that is complementary. Never use more than three different essential oils in one batch of potpourri.

MAKING DRY POTPOURRI

Here's a basic recipe for potpourri.

10–20 drops essential oil
2–4 tablespoons dried orris or calamus root or 1 cup dried oak moss
4 cups (⅓ lb.) dried flowers and herbs
1–3 tablespoons crushed spices
1½ teaspoons powdered gum resin
½ cup dried, crushed citrus peel (optional)
½ cup cedar or sandalwood chips (optional)

1. Prepare for potpourri making at least two days in advance by sprinkling essential oil over the orris, calamus root, or oak moss in a small glass jar and capping tightly.
2. In a large glass, enameled, ceramic, or stainless steel bowl, combine the dried flowers and herbs, crushed spices, and gum resin with the citrus peel and wood chips (if using).
3. Sprinkle on the oil and fixative mixture and stir in thoroughly.
4. Pour the mixture into a large wide-mouthed glass jar and cap tightly. Make sure the jar is big enough so you can shake and mix the potpourri.
5. Put the jar in a warm, dark place. About twice a week, turn the jar end for end and shake gently to redistribute the ingredients. The potpourri should be well blended in about four weeks.

Focus on Fixatives

Potpourris release their fragrance as the oils evaporate. To get these oils to last as long as possible, certain materials, called fixatives, are added to slow evaporation. The best fixatives for potpourri are derived from plants. Buy them from craft shops or potpourri suppliers; orris and calamus can be grown in the garden.

Orris root (*Iris* × *germanica* var. *florentina*) has a delicate, violetlike scent. It is the most popular fixative, blending well with woodsy and oriental-type mixtures. Calamus root (*Acorus calamus*), or sweet flag, grows in boggy ground. It goes well with spicy, earthy, and vanilla-scented potpourris. Oak moss is actually a lichen. It blends well with lavender, makes citrus and floral blends smell fresher, and adds depth to potpourris containing patchouli, vanilla, and tonka bean.

For dry potpourris, use the fixatives in chopped form, if possible. To make your own, scrub the roots of orris or calamus well, dice into ¼″ pieces, and allow to dry thoroughly in a warm, dark, well-ventilated place.

Gum resins such as gum arabic, gum benzoin, frankincense, myrrh, and gum styrax unite the different fragrances in potpourri. Add 2 tablespoons of one of them to each gallon of potpourri.

Using and Displaying Potpourri

Once the potpourri has aged and blended to your satisfaction, it's ready to use. Transfer it to smaller containers for use around the house. Although open bowls filled with potpourri are pretty, the scent will soon dissipate. Better to choose containers with covers so that the scent can be released when you choose. Possibilities include ginger jars, ceramic mustard crocks with cork lids, porcelain rice bowls with lids, sugar bowls, soup tureens, and apothecary jars.

Another way to use potpourri is in sachets, pillows, hangers, or other stuffed items. You can also grind it up and add it to melted wax for scented candles, or glue it to polystyrene wreaths and balls or papier-mâché forms for decorations. ❖

PLANT MATERIALS FOR POTPOURRI

You can dry and use both whole flowers and individual petals in potpourri. The classic components of potpourri are lavender flowers and rose petals, which hold their scent best when dried. Other fragrant flowers to consider include chamomile, citrus, jasmines, lilacs, and lilies-of-the-valley. You may wish to choose heliotropes (*Heliotropium* spp.), honeysuckles (*Lonicera* spp.), hyssop (*Hyssopus officinalis*), lindens (*Tilia* spp.), mignonette (*Reseda odorata*), mock oranges (*Philadelphus* spp.), pinks (*Dianthus* spp.), stocks (*Matthiola* spp.), sweet peas (*Lathyrus odoratus*), tuberoses (*Polianthes tuberosa*), or wallflowers (*Cheiranthus cheiri*) as well.

The leaves of many herbs also add special fragrance to potpourri. Those used most often include angelica, basil, bay, costmary, hyssop, marjoram, mint, myrtle, rosemary, sage, scented geraniums, summer savory, sweet woodruff, tarragon, and thyme.

Spices add an exotic undertone to potpourri. Don't use ground spices—they will settle to the bottom and quickly lose their scent. Buy whole spices and lightly crush them with a mortar and pestle. Spices to consider include allspice, anise, caraway, cardamom, cloves, coriander, ginger, juniper berries, nutmeg, sassafras, star anise, and vanilla.

Other plant materials that can contribute fragrance to potpourri include cedar shavings and chips, citrus peels, evergreen needles, sandalwood shavings and chips, tonka beans, and vetiver roots.

Besides the plant materials that contribute scent to the potpourri, you can add colorful flowers for appearance alone. The flowers that retain their color best when dried or have an interesting shape include annual statice, borage, calendulas, delphiniums, feverfew, geraniums, nasturtiums, pansies, sages, primroses, and violets. Also included are bee balms (*Monarda* spp.), coreopsis (*Coreopsis* spp.), cornflowers (*Centaurea cyanus*), larkspurs (*Consolida* spp.), monkshoods (*Aconitum* spp.), and yarrows (*Achillea* spp.). Add hemlock cones to a pine-based potpourri.

Primula

Primrose. Spring-blooming perennials.

Description: Primroses bear rounded, five-petaled flowers in clusters above crowded leaves.

Primula × polyantha, polyanthus primrose, practically hides its 6" paddlelike leaves in early spring under 6"-10" tall, dense clusters of 1½" blooms in rich shades of white, yellow, red, and blue, many with a distinct yellow eye. Best in Zones 5-7; widely grown as annuals elsewhere.

P. sieboldii, Siebold's primrose, carries its 1½" blooms in white, lilac, and magenta-purple shades 8"-10" above spreading masses of scalloped 4" leaves that die down in summer. Zones 4-8.

P. vulgaris, English or common primrose, bears yellow, 1", slightly fragrant blooms just above dense rosettes of 3" leaves. Zones 5-8.

How to grow: Plant in spring or divide after bloom every 2-3 years. Grow in partially shaded, average to fertile, well-drained but moisture-retentive soil enriched with organic matter. They tolerate full sun if the soil remains moist, although common primroses tolerate drier soils than most. Individual plants are usually short-lived, but they self-sow or produce offsets generously. Mulch in summer to retain moisture and in winter to prevent the shallow-rooted plants from being heaved out of the ground by the freezing and thawing of the soil. Handpick or trap slugs and snails; wash spider mites off plants with a strong spray of water.

Landscape uses: Group primroses along paths, at the edge of borders, and in cottage gardens. Combine with bulbs, ferns, and other spring flowers in a wooded area. Make a late sowing of sweet alyssum to fill bare spots left by Siebold's primroses.

Best cultivars: *P. × polyantha:* 'Pacific Giants' cultivars feature the entire color range. *P. sieboldii:* the 'Barnhaven' strain comes in a wide range of colors and petal shapes, some fringed or toothed. ❖

Propagation

Learning to propagate plants—to make new plants from existing ones in your home and garden—is one of the most exciting and rewarding aspects of gardening. Many of the methods are easy, and you don't need fancy or expensive tools. Propagation is cheaper than buying large numbers of plants, so with a little time and effort you can fill your garden quickly at minimal cost. Propagating new plants will keep your house and garden full of vigorous specimens, and you'll probably have plenty to give away, too!

You can reproduce most plants by several methods. There are two major types of propagation: sexual and asexual. Sexual propagation involves seeds, which are produced by the fusion of male and female reproductive cells. Asexual propagation methods use the vegetative parts of a plant: roots, stems, buds, and leaves. Division, cuttings, layering, budding, and grafting are all asexual methods. Spores (produced by ferns and mosses) may look like seeds, but they are technically asexual structures, because they have a specialized way of forming new plants.

Select a technique by considering the plant you are working with, the materials you have, the season, and the amount of time you are willing to wait for a new plant.

Seeds: Growing from seed is an inexpensive way to produce large numbers of plants. Annuals, biennials, and vegetables are almost always reproduced by seed. You can also grow perennials, shrubs, and trees from seed, although the seedlings they produce may not resemble the parent plants. Raising seeds requires few materials: a container, a growing medium, and seeds. The time to sow seeds depends on the type of plant. For most garden plants, you can sow seeds indoors in late winter or outdoors in spring. Tree and shrub seeds may need a cold period or other treatment before they will germinate. Depending on the type of plant, it could take anywhere from weeks to years to get a garden-sized specimen. For complete information on growing plants from seeds, see the Seeds and Seedlings entry.

Spores: Spores are the reproductive structures of ferns and mosses. To produce new plants, sow these dustlike "seeds" on a sterile medium and cover them to maintain humidity and prevent contamination. Clear plastic shoe boxes or cups are ideal containers for propagation. You can collect spores from your own ferns or buy them from specialty catalogs. You can sow spores whenever they are available. The new plants will be ready for the garden after a period of months or years.

Division: Division is an easy way to produce more plants with almost 100 percent success. This method involves digging up an established plant and separating it into several pieces. Division is used for bulbs and mat-, clump-, or crown-forming plants, including ferns, bamboos, bugleweed, daylilies, and hostas. Single-stemmed plants like trees cannot be divided.

All you'll need for division is a tool to dig up the plant, and your hands or a sharp implement to separate the pieces. You can divide most plants in either spring or fall. Division produces full-sized plants that can be placed directly in the garden. For more information, see the Division entry.

Cuttings: Cuttings are pieces of leaves, stems, and roots that are separated from a parent plant. When placed in the proper conditions, these pieces form new roots and shoots. Stem cuttings are used for a wide range of plants, including geraniums, pachysandra, and privet. Use root cuttings for plants such as bleeding heart and goldenrain tree. You can also try leaf petiole cuttings, used for African violets and peperomias, and leaf pieces, used for such plants as gloxinias and snake plant.

The materials you'll need depend on the plant and the method you are using. Leaf petiole cuttings of African violet will root in a simple glass of water. You can stick stem and root cuttings in a pot or flat of regular potting soil. A plastic bag or other clear cover will help to maintain high humidity around the cuttings. More complicated structures, such as cold frames and mist boxes, are good for hard-to-root shrub and tree cuttings. Plants reproduced by cuttings can be ready for the garden in a matter of weeks or months. See the Cuttings entry for more details on this method.

Layering: Layering is a way to get stems to root while they are still attached to the parent plant. Some plants produce layers naturally. Strawberries form rooted plantlets on runners; raspberries produce new plants where the stem tips touch the ground. The technique of simple layering involves bending a low-growing stem to ground level and burying a few inches of the stem behind the tip. Simple layering is an easy way to reproduce such plants as camellias, forsythias, and magnolias. To air-layer, you shallowly wound a stem a few inches below the tip to stimulate root production, and then wrap moist sphagnum moss around the stem. Covering the moss with a thin sheet of plastic holds in moisture and secures the moss to the stem. Weeping fig trees, rubber plants, and witch hazels are all good candidates for air layering.

You don't need much equipment to try these techniques. A trowel (for digging the trench) is sufficient for simple layering. For air layering, you'll need sphagnum moss, waterproof tape, a piece of thin plastic, and a knife. Early spring is the best time for simple layering. For outdoor plants, you can set up air layers in spring or late summer. Indoor air layers can be started anytime. It will probably take several months to a year to get a new well-rooted plant. For more information, see the Layering entry.

Grafting: Grafting is a more advanced propagation technique. It involves joining a stem piece of one plant (the scion) to the root system of another plant (the rootstock) in such a way that the parts unite and continue to grow. You can reproduce many types of trees by grafting,

including pines and rhododendrons, and even some herbaceous plants, such as cacti. Grafting has several advantages over other propagation methods. It allows you to propagate plants that are difficult to raise from seeds or cuttings. Through grafting, you can produce a plant adapted to your particular needs. Some rootstocks have a dwarfing effect, while others encourage vigorous top growth. They can also provide tolerance to soilborne insects and diseases, or less-than-perfect soil conditions.

The most important grafting tool is a sharp knife. You may also need string or tape (to keep the graft pieces together) and grafting wax (to prevent water loss and avoid contamination). You'll have to have suitable rootstocks, too. You can raise your own from seeds or cuttings, or buy them from a specialty catalog or nursery. Spring is the most common time for grafting. Herbaceous plants will join successfully in a few weeks; woody plant grafts usually take a month or two to unite firmly and begin growing. See the Grafting entry for more details on this technique.

Budding: Budding is a particular type of grafting. In this method, you use only a single bud from the desired plant. Budding is commonly used to propagate fruit trees as well as ornamentals, such as hybrid tea roses. For the home gardener, the advantages of budding are similar to those of grafting. In some cases, budding is more successful than grafting because it is easier to get close contact between the bud and the rootstock. Budding also allows you to propagate more plants if you have a limited amount of scion material.

For this technique you'll need a sharp knife and some string or tape to secure the bud to the stem. As with grafting, compatible rootstock plants are necessary. Budding is best done in late summer or early fall. Buds inserted at this time will produce new growth the following spring. See the Budding entry for a more complete discussion of this technique. ❖

Pruning and Training

Pruning is both a science and an art—and probably the least-understood gardening practice. A properly pruned landscape shows off each plant at its best. Well-pruned plants produce more or better fruit and flowers. Pruning can improve the health of an ailing plant, make trees stronger and safer, channel growth away from buildings or traffic, and restore a sense of order to an overplanted or overgrown yard.

Pruning Cuts

Many gardeners think pruning is a complicated task; however, most pruning comes down to making one of two kinds of pruning cuts: thinning cuts and heading cuts. "Making Pruning Cuts" on the opposite page shows the differences between these two kinds of cuts.

Thinning cuts: Thinning cuts remove branches totally. They open up a plant but don't make it shorter. Thinning directs growth into alternate patterns. Use thinning cuts to establish good structure of young trees and shrubs, to allow sunlight to reach the plant interior, to remove wayward branches or those that block a view, and to make a plant less likely to break under a heavy snow load.

Heading cuts: Heading cuts shorten plants and stimulate latent buds behind the cut to grow, making the plant more dense. Nonselective heading is the technique used to shape formal hedges and topiary. Branches are cut back partway along the stem, resulting in rapid, bushy regrowth just below the cut. Nonselective heading is often misapplied—resulting in forlorn lollipop-shaped shrubs or trees that would look more attractive, and would likely be healthier, if pruned to follow their natural form.

Selective heading, on the other hand, reduces overall size or height of a plant without changing its natural shape. The plant suffers less stress and doesn't regrow as vigorously. Selective heading combines the best of thinning and heading, but it can't be applied to all plants. The older, larger, and woodier the plant, the fewer selective heading cuts should be used.

Pruning Do's and Don'ts

Proper technique: Prune from the bottom up and, in the case of large plants, from the inside out. Prune out all dead wood first—an important step for health and good looks. Dead

---

Key Words
PRUNING AND TRAINING

Branch collar. The part of the trunk that helps hold the branch to the trunk, often recognizable as a bulge at the base of the branch.

Branch crotch. The angle where a tree branch meets the trunk or parent stem.

Break bud. When a latent bud is stimulated into growing out into a leaf or twig, it is said to break bud.

Cane. A long, slender branch that usually originates directly from the roots.

Leader. The main, primary, or tallest shoot of a tree trunk. Trees can be single-leadered, such as birch, or multiple-leadered, such as vine maple.

Pinching. Nipping out the end bud of a twig or stem with your fingertips to make the plant more compact and bushy.

Thinning cut. Cutting a limb off at the base, either at ground level or at a branch collar.

Heading cut. Cutting a branch back to a side bud or shoot.

Skirting or limbing up. Pruning off the lower limbs of trees.

Sucker. An upright shoot growing from a root or graft union; also, in common usage, straight, rapid-growing shoots or watersprouts that grow in response to wounding or poor pruning.

Topiary. Plants sculpted into tightly sheared geometric shapes or likenesses of animals or people.

wood is easiest to spot in the summer because the branches have no green leaves.

Next look for a few of the worst rubbing, crossing branches. Leave the best-placed one of any pair. Try to keep branches that head up and out from the center or that fill an otherwise empty space.

Prune to open up center areas and to clean up the base of shrubs. This improves plant health by admitting light and increasing air circulation. It also has a large impact on the beauty of a plant.

Selectively thin or head back misplaced branches: those that touch the ground, lay upon or crowd other plants, or come too close to the house, windows, and walkways.

Save any heading cuts until the end of a pruning job. Locate the longest, most unruly branch first, follow it down inside the shrub, and cut it off to a side branch or a bud. Next year's new growth will be channeled into the bud or side branch.

Pruning mistakes: The most common prun-

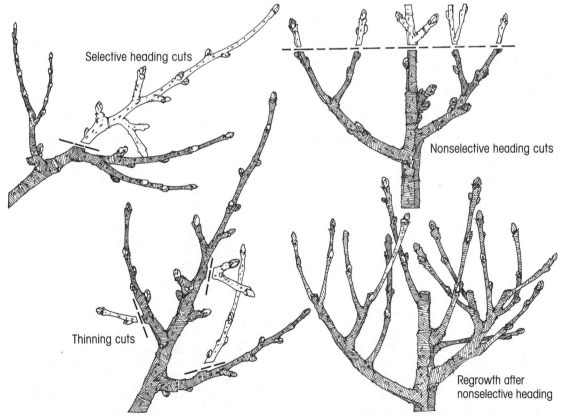

Selective heading cuts

Nonselective heading cuts

Thinning cuts

Regrowth after nonselective heading

Making pruning cuts. (1) Make thinning cuts at the branch collar where the branch originates. Avoid making a flush cut; leave the branch collar intact, but don't leave a stub. (2) Make selective heading cuts back to a point directly above a bud or side branch of significant size that faces the direction you want new growth to take. (3) Make nonselective heading cuts anywhere on the stem to shear branches to a uniform surface.

ing mistake is to cut back everything in the yard in an ill-fated attempt to make it all smaller again. This stimulates an upsurge of messy regrowth, making the final solution more difficult. Tree topping, indiscriminate shearing, and overthinning are the three major forms of "malpruning."

The cure for badly pruned plants is time. Most will reestablish their natural habits given a few years to recover. Rehabilitative pruning can hasten the process and make plants look better. Meticulously prune all dead wood, removing all stubs. Use thinning cuts to simplify tangled branch ends. Take out entire canes. If treelike shrubs have rampantly produced suckers because of heading cuts, slowly remove the worst of them over a period of years. Let the strongest and best-placed suckers grow back into branches. Some plants, such as cane-growers like weigela, can be radically renovated by cutting them entirely to the ground. In about three years they'll regrow to mature size and bloom again. Many lovely but rampant vines, such as autumn clematis, are treated this way to good effect.

The majority of needled evergreens will not green up once they are cut back to unneedled wood. This makes their size difficult to control and radical renovation impossible.

Pruning Timetable

Plan your pruning schedule depending on what you want to accomplish. General thinning can be done in any season. Follow these seasonal guidelines:

• Spring pruning stimulates the most rapid regrowth, so it's a good time for heavy pruning. Prune evergreens in spring, but avoid pruning deciduous trees as they leaf out. Prune spring-flowering shrubs such as azaleas, daphnes, and forsythias when they finish blooming, so they'll have time to grow and set new buds during summer. This is essential if you are heading back all the branches to force more blooms.

• Summer pruning has a less stimulating

effect on growth. Hot or dry weather is extremely stressful for plants, so avoid heavy pruning. This is a good time to tidy up plants and remove suckers and to prune summer-flowering shrubs after they bloom.

• In mid- to late fall, make only thinning cuts. Heading cuts made late in the season can stimulate soft new growth that is easily damaged in fall freezes. Don't prune plants during the period when their leaves are falling.

• Late winter is the traditional time to prune dormant plants; leaves have dropped and it's easy to see plant form. Winter pruning stimulates growth, but the results are delayed until

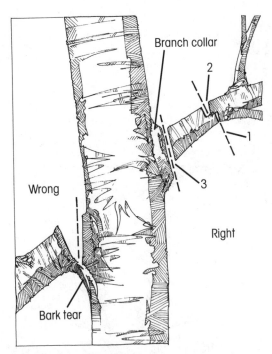

Pruning large limbs. Sawed from above, a large branch will tear bark from the trunk as it falls. Use the three-cut method to prevent damage. (1) About 1' out from the trunk, cut halfway through the branch from underneath. (2) A few inches in from the first cut, saw off the branch from the top. (3) Remove the stub by cutting along, but never into, the branch collar. On tight crotches, saw from the bottom up.

<table>
</table>

More On
PRUNING

You'll find specific pruning instructions for various types of plants in the following entries: Blueberry, Brambles, Citrus, Clematis, Currant, Elderberry, Espalier, Evergreens, Fruit Trees, Grape, Hedges, Herbs, Lonicera (honeysuckle), Nut Trees, Rosa (rose), Shrubs, Trees, Vines, and Wisteria.

spring. This is a good time to prune fruit trees, brambles, grapes, roses, and summer-blooming shrubs, such as butterfly bushes and hydrangeas, that form flowers on the current year's wood.

Good Tools for Good Cuts

Choose pruning tools that cut cleanly and easily. Keep the cutting edges sharp. You'll probably need only three pruning tools: pruning shears for stems and twigs, lopping shears for branches that are finger-size and larger, and a pruning saw for larger branches and crowded areas.

Pruning shears are available in two types. Anvil pruners cut with a sharp blade that closes against a metal plate, or anvil; bypass pruners work like scissors. A leather holster is a wise investment: Your hands are free, but the shears are always handy.

Lopping shears have long handles that extend your reach and give you leverage for more cutting strength. A small rubber shock absorber is a welcome addition on some models. Folding pruning saws fit nicely into a back pocket. New ARS-type saws have multifaceted blades and cut twice as easily as traditional blades. Pole pruners can be used for overhead work, but be careful of overhead wires. The pruning head can consist of either a saw or a cord-operated hook-type shear, or a combination of the two. You may find hedge shears useful for keeping formal hedges neat. ❖

Prunus

Ornamental cherry, plum, almond.
Deciduous or evergreen spring-flowering trees or shrubs.

Description: Many members of this genus produce edible fruit; you'll find more information on planting, maintenance, and pest control in the Cherry, Peach, and Plum entries.

Prunus cerasifera, Myrobalan plum, is a deciduous shrub or small tree with a rounded, spreading habit and a mature height of 15'-25'. Pale to deep pink flowers precede the leaves, which are purple on most cultivars. Zones 4-8.

P. glandulosa, dwarf flowering almond, is a diminutive shrub of 3'-5' with slender twigs and a delicate, open branching habit. Single or double pink or white flowers appear before the leaves in early to mid-spring. Zones 4-8.

P. laurocerasus, cherry-laurel, is an evergreen shrub that bears white flowers in early to mid-spring. Leaves are shiny and leathery; fruits are black. Zones 6-8.

P. serrulata, Japanese flowering cherry, grows 20'-25' tall and is vase-shaped; single or double blooms are white to pink. Zones 5-7.

P. subhirtella, Higan cherry, grows 25' tall and bears pale to deep pink single or double flowers before leaves appear. Zones 5-9.

How to grow: Except for the cherry-laurels (which prefer shade), most species need full sun and well-drained soil. Protect the thin bark from lawn mower injuries. Prune after flowering.

Landscape uses: Most tree cherries make fine focal points or groupings in a sunny area. Cherry-laurels work well in shade individually or grouped. Most *Prunus* attract birds.

Best cultivars: *P. cerasifera* 'Atropurpurea', purple-leaf plum. *P. serrulata* 'Kwanzan', upright form with deep pink double flowers borne before the leaves, orange and red fall colors. *P. subhirtella* 'Pendula', weeping habit, single pink flowers in mid-spring. ❖

Pumpkin

Cucurbita spp.
Cucurbitaceae

Fun-to-grow pumpkins produce rounded orange fruits that are popular for pies and Halloween decorations. Pumpkins are closely related to winter squash, and their growing requirements are the same. For cultural information, see the Squash entry. ❖

Pyracantha

Pyracantha, firethorn. Spring-blooming evergreen or semi-evergreen shrubs.

Description: *Pyracantha coccinea,* scarlet firethorn, is an upright, irregular, spiny shrub reaching 15' tall. It has oval, 1"-1½", dark to medium green leaves, clusters of small white flowers in spring, and showy orange-red berries that persist through fall. Zones 6-8.

How to grow: Provide full sun and good drainage. In Southern climates, site firethorns where air circulation will be good; in the North, site them out of the winter wind. Once established, they need little supplemental water. Prune diligently to remove watersprouts and suckers and to maintain shape. A neglected firethorn is soon out of control. Once overgrown, it is difficult to coax back to size without some awkward pruning cuts.

Landscape uses: Scarlet firethorn makes an attractive espalier—its flowers and berries are set off by a wall or trellis. You can also use firethorn as a hedge; it makes a nearly impenetrable barrier. Plant it to attract berry-eating birds in winter.

Best cultivars: When choosing a cultivar, look for resistance to fire blight and scab. *Pyracantha* × 'Mohave' (a *P. coccinea* hybrid) is a good choice. ❖

Pyrus

Pear. Spring-flowering deciduous trees.

Description: Members of this genus produce edible fruit; you'll find information on planting, maintenance, and pest control in the Pear entry.

Pyrus calleryana, Callery pear, is familiar in city landscapes because its cultivar 'Bradford' has been widely planted as a street tree. This popular cultivar is pyramidal when young and rounded with maturity, with a dense crown. It attains a mature height in the range of 25'-40'. Its winter buds are a woolly buff color, and its white, malodorous flowers appear in early to mid-spring before the leaves, which are a shiny dark green. Spectacular fall leaf colors of reds, russets, oranges, and yellows are reliable most years, especially in the North. Small (½"), round pears appear in the fall. Zones 5-8.

How to grow: Provide full sun and good drainage. Pears can have serious problems with fire blight, a bacterial disease, during wet summers. Watch for branches forming fire blight's distinctive "shepherd's crooks" at their tips following warm, wet weather during periods of rapid growth. However, the popular cultivar 'Bradford' shows good resistance to fire blight. Callery pears have naturally narrow (and therefore weak) crotch angles that often break under the weight of mature (perhaps snow-laden) branches. Watch the marketplace for improved Callery pear cultivars with wider crotch angles.

Landscape uses: Callery pears look nice when massed or as a focal point, especially for an early splash of white flowers. Their tolerance of urban conditions, combined with abundant flowers, attractive foliage, and small- to mid-sized cultivars, makes them a common sight along the sidewalks of many American cities.

Best cultivars: 'Aristocrat' is less dense than 'Bradford' and has wider crotch angles. Its dominant fall foliage color is burgundy. ❖

Quercus

Oak. Large deciduous or evergreen trees.

Description: Large shade trees with toothed or lobed leaves, oaks are pyramidal trees when young, developing a rounded to spreading habit with age.

Quercus acutissima, sawtooth oak, grows 35'-45' in the landscape. Its oblong leaves with bristlelike teeth usually turn brown and persist through the winter. Zones 6-8.

Q. alba, white oak, grows 60'-80' in the landscape; its most outstanding feature is the ash-gray bark layered on its trunk. The leaves have rounded lobes and turn to shades of red and russet late in the fall. Zones 3-8.

Q. imbricaria, shingle oak, has oblong, leathery, deep green leaves that turn brown in autumn and often persist on the tree well into the winter, rattling in the wind. This native tree tolerates limestone soils well. Zones 5-7.

Q. macrocarpa, bur oak, is a massive native of the North American prairie. Growing 70'-80' tall, it has imposing limbs, a wide trunk, and deeply furrowed bark. The leaves have rounded lobes and can grow to 10" long. The cup on the acorn is fringed. Bur oak also performs well in limestone soils. Zones 2-7.

Q. palustris, pin oak, is a popular lawn tree with a strongly pyramidal form and a mature height of 60'-70'. The leaves are sharply lobed and may develop chlorosis (yellowing) when the tree is grown in limestone soils. Zones 5-8.

Q. phellos, willow oak, is similar in form, size, and popularity to pin oak, but has smooth, narrow leaves about 4" long. Some consider its leaf size and shape to make for easier cleanup in the fall because the leaves don't mat and tend to disappear amid groundcovers. Zones 6-9.

Q. robur, English oak, is a sturdy tree with a short trunk, deeply furrowed, dark gray bark, and a broadly spreading to rounded crown. Dark green, alternate leaves are 2"-5" long with rounded lobes; like other oaks native to Europe, fall color is not significant. English oak reaches heights of 40'-60'. Zones 5-8.

Q. rubra, red oak, is a vigorous tree that matures to 60'-75' in the landscape. Lobes are sharply pointed to rounded on shiny dark green leaves; red fall color is not always strong. Red oak tolerates air pollution but may show leaf chlorosis in limestone soils. Zones 4-8.

Q. virginiana, live oak, is an evergreen native of the southeastern coastal forest. Massive and sprawling, live oak grows 40'-80' in the landscape and often larger in the wild. Its elongated oval leaves are shiny dark green above and felted beneath. The huge boughs often host other plants such as Spanish moss and mistletoe. Coastal areas of Zones 7-10.

How to grow: Choose a site with full sun, well-drained, humusy soil, and plenty of room. Although adaptable to a variety of soil conditions, oaks generally perform better in acidic soils. Prune oaks during dormancy to avoid spreading oak wilt, a fungal disease that causes leaves to curl, brown, and droop. Oak wilt moves rapidly through a tree, often killing it within a year. Susceptibility varies among species; white, bur, English, and live oaks show resistance. The disease is more likely to be fatal to red, pin, sawtooth, shingle, and willow oaks. The fungus travels via root grafts; dig a trench between infected and healthy trees to destroy root connections. There is no cure for oak wilt.

The foliage of oaks is a favored food of gypsy moth larvae. Identified by the rows of blue and red stripes along their backs, these 2½" hairy gray caterpillars often occur in sufficient numbers to defoliate a tree; repeated leaf loss causes severe decline and death. Egg masses appear as tan or buff fluffy patches on tree trunks and branches, buildings, and fences; scrape these off into a bucket of soapy water. Tie bands of burlap around tree trunks to capture climbing larvae; crush or handpick trapped caterpillars. Spray BTK (*Bacillus thuringiensis* var. *kurstaki*) to control young caterpillars.

Homeowners are often alarmed by unusual swellings of their oak's leaves, floral parts, or twigs; such galls are caused by various insects and mites. Not all galls injure their hosts, but some kill twigs and branches. Remove and destroy galls to limit further infestation. Spray with dormant oil or lime sulfur in late winter to kill overwintering gall-forming pests.

Landscape uses: Use any of these oaks as long-lasting shade trees; in a large-scale situation, they make fine focal points as well. Most bear acorns that attract wildlife. Good street-tree choices are sawtooth and willow oaks. Look to native oaks if your landscape needs include colorful autumn leaves. ❖

Quince

Cydonia oblonga
Rosaceae

Quince trees are related to apples and pears. They have beautiful pale pink flowers and large green leaves with silvery undersides. The fruit makes excellent preserves, wines, and baked goods. The Fruit Trees entry covers many important aspects of growing quinces and other tree fruits; refer to it for more information on planting, pruning, and care.

Selecting trees: Quinces are self-pollinating. Some flowering quinces (*Chaenomeles* spp.) set small, edible fruit when cross-pollinated. See the Chaenomeles entry for more information on flowering quinces. Quince fruit is yellow to orange, tart, very firm, and often irregularly shaped. Cultivars 'Champion', 'Pineapple', and 'Orange' are good.

Planting and care: Quince trees grow 15'-25' tall, or less when pruned. Their roots are shallow and adaptable to almost all soils.

Quince trees are hardy to −15°F. They bloom late and usually avoid late frost damage. Mulch to retain moisture. Water if soil is dry, especially while the fruit is developing. Limit nitrogen fertilizer to control suckering.

Pruning: Train quinces to an open center shape, or let them develop into a multi-trunk bush. Most of the fruit production will be on young fruiting spurs. Cut out old wood and thin back long branches to encourage more short lateral branches to sprout. Remove suckers.

Problems: See "Fruit Tree Insects and Diseases" on page 256 and the Apple and Pear entries for descriptions and controls of problems. Fire blight can be severe on quince.

Harvesting: Fruit is ripe when the skin changes from green to yellow. A light frost won't hurt them. Quinces bruise easily; handle fruit gently. Refrigerate until you are ready to cook or process them. ❖

Radish

Raphanus sativus
Cruciferae

Colorful and crisp, radishes are a popular addition to vegetable salads. Radishes mature very quickly—some in as little as three weeks. Use them to mark the rows of slow-germinating crops such as carrots and parsnips.

Planting: Dig the soil to a depth of 6″ for quick-growing radishes and up to 2′ for sharper-tasting, slower-growing winter types. Space seeds ½″ deep and 1″ apart; firm the soil and water gently. Make weekly spring sowings as soon as you can work the soil (4-6 weeks before the last expected frost) until early summer; start again in late summer. Sow winter radishes in midsummer for a fall harvest.

Growing guidelines: Thin seedlings to 2″ apart, 3″-4″ for the larger winter types. Mulch to keep down weeds. For quick growth and the best flavor, water regularly.

Problems: Cabbage maggots are attracted to radishes but seldom ruin a whole crop; for controls, see "The Top Ten Garden Insect Pests in America" on page 344.

Harvesting: Pull as soon as the roots mature. Oversized radishes are cracked and tough. ❖

Raised Bed Gardening

The image of an ideal organic food garden typically includes lush crops growing in raised beds. Raised gardening beds are higher than ground level, and separated by paths. Plants cover the bed areas; gardeners work from the paths. The beds are 3′-5′ across to permit easy access and may be any length. You can grow any vegetable in raised beds, as well as herbs, annual or perennial flowers, or berry bushes.

You may wonder whether it's worth your while to build raised beds. In many cases, the answer is a resounding yes. Raised beds can: solve problems of difficult soils; improve production; save space, time, and money; and improve your garden's appearance and accessibility. While that sounds like a tall order, raised beds can do it all. Crops produce better because they grow in deep, loose, fertile soil that is never walked upon. And you can grow twice as many crops in the same space: In a row garden, the crops occupy only ⅓ of the garden area; the paths, ⅔. In a raised bed garden, the proportions are reversed.

Raised beds save time and money because you need only dig, fertilize, and water the beds, ignoring the soil in the paths. You don't need to weed as much when crops grow close together, because weeds can't compete as well. Gardeners with limited mobility find raised beds the perfect solution—a wide sill on a framed raised bed makes a good spot to sit while working, and a high frame puts plants in reach of a gardener using a wheelchair.

The quickest and easiest way to make a raised bed is simply to add lots of organic matter, such as well-rotted manure or compost, to your garden soil to mound up planting beds. However, the traditional way to make a raised bed is to double dig. This process involves removing the topsoil layer from a bed, loosening the subsoil, and replacing the topsoil, mixing in organic matter in the process. Double digging has many benefits, but can be time-consuming and laborious. See the Double Digging entry for details.

If your garden soil is difficult—heavy clay, very alkaline, or full of rocks—you may want to mix your own soil from trucked-in topsoil, organic matter, and mineral amendments. Then you can build beds up from ground level, without disturbing or incorporating the native soil. You may also need to add extra materials to raised beds if you want them to be tall enough for a gardener in a wheelchair to reach easily.

Shape the soil in an unframed bed so that it is flat-topped, with sloping sides (this shape helps conserve water), or forms a long, rounded mound. Frames prevent soil from washing away and allow you to add a greater depth of improved soil. Wood, brick, rocks, or cement blocks are popular materials for framing. Choose naturally rot-resistant woods such as cedar, cypress, or locust. If you don't use rot-resistant woods, you may eventually need to replace the frame. Another option is to use wood treated with borax-based preservatives. This natural mineral is toxic to insects and fungi but relatively nontoxic to humans. For information about these preservatives, write to U.S. Borax, 3075 Wilshire Boulevard, Los Angeles, CA 90010. ❖

Ranunculus

Buttercup. Spring-blooming perennials.

Description: Buttercups bear cheerful, shiny golden yellow, ¾″-1″ blooms above low masses of dark green cut leaves. *Ranunculus acris* 'Flore Pleno', yellow bachelor's buttons, produces double blooms on sparsely branched 3′ stems.

How to grow: Plant or divide buttercups in spring or fall. Buttercups thrive in sun or partial shade with average, moist to nearly boggy soil, but they will tolerate denser shade and drier soil. Divide every 3-4 years.

Landscape uses: Yellow bachelor's buttons are pretty in a spring border or cutting garden. You can also naturalize them in wet areas and woods.

Best cultivars: 'Plenus', 'Plena', and 'Multiplex' are synonyms for 'Flore Pleno'. 'Stevenii' bears larger single or semi-double flowers. ❖

Raspberry

Rubus spp.
Rosaceae

A few raspberry plants will reward you with luscious fruit for many years with a small investment of time and effort. Fresh raspberries are marvelous eaten straight from the bush or made into jam to spread on toast in midwinter for a burst of summer. They thrive in Northern areas, and there are also cultivars suitable for all but the hottest areas of the country.

Summer-bearing cultivars are available in red, black, yellow, and purple. Fall-bearing cultivars are only red or yellow.

Raspberry plants have perennial roots and biennial canes. They grow best when trained on a trellis or other support. For information on care, maintenance, and pest control for raspberries, see the Brambles entry. ❖

Recycling

Using something you have to make something you need: It's an old-fashioned concept that's suddenly fashionable again. Reusing and recycling household materials is one of the best individual actions people can take to help solve environmental problems.

Recyling around the yard and garden is easy, too. Leaves, pine needles, wood chips, and black-and-white newspaper are ideal for mulch and for keeping paths weed-free. Grass clippings, vegetable trimmings, sawdust, and other organic materials go into the compost pile, perhaps the ultimate transformer of waste to useful resource. Tin cans, waxed-cardboard milk cartons, paper or styrofoam cups, scooped-out grapefruit or orange halves, eggshells, and plastic yogurt cups all make fine containers for starting seedlings. "Recycling in the Garden" on page 205 shows several other ways to recycle materials around the yard and garden. You'll also find more information about recycling in the Composting, Environment and Gardening, and Mulch entries. ❖

Regeneration

It all started with an observation of nature's uncanny ability to bounce back from disaster, natural or man-made. "The essence of regeneration is to look at a given area and see how it can help itself," explained Robert Rodale, founder of the concept.

There are seven tendencies that occur when damaged agricultural land is left to regenerate, when depressed communities begin to regenerate, and when an individual grows toward spiritual regeneration: pluralism (diversity), protection, purity, permanence, peace, potential, and progress.

Picture the changes that gradually happen when a field that's been continually planted to a single crop and managed with synthetic fertilizers and pesticides is left "idle." First, without herbicides and cultivation, many species of plants will begin to grow instead of one crop species (pluralism). As this plant community covers the soil surface, erosion will end and populations of soil microorganisms near the surface will increase (protection). Plant life and soil life will flourish without the detrimental effects of synthetic chemicals (purity). More perennial species and other plants with vigorous root systems will begin to grow (permanence). Natural interactions of beneficial species and pest species will increase, reducing plant pest problems (peace). As plants grow, die, and decay, nutrients will accumulate in surface soil layers, increasing soil fertility (potential). Without mechanical tillage, soil structure, organic matter content, and water-holding capacity will improve (progress). Over the course of years, land that could only sustain plants when given artificial supplements will regenerate its own fertility and balance.

Rodale often referred to the regeneration principles collectively as our "internal resources," because they come from nature and from within ourselves. The key to regeneration is utilizing our tremendously powerful internal resources—the land itself, sun, air, rainfall, plants, animals, and people. Together, they have tremendous healing power, much more than external inputs such as chemical pesticides and fertilizers or subsidies that come from a store or the government.

"We have to start looking at our capacity to help ourselves and how we can make that capacity better," Rodale said. "People do better when they focus on their capacity and less on their needs."

Whether you're involved with agriculture, transportation, education, housing, science, medicine, business, or even politics, carefully cultivating your internal resources can help develop a truly regenerative solution. ❖

Rhododendron

Rhododendron, azalea. Spring- or summer-blooming broad-leaved evergreen or deciduous shrubs.

Description: *Rhododendron arborescens,* sweet azalea, is an upright, horizontally layered deciduous shrub growing to 10'. Fragrant, trumpet-shaped white flowers appear in late spring. The leaves usually turn red before they fall. Zones 5-8.

R. calendulaceum, flame azalea, is an upright, layered native growing 5'-10' tall. Its orange-yellow to red flowers appear in spring either before or with the deciduous medium green leaves. Zones 5-8.

R. schlippenbachii, royal azalea, is a deciduous species that blooms in late spring. Flowers are fragrant, pale to rose pink, and spotted in the throat with light red-brown. Grows to 15'; turns yellow to orange-red in the fall. Zones 5-8.

R. vaseyi, pinkshell azalea, is a native deciduous species with an upright, vase-shaped habit growing to 4'-12'. The fragrant flowers are rose with brown specks, appearing in spring before the leaves. The leaves turn reddish in the fall. It tolerates wet soils. Zones 5-8.

R. catawbiense, catawba rhododendron, is a spreading evergreen with thick, leathery leaves, sometimes growing 15' or more, though usually closer to 6'. This native bears large trusses of lilac-colored blooms in late spring. Zones 4-7.

R. maximum, rosebay rhododendron, normally grows 6'-8', though it can reach 30'. The pink flowers (usually with green spots in the throat) are borne in trusses after the new leaves grow out. Zones 5-6.

R. mucronulatum, Korean rhododendron, is a deciduous shrub growing to 8'. The purple flowers appear in late winter or early spring before the leaves. Zones 5-7.

R. yakusimanum, Yaku rhododendron, is an evergreen with a mounded, compact habit, growing 3' tall and wide. Pink or white flowers appear in late spring. Zones 6-7.

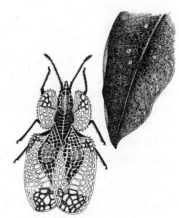

Lace bugs. Azalea lace bugs (pictured here at 10 times their actual size) damage foliage by sucking sap from the undersides of leaves. Leaves become splotched and grayish above, rusty below. Adult lace bugs are only ⅛" long with brown and black markings on their wings. Tiny nymphs are black and spiny. Lace bugs are especially troublesome in sunny sites. Control with repeated use of soap sprays.

How to grow: Provide azaleas and rhododendrons with partial shade, good drainage, even moisture, and humus-rich soil. Site evergreen rhododendrons out of direct wind and deadhead them when the blooms are spent, pruning only to remove dead wood or to correct stray branches. Deciduous azaleas rarely need pruning (except to remove dead wood), but evergreen azaleas usually need post-bloom pruning to keep their size in scale. Fungi can attack rhododendron and azalea flowers and foliage, especially when conditions are wet or humid. Minimize these with good sanitation (fungal diseases often overwinter in ground litter) and by removing infected parts with pruners sanitized between cuts.

Landscape uses: Azaleas and rhododendrons are great in a woodland garden setting, either as specimens or in massed plantings.

Best cultivars: There are hundreds of hybrid azaleas and rhododendrons. Visit a local botanical garden or arboretum, or look for a local chapter of the Azalea Society of America or the American Rhododendron Society for guidance on the best choices for your area. ❖

Rhubarb

Rheum rhabarbarum
Polygonaceae

Rhubarb is one of spring's earliest vegetables. Weeks before the first strawberry ripens, you can enjoy the fresh, tart yet sweet flavor of rhubarb's red or green, celerylike leaf stalks in pies, jams, and jellies. Don't eat the foliage, though: It's poisonous.

Rhubarb needs at least two months of cold weather and does best in areas with 2″-3″ deep ground-freezes and moist, cool springs.

Planting: Grow rhubarb from root divisions, called crowns, rather than from seed, which can produce plants that are not true to type. Three to six plants are adequate for most households.

Choose a sunny, well-drained, out-of-the-way spot for this long-lived perennial. Dig planting holes 3′ wide and 3′ deep to accommodate the mature roots. Mix the removed soil with generous amounts of aged manure and compost. Refill each hole to within 2″ of the top, and set one crown in the center of each hole. Top off with the soil mix, tamp down well, and water thoroughly.

Growing guidelines: Once plants sprout, apply mulch to retain soil moisture and smother weeds. Renew mulch when the foliage dies down in the fall to protect roots from extremely hard freezes. Provide enough water to keep roots from drying out, even when they're dormant. Sidedress with compost or aged manure in midsummer and again in fall. Remove flower stalks before they bloom to encourage leaf stalk production. After several years, when plants become crowded and the leaf stalks are thin, dig up the roots in the spring just as they sprout. Divide so that each crown has 1-3 eyes (buds); replant.

Problems: Rhubarb is usually pest-free. Occasionally it's attacked by European corn borers and cabbage worms; see "The Top Ten Garden Insect Pests in America" on page 344 for control ideas. A more likely pest is rhubarb curculio, a ¾″ long, rust-colored beetle that you can easily control by handpicking. To destroy its eggs, remove and destroy nearby wild dock in July.

Diseases are even rarer, but rhubarb can succumb to Verticillium wilt, which yellows leaves early in the season and can wilt whole plants in late attacks. Crown rot occurs in shady, soggy soil. For either disease, remove and destroy infected plants; keep stalks thinned to promote good air circulation, and clean up thoroughly around crowns in fall. If stands become seriously diseased, destroy the entire stand. Replant disease-free stock in a new location.

Harvesting: In spring when the leaves are fully developed, twist and pull stalks from the crowns. Don't harvest any the first year, though, and take only those that are at least 1″ thick the second year. By the third year, you can harvest for 1-2 months. After that, pick all you can eat.

Best cultivars: 'Victoria', deep red and fairly reliable from seed; 'Cherry Red', very sweet and a heavy producer. ❖

Robinia

Locust. Deciduous shrubs or single-trunked trees.

Description: *Robinia pseudoacacia,* black locust, is an upright tree that grows 30′-50′ tall. The alternate leaves are dull blue-green and compound, with 7-19 oval leaflets. Drooping clusters of edible pealike white flowers begin to appear mid-spring in the South, early summer in the North. Watch for paired spines on the branches and for feeding honeybees if you are tempted to sample the blossoms. Zones 4-8.

How to grow: Choose a sunny site with evenly moist, well-drained soil. Black locust tolerates adverse soil conditions such as drought, high pH, and salinity, but it dislikes wet soils.

Landscape uses: Naturalize black locust in problem areas where other trees won't thrive; its very light shade allows other plants to grow beneath it. ❖

Rock Gardens

A rock garden can add natural beauty to a landscape in a way few other gardens can. The best rock gardens start with a natural-looking construction of rocks planted with a wide variety of tiny, low-growing plants with colorful flowers.

There are many ways to incorporate a rock garden in your landscape:

• Build one on a natural slope, like a steep bank that's awkward to mow.

• Use rocks to build a slope and add interest to a flat yard.

• Design one near a pond.

• Use dwarf evergreens or a clump of birches as a background for a rock garden.

• Plant a rock garden on a rock outcrop or in a woodland area.

• Make a raised bed for rock plants edged with stone or landscape ties.

Design and Construction

A site with full sun or dappled afternoon shade is best. If your property is mostly shaded, you still can have a lovely rock garden—choose shade-loving wildflowers and ferns. Good drainage is an important concern: Most rock plants grow best in very well drained soil high in organic matter—a mixture of equal parts topsoil, humus, and gravel, for example. Plants like moisture about their deep roots but can't tolerate constantly wet soil.

Stone native to your area will look most natural and will be easiest and cheapest to obtain. Stick to one type of rock, repeating the same color and texture throughout to unify the design. Weathered, neutral gray or tan rocks are ideal. Limestone and sandstone are popular.

If you don't have enough rocks in your own yard, other good sources are nearby landowners, rockyards, and quarries. Try to pick out the rocks yourself. Choose mostly large, irregular shapes. Keep in mind you'll need smaller sizes, too.

Plan your garden before you start moving rocks, although you'll modify the design as you build. A good way to visualize your plan is to make a 3-D scale model with small stones and sand on a large tray. Mound the sand and arrange your rocks in the model. You might start with a photograph of a favorite mountain scene. Decide how many rocks—and what sizes—you'll need, and plan for a path or large rock stepping stones for working in the garden. Keep working until you find a design you like. The key to a successful rock garden—one that is harmonious and natural looking—is studied irregularity.

To begin construction, mark out the area you've selected, remove any weeds or sod, and excavate to a depth of a foot or so. Save the soil for fill. You'll need extra topsoil for filling in between rocks and building up level areas. If you need to improve drainage, lay in about 8″ of rubble or small rocks, and cover it with coarse gravel. You may have to remove more soil to accommodate this layer.

You'll need a garden cart or small dolly to move good-sized rocks, or use iron pipes about 4″ in diameter as rollers. Use a crowbar for a lever and a block of wood for a fulcrum to position rocks. For massive rocks, a professional with a backhoe might be the answer.

On a flat site, first place large stones on the perimeter to form the garden's foundation. On a sloping site, place the largest, most attractive rock, the keystone, first. As you work, be sure each rock is stable. Place the wider, heavier part down, and angle rocks to channel water back into the garden. When placing rocks, dig a hole larger than the rock to allow room for moving it into the best position. For the most natural look, lay the rocks so lines in them run horizontally and are parallel throughout the garden.

After positioning each rock, shovel soil around it, ramming it in with a pole so each rock is

PLANTS FOR ROCK GARDENS

There are literally hundreds of easy-to-grow rock garden plants. The following are good choices for a garden in full sun.

Dwarf shrubs: Consider dwarf and low-growing forms of evergreens such as false cypresses (*Chamaecyparis* spp.), junipers (*Juniperus* spp.), spruces (*Picea* spp.), pines (*Pinus* spp.), and hemlocks (*Tsuga* spp.). Or look for dwarf or creeping barberries (*Berberis* spp.), cotoneasters (*Cotoneaster* spp.), and azaleas (*Rhododendron* spp.).

Perennials: Perennials with evergreen foliage also add winter interest. Consider sedums (*Sedum* spp.), hens-and-chickens (*Sempervivum* spp.), and candytuft (*Iberis sempervirens*). Spring- and summer-blooming perennials include basket-of-gold (*Aurinia saxatilis*), creeping phlox (*Phlox subulata*), dwarf bellflowers (*Campanula* spp.), pinks (*Dianthus* spp.), catmints (*Nepeta* spp.), and thymes (*Thymus* spp.). Windflowers (*Anemone* spp.), primroses (*Primula* spp.), and columbines (*Aquilegia* spp.) are fine choices, too. Consider ferns, hostas, shade-loving wildflowers, and hardy bulbs for a garden in a shady spot. There are many diminuitive hardy bulbs for rock gardens in sun or shade, including dwarf narcissi (*Narcissus* spp.), squills (*Scilla* spp.), and snowdrops (*Galanthus* spp.).

Visit local rock gardens—especially in spring—to give you ideas about what will grow in your area. Garden catalogs, books, and magazines are good sources, too. The American Rock Garden Society has an excellent publication, a seed exchange, regional meetings, and also local chapters, many of which hold annual plant sales. Membership is $25 per year; write Secretary, ARGS, P.O. Box 67, Millwood, NY 10546 for information.

firmly anchored. Bury a good portion of each rock—two-thirds is traditional—for a natural effect.

Continue adding tiers of rocks in the same manner until you've reached the top of the garden. As you work, try to create miniature ridges and valleys and intersperse small, level areas to make an interesting design and provide space for plants. End with a series of flat ledges at different levels rather than a peak.

After you've placed all the rocks, shovel soil mix under and around them, making deep planting pockets. A good basic mix is ⅓ topsoil, ⅓ humuslike screened leaf mold, and ⅓ gravel. Tamp it in, wait a week for the soil to settle, and add more to fill to the desired level.

Planting and Care

Plan your planting scheme with tracing paper over a scale drawing of your rock garden, or use labeled sheets of paper and lay out your "plants" right where they'll grow in the garden. Adjust your design as you visualize it for each season. Record your decisions on paper. Allow low, creeping plants like small bellflowers (*Campanula* spp.) and thymes (*Thymus* spp.) to cascade over rocks. Wedge rosette-forming plants such as hens-and-chickens (*Sempervivum* spp.) into vertical crevices. Fill open spaces with mats of ajuga (*Ajuga reptans*), pussy-toes (*Antennaria* spp.), or sedums (*Sedum* spp.). Use dwarf shrubs to soften the harshness of rocks.

Once planted, all the garden requires in return is faithful weeding, watering during extended droughts, and light pruning. A 1″ layer of pea gravel helps conserve moisture, keeps the soil cool, reduces weeds, keeps soil off foliage, and prevents crown rot. Spread the gravel up to, but not over, the crown of each plant. Use chopped leaves for woodland gardens. ❖

Rodale

An IRS accountant turned industrialist, Jerome Irving Rodale (1898-1971) was never quite content with the world as it was. He always had a vision of how the world *could* be.

J. I. Rodale started Rodale Press in 1930 in a back room of the family's electrical switch factory in Emmaus, Pennsylvania. First came a series of short-lived health and humor magazines and books. In 1942, he launched a controversial magazine to teach people how to raise healthy food by having healthy soil. *Organic Gardening* magazine is now the most widely read gardening magazine in the country. He also founded the nonprofit Soil and Health Foundation, now known as the Rodale Institute.

J. I. was an advocate of preventive health care. Why, he asked, do we depend on medicine for *cures?* Why not develop systematic ways of *preventing* illness and disease? People can live longer, healthier, and happier lives simply by improving the way they live. In 1950, that thinking gave birth to *Prevention,* the nation's largest health magazine.

Robert David Rodale (1930-1990) carried on his father's mission. He added many other magazines, including *Bicycling, Runner's World, Backpacker, American Woodworker, Men's Health,* and *The New Farm.* The Rodale Book Division produces about 50 books each year on health, fitness, homes, and gardens.

Bob's vision was worldwide. He popularized grain amaranth—a famine-*prevention* crop, as he called it—and spread his can-do vision throughout Africa, Central America, China, and the Soviet Union. Bob was in the Soviet Union to launch yet another magazine—*Novii Fermer* (Russian for *New Farmer*)—when he died in an auto accident on September 20, 1990.

The Rodale family continues to see the world as it could be: "Our mission is to show people how they can use the power of their bodies and minds to make their lives better. 'You can do it,' we say on every page of our magazines and books." ❖

Roots

Experienced gardeners know that the health and yield of the aboveground parts of their plants depend on vigorous roots to supply water and nutrients, provide support, and anchor the plants in the soil.

Root development: The first root that emerges from a sprouting seed is the taproot or primary root. It tends to grow straight down and may penetrate several inches or more into the soil before the developing shoot emerges aboveground. Sometimes the taproot remains dominant throughout a plant's life. Dandelions, carrots, and spinach are common plants with taproots.

Usually, a plant's root system changes as the plant grows. Grasses and related plants such as corn, onions, daffodils, and lilies replace the initial taproot with fibrous root systems. In most broad-leaved plants, ranging from flowers such as petunias or phlox to shrubs and trees such as roses or maples, a series of lateral (side) roots branches out from the original taproot. Often the lateral roots branch and rebranch into a bushy mass of rootlets.

Key Words
ROOTS

Taproot. The first root to develop from a germinating seed; also called the primary root; a single, central, vertical root.

Fibrous roots. Slender, mostly unbranched roots that look like fine string or yarn.

Root hairs. Tiny projections from the surface cells of a root that extend through the soil around the root.

Adventitious roots. Roots that grow from stems or leaves of a plant.

Mycorrhiza. A symbiotic association of a fungus with the roots of a plant.

Contractile roots. Roots that can change in length and thickness, pulling shoots closer to the ground or deeper into the soil.

Plants can also sprout adventitious roots from stems, runners, and even leaves. This is a natural occurrence which gardeners can stimulate by taking cuttings, layering, or dividing.

Roots get broken or disturbed whenever you transplant, divide, or cultivate around a plant. This can affect root development. For example, studies show that many trees never develop a deep taproot once the original taproot is broken during transplanting. This means that trees you buy from a garden center and replant may not anchor as deeply and securely as trees that grow in place from seedlings.

Root function: The most important function of roots is collecting water and nutrients from the soil. This job is the task of the youngest, most tender parts of the root system—the growing root tips and root hairs. As roots grow, these tips and hairs are continually exploring new soil and mining it for nutrients. Water and nutrients absorbed by the roots are pumped up into the stems and leaves through a pipelike system of hollow cells called the xylem. Similarly, dissolved sugars and other substances produced in the leaves and shoots circulate down to the roots through a second circulatory system called the phloem. The sugars supply the energy that roots need in order to grow and function.

The roots of many kinds of plants grow in symbiosis with one or another kind of fungus. The fungus absorbs dissolved minerals, particularly phosphorus, from the soil and passes them into the plant roots in return for sugars and other organic compounds. These mycorrhizal associations benefit both the plants and the fungi.

Some plants, particularly members of the legume family such as beans and clover, host bacteria in their roots. Infected roots have characteristic round swellings called nodules. Even though the bacteria consume a share of the plant's sugars, the plant benefits because these bacteria can gather nitrogen from the air and convert it into compounds that roots can absorb.

Other types of roots: Roots hold plants upright and in place. The obvious example is

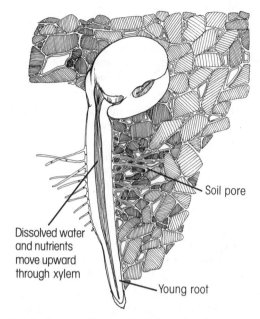

How roots grow. Roots extend through soil pore space, absorbing water and nutrients from the solution of water, dissolved minerals, and organic compounds that lines or fills soil pores. In compacted soil, root growth is retarded or stopped because of lack of pore spaces.

tall trees that can remain erect despite fierce winds. Bulbs, such as tulips and daffodils, and perennials, such as hostas and daylilies, have contractile roots that pull the plant down closer to or deeper into the soil.

Not all roots grow under the ground. Orchids, philodendrons, and other tropical plants that grow in trees all have clinging roots. Like underground roots, their aerial roots serve dual roles. They hold the vine or plant in place and also absorb water during rainy or foggy weather.

Many biennials and perennials, including carrots, beets, and dahlias, deposit sugars and starches in special storage roots. However, some things look like roots but aren't. Onion and daffodil bulbs, canna rhizomes, gladiolus corms, and other storage organs develop from leaves or stems, not roots. For more information on storage organs, see the Bulbs entry. ❖

Rosa

The rose is the best-loved flower of all time, a symbol of beauty and love. Roses have it all — color, fragrance, and great shape. Many roses produce flowers from early summer until frost, often beginning the first year of planting.

Over the years, roses have gained a reputation for being difficult to grow. But many of the "old roses," plus a great number of the newer cultivars, are disease-resistant, widely adaptable plants able to withstand cold winters and hot summers.

Selecting Roses

The members of genus *Rosa* are prickly stemmed shrubs with a wide range of heights and growth habits. There are as many as 200 species and thousands of cultivars. With so many roses available, deciding on the ones you want may be the hardest part of growing roses. This large, diverse genus can be divided into four major types: bush, climbing, shrub, and ground-cover roses.

Bush roses: Bush roses form the largest category, which has been divided into seven subgroups: hybrid tea, polyantha, floribunda, grandiflora, miniature, heritage (old), and tree (standard) roses.

• Hybrid tea roses usually have narrow buds, borne singly on a long stem, with large, many-petaled flowers on plants 3'-5' tall. They bloom repeatedly over the entire growing season.

• Polyantha roses are short, compact plants with small flowers produced abundantly in large clusters throughout the growing season. Plants are very hardy and easy to grow.

• Floribunda roses were derived from crosses between hybrid teas and polyanthas. They are hardy, compact, easily grown plants with medium-sized flowers borne profusely in short-stemmed clusters all summer long.

• Grandiflora roses are usually tall (5'-6'), narrow plants bearing large flowers in long-stemmed clusters from summer through fall.

• Miniature roses are diminutive, with both flowers and foliage proportionately smaller. Most are quite hardy and bloom freely and repeatedly.

• Heritage (old) roses are a widely diverse group available prior to 1867, the date of the introduction of the first hybrid tea rose. Plant and flower forms, hardiness, and ease of growth vary considerably; some bloom only once, while others flower repeatedly. Among the most popular are the albas, bourbons, centifolias, damasks, gallicas, mosses, and portlands. Some species roses are also included in this category.

• Tree (standard) roses are created when any rose is bud-grafted onto a specially grown trunk 1'-6' tall.

Climbing roses: Roses don't truly climb, but the long, flexible canes of certain roses make it possible to attach them to supports such as fences, posts, arbors, and trellises. The two main types are large-flowered climbers, with thick, sturdy canes growing to 10' long and blooms produced throughout the summer, and ramblers, with thin canes growing 20' or more and clusters of smaller flowers borne in early summer.

Shrub roses: Shrub roses grow broadly upright with numerous arching canes reaching

Smart Shopping
ROSES

Whether they're sold locally or by mail order, roses are sold by grade, which is based on the size and number of canes. Top-grade #1 plants grow fastest and produce the most blooms when young; #1½-grade plants are also healthy and vigorous; avoid #2-grade plants, which require extra care.

You can buy either dormant, bareroot roses or container-grown plants. Both mail-order companies and local outlets sell dormant plants, offering the widest range of cultivars. Healthy dormant plants have smooth, plump, green or red canes; avoid plants with dried out, shriveled, wrinkled, or sprouted canes.

4'-12' tall. Most are very hardy and easily grown. Some only bloom once in early summer, while others bloom repeatedly. Many produce showy red or scarlet fruits called hips. Some species roses are considered shrub roses.

Groundcover roses: Groundcover roses are sometimes included with shrub roses. These have prostrate, creeping canes producing low mounds; there are once-blooming and repeat-blooming cultivars.

Using Roses in the Landscape

To grow well, roses need a site that gets full sun at least 6 hours a day, humus-rich soil, and good drainage. If these conditions are met, you can use roses just about anywhere in the landscape. Try roses in foundation plantings, shrub borders, along walks and driveways, surrounding patios, decks, and terraces, or in flower beds and borders. Combine roses with other plants, especially other shrubs or perennials.

Use climbing roses to cover walls, screen or frame views, or decorate fences, arbors, trellises, and gazebos. Grow groundcover roses on banks or trailing over walls. Plant hedges of shrub, grandiflora, and floribunda roses.

You can also grow roses in containers. For all roses except miniatures, choose a container at least 14" deep and 1½' wide. You can grow miniatures in pots as small as 6" in diameter. Use a soilless potting mix; fertilize and water regularly. In all but frost-free climates, overwinter pots in an unheated garage or basement.

Growing Good Roses

The key to growing roses is to remember they need plenty of water, humus, and nutrients.

Soil: Prepare a new site in fall for planting the following spring, or in summer for fall planting. If you plan to grow roses with existing plants, then no special preparation is needed. For a new site, dig or till the soil to a depth of at least 1'. Evenly distribute a 4" layer of organic material such as peat moss, compost, leaf mold, or dehydrated cow manure over the soil surface. Also

spread on fertilizer. A general recommendation is to add 5 lb. of bonemeal and 10 lb. of greensand or granite dust per 100 square feet. Dig or till the fertilizer and soil amendments into the soil.

Planting: For much of the West Coast, South, and Southwest, or wherever winter temperatures remain above 10°F, plant bareroot roses in January and February. In slightly colder areas, fall planting gives roses a chance to establish a sturdy root system before growth starts. In areas with very cold winters, plant bareroot roses in spring, several weeks before the last frost. For all but miniature and shrub roses, space roses 2'-3' apart in colder areas, 3'-4' apart in warmer regions where they'll grow larger. Space miniatures 1'-2' apart, shrub roses 4'-6' apart.

To plant bareroot roses, dig each hole 15"-18" wide and deep, or large enough for roots to spread out. Form a soil cone in the planting hole. Removing any broken or damaged roots or canes, position the rose on the cone, spreading out roots. Place the bud union (the point where the cultivar is grafted onto its rootstock) even with the soil surface in mild climates and 1"-2" below the soil surface in areas where temperatures fall below freezing.

Add soil around the roots, making sure there are no air pockets, until the hole is ¾ full. Fill the hole with water, allow it to soak in, and refill. Make sure the bud union is at the correct level. Finish filling the hole with soil and lightly tamp. Trim canes back to 8", making cuts ¼" above an outward-facing bud and at a 45° angle. To prevent the canes from drying out, lightly mound moist soil over the rose bush. Gently remove it when growth starts in 1-2 weeks.

Plant container-grown roses as you would any container plant. For more on this technique, see the Planting entry.

Water: Ample water, combined with good drainage, is fundamental to rose growth. The key is to water slowly and deeply, soaking the ground at least 16" deep with each watering. Water in the early morning, so if foliage gets wet, it can dry quickly. Use a soaker hose, drip irriga-

Aphids. These ⅛" green, red, or black insects cluster on new growth, causing deformed or stunted leaves and buds with sticky residue. Control with insecticidal soap, pyrethrins, or rotenone.

Borers. Larvae of rose stem girdler, rose stem sawfly, or carpenter bees bore holes in canes; new growth wilts. Prune off damaged canes and seal ends with putty, paraffin, or nail polish.

Beetles. Japanese and other beetles chew leaves and flowers. Remove and destroy by hand, treat soil with milky disease or control with pyrethrins, rotenone, or ryania.

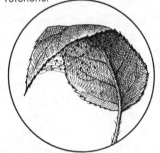

Spider mites. These tiny green, red, or brown spiderlike creatures cause yellowed, curled leaves with fine webs on undersides. Spray all leaf surfaces in early morning with a strong jet of water for three days, or use insecticidal soap or ryania.

Powdery mildew. Disease causes white powder on deformed growth; worst in hot, dry weather with cool nights. Provide good air circulation, prune off infected plant parts, apply lime sulfur to dormant plants, and treat with fungicidal soap.

Rose midges. Very tiny white maggots cause deformed, blackened buds and leaves. Prune and destroy all damaged parts.

Blackspot. Disease causes black spots on yellow leaves; defoliation is worst during wet weather. Prune off all damaged plant parts, don't splash foliage when watering, water in morning, and spray with fungicidal soap.

Rust. Disease causes red-orange spots on undersides of leaves and yellow blotches on top surfaces. Prune off infected plant parts; spray with fungicidal soap.

Rose pests and diseases. Your best defense against rose problems is to buy healthy, disease-resistant roses and be diligent about preventive maintenance, such as destroying diseased foliage and flowers immediately and cleaning up around roses in the fall. Control pests as soon as you see them. When dusting or spraying, apply controls early in the morning and cover both sides of the leaves.

tion system, or a hose with a bubbler attachment on the end. Water roses grown in containers much more frequently. Check containers daily during the summer.

Mulch: An organic mulch conserves moisture, improves the garden's appearance, inhibits weed growth, keeps the soil cool, and slowly adds nutrients to the soil. Spread 2″-4″ of mulch evenly around the plants, leaving several inches unmulched around the stem of each rose.

Fertilizing: Feed newly planted roses 4-6 weeks after planting. After that, for roses that bloom once a year, fertilize in early spring. Feed established, repeat-blooming roses three times a year: in early spring just as the growth starts, in early summer when flower buds have formed, and about six weeks before the first fall frost. The last feeding should have no nitrogen.

Use a commercial, balanced organic plant food containing nitrogen, phosphorus, and potassium, or mix your own, combining 2 parts blood meal, 1 part rock phosphate, and 4 parts wood ashes for a 4-5-4 fertilizer. Use about ½ cup for each plant, scratching it into the soil around the plant and watering well. As an alternative, apply dehydrated cow manure and bonemeal in the spring and use fish emulsion or manure tea for the other feedings. For instructions on making and using manure tea, see the Manure entry.

Pruning: Prune in early spring to keep hybrid tea, grandiflora, and floribunda roses vigorous and blooming. Many of the newer, shrub-type roses need very little pruning. Heritage, species, and climbing roses that bloom once a year bear flowers on the previous year's growth. Prune these as soon as blooming is over, cutting the main shoots back ⅓ and removing any small, twiggy growth. Remove suckers coming up from the rootstock of any rose whenever you see them.

In the first pruning of the season, just as growth starts, remove any dead or damaged wood back to healthy, white-centered wood. Make each pruning cut at an angle ¼″ above an outward-facing bud eye, which is a dormant growing point at the base of a leaf stalk. This stimulates

More On
ROSES

For more on roses, contact the American Rose Society, P.O. Box 30,000, Shreveport, LA 71130-0030. They also publish the *Handbook for Selecting Roses,* updated yearly, with a listing of rose cultivars rated for quality. The *Combined Rose List* lists all roses available, with their sources. For a current price, write to Beverly Dobson, 215 Harriman Road, Irvington, NY 10533.

outward-facing new growth. Also remove any weak or crossing canes. Later in the season, remove any diseased growth and faded flowers on repeat-blooming roses, cutting the stem just above the first five-leaflet leaf below the flower.

Winter protection: Many shrub roses as well as some of the polyanthas, floribundas, and miniatures need only minimal winter protection. Hybrid teas, grandifloras, and some floribundas and heritage roses usually require more.

In areas with winter temperatures no lower than 20°F, no winter protection is necessary. Elsewhere, apply winter protection after the first frost and just before the first hard freeze. Remove all leaves from the plants and from the ground around them and destroy them. Apply a fungicidal soap spray containing sulfur. Apply ¼ cup of greensand around each plant and water well. Prune plants to ½ their height and tie canes together with twine.

Where winter temperatures drop to 0°F, make an 8″ mound of coarse compost, shredded bark, leaves, or soil around the base of each plant. In colder areas, make the mound 1′ deep. Provide extra protection with another layer of pine needles or branches, straw, or leaves. Where temperatures reach −5°F or colder, remove the canes of large-flowered, repeat-blooming climbers from supports, lay them on the ground, and cover both the base and the canes. ❖

Row Covers

It is the rare gardener who finds the growing season long enough. Fortunately, gardeners can satisfy the itch to plant early and to keep crops producing through the fall by using row covers. Made of light, permeable material, usually polypropylene or polyester, row covers can be laid loosely on top of plants or supported with wire hoops. Row covers block out about 20 percent of the sun's rays but let in rain and air. The few degrees of frost protection that row covers provide give young plants an early start. For more on season extenders, see the Cloches, Cold Frames, and Season Extension entries.

Often described as "floating," these mainstays of organic pest management give seedlings excellent protection from insects and birds. Placed over plants before infestation occurs, row covers exclude certain pests throughout the growing season. The Organic Pest Management entry has more on this use of row covers. ❖

Rudbeckia

Coneflower. Summer-blooming annuals and perennials.

Description: Summer-blooming annual *Rudbeckia hirta,* black-eyed Susan, bears single yellow, dark-centered daisies on 3' stems.

Perennial *R. fulgida,* orange coneflower, bears 3"-4" single, dark-centered gold daisies on 3' plants in late summer and autumn. Zones 3-8.

How to grow: Coneflowers need a sunny spot with average to rich, well-drained soil. Sow annuals indoors in spring to set out after frost. Plant perennials in spring or fall. Divide every 3-4 years; deadhead to avoid self-seeding.

Landscape uses: Mass in borders, informal plantings, and cutting gardens.

Best cultivars: *R. hirta* 'Gloriosa Daisy', large blooms in yellow, orange, bronze. *R. fulgida* var. *sullivantii* 'Goldsturm', golden blooms, 2½' plants. ❖

Rutabaga

Brassica napus, Napobrassica group
Brassicaceae

The rutabaga, a turnip-cabbage cross, is commonly used like a turnip. Cook the strong-flavored tops as greens. Use the yellow- or white-fleshed roots, which can grow as large as 6-7 lb., whole or mashed—as side dishes, in soups and stews, or sliced raw for dips.

Planting: Rutabagas take a month longer than turnips to grow and need cool nights as they mature. For these reasons, it is best to grow rutabagas as a fall crop. Plant directly outdoors in the late spring or summer, around 15 weeks before the first expected frost, so the roots will mature in cool autumn weather. Rutabagas do best in medium-heavy soils cultivated to a depth of 6".

Sow seeds ½" deep and ½" apart in rows spaced 1½' apart. Don't pack down the soil.

Growing guidelines: As soon as the seedlings are up, thin to 1" apart; thin again two weeks later to 8" apart. Then mulch heavily to keep down weeds and to conserve moisture. Soil moisture is particularly critical as the plants mature, so water when necessary. Otherwise, the crop is very self-sufficient.

Problems: Rutabagas, while usually pest- and disease-free, are subject to the same problems as cabbage. See the Cabbage entry for controls.

Harvesting: Harvest roots or tops anytime they are large enough to use. Light frosts can improve the taste and texture of rutabaga roots, but a freeze shortens their storage life. To harvest, use a spading fork to loosen the earth around the plants, and then pull gently. Store the roots in a cool place, such as a cellar. They will also keep in the ground if you apply enough mulch to keep the soil from freezing.

Best cultivars: 'Laurentian', dependable; 'American Purple Top', creamy yellow flesh. ❖

Sage

Salvia officinalis
Labiatae

Description: Culinary garden sage is a small, 2'-3' shrub with woody stems. It has pebbly, grayish leaves, spikes of lavender flowers, and a warm spicy flavor. For information on ornamental sages, see the Salvia entry.

How to grow: Garden sage craves sun, good drainage, and average, not overly rich soil. Grow it from seed, or divide plants that are at least two years old. Prune in spring to keep plants shapely and strong.

Harvesting: Clip off leaves and stems throughout the growing season. Avoid cutting back drastically in the fall.

Uses: Try sage with poultry, in sausage and stuffing, with veal, fish, and liver, and in cheese and egg dishes. Perk up cooked vegetables like carrots, asparagus, tomatoes, and cabbage with a crumbling of dried leaves. If you drink tea made with dried sage leaves, according to the herbalists, you will never grow old. The dried leaves, if left on their branchlets, are wonderful in herb wreaths.

Best cultivars: 'Aurea', striking green-and-gold leaves; 'Purpurea', elegant purple foliage; and 'Tricolor', with leaves variegated in rose, cream, gray-green and purple. ❖

Salix

Willow. Deciduous single- or multiple-stemmed trees or shrubs.

Description: This genus is best known for "weeping willows," a term applied to several species and cultivars with pendulous branches.

Salix alba, white willow, is an upright tree growing to 75'. Its slender, pliant branches turn an intense yellow as sap rises in spring. Leaves and catkins follow. Zones 2-8.

S. caprea, goat willow, is often confused with *S. discolor,* pussy willow. Both species bear the fuzzy male catkins for which pussy willow is named; both are shrubby small trees that can grow to 25' tall and 15' wide. Zones 4-8.

S. matsudana, Pekin willow, grows to 40'. It is best known for the cultivar 'Tortuosa', corkscrew willow, which has contorted branches and a gnarled appearance. Zones 5-8.

How to grow: Willows grow naturally at streamside and perform best in sunny, moist locations. Willow wood is brittle, and branches often break under ice or snow. Plant where invasive roots can't reach sewers and drains.

Landscape uses: Willows make fine accent plants and mood-setters for watery areas.

Best cultivars: *S. alba* 'Tristis' is golden weeping willow, a hardy, gracefully pendulous tree with yellow twigs and small branches. ❖

Salvia

Sage. Summer- and fall-blooming annuals and perennials.

Description: Annual *Salvia splendens,* scarlet sage, flaunts brilliant red dragon-mouth blooms in spikes 8″-30″ over dark green leaves.

Perennial *S.* × *superba,* violet sage, bears smaller blue-purple flowers in thin spikes to 2′ above mounded leaves. Zones 4-7.

See the Sage entry for information on the culinary species.

How to grow: Sages grow best in full sun to very light shade and average, well-drained soil. Sow scarlet sage in early spring to plant out after the last frost, or buy plants. Plant or divide violet sage every third year in spring or fall. Deadhead for rebloom.

Landscape uses: Plant a solid bed of scarlet sage or group with other bright colors in a border. Use perennials in a border or cottage garden. ❖

Scabiosa

Pincushion flower. Summer- to fall-blooming annuals; summer-blooming perennials.

Description: Annual *Scabiosa atropurpurea,* sweet scabious, bears 2″-3″ round heads in shades of white, pink, red, blue, and purple with white pinlike stamens on 1½′-3′ stems.

Perennial *S. caucasica,* pincushion flower, produces similar 3″ blooms in shades of white, blue, and lavender 1½′-2′ above gray-green leaves. Zones 3-7.

How to grow: Direct-sow annuals or start 6-8 weeks before the last frost. Plant perennials in spring; divide every 3-5 years. Site both kinds in a sunny spot with loose, average, moist but well-drained soil. Both prefer cool areas and suffer in high humidity. Deadhead for rebloom.

Landscape uses: Group in borders and informal gardens; use as long-lasting cut flowers. ❖

Season Extension

Gardeners can't control the weather, but they can work around it. Many gardeners have discovered ways to make their wish for a longer gardening season come true, using materials as simple as a plastic milk jug or as grand as a greenhouse.

Starting seeds indoors in pots or flats is a type of season extension that any gardener with a sunny window can try. For full information on indoor seed starting, see the Seeds and Seedlings entry. Protecting young plants from cold temperatures outdoors in a cold frame or under row covers is a tried-and-true technique for extending the season. And if you like, you can keep gardening year-round indoors; you'll find ideas in the Houseplants, Container Gardening, and Greenhouse Gardening entries.

Season extenders are materials or structures used to keep the air and soil around plants warmer. There are many different types of season extenders you can make or buy. Backyard gardeners have used cold frames, cloches, and hotcaps for many years. Even commercial vegetable growers use season extenders to lengthen short growing seasons and get an earlier and larger crop to market.

Cold frames. The best-known season extender is the cold frame. This type of structure, usually made of wood with a transparent glass or plastic top, relies on solar energy to warm the air and soil. Use cold frames to trap the sun's energy and keep transplants and seedlings warm at night. Hotbeds are cold frames with an auxiliary heat source. Manure, compost, a heating cable, or some other heating source maintains warm temperatures in the frame. The Cold Frames entry explains how to maintain and use cold frames and hotbeds in many ways throughout the year.

Cloches. Cloches are small plant coverings that trap the sun's warmth, raising the air temperature around an individual or small group of plants. You'll see examples of several types of cloches in the Cloches entry.

Row covers. A row cover is a versatile season extender that you can use to protect rows, small garden areas, or the whole garden from frost or cold temperatures. Row covers are sheets of transparent plastic or fabric. They are made of permeable and impermeable plastic, slitted plastic, or spun, bonded, or woven fabric, and are available in many widths. Row covers can provide from 2°-7°F frost protection at night; during the day, temperatures under row covers can be 5°-30°F higher than the surrounding air. Using row covers in spring and fall can add a month or more of growing time to most garden seasons.

Plastic row covers keep air temperatures warmer during the day and night than other row cover fabrics. You will need to vent them on warm days and close them back up at night. Slitted plastic row covers don't require venting. Colored or shaded plastic covers are available for Southern gardeners. The coloring blocks out some of the sunlight, reducing the heat inside the tunnel.

Suspend plastic row covers over the row with metal, plastic, wire, or wooden hoops to prevent injuring plants. Anchor row cover edges securely in place with soil, boards, pipes, or similar material.

Floating row covers made of spun-bonded synthetic fabric can be laid right on plants and soil. They provide only a few degrees frost protection. Loosely cover the row or garden area. Allow enough slack for 4-6 weeks of plant growth. Secure the row cover edges with soil, pipes, or boards.

Prewarming soil. Season extenders such as cloches and row covers are most effective if you prewarm the garden soil before planting. Seeds will not germinate and transplants will suffer in cold soil, even if the air temperature is high enough. To warm the soil, put the season extender in place 1-2 weeks prior to planting, or cover the soil with clear or black plastic several weeks before planting. ❖

Sedum

Sedum, stonecrop. Perennial flowers or groundcovers.

Description: All sedums have succulent green leaves in trailing rosettes or upright mounds. Leaves of many species turn red in late fall. Many sedums have showy pink, red, or purple flowers in fall. Others bloom from May through August with white or yellow flowers. The best sedums for the perennial garden are hybrids. *Sedum* × 'Autumn Joy' grows upright, producing 2' bushy plants. Flower clusters bear starry blooms that open coral pink in summer, then deepen to copper in fall, while the leaves turn brilliant red. *S.* × 'Ruby Glow' grows 1'-1½' tall, producing pink to ruby red flower clusters in late summer and fall, and has bluish green leaves that turn burgundy red. *S.* × 'Vera Jameson' grows 9"-12" tall, with blue-green leaves and pink flower clusters borne in late summer. Zones 3-10.

Some species sedums make good groundcovers. *S. kamtschaticum* is a 4" trailer with yellow starlike flowers that appear in May, complementing its light green leaves. *S. album* is trailing, with short leaves that turn a reddish color in winter. The flowers open white to pink in late summer. *S. reflexum* grows to 1½' and has yellow blossoms that contrast pleasantly with its bluish green leaves. Zones 3-10.

How to grow: Sedums are easy to grow in any well-drained, average soil in sun or light shade. They are tolerant of poor soil and hot, dry weather. Propagate them in spring or summer by division or cuttings.

Landscape uses: Use the smaller species as groundcovers for banks, or plant in pots, rock gardens, and the front of borders. They also look wonderful trailing over a stone wall. The taller species are striking in beds and borders. 'Autumn Joy' is a useful all-season plant; its flower heads add interest to the winter garden. Feature it with ornamental grasses and other tough perennials like daylilies and *Rudbeckia fulgida* 'Goldsturm'. ❖

Seeds and Seedlings

Seeds come in an amazing variety of forms and sizes, from the dustlike seeds of begonias to the hefty coconut. But all seeds have one quality in common: They are living links between generations of plants, carrying the vital genetic information that directs the growth and development of the next plant generation. Seeds are alive. They even carry on respiration—absorbing oxygen and giving off carbon dioxide.

As long as a seed is kept cool and dry, its life processes hum along on low. Most seeds remain viable for 1-3 years after they ripen on a plant. Some, such as parsnip seed, can't be counted on to sprout after more than one year, but others, like muskmelon seeds, can germinate after five years or more if storage conditions are favorable. In fact, certain seeds recovered from archaeological digs have sometimes proven to be viable after many hundreds of years.

Growing your own plants from seeds can be one of the most satisfying and intriguing aspects of gardening. Almost all gardeners have grown vegetables from seeds. But if you're interested in a challenge, you can start your own perennials, herbs, and even trees from seed. For tips on buying seeds, see "Smart Shopping: Buying the Best Seeds" on the opposite page.

Seed Germination

Moisture and warmth encourage seeds to germinate. When the seed absorbs water, its

Key Words
SEEDS AND SEEDLINGS

Seed. A plant embryo and its supply of nutrients, often surrounded by a protective seed coat.

Seed germination. The beginning of growth of a seed.

Viable. Capable of germinating; alive.

Dormancy. A state of reduced biochemical activity that persists until certain conditions occur that trigger germination.

Seedling. A young plant grown from seed. Commonly, plants grown from seeds are termed seedlings until they are first transplanted.

Cotyledon. The leaf (or leaves), present in the dormant seed, that is the first to unfold as a seed germinates. Cotyledons often look different than the leaves that follow them. In seeds such as beans, they contain stored nutrients. Also called seed leaves.

Endosperm. Specialized layer of tissue that surrounds the embryo.

Scarification. Nicking or wearing down hard seed coats to encourage germination.

Stratification. Exposing seeds to a cool (35°–40°F) moist period to break dormancy.

Damping-off. A disease caused by various fungi that results in seedling stems that shrivel and collapse at soil level.

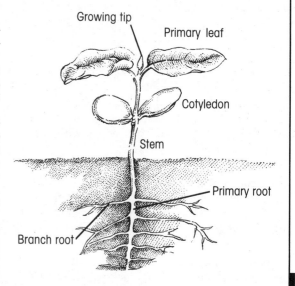

internal pressure rises, rupturing the seed coat. Growth hormones within the seed go into action, directing vital compounds to where they are needed and encouraging the growth of new tissue.

All of these changes depend on temperature as well. Most garden seeds started indoors germinate best at a soil temperature of 75°-90°F. Sprouting seeds also need air. A porous soil kept evenly moist (but not swampy) will provide enough air to support the germination process. Seeds often rot if they are submerged in water for days or if they are planted in completely waterlogged soil.

After the germination process has been in action for several days (or, in some cases, for a week or more), the seed will change in ways that we can see. The root emerges and starts to grow, the stem grows longer, and then the cotyledons unfold. Once germination has begun, you can't reverse the process. If the sprouted seed continues to receive moisture, warmth, air, and light, it keeps growing. If not, it dies.

Most seeds have no specific light requirement for germination. However, some kinds of seeds need light to break dormancy and germinate, including many tiny seeds, such as begonia, columbine, snapdragon, and petunia seeds. Some larger seeds such as impatiens, spider flower, sweet alyssum, and dill are also best left uncovered. Sow light-sensitive seeds on the surface of fine, moist soil or seed-starting mix. Cover them loosely with clear plastic to retain moisture, or mist frequently.

A few seeds require darkness to germinate. For example, Madagascar periwinkle (*Catharanthus roseus*) will germinate far better if the flat is covered with black plastic or kept in a dark closet until seeds sprout.

Other seeds will germinate readily only if planted soon after they ripen. Angelica, hawthorn, and Solomon's-seal are three types of seed best sown soon after they are collected.

Check seed packet information to find out whether the seeds you want to raise have special germination requirements.

Smart Shopping
BUYING THE BEST SEEDS

Here are some tips to help you to get the most from your seed order:

● Send for several seed catalogs so you can compare offerings and prices.

● Keep seed catalogs for reference.

● Some companies offer small seed packets at reasonable prices. Seed mixtures give you a wide variety of plants from a single packet.

● Days to maturity is an average—the actual days in your area may be different.

● Hybrids may offer advantages such as early harvest or high yields but are usually more expensive. Open-pollinated cultivars may taste better and produce over a longer season, and they tend to be cheaper.

● Some seed is routinely treated with synthetic chemical fungicide. Specify untreated seed if you prefer it.

● Read descriptions and choose cultivars with qualities that are important to you.

● Certain catalogs specialize in plants suited to specific regions of the country.

● All-America Selections seeds grow and produce well over a wide range of conditions.

Pretreating Seeds

Some kinds of seeds require certain treatments before they'll start to germinate. No matter how ideal conditions are for germination, the seeds will remain dormant if the pre-germination requirements have not been met. This characteristic, called innate dormancy, helps ensure survival in nature, because the seeds wait out the winter or the dry season before sprouting.

Certain seeds require a period of moist cold. This mechanism is common in plants native to climates with cold winters, especially perennials, trees, and shrubs. Other seeds have chemicals in their seeds coats that must be soaked away before the seeds will germinate. Some seeds are slow to absorb enough water to start germination because of thick or impermeable seed coats. Plants native to areas with seasonal dry spells often have this type of dormancy. If you understand these dormancy mechanisms, you can work around them and coax the seeds to germinate.

Even seeds that don't have dormancy requirements may be slow to germinate. Appropriate pretreatment can significantly increase germination rate and reduce germination time.

Stratification: Some seeds must be exposed to cold for a certain period before they will break dormancy and germinate. Stratification simulates natural conditions when a seed overwinters

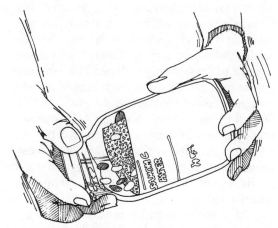

Quick seed scarifying. A sandpaper-lined jar works well for processing many seeds at a time. Slip a sheet of coarse-grit sandpaper inside the jar, add seeds, screw on the lid, and shake until the seed coats wear down.

Stratifying seeds. To stratify seeds, put them in damp sphagnum moss, peat moss, or vermiculite and keep them in a cold place (34°-40°F) for 1-4 months. Layer large seeds between damp sphagnum moss in a covered container. Mix smaller seeds with damp moss or other seed-starting medium in a plastic bag and close with a twist tie. Be sure to label the seeds with name and date.

in cold, moist ground.

Seeds of various perennials, including wild bleeding heart, gas plant, and cardinal flower, need a cold period. You can plant them outdoors in fall, or spring plant after giving them a cold treatment. "Stratifying Seeds" on this page shows how to prepare seeds for cold treatment. Many woody plant seeds also require stratification, including birch, dogwood, false cypress, and spruce. Some tree and shrub seeds, including arborvitae, cotoneaster, and lilac, are double dormant, which means they require a warm, moist period followed by a cold period to germinate. If planted outdoors in fall, these seeds may not germinate for two years.

Scarification: Some seeds, such as morning-glory, sweet pea, okra, and others, have hard seed coats that inhibit water absorption. To make a hard-coated seed absorb water more readily, nick the seed coat. Be careful not to damage the embryo inside the seed. On large seeds, use a knife to cut a notch in the seed coat, or make several strokes with a sharp-edged file. Scarify medium-sized or small seeds by rubbing them between two sheets of sandpaper. "Quick Seed Scarifying" on the opposite page illustrates a handy method for scarifying large numbers of seeds fast. After scarifying, soak seeds in lukewarm water for several hours before planting.

Presoaking: Even seeds that have thin seed coats can benefit from a soak in lukewarm water for several hours before planting. Large seeds such as peas and okra will germinate faster if soaked overnight first. Before planting, drain the seeds and dry them briefly on paper towels to make them easier to handle.

Presprouting: Presprouting takes seeds one step further than presoaking. It's a good way to handle such seeds as melons, squash, and their relatives, which need plenty of warmth for germination. Because sprouted seeds can tolerate cooler temperatures, you can concentrate your population of germinating seeds in one warm place and farm out the presprouted seedlings to cooler spots, where they will receive plenty of light. "Presprouting Seeds" on this page gives step-by-step instructions for this technique.

Presprouted seeds are fragile; handle them with great care. Be sure to plant them before their roots grow together and tangle. Plant sprouted seeds in individual containers of premoistened potting mix. Cover them gently but firmly with potting mix and treat them as you would any container-raised seedling. Presprouted seeds may be planted directly in the garden, but it is better to keep them in containers until the roots become established.

Starting Seeds Indoors

Starting seeds indoors will give you earlier vegetables and flowers, and your cultivar choices will be endless. The process of germination may seem awesomely complex, but the act of seed planting is reassuringly simple. Just take it step-by-step, and you'll soon be presiding over a healthy crop of seedlings.

Select your work area—a surface at a comfortable height and close to a water supply where you'll have room to spread things out. Assemble your equipment: seed-starting containers, starting medium or soil mix, watering can, labels, marking pen, and seed packets.

Choosing Containers

You can start seeds in almost any kind of container that will hold 1"-2" of starting medium and won't become easily waterlogged. Once seedlings form more roots and develop their true leaves, though, they grow best in containers that

---

PRESPROUTING SEEDS

Sprouting seeds before you plant them can boost germination rates and give you more control when working with expensive or scarce seeds. Here's how to presprout seeds:

1. Spread a double layer of damp paper towels on a flat surface.
2. Evenly space seeds 1" or so apart on the moist towels.
3. Roll up the towels, being careful to keep the seeds from bunching up.
4. Label the seed roll and enclose it in a plastic bag. Close the bag loosely—germinating seeds need some air. You can put several rolls in one plastic bag.
5. Put the seeds in a warm place—near a water heater or on top of a refrigerator. Make a note on your calendar to check them in 2–3 days.
6. After the first inspection, check the seeds daily for signs of sprouting.

Plant sprouted seeds in individual containers using a fine, loose potting soil mix, or plant them directly in the garden. Handle them gently. The fleshy roots and stems are easily broken. Then treat as you would other newly germinated seedlings.

provide more space for root growth and have holes for drainage.

You can start seedlings in open flats or in individual sections or pots. Individual containers are preferable, because the less you disturb tender roots, the better. Some containers, such as peat pots, paper pots, and soil blocks, go right into the garden with the plant during transplanting. Other pots must be slipped off the root ball before planting.

Square or rectangular containers make better use of space and provide more root area than round ones do. However, individual containers dry out faster than open flats. Many gardeners start seeds in open flats and transplant seedlings to individual containers after the first true leaves unfold. Choose flats and containers to match the number and types of plants you wish to grow and the space you have available.

Excellent seed-starting systems are available from garden centers and mail-order suppliers. You can also build your own wooden flats. If you raise large numbers of seedlings, it's useful to have interchangeable, standard-sized flats and inserts.

You can reuse your seedling containers for many years. To prevent problems with damping off, you may want to sanitize flats at the end of the season by dipping them in a 10 percent solution of household bleach (1 cup of bleach plus 9 cups of water).

Homemade containers: You can recycle milk cartons and many types of plastic containers as seed-starting pots. Just be sure to poke a drainage hole in the bottom of each. Plastic wrap or plastic bags make good mini-greenhouses for starting seeds. "Homemade Seeding Flats" on this page shows one idea for a homemade seed-starting system.

Two make-at-home seed-starting containers are newspaper pots and soil blocks. To make pots from newspaper, begin by cutting bands of newspaper about twice as wide as the desired height of a pot (about 4″ wide for a 2″ high pot).

Wrap a band around the lower half of a jar a few times, and secure it with masking tape. Then form the bottom of the pot by creasing and folding the paper in around the bottom of the jar. You can also put a piece of tape across the pot bottom to hold it more securely in place. Slip the newspaper pot off the jar. Set your pots in high-sided trays with their sides touching. When you fill them with potting mix, they will support one another. There are also commercial molds for making newspaper pots.

Soil blocks encourage well-branched roots and produce good seedlings. You can buy molds to make soil blocks, but making them is a messy, labor-intensive process.

Begin by mixing a wheelbarrow-load of potting soil. Use plenty of peat moss and lots of water to make a thick, wet, gummy mass with the texture of peanut butter. Jam the soil-block mold into the block mix. Press the mold hard against the bottom of the wheelbarrow, and then

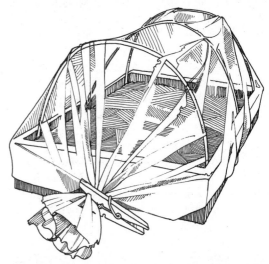

Homemade seeding flats. Construct a four-sided wooden frame 3″-4″ deep to fit your growing area. Nail slats across the bottom, leaving ⅛″-¼″ spaces between them. Fill the flat with potting mix and sow seeds. Bend three lengths of wire coat hanger and insert them in the mix to support a plastic bag that encloses the entire flat. Close the bag with a twist tie.

lift and eject the blocks from the mold onto a tray. Then arrange the blocks in flats and plant directly into them. Don't let soil blocks dry out: Because of their high peat content, they don't absorb moisture well once they have become dry. Water from the bottom or mist gently until roots grow. Once roots fill the blocks, they become solid and easy to handle.

Seed-Starting and Potting Mixes

Seeds contain enough nutrients to nourish themselves through sprouting, so a seed-starting mix does not have to contain nutrients. It should be free of weed seeds and toxic substances, hold moisture well, and provide plenty of air spaces. Don't use plain garden soil to start seedlings; it hardens into a dense mass that delicate young roots can't penetrate.

The following soil-free materials are good for starting seeds. Try them alone, or mix two or more together: vermiculite, milled sphagnum moss, peat moss, perlite, and compost. Let your seedlings grow in such a mixture until they develop their first true leaves, and then transplant into a nutrient-rich potting mix.

Some gardeners prefer to plant seeds directly in potting mix and eliminate transplanting. Planting in large individual pots is ideal for plants such as squash and melons that won't grow well if their roots are disturbed. You can use a commercial potting mix (which may contain synthetic chemical fertilizer) or make your own.

To make your own potting mix, combine equal parts compost and vermiculite. For more recipes for mixes, see the Houseplants entry.

Moisten the planting mix before you fill your containers, especially if it contains peat moss or sphagnum moss. Use warm water, and allow the mix time to absorb it. When you squeeze a handful of mix it should hold together and feel moist, but it shouldn't drip.

If you're sowing directly in flats, first line the bottom with a sheet of newspaper to keep soil from washing out. Scoop premoistened planting medium into the containers, and spread it out. Tap the filled container on your work surface to settle it in, and smooth the surface with your hand. Don't pack it down tightly.

Sowing Seeds

Space large seeds at least 1" apart, planting 2-3 seeds in each pot (snip off the weaker seedlings later). Plant medium-sized seeds ½"-1" apart, and tiny ones about ½" apart. If you're sowing only a few seeds, use your fingertips or tweezers to place them precisely. To sprinkle seeds evenly, try one of these methods:

• Take a pinch of seeds between your thumb and forefinger and slowly rotate thumb against finger—try to release the seeds gradually while moving your hand over the container.

• Scatter seeds from a spoon.

• Sow seeds directly from the corner of the packet by tapping the packet gently to make the seeds drop out one by one.

• Mix fine seeds with dry sand, and scatter the mixture from a saltshaker.

To sow seeds in tiny furrows or rows, just make shallow ¼"-½" deep depressions in the soil with a plant label or an old pencil. Space the seeds along the bottom of the furrow.

Cover the seeds to a depth of three times their thickness by carefully sprinkling them with light, dry potting soil or seed-starting medium. Don't cover seeds that need light to germinate. Instead, gently pat the surface of the mix so the seeds and mix have good contact.

Write a label for each kind of seed you plant and put it in the flat or pot as soon as the seeds are planted, before any mix-ups occur.

Set the flats or pots in shallow containers of water and let them soak until the surface of the planting medium looks moist. Or you can gently mist the mix. If you water from the top, use a watering can with a rose nozzle to get a gentle stream that won't wash the seeds out of place.

Cover the container, using clear plastic or a floating row cover for seeds that need light, or black plastic, damp newspaper, or burlap for those that prefer the dark.

Finally, put the containers of planted seeds in a warm place where you can check them daily. Unless the seeds need light to germinate, you can save space the first few days by stacking flats. Just be sure the bottom of a flat doesn't actually rest on the planting mix of the flat below. Check the flats daily; unstack as soon as the seeds start to sprout. Keep the soil moist but not waterlogged. As soon as you notice sprouts nudging above the soil surface, expose the flat to light.

Raising Healthy Seedlings

Seedlings need regular attention. Provide the right amount of light, heat, and humidity to grow robust, healthy seedlings.

Light: Seedlings need more intense light

SOWING TIMETABLE

To plan the best time to start seedlings indoors in spring, you need to know the approximate date of the average last spring frost in your area. Count back from that date the number of weeks indicated below to determine the appropriate starting date for various crops. An asterisk (*) indicates a cold-hardy plant that can be set out 4–6 weeks before the last frost.

- 12–14 weeks: onions*, leeks*, chives*, pansies*, impatiens, and coleus
- 8–12 weeks: peppers, lettuce*, cabbage-family crops*, petunias, snapdragons*, alyssum*, and other hardy annual flowers
- 6–8 weeks: eggplants, tomatoes
- 5–6 weeks: zinnias, cockscombs, marigolds, other tender annuals
- 2–4 weeks: cucumbers, melons, okra, pumpkins, squash

than full-grown plants. If they don't get enough light or if the light isn't strong enough, they will become spindly and leggy. Sixteen hours of light a day is ideal, 14 hours is acceptable, and plants can get along with 12 hours in a cool location. Up to 18 hours will do no harm, but most plants won't thrive in continuous light.

Windowsills are a popular spot for starting seedlings. Wide windowsills of old houses are ready to use, but you can also widen narrow windowsills by installing shelf brackets and boards. Keep in mind that the air close to the window glass can be too cold for some tender seedlings, especially at night. Pull curtains or prop up cardboard next to the glass at night for protection. Short winter days provide inadequate light for many plants. Turn plants regularly to prevent them from developing a one-sided leaning, or rig up a mirror or a reflector made of aluminum foil and cardboard. A sunporch offers more room and often longer exposure to the sun than do windowsills, and the cooler temperatures in a sunporch can be great for cold-loving plants.

If you have a greenhouse, you can easily raise high-quality seedlings in quantity. Cold frames can shelter small batches of cold-hardy seedlings like pansies and broccoli early in the season, followed by tomatoes and annual flowers as the season progresses. The addition of heating can transform a cold frame into a hotbed. For more information on greenhouses, cold frames, and hotbeds see the Greenhouse Gardening and Cold Frames entries.

Fluorescent lights use energy and will raise your electric bill, but they *do* help in raising good seedlings. Special plant growth lights, often called grow-lights, are expensive. The light from less-expensive cool-white tubes produces comparable plants. Light from incandescent lightbulbs will not stimulate growth as well as grow-lights or cool-white fluorescent tubes do.

Water: Seedlings need a steady supply of moisture. Dry air in a heated house can suck moisture rapidly from the shallow soil in seedling flats. Check for dryness by poking your finger into the soil and by lifting the flats. A flat with dry soil weighs less than one that's well watered. For delicate seedlings, bottom watering is best, since it does not disturb roots and helps prevent disease problems such as damping-off. Use tepid water rather than cold water to water seedlings, especially warmth-loving plants like okra, eggplant, and melons. In a warm, dry house, seedlings may need to be watered every 2-3 days or even more frequently.

Temperature: Young plants require less warmth than germinating seedlings. Average room temperatures of about 60°-70°F, dropping by about 10°F at night, will keep most seedlings growing steadily. Slightly lower temperatures will make seedlings stocky but more slow-growing. Cool-weather plants such as cabbage and lettuce prefer cooler temperatures.

Temperatures of 30°-45°F can cause chilling injury in some warmth-loving flowers and vegetables. Temperatures higher than about 75°F tend to produce weak, spindly plants that are vulnerable to harsh outdoor conditions.

Ventilation: Remove any plastic or other coverings as soon as seeds sprout. Lack of air circulation can lead to the development of damping-off.

Fertilizer: Seedlings growing in a soilless or lean mix will need small doses of plant food, starting at the time the first true leaves develop. Use a half-strength fertilizer solution once a week for the first three weeks. Fish emulsion and compost or manure teas are good. After that, use a full-strength solution every 10-14 days. Seedlings grown in a potting mix that contains compost or other nutrients may not need supplementary feeding for several weeks. If the seedlings start looking pale, feed as above. For recipes for making compost tea or manure tea, see the Composting or Manure entries.

Transplanting: Most gardeners tend to sow seeds thickly, but seedlings grow faster, develop better, and are less prone to disease if they have plenty of space and good soil. Transplanting gives you a chance to select the best seedlings and to move them into a larger container of richer soil. You can transplant seedlings from their nursery flat to another flat with wider spacing, or you can move them to individual pots. Seedlings are ready for transplanting when they have developed their first set of true leaves. For details on how to handle seedlings see the Transplanting entry.

Planting Out

Before you can plant your seedlings in the garden, you must prepare them for life outdoors. Sheltered plants are unaccustomed to wind, strong sun, cold air, and varying temperatures. They will do better if you help them develop tougher

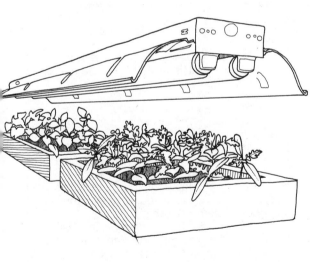

Grow-lights. Use cool-white florescent tubes or grow-lights to light indoor seedlings. Keep tubes close to the seedlings—no more than 3" away—for their first few weeks. Then raise the lights to 4"-6" above seedlings.

tissues gradually, before you plant them outside.

When it's time to plant the hardened-off seedlings in the outdoor garden, wait for an overcast or drizzly day, or plant them in the late afternoon. Seedlings will suffer less stress if they are not set out during a hot, sunny day. If you plant transplants out just before a rain, they'll get off to a good start, and you'll have less watering to do.

After planting out, you may want to put berry baskets or cut-open plastic jugs over seedlings or drape the row with a floating row cover to protect them from sun, wind, or frost. If the sun is strong or the plants are in an exposed location, water the soil around them several times during their first week in the ground, until their roots take hold. If plants wilt, water the soil promptly and shade the plants from the sun for a day or two.

For more information on hardening off and planting out seedlings, see the Transplanting entry.

Starting Seeds Outdoors

You can plant seeds of many flowers, herbs, and vegetables directly in the garden. If you live where winters are mild, you can sow seeds outside pretty much year-round. In cold-winter areas, the outdoor seed-sowing season begins in spring when the ground thaws and continues until early autumn.

When the soil is soft enough to dig and dry enough to crumble readily in your hand, you can make your first outdoor plantings. Don't try to work the soil while it is wet. Start with the hardiest seeds, such as peas and radishes, and gradually work up to more tender crops as the season progresses and frost danger diminishes and finally disappears.

Avoid stepping on the seedbed; compacted soil lacks the air spaces so necessary for good root growth. Sprinkle seed thinly over the entire bed, or plant in straight rows, using a string stretched between two sticks to help you mark out the rows. Follow seed packet directions for seed spacing: Thick stands of seedlings compete with each other just like weeds and are more prone to disease problems such as damping-off. After you have sown the seeds, mark the spot with a label, and record the planting on your garden calendar or plan. For more detailed instructions on outdoor seed sowing, see the Planting entry.

To figure the latest possible planting date for late-summer seed sowing, subtract the average days to maturity for the crop from the average date of your first hard frost. Subtract 5-10 extra days to compensate for cooler fall nights and slower growth. If frost comes in mid-October, for instance, make a final planting of 50-day lettuce in early to mid-August. If you use season extenders like floating row covers, delay the final planting date a few weeks.

TROUBLESHOOTING

If your seeds fail to germinate or if only a few sprout, it is probably due to one or more of these factors:

- Old seed that is no longer viable
- Seed produced under poor growing conditions and is not viable
- Seed that is damaged
- Too much or not enough moisture
- Temperature too high or too low
- Germination-inhibiting substances in the soil (herbicide residues, for example) or high salt content in soil
- Top watering or heavy rain washed seeds out of soil mix or covered them too deeply, or seed was planted too deeply to start with
- Damping-off disease
- Seeds not in good contact with soil
- Lack of light or lack of darkness for seeds that need these for germination
- Dormancy requirement not met

Saving Seeds

Saving seeds is fun, and you can save a bit of money by doing it. You can save seeds from individual plants with traits you desire, such as earliness, disease resistance, high yield, or flower color. By carefully selecting individual plants each year and saving their seed, you can develop strains that are uniquely suited to your growing conditions.

Seed saving is also an important way to perpetuate heirloom plants that are in danger of becoming extinct. For further information, see the Heirloom Plants entry.

Selecting seed to save: Only save seed from plants grown from open-pollinated seed. Open-pollinated cultivars produce seed that comes true—the seedlings are very like the parents. They also are somewhat variable by nature, and repeated selection for a particular character will yield a strain that is slightly different than the original one. Seed harvested from hybrid plants produces seedlings unlike the parents and in most cases inferior to them.

When selecting plants to save seed from, choose those that are vigorous, disease-free, and outstanding in whatever qualities you wish to encourage. Mark chosen plants with a stake or colored string so you won't forget and harvest them for other purposes by mistake.

Some garden plants, such as tomatoes, peas, and lettuce, are self-pollinated. Each flower pollinates itself. You don't have to take any precautions to prevent one cultivar from crossing with another—just let the seed mature, and harvest it.

Others, such as corn and plants of the pumpkin, squash, and cabbage families, are cross-pollinated and can cross with other cultivars of the same plant. To keep a strain pure, keep plants from which you want to save seed separate from other blooming cultivars of the same species by at least 200'. Or use bags to cover the blooms you plan to harvest seed from before they open, and pollinate them by hand with flowers of the same cultivar.

As you become more interested in seed saving, you may want to try your hand at making some controlled crosses of your own by pollinating protected blossoms with flowers from a different cultivar. For more information on how to hand-pollinate and make controlled crosses, see the Plant Breeding entry.

Certain garden plants normally grown as annuals, such as carrots and lettuce, are biennials—these crops will not produce seed the first year. Select superior plants and allow them to overwinter in place if possible. If you can't work around them, transplant them carefully to a new location.

Harvesting: Pick seed pods when they have turned dry and brittle but before they break open and scatter the seed. Some plants have very fragile seed pods or ripen unevenly. Cover the pods of these plants with a bag before the seeds ripen completely, and tie it snugly to the stem so seeds can't escape. Remove the seeds from the pods after harvesting. You can split the pods by hand or thresh the seeds out by beating them with a stick onto a large piece of plastic.

Allow fleshy fruits like tomatoes, squash, and cucumbers to get a little overripe on the plant before harvesting them, but don't allow them to start to rot. Separate the seeds from the flesh and wash them clean in water. Some seeds are covered with a thick, jellylike coating. Clean the seeds by removing as much flesh as possible by letting them sit in water in a jar for a few days. The seeds will sink to the bottom of the jar and the pulp will float. Pour off the pulp and dry the seeds.

Drying and storing: After gathering seeds, spread them on newspaper and let them air dry for about a week. Write seed names on the newspaper so you don't get them confused. Then pack them away in airtight jars and keep them in a cool, dry place. Remember that heat and dampness will shorten the seed's period of viability. Label packaged seeds with cultivar, date, and any other pertinent information. ❖

Sempervivum

Hens-and-chickens, houseleeks. Succulent perennials; evergreen groundcovers.

Description: Hens-and-chickens get their name because they increase by forming new clusters of offsets around each parent plant. Their fleshy, pointed leaves are borne in small rosettes. During summer the rosettes bloom, bearing asterlike flowers in colors of white, green, yellow, pink, or red. Once these blossoms are spent, the parent rosettes die back.

Sempervivum arachnoideum, cobweb houseleek, has very attractive 4″ tall rosettes with grayish green leaves connected by fine, cobweblike hairs. The plants sporadically produce showy, bright red flowers on 4″ stalks. *S. tectorum,* hens-and-chickens or common houseleek, has 4″-6″ rosettes and spreads rapidly by producing new offsets. Its leaves are grayish green with reddish brown, pointed tips. The red flowers are borne on stalks that can reach 1′ tall. Zones 3-10.

How to grow: Hens-and-chickens are easy to grow and need little care. During extended dry periods, plants may require some watering to keep them from shriveling. Afterwards, the shriveled plants will perk right up. These plants thrive in well-drained, humus-rich soil in full sun. They will also flourish in rocky soils or porous rocks, where they creep and multiply in any available nook and cranny. Cobweb houseleeks are slow spreaders that prefer slightly acid soil. Propagate by removing offsets and planting them elsewhere in the garden.

Landscape use: Hens-and-chickens are popular in rock gardens, on rock walls, and in beds or containers. Their interesting shapes and colors make them perfect for patterned borders. They can also be potted up and taken indoors during the winter months. However, don't take plants indoors until after January, as they need a cold dormancy period. ❖

Shade Gardening

Gardening in the shade challenges the talents of many gardeners because they fight the shady conditions rather than adapting to them. You can't grow a lovely lawn or an English flower border under trees. But you *can* grow a diverse, beautiful garden. Instead of struggling to grow sun-loving flowers and lawn grass in a shady site, why not design a garden that will actually thrive in shade? By carefully choosing flowering shrubs, perennials, annuals, groundcovers, and ferns adapted to shady conditions, your garden will be not only colorful and interesting but also easy to care for!

The Challenges of Shade Gardening

Study your shady site to decide if you have dense, light, or partial shade. In partial shade, where some direct sun shines for a few hours a day, you'll be able to grow a wider selection of plants. Light or dappled shade also allows a wider selection than dense all-day shade cast from a thick-foliaged tree. If tree shade is very dense, you might want to thin out a few tree branches (cut them off at the trunk) so that more light reaches the ground, creating a light or filtered shade. You may have to thin out branches every few years.

Working with shade means understanding that in many cases, poor, dry soil limits plant growth more than lack of light. Shady spots under trees can often be remarkably dry, because the trees' surface roots suck up all the available moisture and nutrients. The lack of moisture, not the shade, often limits your endeavors. You'll know if dry, root-clogged soil poses a problem because the ground will feel hard and compacted; you'll have trouble digging a hole with a trowel.

If the soil in your shady spot is hard and compacted, you can layer chopped-up leaves and twigs over the area. In a year or so, they will

PLANTS FOR SHADY GARDENS

The wide selection of plants listed here will brighten up any shady corner. Most prefer partial or filtered shade, but some can do well even in dark shade. Check plant hardiness of perennials, groundcovers, and shrubs, and choose plants that are hardy in your area. If you have room, consider flowering understory trees like dogwoods and redbuds that do well in woodland conditions. For more plants that tolerate shady conditions, see the Ferns entry, "Annuals for Shade" on page 19 and "Best Perennials for Shade" on page 454.

Annuals

Begonia Semperflorens-Cultorum Hybrids (wax begonias)
Browallia speciosa (browallia)
Coleus × *hybridus* (coleus)
Impatiens wallerana (impatiens)
Myosotis sylvatica (garden forget-me-not)
Torenia fournieri (wishbone flower)
Viola × *wittrockiana* (pansy)

Perennials

Astilbe spp. and cultivars (astilbes)
Dicentra eximia (fringed bleeding heart)
Dicentra spectabilis (common bleeding heart)
Digitalis purpurea (common foxglove; reseeding biennial)
Filipendula ulmaria (queen-of-the-meadow)
Helleborus spp. (hellebores)
Hemerocallis spp. and cultivars (daylilies)
Hosta spp. and cultivars (hostas)
Mertensia virginica (Virginia bluebells)
Osmunda cinnamomea (cinnamon fern)
Phlox divaricata (wild blue phlox)
Phlox stolonifera (creeping phlox)
Primula spp. (primroses)
Pulmonaria spp. (lungworts)
Tiarella cordifolia (Allegheny foamflower)

Groundcovers

Ajuga reptans (ajuga)
Asarum spp. (wild gingers)
Galium odoratum (sweet woodruff)
Epimedium spp. (epimediums)
Euonymus fortunei (wintercreeper)
Hedera helix (English ivy)
Lamium maculatum (spotted lamium)
Liriope spp. (lilyturf)
Mitchella repens (partridgeberry)
Pachysandra terminalis (Japanese pachysandra)
Vinca minor (vinca)

Shrubs

Calycanthus floridus (Carolina allspice)
Daphne cneorum (rose daphne)
Ilex crenata (Japanese holly)
Kalmia latifolia (mountain laurel)
Kerria japonica 'Variegata' (variegated Japanese kerria)
Leucothoe spp. (leucothoes)
Mahonia spp. (mahonias and Oregon grapes)
Nandina domestica (heavenly bamboo)
Prunus laurocerasus (cherry-laurel)
Rhododendron spp. and cultivars (rhododendrons and azaleas)
Ribes alpinum (alpine currant)
Sarcococca hookerana (Himalayan sarcococca)
Skimmia japonica (Japanese skimmia)

---

decompose into a rich humus. Chop the dry leaves to the size of fifty-cent pieces with a bagging lawn mower, and spread them several inches deep beneath the tree boughs. Sprinkle the leaves with a compost activator and keep them moist. Repeat this procedure annually until the leaves have rotted into a deep humus. By then, earthworms will have moved in and begun to loosen up the subsoil. Only when you have a loose, friable soil can you begin installing a diverse shade garden, though tough groundcovers such as English ivy (*Hedera helix*) and Japanese pach-

More On
SHADE GARDENS

For ideas on what to do with your shady site, see the design for a shady woodland garden in the Natural Landscaping entry. Two excellent references for shade gardeners are George Schenk's *The Complete Shade Gardener* and Harriet K. Morse's *Gardening in the Shade*.

ysandra (*Pachysandra terminalis*) will grow in dense tree shade and poor soil.

Sometimes tree roots interfere with digging a planting hole for a shade-loving shrub. When this happens, dig an extra-large planting hole and sever all interfering tree roots smaller than 1″ in diameter. Mulch the soil with compost to nourish the young shrub. The large planting hole should give the shrub enough growing room to get established before tree roots return.

Designing a Shade Garden

Arrange plants from tallest to shortest. You might start by planting a shade-loving understory tree, then arranging groups of broad-leaved evergreen shrubs. After these woody plants are in place, add large groups of flowering perennials and underplant them with a groundcover to keep the soil cool and moist. Spring-flowering bulbs often flourish beneath trees, soaking up all the sun they need in spring before the tree leaves emerge. Plant them in large drifts together with the perennials.

Choose white and pastel-colored flowers as well as white- or yellow-variegated foliage plants for your shady site. These light colors pop out of the shadows rather than receding into the gloom like red or purple flowers tend to do. With a careful selection of plants, you can transform your dim spot into a cool, flowery retreat that just might be the best-looking part of your yard. ❖

Shrubs

Some of the most familiar and beautiful plants around our homes are shrubs. The graceful sweep of forsythia and the stately form of a privet hedge show the diversity of these woody perennials. Shrubs have multiple stems and range in height from a few inches to approximately 15′ at maturity, although individual shrubs may grow as high as 30′. A shrub trained to a single stem, called a standard, resembles a miniature tree.

It's hard to imagine a home landscape without shrubs. Their combined features of easy care, interesting forms, and attractive flowers and foliage make them a great asset to all gardeners.

Types of Shrubs

Deciduous shrubs drop their leaves at the end of each growing season and grow new leaves the following spring. Leaves may first change color, but after leaf fall, the shrub enters winter dormancy.

Evergreen shrubs have leaves year-round. They do drop some or all of their old leaves each year, but always have new leaves to keep them looking green. Narrow-leaved or needle evergreens, such as junipers and false cypress, have needle or scalelike leaves. Broad-leaved evergreens such as boxwoods and rhododendrons have wide, generally thick leaves.

Semi-evergreen shrubs keep at least part of their leaves well into the winter. Shrubs such as glossy abelia are evergreen in the South and semi-evergreen further north.

A few groups of shrubs have both deciduous and evergreen species. For example, the evergreen leaves of American holly hide many of its berries. But when the leaves drop from the deciduous winterberry, clusters of bright red berries are revealed.

Landscaping with Shrubs

There are shrubs for every possible situation in your landscape. For single-specimen accent plants, use individual shrubs with colored leaves, large flowers or fruits, or unusual stems or bark. "Showy Shrubs" on page 538 lists many excellent accent shrubs.

Plant shrubs close together to form an unbroken line or a group in screens and hedges. Privet (*Ligustrum* spp.) is a classic, but many others also make good hedges. A low-growing hedge, such as common boxwood (*Buxus sempervirens*), can direct traffic around walkways and define borders of flower and herb beds. Plant larger shrubs, such as spireas (*Spiraea* spp.) and viburnums, singly or in groups. They can frame outdoor spaces, provide privacy, hide unsightly views, and buffer against wind and noise.

Use ground-covering shrubs, such as rockspray cotoneaster (*Cotoneaster horizontalis*) or shore juniper (*Juniperus conferta*), to control erosion and ease maintenance on steep banks.

Low-growing Japanese hollies (*Ilex crenata*) or abelias (*Abelia* spp.) make good foreground plants for foundation plantings. Medium and tall shrubs, such as yews (*Taxus* spp.) and Chinese junipers (*Juniperus chinensis*), serve as background plants for foundation plantings, as well as for perennial beds.

Many medium- and tall-growing shrubs have naturally occurring or cultivated forms that are smaller and slower-growing. These dwarf and miniature forms, such as dwarf nandina (*Nandina domestica* 'Nana') and dwarf mugo pine (*Pinus mugo* var. *mugo*), generally do not grow more than 3′ tall. Use them when your planting site is small, or when you want less pruning maintenance.

Try shrubs with edible fruits, such as blueberries and bush cherries. Plant hollies and viburnums for berries that will attract birds and other wildlife.

For ideas on using shrubs in the landscape, see the Espalier, Hedges, Landscaping, Natural Landscaping, and Rock Gardens entries.

Selecting Shrubs

Before you head to the nursery or garden center to buy shrubs, make a list of desired features. What should the shrubs do—form a windscreen, complete your foundation planting, or serve as a specimen? How big can the shrub get, how often will you have time to prune it, and what showy features do you want?

Make a second list of the conditions of your site—soil, water, and exposure. For healthy, vigorous shrubs, match the plant to the site. Combine your two lists to discover the shrubs that best fill your needs.

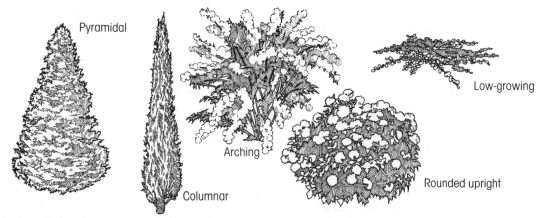

Pyramidal

Columnar

Arching

Low-growing

Rounded upright

Shrub shapes. Tall, short, round, angular—there are shrubs of every shape and size. Consider how tall or wide a shrub will be at maturity before you plant, and be sure that the shrub will have room to grow. Shrubs will be healthier and more attractive in their natural form, and easier to maintain without the need for repeated pruning.

SHOWY SHRUBS

Shrubs are a highlight during their blossom time, but they have other features that can add color and diversity throughout the year. Many have attractive foliage in summer and/or fall, some have colorful berries, and others have unusual bark. To add four-season interest to your home landscape, try planting a few of the plants from this list. Plant name is followed by features and seasons of interest.

Berberis spp. (barberries): summer and fall foliage, flowers, fruit; all seasons
Cornus sericea (red-osier dogwood): flowers, bark; spring, winter
Corylus avellana 'Contorta' (Harry Lauder's walking stick): leaves, flowers, twisted stems; all seasons
Cotinus coggygria (smoke tree): leaves, flowers; all seasons
Cotoneaster horizontalis (rockspray cotoneaster): flowers, fruit, growth habit; all seasons
Euonymus alata (burning bush): fall foliage, winged bark; fall, winter
Hydrangea quercifolia (oakleaf hydrangea): leaves, flowers; all seasons
Lagerstroemia indica (crape myrtle): flowers, fruits, bark; all seasons
Mahonia spp. (mahonias, Oregon grapes): evergreen leaves, flowers, fruits; all seasons
Pieris spp. (pieris): flowers, evergreen foliage; all seasons
Rosa rugosa (rugosa rose): flowers, fruits; spring, summer, fall
Vaccinium spp. (blueberries): flowers, fruits, autumn color; summer, fall
Viburnum spp. (viburnums): flowers, fruits; spring, fall

With your list in hand, you're ready to buy. Remember that shrubs are a long-term feature of the home landscape. It's well worth your time and money to seek out and buy good-quality shrubs. Don't base your selection on price alone.

Follow these guidelines when you shop:
• Choose healthy plants. Look for plump, firm buds and leaves that are the correct size and color.
• Reject shrubs with broken branches or scratched bark, dry or brown leaf margins, or dry root balls.
• Read tags and labels, and don't buy unlabeled plants. Be sure the flowers, fruit, and form of the plant are what you want. Check if the plant will grow well in the site you have chosen.
• Buy bareroot shrubs only when they're dormant and only if the roots have been kept moist.
• Inspect container-grown shrubs, and don't buy rootbound plants. Many large roots on the outside of the root ball or protruding from drainage holes mean the plant may be stunted by growing in a too-small container.
• Select balled-and-burlapped shrubs with firm, well-wrapped root balls.

Planting and Care

Plant bareroot shrubs while dormant, from late fall until early spring. Plant container- and field-grown shrubs all year, except when the ground is frozen. If you transplant shrubs from one location to another in your yard, move them while they are dormant. Slide the root ball onto a piece of burlap so it stays intact during the move. For complete instructions on how to plant shrubs, see the Planting entry.

Newly planted shrubs require more care than shrubs with well-established roots. Water your shrubs well when you plant or transplant them. Continue to water them each week when less than 1″ of rain falls, especially in summer and fall. A layer of mulch helps retain water. Keep mulch away from the stems to discourage mice and prevent extra moisture that may cause rot.

Pruning: As your shrubs grow, you'll need to prune them to control their size, rejuvenate old plants, repair damage and remove pests, and control flowering and fruiting. See the Pruning and Training entry for basic information on making proper pruning cuts.

Maintain the natural form of your shrubs by pruning back to outward-facing buds or removing whole branches. Shearing is faster than naturalistic pruning, but it destroys the natural beauty of the plant—and you'll need to do it often. Learn to read the natural shape and type of a plant and prune accordingly. Many plants combine characteristics and may need more than one pruning technique.

Cane-growers are often fountain shaped. They renew themselves by sending up new canes from the base. Make heading cuts to stimulate lower growth where desired. Thin some branches to maintain an open, uncluttered form.

Mounding shrubs are generally rounded and have fine or supple branches and small leaves. Mounding shrubs are the easiest type to reduce in size and keep at a given height. Remove up to ⅓ of the foliage in a year.

Treelike shrubs with stiff, woody branches are the most difficult to control in size. Don't remove more than ¼ of the greenery in a year.

Prune spring-flowering shrubs in the spring shortly after they finish blooming, and summer-flowering shrubs from late fall until spring bud break. Flower buds form on old wood on spring-flowering shrubs but on new wood for summer-flowering shrubs.

Prune evergreens year-round, except in late summer and early fall. Pruning late in the growing season encourages new growth that may be killed by frosts.

Growing tips: Inspect your shrubs often to minimize problems with insects and diseases. Aphids feed on the new growth and flower buds of almost any shrub. Various caterpillars and beetles chew holes in the leaves, while whiteflies feed on leaf undersides. Scales feed on leaves and stems. Shrub diseases range from leaf spots and blights to stem cankers and root rots.

Avoid problems by selecting insect-tolerant or resistant shrubs. Be sure your plants have well-drained soil, sufficient light, and good air circulation to help prevent pest and disease problems before they start. Handpicking, putting out pheromone traps, and spraying insecticidal soap or BT (*Bacillus thuringiensis*) are all useful insect controls. For more on pest and disease control, see the Organic Pest Management entry.

Heavy ice or snow can sometimes injure dense shrubs, and winter winds can dry out evergreen leaves. For special winter protection, build a temporary structure of boards and burlap.

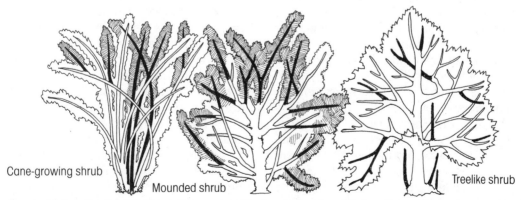

Cane-growing shrub

Mounded shrub

Treelike shrub

Pruning strategies. Renew and control cane-growing shrubs such as forsythia, nandina, and roses by removing older canes at ground level. Neaten up and shorten mounding shrubs such as abelias and barberries by using mostly selective heading cuts to remove unruly and overly long branches, hiding cuts in the shrub interior. Prune rhododendrons, witch hazels, viburnums, and other treelike shrubs with thinning cuts to remove dead wood or interfering branches, reduce bulk and clutter, and create definition.

More On
SHRUBS

You'll find descriptions, growing information, best uses, and best cultivars in the entries for the following shrubs: Abelia, Aesculus (horse chestnut), Amelanchier (serviceberry), Arctostaphylos (bearberry), Berberis (barberry), Buddleia (butterfly bush), Buxus (boxwood), Camellia, Chaenomeles (flowering quince), Cornus (dogwood), Cotoneaster, Daphne, Deutzia, Eucalyptus, Euonymus, Forsythia, Gardenia, Hamamelis (witch hazel), Hibiscus, Hydrangea, Ilex (holly), Jasminum (jasmine), Juniperus (juniper), Kalmia (laurel), Lagerstroemia, Ligustrum (privet), Magnolia, Mahonia (Oregon grape), Malus (crab apple), Palms, Philadelphus (mock orange), Picea (spruce), Pieris, Pinus (pine), Potentilla (cinquefoil), Prunus (flowering cherry), Pyracantha, Rhododendron (azalea and rhododendron), Robinia (locust), Rosa (rose), Salix (willow), Spiraea (spirea), Syringa (lilac), Taxus (yew), Thuja (arborvitae), Viburnum, and Weigela.

Spray the leaves of evergreen shrubs with an antidesiccant or antitranspirant, a protective coating that keeps the leaves from drying.

Small, yellow leaves or too few flowers or fruits may indicate a nutrient deficiency. A dose of organic fertilizer should help matters, unless it's a case of the right plant in the wrong place. See the Plant Nutrition and Fertilizers entries for more information.

Propagating: Starting shrubs from seed is an iffy proposition—plant form and flower and leaf color and size can be quite unlike the parent shrub. Making stem or root cuttings or layering are more reliable methods. Almost any shrub can be propagated using stem cuttings. Forsythia, winter jasmine, and others are easy to propagate by layering. See the Cuttings, Grafting, and Layering entries for particulars. ❖

Slugs and Snails

Slugs and garden snails have an appetite for so many fruits, vegetables, and ornamentals that they are among the most damaging home garden pests. Not insects, they are mollusks, with soft, muscular bodies that secrete slime. Several species, ranging in size from less than 1″ to more than 4″, feed on garden plants.

Slugs and snails need moist surroundings and will hibernate during dry periods. They hide under rocks, garden debris, and mulches during the day. At night, they emerge and chew large ragged holes in leaves. You may find shiny slime trails and damaged plants without ever spotting a slug. For every slug you find, there may be 20 more you don't see. Damage usually is worst in spring, when soil is moist and plants are young. Follow these guidelines to control slugs and snails:

• Create a diverse garden ecosystem to encourage biological controls. Ants, beetle grubs, earwigs, flies, birds, snakes, toads, and turtles prey on slugs.

• Don't plant dense groundcovers or lay mulch near plants you want to protect.

• Armed with a flashlight, handpick slugs and snails from plants at night and drop them in a bucket of soapy water.

• Set out boards or inverted flowerpots as traps. Check the traps daily and kill the slugs or snails hidden there.

• Sink shallow containers of beer in soil near your plants. Snails and slugs are attracted to the beer and will drown after they climb in to drink it.

• Sprinkle dry soil or diatomaceous earth around the stem bases of your plants.

• Make a slug-proof barrier around garden beds by edging them with copper-based strips. Be sure to remove any slugs that are already in the bed when you put up the barrier.

• Traditional organic controls include repelling the pests with an oak leaf mulch and drenching the soil with wormwood tea. ❖

Soil

Healthy soil is the key to successful organic gardening. The basic principle that organic gardeners live by is to feed the soil, and let the soil feed the plants. The challenge for organic gardeners is to balance the soil so that it provides all the conditions plants need to thrive.

You may wonder why the soil in your yard and garden would be out of balance. There are several possible reasons:

• The surface soil around many homes may have been disturbed—or even removed—during construction, and nothing done to restore the soil afterward.

• Driving equipment, such as a lawn tractor, or repeatedly walking on soil compacts it, harming its structure.

• Your soil's natural characteristics may not be favorable for gardening. For example, you may have a soil that is so sandy that it does not hold sufficient water and nutrients to support vigorous plant growth. Or your soil's pH may be so acidic many kinds of plants won't thrive.

• Unless you're a longtime organic gardener, the soil may be depleted by years of cropping without replenishing organic matter, the soil's natural storehouse of nutrients.

• If you've used chemical fertilizers, the soil microorganisms that play an important role in maintaining natural fertility may have died off.

The first step in the process of improving your soil organically is to learn about its characteristics. There are many tests that will help you analyze your soil. After testing, you'll know what problems your soil has, and you can take steps to remedy them. Your soil improvement process will include adding organic matter and other soil amendments. While you work on improving your soil, you may want to use organic fertilizers to boost plant performance.

How Soil Works

Organic gardeners know that soil is much more than just dirt. Soil is an intricate mix of

Key Words
SOIL

Sand, silt, and clay. Tiny fragments of rock or minerals that make up nearly half the material in the soil. They are distinguished from one another by size. Sand particles are from 0.05 to 2.0 millimeters in diameter, silt particles are from 0.002 to 0.05 millimeters, and clay particles are less than 0.002 millimeters in diameter.

Soil texture. The relative proportions of sand, silt, and clay in the soil.

Soil structure. The arrangement of soil particles in the soil.

Loam. Soil that has moderate amounts of sand, silt, and clay. Loam soils are generally considered the best garden soils.

Soil pH. A measurement of the acidity or alkalinity of the soil.

Organic matter. Various forms of living or dead plant and animal material.

Microorganisms. Animals and plants that are too small to be seen clearly without use of a microscope.

Decay cycle. The changes that occur as plants grow, die, and break down in the soil. The action of soil animals and microorganisms breaks down plant tissues to release nutrients that new plants then take up to fuel their growth and development.

Nitrogen cycle. The transformation of nitrogen from an atmospheric gas to organic compounds in the soil to compounds in plants, with eventual release of nitrogen gas to the atmosphere.

Humus. A dark-colored, stable form of organic matter that remains after most of the plant and animal residues in it have decomposed. When soil animals and microbes digest organic matter, such as chopped leaves or weeds, humus is the end product.

Erosion. The wearing away of soil by running water, wind, ice, or other geological forces. Erosion can be accelerated by the activity of people or animals.

fine rock particles, organic matter, water, air, microorganisms, and other animals. A healthy

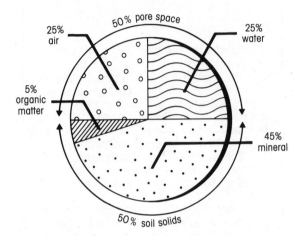

25% air

50% pore space

25% water

5% organic matter

45% mineral

50% soil solids

Soil components. Soil is nearly half minerals and half water and air. Organic matter makes up only a small percentage of the soil. But for successful gardeners, maintaining organic matter content is critical. Soil life, including mammals, reptiles, insects, and microorganisms, transforms organic matter into nutrients that can be taken up by your plants.

soil is full of living things: plant roots, animals, insects, bacteria, fungi, and other organisms. Managing your soils to keep this living system thriving can make the difference between gardening success and failure.

Texture and Structure

Although we might assume that the size differences between soil particles—sand, silt, or clay—are too small to have any significance, they are actually of great importance. The relative proportion of these tiny rock fragments— referred to as soil texture—influences soil water retention, air drainage, and fertility. The tiny spaces between these particles are the holding areas for soil water, and for the dissolved nutrients that can be absorbed by roots.

The spaces between sand particles are comparatively large, so they do not tend to granulate, or stick together. Thus, sandy soils often do not hold enough water to support the growth of many kinds of plants. Sandy soils may also tend to be less fertile because they have less surface area where nutrients can be held.

Clay soils are rich in very tiny particles that are attracted to each other when wet. While these clay particles can hold large reserves of water and dissolved nutrients, too much clay also can create problems. When clay particles dry, they stick together and form a hard layer. Clay soils tend to form surface crusts that water cannot penetrate easily. A clay layer deeper in the soil can form a hardpan that impedes water drainage.

It takes a huge effort to change soil texture. For example, to have a beneficial effect on clayey soil in a 20′ × 50′ garden bed, you'd have to add about 3-5 tons of sand to the top 6″ of soil.

Fortunately, there are steps you can take to improve another important characteristic, soil structure. Soil structure determines how well water is retained in the soil and how well it drains, how much air is available in the soil, and how easily nutrients are released for uptake by plant roots.

Many factors contribute to the creation of soil structure. Soil water freezes and thaws, plant roots grow and die, earthworms move through the soil. All these processes contribute to formation of soil pores and formation of soil clumps, or aggregates. Soil structure is also affected by soil pH, the amount of humus in the soil, and the combination of minerals in the soil. The ideal soil is friable—the soil particles clump together in clusters with air spaces between them. This allows water to drain through, and oxygen and carbon dioxide can easily move from the air above into the spaces below. Pore space can vary from 30 to 50 percent of soil volume.

The best way to improve soil structure is to add organic matter—lots of it. You'll read more about adding organic matter later in this entry.

All too often, gardeners also unthinkingly harm soil structure by tilling excessively, or by walking on or working soils that are too wet.

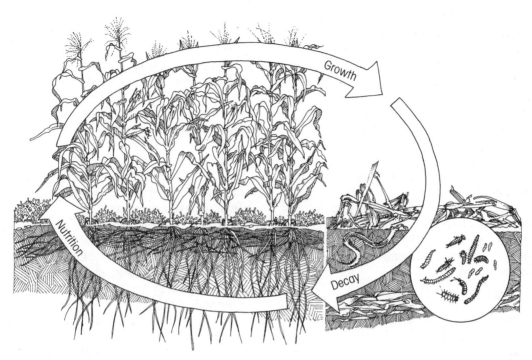

The decay cycle. In nature, when plants die, they literally are returned to the soil via the decay process. Mites, beetles, millipedes, earthworms, bacteria, and fungi feed on the dead and dying tissues. These organisms physically and chemically break the plant tissues down into simpler components. The waste products and, in their turn, the dead bodies of the soil-dwelling animals and microorganisms become part of soil organic matter. Proteins are converted to simple nitrogen compounds that can be absorbed by plant roots. Minerals such as phosphorus, potassium, and calcium are also changed into soluble compounds that are then absorbed by root cells and used by new growing plants.

These activities can ruin soil structure, and the damage done is not easily undone.

Air and Water

Oxygen is critical in the soil because many beneficial soil organisms cannot live without it. Gaseous nitrogen, another component of soil air, is a raw material for nitrogen-fixing bacteria that manufacture protein materials. These are later broken down to yield nitrogen compounds that can be absorbed by plant roots. Plant roots also "breathe" and need good air exchange between soil air and the atmosphere for good development.

Water also occupies soil pore space. Plant roots absorb this water and pass it on to leaves and stems, where it serves as a nutrient, a coolant, and as an essential part of all plant cells. Water is also the carrier for mineral nutrients, allowing them to enter plant roots and be transported through the plants. If soil doesn't drain well, water occupies all the soil pore space. This suffocates the plants because their roots cannot get the air they need.

Soil pore spaces should vary in size and be evenly distributed. Soil with sufficient organic matter will have this quality. Walking on the soil or driving yard and garden equipment over it can cause these pore spaces to collapse.

Organisms

Although only a minute portion of the soil by weight and volume, the living organisms in soil play a vital role. Soil microorganisms power the decay cycle—nature's perfect system for recycling organic matter and maintaining healthy soils.

Soil microorganisms include nematodes, protozoa, fungi, bacteria, and actinomycetes (threadlike bacteria). These microorganisms convert plant material into humus. "The Decay Cycle," illustrated on page 543, explains how.

Earthworms serve as natural "tillers" and soil conditioners. You can learn more about earthworms and their role in soil by reading the Earthworms entry.

Many soil-dwelling insects are parasites and predators of insects that harm crop plants. And soil animals, including the much-maligned mole, also help improve soil aeration and eat some harmful insects.

Investigating Your Soil

One question home gardeners frequently ask is, "Should I be adding anything to the soil this spring?" The best way to answer that question is to investigate your soil—to learn about its structure and content by observation and testing.

There are several simple tests you can do yourself to learn about your soil's structure, drainage, and earthworm activity (earthworms are a key indicator of soil health). You can also submit soil samples from your yard for soil analysis. Privately run soil testing laboratories and the Cooperative Extension Service perform soil analyses for home gardeners and offer recommendations on soil improvement based on the results of their tests.

Preparing a Soil Sample

You may want to collect many samples from around your yard and combine them to submit for a single test and report. Or you may want to prepare separate samples from your vegetable garden soil, your lawn, and an area where you hope to create a flower border, for example. However, you'll have to pay three times as much to get the three separate sets of recommendations.

Follow these steps to prepare a sample that will accurately reflect the content of your soil:

1. Scrape away any surface litter or plant growth from a small area of soil. Use a soil probe to cut a core of soil, or dig a hole with a stainless steel trowel or other tool (if you don't have stainless steel tools, use a large stainless steel spoon) and collect a slice of soil from the side of the hole. For cultivated areas, collect a core or slice to a depth of 6″. For lawns, collect your samples only from the top 4″ of soil.

2. Repeat the sampling procedure at 10-15 different locations around your yard or the particular area you are sampling.

3. Mix the soil cores or slices in a clean plastic or stainless steel container.

4. Place some of the mixed sample in a plastic container or bag, and put it in the bag supplied by your Cooperative Extension Service or the soil testing laboratory for shipment.

Don't touch the sample with soft steel, galvanized, or brass tools, or with your bare skin. The content of some minerals in soil is so small that minerals picked up from these metals or your skin could throw off test results.

You'll send your sample, along with an information sheet concerning your soil's history and your future gardening plans, to the testing laboratory by mail. Be sure to write on the information form that you want recommendations for organic soil amendments.

Interpreting Recommendations

After analyzing your soil, the test lab will send you a report on the results of their analysis and recommendations for improving your soil.

Test results may include: soil pH, organic matter content, and content of calcium, magnesium, nitrogen, phosphorus, potassium, sodium, sulfur, and trace minerals.

Soil labs make recommendations based on results of their research programs on plant responses to additions of mineral amendments. Making the recommendations is an imprecise science because the researchers must try to relate the data from the research soils they study to

SOIL TESTS: WHICH ONE, WHEN?

How can gardeners tell when they should go to the effort and expense of having their soil tested? And if they need a test, should they do it themselves or have a lab do the work?

Cooperative Extension soil tests: Extension soil tests are generally inexpensive (or free in some states). Soil test kits are available from your local Cooperative Extension Service office or at many garden centers. Their analysis will probably not be as complete as that offered by private testing labs.

Private laboratory soil tests: Private soil test labs usually charge $30 or more for their analyses. However, the extra money you spend often will translate to a more complete soil test and final report. It may also be easier to find a soil lab familiar with making organic, rather than chemical, fertilizer recommendations.

Commercial home test kits: Results from home test kits will be less accurate than those from a soil lab, because soil labs factor in individual differences in soil samples, such as moisture content and soil density, when doing analyses. The more sophisti-cated (and expensive) home test kits will give fairly accurate results. If your home results indicate soil imbalances, you may want to confirm the results with a professional soil test.

When to test: When is it worthwhile for you to pay for a private soil test lab? Answer that question by thinking about the general picture of your garden's health. Are your plants growing vigorously? If you've had plant problems, have they been limited to just one area or to a few types of plants? If yields have been disappointing, the lawn is filled with weeds, or many plants suffer from repeated disease problems or show deficiency symptoms, consider testing your soil. Some deficiency or combination of deficiencies may well be at the heart of the problem.

Also, if your observations or home tests indicate an imbalance that could be corrected by adding mineral amendments such as rock phosphate, lime, or gypsum, get a professional test before you act. If you add too much of any of these materials, you can create problems that won't be easy to correct. If you add too little, you won't fix the problem.

your individual soil. However, all soils are different. They do not all respond equally to applications of minerals or organic materials.

Typically, soil fertility studies are performed on soils that have low organic matter content. Analysis of such low organic matter soils may be more accurate because organic matter makes the soil more biologically diverse and complex.

If you have built up your soil's organic matter content, the test results and recommendations you receive may be less than fully accurate. In general, if you have been adding organic matter regularly to your soil for years and had healthy crops and good yields, don't add as much nitrogen, phosphorus, and potassium as recommended. Soil with high organic content uses soil amendments more efficiently. Also, organic soil amendments are less likely to leach quickly out of the root zone. You can reduce the amounts recommended by soil labs by as much as 75 percent. For example, if the recommendation you receive is for 2.5 lb. of nitrogen per 1,000 square feet of garden, you could add 1 lb. per 1,000 square feet.

If you are just beginning an organic soil management program, be prepared to add soil-building materials in the amounts recommended by the testing service. Ask clearly for recommendations for organic amendments. That way, you won't have to guess whether to add smaller amounts than those on the lab report.

Do-It-Yourself Tests

Another way to learn about your soil's condition is to try simple tests that rely not on precise chemical analysis, but rather on your observations of the soil. With these tests, there is little or no cost and no waiting for results.

The squeeze test: This test helps you determine soil texture. Do this test two or three days after a rainy spell. Take a loose ball of soil about the size of a Ping-Pong ball in the palm of your hand. Gently squeeze it between the ball of your thumb and the lower outside edge of your index finger. Sand feels gritty, silt feels like moist talcum powder, and clay feels slippery.

Squeeze the ball in your hand, and release. If it crumbles, it has a reasonably balanced texture. If the soil ball can hold its shape, it has a substantial percentage of clay. If you can roll it into a sausage shape, it has even more clay.

Run the palm of your other hand firmly over the handful of soil. If you see scratch marks on the surface of the soil, there is a sizable proportion of sand present. If the soil feels greasy, this indicates silt.

The perc test: This test is an easy way to assess water drainage through your soil. Dig a hole 6″ across and 1′ deep. Fill the hole with water and let it drain. As soon as the water has drained completely, fill it again. This time, keep track of how long it takes for the hole to drain. If it takes more than 8 hours, you have a drainage problem that needs attention.

The watering test: A variation on the perc test will tell you if your soil drains too rapidly. Start by watering a small area of your lawn or garden bed very thoroughly. Two days later, dig a small hole 6″ deep where you watered. If the soil already is dry to the bottom of the hole, your soil likely doesn't retain enough water for good plant growth.

Another way to monitor soil moisture is to use a manual or automatic moisture sensor. These are small, electronic devices that measure available water in the soil, letting you know how long water levels are adequate for your plants' needs. If a meter indicates that the soil needs rewatering only a few days after you've watered thoroughly or after a soaking rain, then you need to improve the soil's water-retention capacity.

The undercover test: The best way to learn about some aspects of your soil is to get right down into it. If you plan to plant a new tree or shrub, kill two birds with one stone and check out your soil as you prepare the hole. Your new plant will benefit from the extra-large planting hole, and you'll get valuable information about what's happening beneath the soil surface.

Dig a hole at least 2′ deep and 2′ across so you can get a view down into it. Pile soil on a ground cloth as you dig, so you can neatly refill the hole when you're done. Then observe your soil closely. For some ideas on what to look for, see "A Worm's-Eye View" on the opposite page.

Other Tests

If you have your soil tested, the test results will include a measurement of your soil's pH. However, pH is something you may want to measure separately from the mineral content. For example, if you plan to plant blueberries, which require acid soil, you may want to quickly check pH at several sites to see if the soil pH needs adjusting. For more information about pH testing and changing soil pH, see the pH entry.

An indirect way to find out about nutrient levels in your soil is to analyze the content of the plants growing in it. Plant analysis is not a do-it-yourself test. Many Cooperative Extension Service offices and some private labs will analyze samples of leaf tissue for nutrient content. This type of testing may give more accurate results for certain nutrients, including nitrogen, than soil analysis does. The labs analyze the nutrient content in the samples and compare the readings with compiled research data that show the normal range of nutrients required for optimal growth of that species. Based on that comparison, they make recommendations for treatment.

Improving Your Soil

There are no overnight or even single-season organic solutions for an imbalanced soil. Unlike gardeners who rely on soluble synthetic chemical fertilizers to keep their plants green and

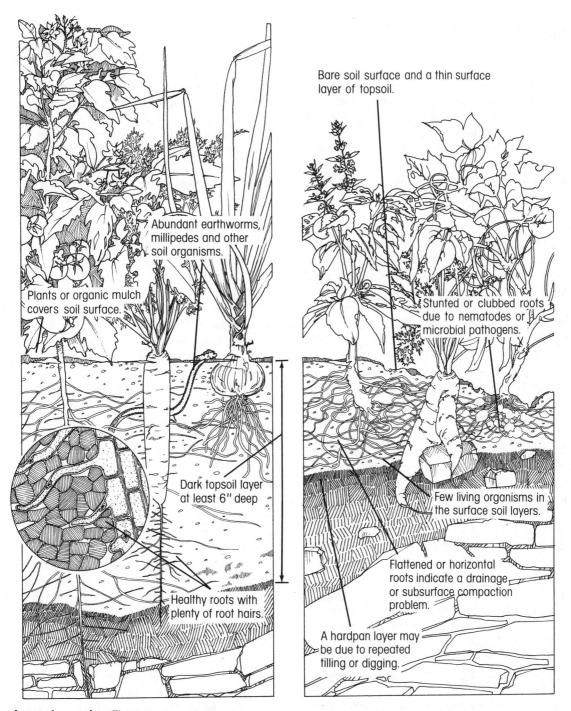

Bare soil surface and a thin surface layer of topsoil.

Abundant earthworms, millipedes and other soil organisms.

Plants or organic mulch covers soil surface.

Stunted or clubbed roots due to nematodes or microbial pathogens.

Dark topsoil layer at least 6" deep

Few living organisms in the surface soil layers.

Flattened or horizontal roots indicate a drainage or subsurface compaction problem.

Healthy roots with plenty of root hairs.

A hardpan layer may be due to repeated tilling or digging.

A worm's-eye view. There are many clues both above and below ground level about the health of your soil. Vigorous plants with strong, deep root systems are among the best indicators of soil health. Soil color is also important. Generally, dark browns, reds, and tans indicate good soils. Soils that have a high humus content will usually be darker in color than soils low in humus. Soil color is also a clue to drainage. Tinges of blue and gray indicate poor aeration, often the result of poor water drainage. Generally, brown soils will drain much better than gray-colored soils. Brown and red colors reflect the oxidized iron content of the soil.

growing, organic gardeners boost the soil's natural fertility through a two-, three-, or four-year program that results in a fertile, rich soil. However, your plants don't have to suffer during the soil-building years. You can supplement your soil-building program with organic fertilizers to meet your plants' needs for nutrients.

Adding Organic Matter

The single most important step you can take to improve your soil is to increase its organic matter content. Adding organic matter will help improve your soil's structure and biological activity. Organic material stimulates the growth and reproductive capacity of the bacteria and other microorganisms that help create a vital and productive soil. Adding finished compost or other partially decayed organic material can also go a long way toward helping solve mineral deficiencies in your soil and can even modify soil pH.

There is a wide range of organic materials available to gardeners. The best of these is compost—a mixture of decayed organic materials. Other good organic materials include aged manure, chopped leaves, straw, grass clippings, and peat moss. To learn how to make and use compost, read the Composting entry.

How to add organic matter: You can add organic matter by digging or tilling it into the surface of the soil, by planting green manure crops, or simply by applying mulches and allowing them to break down over time. For more information on these methods, see the Double Digging, Green Manure, and Mulch entries.

It's relatively easy to increase the humus content of vegetable gardens because they are usually cleared of plants every year. But how do you increase the organic material under an existing lawn? Or around trees and shrubs? Wherever you have existing plants, including lawn grass, shrubs, or perennials, you can lay compost or other decayed organic material on the surface. In a few months, the soil organisms will have begun to work that organic material down into the soil. The other method for gardens and

around trees and shrubs is to use some kind of organic mulch and let it break down naturally, giving the soil an organic material boost as it does. You can do this at any convenient time of year. Remember, a soil filled with plants also is gaining organic matter from the growth and decay of the plant root systems. However, that may not be adequate to give the soil the amount of organic material it needs.

How much to add: Five percent organic matter is a good goal to strive for in your soil. One inch of compost or other fine-textured organic material spread over the soil surface equals about 5 percent of the volume of the first foot of soil. As a rule of thumb, if you add about 1″ of fine organic matter to a garden every year, you will gradually increase that soil's organic matter content to a desirable level. If you use a bulkier material such as chopped leaves or straw, you will have to apply a thicker layer, because there is less actual organic matter per volume. A 4″ layer of bulky organic material is equivalent to a 1″ layer of fine material.

In the South, it's more difficult to maintain soil organic matter levels. Microorganisms break down organic matter, and microbial populations grow faster (and so eat more) in warmer temperatures. Organic material can break down twice as fast in hot Southern soils as it does in cooler Northern soils.

Fresh vs. dry: On the average, fresh organic matter—such as grass clippings, kitchen waste, and green weeds—worked into the soil will be 50 percent decayed in just two months. The material will be 75 percent decayed after 4 months, and about 87 percent decayed after 6 months.

Dry materials decompose more slowly than moist. For example, if you dig chopped dried leaves into your garden, it may take 4-5 months for them to be halfway along the path of transformation to humus.

The decay process works best if there is a constant supply of food for the soil microorganisms that act as the decay "machine." So it's a good idea to mulch areas where you've incorporated partially decayed material with dry organic matter that will decompose slowly. The mulch serves two functions. It protects the decomposing organic matter from excessive heat, which can cause some organic compounds to volatilize and be lost. It also provides a longer-term food source for the soil microorganisms that are stimulated by the dug-in organic matter.

The rule of mulch: There is one cardinal rule in your efforts to increase the organic content of your soil. Once you've added whatever material your soil needs, there should not be one square inch of bare soil left anywhere on your property. It should be covered with grass, a groundcover, plants, or mulch. Bare soil loses humus much faster than covered soil because the nutrients created by the decomposition of the organic matter are leached away more readily. In addition, the impact of raindrops on bare soil can destroy the loose soil structure you have worked to obtain. Covered soil is also much less prone to surface erosion by wind or water.

Adding Microbes

If you're a gardener who's switching to organic methods from chemical methods, or if you've inherited a garden that's been treated with pesticides, you may have soils with very low biological activity. Give some extra help to the struggling microbial populations by applying bacterial cultures that give your soil and compost piles a biological boost. Some of these cultures are in a dry, dormant, powdered form. After you spread this material over your soil or into a compost pile, the microbes become activated and biological activity accelerates. Keep in mind that you must keep adding sufficient organic matter to feed the increased populations of soil microbes, or you won't get any lasting benefit from your investment.

If your earthworm count is low, don't despair. Once you provide more organic material to feed them, they will usually return. Earthworm egg casings can lay dormant as deep as 20' in the soil for as long as 20 years.

PROBLEM SOILS

Two of the most common problems gardeners face are soils that are high in clay and soils that don't drain well.

Clay soils: If you have heavy clay soil that is low in organic matter, you will have to add considerable amounts of organic material and energy to make that soil as loose and friable as you can. Double digging is your best option. Some gardeners will add sand along with the organic material to heavy clay soils in beds where they want to grow root crops or flower bulbs. A lot of sand is required to make a significant difference, though. Adding small amounts of sand may actually cause your soil to harden, worsening its condition. To boost the sand component to the top 6''-8'' of the soil by 5-10 percent, you will need about 3-5 tons per 1,000 square feet of garden. If you have a close and convenient source of sand, it may be worth the effort to spread and till in the sand. However, adding sand alone will not remedy problems with heavy clay. Using green manures and incorporating organic matter are the best long-term solution.

Poorly drained soils: If your soil tests and observations have alerted you to a drainage problem in your yard, you have three options. Your first option could be to accept the wet spot and create a small bog garden. If you have other plans for the site, you'll have to find a way to improve drainage.

The drainage problem may be due to a hardpan somewhere in the top 2' of soil. You may be able to break up the compaction layer by double digging. If the layer is deeper than you can reach by double digging, try planting deep-rooted sweet clover in spring and allow it to grow for two full growing seasons. The roots may penetrate the deep hardpan and naturally create better drainage.

Another way to sidestep a drainage problem is to create a raised bed in the wet area. You'll have to bring in extra topsoil and build up sides, essentially creating a layer of soil with good drainage for plants to grow in above the poorly drained area.

Lastly, you can install a drainage system, but this is a project for which you'll probably need professional help.

Dry or granular, fast-acting chemical fertilizers can repel earthworms when they dissolve in soil water and leach down into the soil. Earthworms are highly sensitive to changes in the physical and chemical environment and will avoid the salty conditions created by the chemical fertilizers. If you are making the transition from chemical fertilizers to organic soil amendments and fertilizers, have patience. As your soil reaches a healthy balance, you will see more earthworm activity.

Adding Minerals

There are several organic soil amendments you can add to correct specific pH and mineral imbalances. In most cases, you should only add these amendments according to recommendations from soil tests or plant analyses. If you add too much of a natural mineral supplement such as rock phosphate, you can create an excess of a particular nutrient. The excess may damage plants or may interfere with uptake of some other nutrients. For more information on soil amendments, see the Fertilizers entry.

Working the Soil

To many gardeners, working the soil means using a rotary tiller. While a tiller is a powerful and helpful tool, it's not the only, or the best, way to work the soil.

Many gardeners use their rotary tillers several times during the season. They may till in a green manure crop in early spring, and then till again a few weeks later to make a fine seed bed for planting. During the season, they may get out a smaller tiller for weed control, and then till the garden under again in fall. While tillers are valuable, time- and back-saving machines, their use does have a cost to your soil's health.

Tilling or hand digging, no matter how carefully done, has a major impact on soil microorganisms. When you turn the soil, you add an enormous amount of oxygen to it. This creates an environment primed for an explosion of microbial activity. In most soils, more than 80

EROSION ON THE HOME FRONT

The loss of topsoil through erosion isn't just a problem on farms and at construction sites. Erosion can happen in our own front- and back-yards. Take these steps to minimize soil erosion around your home:

● On slopes, build terraced garden beds, or at the least, be sure your garden rows run across the slope, not up and down.
● Don't leave sloping areas unplanted. Plant groundcovers, vines, or other plants with spreading roots and top growth that will hold soil in place.
● Mulch permanent pathways with stone or a thick layer of organic mulch, or plant a durable groundcover or lawn grass.
● In fall and winter, mulch bare vegetable or flower beds, or plant a cover crop to prevent wind or water erosion.
● Keep areas cleared for construction well mulched with straw. Try to minimize the use of heavy equipment. Soil compacted by machinery cannot absorb water well; the runoff will carry valuable soil with it.

percent of the aerobic bacteria are present in the top 6"; more than 60 percent are in the top 3"-4". If you add organic matter as you till, you supply fuel for the population explosion, and your soil will remain in balance. If you till repeatedly without supplying more food for the rapidly increasing microbial population, you'll speed the decomposition of your soil's organic reserves. Soil organic matter levels will decrease.

Cultivating the soil when it is too wet or too dry is even more harmful. Tilling or digging at these times is disastrous for soil structure. Wet soils will form large clumps when tilled. The clumps will dry hard and solid, without the many tiny pores that hold soil water and air. Dry soils can turn to fine dust when tilled. So for your soil's and plants' sakes, reserve the tiller for when you really need it. Use mulches to reduce weed problems and conserve soil moisture, avoid walking on growing beds to reduce compaction, and cultivate shallowly when weeds are small. ❖

Solidago

Goldenrod. Summer- and fall-blooming perennials.

Description: There are many species of our native goldenrod that are fine for naturalizing, but hybrids are better garden plants. Hybrid goldenrods bear tiny yellow and gold flowers in showy 4"-12" clusters over upright to V-shaped clumps. Elongated leaves spiral up the stiff, 1'-3' stems. Zones 3-8.

How to grow: Plant or divide in spring or fall in a sunny or lightly shaded spot. Goldenrods do best in average, moist, well-drained soil, though most tolerate fairly dry soil. Divide every three years.

Landscape uses: Grow goldenrods in small groups in borders; mass in fields and meadow gardens. Combine with asters, other fall-blooming perennials, and grasses. Remember, it's ragweed that causes hayfever, not goldenrod.

Best cultivars: 'Golden Thumb', 1'; 'Peter Pan', 2'-2½'; 'Goldenmosa', to 3'. ❖

Sorbus

Mountain ash. Deciduous spring-blooming trees.

Description: Mountain ashes are small- to medium-sized trees that bear late-spring clusters of white flowers and persistent red-orange berries in fall. *Sorbus alnifolia,* Korean mountain ash, grows 40'-50' and has alternate simple leaves. Zones 4-6. *S. americana,* American mountain ash, grows to 30' and has alternate compound leaves. Zones 2-6.

How to grow: All mountain ashes need full sun and good drainage. Korean mountain ash resists borer injury better than other species. If fire blight is a problem, prune to remove infected twigs and improve air circulation. Sanitize pruning equipment between cuts.

Landscape uses: Mountain ashes make fine shade trees; wild animals feed on the berries. ❖

Spinach

Spinacia oleracea
Chenopodiaceae

Spinach's reputation as a health food is well deserved. It has the highest amount of vitamins A and B_2 of any common vegetable and is loaded with iron, calcium, and protein. It's excellent as a salad or cooking green. Unlike regular spinach with its dark, crinkly leaves, New Zealand spinach (*Tetragonia tetragonioides*) has light green, smooth leaves. It is not a true spinach but tastes much the same and is excellent for growing in warm climates.

Planting: Spinach does best when provided with plenty of moisture and nitrogen. Spinach has a deep taproot, so cultivate the soil at least 1' deep before planting.

Treat this cool-weather crop like an early lettuce. Lengthening days cause plants to quickly bolt and go to seed, so plant as early as eight weeks before the last frost or as soon as you can work the soil. Prepare the soil the previous autumn, and you can drop the seeds in barely thawed ground. In areas with a long, cool spring, make successive plantings every 10 days until mid-May.

In warm climates, plant spinach in the shade of tall crops such as corn or beans. The young plants will be spared the hottest sun and be ready for harvest in fall or winter. Using cold frames, you can grow spinach all winter in many parts of the country. Try planting it in February for a March harvest.

Buy fresh seeds every year and soak them for 24 hours before planting. Sow them ½" deep and 2" apart in beds or rows. If the weather isn't extremely cold, seeds will germinate in 5-9 days. For fall crops, plant in August, keeping in mind that the germination rate drops to about 50 percent in warm weather. In such conditions, it helps to freeze the seeds for a few days, then moisten and refrigerate them for a few more days before sowing. Shade the soil until the seeds germinate.

Growing guidelines: Overcrowding stunts growth and encourages plants to go to seed, so thin to 4"-6" apart when seedlings have at least two true leaves. Fertilize with manure tea or fish emulsion when the plants have four true leaves. (For instructions on making manure tea, see the Manure entry.) Weeding can harm spinach roots, so lay down a light mulch of hay, straw, or grass clippings to eliminate this task and to retain moisture. Dry soil will encourage plants to bolt, so provide enough water to keep the soil moist but not soggy. Cover the crop with shade cloth if the temperature goes above 80°F.

Problems: Since most spinach grows in very cool weather, pests are usually not a problem. Handpick and destroy any spotted cucumber beetles (¼" long, black-spotted, greenish yellow insects); dust heavy infestations with pyrethrins. Leafminer larvae can burrow inside leaves and produce tan patches. Remove and destroy affected leaves to prevent adult flies from multiplying and further affecting the crop. For information on controlling aphids and cabbage loopers, see "The Top Ten Garden Insect Pests in America" on page 344.

Spinach blight, a virus spread by aphids, causes yellow leaves and stunted plants. Downy mildew, which appears as yellow spots on leaf surfaces and mold on the undersides, occurs during very wet weather. Reduce the spread of disease spores by not working around wet plants. Avoid both of these diseases by planting resistant cultivars.

Harvesting: In 6-8 weeks you can start harvesting from any plant that has at least six leaves 3"-4" long. Carefully cutting the outside leaves will extend the plants' productivity, particularly with fall crops. Harvest the entire crop at the first sign of bolting by using a sharp knife to cut through the taproot just below the ground.

Best cultivars: 'Bloomsdale Long Standing', cold-resistant, good for fall or winter crops; 'Tyee', high-yielding, slow to bolt. ❖

Spiraea

Spirea, bridalwreath. Deciduous, spring-blooming shrubs.

Description: *Spiraea bullata,* crispleaf spirea, is a 12"-15" tall groundcover shrub with blue-green, crinkled leaves and 1½"-3" rosy red flower clusters in summer. Zones 4-8.

S. × bumalda, bumald spirea, has a low, rounded, twiggy form and grows about 2' tall. It has 1"-3", oval or lance-shaped, toothed, dark green leaves. The small white to deep pink flowers bloom in flat 4"-6" clusters during late spring or early summer. Zones 4-8.

S. prunifolia, bridalwreath spirea, has an upright, rounded form, growing to about 10'. Its slender oval, shiny dark green leaves are 1"-2" long. The flowers are pure white and double, blooming in profusion along each branch in spring. For fall color, bridalwreath is one of the most reliable spireas, usually turning soft orange-red. Zones 5-8.

S. × vanhouttei, vanhoutte spirea, has an arching form that's narrow and bare at the base, reaching 6'-8' tall and 10'-12' wide. It bears white flowers in flat clusters along the branches in late spring, and blue-green, ¾"-1¾", fine-textured foliage. Zones 3-8.

How to grow: All spireas need full sun and good drainage. Promote vigorous growth by removing ⅓ of the oldest branches to a few inches above ground level after bloom time. If drastic renewal is needed, cut the entire shrub in this way.

Landscape uses: Because of its compact form, bumald spirea makes a fine foundation plant. All spireas are useful for massed plantings, specimens, and borders.

Best cultivars: *S. × bumalda:* 'Anthony Waterer' blooms sporadically through the summer following its usual flush of spring flowers; 'Crispa' has incised, twisted leaf margins; 'Gold Flame' has new foliage that opens golden yellow, then turns green. ❖

Squash

Cucurbita spp.
Cucurbitaceae

From acorn squash to zucchini, the group of vegetables we call squash has a delightful range of shapes, sizes, colors, and flavors. These frost-tender plants need warm weather, lots of sun, and plenty of room.

Types: Squash come in two main types: summer squash and winter squash. While there's not much difference in the taste and texture of summer squash, winter cultivars come in a mind-boggling array of sizes and flavors.

Summer squash, *Cucurbita pepo,* produces prolifically from early summer until the first frost. This group includes both green and yellow zucchini, most yellow crookneck and straightneck squash, and scallop (or pattypan) squash that come in white and yellow versions. Most summer squash are ready to harvest in 60-70 days, but some are eating-sized in 50 days. You can use them raw for salads and dips or cook them in a wide variety of ways, including squash "french fries" and such classics as zucchini bread.

Summer squash blossoms, picked just before they open, are delicious in soups and stews, or try them sautéed, stuffed, or dipped in batter and fried. (You'll want to use mostly male flowers for this purpose, though, and leave the female flowers to produce fruit. "Identifying Male and Female Flowers" on page 554 shows how to tell the flowers apart.) Summer squash keep for only a week or so in the refrigerator, so you'll probably want to freeze most of the crop.

Winter squash is a broad category—*C. maxima, C. mixta, C. moschata,* and *C. pepo*—that includes butternut, acorn, delicious, hubbard, banana, buttercup (or turban), and spaghetti squash. Pumpkins are also in this group, but their flesh is often less sweet than other winter squash. Most winter squash take 75-120 days to mature.

Steam the young fruits, or harvest and bake the squash when they're fully mature. Dry and roast the nutritious seeds. Winter squash are even more nutritious than their summer kin, but the sprawling vines, which can grow 10'-20' long, require more space. If this is a problem, try one of the bush or semibush cultivars.

Butternuts produce rampant vines and 1' long fruits with tan skins and orange flesh. Acorn squash have dark green to yellow fruits that are round and usually furrowed; they generally weigh 1-2 lb. Acorns don't store as well as most winter squash, but they are very productive.

Delicious squash can take more than 100 days to mature, but the wait is worth it; the wide-spreading vines produce wonderfully sweet fruit. Hubbards are best for storing, but standard cultivars can weigh up to 30 lb., which is a lot of squash to eat. Pink-skinned banana squash can grow up to 75 lb. Buttercup, or turban, squash have a sumptuous taste that make them a winter squash favorite.

Planting: These sun lovers are sensitive to

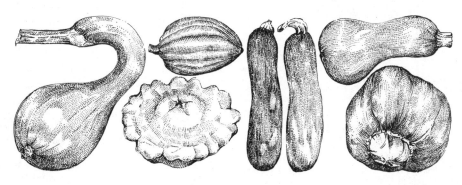

cold, though winter squash tolerate light shade and cooler nighttime temperatures better than summer squash can.

Both types of squash are heavy feeders and need a light and well-drained but moisture-retentive soil. You can give them exactly what they need by planting them in specially pre-pared hills. See the Melon entry for details on creating super-charged planting hills. Space the hills 3' apart for summer squash; vining winter squash need 6'-8' between hills.

Summer squash can cross-pollinate with various cultivars of both summer and winter squash, as well as with several types of pumpkins. This won't affect the current season's fruit but can alter the next crop if you save seeds. If you want to save seed, be careful not to let crops cross-pollinate. Otherwise, the seed won't be

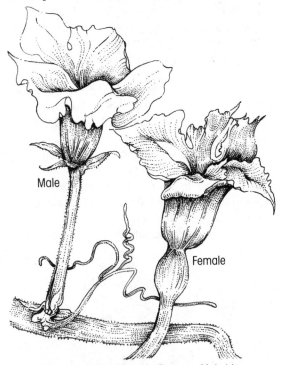

Identifying male and female flowers. Male blossoms, each with a single stamen in its center, appear first. They are followed about a week later by female flowers, which have a large swelling (the ovary) just beneath the blossom and a four-part pistil in the flower's center.

true to type, and the following season's crop will be some strange-looking hybrid.

A week after the last frost date, or when the soil temperature is at least 60°F and the weather has settled, sow six seeds ½" deep in a circle on the top of each hill. Thin to the two strongest seedlings per hill.

If planting in rows, space vining cultivars 3'-4' apart in rows 8'-12' apart; space bush types 2'-3' apart in rows 4'-6' apart. You can also intersperse squash with corn, so the vines can use the cornstalks as climbing poles. If gar-den space is limited, tie three long poles together at the top and spread the legs to form a tripod; plant a squash seed at the base of each pole. You can also grow vining types on fences and well-supported growing nets.

In areas with short growing seasons, sow the seeds indoors a month before the last frost date. Put two seeds in a peat pot and clip off the weaker seedling after seedlings emerge. Water well just before transplanting, and disturb the roots as little as possible. Full-grown plants can tolerate cold weather, but seedlings are very cold-sensitive. Use hotcaps or cloches to protect them until the weather turns hot.

Summer squash will produce more heavily than winter squash. In either case, unless you plan to preserve or store a great deal of your crop, two vines of either summer or winter squash are probably adequate to feed four people. Unused seeds are viable for 4-5 years.

Growing guidelines: Give seedlings lots of water and keep the planting area moist through-out the growing season. To avoid such diseases as mildew, water the soil, not the foliage, and don't handle plants when they are wet. Dig weeds by hand until the squash vines begin to lengthen, then put down a thick mulch of hay, straw, or leaves.

About six weeks after germination, male blossoms will appear, followed by the first of the female flowers. Since squash depend on bees for pollination, female blooms that drop off without producing fruit probably weren't fertilized. You can transfer pollen from the male stamen to the female pistil yourself with a soft brush. Or simply pluck a male flower, remove the petals, and whirl it around inside a female flower. Sidedress plants with compost or fertilize with manure tea when the first fruits set. For instructions on making manure tea, see the Manure entry.

When vines grow to about 5', pinch off the growing tips to encourage fruit-bearing sideshoots. By midsummer, winter squash will have set all the fruit they will have time to mature; remove all remaining flowers so the plant can put its energy into ripening the crop. To avoid rot, keep maturing fruit off the soil with a board or a thick mulch. This is particularly important with winter squash, which take a long time to ripen.

Problems: Well-cultivated squash are usually trouble-free. The two pests most likely to attack are squash vine borers and squash bugs.

Squash vine borers, which do the most damage to winter squash, look like 1" long, white caterpillars. They tunnel into stems and can go undetected until a vine wilts. Keep a constant lookout for entry holes at the base of the plants, surrounded by yellow, sawdustlike droppings. Cut a slit along afflicted stems and remove and destroy the larvae inside, or inject the stems with BTK (*Bacillus thuringiensis* var. *kurstaki*). Hill up soil around such stem wounds so the plant can reroot.

Better yet, keep an eye out for the adult borer, an orange-and-black, wasplike moth; it lays eggs at the base of the stem in late June or early July in the North, or in April to early summer in the South. During these times, check the base of the stems and just below the surface of the soil regularly for very tiny— $^1/_{25}$ of an inch—red-and-orange eggs. Rub and destroy as many as you find. When many vine borer eggs turn up, try dusting the base of the plants with pyrethrins every 2 days for a week.

Handpick all ¾" long, grayish brown squash bugs. Also destroy their red-brown egg clusters on the undersides of leaves. To trap adults, lay boards on the soil at night; the squash bugs will

Squash bug. Squash bug feeding causes leaves to wilt and blacken. These pests are often called stink bugs because of the odor given off when they're crushed.

tend to congregate beneath them, and you can destroy the pests the next morning. Nearby radishes, nasturtiums, or marigolds can repel squash bugs.

Striped and spotted cucumber beetles may also attack squash plants. These 1" long, black-headed beetles with green or yellow wings usually aren't as troublesome as squash bugs and vine borers, but they can carry bacterial wilt. Since these are spring pests, you can plant squash later in the season when cucumber beetles are less prevalent. Or protect young plants with a floating row cover, which should be removed when the plants start to flower to allow for pollination. For serious infestations, dust plants with pyrethrins.

In most cases, you can avoid squash diseases by choosing resistant cultivars, rotating crops, and choosing planting sites with good air circulation. Here are some diseases to watch for:

• Anthracnose, a soilborne fungus, causes leaves to develop hollow, water-soaked spots that eventually grow large and brown.

• Bacterial wilt is a disease that wilts and quickly kills plants.

• Downy mildew produces yellow-brown

spots on leaf surfaces and downy purple spots on the undersides. These spots eventually spread, and the leaves die.

• Mosaic, a viral disease that results in rough, mottled leaves, stunted growth, and whitish fruit, is spread by cucumber beetles and aphids. Reduce the chance of disease by controlling problem insects. (For aphid control measures, see "The Top Ten Garden Insect Pests in America" on page 344.)

• Powdery mildew causes fuzzy white spots on leaves. Affected leaves are distorted, and the plant may appear stunted.

Immediately remove and destroy vines affected with any of the above diseases, or place them in sealed containers and dispose of them with household trash.

Harvesting: Pick zucchini and crookneck cultivars at a tender 6"-8" long and rounder types at 4"-8" in diameter. Summer squash will continue setting buds until the first frost, but only if you pick the fruit before it matures—that is, just as its blossom drops off the tip. If you miss even one fruit, the whole plant will quit producing. Enjoy summer squash fresh, or preserve them by canning or freezing; they can also be dried, pickled, or turned into relish.

Winter squash taste bland and watery and won't store well unless you allow them to fully ripen on the vine. Wait until the plants die back and the shells are hard. A light frost can improve the flavor by changing some of their starch to sugar, but it will also shorten their storing quality. It's better to pick all ripe fruits before an expected frost and cover any unripe ones with a heavy mulch. You can even carefully gather the vines and fruit close together and protect them with tarps or blankets.

Harvest during dry weather. Use a sharp knife to cut the fruit from the vine, leaving 3"-4" of stem. Pulling the fruit off may damage the stem, and the whole fruit may soon rot from that damaged end. (For that same reason, never carry squash by their stems. If a stem breaks off accidentally, use that fruit as soon as possible.) Clean your harvesting knife between cuttings to avoid spreading diseases. Handle squash carefully, because bruised fruit won't keep.

Never wash any winter squash that you intend to store. Dry all types in the sun until the stems shrivel and turn gray; the exception is acorn squash, which doesn't need curing. If placed in a cool, dry area with temperatures of 45°-50°F and with 65-70 percent humidity, winter squash will keep for up to five months. Only acorn squash needs a slightly cooler and moister storage area.

Mildew may be a problem on squash if storage areas aren't dry enough. Before you store squash, wipe the fruits with a solution made of 1 part chlorine bleach and 9 parts water, then dry them and rub with salad oil; this will prevent mildew.

Best cultivars: Summer squash: 'Aristocrat', a popular hybrid zucchini, takes only 48 days to mature; 'Benning's Green Tint', pale green, disc-shaped fruits with scalloped edges, best eaten when very small; 'Scallopini', a cross between scallop and zucchini types, bright green fruits; 'Seneca Prolific', a very early cultivar, produces high yields of smooth, creamy yellow fruits.

Winter squash: 'Butterbush', butternut type, compact growth habit; 'Table King', acorn type, a popular green cultivar; 'Jersey Golden Acorn', yellow fruit, semibush habit with sweet, orange flesh, good in containers; 'Golden Delicious', sweet golden flesh extra high in vitamin C; 'Golden Hubbard', orange-red shells with deep orange flesh; 'Sweet Mama', buttercup type, bush habit, resistant to Fusarium wilt and vine borers; 'Vegetable Spaghetti', yellow fruits, cooked flesh forms spaghetti-like strands that taste like squash but are used like pasta.

Pumpkins: 'Autumn Gold', early ripening, 7-10 lb. fruits; 'Ghost Rider', deep orange, 15-20 lb. fruits; 'Big Max', can grow 70-100 lb. fruits; 'Small Sugar', good for cooking. ❖

Staking

Staking plants in the flower and vegetable garden is a job that busy gardeners sometimes overlook. In most cases, however, the time you spend staking will be amply rewarded by the improved health and appearance of your garden.

Vining plants virtually require stakes or other support. Top-heavy, single-stemmed flowers like delphiniums, lilies, and dahlias benefit from support. Left unstaked, they are apt to bend unattractively and may snap off during heavy storms. Staking also improves the appearance of plants with thin floppy stems that flatten easily.

Choose stakes and supports that match the needs of the plant and of you as a gardener. They must be tall enough and strong enough to support the entire mature plant when wet or windblown, and they must be firmly inserted in the soil. A stake that breaks or tips over can cause more damage than using none at all. Take care not to damage roots when inserting a stake, and avoid tying the shoots too tightly to the stake. Install the supports as early in the growing season as possible, so that the plants can be trained to them as they grow, not forced to fit them later on. When growing plants from seed, install the support before planting.

In the flower garden, choose supports that are as inconspicuous as possible. Thin, slightly flexible stakes that bend with the plant are less conspicuous and may be better than heavier, rigid ones. In general, select stakes that stand about ¾ of the height of the mature plant. Insert them close to or among the stems so that as the plant grows, the foliage will hide the supports. Choose colors and materials that blend with the plants. Bamboo stakes tinted green are available in a variety of sizes and are a good, inexpensive choice for many plants. You can also buy wood, metal, and plastic stakes and trellises, and a wide assortment of metal rings and support systems. Green twine or plastic-covered wire are inconspicuous ways to fasten plants to their supports.

In the vegetable garden, sturdiness is more important than appearance. Staking vegetables like tomatoes, peppers, and beans makes them easier to cultivate and harvest. It increases yields by preventing contamination with soilborne diseases and allowing for more plants in a given area. Choose tall, sturdy stakes or cages that can support the plant even when it is heavy with fruit, and insert stakes firmly into the ground. Use narrow strips torn from rags or bands cut

Individual plant stakes. Sink stake firmly near the stem when plant is 6"–8" high. A loose figure-eight tie connects stem to stake securely, yet maintains the plant's natural form and prevents damage to the stalk. As the plant grows, add ties every 8"–10". Two closely spaced plants can be tied to one stake if it is placed between them. Top-heavy flowers like this lily need stakes almost as tall as the mature plant.

Pea brush. For plants such as peas, coreopsis, and baby's-breath, try "pea sticks." Cut lengths of sturdy, twiggy brush or branches to the final height of the plants, and push them 6" into the ground between the young plants.

Wire grid supports. The shoots of this young poppy plant have grown through the circular metal grid support, which is now barely visible. The natural form of the plant is enhanced, not disrupted.

Stakes and strings. Insert four stakes into the corners of the bed when shoots are a few inches high. Tie string (or wire) from stake to stake to form a box about 6"–8" off the ground. Add strings as needed. Run additional strings across the bed or weave them back and forth to keep plants from falling inside the bed.

from stockings to gently fasten plants to supports. See individual entries for more detailed information on staking specific vegetable crops.

Perennial vines such as roses and grapes are commonly grown on trellises or on wires between sturdy posts. For more information on trellises, see the Vines entry. Raspberries and other brambles are also trellised; see the Brambles entry for ideas.

Trees and tall shrubs are commonly staked temporarily at planting to help hold them upright until their roots become established. Fruit trees on dwarfing rootstocks may need to be permanently staked. For more information on staking trees, see the Trees entry. ❖

Strawberry

Fragaria × ananassa, F. vesca
Rosaceae

Strawberries are justly celebrated each spring in festivals all over America. Fresh strawberry shortcake, strawberry ice cream, strawberry pie, and even plain red ripe strawberries are hard to beat. The plants are inexpensive, bear a full crop within a year of planting, and are relatively simple to grow.

Selecting Plants

Garden strawberry cultivars (*F. × ananassa*) are divided into three types: Junebearers, everbearers, and day-neutrals, which flower at different times in response to day length.

Junebearers: These bear fruit in June or July, or as early as April in Florida and California. They produce a single large crop over 3-4 weeks. If you want to freeze lots of fruit at one time, plant Junebearers. There are early-, mid-, and late-season cultivars. Junebearers produce many runners and spread rapidly.

Everbearers: These produce a moderate crop in June, scattered berries in summer, and a small crop in late August. They are especially productive in Northern areas with long summer days. The total harvest for everbearers is much less than the total harvest for Junebearers. Plant everbearers if you want berries for fresh eating all season. They produce fewer runners than Junebearers and so are easier to control.

Day-neutrals: These are unaffected by day length. They are extremely productive and bear fruit from June through frost in Northern areas, or January through August in milder climates. Unfortunately, day-neutrals require pampering. They are fragile and sensitive to heat, drought, and weed competition. If you are willing to give them the care they need, they'll reward you with a generous supply of berries throughout the season from relatively few plants. They produce few runners, so they rarely get out of control.

Alpine strawberries: Alpine strawberries (*F. vesca*) are one of the parent species of the garden strawberry. They produce small, aromatic berries from early summer through frost. Alpines are grown from seed or divisions and produce no runners. They are care-free and make good ornamental edgings.

Planting

Strawberries do best in full sun, sandy loam, and a pH of 6.0-6.5, although they'll tolerate less-than-ideal conditions, provided they have good drainage. Prepare a planting bed by tilling in 3"-4" of compost.

Plant strawberries in spring, as soon as the ground has warmed. In the South, you can plant them in the fall as well.

If you buy plants, or receive them through the mail, and can't plant them immediately, you can store them in the refrigerator for a few days. Be sure the packing material is moist but not soggy. When planting, place the plants in a bucket of water and carry it to the garden with you. This lets plants rehydrate and keeps them from drying out while you're planting.

Dig a hole deep enough so the roots will not be bent, and make a cone-shaped pile of soil in the bottom. Arrange the roots over the soil cone and gently fill the hole with loose soil. Hold the crown while you work to make sure it remains level with the soil line. Double-check to make sure the crown is neither protruding above the soil nor buried too deeply, and firm the soil with your hand. "Proper Planting Level" on page 561 shows you how.

Bed Layout

Most strawberries spread aggressively by producing runners—long slender shoots with a cluster of leaves at the tip. The tips root when they touch the ground, forming daughter plants. Each daughter plant sends out its own runners, often in the same season it was formed.

There are three traditional methods for managing strawberries: matted rows, hills, and spaced rows. The methods differ in how runners are managed, and how the plants are renewed.

Matted row system: Space plants 1½'-2' apart in rows, with 4' between rows. Allow the runners to grow in all directions, so the daughter plants fill in between the mother plants to form a wide, solid row. Remove all flowers that appear in the first 3-4 months after planting to give the plants a good start.

The second and subsequent years, rejuvenate the bed immediately after the harvest is finished. Set your lawn mower blade at 2½", mow the entire bed, and rake up all the debris. Then till or turn under the edges of the rows to leave a 1' strip down the center with the original mother plants in it. Spread several inches of compost or well-rotted manure over the bed and work it in on either side of the remaining plants. Then water the bed well and renew the mulch between the rows. The undamaged crowns of the strawberry plants will vigorously send out runners throughout the rest of the summer and produce a great crop the following year.

In most areas, even strawberries given the best of care will decline and produce low yields after as few as three seasons. It pays to start a fresh patch in a new location with new plants every few years, so as one declines, the next one is ready to produce.

The matted row system is well suited to Junebearers. For everbearers and day-neutrals, reduce the initial spacing within the row.

Hill system: Space plants 1' apart in rows, with 2'-3' between rows. Remove all flowers the first 3-4 months after planting to give the plants a good start. Ruthlessly remove every runner so plants channel all their energy into producing fruit. You'll get luscious, large berries and fewer disease problems because the crop will get good air circulation.

Renew the bed the third year by allowing enough runners to root in the row to replace the mother plants, which will be less productive

because they have formed multiple crowns. Remove the mother plants in the fall after harvest.

The hill system is well suited to everbearers, since they produce fewer runners than Junebearers. It's a lot of work to keep up with runner removal with Junebearers.

Modified hill system for day-neutrals: Space plants 7" apart each way in double, staggered rows. Allow 3½'-4' aisles between rows. Remove all flowers for the first six weeks after planting and all runners during the first growing season. Side-dress with compost or well-rotted manure once a month during the growing season. Mulch around plants to conserve moisture and smother weeds. Renew as for the hill system.

Spaced runner system: The spaced runner system is intermediate between the matted row and the hill systems. Space plants as for the matted row, and allow only a few runners to remain. Pin down the tips so the new plants will be spaced about 8" apart each way. Renew and care for as for matted row.

An interesting variation of renewing matted or spaced rows is to preserve a 1' strip of plants next to, but not including, the mother plants each year. This may add a few years to the productivity of your patch.

Care

Vigilant weed control is essential to prevent aggressive perennial weeds from out-competing shallow-rooted strawberry plants. It helps to lay down a thick mulch of straw around the plants during summer.

Strawberries need 1" of water per week throughout the growing season. Drip irrigation works best; for information on installing a drip irrigation system, see the Irrigation entry.

After the ground has frozen, cover the plants with fresh straw, pine boughs, or spun-bonded fabric to protect them from alternate freezing and thawing, which can heave plants from the soil. (In climates where a snow cover remains through the winter, strawberries need no special

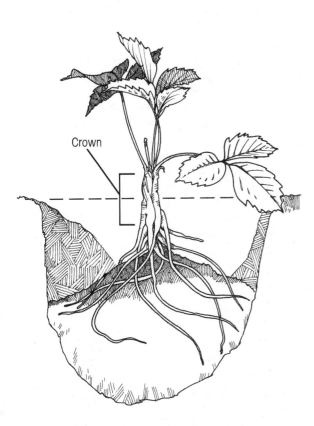

Proper planting level. It is important to spread out the roots of your new strawberries as you plant. Set the middle of the crown level with the soil surface.

Crown

winter mulch.) Pull the mulch away from the plants in early spring so the ground can warm up. Reapply fresh mulch around the plants to smother early weeds. Leave spun-bonded fabric on over winter and into spring for slightly earlier harvests. Remove it when flowers open so bees can pollinate the blossoms.

Harvesting

Spring-planted Junebearers won't provide a harvest until a year after planting. Everbearers will produce a sizable late-summer crop, and day-neutrals will produce from midsummer through fall the year they're planted. Fall-planted berries will bear a full harvest the next growing season.

Harvest berries by pinching through the stem rather than pulling on the berry. Pick ripe berries every other day; always remove *all* ripe berries and any infected or malformed ones from the patch to prevent disease problems. During wet or humid weather, pick out diseased berries every day. Cull the moldy berries, wash your hands, and then pick the ripe berries. At the least, carry a second basket or a plastic bag to put moldy or damaged berries in while you pick.

Problems

Verticillium wilt and red stele infect the roots. They are often carried in on new plants and made worse by heavy, wet soil. Remove and destroy infected plants. Replant new plants in a new location or choose resistant cultivars. Vegetables like tomatoes and potatoes are also infected by Verticillium wilt, so grow only resistant cultivars where these vegetables have grown in the last three years, and vice versa.

Gray mold rots the berries. Wet, humid weather and overcrowded beds with poor air circulation invite it. Keep rows narrow, thin out crowded plants, and remove moldy berries from the plants immediately to control gray mold.

Berries injured by the tarnished plant bug don't grow or ripen properly, but remain small and woody or form hard, seedy tips. "The Top Ten Garden Insect Pests in America" on page 344 gives controls. Birds love strawberries; cover plants with netting, and see the Animal Pests entry for other suggestions. Slugs can take a bite out of your ripe berries; the Slugs and Snails entry lists controls.

Cultivars: Choose disease-resistant cultivars adapted to your climate and day length; check catalogs or your local extension office for recommendations. Certified virus-indexed plants are worth the extra cost because the plants are more vigorous and productive. ❖

Sulfur

Sulfur is an important nutrient for plant growth. Cabbages, legumes, onions, and turnips require high amounts of sulfur, whereas corn, cereals, and other grasses are rarely lacking. Deficiencies may appear as yellowing leaves, small spindly growth, or delayed ripening. However, in a balanced, humus-rich soil, sulfur deficiency is usually not a problem. Adding sulfur to soil is a common way to decrease the pH of alkaline soils.

Organic gardeners spray or dust elemental sulfur or sulfur compounds to help prevent many fungal diseases on crops. However, applying sulfur may harm beneficial insects, soil microorganisms, and the plants themselves; save it for the last resort in combating disease problems. For more information on using sulfur, see the pH, Fertilizers, and Fungicides entries. ❖

Sunflower

Helianthus annuus
Compositae

While often admired as ornamentals, sunflowers have an amazing variety of uses. They make a good fodder for poultry and livestock, dyes come from the petals, and paper can be made from the stalk pith. Its seeds and seed meal feed countless people, animals, and birds; sunflower-seed oil is used in cooking and in soaps and cosmetics. In the garden, you can grow sunflowers as windbreaks, privacy screens, or living supports for pole beans.

Sunflowers also come in a wide assortment of sizes. Some cultivars grow as tall as 15', and the flower heads can be as big as 1' across; dwarf types, however, are only 1½'-2' tall. There are also early, medium-height sunflowers that stand 5'-6' tall but have heads that are 8"-10" across. Some cultivars produce a single large flower; others form several heads.

Planting: If possible, choose a site in full sun on the north side of the garden, so the tall plants won't shade your other vegetables. Sunflowers aren't fussy about soil.

Seedlings are cold-resistant, so short-season growers may want to get a head start by planting several weeks before the last frost. In most areas, though, it's best to wait until the soil is warmer, around the last frost date. Sow seeds 1" deep and 6" apart. Thin large types to 1½' apart and dwarf or medium-sized cultivars to 1' apart. Water well after planting.

Growing guidelines: Apply a 3"-4" layer of mulch to conserve moisture and keep down weeds. Sunflowers are drought-resistant, but they'll grow better if you water regularly from the time the flowers begin to develop until they're mature.

Problems: Sunflowers are remarkably trouble-free, but for details on controlling aphids, see "The Top Ten Garden Insect Pests in America" on page 344. Rotate the crop if leaf mottle, a soil fungus that produces dead areas along leaf veins, becomes a problem. An early autumn may interfere with pollination and cause the plant to form empty seeds; plant earlier the next year. To protect seeds from birds, cover the flowers with mesh bags, cheesecloth, old pantyhose, or perforated plastic bags.

Harvesting: Harvest as soon as seeds start to turn brown or the backs of the seed heads turn yellow. The heads usually droop at this time. Cut them along with 2' of stem and hang upside down in a dry, well-ventilated place, such as a garage or attic, until fully dry. Rub two seed heads together to extract the seeds, or use a wire brush or similar tool. Spread out damp seeds on a rack until fully dry; store in plastic bags for birds and animal food. To eat, soak overnight in water (or in strong salt water, if a salty flavor is desired), drain, spread on a shallow baking sheet, and roast for 3 hours at 200°F or until crisp. ❖

Sweet Potato

Ipomoea batatas
Convolvulaceae

This warm-weather crop is remarkably nutritious and versatile. Each fleshy root contains large amounts of vitamins A and C, along with protein, calcium, magnesium, iron, and carotene. Use them raw, boiled, fried, or baked, in soups, casseroles, desserts, breads, or stir-fries.

In addition to being a productive garden vegetable, sweet potatoes also grow attractive vines and leaves. Try them as a temporary groundcover or a trailing houseplant. In a patio planter, it will form a beautiful foliage plant that you can harvest roots from in the fall.

Sweet potato flesh is classified as moist or dry. Moist, deep orange types are sometimes called yams, but true yams are native African plants raised only in tropical climates. Sweet potatoes are grown worldwide, from tropical regions to temperate climates.

Planting: Grow sweet potatoes from root sprouts, called slips, that are available from nurseries. Or see "Starting Sweet Potato Slips" on this page for details on starting your own slips.

Sweet potatoes will grow in poor soil, but roots may be deformed in heavy clay or long and stringy in sandy soil. To create the perfect environment, build long, wide, 10" high ridges spaced 3½' apart. (A 10' row will produce 8-10 lb. of potatoes.) Work in plenty of compost, avoiding nitrogen-rich fertilizers that produce lush vines and stunted tubers. In the North, cover the raised rows with black plastic to keep the soil warm and promote strong growth.

Sweet potatoes mature in 90-170 days and are extremely frost-sensitive. Plant in full sun 3-4 weeks after the last frost when the soil has warmed. Make holes 6" deep and 12" apart. Bury slips up to the top leaves, press the soil down gently but firmly, and water well.

Growing guidelines: If you're not using black plastic, mulch the vines two weeks after planting to smother weeds, conserve moisture, and keep the soil loose for root development. Occasionally lift longer vines to keep them from rooting at the joints, or they will put their energy into forming many undersized tubers at each rooted area rather than ripening the main crop at the base of the plant. Otherwise, handle plants as little as possible to prevent wounds that might be invaded by disease spores.

If the weather is dry, provide 1" of water a week until two weeks before harvesting, then let the soil dry out a bit. Don't overwater, or the plants—which can withstand dry spells better than rainy ones—may rot.

Problems: Southern gardeners are more likely to encounter pest problems than garden-

Starting sweet potato slips. To grow your own slips, save a few tuberous roots from your last crop, or buy untreated ones; store-bought sweet potatoes are often waxed to prevent sprouting. Some six weeks before transplanting, place them in a box of moist sand, sawdust, or chopped leaves, and keep at 75°-80°F. When shoots are 6"-9" long, cut them off the tuberous root. Remove and dispose of the bottom inch from each slip, which sometimes harbors disease organisms.

ers in Northern areas.

Sweet potato weevils—¼″ long insects with dark blue heads and wings and red-orange bodies—puncture stems and tubers to lay their eggs. Developing larvae tunnel and feed on the fleshy roots, while adults generally attack vines and leaves. They also spread foot rot, which creates enlarging brown to black areas on stems near the soil and at stem ends. Since weevils multiply quickly and are hard to eliminate, use certified disease-resistant slips and practice four-year crop rotation. Destroy infected plants and their roots, or place in sealed containers and dispose of them with household trash.

Fungal diseases include black rot, which results in circular, dark depressions on tubers. Discard infected potatoes, and cure the undamaged roots from the same crop carefully. Don't confuse this disease with less-serious scurf, which creates small, round, dark spots on tuber surfaces but doesn't affect eating quality. Stem rot, or wilt, is a fungus that enters plants injured by insects, careless cultivation, or wind. Even if this disease doesn't kill the plants, the harvest will be poor. Minimize the chances of disease by planting only healthy slips; avoid black and stem rot by planting resistant cultivars. Reduce the incidence of dry rot, which mummifies stored potatoes, by keeping the fleshy roots at 55°-60°F.

Harvesting: You can harvest as soon as leaves start to yellow, but the longer a crop is left in the ground, the higher the yield and vitamin content. Once frost blackens the vines, however, tubers can quickly rot.

Use a spading fork to dig tubers on a sunny day when the soil is dry. Remember that tubers can grow a foot or more from the plant, and that any nicks on their tender skins will encourage spoilage. Dry tubers in the sun for several hours, then move them to a well-ventilated spot and keep at 85°-90°F for 10-15 days. After they are cured, store at around 55°F, with a humidity of 75-80 percent. Properly cured and stored sweet potatoes will keep for several months. ❖

Syringa

Lilac. Deciduous, spring-blooming shrubs or trees.

Description: *Syringa laciniata,* cutleaf lilac, has a rounded, arching form and grows to a mature height of about 6′. Its leaves are opposite, often deeply lobed. Fragrant, lavender flowers are borne in 3″ long, loose clusters along the branches in spring. Cutleaf lilac is one of the few lilacs to flower reliably in the South. Zones 5-8.

S. meyeri, Meyer lilac, is a broad shrub, 4′-8′ tall. It bears ¾″-1¾″, dark green, oval leaves. Violet purple, fragrant flowers are borne in 4″ clusters in spring, covering the plants. Zones 4-8.

S. reticulata, Japanese tree lilac, is a large shrub or small tree with a rounded crown, growing to a mature height of 30′. The 5″, dark green leaves are broad and nearly heart-shaped. Plants bloom in summer, bearing yellowish white flowers in loose, generous 6″-12″ clusters at the branch tips. Zones 3-7.

S. vulgaris, common lilac, is an upright, vase-shaped shrub that can grow to a mature height of 20′. Dark green, 2″-5″ leaves are basically heart-shaped. The flowers are purplish or white, fragrant, and borne in 4″-8″ terminal clusters in the spring. Zones 3-7.

How to grow: Provide lilacs with full sun and good drainage. Once established, they need minimal watering. Remove spent blooms, or flower bud formation for the following year may be inhibited by seed development. Prune immediately after bloom by removing a few of the oldest stems a few inches above ground level each year. This will keep the plant growing vigorously. Powdery mildew can be a problem. Choose cultivars that are resistant to this fungal disease, and don't plant them in shade. Meyer lilac is mildew-resistant.

Landscape uses: Japanese tree lilac makes a fine street tree. The other lilacs are useful as hedges, specimens, or massed plantings. ❖

Tagetes

Marigold. Summer- and fall-blooming annuals.

Description: French marigolds, derived from *Tagetes patula,* include most of the dwarf cultivars, while the generally taller African cultivars arose from *T. erecta.* Hybridizing has also produced many cultivars with intermediate characteristics. As a group, marigolds grow 8"-42" tall, as low mounds or erect bushes. The 1"-4" flowers may be rounded, tufted, or shaggy puffs in shades of white, yellow, orange, and rust. Dark green leaves are dense, ferny, and often strongly scented. Other worthy marigolds include the signet group from *T. tenuifolia,* which has 8" mounds of lacy, lemon-scented leaves and ½" red, orange, or yellow single flowers. *T. filifolia,* Irish lace marigold, is grown for its dense 1' mounds of delicate foliage.

How to grow: Marigolds are so easy to grow that they're often a child's first garden success. Given warmth, they grow quickly. Sow seed indoors a few weeks before frost (especially recommended for the taller cultivars) or direct-seed when the soil is warm. Give them full sun in average soil and moisture for best results, but don't worry if the soil is poor or dry. Excess fertility may promote lush growth and soft stems, especially in the tall cultivars, which then need to be staked. Wash spider mites off with regular, strong hosings or control with soap spray. Remove spent flowers regularly to encourage more blooms.

Landscape uses: Marigolds form the backbone of many plantings because of their diversity and adaptability. Use them freely in beds, borders, edges, pots, and boxes. Disguise dying bulb foliage with marigolds, or fill gaps left by discarded spring-blooming annuals and biennials. They also make long-lasting cut flowers, excellent for informal arrangements.

Best cultivars: Dwarfs, all 8"-12" spreading mounds with 1"-1½" flowers: 'Janie', 'Boy', 'Crush', 'Sophia', 'Nugget', and 'Disco'. Mid-height, from 1'-1½' upright-mounded plants with 3"-4" blooms: 'Inca', 'Galore', and 'Lady'. Tall, upright growers with flowers 4" or more: 'Jubilee', 'Toreador', and 'Climax'. Signet cultivars include 'Lemon Gem' and 'Golden Gem'. The 'Nemagold' mix will rid your vegetable garden of nematodes when planted as a cover crop. All of these are mixes. ❖

Taxus

Yew. Needle-leaved evergreen shrubs or trees.

Description: *Taxus baccata,* English yew, is a tree or shrub with deep green foliage. The shrubby cultivars usually mature under 4' tall, while the trees grow 15'-25'. Weeping forms are available. The bark is cinnamon brown and sinewy. Zones 6-7.

T. cuspidata, Japanese yew, is a shrub or tree ranging from 4' to 40' when mature, depending on the cultivar. As with the other yews, the needles are flattened and green, having two white lines on the (usually) lighter green undersides. Zones 4-7.

T. × media, Anglojapanese yew, has cultivars in numerous shapes and sizes, from 2'-20' tall; like the other yews, it has dark green needles and bears seeds with fleshy red coats in fall. Zones 5-7.

How to grow: Provide good drainage, as yews cannot tolerate standing water for any length of time. In the North, site yews out of direct wind; in the South, plant out of direct sun. Provide even moisture and mulch. Yews don't need much supplemental water once they're established. Black vine weevil occasionally feeds on yew, leaving C-shaped notches on the needles. Note that all parts of the yew are poisonous when eaten.

Landscape uses: An exceptional specimen can make a striking focal point, but yews are useful mostly for hedges, massed plantings, and foundation plantings.

Best cultivars: *T. baccata:* 'Fastigiata' is rigidly upright, 15'-30' tall, with blackish green needles; 'Repandens' grows low (to 3') and wide (to 12'), with a handsome, gracefully weeping form. *T. cuspidata:* 'Capitata' is a cone-shaped plant that lends itself well to a formal setting. *T. × media:* 'Tauntonii' is low (3'-4' tall), with resistance to winter burn and good heat tolerance. ❖

Thalictrum

Meadow rue. Spring- and summer-blooming perennials.

Description: Meadow rues bear many ½"-1" flowers over layered mounds of foliage. *Thalictrum aquilegifolium,* columbine meadow rue, bears clusters of powder-puff flowers in white, pink, or purple on 2'-3' plants in late spring. Zones 5-8. *T. delavayi,* Yunnan meadow rue, bears lilac flowers in open clusters on 3'-6' plants in late summer. Zones 4-7.

How to grow: Plant or divide in full sun and average, moist but well-drained soil out of wind. Plant in partial shade in warmer, drier areas. Support tall cultivars. Divide every 4-5 years.

Landscape uses: Feature in borders; use the foliage as a backdrop for other flowers. Try a group in a lightly shaded woodland.

Best cultivars: *T. delavayi:* 'Hewitt's Double', longer-lasting double flowers. ❖

Thuja

Arborvitae. Scaly-leaved evergreen trees or shrubs.

Description: *Thuja occidentalis,* American arborvitae or eastern white cedar, is a pyramidal tree that can grow 40'-60' tall. Its medium to light green foliage is fanlike, rather vertical, and aromatic when crushed. Zones 3-7.

T. plicata, giant arborvitae or western red cedar, also has a pyramidal form and can reach a mature height of 50'-70'. It has darker green, glossier foliage than American arborvitae and is more aromatic when crushed. Zones 4-6.

How to grow: Provide arborvitaes with full sun, good drainage, and even moisture. Pruning is rarely necessary except where these plants are used as a formal hedge. Watch for damage from bagworms; remove these pests before they become a problem. If you attempt to tear the bag away, you'll almost certainly leave a coil of tightly wound silk ready to girdle the twig. To avoid this hazard, use a knife to cut the silk from the branch or twig. Spider mites may be a problem in hot weather; control by hosing the plant with water or using a soap spray.

Landscape uses: Use arborvitaes as a hedge, specimen, windbreak, or screen.

Best cultivars: *T. occidentalis:* 'Canadian Green' is rounded, to 3′, with bright green foliage; 'Emerald' has a conelike form, to 15′, with bright emerald green foliage borne in vertical sprays and good heat- and cold-tolerance; 'Filiformis' has a weeping habit; 'Techny', to 15′, has deep green foliage and a strongly pyramidal, vigorous habit, excellent for Northern gardens. *T. plicata:* 'Atrovirens' has lustrous dark green foliage and good pyramidal form; 'Canadian Gold' has bright gold foliage; 'Zebrina', to 30′, is broadly pyramidal with yellow-striped foliage, giving the tree a yellow-green color. ❖

Thunbergia

Thunbergia. Tender perennial vines.

Description: *Thunbergia alata,* black-eyed Susan vine, is a tender twining vine to 6′ long with heart-shaped leaves. The orange-yellow flowers have narrow trumpets with five flat petals and are 1″-2″ wide. The vine blooms in summer. A tropical perennial, it is grown as an annual in most of the United States.

How to grow: Start seed indoors 6-8 weeks before the last frost. In mild climates, sow seed in early spring. Seed will germinate in two weeks at soil temperatures of 70°-75°F. Plant in well-drained, moist soil in full sun. Provide a support for the vine to twine around.

Landscape uses: Black-eyed Susan vine will quickly cover a fence, trellis, or arbor. Use it as a colorful screen or on a porch, or grow it on a tripod to create a child's hideaway. It also is eye-catching in hanging baskets. ❖

Thyme

Thymus spp.
Labiatae

Description: Versatile and beautiful, thymes should have a place in every herb garden. All thymes bear very small leaves and tiny flowers ranging in color from white through pink to deep rose-magenta. The creeping types, such as mother-of-thyme (*Thymus serpyllum*), will cover bricks and stones or low walls and can tolerate a certain amount of foot traffic. The bush forms are 6″-8″ high and have woody, wiry stems and branches.

Common thyme (*T. vulgaris*) is the type of thyme most frequently used for cooking. Most thymes are very fragrant, with aromas reminiscent of coconut, orange, balsam, oregano, or nutmeg. Golden lemon thyme (*T. × citriodorus* 'Aureus') has yellow-edged leaves and a strong lemon odor.

How to grow: Thymes need full sun and a dry, gritty soil. Plant the seed outdoors in a prepared bed in fall or spring, or start your seeds in flats indoors. Bush thymes (except for variegated cultivars) often seed themselves freely, so there should be no shortage of new plants if the old ones don't come through a hard winter. To propagate cultivars, separate rooted pieces or take cuttings. In the North, protect plants from winter damage with a covering of evergreen boughs.

Harvesting: When plants are beginning to flower, cut off the top half and hang to dry in a shady place. You may harvest pieces from thyme plants all summer, but don't cut them back severely in the fall.

Uses: One of the essential oils in thyme is thymol, still used by pharmacists, especially in cough remedies. Thyme is antiseptic, as well as an aid to digestion. In the kitchen, thyme is a wonderful addition to stews, stuffings, meat loaf, and soups and is especially good with poultry, fish, and eggs. ❖

Tilia

Linden, basswood. Large summer-flowering trees.

Description: Pyramidal in youth, lindens grow rounded with age, reaching heights of 50'-80' in the landscape. Fragrant flowers dangle from leafy bracts in early summer.

Tilia americana, basswood or American linden, grows to a height of 60'-80'. The bark is deeply furrowed, and the floppy heart-shaped leaves usually turn yellow in the fall. Remove the sprouts arising from the base of the tree that are typical of this species. Zones 2-7.

T. cordata, littleleaf linden, resembles basswood in size and shape, but its smaller heart-shaped leaves provide a finer texture. Yellow fall color is less reliable. Zones 3-7.

T. tomentosa, silver linden, grows 50'-70' tall. The silvery undersides of its leaves distinguish it from other lindens. Zones 5-7.

How to grow: Plant lindens in full sun or partial shade in rich, moist but well-drained soil. Lindens are adaptable to a range of soil pH conditions; littleleaf and silver lindens will endure urban conditions. A variety of leaf-eating caterpillars feed on lindens and can disfigure and damage trees by nearly defoliating them. Use sprays of BTK (*Bacillus thuringiensis* var. *kurstaki*) for control. Aphid infestations and their accompanying sticky honeydew are common on lindens, especially when stressed; use a forceful spray of water to knock them from trees, or spray with insecticidal soap.

Landscape uses: Beekeepers will be interested in basswood and littleleaf lindens, as they are good nectar sources. Littleleaf and silver lindens tolerate pollution well and are good street tree choices; use either as an attractive shade tree. Use basswood in shadier situations and for naturalizing in large-scale settings.

Best cultivars: *T. cordata* 'Greenspire' is a good, symmetrical street tree. ❖

Toads

Like ladybugs and earthworms, toads are humble heroes in the garden. One toad will eat 10,000-20,000 insects a year (that's 50-100 every night from spring until fall hibernation). Toads will clean up slugs, flies, grubs, wood lice, cutworms, grasshoppers, and anything else that's smaller (and slower) than they are. And unlike many part-time garden allies, toads won't do an about face and head for your vegetables and flowers as dessert.

To encourage toads to make your garden their home, provide shelter and water and, above all, use only the least-toxic organic pesticides. Toads like to live in places that are fairly light, humid, and out of the wind; you might find them in a rock garden or an old stone wall. Make your own shelters by digging shallow depressions in the garden (just a few inches deep) and loosely covering them with boards. (Leave the toad room to get in!) A plant saucer or ground-level birdbath will provide water for your toads. Set it near rocks or plants where the toads can take shelter from predators. Once a toad has found your garden, it may live there for decades. Remember, too, that toads, like frogs, lay their eggs in ponds. Adding a water garden to your yard may provide a breeding ground for future generations of toads.

The toads most likely to find a home in your garden in the East are the American toad, a brown, rusty, or tan amphibian that's 2"-4½" long, and the Eastern spadefoot toad, which is 1¾"-4" long with pale lines running down its back. In the South, the Southern toad, which may be brown, gray, or brick red and is 1½"-4" long, is the common species. Gardeners in the West will find the Western spadefoot toad, which is 1½"-2½" long. There's also a Midwestern species, the Plains spadefoot, a plump toad that is 1½"-2½" long. Spadefoot toads are burrowers that dig their homes in dry soil. They are brown and comparatively smooth-skinned. ❖

Tomato

Lycopersicon esculentum
Solanaceae

Tomatoes are America's favorite garden vegetable. There are hundreds of different tomato cultivars, ranging from cherry-size to huge beefsteak tomatoes, in yellow, red, orange, and pink versions. You can also pick between early cultivars and main-season types, and those bred for special climates and for disease resistance. Some have been developed especially for slicing, canning, juicing, or stuffing.

Types: The tomato cultivars that turn out to be your favorites will depend on your climate and personal taste and may involve a great deal of experimenting. Most early types produce a harvest in around 68 days, while the main-season cultivars can take up to 80 days. To extend your harvesting season, be sure to plant some of each type.

Tomatoes are often classified by their uses. Most standard cultivars are adapted for a variety of uses, including slicing, canning, and salads. The large, meaty fruits of beefsteak tomatoes are especially popular for slicing. Pear-shaped, thick-skinned, and nearly seedless tomatoes, often called Italian or paste tomatoes, are favorites for cooking, canning, and juicing. Try small-fruited cherry tomatoes in salads or as snacks.

Tomatoes come in determinate and indeterminate types. The vines of determinate, or bush, tomatoes grow 1'-3' long, and the main stem and suckers produce about three flower clusters each. Once flowers form at the vine tips, the plant stops growing. This means determinate types set fruit once and then stop, which makes them excellent choices for canning. You may still want to stake and prune them, though pruning back suckers will cut down on fruit production. Generally speaking, the flavor of bush-type fruits is not as quite as good as that of indeterminate cultivars.

Indeterminate tomatoes have sprawling vines that grow 6'-20' long. They make up ¾ of all tomato cultivars, and most produce about three flower clusters at every second leaf. They keep growing and producing unless stopped by frost or disease, which means you can keep picking fresh tomatoes the whole season. Pruning is necessary, however, or they will put too much energy into vine production.

Planting: The tomato transplants that are available from nurseries are usually dependable, disease-resistant hybrids. But if you want to take advantage of the full range of available cultivars, you'll have to grow tomatoes from seed. Unless you plan to preserve a lot of your crop, 3-5 plants per person is usually adequate. Unused seeds are good for three years.

Six to eight weeks before the average last frost, sow seeds ¼″ deep and 1″ apart in well-drained flats. Use a sterile potting mix to avoid disease problems. Seeds will germinate in about

one week when the soil temperature is 75°-85°F; at 60°F the germination process can take two weeks.

In most places, a sunny spot indoors, such as a south-facing window, provides the warm, humid environment young seedlings need. If you don't have sunny windows, use a heating coil for bottom heat and a fluorescent or grow-light overhead. Lack of adequate light will make seedlings leggy and weak. Also, if you cook or heat with natural gas, be aware that even a small amount of gas will harm or kill young tomato plants.

Once the seedlings emerge, keep the temperature no higher than 70°F, and water regularly. Once a week, feed with manure tea or fish emulsion, and discard any weak or sick-looking seedlings. (For instructions on making manure tea, see the Manure entry.) When the second set of leaves—the first true leaves—appear, transplant to individual 4″ peat pots, burying the

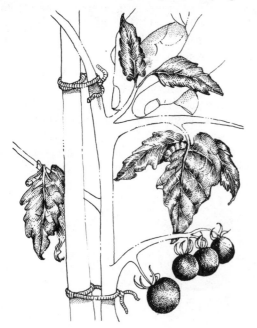

Pruning tomato plants. Use your fingers to snap off suckers—the sprouts that grow between the main stem and the leaf axils. If you need scissors or pruning shears to do the job, you're waiting too long to prune.

stems slightly deeper than they stood previously. Unless store-bought transplants are going directly into the ground, they, too, should be transplanted to individual pots; otherwise, they are likely to get rootbound and produce flowers but a minimum of fruits.

After this initial transplanting, give the seedlings less water and more sun. As the weather warms, harden off the plants before planting them in the garden. Again, discard any weaklings that might harbor disease.

Except in extremely hot climates, plant tomatoes where they will get full sun. To lessen shock, though, transplant seedlings on a cloudy day. Make the planting holes larger than normal for each seedling; cover the bottom of the hole with several inches of sifted compost mixed with a handful of bonemeal. For magnesium, which promotes plant vitality and productivity, sprinkle 1 teaspoon of Epsom salts into each hole. Disturb the soil around seedling roots as little as possible when you set them in contact with the compost.

Set the transplant so the lowest set of leaves is at soil level; fill the hole with a mixture of compost and soil. Or you can bury the stem horizontally in a shallow trench so that only the top leaves show; make sure you strip off the leaves along the part of the stem that will be buried. Many growers claim this planting method produces higher yields. Press down the soil gently but firmly to remove air pockets, and water well.

Spacing between planting holes depends on how you grow your tomatoes. If you're going to stake and prune the plants or train them on trellises, space the seedlings 1′-2′ apart. If you plan to let them sprawl, space them 3′-4′ apart.

Letting plants sprawl involves less work, and the vines often produce higher yields. They do, however, consume more garden space. Unless protected by a very thick mulch, the plants and fruits are also more subject to insects and diseases from contact with the soil—not to mention being more accessible to four-legged predators, such as chipmunks.

Though staked plants produce fewer tomatoes, the fruits are usually richer in vitamin C from having received more sunshine. If you plan to train the plants, put 5'-7' long stakes 6"-8" in the ground *before* planting, so you won't damage the tomato roots. As the vines grow on staked tomatoes, tie them loosely to the stakes at 6" intervals with strips of cloth, soft twine, or panty hose.

There are also ready-made tomato cages, but they are expensive to buy and usually aren't tall enough. For details on making your own tomato cages, see "Lifetime Tomato Cages" on this page.

Any slight frost will harm young tomato plants, and nighttime temperatures below 55°F will prevent fruit from setting. In case of a late frost, protect transplants with cloches or hotcaps; any cold damage early in a tomato's life can reduce fruit production for the entire season.

Growing guidelines: Cultivate lightly to keep down any weeds until the soil is warm, then lay down a deep mulch to smother the weeds and conserve moisture. Give the plants at least 1" of water a week, keeping in mind that a deep soaking is better than several light waterings. Avoid wetting the foliage, since wet leaves are more prone to diseases.

A weekly dose of liquid seaweed will increase fruit production and plant health. When plants flower, side-dress with compost. When small fruits appear, feed with manure tea. For instructions on making manure tea, see the Manure entry.

If you stake your plants, you may want to prune them to encourage higher yields. Pruned tomatoes take up less space and are likely to produce fruit two weeks earlier than unpruned ones; they do, however, take more work. "Pruning Tomato Plants" on the opposite page shows how to remove unwanted suckers.

Leave a few suckers on the middle and top of the plant to protect the fruit from sunscald, which produces light gray patches of skin that are subject to disease. When the vine reaches the top of the stakes, pinch back the tip to encourage more flowering and fruit.

Problems: The tomato hornworm—a large, white-striped, green caterpillar—is an easy-to-spot pest. Just handpick and destroy, or spray plants with BT (*Bacillus thuringiensis*). If you're handpicking, check to see whether hornworms have been attacked by parasitic wasps first—"Hornworms as Hosts" on page 572 shows you

LIFETIME TOMATO CAGES

The same welded steel mesh that gives reinforced concrete its strength is just the thing for making tomato cages that will last a lifetime. You can buy it at just about any building supply center. Although the mesh comes in 100' rolls, the sales clerk will cut off the amount you need. Figure on buying at least 16'—enough for two cages.

The only tools you need are a small pair of bolt cutters to cut the heavy wire and a good pair of pliers. Or if you have a very strong grip, just a pair of pliers with a good wire cutter will do. Be sure to wear work gloves to avoid cuts and blisters.

Building a cage is easy. Lay the mesh strip flat on the ground. Measure an 8' piece by counting off 16 sections of the mesh (each section of mesh is 5¼" × 6"). In the middle of the 16th section, cut each cross wire in the middle. You'll use those loose ends later to fasten the cage together.

Next, trim off the bottom horizontal wire to create a row of 5" tines along the base of the cage. Now gently bend the prepared mesh section into a circle. Pull the clipped ends together, and use your pliers to twist them around each other to form the cage.

Set the cage upright around the plant, and push the tines into the ground to anchor it. Even high winds and bumper crops have a hard time toppling these cages. At the end of the season, clear off old vines and store the cages for winter, or leave the cages standing and have them double as compost bins. Fill them with organic material, and you'll have plenty of good organic fertilizer ready for next summer's tomato crop.

what to look for. Also, plant dill near your tomatoes. It attracts hornworms, and they're easier to spot on dill than they are on tomato plants.

Aphids, flea beetles, and cutworms may also attack your tomato plants. See "The Top Ten Garden Insect Pests in America" on page 344 for details on controlling these pests.

Hard-to-spot spider mites look like tiny red dots on the undersides of leaves. Their feeding causes yellow speckling on leaves, which eventually turn brown and die. Knock these pests off the plant by spraying with water, or control with insecticidal soap.

If you are new to growing tomatoes, check with your county extention agent to find out what diseases are prevalent in your area, and buy resistant cultivars. Such resistance is generally indicated by one or more letters after the cultivar name. The code "VFNT," for example, indicates that the cultivar is resistant to Verticillium (V) and Fusarium (F) wilts, as well as nematodes (N) and tobacco mosaic (T).

Nematodes, tiny wormlike creatures, attack a plant's root system, stunting growth and lowering disease resistance. The best defenses against nematodes are rotating crops and planting resistant cultivars.

Verticillium wilt and Fusarium wilt are two common tomato diseases. Should these wilts strike and cause leaves to curl up, turn yellow, and drop off, pull up and destroy infected plants, or put them in sealed containers and dispose of them with household trash.

Another disease, early blight, makes dark, sunken areas on leaves just as the first fruits start to mature. Late blight appears as black, irregular, water-soaked patches on leaves and dark-colored spots on fruits. Both blights tend to occur during cool, rainy weather. To avoid losing your whole crop, quickly destroy or dispose of affected plants. The best defense is to plant resistant cultivars.

Blossom drop, where mature flowers fall off the plant, is most prevalent in cool rainy weather or where soil moisture is low and winds are hot and dry. It can also be from a magnesium deficiency or from infection by parasitic bacteria or fungi. Large-fruited tomatoes are particularly vulnerable. Fruit set can sometimes be encouraged by gently shaking the plant in the middle of a warm, sunny day or by tapping the stake to which the plant is tied.

Blossom-end rot appears as a water-soaked spot near the blossom end when the fruit is about ⅓ developed. The spot enlarges and turns dark brown and leathery until it covers half the tomato. This problem is due to a calcium deficiency, often brought on by an uneven water supply. Blossom-end rot can also be caused by damaged feeder roots from careless transplanting, so always handle seedlings gently. Try to keep the soil evenly moist by using a mulch and watering when needed.

Prolonged periods of heavy rainfall that keep the soil constantly moist can cause leaf roll, which can affect more than half the foliage and cut fruit production significantly. At first, the edges of leaves curl up to form cups; then the edges overlap and the leaves become firm and

Hornworms as hosts. Don't destroy cocoon-covered hornworms; those white pouches contain eggs of the beneficial braconid wasp that will hatch and kill their host naturally. The larvae feed on the worm, eventually growing into adults that then prey on many other pest insects.

leathery to the touch. Keeping soil well drained and well aerated is about the only method of preventing this problem.

Fruit with cracks that radiate from the stems or run around the shoulders are often caused by hot, rainy weather. Such cracks, aside from being unsightly, attract infections. To avoid them, make sure you don't overwater.

Tomatoes—like eggplants, potatoes, and peppers—are related to tobacco and subject to the same diseases, including tobacco mosaic. Therefore, don't smoke around such plants, and wash your hands after smoking before handling them. Plan your garden so nightshade-family crops such as peppers and tomatoes are separated by plants from other families.

Harvesting: Once tomatoes start ripening, check the vines almost daily in order to harvest fruits at their peak. Cut or gently twist off the fruits, supporting the vine at the same time to keep from damaging it.

Most plants can survive a light frost if adequately mulched, but at the first sign of a heavy frost, harvest all the fruits, even the green ones. To continue enjoying fresh tomatoes, cut a few suckers from a healthy and preferably determinate plant and root them. Plant in good potting soil in 3-gallon or larger containers. Keep in a warm, sunny spot, and with a little luck and care, you can enjoy fresh tomatoes right through the winter.

Ripe tomatoes will keep refrigerated for several weeks, and green ones will eventually ripen if kept in a warm place out of direct sunlight. To slowly ripen green tomatoes, and thereby extend your harvest, wrap them in newspaper and place in a dark, cool area, checking frequently to make sure that none rot. Sliced green tomatoes are delicious when lightly dipped in egg, then in flour or cornmeal and black pepper, and fried.

Best cultivars: Transplants: 'Burpee's Big Boy', red, thick-walled fruits; 'Better Boy VFN', large red fruits; 'Burpee's Big Girl VF', delicious, crack-resistant; 'Ultra Girl VFN', an early, disease-resistant transplant.

TOMATOES IN SMALL SPACES

Even if you don't have much room to grow vegetables, you can still enjoy the taste of a fresh-picked tomato. Tomatoes are easy to grow in containers, making them perfect for decks, patios, or balconies. If you have the space, try growing full-size tomatoes in large fiberglass tubs or wooden barrels. For people with less room, there are dwarf cherry tomato cultivars, such as 'Tiny Tim' and 'Pixie Hybrid II', that can grow in 6″ deep pots.

All container tomatoes need lots of sun, plenty of water, and a rich, well-drained potting mixture. Compensate for the restricted root zone by applying liquid fertilizer, such as manure tea, lightly but frequently, increasing both water and nutrients as the plants grow. For instructions on making manure tea, see the Manure entry.

Early types (best for growing in short-season areas): 'Cold Set', deep red fruit, good for canning, tolerates direct-seeding; 'Sub-Arctic Plenty', determinate, very early, good for cold climates.

Main-crop types: 'Celebrity VFNT', vigorous, flavorful; 'Caro Rich', high in vitamin A; 'Orange Queen', mild-flavored, low-acid fruits, good for Northeast, Midwest, and Northwest climates; 'Moira', deep red, firm, delicious fruits; 'Burpee's Supersteak Hybrid VFN', meaty, deep red fruits; 'Burpee's Long-Keeper', fruits will keep for 6-12 weeks.

Italian or paste tomatoes: 'Roma VF', firm, medium-sized, plum-shaped fruits; 'San Marzano', deep red fruit; 'Veeroma VF', medium red fruits, crack-resistant.

Cherry tomatoes: 'Patio', sturdy, productive plants with delicious fruits; 'Red Cherry', deep red fruits, great for salads; 'Sweet 100', very prolific; 'Cherry Grande', high-yielding, firm fruits; 'Golden Hybrid', a fine gold cherry type; 'Small Fry', compact plants, large clusters of 1″ fruits; 'Yellow Pear', prolific, bright yellow fruits; 'Yellow Plum', small-fruited, very high-yielding. ❖

Tools and Equipment

The wise gardener starts with a small collection of basic tools and builds from there. Stores and catalogs are packed with both familar and outlandish-looking hand tools. And if that weren't enough, there are also gas- or electric-powered versions of many tools. Deciding which tools you need isn't easy. The ideal collection depends on your gardening style and scope.

Your starter collection will include a fork or spade for digging, a garden rake for smoothing the soil and preparing beds, a hoe for cultivating and weeding, and a trowel for working closely around plants. Pruning tools and a lawn mower round out a basic tool collection.

Whenever it's practical, use hand tools rather than power tools. Power tools are expensive and contribute to both our air and noise pollution problems. Designing your yard to be low-maintenance will reduce your tool needs and increase your enjoyment of the garden. For more details on low-care landscapes, see "Reducing Landscape Maintenance" on page 361.

Hand Tools

Hand tools form the basis for a garden tool collection. If you keep them sharp, good-quality hand tools will make your garden work go quickly and easily.

Hoes: You can use hoes to lay out rows, dig furrows, cultivate around plants to loosen the soil and kill weeds, create hills and raised beds, break up clods, and prepare bare spots in lawns for reseeding.

The standard American pattern hoe is a long-handled tool that allows you to work without too much bending. It has a broad, straight blade, a little larger than 6″ wide and 4″ deep. However, many gardeners prefer a nursery hoe, which is lighter and has a 2″-3″ deep blade.

Use an oscillating hoe to slice weeds just below the soil surface. It cuts on both the push and the pull stroke. On modern variations, often called "hula" or action hoes, the slicing blade moves back and forth to cut while being pulled or pushed.

Narrow hoe blades utilize your arm power more efficiently than wider blades. The hoe handle should be at least 4½′ long so you can work without bending over and straining your lower back muscles. In general, when working with hoes, try to remain standing upright and run the hoe blade below and parallel to the soil surface. Keep your hoe sharp so it will cut through weeds rather than yank them out.

Shovels: A standard American long-handled shovel is good for mixing cement and for scooping up soil, gravel, and sand. You can also use it to pry rocks and root clumps from the soil. You can use a shovel to dig rounded planting holes, but a garden fork or a spade generally works better for most digging.

The standard shovel handle is about 4′. The shovel handle should come to shoulder height or higher. Shovels should also have a turned edge or footrest on the shoulders of the blade to protect your feet when you step on the tool.

Spades: Spades have a flat, rather than scooped, blade with squared edges. With a spade, you can cut easily through sod and create straight edges in soil. Use a spade for digging planting holes, prying up rocks, dividing and moving perennials, cutting unwanted tree and shrub roots, tamping sod, and digging trenches.

A spade handle is generally shorter than a shovel handle, usually ranging from 28″ to 32″. Like shovels, spades should also have a turned edge or footrest on the shoulders of the blade.

Forks: Spading forks cut into soil, usually more easily than solid-bladed tools can. A spading fork is handy for mixing materials into the soil and for harvesting potatoes, carrots, and other root crops. The tines of a standard spading fork are broad and flat; those of the English cultivating fork are thinner and square. The English version is better for cultivating and aer-

Smart Shopping
TOOLS

The first rule of tool buying is to avoid cheap tools at all costs. They are poorly designed and constructed, they don't do the job well, and they break easily. Also, don't buy cheap tools for children; they won't learn to love gardening if the first tools they use don't work well.

● The best wood for the handle of a shovel and all long-handled garden tools is North American white ash, which is strong, light, and resilient. Hickory is stronger but heavier and is ideal for hammers and other short-handled tools.

● Examine the lines (rings) in a wooden handle; they should run straight down the entire length of the handle, with no knots. Avoid tools with painted handles; the paint often hides cheap wood.

● The attachment of the metal part of the tool to its handle affects durability. Buy tools with solid-socket or solid-strapped construction, forged from a single bar of steel that completely envelops the handle, thus protecting it and adding strength.

● If you buy a one-piece cast aluminum trowel, select one with a plastic sleeve over the handle to prevent your hands from blackening from contact with the aluminum.

● A rotary tiller is an important investment. Borrow or rent various models as a test before buying one. Wheeled tillers are always easier to operate than those without wheels, and large wheels provide more maneuverability than small ones. Look for heavy, heat-treated carbon steel blades.

ating soil. Remember that forks are used to loosen soil, not to lift it. Use a pitchfork (3 tines) or a straw fork (5-6 tines) for picking up, turning, and scattering hay mulch, leaf mold, and light compost materials.

The standard handle length for a spading

fork is 28″. Very tall gardeners may prefer a 32″ handle. Short gardeners, including children, should use a border fork, which has shorter tines and handle.

Trowels: A garden trowel is a miniature version of a shovel. Use it to dig planting holes for small plants and bulbs, for transplanting seedlings, or for weeding beds and borders.

Some trowels are made from forged steel and fitted with hardwood handles; good ones are also available in unbreakable one-piece cast aluminum. Trowels come with a variety of blade widths and lengths. Choose one that feels comfortable in your hand.

Rakes: Rakes generally fall into one of two categories: garden rakes and leaf rakes. Garden rakes are essential for leveling ground, creating raised beds, killing emerging weeds, gathering debris from rows, covering furrows, thinning seedlings, working materials shallowly into the soil, erasing footprints, and spreading mulch. Garden rakes come in many widths, with long or short teeth that are widely or closely spaced. The handle should be long (4½'-5') and the head should be heavy enough to bite into the soil easily. If you have rocky soil, choose a rake with widely spaced teeth.

Lawn or leaf rakes, also called fan rakes, are good for gathering up leaves, grass clippings, weeds, and other debris and for dislodging thatch from the lawn. Metal lawn rakes last longest and are the springiest, although many gardeners prefer the action and feel of bamboo tines, and some prefer plastic or rubber.

Pruning tools: There are two types of pruning shears: the anvil type, with a straight blade that closes down onto an anvil or plate, and the bypass type, which cuts like scissors. Anvil pruners are often easier to use, requiring less hand pressure to make a cut. Bypass shears make a cleaner cut, can work in tighter spaces, and can cut flush against a tree trunk or branch (anvil pruners leave a short stump). Most models of

CLASSIC TOOLS

These days, you can buy a high-powered, gasoline-guzzling tool to do everything from tearing weeds out of your garden to blowing leaves off of your driveway. But why spend all that money and fight engine noise and exhaust fumes to boot?

Some of the best garden and yard tools are the ones that let you get the job done while providing good exercise and letting you enjoy the sights and sounds of nature.

So if you have a small yard, think about buying a push-type reel lawn mower instead of a $400 gasoline-powered mower. An ordinary hoe will do the work of a $300 power cultivator. A spading fork can do the same job as a garden tiller. And a good tool for those leaves in your driveway? It's still hard to beat a good, old-fashioned, spring-tine rake! Hand tools aren't any less effective— they're just slower.

Scythes and sickles are perfect examples of classic tools. A scythe is a traditional hand tool used for mowing grain crops or tall grass and weeds. The mechanical reaper, invented in 1831, and subsequent modern machinery have made the scythe nearly obsolete for agricultural use. However, gardeners may still find a scythe handy for mowing grass on steep slopes or in rocky areas.

Sickles, also called grass hooks, are handy for chopping down grass and weeds wherever other tools can't reach—along fencerows, against buildings, or around trees.

Check your local hardware store. You may be surprised at the unusual items they have in the back room or can easily order. Probably the best source for classic, non-powered equipment is where many Amish people buy their tools: Lehman's Hardware, Box 4111A, Kidron, OH 44636. Lehman's catalog offers more than 1,000 such items.

Scythe

Sickle

Using scythes and sickles. To mow with a scythe, stand with your feet spread moderately apart, and hold one nib (handhold) of the scythe in each hand. Sweep the tool in an arc from right to left in front of you, parallel to the ground, to cut a swath. Swing the tool back from left to right to prepare to cut the next swath. Take small steps as you work, in rhythm with the swinging blade.

Cut with a sideways motion when using a sickle. Hold a stick in your other hand and use it to hold back overhanging grass so you can cut near the stem bases. If the grass is wet, hold the stick upright with one end touching the ground to act as a barrier in case the sickle slips on the wet grass as you swing.

either type will cut hardwood branches up to ½″ in diameter.

Lopping shears, also called loppers, are heavy-duty pruners with long handles. Both anvil and bypass loppers can cut branches up to 2″ in diameter. Hedge shears have long blades and relatively short handles. They can cut branches up to ½″ thick. Pruning saws cut through most branches that are too thick for shears.

Push mowers: Push mowers have several revolving blades that move against a single fixed blade, producing a neat trim. They do a fine job, cutting evenly and quietly. For those with small, level lawns, the push mower is the ideal lawn-cutting instrument. It is inexpensive, not difficult to push, nonpolluting, quiet, and produces a neat-looking lawn.

Power Tools

In some cases, you may need the extra power of engine-driven equipment. It's tempting to use these machines on a regular basis because they get the job done quickly. Keep in mind, though, that handwork can be part of the pleasure and relaxation of gardening. If you routinely use power tools to speed through garden chores, you'll miss the opportunity to observe the growth of your plants and to watch for the beginning of disease or insect problems.

Power mowers: Gas-powered rotary mowers have a single blade that revolves at a high speed, literally ripping the tops off grass plants. Unlike push mowers, power mowers can handle rough terrain and knock down high weeds. Mulching mowers blow finely cut grass pieces back into the lawn, building up soil organic matter while removing the need to rake or bag clippings.

Tillers: Rotary tillers can make short work of turning and churning garden soil, breaking new ground, cultivating, aerating, weeding, and mixing materials into the soil. The rotary tiller is a gasoline-powered machine equipped with steel blades that rotate on a central spindle.

Chipper/shredders: After a lawn mower and a rotary tiller, the favorite large power tool of gardeners is often a chipper/shredder. This machine, powered with gasoline or electricity, reduces leaves, pruned branches, and plant debris to beautiful mulch or compost material. Shredders are better for chopping up weeds and other soft plant material; chippers can handle heavier, woody materials.

Keeping Tools in Shape

After making the considerable investment in good-quality tools, it is wise to spend some time to keep them in good shape.

Routine care: Clean, dry, and put away all hand tools after each use. Keep a large plastic kitchen spoon handy to knock dirt off metal blades. Don't use a trowel or other metal tool, as you could damage the blades of both tools. A 5-gallon bucket of sharp builder's sand in the toolshed or garage is useful for cleaning tools. Dip the metal blade of each tool into the sand and plunge it up and down a few times to work off any clinging soil. Use a wire brush to remove any rust that may have formed. Keep power equipment in good repair and properly adjusted.

Handles: Regularly varnish and sand wooden handles to maintain their resilience and good looks. If you buy a good-quality tool secondhand and it has a weather-beaten handle, refresh it with several coats of varnish, sanding between each coat. You can repair split handles temporarily with tape and glue, but replace broken handles as soon as possible.

Sharpening: Sharp-bladed hand tools will perform efficiently and with ease only if you keep them sharp. Take the time to study the angle of the bevels on all your tools, then sharpen each, as needed, to keep the proper bevel. If you have tools that are especially difficult to sharpen, take them to a professional for sharpening.

Winter care: At the end of the season, polish all metal parts of hand tools with steel wool, oil them to prevent rust, and store them in a dry place. Lubricate all tools that have moving parts. This is also a good time to take hard-to-sharpen tools to the sharpening shop. ❖

Tradescantia

Spiderwort. Late-spring- to summer-blooming perennials.

Description: *Tradescantia × andersoniana,* common spiderwort, produces triangular 1½″ blooms in white, red, blue, and violet. Clustered buds open one by one at the tops of angular 2′ stems with 1′ straplike leaves. Foliage declines after bloom. Plants form loose mounds. Zones 3-8.

How to grow: Plant or divide in spring or fall in a sunny site with average, moist to wet soil. Cut back 6″-8″ from the ground after flowering to promote new growth and rebloom. Divide every 3 years.

Landscape uses: Grow spiderworts in borders among other plants to disguise their declining foliage. Naturalize in wet spots.

Best cultivars: 'Blue Stone', rich blue; 'Pauline', mauve pink; 'Red Cloud', purple-red; 'Iris Pritchard', white brushed with blue-violet; 'Snowcap', white. ❖

Transplanting

Transplanting simply means moving a rooted plant from one place to another. If you prick out tiny parsley seedlings from a flat into individual pots, you're transplanting. If you move tomato plants from your windowsill into the garden, you're transplanting. And if you decide the big forsythia would really look better in the backyard, you're transplanting, too.

For information on planting seeds, see the Seeds and Seedlings entry. Instructions for planting perennials, shrubs, and trees are in the Planting entry.

Transplanting to containers: If you start seeds in flats, transplant when seedlings are still very young. Watch for the emergence of the first pair of true leaves and transplant soon after. The choice of planting containers ranges from homemade newspaper cylinders to plastic cell packs and clay pots. Peat pots are a favorite of many gardeners, because the pots can be transplanted with the plant. Plastic and clay containers are reusable.

Before you start, collect your transplanting supplies and put down a layer of newspaper to catch spills. Follow these steps:

1. Fill the containers with soil mix. You'll find recipes for mixes in the Seeds and Seedlings entry. The depth of the soil depends on seedling size: Fill nearly to the top for small seedlings; add only 1″ of soil for large ones.

2. Pour warm water onto the soil mix, and let it sit for an hour to soak in. Moist potting soil prevents seedling roots from drying out.

3. Carefully dig out either individual seedlings or small groups of seedlings. A Popsicle stick makes a good all-purpose tool for digging, lifting, and moving tiny plants. A tablespoon or narrow trowel works well for larger transplants.

4. Hold the seedling by one of the leaves, not by (or around) the stem: You could crush the tender stem, or if you grasp the stem tip, you could kill the growing point and ruin the seedling's further growth.

5. For very young seedlings, poke small holes into the soil mix with a pencil. For larger seedlings, hold the plant in the pot while you fill in around the roots with soil. Firm the soil with your fingertips.

6. Return the seedlings to the window, light rack, or cold frame. If seedlings wilt from the stress of transplanting, mist lightly with water and cover loosely with a sheet of plastic wrap. Keep them cool and out of direct sun for a day or two, then remove wrap and return to light.

7. Keep soil lightly moist but not soggy by pouring water into the tray holding the containers. Feed regularly with a weak solution of water-soluble organic fertilizer.

8. As the plants grow, pinch or snip off any extra seedlings, leaving only the strongest one.

If you miscalculated the seed-starting date or if the weather turns nasty, you may need to transplant your plants again to larger containers so plants won't stop growing and become stunted.

Roots pushing through drainage holes are a clue that it's time to transplant.

Transplanting to the garden: Toughen your plants for outdoor growing conditions by hardening off. Two weeks before outdoor transplanting time, stop feeding and slow down on watering. About a week before you plan to plant out the seedlings, put them outdoors in a protected area, out of direct sun and wind. Leave them outdoors for only 1 hour at first, then 2 hours, then a morning, until they are used to a full day. Water frequently.

Transplant on a cloudy or drizzly day or in early evening to spare transplants from the sun's heat. Water the plants before you start. Follow these steps for best results:

1. Dig a hole slightly wider than and of the same depth as the container. (Plant tomatoes deeper, so that roots form along the stem. See the Tomato entry for details.)

2. If your transplants are in plastic or clay pots, turn the pots upside down and slide out the

Transplanting peat pot plants. Slit the sides and remove the bottom of the peat pot before transplanting unless many roots have already penetrated. Always tear off the rim above the soil line. If even a small piece of peat pot is exposed after transplanting, it will draw water from the soil surrounding the transplant's roots, leaving the plant in danger of water stress.

plants. Whack the pot with your trowel to dislodge stubborn ones. Plants in peat or paper pots can be planted, pot and all.

3. Gently place the plant in the hole, and spread out roots of plants that aren't in pots. "Transplanting Peat Pot Plants" above shows how to open up peat pots for better root penetration after planting.

4. Fill and tamp with your hands, forming a shallow basin to collect water.

5. Slowly pour plenty of water—at least a quart—at the base of the transplant. Keep well watered until transplants become established and start showing new growth.

Transplanting large plants: Sometimes a favorite tree or shrub gets too big for its place or is threatened by construction. Or maybe you just want to move a certain plant to a different spot in the landscape. If hard work doesn't scare you off, consider transplanting. See the Trees entry for the particulars. ❖

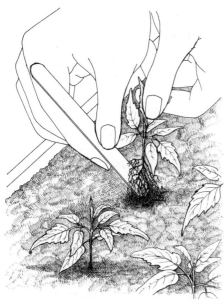

Handling seedlings. Hold and move seedlings by grasping a leaf between thumb and forefinger. Yanking up seedlings by their stems will damage roots. Also avoid touching the delicate growing tip of the stem.

Trees

Trees dominate the landscape. They're the biggest, longest-lived plants, and often a considerable monetary investment. Versatile trees provide privacy and food, protect you from sun and wind, and add beauty. A landscape without trees looks bare and uninviting; the presence of trees softens the look of house and surroundings.

Trees cool your house and yard with shade in summer and buffer it from winter winds. They intercept glare off buildings and paved surfaces and soak up noise. Their leaves soften the impact of rain, reducing soil erosion, and act as air purifiers by absorbing pollutants and releasing oxygen.

Trees enhance your home, but not only in terms of monetary value or ecological good sense. You also benefit psychologically when trees are present, with an improved sense of well-being that's very important in our stressful world.

Types of Trees

Trees are woody perennials, usually with a single trunk, ranging in height at maturity from 15' to giants exceeding 100'. A plant thought of as a tree in some parts of the country may be considered a shrub in others. Crape myrtle (*Lagerstroemia indica*) exceeds 15' in the South, where it is grown as a small flowering tree, but in the mid-Atlantic area, it may die back to the ground after cold winters and only reach shrub heights.

Deciduous trees drop all of their leaves at the end of the growing season and grow new leaves the following spring. They are good choices for fall color. Once your trees drop their leaves, with the exception of some limited root growth, they generally have gone dormant for the winter.

Evergreen trees hold most of their leaves year-round. Needled evergreens like pines and spruces are also known as conifers because they bear cones. But not all coniferous trees are evergreen: Larches (*Larix* spp.) and bald cypress (*Taxodium distichum*) are deciduous conifers. See the Evergreens entry for more about evergreen conifers. Evergreens with wide, generally thick leaves, such as Southern magnolia (*Magnolia grandiflora*) and live oak (*Quercus virginiana*), are called broad-leaved evergreens.

If you live in a warmer area, you may be able to select a third type of "evergreen" tree. Palms are categorized as evergreens, although they are monocots, not dicots like other trees. A dicot forms annual growth rings that increase the trunk's diameter, and their crown is formed of branches. Palms don't form annual growth rings, and they generally don't branch—their crowns are made up entirely of their large leaves.

A few trees, such as certain cultivars of Chinese or lacebark elm (*Ulmus parvifolia*), keep many of their leaves well into the winter. These trees are called semi-evergreen; they may be fully evergreen in the South.

Selecting Trees

Your trees will be a part of your life for a long time. Choose them with care. Think about what you want from a tree. Will it shade your house, serve as an accent for a flower garden, provide food for wildlife? Would you rather have a display of flowers in spring, brightly colored leaves in fall, showy bark, or persistent fruit in the winter?

Use groups of trees to block unwanted views or accent desirable ones, both on and off your property, and to give privacy. Evergreens provide year-round concealment. A unified group of trees in a single bed looks better than a widely separated planting, and the arrangement helps protect the trees from lawn mower nicks and gouges.

Specimen or accent trees are used alone to call attention to an attractive feature such as the finely cut leaves of full-moon maple (*Acer japonicum*), or the showy flowers of saucer magnolia (*Magnolia* × *soulangiana*). Unusually textured bark, bright fall color, or an interesting

Key Words
TREE SHAPES

Clump. A tree grown with several closely growing trunks. Birches are often sold as clumps.

Vase-shaped. A tree with upswept branches, narrower in silhouette near the base than at the top, such as American elm.

Globe-shaped. A tree with a rounded, usually low-growing silhouette, such as crab apple.

Oval. A tree with branches that form an oval silhouette, such as 'Bradford' flowering pear.

Columnar. A tall, somewhat narrow form, such as 'Columnare' Norway maple.

Pyramidal. A cone-shaped tree, such as spruces or American arborvitae.

Conical. Cone-shaped, but with a narrower profile than a pyramidal tree, such as 'Wichita Blue' juniper.

Weeping. A tree with branches that droop toward the ground, such as a weeping willow.

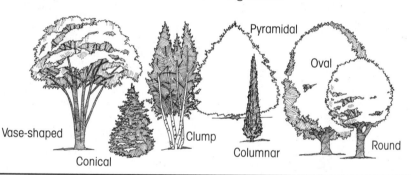

shape are other good reasons to showcase a tree as a specimen plant.

Trees supply food, shelter, and nesting sites for birds and other wildlife. Those with berries or other fruits are especially welcome.

You may want to add trees to your landscape that will provide food for you, not just for wildlife and birds. Many common fruit trees, such as apples, pears, peaches, and plums, are available in dwarf sizes that fit neatly into a small corner or even a large container. Use the entries for specific fruits and the Fruit Trees entry to guide your selection. Many lesser-known trees also produce good food.

• For fleshy fruit to be eaten fresh or cooked, try pawpaw (*Asimina triloba*), common persimmon (*Diospyros virginiana*), and Japanese persimmon (*D. kaki*).

• For small, fleshy fruits for jams and jellies, try cornelian cherry (*Cornus mas*), crab apples (*Malus* spp.), hawthorns (*Crataegus* spp.), and wild cherries and plums (*Prunus* spp.).

• For nuts, try hickories (*Carya* spp.), walnuts and butternuts (*Juglans* spp.), pecans (*Carya illinoinensis*), filberts (*Corylus* spp.), and chestnuts (*Castanea* spp.). See the Nut Trees entry for advice on selecting and growing nut trees.

• For beekeepers interested in a new taste to their honey, try sourwood (*Oxydendrum arboreum*), lindens (*Tilia* spp.), and water tupelo (*Nyssa aquatica*).

Be realistic about the amount of maintenance you're willing to do. Do you want to plant trees and forget them, as you can do with many evergreens? Or do you enjoy pruning and raking up baskets of leaves on a brisk fall day? For some

SMALL FLOWERING TREES

Don't forget that trees can also add the beauty of flowers to your landscape. The list that follows is arranged by time of bloom, beginning with trees that flower in early spring and progressing through summer-blooming trees such as Japanese pagoda tree and golden-rain tree. Plant name is followed by flower color.

Amelanchier spp. (serviceberries): white
Cornus mas (cornelian cherry): yellow
Cercis canadensis (Eastern redbud): pink
Cercis chinensis (Chinese redbud): magenta
Magnolia stellata (star magnolia): white to pale pink
Magnolia × soulangiana (saucer magnolia): white to wine
Cornus florida (flowering dogwood): white, pink
Pyrus calleryana (callery pear): white
Malus spp. (crab apples): white, pink, red
Halesia carolina (Carolina silverbell): white
Cornus kousa (kousa dogwood): white
Chionanthus virginicus (white fringe tree): white
Styrax japonicus (Japanese snowbell): white
Laburnum × watereri (golden-chain tree): yellow
Syringa reticulata (Japanese tree lilac): white
Koelreuteria paniculata (golden-rain tree): yellow
Sophora japonica (Japanese pagoda tree): creamy white
Lagerstroemia indica (crape myrtle): white, pink, lavender
Oxydendrum arboreum (sourwood): white
Stewartia pseudocamellia (Japanese stewartia): white
Franklinia alatamaha (franklinia): white

gardeners, the beauty of the tree or the bounty of the crop outweighs the extra work. See "Nuisance Trees" on page 585 for information on trees that require extra work to maintain.

Match Tree to Site

Consider the characteristics of your tree-planting site before you head for the nursery. Refer to the map on page 651 to determine your hardiness zone, and make sure the tree you want is compatible. While most nurseries stock plants that are hardy in their area, borderline-hardy plants are sometimes offered with no warnings. It's always a good idea to ask. Remember to check catalogs for hardiness information.

Know your soil—its pH, fertility, and consistency. Take a close look at drainage; choose another site if you see standing water at any season. Check the amount of light the tree will receive. Be sure to scout out overhead wires, nearby walkways, or other limiting factors. Think about the size of your tree in 5, 10, or 20 years.

As a tree grows, so does the area of ground that it shades. Some trees, such as thornless honey locust (*Gleditsia triacanthos* var. *inermis*), produce only light or filtered shade; grass and other plants generally have enough light to grow under or in the shade of these trees. Other trees, like the sugar and Norway maples (*Acer saccharum* and *A. platanoides*), produce very dense shade in which even shade-tolerant grasses have trouble growing. You'll need to use shade-lovers such as ivy, hostas, or ferns or a mulch to cover the ground beneath such trees.

Even shade-tolerant plants may have difficulty growing under or near a tree, particularly a large one. If the crown of the tree is dense, as with maples, most rain is shed off the canopy of the tree. The ground immediately below may be dry even after a rain. Tree roots absorb much of the available water from surrounding soil. See "Groundcovers for Dry Shade" on page 301 for a list of plants that will tolerate these conditions.

City-Smart Trees

City trees must contend with constricted root space, compacted soil, wind tunnels between buildings, limited moisture and nutrients, high temperatures, and pollutants.

Trees used along streets, in raised planters, in median strips, or in parking lots must survive in the harshest and most stressful of any landscape environment. These often-neglected trees face all the hazards of city trees and must put up with drought, paving heat, and human vandalism. Despite relentless pruning to make them fit under overhead utility lines or within narrow corridors, and even when main branches are whacked off to permit people and cars to pass by, street trees manage to survive. But all these stresses take their toll: On average, street trees live only 10-15 years.

In addition to resisting insects and diseases, good street trees also share other characteristics. They should be "clean" trees with no litter problems, such as dropping large leaves or fruit, although sometimes, as with sycamores (*Platanus* spp.) and oaks, the litter is overlooked because of other good qualities. Avoid trees with dangerous thorns or spines, such as hawthorns (*Crataegus* spp.); shallow-rooted trees, such as silver maples (*Acer saccharinum*), that buckle paving; and thirsty trees, like weeping willows (*Salix babylonica*), whose roots seek water and sewer lines. Trees with branches that angle downward, such as pin oaks, also don't make the best street trees, unless they are limbed up high enough for pedestrians and traffic to pass easily. See "Street Trees" on page 586 for a list of city-smart trees to consider.

Buying Trees

Trees are sold bareroot, balled-and-burlapped (B&B), or in containers. The heeling-in technique, described in the Planting entry, is a good way to hold bareroot or B&B stock until you're able to plant.

Buy small- to medium-sized trees. Big trees are difficult to move and plant. They take longer to get established than smaller trees, because

TREES FOR FALL COLOR

Enhance your landscape with bright fall colors from these deciduous trees.

Yellow

Acer saccharum (sugar maple)
Betula spp. (birches)
Cercis canadensis (Eastern redbud)
Cladratis lutea (American yellowwood)
Fraxinus spp. (ashes)
Ginkgo biloba (ginkgo)
Larix spp. (larches)
Gleditsia triacanthos var. *inermis* (thornless honey locust)
Liriodendron tulipifera (tulip tree)

Orange to rust

Acer saccharum (sugar maple)
Taxodium distichum (bald cypress)

Red

Acer rubrum (red maple)
Cornus florida (flowering dogwood)
Nyssa sylvatica (black tupelo)
Oxydendrum arboreum (sourwood)
Pistacia chinensis (Chinese pistache)
Quercus coccinea (scarlet oak)
Q. rubra (Northern red oak)

Mixed colors

Cotinus coggygria (smoke tree)
Lagerstroemia indica (crape myrtle)
Liquidambar styraciflua (sweet gum)
Pyrus calleryana (callery pear)
Sassafras albidum (sassafras)

more of their roots were lost when they were dug. Buy only trees that are clearly tagged or labeled with the botanical and common names to make sure you get the flowers, fruits, and crown shape you want.

Look for a relatively straight trunk with a slight natural flare at its base—if no flare exists, the tree has had too much soil placed atop its roots. Buy trees with widely spaced, even branches, not trees with branches that are tightly spaced and mostly at the top of the trunk. Buy trees from retailers who offer guarantees, and find out the terms of the guarantee.

Sometimes a low-priced tree is no bargain. And sometimes higher-priced trees aren't worth their price tag. Know how to spot a good buy when you go tree-shopping. Look for healthy trees, with plump buds. Watch out for broken branches or scratched bark, dry or brown leaf margins, or dry root balls. B&B or container-grown trees may be putting out new leaves; check for healthy growth. Examine leaves and bark for pests and diseases.

Buy bareroot trees only when they're dormant, and only if the roots have been kept moist. Roots that are evenly spaced around the base of the stem make a secure anchor. On B&B trees, look for a well-wrapped, secure root ball. Container-grown trees may be rootbound, with crowded roots wrapped around the root ball. Avoid trees that pull easily from the container, leaving the potting soil behind. Also avoid those whose roots have left the container and anchored themselves firmly in the soil beneath.

Planting Trees

Plant a bareroot tree while it is dormant, either in fall or early spring. A few trees have roots so sensitive to disturbance that you should not buy or transplant them bareroot. Your chances of success are best when these trees are container-grown: Kentucky coffee tree (*Gymnocladus dioica*), crape myrtle (*Lagerstroemia indica*), sweet gum (*Liquidambar styraciflua*), black tupelo (*Nyssa sylvatica*), white oak (*Quercus alba*), and sassafras (*Sassafras albidum*).

You can plant most B&B or container-grown trees any time of year except when the ground is frozen. There are a few exceptions, however. A few trees, especially those with thick and fleshy roots, seem to suffer less transplanting shock if planted in the spring in areas where the soil freezes deeply during the winter. Though tree roots will continue to grow until the soil temperature drops below 40°F, these trees are slow to get established and are best reserved for spring planting: dogwoods (*Cornus* spp.), golden-rain tree (*Koelreuteria paniculata*), tulip tree (*Liriodendron tulipifera*), magnolias (*Magnolia* spp.),

TREES WITH ATTRACTIVE BARK

For adding interest and color to the landscape in winter—or any season of the year—there's nothing like trees with ornamental bark. For most gardeners, the white flaking bark of birches—especially canoe birch (*Betula papyrifera*) and European white birch (*B. pendula*)—represents the epitome of ornamental bark. But white-barked birches are prone to insect problems and are not good choices for dry sites. 'Heritage' river birch (*B. nigra* 'Heritage') is a good substitute: It has tan, flaking bark and resists common birch pests.

The smooth, gray bark of trees such as beeches (*Fagus* spp.) and American yellowwood (*Cladrastis lutea*) is ornamental, too, as is the blocky gray bark of flowering dogwood (*Cornus florida*), which resembles alligator's hide. The following trees have exfoliating or flaking bark in a variety of colors, including red, brown, or combinations of cream, gray, and brown.

Acer griseum (paperbark maple)
Betula nigra (river birch)
Cornus kousa (kousa dogwood)
Lagerstroemia indica (crape myrtle)
Prunus spp. (flowering cherries)
Pinus bungeana (lacebark pine)
Pinus densiflora (Japanese red pine)
Platanus spp. (sycamores or plane trees)
Stewartia spp. (stewartia)
Ulmus parvifolia (Chinese or lacebark elm)

black tupelo (*Nyssa sylvatica*), ornamental cherries and plums (*Prunus* spp.), most oaks (*Quercus* spp.), and Japanese zelkova (*Zelkova serrata*).

A close examination of the roots of your new tree will prevent problems that can limit growth. Trim any mushy, dead, or damaged roots. Comb out potbound roots and straighten or slice through roots that circle the root ball before you set the plant in its hole. Look carefully for girdling roots, which can strangle the tree by wrapping tightly around the base of its trunk. This stops the upward movement of water and nutrients absorbed by the roots and needed by the leaves and branches.

Traditional planting advice once called for digging the biggest hole you could dig and filling it with a rich mixture of topsoil and compost. Now gardeners have learned that the best way to plant is to dig a hole just deep enough for the roots, widening toward the top, and filled with the same soil you took out. While the "big and rich" idea did indeed get the tree off to a good start, the tree roots had no inclination to leave the hole. Eventually such trees became top-heavy and subject to windthrow — toppling over during high winds. It is a good idea to encourage roots to reach out beyond the planting hole by loosening ground surrounding the hole. Plunge a garden fork in as deep as the tines allow, and wiggle it slightly to break up compacted soil. Repeat every 1'-1½' to a distance of 5' or more on all sides.

Water your trees well after planting. Apply a layer of mulch, but don't overmulch: 2"-3" is plenty. See the Planting entry for more details on settling your new tree into your home landscape.

Staking

Staking is done to straighten or strengthen the trunk, or to prevent root movement and breakage before the tree anchors itself in the soil. Trees under 8' with small crowns, which aren't

NUISANCE TREES

Some trees create problems that outweigh their contributions. Many of the following trees are considered nuisance trees and are even banned or illegal to plant in many cities. Plant name is followed by the nuisance features of the the tree.

Acer negundo (box elder): weak wood, pest problems
Acer saccharinum (silver maple): shallow roots, weak wood, seeds prolifically
Aesculus hippocastanum (common horse chestnut): poisonous fruit, disease problems
Ailanthus altissima (tree-of-heaven): invasive grower, seeds prolifically, leaves and male flowers are foul-smelling
Albizia julibrissin (mimosa): insect and disease problems
Ginkgo biloba (ginkgo): female trees have foul-smelling fruit; plant only males
Gleditsia triacanthos (thorned honey locust): dangerous thorns; plant only thornless cultivars (*G. triacanthos* var. *inermis*)
Juglans nigra (black walnut): produces toxin that poisons many other plants
Morus spp. (mulberries): messy fruit
Populus deltoides (Eastern cottonwood): messy fruit, weak wood
Populus nigra 'Italica' (lombardy poplar): incurable canker disease kills top
Robinia pseudoacacia (black locust): seeds prolifically, insect problems
Ulmus americana (American elm): insect and disease problems

located in windy sites, usually don't need staking.

Avoid rigid staking. Allow the trunk to flex or move slightly when the wind hits it. This movement encourages the tree to produce special wood that will naturally bend when the wind hits it. A tree that is rigidly staked will often bend over or break after it is unstaked. Given a choice, avoid buying staked, container-grown trees—you will generally be buying a weak stem.

Unstake all trees one year after planting. Any tree that had an adequate root system and was properly planted will by then be able to stand on its own. If you want to leave the stakes in place to keep lawn mowers and other equipment from hitting the trunk, remove the guy wires or ropes but leave the stakes for a barrier.

Care and Maintenance

Carefully selected and planted trees need only occasional attention, especially once they become well established.

During the first year after planting, water each week when less than 1" of rain falls, especially in summer and fall. Water to thaw the ground, and provide water for the leaves of evergreen trees during warm winter weather.

The mulch you applied at planting time will gradually decompose. Replenish it as needed, but only use a few inches. To avoid rodent problems and to encourage good air circulation, keep the mulch away from the trunk. To find out more about using mulch to conserve moisture and reduce maintenance, see the Mulch entry.

Small, yellow leaves, premature fall coloration, stunted twig growth, or too few flowers or fruits often indicate a nutrient deficiency. Your trees will generally receive enough fertilizer if they are located in a lawn that you regularly fertilize. If your trees are located in isolated beds, in areas surrounded by paving, or in containers, you may need to apply compost or a balanced organic fertilizer. Simply broadcast the needed fertilizer on the soil surface. See the Fertilizers entry for more information about blended organic fertilizers.

Most trees are too large for you to provide them with special winter protection such as a burlap enclosure. If snow or ice loads bend the trees' branches, avoid vigorously shaking the branches to remove the ice or snow. Frozen, brittle branches can easily break. Either allow the ice or snow to melt away naturally or very gently sweep it off.

STREET TREES

These trees are tough enough to tolerate the difficult growing conditions of city streets. All will tolerate poor soil, pollution, and droughty conditions.

Small trees

Acer buergeranum (trident maple)
A. campestre (hedge maple)
A. ginnala (amur maple)
A. tataricum (tatarian maple)
Crataegus crus-galli var. *inermis* (thornless cockspur hawthorn)
Koelreuteria paniculata (golden-rain tree)
Prunus sargentii (sargent cherry)
Pyrus calleryana 'Aristocrat' and 'Red Spire' (flowering pears)
Syringa reticulata 'Ivory Silk' and 'Summer Snow' (Japanese tree lilacs)

Medium to large trees

Acer pseudoplatanus (sycamore maple)
Carpinus betulus 'Fastigiata' (upright European hornbeam)
Celtis occidentalis 'Prairie Pride' (hackberry)
Ginkgo biloba 'Fastigiata' (upright ginkgo)
Gleditsia triacanthos var. *inermis* 'Skyline' and 'Shademaster' (thornless honey locusts)
Platanus × *acerifolia* 'Bloodgood' (London plane tree)
Quercus acutissima (sawtooth oak)
Q. phellos (willow oak)
Q. robur 'Fastigiata' (upright English oak)
Sophora japonica (Japanese pagoda tree)
Taxodium distichum (bald cypress)
Tilia tomentosa (silver linden)
Ulmus parvifolia (Chinese or laceback elm)
Zelkova serrata 'Green Vase' and 'Village Green' (Japanese zelkovas)

Pruning and Training

Prune young trees at planting time and as they grow, to correct structural problems and improve their form. Training a young tree with several years of judicious pruning leads to a structurally sound, well-shaped mature tree. Remove crossing and rubbing branches and suckers or watersprouts. Remove branches with narrow crotch angles. Repair storm and vandalism damage immediately after it occurs to reduce wound injury and subsequent decay. See the Pruning and Training entry for information on how to make pruning cuts.

After a few years, begin the limbing-up process if the tree is planted where passersby will walk below it. Remove the lowest branch or two by sawing through the limb just before the branch collar. Repeat every year until the lowest branches are high enough to permit easy passage. About 5-6 years after planting, thin to open up the canopy, reducing wind resistance and allowing light to reach the interior. If your tree is intended to block an undesirable view, use heading cuts to encourage denser branching.

Trees can generally be pruned at any time of year, but avoid spring pruning of beeches (*Fagus* spp.), birches (*Betula* spp.), elms (*Ulmus* spp.), and maples (*Acer* spp.), which tend to bleed if pruned in spring. Spring-pruning these trees can increase certain disease and insect problems. If you grow trees for their flowers or fruits, prune them before the next year's flower buds develop. A good time to prune broad-leaved evergreen trees or thin needle evergreens is during the winter, especially if you can use the leaves, such as those on hollies (*Ilex* spp.) and Southern magnolia (*Magnolia grandiflora*), for Christmas greenery.

Transplanting Trees

It's a little harder to move a tree than it is to shove the sofa around in the living room. But if you redo your landscape, or if a tree gets in the

Smart Shopping
BUYING MAIL-ORDER TREES

It's often difficult to find a new or unusual tree you read about because your local garden center doesn't stock it. Although they may be more expensive than commonly sold species, you can buy many new or unusual trees from specialty mail-order nurseries. They're often well worth the extra effort it takes to search them out.

Most trees from mail-order nurseries are less than 6' and are sold bareroot to reduce shipping costs. Here are some tips to help you use mail-order with success:

● Buy from reputable firms. Check with friends, ask a local nursery owner or your extension agent, look for the Mailorder Association of Nurseries (MAN) logo in catalogs, or order from sources recommended by gardening magazines.
● Read the catalog descriptions carefully. Be sure the tree will have the features you want and will grow in the conditions in your landscape. If the prices or the claims about the trees sound too good to be true, they probably are: Avoid them.
● Be sure a guarantee is offered, and know what to save should the tree grow poorly or die. Some nurseries will take your word; others insist you ship them the tree (at your expense). Find out if a refund or only a replacement is offered.
● Have the tree shipped during the best time of year to plant in your area (especially if the tree will be shipped bareroot). If you work outside the home, consider delivery to your workplace to avoid having it left on your doorstep, where it could be exposed to cold, wind, and sun.
● For new species or cultivars, order early to avoid receiving a "sold out" notice or an inferior substitute. Specify "no substitution" if you won't accept one.
● When your tree arrives, unpack it immediately. Read the label to be sure the correct tree was shipped. Check the plant's condition: If roots are totally dry, or the plant is broken, repackage and return it.

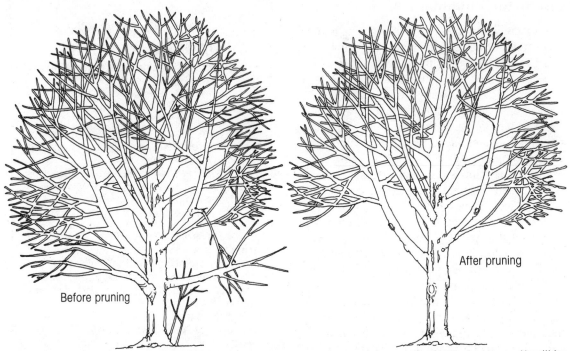

Before pruning

After pruning

Pruning a mature tree. If you've inherited a mature tree, some judicious pruning can make it better looking and healthier. If you're not an experienced tree-climber, hire an arborist to rejuvenate your tree. *Before:* Dead and diseased branches, watersprouts, tight crotch angles, and rubbing or crossing branches weaken the tree's structure and make it look neglected. *After:* The tree has been rejuvenated and thinned out, and branches have been headed back to encourage dense new growth.

way of a planned addition or pool or driveway, it may be worth a try.

Be realistic about the size of tree you can move yourself. Very young deciduous trees may sometimes be successfully moved bareroot. But the bigger the root ball you can dig and move, the more successful your transplanting operation will be. Earth is heavy — very heavy. Figure on a root ball at least 1½' across and 1' deep for every inch of trunk. If you want to move a tree with a 2" trunk, that's a ball of earth roughly 3' across and 2' deep—and that will weigh a few hundred pounds! If your back aches just thinking about it, consider hiring a nursery owner or

arborist to dig and transplant the tree.

When you transplant a tree, you cut many of its roots, leaving them behind in their old location. Transplanting while the tree is dormant lessens the chance of leaves drying out while new roots are growing. Root pruning in advance of the move encourages the remaining roots to branch and makes it easier for the tree to become reestablished. Six months to a year before transplanting, slice through the soil around the tree to a depth of 8"-12", outlining the root ball. Make a narrow trench and fill it with sphagnum moss, so that any roots that regrow will be easy to lift. Prune the tree, thinning out about ⅓ of the branches, so there is less topgrowth for the roots to support.

When you're ready to move the tree, widen the trench, digging outward until it is at least 1½' wide around the full diameter of the root ball. Slice through any small roots that have grown beyond the original cut. Deepen the trench until you get to a depth where the soil contains few roots. Then begin digging under to shape the ball.

If your soil has enough clay to hold the ball together well, completely undercut the ball. If you can lift the tree and ball—lifting from under the ball—put it into a large container to move it. If the tree is too heavy to lift, gently tip the ball, then position a piece of burlap or other covering material under the ball. Gently work the material under and around the ball, and secure it with rope or nails.

If your soil is sandy, prior to undercutting the ball, wrap the top of the ball with burlap or other strong material, and secure it with heavy cord or twine as close to the base as possible. Then undercut the ball, gently tip it over, and secure the rest of the covering material across the bottom of the ball.

Get help lifting the tree out of its hole, levering it out from below. Then transport it to its new location and replant. Water well and mulch.

Trees and Construction

In some cases, you may find it more practical or desirable to leave large trees in place and build around them, rather than transplanting them elsewhere. Be sure that you—and your construction crew—do everything you can to minimize direct and indirect damage to the trees.

Direct tree damage occurs when you cut roots; damage or tear away trunk bark; break, tear away, or incorrectly prune off branches; or tie or nail items to the trees. Indirect tree damage occurs when you strip away topsoil and leaf

---

WHERE ARE THE ROOTS?

Contrary to old beliefs, tree roots don't stop where the tree canopy stops—the "drip line"—nor do they penetrate to great soil depths. The roots of almost all trees, both in wooded and in open areas, spread out 1–3 times beyond the canopy. For this reason, if possible, apply fertilizer over this entire area, and protect it from soil compaction and other stresses that damage roots.

Most of the roots of your trees are located in the top few inches of soil. Only a limited number of trees in native stands have deep roots called taproots. Most other trees have no taproots—they stopped either due to limited soil oxygen or because they were cut off when the nursery dug the trees.

---

litter, compact the soil, dump additional fill soil atop the roots, and burn or bury waste materials near the trees. You also indirectly damage the trees by paving over open areas that absorbed rainfall, removing neighboring plants that provided wind and sun protection, and creating new drainage patterns for rainwater and runoff.

Your top priority is to preserve the natural root environment. If you keep people and equipment away from the tree, you will minimize the chances of damage being done to the tree trunk and branches. If possible, erect fences around the drip line of trees before construction begins to keep vehicles and piles of building materials away from the sensitive root zone and trunk. Once construction is completed, apply mulch to replace leaf litter that was removed, prune structurally weak branches, and provide water and fertilizer to help stimulate new roots.

Pests and Problems

Frequent inspection of your trees will help minimize problems. Your best defenses are to

LOLLIPOP TREE SYNDROME

If you need to reduce the size of a tree, remove branches back to the main branches from which they originated, or back to the tree trunk. Topping your tree by chopping branches off in the middle leaves large branch stubs and destroys the natural crown shape of your tree, making it look like a lollipop. It stimulates the growth of watersprouts, which are upright-growing, unbranched stems that develop very quickly and never return to the normal branch pattern of your tree. Topping also weakens your tree, turning it into a liability or a potential hazard in your landscape.

When large branches are topped, the branch stub that is left begins to die. As the wood dies, decay fungi and insects can get into the wood, further weakening the tree. During wind, ice, and snow storms, these weakened branch stubs break from the tree more easily than healthy branches that have been properly pruned.

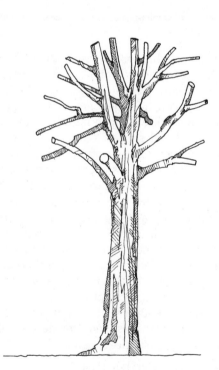

Tree form just after topping

Regrowth after topping

buy good-quality, pest-free trees to avoid introducing pests or disease; to plant your trees in proper environments to encourage vigorous growth; to use good maintenance practices; and to minimize environmental stresses.

Biotic or pathological problems are caused by living organisms—insects, mites, fungi, bacteria, viruses, nematodes, and rodents. Abiotic or physiological problems are caused by nonliving things—improper planting and maintenance, poor soil conditions, air pollution, injury, compacted soil, construction damage, and lightning.

Far more tree problems are caused by abiotic problems, which weaken trees, allowing boring insects and decay fungi to attack. If your tree shows signs of ill health, check for poor conditions that may have allowed the pest or disease to get a foothold.

The plant family bothered by the greatest number of insect and disease problems is the rose family. This large family includes such trees as crab apples, flowering pears, cherries, peaches and plums, hawthorns, serviceberries, and mountain ash. Crab apples are particularly susceptible to problems; buy only those cultivars that are resistant to the diseases rust, scab, powdery mildew, and fire blight. (See the Malus entry for a list of disease-resistant crab apples.) Other trees, such as flowering dogwood, maples, sycamores, birches, elms, locusts, and oaks, may also have numerous pest or disease problems. Ask your nursery owner for advice before making the purchase.

Whenever a disease or insect problem is seen, try to control it by removing the pest or the affected plant part. Don't compost or burn infected plants. Remember to sanitize tools after pruning infested or infected wood by cleaning them with a 10 percent bleach solution.

Insects

Most insect problems of trees are caused by a relatively small number of insects and mites (technically classed as arachnids). These pests have their preferences: Some primarily damage leaves, and others primarily damage branches and trunk.

Insects eat leaves and suck plant sap from them. The larvae of moths and butterflies, such as bagworms, cankerworms, webworms, tent caterpillars, and gypsy moths, are especially voracious leaf-eaters. Highly noticeable webs of Eastern tent caterpillars and fall webworms protect the larvae from predators while they munch your leaves. Although the nests are unsightly, trees usually recover from infestations. Remove and destroy any webs you can reach.

Gypsy moth populations rise to a peak in cycles of several years, causing almost complete defoliation in areas of heavy infestation. Handpicking and spraying BT (*Bacillus thuringiensis*) are the best defenses against severe attacks of gypsy moths. In winter, check your trees for the light brown egg masses and scrape them off into a container of ammonia.

Other major insect pests that damage leaves are aphids and adelgids, various beetles and bugs, miners, scales, and spider mites.

Insects are always present on trees. Populations must be extreme before the tree suffers any real damage. Don't rush to the sprayer as soon as you spot a caterpillar or two. Remember, the goal is a healthy tree, not complete insect annihilation. Learn to recognize harmful pests and the signs of infestation: curled leaves, stunted growth, deformed flowers.

Try handpicking and pruning off affected branches before you reach for other controls. Even BT is not innocuous. It does kill gypsy moth larvae, tent caterpillars, and other undesirables—but it will also kill any other caterpillar that happens to eat a tainted leaf, including the beautiful luna moth, giant silk moths, and dozens of others.

Stems are damaged when insects such as borers and scales either bore into them or feed on them. Cicadas cause stem damage when they

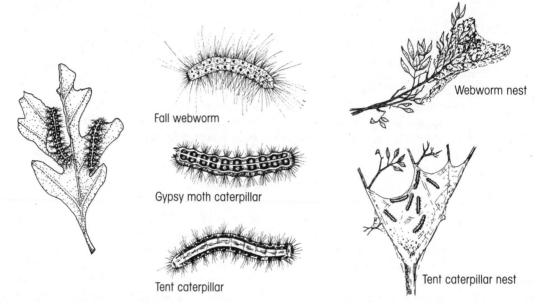

Fall webworm

Gypsy moth caterpillar

Tent caterpillar

Webworm nest

Tent caterpillar nest

Common tree pests. Three of the most troublesome pests of deciduous trees are chewing caterpillars. Look for tent caterpillar nests in spring in the crotches of cherries and other trees; fall webworms appear in late summer, their webs festooning branch tips of walnuts and other trees. Hairy gypsy moth caterpillars are hard to overlook in peak years of infestations.

lay their eggs into slits in twigs. Microscopic, wormlike nematodes also cause problems on the roots of many trees.

Turn to the Insects, Insecticides, and Organic Pest Management entries to find out more about controlling insect problems.

Diseases

Tree diseases occur on leaves, stems, and roots. Many pathological diseases are difficult to distinguish from physiological problems. For instance, while fungi and bacteria can cause leaf spot diseases, spots on tree leaves can also be caused by nutrient deficiencies, improperly applied pesticides, road salts, and even drought. Be careful to properly identify a tree problem before you look for a control or corrective measure.

Most tree diseases are caused by fungi,

although a few major diseases, such as fire blight on pears and other members of the rose family, are caused by bacteria. Flowering peaches and plums are also bothered by viral diseases.

Diseases of tree leaves are generally spots, anthracnoses, scorches, blights, rusts, and mildews. You will see them on your trees most frequently during moist weather and when plants are under environmental stress. Diseases of tree stems are generally cankers, blights, and decays. You will see these diseases when trees have been damaged by improper pruning, mechanical injury, and other maintenance and environmental factors. The major diseases of tree roots are root rots. Root rots occur when soils are poorly drained and may be intensified if roots have been injured by such things as construction damage and trenching. Refer to the Disease and

Organic Pest Management entries for more information on disease prevention and control.

Physical Damage

You can damage a tree by nailing items to it or gouging it with a lawn mower. Animals also

More On
TREES

You'll find more information about caring for trees in the Christmas Trees, Evergreens, Fruit Trees, and Nut Trees entries.
The following individual tree entries include descriptions, landscape use suggestions, care information (including thinning and harvesting for food-crop trees), and cultivar listings: Abies (fir), Acer (maple), Aesculus (horse chestnut), Albizia, Amelanchier (serviceberry), Apple, Apricot, Avocado, Betula (birch), Buxus (boxwood), Camellia, Carpinus (hornbeam), Cedrus (cedar), Cherry, Citrus (oranges and other citrus fruits), Cornus (dogwood), Crataegus (hawthorn), Eucalyptus, Fagus (beech), Fig, Fraxinus (ash), Ginkgo, Gleditsia (honey locust), Halesia (silverbell), Hamamelis (witch hazel), Hibiscus (mallow), Hydrangea, Ilex (holly), Juglans (walnut), Juniperus (juniper), Lagerstroemia (crape myrtle), Larix (larch), Ligustrum (privet), Liquidambar (sweet gum), Liriodendron (tulip tree), Magnolia, Malus (crab apple), Nyssa (tupelo), Ostrya (hop hornbeam), Palms, Peach, Pear, Persimmon, Picea (spruce), Pinus (pine), Platanus (planetree), Plum, Populus (poplar), Prunus (flowering cherry), Pyrus (flowering pear), Quercus (oak), Quince, Robinia (locust), Salix (willow), Sorbus (mountain ash), Syringa (lilac), Taxus (yew), Thuja (arborvitae), Tilia (linden), Tsuga (hemlock), Ulmus (elm), Viburnum, and Zelkova.

damage trees. Birds may occasionally break branches or drill branches, looking for sap or insects. Moles damage your trees by cutting the roots as they tunnel, and voles actually feed on the roots. Mice and rabbits damage trees by feeding on the bark. Deer damage trees by browsing on young branch tips and by rubbing their antlers on the trunks and branches.

Handle your trees gently. Avoid lawn mower damage by using mulch or beds of groundcovers to surround the trunk. A cat that patrols outdoors now and then is one way to control rodents. Fence to keep out deer. For more on controlling animals, see the Animal Pests entry.

Propagating Trees

Tree seeds are often notoriously slow to germinate, and many need special treatment to break dormancy. Variations in plant form, or in flower and leaf color or size, may occur with seed propagation. A good example is the range of needle colors, from pale blues to grayish and greenish blues, that develop on seed-propagated Colorado spruce (*Picea pungens*). But if you have the space for a small nursery bed, and plenty of time and patience, you might enjoy the challenge of growing from seed. The Seeds and Seedlings entry will help you start seeds successfully.

When you take cuttings or use the layering method, you preserve the exact characteristics of the parent tree. Some trees can be propagated from stem cuttings, and some, from cuttings from the roots. Timing and technique are important. The Cuttings, Layering, and Propagation entries will give you a start.

More complicated techniques such as grafting and tissue culture also produce an exact duplicate of the parent tree. Try your hand at grafting with a flowering dogwood (*Cornus florida*) or a crab apple (*Malus* spp.) See the Grafting entry for more details. ❖

Tropaeolum

Nasturtium. Summer- and fall-blooming annuals; edible flowers.

Description: Fragrant, cup-shaped, 2″ flowers in yellow, orange, and red bloom among round, yellowish green leaves on short vines or 1′ mounds.

How to grow: Because they transplant poorly, sow seeds directly where they are to bloom after the soil has warmed up. Nasturtiums thrive in sunny, cool areas in average soil, but they adapt fairly well to heat. Provide support for the climbers. Control aphids with soap spray.

Landscape uses: Nasturtiums look pretty in beds, borders, edges, pots, and hanging baskets, and on short trellises.

Best cultivars: 'Double Dwarf Jewel', 1′ mix; 'Alaska', single, 1′, creamy variegated leaves. ❖

Tsuga

Hemlock. Needle-leaved evergreen trees.

Description: *Tsuga canadensis,* Canada or Eastern hemlock, has soft, fine-textured foliage and a loosely pyramidal form. It grows 40′-75′ tall. Zones 3-8.

T. caroliniana, Carolina hemlock, has needles that are somewhat darker green and blunter; it can reach 70′. Zones 5-7.

Both species produce decorative tiny (1″) cones.

How to grow: Hemlocks grow naturally in cooler mountain climates in rocky, shallow soil. In the landscape, they do best with shaded roots, even moisture, and a deep mulch. Hemlocks can grow in full sun in the North and rarely need pruning.

Landscape uses: Hemlocks make charming specimens or effective informal screens or hedges. Canada hemlock can also be sheared to make a formal hedge. ❖

Tulipa

Tulip. Spring-blooming bulbs.

Description: The most familiar tulips are hybrids that bear oval to cuplike blooms on long stems, but within the genus are flowers from barely 1″ to over 8″ wide, resembling stars, bowls, or eggs; some are double and resemble peonies, while others look like lilies and water lilies. The most exotic bear fanciful fringes on the petal tips, or their petals are deeply cut and feathered like tropical parrots. Colors cover virtually the entire range except blue. Some have subtly blended colors, while others offer strikingly striped or edged patterns.

Although generally not fragrant, a few, especially the parrots, have a sweet, fruity perfume. They bloom singly or (rarely) in clusters on gracefully curving to strictly upright stems, reaching from 3″-36″ above broad, fleshy green to blue-green leaves, some (mostly the Greigii cultivars) beautifully lined with dark purple. The species typically produce much smaller leaves than their hybrid relatives.

Species worth trying include *Tulipa acuminata,* horned tulip, with red-and-yellow blooms; *T. chrysantha,* golden tulip, with red-and-yellow flowers; *T. clusiana,* lady or peppermint stick tulip, with red-and-white blooms; and *T. praestans* 'Fusilier', a cluster bloomer in bright red-orange. Most tulips are hardy to Zone 3; they do poorly in Zones 8-9.

How to grow: Virtually all tulips are easy to grow. Plant in fall before the ground freezes, in a sunny to partly shady spot with average, well-drained soil. Bury bulbs at a depth 2-3 times their width, measuring the depth from the top of the bulb. You should plant many of the cultivars even deeper to help encourage the bulbs to remain blooming-sized. Shallow planting usually results in good bloom the first year, followed by progressively disappointing displays in succeeding years. Fertilize like daffodils (see the Narcissus entry) to prolong the useful life of

CHOOSING TERRIFIC TULIPS

It's easy to get lost among the hundreds of beautiful tulips offered. How can you choose the best? First, decide whether you want bloom throughout the season or just a big show for a few weeks in mid- to late spring. Then choose tulips that bloom when you want a show, or select some from each group for a long bloom season.

Here are some popular tulip types listed according to bloom season. Species tulips bloom early or during mid-season.

Early-Blooming Tulips

Single early: 2''–4'' flowers; 12''–14'' stems; often fragrant.
Double early: 3''–4'' many-petaled flowers; 12''–14'' stems.
Greigii: 3'' long flowers; 6''–12'' stems; purple-striped foliage.

Kaufmanniana: 3'' long flowers; 4''–8'' tall; called waterlily tulips because of the flower shape; foliage sometimes mottled.
Fosteriana: 4'' long flowers; 1' stems; includes 'Emperor' strain tulips.

Mid-Season Tulips

Darwin hybrid: 3''–4'' flowers; 3' stems.
Triumph: 2''–4'' flowers; 15''–18'' stems.

Late-Season Tulips

Lily-flowered: 2''–4'' flowers with curved, spreading petals; 20'' stems.
Single late: 3''–4'' long, egg-shaped flowers; 1½'–2' stems.
Parrot: 6'' wide feather-edged flowers, often with contrasting colors; 20'' stems.
Double late: 6'' wide, peony-like flowers; 20'' stems; the last tulips to bloom.

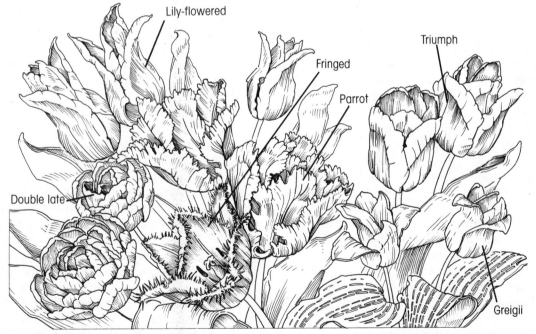

Tulip flower forms. Tulips come in a striking variety of flower forms and sizes, from the tiny species tulips to 6'' wide double late cultivars. Some of the most popular are shown here.

your tulips. If you are bedding them out and plan to remove them after they fade, or if you are growing them as annual cut flowers, don't fertilize—the bulb contains everything the flower needs to bloom its first year. Water if spring rains amount to less than 1″ or so per week. Deadhead tulips after bloom if you want them to remain for another display the next year, but expect the flowers to be smaller and on shorter stems. Don't remove the foliage until it has turned quite yellow and starts to die down. If you need to divide a clump, do so as you would for daffodils.

Control tulip fire (a fungal disease that will spread rapidly through an infected planting) by deep planting and immediate destruction of plants that wilt suddenly. Botrytis sometimes attacks the flowers, turning them into a twisted or collapsed mess; remove and destroy the flowers as soon as you notice it. Mice, squirrels, and chipmunks eat the bulbs with gusto. Planting a small group of bulbs in baskets made of ⅓″-½″ wire mesh should discourage them; so will a large piece laid 1″ over the bulbs in a larger planting. Rabbits may nibble the leaves and flowers; a few deer can eat a planting to the ground overnight. Scatter blood meal or lime to help repel these pests.

Landscape uses: Grow small to large masses of tulips throughout a border in between perennials and annuals, which will disguise the yellowing foliage. Plant them in formal beds and in sweeps in lawns, removing them after bloom and replacing with annuals. They look marvelous against an evergreen hedge and in groups at the edges of patios. Smaller species are perfect for rock gardens, and many are wonderful forced in pots, particularly the early bloomers. All combine nicely with phlox (*Phlox* spp.), pansies, bleeding hearts (*Dicentra* spp.), rock cress (*Aubrieta* spp.), candytuft (*Iberis* spp.), irises, azaleas (*Rhododendron* spp.), and lilacs. You can enjoy 6-8 weeks of bloom from the earliest tiny species to the last giant cultivars. ❖

Turnip

Brassica rapa, Rapifera group
Cruciferae

Fast-growing turnips thrive in cool temperatures; hot weather makes the leaves tough and the roots woody and bitter. Ample moisture and temperatures of 50°-70°F encourage rapid growth and a high-quality crop. Enjoy the roots and tops either raw or cooked.

Planting: Turnips thrive in well-drained, deeply worked soil on a sunny site.

Plant seeds outdoors three weeks before the last frost in the spring or—for a usually better-tasting and more productive fall crop—plant in midsummer about two months before the first frost. The soil must be at least 40°F for germination, which takes from 7-14 days.

Sow spring crops ¼″ deep and fall crops ½″ deep. Broadcast the seeds, and later thin them to 3″-4″ apart, or plant seeds in rows spaced 1½′ apart.

Growing guidelines: Keep the soil evenly moist to promote fast growth and the best flavor. When plants are 5″ tall, apply a mulch at least 2″ thick. No extra fertilizer is necessary in well-prepared soil.

Problems: See the Cabbage entry for details on pest and disease control.

Harvesting: Harvest greens when they're large enough to pick, leaving at least a few of the tops to keep the root alive. Loosen the earth at the base of the leaves with a spading fork before harvesting roots. Small roots are the most tender, so pull when they are 1″-3″ in diameter. To store the roots, twist off the tops, leaving ½″ of stem. Place undamaged roots in a cool, dark place, such as a basement or root cellar. Don't wash off soil that clings to roots; it helps protect roots in storage. They will keep for several months. In mild areas, you can overwinter roots in the ground by covering them with a thick mulch. ❖

Ulmus

Elm. Deciduous trees.

Description: *Ulmus alata,* winged elm, has a pyramidal form and is 30'-40' tall. It flowers inconspicuously in spring and bears small, fuzzy, waferlike fruits. The small (2½") leaves turn soft reds and oranges most years. Thin twigs sport corky wings. This Southeastern native elm can be weedy and is considered undesirable by some, but it grows beautifully in poor, compacted soils. Zones 6-8.

U. americana, American elm, is the stately 60'-80', vase-shaped tree that for many years shaded North American campuses and avenues. Much publicized in the wake of the Dutch elm disease (DED) epidemic that decimated huge numbers of this species, American elm is a beautiful, but no longer recommended, shade tree. Zones 2-8.

U. parvifolia, Chinese or lacebark elm, is a handsome tree with flaking bark that exposes patches of tan, green, and cream. Growing 40'-50', Chinese elm has inconspicuous, late-summer flowers and small (1"-3") leaves that turn yellow or purple shades when conditions favor good autumn color development. Zones 5-8.

U. pumila, Siberian elm, is a fast-growing, weak-wooded tree with few assets beyond its hardiness and ability to grow on very poor sites. It has an irregular, open form and a landscape height of 50'-70'. During dormancy, Siberian elm's round black buds distinguish it from the highly desirable Chinese elm, which has relatively flat buds. Zones 2-8.

How to grow: Elms are adapted to a variety of soil types but require good drainage and full sun. While many American elms still stand, far more have fallen to DED. Control programs are somewhat effective, but until DED is controlled, admire American elms, but don't plant them. Breeding programs continue to search for DED-resistant American elm cultivars, often crossing it with Asian elm species. No reliably resistant trees have yet been selected that have American elm's desirable features.

Elm leaf beetles will feed on all elms, but seem to prefer Siberian elm. The ½" long adults are drab yellow-green, black-striped beetles that eat round holes in young elm leaves in spring, then lay eggs that hatch into leaf-skeletonizing larvae. The result is an unhealthy-looking tree with brown foliage. Elms often respond with another flush of growth just in time for the next generation of beetles. Adults also overwinter in nearby buildings. Spray BTSD (*Bacillus thuringiensis* var. *san diego*) after eggs hatch (late May through June) to control larvae.

Landscape uses: Naturalize winged elm among other trees. Use Chinese elm for shade and as a focal point, much as you would American elm; plant Siberian elm hybrids on difficult sites. ❖

597

Urban Gardening

Urban gardeners face different challenges than their rural and suburban counterparts. Urban gardeners need ingenuity to garden in small spaces with blocked sunlight, poor soil, and unreliable water sources. Soil and air pollutants, theft, vandalism, and politics further complicate city gardening.

A near absence of wildlife damage helps to balance the disadvantages of urban planting. Another benefit is a frost-free season as much as one month longer than that in surrounding areas, due to the warming effects of buildings and pavement. Easily managed smaller gardens demand less time but inspire creativity in the quest for productive beauty. City farmers turn yards, rooftops, fire escapes, and a variety of containers into fields of plants.

In 1976, Congress established urban gardening programs through the Cooperative Extension Service. The not-for-profit American Community Gardening Association (ACGA) also promotes gardening nationwide. See the Community Gardens entry for more information on ACGA programs.

Urban Concerns

The key to city gardening success is adapting traditional gardening methods to suit the limits imposed by an urban environment.

Space: Design your garden to maximize growing area while preserving living space. Make the most of your garden space by growing compact (bush-type) cultivars. To utilize vertical space, build trellises or fences for vines. Interplant fast- and slow-growing vegetables. See the Container Gardening and Intensive Gardening entries for more information on these techniques.

Light: Select plants and a design to suit each location, based on the total light it receives. Most plants need at least 6 hours of daily sunlight to produce flowers and fruits.

Soil: Most urban soils are compacted and clayey, and have a high heavy-metal content.

Improve such soils by adding compost, peat moss, aged sawdust, or other types of organic matter. Many cities make compost or mulch from tree trimmings and leaf pickups. Contact local parks or street departments about these often free soil amendments.

Sometimes soil is absent or so poor it can't quickly be improved. An alternative to amending existing soil is to bring in soil for raised beds or containers.

Theft and vandalism: Most urban gardening takes place in densely populated or publicly accessible places. Theft and vandalism can be a frustrating reality. Fences keep honest people honest, but involving area youth and adults in gardening is a more effective tactic. Share garden space and/or knowledge with your neighbors.

To reduce vandalism and theft, keep your garden well maintained, repair damage immediately, harvest ripened vegetables daily, and plant more vegetables than you need. Grow ornamentals in the garden to hide ripening vegetables.

Soil contaminants: Excessive lead, cadmium, and mercury levels are common in urban soils. Sources of such pollution include leaded paint, motor vehicle exhaust, and industrial waste. Poisoning from eating contaminated produce can affect all gardeners, especially young children whose bodies are actively growing and who tend to put their hands in their mouths.

You can reduce the amount of lead that plants absorb from soil and also keep down dust that may carry lead by adding organic matter to soil and mulching heavily. Planting food crops away from streets and keeping soil pH levels at 6.7 or higher will also help prevent plants from taking up lead. If contaminant levels are too high, garden in containers filled with clean soil and wash crops thoroughly before eating them.

Testing to monitor soil contaminants is strongly urged for city gardens, particularly those used by children. Contact your local extension service office to find out what soil tests are available. ❖

Vegetable Gardening

Fresh-picked sweet corn, tomatoes, and snap peas are a taste treat you can only get from your backyard vegetable garden. The quality and flavor of fresh vegetables will reward you from early in the growing season until late fall. And when you garden organically, you know that your harvest is free of potentially harmful chemical residues.

Vegetable gardens are ideal sites for putting organic soil improvement and pest management techniques into practice. Since you're working the soil each year, you'll have lots of opportunities to add organic matter and soil amendments that help keep the soil naturally balanced. As you make your yearly plan for planting and caring for your garden, you can incorporate crop rotation and other cultural pest prevention techniques. And there's a broad range of organically acceptable pest control methods and products for vegetable crops.

Although the plants grown in vegetable gardens are a diverse group from many different plant families, they share broad general cultural requirements. Most will thrive in well-drained soil with a pH of 6.5-7.0. Some will tolerate frost; others will tolerate some shade. If you pick an appropriate site, prepare the soil well, and keep your growing crops weeded and watered, you should have little trouble growing vegetables successfully.

This entry will serve as your guide to planning, preparing, and tending your vegetable plot through the seasons. Many other entries in this encyclopedia provide detailed information on topics such as soil improvement and pest control that you'll find helpful. See "Putting It All Together" on page 600 if you want facts about individual crops and see "More On : Vegetables" on page 618 for a listing of vegetable crops that have separate entries.

Planning Your Garden

Planning your garden can be as much fun as planting it. When you plan a garden, you'll balance all your hopes and wishes for the crops you'd like to harvest against your local growing conditions, as well as the space you have available to plant. Planning involves choosing a site (unless you already have an established garden), deciding on a garden style, selecting crops and cultivars, and mapping your garden.

Site Selection

Somewhere in your yard, there is a good place for a vegetable garden. The ideal site has these characteristics:

1. Full or almost full sun. In warm climates, some vegetables can get by on 6 hours of direct sunshine each day, while a full day of sun is needed in cool climates. The best sites for vegetable gardens usually are on the south or west side of a house, where sunshine is most abundant. If part of the site you select is too shady for planting, put your compost pile there.

2. Good drainage. A slight slope is good for vegetable gardens. The soil will get well soaked by rain or irrigation water, and excess will run off. Avoid low places where water accumulates; these are ideal breeding places for diseases.

3. Limited competition from nearby trees. Tree roots take up huge amounts of water. Leave as much space as possible between large trees and your garden. Plant shade-tolerant shrubs or small fruits between trees and your garden.

4. Easy access to water. If you can't get a hose or irrigation line to a prospective garden site, don't plant vegetables there. No matter what your local climate is, you'll most likely have to provide supplemental water at some point in the growing season, or your harvest will suffer.

5. Accessibility. Organic gardens need large amounts of mulch, plus periodic infusions of other bulky materials such as well-rotted manure or rock fertilizers. If you have a large garden, you should be able to drive a truck up to its edge for easy unloading. In narrow city lots, the garden access path should be wide enough for a cart or wheelbarrow.

PUTTING IT ALL TOGETHER

Vegetable gardeners will find helpful information to fine-tune their gardens throughout this encyclopedia. Here's a summary of other entries to refer to for additional information.

Preparing the soil: The Soil entry offers detailed instructions for evaluating and improving garden soil. Under Green Manure you'll find instructions for seeding and working with green manure crops. Mulch gives a rundown of the characteristics and uses of many kinds of mulch. Fertilizers suggests specific materials to use for balancing the soil and feeding plants. The pH and Plant Nutrition entries explain the roles of various nutrients in plant growth.

Planting: For more information on starting and planting vegetable seeds, see Seeds and Seedlings, Transplanting, and individual vegetable entries. Companion Planting offers suggestions on planting flowers and herbs among your vegetables to help attract beneficial insects or repel pests.

Care during the season: Weeds offers tips on the right tools and techniques for controlling weeds. Fertilizers explains how to apply dry and foliar fertilizer materials for best results. Organic Pest Management outlines the strategies and techniques you can apply to help prevent and control insects and diseases. Insecticides, Insects, Beneficial Insects, and Disease offer details on control methods.

Harvesting and storage: For information on processing vegetables, see the Canning, Drying Food Crops, and Freezing entries.

Once you find a site that has these characteristics, double-check for hidden problems. For example, don't locate your garden over septic-tank field lines, buried utility cables, or water lines.

Garden Layout

Once you've decided on a site, think about the type of vegetable garden you want. Possible layouts range from traditional row plantings to intensive raised beds and container gardens.

Row planting: A row garden, in which vegetables are planted in parallel lines, is easy to organize and plant. However, it's not as space efficient as more intensive methods, such as raised beds. You may spend more time weeding unless you mulch heavily and early between rows. Also, you'll get less yield per area than you would from an intensively planted garden. Row planting is quick and efficient for large plantings of crops such as beans or corn.

You can enhance the appearance and productivity of a row garden by making a raised bed along the front edge and planting it with herbs and flowers. "Sod Strips Save Work" on page 604 describes an easy way to start a row garden.

Beds: Productivity, efficient use of space, less weeding, and shading the soil are all benefits of intensively planted beds. Beds are raised planting areas, generally with carefully enriched soil, so they can be planted intensively. While they require more initial time to prepare, they save time on weeding or mulching later in the season. Because they're more space efficient, you'll also get higher yields per area than from a traditional row garden.

Beds for vegetables should be no more than 4' wide so you can easily reach the center of the bed to plant, weed, and harvest. See the Raised Bed Gardening entry for directions on making raised beds. "Topping Off Your Beds" on page 602 shows interesting ways to adapt beds to your needs.

Spot gardens: If your yard is small, having no suitable space for a separate vegetable garden, look for sunny spots where you can fit small plantings of your favorite crops. Plant a small bed of salad greens and herbs near your kitchen door for easy access when preparing meals. Tuck vegetables into flower beds. You can dress up crops that aren't ornamental, such as tomatoes, by underplanting them with annuals such as nasturtiums and marigolds. For ideas on incorporating vegetables into your landscape, see the Edible Landscaping entry.

Containers: You may not be able to grow all your favorite vegetables in containers, but many dwarf cultivars of vegetables will grow well in pots or planters. Garden catalogs include dwarf tomato, cucumber, pepper, and even squash cultivars suitable for container growing. Vegetables that are naturally small, such as loosehead lettuce, scallions, and many herbs, also grow nicely in containers. See the Container Gardening entry for details on choices of containers and soil mixes.

Crop Choices

Generally, vegetables can be divided into cool-weather, warm-weather, and hot-weather crops. "Some Like It Hot" on page 606 lists popular vegetables in these categories.

Consider the length of your growing season (the period of time between the last frost in spring and the first one in fall), seasonal rainfall patterns, and other environmental factors when choosing vegetables. There are many new fast-maturing and heat- or cold-tolerant cultivars that make it easier for Northern gardeners to grow hot-weather crops such as melons and for Southern gardeners to be able to enjoy cool-loving crops such as spinach. See "Smart Shopping: Making the Right Choices" on page 603 for more ideas on how to make good crop and cultivar choices for your garden.

Have some fun when you choose plants for your vegetable garden as well. Make some of your selections for beauty as well as flavor. Beans with purple or variegated pods are easy to spot for picking and lovely to behold. Swiss chard with red ribs makes a dramatic statement, and purple kohlrabi is oddly eye-catching. Small-fruited Japanese eggplants make wonderful container subjects. Try some historical heirlooms or little-known imports. Cultivars endorsed by All-America Selections (AAS) also are good bets. For more details, refer to the Heirloom Plants and All-America Selections entries.

SMALL GARDEN STRATEGIES

If your appetite for fresh vegetables is bigger than the space you have to grow them in, try these ways to coax the most produce from the least space:

● Emphasize vertical crops that grow up rather than out: trellis snow peas, shell peas, pole beans, and cucumbers.

● Interplant fast-maturing salad crops (lettuce, radishes, spinach, and beets) together in 2' square blocks. Succession plant every two weeks in early spring and early fall.

● Avoid overplanting any single vegetable. Summer squash is the number one offender when it comes to rampant overproduction. Two plants each of zucchini, yellow-neck, and a novelty summer squash will yield plenty.

● Choose medium- and small-fruited cultivars of tomatoes and peppers. The smaller the fruits, the more the plants tend to produce. Beefsteak tomatoes and big bell peppers produce comparatively few fruits per plant.

● Experiment with unusual vegetables that are naturally compact—such as kohlrabi, bok choy, and Oriental eggplant. Experiment with dwarf cultivars of larger vegetables.

● Maintain permanent clumps of perpetual vegetables such as chives, hardy scallions, and perennial herbs. Even a small garden should always have something to offer.

Garden Mapping

As you fill in seed order forms, it's wise to map planned locations for your crops. Otherwise, you may end up with far too little or too much seed. Depending on the size of your garden, you may need to make a formal plan drawn to scale.

Consider these points as you figure out your planting needs and fill in your map:

● Are you growing just enough of a crop for fresh eating, or will you be preserving some of your harvest? For some crops, it takes surprisingly little seed to produce enough to feed a family. You can refer to seed catalogs or check individual vegetable entries for information on how much to plant.

• Are you planning to rotate crops? Changing the position of plants in different crop families from year to year can help reduce pest problems.

• Are you going to plant crops in spring and again later in the season for a fall harvest? Order seed for both plantings at the same time.

For more ideas to help you create your own garden map and plan, see "Vegetable Garden Planning" on page 605.

Preparing the Soil

Since most vegetables are fast-growing annuals, they need garden soil that provides a wide range of plant nutrients and loose soil that plant roots can penetrate easily. In an organic vegetable garden, soil with high organic matter content and biological activity is paramount in importance. Every year when you harvest vegetables, you're carting off part of the reservoir of nutrients that was in your vegetable garden soil. To keep the soil in balance, you need to replace those nutrients. Look for every opportunity to incorporate different forms of organic matter into your soil.

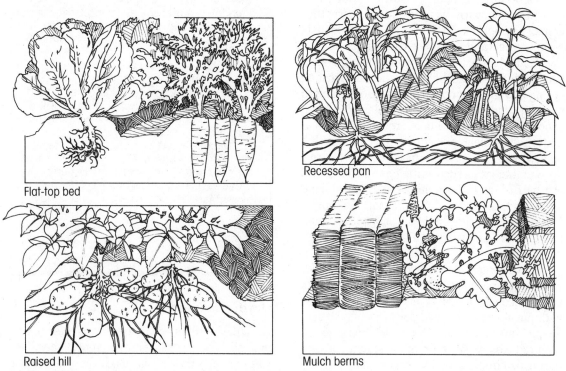

Flat-top bed

Recessed pan

Raised hill

Mulch berms

Topping off your beds. When shaping soil into beds or rows, consider the needs of the vegetables you will be planting. Flat-top beds are best for small-seeded crops that need lots of water, such as lettuce and other leafy greens, carrots, and cabbage-family plants. Use raised hills or rows when planting crops that may be prone to foliar diseases, such as cantaloupes, cucumbers, potatoes, corn, and squash. Recessed pans help slow evaporation of soil moisture; use in hot climates for crops such as beans, okra, and eggplant. Put up mulch berms made of hay bales or layers of soil and mulch alongside beds in arid climates to retain soil moisture and protect plants from drying winds.

Seed catalogs and seed racks present a dazzling array of choices for the vegetable gardener. They all look tasty and beautiful in the pictures, but here's how to choose:

● If you're a beginning gardener, talk with other gardeners and your local extension agent. Ask what vegetables grow best in your area, and start with those crops. Most extension service offices also provide lists of recommended cultivars.

● Seek out catalogs and plant lists offered by seed companies that specialize in regionally adapted selections.

● Match cultivars to your garden's characteristics and problems. Look for cultivars that are resistant to disease organisms that may be widespread in your area, such as VF tomato cultivars—which are resistant to Verticillium and Fusarium fungi.

● If you buy seeds by the packet, take note of how many seeds you're getting. Seed quantity per packet varies widely. Some packets of new or special cultivars may contain fewer than 20 seeds.

● When buying transplants at local garden centers, always check for disease and insect problems.

● Ask whether the transplants you're buying have been hardened off yet. If the salesperson doesn't know what you're talking about, take the hint, and buy your transplants from a more knowledgeable supplier.

● Remember, with tranplants, larger size doesn't always mean better quality. Look for stocky transplants with uniform green leaves. Don't buy transplants that are already flowering—they won't survive the shock of tranplanting as well as younger plants will.

Assessing Your Soil

If you're starting a new vegetable garden or switching from conventional to organic methods (or if you've just been disappointed with past yields or crop quality), start by testing your soil. Soil acidity or alkalinity, which is measured as soil pH, can affect plant performance. Most vegetables prefer soil with a pH of 6.5-7.0. Overall soil fertility also will influence yield, especially for heavy-feeding crops such as broccoli and tomatoes. A soil test will reveal soil pH as well as any nutrient imbalances. The Soil entry explains how to collect a soil sample and have it tested; the pH and Plant Nutrition entries explain more about pH and nutrient requirements of plants.

New Gardens

If you're just starting out, you'll probably be tilling under sod, or possibly bare ground, to start your garden. Using a rotary tiller may be the only practical way to work up the soil in a large garden. But whether you're working with a machine or digging by hand, use care. Don't work the soil when it's too wet or too dry. It will have serious detrimental effects on soil structure and quality. "Sod Strips Save Work" on page 604 explains a simple method for creating a new garden in a lawn area.

If you're ambitious, a great way to start a vegetable garden is by double digging the soil. This process thoroughly loosens the soil, so it will retain more water and air, have better drainage, and be easier for roots to penetrate. For step-by-step instructions, see the Double Digging entry.

Depending on the results of your soil tests, you may need to work in lime to correct pH or rock fertilizers to correct deficiencies as you dig your garden. In any case, it's always wise to incorporate organic matter as you work.

Soil Enrichment

If you're an experienced gardener with an established garden site, you can take steps to replenish soil nutrients and organic matter as soon as you harvest and clear out your garden in the fall. Sow seed of a green manure crop in your garden, or cover the soil with a thick layer of organic mulch. Both green manures and mulches will protect the soil from erosion and will improve organic matter content. In the spring, you'll be ready to push back or incorporate the mulch or green manure and start planting.

If you don't plant a green manure crop, spread compost or well-rotted manure over your garden in spring and work it into the soil. You can add as much as a 6″ layer of organic material, if you're fortunate enough to have that much on hand. The best time to do this is a few weeks before planting, if your soil is dry enough to be worked. You can cultivate with a rotary tiller or by hand, using a turning fork and rake. Never cultivate extremely wet soil, or you will be compacting it instead of aerating it. Be conservative when you work the soil. While some cultivation is necessary to prepare seedbeds and to open up the soil for root growth, excess cultivation is harmful. It introduces large amounts of oxygen into the soil, which can speed the breakdown of soil organic matter. And if soil is too wet or too dry, cultivating it can ruin soil structure.

Other opportunities for improving your soil will crop up at planting time, when you add compost or other growth boosters in planting rows or holes, and during the growing season, as you mulch your developing plants.

Planting

Planting season can be the busiest time of year for the vegetable gardener. Some careful planning is in order. To help you remember what you have planted and how well cultivars perform in your garden, keep written records. Fill in planting dates on your garden map as the season progresses. Later, make notes of harvest dates. If you would like to keep more detailed records, try keeping a garden journal, or set up a vegetable garden data file on index cards. With good records, you can discover many details about the unique climate in your garden, such as when soil warms up in spring, when problem insects emerge, and when space becomes available for replanting.

SOD STRIPS SAVE WORK

When transforming a plot of lawn into a vegetable garden, try cultivating strips or beds in the sod. You'll only have to contend with weeds in the beds. Plus, you'll have excellent erosion control and no mud between the rows, which makes picking easier and more enjoyable.

Tilling the bed: Overlap your tilling so that the finished bed is 1½–2 times the cutting width of your tiller. Start out with a slow wheel speed and shallow tilling depth. Gradually increase speed and depth as the sod becomes more and more workable. Make the beds as long or as short as you want, but space the beds about 3′ apart. Depending on how tough the sod and your tiller are, you may have to retill in a week or two or hand-dig stubborn grass clumps to make a proper seedbed.

Weed control: You can control weeds easily in the rows with a wheel-hoe cultivator or hand hoe or by hand-weeding. What about weeds along the outside edges of the beds? Just mow them down with your lawn mower when you mow the grassy areas between the beds. You'll be rewarded with a ready supply of grass clippings for compost or mulch.

Caution: Before mowing, be sure to pick up all of the larger rocks that your tiller brought to the surface. Rocks will quickly dull and chip your mower blade, and they're downright dangerous to people, pets, and property when your mower kicks them up and hurls them through the air.

Once your garden is finished for the season, sow a green manure crop such as buckwheat, clover, or ryegrass in the beds. The following spring, just till the strips that were in sod. It's crop rotation made easy! Or let your sod strips be permanent pathways. Over time, as the soil in the tilled strips improves, they naturally evolve into raised beds.

Getting Set to Plant

Once the soil is prepared, lay out your garden paths. Then rake loose soil from the path-

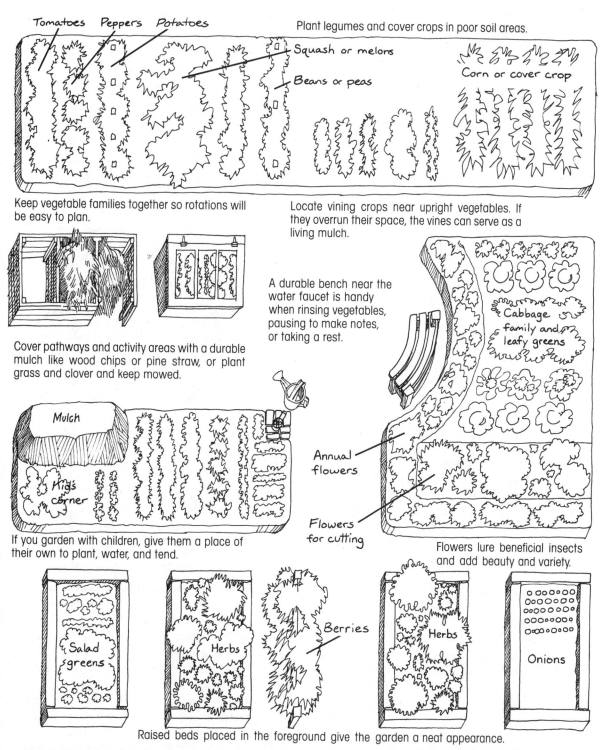

Tomatoes Peppers Potatoes

Plant legumes and cover crops in poor soil areas.

Squash or melons

Beans or peas

Corn or cover crop

Keep vegetable families together so rotations will be easy to plan.

Locate vining crops near upright vegetables. If they overrun their space, the vines can serve as a living mulch.

A durable bench near the water faucet is handy when rinsing vegetables, pausing to make notes, or taking a rest.

Cover pathways and activity areas with a durable mulch like wood chips or pine straw, or plant grass and clover and keep mowed.

Mulch

Kid's corner

Cabbage family and leafy greens

Annual flowers

Flowers for cutting

If you garden with children, give them a place of their own to plant, water, and tend.

Flowers lure beneficial insects and add beauty and variety.

Salad greens

Herbs

Berries

Herbs

Onions

Raised beds placed in the foreground give the garden a neat appearance.

Vegetable garden planning. It pays to plan your vegetable garden for ease of watering and harvesting crops. Add features to attract birds and beneficial insects. Interplant crops to help reduce pest problems and to make the garden more attractive. Rotate crop families if possible.

ways into the raised rows or beds. As soon as possible, mulch the pathways with leaves, straw, or another biodegradable mulch. Lay mulch thickly to keep down weeds. If you live in a region that has frequent heavy rain, place boards down the pathways so you'll have a dry place to walk.

You can prepare planting beds and rows as much as several weeks before planting. However, if you plan to leave more than three weeks between preparation and planting, mulch the soil so it won't crust over or compact.

Plant arrangement: There are practically no limits to the ways you can arrange plants in a vegetable garden. In a traditional row garden, you'll probably plant your crops in single rows of single species. If you have raised rows or raised beds, you can interplant—mix different types of crops in one area—and use a variety of spacing patterns to maximize the number of plants in a given area. See "Topping Off Your Beds" on page 602 and "Spacing and Interplanting" on the opposite page for ideas on planning the layout of your garden crops.

Planting combinations: Frequently you can practice succession cropping—growing two vegetable crops in the same space in the same growing season. You'll plant one early crop, harvest it, and then plant a warm- or hot-season crop afterward. To avoid depleting the soil, make sure one crop is a nitrogen-fixing legume, and the other a light feeder. All vegetables used for succession cropping should mature quickly. For example, in a cool climate, plant garden peas in spring, and follow them with cucumber or summer squash. Or after harvesting your early crop of spinach, plant bush beans. In warm climates, try lettuce followed by field peas, or plant pole beans and then a late crop of turnips after the bean harvest.

Seeds and Transplants

Some vegetable crops grow best when seeded directly in place. Other crops will benefit from

---

SOME LIKE IT HOT

Because vegetables differ so much in their preferred growing temperatures, planting the vegetable garden isn't a one-day job. Be prepared to spend several days over the course of early spring to early summer planting vegetable seeds and plants. You'll plant cool-weather crops a few weeks before the last spring frost. Set out warm-weather crops just after the last spring frost. Hot-weather crops cannot tolerate frost or cold soil. Unless you can protect them with a portable cold frame or row covers, plant them at least three weeks after the last spring frost. In warm climates, plant cool-weather crops again in early fall so that they grow during the fall and winter. Here is a guide to the temperature preferences of 30 common garden vegetables.

Cool Weather	Warm Weather	Hot Weather
Beets	Canta-	Eggplant
Broccoli	loupes	Field peas
Cabbage	Carrots	Lima beans
Cauliflower	Chard	Okra
Celery	Corn	Peanuts
Garden	Cucumbers	Shell beans
peas	Peppers	Sweet
Lettuce	Potatoes	potatoes
Onions	Pumpkins	Watermelons
Radishes	Snap beans	
Spinach	Squash	
Turnips	Tomatoes	

---

being coddled indoors during the seedling stage, and will grow robustly after transplanting.

Direct seeding: You can plant many kinds of vegetable seeds directly into prepared soil. However, even when you follow seed-spacing directions given on the seed packet, direct-seeded crops often germinate too well or not well enough. When germination is excellent, thin plants ruthlessly, because crowded vegetable plants will not mature properly. When direct-seeding any

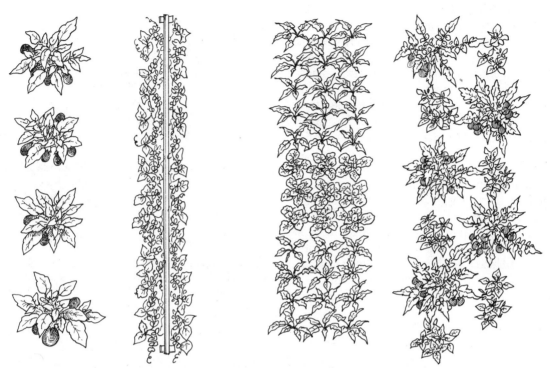

Spacing and interplanting. There are many good ways to combine and configure vegetable plants. Single rows are good for upright bushy plants and those that need good air circulation such as tomatoes and summer squash. Use double rows for trellised plants such as pole beans and cucumbers and for compact bushes such as snap beans and potatoes. Matrix planting is good for interplanting leafy greens such as lettuce and spinach and root crops such as carrots and onions. A zigzag arrangment works well for interplanting vegetables and flowers.

vegetable, set some seeds aside so you can go back in two weeks and replant vacant spaces in the row or bed.

Soil temperature and moisture play important roles in germination of vegetable seeds. Very few vegetable seeds will sprout in cold soil. High soil temperatures also inhibit germination. Also, be sure to plant seeds at the recommended planting depth, and firm the soil with your fingers or a hand tool after planting to ensure good contact of seed and soil.

Starting seeds indoors: To get a head start on the growing season, escape poor outdoor germination conditions, or try rare and unusual cultivars, many gardeners start seeds indoors.

Tomatoes, peppers, eggplant, cabbage, broccoli, cauliflower, brussels sprouts, onions, and celery are almost always handled this way, and cold-climate gardeners might add lettuce and members of the squash family to this list.

Keep in mind that most vegetable seedlings need sun to grow well. A sunny windowsill is adequate for vegetable seedlings, but natural sun and supplemental artificial light is best. Also remember that vegetables started indoors receive very little exposure to stress factors present outdoors, such as wind, fluctuating temperatures, and intense sunlight. One week before you plan to transplant, begin hardening off vegetable plants by exposing them to these natural elements. Move them to a protected place outdoors, or put them in a cold frame.

If temperatures are erratic or windy weather is expected, use cloches to protect tender seedlings from injury for 2-3 weeks after transplanting. Remove cloches when the plants begin to grow vigorously—a sign that soil temperature has reached a favorable range and roots have become established. See the Cloches entry for illustrated examples of good cloches for vegetable transplants.

In late summer, sun and heat can sap moisture from the new transplants of your fall crops faster than the roots can replenish it. Protect seedlings and transplants with shade covers instead of cloches. You can cover plants with cardboard boxes or flowerpots on sunny days for one week after transplanting, or you can cover them with a tent made of muslin or some other light-colored cloth.

Care during the Season

After the rush of planting, there's a lull while most of your crops are growing, flowering, and setting fruit. But regular plant care is important if you want to reap a good harvest later in the season. Get in the habit of taking regular garden walks to thin crops, pull weeds, and check for signs of insect and disease problems.

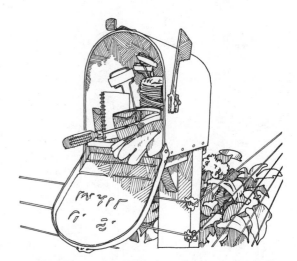

Handy storage. A mailbox mounted on a post in the vegetable garden makes a handy place for storing small tools, a notepad and pencil, or seeds that won't fit in your pockets.

Weeding

Start weed control early and keep at it throughout the season. Remove all weeds within 1' of your plants, or they will compete with the vegetables for water and nutrients. If you use a hoe or hand cultivator, be careful not to injure crop roots.

Some vegetables benefit from extra soil hilled up around the base of the plant. When hoeing around young corn, potatoes, tomatoes, and squash, scatter loose soil from between rows over the root zones of the plants. Once the garden soil has warmed (in late spring or early summer), mulch around your plants to suppress weeds and cut down on moisture loss. If you have areas where weeds have been a problem in the past, use a double mulch of newspapers covered with organic material such as leaves, straw, grass clippings, or shredded bark.

Another solution to weed problems is to cover beds with a sheet of black plastic. The

---

PLANTING BY THE THERMOMETER

Soil temperature can be a good indicator of seed-sowing times. Follow these guidelines:

45°-60°F. Sow beets, carrots, garden peas, lettuce, parsley, radishes, and spinach.

65°-80°F. Sow beans, corn, cucumbers, melons, and squash.

80°-90°F. Sow field peas, okra, peanuts, and shell beans.

plastic can help warm up cold soil, and it is a very effective barrier to weeds. If you do use black plastic, buy the thickest sheets you can find, and use them over and over again. Don't leave the plastic in place in the garden any longer than necessary, as exposure to sunlight will quickly degrade it. As soon as you remove the crop, rinse off and store plastic sheeting in a cool place. See the Mulch entry for more information about using black plastic.

Watering

In the vegetable garden, some supplemental water is invariably needed, especially from midsummer to early fall. Most vegetables need ½"-1" of water each week, and nature rarely provides water in such regular amounts. Dry weather can strengthen some vegetable plants by forcing them to develop deep roots that can seek out moisture. However, the quality of other crops suffers when plants get too little water. Tomatoes and melons need plenty of water early in the season when they're initiating foliage and fruit. However, as the fruit ripens, its quality often improves if dry conditions prevail. The opposite is true of lettuce, cabbage, and other leafy greens, which need more water as they approach maturity.

When to water: How can you tell when your crops really need supplemental water? Leaves that droop at midday are a warning sign. If leaves wilt in midday and still look wilted the following morning, the plants are suffering. Provide water before soil becomes this dry.

If you don't water in time and the soil dries out completely, replenish soil moisture gradually, over a period of 3 days. If you soak dry soil quickly, your drought-stressed crops will suddenly take up large amounts of water. The abrupt change may cause tomatoes, melons, carrots, cabbage, and other vegetables to literally split their sides, ruining your crop.

Watering methods: Watering by hand, using a spray nozzle on the end of a hose, is practical in a small garden but can be too time-consuming in a large one. Sprinklers are easier to use but aren't water efficient. Some of the water from a sprinkler may fall on areas that don't need watering. And on a sunny day, some water evaporates and never reaches your plants' roots. Using sprinklers can saturate foliage, leading to conditions that favor some diseases, especially in humid climates. The one situation in which watering with a sprinkler may be the best option is when you have newly seeded beds, which need to be kept moist gently and evenly.

In terms of both water usage and economy of labor, the best way to water a vegetable garden is to use a drip irrigation system. You can buy several different types, including versatile systems that "weep" water into soil via porous tubing or pipes. These systems are most efficient when you install them between soil and mulch and use them at low pressure. Water seeps slowly into the soil, and there is very little surface evaporation. See the Irrigation entry for more information on drip irrigation systems.

Many gardeners make their own irrigation lines by punching holes into short lengths of garden hose or plastic pipe. You can also drip water to your vegetables by punching small holes in the bottoms of plastic milk jugs, filling the jugs with water, and placing them over the roots of thirsty plants.

Irrigation pipes do not take the place of a handy garden hose—you need both. Buy a two-headed splitter at the hardware store, and screw it onto the faucet you use for the vegetable garden. Keep the irrigation system connected to one side, leaving the other available for hand-watering or other uses.

Staking

Many vegetables need stakes or trellises to keep them off the ground. Without support, the leaves and fruits of garden peas, tomatoes, pole beans, and some cucumbers and peppers easily become diseased. Also, many of these crops are

WEED CONTROL: LONG-TERM STRATEGIES

Over a period of years, you can effectively reduce the number of weed seeds present in your vegetable garden. Here's how:

● Mulch heavily and continuously to deprive weed seeds of sunlight.
● Remove all weeds before they produce seeds.
● Plant windbreaks along any side of the garden that borders on woods or wild meadows. Shrubs and trees can help filter out weed seeds carried by the wind.
● Grow rye as a winter cover crop. Rye residue suppresses weed germination and growth.
● Solarize soil to kill weed seeds in the top 3" of prepared beds.

easier to harvest when they're supported because the fruits are more accessible. You'll find many handy tips for staking and supporting crops in the individual vegetable entries.

Fertilizing

Keeping your soil naturally balanced with a good organic matter content will go a long way toward meeting the nutrient needs of your crops. Crops that mature quickly (in less than 50 days) seldom need supplemental fertilizer when growing in a healthy soil, especially if they're mulched. But vegetables that mature slowly (over an extended period) often benefit from a booster feeding in midsummer.

Plan to fertilize tomatoes, peppers, and corn just as they reach their reproductive stage of growth. Sprinkle cottonseed meal or a blended organic fertilizer beneath the plants just before a rain. Or rake back the mulch, spread a ½" layer of compost or rotted manure over the soil, and then put the mulch back in place. When growing plants in containers, feed them a liquid fertilizer

such as manure tea every 2-3 weeks throughout the season. You can also use manure tea to feed vegetables grown in the ground. For instructions on making and using manure tea, see the Manure entry.

Foliar fertilizing—spraying liquid fertilizer on plant leaves—is another option for mid-season fertilization. Kelp-based foliar fertilizers contain nutrients, enzymes, and acids that tend to enhance vegetables' efforts at reproduction. They're most effective when plants are already getting a good supply of nutrients through their roots. Use foliar fertilizers as a mid-season tonic for tomatoes, pole beans, and other vegetables that produce over a long period.

Pollination

You'll harvest leafy greens, carrots, and members of the cabbage family long before they flower. But with most other vegetables, the harvest is a fruit—the end result of pollinated blossoms. A spell of unusually hot weather can cause flowers or pollen grains to develop improperly. Conversely, a long wet, cloudy spell can stop insects from pollinating. Either condition can leave you with few tomatoes, melons, or peppers, or with ears of corn with sparse, widely spaced kernels. The blossom ends of cucumbers and summer squash become wrinkled and misshapen when pollination is inadequate.

To prevent such problems, place like vegetables together so the plants can share the pollen they produce. Two exceptions here are hot and sweet peppers, and super-sweet and regular hybrid corn: Separate these by at least 25' to limit the amount of cross-pollination that takes place, or your harvest may not be true to type.

Tomatoes, corn, and beans are pollinated primarily by wind, though honeybees and other insects provide a little help transporting pollen about the plants. The presence of pollinating insects is crucial for squash, cucumbers, and melons. Plant flowers near these crops to lure bees in the right direction. You'll find more sug-

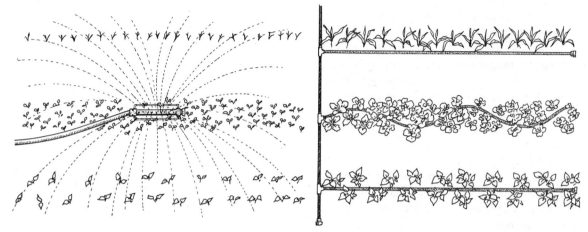

Easy irrigation. At planting time, use a sprinkler to keep the seedbed constantly moist. Remove when seeds have germinated and plants are ready to thin and weed. Before mulching growing crops, arrange soaker hoses or tubing down rows. Cover with mulch to protect irrigation lines from sun and to slow surface evaporation.

gestions for helping with pollination in individual vegetable entries.

Pest Management

Pests and diseases of vegetable crops include insects, fungi, bacteria, and viruses, as well as larger animals such as raccoons and deer. Fortunately for organic gardeners, there are ever-increasing numbers of vegetable cultivars that are genetically resistant to insects and diseases. If you know a pest or disease has been a problem in your garden, seek out and plant a resistant cultivar whenever possible.

Prevention can go a long way toward solving insect and disease problems in the vegetable garden. An important part of your continuing care for your garden is to practice the principles of organic pest management. It's important to realize that a weed-free or insect-free environment is not a natural one. If your garden is a diverse miniature world, with vigorous plants nourished by a well-balanced soil and an active population of native beneficial insects and microorganisms, you'll likely experience few serious pest problems.

Insects: However, when insects threaten to remove more than 20 percent of the leaves on any vegetable plant or are known to carry viral diseases, it is time for you to intervene. See the Organic Pest Management entry to plan a control strategy. In most cases, once you've identified the pest that's damaging your crop, you'll be able to control it by implementing one of the following five treatments:

• Handpick or gather the insects with a net or hand-held vacuum. As you gather them, put the bugs in a container filled with very hot water or alcohol. Set the container in the sun until the bugs die.

• Use floating row covers as a barrier to problem insects. Row covers are particularly useful in protecting young squash, cucumber, and melon plants from insects. Remember to remove the cover when the plants begin to flower. You can also wrap row covers around the outside of tomato cages to discourage disease-carrying aphids and leafhoppers.

• BT (*Bacillus thuringiensis*) gives excellent control of leaf-eating caterpillars. It is often indispensable when you're growing members of the cabbage family, which have many such pests, and when hornworms are numerous enough to seriously damage tomatoes. A special strain— BTSD (*B.t.* var. *san diego*)—is available that is effective against the most common enemy of potatoes, the larvae of Colorado potato beetles.

• Spraying insecticidal soap is effective against aphids on leafy greens, thrips on tomatoes, and several other small soft-bodied pests.

• As a last resort, neem, an extract of a tropical tree, controls at least 75 kinds of pests. You can apply it as a spray or drench. Neem's toxicity is considerably lower than that of other plant-derived pesticides, such as rotenone and ryania.

Diseases: Vegetable crop diseases are less threatening in home gardens than they are in farm fields, where crops are grown in monoculture. When many different plants are present, diseases that require specific host plants have a hard time gaining a firm foothold. Plus, a healthy, natually balanced soil contains many beneficial microorganisms capable of controlling those that are likely to cause trouble.

Two of the best techniques for combating disease problems in the vegetable garden are rotating crops and solarizing the soil. Rotate crops by planting them in different places in the garden from one year to the next. When you plant the same vegetable continuously in the same spot, disease organisms that feed on that plant flourish. When crops change from year to year, the disease organisms don't have a host plant and will not build up large populations. "Rotating Vegetable Families" on the opposite page presents many helpful suggestions for planning crop rotation in your garden.

Where diseases, weeds, soil-dwelling insects, or root knot nematodes seriously interfere with plant health, you can often get good control by subjecting the soil to extreme temperatures. Leave the soil openly exposed for a few weeks in the middle of winter. In the hottest part of summer, a procedure known as solarization can kill most weed seeds, insects, and disease organisms present in the top 4″ of soil. See the Organic Pest Managment entry for step-by-step instructions for solarizing soil.

Animal pests: Rabbits, woodchucks, deer, and other animals can wreak havoc in a vegetable garden. A sturdy fence is often the best solution. For tips on controlling animal pests, see the Animal Pests and Fencing entries.

Harvesting and Storage

As a general rule, harvest your vegetables early and often. Many common vegetables, such as broccoli, garden peas, lettuce, and corn, are harvested when they are at a specific and short-lived state of immaturity. Also be prompt when harvesting crops that mature fully on the plant, as do tomatoes, peppers, melons, and shell beans. Vegetable plants tend to decline after they have produced viable seeds. Prompt harvesting prolongs the productive lifespan of many vegetables. See individual vegetable entries for tips on when to harvest specific crops.

Use "Days to Maturity" listed on seed packets as a general guide to estimate when vegetables will be ready to pick. Bear in mind that climatic factors such as temperature and day length can radically alter how long it takes for vegetables to mature. Vegetables planted in spring, when days are becoming progressively longer and warmer, may mature faster than expected. Those grown in the waning days of autumn may mature 2-3 weeks behind schedule.

In summer, harvest vegetables in mid-morning, after the dew has dried but before the heat of midday. Wait for a mild, cloudy day to dig potatoes, carrots, and other root crops so they won't be exposed to the sun. To make sure your homegrown greens are as nutritious as they can be, harvest and eat them on the same day whenever possible.

Rotating Vegetable Families

Susceptibility to pests and diseases runs in plant families. Leave at least two, and preferably three or more, years between the times you plant members of the same crop family in an area of your garden. When planning your rotations, keep in mind that some crops are heavy feeders, taking up large amounts of nutrients as they grow, while others are light feeders. Balance plantings of heavy feeders with soil-restoring legumes or green manure crops. Here are the seven family groups most often planted in vegetable gardens and ideas for rotating them.

Family Name	Common Crops	Rotation Relations
Cruciferae	Broccoli, brussels sprouts, cabbage, cauliflower, kale, radishes, turnips	High level of soil maintenance required for good root health. Heavy feeders. Precede with legumes; follow with open cultivation and compost.
Cucurbitaceae	Cucumbers, melons, squash, pumpkins, watermelons	For improved weed and insect control, precede with winter rye or wheat. Follow with legumes.
Gramineae	Wheat, oats, rye, corn	Plant before tomato- or squash-family crops to control weeds and improve soil's ability to handle water.
Leguminosae	Beans, peas, clovers, vetches	Beneficial to soil and have few pest problems. Rotate alternately with all other garden crops whenever possible.
Liliaceae	Onions, garlic	Rotate with legumes, but avoid planting in soil that contains undecomposed organic matter.
Solanaceae	Eggplant, peppers, potatoes, tomatoes	Heavy feeders with many fungal enemies. Precede with cereal grain or grass; follow with legumes.
Umbelliferae	Carrots, parsley, dill, fennel, coriander	Moderate feeders. Precede with any other plant family, but condition soil with compost before planting. Follow with legumes or heavy mulch.

Refrigerate vegetables that have a high water content as soon as you pick them. These include leafy greens, all members of the cabbage family, cucumbers, celery, beets, carrots, snap beans, and corn. An exception is tomatoes—they ripen best at room temperature.

Some vegetables, notably potatoes, bulb onions, winter squash, peanuts, and sweet potatoes, require a curing period to enhance their keeping qualities. See individual entries on these vegetables for information on the best curing and storage conditions.

Bumper crops of all vegetables may be canned, dried, or frozen for future use. Use only your best vegetables for long-term storage, and choose a storage method appropriate for your climate. For example, you can pull cherry tomato

(continued on page 618)

Unusual and Oriental Vegetables

There's always room for at least one new crop in most vegetable gardens. Why not grow a crop you won't find in the local grocery store? If you're looking for new tastes and textures, try some of the uncommon and Oriental vegetables listed here. The listings include descriptions, growing guidelines, and suggested uses for a potpourri of Asian and unusual vegetables.

Plant Name	Description	Cultural Requirements	Comments
UNUSUAL VEGETABLES			
Arugula (*Eruca vesicaria* subsp. *sativa*) Cruciferae	Also known as rocket, roquette, and rugula. An annual grown for its flavorful green lobed leaves. Matures in 6–8 weeks. Easy to grow.	Sow seed in rich soil in early spring and autumn. Space 4"–6" between plants and 10" between rows. Needs cool weather and lots of water.	Add young leaves to salads and soup for a distinctive nutty and spicy flavor. Use the piquant flowers as a garnish or add them to salads.
Basella (*Basella alba* and *B. alba* var. *rubra*) Basellaceae	Also known as Malabar spinach, vine spinach, and summer spinach. A 6' perennial vine from India. Heat tolerant and ornamental. Thick, dark green leaves can be harvested all season.	Start plants indoors and transplant outdoors in rich soil after frost danger is past. Trellis to maximize garden space. Space plants 6" apart in the row with 1' between rows. Requires warm weather and plenty of moisture.	Harvest sparingly until plants branch. Substitute the mild-flavored greens for spinach. Steam, stir-fry, add to soup, or use fresh in salads. Rich in calcium, iron, and vitamins A and C.
Broccoli, Romanesco (*Brassica oleracea*, Botrytis group) Cruciferae	A delicately flavored broccoli variety grown extensively in Italy. Chartreuse, symmetrical cone-shaped heads are a robust 7"–8" in diameter. Rich in potassium and calcium, and low in calories.	Performs best in cool weather. Start indoors six weeks before planting outdoors for an early spring crop or a fall crop. Space 1½' between plants in the row with 2' between rows.	Harvest before florets start to open. Cooks in shorter time than regular broccoli. Serve steamed, stir-fried, baked in casseroles, cooked in soups, and raw in salads.
Burdock (*Arctium lappa*) Compositae	Also referred to as gobo. Prepare young leaves and stems as you would spinach. The vigorous 3' long and 1" wide brown roots also are eaten. A biennial, burdock will go to seed the second year.	Plant seed in spring in a raised bed that has been enriched with compost for ease of harvest. Plant seed ¼" deep. Thin seedlings to 8" apart. Harvest roots (mature 4–5 months) the first season.	Scrape the root prior to cooking as you would a carrot. Stir-fry or add to soups for interesting flavor and texture, or fry in a tempura batter. Wild burdock (*A. minus*) is also edible, but rather bitter.

Plant Name	Description	Cultural Requirements	Comments
Cardoon (*Cynara cardunculus*) Compositae	This 4'–6' ornamental is a relative of the globe artichoke. Spiny gray-green stalks are peeled before eating; taste is similar to that of globe artichoke. Treat as an annual in the North, a perennial in the South.	Start seed indoors. Plant outdoors after last frost date in rich soil. Space 2' between plants. Mulch well to keep soil moist. In midsummer, gather the leaves together and wrap the stalks with burlap or newspaper for a month.	A blanched plant looks like an overgrown celery bunch. Prepare the stalks by removing the fibrous outside skin and strings. Preblanch in lemon to remove the acrid flavor. Add to stews, french fry, steam, or marinate.
Celeriac (*Apium graveolens* var. *rapaceum*) Umbelliferae	The bulbous, knobby root is white fleshed and has a crisp texture and sweet celery-like taste. Celeriac reaches a height of 10"–12". Celeriac is hardier than celery, and easy to grow.	Start celeriac in flats or direct-seed outdoors after last frost date. Requires a long season to mature. Keep the soil moist until germination, which may take 14 or more days. Thin to 6" between plants and 8"–10" between rows.	Harvest root when 2"–4" in diameter. Add the raw root to salads, or braise, cream, sauté, or add to soups. Use the foliage for celery flavor, too. Celeriac roots store well for winter use.
Corn salad (*Valerianella locusta*) Valerianaceae	This popular European salad green is also known as mache. It is an annual and grown as a speciality crop in the United States. The rosette of dark green, rounded leaves is thick textured and has a gourmet nutlike flavor.	Sow seed indoors in late winter and transplant outdoors or direct-seed in early spring. Plant ½" deep and space 4"–6" apart. Matures in 40–70 days. Resists bolting. Cold-tolerant; frost enhances flavor.	Harvest individual leaves or an entire head. Use the young leaves in a mixed salad and flavor with your favorite herbs and salad dressing.
Elephant garlic (*Allium ampeloprasum*) Liliaceae	Also known as great-headed garlic and levant garlic. A mild garlic-flavored ½–1 lb. bulb closely related to the leek. Plants mature to 3'–4' in height.	Prepare a deep bed with compost or aged manure. Plant cloves 8" apart in fall or late summer. Mulch well in the North. Harvest bulbs the following season when tops die back. Dry in shade and store in a cool, dark, dry place.	Use cloves in salads or meat entrées. Use whole bulbs in vegetable casseroles or plain in a sauce. Use the greens for seasoning. Herbalists recommend garlic for the common cold, digestive problems, and high blood pressure.

(continued)

Unusual and Oriental Vegetables—*Continued*

Plant Name	Description	Cultural Requirements	Comments

UNUSUAL VEGETABLES—*Continued*

Ground cherry
(*Physalis pruinosa*)
Solanaceae

Also known as dwarf Cape gooseberry. Low 6″–8″ sprawling plants produce sweet, marble-size, golden yellow fruit encased in a papery husk. Will self-sow.

Start seed indoors or sow outdoors in rich soil after last spring frost. Space 2′ between plants. Harvest when the tan husks turn papery thin.

Add to vegetable and fruit salads for a sweet exotic flavor. Makes delectable pies and jams. Freeze or dry to preserve.

Hyacinth bean
(*Dolichos lablab*)
Leguminosae

This vining legume has lovely 1″ lavender flowers and deep burgundy pods on purple stems. Use to cover trellises in the ornamental garden.

Start seed indoors or direct-seed outdoors after frost danger has passed. Space 4″ between plants in rich soil. Grow as you would pole lima beans.

Use flowers in salads and dips. Prepare the young pods, up to 2″ long, like string beans, or use fresh in salads. Prepare older beans as you would green shell beans.

Jicama
(*Pachyrhizus tuberosus*)
Leguminosae

Looks much like a sweet potato plant; produces crisp-fleshed, irregularly shaped 5 lb. roots. Requires a long growing season. Grown as an annual.

Start seed indoors and transplant outdoors after last frost date in fertile, well-drained soil. Space 1′–2′ apart. Harvest roots after vines die.

Roots have a sweet flavor and texture similar to water chestnuts. Use fresh in salads or stir-fry. Foliage, ripe pods, and seeds are toxic.

Sea kale
(*Crambe maritima*)
Crucifererae

This large perennial boasts celerylike stalks with frilly green leaves toward the top of the plant. The tender shoots are harvested in the spring when 5″–8″ tall.

Grown from seed, divisions, or cuttings. Sow seed in spring in warm soil enriched with compost. Space and thin to 8″ between plants. Maintain plants as you would rhubarb. Takes two years to yield from seed.

To tenderize shoots, place a basket or pot over them when they appear in spring. Prepare the young shoots like asparagus or serve raw in a salad. The flavor is slightly bitter, with a hint of the savory hazelnut.

Sorrel, French
(*Rumex scutatus*)
Polygonaceae

A hardy perennial that forms a loose rosette of succulent, lemony greens. High in vitamin C, sorrel has been used historically to treat numerous maladies, such as scurvy, and as a diuretic and blood cleanser.

Start from seed or buy plants from a nursery. Sorrel prefers rich, well-drained soil in full sun or partial shade. Space 1′ between plants. Harvest after established. Remove seed heads to prevent leaves from becoming bitter and fibrous.

Harvest delicate greens in early spring. Mix with other leafy greens for pleasant salads. Add leaves to hearty winter soups. Add to chicken and fish entrées for zestful flavor.

Plant Name	Description	Cultural Requirements	Comments

ORIENTAL VEGETABLES

Chinese celery cabbage
(*Brassica rapa*, Pekinensis group)
Cruciferae

A compact, delicately flavored, cabbage also known as michihli, tientsin, and napa. Savoyed green leaves on light green stalks reach 13"–16".

Grow like other cool-weather cabbage. Space 1'–1½' between plants in the row with 1½' between rows. Keep well watered. Matures in 75 days.

Use in coleslaw or stir-fry for crisp texture. Traditionally pickled. Will store 2–3 months in a cool environment.

Chinese okra
(*Luffa acutangula* and *L. aegyptiaca*)
Cucurbitaceae

Also known as luffa (loofah) or sponge gourd. Young fruit, leaves, blossoms, and seeds have culinary value. Mature fruits are dried and skinned to make sponges.

Start seed indoors and transplant outdoors when frost danger has passed. Grow as you would other gourds. Harvest fruit when 6" long for eating. For sponges, allow to mature and dry on vines.

Immature fruits (okra) are sweet. Use like zucchini—raw, cooked, baked, stuffed with rice, or stir-fried. Luffa sponges are valued for bathing and general cleaning.

Daikon
(*Raphanus sativus* var. *longipinnatus*)
Cruciferae

Also called Chinese radish. Immense, distinctively shaped radishes in a wide variety of colors. The flesh has a crisp texture and flavor.

Plant in deep, rich soil and cultivate like a common radish. Space according to cultivar. Read seed packet for best season to plant. Stores well.

Root adds mildly spicy flavor to salads, Chinese sauces, and stir-fried seafood. Steam peppery leaves or add to clear soup.

Japanese parsley
(*Cryptotaenia japonica*)
Umbelliferae

Leaves similar in appearance and flavor to Italian parsley, with small white flowers. Seed pods are ribbed and ¼" long.

Plant in moist neutral soil, early spring. Space 6" between plants and 10" between rows. Shade-tolerant, prefers cool weather.

Harvest outside leaves or entire plant. Seeds, leaves, stems, and roots are used raw and cooked to flavor salads, soups, and dips.

Mizuna
(*Brassica juncea* var. *japonica*)
Cruciferae

Known as Japanese greens in China. Attractive, compact green plant matures in 35 days, tolerates heat, and is easy to grow. Serrated leaves are used fresh and cooked.

Sow seed in early spring; grow like spinach. Space plants 6" apart in the row and 8"–10" between rows. Make successive plantings. Harvest leaves or entire plant.

Blend with lettuce and crisp vegetables for an unusual, nutritious salad. Stir-fry with Oriental vegetables. Add to cream and clear soups for flavor and texture.

Winter melon
(*Benincasa hispida*)
Cucurbitaceae

Also known as wax gourd, Chinese preserving melon, and white gourd. The oblong melons are 10"–12" long and weigh 10–15 lbs.

Start seed indoors and transplant outdoors when frost danger has passed. Grow as you would any vining melon.

Traditionally, the waxy rind is carved, and the melon hollowed out, then filled with vegetables, meat, and broth. It is steamed before serving.

plants and hang them upside down until the fruits dry in arid climates, but not in humid climates. In cold climates, you can mulch carrots heavily to prevent them from freezing and dig them during the winter. In warm climates, car-

CROPS THAT WAIT FOR YOU

Few things are more frustrating than planting a beautiful garden and then not being able to keep up with the harvest. Leave your sugar snap peas on the vine for a few too many days, and you might just as well till them under as a green manure crop.

Fortunately, there are a host of forgiving crops that will more or less wait for you. They include onions, leeks, potatoes, garlic, many herbs, kale, beets, popcorn, sunflowers, hot peppers (for drying), horseradish, pumpkins, winter squash, and carrots. You can measure the harvest period for these crops in weeks or even in months.

To keep your harvest from hitting all at once, stagger plantings. Make a new sowing every 10 days to two weeks. Mix early, mid-season and late cultivars. Bok choy and other Oriental greens can be harvested through Thanksgiving.

Never have time to pick all of your fresh snap or shell beans at their prime? Relax. Plant cultivars meant for drying, and enjoy hearty, homegrown bean dishes throughout winter.

You can pick leeks young and small or wait the full 90–120 days until they mature. Leeks have excellent freeze tolerance. When protected by mulch, they can be harvested well into winter. In mild winter areas where hard freezes are few and far between, winter is the best time to grow collards, spinach, turnips, carrots, and onions.

In all climates, be prepared to protect overwintering vegetables from cosmetic damage by covering them with an old blanket during periods of harsh weather. Or you can try growing cold-hardy vegetables such as spinach and kale under plastic tunnels during the winter months.

More On VEGETABLES

You'll find planting and growing guidelines, solutions to pest problems, harvesting instructions, and suggested cultivars in the entries for the following vegetables: Amaranth, Artichoke, Asparagus, Bean, Beet, Broccoli, Brussels Sprouts, Cabbage, Carrot, Cauliflower, Celery, Collard, Corn, Cucumber, Eggplant, Endive, Garlic, Gourd, Horseradish, Jerusalem Artichoke, Kale, Kohlrabi, Leek, Lettuce, Melon, Okra, Onion, Parsnip, Pea, Peanut, Pepper, Potato, Radish, Rhubarb, Rutabaga, Spinach, Squash, Sunflower, Sweet Potato, Tomato, and Turnip.

rots left in the ground will be subject to prolonged insect damage.

Off-Season Maintenance

After you harvest a crop in your vegetable garden, either turn under or pull up the remaining plant debris. Many garden pests overwinter in the skeletons of vegetable plants. If you suspect that plant remains harbor insect pests or disease organisms, put them in sealed containers for disposal with your trash, or compost them in a hot (at least 160°F) compost pile.

As garden space becomes vacant in late summer and fall, cultivate empty spaces and allow birds to gather grubs and other larvae hidden in the soil. If several weeks will pass before the first hard freeze is expected, consider planting a green manure crop such as crimson clover, rye, or annual ryegrass. See the Green Manure entry for instructions on seeding these crops.

Another rite of fall is collecting leaves, which can be used as a winter mulch over garden soil or as the basis for a large winter compost heap. If possible, shred the leaves and wet them thoroughly to promote leaching and rapid decomposition. You can also till shredded leaves directly into your garden soil. ❖

Verbascum

Mullein. Late-spring- to summer-blooming biennials and short-lived perennials.

Description: Biennial *Verbascum bombyciferum* displays scattered 1″ yellow flowers on woolly, narrow 5′ spikes above a rosette of broad, felty leaves.

Perennial *V. × hybridum* cultivars bear more numerous flowers in yellow, white, pink, and red shades on 2½′-4′ spikes over rosettes of less-hairy leaves. Zones 4-8.

How to grow: Sow biennials in late spring to summer in pots and set out plants in fall, or sow directly where they are to bloom. Plant mulleins in full sun and average, very well drained soil. Perennials are short-lived but, like the biennials, will self-sow. All tolerate drought.

Landscape uses: Mix upright mulleins with mounded and spreading border plants. ❖

Veronica

Speedwell. Spring- and summer-blooming perennials.

Description: Speedwells bear small flowers in spikes above lance-shaped leaves. *Veronica incana*, woolly speedwell, bears pink or blue-violet flowers on 1′-1½′ spikes above spreading 6″ gray mats in summer. Zones 3-7. *V. spicata*, spike speedwell, and *V. longifolia*, longleaf speedwell, produce white, pink, or blue spikes on 1½′-3′ upright plants in summer. Zones 3-8.

How to grow: Plant or divide in spring or fall in sun or very light shade and average, well-drained soil. Support tall plants with thin stakes. Divide every 3-4 years.

Landscape uses: Group in borders and cottage gardens. Try woolly speedwell in a rock garden. Spike and longleaf speedwells make good cut flowers. ❖

Viburnum

Viburnum, arrowwood. Deciduous or evergreen spring-blooming shrubs or small trees.

Description: Viburnums are excellent shrubs for the landscape. These are just a few of the dozens of outstanding species and cultivars available.

Viburnum dentatum, arrowwood viburnum, has an upright habit, arching with age, and grows to a mature height of 6′-8′. Its oval or round, 2″-3″ leaves are coarsely toothed and turn red in the fall. Flowers appear in spring, borne in flat, creamy white, 3″ clusters followed by berries turning from blue to black. Zones 4-8.

V. plicatum var. *tomentosum,* doublefile viburnum, is a deciduous, rounded shrub with a horizontally layered habit, growing 8′-10′ tall. Dark green, deeply veined, 2″-4″, toothed leaves turn reddish purple in fall. Flowers are borne in spring in flat, 3″ clusters with larger, sterile flowers ringing a center of smaller, fertile flowers. These white clusters appear in pairs along the horizontal branches, inspiring the common name. Fruit follows bloom on the fertile flowers, changing from red to black as autumn progresses and the foliage turns dull red. Zones 5-7.

V. prunifolium, black haw, is a small (12′-15′) tree with a single trunk and a round-headed habit. Broadly oval, finely toothed, 2″-3″ leaves turn shades of purple and crimson in the fall. White flowers are borne in 4″ clusters in spring, followed by blue-black fruits. Zones 3-8.

How to grow: Site viburnums in partial shade, with good drainage and even moisture. Prune black haw for form. Doublefile viburnum has vertical watersprouts that ruin the graceful lines of this shrub; remove them annually. Prune the other viburnums for vigorous growth, removing some of the oldest branches a few inches above ground level each year after bloom.

Landscape uses: Plant viburnums in woodland gardens, where their berries are great wildlife food. Viburnums also do well as specimens, hedges, and massed plantings. ❖

Vinca

Periwinkle, vinca, myrtle. Evergreen perennial groundcovers.

Description: Periwinkles are hardy, trailing vines that root along the stems. *Vinca major,* big periwinkle, has glossy oval 1″-3″ leaves on 2′ long stems. The foliage is a lustrous dark green. The abundant blue, red-purple, or white flowers bloom in mid-May and are 1″-2″ wide. Zones 7-9. *V. minor,* common periwinkle or creeping myrtle, is similar to big periwinkle, but on a smaller scale. The 1½″ leaves are more oblong and grow on 6″ stems. The plants produce a profusion of 1″ wide blue, blue-purple, red-purple, or white flowers in spring. Zones 4-9.

How to grow: Periwinkles are easy to grow in shade or full sun but will not tolerate hot, dry locations. Plant in ordinary soil or prepare new beds with a mixture of peat moss and well-rotted leaf mold. Space plants about 1′ apart. Once a year, apply an organic fertilizer, but don't over-fertilize or you'll encourage fungal diseases. In the spring, propagate plants by cuttings or division. Prune back the rooted cuttings to encourage dense new growth.

Landscape uses: Use periwinkles in planters, beds, and borders. Or plant them as a groundcover on steep slopes and banks or under trees. A favorite combination is periwinkles interplanted in drifts of white or yellow daffodils. Or plant them alone for the attractive starlike flowers. Variegated big periwinkle is often planted in window boxes in the South; in the North, it is commonly treated as an annual.

Best cultivars: *V. major:* 'Variegata' (sometimes called 'Elegantissima'), rich, variegated creamy white leaves, blue flowers. *V. minor:* 'Alba', large white flowers; 'Bowles' Variety', 1¼″ light blue flowers; 'Jekyll's White', white flowers; 'Sterling Silver', white-edged foliage and dark blue flowers; 'Variegata', yellow-variegated leaves and pale blue flowers. ❖

Vines

Versatility is the hallmark of vines. All scramble or climb, but that's where their similarity ends. You can grow vines for shade, for food, or for beauty of foliage, bloom, or fruit. Vines range from tough, woody grapes and wisterias to annuals like morning-glories and garden peas. Other favorite vines include climbing roses, clematis, Boston and English ivies, Virginia creeper, climbing hydrangea, bittersweet, and passionflowers.

You can find a vine for almost any kind of site—sun, shade, loam, or sand, boggy or dry, fertile or poor soil. You're better off matching the vine to the situation than trying to alter the environment to suit the plant. In general, most vines are tolerant of a wide range of cultural conditions. It is the exception, such as clematis (which requires cool soil around its roots), that has specialized requirements. Be sure to check the specific needs of any plant before adding it to your garden. For basics on planting, propagating, and pest control, see the Planting, Propagation, and Organic Pest Management entries.

Landscaping with Vines

Vines' growing habits let you merge boundaries and soften harsh edges. Planting annual vines on fences, gates, and other structures quickly brings an established look to a young garden where the plants have yet to fill in. Use vines to define a garden room: Create green walls by covering fences, mark an entrance with a covered arbor, or provide overhead shade with a pergola.

Vines soften and connect the hard edge between the structures and the plants in a garden. Plant Boston ivy or wisteria to climb up a wall of your home, and you'll link the house and garden. Vines also make the house wall more attractive, provide seasonal interest (in our example, Boston ivy has fall color and berries, and wisteria has early-summer bloom), and if planted on the south side of the house, the vines will help cool it.

How vines climb. All vines climb, but not all climb the same way. You need to know how a vine climbs so you can choose the best support for it. Some vines climb by twining around a support—garden and sweet peas wrap a tendril around a slender pole (1), while the entire stem of vines like wisteria twines around the support (2). Others attach themselves with adhesive holdfasts—English ivy and wintercreeper have adhesive rootlets (3), while Boston ivy and Virginia creeper have adhesive discs at the ends of tendrils (4). All these vines are useful for covering masonry and brick walls because they stick to them. Other vines, like climbing roses, have no real way of holding on to a support; for them to climb rather than sprawl, weave them through a trellis or tie them to their support (5).

Plant vines to screen unsightly walls or views. A planting of wintercreeper will make an ugly concrete wall into a feature rather than an eyesore. A chain-link fence can become an asset if you cover it with trumpet vine (*Campsis radicans*) with its showers of brilliant red-orange blooms in midsummer.

Versatile vines have many other uses as well. Clematis or other vines planted next to lampposts and pillars add interest to any garden. Make the most of a small garden or terrace by "growing up." Grow vines over railings and along windows and door frames to create a magical hideaway. Annual vines can be grown in window boxes and are useful on terraces. Morning-glories (*Ipomoea* spp.), scarlet runner beans (*Phaseolus coccineus*), and black-eyed Susan vines (*Thunbergia alata*) are good window-box choices. And don't forget attractive vines with edible parts such as cucumbers, pole beans, and peas.

Pruning and Training Vines

Pruning is your opportunity to train and control a vine. Look hard at the plant before cutting. The first step in any pruning operation is removal of dead, damaged, and diseased wood. Always use a sharp tool—a hand pruner, lopper, or saw—and make the cut just above a live bud or nearly flush with the stem. Only after "cleaning up" the plant should you start on the live wood.

Prune live wood after the vine has finished blooming for the season. This means you'll prune spring bloomers in early summer, summer bloomers in early fall, and fall bloomers in winter or early spring. Remove dead wood anytime. Shape and control annuals by pinching early in the season. Pruning depends on the growth habit of the plant. Clinging vines like English ivy (*Hedera helix*), wintercreeper (*Euonymus fortunei*), and Virginia creeper (*Parthenocissus quinquefolia*) merely need trimming to keep them in bounds. Other vines like wisteria, clematis, and grapes will need annual pruning. For more on pruning techniques, see the Pruning and Training and Grape entries. ❖

Viola

Pansy, violet. Mostly spring- and fall-blooming biennials and perennials.

Description: Cheerful biennial *Viola × wittrockiana,* pansy, bears long-stemmed, five-petalled 1½"-3" wide, flat blooms in a range of solid colors and combinations, many marked with a dark "face". They begin to bloom in early spring on tight clumps of spatula-like leaves; most types reach less than 1' tall. Zones 5-9.

Perennial *V. cornuta,* horned violet, produces smaller flowers to 1½" with a little curved spur (the "horn") at the back of the flower. Blooms come in many colors, often marked with a black or yellow blotch in the center. Spreading evergreen plants grow to 1' tall. Zones 6-9.

How to grow: For pansies, buy plants or sow seeds indoors (in late winter in the North for spring planting, or in midsummer to fall in the South for late-fall planting). Plant in full sun to light shade and average, moist but well-drained soil loosened with organic matter. Plant no more than 6" apart for a good show. Deadhead regularly and water if dry. Older types die out when hot weather approaches, but many newer cultivars will live on to bloom again in fall.

Plant horned violets in spring or fall; divide every 3-4 years. They like the same conditions as pansies but tolerate heat better. They usually bloom when cool weather returns.

Landscape uses: Grow pansies in beds, borders, and containers for a splash of early color. They combine well with other early-spring flowers, like forget-me-nots and primroses. Use horned violets in the same way or as a colorful groundcover for smaller areas. These late-blooming flowers also add color to rock gardens.

Best cultivars: *V. × wittrockiana* (all mixed colors): 'Crystal Bowl', 'Majestic Giants', and 'Universal'. *V. cornuta:* red with black center 'Arkwright Ruby', apricot 'Chantreyland', purple 'Jersey Gem', and 'White Perfection'. ❖

Walkways and Paths

Some garden walkways and paths exist mainly to get you efficiently from here to there. Others also provide access to views or to garden areas that are worth seeing. And some paths provide a place to stand or kneel while tending your plants. When planning paths, think about their purpose as well as their appearance. You will need to consider each path's route, its width, and the best material for its surface.

Planning the Path

To plan the route of a path, walk it. Decide which places the path is to connect, and then walk between them. If the path is a utilitarian one, such as the route from the house to the garage, a fairly direct path is best. You won't use a route that meanders through the garden when dashing from your car to your house on a rainy day! But you needn't make such paths exactly straight. A straight path is formal, a curved one less so. For an informal effect, you can gently curve the most utilitarian of paths, as long as it's direct enough to travel quickly.

Paths for pleasure strolls can be quite indirect. In a formal setting, a path can take right angles to go around a fountain or a rose garden. In an informal one, it can curve prettily through the shrubbery. To plan a strolling path, search out a route through your garden that provides the best views of garden features and nearby scenery. All but the shortest paths should pass interesting features or have stopping places along their routes. Make sure the path has a destination, such as an attractive view or a small garden bench.

A path to your front door should be 4'-5' wide, so two people can walk comfortably side by side. Most other paths should be 2'-3' wide. Paths that allow you to tend plants in raised beds may be as narrow as 1', but some should be wide enough for a wheelbarrow to pass through. See the Vegetable Gardening entry for information on vegetable garden paths.

Choosing the Right Material

Path surfaces should be both attractive and functional. Choose materials that echo or complement those on the exterior of the house or elsewhere in the garden and that are easy to walk on in any weather.

In less-formal gardens, try paths of shredded bark, gravel, pine needles, crushed seashells, or decomposed granite. Earth concrete, made by mixing concrete into the topsoil, offers a firm surface the color of your native soil. In a more formal setting, brick, flagstones, concrete pavers, or poured concrete are good choices for path surfaces. Concrete can be dressed up with skillful surfacing. One of the nicest is inlaid pebbles, known as an exposed aggregate finish. Renew existing concrete by covering it with special brick pavers—thin blocks of brick—or by applying epoxy-based surfacing compounds.

Be sure the surface you select is suited for the use you intend. Strolling can be done on many surfaces, soft or firm. If someone in your household wears high-heeled shoes regularly, the surface of the path to the garage or sidewalk should be solid and smooth. Children's wheeled toys require a smooth-surfaced path that takes heavy wear; a wheelbarrow is easier to push if the surface is firm and flat.

Consider soil texture, drainage, and rainfall. Most paths can be laid on any kind of soil, but earth concrete works best in a sandy soil. In low-rainfall areas, paths with a porous surface help replenish soil moisture. In areas of high rainfall, choose surfaces that won't become waterlogged or wash away. To improve drainage, lay a base of sand or gravel at least 2" thick before you lay the final surface. For brick paths that will be in contact with earth, it's best to use bricks rated SW (severe weather). SW brick holds up better under freezing and thawing and generally wears better than other brick.

Laying and Maintenance

You can lay many kinds of paths yourself, including soft-surfaced ones, earth concrete, and bricks or concrete pavers set in sand. Poured concrete requires heavy work done very quickly, so be sure you can muster a volunteer crew large enough to do the job. Setting bricks, flagstones, or concrete pavers in mortar is probably best left to experts. While you can probably lay brick pavers over an old concrete path yourself, hire professionals to apply epoxy-based concrete surfacing compounds.

If you're laying a brick path yourself, you may want to try using dry mortar. To make dry mortar, mix 4 parts portland cement, 1 part lime, and 12 parts dry sand. Set bricks ⅛" apart, then force the dry mortar into the cracks. Tamp it down with a thin board. Sweep excess dry mortar away carefully, so it won't stain the bricks. Dampen with a fine mist water spray. Repeat in 15 minutes, then intermittently for the next 3 days.

If you're planning an earth concrete path, do a test mix first, because the amount of concrete you need to add to your soil will vary according to soil texture. Mix 1 part cement to 8 parts soil and wet it until it feels like bread dough. Tamp it solidly into a box or form. Keep it damp for a few days, and then let it dry in the sun. If it doesn't set, repeat the process using a larger proportion of concrete. Once you find the right porportions, thoroughly dig and break up the top 6" in the area of the planned walkway, and set the edges with brick or wood. Spread the cement, rake it in, and mix it with the soil. Wet it with a fine spray. Let it dry, and roll it smooth several times with a heavy roller. Then spray again with water and keep the surface damp for several days while the cement sets.

Use edgings of wood or brick to hold in soft materials, to keep pavers set in sand from separating, and to discourage encroaching weeds or garden plants. Weeds will invade soft surface paths at first, but will do so less as the surface settles and compacts. Reduce weed invasions in soft paths, or those with sand between pavers, by laying plastic or weed-resistant fabric mulch under the sand or gravel base of the path. Puncture plastic every few feet to improve drainage.

You can control annual weeds in a path by using a soap-based weed killer such as Sharp-Shooter. If your brick path becomes slippery due to growth of moss and algae, there are also soap-based products such as Safer Moss & Algae Killer that will remove them. ❖

Water

Water covers nearly ¾ of the earth's surface. But only about 3 percent of that water is fresh water fit for use by humans and animals or for watering plants. And the world's existing sources of fresh water are being stretched to their limits.

Think of it this way: Surface water—reservoirs, lakes, and streams—is your checking account, while groundwater wells are your savings account. Normally, the checking account is adequate to meet your needs. But when you go on a spending binge—as when increasing demand for water is coupled with prolonged drought—you have to start dipping ever deeper into your savings account. Dig too deeply into your savings account—or go back to the well too many times—and neither will recover quickly, if at all.

That's bad news for gardeners because water is the best fertilizer there is. Adequate water is simply essential for plant growth. Just as the adult human body is up to 65 percent water, plant cells are made up largely of water. Lack of water affects growth mainly by inhibiting cell enlargement, resulting in stunted, weak plants. You can have the best soil, seed, and intentions in the world, but without water, nothing will grow.

Plants use—and lose—water continuously. Water loss is lowest at night, highest at midday. Soil acts as a moisture reservoir when moisture is not replaced by rainfall or irrigation. How much water the soil can hold depends on its texture and organic matter content. The best way to increase soil water-holding capacity is to add organic matter.

Organic gardeners should strive to minimize the need for supplemental watering. Fortunately, there are many things we can all do to reduce water consumption in our gardens. For more information on reducing water use in the garden, see the Irrigation, Mulch, Soil, and Xeriscaping entries. ❖

Water Gardens

Water is calming and refreshing—the most magical garden feature. And it's possible to have a water garden in even the smallest yard. You can choose a wall fountain, barrel, pool, or pond. Water gardens can be formal or informal. Formal pools have geometric shapes and can be made of precast fiberglass liners or concrete. Concrete pools require a professional for proper construction, so most gardeners use fiberglass for formal pools. But for most backyard gardeners, an informal, do-it-yourself water garden is more practical and better suited to today's yards and lifestyles. To decide whether you'd perfer a formal or informal pool style, see "Design Styles" on page 262.

If you are starting a water garden from scratch, your first task is to choose a site. Select a level spot that receives at least 6 hours of sun daily. (You can create a water garden in a shaded spot, but you won't be able to grow water lilies.) An informal pool looks best against a background. Site a large pool where plantings of shrubs and flowers will serve as a backdrop. You can site smaller pools against a wall or fence. If you want a waterfall, blend it into the landscape with background plantings. Avoid vigorous fountains; most water plants prefer still water.

Installing a Water Garden

When planning your water garden, you can choose a flexible liner made of PVC (polyvinyl chloride) plastic or butyl rubber, or a rigid fiberglass liner for the pool. All three types are available from water garden supply companies. A PVC or butyl rubber liner will adapt to any shape pool you want to dig; fiberglass pools are preshaped, so you have to dig a hole that's the same shape as your liner. Both flexible liners and rigid liners are easy to install.

If you opt for a flexible liner, consider its lifespan when ordering, and choose the best liner you can afford. Butyl rubber liners are stretchy and last longest—up to 30 years—but are also most expensive. The thicker the PVC liner, the better it is. PVC-liner thickness is measured in mils. A 32-mil PVC liner will last 15-20 years and is the next best choice, followed by 20-mil PVC, which must be replaced every 7-10 years. Imagine digging up the whole pond, and choose accordingly!

Plastic and rubber liners: First, draw the shape and dimensions of your garden pool on graph paper. Make the pool as large as you can to set off the water plants—$3' \times 5'$ is a nice minimum size. Give the pool a natural shape, with smooth, flowing curves; avoid tight angles. Keep it simple, like a kidney or amoeba shape. Make your pool $1\frac{1}{2}'$-$2'$ deep for water lilies and lotuses.

To determine the size liner to buy, add the width of the pool to 2 times the depth, and then add 2 more feet for the edges. (So, if your pool is $3'$ wide and $2'$ deep, multiply 2 by $2' = 4'$, add $3' = 7'$, plus $2' = 9'$ for the liner width.) Do the same, substituting length for width, to get the overall dimensions.

Use a tape measure and a garden hose to recreate your chosen shape on the garden site. Strip the sod inside the marked area with a flat-bottomed shovel. Excavate the hole 20″-24″ deep, sloping the sides gradually and keeping the bottom as flat as possible. Pile the excavated soil on a tarp or in a wheelbarrow. Make shelves about 9″ wide along the pool sides to accommodate shallow-water plants. A good shelf depth is 9″-12″, depending on the plant and pot size. Check to make sure the pool sides are level by placing a $2' \times 4'$ board over the opening. Use a builder's level on the board to check for high spots. Remove or add soil as necessary to make the rim even.

Remove rocks, sticks, and other sharp objects, then line the entire hole with an old carpet pad. If you can't get a carpet pad, use 1″-2″ of builder's sand, packed down firmly. Then gently place the pool liner over the hole, with the center at the deepest point. Let the liner sink into the hole

PLANTS FOR WATER GARDENS

There are plants for the shallow edges of a water garden as well as the deeper water in the center. Here are some of the best hardy plants for your water garden along with information on water depth preferences.

There are many plants to choose from for growing along the water's edge or in up to 6″ of water. Blue flag (*Iris versicolor*), red iris (*I. fulva*), and yellow flag (*I. pseudacorus*) have clumps of sword-shaped leaves and showy flowers. Sweet flag (*Acorus calamus*), arrowhead (*Sagittaria latifolia*), golden club (*Orontium aquaticum*), and pickerel weed (*Pontederia cordata*) are other fine plants for the pool's edge.

Other aquatics need deeper water—3″ to 12″—and will float their foliage on the water surface. These include plants such as water clover (*Marsilea* spp.), parrot's feather (*Myriophyllum aquaticum*), white snowflake (*Nymphoides indica*), and floating heart (*Nymphoides peltata*). Grow them along the pond edges or with pots set on bricks in the center of the pool.

Lotuses (*Nelumbo* spp.) are hardy perennials that grow in about 4″ of water. They bloom in summer and hold their leaves above the water's surface. Prop the tubs in which they are growing on bricks to provide them with the proper depth.

Water lilies (*Nymphaea* spp.) grow in up to $2'$ of water and float their rounded or heart-shaped leaves on the water's surface. Flowers rest on or above the water and come in a wide variety of colors. They may be hardy or tropical, which are overwintered indoors or replaced annually. For more on water lilies, see the Nymphaea entry.

Every pond should contain submerged plants that help trap debris in the leaves and also compete with algae for dissolved nutrients in the water, thus helping to keep the water clear. These include cabomba (*Cabomba caroliniana*), elodea (*Elodea canadensis*), and vallisneria (*Vallisneria americana*).

Hardy water garden plants—plus many tropical water plants— are available from companies specializing in water gardening.

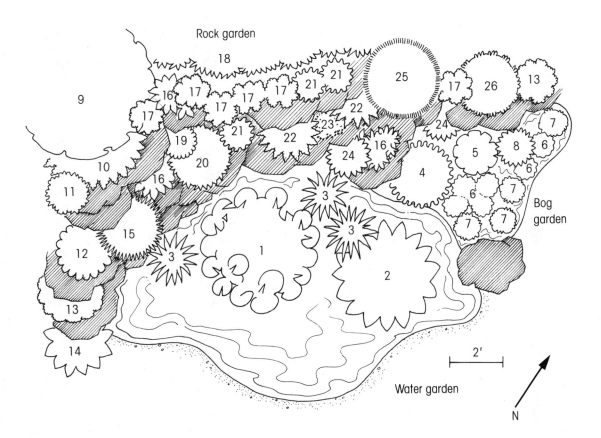

Rock garden

Bog garden

Water garden

2'

N

Water, bog, and rock gardens. A bog garden forms a natural transition between this lovely water garden and dry land. Rocks go beautifully with water, and this rock garden frames the pool and bog garden.

Water Garden

1. Lotus (*Nelumbo nucifera* or *N. lutea*)
2. Water lily (*Nymphaea* hybrid)
3. Yellow flag (*Iris pseudacorus*)

Bog Garden

4. Pickerel weed (*Pontederia cordata*)
5. Turtlehead (*Chelone lyonii*)
6. Japanese primrose (*Primula japonica*)
7. Marsh marigold (*Caltha palustris*)
8. Marsh fern (*Thelypteris palustris*)

Rock Garden

9. Harry Lauder's walking stick (*Corylus avellana* 'Contorta')
10. Creeping juniper (*Juniperus horizontalis*)
11. Penstemon (*Penstemon barbatus*)
12. 'Vera Jameson' sedum (*Sedum* × 'Vera Jameson')
13. Heartleaf bergenia (*Bergenia cordifolia*)
14. Yellow-flowered dwarf daylily (*Hemerocallis* 'Happy Returns' or 'Bitsy')
15. Golden-variegated hakonechloa grass (*Hakonechloa macra* 'Aureola')
16. Lady's-mantle (*Alchemilla mollis*)
17. Candytuft (*Iberis sempervirens*)

18. Cinnamon fern (*Osmunda cinnamomea*)
19. Lavender (*Lavandula* spp.)
20. Thyme (*Thymus* spp.)
21. Carpathian harebell (*Campanula carpatica*)
22. Maiden pinks (*Dianthus deltoides*)
23. Hens-and-chickens (*Sempervivum* spp.)
24. 'Autumn Joy' sedum (*Sedum* × 'Autumn Joy')
25. Moor grass (*Molinia caerulea*)
26. Dwarf goldenrod (*Solidago* 'Peter Pan' or 'Goldenmosa')

and then slowly add water to the new pool. The liner will be pushed snug against the sand or carpet pad lining as the pool fills. Adjust the liner as the pool fills to remove wrinkles and reshape the sides.

Give the filled pool a day to settle, then cut off the excess liner, leaving at least a 6" lip along the level edge. Disguise the rim with flagstones, bricks, or rocks. Bury any edges that aren't covered by the border stones.

Fiberglass liners: Follow a similar procedure for a rigid fiberglass pool. Dig the hole larger than the pool and line it with 1"-2" of sand. Place the liner into the hole, leaving the rim just above ground level. Place a builder's level across the top and make any necessary adjustments so the pool edge is absolutely level. Fill the pool slowly, backfilling with sand as the liner settles into the hole. Disguise the rim the same way you would for a flexible liner.

Growing Aquatic Plants

The amount of water a plant requires or tolerates determines where you can grow it. Moisture-loving plants such as cardinal flower (*Lobelia cardinalis*) and Siberian iris (*Iris sibirica*) prefer to grow on the land around a pond, with their roots penetrating into the wet soil. See "Plants for Water Gardens" on page 626 for more plants to grow in or around your water garden.

You can create an exciting landscape around your water garden, but use restraint when choosing plants for the pool itself. One of the chief pleasures of water gardening is enjoying reflections in the water, so you don't want to completely cover the surface with water plants. Strive for a balance of ⅓ open water to ⅔ plant cover. Consider the mature spread of the plants you plan to order. Plant water lilies 3'-5' apart to give them room to spread out in their typical bicycle-spoke pattern.

Wait at least a week after filling your pool before adding plants or fish, so the chlorine can evaporate and the water can warm up. If your community uses chloramine (a chlorine-ammonia compound) to treat its water, it won't evaporate. Use a product such as DeChlor or Aqua Safe to neutralize the chloramine before adding plants or fish. Plant water plants in containers before placing them in the water garden. Use black or brown plastic tubs or pails. The best soil is heavy garden loam, with some clay mixed in for stability, and well-rotted (not dried) cow manure added for fertility. (Mix 1 part cow manure for 5 parts soil.) Do not use commercial potting mixes with lightweight peat and perlite that will float to the water's surface.

Fill containers ½-⅔ of the way with soil, depending on the size of the rootstock. Position the roots around a cone of soil with the crown 2" below the rim of the pot. Fill the remainder of the container with soil up to the crown of the plant. Cover the top of the soil with 1" of pea gravel. Do not bury the growing points. Fill the container with water and allow it to settle. Refill and allow a gentle stream of water to run over the rim of the container until it runs clear. Sink the pots to the proper depth in the pool. In 2-4 weeks your plants will have adjusted and will be growing vigorously.

Water Garden Maintenance

Water gardens need routine maintenance. To avoid the buildup of decaying plant material, remove yellowing leaves and spent flowers of water garden plants. Weed the banks and edges regularly, too. Divide plants every 1-2 years; potbound plants will quickly lose vigor. For more on the care of wetland plants, see the Bog Gardens entry.

Winter protection is important. If you live in moderate climates, you can leave hardy plants in the pool over the winter. (In severe climates, where the water may freeze to the bottom of the pool, store hardy plants indoors as you would tropical ones.) Make sure the pots are below the ice at all times. You can use a stock tank de-icer, available from water garden specialists or farm stores, that floats directly in the pool to keep the water from freezing if you like. Lift tropical water lilies each fall, and store them in a frost-free place. Place the containers in a cool spot and keep the soil evenly moist throughout the storage period. A cellar or cool greenhouse is ideal.

Maintaining a balanced environment is essential to keep algae from covering the pond with green scum. Algae need nitrogen and sunlight to grow. Grooming water plants will reduce the buildup of excess nitrogen in the water, while shade from their foliage will reduce sunlight.

Plants that grow entirely underwater are good natural filters. They absorb excess nitrogen and are important for maintaining a balanced pool. Freshwater clams, which are filter feeders, and black Japanese or trapdoor snails, which are scavengers, are available from water garden suppliers and will also help keep your water clear. So will the tadpoles that may appear in spring.

Goldfish and koi add color and movement to the water garden. Though they may stir up the pond bottom in search of food, they'll also keep the water free of mosquito larvae. Fish are also great biological controls for plant pests—if your water plants are bothered by aphids or caterpillars, hose the pests into the water and the fish will finish them off.

If the water becomes cloudy despite your best efforts, or if you have fish in your pool, you may need to install a recirculating pump and filtering system. A recirculating pump will enable you to lift water to a height from which it can fall, adding oxygen (which the fish need) to the water but also adding the lovely sound of moving water. Pumps and filters are available from companies specializing in water gardening. ❖

Watermelon

Citrullus lanatus
Cucurbitaceae

Sweet and succulent, this summertime favorite loves warm temperatures, well-drained soil, and lots of moisture. Once considered a Southern crop, watermelons are now available in small-fruited "icebox" cultivars that are suited for cooler climates. For cultural information, see the Melon entry. ❖

Weather

Weather affects not only the health and growth rates of your crops but also determines to a large extent which types and cultivars can be raised in your area. Understanding the relationships between plants and the elements can help you plan and take care of your garden.

Cold Hardiness

Hardiness is the ability of a plant to survive in a given climate. In the strictest sense, this includes not only a plant's capacity to survive through the winter, but also its tolerance of all the climatic conditions characteristic of the area in which it grows. Still, most gardeners refer to a hardy plant as one capable of withstanding cold and to a tender plant as one that's susceptible to low temperatures and frost.

In order to help growers determine which plants are best for their regions, the USDA's Agricultural Research Service has developed a Plant Hardiness Zone Map. An updated version was released in 1990. It divides the United States and southern Canada into 11 climatic zones, based on the average annual minimum temperature for each zone. Zone 1 is the coldest, most northerly region, and Zone 11 is the warmest, most southerly. If you live somewhere in Zone 6 and a plant is described as "suitable for Zones

5-9" or "hardy to Zone 4" you can expect the plant to do well in your area. If you live in Zone 3, on the other hand, you should select a more cold-tolerant plant. You can find out which zone you live in by referring to the map on page 651.

Keep in mind that there are climatic variations within each region and even within each garden. Your garden's immediate climate may be different from that of the region overall. Many factors—altitude, wind exposure, proximity to bodies of water, terrain, and shade—can cause variations in growing conditions by as much as two zones in either direction.

Frost

Many food and ornamental plants are native to warm climates and can't withstand freezing temperatures. Others go dormant for the winter. So the primary growing season for North American gardeners is between the last frost in the spring and the first killing frost of fall.

Air temperature is only one of the factors that determines whether or not plants will be damaged by a frost. Sometimes when the temperature dips a little below freezing, the air is sufficiently moist for water vapor to condense (in the form of ice crystals) on the ground and on plants. When water condenses, it gives off heat and warms the air around plants, protecting them from extensive damage. On clear, windless, star-filled nights when near- or below-freezing temperatures are forecast, it's wise to protect plants. Heat is lost rapidly under such conditions, and frost damage often occurs. When temperatures fall more than a few degrees below freezing, frost damage to growing leaves and shoots is likely no matter how humid conditions are.

Frost damages plants when the water in the plant's cells freezes and ruptures the cell walls. Different plants and parts of plants have different freezing points. Plants that are native to Northern regions have many ways of protecting themselves from the cold. Many perennials die down each fall. The roots buried in the insulat-

ing soil remain alive to sprout again the next season. Some plants such as kale have cold-tolerant leaves that will survive unharmed under a blanket of snow, but not when exposed to drying winds. Deciduous shrubs and trees drop their leaves each fall and form leaf and flower buds that stay tightly wrapped in many layers and go dormant until spring comes again. They may also have a natural antifreeze in their sap that helps prevent them from cold injury, as do hardy plants with evergreen leaves.

Frost heaving of soil can also cause problems for gardeners. Soil moves as it freezes, thaws, and refreezes. This action can push newly planted perennials, shrubs, or other plants that don't have established root systems out of the soil. Mulch heavily around such plants after the soil freezes to prevent thawing during sudden warm spells in winter or early spring.

Other Factors

Rainfall: Natural rainfall is an important factor in what crops you can grow and how you need to take care of those you do grow. Keep track of the rainfall in your garden with a rain gauge. You can buy a gauge, or simply use an empty tin can and a ruler. An inch of rain in the can equals an inch of rain on the garden.

Sunlight: All plants, except mushrooms and other fungi, require light. The amount of sunshine your region (and your garden in particular) receives will determine which plants will do well for you. In shady or cloudy locations, crops such as tomatoes, peaches, sweet corn, and melons won't ripen well. Lots of sunshine will warm the soil and air, which can prompt cool-season vegetables such as cabbage, lettuce, and spinach to bolt prematurely and go to seed.

Wind: Wind is another factor that influences plant growth. Too much wind can dry out plants and soil, stunt seedling growth, and knock over tall, shallow-rooted crops such as corn. However, in humid areas, some air movement is desirable and will help reduce disease problems. ❖

Weeds

Fast, tough, and common—that's all it takes to earn a plant the name of weed. But any plant growing in the wrong place—especially if it's growing there in abundance—is a weed. Maple tree seedlings that sprout between the lettuce and radishes are weeds. So is the bermudagrass that keeps invading your perennial beds from the lawn.

Some weeds become desired plants when we find uses for them. Purslane is a nuisance in the vegetable garden, yet you can eat leaves of this weed in salads. The cultivated species of purslane—known as rose moss (*Portulaca grandiflora*)—has large, colorful flowers and is prized as a bedding plant for warm, sunny places. Honeysuckle vines can cause considerable damage as they twine around your trees, yet they might be a good groundcover for a bank that's too steep to mow.

Weeds make a lawn, garden, or landscape look untidy and neglected. But aesthetics aside, there are better reasons for keeping your weeds in check. Weeds compete for water, nutrients, light, and space. The competition can weaken your plants and reduce your harvest. They grow fast, shading out less vigorous plants. Weeds serve as alternate hosts or habitats for insects and diseases. For example, aphids and Japanese beetles on smartweed or powdery mildew fungus on red clover can move from the weeds onto your food and landscape plants.

Some weeds are a nuisance because they have poisonous parts, such as pokeweed berries or poison ivy leaves, stems, and roots. A few weeds secrete chemicals from their roots that are toxic to other plants, such as the well-known effect of the toxin juglone produced by black walnut trees.

The Life of a Weed

Just like flowers, weeds may be annuals, biennials, or perennials. Annual weeds, the easiest to control, complete their life cycles in a year or less. Summer annuals sprout in spring and go to seed in fall; winter annuals sprout in fall, live over winter, and go to seed by spring or summer. Summer annuals such as crabgrass, giant foxtail, pigweed, and lamb's quarters will be your biggest weed problem in the vegetable garden. As your fall plantings of lettuce and radishes sprout, so too will the seeds of winter annuals, such as chickweed and henbit. By the time you get ready to plant the following spring, these weeds will be dying out and can be easily turned under.

Biennial weeds, such as Queen-Anne's-lace, form only roots and a rosette of leaves the first year, then flower and set seed the second year. Perennial weeds, which live for more than two years, reproduce not only by seed, but also by roots, stems, and stolons. Gardeners dread perennial weeds such as quackgrass or ground ivy, which spring into new life from an overlooked fragment of stem or root.

A Waiting Horde

A single weed can produce as many as 250,000 seeds. Though some seeds are viable for only a year, others can lie dormant for decades, just waiting for their chance to grow. Buried several inches deep, the lack of light keeps them from germinating. But bring weed seeds to the surface, and they'll germinate right along with your flower and vegetable seeds.

Even if you're diligent at hoeing and pulling weeds, more seeds arrive—by air, by water runoff, and in bird droppings. You may accidentally introduce weeds by bringing seeds in on your shoes, clothing, or equipment or in the soil surrounding the roots of container-grown stock. Even mulches put down to restrict weeds or straw that's spread to protect new grass may be contaminated with weed seed. Grass seed itself, unless certified weed-free, may contain seeds of undesirables.

An Ounce of Prevention

Gardeners, especially organic gardeners, should remember that keeping weeds from getting started is easier than getting rid of them. Here's how:

• After preparing garden soil for planting, let it set for 7-10 days. Then slice off newly emerged weeds with a hoe, taking care to disturb the soil surface as little as possible. If you have time, wait another week or so and weed again. This tactic puts a considerable dent in the reservoir of surface weed seed that could germinate and cause problems later in the season.

• Cover the soil with black plastic to kill existing weeds and stop seeds from germinating. (Don't leave plastic in place for more than a few months; soil needs air and water to remain healthy.)

• Use weed-free mulches like pine bark or grass clippings. See the Mulch entry for more information on mulches.

EAT THEM UP

The roots, stems, leaves, flowers, and fruits of many common weeds are edible. However, always be sure to carefully identify any wild-growing plant before you eat it. Here is a sampling to try:

● Add leaves of lamb's quarters (*Chenopodium album*), purslane (*Portulaca oleracea*), watercress (*Nasturtium officinale*), and sheep sorrel (*Rumex acetosella*) to salads, soups, and stews.

● Germinate green amaranth (*Amaranthus hybridus*), great burdock (*Arctium lappa*), red clover (*Trifolium pratense*), dandelion (*Taraxacum officinale*), broadleaf plantain (*Plantago major*), or wild garlic (*Allium canadense*) seeds for salad sprouts.

● Dip American elderberry blossoms (*Sambucus canadensis*) in batter and fry them; stir-fry or pickle tawny daylily buds (*Hemerocallis fulva*).

● Make jelly or jam from fruits of wild strawberries (*Fragaria virginiana*), grapes (*Vitis* spp.), roses (*Rosa* spp.), and huckleberries (*Gaylussacia* spp.).

• Put down landscape fabric to prevent weeds from getting a foothold, and top it with a thin layer of mulch.

• Use vertical barriers, such as wood or metal edgings, between lawn and garden areas to prevent grass from infiltrating.

• Be a good housekeeper in the garden. Pull weeds before they set seed. Police nearby areas, not just the garden; they may be reservoirs of weed seeds just waiting to blow into your freshly prepared seedbed.

• Let the sun's heat weed your vegetable garden by solarizing the soil. Covering bare soil tightly with clear plastic for several weeks can kill weed seeds in the top few inches of the soil. For details on this technique, which also helps reduce soilborne diseases and pests, see the Organic Pest Management entry.

Getting Rid of Weeds

The bigger your weeds get, the more difficult they are to control. Get into the habit of a once-a-week weed patrol to cut your weed problem down to size. Using the right tools and techniques also will help to make weeding a manageable—maybe even enjoyable—task.

Weeding by Hand

Hand-pulling weeds is simple and effective. It's good for small areas and young or annual weeds such as purslane and lamb's quarters. Using your hands allows you to weed with precision, an important skill when sorting the weeds from the seedlings. For notorious spreaders like ground ivy, the only choice for control is to patiently hand-pull the tops and sift through the soil to remove as many roots as you can find.

Short-handled tools such as dandelion forks (sometimes known as asparagus knives), pronged cultivators, and mattocks are good for large, stubborn weeds, especially in close quarters such as among perennials. Use these tools to pry up tough perennial weeds. Hand weeders come in all shapes, and everybody has a favorite. If one type feels awkward, try another.

If the weeds you pull haven't yet set seed, recycle them: Leave the weeds upside down on the soil to dry, then cover with soil or mulch. If they have gone to seed, only add them to the compost pile if you keep the pile temperature high (at least 160°F). Otherwise the weed seeds will survive the composting process, and you'll spread weed problems along with your finished compost. See the Composting entry for instructions on keeping a compost pile hot.

Hoeing

A hoe is the best tool for weeding larger areas quickly and cleanly. Use it to rid the vegetable garden of weeds that spring up between rows. When you hoe, slice or scrape just below the soil surface to sever weed tops from roots. Don't chop into the soil—you'll just bring up more weed seeds to germinate. Keep the hoe blade sharp. Hoeing kills most annual weeds, but many perennial weeds, such as dandelions, will grow back from their roots. Dig out these roots with a garden fork or spade. See the Tools and Equipment entry for help in picking the right tools.

In gardens with wide spaces between plant rows, you may be able to handle most of your weeding chores with a wheel hoe—an oscillating or stationary hoe blade mounted on a wheel with two long handles—or a rotary tiller. But keep in mind that, while a tiller makes fast work of weeds, tilling can have detrimental effects on your soil structure and will bring up more weed seeds in the process. Also, tilling perennial weeds can chop their rhizomes into small pieces, each of which will then sprout into life, worsening your weed problem.

Mulching

One of the best low-effort ways to beat weeds is to block their access to light and air by mulching bare soil areas. A 3"-4" layer of mulch smothers out many weeds, and weeds that manage to

NOT ALL BAD

When weeds overwhelm you, and your aching back says it never wants to see another wheelbarrow of mulch, think of the good side of weeds:

● Weeds produce quick cover for land devastated by fire, flood, or construction.
● Weedy areas provide a haven and an alternate food source for many of the beneficial insects that prey on garden insect pests.
● Songbirds and other wildlife depend on weed seeds as a food source.
● Weeds are sources of drugs and dyes. Ragweed produces a green color; dock and smartweed, yellow. Coltsfoot is used for cough syrup, castor bean for castor oil. Oil from jewelweed soothes poison ivy rash.
● Dried flowers, seed pods, and stems of many weeds, especially weedy grasses, make attractive fall and winter bouquets.

poke through are easier to pull.

Black plastic mulch can practically eliminate weeding in the vegetable garden. Cut slits for plants and water to penetrate. Remove the plastic at the end of the growing season to let the soil breathe. You can use biodegradable materials, such as newspaper or corrugated cardboard, to temporarily suppress weeds, tilling them into the soil at the end of the season. See the Mulch entry for more information on organic and black plastic mulches.

A living mulch of a low-growing grass or legume crop seeded between rows of plants in your vegetable garden can keep down weeds and improve soil organic matter content at the same time. See the Green Manure entry for suggestions on planting living mulches in your garden.

Even tough perennial weeds will succumb eventually to a thick layer of mulch. "Mulching Perennial Weeds" on page 634 shows how to

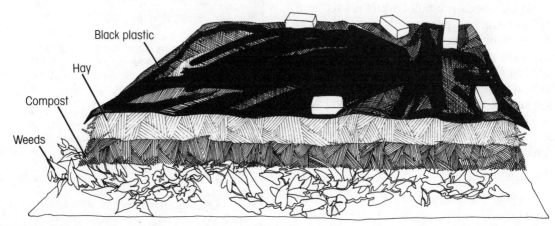

Black plastic

Hay

Compost

Weeds

Mulching perennial weeds. Wipe out stubborn perennial weeds such as poison ivy or field bindweed with a multilayered mulch treatment. Spread lime or rock fertilizers if needed, then put down compost or manure. Next, spread a thick layer of organic mulch such as hay, wood chips, or shredded leaves. Top the mulch with an opaque, impenetrable cover: Black plastic, old carpeting, or a 2" thick layer of newspaper work well. Leave the mulch and heavy cover in place for the season. The following spring, remove the cover and mulch, and check in the soil for weed roots. If the roots aren't dead yet, re-cover the area. Two years under this kind of cover will kill virtually any weed.

layer on mulches to solve tough weed problems.

Try porous but tightly woven landscape fabrics around trees and shrubs. Look for a "closed space" fabric with a low number of open spaces in the weave. The final word is not yet in on the value of landscape fabrics. Recent observations point to problems with those of looser weave: Roots of desirable plants may grow up into the fabric, reaching for the loose mulch on top. Then, in times of drought, the plant suffers. Some of these materials degrade in sunlight, so cover them with a 1" mulch layer. Before you invest heavily in modern miracle fabrics, try your own experiments to see how they perform in your garden.

Shading Out Weeds

Just as weeds compete with your garden and landscape plants for water, food, and growing space, your plants use the same method to crowd out weeds. As your plants grow, they will shade the ground, reducing weed germination and growth. Space vegetable and flower plants closely in beds to decrease the time until the leaves form an effective light-blocking canopy.

Reduce weed growth in your lawn by setting your lawn mower blade a notch or two higher. Taller grass is generally healthier and lets less light reach the soil.

Using Herbicides

In some cases, fatty-acid-based herbicides such as Safer SharpShooter can help control weeds. These herbicides provide effective spot control for annual weeds, but perennial weeds will spring up anew from the unharmed roots. Some organic gardeners have traditionally relied on vinegar or salt to kill weeds. However, these substances will affect soil balance and can harm your garden plants as well. Only use them in areas where you don't want *any* plants to grow, such as between cracks in a patio. ❖

Weigela

Weigela. Deciduous spring-blooming shrubs.

Description: *Weigela florida,* old-fashioned weigela, has an oval, spreading habit, and grows 8'-10' tall. Slender oval, 2"-4½" long leaves are medium green. Bell-shaped, 1½", rose-colored flowers appear in the spring. Zones 6-8.

How to grow: Provide full sun to partial shade and good drainage. Prune to maintain the form by removing stray and internally crossing branches.

Landscape uses: Plant weigela in foundation areas and massed plantings, or as a specimen.

Best cultivars: 'Bristol Snowflake' has white flowers; 'Bristol Ruby' bears bright red flowers that may continue to open sporadically through the summer; 'Dropmore Pink' has dusty rose flowers and shows remarkable cold-hardiness (to Zone 3). ❖

Wildflowers

Wildflowers are among America's favorite garden plants. They are at home in informal shade gardens, sunny meadows, and formal borders. Some native wildflowers such as garden phlox (*Phlox paniculata*), bee balm (*Monarda didyma*), and purple coneflower (*Echinacea purpurea*) have been grown widely for years. But others weren't commonly cultivated in this country until recently, although they were widely grown and hybridized in Europe. Ironically, today we grow European-produced cultivars of many American wildflowers.

When You Buy Wildflowers

When you're shopping for wildflowers, remember that more is at stake than your checkbook balance and the plants' health. Wildflowers are available as containerized or bareroot plants from nurseries across the country. While most of these nurseries propagate the plants they sell, some offer plants collected from the wild. If you buy collected wildflowers, you could be depleting plants in the wild. Use this checklist to make sure you're buying nursery-propagated plants:

• Don't buy plants that look like they were just dug out of the ground and stuffed into nursery pots. Battered or wilted leaves, leaves growing in unlikely directions, and plants that are too big for their pots but are not potbound are a few telltale signs. Before you buy such a plant, verify its source.

• Beware of the phrase "nursery-grown." It doesn't necessarily mean that the plants are nursery-propagated; they may have been collected, then grown on in the nursery for a couple of years. Do not buy wildflowers unless you are sure that they were propagated by the nursery or purchased by a garden center from a nursery that propagates them.

• Wildflowers that take a long time to propagate are the most likely victims of wild-collection. Be especially careful to determine the source of trilliums, trout lilies, and other spring woodland wildflowers.

Key Words
WILDFLOWERS

Wildflower. An herbaceous (nonwoody) flowering plant capable of reproducing and becoming established without cultivation.

Native wildflower. An herbaceous flowering plant indigenous to a particular region, state, or country.

Indigenous plant. A plant that originated in a given area and grows there naturally.

Spring ephemeral. A woodland wildflower that grows, blooms, sets seed, and dies back in spring before the forest trees leaf out and create summer shade.

• Don't buy native orchids such as lady's-slippers. They can't be propagated in commercial quantities and are wild-collected.

• Cultivars, like *Echinacea purpurea* 'Bright Star', are always nursery-propagated. To be safe, buy the cultivar (rather than the species) if one is offered.

• Be wary of inexpensive wildflowers or quantity discounts offered by mail-order nurseries. These plants are probably wild-collected. You should expect to pay the same price for a well-grown wildflower as you would for a garden perennial.

Growing Wildflowers

Success with wildflowers depends on matching the plants' native environment. Prairie plants will pine away in a shaded garden, and plants from cool mountains are unsuitable for hot Southern gardens. The right light, moisture, and soil type are essential.

If you can match conditions of light and moisture, you can amend the soil to support a

wide variety of species. Woodland plants like moist, humus-rich soils. Canada wild ginger (*Asarum canadense*), Jacob's ladder (*Polemonium caeruleum*), bloodroot (*Sanguinaria canadensis*), and Virginia bluebells (*Mertensia virginica*) are a few examples of these beautiful plants. They are perfect for growing in a shade garden with hostas, ferns, astilbes, and woodland phlox.

Prairie plants like gayfeathers (*Liatris* spp.) and queen-of-the-prairie (*Filipendula rubra*) need deep, loamy soils. Meadow and old-field species like butterfly weed (*Asclepias tuberosa*) and goldenrods (*Solidago* spp.) can survive in thin, poor soil. Mountain soils are often thin on slopes of scree (loose rock) and humus-rich under trees. Most mountain wildflowers, including some phlox (*Phlox* spp.), gentians (*Gentiana* spp.), and lupines (*Lupinus* spp.), grow best in rock gardens.

Propagate wildflowers just like other garden flowers. Collect seed from the garden or in small quantities from the wild. If sowing outside, plant the seeds as soon as you collect them. It's especially important to sow seeds of spring ephemerals such as spring beauties (*Claytonia virginica*), trout lilies (*Erythronium* spp.), and bloodroot right away—if these seeds are allowed to dry out, they enter a dormancy that is very difficult to overcome. If you plan to raise seedlings under lights or in a greenhouse, clean the seeds and store them in moist sphagnum or peat moss in the refrigerator for early spring sowing. For more on growing plants from seed, see the Seeds and Seedlings entry.

You can grow many perennial wildflowers easily from cuttings. Or divide clumps of established perennial wildflowers. For more on taking cuttings and making divisions, see the Cuttings and Division entries.

Wildflowers growing in their native habitats have evolved to cope with local pests and diseases. If yours are struck by an occasional outbreak, see the Organic Pest Management entry for help. ❖

Wildlife

While wild birds have been welcome backyard and garden visitors for decades, other forms of wildlife have generally been greeted with much less warmth. But growing numbers of gardeners across the country are turning to a new attitude toward squirrels, rabbits, mice, toads, salamanders, crickets, and all the rest the neighborhood ark might hold.

Across the country, backyards are being transformed into habitats to attract wild creatures by supplying their four basic needs: food, water, shelter, and a safe place to produce and raise the next generation. With careful planning, you can develop even a tiny yard to attract a surprising array of wildlife. Of course, the bigger the space you have to work with, the better the potential of your backyard.

Food, Shelter, Water

Look at your backyard from a new perspective—one of wildlife in search of food, water, cover, and a safe place for their young. When viewed in this light, tangled brush, tall weeds, and dead trees take on a much more essential role than manicured lawns and rows of flowers.

Smaller occupants, such as rabbits, squirrels, and birds, can become near-permanent breeding residents. Animals with larger territories, such as deer, raccoons, and foxes, may appear for a visit as their travels through their ranges come to include your backyard as a regular stop.

To make your sanctuary attractive to a number of species, you'll need to include a variety of plants. The cottontail rabbit, for example, eats herbaceous plants such as grasses and clovers for much of the year and in winter adds the twigs and bark of young trees and shrubs. The Eastern gray squirrel is most decidedly a nut eater—primarily acorns, hickory nuts, and beechnuts—but corn is also a great attraction. Birds depend on insects as their mainstay but also eat seeds, berries, and fruits. The browsing diet of the white-tailed deer consists largely of twigs from trees and shrubs but is supplemented in spring and summer by many of the same herbaceous plants cottontail rabbits eat.

Raccoons relish crayfish, grasshoppers, frogs, and birds' eggs, but almost any living creature that is smaller and slower than a coon will find its way into its diet. Acorns, corn, and fleshy fruits also are favorite raccoon foods. Most of the diet of the red fox is small rodents, such as mice, voles, and rabbits. In summer and fall, fox diets also include as much as 25 percent fleshy fruits.

Tall and mid-sized trees, shrubs, tall herbaceous plants, grasses, and groundcovers all provide for varying needs of different species. Weeds and wildflowers also play their part where local

More On
WILDLIFE

In 1991, the National Wildlife Federation registered its ten-thousandth backyard habitat. That number represents only those gardeners who took the time and trouble to officially register the wildlife-friendly habitats they had developed. Millions of others— the Federation estimates more than 12 million—are enjoying the fruits of attracting wildlife into their backyards without any official recognition whatsoever. For information on registering your backyard, write to Backyard Wildlife Habitat Program, National Wildlife Federation, 1400 16th Street NW, Washington, DC 20036-2266.

You'll find more information on backyard wildlife in the following entries: Beneficial Animals, Beneficial Insects, Birds, Butterfly Gardening, Earthworms, and Toads. See the Water Gardens entry for details on backyard pond making, and for information on controlling unwanted wildlife, see the Animal Pests and Insects entries.

Nesting or roosting boxes for birds and bats are a good project for winter weekends.

Berry bushes supply a banquet for birds, raccoons, chipmunks, and other creatures. Toads, turtles, and even snakes relish low-growing strawberries.

Be sure to place feeders, birdbaths, and shallow ponds in easy view of a favorite window.

Flowers and meadow grasses bring nectar-seeking insects and insect-eating birds. In fall, seed-eating birds scour the flower heads, while mice and chipmunks scavenge the ground below.

A plank or log in the pond is perfect for sunbathing turtles. Frogs often hide among the stems of water plants or the floating leaves of water lilies.

Backyard wildlife. A garden alive with wild creatures is interesting in all seasons. Make your yard a haven for wildlife by supplying the essentials—food, water, and shelter.

ordinances and neighbors will allow.

Consider seasonal diversity, too. Different plants produce their buds, fruits, and seeds at different times of the year. Some plants, such as evergreens, supply shelter year-round. The brambly interior of a blackberry patch makes a good escape route for rabbits, even in winter.

You'll attract the most wildlife by mimicking the plantings of nature. Wild animals stay safe from predators by moving from place to place through protective cover. An isolated berry bush may attract a migrating group of cedar waxwings, but a grouse who tries to reach it could soon become hawk food. If you add another few bushes, and perhaps a hemlock (*Tsuga* spp.), and front the shrubs with meadow grasses and wildflowers, you'll make the planting attractive to a variety of wild creatures.

To this living landscape, add snags, logs, brush piles, and rock piles to provide places for smaller creatures to hide and to rear their young. You can camouflage these elements by planting vines like wild grapes or Virginia creeper (*Parthenocissus quinquefolia*) to trail over them. In the process, you'll provide additional food sources.

Water is the most overlooked aspect of backyard wildlife habitats. Food and cover preferences vary widely, but nearly all creatures need water. A birdbath will serve many birds, many insects, and some mammals. A ground-level fountain will provide for even more drinkers and might also attract some amphibians. A small pond of varying depth will find use by nearly every creature that you can expect to draw into the backyard and can even provide a permanent home for frogs and turtles. ❖

Wisteria

Wisteria, wistaria. Spring-blooming woody vines.

Description: Wisterias are vigorous woody vines that can grow more than 10′ a year, ultimately reaching over 30′ long. The deciduous, dark green, compound leaves drop in late fall, revealing gray trunks that become twisted with age. Showy, drooping, violet-blue flower clusters (12″-20″ long) appear in April or May. Cultivars have reddish violet, pink, and white blooms. Clusters of velvety brown pods follow the blooms and remain after leaf drop, adding winter interest. The two most common species in cultivation both match this description. *Wisteria sinensis,* Chinese wisteria, blooms in May and is the most commonly grown. Zones 5-9. The earlier-blooming *W. floribunda,* Japanese wisteria, has larger flower clusters and is slightly hardier (to Zone 4).

How to grow: Wisterias prefer full sun. Transplant container-grown plants to well-drained, fertile soil. Make sure you buy cutting-grown plants from wisterias known to flower. Both species require strong support—metal is best because the heavy vines can crush wood supports. The most frequent problem of wisteria is failure to bloom, usually due to an abundance of nitrogen (which promotes vegetative growth rather than bloom) and a phosphorus deficiency. To avoid this situation, amend the soil in the fall with ½ lb. of colloidal phosphate or bonemeal per 1″ of main trunk diameter. Be aware that it may be several years after planting before the vine blooms. Root-pruning of established plants may encourage shy bloomers to perform. Prune wisteria severely after blooming to encourage bloom and control rampant growth; cut all new growth back to three buds.

Landscape uses: Wisteria is dramatic growing up the side of a building or on an arbor shading a patio or walkway. It may also be trained to grow in a tree form called a standard. ❖

Witch's Brooms

Witch's brooms are dense clusters of twigs that form on the tips of various woody plants. Most common on needle-leaved evergreens, they may also appear on deciduous trees like hackberries (*Celtis* spp.). Witch's brooms can occur for any of several reasons, including a fungal infection, a mite infestation, or invasion by mistletoe. When these or other factors overstimulate a growing point on a plant, the mutated bud produces a bushy outgrowth of stems. You may want to prune off witch's brooms if they are unsightly; otherwise, they're generally harmless. Many dwarf evergreens are actually witch's brooms that nurseries have propagated by cuttings or grafting. ❖

Wreathmaking

Wreaths let you create a wealth of decorating possibilties with a minimum of expense and time. In addition to the traditional wall or door display, you can lay wreaths flat on a table as a centerpiece or other decoration.

Four basic wreath bases are used for wreathmaking—grapevine, wire, straw, and polystyrene. You can buy all these bases at craft or hobby shops, or make your own grapevine or straw wreaths.

Making grapevine wreaths: To make a grapevine wreath, start with freshly cut vines, which are naturally pliable, or soak the grapevines for at least 30 minutes in a large tub or sink of warm water. Make a circle with a vine, adding more pieces as necessary to get the thickness you want—about 12 times around is average.

If you want a perfect circle, wrap the vines around a bucket or other cylindrical object. Tuck in the ends to secure, or tie with #22-gauge floral wire. Decorate as desired.

Making evergreen wreaths: Evergreen wreaths are simple and inexpensive, especially when made from greens pruned from your own shrubs and trees. Fir, pine, yew, juniper, and false cypress branches hold their needles best.

To make an evergreen wreath, use pruning shears to cut 4"-6" long pieces of evergreen branch tips. Use wire cutters to cut a number of 6" lengths of #24-gauge floral wire. Gather 3-4 of the evergreen sprigs with the stem ends together. Lay these on a 15" three-wire wreath form. Bind the stems securely to the frame, with the floral wire.

Continue this procedure around the frame on each of the three wires of the frame, overlapping the groups like shingles on a roof. To finish attaching the greens, gently pull back the first sprigs and bind in the last bundle. Add ribbon, cones, berries, or other ornaments, attaching

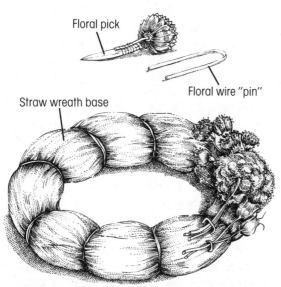

Floral pick

Floral wire "pin"

Straw wreath base

Making a straw-based wreath. Cover the wreath with artemisia or another background material by attaching as many as five 3"-5" stems in a cluster with a floral pin. Start on the inside of the wreath and work around, overlapping the stems of the previous cluster. When the wreath is covered, add colorful dried flowers, pods, herbs, and berries by attaching them to floral picks.

each decoration with its own piece of wire.

Making dried flower and herb wreaths: Straw wreaths form the base of most dried flower and herb wreaths. Many sizes are available, but 12", 14", or 16" wreaths are most popular. To make a wreath from a straw wreath base, first make a hanger by bending a length of #22-gauge floral wire in half, knotting the two ends together, then pulling the knot tight with needle-nose pliers. Loop the wire around the wreath, putting one end through the other. Pull it tight on the back of the wreath.

Next, cover the wreath with a background material, such as artemisias, baby's-breath, statice, goldenrods, hydrangeas, yarrows, or pearly everlasting. Start on the inside of the wreath, working around in one direction, overlapping and covering the stems of the previous cluster. When you get to your starting place, gently lift the first cluster and tuck in the stems of the last. Next, do the front of the wreath, and finally, the outside edge, following the same procedure. To make a cornshuck wreath, attach loops of cornshuck with floral pins.

Add accent materials such as flowers, berries, and pods next. You can attach them by wrapping the wire on a floral pick around the base or stem of the accent material and inserting the pick into the wreath. Another way is to glue the accent material directly to the background, using either white household glue or a hot glue gun with clear glue sticks.

Spray the finished wreath with clear plastic sealer to keep the dried flowers from shattering or absorbing moisture.

You can also use a polystyrene wreath as a base for dried flowers. First, conceal the white base by covering with pieces of either dried Spanish moss or dried sheet moss, attaching them with clear hot glue. Attach ribbon or wire for a hanger. Then, hot-glue individual dried blossoms, such as strawflowers, or seed pods to the wreath, as desired. When completed, spray with clear plastic craft sealer. ❖

Xeriscaping

In areas of the country where drought is measured in years—years in which winter rain did not replenish the reservoirs—xeriscaping is becoming a way of life in the garden. This method depends on basic water-saving principles, such as increasing soil organic matter content and mulching, as well as on using native plants and reducing areas of thirsty lawn grass.

A xeriscape (from the Greek *xeros* meaning dry) is a water-saving garden designed for a dry region. Xeriscaping is especially useful in the western half of the country where little rain falls in summer and gardeners depend heavily on irrigation. Savvy gardeners have been incorporating some of the same principles for years in their own gardens. The idea gained more widespread notice, and an official name, in 1981 when the Denver Water Department developed the concept and the policy of xeriscaping as a way to deal with the West's chronic water shortages. Even Eastern gardeners can benefit through an offshoot called mesiscaping, planning a garden that is only moderate in water use in areas of relatively dependable rainfall.

Principles

Xeriscapes do not have to be desert gardens. Xeriscapers emphasize that these gardens can be lush and colorful. Anyone can use the seven principles of xeriscaping in designing or rejuvenating a garden.

1. Incorporate water savings into your planning and design. Map your yard's microclimates and soil types, paying special attention to the places that stay moist longest and those that dry out fastest or are most difficult to irrigate. In your design, plan zones of high, moderate, and low water use, based on your map. Group plants with similar water needs in these zones. Put your high-water-use plants where you'll appreciate them most, for example, near an entryway or patio.

2. Improve your soil or use adapted plants. For plants with high or moderate water needs, dig the soil deeply and add plenty of organic matter. Many drought-tolerant plants prefer unimproved soil. Group these and leave their soil unamended. See the Soil entry for more information on improving your soil organically.

3. Limit the area in lawn. Lawns are high-water-use areas. Although some grasses tolerate drought better than others, all lawn grasses need similar amounts of water to look good and stay healthy.

Design your lawn to be a small oasis of green. Xeriscape experts calculate that the average single-family garden needs no more than 800 square feet of lawn. Site your lawn next to a patio or driveway, so activities can spill over from one into the other.

Keep edges rounded, and avoid irregularly shaped areas or narrow strips of lawn. Irregular shapes and peninsulas have more edge area that will abut pathways or areas of bare soil that heat up quickly; the heat will promote faster moisture loss from the lawn. Plant lawns only on level ground to reduce runoff. Select grasses that are drought-tolerant and adapted to your region and soil type.

4. Use mulches. Mulch any unplanted soil areas with 2″-3″ of organic mulch or a thick mulch of gravel or stone. Either can be laid over weed-resistant landscape fabric. The little rain that does fall will be able to soak through these porous mulches. Keep overall design in mind: You don't want such a large area of mulch that your garden is no longer a green landscape. See the Mulch entry for details on using mulch.

5. Irrigate efficiently. If you water by hand, test the soil before you water. Water established plants only if the soil is dry several inches below the surface. Better yet, construct a water-efficient irrigation system. Plan it to allow different watering schedules for areas of high, moderate, and low water use. Lawns require sprinklers, but water other plants with soaker hoses or drip irrigation. See the Irrigation entry for more information.

6. Use plants that don't demand as much water. There is no one best list of plants for a xeriscape. Plant lists for Denver, for instance, include native Colorado maples (*Acer* spp.), but California is so dry that no maples are recommended. Another plant, Catalina lilac (*Ceanothus arboreus*), is an excellent choice for California gardens but would be killed by Denver's higher summer rainfall and colder winters. Xeriscapers often turn to plants native to a particular region or to regions with similar climates and soils. Many familiar landscape plants are also adaptable. Water even drought-tolerant plants until well established.

7. Maintain the garden in ways that save water. Tend your garden well, fertilizing and pruning when needed, and checking for pests. Inspect your irrigation system frequently for leaks or other malfunctions. Adjust the timing so that the system releases more or less water as needed during drier and wetter seasons of the year.

Planning a Xeriscape

One of the best ways to learn more about xeriscaping is to visit a demonstration garden. Denver built the first of such gardens, which now bloom in a number of Western cities. To find out the location of the one nearest you, call your local water department or botanical garden.

When you're ready to select plants, learn as much as you can about the ones you're considering. Watching a plant grow for a year is the best way to judge, but you can also get recommendations from nurseries. Plant lists in books and water department publications can help you decide if a plant is suited to your region. Books and other publications will provide details such as height, bloom season, and any potential problems. Another easy way to choose is to observe your neighborhood and note plants that thrive without irrigation. ❖

More On
XERISCAPING

Many municipal and state water departments publish low-cost or free guides for the beginning xeriscaper. Check your library, bookstore, or the government listings in your phone book to read more about planning a xeriscape.

Among the many books about water-conserving gardening are *Sunset Waterwise Gardening* and *Taylor's Guide to Water-Saving Gardening*.

Publications on xeriscaping are also available from the National Xeriscape Council, P.O. Box 163172, Austin, TX 78751-3172.

Yucca

Yucca, Adam's-needle. Summer-blooming woody perennials.

Description: Massive, dramatic *Yucca filamentosa,* Adam's-needle, bears creamy white 2″ hanging bells in giant spikes up to 10′. Plants have mounded, evergreen, 2½′ dark green sword-like leaves with sharp tips and curly-haired edges. Zones 4-9.

How to grow: Plant in spring or fall from containers in a sunny spot with average to poor, very well drained soil. Heavier soils may cause rotting during wet winters. Sandy soil, drought, heat, high humidity, and pests don't bother these rugged plants.

Landscape uses: Yuccas are unequaled as specimens or in small groups among rocks or around buildings and pools. Grow in irregular groups on grassy slopes or in hot corners.

Best cultivars: 'Bright Edge', creamy yellow-edged leaves; 'Golden Sword', yellow-striped leaves; both 4′-5′ in bloom. ❖

Zelkova

Zelkova. Deciduous trees.

Description: *Zelkova serrata,* Japanese zelkova, has a vase-shaped form and a height in the landscape of 50′-80′. The alternate leaves are simple and sharply toothed. In autumn they turn yellow-orange to red before falling. With age, the bark on this tree exfoliates, leaving mottled patches. Zones 6-8.

How to grow: Plant Japanese zelkova on a site with full sun, good drainage, and even moisture. Established trees tolerate dry conditions. This fast-growing member of the elm family resists the elm leaf beetles and Dutch elm disease that plague its relatives.

Landscape uses: Japanese zelkovas are suitable for use as shade or street trees. Their elmlike shape makes them a suitable replacement for elms in the landscape. ❖

Zinnia

Zinnia. Summer- and fall-blooming annuals.

Description: Flower colors include white, cream, yellow, orange, red, green, and bronze, plus combinations. Flowers range from less than 1″ to over 6″ wide with rounded or pointed petals in single, semidouble, and double forms. Cultivars may be 6″-36″ tall, forming low mounds or upright bushes. All zinnias have dull green leaves.

How to grow: Start indoors no more than three weeks before the last frost, or direct-seed outdoors when the ground is warm. Give them full sun in average soil and water only when very dry. Keep the flowers cut to encourage more bloom.

Powdery mildew is a fungal disease that causes dusty white spots on leaves and flowers. The disease is most prevalent in hot, humid weather and when plants are grown close together. Good air circulation and antidesiccant sprays help control mildew.

Landscape uses: Use zinnias in masses in beds, borders, and edges, as cut flowers, or to screen dying bulb foliage.

Best cultivars: Mixes: 'Thumbelina', 6″ tall; 'Peter Pan', 10″-12″; 'Sun' and 'Splendor', 20″; 'Zenith' and 'Ruffles', 2½′. Try 20″ tall 'Candycane' and 'Whirligig', with striped and splashed blooms in many color combinations. ❖

Zucchini

Cucurbita pepo
Cucurbitaceae

One of the most prodigious producers of the summer garden, zucchini is a delicious and dependable crop. You may, however, want to exercise some self-restraint in planting these easy-to-grow summer squash; otherwise you'll have more fruit than you can possibly eat! For helpful zucchini know-how, see the Squash entry. ❖

Common and Botanical Names

This encyclopedia lists ornamentals—annuals, perennials, biennials, trees, shrubs, groundcovers, and vines—by botanical name. Here, you'll find common names of plants with individual entries and the botanical name under which they're listed. If you don't find a plant here, check the index for common and botanical names of all plants mentioned in the book.

Abelia, *Abelia*
Adam's-needle, *Yucca*
Ageratum, *Ageratum*
Ajuga, *Ajuga*
Albizia, *Albizia*
Allium, *Allium*
Almond, *Prunus*
Alumroot, *Heuchera*
Amaranth, *Amaranthus*
Amaryllis, *Hippeastrum*
Anemone, *Anemone*
Arborvitae, *Thuja*
Arrowwood, *Viburnum*
Artemisia, *Artemisia*
Ash, *Fraxinus*
Aspen, *Populus*
Aster, *Aster*
Astilbe, *Astilbe*
Avens, *Geum*
Azalea, *Rhododendron*
Baby's-breath, *Gypsophila*
Balloon flower, *Platycodon*
Baptisia, *Baptisia*
Barberry, *Berberis*
Basswood, *Tilia*
Bearberry, *Arctostaphylos*
Beardtongue, *Penstemon*
Bee balm, *Monarda*
Beech, *Fagus*
Begonia, *Begonia*
Bellflower, *Campanula*
Bergenia, *Bergenia*
Birch, *Betula*
Bishop's hat, *Epimedium*
Blanket flower, *Gaillardia*
Blazing-star, *Liatris*
Bleeding heart, *Dicentra*
Bluebells, *Mertensia*
Boxwood, *Buxus*
Bridalwreath, *Spiraea*
Buckeye, *Aesculus*
Bugbane, *Cimicifuga*

Bugleweed, *Ajuga*
Buttercup, *Ranunculus*
Butterfly bush, *Buddleia*
Butterfly weed, *Asclepias*
Caladium, *Caladium*
Calliopsis, *Coreopsis*
Camellia, *Camellia*
Campion, *Lychnis*
Candytuft, *Iberis*
Canna, *Canna*
Cape jasmine, *Gardenia*
Carnation, *Dianthus*
Catchfly, *Lychnis*
Catmint, *Nepeta*
Cedar, *Cedrus*
Cherry pie, *Heliotropium*
China aster, *Callistephus*
Chrysanthemum, *Chrysanthemum*
Cinquefoil, *Potentilla*
Clematis, *Clematis*
Cockscomb, *Celosia*
Coleus, *Coleus*
Columbine, *Aquilegia*
Coneflower, *Rudbeckia*
Coral bells, *Heuchera*
Coreopsis, *Coreopsis*
Cornel, *Cornus*
Cosmos, *Cosmos*
Cotoneaster, *Cotoneaster*
Cottonwood, *Populus*
Crab apple, *Malus*
Cranesbill, *Geranium*
Crocus, *Crocus*
Daffodil, *Narcissus*
Dahlia, *Dahlia*
Daphne, *Daphne*
Daylily, *Hemerocallis*
Dead nettle, *Lamium*
Delphinium, *Delphinium*
Deutzia, *Deutzia*
Dogwood, *Cornus*
Elm, *Ulmus*

Epimedium, *Epimedium*
Eucalyptus, *Eucalyptus*
Euonymus, *Euonymus*
Evening primrose, *Oenothera*
False indigo, *Baptisia*
False spirea, *Astilbe*
Fennel flower, *Nigella*
Fir, *Abies*
Firethorn, *Pyracantha*
Flag, *Iris*
Flame nettle, *Coleus*
Flax, *Linum*
Flossflower, *Ageratum*
Flowering quince, *Chaenomeles*
Flowering tobacco, *Nicotiana*
Forsythia, *Forsythia*
Foxglove, *Digitalis*
Fuchsia, *Fuchsia*
Funkia, *Hosta*
Garden balsam, *Impatiens*
Garden geranium, *Pelargonium*
Garden mum, *Chrysanthemum*
Garden petunia, *Petunia*
Gardenia, *Gardenia*
Gas plant, *Dictamnus*
Gayfeather, *Liatris*
Ginkgo, *Ginkgo*
Gladiolus, *Gladiolus*
Glads, *Gladiolus*
Globe thistle, *Echinops*
Golden-ray, *Ligularia*
Goldenrod, *Solidago*
Gum tree, *Eucalyptus*
Harebell, *Campanula*
Hawthorn, *Crataegus*
Heliotrope, *Heliotropium*
Hellebore, *Helleborus*
Hemlock, *Tsuga*
Hens-and-chickens, *Sempervivum*
Holly, *Ilex*
Hollyhock, *Alcea*
Honey locust, *Gleditsia*

Honeysuckle, *Lonicera*
Hop hornbeam, *Ostrya*
Hornbeam, *Carpinus*
Horse chestnut, *Aesculus*
Hosta, *Hosta*
Houseleeks, *Sempervivum*
Hyacinth, *Hyacinthus*
Hydrangea, *Hydrangea*
Impatiens, *Impatiens*
Iris, *Iris*
Ivy, *Hedera*
Jasmine, *Jasminum*
Jonquil, *Narcissus*
Joseph's-coat, *Amaranthus*
Juneberry, *Amelanchier*
Juniper, *Juniperus*
Knapweed, *Centaurea*
Lady's eardrops, *Fuchsia*
Lagerstroemia, *Lagerstroemia*
Lamium, *Lamium*
Lantana, *Lantana*
Larch, *Larix*
Laurel, *Kalmia*
Lavender, *Lavandula*
Ligularia, *Ligularia*
Lilac, *Syringa*
Lily, *Lilium*
Lily-of-the-valley, *Convallaria*
Lilyturf, *Liriope*
Linden, *Tilia*
Liriope, *Liriope*
Lobelia, *Lobelia*
Locust, *Robinia*
Loosestrife, *Lysimachia*
Love-in-a-mist, *Nigella*
Lupine, *Lupinus*
Magnolia, *Magnolia*
Mahonia, *Mahonia*
Maidenhair tree, *Ginkgo*
Mallow, *Hibiscus*
Mallow, *Malva*
Manzanita, *Arctostaphylos*
Maple, *Acer*
Marigold, *Tagetes*
Meadow rue, *Thalictrum*
Michaelmas daisy, *Aster*
Milkweed, *Asclepias*
Mimosa, *Albizia*
Mock orange, *Philadelphus*

Moonflower, *Ipomoea*
Morning-glory, *Ipomoea*
Moss rose, *Portulaca*
Mountain ash, *Sorbus*
Mugwort, *Artemisia*
Mullein, *Verbascum*
Musk mallow, *Malva*
Myrtle, *Vinca*
Narcissus, *Narcissus*
Nasturtium, *Tropaeolum*
Oak, *Quercus*
Oregon grape, *Mahonia*
Ornamental cherry, *Prunus*
Ornamental onion, *Allium*
Pachysandra, *Pachysandra*
Pansy, *Viola*
Pasqueflower, *Anemone*
Passionflower, *Passiflora*
Patient Lucy, *Impatiens*
Pear, *Pyrus*
Penstemon, *Penstemon*
Peony, *Paeonia*
Periwinkle, *Vinca*
Phlox, *Phlox*
Pieris, *Pieris*
Pincushion flower, *Scabiosa*
Pine, *Pinus*
Pinks, *Dianthus*
Planetree, *Platanus*
Plantain lily, *Hosta*
Plum, *Prunus*
Poplar, *Populus*
Poppy, *Papaver*
Portulaca, *Portulaca*
Pot marigold, *Calendula*
Primrose, *Primula*
Privet, *Ligustrum*
Purple coneflower, *Echinacea*
Purple loosestrife, *Lythrum*
Pyracantha, *Pyracantha*
Red-hot poker, *Kniphofia*
Rhododendron, *Rhododendron*
Rock cress, *Arabis*
Rose, *Rosa*
Sage, *Salvia*
Sagebrush, *Artemisia*
Sea-pink, *Armeria*
Sedum, *Sedum*
Serviceberry, *Amelanchier*

Shadbush, *Amelanchier*
Silk tree, *Albizia*
Silverbell, *Halesia*
Snakeroot, *Cimicifuga*
Snapdragon, *Antirrhinum*
Speedwell, *Veronica*
Spiderwort, *Tradescantia*
Spindle tree, *Euonymus*
Spirea, *Spiraea*
Spruce, *Picea*
Spurge, *Euphorbia*
Spurge, *Pachysandra*
Stonecrop, *Sedum*
Sundrops, *Oenothera*
Sunflower, *Helianthus*
Sweet alyssum, *Lobularia*
Sweet gum, *Liquidambar*
Sweet pea, *Lathyrus*
Sycamore, *Platanus*
Thrift, *Armeria*
Thunbergia, *Thunbergia*
Tickseed, *Coreopsis*
Torch lily, *Kniphofia*
Tulip poplar, *Liriodendron*
Tulip tree, *Liriodendron*
Tulip, *Tulipa*
Tupelo, *Nyssa*
Viburnum, *Viburnum*
Vinca, *Vinca*
Violet, *Viola*
Walnut, *Juglans*
Water lily, *Nymphaea*
Weigela, *Weigela*
Wild ginger, *Asarum*
Wild indigo, *Baptisia*
Willow, *Salix*
Windflower, *Anemone*
Wistaria, *Wisteria*
Wisteria, *Wisteria*
Witch hazel, *Hamamelis*
Woodbine, *Parthenocissus*
Wormwood, *Artemisia*
Yarrow, *Achillea*
Yellow poplar, *Liriodendron*
Yew, *Taxus*
Yucca, *Yucca*
Zelkova, *Zelkova*
Zinnia, *Zinnia*
Zonal geranium, *Pelargonium*

Suggested Reading

Armitage, Allan M. *Herbaceous Perennial Plants*. Athens, Ga.: Varsity Press, 1989.

Barton, Barbara J. *Gardening by Mail 3: A Source Book*. 3rd ed. Boston: Houghton Mifflin Co., 1990.

Brickell, Christopher. *Pruning*. New York: Simon & Schuster, 1988.

Brickell, Christopher, ed. *The American Horticultural Society Encyclopedia of Garden Plants*. New York: Macmillan Publishing Co., 1989.

Bubel, Nancy. *The New Seed Starter's Handbook*. Emmaus, Pa.: Rodale Press, 1988.

Carr, Anna. *Good Neighbors: Companion Planting for Gardeners*. Emmaus, Pa.: Rodale Press, 1985.

————. *Rodale's Color Handbook of Garden Insects*. Emmaus, Pa.: Rodale Press, 1979.

Carr, Anna, et al. *Rodale's Chemical-Free Yard and Garden*. Emmaus, Pa.: Rodale Press, 1991.

————. *Rodale's Illustrated Encyclopedia of Herbs*. Emmaus, Pa.: Rodale Press, 1987.

Clausen, Ruth Rogers, and Nicolas H. Ekstrom. *Perennials for American Gardens*. New York: Random House, 1989.

Coughlin, Roberta M. *The Gardener's Companion: A Book of Lists and Lore*. New York: HarperPerennial, 1991.

Cox, Jeff. *Landscaping with Nature*. Emmaus, Pa.: Rodale Press, 1991.

Dirr, Michael A. *Manual of Woody Landscape Plants*. 4th ed. Champaign, Ill.: Stipes Publishing Co., 1990.

Elias, Thomas S. *The Complete Trees of North America Field Guide and Natural History*. New York: Crown Publishers, 1987.

Ellis, Barbara W., ed. *Rodale's Illustrated Encyclopedia of Gardening and Landscaping Techniques*. Emmaus, Pa.: Rodale Press, 1990.

Flint, Mary Louise. *Pests of the Garden and Small Farm: A Grower's Guide to Using Less Pesticide*. Oakland, Calif.: ANR Publications of the University of California, 1990.

Gershuny, Grace, and Joseph Smillie. *The Soul of Soil: A Guide to Ecological Soil Management*. 2nd ed. St. Johnsbury, Vt.: GAIA Services, 1986.

Halpin, Anne Moyer. *Rodale's Encyclopedia of Indoor Gardening*. Emmaus, Pa.: Rodale Press, 1980.

Halpin, Anne Moyer, and the editors of Rodale Press. *Foolproof Planting: How to Successfully Start and Propagate More Than 250 Vegetables, Flowers, Trees, and Shrubs*. Emmaus, Pa.: Rodale Press, 1990.

Heriteau, Jacqueline, et al. *The National Arboretum Book of Outstanding Garden Plants*. New York: Simon and Schuster, 1990.

Hill, Lewis. *Fruits and Berries for the Home Garden*. Rev. ed. Pownal, Vt.: Garden Way Publishing, 1992.

Hunt, Marjorie B., and Brenda Bortz. *High-Yield Gardening*. Emmaus, Pa.: Rodale Press, 1986.

Hupping, Carol, et al. *Stocking Up III*. Emmaus, Pa.: Rodale Press, 1986.

Jacobs, Betty E. *Flowers That Last Forever: Growing, Harvesting, & Preserving*. Pownal, Vt.: Garden Way Publishing, 1988.

Lathrop, Norma. *Herbs: How to Select, Grow, and Enjoy*. Los Angeles: Price Stern Sloan, HP Books, 1981.

Leighton, Phebe, and Calvin Simonds. *The New American Landscape Gardener*. Emmaus, Pa.: Rodale Press, 1987.

Loewer, Peter. *The Annual Garden*. Emmaus, Pa.: Rodale Press, 1988.

Logsdon, Gene. *Wildlife in Your Garden*. Emmaus, Pa.: Rodale Press, 1983.

Martin, Deborah L., and Grace Gershuny, eds. *The Rodale Book of Composting*. Emmaus, Pa.: Rodale Press, 1992.

Martin, Laura C. *The Wildflower Meadow Book*. 2nd ed. Chester, Conn.: The Globe Pequot Press, 1990.

Niering, William A., and Nancy C. Olmstead. *The Audubon Society Field Guide to North American Wildflowers*. New York: Alfred A. Knopf, 1979.

Oster, Maggie. *Gifts & Crafts from the Garden: Over 100 Easy-to-Make Projects*. Emmaus, Pa.: Rodale Press, 1988.

Reich, Lee. *Uncommon Fruits Worthy of Attention*. Reading, Mass.: Addison-Wesley Publishing Co., 1991.

Roth, Susan A. *The Weekend Garden Guide*. Emmaus, Pa.: Rodale Press, 1991.

Schultz, Warren. *The Chemical-Free Lawn: The Newest Varieties and Techniques to Grow Lush, Hardy Grass*. Emmaus, Pa.: Rodale Press, 1989.

Smith, Miranda, and Anna Carr. *Rodale's Garden Insect, Disease & Weed Identification Guide*. Emmaus, Pa.: Rodale Press, 1988.

Taylor, Norman. *Taylor's Guide to Annuals*. Rev. ed. (Taylor's Guides to Gardening Series). Boston: Houghton Mifflin Co., 1986.

———. *Taylor's Guide to Perennials*. Rev. ed. (Taylor's Guides to Gardening Series). Boston: Houghton Mifflin Co., 1986.

Taylor's Guide Staff. *Taylor's Guide to Ground Covers, Vines & Grasses* (Taylor's Guides to Gardening Series). Boston: Houghton Mifflin Co., 1987.

———. *Taylor's Guide to Shrubs* (Taylor's Guides to Gardening Series). Boston: Houghton Mifflin Co., 1987.

———. *Taylor's Guide to Trees* (Taylor's Guides to Gardening Series). Boston: Houghton Mifflin Co., 1988.

Westcott, Cynthia. *Westcott's Plant Disease Handbook*. 5th ed., rev. by R. Kenneth Horst. New York: Van Nostrand Reinhold Co., 1990.

Whealy, Kent, ed. *Fruit, Berry & Nut Inventory*. Decorah, Iowa: Seed Saver Publications, 1989.

———. *Garden Seed Inventory*. 2nd ed. Decorah, Iowa: Seed Saver Publications, 1988.

Wilson, Jim. *Landscaping with Container Plants*. Boston: Houghton Mifflin Co., 1990.

Credits

Contributors

Bonnie Lee Appleton is associate professor of horticulture and Extension nursery specialist at the Hampton Roads Agricultural Experiment Station, Virginia Polytechnic Institute and State University. (*Planting, Shrubs, Trees, and Weeds entries*)

Helen Atthowe has a master's degree in horticulture from Rutgers University and has worked with the Rutgers University Fruit IPM Program, Rutgers Cooperative Extension, New Jersey. (*technical review and pest control information for individual fruit entries and for pest table in Fruit Trees entry*)

Cathy Barash is the author of *Roses* and is a freelance garden writer and photographer. (*Container Gardening and Edible Landscaping entries*)

Nancy Bubel is the author of *The New Seed Starter's Handbook* and *52 Weekend Garden Projects*. (*Seeds and Seedlings entry*)

Rita Buchanan is the author of *A Weaver's Garden* and former editor at *Fine Gardening* magazine. (*Botanical Nomenclature, Flowers, Leaves, and Roots entries*)

C. Colston Burrell is an author, photographer, lecturer, and garden designer in Minneapolis. He is the former curator of plants at the Minnesota Landscape Arboretum and former curator of native plants at the U.S. National Arboretum. (*Annuals, Biennials, Bog Gardens, Ferns, Groundcovers, Natural Landscaping, Perennials, Water Gardens, and Wildflowers entries*)

Pat Corpora is president of the Book Division of Rodale Press and an avid fig grower. (*Fig entry*)

Peggy Walsh Craig is a freelance garden writer whose work appears in *Horticulture Review*. (*Espalier, Horticultural Therapy, and Plant Breeding entries*)

George DeVault is editor of *Novii Fermer* magazine and former editor of *New Farm* magazine. (*Irrigation, Regeneration, Rodale, and Water entries*)

Alexander Eppler owns a nursery specializing in *Ribes* and is vice president of the International Ribes Association. (*Currant and Gooseberry entries*)

Peggy Fisher is the owner of Flowerscapes, a flower arrangement and landscape firm in Eugene, Oregon. She has contributed to several books, including *Essential Flowering Shrubs*. (*Poisonous Plants entry and individual groundcover entries*)

Stephen Flickinger is a branch manager for Frank's Nursery and Crafts and has more than 15 years of experience in the nursery business. (*Christmas Trees and Evergreens entries*)

Grace Gershuny, coauthor of *The Soul of Soil* and an editor of *The Rodale Book of Composting,* is also an organic agricultural consultant. (*Composting entry*)

Linda Gilkeson, coauthor of *Rodale's Chemical-Free Yard and Garden,* holds a doctorate in entomology from McGill University, Montreal, and is an IPM coordinator in the Ministry of Environment for the province of British Columbia. (*Beneficial Insects, Insects, Nematodes, and Organic Pest Management entries*)

John Greenlee is the owner of Greenlee Nurseries and John Greenlee and Associates Design in Pomona, California. (*Bamboo and Grasses entries*)

Brent Heath and his wife, Becky, own the Daffodil Mart in Gloucester, Virginia, which grows the largest selection of bulbs in the United States. They also give lectures across the country. (*Bulbs entry*)

Lewis Hill is the author of *Fruits and Berries for the Home Garden.* He owns Vermont Daylilies in Greensboro, Vermont. (*Blueberry and Elderberry entries*)

L. Patricia Kite is the author of *Controlling Lawn & Garden Insects* and *The Home Gardener's Problem Solver.* (*Avocado, Citrus, Companion Planting, Earthworms, and Plant Disorders entries*)

Terry Krautwurst is editor of *Back Home* magazine and former senior editor of *Mother Earth News* magazine. (*Bees and Beekeeping, Birds, Fencing, Grains, Intensive Gardening, and Weather entries*)

Hiram Larew is research entomologist for the Agency for International Development in Washington, D.C. (*Galls entry*)

B. Rosie Lerner is Cooperative Extension consumer horticulture specialist at Purdue University and state coordinator of the Indiana Master Gardener Program. (*pH and Plant Nutrition entries*)

Cheryl Long is research editor for *Organic Gardening* magazine. (*Houseplants entry*)

Bill and Diana MacKentley own St. Lawrence Nurseries, a nursery specializing in Northern-hardy fruits and nuts, in Potsdam, New York. (*Nut Trees entry*)

Leslie May has a master's degree from the Longwood Program. She is a coauthor of *Rodale's Book of Practical Formulas*. (*Forcing, Heirloom Plants, Historical Gardens, and Staking entries*)

Sally McCabe is an education specialist at the Pennsylvania Horticultural Society. (*Community Gardens and Urban Gardening entries*)

Susan McClure, coauthor of *All About Pruning,* holds a master's degree in botany and is a widely published freelance gardening writer. (*Fruit Trees entry and individual fruit tree entries*)

Scott Meyer is copy editor at *Organic Gardening* magazine. (*Bonsai entry*)

Pat Michalak has a master's degree in entomology from Michigan State University. She is a freelance garden writer and organic market gardener in Kempton, Pennsylvania. (*Animal Pests, Disease, Fungicides, Herbicides, Insecticides, Organic Farming and Gardening, Parasitic Plants, and Pesticides entries.*)

Susan C. Milius is senior editor of *National Wildlife* and *International Wildlife* magazines. (*Beneficial Animals entry*)

Carol Munson is a freelance writer and editor and former senior editor at Rodale Press. (*Canning, Drying Food Crops, and Freezing entries*)

Melinda Myers is home horticulture director for Milwaukee County Cooperative Extension in Wisconsin. (*All-America Selections, Cooperative Extension Service, Government Agencies, Master Gardeners, and Season Extension entries*)

Ellen Ogden is co-owner of the Cook's Garden, a mail-order seed company in Londonderry, Vermont. (*Children and Gardening and Food and Nutrition entries*)

Maggie Oster is a garden writer, photographer, and landscape designer. She is the author of *Gifts and Crafts from the Garden, Flowering Herbs, 35 Garden Blueprints,* and *Perennials.* (*Crafts from the Garden, Cut Flower Gardening, Dried Flower Gardening, Flower Arranging, Potpourri, Rosa, and Wreathmaking entries*)

Paul Otten is general manager of North Star Gardens, a nursery specializing in raspberries, in Marine on St. Croix, Minnesota. (*Brambles entry*)

Sara Pacher is a freelance garden writer and former senior editor for *Mother Earth News* magazine. (*individual vegetable entries*)

Pam Peirce is a freelance garden writer, photographer, and photo editor. She is also author of *Environmentally Friendly Gardening: Controlling Vegetable Pests.* (*Raised Bed Gardening, Walkways and Paths, and Xeriscaping entries*)

Cass Peterson is the co-manager of the Flickerville Mountain Farm and Groundhog Ranch and a former environmental writer for the *Washington Post.* (*Environment and Gardening entry*)

C. Robert Phillips III is professor of classics and ancient history at Lehigh University and an accredited judge with the American Orchid Society. (*Orchids entry*)

Barbara Pleasant is the author of *The Handbook of Southern Vegetable Gardening* and is contributing editor for *Organic Gardening* magazine. (*Lawns, Permaculture, and Vegetable Gardening entries*)

Frank Pollock raises organic garlic and other fruits and vegetables at Rolling Hills Farm in Saylorsburg, Pennsylvania. (*Garlic entry*)

Joanna Poncavage is senior editor for *Organic Gardening* magazine. (*Organic Certification entry*)

Sarah F. Price, curator of the Conservatory Garden in Central Park, has a master's in public garden management from the Longwood Program and is a former associate editor of *Organic Gardening* magazine. (*Vines entry and individual vine entries*)

Lee Reich is the author of *Uncommon Fruits Worthy of Attention* and a former fruit researcher for Cornell University and the U.S. Department of Agriculture. (*Fruit entry*)

Raymond J. Rogers is a horticulturist, consultant, and lecturer. He is a former curatorial assistant at the Morris Arboretum of the University of Pennsylvania and a former education supervisor/horticulturist at the American Horticultural Society. (*individual annuals, biennials, bulbs, and perennials entries*)

Susan A. Roth is a freelance writer, editor, and photographer specializing in gardening and landscape design. She has a master's degree in ornamental horticulture from Cornell University and is the author of *The Weekend Garden Guide.* (*Cottage Gardening, Curbside Gardens, Kiwi, Meadow Gardens, Mulch, Shade Gardening, and Strawberry entries*)

Marcus Schneck is a freelance nature writer and the author of *Butterflies.* (*Butterfly Gardening and Wildlife entries*)

E. H. Sheldon is a freelance horticultural writer and the author of *A Proper Garden*. (*Herbs entry and individual herb entries*)

Miranda Smith is coauthor of *Rodale's Chemical-Free Yard and Garden* and author of *Greenhouse Gardening*. (*Greenhouse Gardening entry*)

Nancy Tappan is a freelance garden writer who raises grapes in western Oregon. (*Astrological Gardening, Folklore, and Grape entries*)

Kris Medic Thomas is landscape manager and arborist for the city of Columbus, Indiana. She has a master's degree in ornamental horticulture/public horticulture administration from the Longwood Program. Kris is former staff horticulturist/trails manager at Callaway Gardens in Georgia. (*individual shrub and tree entries*)

Cass Turnbull is the founder of PlantAmnesty, a private nonprofit organization that strives to educate commercial landscapers and home gardeners on proper pruning practices. (*Hedges and Pruning and Training entries*)

Eileen Weinsteiger is the garden project manager at the Rodale Research Center and has more than ten years of experience with organic vegetable culture. (*table in Vegetable Gardening entry*)

Bill Wolf is the founder and president of the Necessary Trading Company in New Castle, Virginia. (*technical review of Fertilizers, Green Manure, Organic Matter, and Soil entries*)

Editors

Fern Marshall Bradley has a bachelor's degree in plant science from Cornell University and a master's degree in horticulture from Rutgers University. She has managed an organic market garden and is an editor at Rodale Press.

Barbara W. Ellis has a bachelor of arts degree from Kenyon College and a bachelor's degree in horticulture from the Ohio State University. She is a former publications director/editor for *American Horticulturist,* the publication of the American Horticultural Society, and is a senior editor at Rodale Press.

James E. Farrell is an intern at Rodale Press and is studying landscape architecture at Temple University.

Deborah L. Martin has a bachelor's degree in horticultural writing from Purdue University and has worked as a Cooperative Extension agent for urban gardeners in Indianapolis. She is an associate editor at Rodale Press.

Jean M. A. Nick has a bachelor's degree in biology from Smith College and a master's degree in horticulture from Rutgers University. She has extensive experience in the commercial greenhouse industry and is an associate editor at Rodale Press.

Nancy J. Ondra has a bachelor's degree in agronomy from Delaware Valley College and is an assistant editor at Rodale Press. In addition to editing, she wrote the Budding, Cuttings, Division, Grafting, Landscaping, Layering, and Propagation entries.

Ellen Phillips has a master's degree in creative writing from Indiana University and a master's degree in horticulture from the University of Kentucky. She is a former senior editor of *Organic Gardening* magazine and is an editor at Rodale Press.

Sally Roth is a freelance garden writer and editor and is coeditor of *Letter from the Country.*

Heidi A. Stonehill has a bachelor's degree in biology from Colby College. She is a senior research associate and photo editor at Rodale Press.

Special Thanks

Bruce Barritt, horticulturist at Washington State University, for information on proper pruning of fruit trees.

Sandra Corpora, artist/designer, for sketches for the fig-overwintering illustration.

Robert Cotts, professor of physics at Cornell University, for information on drying herbs in microwave ovens.

Frank Fretz, freelance illustrator, for design of anchored plastic jug cloche.

Glen Grantham, freelance illustrator, for sketches for pruning illustrations.

Paul Heller, professor of entomology at Penn State Cooperative Extension, for information on control methods for insect pests of evergreens.

USDA PLANT HARDINESS ZONE MAP

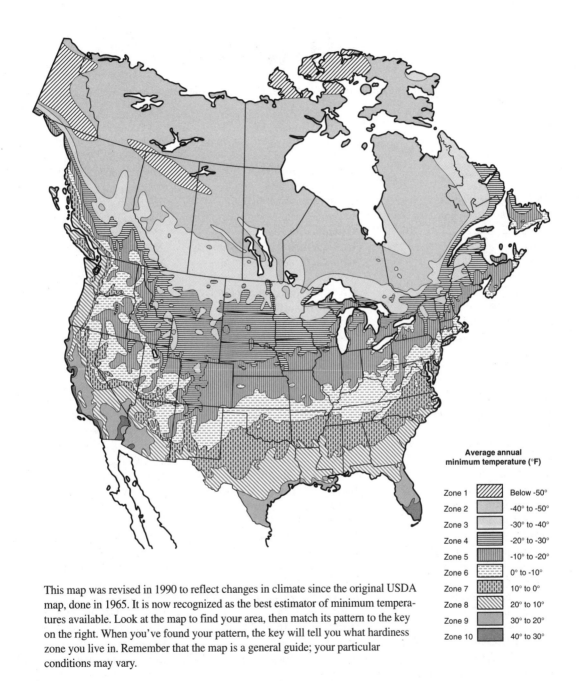

Average annual minimum temperature (°F)

Zone 1		Below -50°
Zone 2		-40° to -50°
Zone 3		-30° to -40°
Zone 4		-20° to -30°
Zone 5		-10° to -20°
Zone 6		0° to -10°
Zone 7		10° to 0°
Zone 8		20° to 10°
Zone 9		30° to 20°
Zone 10		40° to 30°

This map was revised in 1990 to reflect changes in climate since the original USDA map, done in 1965. It is now recognized as the best estimator of minimum temperatures available. Look at the map to find your area, then match its pattern to the key on the right. When you've found your pattern, the key will tell you what hardiness zone you live in. Remember that the map is a general guide; your particular conditions may vary.

Index

Note: Page references in *italic* indicate illustrations. **Boldface** references indicate tables.

W

Waldsteinia fragarioides, 161
Walkways, 623-24
Wallo'Water, *130*
Walnut, **403**, 581. *See also Juglans*
　black, 400, **403** (*see also
　　Juglans nigra*)
　English, 356
　Persian, 403 (*see also Juglans
　　regia*)
Warm-season grass, definition of,
　366
Washingtonia filifera, 435
Wasps
　as beneficial insects, 57, **58**
　gall, 262
　parasitic, as beneficial insects,
　　57
Waste, recycling, *205, 209*
Water, 625
　for birds, 69
　conservation of, 206, 207,
　　351, *352,* 353
　gray, 207
　for seedlings, 530-31
Water gardens, 625-29
　formal vs. informal, 625
　growing aquatic plants in,
　　628
　installation of, 625-26, 628
　maintenance of, 628-29
　perennials for, 456
　plants for, 626
　sites for, 625
Watering. *See* Irrigation
Watermelon, 387, 389, 629
Water pollution, 206, 208
Watersprouts, definition of, 249
Water traps, yellow, 430
Weather, 629-30
　disease and, 178
　season extension and, 522-23
Weather lore, 233-34

Webworms, *592. See also specific
　plants affected*
Weeds, 631-34
　benefits of, 633
　control of, 604, 608, 610
　edible, 632
　elimination of, 632-34, *634*
　life cycle of, 631
　in meadow gardens, 386
　prevention of, 631-32
Weeping tree, definition of, 581
Weeping willow. *See Salix
　babylonica*
Weevils, **257**. *See also specific
　types and specific plants affected*
Weigela, 635
Weigela florida, 635
Western predatory mite, **59**
Wheat, 156, 282
Wheat rust, 181
Whip, definition of, 249
Whip-and-tongue graft, 278-79,
　279
Whiteflies, 333, 428. *See also
　specific plants affected*
Whitefly parasite, **59**
White grubs, *343*
White pine blister rust, 181. *See
　also specific plants affected*
Whorled leaf, definition of, 371
Wildflowers
　bulbs with, 90
　definitions, 635
　growing, 636
　for meadow garden, 386
　purchase of, 635-36
Wildlife, 637-38, *638*
Willow. *See Salix*
Willow, desert. *See Chilopsis
　linearis*
Willow water, 167
Wilts, 181. *See also specific types
　and specific plants affected*
Wind, 630
Wind damage, 183

Windflower. *See Anemone*
Windrow, definition of, 140
Winterberry. *See Ilex verticillata*
Wintercreeper. *See Euonymus
　fortunei*
Wintergreen, 315. *See also Gaul-
　theria procumbens*
Wireworms, 431. *See also specific
　plants affected*
Wishbone flower. *See Torenia
　fournieri*
Wisteria, 241, 620, *621,* 639
Wisteria floribunda, 639
Wisteria sinensis, 639
Witch hazel. *See Hamamelis*
Witch's brooms, 639
Wood ashes, 140-41, **228**, 472
Woodbine. *See Parthenocissus*
Woodchucks, 14
Wood rots, 180-81
Woodruff, sweet, 315, 316, 323
Woodwardia, 220
Woody perennial, definition of,
　453
Worm castings, **228**
Worms, 191-92, 428, 431
Wormwood. *See Artemisia*
Wreathmaking, 155-56, 639-40,
　640

X

Xanthomonas pruni. See Bacte-
　rial leafspot
Xeranthemum annuum, 186
Xeriscaping, 300, 641-42

Y

Yam. *See* Sweet potato
Yarrow. *See Achillea*